You only see what you know.
Goethe

Wind Speed

MPH	Knots
1 - 2	1 - 2
3 - 8	3 - 7
9 - 14	8 - 12
15 - 20	13 - 17
21 - 25	18 - 22
26 - 31	23 - 27
32 - 37	28 - 32
38 - 43	33 - 37
44 - 49	38 - 42
50 - 54	43 - 47
55 - 60	48 - 52
61 - 66	53 - 57
67 - 71	58 - 62
72 - 77	63 - 67
78 - 83	68 - 72
84 - 89	73 - 77
119 - 123	103 - 107

knots x 1.15 = miles per hours

Conversion Formulas

Millimeters (mm)
millimeters x 0.03937 = inches

Centimeters (cm)
centimeter x 0.3937 = inches

Meters (m)
meters x 3.281 = feet
meters per second x 3.281 = feet per second
square meters x 10.76 = square feet
square meters x 1.196 = square yards
square meters x 0.0002471 = square acres
cubic meters x 35.31 = cubic feet
cubic meters x 1.308 = cubic yard
cubic meters x 0.0008107 = acre-feet
cubic meters / second x 35.31 = cubic feet /second
cubic meters / second x 15,850.00 = gallons / minute

Kilometers (km)
kilometers x 0.6214 = miles
square kilometers x 0.3861 = square miles
cubic kilometers x 0.2399 = cubic miles

Inches (in)
inches x 25.4 = millimeters
inches x 2.54 = centimeters
square inch x 6.4516 = square centimeters

Feet (ft)
feet x 0.3048 = meters
square feet x 0.09294 = square meters
cubic feet x 0.02832 = cubic meters
acre-foot x 1233 = cubic meters

Yard (yd)
yard x 0.9144 = meters

Miles (mi)
miles x 1603.3 = meters
miles x 1.609 = kilometers
square miles x 2.590 = square kilometers
cubic miles x 4.168 = cubic kilometers

Acre-foot (acre-ft)
acre-ft x 1233 = cubic meters

Microradian
microradian x 0.02 = second of arc

Temperature Conversions

°Fahrenheit (°F)
(°F - 32) x 5/9 = °C

°Celsius (°C)
(°C x 1.8) + 32 = °F
(°C x 2) - (°C x 2 x 0.1) + 32 = °F
*a) double the Celsius temperature b) subtract 10%
of the doubled temperature c) add 32*

Time

Standard to UTC (Z)
UT is the time at 0° longitude (Greenwich, England)

Newfoundland+ 3.5 hr = UTC
Atlantic + 4 hr = UTC
Eastern + 5 hr = UTC
Central + 6 hr = UTC
Mountain + 7 hr = UTC
Alaskan + 8 hr = UTC
Hawaiian + 10 hr = UTC
Add one less hour for Daylight Savings Time

More conversions on page 624.

CAMPING & SURVIVAL

PAUL TAWRELL

The Ultimate Outdoors Book

EXXA

LEBANON, NEW HAMPSHIRE

OCLC 8/27/14

CAMPING & SURVIVAL

The Ultimate Outdoors Book

Graphic Design
Ler Watt

Illustrations
Melita Fechner

Copyright © 2011 Leonard Paul Tawrell
All rights reserved. No part of this publication may be reproduced, transmitted, in any form or by any means, electronic or mechanical, ebook, including xerography, recording, or stored in a retrieval system, without prior written permission from the publisher.

Printed in Canada

ISBN 978-0-9740820-5-9

Notice

The aim of this book is to entertain its readers, to alert readers to the potential dangers and emergencies that might occur in the wilderness and how to avoid them. This knowledge might help a person survive or avoid a difficult situation. *Some of the activities and survival methods may be inappropriate for certain individuals due to their lack of forest and outdoor skills, material, physical condition, or other handicaps.* Local laws and private property should be respected and the security of other outdoor travelers should always be kept in mind. *Some of the techniques outlined in this book can cause serious injury and the publisher and author disclaim any liability.* Readers are advised to read and follow usage instructions included with camping and survival products that they buy.
A First Aid course is a *must* for a well rounded knowledge of the outdoors and this book does not attempt to replace this course nor the techniques taught in a First Aid course.

CONTENTS

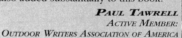

My goals in writing this guide have been to help you acquire and sharpen the skills required to safely enjoy the wilderness. You will find details on how to travel, "make a camp", choose suitable equipment, and understand your environment. You will learn how to search for food and water, as well as how to take shelter from the weather and how to care for yourself if you become injured or ill while in the wilderness. Mastering these tools will ensure that you are well prepared in the case of an emergency. There are general topics, such as Signals, Animals, and Weather as well as sections devoted specifically to special activities, such as Summer Hiking, Desert Travel, Water Travel, and Car Travel. Individual chapters, for example, Maps and Compasses, First Aid, and Mountain Climbing, provide a good foundation on which to build your knowledge of the outdoors. The information contained in this book will help you enjoy the outdoors while at the same time alert you to the dangers that you might encounter. There are a multitude of facts about Woodcraft, Fire Making, Food and Water, Shelter, and Navigation, and many survival topics are covered in detail. The book gives you a wide overview of nature and your surroundings so that your ability to improvise and respond to your immediate situation is improved.

I hope that my appreciation and respect for the great outdoors will be transmitted to you, the reader. I believe that you can remain alive anywhere in the world if you keep your wits about you. Nature and the elements are neither your friend nor your enemy, but it is your determination to survive and your ability to make nature work for you that are the deciding factors. *Camping & Survival* attempts to give you and your family the means with which to safely enjoy the outdoors.

I owe thanks to the United States government for making freely available countless articles, maps, and other publications from which I was able to find useful information to enhance the quality of this book. Special appreciation is due to the United States Center for Disease Control in whose publications I discovered abundant medical information that helped to make the chapter on First Aid a comprehensive "how-to" guide. Research and data from NOAA also added substantially to this book.

PAUL TAWRELL
ACTIVE MEMBER:
OUTDOOR WRITERS ASSOCIATION OF AMERICA
OUTDOOR WRITERS OF CANADA

CONTENTS

Third Printing 2014

CampingBook.com

The will to survive is the key to survival

01 LOST ?

Panic can cause a person to act without thinking.

Knowledge is the first step in overcoming fear.

Knowledge can be amplified by the confidence in your equipment, use of the equipment, group interaction, and survival techniques. The understanding of the smells, noises, physical characteristics of land, weather, and your relationship with them will also be of great help.

It is easy to get lost and this book is intended to give you an overview of the wilderness, an understanding of your environment, and how you can use the material available to survive.

Before entering a wilderness area or abandoning your car. Tell someone where you are going or leave a note indicating where you have gone, which path you are taking, and when you will be back. Do it every time even if entering a familiar area for a short period. You can break a leg a few hundred feet from home as well as 10 miles (16 km) from camp.

Always carry survival tools as a knife, compass, matches in a waterproof container, and a windbreaker or poncho.

For longer trips always have a survival kit to prepare for any eventuality.

FEAR & PANIC

- To feel fear is normal and necessary. It is nature's way of giving you that extra shot of energy. A caveman would sleep and at the first unusual sound would bound up and get out of danger's way. This rapid response is due to an extra charge of adrenaline and it is released by the body because of fear.
- Undue fear is usually caused by the unknown. Look carefully at a situation to determine if your fear is justified. Upon investigation you will usually find many of your fears are unreal. The dangerous noise might be a squirrel dropping a nut falling from a tree and bouncing through the leaves.
- If you are injured pain might turn fear into panic. Panic can cause a person to act without thinking and go running off into the forest.
- Panic can be caused by loneliness which can lead to hopelessness, thoughts of suicide and carelessness.
- Keep your mind busy and plan for survival. Recognizing the signs of fear and panic will help you overcome their devastating effect. Develop a plan for the next few days. This will raise your morale. Make sure that your doorway faces east towards the rising sun. Get up as soon as it is light and get busy.

AVOID GETTING LOST

When traveling make it a habit to...
- Check your approximate location on the map and try to compare its markings with your surroundings. Do this every 15 to 20 minutes. If you are using a GPS check against a map and also recall your surroundings.
- Direction of the wind.
- Watch where you cast a shadow to make sure you are not walking in circles and that you are not misreading the direction on your compass.
- How long have you traveled and estimate the distance covered.
- How do the contours of the land compare to the contours on the map?
- Major landmarks as large hills, rivers or large trees, that have been passed.
- If following a trail and somehow you lose your direction, do not just walk back but remember your "lost" position by looking for an identifiable landmark and head back. Leave markings as broken branches or blazes at "lost" position to find your way back. Make sure that you are following a blaze and not an abrasion on a tree caused by a falling branch or gnawed by an animal as a moose or bear. Man made blazes will usually have a mechanical feature as a straight cut, etc. *See Signal Chapter.*

Self confidence can be established by the knowledge of survival techniques and understanding the wilderness. This knowledge serves to lessen fear and prevent panic and irrational panic decisions from being made.

LOST?

YOU GET LOST & ARE ALONE

- The shock of realizing that you are lost can be mentally crippling but you have to hope for the best and plan for the worst. Recall survival techniques or training and expect them to work as it will increase your chances for success by increasing your confidence in that you can survive.
- Stay "Put". If you're not sure of the way out and people know you are missing.
- Remain calm. Usually it is best to stay where you are and build a shelter. This is especially true if you are lacking food or are injured. Staying will give you a chance to conserve your energy.
- Carefully study your surroundings.
- Find water, if possible an open area for a signal fire, a sheltered area for a camp, and wood. If the wood supply permits, keep a small fire going, at all times, for a signal fire.
- Build a simple safe comfortable shelter and fire as quickly as possible.
- Once well sheltered and warm form a plan. A survival plan will alleviate your fear. Your confidence and morale will increase.
- Be calm. Take it easy and think of how to implement your action plan. Establish where you are by identifying landmarks and compass directions.
- Take stock of your situation once your signal fire has been built, your campfire, and shelter is ready. Mentally list everything you have on you. Empty your pockets and use your imagination to discover how your belongings can be used. This book gives many original survival ideas which are based upon common items in your pockets.
- Any shiny object can be used to attract the attention of passing aircraft. *See Signal Chapter.*
- Do not be too eager to find your way out until you have adapted to your environment and have the basic survival necessities of food, water, and shelter. Unnecessary risks will be taken if you are careless and impatient.

FOOD RATIONING

Immediately start rationing and do not eat any food on the first day. Limit the intake of water if it is not readily available . Eat food in small amounts at a time and eat slowly. Trap small animals, catch insects, and find edible plants to supplement your rations.

IF IN A GROUP

- A group should chose a leader and assign responsibilities to all individuals so that all have a responsibility for the rescue of the group. Always try to determine and use special skills offered by members of the group. The leader can consult with the group but he has to make the decisions. Above all, the leader must at all times avoid the appearance of indecision.
- Make sure that no member of the group is left on his own as he might be in a depression. Negative ideas should be squashed as soon as possible.
- Panic, confusion, and disorganization are minimized by good leadership.
- Problems usually occur in a group. These problems can be due to fatigue, hunger, close quarters, cold, and strategic decisions that have to be made.
- Develop a feeling of team work and stress that each man depends on the other individuals for survival. Teamwork fosters higher morale and unity as each member feels the support and strength of the group.

USE IMAGINATION & IMPROVISE

- Improvise to improve the situation. This will give you more control and raise your morale.
- Remember your goal is to get out alive. Raise your morale by "dreaming" of the time after you "get out alive" will help you value life now.
- Conserve your health and strength. Illness or injury will greatly reduce your chance of survival.
- Hunger, cold, and fatigue lower your efficiency, stamina, and will make you careless. You will realize that your low spirits are the result of your physical condition and not danger.
- Improvising includes eating insects and other unusual foods.

Don't just sit there. Do something!

SUNBURN & WINDBURN

Severe sunburn can occur summer or winter. In the late winter months the sun can produce a severe burn in a short time. Wear a hat, sunglasses, long sleeved clothing and take advantage of the shade.

INTESTINAL SICKNESS

Common diarrhea, food poisoning, and other intestinal diseases are common if you are in the wilderness especially if you are trying to survive on a limited diet and primitive storage conditions.
To guard against discomfort...
- Keep the body and hands clean. Keep fingers out of your mouth. Avoid handling food with your hands. Wash hands after handling wild foods.
- Avoid eating raw foods, especially those grown on or in the ground. Wash and peel fruit. See Cooking Chapter on how to store food. Eat food right after preparation especially meat and fish. Cook all food well done.
- Purify drinking water. *See Finding Water Chapter.*
- Sterilize eating utensils by boiling in water or heating over a flame.
- Keep insects and other vermin off your food and drink.
- Keep camping area clean and food away from camp.
- Human waste should be kept away from camp site and water supply.

If you develop vomiting or diarrhea rest and stop eating solid foods. Drink water in small amounts at frequent intervals. Maintain normal salt intake.

See the First Aid Chapter for information on salt requirements. Page 591.

Water Container

Fire Starter

... the trees all look the same!

HYGIENE

Good physical health is essential to survival.

- The Cooking and Fishing Chapters outline methods of catching, cooking and storing food.
- The First Aid Chapter highlights insect stings, snake and animal bites, cleanliness, drowning, etc. The *First Aid Chapter* also outlines methods to prevent disease and treatment of injuries.
- **Injuries:** Even minor injuries are potentially serious as they can become infected. Carefully treat every cut, sprain, or bruise.
- **Bleeding:** Limit bleeding by the methods outlined in the *First Aid Chapter.*
- **Blisters:** Avoid blisters on your feet as they will restrict your movement. Never miss a chance to dry your socks by the fire.
- **Insects:** The ferocity, persistence and quantity of insects in the bush are always an insurmountable surprise. Small insects as black flies can be a major problem. Short exposure to them can make life unbearable.
- Follow the simple rules of personal hygiene to protect yourself against disease and injury.
- Brush your teeth using table salt or baking soda as a substitute for toothpaste. If you do not have a toothbrush chew a green twig to a pulpy consistency. Rinse your mouth after each meal.
- Use soap and water to keep clean. Special attention should be given to areas on your body that are susceptible to rash and fungus infection; between your toes, your crotch and scalp. If soap is not available use wood ash as a substitute. A daily shower with hot water and soap is ideal. If this is impossible, keep your hands as clean as possible and sponge and dry your face, armpits, crotch, and feet at least once a day.
- Keep your clothing, especially your underclothing and socks, as clean and dry as possible. If laundering is impossible shake out your clothing and expose them to the sun and air every day. Clothing should be kept clean as clean clothing does not wear out as fast and cleanliness will reduce your exposure to rashes and infections.
- Have up to date immunization before you travel.
- Guard against heat illness, cold, windchill, hypothermia and fatigue.

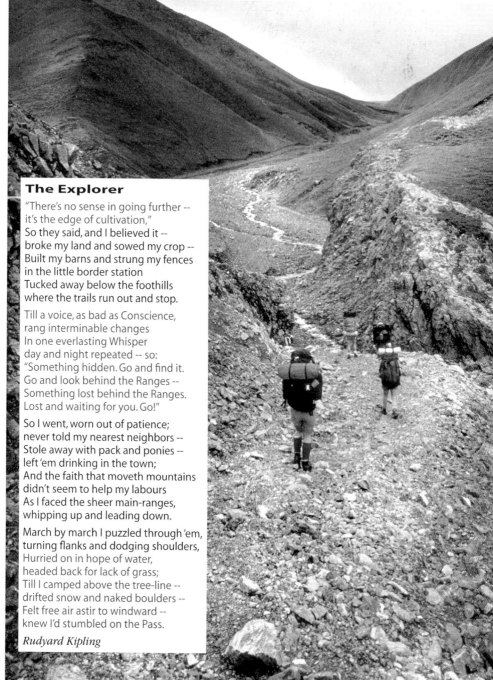

The Explorer

"There's no sense in going further --
it's the edge of cultivation,"
So they said, and I believed it --
broke my land and sowed my crop --
Built my barns and strung my fences
in the little border station
Tucked away below the foothills
where the trails run out and stop.

Till a voice, as bad as Conscience,
rang interminable changes
In one everlasting Whisper
day and night repeated -- so:
"Something hidden. Go and find it.
Go and look behind the Ranges --
Something lost behind the Ranges.
Lost and waiting for you. Go!"

So I went, worn out of patience;
never told my nearest neighbors --
Stole away with pack and ponies --
left 'em drinking in the town;
And the faith that moveth mountains
didn't seem to help my labours
As I faced the sheer main-ranges,
whipping up and leading down.

March by march I puzzled through 'em,
turning flanks and dodging shoulders,
Hurried on in hope of water,
headed back for lack of grass;
Till I camped above the tree-line --
drifted snow and naked boulders --
Felt free air astir to windward --
knew I'd stumbled on the Pass.

Rudyard Kipling

Basic Wilderness Emergency Kit

- Brass wire • Candle or lantern
- Brown sugar • Canteen • Compass
- Emergency blanket (poncho)
- Extra pair of prescription glasses
- Fire starter • First aid kit • Flare
- Fishing kit • Flashlight & batteries
- GI can opener • Heavy knife or ax
- High energy food • Poncho • String
- Mess kit • Razor blades • Sewing kit
- Rope 12'-24' (4-8 m) • Signal mirror
- Small pot • Tea bags, broth cubes
- Tube tent • Water bottle • Whistle
- Waterproof matches
- Waterproof match container
- Water purifying tablets or filtration system

Camping

- Air mattress • Backpack • Compass
- Bottle opener • Can opener • Knife
- Candle/lantern • Cutlery • Foam pad
- Cookware and utensils • Nylon cord
- Day pack or small fanny pack.
- Disposable butane lighter • Tent
- Drinking cup • First aid kit • Towel
- Flashlight/extra batteries
- Plastic bags for storage
- Plastic bags (re-sealable)
- Plastic containers • Pot gripper
- Repair kits • Scissors • Sewing kit
- Signal mirror • Sleeping bag
- Stove / fuel • Waterproof matches
- Tarpaulin, ground sheet, or poncho
- Washing liquids • Whistle
- Water bottle • Waterproof pouch
- Water purifier or tablets

Rock Climbing

- Helmet • Rock hammer • Carabiners
- Hammer holster • Chocks and nuts
- Pitons • Kletterschuhe • Swami belt
- Rope

Ice & Snow Climbing

- Helmet • Cagoule (Balaclava)
- Extra socks • Gaiters
- Mittens, Fingerless mittens
- Slings, rappel anchors, runners, seats, etc. • Down jacket
- Rock pitons • Tubular ice screws
- Rucksack • Emergency shelter
- Crampons • Boots • Rope
- Carabiners • Alpine hammer
- Hammer holster • Ice ax

Before Leaving Home

- Leave keys and itinerary with a friend.
- Obtain permits (fishing, camping, hunting).
- Passport and visas.
- Fill prescriptions and have copies.
- Mail on hold at Post Office
- Stop newspaper delivery.
- Traveler's medical insurance.
- Vaccinations and/or inoculations.

Take With You

- Address book • Binoculars • Camera and film
- Credit cards • Drivers license • Flashlight
- Electrical converter or adapter
- Itinerary • Maps • Money belt •Padlock • Pen
- Soap • Charged cell phones might.
- Wallet • Walking shoes

Summer Travel

- Cotton hat • Light colored cotton shorts & shirt
- Insect repellent • Light walking shoes
- Sunglasses • Sun lotion • Towels

Cold Weather Travel

- Balaclava • Emergency blanket • Scarf
- Outerwear (poncho) • Survival candles
- Thermal underwear • Warm hat
- Warm parka • Warm waterproof boots
- Wool gloves • Wool socks • Wool sweater

Food

- Chocolate bars • Freeze dried food • Salt
- Raisins & brown sugar • Tea & broth cubes
- Water treating tablets

Personal Items

- Aspirin • Baking Soda • Cold medication
- Dental floss • Diarrhea medication
- Ear plugs • Extra glasses • Laxative
- Moleskin for feet • Personal hygiene items
- Motion sickness medication • Shampoo
- Personal medications • Prescription drugs
- Shaving kit • Biodegradable Soap
- Toiletries • Toothbrush and paste • Vitamins

Camping Gear

- Back Pack • Citronella candle • Cot or mat
- Compass and maps • Emergency candles
- Fire starter • Flashlight or lantern
- Pocket knife • Sleeping bag & pad • Tent pegs
- Shelter (tube tent) • Stove & fuel

Cooking Gear

- Canteen & mess kit • Knife • GI can opener
- Plastic bags • Utensil kit

Emergency Fishing Kit

- Plastic pill containers to store fish hooks, floats, sinkers, strand of monofilament.
- Different sized hooks.
- 15' of monofilament line 10 lb test.
- Rubber bands • Sinkers • Sewing needle
- Waterproof emery paper to sharpen hooks.

Winter Driving

The leading cause of death during winter storms is transportation accidents. Preparing your vehicle for the winter season and knowing how to react if stranded or lost on the road are the keys to safe winter driving.

Before:

Have a mechanic check the following on your car.

- Battery • Antifreeze • Ignition system
- Wipers & windshield washer fluid • Thermostat
- Lights • Heater • Brakes • Defroster
- Flashing hazard lights • Exhaust system
- Oil level (if necessary, replace existing oil with a winter grade oil)

Winter Car Kit

Keep these items in your car:

- Flashlights with extra batteries
- First aid kit with pocket knife
- Necessary medications • Several blankets
- Sleeping bags • Extra newspapers for insulation
- Plastic bags (for sanitation) • Matches
- Extra set of mittens, socks, and a wool cap
- Rain gear and extra clothes
- Small sack of sand for generating traction under wheels • Small shovel • Booster cables
- Small tools (pliers, wrench, screwdriver)
- Set of tire chains or traction mats
- Brightly colored cloth to use as a flag
- Canned fruit and nuts • Nonelectric can opener
- Bottled water FEMA LIST

02 LIST OF LISTS

REDUCE EXPOSURE TO BITING INSECTS

- Stay away from breeding areas. Usually slow flowing or stagnant bodies of water.
- Avoid areas with high grass or dense vegetation.

Insure that you:

- Have a good bed net.
- Your immunizations are current.
- Laundry and bathing facilities are available.
- Shirt is buttoned.
- Sleeves are rolled down.
- Pants tucked inside boots.
- Bathe or shower regularly.
- Have clean clothing.
- Use insect repellent.
- Take malaria pills if prescribed.

Preventing Skin Infections

Bathe frequently. If showers or baths are not available, wash the following with a wash cloth every day.

- Your genital area.
- Your armpits.
- Your feet and between toes.
- Other areas where you sweat or that become wet such as: between thighs or (for females) under the breasts.

Keep the Skin Dry

- Use foot powder on your feet, especially if you have had previous fungal infections on the feet.
- Use talcum powder in areas where wetness is a problem, such as: between the thighs or (for females) under the breasts.

Wear Proper Clothing

- Wear loose fitting clothing as this allows for better ventilation. Tight fitting clothing reduces blood circulation and ventilation.
- Do not wear nylon or silk undergarments; cotton undergarments are more absorbent and allow the skin to dry.

For Females

- Wash your genital area each day.
- Do not use perfumed soaps or feminine deodorants in the field as they cause irritation and attract insects.
- Do not douche unless directed by a doctor.
- Drink extra fluids, even when it is not hot. Some individuals do not drink enough fluid and tend to hold their urine due to the lack of privacy. Urinary tract infections are one of the most frequent medical problems females face in the field. Drinking extra fluids will help prevent these infections.

US Army Insect Bar *(Bed Net)*

An insect bar should be used in all malaria areas. You must take care not to come in contact with the net as insects can bite through it.

There are places in the tropics where 20% of the US troops have become ill with malaria as the result of being exposed to mosquitoes for one night without the protection of an insect bar.

Voltage While Traveling

The voltage, cycle, and electrical plug can vary from country to country and sometimes even within the country. Buy the required adaptor or adaptor kit before you leave on your trip.

Area	Voltage
North America	110V
Caribbean	110V-220V
Europe	220V
except Andorra	125V
Canary Is.	110V
Turkey	220V
Former Yugoslavia	220V
Former USSR	220V

DESERT SURVIVAL
Planning a Day Trip

Plan an Itinerary

Make a detailed plan as to where you are going and where you plan to stay. Leave a copy of the plan with someone and tell them when you will report back to them. If you do not report back on time they will report you as "lost" to the authorities. When traveling do not leave the road or track because you will find that cacti and rocks all look the same if you are lost. If you have any problems en route or change your plan inform your contact.

Food & Water

Bring at least two or three days of water.
4 quarts per person per day and use it sparingly.

Clothing

Wear the right clothing and be prepared for cold nights.

Accessories

Bring sunscreen (use at least SPF 30), hats, bandana, and sunglasses. For tent anchors use "Ziploc" bags filled with sand. Place them inside self standing tents to hold them down.

Car Supplies

Gasoline in a five gallon jerry can and make sure that the inside of the can is not rusted as the rust flakes might block your fuel system. Extra radiator fluid, fan belt, radiator hose, distilled water for the battery. Shovel with at least a three foot handle. A hydraulic jack, pulley and rope to disengage the car. If you are driving off the road you will encounter sand and you will require high-axles, wide tires and preferably a four wheel drive car.

Walking

Walking on sand is difficult as you have the tendency to slide back. The energy required for one mile on sand is equivalent to two miles on regular terrain. Wear boots and heavy socks as the sand is so hot that it can cause burns.

DESERT SURVIVAL
Survival items for the desert:

- Mirror for signaling.
- Magnifying glass to a start fire.
- Water purification tablets.
- Brass wire for trapping.
- Collapsible water container.
- 4 quarts of water per person per day.
- Fishing line to construct shelter out of brush.
- Hat with a wide brim. Sunglasses.
- Loose fitting light colored clothing that will cover the body and arms. Clothing made of natural materials as cotton or wool. Wool blanket.
- Sturdy boots with wool socks.

First Aid Kit
See your physician for advice...

- First Aid kit • Snakebite kit • Insect repellent
- Moleskin for sore feet • Salt tablets • Baking soda
- Table salt • Distilled water • Rubbing alcohol
- Cotton applicators • Bandages • Petroleum jelly
- Aspirin • Mild antiseptic • Tweezers • Scissors
- Thick blunt needle • Feminine napkins • Aspirin
- Medical thermometer • Nausea or vomiting tablets
- Sterile gauze dressings, individually wrapped (2"x2" and 4"x4"). • Oral antibiotics for infections
- Piece of clean folded old bed sheet
- Roll of 1/2" wide adhesive tape
- Motion sickness tablets • Diarrhea medication
- Pepto Bismol - for traveler's diarrhea (turista)
- Aromatic spirits of ammonia • Mild antiseptic
- Steristrips for cuts (hold edges of cut together)
- Suturing kit (see your physician)

HEAT DISORDERS
Sunburn

Symptoms: Skin redness and pain, possible swelling, blisters, fever, headaches.
First Aid: Take a shower, using soap, to remove oils that may block pores preventing the body from cooling naturally. If blisters occur, apply dry, sterile dressings and get medical attention.

Heat Cramps

Symptoms: Painful spasms usually in leg and abdominal muscles. Heavy sweating.
First Aid: Firm pressure on cramping muscles or gentle massage to relieve spasm. Give sips of water. If nausea occurs, discontinue.

Heat Exhaustion

Symptoms: Heavy sweating, weakness, skin cold, pale and clammy. Weak pulse. Normal temperature possible. Fainting, vomiting.
First Aid: Get victim to lie down in a cool place. Loosen clothing. Apply cool, wet cloths. Fan or move victim to air-conditioned place. Give sips of water. If nausea occurs, discontinue. If vomiting occurs, seek immediate medical attention.

Heat Stroke (Sun Stroke)

Symptoms: High body temperature (106°+). Hot, dry skin. Rapid, strong pulse. Possible unconsciousness. Victim will likely not sweat.
First Aid: Heat stroke is a severe medical emergency. Call 9-1-1 or emergency medical services or get the victim to a hospital immediately. Delay can be fatal. Move victim to a cooler environment. Try a cool bath or sponging to reduce body temperature. Use extreme caution. Remove clothing. Use fans and/or air conditioners. DO NOT GIVE FLUIDS. *FEMA*

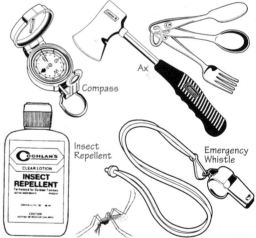

Compass   Ax   Insect Repellent   Emergency Whistle

Do not forget your sunglasses.

TORNADO DANGER SIGNS

Learn these tornado danger signs:
- An approaching cloud of debris can mark the location of a tornado even if a funnel is not visible.
- Before a tornado hits, the wind may die down and the air may become very still.
- Tornadoes generally occur near the trailing edge of a thunderstorm. It is not uncommon to see clear, sunlit skies behind a tornado.

DURING A TORNADO

If at home:
- Go at once to a windowless, interior room; storm cellar; basement; or lowest level of the building.
- If there is no basement, go to an inner hallway or a smaller inner room without windows, such as a bathroom or closet.
- Get away from the windows. Go to the center of the room. Stay away from corners because they tend to attract debris.
- Get under a piece of sturdy furniture such as a workbench or heavy table or desk and hold on to it.
- Use arms to protect head and neck.
- If in a mobile home, get out and find shelter elsewhere.

If at work or school:
- Go to the basement or to an inside hallway at the lowest level.
- Avoid places with wide-span roofs such as auditoriums, cafeterias, large hallways, or shopping malls.

If outdoors:
- If possible, get inside a building.
- If shelter is not available or there is no time to get indoors, lie in a ditch or low-lying area or crouch near a strong building. Be aware of flying debris. FEMA

TORNADOES
Page 465

DURING A HURRICANE

- Listen to a battery-operated radio or television for hurricane progress reports.
- Check emergency supplies and fuel car.
- Bring in outdoor objects such as lawn furniture, toys, and garden tools and anchor objects that cannot be brought inside.
- Secure buildings by closing and boarding up windows. Remove outside antennas.
- Turn refrigerator and freezer to coldest settings. Open only when absolutely necessary and close quickly.
- Store drinking water in clean bathtubs, jugs, bottles, and cooking utensils.
- Review evacuation plan.
- Moor boat securely or move it to a designated safe place. Use rope or chain to secure boat to trailer. Use tiedowns to anchor trailer to the ground or house.
- Store valuables and personal papers in a waterproof container on the highest level of your home.

If at home:
- Stay inside, away from windows, skylights, and glass doors.
- Keep a supply of flashlights and extra batteries handy. Avoid open flames, such as candles and kerosene lamps, as a source of light.
- If power is lost, turn off major appliances to reduce power "surge" when electricity is restored.

If evacuation is necessary:
- Leave as soon as possible. Avoid flooded roads and watch for washed-out bridges.
- Unplug appliances and turning off electricity and the main water valve.
- Tell someone outside of the storm area where you are going.
- If time permits, and you live in an identified surge zone, elevate furniture to protect it from flooding or better yet, move it to a higher floor.
- Take blankets and sleeping bags to shelter.
- Bring pre-assembled emergency supplies and warm protective clothing. FEMA

HURRICANES
Page 472

TSUNAMIS

A tsunami is a series of waves that may be dangerous and destructive. When you hear a tsunami warning, move at once to higher ground and stay there until local authorities say it is safe to return home.

Before:
- Find out if your home is in a danger area.
- Know the elevation of your street above sea level and the distance of your street from the coast. Evacuation orders may be based on these numbers.

Be familiar with the tsunami warning signs...
Because tsunamis can be caused by an underwater disturbance or an earthquake, people living along the coast should consider an earthquake or a sizable ground rumbling as a warning signal. A noticeable rapid rise or fall in coastal waters is also a sign that a tsunami is approaching.
- Make sure all family members know how to respond to a tsunami and prepare evacuation plans.
- Pick an inland location that is elevated. After an earthquake or other natural disaster, roads in and out of the vicinity may be blocked, so pick more than one evacuation route.
- Teach family members how and when to turn off gas, electricity, and water.

Have disaster supplies on hand.
- Flashlight & extra batteries
- Portable, battery-operated radio & extra batteries
- First aid kit • Emergency food and water
- Nonelectric can opener • Sturdy shoes
- Essential medicines • Cash & credit cards
- Develop an emergency plan.

During:
- Listen to a radio or television to get the latest emergency information, and be ready to evacuate if asked to do so. If you hear an official tsunami warning or detect signs of a tsunami, evacuate at once. Climb to higher ground. A tsunami warning is issued when authorities are certain that a tsunami threat exists.
- Stay away from the beach. Never go down to the beach to watch a tsunami come in. If you can see the wave you are too close to escape it.
- Return home only after authorities advise it is safe to do so.
- A tsunami is a series of waves. Do not assume that one wave means that the danger over. The next wave may be larger than the first one. Stay out of the area. FEMA

Protect your head if there is a tornado, hurricane, or earthquake.

LANDSLIDES & MUDFLOWS

Landslide and mudflows usually strike without warning. The force of rocks, soil, or other debris moving down a slope can devastate anything in its path.

Take the following steps to be ready.

Before:
- Get a assessment of your property on areas vulnerablity to landsliding. Consult a geotechnical expert for advice on landslide problems and on corrective measures you can take.
- Minimize home hazards.
- Plant ground cover on slopes and build retaining walls.
- In mudflow areas, build channels or deflection walls to direct the flow around buildings.

Remember: If you build walls to divert debris flow and the flow lands on a neighbor's property, you may be liable for damages.

Landslide Warning Signs
- Doors or windows stick or jam for the first time.
- New cracks appear in plaster, tile, brick, or foundations.
- Outside walls, walks, or stairs begin pulling away from the building.
- Slowly developing, widening cracks appear on the ground or on paved areas such as streets or driveways.
- Underground utility lines break.
- Bulging ground appears at the base of a slope.
- Water breaks through the ground surface in new locations.
- Fences, retaining walls, utility poles, or trees tilt or move.
- You hear a faint rumbling sound that increases in volume as the landslide nears. The ground slopes downward in one specific direction and may begin shifting in that direction under your feet.

Make evacuation plans: Plan at least two evacuation routes since roads may become blocked or closed.

During a Flood
If outdoors:
- Climb to high ground and stay there.
- Avoid walking through any floodwaters. If it is moving swiftly, even water 6inches deep can sweep you off your feet.

If in a car:
- If you come to a flooded area, turn around and go another way.
- If your car stalls, abandon it immediately and climb to higher ground. FEMA

Many deaths have resulted from attempts to move stalled vehicles.

Rope

First Aid Kit

Teach children how and when to call 9-1-1, police or fire department, and which radio station to listen for official information.

A lava flow blocking a road.

VOLCANOES & HAWAII LAVA HIKING
Page 69

VOLCANOES
Volcanic eruptions can hurl hot rocks for at least 20 miles. Floods, airborne ash, or noxious fumes can spread 100 miles or more. If you live near a known volcano, active or dormant, be ready to evacuate at a moment's notice. Learn about your community warning systems.

Be prepared for disasters that can be spawned by volcanoes.
- Earthquakes • Flash floods • Tsunamis
- Landslides and mudflows • Thunderstorms

STORING EMERGENCY WATER
Store water in plastic containers such as soft drink bottles. Avoid using containers that will decompose or break, such as milk cartons or glass bottles. A normally active person needs to drink at least two quarts of water each day. Hot environments and intense physical activity can double that amount. Children, nursing mothers and ill people will need more.

Basic Items to Stock in your Home
- Water   • Tools & emergency supplies
- Food   • Extra clothing & bedding
- First aid supplies

Keep the items that you would most likely need during an evacuation in an easy-to-carry container - suggested items are marked (*). Possible containers include a large, covered trash container, camping backpack,
- Store one gallon of water per person per day (two quarts for drinking, two quarts for food preparation/sanitation)*
- Keep at least a three-day supply of water for each person in your household.

Emergency Stored Food
Store at least a three-day supply of non-perishable food. Select foods that require no refrigeration, preparation or cooking and little or no water. If you must heat food, pack a can of sterno. Select food items that are compact and lightweight. *Include a selection of the following foods in your Disaster Supplies Kit:

- Foods for infants, elderly persons or persons on special diets   • Vitamins
- Comfort/stress foods - cookies, hard candy, sweetened cereals lollipops, instant coffee, tea bags
- Sterile adhesive bandages in assorted sizes
- 2 inch sterile gauze pads (4-6)
- 4 inch sterile gauze pads (4-6)
- Hypoallergenic adhesive tape
- Triangular bandages (3)
- 2 inch sterile roller bandages (3 rolls)
- 3 inch sterile roller bandages (3 rolls)
- Tweezers   • Needle   • Scissors
- Moistened towelettes • Antiseptic
- Thermometer   • Tongue blades (2)
- Tube of petroleum jelly or other lubricant
- Ready-to-eat canned meats, fruits & vegetables
- Canned juices, milk, soup (if powdered, store extra water)
- Staples - sugar, salt, pepper
- High energy foods - peanut butter, jelly, crackers, granola bars, trail mix
- Assorted sizes of safety pins
- Cleansing agent/soap • Latex gloves (2 pair)
- Sunscreen Adapted from the CDC & Red Cross.

DURING A VOLCANIC ERUPTION
Avoid areas downwind of the volcano.

If indoors:
- Close all windows, doors, and dampers.
- Put all machinery inside a garage or barn.
- Bring animals and livestock into closed shelters.

If outdoors:
- Seek shelter indoors.
- If caught in a rockfall, roll into a ball to protect the head.
- Avoid low-lying area where poisonous gases can collect and flash floods can be most dangerous.
- If caught near a stream, beware of mudflows.

Protect yourself:
- Wear long sleeved shirts and pants.
- Use goggles to protect eyes.
- Use a dust-mask or hold a damp cloth over the face to help breathing.
- Keep car or truck engines off.
- Stay out of the area. A lateral blast of a volcano can travel many miles from the mountain. Trying to watch an erupting volcano is a deadly idea.

MUD FLOWS
Mudflows are powerful "rivers" of mud that can move faster than people can walk or run. Mud flows occur when rain falls through ash-carrying clouds or when rivers are damed during an eruption. They are most dangerous close to stream channels. When you approach a bridge, first look upstream. If a mudflow is approaching or moving beneath the bridge, do not cross the bridge. The power of the mudflow can destroy a bridge very quickly.

AFTER AN ERUPTION
- Listen to a battery-powered radio or television for the latest emergency information.
- Stay away from volcanic ashfall.

When outside:
- Cover your mouth and nose. A number of victims of the Mount St. Helens volcano died from inhaling ash.
- Wear goggles to protect your eyes.
- Keep skin covered to avoid irritation or burns.
- If you have a respiratory ailment, avoid contact with any amount of ash. Stay indoors until local health officials advise it is safe to go outside.
- Avoid driving in heavy ash fall. Driving will stir up more ash that can clog engines and stall vehicles.
- Clear roofs of ash fall. Ash fall is very heavy and can cause buildings to collapse. FEMA

It is not right for trees to grow so near to the road!

03 CAR TRAVEL

- Cell telephone with charged batteries, a car battery charger and a compact solar charger.
- A quality car jack can have many uses.
- Chains for tires especially in sandy, muddy and snowy areas.
- Warm clothing and boots.
- Methyl hydrate added to water to make windshield washer.
- Tire pump, either electric or a quality foot pump.
- Flares, rectangular reflectors, and a flashlight.
- First aid kit which should be inside the car and not in the trunk.
- Fire extinguisher.
- Dried fruit and chocolates.
- Maps and car repair manual.
- First Aid Kit.
- Booster cables.
- Shovel made of metal which can be used as a shovel or for traction for a skidding tire.
- Set of wrenches, screwdrivers, tire repair kit, one inner tube.
- Oil for car and a jerry can of gasoline.
- Gas antifreeze or methyl hydrate in cold areas.

Whistle

Warning
Static electric spark is an explosion hazard.

Always place containers on the ground. Keep nozzle in contact with container while filling. Never fill portable containers that are in or on a vehicle.

Static Electric Spark
A static electric spark can occur when filling portable containers sitting on truck bed liners, or on any vehicle's carpeting or floor matting. This spark will explosively ignite a gasoline vapor fire and cause serious injury or death.

Estimating Distance while Driving
Objects look much closer than they actually are when...
- Looking up or down a hill.
- There is a bright light on the object being looked at.
- Looking across water, snow or flat sand.
- The air is clear.

Objects look much farther away than they actually are when...
- The light is poor.
- Color of the object blends with the background.
- The object is at the end of a long avenue or highway.
- You are looking over undulating ground.

Chemical Burns
While traveling the most probable cause of an acid burn would be from the car battery or from cleaning fluids. See the First Aid Chapter for more information.

Electrical Burns
Electrical burns do not look too serious but the tissue under the small skin wound can have been destroyed. See the First Aid Chapter for more information.

HIGHWAY BREAKDOWN
If you have a sign of trouble...
1 Take foot off the accelerator.
2 Do not brake hard or suddenly.
3 While signalling work your way through any traffic to the breakdown lane. Avoid going into the median.
4 If possible, try to drive towards an exit.
5 If not possible to drive to an exit make sure you car is safely out of the traffic lane and that the car is visible and the emergency flashers are on. If possible light flares, mount warning flags or reflectivities triangles. Put on the dome light in the car at night.
6 Do not try to flag down other vehicles. Put a something on your antenna and raise you hood to signal your need of help.
Changing Flat Tire: Make sure that it can be changed safely without endangering yourself.

Car Crash
If in a car crash follow the procedures outlined by your insurance company or your local authorities.

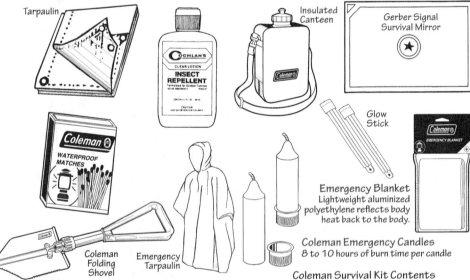

Tarpaulin

Insulated Canteen

Gerber Signal Survival Mirror

COGHLAN'S CLEAR LOTION INSECT REPELLENT

Glow Stick

Coleman WATERPROOF MATCHES

Coleman EMERGENCY BLANKET

Emergency Blanket
Lightweight aluminized polyethylene reflects body heat back to the body.

Coleman Folding Shovel

Emergency Tarpaulin

Coleman Emergency Candles
8 to 10 hours of burn time per candle

Coleman Survival Kit Contents
- First Aid Kit (10 small adhesive bandages, 6 medium adhesive bandages, 1 large adhesive bandage, 1 knuckle bandage, 4 adhesive strips, 3 gauze pads, 3 alcohol pads, 3 antiseptic pads, 1 moleskin, 2 travel towels, 1 steel needle)
- Stainless steel scissors
- Emergency blanket
- Signal Whistle
- 2 glowsticks
- Zipper pull compass thermometer
- Waterproof matches (2 boxes)

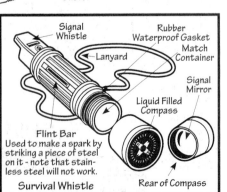

Signal Whistle

Rubber Waterproof Gasket

Lanyard

Match Container

Signal Mirror

Liquid Filled Compass

Flint Bar
Used to make a spark by striking a piece of steel on it - note that stainless steel will not work.

Rear of Compass

Survival Whistle

CAR FIRE
What to Do
If in moving traffic...
1 Try to get to breakdown lane.
2 Stop and shut off the engine.
3 Get far away from vehicle - warn oncoming traffic.
4 Call the fire department.
Do not attempt to put the fire out.
Car immobile...
1 Shut of engine.
2 Get far away from vehicle - warn oncoming traffic and pedestrians.
3 Call fire department.

POSSIBLE CAUSE
The cause of every car fire is different:
The majority of car fires are caused by mechanical or electrical problems. These are usually caused by a lack of proper maintenance especially in older cars. Fires can also happen in collisions or roll overs - if you are wearing a seat belt the odds are that you will be not as severely injured and be able to safely leave the car.
Older Cars: In older cars it might be faulty brittle wire covering that exposes live wires. The hoses, especially the ones coming from the gas tank might be leaking. If this gasoline comes in contact with a hot surface or spark it might ignite.
Oil Leaks: Oil might leak onto the engine or other hot parts. Clean any oil spills that might occur during maintenance. Do not try to put out an oil fire with water as the fire might spread.
Running out of Gasoline: Only put gasoline in the tank and do not put a few drops the carburetor. The gasoline in the carburetor might ignite when you turn the ignition - starting an engine fire. This would also apply to lawn mowers. This would not apply to fuel injection systems.
Car on Fire: Many parts of a burning car might burn or explode.
- **Explode:** tires, plastic bumpers (some bumpers are fluid filled), shook absorbers.
- **Burn:** plastics on modern cars, the liquids that might flow from a damaged burning car, fabrics, and plastics.
- Stand upwind from a burning car to avoid inhaling dangerous fumes.

STOPPING CAR FIRE
If you have and know how to work an extinguisher only try to extinguish a small fire. In general do not attempt to put the fire out.

AVOID CARJACKING
- Watch your environment while driving. Frequently check mirrors for potentially dangerous situations. Keep your distance for other vehicles and keep an escape route open.
- Avoid driving alone in dangerous areas. Plan you route and do not get lost.
- Drive with windows up and doors locked.
- If crashed from behind signal other driver to follow you to nearest police station - if you feel insecure call 9-1-1 on your cell phone.
- If car breaks down - this is when you wish that your battery is charged on your cell phone - pull a safe distance out of moving traffic - if safe tie something to your antenna - then keep your door locked. If you are offered assistance ask individual to call the police of a towing service. Be sure that an approaching officer is genuine.
- Give up your car if confronted by an armed individual.

Wonder what happened?

DRIVING & SURVIVING
Drive slowly on back roads especially if your car is low as you might pierce your oil pan while going over boulders.
To drive over soft spots and to increased traction you might have to slightly deflate your tires. When you park cover your car with a blanket as this will reduce the heat inside the car. When sunlight goes through glass the wavelength changes and the heat waves from this light cannot leave the inside of the car. For this reason a cover should be placed on the outside of the glass to keep the inside cool. Do not leave animals in a car.
In general if your car breaks down on a traveled route stay with it as it:
- Contains your survival tools and water.
- Has items that can be used for survival.
- Side mirrors for signaling.
- Hubcaps to collect water and cooking.
- Spare tire to burn as a rescue signal because black smoke can be seen over a large distance.
- Seats can be used as a bed.
- Car provides shade.
- Battery can be used to light a fire with the cigarette lighter or two wires.
- If car still works or battery is strong headlights can be used for night time signaling.
- Battery can be used to magnetize a needle to use as a compass.

If you leave your car make sure of your route and where you will get your next drink of water. Scavenge your car before you leave but do not take too many heavy things.
Take...
- Water.
- Mirrors for signaling.
- Seat covers to cover head or use as blanket.
- Leave a note in the car to indicate direction of travel and leave blazes on your route.
- Fuel to help you start a fire during the desert's cold nights.
Do not leave the car during the heat of the day.

VW Thing 1973

VW Camper

Jeep CJ5

Jeep Commando

VW Beetle

Blind spots for truck drivers.

Land Rover

15

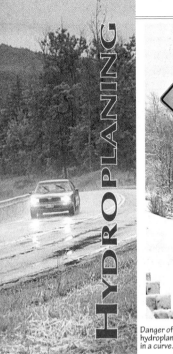

BRIDGES FREEZE BEFORE ROAD

Danger of hydroplaning in a curve.

HYDROPLANING

DRIVING IN THE RAIN

Realize that your car handles very differently in the rain and that quick stops are longer.

Water Damming   Hydroplaning

Rain Starts: Trucks and cars leave a layer of oily deposits on the road surface and this accumulates when the road is dry. When it starts to rain the oily layer will float on the water and be extremely slippery.

Hydroplaning: Normally a cars weight pushes the rainwater away from below your tires. During a heavy rainstorm or when you hit a puddle or water filled grove on the road the water in front of you tires will build up faster than it can be dissipated. This will cause your car to rise up on the water surface and you will slide on the water. If all tires are off the surface you will be hydroplaning and you will have lost all contact with the road. If you are in a curve or turning you will slide into the other lane, a ditch, or tree. You will never forget this experience.

Preventing Hydroplaning: Have tires that are not too worn and slow down especially in a curve. Apply the brakes very lightly and in short intervals. If you do not have anti-lock brakes, avoid using your brakes - because the car might skid sideways. With anti-lock brakes brake normally and the computer on the car will automatically pump in short intervals.

If Hydroplaning: Ease the pressure on the gas pedal and steer the car into the direction you want to go. Do not brake or turn suddenly.

DRIVER FATIGUE

A major symptom is - the few second snooze and suddenly waking up while you are driving. This can be fatal.

- When you drive stop frequently and stretch your legs and have a snack.
- Have someone drive with you on long-distance trips.

- Keep the temperature of your car on the cooler side so that you do not get to comfortable. Make sure that there is good fresh air circulation. This will keep you more alert and also expel any car fumes that might build up during long drives.
- Do not use cruise control as you might get too comfortable. Watch your posture with legs not fully extended in a relaxed position - your body might think it is in a bed! Change your position frequently - chew gum - stretch your neck - move your eyes, etc.
- If possible try to do your long distance driving during daylight hours especially if this follows you regular sleep routine. During the day there is less glare and the road is visible and more interesting to keep you alert.
- At night avoid letting your eyes become hypnotized by the white lane lines (especially if you drive on the line).

If you feel fatigue - get some sleep at a rest area. If it is late at night find a motel and get a good rest in a bed and then you will be much more alert that next day.

DRIVING AT NIGHT

Problems when driving at night...
- Lack of color that helps in differentiating different obstacles. The curb from the road.
- Limited depth perception.
- The angle of vision is reduced by the limited light from the head lights.
- Older drivers have a lower light sensitivity in their eyes.
- Darkness might cause drowsiness and it is more difficult to concentrate and also reduces the reaction time.

Improve Night Time Visibility
- Keep headlights, taillights, signal lights and windows (inside and out) clean.
- Make sure that your headlights are properly aimed to maximize the light on the road. You have to realize that if your truck is loaded your high beams will be aiming above the road.
- Keep your headlights on low beams when following another car.
- Light your lights at dawn, dusk, and during rainstorms as this will help other drivers to see you.
- Reduce your speed at night and make sure you do not overdrive your headlights. Always consider your possible reaction time to anything that might pop up - and can you stop on time - or have a blind crash.

FALLEN POWER LINES

Power lines by themselves are not dangerous as long as the object touching them is not grounded. You can see birds sitting on power lines and not getting a shock. If someone touches a "hot" power line and at the same time is standing on wet ground or is 'grounded', they complete the circuit and the electricity flows through the person causing an electrical shock.

Fallen Power Line on a Car
If a power line has fallen across a car assume that the line is live. The rubber tires of the car form a satisfactory insulation between the fallen wire and the ground. The people in the car are safe as long as they do not touch the metal frame of the car and the ground - at the same time. This would bypass the insulation of the car's tires. The person should stay in the car if help is on its way. If the car is on fire, in a dangerous location, or no help is on the way then the occupants can jump clear of the car making sure that they are not touching the car and the ground at the same time.

BRAKE FAILURE
First sign of brake problems...
- Do not to panic.
- Work car into the shoulder of the road while watching your mirrors and the traffic around you. Use your directional signal.
- When in the right lane turn on your emergency hazard lights.
- Take your foot off the gas pedal and steer as your car slows and then shift the car into a lower gear to let the engine help slow the car.
- Shift into neutral and gradually apply the hand brake until the vehicle stops.

(If hand brake has also failed, direct the car onto a soft shoulder or rub the wheel against a curb which will help you to slow down.)

DRIVING IN A SANDSTORM
- Pull off the road and out of the way of traffic.
- Turn off the engine as you will clog your air filter with sand.
- If possible cover your windshield because a violent sand storm can 'sand' the glass.
- Park your car so that the engine does not face into the wind as sand will infiltrate into all parts of the engine.

DRIVING IN DESERT COUNTRY
Before leaving on a trip in the desert, check:
- Battery.
- Radiator and coolant quality and level.

Take:
- First Aid Kit. • Flares • Extra radiator coolant.
- Cooling hoses • Spare fan belts • Set of tools.
- Fire extinguisher.
- Spare tire(s), tubes, and repair kits.
- Air pump and small hydraulic jack.
- Extra motor oil and check the manufacturers specifications as to SAE for hot weather.
- Extra air filters as you might want to change it every few hundred miles if it is dusty.
- Spot light for night repairs or signalling.

EQUIPMENT FOR DESERT TRAVEL
- Shovel and ax • Wool blanket.
- Sturdy car cover.
- Winch with a heavy rope.
- Wide tires.
- 4 quarts of water per person per day.
- Two planks to help in releasing the car from soft sand.

Visibility problems during a rainstorm.

WINTER TRAVEL

- Check the latest forecasts and road conditions.
- Dress for the outdoor conditions.
- Fully winterize and check your vehicle including such things as the battery, heating system, and belts.
- Have a winter survival kit.
- Leave a route plan and indicate approximate time of arrival.
- Keep your gas tank as full as possible.

Trapped in Car During Blizzard

- If stranded, stay with your vehicle and don't try to walk to safety. Try to make sure that you are parked in a safe spot - especially during a snowstorm or whiteout.
- Do not search for assistance unless help is visible within 100 yards. You may become disoriented and lost is blowing and drifting snow.
- Run the motor for about 10 minutes each hour for heat. Slightly open a window, on the leeward side, for fresh air. Light the survival candle from your winter kit. Remember the dangers or Carbon Monoxide poisoning. Also, turn on the car's dome light when the car is running.
- Make sure the exhaust pipe is not blocked. It will cause a problem with fumes and stall the engine.
- Tie a colored cloth (preferably bright) to the antenna and turn on the dome light at night when the motor is running. This will make your vehicle more visible to rescuers. Raise your hood to indicate trouble - not during a major snowstorm as the engine compartment might get clogged and stall the engine.
- All the occupants should not sleep at the same time. Exercise from time to time by vigorously moving arms, legs, fingers, and toes to keep blood circulating and to keep warm. Try not to stay in one position for too long. For warmth, huddle together.
- Avoid overexertion. Cold weather puts an added strain on the heart. Unaccustomed exercise such as shoveling snow or pushing a car can bring on a heart attack or make other medical conditions worse.
- Watch for signs of frostbite and hypothermia.
- Be aware of symptoms of dehydration.
- Use newspapers, maps, and even the removable car mats for added insulation. Also use the mat from the trunk.

Some cars spend a lot of time off the road.

DEER ON THE ROAD

Peak periods of seeing deer are at sunrise and sunset and during the spring and fall. Watch for deer crossing signs - they are there because this is where deer - car accidents have happened. If you see deer slow down - if you see one the odds are that others are following.

At night car lights will brilliantly reflect back from a deer's eyes.

Flashing your high beams or blowing your horn alert the deer or make it move.

Do not swerve to avoid a deer. When travelling at highway speeds by avoiding the deer you might hit another car, go off the road and hit a tree, or go into a steep ditch and roll over.

Apply you brakes. Firmly hold your steering wheel and come to a controlled stop - even if you hit the deer. Your seat belt should be attached.

Do not touch the deer. It might still be alive and might kick you with its sharp hooves.

MOOSE & DRIVING
Page 558

WIND CHILL

"Wind chill" is a calculation of how cold it feels outside when the effects of temperature and wind speed are combined. A strong wind combined with a temperature of just below freezing can have the same effect as a still air temperature about 35° colder.

Winter Storm Watches & Warnings

Winter Storm Watch: indicates that severe winter weather may affect your area. A winter storm warning indicates that severe winter weather conditions are definitely on the way.

Blizzard Warning: means that large amounts of falling or blowing snow and sustained winds of at least 35 miles per hour are expected for several hours.

Frostbite & Hypothermia

Frostbite: is a severe reaction to cold exposure that can permanently damage its victims. A loss of feeling and a white or pale appearance in fingers, toes, or nose and ear lobes are symptoms of frostbite.

Hypothermia: is a condition brought on when the body temperature drops to less than 90° F. Symptoms of hypothermia include uncontrollable shivering, slow speech, memory lapses, frequent stumbling, drowsiness, and exhaustion. If frostbite or hypothermia is suspected, begin warming the person slowly and seek immediate medical assistance. Warm the person's trunk first. Use your own body heat to help. Arms and legs should be warmed last because stimulation of the limbs can drive cold blood toward the heart and lead to heart failure. Put person in dry clothing and wrap their entire body in a blanket. Never give a frostbite or hypothermia victim something with caffeine in it (like coffee or tea) or alcohol. Caffeine, a stimulant, can cause the heart to beat faster and hasten the effects the cold has on the body. Alcohol, a depressant, can slow the heart and also hasten the ill effects of cold body temperatures.

Some of this chapter is based on FEMA information.

Dress warmly: Wear layers of loose-fitting, layered, lightweight clothing.

Carry food & water: Store a supply of high energy "munchies" and several bottles of water.

Animals on the Road are Hard to See
When driving in the summer watch for large animals as deer and moose. They might wander across a road or highway especially at night. Hitting a moose at high speed will demolish your car and you might get killed. In some states and provinces the local authorities, especially in state parks, might charge you, per pound, for the dead animal and you do not get to keep it.

PREPARING FOR WINTER

The leading cause of death during winter storms are road accidents. Preparing your vehicle for the winter season and knowing how to react if stranded or lost on the road are the keys to safe winter driving.
Fully check and winterize your vehicle before the winter season begins. Keep your gas tank near full to avoid ice in the tank and fuel lines. Try not to travel alone. Let someone know your timetable and primary and alternate routes.

Before...
Have a mechanic check:
- Battery • Antifreeze • Thermostat
- Ignition system • Exhaust system
- Lights • Flashing hazard lights
- Heater • Brakes • Defroster
- Wipers & windshield washer fluid

Oil level (if necessary, replace existing oil with a winter grade oil or the SAE 10w/30 weight variety)

WINTER CAR SURVIVAL KIT

- Cloths, blankets & sleeping bags
- Flashlight with extra batteries
- First-aid kit & pocket knife • Tool kit & tow rope
- Survival candle & matches
- High-calorie, non-perishable food
- Large empty can and plastic cover with tissues and paper towels for sanitary purposes
- Small can to melt snow for drinking water
- Sack of sand (or cat litter) for traction
- Shovel & booster cables
- Windshield scraper & brush
- Compass and road maps • Necessary medications
- Brightly colored cloth to use as a flag

WINTER TIRES

Make sure the tires have adequate tread. All-weather radials are usually adequate for most winter conditions. However, some jurisdictions require that to drive on their roads, vehicles must be equipped with chains or snow tires with studs.

Additional Precautions...

- Keep a windshield scraper and small broom for ice and snow removal.
- Maintain at least a half tank of gas during the winter season.
- Plan long trips carefully.
- Listen to the radio or call the state highway patrol for the latest road conditions. Always travel during daylight and, if possible, take at least one other person.
- If you must go out during a winter storm, use public transportation.

FIRST TRIP WITH A CHILD

Plan a child's first hiking trip so that it is enjoyable.

- Make the trip short and within the physical abilities of the child. Have numerous stops and points of interest (e.g. pond with frogs).
- Show the child a map of the planned trip and the progress of the trip.
- Do not walk too fast. Give the child a chance to look around.
- If you fall behind on your trip do not push your child to go faster. An excursion should be well planned so that you can reach your destination point long before dusk.
- Keep safety in mind by explaining all your activities. For example, choice of a fire site, how to cross a stream, etc. Always explain the dangers involved in these activities without scaring the child.
- Develop games en route for the child. These games should help the child to appreciate nature. Some games: not walking on ants, roots; seeing wild animals, birds, and looking for toads.
- Along the way, give the child healthy snacks.
- Listen to the child and explain all noises and dark spots so that he is not afraid.
- Explain the hiking environment to the child and the positive ecological features.

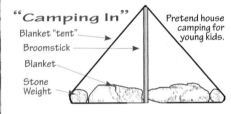

"Camping In" — Blanket "tent", Broomstick, Blanket, Stone Weight — Pretend house camping for young kids.

BIKE SAFETY TIPS

- Be sure that a child is ready to learn to bicycle on a two-wheeler - and that you have the patience to teach the child.
- A bicycle should be the correct size or the child might lose control. Oversized bikes can be dangerous.
- Always wear a bike helmet. Adults are important role models for children and should always wear a bike helmet. Children should always keep the helmet straps buckled when riding.
- Buy a helmet that is the right size, sits on top of the head in a level position, not tilted back on the head. Make sure that the straps can be adjusted for a snug and comfortable fit. The bike helmet should meet national safety standards.
- Obey traffic signs, signals, and other rules of the road when cycling with children. Teach a child the correct hand signals. Stop and look both ways before entering a street
- Do not cycle against the direction of the road traffic. Yield the right-of-way to pedestrians and skaters.
- Children should ride on sidewalks and paths until they are at least 10 years old. Before riding on the road they should show good riding skills, observe the basic rules of the road, and realize the speed that a bicycle can achieve.
- Children (and adults) should always wear bright clothing to stand out from the surroundings. At dawn, at dusk, or at night, reflective clothing should be warn. The bike should have a headlight and a rear reflector.
- Check the brakes frequently. Make sure that the wheels are tightly attached.

CHILDREN TRAVELING IN CARS

- Always use a child safety seat, even on short trips, as most crashes occur on short trips at low speeds. Do not keep children on the laps of adults - the child is apt to be thrown forward towards the back of the front seat or, if in the front seat, towards the dashboard or windshield.
- In a car, the safest place for a child safety seat is in the center of the back seat. This area offers more protection from being hit on either side. An adult can sit next to the child in the back seat if he has to be entertained.
- Choose an approved child safety seat and follow the manufacturer's positioning and installation instructions. Make sure that weight and size of the child is considered when choosing a child's safety seat.
- If there are numerous children, make sure that they are all seated securely.
- Children over 80 pounds and eight years usually can fit correctly in lap/shoulder belts (always in the back seat). Have an entertainment kit to keep them busy. The items should be light weight so that they do not become flying projectiles during a crash.
- Always have some snacks available.

EQUIPMENT FOR A CHILD

Clothing

Clothing should be layered so that the individual items can be gradually removed when it gets warm or applied if it gets cool. A waterproof, slightly oversize shell jacket is important as it will protect the child from the sun, rain, scratches, insects and abrasions.
A wide-brimmed hat with a built-in mosquito net. Rain gear is needed for rainy days. Have an extra pair of socks as one pair will certainly get wet. The clothing should be bright colored so that the child can be easily seen on the track or in the woods.

Footwear

Should be sturdy, well fitting, and broken in. The footwear should be lightweight, offer good support and be comfortable.

Backpacks

The day pack should fit the child. The weight the child carries should, in general, not exceed 20% of his weight. Give the child some responsibility and let him carry an important item.

"CAMPING IN"

To give the kids a test run of an ideal camping environment set up a tent and the required paraphernalia in the living room.

Items that can be used...

- King sized sheet to make a tent - if a small kid's tent is not available.
- Sleeping bags if available - or use wool blankets.
- Flashlights.
- Backpacks to store inside the tent.
- When it is dark, create a "fire" by shinning a flashlight on some crumpled red foil from Christmas packaging.

When dark, make forest sounds by playing a CD with new age music of forest sounds. When the kids are asleep, add some excitement by playing a CD of rain and a thunderstorm. Then when you have a real camping experience the children will find it quite boring - except if a skunk wanders through the campsite.

Adrien wearing a hat and with his body covered with sun protective lotion.

The objective of this book... is to make sure... that a child... (and parent) will see, enjoy and... understand the outdoors.

KID'S BACKPACK

A child's pack should contain:

- Whistle to use in case of emergency.
- Water and snacks: Teach the child to keep some for an emergency.
- Child sun block.
- Quality sunglasses.
- Insect repellent: Try to use a natural repellent. Make sure that any repellent does not have higher than 30% DEET content for children.
- Flashlight: A model that is easy to switch on and off.
- **First Aid Kit:** If a child gets scratched, have him use his own kit. This will give the child a sense of pride and he will want to know how to use the items in his kit.
- Toilet paper and small garbage bags. The garbage bag can be used as a poncho if you encounter a sudden downpour. Make sure that the child does not suffocate in the bag.
- Simple sturdy compass.
- **Watch:** This will teach the adolescent the time factor in the trip and the need to get back before dusk.
- Map of the trail showing the route and the destination point. Identify the main features (bridges, streams, hills) on the map and show them to the child while traveling.
- Tube tent so the child can take a planned nap in his own tent.
- A digital camera, if the child is old enough.

WATER & CHILDREN

- Watch the local weather forecast before taking children to the beach - especially on large bodies of water. If thunderstorms and strong winds are imminent it might be difficult to "convince" the children to leave the water's edge - and you might be in danger due to the inclement weather.
- Changing weather on large bodies of water can make the direction and force of currents unpredictable.
- Watch for dangerous waves which might occur in between regular waves. Rip currents are very dangerous - they can sweep even a strong person off his feet. Signs of rip currents are choppy, foamy, debris-filled, and discolored water.
- Make sure an adult is constantly watching the children swimming, playing, or bathing in or near water. Do not get distracted by reading, playing cards, or talking on the phone.
- To prevent choking, never chew gum or eat while swimming, diving, or playing in water.
- Learn CPR (cardiopulmonary resuscitation). This always helps in a water emergency.
- Stay in designated swimming areas, usually marked by buoys or within sight of a life guard.
- Use U.S. Coast Guard-approved personal flotation devices (life jackets) when boating.

Watch where you poke s stick!

CHILDREN'S LIFE JACKETS & PRESERVERS

Personal flotation devices (PFDs) should be used on all boats.
Child PFD's are chosen based on the child's weight. The user weight is on the label.

Life Jackets

TYPE 1: This jacket floats the best.
- Will turn most victims who are unconscious from the face-down position to an upright and slightly backward position.
- The victim will stay in the above-mentioned position for a long time.
- For open water and oceans.

In two sizes: adult size more than 90 pounds and one child size for less than 90 pounds.

TYPE 2: Turns a victim upright and slightly backwards but not as much as the Type 1 jacket.
- It may not always help an unconscious victim to float face up.
- Comes in many sizes for children.

TYPE 3: For conscious victim in calm, inland water.
- Very comfortable - in many styles.
- Used for water sports.
- Used only when the rescue can be done quickly.

CHILDREN & LIFE JACKETS

- Children should always wear life jackets when on boats or near bodies of water. Adults should wear life jackets as a good role model for children.
- Make sure that the life jacket is the correct size for the child. It should not be to loose and the straps should be attached correctly.
- To give the child a sense of involvement, the child should learn how to put on his or her life jacket.
- Do not use beach toys such as air mattresses, rafts, beach balls, etc. as a temporary replacement for a suitable life jacket.

This article is not meant to replace the manufacturer's instructions as to use and fitting of a life jacket.

LIFE PRESERVERS

TYPE 4: A cushion or ring and is not meant to be worn.
A: Grasped and held until the victim is rescued,
B: Thrown to victim in the water, and held by victim, until he or she is rescued.

Should only be used in rescue situations and not used as a beach toy.

Looking at Critters

Axel removing sand from shoes.

Axel with favorite bear and a stick.

Mathilde

05 SUMMER HIKING

> **Preparation…**
> *If I always appear prepared,*
> *it is because before entering on*
> *an undertaking, I have meditated for*
> *long and foreseen what may occur.*
> Napoleon Bonaparte, 1769-1821

KNOW HOW TO FALL

When traveling, assume that a problem lies ahead and prepare for any eventuality. When descending a hill or steep bank make sure that you are balanced so that you will fall backwards and into a position in which you can slide. Your fall might disengage loose rocks, earth or snow which you will have to ride downhill. Be prepared to jettison your backpack when traveling downhill.

Problems you can encounter are…
- Slippery, slimy, and moving stones while crossing a stream.
- Moss growth on rocks.
- The earth on or below a rock might give way.
- Morning dew can make rocks, logs, and grass slippery.
- Morning hoar frost can bring surprises the same as morning dew.
- Be careful when crossing a stream on a fallen log because the log might break, move, be slippery, or the rotten bark on a log might slip off.
- You might sprain your ankle.

Ancient Greek Army Ration
Philon of Byzantium in 150 BC developed a ration pill for his soldiers. This pill was the size of an olive and consisted of: sesame seeds, honey, opium, poppy and squill (a root plant). These pills provided protein (sesame), hydrocarbons (honey), alleviated pain from hunger and discomfort (opium), and a general tonic (squill). Most likely white squill which acts as an expectorant, diuretic and cough remedy (large doses of squill cause severe vomiting). Active soldiers were given two pills daily, one at 8 am and one at 4 pm.

THE ART OF HIKING
- Plan your trip on a map and indicate rest points and your destination for the day. This destination should have shelter for the group. If not, you should plan to arrive early enough to pitch camp. The route should be chosen so that everyone can muster the require energy to have a pleasant trip. Make sure that all members of the group agree and have the physical stamina and experience to reach these objectives. Have an alternative plan in case of an emergency. Leave your itinerary with a responsible person and indicate when you will check back.
- Have a check list of all items required for the trip. These should include a first aid kit and other emergency material specific to the area, e.g. extra water in a dry area. Make sure that some individuals do not overpack.
- Start slowly so that your body gets warmed up, your feet get coordinated, your shoes are well adjusted, and your backpack is comfortable and well balanced.
- Wear comfortable and loose clothing. Have sufficient head cover. Make sure that you have the right clothing for the trip and upcoming weather.
- Pace your trip and do not rush.
- Stop periodically, remove your pack, stretch, swing your arms and check your progress on the map. If you see that you are falling behind on your trip because of difficulties in the terrain or a slow individual revise your destination for the day. Consider returning to the base camp if there are any critical problems or your ultimate destination cannot be reached in the required time. Remember if you are having difficulties at the start of a long trip things will probably get worse. A problem trip should be aborted if the moral of the group is not too positive.
- Walk in a zigzag up steep slopes. This will minimize your effort and you will be able to walk further and have less strained muscles the next day.
- When going uphill, check your footing, first place your right foot keeping your weight on your left foot. When the right foot is well and securely placed, transfer your weight to the right foot and move uphill.
- When going downhill, tighten the shoulder straps on your pack because if the pack shifts it might destabilize you. Check your boots making sure that the laces are tight enough so that your toes do not touch the front of the boot. If adjustment is difficult you might want to wear an extra pair of socks.

ACCLIMATIZATION: LONG DIFFICULT HIKE

You must be physically and mentally conditioned to participate in a long difficult hike.

- Different types of terrain and climate require different acclimatization procedures. If a major mountain hike is planned high-altitude acclimatization of 10 to 14 days is required.
- Any psychological fears of individual members of the group have to be considered. These fears can be of: animals, insects, height, cold, or isolation.

WALKING RHYTHM

During the hike, avoid delays that keep the group standing. Delays can increase fatigue and cause legs to stiffen, making it more difficult to resume the walk.

- Maintain a steady rate of walking- too rapid or too slow a rate induces fatigue.
- Ensure that any stragglers to the rear of the receive a full break time.
- All members of the group should be of more or less equal stamina so that the stronger of the group do not have to slow their stride for the slow.
- Adequate water at rest stops.

INDIVIDUAL CARRYING LOAD

Make sure that the individual carrying load is kept at a minimum - but should include the basic survival equipment. An in shape male might be able to carry up to 72 pounds. These load weights include all clothing and equipment that are worn and carried. The primary consideration is not how much you can carry, but how much you can carry and still enjoy your trip.

HALTS

In hot weather start your hike early and end early to rest and have time to prepare for the next day's activities. Midday heat can require a long daylight halt or consider night travel. Under normal conditions, a 15-minute halt provides rest after the first 45 minutes of travel. Following the first halt, a 10-minute halt for every 50 minutes of travel. You should remove or loosen your gear and sit or lie down with your feet elevated for optimum relaxation.

ACCORDION EFFECT

An accordion effect in single file travel is caused by changes in the rate of travel and most often occurs as lead members of the column ascend or descend terrain, or pass through rougher terrain on the route. A change in the rate of march increases as it passes down the column, so that the rear members must either double time to maintain the distance or be left far behind. Thus, a minor change of rate at the head of the column becomes magnified by the time it reaches the tail of the column. The best method for reducing the accordion effect is for lead members to slow their rate of travel after passing obstacles to permit rearward elements to maintain distances without running.

EFFECTS OF WEATHER & TERRAIN ON HIKE

The varying types of terrain on a long hike present different problems with the weather conditions being an added variable.

- Hiking under adverse climatic conditions follows the same principles as under normal conditions although extra precautions have to be considered - slippery mud, wet clothing, limited visibility, etc.
- Extreme weather and terrain might require a major change in plans.
- The difficulties encountered might make the trip take longer than "planned" thus causing problems such as lack of water and food.

WATER DISCIPLINE

Water discipline must be observed by all members of the group - especially on long trips.

- Drink plenty of water before each leg of hike.
- Drink only treated water from secure sources.
- Drink water often. Water should be consumed before, during, and after the hike.
- Drink small quantities of water rather than gulping or rapid intake.
- Drink water even when not thirsty.
- Drink water slowly to prevent cramps or nausea.
- Avoid spilling water.
- Refill canteens at every opportunity.
- The human body does not operate efficiently without adequate liquid intake. In strenuous activities, excessive amounts of water and electrolytes are lost through perspiration. More water is lost through normal body functions such as respiration and urination, which can create a liquid imbalance in the body. As a result, dehydration could occur unless this loss is immediately replaced and you rest before continuing your activities. Deficient liquid and salt intake during hot weather can also result in heat injuries.
- The danger of dehydration is as prevalent in cold regions as it is in hot, dry areas. The difference is that in hot weather you are aware that your body loses liquids and salt through perspiration. In cold weather, when you are bundled up in many layers of clothing, it is difficult to know that this condition exists since perspiration is rapidly absorbed by heavy clothing or evaporated by the air - it is rarely visible on the skin.
- Salt in food compensates for the daily salt requirement. Additional intake of salt should be under supervision of a physician.
- If pure water is not available, water in canteens can be purified.

Fire Starter Sticks
Lights even when wet.

Average Pace per Mile	
Average terrain	2112 paces per mile (1.6 km)
Rough terrain	2800 paces per mile (1.6 km)
People can Hike	
Level ground	2.5-4 mph (4-6.4 km/h)

HIKING TRAIL HEAD BREAK-INS

Break-ins and car vandalism are a potential problem in the parking area at the head of a trail. Precautions for trail head problems are:

- Check to see if the trail head has a high break-in or vandalism problem. If so do not use the facilities in that area. This might motivate the local authorities to provide better protection.
- Park your car(s) in a safe spot such as a garage or ranger station and use one car (the oldest), shuttle service or taxi to deposit you at the trail head.
- Check the parking area for evidence of vandalism and broken glass from car windows.
- If the trail head has little traffic or is close to a main road the probability of a problem is relatively high.
- Park with the tail of the car facing the parking area. This will expose any potential tampering to other hikers who might be present.
- Remove all valuables, open the glove compartment and do not cover or seem to cover anything in the car.
- Do not hide objects in the car when you have parked as it would be obvious for anyone observing you from the woods. Do not hide car keys, wallets with credit cards, in the car.
- Plan your baggage, at home, so that everything can fit into your bags and leave nothing of value in your car.

CALIFORNIA CYCLIST
Beats Off Cougar

Los Angeles, California

The 27 year old cyclist, Scott Fike, said of the attack: "It was very much a shock. 'Don't think it can't happen' is what you should probably tell people."

Mr. Fike was alone and riding on a trail in the Angeles National Forest when a cougar loped up alongside. He stopped and tried to use the mountain bike as a shield but the mountain lion chewed on the bike tire, clawed the spokes and maneuvered around the cycle. Mr. Fike fell but managed to beat off the cougar with rocks, gaining enough time to get away. Mr. Fike was bitten and cut but not seriously injured and declined hospital treatment.

"It ended up with a few wounds itself," Mr. Fike said of the cougar.

Hunters are trying to find the animal. If found, animals that attack humans in the wild are usually killed.

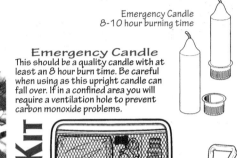

Emergency Candle
8-10 hour burning time

Emergency Candle
This should be a quality candle with at least an 8 hour burn time. Be careful when using as this upright candle can fall over. If in a confined area you will require a ventilation hole to prevent carbon monoxide problems.

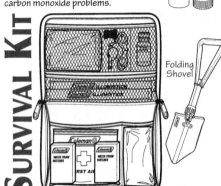

SURVIVAL KIT

Folding Shovel

Folding Shovel & Case

Scout Canteen

Fer de Lance Rattlesnake

SNAKE BITE KIT
Ideal for pocket or pack complete and easy to use
• CAMPERS • HIKERS • HUNTERS • HOME

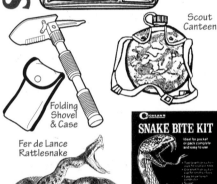

Flint Bar
Match Box
Lanyard
Closed Survival Whistle
Lanyard
Luminous Dial
Signal Whistle
Signal Whistle
Rubber Water-proof Gasket
Mirror
Liquid Filled Compass

Survival Whistle/Compass/Match Box/Flint Bar/Mirror

GI Can Opener

Can Opener

Ax

Swiss Army Knife

BASIC EMERGENCY TRAVEL KIT

Survival Items
- Compass • Penknife • Fishing kit • Brass wire
- Poncho or emergency blanket
- Waterproof container of matches
- Water bottle and purifying tablets

Bandage
- A box of bandage(s) • Moleskin for sore feet.
- Steristrips for cuts (To hold the edges of a cut together)
- Sterile gauze dressing (2"x2" & 4"x4") and a 2" wide roll
- Roll of 1/2 " wide adhesive tape
- Cotton applicators
- Suturing kit *(see your physician)*

Brass Scout Whistle

Medication *(see your physician for advice)*
- Oral antibiotics for infections • Aspirin
- Nausea or vomiting tablets
- Motion sickness tablets • Diarrhea medication
- Pepto Bismol - for traveler's diarrhea *(turista)*
- Aromatic spirits of ammonia
- Mild antiseptic • Snakebite kit

General
- Petroleum jelly
- Rubbing alcohol
- Medical thermometer
- Tweezers
- Salt tablets
- GI can opener
- Insect repellent
- Baking soda
- Scissors & sewing kit
- Distilled water

Food
- Raisins in sealed packages
- Brown cane sugar in sealed packages

Nor'easter Hat

Metal Whistle

Money Belt

Waterproof Matches

Collapsible Cup

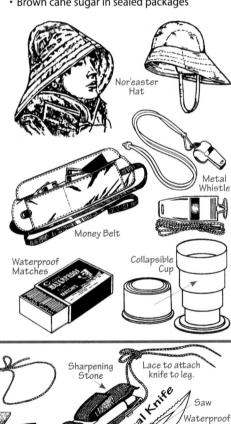

Sharpening Stone
Lace to attach knife to leg.
Compass
Saw
Waterproof Matches
Saw Holders
Sandpaper
Survival Knife
Survival Saw
Rubber waterproof grommet
Compass
Storage in handle.
Fish Line + Hooks
Sinkers
Tweezers

MINIMUM AIR FORCE SURVIVAL KIT

- High quality pocket knife with at least two cutting blades.
- Match safe with matches. • Pocket compass.
- Plastic or container. • Snare wire - small hank.
- Waterproof kitchen-type matches *(cushion heads against friction)*, or waterproof matches rolled in paraffin-soaked muslin in an easily opened container such as small soap box, toothbrush case, etc.
- Needles - sail maker's, surgeon's, and darning - at least one of each.
- Assorted fishhooks in heavy foil, tin, or plastic holders.
- Needle-nosed pliers with side cutters; high quality.
- Bar of surgical soap or hand soap
- Small fire starter of pyrophoric metal *(some plastic match cases have a strip of the metal anchored on the bottom outside of the case).*
- Personal medicines. • Bandaids®.
- Water purification tablets. • Insect repellent.

Secondary Items
- Colored cloth or scarf for signaling.
- Plastic water bottle. • Flexible saw *(wire saw)*.
- Sharpening stone. • Safety pins *(several sizes)*.
- Small steel mirror. • Aluminum foil.

Additional Items
- Travel toothbrush • Surgical tape.
- Penlight with batteries. • Clear plastic bags.
- Fish line - mono filament. • Fishing sinkers.
- Emergency ration can opener. • Gill net.
- Small, high quality candies.

Personal Medical Kit
- Sterile gauze compress bandage.
- Antibiotic ointment • Skin antiseptic.
- Aspirin tablets.

Reversible Poncho

Emergency Blanket Lightweight aluminized polyethylene that reflects heat back to body.

Cotton Hat

Poncho Sleeping cover and groundsheet

Backpack Poncho

SEAM SEAL

Tent Repair

Filleting Knife

Hip Pouch

Folding Saw

Stainless Coffee Cup

Hand Warmers Activated by removing from pouch and shaking. Can last up to six hours. Put in gloves or pockets.

Glowsticks Low power light. Last up to 12 hours. Weatherproof.

Tarpaulin

Camping Egg Container

Sierra Cup

Cotton Shorts

Tweezers + Magnifying Glass To remove splints or look for ticks.

Military Folding Shovel

FIRST AID

...are Air Mattress Plugs

WILDERNESS EMERGENCY KIT

Signaling and Orientation
- Signal mirror
- Compass
- Whistle
- Flare
- Waterproof match container

Shelter and Warmth
- Poncho or emergency blanket.
- Warm parka for cold nights.
- Warm waterproof boots. • Tube tent.

Food
- Pot to cook, collect water etc.
- Maple sugar or brown sugar to give you strength for 4 days.
- Tea bags and broth cubes.
- Water purification tablets or filtration system.
- Canteen or water bottle. • Mess kit

Tools
- Ax or heavy knife
- Sewing kit
- Brass wire for snares
- Fishing kit
- String / leather thong for emergency repairs.
- Rope 12' to 24' long • Flashlight & batteries.
- Gun not of prime importance.

First Aid
- First aid kit
- Snakebite kit
- Insect repellent
- Moleskin for sore feet.
- Salt tablets
- Baking soda
- Table salt
- Bottle of distilled water
- Rubbing alcohol
- Cotton applicators
- Bandages
- Tube of petroleum jelly
- Aspirin
- Mild antiseptic
- Tweezers
- Thick blunt needle
- Feminine napkins
- Scissors
- Sterile gauze dressings, individually wrapped (2"x2" & 4"x4").
- Piece of clean folded old bed sheet
- Roll of 1/2" wide adhesive tape
- Small bottle of aromatic spirits of ammonia.

First Aid Kit

Water Purifier

Dynamo Flashlight

Water Purification Tablets

Survival Candle

Signal Mirror Gerber®

Compact Binoculars

Map Compass

EMERGENCY KITS

Tube Tent

Pocket Compass

Sportsman's Plus 50 Soap

Sewing Kit

Army Canteen Wet the covering material and when the water evaporates the water in the flask will cool.

Ground Sheet or Tarpaulin

Flint
Striker Pin

Making the spark.

Flint Fire Starter

Ax + Case

Magnesium Fire Starter

Flint Bar

Pepper/Salt Shaker made from a 35mm film canister

Rope

Bungee Cord

Warm Blanket

Hot/Cold Insulated Canteen

Fire Starter — COGHLAN'S FIRE PASTE Quick Clean Fire Starter — Squeezes on starts campfires barbecues fireplaces Primes stoves — NET WEIGHT 3.75 oz.

Bungee Cord

Folding Saw

Mother didn't put me wise on flannel washing

MOSQUITOES

Some of the latest studies on mosquitoes show the following:

- Mosquitoes seem to be attracted to taller people and ones that are fidgety. Tall and fidgety people exhale more carbon dioxide which attracts mosquitoes. If you are swatting at the mosquitoes and moving all the time you will attract more mosquitoes.
- Mosquitoes do not die after biting but can bite up to six times.
- Only female mosquitoes feed on humans and they will lay 200 eggs after biting.
- Mosquitoes live two weeks and some females up to 5 months.
- Upon biting the mosquito injects saliva into the body to help extract the blood. This saliva causes the itching.
- Mosquitoes can detect humans from as far away as 20 feet (6m). They are attracted by heat, moisture and carbon dioxide. All of these factors are increased if you are moving a lot on a warm day.
- The movement of the wings causes the mosquito to produce the high pitched whine.
- One million malaria deaths are caused by mosquitoes each year.

Best Mosquito Repellent

The best repellents contain "N.N-diet-m-toluamide" known as DEET. This is the most effective long term repellent. Check for children. A natural repellent which is nearly as effective contains oil of citronella.

Home Remedies
Insect Repellent

The pioneers used "Nessmuk Juice" made of:
- 3 oz. (90 ml) pine tar.
- 2 oz. (60 ml) castor oil.
- 1 oz. (30 ml) pennyroyal oil.

Slowly simmer over a low fire until it becomes a pasty substance and smear it on your body. Have your friends do the same or you will have no friends.

FIRST AID

Insect Bites page 598

MOSQUITO REPELLENT

Add 10 drops of oil of thyme and 20 drops of pennyroyal to olive oil, lard or add to your favorite sun block.

To Keep Bugs Away

Pour some sweet sticky syrup or molasses some 20 feet (6 m) upwind from your shelter and most bugs will converge on this spot and not in your living and cooking area.

Sting Stopper

To neutralize the stinging sensation of a mosquito bite wet the area with some saliva or water and pass a bar of soap over the spot. This will usually stop the stinging and itching sensation.

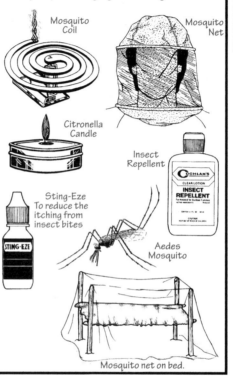

Mosquito Coil

Mosquito Net

Citronella Candle

Insect Repellent

COGHLAN'S CLEAR LOTION INSECT REPELLENT

Sting-Eze To reduce the itching from insect bites

STING-EZE

Aedes Mosquito

Mosquito net on bed.

Protect your OFF!

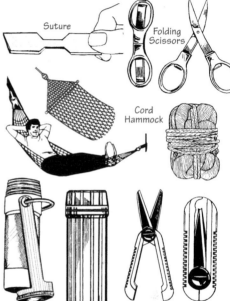

Suture

Folding Scissors

Cord Hammock

Waterproof Match Containers   Folding Scissors

EMERGENCY FISHING KIT

- 35mm film container for storage and as a float.
- Different sized hooks. • Round sinkers.
- Piece of waterproof emery paper to sharpen hooks.
- 15' of mono filament line (at least 10 pound test).
- A sewing needle (use mono filament to do any emergency repairs).
- Rubber bands.

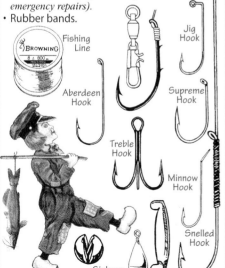

BROWNING 8 ÷ 800

Fishing Line

Jig Hook

Aberdeen Hook

Supreme Hook

Treble Hook

Minnow Hook

Snelled Hook

Sinkers

EMERGENCY KIT

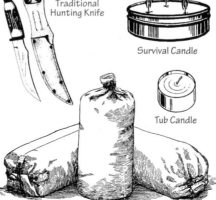

Maglite Flashlight

Maglite Flashlight Camo

Traditional Hunting Knife

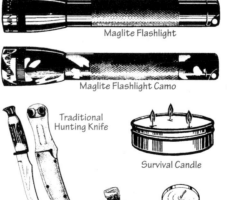

Survival Candle

Tub Candle

BEE & WASP STING RELIEF with BAKING SODA

AFTER STING Gel FAST RELIEF FROM BEE & WASP STINGS SOOTHING GEL FORMULA with natural repellents

BEE & WASP STING GEL

Tender CORPORATION

NEW AfterBite KIDS

TEA TREE OIL EUCALYPTUS OIL ALOE VERA & VITAMINE CREAM FORMULA

SPECIAL CREAM FORMULA

Fast, Gentle Relief from insect bites & other minor skin irritations

Special non-stinging cream formula

AfterBite KIDS

Tender CORPORATION Contents 0.7oz. (20g)

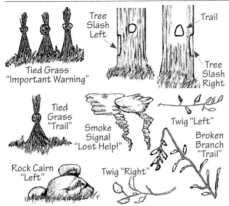

Tree Slash Left

Trail

Tied Grass "Important Warning"

Tree Slash Right

Tied Grass "Trail"

Smoke Signal "Lost Help!"

Twig "Left"

Broken Branch "Trail"

Rock Cairn "Left"

Twig "Right"

TRAILBLAZING

To mark a route in the forest you can:
See Signal Chapter page 394

- Break branches in the direction you are taking.
- Hack marks on trees - one gash in the direction of travel and two gashes on the return side. This method should not be overused otherwise fairly soon every tree will have blazes.
- Break a branch in the direction of the turn in your trail.
- The Indians of the Eastern United States deformed trees in the direction of travel. They would pull a branch of a sapling in the direction of travel and tie it down with vines and this would grow into a permanent marker.
- The Indians of British Columbia used cedar chips, dropped from the back of their boat into the water, to mark their route in the fog.
- The "cairn" is currently used on many trails. These can be made of snow, ice, rocks, and wood.

Insulated Water Canteen

DESERT TRAVEL

Page 79

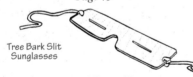

Tree Bark Slit Sunglasses

Protect Your Eyes

Wear sunglasses to prevent sun fatigue or improvise sunglasses (slit goggles) if needed.

INSECTS & ANIMALS

Rabid Animal Attack

When you are attacked by a suspected rabid animal such as a raccoon, wolf, coyote, wild dog, bat, or fox, do not run as you will expose your back, the back of your legs, and your ankles. Grab a stick or use a clenched fist to hit the animal across its snout. This is very painful and the animal might fall to the ground in a stupor or beat a fast retreat.

Animal Repellent

Spray ammonia on your trash. This will keep curious animals away.

Porcupine Repellent

Use moth balls to keep porcupines away from camp areas and the cottage. Porcupines are always looking for salt and will eat through treated wood and leather.

Lice Repellent

Camphor, carried in your pocket, can be used against body lice.

Ant Stopper

Use a piece of white chalk to mark lines on the table legs or eating area. This should keep most non-flying insects away.

Tick Check

Check for ticks and tick bits every day or after walking through grassy areas.

If you find one, cover it with petroleum jelly or oil to kill the tick. Apply hydrogen peroxide to kill any germs at the entry point. If the head remains stuck, see a doctor. *See the article on Lyme Disease in the First Aid Chapter.*

BAKING SODA

This is a standby of campers and hikers.

Major uses are...

- Foot powder   • Toothpaste
- Antacid: 1/2 teaspoon in cup of water.
- Insect Bites: Mix baking soda with a small quantity of water to make a paste. Apply the paste to the bite. Do not apply too much as when it dries it will fall off. A light coating will only crack.
- Eliminate Odor: Use on the body as deodorizer or on coolers or other food containers. Wash hands with soda after cleaning animals or fish to remove any lingering odor. To avoid having a stale odor in canteens, sprinkle some baking soda in them before storing.

Eye Glass Cords

If you wear glasses, this is a required item in the wilds. You will know that your glasses are around your neck and will not be mislaid or sat on. The cord will prevent you from losing your glasses while climbing or fishing.

UV RADIATION

Protection from sun exposure is important all year round, not just during the summer or at the beach. Any time the sun's ultraviolet (UV) rays are able to reach the earth, you need to protect yourself from excessive sun exposure. UV rays can cause skin damage during any season or temperature. Relatively speaking, the hours between 9 a.m. and 4 p.m. are the most hazardous for UV exposure. UV radiation is the greatest during the late spring and early summer in North America. Remember: UV rays reach you on cloudy and hazy days, as well as on bright and sunny days. UV rays will also reflect off any surface like water, cement, sand, and snow.

The level of UV radiation that reaches the earth's surface is dependent on several factors.

Ozone: The stratospheric ozone layer protects all life on earth from excessive exposure to UV radiation from the sun. Ozone depletion, as well as seasonal and weather variations, causes different amounts of UV radiation to reach the Earth at any given time.

Intensity: The sun's intensity varies throughout the day much like visible light. Around noon, the sun is at its highest, so the sun's rays have less distance to travel through the atmosphere and the intensity is highest.

Time of year: Time of year causes the intensity of UV rays to vary.

Geographical location: The sun's rays are strongest at the equator, where the sun is most directly overhead.

Altitude: UV intensity increases with altitude because there is less atmosphere to absorb the damaging rays.

Weather: Cloud cover reduces the amount of UV radiation reaching the earth.

Reflection: UV rays are reflected off surfaces such as snow, water, sand, and concrete.

UV RAYS = SKIN CANCER

Premature Aging • Cataracts

UV exposure appears to be the most important environmental factor in the development of skin cancer and a primary factor in the development of lip cancer. Although getting some sun exposure can yield a few positive benefits, excessive and unprotected exposure to the sun can result in the immediate effect of sunburn but over time premature aging and undesirable changes in skin texture. Such exposure has been associated with various types of skin cancer, including melanoma, one of the most serious and deadly forms. UV rays also have been found to be associated with various eye conditions, such as cataracts, and immune system suppression.

SKIN CANCER

Skin type is the most important factor in determining a person's risk for skin cancer. Skin types range from those individuals that burn easily and never suntan to those who do not burn at all. Some individual characteristics that are risk factors for skin cancer include:

- Fair skin. Blue, green, or hazel eyes.
- Light-colored hair.
- Tendency to burn rather than suntan, history of severe burns, many moles, freckles.
- Family history of skin cancer.

Even people with dark complexions can get a sunburn. No one is exempt from the possibility of getting skin cancer or other serious health problems from the sun's UV rays.

SUNGLASSES

Feature	Type/Color	Notes
Protection from sunlight	99% UV elimination/any color	A required feature.
To drive		Sunglasses that are not too dark.
High contrast	Yellow, amber, rose	Increase perception of details, for hunting, skiing, mountain biking.
See through water surface	Polaroid	Eliminate reflections. For fishing.
Shadow and sunlight	Photochromics/variable density	Hiking, general use.
Bright snow and sun	Slit glasses (Inuit). Dark top and bottom, light centre.	For skiing, winter hiking.
Limited color distortion	Gray or green	Photography, painting, seeing nature.
Plastic lenses	Will not shatter	Easily get scratched.
Frames	Quality plastic	Stand up better than thin metal frames.
Lens size	Get largest possible	Wider angle of vision.
Glass lenses	Better quality	High optical grinding, distortion free and scratch resistant.

SNAKES & CAMPING

Except for a few species, snakes tend to be shy or passive. Unless they are injured, trapped, or disturbed, snakes usually avoid contact with humans. The harmless species are often more prone to attack. All species of snakes are usually aggressive during their breeding season.

Land Snakes

Many snakes are active during the period from twilight to daylight. Avoid walking as much as possible during this time.

- Keep your hands off rock ledges where snakes are likely to be sunning.
- Look around carefully before sitting down, particularly if in deep grass among rocks.
- Attempt to camp on clean, level ground.
- Avoid camping near piles of brush, rocks, or other debris.
- Avoid swimming in areas where there are many snakes.
- Sleep on camping cots or anything that will keep you off the ground. Avoid sleeping on the ground if at all possible.
- Avoid walking about an area during the period from dusk to complete daylight, as many snakes are active during this period.
- Check the other side of a large rock before stepping over it. When looking under any rock, pull it toward you as you turn it over so that it will shield you in case a snake is beneath it.
- Try to walk only in open areas. Avoid walking close to rock walls or similar areas where snakes may be hiding.
- Determine when possible what species of snakes are likely to be found in an area which you are about to enter.

Hike with another person.
Avoid hiking alone in a snake-infested area. If bitten, it is important to have at least one companion to perform lifesaving first aid measures and to kill the snake. Providing the snake to medical personnel will facilitate both identification and treatment.

Handle freshly killed venomous snakes only with a long tool or stick. Snakes can inflict fatal bites by reflex action even after death.

Wear heavy boots and clothing for some protection from snakebite. Keep this in mind when exposed to hazardous conditions.

Eliminate conditions under which snakes thrive: brush, piles of trash, rocks, or logs and dense undergrowth. Controlling their food (rodents, small animals) as much as possible is also good prevention.

ARTHROPODS & ANIMALS
Spiders, Scorpions & Centipedes

In many locations worldwide, centipedes are more of a problem than scorpions.

- Remove spiders from tents.
- Shake out and inspect clothing, shoes, and bedding before use.
- Clear the campsite of scrap wood and other debris to eliminate the resting/ hiding areas of spiders and scorpions.
- Thoroughly clean beneath and behind large items; spiders and scorpions may be resting in these areas.
- Check outdoor latrines before use; run a small stick under the rim of the latrine hole to dislodge any spiders or scorpions. Spiders and scorpions may rest under toilet seat or inside latrine box.
- Wear gloves when handling paper, cloth, lumber, or other items that have been stored for long periods.
- Check around rocks and logs before resting against them.
- Use a long-handled tool or stick to turn over debris before removing it.
- Wear leather gloves to remove rocks, lumber, and such from the ground.

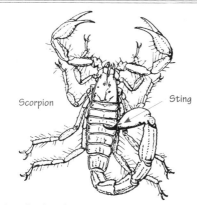

Scorpion   Sting

Meeting a Rattlesnake

SNAKE BITES

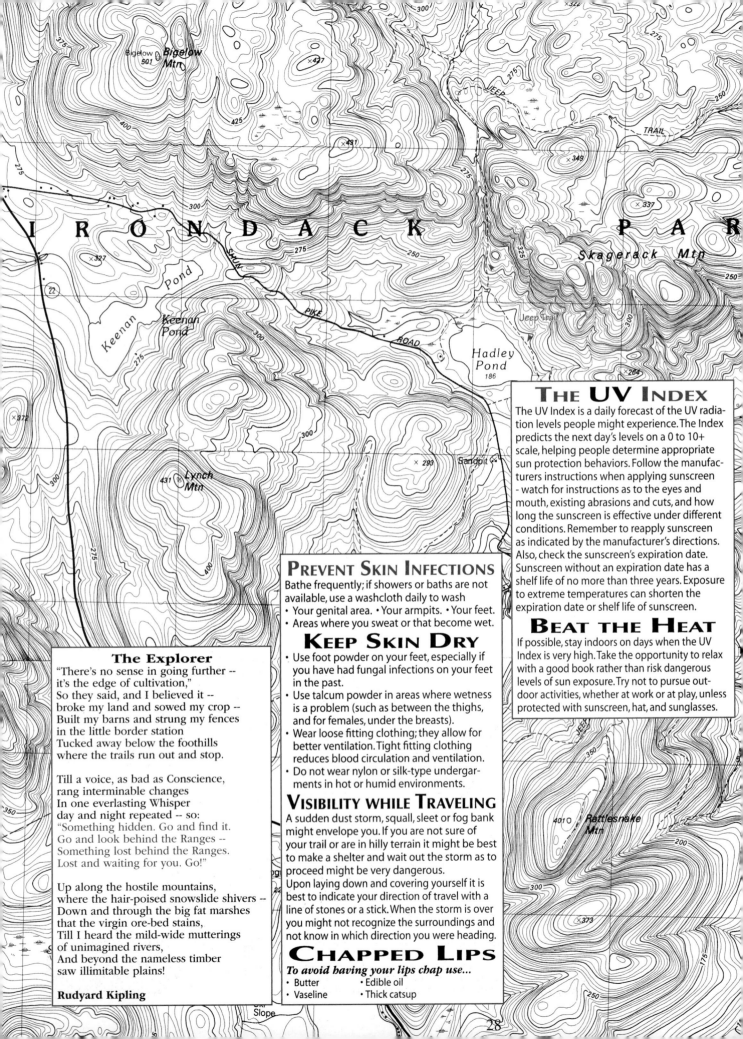

The UV Index

The UV Index is a daily forecast of the UV radiation levels people might experience. The Index predicts the next day's levels on a 0 to 10+ scale, helping people determine appropriate sun protection behaviors. Follow the manufacturers instructions when applying sunscreen - watch for instructions as to the eyes and mouth, existing abrasions and cuts, and how long the sunscreen is effective under different conditions. Remember to reapply sunscreen as indicated by the manufacturer's directions. Also, check the sunscreen's expiration date. Sunscreen without an expiration date has a shelf life of no more than three years. Exposure to extreme temperatures can shorten the expiration date or shelf life of sunscreen.

Beat the Heat

If possible, stay indoors on days when the UV Index is very high. Take the opportunity to relax with a good book rather than risk dangerous levels of sun exposure. Try not to pursue outdoor activities, whether at work or at play, unless protected with sunscreen, hat, and sunglasses.

Prevent Skin Infections

Bathe frequently; if showers or baths are not available, use a washcloth daily to wash
- Your genital area. • Your armpits. • Your feet.
- Areas where you sweat or that become wet.

Keep Skin Dry

- Use foot powder on your feet, especially if you have had fungal infections on your feet in the past.
- Use talcum powder in areas where wetness is a problem (such as between the thighs, and for females, under the breasts).
- Wear loose fitting clothing; they allow for better ventilation. Tight fitting clothing reduces blood circulation and ventilation.
- Do not wear nylon or silk-type undergarments in hot or humid environments.

Visibility while Traveling

A sudden dust storm, squall, sleet or fog bank might envelope you. If you are not sure of your trail or are in hilly terrain it might be best to make a shelter and wait out the storm as to proceed might be very dangerous.
Upon laying down and covering yourself it is best to indicate your direction of travel with a line of stones or a stick. When the storm is over you might not recognize the surroundings and not know in which direction you were heading.

Chapped Lips

To avoid having your lips chap use...
- Butter   • Edible oil
- Vaseline   • Thick catsup

The Explorer

"There's no sense in going further --
it's the edge of cultivation,"
So they said, and I believed it --
broke my land and sowed my crop --
Built my barns and strung my fences
in the little border station
Tucked away below the foothills
where the trails run out and stop.

Till a voice, as bad as Conscience,
rang interminable changes
In one everlasting Whisper
day and night repeated -- so:
"Something hidden. Go and find it.
Go and look behind the Ranges --
Something lost behind the Ranges.
Lost and waiting for you. Go!"

Up along the hostile mountains,
where the hair-poised snowslide shivers --
Down and through the big fat marshes
that the virgin ore-bed stains,
Till I heard the mild-wide mutterings
of unimagined rivers,
And beyond the nameless timber
saw illimitable plains!

Rudyard Kipling

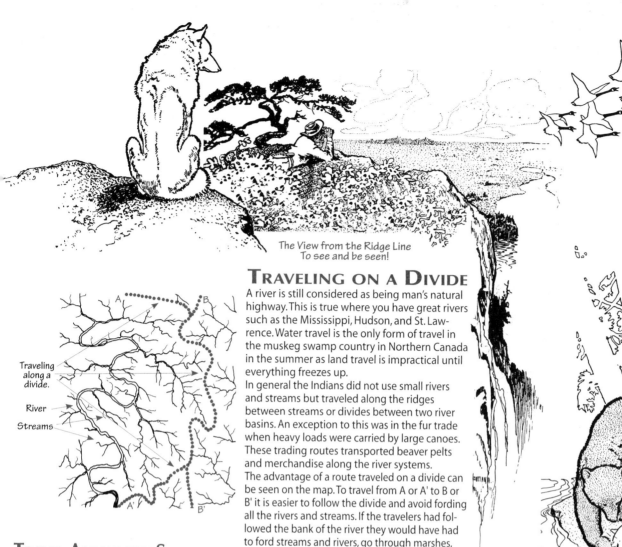

The View from the Ridge Line
To see and be seen!

Traveling along a divide.

River

Streams

TRAVELING ON A DIVIDE

A river is still considered as being man's natural highway. This is true where you have great rivers such as the Mississippi, Hudson, and St. Lawrence. Water travel is the only form of travel in the muskeg swamp country in Northern Canada in the summer as land travel is impractical until everything freezes up.

In general the Indians did not use small rivers and streams but traveled along the ridges between streams or divides between two river basins. An exception to this was in the fur trade when heavy loads were carried by large canoes. These trading routes transported beaver pelts and merchandise along the river systems.

The advantage of a route traveled on a divide can be seen on the map. To travel from A or A' to B or B' it is easier to follow the divide and avoid fording all the rivers and streams. If the travelers had followed the bank of the river they would have had to ford streams and rivers, go through marshes, swamps, dense thickets and also have to face the 'friendly' mosquitoes and blood suckers.

On ridges or divides, between two major river watersheds, the footing is usually better, vegetation is thinner, fallen trees are smaller, there is no mud or bog, and a better view of the surrounding area to help find your direction. In windblown areas there will hardly be any mosquitoes. If following a divide plan your trip, or take frequent sightings (climb a high tree), so that you do not end up in a dead end from which you have to descend to the lowlands.

Hiking & Climbing
Hikers in good condition can climb 1000 feet (300 meters) per hour. This varies with the type of terrain. On level ground the speed would be 2.5 - 4 miles per hour (4 - 7 km).

TRAVEL ALONG THE SHORELINE
OCEAN & SEA SHORES

Oceans are large bodies of water that are affected by tides and winds. If you are following the shore be careful of incoming waves. If an unexpected big wave arrives hold your footing, do not attempt to run. You will not be sure of your footing or the depth of the water. You might be caught in an undertow and be swept into deep water and drown. In general it is quite easy to follow the sea shore as there is usually a beach that has been created by the incoming waves and tides. Difficulties might be encountered when you are in an area where a river flows into the sea as it might be swampy with many islands. *See Rafting.*

RIVER & LAKE SHORES

The tributaries of rivers that run through a wide bottomland are likely to be deep or run over fathomless mud, sometimes quicksand and require long detours or be crossed with a raft or boat. The vegetation, in these areas, up to the very bank of the river can be exceedingly thick, a wretched tangle of bushes, vines, briers, tall grass, and fallen trees. In periods of heavy rain the river might rise out of its banks and maroon you on a high piece of land.

Rivers in mountain areas are swift and usually in gorges or steep valleys which would lead to numerous impassable dead ends. Each bend in the river will be a surprise and for this reason it would be best to cross the area on the divide.
See the article about traveling along a divide.

QUICKSAND

The sign of quicksand is the presence of water oozing upwards. This water keeps the sand and muck in suspension. There might be a thin crust on the surface.

If you step into quicksand or mire:
- Do not struggle.
- Trying to lift one foot makes the second foot sink deeper as all the weight is on one foot.
- Drop to your hands and knees and try to crawl slowly. The surface of your hands, knees and legs will distribute your weight over a wider area.
- If the mire is too soft and you feel that you are still sinking, lie flat on your stomach and move only one part of your body at a time. Try to float out of the quicksand by using snake like movements.

Divide or Ridge Line   Best route to take.

On ridges or divides, between two major river watersheds, the footing is usually better, vegetation is thinner, fallen trees are smaller, there is no mud or bog, and there is a better view of the surrounding area to help find your direction.

Coral Snake

CAMPING GEAR

To Choose a Bag

A good bag should distribute the weight of the cargo over your shoulders and hips. Meet your travel needs and be large enough.
See article for women.

Factors to consider...

Volume: To determine the size of bag required assemble everything that you will take for the trip. Place these items in a large garbage bag and measure, in inches or centimeters, the height, width and length of the filled bag. Multiply these numbers and you will have the number of cubic inches or centimeters of volume you require for your bag. Buy a bag with this volume.

Torso Length: Every person has a different "drop". The "drop" is the length from the bottom of your neck to the hollow in your back (waist). The bag should have adjustments on the back panel to accommodate your torso length.

Width of Back: Your bag should be narrow enough for your elbows, while hiking, to swing back and forth with limited interference.

Adjustments: There should be a range of adjustments on the harness to adapt the bag to fit comfortably to your body.

Harness: Select a well padded harness.

Hip Belt: The hip belt should be cushioned and have adjustment straps ("trim straps") on the sides. These will let you adjust the belt to hug your waist without pressing your stomach. The hip belt should support 2/3 of the bag's weight.

Pockets: Check that pockets, strap attachments, add-on pouches are what you require.

Filling a Backpack

- Place no hard objects against your back.
- Place all small items in transparent plastic bags so that they will not fall to the bottom, or place them in the side pockets.
- Place heavy items at the upper center of the back and close to the body. The lighter items are placed further from the back.
- Backpack should be internally divided to help separate and organize items.

The vertical location of heavy items varies upon the type of terrain. If the terrain is smooth place the heavy items higher in the bag. This will raise the center of gravity of the bag and more weight will be carried by the hips. If the terrain is uneven or you are traveling with reduced visibility pack heavy items at the bottom and close to the body. This also applies to skiing, biking and mountain climbing. This will lower the center of gravity.

- Women have a different weight distribution than men (a heavier posterior) and therefore should pack heavy objects at a lower level.
- Items such as maps, cameras, water bottles, compass, some food should be packed in an accessible location. Make efficient use of the pockets and partitions in the backpack.
- Items such as wet clothing and fuel bottles should be placed in plastic bags to avoid leakage.

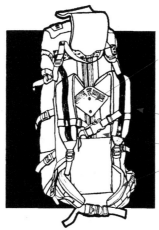

Torso Suspension
To adjust the shoulder strap fit to the length from nape of neck to the waist of the individual.

Curved Shoulder Straps

Sternum Strap

Waist Suspension

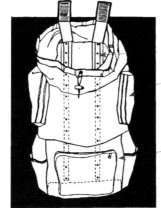

Pre-contoured Stays

Side Pockets

Zippered opening to lower pouch.

Internal Frame Backpack

Modern backpacks have a curved back (or one that can be adapted to the back by bending the aluminum support rods). There also is a padded waist strap that, when attached and adjusted for your body, carries 2/3 the weight of the bag on your hips. This relieves your shoulders and backbone of some weight.

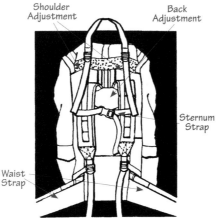

Shoulder Adjustment

Back Adjustment

Sternum Strap

Waist Strap

Spindrift Collar

Accessory Patch

Divider

Compression Straps

Ice Ax Loop

Kelty Backpack

Shoulder Adjustment

Back Adjustment

Waist Strap

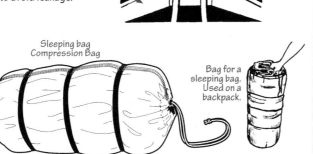

Strap to attach sleeping bag to a backpacks.

Luggage Strap

Sleeping bag Compression Bag

Bag for a sleeping bag. Used on a backpack.

Internal Frame Backpack

Bag Damage

Check the bag for damage before and after use. Check that:

- No buckles are missing or bent.
- Straps and seams are not torn or parting.
- No parts are rubbing the body of the bag. These can be the internal frame, external frame, ice ax, etc.
- Hot embers have not burnt holes into the bag. Fix the problem before the material unravels.

Spare Buckles

Frames should be strong, lightweight with deeply curved cross members. The curves should follow your back's contour and bring the center of gravity closer to your body. If a bag is not comfortable and cannot be adjusted - do not buy it.

Padded hip belt to adapt to your unique shape.

Good selection of outside pockets for items that have to be accessible.

Mesh back bands for good ventilation and adjust to the shape of the back.

Packs should be internally divided to help separate and organize items.

Lash points let you attach optional bags, sleeping pads or other accessories.

EXTERNAL FRAME BACKPACK

Stretch Cord

Baby Pack External Frame

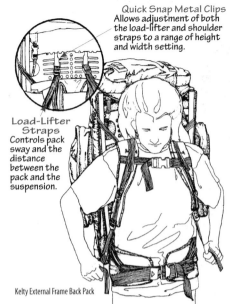

Quick Snap Metal Clips
Allows adjustment of both the load-lifter and shoulder straps to a range of height and width setting.

Load-Lifter Straps
Controls pack sway and the distance between the pack and the suspension.

Kelty External Frame Back Pack

Insulation Mat

Bungee Cord
Always useful on a trip.

Quick Snap Metal Clips
Allows adjustment of both the load-lifter and shoulder straps to a range of height and width setting.

Load-Lifter Straps
Controls pack sway and the distance between the pack and the suspension.

Breathable Mesh Back Band
Adjusts in tension to allow the body to settle deeply into the frame, making the pack stable and keeping the weight off the shoulder and over the legs.

Shoulder Straps
Curved and tapered, with all seams on top to reduce chafing.

Sternum Strap
Adjusts in height with quick-release Velcro and has a thin profile to reduce arm chafe.

D-Rings On Shoulder Straps
Allows a camera or canteen to be carried without dangling it around the neck.

Shoulder Strap Tightening Buckle
Located on top of foam so it isn't pressing into wearer's sides.

Sway Control Straps
Controls the amount of independent motion between the waist belt and the pack.

Tri-Layer Sculpted Waist Belt
Combines two types of foam with an outer polyethylene laminate to give a sculpted belt that transfers the pack's weight over the tops and sides of the hip bones positively and painlessly. The removable belt comes in three sizes: Women's, Regular, Extra Large.

Waist Belt's Conical Flare Adjustment Strap
Fine-tunes the waist belt to individual hip shapes.

Small-Of-Back Adjustment Straps
Controls the tension with which the waist belt is held to the frame at its top, middle and bottom points. This in turn controls the fit of the waist belt in the small of the back.

Kelty Backpack

TYPES OF BACKPACKS
Day Pack & Rucksack
For day trips and rock climbing. Choose one that is small and well balanced. It should be easy to load with some external pockets, some lash points for extra items, padded shoulders and a waist strap for stability.
External Frame
Is made to carry heavy loads on long excursions. Most of the weight is carried on the hips. As the frame keeps the bag off your back you will be more comfortable on a hot day (see First Aid on prickly heat). Additional items can be attached to the framing and the frame can include a head strap to help balance a heavy load.
Internal Frame
Rides closer to the back giving you a better balance and usually slimmer and easier to maneuver on tight trails. In difficult terrain, biking, skiing or mountain climbing, an internal frame has a tighter fit and a lower center of gravity - have less tendency to shift. When carrying a smaller load, at the end of the trip, the bag can be easily adjusted.
Convertible Luggage
Can be either a backpack or a suitcase. The harness can be covered with a zippered cloth panel which is useful when the bag is checked as airplane luggage.
Pack Board
Used to carry very heavy objects such as boat motors or batteries. It is very flexible because anything can be lashed onto it.
See US Army Pack Board - Page 33.

BACKPACKS FOR WOMEN
Women have to choose a backpack to fit their physique. Some companies manufacture women's models.
Torso Length or Drop
Women usually have shorter torsos than men so that a man's backpack and hip straps will ride too low and the women's shoulders will have to carry most of the load.
Shoulder Harness
Women usually have narrower shoulders and regular shoulder straps will slip off especially when going up or down hills.
Harness Pads
Unisex pads are usually too wide, and lack the required curvature. They cause chafing at the armpits. This is because the up and down movement of the arms. Wide pads will also restrict the breasts.
Hip Belts
Men's hip belts do not accommodate a woman's profile. The bottom of the pad digs into the woman's hip.

WELL BALANCED BAG

Center of Gravity

Center of Gravity

Well Balanced Pack

Badly Packed

US Army Frame Pack

This frame pack is of a modular design to which you can add adjustable shelves and pouches.

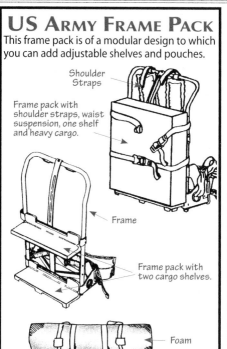

Frame pack with shoulder straps, waist suspension, one shelf and heavy cargo.

Shoulder Straps

Frame

Frame pack with two cargo shelves.

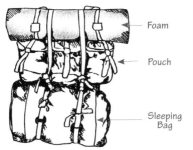

Foam

Pouch

Sleeping Bag

Frames with pouches, sleeping bag, and sleeping bag foam. Note two ways of carrying sleeping gear.

Pouch

Foam

Sleeping Bag

US Army Pack Board

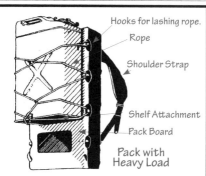

Hooks for lashing rope.
Rope
Shoulder Strap
Shelf Attachment
Pack Board

Pack with Heavy Load

Excellent for carrying heavy items that can be lashed down. The bag has a waist belt and also a forehead band for extra carrying power. The pack board is carried vertically with a light load but with a heavy load it is carried tilted forward so that the weight is spread over the back and on the forehead. This pack can carry 200 pounds (90 kg).

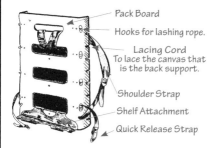

Pack Board
Hooks for lashing rope.
Lacing Cord
To lace the canvas that is the back support.
Shoulder Strap
Shelf Attachment
Quick Release Strap

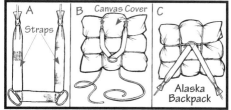

A
Straps
B   Canvas Cover
C
Alaska Backpack

Backpack Poncho

Hiker from the 1870's

Indian Head Pack

This pack was made of a tanned deer skin. The whole hide was used as one piece. Cargo was put in the opening and the front legs (legs near the opening) were also stuffed into the opening. The hind legs were tied together and carried on the forehead.

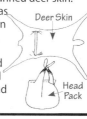

Deer Skin

Head Pack

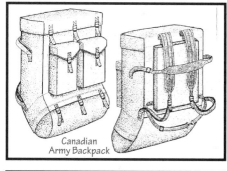

Canadian Army Backpack

US Army Duffel Bag

These heavy canvas bags can be used to carry tents, tent poles, and pots. The material is strong so that it will not split. The bags close securely. The bags can be easily transported in the car, a camper, by boat, by airplane, by snowmobile, dragged or as a backpack.

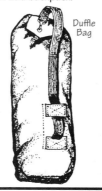

Duffle Bag

Duffle Bag with shoulder straps.

Portaging Bag

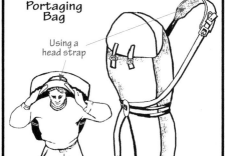

Using a head strap

Resting

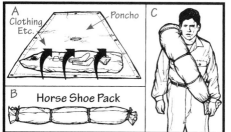

A
Clothing Etc.
Poncho
C

B   Horse Shoe Pack

Shorten Nylon Strap

Cut with scissors or knife and then seal cut edge by holding a match to the end. This will fuse the frayed edge.

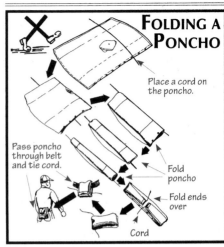

FOLDING A PONCHO

Place a cord on the poncho.

Pass poncho through belt and tie cord.

Fold poncho

Fold ends over

Cord

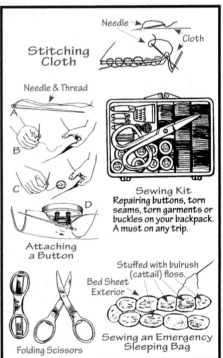

Stitching Cloth

Needle

Cloth

Needle & Thread

A

B

C

D

Sewing Kit
Repairing buttons, torn seams, torn garments or buckles on your backpack. A must on any trip.

Attaching a Button

Stuffed with bulrush (cattail) floss.

Bed Sheet Exterior

Sewing an Emergency Sleeping Bag

Folding Scissors

Day Packs

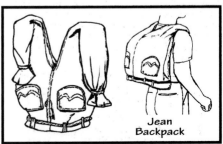

Jean Backpack

CHOICE OF FOOT GEAR

Your feet are extremely sensitive, especially when walking. Frequently the shoes are the problem.

- **Size of shoe:** If too small it will restrict the movement of your bones and muscles. Poor circulation of the blood will cause your feet to be cold. If too large or too wide the heel will move, up and down or laterally, and you will not be sure of your footing.
- When wearing boots try to buy socks for your foot size.
- **Sole material:** Leather can be very slippery in the woods. A better choice is a well indented rubber composite sole.
- **Upper of shoe or boot:** Avoid rubber boat shoes or hunting boots that have a high rubber foot. Rubber does not breath and humidity will build up in the boot. It will be too hot and you will literally cook your feet or in cooler weather, with the accumulation of humidity, you will have cold and clammy feet.
- **Shoelace:** The Canadian Army uses a loose woven round nylon shoelace that stretches and contracts depending upon the fit of the boot. The lace does not undo as it is always under tension. The stretching also helps when the foot is swelling.
- The best choice for the top of a boot is leather or a modern breathable synthetic material.
- **Waterproofing:** Sole should be fused onto the upper of the shoe. Avoid too many stitches on the upper part of the boot. They can leak or break open.
- The boot should have a steel shank to give you long term support at the arch.

Well rounded top so that it does not cut into the calf.

Tongue

Traction Ribs on Soles

Leather Inner Lining

Quality Laces
Laces that tie easily and do not slip.

Leather Uppers
With a minimum of seams.

Heel
Well formed to offer good support.

Steel Shank

Oil Resistant Sole

FOOT CARE

Foot care involves good hygiene measures such as bathing frequently, using foot powder, wearing properly fitted footwear to allow for ventilation, and correctly trimming toenails.

Foot Hygiene

The care of minor foot ailments should be given the utmost attention. Many major conditions requiring hospitalization and disability have resulted from neglected or maltreated minor conditions.

Walk Conditioning

Conditioning is accomplished by progressively increasing the distance to be walked from day to day. Walking is a good way to strengthen the feet and legs; running alone will not suffice. The arch, ankle, and calf can be conditioned by performing simple exercises - for example, rising high on the toes or placing the feet on towels and using the toes to roll the towel back under the arch.

AVOIDING FOOT PROBLEMS

Certain preventive measures can be implemented to avoid painful foot problems.

Before Major Hikes: Trim toenails at least every two or three weeks, depending upon individual needs. Cut toenails short and square, and straight across. Keep feet clean and dry, and use foot powder. Wear clean, dry, unmended, good-fitting socks (preferably cushion-soled) with seams and knots outside. A nylon or polypropylene sock liner can reduce friction and add protection. Carry an extra pair of socks. Carefully fit new boots. When getting used to a new pair of boots, alternate with another pair; tape known hot spots before wearing.

During Halts: Lie down with the feet elevated during each halt. If time permits, massage the feet, apply foot powder, change socks, and medicate blisters. Cover open blisters, cuts, or abrasions with absorbent adhesive bandages. Obtain relief from swelling feet by slightly loosening bootlaces where they cross the arch of the foot.

After Hiking: Repeat procedures for the care of feet, wash and dry socks, and dry boots. Medicate blisters, abrasions, corns, and calluses. Inspect painful feet for sprains and improper fitting of socks and boots. Feet can develop red, swollen, tender skin along the sides of the feet from prolonged marching, which could become blisters. Therefore, feet require aeration, elevation, rest, and wider footwear. Prevent major foot problems by keeping the feet clean. The formation of blisters and abrasions with dirt and perspiration can cause infection and serious injury. If possible, give the feet a daily foot bath. In the field, cool water seems to reduce the sensation of heat and irritation. After washing, dry the feet well.

FOOT GEAR

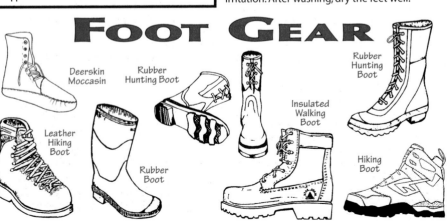

Deerskin Moccasin

Rubber Hunting Boot

Rubber Hunting Boot

Leather Hiking Boot

Rubber Boot

Insulated Walking Boot

Hiking Boot

Foot Injuries
Blisters & Abrasions

Common causes of blisters and abrasions are improperly conditioned feet, ill-fitting footwear and socks, improperly maintained footwear, heat, and moisture. They are normally caused by friction or pressure, as opposed to impact.

- To clean a blister, wash gently around it with soap and water, being careful not to break the skin. If unbroken, use a sterilized needle or knife point to prick the lower edge of the blister to remove fluid. (To sterilize needle or knife point, hold in a flame.) Do not remove the skin; cover the blister with an absorbent adhesive bandage or similar dressing, extending beyond the edge of the blister. After applying the dressing, dust the outside of the dressing and entire foot with foot powder.
- Use just enough foot power since it can harden and become irritating. Foot powder lessens friction on the skin and prevents the raw edges of the adhesive plaster from adhering to socks. The adhesive plaster should be smooth so it can serve as a "second skin." Check the blister periodically for proper drying. After the blister has dried, remove the adhesive plaster. Carefully inspect the foot for other problem areas that are red and tender that may need the protection of an adhesive plaster. Cover abrasions and cuts on the foot with absorbent adhesive bandages for rapid healing. In an emergency get medical attention.

Perspiration Problems

When feet perspire, the secretion decomposes and causes a foul odor. The skin between the toes usually becomes white and soft, rubs off easily, and is prone to abrasions. Treatment consists of washing and thoroughly drying the feet, and carefully painting the affected area with a cotton swab and a solution and application instructions provided by your pharmacy.

Athlete's Foot

Athlete's foot usually occurs between the toes, on the sole of the foot, and at points of contact between skin and footwear. This and other mild chronic cases of fungus infection may respond to daily foot powder applications. If fungicidal ointment is available, it can be used in addition to foot powder. Ointment should be used as directed and while the feet are at rest. If applications of foot powder and ointment do not heal the infection, *get medical attention.*

Protect Your Feet
You Need Them!

In all types of foot gear, feet perspire more and are generally less well ventilated than other parts of the body. Moisture accumulates in socks, decreasing their insulating quality. The feet are susceptible to cold injury and are less frequently observed than the remainder of the body.

- Bring several pairs of socks with you.
- Keep socks clean and dry. Change wet or damp socks as soon as possible. Socks can become wet from sweating.
- Apply foot powder on feet and in boots when changing socks.
- Avoid tight socks and boots (completely lace boots up as loosely as possible).
- Wash your feet daily.

Care of Footwear

Boots must be dried after use to avoid losing shape and hardening of the leather. This can be done by placing a warm cloth in the boot or by any method that avoids rapid drying. To prevent moist leather from freezing during winter, boots should be placed inside a sleeping bag or used as a headrest.

Boot Fitting

When buying boots or shoes remember that your feet will swell while traveling. If too large or too wide the heel will move, up and down or laterally, and you will not be sure of your footing. Two important factors in fitting boots are: the space between the end of the great toe and the toe of the boot should be the width of the thumb; and, in the unlaced boot, there should be enough space under the lower edge of the tongue to insert an index finger

- Poorly fitted boots can cause blisters, abrasions, calluses, and corns. Pressure is caused by boots being too small; friction is caused by boots being too large. If the tops of the toes are involved, the cap is too low or too stiff. If the ends of the toes are affected, the boot is too short or too loosely laced. If the sides of the big and little toes become irritated, the boot is too narrow. Irritation at the heel is caused by boots being too long, too loosely laced, or too wide a heel space.
- Proper lacing of boots not only prevents blisters but also prevents improper blood flow in the foot. Laces can assume a seesaw action, which can produce a long blister across the instep. To prevent blistering, lacing over the instep can be avoided. If possible, broad laces should be used and an extra pair should be carried.

Reduce Pain by Correct Lacing

Lacing Hiking Boots: The way you lace your hiking boot changes the pressure points in your boot and changes the feel of your boot.

Pressure Point that Hurts: Bypass the eyelets that are near that spot.

High Arch: Tie the laces so that the lower layer does not cross from side to side but goes up on the side.

Pressure on the Toe: Run one side of the lace back and forth and the second lace goes up diagonally. This method is frequently used for army boots.

Improve the Fit of the Heal: To remove the pressure from the heal lace the boot but do not lace the last top hole or holes.

Boot Liners

Remove the felt liners from winter boots when not in use as this will let them dry out. The best type of felt liners are those that are made of woven wool which are then cooked in boiling water which mats the wool and it looks like felt. Boots having this type of lining are used by the Canadian Army and are rated to -58°F (-50°C).

Boots should be large enough so that the toes can wiggle. Check fit while standing up.

Trim toenails before going on a hike. This will save your socks and avoid rubbing against the upper inside of your boots.

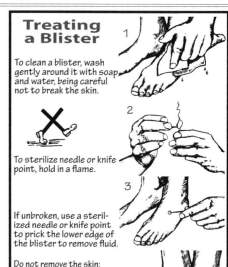

Treating a Blister

To clean a blister, wash gently around it with soap and water, being careful not to break the skin.

To sterilize needle or knife point, hold in a flame.

If unbroken, use a sterilized needle or knife point to prick the lower edge of the blister to remove fluid.

Do not remove the skin; cover the blister with an absorbent adhesive bandage or similar dressing, extending beyond the edge of the blister. After applying the dressing, dust the outside of the dressing and entire foot with foot powder.

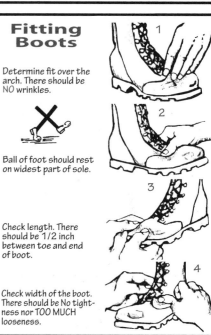

Fitting Boots

Determine fit over the arch. There should be NO wrinkles.

Ball of foot should rest on widest part of sole.

Check length. There should be 1/2 inch between toe and end of boot.

Check width of the boot. There should be No tightness nor TOO MUCH looseness.

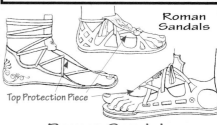

Top Protection Piece

Roman Sandals

Roman Sandals

They were made of different types of leather. The soles were stitched heavy leather layers with the softer sides inserted between the hard sole layers. The tops were soft leather. The special feature is the top piece that protects the foot from the pressure of the laces.

Indian Moccasins

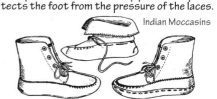

Breathing Holes

Jungle Boots

Combat Boots

Deep threads for mud.

Threads for regular walking.

Socks should not be too loose or tight. Avoid socks with heavy ribbing because they might cause boils.

SHOE THREADS

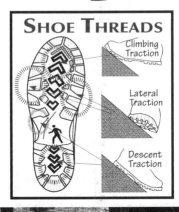
Climbing Traction

Lateral Traction

Descent Traction

LEATHER BOOT CARE

- Break in your boots on leisurely walks.
- Do not apply too much oil that will decompose the leather. Do not over-wax your boots.
- Do not walk on machine oil as this will deteriorate your soles.
- Wash salt and perspiration stains off your boots with warm water. Let boots dry for a few days before applying Neat's foot oil.
- Do not leave your boots in the sun.
- Store your boots on a shoe tree.
- Do not store boots in plastic bags as they have to breath.
- Vary the tension of the lacing on your boots. At the top of the boot and in the shoe area it should be tight. Around the ankle it should be loose.
- When on a trip, always turn your boots upside down and shake them to remove any visitors before putting them on. The visitors can be scorpions.
- To avoid having the boot laces untie roll your socks over the knots of your laces.

Treating Leather Boots & Clothing

If leather gets wet do not place it too close to heat as it will get hard and brittle. After the leather is dry, wipe it with Neat's foot oil (or any oil that you can render from the hoofs and feet of moose, antelope, cow). Do not apply too much oil as you will fill the air pores in the leather and the garment or shoes will not retain heat.

Neat's Foot Oil

This oil, which is derived from boiling the feet and shinbone of cows and other hoofed animals, is used to nourish and soften leather. Using it on straps, leather jackets, or boots will prolong their useful life.

Humid Boots

Have a few pair of socks and change your socks at regular intervals during the day. The socks will accumulate unwanted humidity and your boots will stay fairly dry. Do not store your socks in your boots overnight as the boots cannot dry.
Shake your boots before putting them on, especially in the desert or dry areas, as insects might be sheltered in the humid boots. Humid boots are a likely refuge for scorpions and spiders.

SOCKS

Wear wool or cotton socks - they will absorb perspiration. Buy quality socks because a loosely wound yarn will wear out. Do not store your socks in your boots overnight as the socks and boots will not be able to dry. Have a second pair of socks and change them every few hours. Tie your humid socks to your backpack so that they can dry. To check the fit of socks, stand with your weight evenly distributed on both feet. If the socks fit correctly, no tightness or fullness should exist. The wool cushion-sole sock is best because it offers good foot protection.

- Allow 3/8 of an inch for shrinkage of new socks. Those that are too large wrinkle inside the shoe, rub the feet, and cause blisters and abrasions. Socks that are too small wear quickly and reduce blood flow in the foot. When wearing two pairs of socks, wear an outer pair at least a half-size larger than usual. Socks must be changed daily - dirty socks are conductors of heat and allow warmth to escape. They should be washed in lukewarm water to preserve the fiber of the sock since hot water can cause them to shrink.
- When socks become damp, they can be dried by placing them inside a shirt next to the body. Socks should be completely dry before wearing. If it is not possible to wash the socks, they should be changed; the dirty socks should be dried and kneaded with the hands to remove dirt and hardness.

Extending the Life of Socks

If your socks have given up and your soles are getting thin, make a new insole with several sheets of birch bark. To replace or add to the soles of the socks you can use some soft grass, the fluff from milkweed seeds, or the fluff from cattails in the fall and winter. Milkweed seeds and cattail fluff are excellent insulators which should be replaced at regular intervals.

PUTTEES

Are gaiters used by armies all over the world for many centuries. They were used by the British, Canadian, and American forces up to the First World War and partially in the Second World War. The French Foreign Legion still uses them in Africa. Puttees were made of wool or cotton ribbons that were wound around the legs to cover the top of the boots and in some cases to below the knee. Wool puttees were used in the winter and the cotton ones in the summer and in desert areas.

Putties

SLEEPING BAG DESIGN

The design of a bag should match your needs.

Shape of a Bag

There are a wide range of shapes from a tight mummy bag up to a rectangular bag.

Rectangular Bag: The rectangular bag is the least efficient but it has many uses. It is a good family bag as it can be used by a child or adult or as a bed cover. Two rectangular bags can be zippered together to have a "family format". To increase the efficiency of a rectangular bag use a cotton flannel sleeping sack inside the bag to reduce the air cavities. A rectangular bag weighs an extra pound because of its shape. A rectangular bag has no hood so air will circulate over the head and shoulders. The bag is bulkier and cannot easily be compressed. Usually weighs much more than a mummy bag. Cold air comes in by way of the long zipper.

Semi-Rectangular: Slightly tapered but not as much as a semi-mummy bag.

Semi-Mummy Bag: A regular mummy bag is not too comfortable as it restricts the movement of the body. A semi-mummy bag is the choice if you need more room.

Mummy Bag: The mummy bag is the most efficient as there is limited airspace to heat. A well insulated tight mummy bag, with a short well covered zipper, a hood with a drawstring is very warm. You can get cramps as you will not be able to move your body in a tight mummy bag. It is difficult to enter the bag because of the tight fit and short zipper.

Hood

A hood covers your head and shoulder area. At least 85% of your body heat can be lost by this area. Hoods come with different fits, tight or loose. A tightly formed hood is very efficient but can be too warm for a summer bag. You will have to become used to a tight shoulder area. A hood is required if the tent has draft or convection currents (which occur in large tents) or you are sleeping outdoors.

Zippers

They must be strong, have pull tabs inside and outside, two way if possible, not jam easily, and be easy to maintain. The zipper opening should be covered by at least one wind baffle. Ideally there should be two or three baffles that can be buttoned down. A two way zipper on a bag can zip up from the bottom to cool the feet without exposing the chest. A half-length zipper on an efficient mummy bag can leave the feet too hot.

Two rectangular bags can be zipped together to make a large bag. To do this you need a right hand and left hand zipper to mate two bags together.

Cover Head

Insulating the body to retain heat.

SLEEPING BAGS

SELECTING A SLEEPING BAG

A sleeping bag does not warm you but it retains the heat that your body generates.

The heat is retained by the air trapped inside the insulation of the bag. The more loft in the bag the more air space and the warmer the bag. A quality bag, for its weight, lets the minimum heat leave the body area. Sleeping bags are chosen with a temperature rating. The rating you choose should be the temperature at which you will camp. You can buy a summer bag, three season bag, winter bag, or a multilayer four season bag.

Features of a Sleeping bag

- Temperature rating
- Bulk
- Type of construction
- Size
- Insulation material
- Weight
- Design or Shape

D.T. Abercrombie Sleeping Bag

This is the ultra light weight sleeping bag and weather protection made for D.T. Abercrombie for the ultimate camper-hiker of the 1890's. At that time a camping-hiking-mountain climbing-nature craze swept North America and Europe. Wealthy people bought quality equipment that had the lowest weight and left for long excursions in the woods and mountains. Abercrombie was a high end supplier who had exotic products such as Egyptian cotton tents, British Hardy fly rods, rucksacks, etc. These quality products have hardly been matched and are in high demand by collectors.

Sleeping Bag Pads

These are an excellent investment as they will let you sleep more comfortably and they will reduce the transmission of humidity and cold from the ground. A quality foam pad will have closed air cells that will retain their spring and not let water pass through like a sponge.

BODY HEAT LOSS

Radiation
Heat from the face that is not totally covered.
Respiration
Inhaling cold air and exhaling warm air.
Evaporation
Body cooling system releases 1 1/2 pt (1 L) of water in 8 hours.
Convection
From movement of air over exposed parts of the body.
Transmission
Heat that is lost through contact with the cold ground.

Shaking out a down filled sleeping bag - to redistribute the down as it will tend to migrate. In the winter you would want to shake out the frost that might have accumulated on the bag.

Compact Folding Camp Cot

Sleeping on a cot is more comfortable than on sleeping bag pads. In cool weather you will need a heavy blanket on the cot to keep you warm. The insulation offered by a sleeping bag is not as effective on the bottom as the weight of the body reduces the loft of the sleeping bag.

MOUNTAINEERS

Mountaineers might choose a quality child's bag instead of an adult bag. A child's bag is lighter to carry, has less bulk and is only required to cover the legs and thighs of the traveler. The mountaineer's heavy winter parka with its hood covers the upper part of the body.

Backpack

Scarf

Sleeping Bag Storage Bag

Sleeping Bag Pad closed cell foam.

Air Stopper Plugs

Buckle End

Tubing

Attaching sleeping bag strap to external frame.

Self Inflating Sleeping Mat

Sleeping Bag Strap

Assembled Metal Frame Cot

INSULATION MATERIAL

White Goose Down Filled

It retains the most warmth for the least weight. A down bag can be packed tighter than a synthetic bag and takes less space. A disadvantage of down is that it does not retain its loft if wet and it takes a long time to dry. Sleeping bags are usually used in tents so rarely get wet. The best down is white goose down as it has the highest heat retention to weight ratio. The main difference between duck down and goose down is the fact that the down in geese has a hard spin which helps in maintaining a high loft. Duck down has a soft spine so requires more down (more weight) for the same loft. Some other exotic products are used for insulation - silk cocoons, Asian camel hair, Tibetan goat hair.

Synthetic Fill

All better quality synthetics are nearly the same. There is a whole array of man-made insulation material available. They usually are easy to maintain and dry.

Sleeping Bag Liner

A cotton liner for your sleeping bag will eliminate the clamminess in a nylon blend sleeping bag. The liner will hug the body and reduce the heating energy required to keep you warm.

Sleeping Bag Cover

Improves the insulating characteristic of the bag when camping with no tent. The bottom of the bag is waterproof material, the top of the bag can be cotton or other breathable material.

Storage & Maintenance

Hang a bag or roll it loosely but never store it in its stuff sack. Hand wash the bag in a large tub with mild soap and water. Rinse to remove all soap. Do not lift a wet bag by one end but lift it altogether as the wet weight of the bag might tear some of the baffling. Let the bag dry on a board inclined at an angle.

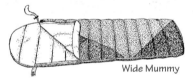
Wide Mummy

US Army
Intermediate Cold Down Filled
Note: The tight space for the feet. Length wise quilting so the down should be shaken out of the feet every day.

Face Area

Zipper down to the feet.

No hood.

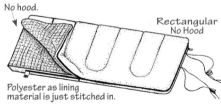

Rectangular
No Hood

Polyester as lining material is just stitched in.

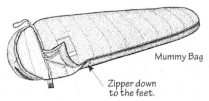
Mummy Bag

Zipper down to the feet.

BAFFLES

Quilt

- Polyester or down.
- Cold at stitching.

Double Quilt

- Polyester or down.
- More material than filling by weight.

Box

- Good for heat retention.

Slant & Off Set Construction

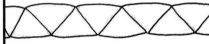

- Down only.
- Better than Box construction.

V-Tube Construction Overlapping Tube

- Down only.
- Excellent for cold weather.

You can check the baffle type by moving the outside shell and inner shell up and down to feel the construction.
Verify...

- The foot baffle and space for your feet.
- Stitches should be double sewn at stress points.
- Avoid length wise baffles as the down accumulates in the feet.

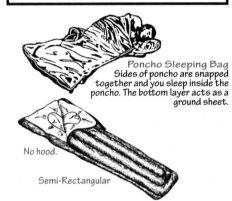

Poncho Sleeping Bag
Sides of poncho are snapped together and you sleep inside the poncho. The bottom layer acts as a ground sheet.

No hood.

Semi-Rectangular

Direction to Place a Sleeping Bag
When sleeping under the stars, place your sleeping bag so that your feet point into the direction of the wind. This will have the wind blow around you and not into the bag. You can also sleep behind a windbreak.

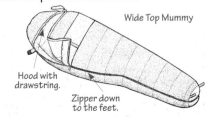

Wide Top Mummy

Hood with drawstring.

Zipper down to the feet.

Temperature Rating

This is the lowest temperature at which the bag will keep you warm. The rating is established by the manufacturer.

Size

The size of a bag should match the size of your body but also depends upon your other requirements. Ideally you want a bag as small as possible as it is easier to heat with your body.

Weight

The ideal is the minimum weight with the least bulk when backpacking. The bag should still meet your temperature rating and size requirements. If you are traveling in a car you can buy a cheaper bulkier bag. The weight of a bag depends upon the temperature rating, size, insulation material, design, weight of material used in the construction, and the fixture such as zippers.

Bulk

The bulk of a bag depends upon the temperature rating and the heat retention factor of the insulation. A quality insulation has the least weight and the least bulk while being transported and the highest loft for maximum retained heat. The insulation that has these best qualities is white goose down.

Construction

The construction of a sleeping bag includes:
Baffles: The baffling keeps the insulation material well distributed inside the bag. Well designed baffling reduces cold spots.
Different types of baffling:
Down filled bags have slant box baffles.
See the adjacent article.

Synthetic Bags

- Shingle construction (louvered) is the most efficient.
- Double quilt sandwich is used in cheaper bags.
- Sewn through quilting is used in cheaper bags.

Cut of Material: The standard cut is called the space filler cut and its advantage is that the inner shell falls onto the body and reduces the airspace. In the standard cut the inside liner is the same size as the outer shell.
The inside liner can be cut smaller than the outside shell. This is called a differential cut. This cut stops the elbow or other body parts from touching the outer shell which reduces the loft.
Shell: The shell should not be waterproof as it should breath to reduce moisture accumulation inside the bag. If moisture accumulates the sleeper becomes damp and cold. The material should allow 1 1/2 pints of water to escape in 8 hours. A sleeping bag should be well aired after and before use.

Compression Sleeping Bag Bag
Once the sleeping bag is in the storage bag tighten the belts to force out the excess air that creates the heat retaining loft in the bag.

Air Stopper

Pneumatic Sleeping Pad
Comfortable but heavy and can leak.

Foot Pump
For pneumatic sleeping pad.

USING A TENT

Ground Preparation

Make sure the ground is free of sharp twigs and rocks.

Ground Sheet

A ground sheet placed under the floor of the tent will prolong the life of the tent. Make sure that the footprint, of the tarpaulin, is smaller than the tent's to avoid water collecting below the tent. A ground sheet can also be placed in the tent to reduce the humidity that wicks through the floor. Never wear shoes in a tent as they will apply too much pressure on the soft flooring and pierce holes.

Drainage Trench

Dig a small trench around the tent, especially on the up slope side of the tent.

Fly

This is the outer protective shell of the tent. It should not touch your tent's surface but offer sufficient space for currents of air to keep your tent cool. It is usually made of nylon taffeta or rip stop nylon that is made waterproof with a polyurethane coating. Always use your rainfly to protect your tent against ultra violet rays. A nylon tent left erect for a long time in the sun can be damaged by UV rays. If camping in one spot for a long time pick a shaded campsite. Always have the possibility of lightning on your mind.

Cooking Fires and the Tent

Do not cook with open flames inside or near your tent. Never store flammables or refuel any appliance in your tent. All campfires should be built at a distance from the tent and downwind to avoid embers from blowing onto the tent. Tents are fire retardant but not fireproof and the retardant loses its effect over time.

Oils, Insect Repellent, etc.

Do not put any oils, insect repellent or other liquids on the surface of your tent or fly.

TO CHOOSE A TENT

A tent should keep you dry, cool in the summer (summer tent), warm in the winter (winter tent), be of a reasonable weight and easy to setup.

- Functional design and easy setup.
- High quality material and design.
- The stitching should be sturdy, well placed, and possibly waterproofed. The adjacent material can have some form of overlapping.
- No-see-um mesh in the windows and doors to protect you from insects.
- Tub style waterproof floors to raise the floor seams above the ground to prevent leaking. In better quality tents the floor seams are fully taped for extra protection against moisture.
- Each individual, including children, needs approximately 3x8 feet (1x2 m) or 24 square feet (2 m²).
- Two or three windows that have zip closed flaps and bug netting to let the air circulate.
- A high doorway for easy access. The door can also have an awning cover for inclement weather and protection against the sun.
- Mesh side storage pockets.
- Quick attaching rainfly with sealed seams.
- Vestibule for extra gear storage.
- Tempered aluminum shock-corded poles. Spun aluminum with no welding seams.
- Correct pegs for the camping site.

Marquee Tent
A tent for desert and beach areas.

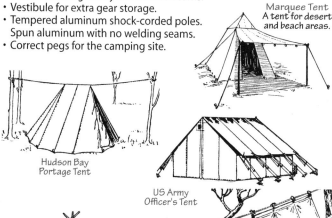

Hudson Bay Portage Tent

US Army Officer's Tent

Wedge Tent

Compact Tent
For 2 people and their packs. Weighs only 3.75 lbs, with rope, and rolls into a 16x4 inch parcel.

Wall Tent with side bars.

US Army Conical Tent
Good for 8 people (up to 12) and a stove. Chimney hole is in the centre.

Tropical Tent
With a large fly to protect travelers from heavy thunderstorms.

Wall Tent & Fly

TENTS 1860's-1920's

Tents for Forest Cruisers (Hikers!)

George Tent 1900's

A 2 person tent. Floor dimensions were 7x7x7 feet (2x2x2 m). It was made of "waterproof balloon silk" and weighed 5.25 lbs (2.4 kg), including pegs, and packed into a 12x5 inch (30x13 cm) parcel. In cold weather the front was left open and the sloping back and sides reflected the heat of the camp fire down upon the occupants. A camper could stand up in the door area. These tents were well suited for "canoeists" and "forest cruisers".

George Tent

DANGER WATER RISES RAPIDLY DAM UPSTREAM

Watch for warning signs BEFORE selecting a campsite.

TREATING A NEW TENT

Seal the Seams

Use a seam sealer to seal the needle holes that can wick water through the seams of a tent. Reapply the sealer as necessary. Most leakage will usually occur along a stitched seam. Apply sealer on both the outside and inside seams of the tent.

Waterproofing

Exposure to heat, cold, UV radiation, stress on the seams, folding during storage, and bad storage conditions can all affect the material and waterproofing of a tent.

USE OF TENT

Accessories

Aluminum and fiberglass poles and pegs should be kept clean and dry. Poles with shock cords are fragile especially at the interlocking edges between the pole sections. They can be bent, stepped on, or damaged by the shock card. Lubricate the ends of the pole sections with soap or wax to reduce any resistance when assembling them. Do not snap fiberglass poles together as the ends can be easily damaged.

Zippers

Lubricate the zippers with a mild soap or paraffin wax. Do not use oil as it will attract grit and make the nylon deteriorate. Never force a zipper as it can damage the slider or teeth. Keep sand off the zipper.

Repairs

Small holes can be closed by using seam sealer or nail polish. Ripstop repair tape can repair small tears.

Cleaning the Tent

Erect your tent before hand washing it. Wash it with a sponge and a mild soap. Do not use detergent, machine wash or dry clean. Do not fold your tent, for storage, when wet or on very humid days. Store it in a cool dry spot (not in the sunlight near the window). Nylon can be damaged when in the proximity of acids and caustic solutions. Avoid car batteries, acidic fruit juices, insect repellents, and hair sprays.

Storage

Make sure that your tent is clean and dry before storing. If your tent was taken down on a humid or rainy day re-erect at your house, wipe it down and let it dry. Store the tent in a cool, dark and dry spot. Do not store on a concrete floor as moisture and released chemicals from the cement can damage nylon. If stored in a damp environment there might be color transfer from the dark to light areas.

FEATURES OF A TENT

Size

Take a tent one person larger than you expect in the tent. You will appreciate the extra room.

Season

The season category of the tent you choose depends upon in which season you will travel and at what altitude. It can be very cold at night. For cold regions get a sturdy (to carry some snow) tight fitting tent. In warm areas you need ventilation and insect screens.

Poles

Aircraft aluminum poles are sturdy, light and will not corrode. Metal tipped fiberglass is more economical. Most poles have shock cords.

Pegs

Some tents are free standing but they should be pegged down as they might blow away. The type of pegs you choose depends upon the type of ground. Special pegs exist for snow and loose sand.

Tent Models

Many different models of tents are available each one for a specific market.

Tent Materials

A tent is usually made of nylon or rip stop nylon. A three season tent has nylon mesh doors and windows to keep the tent cool, improve ventilation and keep out the insects. Tents have waterproof floors which sometimes rise up the sides. This tub style floor keeps out the water from a downpour but makes the tent more difficult to pack. Tents can also have flat floors with waterproofed and taped edge seams.

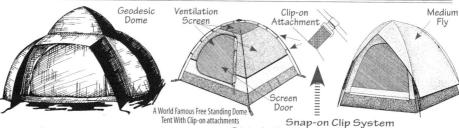

Medium Fly
Helps to keep tent cooler in sunny areas. Also additional protection against strong rain.

Fly Overhang
Protects against rain.

Rear Screen
Window to help in the ventilation of the tent.

Zip close screen as protection from insects.

Elevated floor edge - as protection from water draining into the tent.

Geodesic Dome

Ventilation Screen

Clip-on Attachment

Medium Fly

Screen Door

A World Famous Free Standing Dome Tent With Clip-on attachments

Snap-on Clip System
This is the ideal system to attach the tent material to the self supporting poles. It is very convenient as you do not have to feed the poles through the long tubes as on regular tents.

DOME TENT

A dome tent has straight walls and more usable interior space. Most models are self supporting and have easy access. As the tent is freestanding it can be installed on hard ground and weigh it down with some heavy rocks on the inside. Its weight/ sleeping area ratio is much less than the "A" Frame. A vestibule which is part of the rain fly can be added to a dome tent to enlarge the storage area.

External Frame Tent
An external frame tent is roomy and has no framing obstructions in the tent. The frame of ridged aluminum is different than the frame on the dome tents which is flexible. The frame is mounted and then the tent is attached from below the frame. In a dome tent the structure is self standing with the tent material and the flexible poles re-enforcing each other.

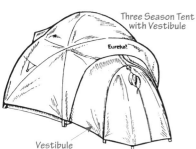

Three Season Tent with Vestibule

Eureka!

Vestibule

Fly Overhang
Protects against rain.

Small Fly

Full Fly

Dome tent without fly.

'A' Framed tent living in the 1940's.

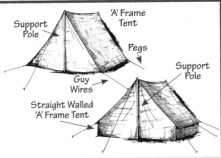

Support Pole — 'A' Frame Tent — Pegs — Support Pole — Guy Wires — Straight Walled 'A' Frame Tent

'A' Frame Tent

This is the traditional tent design with two poles on the inside (one partially blocking the doorway) and guy cords. The biggest disadvantage is the lack of headroom and the difficulty to stand up. To improve upon the headroom larger models have vertical walls on the sides and the roof has a flatter pitch.

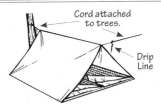

Cord attached to trees. — Drip Line

Emergency Tube Tent

Simple emergency shelter for two people. Orange tent can be cut into panels for signaling in an emergency. One of the best camping and general outdoor travel tents available.

- Lightweight, only a few ounces.
- Easy to mount, requires one support line.
- No ground sheet required. If you plan to camp for a longer time get a ground sheet to reduce the humidity wicking through the floor. If you are in a survival situation place a layer of evergreen boughs below the tent. Make sure that no sharp branches are poking through the floor.
- Material should be 4 mil or thicker.
- Rope 24' (7 m) long, add stick or drip line to stop water from running along the support cord.

Fly is put over the tent. — Hoop Frame — Screen — Door — Tapered at feet.

Tunnel Hoop Tent

This tent is like a spider covered with material. It is straight walled but tapers at the feet. It sleeps one or two but is very tight. It is very light and excellent for cycling.

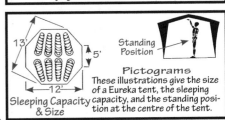

13' — 5' — 12' — Standing Position

Pictograms

Sleeping Capacity & Size — These illustrations give the size of a Eureka tent, the sleeping capacity, and the standing position at the centre of the tent.

Leak in Tent

Attach a string to the hole and the water will flow along the string into a container.

Close-up — Drops of water — Leak — Stone to weigh down string. — Drops of water

Tarpaulin

Ax

WAX STICK — SEALS SEAMS ON TENTS TARPAULINS BOAT COVERS BOOTS

Nylon Repair Tape — FOR EASY INSTANT REPAIR OF TORN NYLON FABRICS

Coleman EMERGENCY BLANKET

Survival Blanket

Coleman PRO-TECHT WATER REPELLENT

Rope

Coleman SEAM SEALER & OUTDOOR REPAIR

Coleman's SEAM SEAL & OUTDOOR REPAIR

TENT REPAIR KIT — CONTENTS

Tent Repair Kit — CANVAS CEMENT

Screening — Mosquito Coil — Mosquito Screen Tent — Culex Mosquito — Screening — Tent Area — Frame Outside — Screen — External Frame Family Tent — Screen Tent & Tent Combo

SEAM SEAL

Trowel

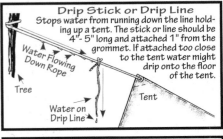

Drip Stick or Drip Line

Stops water from running down the line holding up a tent. The stick or line should be 4"- 5" long and attached 1" from the grommet. If attached too close to the tent water might drip onto the floor of the tent.

Water Flowing Down Rope — Tree — Water on Drip Line — Tent

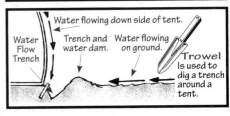

Water flowing down side of tent. — Water Flow Trench — Trench and water dam. — Water flowing on ground. — Trowel Is used to dig a trench around a tent.

External Frame Tent 1960's

Cord at ground level

Very stable to lateral movement.

Double Peg if ground is soft.

Use boulder to reinforce peg if it cannot enter the ground.

Force Direction

Cord at ground level.

Correct way to enter peg.

90°

PLACING PEGS

The way you place your pegs is important as well placed pegs will:
- Reduce tent flap in the wind.
- Make sure that your tent will stay up in a storm.
- Note that the cord should be placed at ground level to minimize the leverage exerted on the peg.

Loose Sand or Snow Tent Peg
One can be made by using a regular wire peg and a squashed tin can.

Tin Can

Aluminum pegs with spiral.

Homemade wood pegs.

Peg Puller

Metal Peg with plastic top.

Metal Pegs

Snow or Loose Sand Peg
Military metal peg which is used in snow or desert sands. It is made of pressed sheet metal and stacks well.

Steel Pegs
For stony and hard packed ground.

Heavy Duty Metal Pegs

Molded Plastic Peg that has a large head to help drive the peg with the foot.

Emergency Pegs
A buried log peg that can be used in a desert.

Stones used as pegs when the earth is frozen or too hard.

Peg that is put into a hole in the ice. The hole will freeze over.

Peg that is put in a hole in the snow and covered with water - that freezes.

Metal Grommet Repair Kit

Metal Snap Repair Kit

Punch

Metal Guy Wire Attachment
It eliminates having to tie a knot around a peg. It can be tightened or loosened as required.

Rubber Guy Wires
They are attached to pegs and to the guy ropes coming from the tent. They are elastic and absorb the push and pull of the wind on the tent and help reduce tent flap noise.

Sliding Hitch
Can be used to attach a part of the tent when you want to vary the tension. As on the flap.

Enamel Coffee Pot

Enamel Frying Pan

Pepper/Salt Shaker

Insect Food Cover

Tripod Stool

Dunk Bag

Mosquito Hat

Collapsible Water Bag

Collapsing Cup

Folding Grill

OUTDOORS COOKING

Camp Toilet

Biodegradable Soap

Insulated Canteen

Butane Stove Lighter

Grill Stove

FIRE PASTE
Quick Clean Fire Starter

INSECT REPELLENT

Wash Your Mess Kit
A sure way to get diarrhea is to use a dirty mess kit or eating utensils. Protect yourself by washing your mess kit/ eating utensils

Coleman® Mess Kit

Coleman® cooking mess kit.

Coleman® Ultra Light Stove

Machete

Mini Storage Hammock

Carbon Element

Membrane

Ceramic Filter Pump

Illustrations courtesy of: Camping Gaz, Coghlan's, Coleman, Eureka!, Gerber, Katadyn, Kelty, Leatherman Tool, Mag Int'l, msr, Opinel, Optimus, Outbound, PentaPure, Petzl, Pur, Silva, SOG, Wenger SA, World Famous Sales of Canada.

Toilet Seat Covers

Frying Tray

Toothbrush Cover

Cooking Reflector & Wind Deflector

Dromedary Water Bag

Pocket Knife

Folding Shovel with case. Coleman®

Folding Frying Pan

Flashlight

Plastic Match Container

Insulated Canteen

Knife Tool

Plastic Water Flask

MSR Minicook Set

MSR Cook set

Stainless Steel Coffee Cup

GI Can Opener

DRINKING WATER TABLETS

Drinking Water Tablets

Camping Light

Coleman® Plastic Dinnerware Set

44

CAMPING STOVE FUELS
White Gas

This is the best fuel for avid campers, hikers and mountaineers. The flame blows like a pressurized blow torch and because of this it is quite wind proof. It is efficient at all temperatures and cooks fast but sometimes it is difficult to have a low enough setting to "simmer". The fuel is easy to find.

Maintenance
A white gas stove requires attention.

- The air pressure pump has to be pumped to pressurize the fuel. When lighting the stove there might be a temporary flare-up (light it from the side). The stove has to be kept clean, especially the jet assembly.
- Keep it clean, oil the pump. Replace the gasket rings if the pump leaks. If a replacement gasket is not available cut one out of a piece of leather. Oil the leather and this will serve as a temporary gasket.
- Disassemble the jet section (it is simple) if your stove sputters. It is time to soak it in white gas and wipe it clean with a soft tissue.
- Do not use old fuel (one which has been opened or is in the stove) as the fuel decomposes after a few months, and forms soot in the jet system.

Gasoline or Kerosene
If traveling to a remote area or overseas buy a "dual fuel" stove that can use white gas, gasoline or kerosene. When using gasoline or kerosene clean your stove at frequent intervals. These fuels being dirty will deposit carbon soot on your stove and reduce its heating capacity.

Alcohol
Alcohol burns at low temperatures, therefore takes longer to heat your meal. Stoves using alcohol require minimal maintenance. The fuel is easy to find. You can use denatured alcohol, methyl alcohol (wood alcohol) or isopropyl alcohol (rubbing alcohol). In general alcohol stoves are simple to operate.

Butane/Butane-Propane Mixture
These stoves are easy to operate and require minimal maintenance. Butane comes in small (usually blue) replaceable canisters. These canisters cannot be refilled but are usually easy to find. Their major drawback is that pure butane will not vaporize (go from liquid state to a gas state) below 32°F (0°C). For lower temperatures: at 20°F (-7°C) you will need a mixture of butane-propane and at 10°F (-12°C) you will need ISO butane. If the canister is not well mounted it might leak gas when not in use. A butane tank is filled with liquid gas topped off with a layer of lighter vaporized gas. Do not shake the tank before using as some of the liquid gas might come out with the vaporized gas when you light the stove.

Maintenance
Liquid butane to vaporize into gas requires heat to make the transition from a liquid to a gas state. This heat partially comes from the surroundings of the butane tank and from the remaining liquid butane. (This is similar to the workings of a refrigerator or when sweat on your forehead dries (becomes a gas) and cools your forehead). If the outdoor temperature is cold water will condense on the outside of the butane tank and the liquid gas, inside, has also become colder. This reduces the liquid butane conversion to gas and the flame pressure will decrease. Keep a spare tank in a warm place and change tanks or warm your cold tank in your hands. Do not place a canister in hot water or over a fire as it might explode.

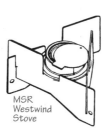

MSR
Westwind
Stove

Iso Butane
Fuel

MSR
Rapid Fire
Stove

Find a reliable stove, one that has easily available fuel, works in all weather conditions and at high and low altitudes.

Plastic Cutting Board
When camping use a plastic cutting board because it is light and does not retain odors when washed so that it will not attract animals.

Large Size
Propane
Tank

MSR
IsoButane

White
Gas

MSR Fuel
Bottles

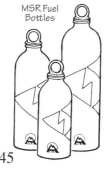

OUTDOORS COOKING

MSR
XGK Stove

Marine
Stove

Whisperlite
White Gas Stove

MSR XPD
Cooking Set

GI's Using a Coleman Pocket Stove in the World War II

06 SWAMPS, MARSHES & BOGS

In a swamp you are always being watched.

Map labels

Exiting Stream

Marsh

Ponds that will gradually be covered and become bogs.

Marsh

Winona Lake
467

Marsh Hawk

Marsh

Intermittent Streams
Only flow during the wet season. Note that they are indicated by a dashed line.

Incoming Streams

500 foot Topographic Elevation Line

BM 525

05

500

SWAMPS

A swamp is a damp, wet lowland saturated with water not usually covered by standing water. More than 50% of the area is covered with woody plants as trees, brush, vines, etc.

It is caused by some interference with the run-off of water, such as a very gentle slope, the growth of water absorbing swamp vegetation that clogs the natural water drainage channels, or damming by beavers. One of the most common causes of swamps is the natural filling of lakes, which forms a level humid surface that encourages the growth of swamp plants. These plants retain water and retard the drying of the extinct lake surface. During the stages of lake filling, swamps are formed on deltas, in bays, and, if the lake is small, even along the shores; when completely filled, the lake is replaced by a swamp.

Swamps form...

• Along meandering rivers (Mississippi).
• As a result of glacial damming of the natural water flow system (around the Great Lakes).
• The receding oceanfront (Okefenokee Swamp).
• Areas behind dune deposits at the seashore (Atlantic shore line).
• Created by the depressions caused by fallen meteorites (Carolina Bays).
• Damming by beavers.
• Tidal and intertidal areas.

INTERTIDAL ZONE

Page 494

INTERTIDAL ZONE

Overlap the characteristics of the saltwater marshes but are areas between the high and low tide. Travel is difficult due to the tides and constantly changing landscape. If entering this area, special consideration has to be given to the turbulent movement of the water when the tide comes in and goes out. In the zone you have to know when the tide comes in and also where the high ground is because what you consider high ground might be covered or wave swept during high tide.

When in Intertidal Zones:

• Know where the high water mark is. (What's wet, what's not).
• Direction of the tide. What is the extreme high and low of the day?
• How the incoming tide changes affect the shoreline. You might be stranded (thinking it is sufficiently elevated) on an elevated area that will be flooded at high tide.
• Watch the wave patterns if you are near the water. Observe how large and how close together the waves are within a set of waves. Watch the interval (or lulls) between sets of waves. There might be a wave surge coming in if you see the water withdraw in an unusual way. Watch the swell. As the swell increases in size, the dynamics of the ocean become stronger resulting in strong currents, riptides and sometimes undertow. Learn about the characteristics of these currents - they can easily kill you.
• Always keep in mind that you have to be prepared to swim to shore.

Salt Marsh

Freshwater marsh in Vermont.

Freshwater marsh in the Everglades.

SALTWATER MARSHES

Saltwater marshes are usually created by tidal activity, are areas with high saline or alkaline content in the soil, and usually located near the oceans and in the deltas of rivers. They are covered with grass like plants and hardly any bushes or trees. Also might occur in the intertidal zone.

SWAMPS - COAST PLAIN

Level coastal plains often have so gentle a slope that the water cannot run off. Dense swamp vegetation will also hinder the drainage. Coastal plain swamps are found on the coastal plain of Texas and in Florida, the Everglades region, and the Dismal Swamp on the coastal plain of Virginia and North Carolina.

SALT SWAMPS

There are few swamps in arid lands, but some are found near springs and on the river floodplains. There are also marshy places - alkali flats and salines in which only a few species of plants can grow. During flooding they may become shallow, muddy lakes. During the dry season evaporation changes them to hardened mud, crusted over with alkali and salt. When wet, the deep, sticky mud often makes them quite impassable.

Mosquito Bed net on a Camping Cot

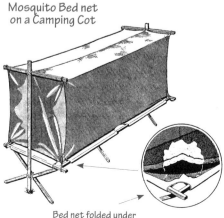

Bed net folded under blanket or mattress

FRESHWATER MARSHES

Are marshes whose source of water are freshwater creeks, streams, rivers and lakes. The water level, for most of the year, ranges from 1 to 6 feet. In the United States the biggest freshwater marsh are in parts of the Florida Everglades.

Damage Caused by ATVs in a Marsh

The vegetation surface of a swamp is very sensitive as it has a weak root structure and the soil base is not too stable. This areal photograph shows the damage caused by ATVs speeding across the sensitive surface. From the track marks, it is obvious that these travelers were out on a joy-ride.

Swamps - Floodplain

The overflow of rivers causes swamps on low areas behind the natural levees on floodplains. These swamps have dense forests of cypress and black gum. Swamps are also found along the lower courses of rivers, where the river water is backed up by the tide and caused to overflow the adjacent lowland.

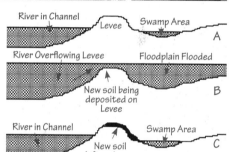

Natural Levee Formation

A natural levee is formed by the overflow of rivers during flooding.

A: The river is within its channel. When the river starts to rise during the flood season it flows faster and picks up more soil.

B: When the river overflows its bank it is carrying much soil. Upon overflowing, the water from the river expands on the floodplain, it decelerates and drops some of the soil - this soil accumulates and builds up the levee.

C: The river recedes into its channel, leaves water in the marsh area, and the levee is higher than before the flood.

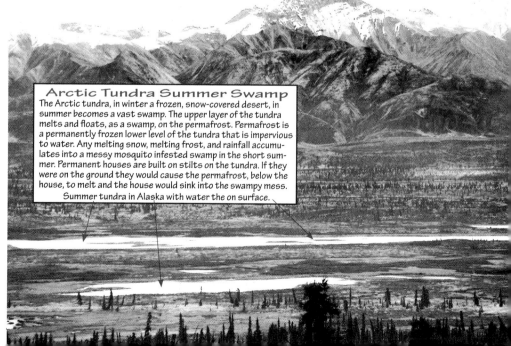

Arctic Tundra Summer Swamp

The Arctic tundra, in winter a frozen, snow-covered desert, in summer becomes a vast swamp. The upper layer of the tundra melts and floats, as a swamp, on the permafrost. Permafrost is a permanently frozen lower level of the tundra that is impervious to water. Any melting snow, melting frost, and rainfall accumulates into a messy mosquito infested swamp in the short summer. Permanent houses are built on stilts on the tundra. If they were on the ground they would cause the permafrost, below the house, to melt and the house would sink into the swampy mess.

Summer tundra in Alaska with water the on surface.

Traveling in a narrow "Johnboat"

BOGS

Are the dying and rotting plant root congested remains of ponds or lakes. These deposits build up around the edge of the usually stagnant water. When a bog forms, it is covered with mosses, ferns, and lichens. When you step on a bog, your feet will feel like stepping on a wet sponge and water will ooze up around your feet. This happens because the bog has overgrown the water.

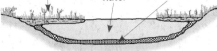

Growth of sphagnum moss, weeds, and other plants out from the shore.

Stagnant Water

Decayed materials covering the entire bottom with muck.

Formation of a Bog

This cross section of a pond shows the growth of sphagnum moss, weeds, and other plants out from the shore, forming a "quaking bog." In time the moss from the sides will meet, completely enclosing the pond, and by its decay, covering the entire bottom with muck.

Permanent Semenola shelter in Florida

Sleeping area is OFF the ground.

SPHAGNUM MOSS

In cool, damp, temperate climates, the most important swamp-producing plant is the sphagnum moss, which forms peat bogs. Sphagnum often grows out from the shores of small, shallow ponds, floating on the surface, and, by the decay of its lower parts, causing a deposit of vegetable muck on the bottom.

QUAKING BOG

Eventually the sphagnum may reach entirely across a pond, with growing plants above and a thick, liquid mass of decaying vegetation below. It is then called a quaking bog, because it trembles, or quakes, under the foot.

If one sinks into the muck below, escape is nearly impossible. This is especially true when the water below the moss is very deep. The sphagnum moss deposit forming the edge of the hole, you have fallen into, does not offer much of a handhold. Some peat bogs (dense sphagnum moss deposits) have revealed perfect remains of extinct animals, and even of men. The decaying vegetation of a bog form preserving acids which interfere with the decay of organic material.

CLIMBING BOG

Swampy or boggy places are common on hillsides where springs appear, encouraging the growth of sphagnum and other swamp plants. Sphagnum holds water like a sponge, and is thus able to grow some distance from the spring; in fact, it may even climb the hillside, making a climbing bog. A climbing bog sometimes becomes so heavy with water that it slides downhill, becoming a "bursting bog." This slippage can be dangerous to anyone caught below this wet mass.

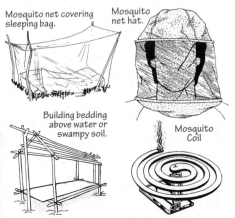

Mosquito net covering sleeping bag.

Mosquito net hat.

Building bedding above water or swampy soil.

Mosquito Coil

FEAR OF SWAMPS

Few swamps exist in the British Isles and Western Europe, the origins of the pioneer settlers, so that they had a fear or swamps. Most of the swamps, in Europe, have been drained or dried up to form peat moss deposits. In the southern parts of Europe swamps were breeding spots for the malaria carrying mosquito - this was a major problem around Rome in Italy. Peat moss in some areas is used for heating fires. The native Indians realized this innate fear of the unknown and spoke of the dangers of snakes, insects, quicksand, panthers, bears, and getting lost. Swamps were the last refuge, for the native Indians and the escaped slaves, from the white man.

SWAMP TRAVEL

The ideal method of travel is a narrow boat with a shallow draft that can go forwards and backwards. The directions of travel are important because a boat has to be able to back out of a dead end in the waterways. It is important that a boat carry a balanced load, the load is well tied down to avoid shifting, and use waterproof bags in case of a spill. Every member of the party should have a personal flotation device. Have a rope, trail cutting machete, and extra paddle easily available. Remember, you cannot walk out of a swamp if your boat has a problem. If you have an emergency it will be difficult to leave at any great speed. You might feel secure with a cellular telephone but because a swamp has no prominent features it will be difficult to give your location without a GPS. Pay special attention to the debris in the water as it might damage your boat.

It is as easy to drown in a swamp as in any body of water. Swamps might not look deep but the water can be 3 feet deep but the soft bio-silt might be another 3 feet.

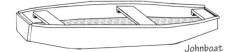

Johnboat

Johnboat: Is a long, narrow, flat-bottomed traditionally wooden boat (now of aluminum or fiberglass) designed so that it is stable, has a shallow draft, and can easily be maneuvered in tight areas. It floats with the current and is paddled by one person in the back using a lightweight paddle. It can be loaded with a week's supply of gear and using a 5 hp motor it can slowly reach its destination. Poles can be used in shallow water. It can pass over sandbars and logs because its draw less than 5 inches of water.

Canoe: has the same quality as a johnboat but is narrower and so can be maneuvered into tighter spots. In general a johnboat is more stable and a motor can be attached. Canoes have an advantage when going through swamp growth as lilies. If required it can easily be pulled over a log obstruction.

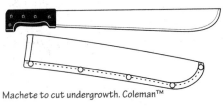

Machete to cut undergrowth. Coleman™

Avoid Getting Wet & Avoid Insects

The basic camping gear is the same as on any camping trip. As you will usually approach a remote site by a small shallow draft boat, you will have to limit the amount and size of your supplies.

SWAMP CAMP SITE

- Look for the driest site possible.
- Look for the highest breezy site so that the insects get blown away.
- Trees are not well anchored in the wet swamp soil; avoid camping near trees that do not look stable.
- Look for an open site or remove the over-grown grasses as this will remove the cover for snakes or other pests.

Sleeping Bag: Make sure that the sleeping bag is the right weight for the season

Sleeping Mattress: A sleeping mattress has two purposes in a swamp. It should give you a com-fortable sleep and not let the humidity from the ground rise through it into the insulation below your body. The foam mattress should be made of closed-cell pores and you might want to put a sheet of plastic below the mat if sleeping on the ground. This plastic sheet will keep the mat from getting muddy if the humidity rises from the ground during the night.

Swamp Toilet: Select a site at least 50 feet from the campsite and some distance from the water. If nature calls, dig a hole 10 inches in diameter and not more than 8 inches deep. The reason that you do not want to dig too deep is that the bacteria that will decompose any deposits are in the topsoil. Cover the hole with loose soil and tramp on it. Biological decomposition in the hu-mid swamp is very active so trace of degradable waste will be gone in a short time.

SWAMP TRAVEL KIT

- First Aid Kit in snake country should include a snakebite kit. Do not forget the insect repellent.
- Waterproof storage bags- for the sleeping bag, tent, food, clothing, etc.
- Quality 3-4 inch blade knife with a lanyard attached to your belt. It is easy to lose your knife during rugged swamp travel. You have to choose if you want a fixed blade knife or a folding knife. If you chose a folding blade make sure that you keep it clean of sand.
- Machete to help you clean a campsite, cut wood, and help open up a trail.
- Folding saw to help in opening a trail in an overgrown swamp.
- Citronella candles to be used to keep flying pests away during the mosquito season.
- Lightweight food would include the staples in freeze-dried form and possibly some jerky and pemmican if you want to have an original travel experience. Lewis and Clark used pem-mican as their staple trail food.

Swamp camping in Florida

CAMPING IN A SWAMP

SWAMP SHELTER

- Lean-to is only the last resort as you will be sleeping on the damp ground and the shade of the lean-to will attract insects.
- Sleeping in a canoe will not be restful and you will be exposed to the insects. If a summer rainstorm occurs you and your sleeping bag will be afloat.
- The ideal shelter and sleeping shelter is a tent that is insect-proof, with a waterproof bottom and a waterproof ground sheet below the tent. The tent should be high enough so that you can dress in the tent. This will help you avoid getting bitten by the insects outside the tent. A dry flat site has to be found to set the tent and the tent cords can be attached to trees and roots. Remove all sticks and stones before pitch-ing the tent. In some areas the best sites will be on sandbars. In this case a freestanding dome tent is the best choice because pegs will not hold in sand deposits – especially in a windy area. If camping on a sandbar, always remember that a distant downpour might cause a flash flood. If this is a tidal swamp you might be below the high tide level.
- A compact portable shelter is a jungle ham-mock, with insect netting, that can be supported between two or three trees. Three or four well-placed trees are the best because in a two-tree setup it is very difficult to keep the hammock stable when embarking or disembarking. The fact that the bottom of the hammock is exposed it is difficult to stay warm in cold weather. The weight of the body will compact the bottom (remove the airspaces) of a sleeping bag so that there will be a major heat loss.
- An insect bar on a sleeping cot will have similar heat retention problems as the jungle hammock.

SWAMP CLOTHING

Warm, wet, and sweaty clothing attracts insects. Make sure that you remain dry. Try keeping your clothing clean to minimize the accumulation of body odors.

Shirts & Pants: Wear loose long sleeved shirts with a button-down collar and cuffs. Long loose pants with draw strings on the legs. Make sure that the cloth material is the right weight for the season and that it will dry easily if you have a spill.

Hat: During the prime insect season wear a clean head net to give you some protection.

Boots: In the summer, the odds are that you will be walking through wet muddy areas. The ideal boot is the lightweight Vietnam Jungle Boot. It has a lightweight canvas top, leather side support, and lug soles. The original feature is that they have two meshed breather holes near the arch to permit the water in the boot to escape. The boots are quite high protecting you from mosquitoes and the undergrowth. In the summer you might want to go barefoot but you might sprain your ankle when wading through roots in the water. Boots might partially protect you from leeches and snakebites. Duck hunters usually will use waders in swampy areas.

Temporary Semenola shelter in Florida

Black Rat Snake

WILD SWAMP FOOD

See the Cooking Chapter for cooking hints.

Fish: are abundant and should be eaten right away as they will rapidly spoil in a warm climate. If you have caught some fish and do not want to eat them right away, you should clean them *and* wipe the body cavity with a paper towel. If the fish was washed with water – dry the complete fish. *The importance of drying the fish is that moisture and the heat of the summer will cause bacteria to grow.* Keep the fish in a cool place or if it is very hot wrap the fish in papers and wrap them in blankets or other insulation. Once the fish are dry, you can put them in a plastic bag and cover the bag with a *wet* cloth. The water from the wet cloth will evaporate and cool the fish in the plastic bag.

Berries: there are many berries and other edible plants to satisfy your taste. Learn to recognize the plants of your favorite swamp area – and then you can travel light – as your food is all around you.

Crawfish: In the southern states you can catch crawfish that are abundant in swampy areas. To catch crawfish, cut a few long poles and attach an 8 -foot long fish line to each pole. Tie a piece of raw meat (1" square) to the end of each line and drop into the water. Wait ten minutes and slowly lift the bait just below the surface to see if a crawfish is clinging to the meat – do not raise the crawfish out of the water or else it will escape. Place a net in the water, below the crawfish and then raise the bait to the surface and the crawfish will escape into your net. Place your catch in a water-filled container or a wet cloth bag. When you have enough for a meal, drop your catch into salted boiling water for 5 minutes.

SWAMP FOOD STORAGE

There are many swamp animals waiting to share your meal – skunks, squirrels, bears, opossums, mice, etc. so keep the food out of reach and well packed.

SWAMP FIRE

Swamp fires are the same as any camping fires but you will want to build a platform for the fire if on wet ground. There usually is peat moss (accumulation of dead plants and other growth) in swampy areas and a fire *should not* be made on a peat moss accumulation. The peat moss might catch fire and slowly burn underground and after a week or two burst out into a major swamp fire. *See the Fire Chapter 51.*

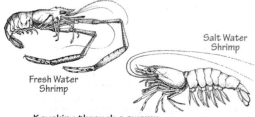

Fresh Water Shrimp

Salt Water Shrimp

Kayaking through a swamp.

SWAMP - DRINKING WATER

One of the factors in the quality of swamp water depends upon how or why the water accumulates.

Assume that all swamp water is polluted.

QUALITY OF SWAMP WATER

Flood Plain Swamps: These are found in the area where a riverbed meanders and overflows during the flood season. There can be small oxbow lakes, swamps, and marshes. An example would be along the Mississippi. In the upper reaches of the river the adjacent swamp water might be safe (the odds are that they are not), and in the lower river areas you can assume that the water has passed through industrial areas and is polluted.

Natural Depression Swamps: Are usually formed by water accumulating because of water runoff after rainfalls. This water is stagnant and will usually have bacteriological contamination.

SWAMPS FROM DAMMING

- A swamp might be caused by man-made damming, as when a highway passes through a wilderness area and changes the natural water runoff pattern. The water that accumulates in this process will contain leaching and sediment from the fill used in the highway construction. The leached material can include arsenic and elements that have long been underground. These waters can be very dangerous even when treated.
- Beavers might have dammed a stream and caused a swamp area to form upstream from the dam. These waters can be very dangerous for human consumption as the dammed water can build up the concentration of contaminants from upstream and the water is contaminated by the urine from beavers and can transmit tularemia.

(Rabbit Fever - First Aid Chapter Page 608)

POISONOUS PLANTS

The poisonous plants that can be found in swamps are Poison Ivy, Poison Sumac, and Oak leaf Poison Ivy.

Poison Ivy Swamp poison ivy is hard to detect because it can grow mixed in with other vines which have a similar appearance. The leaves are hard to identify because the leaves have a wide range of shapes and colors – but they always grow in threes.

Poison Sumac Grows as a coarse woody shrub and never as a vine. It occurs in swamps and bogs and can grow up to 25 feet high. The green fruit of the poison sumac hangs down while other sumacs have red fruit that grow upwards.

Oak leaf Poison Ivy Usually grows as a shrub, not as a vine.

SURVIVAL CRAYFISH TRAP

String or Cord

Wooden Stick to float the strings that support the net.

Bait fastened to the center.

Net or Porous Cloth

SWAMP NAVIGATION

Swamps usually have no distant point of reference, as there is limited long distance visibility. The trees are nearly all the same color, green of plants is green, and water is stagnant and has no sense of direction. You need a swamp topographic map with the water channels, compass, and GPS or an experienced guide. Swamp maps are not very accurate as the water channels might shift with the seasons and aerial photography has difficulty photographing through the tree canopy. Your location on the map is important as a dense swamp has a numerous water routes, which you have to follow, and you cannot just take a shortcut. A GPS will give you your global position but will not indicate the unobstructed water channel to leave the swamp, and without a viable route, a swamp can be like a maze.

Before you set out on a trip...

- Talk to the locals as to the best unobstructed channels and campsites.
- Ask about any special water currents in channels that might give you a sense of direction. These faster currents might even take you further than expected.
- Ask about any seasonal changes that might not be correctly indicated on your map. An example would be excessive rainfall this year might have flooded some channel islands that you will use as direction indicators.
- Leave a route plan and information as to when you expect to return.
- Consider using a guide, at least for the first trip.

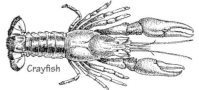

Crayfish

Cutting canebrake.

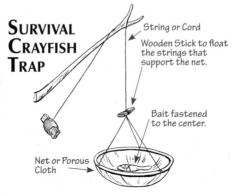

Alligators
There are not many alligators in the wild but if you see one sunning give it a respectful space. Be observant when you approach the shore and you should have no problems.

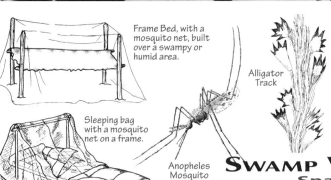

Frame Bed, with a mosquito net, built over a swampy or humid area.

Sleeping bag with a mosquito net on a frame.

Alligator Track

Anopheles Mosquito

If the mire is too soft and you feel that you are still sinking, lie flat on your stomach and move only one part of your body at a time. Try to float out of the quicksand by using snake like movements.

SWAMP WILDLIFE
Snakes

Swamps are not full of snakes but precautions should be taken to limit any potential problems. Keep your campsite clean and your gear off the ground so that snakes have no places to crawl. As a snake is well camouflaged, it is easier to see when in an exposed area, as its body will cast a shadow on a sunny day. When righting your boat in the morning do so slowly and watch where you place your hands. There might be a snake underneath the boat or coiled up below the bow. You might only realize it is there when you cast off. The poisonous snakes that might be encountered in a swamp are: Cottonmouth (Water Moccasin), Copperhead, Massasauga Rattlesnake, Eastern Diamondback Rattlesnake, and the Canebreak Rattlesnake. *See Rattlesnakes page 540 & 608.*

Cottonmouth (Water Moccasin) Is a curious snake and will stand its ground. Follow the basic poisonous snake precautions but also, while traveling in a boat through a swamp, watch for overhanging branches and sunny areas adjacent to the water where snakes might be sunning. They are excellent swimmers.

Copperhead Is well camouflaged so is hard to see. *Page540 & 608.*

Massasauga Rattlesnake This snake is small and hard to see.

Eastern Diamondback Rattlesnake Usually are found on the high ground and on islands in swampy areas.

Canebrake Rattlesnake (Timber Rattler) Lives in dark moist areas and also cane growth after which it is named. They are active both day and night in cool but not cold weather. During hot summer months, they are most active at night.

QUICKSAND

The sign of quicksand is the presence of water oozing upwards. This water keeps the sand and muck in suspension. There might be a thin crust on the surface.
Quicksand is gravel, sand, and silt that are super saturated with water rising up through the sand. This rising water causes the sand particles to float and in effect has no vertical strength to support any weight. The cause of this water accumulation can be due to the presence of a slow flowing spring, which has no obvious drainage system. The water rises up and floats the sand particles. This surge of water can be so slow that the exposed surface will actually have a dry crust that cannot support much weight. Some bogs might even have characteristics of quicksand because of the mucky depth of the bog and a dry surface that hides its instability.

If you step into quicksand or mire:
• *Do not struggle.*
• Trying to lift one foot makes the second foot sink deeper as all the weight is on one foot.
• Drop to your hands and knees and try to crawl slowly. The surface of your hands, knees and legs will distribute your weight over a wider area.
• If the mire is too soft and you feel that you are still sinking, lie flat on your stomach and move only one part of your body at a time. Try to float out of the quicksand by using snake like movements.

Quicksand !!

Massasauga Rattlesnake   Cottonmouth Snake

Cottonmouth are very good swimmers and might board your boat.

51

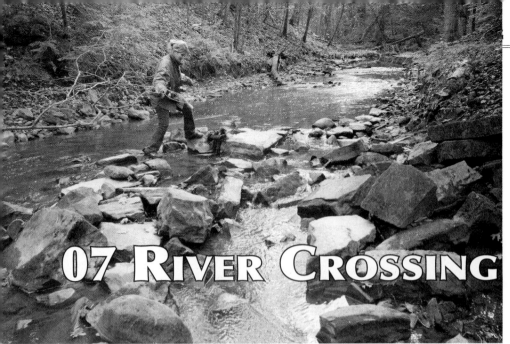

07 RIVER CROSSING

RIVER CROSSING

Rivers form unique obstacles. They are generally linear and extensive and normally cannot be bypassed. Meandering bends in rivers do not let you see very far so it is difficult to choose the ideal crossing point.

CURRENTS & CROSSING

The current of a river is a major limiting factor. It imposes limits to how you cross, what type of flotation methods (rafts) you use for transporting backpacks, and what type of support roping might be used as a bridge. The current's velocity determines the amount of materiel can be carried per trip and if the river can be crossed at all. Current affects the distance that the floating items will drift downstream. You must either select an offset starting point upstream to reach a desired point on the far shore or take additional time to fight the current. High current velocities make control of a heavy raft difficult. Current causes water pressure against floating bridges. Current can be measured easily (for example, by timing a floating stick) but is normally not constant across the width of the river. Generally, it is faster in the center than along the shore. It is also faster on the outside of a curve than on the inside.

CROSSING RIVERS & STREAMS

The method used to cross depends on the width and depth of the water, the speed of the current, the time and equipment available.

There is always a possibility of rope failure. For this reason, every member of the group should be able to swim. In all water crossings several strong swimmers should be stationed either at the water's edge or, if possible, in midstream to help anyone who gets into trouble. If you accidentally fall into the water, you should swim *with the current to the nearer bank.* Swimming against the current is dangerous because the swimmer is quickly exhausted by the force of the current.

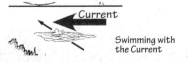

Swimming with the Current

DEPTH OF WATER & CROSSING

The depth of the water influences river crossing. If the water is shallow enough and the riverbed will support traffic, fording is possible.

The depth of the water is not constant across a river. It is generally deeper in the center and in high-velocity areas.

WAVE ACTION, TIDES & CROSSING

A swell is the wave motion found in large bodies of water and near the mouths of rivers. It is caused by normal wave action in a larger body, from tidal action, or from wind forces across the water. A swell is a serious consideration for swimming heavy rafts. Note that a swell changes over time with changing tide and weather conditions. Tidal variation can cause significant problems. The depth and current of water change with the tide and may allow crossings only during certain times. Tidal variation is not the same every day, as it depends on lunar and solar positions and on the current's velocity. Another tidal phenomenon found in some estuaries is the tidal bore, which is a dangerous wave that surges up the river as the tide enters. It seriously affects water crossings as this reverse flow may push the raft in an unexpected direction and even swamp it against a docking area. Rivers may be subject to sudden floods due to heavy rain or thawing upstream. This will cause bank overflow, higher currents, deeper water, and significant floating debris.

It is safer to wade through water and avoid the risk of jumping between slippery logs and stepping stones and spraining your ankle.

LEAPING

When leaping, the point of departure and the landing spot have to be considered. The point of departure because you will be exerting additional pressure on the ground below you. If it is a river bank it might slide and collapse. The landing point has to be stable enough to take your weight, the additional pressure of your landing (which might be double your weight) and the fact that you are landing at an angle. This might cause a rock or trunk to roll.

RIVER OBSTRUCTIONS

Most rivers contain sand or mud banks. They are characteristic of low-current areas along the shore and on the inside of the curves of a river, but they can be anywhere. They can be a surprise if your raft lurches to a sudden halt upon striking a sandbar or rocks.

CROSSING SITES

- Each river crossing has its unique set of problems and solutions. Characteristics vary per location and season.
- Availability and your capabilities of methods of crossing. This is an important factor in selecting a site because it strongly depends upon the abilities of the group.
- Narrow segments of the river might be tempting as a crossing point but the higher current velocities may offset any short distance advantage. As the current's velocity increases the difficulty of rafting or even wading across might make it impossible.
- Ford banks may be steep and rugged and substantially add to the effort of crossing.

MEASURING CURRENT'S VELOCITY

Throw a stick into the water and pace beside it on the shore. Count your paces and time yourself in seconds. If your average pace is 30" then:

120 steps per minute (60 seconds)
= 5 feet / second (fps)
= 3.5 miles/hour (mph)
= 5.5 kilometers/hour (kph)

So 120 steps per 30 seconds would = 7 mph.

PLANNING A TRIP

- Watch the weather. Sudden rains or thaws can change placid streams into roaring torrents.
- Distant mountain thunderstorms can dramatically raise the level of the water especially in narrow valleys.
- If the stream is fed by melting snow cross in the morning before the sun melts more snow.

MEASURING A RIVER'S WIDTH
Compass Method

A field-expedient means of measuring the river's width is with a compass. While standing at the waterline, fix your sight on a point on the opposite side and note the magnetic azimuth. Move upstream or downstream until the azimuth reading to the fixed point on the opposite bank is 45° different than the original reading. The distance from the original point to the final point of observation is equal to the river's width.

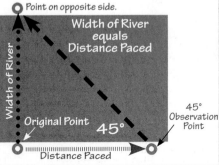

Point on opposite side.

Width of River equals Distance Paced

Width of River

Original Point

45°

45° Observation Point

Distance Paced

FORDING A RIVER
Inspect the River

Inspect the river, potential crossing areas, current, eddies, obstacles, and footing under the water.
- Look for possible natural bridges.
- Look for an area where the current is not as strong. If you are in a canyon or gorge go towards a widening in the river.
- Study the river bed and any potential stepping stones. The bed and stones might be slimy with moss and the stones with a coating of ice.

PREPARE FOR CROSSING
Plan a strategy...
- Which shoes will you wear? Preferably have a pair of canvas running shoes with well notched soles. These shoes will be removed after the fording and carried, to dry, hanging from your backpack.
- How should you cross the river? You might consider fording straight across. This is the shortest distance but you will have to resist the current.
- You might cross at a diagonal in the direction of the current. This will give you potentially better footing because your forward step will be pushed by the current.
- There is a current/body weight strength ratio which, if it is exceeded, will lead to you being pushed over by the current. This fall ratio depends upon how strong you are, how tall, do you have a walking stick support or are you wearing baggy pants that will add to the resistance to the current. A basic rule of thumb is that if the water is up to your knees and the water starts to churn and boil you will not be up for very long. If the water is cold, even cool, you might even suffer muscle cramps.
- The safest might be to build a log raft or other flotation device and float across at a point where the current is deflected to the other side or enters a calm area on the other side.

FORDING STREAMS

When traveling through wilderness areas you may have to ford some streams. These can range from small, ankle-deep brooks to large rivers. Mountain rivers are often so swift that you can hear boulders on the bottom being crashed together by the current.

If streams are of glacial origin, you should wait for them to decrease in strength during the night hours before attempting to ford.

CROSSING STRATEGY

Careful study is required to find a place to safely ford a stream. If available, climb a high vantage point to observe the river. Finding a safe crossing area may be easy if the river breaks into a number of small channels. The area on the opposite bank should be surveyed to make sure travel will be easier after crossing.
- Meandering streams usually flow slowly and can easily be crossed.
- When two streams meet, cross above the meeting point as the current usually is slower due to a lower volume of water.
- Ford a stream further up its course where it is smaller. If you have a choice follow a land divide or ridge while traveling.
- In a forest area trees will have fallen on a stream. These can be used as a bridge.

FALLING IN A SWIFT CURRENT
- Drop your backpack.
- Do not try to stand up but fall onto your back with your feet pointing downstream. You will use your feet to bounce off any obstacles.
- Steer toward shore or a calm eddy so that you can get up.
- Dry yourself and warm up to avoid hypothermia.

Crossing stream with floating boxes.

CROSSING A RIVER WITH THE PENDULUM ACTION OF A RAFT

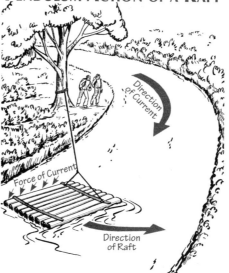

BEFORE CROSSING A STREAM
- Place clothing and sleeping bag in a waterproof bag. Make sure that the contents of your bag are well balanced and firmly attached so that the contents will not shift.
- Watch for bubbly areas behind rocks as the water-air mixture will not have the buoyancy to hold up your body and if you enter this area of turbulence your body might be held down against the rocks.
- If the stream has a strong current chose an entry point where, if you lose your footing, you will be swept to a calm shallow spot or an eddy near the opposite side. Do not cross in areas of cliffs, logs, brush or rapids.
- When crossing wear old running shoes for traction and to help you avoid any sharp objects. The running shoes will also keep your feet warm and you will not wet your hiking boots.
- It is safer to wade through water than the risk of jumping between slippery logs or stepping stones and chance spraining your ankle.
- The shallowest water is usually where the stream is the widest or the current is the fastest as a certain volume of water has to pass a certain point on the river at a certain time.
- Before crossing a stream look for potential rescue points. Use all possible precautions.
- Study the flow of the water for the location of eddies. Eddies are a spiral or circular movement of water and can be relatively calm. A strong eddy can become a whirlpool. These areas are usually behind rocks or where a stream passes into a wider area.
- When possible, select a travel course that leads across the current at about a 45° angle downstream.
- Watch for debris in rapidly flowing water.
- Never attempt to ford a stream directly above, or close to, a deep or rapid waterfall or a deep channel. The stream should be crossed where the opposite side has a shallow bank or sandbars.
- Avoid rocky places, since a fall may cause serious injury. However, an occasional rock that breaks the current may be of some assistance. The depth of the water is not necessarily a deterrent. Deep water may run more slowly and be safer than shallow water.
- Have a plan of action before entering the water to make a crossing.

Indirect Measurement of the Width of a Stream
Width of River: Pace Method

A: Point on Opposite Bank
B: Point from which to Pace

Stream

B — 10 Paces — C

Pace 10 paces from B to C

Stream

B — 10 Paces — C — 10 Paces — D

At C: Look at A and visualize a line from A to E. You could also walk backwards while lining up C with A to approximate the A-C-E line.

Assume 1 Pace = 30 inches

5 Yards

Stream

B — 10 Paces — C — 10 Paces — D

6 Paces

E

From C pace 10 paces to D. At D pace perpendicular to the river until you cross the imaginary A-D-E line at E. In this example there are 6 paces which means that the river is 6 paces wide. An average pace is 30". 6 x 30" = 180" which is 180/12 = 15. The river is 15 feet wide

Using Pole to Cross

Use a pole to probe your advance. Do not put your weight on it, until it is well placed, as it might slip and destabilize you. Only move one

Use pole on upstream side

of the three contact points at a time. When probing move into the current as this will maximize your stability.

Current

Crossing Swift & Narrow Stream

A tangle of trees and bushes

Swift Current — Throw a rope with a weight or heavy log/stick at the end

Raft

Person throwing rope

Weight stuck in bushes

Swift Current — Rope

Raft

Person has moved to raft with the end of the rope.

Throwing location

Raft — Rope

Swift Current

Sits on raft while the rapid current catches the raft and gives it a pendulum swing towards the facing shore.

Heaviest Person acts as anchor for crossing.

Lightest Person on upstream position.

Current

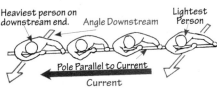

Heaviest person on downstream end. — Angle Downstream — Lightest Person

Pole Parallel to Current

Current

Pole Assisted Crossing

A pole 5 inches in diameter and about 8 feet long can be used as a group anchor point to cross a swift stream. When a group is traversing keep the pole parallel to the current and the direction of travel is gradually downstream.

Wrong way to Cross a Log
If crossing sideways and you fall you will fall OFF the log.

Correct Way to Cross a Log
To successfully cross a log walk straight forwards while looking at your destination point. If you fall, you will fall ON the log and not OFF the log.

WADING ACROSS

- Find a shallow crossing point where the river-bed looks stable and clear.
- If the water is cloudy with silt or debris use a walking stick to probe in front of you.
- Use a pole to probe your advance. Do not put your weight on it, until it is well placed, as it might slip and destabilize you. Only move one of the three contact points at a time.
- Keep your pack lightly attached so that it can be jettisoned if necessary.
- Wade across fast streams into the flow of the water. Deep slow streams are crossed while going downstream as the current will help you angle across.
- Do not tie a rope to a person crossing a stream as the current might make him fall and the secured rope will pull him under the water. The first person (the strongest) wading across should carry the rope loosely in his hand, so that it can be released in case of an emergency. Once he has waded across it can be attached so that the rest of the group can cross while holding onto it on the downside of the current's flow.
- Mountain streams can be very cold and by crossing and getting wet you might expose yourself to hypothermia even on warm days.
- You might consider using a flotation device to float your backpack and to grab if you loose your balance.
- Legs should be dragged through the water, not lifted, so that the force of the current will not throw the you off balance.

GOOD FORDING SITES

- Few large rocks in the river bed. Submerged large rocks are usually slippery and make it difficult to maintain footing.
- Shallow water or a sandbar in the middle of the stream so you can rest or regain your footing on these sandbars.
- Low banks to make entry and exit easier. High banks normally mean deep water. Deep water near the far shore is especially dangerous as you may be tired and less able to get out.
- Cross at an angle against the current. Keep your feet wide apart and drag his legs through the water, do not lift them, so that the current will not throw you off balance. Poles can be used as a probe to help find deep holes and maintain footing.

Crossing on Rocks or Logs

- Make sure that they are well anchored and dry. Sprinkle sand on a wet log before stepping on it.
- Use a walking stick for additional stability.

PIVOT CROSSING

This method can be used by three or more hikers. Hold clothing or backpack straps on each others shoulders and cross the stream in a wheel-like way. One person moves at a time while the others stabilize him. The ideal number of people is three. If the group gets too large it will be difficult to resist the current. The danger of the pivot method is that if one person slips the whole structure could collapse.

TRAVELING ALONG A SHORELINE
OCEAN & SEA SHORES

Oceans are large bodies of water that are affected by tides and winds. If you are following the shore be careful of incoming waves. If an unexpected big wave arrives hold your footing, do not attempt to run. You will not be sure of your footing or the depth of the water. You might be caught in an undertow and be swept into deep water and drown. In general it is quite easy to follow the sea shore as there is usually a beach that has been created by the incoming waves and tides. Difficulties might be encountered when you are in an area where a river flows into the sea as it might be swampy with many islands.

RIVER & LAKE SHORES

The tributaries of rivers that run through a wide bottomland are likely to be deep or run over fathomless mud, sometimes quicksand and require long detours or be crossed with a raft or boat. The vegetation, in these areas, up to the very bank of the river can be exceedingly thick, a wretched tangle of bushes, vines, briers, tall grass, and fallen trees. In periods of heavy rain the river might rise out of its banks and maroon you on a high piece of land. Rivers in mountain areas are swift and usually in gorges or steep valleys which would lead to numerous impassable dead ends. Each bend in the river will be a surprise and for this reason it would be best to cross the area on the divide. See the article about traveling along a divide. *Page 29.*

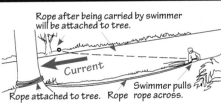

Rope after being carried by swimmer will be attached to tree.

Current

Rope attached to tree. — Rope — Swimmer pulls rope across.

ONE ROPE BRIDGE

The One Rope bridge can be constructed either above or at water level. The bridge rope is pulled around the upstream side of the far side anchor point and temporarily secured without tying a knot. On the near side a slip knot is made on the rope. The far side is firmly attached. The near side of the rope is pulled tight so that no slack is left in the rope and it is firmly attached. Note that the knotting should be well done as the rope will be retrieved and reused.

Far Side

Current

Near Side

Tightening Rope

Construction of One Rope Bridge

ROPE BRIDGES

For crossing streams and small rivers quickly, rope bridges offer a suitable temporary system, especially when there is a strong current. Because of the stretch factor of nylon ropes, they should not be used to cross gaps of more than 60 feet. For larger gaps, manila rope should be used. In order to erect a rope bridge, the first thing to be done is to get one end of the rope across the stream. This task can be frustrating when there is a strong current. To get the rope across, anchor one end of a rope that is at least double the width of the stream at point A. Take the other end of the line upstream as far as it will go. Then, tie a sling rope around the waist of a strong swimmer and, using a snaplink, attach the line to him. He should swim diagonally downstream to the far bank, pulling the rope across.

ONE-ROPE BRIDGE

A one-rope bridge can be constructed either above water level or at water level. The bridge is constructed the same regardless of the level.

Crossing Above Water Level.

Crawl: Lie on the top of the rope with the instep of the right foot hooked on the rope. Let the left leg hang to maintain balance. Pull across with the hands and arms, at the same time pushing on the rope with the right foot. (For safety, tie a rappel seat and hook the snaplink to the rope bridge.)

Monkey Crawl: Hang suspended below the rope, holding the rope with the hands and crossing the knees over the top of the rope. Pull with the hands and push with the legs. (For safety, tie a rappel seat and hook the snaplink to the rope bridge.) This is the safest and the best way to cross the one-rope bridge.

Two-Rope Bridge

Construction of this bridge is similar to that of the one-rope bridge, except two ropes, a hand rope and a foot rope, are used. These ropes are spaced about 5 feet apart vertically at the anchor points. (For added safety, make snaplink attachments to the hand and foot ropes from a rope tied around the waist. Move across the bridge using the snaplink to allow the safety rope to slide.) To keep the ropes a uniform distance apart as men cross, spreader ropes should be tied between the two ropes every 15 feet. A sling rope is used and tied to each bridge rope with a round turn and two half-hitches.

CROSSING AT WATER LEVEL

Hold onto the rope with both hands, face upstream, and walk into the water. Cross the bridge by sliding and pulling the hands along the rope. (For safety, tie a sling rope around your waist, leave a working end of about 3 to 4 feet. You tie a bowline in the working end and attache a snaplink to the loop. You then hook the snaplink to the rope bridge.) To recover the rope, the last person unties the rope, ties it around his waist and, after all slack is taken up, is pulled across.

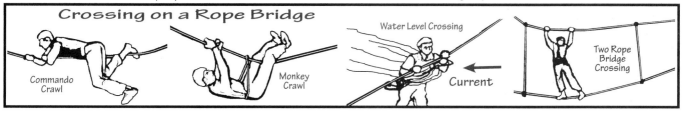

Crossing on a Rope Bridge

Commando Crawl

Monkey Crawl

Water Level Crossing

Current

Two Rope Bridge Crossing

FLOTATION AIDES

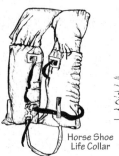 

Two dry logs roped together.

Horse Shoe Life Collar

Waterproof Material

Dry vegetation or branches.

Dry Vegetation or Branch Filling

Waterproof material or plastic sheeting.

Can have a floor to transport clothing or equipment.

 Water Hyacinth

Plastic or Waxed Canvas Bag

Filled with plants that hold air: Water Hyacinth

Pant legs for flotation.

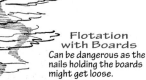

Flotation with Boards
Can be dangerous as the nails holding the boards might get loose.

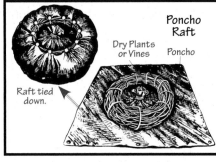

Poncho Raft

Dry Plants or Vines

Poncho

Raft tied down.

Hide or tarpaulin cover.

Wood Frame

Bull Boat

A boat made with a frame of branches attached with leather thongs or rope. These boats traditionally were made of buffalo bull hides and used on the Mississippi River. A tarpaulin can be used to cover frame.

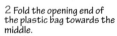

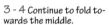

Waterproofing Bag

1 Put articles in plastic bag. Press out the air.

2 Fold the opening end of the plastic bag towards the middle.

3 - 4 Continue to fold towards the middle.

5 Begin to fold the opening end of bag towards the filled part.

6 Continue folding.

7 Apply tape or string on folded end. Now the bag should be quite waterproof for a period of time. Place bundle into a backpack to protect the plastic bag from any tears.

FLOTATION AIDES

When launching any poncho raft or leaving the water with it, take care not to drag it on the ground as this will cause punctures or tears. Floating aids for deeper streams which have little current:

- Log rafts   • A standard air mattress
- Canteen safety belt
- Poncho life belt   • Poncho brush raft
- Water wings   • Poncho raft
- Trousers must be soaked in water before using for flotation.

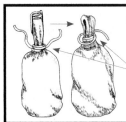

Waterproofing Bag

Tie the top closed and fold over the protruding end. Tie down the protruding end.

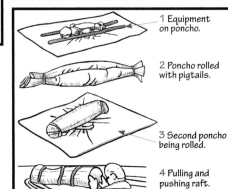

1 Equipment on poncho.

2 Poncho rolled with pigtails.

3 Second poncho being rolled.

4 Pulling and pushing raft.

Attached crates for flotation.

08 JUNGLE TRAVEL

Central American Jungle

Greater Colombian Jungle

Amazonian Jungle

JUNGLES OF THE AMERICAS

Amazonian: Formed by the extended Amazon River basin and its major tributaries, the Amazonian is the world's largest jungle area.

Greater Colombian: This jungle area extends from northern Ecuador (north of the Humboldt Current) through parts of Colombia, Venezuela and into the Isthmus of Panama.

Central American: North from Panama, the Central American jungle spreads to the eastern side of the Sierra Madre Oriental of Mexico and as far north as Tampico. The jungle areas of the Antilles are also included.

JUNGLE SURFACE SOILS

Though varied in many of their properties, the majority of the soils of lowland jungles have certain important common characteristics: in color they are often bright red or yellow; in texture they are frequently clayey, sometimes loamy; and superficial layers are occasionally sandy. In spite of their lush growth (most of which stems from the hothouse environment), soils are generally low in vegetal nutrient content. *Travel is generally poor, especially during rainy periods.*

THE JUNGLE

The jungle is defined as an area located in the humid tropics where the land is covered with a dense growth of trees and other types of associated vegetation. Tropical vegetation in jungle areas includes lowland and highland tropical rain forest, dry deciduous forest, secondary growth forest, swamp forest and tropical savannas. Jungles are confined to three major areas known as the American, the African, and the Oriental jungles.

THE TROPICAL ZONE

The tropical zone lies between the Tropic of Cancer and the Tropic of Capricorn (23.5° North and South of the Equator). Within this zone there are diverse environmental conditions as snow-capped mountains, barren deserts and rain forests. *The jungle is part of the tropics where the temperature and relative humidity remain high throughout the year.*

JUNGLE TRAVEL

Know about:
- Heat disorders
- Jungle climate & survival
- Jungle First Aid
- Health, hygiene & field sanitation
- Proper wearing of clothing
- Prevention & treatment of snakebites & insect bites
- Jungle land navigation
- Jungle terrain characteristics

General: The dominating features of jungle areas are a high and constant temperature, heavy rainfall during the greater part of the year and *oppressive humidity.* Seasonal changes of temperature are insignificant compared with seasonal variation in rainfall, The year has no summer or winter, only cyclic wet and dry seasons. Within complex vegetation environments such as a tropical rain forest, micro climates exist, some of which differ greatly from the standard climate of the same locality.

Temperature: Although seasonal variation in temperature increases gradually as one moves away from the equator, in the lowland humid tropics the mean annual temperature seldom varies for more than 5°F, averaging between 79°F and 82°F with extremes of 64°F and 95°F.

Rainfall: The main factor in all tropical climates is rainfall. In general, the seasonal distribution of rainfall within the tropics is associated with latitude. At the equator, rain falls during all seasons; as the distance from the equator increases, there is a distinct dry and wet season for each year. Although rain occurs during the relatively dry season, it is less in quantity than during the wet season. Rarely gentle or of long duration, tropical rain is often accompanied by thunder and lightening. Tropical rainfall is also relatively constant in its daily timing, usually occurring in the afternoon or early evening. For a given year, rainfall generally totals more than 60 inches.

Atmospheric Humidity: The relative humidity in a tropical rain forest area averages between 65-75% during the day and over 90% (near saturation) at night. The nature of the vegetation, the dank moistness of the surface soil, and *the manner in which books, clothing, shoes, and other materials become moldy unless frequently exposed to wind and bright sunshine*, are all indicators of the high average relative humidity.

Wind: In tropical areas, wind velocities are lower than in temperate areas and violent winds are less frequent. *Mean annual wind velocities average less than 3 mph and seldom exceed 8 mph, and their major influence affects only the upper canopy.* Radical wind variations occur during typhoons, cyclones, and hurricanes; however, such disturbances are confined to certain tropical areas.

Light: The length of tropical day and night are almost equal, varying by little more than an hour at the outer limits of the tropical zone. Near the equator, cloudless days are rare. Cloudiness decreases as one moves north or south of the equator.

Micro Climate: Climatic conditions on the ground, in even a small patch of jungle, way not resemble those above the canopy. In some jungle areas, the canopy is so dense that it provides a cover within which the jungle develops its own miniature climate or micro climate. *In such an environment, the sun may be shining brightly above the canopy, while a brisk shower may be to progress at ground level.* The canopy not only intercepts and redirects a considerable proportion of the rain, it also shelters the jungle from the wind, preventing a sharp rise and fall in temperature. Finally, the canopy diffuses the interior light, tinting it green and rendering it considerably less intense on the forest floor than on the surface of the canopy.

Jungle Terrain & Vegetation

The jungle environment includes densely forested areas, grasslands, cultivated areas, and swamps. Jungles are classified as primary or secondary jungles based on the terrain and vegetation.

Tropical Rain Forest

Are found in areas where the rainfall averages as much as 80 inches during the year. Although a so-called dry season may occur, there is still sufficient rain to sustain the growth of the rain forest. Extensive above-ground root systems and hanging vines are common. These conditions, combined with a wet and soggy surface, make vehicular traffic difficult. *Foot movement is easier in tropical rain forests than in other types of jungle. View of sight is generally limited to about 60 yards.*

Lowland Tropical Rain Forest: occurs in elevations below 2,000 feet and consists mainly of trees, the tallest of which range between 150-180 feet. Trees are usually 10 to 20 feet apart, often appearing to be much closer together because of their buttress roots. The tree trunks are usually straight and slender and without branches for the first 100 feet. Then the branches spread out and interlock to form the upper stratum of the rain forest commonly known as the canopy. In some jungles, the canopy is composed of two or three successive levels of vegetation, which is generally filled with foliage. Beginning at a height of 20-25 feet from the ground such a canopy blots out the sun from the forest floor which, consequently, supports relatively little undergrowth. *Only on river banks or in clearings where more sunlight reaches the ground is there dense undergrowth which is often impenetrable.* However, in the interior of a virgin forest, especially in well-drained areas, movement is less difficult. Horizontal visibility is obstructed by the tree trunks and by the leaves on the thick vines which ascend to the forest canopy like cables. Heavy rainfall throughout the year supports this type of forest; the ground is nearly always wet and slippery, and the humidity remains high even during the hottest part of the day.

Highland Tropical Rain Forest: The gradual transition from lowland to highland tropical rain forest occurs in areas between 1,650-2,300 feet in elevation. Highland tropical rain forest (also known as cloud or moss forest) terminates at various altitudes, depending upon its exposure to wind and rainfall; in continental interiors it may terminate at 13,000 foot elevations. Many characteristics of the lowland tropical rain forests also apply to the highland tropical rain forest. While trees dominate, they are smaller in height and lack buttress roots; there is also extensive fern growth. *Most vegetation, prominent rock formations, and the ground itself are covered with moss or a heavy slippery slime.* Although the temperature may drop to 60°F, the humidity remains high. Animals, insects, and birds are scarce. *Movement in this type of forest is extremely arduous and hazardous since the slopes are usually steep. The ground is slick and deep layers of ground moss often cover hidden chasms and ravines.* At higher altitudes the mountains are often shrouded by a damp mist which substantially reduces visibility.

Jungle Terrain Features

Jungle types are classified by distinct vegetation types. Transition from one type to another tends to be gradual rather than sharp. Vegetation types are numerous, and they tend to intermingle which complicates their classification.

Jungle Types

Lowland Jungles: Located in areas varying from sea level to 2,000 feet of elevation, bordering on bodies of water and consisting of alluvial plains and swamps.

Highland Jungles: Normally found in areas ranging from 2,000 to 13,000 feet above sea level. They are characterized by steep, slippery slopes, and sometimes by steep-sided gullies and ravines which have been cut by torrential rains. The presence of numerous ridges establishes the existence of a many-branched drainage system which, in turn, causes a rugged and complex terrain structure. *The streams and rivers draining these ridges often have steep, almost vertical banks and are swift, deep and difficult to cross. During heavy rains, such streams and rivers may rapidly become raging torrents.* Despite the profusion of heavy vegetation, with few exceptions jungle soil is poor.

Primary Jungles

These are tropical forests. Depending on the type of trees growing in these forests, primary jungles are classified either as tropical rain forests or as deciduous forests.

Secondary Growth Forests

Wherever tropical rain forests or tropical deciduous forests are cleared and later abandoned, a secondary jungle growth results. Because of exposure to sunlight, these areas are rapidly overgrown by dense bushes and shrubs and climbing plants. *Foot movement is extremely slow and difficult. Vegetation may reach to a height of 6 feet. View of sight is generally limited to only a few feet.* Gradually, the composition of this forest becomes more complex, tending to approach its original nature. Because of uncontrolled cultivation, usually by primitive peoples, secondary forests in various stages of development have replaced a substantial percentage of virgin forest in most jungle areas and are invariably more difficult to traverse.

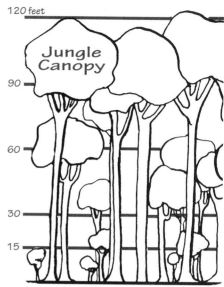

Tropical Deciduous Forest

- In some parts of the tropics there is a true dry season, lasting from three to six months, with almost no precipitation. Most of the trees in this area are deciduous, that is, they shed their leaves for a month or more. Although the leaves begin to fall gradually at the beginning of the dry season, the trees rarely become completely bare.

- The upper canopy of a primary deciduous forest is generally formed by 100 foot trees. Where the canopy is continuous, there is little undergrowth; where the canopy breaks, the undergrowth becomes dense, comprising thorny shrubs, knife-edged and saw-toothed grasses, and spiny vines. Even during the dry season this undergrowth reduces horizontal visibility to 15-60 feet. During the rainy season, climatic and soil conditions within this kind of forest are nearly identical to those in the tropical rain forest. During the dry season, the ground becomes hard and the temperature and humidity fluctuate more than in the tropical rain forest.

Density of Mangrove Roots

Extensive mangrove swamps occur in tropical coastal areas which are subject to tidal flooding. Closely spaced trees with thick root structure that extend as high as 10 feet above the ground form a considerable barrier to movement.

MANGROVE SWAMP

SWAMP FORESTS

Mangrove Swamp: Extensive mangrove swamps occur in tropical coastal areas which are subject to tidal flooding. This type of forest is generally found in the soft mud around river mouths, deltas, inlets, along shallow bays on small islands, and upstream as far as the tidal influence is felt. Closely spaced trees with thick stilt roots (tent shaped) that extend as high as 10 feet above the ground form a considerable barrier to movement. Usually the ground is covered by standing water. *The steeply arching roots hamper horizontal visibility and create an extremely slippery surface.* On the inland periphery where the water is less saline, mangrove swamps are usually bordered in many places by marshes. Mangrove species can usually be identified by the color of their bark, an important factor, since differences involve growth intensity, subjection to flooding and relative size of aerial roots, which have an effect on travel.

Red Mangrove: grows in deeply flooded areas and has both aerial roots which drop to seek water, and ground roots which branch out in a tangled tent-shaped mass, forming a formidable barrier to travel.

Black Mangrove: does not produce the maze of tent-shaped ground roots usually associated with red mangrove swamps, making movement easier than in swamps of red mangrove.

White Mangrove: Of all mangrove species, the white mangrove, which actually appears gray in color, presents the fewest barriers to ground movement. White mangrove generally stands further apart than other species and has no tent-shaped mass of roots.

Palm Swamp: is generally characterized by flooded ground and a sparse canopy of overhanging trees. These swamps have palms and large ferns with the plants being in dense stands.

Catival Swamp: derives its name from the Latin American cative or catival tree. Found in some jungle areas, the catival tree produces a high, closed canopy of branches which shuts out the sunlight and retards the growth of other vegetation. The catival growth is often dry; however, when exposed to flooding, the area is commonly referred to as catival swamp.

Coastal Thicket Swamp: Found along sandy beaches at or near sea level. Dense and difficult to traverse, the coastal thicket is a mixture of scattered coconut palm trees and salt tolerant shrubs

ASSOCIATED TERRAIN & VEGETATION

Marshes: generally are found in areas where the water is not brackish enough for mangrove, yet too wet for most forest trees. Tropical marshes contain tough thick reeds which grow to a height of 15 feet or more. While they offer less resistance to penetration than tree growths, marshes restrict observation at ground level to a few feet. In most cases, the footing in marshes is less secure than in other jungle growths.

Savanna: Tropical savanna grasslands commence along the fringes of tropical forests. Trees are scarce, occurring only in scattered small groves or as isolated specimens. Often comprising the principal vegetation, savanna grass ranges from a height of 15 feet in well watered areas to as low as three feet in drier areas. Although horizontal visibility in the tall grass is reduced to a few feet, the grass offers less resistance to movement than most other types of jungle growth. The highest temperatures in the humid tropics are recorded in savanna areas, and the daily differences in both temperature and humidity are greater than in the other jungle growth.

Bamboo: grows in clumps of varying size throughout the humid tropics. Springy, hollow jointed bamboo stems vary greatly in circumference and length. Some growths attain a height of well over a hundred feet, limiting horizontal visibility to only a few feet. Movement through bamboo is slow and arduous because of its unusual strength of resistance. Bamboo stems usually have to be cut or broken to traverse a growth.

Bamboo growth is very difficult to penetrate.

FARM CULTIVATION IN JUNGLE AREAS

Slash & Burn: Throughout tropical areas farmers till the land in a relatively similar manner. Several acres of trees are cut during the rainy season and the logs and stumps are left in the clearing. These are then burned during the dry season. At the beginning of the rainy season the farmers punch small holes in the ground with pointed sticks, drop a few seeds in each hole, cover the seeds by stamping the ground with their feet, and wait for the crop to grow. After one or two years of use, a clearing is abandoned and a new clearing is made. This is called "slash and burn" agriculture. Abandoned clearings usually contain a dense growth of scrub vegetation in which relics of former crops, such as bananas, may be found.

Wet Rice: Wet rice is grown both in the lowlands and on the hill slopes. In the lowlands rectangular fields separated by dikes two to four feet high are flooded during the growing season through a network of canals and irrigation ditches. On the hill slopes, terraces are constructed on which to grow the rice; dikes surround the terraced fields and the fields are flooded by gravity flow. Since most of these rice fields are fertilized by feces, accidental puncture of the skin while crossing these fields will generally result in an infection.

JUNGLE CLIMATES OF THE AMERICAS

Climate in the Amazon basin and most of the Central American tropics is characterized by high humidity and a lack of seasonal variations. In general, humidity decreases with distance from the Atlantic Ocean. In Panama, humidity often reaches 95% or more at night, and more than 60% during the day. At Manaus, in the heart of the Amazon basin, humidity averages 78%. The highest temperatures prevail along the Guyana and Caribbean coasts. Average temperature along many of the coastal lowland regions of Central America is 80°F. Average temperature variations between the warmest and coolest months in the Amazon basin is 3°F. Lowest temperature in many sections of the Amazon basin are recorded at 4 am., usually in August, when temperatures drop below 60°F. Rainfall over the entire American jungle is generally abundant. In the Amazon basin, rainfall exceeds 80 inches in most areas. The Amazon "winter" (rainy season) lasts from January to June, with almost daily rainfall in the form of local showers that begin and end suddenly. During this period, inhabitants of the region are generally restricted to their homes as roads and trails are inundated and become practically impassable. The lower Amazon experiences a marked dry season from July to September. Nights in the Amazon basin are always brilliantly clear. In Central America, most rainfall occurs along the low, flat stretches of the Caribbean coast, where warm, easterly trade winds annually bring between 125 and 200 inches of precipitation. Most rain falls along the coast between May and November, followed by a drier season lasting from December to April. On the Pacific coast of Central America, rainfall is somewhat less, averaging between 40 and 100 inches annually.

JUNGLE ANIMAL LIFE

Jungle-Tropical Rain Forest: The animal population of jungle areas is abundant and diversified. Some are remarkable for their size, such as 30 foot pythons and anacondas, the quarter ton land tortoises, giant scorpions and beetles, Ants, leeches, spiders, mosquitoes, and other insects are innumerable and are found everywhere from ground level to the tops of the tallest trees, Animal life is most abundant in the forest canopy, decreasing progressively in both species and number as they approach the forest floor. Environment involves five layers: the canopy, the middle tier, the surface of the ground, beneath the ground, and in the waters. Birds such as the parakeet, fruit pigeons, birds of paradise, toucans, and trogans live in the canopy. The forest canopy is also the habitat of monkeys, apes, sloth, iguanas, marsupials, squirrels, and a rich insect and reptilian life including snakes, spiders, centipedes and ants. Because of its unprotected cover, the forest floor supports the least animal life.

Savannas & Secondary Forests: In savannas and secondary forests with good shrub and bush cover, are found large animals such as deer, tapirs, wild pigs, jaguars and anteaters. On the floor of the tropical rain forest only lizards, grubs, termites and ants can survive. With the exception of monkeys, squirrels, snakes and lizards, the jungle canopy is virtually devoid of animal activity from mid-morning until about an hour before sundown. While life exists in the jungle during these hours, practically all wild life is resting under bark or logs, sleeping in the dense masses of vines or in the heads of palms, in holes in the ground, or in the rare patches of tall vegetation, usually near the water. Most animals in the jungle will not attack man unless they are frightened. There are a few exceptions. The jaguar, and peccaries (commonly called wild boars) may attack unprovoked. These animals are in the minority and are rarely encountered. Snakes will not usually attack unless they are molested. The danger of snake bites is commonly exaggerated. Some reptiles, such as the crocodile will attack when provoked, and some fish, such as the piranha of northeastern South America, will attack anything that moves. For the most part, the animals, other than insect types, that inhabit the jungle are not a significant hazard.

AMAZON JUNGLE

The Amazon basin contains about one sixth of the world's jungles. Extending more than 2,000 miles from the South Atlantic to the base of the Andes Mountains, the basin encompasses a land mass nearly as large as the continental United States. The heart of the Amazon basin is the immense Amazon River system, an inland sea, which fans out from the Atlantic coast to the Andes. The Amazon and its tributaries are bordered by an extensive flood plain sometimes varying in width from 50 to 60 miles. Because of low elevation and poor drainage, the plain is frequently flooded, forming numerous swamps, that sometimes cover thousands of square miles of land. The lower Amazon flood plain is usually under water from November through September. Bordering the Amazon flood plain are river bluffs averaging from 150 to 200 feet high. The remainder of the basin containing about 90% of the Amazon region consists of a low plateau of rolling terrain with intervening valleys which gradually slope inward toward the Amazon River. Covered with tropical rain forests and extensive stretches of scrub brush and short grasslands (campos), the Amazon uplands are relatively well drained and generally free of swamps. Facing the Amazon basin, the eastern foothills of the Andes form steep, dissected slopes and narrow valleys. These, together with intermittent swamps and dense vegetation, make land travel extremely difficult.

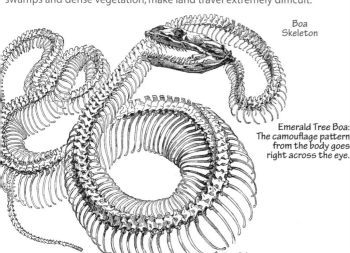

Boa
Skeleton

Emerald Tree Boa:
The camouflage pattern
from the body goes
right across the eye.

61

SURVIVAL IN THE JUNGLE

Jungle life and travel is difficult and you have to be prepared for an interesting experience – as it can be considered as a harsh environment. Most Americans, especially those raised in cities, are far removed from their pioneer ancestors, and have lost the knack of taking care of themselves under all conditions.

If prepared there is little to fear from the jungle environment. In a jungle, as the environment is unusual, the most important thing is to keep your head and calmly think out any situation. Many of the stories written about out-of-the-way jungle places were written by writers who went there in search of adventure rather than facts. Practically without exception, these authors exaggerated or invented many of the thrilling experiences they relate.

THE JUNGLE

- There are about 12 hours of daylight in jungle followed by extreme darkness. Camp preparation should be begun at least two hours prior to nightfall.
- The high humidity will adversely affect physical effort and group should be rested as required.
- Tropical downpours will quickly flood campsites unless they are adequately drained. This should be considered when selecting a site. During the rainy season the location of high ground should be determined.

JUNGLE CLIMATE

The discomforts of tropical climates are often exaggerated, but it is true that the heat is more persistent. In regions where the air contains a lot of moisture, the effect of the heat may seem worse than the same temperature in a dry climate. Many people experienced in jungle travel feel that the heat and discomfort in some US cities in the summertime are worse than the climate in the jungle. Strange as it may seem, there may be more suffering from cold in the tropics than from the heat. Of course, very low temperatures do not occur, but chilly days and nights are common. *In some jungles, in winter months, the nights are cold enough to require a wool blanket for sleeping.*

JUNGLE RAINFALL

Rainfall in many parts of the tropics is much greater than that in most areas of the temperate zones. Tropical downpours usually are followed by clear skies, and in most places the rains are predictable at certain times of the day. Except in those areas where rainfall may be continuous during the rainy season, there are not many days when the sun does not shine part of the time. *People who live in the tropics usually plan their activities so that they are able to stay under shelter during the rainy and hotter portions of the day.* After becoming used to it, most tropical dwellers prefer the constant climate of the torrid zones to the frequent weather changes in colder climates.

JUNGLE ACCLIMATIZATION

If a group is planning an intensive jungle trip the following are required:
- Excellent physical condition and a period of acclimatization. The hikers should be given a minimum of 7 days after arrival in the tropics to become acclimated to the heat and humidity. The acclimation process is automatic and begins the first day of arrival in the tropics. The ease and rapidity with which the body becomes acclimated depends upon degree of temperature change between the two climates involved. Individuals from a southern location in the mid-latitudes will become acclimated easier than members from a place farther to the north.
- Be psychologically prepared for the jungle. The foreboding appearance of the jungle, oppressive humidity and heat, unfamiliar noises and abject feeling, of loneliness that one feels when entering the jungle intensify the already existing fear of the unknown. To overcome these fears and uncertainties, group leaders should condition the member's mind for this new experience.
- The individuals must be given confidence in their ability to live, move and understand the jungle. Members must be trained in techniques of survival so that any potential accident or illness can be faced.

JUNGLE FEATURES & TRAVEL

These are common to all low jungle areas where there is water and poor drainage. There are two basic types of swamps - mangrove and palm.

Mangrove Swamps: are found in coastal areas wherever tides influence water flow. The mangrove is a shrub-like tree which grows 1 to 5 meters high. These trees have tangled root systems, both above and below the water level, which restrict movement to foot or small boats. View of sight in mangrove swamps, both on the ground and from the air, is poor. Easy to get lost.

Palm Swamps: exist in both salt and fresh water areas. Like movement in the mangrove swamps, movement through palm swamps is mostly restricted to foot (sometimes small boats). Vehicular traffic is nearly impossible. View of sight is very limited.

Savanna: is a broad, open jungle grassland in which trees are scarce. The thick grass is broad-bladed and grows 1 to 5 meters high. Movement in the savanna is generally easier than in other types of jungle areas, especially for vehicles. The sharp-edged, dense grass and extreme heat make foot movement a slow and tiring process. Depending on the height of the grass, view of sight may vary from poor to good.

Bamboo: grows in clumps of varying size in jungles throughout the tropics. Large stands of bamboo are major obstacles for vehicles. Foot movement through bamboo is slow and exhausting. You should bypass bamboo stands if possible.

Cultivated Areas: exist in jungles throughout the tropics and range from large, well-planned and well-managed farms and plantations to small tracts cultivated by individual farmers. There are three general types of cultivated areas - rice paddies, plantations, and small farms.

Rice Paddies: are flat, flooded fields in which rice is grown. Flooding of the fields is controlled by a network of dikes and irrigation ditches which make movement by vehicles difficult even when the fields are dry. Foot travel is poor when the fields are wet because you must wade through water about 2 feet deep and soft mud. When the fields are dry, foot travel becomes easier. The dikes, about 2 to 3 meters tall.

Plantations: are large farms or estates where tree crops, such as rubber and coconut, are grown. They are usually carefully planned and free of undergrowth. Travel through plantations is generally easy.

Small Farms: exist throughout the tropics. These small cultivated areas are usually hastily planned. After 1 or 2 years' use, they usually are abandoned, leaving behind a small open area which turns into secondary jungle. Travel through these areas may be difficult due to fallen trees and scrub brush.

Anaconda Snake

SURVIVAL IN THE JUNGLE

VISIBILITY IN JUNGLE

Ground observation in jungle areas varies according to the type of vegetation.

- Tropical rain forest the canopy, which consists of mature trees, is so thick that it cuts off most sunlight, and ground observation is limited to about 60-90 ft.
- Tropical deciduous forest, the tangle of secondary growth may limit ground observation to 15 ft. or less.
- Tropical savanna, commonly called elephant grass, which sometimes grows to a height of 15 feet or more, ground observation may be limited to a few feet.
- Mangrove swamps, ground observation will normally be limited to about 60 feet.

Visibility is be greatly restricted during rainy seasons, not only by the rain itself, but also by the heavy ground fogs which may linger for several hours after sunrise.

- Tops of ridges and hills offer slightly improved visibility because these features usually contain sparser jungle vegetation than is found in the valleys.
- Aerial visibility is generally ineffective because one cannot see activity underneath the jungle canopy and is extremely difficult during the rainy season due to excessive downfall and low hanging clouds plus fog and haze.

So if you get lost it would be extremely difficult to be found or in finding your way out.

OBSTACLES TO TRAVEL

The jungle itself is an obstacle. Major obstacles to movement include: dense vegetation; deep, eroded gullies; steep hills and cliffs; wide and deep rivers; and numerous fast flowing unfordable streams which can become raging torrents during the rainy season. During the rainy season, swamps may become impassable to even foot movement because of the depth of the water.

MOVEMENT IN A JUNGLE

- Cross-country movement in jungle areas is slow and difficult. One may have to cut ones way through continuous thick undergrowth or make detours of impassable swamps. Movement rarely exceeds 2 miles per hour.
- Ridge lines are the most favorable routes and preferable to valley travel which involves the crossing of numerous streams and gullies. On ridge lines, trees are more widely spaced, and tressed roots are less common, and better drainage results in less muddy surfaces. Animal trails and native trails are often found on the ridges. Movement on ridges is usually easier, faster, and less tiring.
- Movement is possible along small, fast flowing streams with traversable beds.
- Movement is poorest along the banks of rivers, because of the dense vegetation, mud, swamp, and tributary streams normally located in the vicinity of rivers.
- It is easier to follow corridors than it is to cross them. In flat jungle areas taking a direct route from one point to another may be convenient; however, in hilly jungle areas, such a route may prove to be the most demanding on the physical condition of traveler.

JUNGLE EQUIPMENT

Insect (mosquito) Bar: The insect bar or net should be used any time you sleep in the jungle. Even if conditions do not allow a shelter, the bar can be hung from trees or brush. No part of the body should touch the insect net when it is hung, because mosquitoes can bite through the netting. The bar should be tucked or laid loosely, not staked down. Although it is very light, it can be bulky if not folded properly.

Machete: The machete is an indispensable aid for jungle travel in moving through thick jungle and for shelter construction purposes.

Knife: A hunting knife is handy as there are always vines or fern like plants to cut.

Magnetic Compass: always carry a compass in the jungle as the viewing distance is restricted by the dense undergrowth. It should be worn high on the shoulder to prevent if from coming in contact with mud and water. It can be secured to the suspenders or backpack by a string.

Climbing Rope & Snap Links: are required for negotiating the numerous obstacles encountered in the jungle.

Canteen: While water is available in the jungle, it is usually of questionable quality. Each hiker should carry two canteens, one being used for drinking while the water in the other is ready to be purified.

Poncho: When the poncho is worn as a raincoat in the jungle, its nonporous structure will cause perspiration and will cause the hike to be more uncomfortable, and wetter, than not attempting to clothe oneself against the rain. Also, the vegetation at times will literally tear the poncho from the wearer's body. The poncho as an expedient has many useful purposes. It can be used to construct shelters and rafts and it can be used as a sleeping bag, or mattress.

Waterproof Map Case or plastified maps

Map Protractor	**Whistle**
Waterproof Flashlight	**Waterproof Watch**

JUNGLES & SOUND

- Dense vegetation tends to muffle sounds.
- To increase the range, sounds which contrast with normal jungle background noises should be used (for example whistling or metallic noises).

JUNGLE RADIO COMMUNICATION

Radio waves are absorbed by the damp and dense vegetation, and it is not unusual for the range of a set operated in the jungle to be reduced by 10-25% of the normal range. Absorption losses are compounded by the greater atmospheric noise levels and instability of the ionosphere typical of the tropics. The jungle environment affects different types of radio propagation. An example the ground wave (used by short range, high frequency AF and FM sets) is quickly absorbed and generally limited to less than one mile.

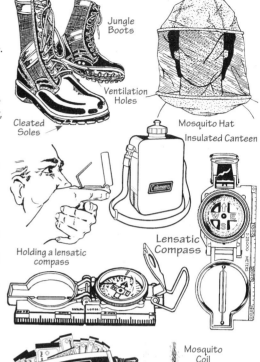

Jungle Boots
Ventilation Holes
Cleated Soles
Mosquito Hat
Insulated Canteen
Holding a lensatic compass
Lensatic Compass

First Aid Kit
Mosquito Coil

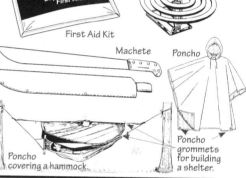

Machete
Poncho
Poncho covering a hammock.
Poncho grommets for building a shelter.

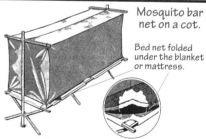

Mosquito bar net on a cot.

Bed net folded under the blanket or mattress.

Mosquito Bar Net

Should be used whenever sleeping the jungle. If conditions prevent construction of a shelter the bar can still be used by tying it to trees or brush. Besides providing protection from insects, the mosquito bar will offer protection from bats, whose bites are a potential source of rabies. Do not allow any portion of uncovered body to contact the mosquito bar when it is hung, as mosquitoes and bats will bite through the net.

Pocket Knife

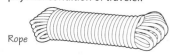

Rope

Electric Eels live only in the Amazon
The electric eel has special muscle cells that act like numerous battery cells that when they add their individual small charges can generate a single strong jolt.

SURVIVAL IN THE JUNGLE

JUNGLE CLOTHING

Clothing for humid, hot and wet environments requires special consideration.

Clothing: preferably heavier fast drying cotton. To provide the best ventilation, the clothing should fit loosely. Shirts or jackets should be worn on the outside of the trousers. Worn or threadbare clothing will not protect from insect bites, brambles, and direct sunlight. Garments should have cuffs and laces to protect against insects. Avoid wearing underwear as it may irritate the skin and reduce ventilation – if warn it should be light weight, loose, and cotton.

Boots: A lightweight jungle boot with cleated sole. Their cleated soles will maintain footing on steep, slippery slopes. The jungle boots usually have drainage holes on the side to let water and mud escape. Boots should be taken off at every opportunity to allow for drying of feet and boots, and for application of foot powder. The ventilating insoles should be washed in mild soap.

Headgear: A brimmed hat is recommended as it will help deflect insects and bugs falling from foliage from falling into the ears or down the neck.

Gloves: are useful when moving through vegetation to provide, protection from thorns, brambles, insect bites and snake bites. Gloves will also protect the hands from blisters when using the machete for prolonged periods of time. Gloves should not be worn, too long, because the skin will soften.

SURVIVAL KNIFE

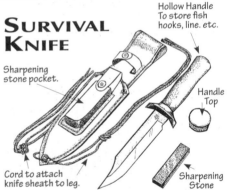

Hollow Handle To store fish hooks, line. etc.

Sharpening stone pocket.

Handle Top

Cord to attach knife sheath to leg.

Sharpening Stone

LEECHES

Leeches are common in many jungle areas. They are found in swampy areas, streams, and moist jungle country. They are not poisonous, but their bites may become infected if not cared for properly. The small wound that they cause may provide a point of entry for the germs which cause tropical ulcers or "jungle sores." Watch for leeches on the body and brush them off before they have had time to bite. If they have taken hold, they should not be pulled off forcibly because part of the leech may remain in the skin. Leeches will release themselves if touched with insect repellent, a moist piece of tobacco, the burning end of a cigarette, a coal from a fire, or a few drops of alcohol. Straps wrapped around the lower part of the legs (" leech straps") will prevent leeches from crawling up the legs and into the crotch area. Trousers should be securely tucked into the boots.

SNAKES

In the jungle you probably will see very few snakes. When you see one, the snake most likely will be making every effort to escape. If you accidentally step on a snake or otherwise disturb a snake, it will probably attempt to bite. The chances of this happening when traveling along trails or waterways are remote if you are alert and careful. Most jungle areas pose less of a snakebite danger than do the uninhabited areas of New Mexico, Florida, or Texas. This does not mean that you should be careless about the possibility of snakebites, but ordinary precautions against them are enough. Be particularly watchful when clearing ground. Treat all snakebites as poisonous.

MARINE LIFE

Hazards in tropical areas are poisonous, venomous, and ferocious fish; crocodiles and cayman; sea urchins; and coral, which can inflict painful cuts. Caution must be exercised in fording and bathing in jungle streams because of the danger posed by cayman and crocodile. Be aware of any water hazards peculiar to an area.

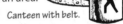

Canteen with belt.

JUNGLE INSECTS

The greatest hazard of the tropics is the insects. The intense heat, high humidity, heavy rainfall and incidence of low swampland coupled with dense vegetation of the jungle constitute an ideal environment for insects. The greatest danger is the ability of insects to transmit diseases through their bites. The bites constitute a serious threat to health by promoting infections as scratching all insect bite will generally cause an infection if no medication is applied. **AVOID SCRATCHING.** Keeping the body well covered will reduce the incidence of insect problems.

Malaria-carrying mosquitoes: are probably the most harmful of the tropical insects. Malaria can be contracted if proper precautions are not taken.

Precautions against malaria include:
- Take the required anti malaria medication
- Using insect repellent
- Wearing clothing that covers as much of the body as possible and use nets or screen at every opportunity
- Avoiding the worst-infested areas

MOSQUITOES

Mosquitoes are most prevalent early at night and just before dawn. You must be especially cautious at these times. Malaria is more common in populated areas than in uninhabited jungle, so be especially cautious when visiting villages. Mud packs applied to mosquito bites offer some relief from itching.

WASPS & BEES

Wasps and bees may be common in some places, but they will rarely attack unless their nests are disturbed. When a nest is disturbed leave the area as fast as you can. In case of stings, mud packs are helpful. In some areas, there are tiny bees, called sweat bees, which may collect on exposed parts of the body during dry weather, especially if the body is sweating freely. They are annoying but stingless and will leave when sweating has completely stopped, or they may be scraped off with the hand.

CENTIPEDES & SCORPIONS

The larger centipedes and scorpions can inflict stings which are painful but not fatal. They like dark places, so it is always advisable to shake out blankets before sleeping at night, and to make sure before dressing that they are not hidden in clothing or shoes.

SPIDERS & ANTS

Spiders are commonly found in the jungle. Their bites may be painful, but are rarely serious. Ants can be dangerous if lying on the ground. Sleep on a platform in an area free of ants.

WILD ANIMALS

Latin America's jungles have the jaguar. Ordinarily, these will not attack a man unless they are cornered or wounded. The larger and more dangerous animals are found in the grasslands along the periphery of the jungle.

One of the jungle's water hazards.

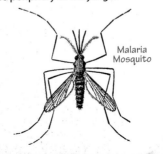

Malaria Mosquito

SURVIVAL IN THE JUNGLE

POISONOUS VEGETATION

An area of danger is that of poisonous plants and trees. For example, nettles, particularly tree nettles, are one of the dangerous items of vegetation. These nettles have a severe stinging that will quickly educate the victim to recognize the plant. The poison ivy and poison sumac of North America can cause many of the same type troubles that may be experienced in the jungle. The danger from poisonous plants in the woods of the eastern seaboard of North America is similar to that of the tropics. Thorny thickets, such as rattan, should be avoided as one would avoid a blackberry patch. Some of the dangers associated with poisonous vegetation can be avoided by keeping sleeves down and wearing gloves. **Importance of Clothing:** Many poisonous plants have thorns that can puncture the skin, introduce poison into the skin, or cause infection. Clothing can serve as a protective barrier for the skin. Clothing can also be a source of exposure if it is not properly cleaned after contact with poisonous plants. Toxic fruits can also cause significant harm, ranging from minor wounds to rapidly fatal poisoning.

- Avoid contact with poisonous plants by being properly covered.
- Avoid areas where poisonous plants grow.
- Only eat plants or parts of plants that are known to be edible. If you do not know, DO NOT eat it.
- DO NOT put grasses or woody twigs or stems in your mouth; they may be poisonous.

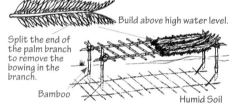

Split the end of the palm branch to remove the bowing in the branch.

Build above high water level.

Bamboo

Humid Soil

Tropical Bed for Swampy Areas

Implant bamboo sticks in the mud. Cross ribbing and horizontals are bamboo which is attached with rope or vines. The size and strength depends upon your weight and height. The bedding is palm branches, long reeds, or bull rushes. With taller vertical supports the structure can be covered with a mosquito net.

JUNGLE SURVIVAL FOOD

Food of some type is always available in the jungle - in fact, there is hardly a place in the world where food cannot be secured from plants and animals. All animals, birds, reptiles, and many kinds of insects of the jungle are edible. Some animals, such as toads and salamanders, have glands on the skin which should be removed before their meat is eaten. Fruits, flowers, buds, leaves, bark, and often tubers (fleshy plant roots) may be eaten. Fruits eaten by birds and monkeys usually may be eaten by man – *but not always* – as they might have a digestive track that neutralizes certain active ingredients.

See First Aid Chapter regarding water and food diseases.

JUNGLE COOKING

There are various means of preparing and preserving food found in the jungle.

- Fish can be cleaned and wrapped in wild banana leaves. This bundle is then tied with string made from bark, placed on a hastily constructed wood griddle, and roasted *thoroughly until done.* Another method is to roast the bundle of fish underneath a pile of red-hot stones.
- Meats can be roasted in a hollow section of bamboo, about 2 feet long. Meat cooked in this manner will not spoil for three or four days if left inside the bamboo stick and sealed.
- Yams, taros, yuccas, and wild bananas can be cooked in coals. They taste somewhat like potatoes. Palm hearts can make a refreshing salad, and papaya a delicious dessert.

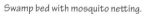

Large jungle leaves.

Swamp bed with mosquito netting.

Insulated Canteen -keeps water cool.

Mosquito net covering a sleeping bag.

JUNGLE WATER SUPPLY

Every effort should be made to obtain water from an approved water point. An abundance of water can be found in the jungle; however, all water obtained from other than an approved source must be purified before it is consumed. Even then be wary! Streams and rivers, water holes, and some vines will furnish water. Banana tree stalks, wrung out like a wet cloth, are a source of water. Bamboo saplings contain a supply of water in the lower sections. Rain is a good source of water, however, the jungle canopy is inhabited by thousand, of creatures. If rainwater is being used one should wait for rain to fall for 15 to 30 minutes to insure that water that falls through the canopy is free from contamination caused by excretion of these creatures.

Jungle Survival Platform

Jungle Shelter

Jungle shelters are used for protection from the harsh elements of the jungle. Shelters are necessary while sleeping and staying out of inclement weather.
- Choose high ground, away from swamps and dry river beds.
- Avoid game tracks and ant infested areas.

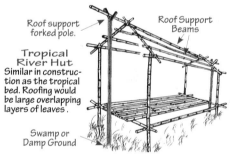

Roof support forked pole.

Roof Support Beams

Tropical River Hut

Similar in construction as the tropical bed. Roofing would be large overlapping layers of leaves .

Swamp or Damp Ground

Jaguar hunting a Tapir.

SURVIVAL IN THE JUNGLE

JUNGLE TRAVEL TIME

Movement in the jungle is calculated in terms of time rather than distance.

The rate of movement will depend on:
- Distance to be traveled.
- Availability of road and trails.
- Soil type and condition.
- Density and type of vegetation and type of terrain (e.g., mountainous, flat, inundated).
- Number and type of obstacles to be traversed.
- Physical condition of group.

TIME-DISTANCE FACTORS

Foot travel: The terrain and prevailing high temperature and humidity limit the rate of foot movement. Hikers tend to tire much faster and heat exhaustion is a common occurrence. Water consumption is high, creating the necessity for each member to carry two canteens.

Tropical rainforest: Average rate of movement is about 1,000 yards per hour, dependent upon the incidence of hills, rivers, and swamps which will slow movement considerably.

Tropical deciduous forests: Average rate is about 500 yards per hour.

Swamps: Average rate is about 100 to 500 yards per hour. During the rainy season some swamps become impassable because of the depth of the water, therefore requiring the use of boats and rafts.

Tropical savanna (elephant grass): Rate of movement is about the same as for tropical deciduous forest, but is more taxing and exhausting.

Bamboo: Extremely slow, dependent upon the size. Bamboo grows in impenetrable clumps which can normally be bypassed.

Rice paddies: During the dry season, the rate of movement is the same as for open terrain. During the rainy season, the average rate is about 1,000 yards per hour.

Road & trails: Average rate of movement is two miles per hour on roads and one mile per hour on trails.

Swamp Bed

In damp areas you need protection from the wet ground. Find four well positioned trees or implant 4 poles, bamboo is preferred if available. This bed can be covered with a mosquito net or poncho.

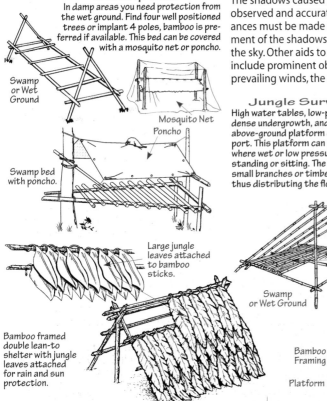

Swamp or Wet Ground

Mosquito Net Poncho

Swamp bed with poncho.

Large jungle leaves attached to bamboo sticks.

Bamboo framed double lean-to shelter with jungle leaves attached for rain and sun protection.

JUNGLE ROUTE SELECTION

In planning the route, consider the following:
- Lines of drift, such as ridge lines, are easy to travel on because they avoid streams and gullies and because they are usually less vegetated.
- Danger areas, such as streambeds and draws, are usually more thickly vegetated. Travel along them is slow and difficult.
- Roads and trails are the ideal selection.

Soil & Seasons: Jungle conditions vary greatly from place to place and season to season.
- Red silt soils tend to break down quickly when wet and become muddy.
- Inundated areas containing yellowish reeds and cloudy water usually have soft bottoms.
- Rice fields, in the dry season, are no problem but in the rainy season fields with standing water may have a soft bottom. Those containing clear water and green vegetation usually have firm ground.
- River and stream bottoms might be soft silt with densely vegetated banks.
- There are steep cliffs caused by soil erosion by the heavy rainfalls.

JUNGLE NAVIGATION

Navigation in thick jungle areas is difficult even for the most experienced. The compass is important but you will never be able to move very fast in the jungle if you had to constantly move along a magnetic azimuth. Movement along a terrain feature, such as a ridge line, is easier as it is the high ground – with no swamps, less dense vegetation, more air currents for cooling and to carry away most flying insects. If you have a map and know what feature or indicated path you are following you would use the compass, map, and also the pace count. The pace count is important as it will let you know how far you have progressed along the path. As there usually is dense vegetation it might be difficult to see reference points that would normally help you position yourself along a path.

The shadows caused by the sun are an easily observed and accurate aid to direction. Allowances must be made for the gradual displacement of the shadows as the sun moves across the sky. Other aids to maintaining direction include prominent objects, the course of rivers, prevailing winds, the stars, and the moon.

Jungle Survival Platforms

High water tables, low-pressure resistance soil, dense undergrowth, and tree roots, often requiring above-ground platform construction for shelter support. This platform can provide a floating base or floor where wet or low pressure resistance soil precludes standing or sitting. The platform is constructed of small branches or timber layered over cross-posts, thus distributing the floor load over a wider area.

Lean-to Bamboo Platform Shelter

Bamboo Framing

Platform

Swamp or Wet Ground

Swamp or Wet Ground

Bamboo Framing

Platform

CHECK MAJOR LAND FEATURES

Major recognizable features (hills, rivers, changes in the type of vegetation) should be noted as they are reached and then identified on the map. Jungle navigators **must be cautious about trails** - the trail on the ground may not be the one on the map.

SPEED OF MOVEMENT

Speed will vary with the physical condition of the group, the load they carry, and the type of jungle growth. The normal error is to **overestimate** the distance traveled.

Pacing

In thick jungle, this is the best way of measuring distance. It is the only method which lets you know how far you have traveled. To be accurate, you must practice pacing over different types of terrain and know your personal pace. Using a GPS has reduced the importance of the pace.

If Lost in the Jungle

Do not panic! Few travelers become permanently lost in the jungle, although many have taken longer to reach their destination than they should. Disoriented navigators should try to answer these questions:
- What was the last known location?
- Have you overshot your destination – due to the limited visibility? This is where the pace count would be important – or GPS location.
- Does the terrain look the way it should? Compare the surroundings with the map, the fall of the shadows, or GPS location.
- What features in the area will help to fix the unit's location? (find these features.)

NIGHT TRAVEL

If you have not gotten back by nightfall you should consider setting camp before it gets dark. Night navigation is the same as day travel. The problem in night movement is one of control, not navigation. In clear weather, through sparse vegetation and under a bright moon, it might be possible to move almost as fast by night as by day. If the sky is overcast, vegetation is thick, or there is little or no moon, movement will be slow and hard to control.

To help in night travel:
- Attach luminous tape to the back of each travelers headgear. Two strips, side by side, are used as they aid depth perception and reduce the hypnotic effect that one strip can cause.
- When there is no light at all, limit the distance between members of the group.
- To prevent the loss of contact, each member should hold on to the belt or the pack of the individual in front of him.
- The leading man should carry a long stick to probe for sudden drop-offs or obstacles.
- Use the compass bezel ring, especially during night navigation. *See Compass Chapter page 363.*

Survival in the Jungle

Navigation Tools

Maps: Because of the isolation of many jungles, the rugged ground, and the presence of the canopy, topographic survey is difficult and is done mainly from the air. Although maps of jungle areas generally depict the larger features (hill, ridges, larger streams, etc.) fairly accurately, some smaller terrain features (gullies, small or intermittent streams, small swamps, etc.), which are actually on the ground, may not appear on the map. Also, many older maps are inaccurate. So, before going into the jungle, check on the accuracy of your maps.

Compass: No one should move in the jungle without a compass. It should be tied to the clothing by a string or boot lace. The keys to navigation are maintaining the right direction and knowing the distance traveled. Skill with the compass (acquired through practice) takes care of the first requirement. Ways of knowing the distance traveled include checking natural features with the map, knowing the rate of movement, and pacing.

Three most common compass reading methods:

- Sighting along the desired azimuth. The compass man notes an object to the front (usually a tree or bush) that is on line with the proper azimuth and moves to that object. *This is not a good method in the jungle as trees and bushes tend to look very much alike.*
- Holding the compass at waist level and walk in the direction of the set azimuth. *This is a good method for the jungle.*
- Set the compass for night use with the long luminous line placed over the luminous north arrow and the desired azimuth under the black index line. There is a natural tendency to drift either left or right using this method. Jungle navigators must learn their own tendencies and allow for this drift. The navigator with the compass is at the rear or the group (if the group is not to large – 'large' depending upon the density of the jungle). Sighting along the desired azimuth and guiding the lead person forward until he is on line with the azimuth. *This is the most accurate method to use in the jungle during daylight hours, but it is slow.* In this method, the compass man cannot mistake the aiming point and is free to release the compass on its string and use both hands during movement to the next aiming point.

Vehicle Travel

Cross-country movement by vehicles is normally impossible. The primary factors that affect the movement capability of wheeled and tracked vehicles are:

- Availability of roads and trails.
- Soil condition.
- Density and type of vegetation.
- Slopes of hills and mountains.
- Weather conditions (dry or rainy)
- Effects of high and low tides on rivers, streams and inundated areas.
- River, stream, and swamp obstacles to be crossed.

Folding Shovel

Although any one of the above factors may affect vehicle movement, a combination of factors, such as weather and soil, slope and vegetation, will normally have to be considered when determining the affect on movement.

Soil & Travel: Soils composed of red clay silt (common in jungle areas) tend to break down when wet. Single tracks may usually be made but repeated passes or sharp turns cause these soils to break down and become impassable. A simple test for this type of soil is to stick a rod into the ground where surface water is standing. If the water drains through the hole, clay is usually present and vehicle travel is not advisable during the rainy season.

Plants & Vehicle Travel

Inundated areas containing yellowish reeds and cloudy water can be expected to have a soft bottom. Watch the water buffalo and similar animals. They do not go where they cannot stand on the bottom. If the bottom supports them, it will usually support the vehicle.

Cross-Country Orienteering

Maintaining direction during cross-country movement in a jungle area is extremely difficult. A position has to be determined and a rout has to be selected with very limited visibility.

Rappelling

Rappelling is a means to move quickly down very steep hills and cliffs. Rappelling involves sliding down a rope which has been anchored around a firm object (anchor point) such as a tree, projecting rock, or piton. *See page 173.*

Jungle Obstacles

Climbing and rappelling might have to be used so you must be familiar with ropes and knots.

Types of Rope & the Jungle

Nylon: Nylon rope is most commonly used in climbing and rappelling. The rope is seven-sixteenths of an inch in diameter. Its dry breaking strength averages 3,840 pounds (± 5%). Strength is reduced by about 20% when the rope is wet. It will stretch about one-third of its length when wet.

Vegetable Fiber: Readily available in jungle areas as it is made primarily from the fibers of tropical plants.

Manila Rope: is made from the fibers of the leaves of a banana tree. The lighter the color of the rope, the better the quality. This rope is superior to nylon rope for suspension traverses and rope bridges because it does not stretch as much as nylon, and it is not weakened when wet.

Hemp Rope: is made from the fibers of the hemp plant. This is the strongest of the fiber ropes. It is usually soaked in tar to preserve the rope from damage caused by dampness, but this tar tends to reduce the rope's strength. Tarred hemp is quite heavy so that it is not too practical.

Breaking Strength: of a rope is always greater than its safe working capacity. The difference is a "safety factor." Individual ropes can vary greatly in minimum breaking strength. Even though a rope may not break under this load, the fibers are stretched beyond their elastic limit. Thereafter the strength of the rope is permanently reduced. Exposure, wear, use, and bending decrease a rope's strength over a period of time. This should be allowed for in estimating the strength of a used rope. The strength of a rope that is slung over a hook or contains a knot is reduced by about 30%; sharp bends over corners will cut strength by 50%; sand or grit between the fibers will quickly cut the fibers, and sharply drop the overall strength of the rope.

Care of Rope

- Clean a muddy rope by washing it in water, but not in salt water.
- Do not pull a rope over sharp edges. Place layers of heavy cloth or grass between the rope and any sharp edge to prevent the cutting of fibers.
- Do not drag a rope through sand and dirt, or step on it, or drive over it.
- Keep a rope dry. If it gets wet, dry it as soon as possible to prevent rotting. (A mildewed rope will have a musty odor and inner fibers will have a dark, stained look.)
- Do not leave a rope knotted or tightly stretched any longer than needed.
- Never splice a climbing or rappelling rope.
- Inspect a rope often, both the outside and the inside. Untwist a few strands at different points to open the rope to check the inside.
- Melted nylon and dark streaks indicate burns. Nylon rope burns when it rubs against other nylon ropes.
- Nylon ropes should never be tied in such away that there is rope-to-rope friction.
- Dirt and sawdust-like material inside the rope indicates damage.
- A rope should be checked at a number of different places - any weak point in it weakens the entire rope.
- Whenever any unsafe conditions are found in a rope, it should be destroyed or cut up in short pieces.

A bamboo raft.

JUNGLE FIRST AID

JUNGLE TRAVEL

When traveling in the jungle the relatively high incidence of disability caused by heat, humidity, and insect borne diseases will require emphasis on health and sanitation measures.

Special precautions have to be taken in the storage of certain medical supplies due to heat and high humidity which can cause deterioration and loss of potency.

WET SKIN DISEASES

Warm Water Immersion Foot: occurs usually where there are many creeks, streams, and canals to cross, with dry ground in between. The bottoms of the feet become white, wrinkled, and tender. Walking becomes painful.

Chafing: This disease occurs when frequently wading through water up to your waist, and the trousers stay wet for hours. The crotch area becomes red and painful to even the lightest touch.

Most skin diseases are treated by letting the skin dry.

PREVENTIVE MEASURES

Each member should to protect themselves from these diseases:

- First and foremost, each member should assume personal responsibility for their own cleanliness and sanitation of the surroundings.
- Inspect the body frequently for lice, ticks, or other insect bites (use the "buddy system").
- Inspect the body for skin breaks, lacerations and scratches, and more important, treat them immediately. Due to the excessive heat and humidity, the body will sweat profusely and this moist condition often causes a minor scratch or skin laceration to become infected and it will not heal.
- Protect the body from insect bites by using the mosquito bar. Use latrines where possible, and keep the camp well separated.
- Bathe often, and air or sun dry the body as often as possible.
- Wear clean, dry, loose-fitting clothing.
- Do not sleep in wet, dirty clothing. If clothing is wet and dirty remove it at night and use it again in the morning. This not only fights fungus, bacterial, and warm water immersion diseases but also prevents night chills and provides for a better rest.
- Avoid wearing underwear if at all possible; this is known as the single layer principle. Humid underwear causes severe chafing.
- Take off boots and message feet as often as possible. Always remove the boots while sleeping.
- Dust feet, socks, and boots with foot powder at every chance.
- Always carry several pairs of socks and change them frequently.
- Keep the hair cut short and shave frequently.
- Sleep off the ground in a hammock or on a platform.
- Individual responsibility for personal health cannot be overemphasized. A group leader should make frequent inspections.

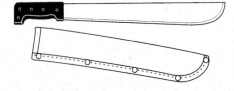

A machete the most important jungle tool.

HEALTH & HYGIENE

The climate in tropical areas and the absence of normal sanitation facilities increases the chance that a traveler may contract a disease. Disease is fought with good sanitation practices and preventive medicine.

Before going into a jungle area:
- Make sure immunizations are current.
- Be in top physical shape.
- Watch your personal hygiene.

Upon arrival in the jungle area:
- Allow time to adjust (acclimate).
- It is very important to replace the fluids lost through sweating.
- Know the sources of possible diseases.

Insects cause: malaria, yellow fever, scrub, typhus.

Dirty food & contaminated water cause: typhoid, dysentery, cholera, hepatitis.

WATERBORNE DISEASES

Water is vital in the jungle and is usually easy to find. However, water from all natural sources should be considered contaminated. Water purification procedures must be used. Germs of serious diseases, like dysentery, are found in impure water. Other waterborne diseases, such as blood fluke, are caused by exposure of an open sore to impure water.

Prevent waterborne diseases by:
- Obtaining drinking water from approved water points.
- When using rainwater; only collect it after it has been raining at least 15 to 30 minutes. This lessens the chances of impurity being washed from the jungle canopy into the water container. Even then the water should be purified.
- Purify all drinking water.
- Do *not* swim or bath in untreated water.
- Keeping the *body fully clothed* when crossing water obstacles.

FUNGUS DISEASES

These diseases are caused by poor personal health practices. The jungle environment promotes fungus and bacterial diseases of the skin and warm water immersion skin diseases. Bacteria and fungi are tiny plants which multiply fast under the hot, moist conditions of the jungle. *Sweat-soaked skin invites fungus attack.* Ringworm, athlete's foot, and trichophytosis, a fungus disease of the hair.

JUNGLE HEAT DISORDERS

These result from high temperatures, high humidity, lack of air circulation, and physical exertion.

Heat injuries are prevented by:
- Drinking plenty of water.
- Using extra salt with food and water.
- Slowing down movement.
- Eat your heavy meal during the cool of the day if this is possible.

First Aid: heat injury treatment Page 590.

Arrow Poison Frog

HYGIENE & SANITATION

Hygiene & Sanitation: In no other type of outdoor activity is sanitation and personal hygiene more important than in the jungle for diseases can quickly bog down the whole hiking party. Before leaving on the trip every member must have at least an elementary knowledge of how to care for his own health, for clinical features, treatment, control and prevention of specific diseases that are prevalent in this area.

Tropical Diseases: All tropical areas, due to their warm and humid climates, favor rapid reproduction, growth, and spread of disease causing germs. Most of these areas have a high rate of endemic diseases; the primitive sanitation systems and great numbers and varieties of disease carrying insects compound this condition. It would not be possible or practical to discuss the subject of tropical diseases at any great length. However, a basic knowledge of the disease conditions, their cause and method of spreading, and their prevention is necessary.

COMMUNICABLE DISEASES

The communicable diseases will be categorized by their method of transmission.

Contact Diseases: As the name implies, these diseases are spread by personal or direct contact as smallpox.

Intestinal Infections: These diseases are usually transmitted by eating contaminated food or drinking untreated water. Contamination of food is common. The contamination may be caused in vegetable products by contact with infected material during growth, such as human excrement used as fertilizer. Contamination of any food may be caused by dirty utensils, flying insects, or by food handlers who have, or are carriers of, intestinal diseases. Some of the parasitic intestinal infections (such as hookworm) are acquired through the skin by walking barefoot.

Waterborne Diseases: These diseases may be transmitted by impure water which is used for drinking, cooking and bathing purposes. Some examples are typhoid fever, salmonellosis, bacillary dysentery, ambiasis, cholera, and schistosomiasis (blood fluke), which may be readily encountered in surface water while bathing (entrance may be through any minute break in the skin) or swimming, and through drinking.

Insect & Animal Borne Diseases: are transmitted from man to man directly through bites of bloodsucking insects or animals. The germ may be introduced into the human bloodstream or tissues by the bite of the infected insect or it may be deposited on the skin by defecation or during the process of biting. In the latter two instances, scratching the insect bite infects the wound with the germs. Diseases transmitted by mosquitoes include malaria, yellow fever, dengue (breakbone) fever, filariasis (elephantiasis), and some forms of encephalitis. Ticks transmit tick born typhus, rabbit fever, tick paralysis, and relapsing fever. Sand flea bites can produce various diseases such as tropical and oriental sores. Fleas may convey the bubonic plague (rat flea) and marine typhus; scrub typhus is transmitted by small mites. Body and head lice may transmit epidemic typhus fever and relapsing fever. Mites, blood sticking flies, kissing bugs, and bats can convey diseases and rabies to human beings by their bite. Insect repellent and impregnated clothing are effective in preventing many of these diseases.

Augastine
Alaska Eruption

09 Hawaii Lava Hiking

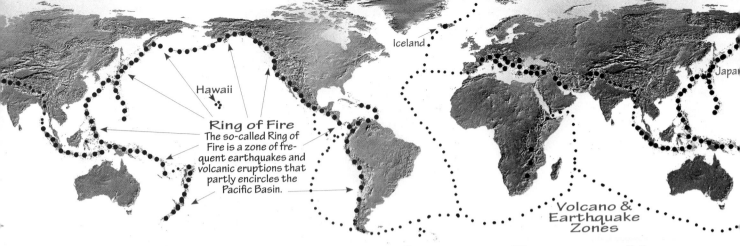

Iceland

Japan

Hawaii

Ring of Fire
The so-called Ring of Fire is a zone of frequent earthquakes and volcanic eruptions that partly encircles the Pacific Basin.

Volcano & Earthquake Zones

EARTH'S SURFACE

Volcanoes have contributed significantly to the formation of the surface of our planet. Volcanism produced the crust we live on and most of the air we breathe by liberating gases in the atmosphere and water in lakes and oceans from the rocks deep beneath the surface of the earth. The fertility of the soil is greatly enhanced by volcanic eruptive products. Land masses such as islands and large sections of continents may owe their existence entirely to volcanic activity.

VOLCANIC ERUPTIONS

Volcanoes occur because the Earth's crust is broken into plates that resemble a jigsaw puzzle. These rigid plates float on a softer layer of rock in the Earth's mantle. As the plates move about, they push together or pull apart. Most volcanoes occur near the edges of plates. When plates push together, one plate slides beneath the other. This is a subduction zone. When the plunging plate gets deep enough inside the mantle, some of the rock on the overlying plate melts and forms magma that can move upward and erupt at the Earth's surface. At rift zones, plates are moving apart and magma comes to the surface and erupts. Some volcanoes occur in the middle of plates at areas called hots pots - places where magma melts through the plate and erupts.

VOLCANIC ERUPTION SAFETY
Page 13

VOLCANO ACTIVITY

There is no consensus among volcanologists on how to define an active volcano. The life span of a volcano can vary from months to several million years, making such a distinction sometimes meaningless when compared to the life spans of humans or even civilizations. For example, many of Earth's volcanoes have erupted dozens of times in the past few thousand years but are not currently showing signs of activity. Given the long life span of such volcanoes, they are very active. Compared to our life span, however, they are not. Complicating the definition are volcanoes that become restless but do not actually erupt.

ACTIVE VOLCANO

Scientists usually consider a volcano active if it is currently erupting or showing signs of unrest, such as unusual earthquake activity or significant new gas emissions. Many scientists also consider a volcano active if it has erupted in historic time. It's important to note that the span of recorded history differs from region to region; in the Mediterranean, recorded history reaches back more than 3000 years but in the Pacific Northwest of the United States, it reaches back less than 300 years, and in Hawaii, little more than 200 years.

Yellowstone caldera in Yellowstone National Park is at least 2 million years old and hasn't erupted for 70,000 years, yet scientists do not consider Yellowstone as extinct. In fact, because the caldera has frequent earthquakes, a very active geothermal system, and rapid rates of ground uplift, many scientists consider it to be a very active volcano.

DORMANT VOLCANO

Is one that is not currently active, but could become restless or erupt again.

EXTINCT VOLCANO

Is one that scientists consider unlikely to erupt again. Whether a volcano is truly extinct is often difficult to determine. For example, since calderas have life spans sometimes measured in millions of years, a caldera that hasn't produced an eruption in tens of thousands of years is likely to be considered dormant instead of extinct.

Based upon data from the U.S. Geological Survey

Lava Flow Deposit   Crater   Shield Volcano   Old Debris Deposit

Lava mounting in vent.   Dike

Shield Volcano

Volcanoes with broad, gentle slopes and built by the eruption of fluid basalt lava. Basalt lava tends to build enormous, low-angle cones because it flows across the ground easily and can form lava tubes that enable lava to flow tens of kilometers from an erupting vent with very little cooling. The largest volcanoes on Earth are shield volcanoes. The name comes from a perceived resemblance to the shape of a warrior's shield. This is the type of structure in Hawaii and the Yellowstone National Park.

Convergent Plate Boundary

The descending ocean (subducting) plate goes below the continental crust causing the formation of major mountain ranges, earthquake zones, and volcanoes. Examples are the Cascades and the Andes.

Shield Volcano

Forms in an area where the magma rises to the surface. Usually forming a series of active areas (islands). This is the type of structure in Hawaii and the Yellowstone National Park.

Divergent Plate Boundary

Fissure volcanoes can form along the oceanic spreading ridge which is formed by divergence of the plate.

Convergent Plate Boundary

Stratovolcanoes form where convergent plate boundaries, such as the Aleutian trench in Alaska, subduction results in a curved chain of submarine volcanoes or volcanic islands (called an island arc) behind the oceanic trench. Extensive island arc-trench systems also exist in much of the western Pacific.

Continental Rift Zone
Young Divergent Plate Boundary
Is an elongate system of crustal fractures associated with an area that has undergone extension (ground has spread apart). The volcanic features on a rift zone may be the rise and eruption of magma from narrow dikes, including eruptive fissures, cinder and spatter cones, spatter ramparts, pit craters, lava flows, ground cracks, and normal faults.

Hawaii Type Structure

Transform Plate Boundary

After Jose F. Vigil US Geological Survey

Island Arc

Stratovolcano

Trench

Shield Volcano

Lithosphere

Hot Spot

Ocean Spreading Ridge

Trench

Oceanic Crust

Continental Crust

Asthenosphere

Subducting Plate

Cross Section Showing the Plate Tectonic Process

VISITING HAWAII'S ACTIVE VOLCANO AREAS

VOLCANIC ASH

Consists of rock, mineral, and volcanic glass fragments smaller than 2 mm (0.1 inch) in diameter, which is slightly larger than the size of a pinhead. It is hard, does not dissolve in water, and can be extremely small - ash particles less than 0.025 mm in diameter are common.

Ash is extremely abrasive, similar to finely crushed window glass, mildly corrosive, and electrically conductive, especially when wet. Volcanic ash is created during explosive eruptions by the shattering of solid rocks and violent separation of magma (molten rock) into tiny pieces. Explosive eruptions are generated when ground water is heated by magma and abruptly converted to steam and also when magma reaches the surface so that volcanic gases dissolved in the molten rock expand and escape (explode) into the air extremely rapidly. After being blasted into the air by expanding steam and other volcanic gases, the hot ash and gas rise quickly to form a towering eruption column directly above the volcano.

ERUPTION CLOUD

A cloud of tephra and gases that forms downwind of an erupting volcano is called an eruption cloud. The vertical pillar of tephra and gases rising directly above a vent is an eruption column. Eruption clouds are often dark-colored - brown to gray - but they can also be white, very similar to weather clouds. Eruption clouds may drift for thousands of kilometers downwind and often become increasingly spread out over a larger area with increasing distance from an erupting vent.

VOLCANIC GAS

Magma contains dissolved gases that are released during eruptions. Gases are also released from magma that either remains below ground (as an intrusion) or rises toward the surface. In such cases, gases may escape continuously into the atmosphere from the soil, volcanic vents, fumaroles, and hydrothermal systems. The most common gases are steam (H_2O), followed by CO_2 (carbon dioxide), SO_2 (sulfur dioxide), (HCl) hydrogen chloride and other compounds.

LAVA ERUPTION

Some volcanic eruptions are explosive and others are not. How explosive an eruption is depends on how runny or sticky the magma is. Gases can escape easily if the magma is thin and runny. When this type of magma erupts, it flows out of the volcano as lava. Lava flows rarely kill people, because they move slowly enough for people to escape. Lava flows, however, can cause considerable destruction to buildings in their path.

The rate of supply of magma relative to the velocity of the lava as it flows from the vent and the external environment through which the lava flows also affect the structure of the solidified lava. Lava may form lava lakes of fluid rock in summit craters or in pit craters on the flanks of shield volcanoes. When the lava issues vertically from a central vent or a fissure in a rhythmic jet-like eruption, it produces a lava fountain.

Based upon data by the U.S. Department of the Interior & U.S. Geological Survey.

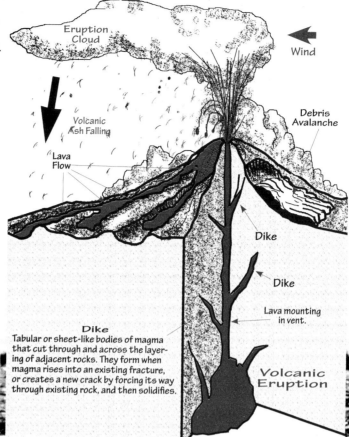

Eruption Cloud

Wind

Volcanic Ash Falling

Debris Avalanche

Lava Flow

Dike

Dike

Lava mounting in vent.

Dike
Tabular or sheet-like bodies of magma that cut through and across the layering of adjacent rocks. They form when magma rises into an existing fracture, or creates a new crack by forcing its way through existing rock, and then solidifies.

Volcanic Eruption

EXPLOSIVE ERUPTION

If magma is thick and sticky, gases cannot escape easily. Pressure builds up until the gases escape violently and explode. In this type of eruption, the magma blasts into the air and breaks apart into pieces called tephra. Tephra can range in size from tiny particles of ash to house-size boulders. Explosive volcanic eruptions can be dangerous and deadly. They can blast out clouds of hot tephra from the side or top of a volcano. These fiery clouds race down mountainsides destroying almost everything in their path. Ash erupted into the sky falls back to Earth like powdery snow. If thick enough, blankets of ash can suffocate plants, animals, and humans. When hot volcanic materials mix with water from streams or melted snow and ice, mudflows form. Mudflows have buried entire communities located near erupting volcanoes.

Because there may be hundreds or thousands of years between volcanic eruptions, people may not be aware of a volcano's dangers. When Mount St. Helens in the State of Washington erupted in 1980, it had not erupted for 123 years. Most people thought Mount St. Helens was a beautiful, peaceful mountain and not a dangerous volcano.

PYROCLASTIC ERUPTIONS

Pyroclastic (fire broken) rocks and rock fragments are products of explosive eruptions. The force that produces explosive eruptions is the release of trapped gas. Ejecta from these explosions may be derived from the magma or from rocks in the vicinity of the volcanic conduit that are blasted out in the eruption. These may be ejected more or less vertically, then fall back to earth in the form of ash fall deposits. Pyroclastic flows result when the eruptive fragments follow the contours of the volcano and surrounding terrain. They are of three main types:

Glowing Ash Clouds: A glowing ash cloud consists of an avalanche of incandescent volcanic fragments suspended on a cushion of air or expanding volcanic gas. This cloud forms from the collapse of a vertical ash eruption, from a direct blast, or is the result of the disintegration of a lava dome. Temperatures in the glowing cloud can reach 1000°C and velocities of 150 km per hour.

Ash Flows: Resemble glowing ash clouds; however, their temperatures are much lower.

Mudflows (lahars): Consist of solid volcanic rock fragments held in water suspension. Some may be hot, but most occur as cold flows. They may reach speeds of 92 km per hour and extend to distances of several tens of kilometers. Large snow-covered volcanoes that erupt explosively are the principal sources of mud flows.

Lava Stone

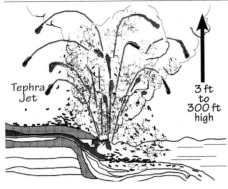

Tephra Jet

3 ft to 300 ft high

Tephra Jet

A tephra jet is the most common type of explosion a hiker is likely to witness when an active lava tube opens to the sea. When waves splash onto molten lava, they "explode" in a cloud of steam, hot water, and tephra (molten splatter, tiny glass fragments, and long glass filaments known as "Pele's hair").

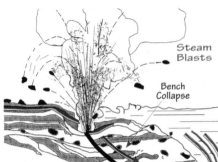

Steam Blasts

Bench Collapse

Steam Blasts

Collapse of a lava bench exposes hot, newly solidified lava flows to sea water. The water heats to steam and can trigger a type of explosion called a steam blast. Hikers standing anywhere near a bench or on cliffs formed by a previous bench collapse can be hit by ballistic projectiles. In 1993, a lava bench at a Kilauea ocean-entry site collapsed, triggering a violent steam explosion. A person standing on the bench died, and twelve others who were nearby needed medical attention after being hit by flying rocks.

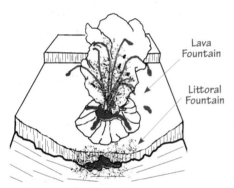

Lava Fountain

Littoral Fountain

Lava Fountain

A jet of lava sprayed into the air by the rapid formation and expansion of gas bubbles in the molten rock is called a lava fountain. Lava fountains erupt from isolated vents, along fissures, within active lava lakes, and from a lava tube when water gains access to the tube in a confined space.

Littoral Fountain

A "littoral fountain" produces bursts of molten lava and steam from a lava tube at or below sea level. As water enters the 2120°F (1160°C) lava tube, it immediately flashes to steam. The resulting explosions of molten lava and bombs and smaller tephra pieces can reach higher than 300 feet (100 m) and build a steep cone on the lava bench.

Based upon data by the U.S. Department of the Interior & U.S. Geological Survey.

Lava Hiking

Common sense is not enough. Eruptions of the volcanoes are noted for their "approachable" flows of molten lava. These "friendly flows" can undergo many rapid and unpredictable changes that can be life-threatening. Without knowledge of Hawaii's volcanic landscapes and the processes that form them, visitors can easily find themselves in danger. Understanding volcano hazards and taking the right equipment are key to safely exploring the volcanic landscape.

Hiking in Lava Areas

- Stay well back from the edge of steep cliffs because they frequently break off. If you fall into the ocean, you cannot climb out because of the irregular sharp shoreline and you may be burned by hot, acidic water.
- Do not venture onto the "benches" (solid cooled areas built by lava entering the sea) as collapsing benches have killed people.
- Move inland quickly if you hear unusual sounds. They may indicate that the ground is about to collapse.
- Do not go near the water because it may be extremely hot, and you could be severely scalded by unexpected waves.

Active Lava Flow Hiking

Kilauea is currently erupting. This eruption started in 1983, when spectacular lava fountaining began at a new vent high on the volcano's east rift zone. Surface flows have been common in the eruption, but most lava from the vent flows are concealed in lava tubes until it reaches the ocean.

Dangers of Lava Bubbles

Lava bubbles occur when seawater enters the lava tube, flashes into steam, and blows lava bubbles through the roof of the tube. A lava bubble fountain is an explosive fountain throwing hot lava spatter and basketball-sized rocks 300 feet (100 m) into the air; the fountain results from a piece of a lava-filled bench collapsing and exposing hot rock to the ocean. Lava flows and lava tubes change frequently.

Warning signs cannot always be posted near hazardous areas, because car-sized bubbles of lava can burst from a lava-formed "bench" at the ocean's edge.

Volcanism in Hawaii

The island of Hawaii has one of the youngest and most diverse landscapes on Earth. Built by countless eruptions of lava and tephra and sculpted by faults, landslides, and water, the Big Island is a remarkable window into the early histories of the other, much older Hawaiian Islands.

Hawaii's volcanoes have more fluid, less gaseous magmas that produce quieter, less hazardous eruptions. Fewer than one hundred people have been killed by eruptions in the recorded history of Hawaii, and only one death has occurred in this century. However, the lava flows are highly destructive to populated and cultivated areas.

Volcanic Hazards

- Bench collapse can kill.
- Tephra jets & littoral fountains hurl hot lava.
- Steam blasts toss rocks.
- Acid fumes and glass particles can irritate eyes and lungs.
- Scalding waves can burn.

Personal Hazards

- Dehydration
- Heat stroke
- Sunburn & sunstroke
- Sprains & abrasions
- Getting lost in the dark

Lava Entering the Sea

When hot lava enters the ocean, it bursts into pieces, building new land at the water's edge from the fragmental material. This pile of rubble is then covered with a veneer of lava flows, forming a "bench" that gives a false impression of solid ground. Lacking years of experience, casual hikers will not be able to recognize potential hazards and may easily underestimate them.

Lava entering the sea on Kilauea Volcano, J.D. Griggs USGS

BENCH FORMATION
(Unstable Land)

A bench is an area of new, unstable land formed where lava enters the ocean, cools, and solidifies. Although most lava activity consists of sluggish submarine flows and mild spattering, the contact of water and molten lava can produce "tephra jets" and "littoral fountains."

•

The bench can collapse, triggering violent explosions that throw lava and rocks 300 feet (100 m) inland.

•

Hardened lava-covered benches look solid from above but can collapse unexpectedly.

•

Be alert to cracking or booming sounds. Avoid "flying rocks"!

•

Stay at least 100 yards (100 m) from the ocean entry.

•

Collapse of a lava bench exposes hot, newly solidified lava flows to sea water. The water heats to steam and can trigger a type of explosion called a steam blast.

•

Visitors standing anywhere near a bench or on cliffs formed by a previous bench collapse can be hit by ballistic projectiles. In 1993, a lava bench at a Kilauea ocean-entry site collapsed, triggering a violent steam explosion (steam blast). A person standing on the bench died and twelve others who were nearby needed medical attention after being hit by flying rocks.

•

After a collapse, lava can build out from the newly formed cliffs giving the illusion that areas behind the cliffs are solid and stable.

•

Large areas can collapse into the ocean with little warning, triggering explosions that blast lava spatter and large rocks into the air and send waves of scalding water onshore.

Volcanic eruption in Hawaii. The smoke (gases) and flowing lava are impressive. In the foreground trees are silhouetted against the lava.

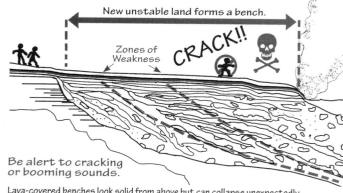

New unstable land forms a bench.

Zones of Weakness

CRACK!!

Be alert to cracking or booming sounds.

Lava-covered benches look solid from above but can collapse unexpectedly.

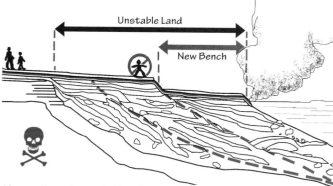

Unstable Land

New Bench

After a collapse, lava can build out from the newly formed cliffs - giving the illusion that areas behind the cliffs are solid and stable.

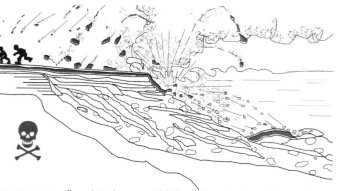

Large areas can collapse into the ocean with little warning, triggering explosions that blast lava spatter and large rocks into the air and send waves of scalding water onshore.

An area of new, unstable land, commonly called a "bench," forms where lava enters the ocean. Although most activity consists of sluggish submarine flows and mild spattering, the contact of water and molten lava can produce "tephra jets" and "littoral fountains." The bench can also collapse, triggering violent explosions that throw lava and rocks 300 feet (100 m) inland.

Lava Vent
Openings in the Earth's crust from which molten rock and volcanic gases escape onto the ground or into the atmosphere. Vents may consist of a single circular-shaped structure, a large elongate fissure and fracture, or a tiny ground crack.

DANGERS!
LAVA ENTERING OCEAN STEAM PLUME - LAZE

Steam plumes are caused by the very hot lava entering the ocean.

- Onshore winds can blow the steam plume into the path of hikers, creating a "whiteout" which limits visibility. This can be disorienting and could cause you to walk into risky areas. The whiteout can hide deep cracks in the ground. Move away from a whiteout when the winds shift. Heavy rain can also produce dense fog that limits visibility.
- Avoid walking under plumes of "laze" (lava haze). Chloride and hydrogen from the water combine to form hydrochloric acid in the plumes. When onshore winds blow clouds of laze inland, "acid rain" can fall on the land and people below. Acid rain has a pH between 1.5 - 3.5 and has the corrosive power of battery acid.
- Plumes of laze also contain tiny glass fragments that can irritate eyes and, in rare cases, cause permanent damage.

SCALDING OCEAN WATER

When hot lava touches the ocean, it heats the surface water to temperatures capable of causing third-degree burns.

- In November 2000, two visitors who had ventured too close to an ocean entry site of lava were found dead, apparently scalded by acid-laced steam on the lava bench. Six years earlier, two people standing near the water's edge by a lava entry site were severely scalded by a sudden wave and had to be hospitalized.
- Sudden releases of hot, acidic steam can occur unexpectedly on a lava bench because of bench collapse or high waves.
- Stay off the bench to avoid being scalded by hot water or burned by acid steam.

VOLCANIC SMOG - VOG

"Vog" is the visible haze that forms when Irritating sulfur dioxide and other volcanic gases combine and interact chemically with oxygen, moisture, dust, and sunlight. Currently Kilauea emits about 2000 tons of sulfur dioxide each day, mainly from the still-open vent at Pu'u'Ö'ö.

VOLCANIC GASES

In Hawaii, trade winds commonly disperse volcanic gases, so that their concentration is not generally hazardous. However, sulfur dioxide fumes can be concentrated near ground cracks along and downwind from lava tubes.

Exposure to concentrated sulfur dioxide fumes puts all people at risk, but particularly those with breathing problems (such as asthma and chronic obstructive pulmonary disease) and heart difficulties, pregnant women, infants, and young children. If sulfur fumes begin to cause physical distress, you should leave the area!

LAVE TUBE - SKYLIGHT

Large volumes of lava move in lava tubes beneath the congealed surface of recent flows. "Skylights" form when the roof of a lava tube collapses, revealing the molten lava flowing beneath. The sight of this flowing hot red lava can be quite impressive. Lava in the tube has a temperature of about 2120°F (1160°C).

It is important to stand well back from these holes, which form where the roof of the tube is thin and the ground unstable. A steam plume forms when the lava from a lava flow enters the ocean.

EFFUSIVE ERUPTIONS OF HAWAII

An eruption dominated by the outpouring of lava onto the ground is often referred to as an effusive eruption (as opposed to the violent fragmentation of magma by explosive eruptions). Lava flows generated by effusive eruptions vary in shape, thickness, length, and width depending on the type of lava erupted, discharge, slope of the ground over which the lava travels, and duration of eruption.

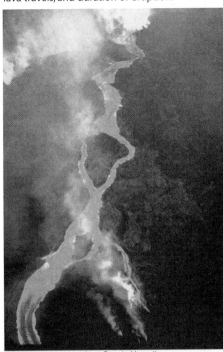

Effusive eruption - a lava flow in Hawaii
Lava flow burning trees in its path.

VISITING A LAVA-FLOW FIELD

Before trying to visit Kilauea's lava-flow field, check with park rangers for current conditions and routes. A hike is not recommend unless you are prepared and well informed of the risks. The area is remote, has no shade or water source, and is seldom patrolled.

WALKING ON COOLED LAVA-FLOWS

The hummocky surfaces (small round bumps) of cooled lava flows are unlike anything most people have walked on. Because of surface irregularities, plan twice the estimated time for the walk. If 3 miles (5 km) consider it the equivalent of walking 5-6 miles (8-10 km) on a smoother surface. If the return trip is uphill, it will be much harder and take longer.

CARRY A FLASHLIGHT

Many people on a "day hike" get caught in the dark. This happens by under-estimating the walking speed, or by being engrossed in the scenery and forgetting the time. Darkness falls more quickly near the equator than in temperate locales. With the setting sun there is less than an hour of twilight left.

Lava-Flow Travel Kit

- Water, 2-3 quarts (or liters) per person
- First Aid Kit
- Sturdy boots/shoes not sandals
- Strong Sunscreen
- Sun hat with brim
- Gloves
- Long pants - not shorts
- Flashlight (1 per person)

CAUSES OF INJURIES
Most injuries at Hawaii's volcanoes are not directly due to the eruptions.

Dehydration, heat exhaustion, sunstroke: Caused by intense sunlight and high temperatures. Air temperatures near lava flows can exceed 120F (49C) depending on cloud cover and wind conditions. Take sun-screen and a hat. Drink more water than you think you need - if you feel thirsty, you are already dehydrated.

Hypothermia: at higher elevations, wind and rain can chill you and lead to hypothermia. Dress in layers.

Falls: These are a common cause of injury. It is easy to break through a thin, overhanging crust of lava or trip on a crack and fall on the abrasive glassy surface of a lava flow. Wear good walking shoes.

Fatigue: be alert when walking down-slope from a moving lava flow.

Unexpected advancing flows: Have an escape route planned to prevent getting caught between two advancing flows.

Injuries from falls are common. It is easy to break through a thin, overhanging crust of lava or trip on a crack and fall on the abrasive, glassy surface of a lava flow. Be alert when walking downslope from a moving lava flow.

The explosive eruption of May 18, 1980, caused the upper 400 meters (1300 feet) of the mountain to collapse, slide, and spread northward, covering much of the adjacent terrain (lower left), leaving a crater atop the greatly shortened mountain.

Subsequent eruptions built a volcanic dome within the crater.

MOUNT SAINT HELENS

The mountain is one of several prominent volcanoes of the Cascade Range. Mount Adams (left background) and Mount Hood (right background) are also seen in this view, which was created entirely from elevation data produced by the Shuttle Radar Topography Mission.

Prior to 1980, Mount Saint Helens had a shape roughly similar to other Cascade peaks, a tall, bold, irregular conic form that rose to 2950 meters (9677 feet). However, the explosive eruption of May 18, 1980, caused the upper 400 meters (1300 feet) of the mountain to collapse, slide, and spread northward, covering much of the adjacent terrain (lower left), leaving a crater atop the greatly shortened mountain. Subsequent eruptions built a volcanic dome within the crater, and the high rainfall of this area lead to substantial erosion of the poorly consolidated landslide material. Eruptions at Mount Saint Helens subsided in 1986, but renewed volcanic activity here and at other Cascade volcanoes is inevitable.

NASA Jet Propulsion Laboratory

To help in Hawaii lava hiking...
VOLCANO GLOSSARY

`A`a Flow: `A`a (pronounced "ah-ah") is a Hawaiian term for lava flows that have a rough bubbly surface composed of broken lava blocks called clinkers. The incredibly spiny surface of a solidified `a`a flow makes walking very difficult and slow. The clinker surface actually covers a massive dense core, which is the most active part of the flow. As pasty lava in the core travels downslope, the clinkers are carried along at the surface. At the leading edge of an `a`a flow, however, these cooled fragments tumble down the steep front and are buried by the advancing flow. This produces a layer of lava fragments both at the bottom and top of an `a`a flow.

Andesite: Is a gray to black volcanic rock. Andesite magma commonly erupts from strato-volcanoes as thick lava flows, some reaching several km in length. Andesite magma can also generate strong explosive eruptions to form pyroclastic flows and surges and enormous eruption columns. Andesites erupt at temperatures between 900 and 1100° C.

Basalt: Is a hard, black volcanic rock with a low viscosity (resistance to flow). Therefore, basaltic lava can flow quickly and easily move >20 km from a vent. The low viscosity typically allows volcanic gases to escape without generating enormous eruption columns. Basaltic lava fountains and fissure eruptions, however, still form explosive fountains hundreds of meters tall. Basalt is erupted at temperatures between 1100 to 1250° C. Basalt is the most common rock type in the Earth's crust (the outer 10 to 50 km). In fact, most of the ocean floor is made of basalt. Huge outpourings of lava called "flood basalt" are found on many continents. Shield volcanoes, such as those that make up the Islands of Hawaii, are composed almost entirely of basalt.

Block: A volcanic block is a solid rock fragment greater than 64 mm in diameter that was ejected from a volcano during an explosive eruption. Blocks commonly consist of solidified pieces of old lava flows that were part of a volcano's cone.

Bomb: Volcanic bombs are lava fragments that were ejected while viscous (partially molten) and larger than 64 mm in diameter. Many acquire rounded aerodynamic shapes during their travel through the air. Volcanic bombs include breadcrust bombs, ribbon bombs, spindle bombs (with twisted ends), spheroidal bombs, and "cow-dung" bombs.

Caldera: Is a large, usually circular depression at the summit of a volcano formed when magma is withdrawn or erupted from a shallow underground magma reservoir. The removal of large volumes of magma may result in loss of structural support for the overlying rock, thereby leading to collapse of the ground and formation

To help in Hawaii lava hiking...

VOLCANO GLOSSARY

of a large depression. Calderas are different from craters, which are smaller, circular depressions created primarily by explosive excavation of rock during eruptions.

Cinder Cone: Is a steep, conical hill of volcanic fragments that accumulate around and downwind from a vent. The rock fragments, often called cinders or scoria, are glassy and contain numerous gas bubbles "frozen" into place as magma exploded into the air and then cooled quickly. Cinder cones range in size from tens to hundreds of meters tall. Cinder cones usually erupt lava flows, either through a breach on one side of the crater or from a vent located on a flank. Lava rarely issues from the top (except as a fountain) because the loose, non-cemented cinders are too weak to support the pressure exerted by molten rock as it rises toward the surface through the central vent.

Dacite: Dacite lava is most often light gray, but can be dark gray to black. Dacite generally erupts at temperatures between 800 and 1000°C. It is one of the most common rock types associated with enormous Plinian-style eruptions. When relatively gas-poor dacite erupts onto a volcano's surface, it typically forms a thick rounded lava flow in the shape of a dome.

Debris Avalanche: moving mass of rock, soil and snow that occurs when the flank of a mountain or volcano collapses and slides downslope. As the moving debris rushes down a volcano and into river valleys, it incorporates water, snow, trees, bridges, buildings, and anything else in the way. Debris avalanches may travel several km before coming to rest, or they may transform into more water-rich lahars, which travel many tens of km downstream.

Dike: Tabular or sheet-like bodies of magma that cut through and across the layering of adjacent rocks. They form when magma rises into an existing fracture, or creates a new crack by forcing its way through existing rock, and then solidifies.

Effusive Eruption: An eruption dominated by the outpouring of lava onto the ground is often referred to as an effusive eruption (as opposed to the violent fragmentation of magma by explosive eruptions). Lava flows generated by effusive eruptions vary in shape, thickness, length, and width depending on the type of lava erupted, discharge, slope of the ground over which the lava travels, and duration of eruption.

Eruption Cloud: A cloud of tephra and gases that forms downwind of an erupting volcano is called an eruption cloud. The vertical pillar of tephra and gases rising directly above a vent is an eruption column. Eruption clouds are often dark-colored brown to gray but they can also be white, very similar to weather clouds. Eruption clouds may drift for thousands of kilometers downwind and often become increasingly spread out over a larger area with increasing distance from an erupting vent.

Fault: Are fractures or fracture zones in the Earth's crust along which one side moves with respect to the other. A fault scarp is a cliff or steep slope that sometimes forms along the fault at the surface. There are many types of faults (for example, strike-slip, normal, reverse, and thrust faults) ranging in size from a few tens of meters to hundreds of kilometers in dimension.

Fissure: In geology, a fissure is a fracture or crack in rock along which there is a distinct separation; fissures are often filled with mineral-bearing materials. On volcanoes, a fissure is an elongate fracture or crack at the surface from which lava erupts. Fissure eruptions typically dwindle to a central vent after a period of hours or days. Occasionally, lava will flow back into the ground by pouring into a crack or an open eruptive fissure, a process called drainback; sometimes lava will flow back into the same fissure from which it erupted.

Fumarole: Are vents from which volcanic gas escapes into the atmosphere. Fumaroles may occur along tiny cracks or long fissures, in chaotic clusters or fields, and on the surfaces of lava flows and thick deposits of pyroclastic flows. They may persist for decades or centuries if they are above a persistent heat source or disappear within weeks to months if they occur atop a fresh volcanic deposit that quickly cools.

Volcanic Gas: Magma contains dissolved gases that are released into the atmosphere during eruptions. Gases are also released from magma that either remains below ground (as an intrusion) or rises toward the surface.
In such cases, gases may escape continuously into the atmosphere from the soil, volcanic vents, fumaroles, and hydrothermal systems. The most common gas released by magma is steam (H_2O), followed by CO_2 (carbon dioxide), SO_2 (sulfur dioxide), (HCl) hydrogen chloride and other compounds.

Geyser: Most geysers are hot springs that episodically erupt fountains of scalding water and steam. Such eruptions occur as a consequence of groundwater being heated to its boiling temperature in a confined space (a fracture or conduit). A slight decrease in pressure or an increase in temperature will cause some of the water to boil. The resulting steam forces overlying water up through the conduit and onto the ground. This loss of water further reduces pressure within the conduit system, and most of the remaining water suddenly converts to steam and erupts at the surface.

Hornito: A small rootless spatter cone that forms on the surface of a basaltic lava flow (usually pahoehoe) is called a hornito. A hornito develops when lava is forced up through an opening in the cooled surface of a flow and then accumulates around the opening. Typically, hornitos are steep sided and form conspicuous pinnacles or stacks. They are "rootless" because they are fed by lava from the underlying flow instead of from a deeper magma conduit.

Lava: Is the word for magma (molten rock) when it erupts onto the Earth's surface. Geologists also use the word to describe the solidified deposits of lava flows and fragments hurled into the air by explosive eruptions (lava bombs or blocks).

Lava Delta: Lava entering the sea often builds a wide fan-shaped area of new land called a lava delta. Such new land is usually built on sloping layers of loose lava fragments and flows. On steep submarine slopes, these layers of debris are unstable and often lead to the sudden collapse of lava deltas into the sea. The partial collapse of a lava delta can be a hazard for people who venture too close to lava entering the ocean.

Lava Dome: Lava domes are rounded, steep-sided mounds built by very viscous magma, usually either dacite or rhyolite. Such magmas are typically too viscous (resistant to flow) to move far from the vent before cooling and crystallizing. Domes may consist of one or more individual lava flows. Lava domes often erupt, however, on the top and sides of stratovolcanoes. Although lava domes are built by nonexplosive eruptions of viscous lava, domes can generate deadly pyroclastic flows. The sides of a dome or an erupting lava flow on a dome can collapse down a steep slope to form a hot avalanche of hot lava fragments and gas (pyroclastic flow). Some domes erupt obsidian, which is volcanic glass that may form in rhyolite or dacite lava flows. Most obsidian is black, but red, green, and brown obsidian is known. Obsidian forms when magma is cooled so quickly that individual minerals cannot crystallize.

Lava Flow: Are masses of molten rock that pour onto the Earth's surface during an effusive eruption. Both moving lava and the resulting solidified deposit are referred to as lava flows. Because of the wide range in (1) viscosity of the different lava types (basalt, andesite, dacite, and rhyolite); (2) lava discharge during eruptions; and (3) characteristics of the erupting vent and topography over which lava travels, lava flows come in a great variety of shapes and sizes.

Characteristics of basaltic lava flows:

- Lava cascades and lava drapery form when lava pours over cliffs.
- In lava channels, standing waves and spillways are common features.
- Surges of lava occur when the supply of lava to a flow front increases.
- Methane gas explosions often occur at the edges of lava flows moving over vegetation, even as far as 100 m in front or to the side of a flow.

Lava Fountain: A jet of lava sprayed into the air by the rapid formation and expansion of gas bubbles in the molten rock is called a lava fountain. Lava fountains erupt from isolated vents, along fissures, within active lava lakes, and from a lava tube when water gains access to the tube in a confined space.

Lava Lake: Is large volumes of molten lava, usually basaltic, contained in a vent, crater, or broad depression.

Lava Tube: Is natural conduits through which lava travels beneath the surface of a lava flow. Tubes form by the crusting over of lava channels and pahoehoe flows. A broad lava-flow field often consists of a main lava tube and a series of smaller tubes that supply lava to the front of one or more separate flows. When the supply of lava stops at the end of an eruption or lava is diverted elsewhere, lava in the tube system drains downslope and leaves partially empty conduits beneath the ground. Such drained tubes commonly exhibit "high-lava" marks on their walls, generally flat floors, and many lava stalactites that hang from the roof. Lava can also erode downward, deepening the tube and leaving empty space above the flowing lava.

Based upon data from the U.S. Geological Survey

To help in Hawaii lava hiking...

VOLCANO GLOSSARY

Kipuka: A Hawaiian term for an "island" of land completely surrounded by one or more younger lava flows. A kipuka forms when lava encircles a hill or a slight rise in the ground as it moves downslope or across relatively flat ground. Because they are surrounded by more recent flows, kipukas are often covered with mature vegetation.

Lahar: An Indonesian word for a rapidly flowing mixture of rock debris and water that originates on the slopes of a volcano. Lahars are also referred to as volcanic mudflows or debris flows. They form in a variety of ways, chiefly by the rapid melting of snow and ice by pyroclastic flows, intense rainfall on loose volcanic rock deposits, breakout of a lake dammed by volcanic deposits, and as a consequence of debris avalanches.

Lapilli: Rock fragments between 2 and 64 mm (0.08-2.5 in) in diameter that were ejected from a volcano during an explosive eruption. Lapilli may consist of many different types of tephra, including scoria, pumice, and reticulite.

Limu: Consists of thin flakes of basaltic glass that sometimes form when pahoehoe lava pours into the ocean. As waves wash atop exposed streams of lava, some water may become trapped and boil, resulting in delicate steam-filled bubbles of lava. Abrupt chilling and continued expansion of the delicate bubble walls form thin plates and shattered pieces of brownish-green to nearly-clear glass.

Littoral Cone: A cone of lava fragments built on the surface of a lava flow pouring into a body of water, usually the sea, is called a littoral cone ("littoral" refers to a shoreline). Lava entering the ocean heats and boils seawater, often generating steam explosions that hurl tephra onto the shore, including spatter, bombs, blocks, ash, lapilli, and, rarely limu. As the various tephra accumulates on the shoreline, a well-developed cone may be created.

Maar: A low-relief, broad volcanic crater formed by shallow explosive eruptions. The explosions are usually caused by the heating and boiling of groundwater when magma invades the groundwater table. Maars often fill with water to form a lake.

Magma: Is molten or partially molten rock beneath the Earth's surface. When magma erupts onto the surface, it is called lava. It consists of:
- a liquid portion (often referred to as the melt).
- a solid portion made of minerals that crystallized directly from the melt.
- solid rocks incorporated into the magma from along the conduit or reservoir, called xenoliths or inclusions.
- dissolved gases.

Mud Volcano: A small volcano-shaped cone of mud and clay, usually less than 1-2 m tall. These small mud volcanoes are built by a mixture of hot water and fine sediment (mud and clay) that either pours gently from a vent in the ground like a fluid lava flow; or is ejected into the air like a lava fountain by escaping volcanic gas and boiling water.

Obsidian: Dense volcanic glass, usually rhyolite in composition and typically black in color. Crystals of iron oxide within the glass cause its dark color. Obsidian is often formed in rhyolite lava flows where the lava cools so fast that crystals do not have time to grow. Glass, unlike crystals, has no regular structure and therefore fractures in smooth conchoidal (curved) shapes. The intersections of these fractures can form edges sharper than the finest steel blades. For this reason, obsidian was used by many native cultures to make arrowheads and blades.

Pahoehoe: Basaltic lava that has a smooth, hummocky, or ropy surface. A pahoehoe flow typically advances as a series of small lobes and toes that continually break out from a cooled crust. The surface texture of pahoehoe flows varies widely, displaying all kinds of bizarre shapes often referred to as lava sculpture.

Pele's Hair: Thin strands of volcanic glass drawn out from molten lava have long been called Pele's hair, named for Pele, the Hawaiian goddess of volcanoes. A single strand, with a diameter of less than 0.5 mm, may be as long as 2 m. The strands are formed by the stretching or blowing-out of molten basaltic glass from lava, usually from lava fountains, lava cascades, and vigorous lava flows (for example, as pahoehoe lava plunges over a small cliff and at the front of an `a`a flow). Pele's hair is often carried high into the air during fountaining, and wind can blow the glass threads several tens of kilometers from a vent.

Pele's Tears: Small bits of molten lava in fountains can cool quickly and solidify into glass particles shaped like spheres or tear-drops called Pele's tears. Jet black in color and are often found on one end of a strand of Pele's hair.

Phreatic Eruptions: Are steam-driven explosions that occur when water beneath the ground or on the surface is heated by magma, lava, hot rocks, or new volcanic deposits (for example, tephra and pyroclastic-flow deposits). The intense heat of such material (as high as 1170°C for basaltic lava) may cause water to boil and flash to steam, thereby generating an explosion of steam, water, ash, blocks, and bombs. Phreatic eruption occurred at the summit of Mount St. Helens, Washington. Hundreds of these steam-driven explosive eruptions occurred as magma steadily rose into the cone and boiled groundwater. These phreatic eruptions preceded the volcano's plinian eruption on 18 May 1980.

Pillow Lava: When basalt erupts underwater, they commonly form pillow lava, which are mounds of elongate lava "pillows" formed by repeated oozing and quenching of the hot basalt.

Pit Craters: Are circular-shaped craters formed by the sinking or collapse of the ground. Fissures may erupt from the walls or base of a pit crater, but pit craters are not constructional features built by eruptions of lava or tephra. Pit craters may also partially fill with lava to form a lava lake. They are common along rift zones of shield volcanoes. They are thought to form as a consequence of the removal of support by withdrawal of underlying magma.

Plinian Eruptions: Are large explosive events that form enormous dark columns of tephra and gas high into the stratosphere (>11 km). Such eruptions are named for Pliny the Younger, who carefully described the disastrous eruption of Vesuvius in 79 A.D. This eruption generated a huge column of tephra into the sky, pyroclastic flows and surges, and extensive ash fall. Many thousands of people evacuated areas around the volcano, but about 2000 were killed, including Pliny the Older. Large plinian eruptions sometimes result in the withdrawal of so much magma from below a volcano that part of it collapses to form a large depression called a caldera. Some plinian eruptions inject such large quantities of aerosols (small liquid droplets) into the stratosphere that surface temperatures on Earth may decrease slightly.

Pumice: Is a light, porous volcanic rock that forms during explosive eruptions. It resembles a sponge because it consists of a network of gas bubbles frozen amidst fragile volcanic glass and minerals. All types of magma (basalt, andesite, dacite, and rhyolite) will form pumice.

Pyroclastic Flow: Is a ground-hugging avalanche of hot ash, pumice, rock fragments, and volcanic gas that rushes down the side of a volcano as fast as 100 km/hour or more. The temperature within a pyroclastic flow may be greater than 500°C, sufficient to burn and carbonize wood. Once deposited, the ash, pumice, and rock fragments may deform (flatten) and weld together because of the intense heat and the weight of the overlying material.

Reticulite: Is basaltic pumice in which nearly all cell walls of gas bubbles have burst, leaving a honeycomb-like structure. Even though it is less dense than pumice, reticulite does not float in water because of the open network of bubbles.

Rhyolite: Is a light-colored rock mainly composed of silica. Rhyolite was named from the Greek "streaming rock" because of its beautiful flow bands, which are made of bubble and crystal-rich layers that form as the lava flows onto the surface and advances. Rhyolite can look very different, depending on how it erupts. Explosive eruptions of rhyolite create pumice, which is white and full of bubbles. Effusive eruptions of rhyolite often produce obsidian, which is bubble-free and black.

Rift Zone: Is an elongate system of crustal fractures associated with an area that has undergone extension (ground has spread apart). On the great shield volcanoes in Hawaii, a rift zone consists of many different features associated with the rise and eruption of magma from narrow dikes, including eruptive fissures, cinder and spatter cones, spatter ramparts, pit craters, lava flows, ground cracks, and normal faults.

Rock: Naturally occurring mixtures of minerals, mineral matter, or organic materials. Three main types occur: sedimentary rocks, formed by weathering and mechanical sorting on the Earth's surface; metamorphic rocks, which are rocks that have been transformed by the effects of high temperature and pressure; and igneous rocks, derived from magma (for example, volcanic rocks).

Sedimentary rocks include sandstone, limestone, and shale. These rocks often start as sediments carried in rivers and deposited in lakes and oceans. When buried, the sediments lose

Based upon data from the U.S. Geological Survey

To help in Hawaii lava hiking…
VOLCANO GLOSSARY

water and become cemented to form rock.
Metamorphic rocks include schist, marble, and gneiss. The sedimentary rock shale (formed mostly of clay sediments) when buried and heated to high temperatures (300-500°C) becomes transformed or metamorphosed into schist.
Volcanic igneous rocks are basalt, andesite, and rhyolite. When magmas crystallize deep underground they look different from volcanic rocks because they cool more slowly and, therefore, have larger crystals. Igneous rocks cooled beneath the Earth's surface are called intrusive rocks.

Scoria: Is a vesicular (bubbly) glassy lava rock of basaltic to andesitic composition ejected from a vent during explosive eruption. The bubbly nature of scoria is due to the escape of volcanic gases during eruption. Scoria is typically dark gray to black in color, mostly due to its high iron content. The surface of some scoria may have a blue iridescent color; oxidation may lead to a deep reddish-brown color.

Shield Volcano: Volcanoes with broad, gentle slopes and built by the eruption of fluid basalt lava. Basalt lava tends to build enormous, low-angle cones because it flows across the ground easily and can form lava tubes that enable lava to flow tens of kilometers from an erupting vent with very little cooling. The largest volcanoes on Earth are shield volcanoes. The name comes from a perceived resemblance to the shape of a warrior's shield.

Spatter: Very fluid fragments of molten lava ejected from a vent that flatten and congeal on the ground are called spatter. Typically, spatter will build walls of solidified lava around a single vent to form a circular-shaped spatter cone or along both sides of a fissure to build a spatter rampart.

Spatter Rampart: Lava fountains that erupt from an elongate fissure will build broad embankments of spatter, called spatter ramparts, along both sides of the fissure. The spatter commonly sticks together, or agglutinates, when it lands and is buried by later spatter. In contrast to these low linear fortifications, spatter cones are more circular and cone-shaped. The only real distinction between the two structures is their shape.

Spatter Cone: Long-lived basaltic lava fountains that erupt spatter, scoria or cinder, and other tephra from a central vent typically build steep-sided cones called spatter-and-cinder cones. The greatest bulk of these cones consists of spatter, but during fountaining a lava flow usually pours down one side of the cone. Eruptions that build spatter and cinder cones are much longer in duration and much more varied in intensity than those that eject only spatter to build spatter cones and ramparts.

Stratovolcano: Steep, conical volcanoes built by the eruption of viscous lava flows, tephra, and pyroclastic flows. Usually constructed over a period of tens to hundreds of thousands of years, stratovolcanoes may erupt a variety of magma types, including basalt, andesite, dacite, and rhyolite. All but basalt commonly generate highly explosive eruptions. A stratovolcano typically consists of many separate vents, some of which may have erupted cinder cones and domes on the volcano's flanks. A synonym is composite cone. Mount St. Helens is the youngest stratovolcano in the Cascades and the most active. Geologists have identified at least 35 layers of tephra erupted by the volcano in the past 3500 years.

Tephra: Is a general term for fragments of volcanic rock and lava regardless of size that are blasted into the air by explosions or carried upward by hot gases in eruption columns or lava fountains. Tephra includes large dense blocks and bombs, and small light rock debris such as scoria, pumice, reticulite, and ash. As tephra falls to the ground with increasing distance from a volcano, the average size of the individual rock particles becomes smaller and thickness of the resulting deposit becomes thinner. Small tephra stays aloft in the eruption cloud for longer periods of time, which allows wind to blow tiny particles farther from an erupting volcano.

Tree Mold: Fluid basaltic lava may preserve the shapes of trees and other objects by solidifying around them. Tree molds are formed when:
• Lava surrounds a tree, chills against it, and then drains away. The standing structure left behind is often called a "lava tree".
• Tree trunks engulfed and incinerated by lava leave cylindrical hollows, or "tree molds", where lava solidified against them.

Tree molds often preserve the original surface texture of the tree. Tree molds are found within standing lava trees and on the surfaces of lava flows. Common in pahoehoe flows and occasionally found in `a`a flows. A tree mold glows several hours after pahoehoe lava surrounds a tree and burns its trunk until the tree falls onto the lava flow.

Tumulus: The surfaces of pahoehoe flows on flat or gentle slopes often exhibit elliptical, domed structures called tumuli. A tumulus is created when the upward pressure of slow-moving molten lava within a flow swells or pushes the overlying crust upward. Since the solid crust is brittle, it usually breaks to accommodate the "inflating" core of the flow. Such fractures generally extend along the length of a tumulus, and are frequently accompanied by smaller irregular cracks down the sides. Lava commonly squeezes out through these fractures, and sometimes drains from the tumulus to leave a hollow shell.

Volcano: A volcano is a vent at the Earth's surface through which magma (molten rock) and associated gases erupt, and also the cone built by effusive and explosive eruptions.

Vulcanian Eruption: Is a type of explosive eruption that ejects new lava fragments that do not take on a rounded shape during their flight through the air. This may be because the lava is too viscous or already solidified. These moderate-sized explosive eruptions commonly eject a large proportion of volcanic ash and also breadcrust bombs and blocks. Andesitic and dacitic magmas are most often associated with vulcanian eruptions, because their high viscosity (resistance to flow) makes it difficult for the dissolved volcanic gases to escape except under extreme pressure, which leads to explosive behavior.

Based upon data from the U.S. Geological Survey

Mount Saint Helen's Eruption

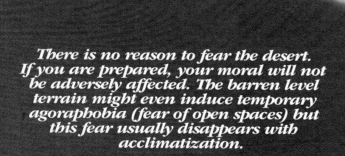

*There is no reason to fear the desert.
If you are prepared, your moral will not
be adversely affected. The barren level
terrain might even induce temporary
agoraphobia (fear of open spaces) but
this fear usually disappears with
acclimatization.*

10 DESERT TRAVEL

DESERT ENVIRONMENT

Deserts cover 20% of the land surfaces of the world. Desert travel requires adapting to the desert environment and to the limitations its terrain and climate impose. Methods of travel and shelter must be modified and adapted to a dusty and rugged landscape where temperatures vary from extreme highs down to freezing and where visibility may change from 30 miles to 30 feet in a matter of minutes. Deserts are arid, barren regions of the earth incapable of supporting normal life due to lack of water. Temperatures vary according to latitude and season, from over 136°F in the deserts of Mexico to the bitter cold of winter in the Gobi (East Asia) and the arctic regions. In some deserts, day-to-night temperature fluctuation exceeds 70°F. Some species of animal and plant life have adapted successfully to desert conditions where annual rainfall may vary from 0-10 inches. Desert terrain also varies considerably from place to place, the sole common denominator being lack of water with its consequent environmental effects, such as sparse, if any, vegetation. The basic land forms are similar to those in other parts of the world, but the topsoil has been eroded due to a combination of lack of water, heat, and wind to give deserts their characteristic barren appearance. The bedrock may be covered by a flat layer of sand, or gravel, or may have been exposed by erosion. Other common features are sand dunes, escarpments, wadis, and depressions. This environment can profoundly affect travel.

Extreme Desert Temperatures

Highest Temperature 136.4°F   Mexico
Coldest Temperature -50°F   Gobi Desert

- Low temperatures can be aggravated by a high windchill factor.
- The sun in the cloudless sky will heat the desert but at night the desert will cool to near freezing.

EXTREME DESERT TEMPERATURES

Night Time: As there is no insulating cover 90% of heat is lost by the ground and only 10% is reflected back by dust particles. This loss of heat causes the sharp temperature drop at night. This is why clothing should not be discarded in the day and you should travel in the early morning, evening or moonlit nights if there are no obstacles.

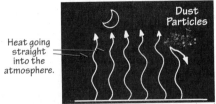

Heat going straight into the atmosphere.

Dust Particles

Daytime: As the desert sky is clear with no clouds, humidity or vegetation cover 90% of the solar rays hit and heat the ground. Only 10% of the rays are deflected by dust particles etc. in the sky. This is why desert areas are so hot in the day.

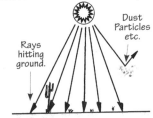

Rays hitting ground.

Dust Particles etc.

Large Deserts of North America

Desert	Location	Square Miles
Sonoran Desert	Arizona extends south into Mexico.	70,000
Colorado Desert	California and Arizona.	7,500
Chihuahuan Desert	Mexico and north into Texas and New Mexico.	140,000
Mojave Desert	California, extends into Nevada and Arizona.	15,000
Great Basin Desert	Utah and Nevada	190,000
Death Valley	Eastern California & SW Nevada.	3,300
Painted Desert	Northern Arizona	150 miles long

TYPES OF DESERT TERRAIN
Mountain Deserts

Mountain deserts are areas of barren hills or mountains separated by flat and dry basins. The high ground can rise to the height of several thousand feet above sea level. Rainfall occurring at high altitudes runs off in flash floods which erode deep gullies and ravines and deposit sand and rocks at their mouths. The water might give life to temporary vegetation, but rapidly evaporates. The land returns to its barren state until the next rainfall. If all the water does not evaporate it might remain in a basin creating a shallow lake like the Great Salt Lake which has a high salt content.

Rocky Mountain Plateau

These plateaus have slight relief interspersed by extensive flat areas with quantities of solid or broken rock at or near the surface. The area might be cut by dry steep walled canyons. Very narrow canyons are very dangerous because of possible flash floods. Their flat bottoms may be attractive as camp sites- but dangerous.

Sandy or Dune Deserts

These deserts are extensive relatively flat areas covered by sand or gravel which can be ancient deposits or modern wind erosion. In some cases the dunes can rise to over 1000 feet and be 10-15 miles long. The plant life is scrub that reaches six feet high. Examples of this type of desert can be seen in parts of California and Mexico.

Insulated Canteen

DESERTS OF THE WORLD

Arabian (Eastern): 70,000 square miles In Egypt between the Nile River and Red Sea, extending southward into the Sudan.
Atacama: 600 miles long In northern Chile.
Chihuahua: 140,000 square miles In New Mexico, Texas, Arizona and Mexico.
Colorado: 7,500 square miles South of Mojave desert, along the Colorado River in southern California.
Death Valley: 3,300 square miles In eastern California and southwest Nevada.
Gibson: 120,000 square miles. In the interior of western Australia.
Gobi: 500,000 square miles In Mongolia and China.
Great Sandy: 150,000 square miles In W Australia.
Great Victoria: 150,000 square miles In western and southern Australia.
Kalahari: 225,000 square miles In southern Africa.
Kara-Kum: 120,000 square miles In Turkmenia.
Kavir: 400 miles long In central Iran.
Kyzl Kum: 100,000 square miles Kazakhstan & Uzbekistan.
Lut: 20,000 square miles In eastern Iran.
Mojave: 15,000 square miles In southern California.
Nafud: 40,000 square miles Near Jawf in Saudi Arabia.
Namib: 800 miles long. Along the southwest coast of Africa.
Nubian: 100,000 square miles In the Sahara in NE Sudan.
Painted Desert: 150 miles long In northern Arizona.
Sahara: 3,500,000 square miles In Northern Africa extending westward to the Atlantic (largest desert in the world).
Simpson: 40,000 square miles In central Australia.
Sonoran: 70,000 square miles In southwest Arizona and southeast California.
Syrian: 100,000 square miles In northern Saudi Arabia eastern Jordan, southern Syria, and western Iraq.

Desert Coyote

DESERT ZONES IN NORTH AMERICA

Life Zone	Inches of rain per year	Location	Elevation above sea level (feet)	Plants	Animals
Arctic-Alpine	30-35	Above the timber line	Above 12,000	Lichens, grasses	Mountain goat
Hudsonian	30-35	High mountains	9,500-12000	Spruce, Alpine fir	Golden eagle, Bighorn sheep
Canadian	25-30	Mountains	8,000-10,000	White & Douglas fir	Black bear, grouse
Transition	19-25	Plateau	7,000-8,000	Ponderosa pine	Mountain lion, Chipmunk
Upper Sonoran*	12-20	Mesas, foothills & Great Basin Desert	3,5000-7,000	Sage brush, Pinyon juniper	Prairie dog, Black-tailed jack rabbit
Lower Sonoran*	3-15	Sonoran, Mojave & Chihuahuan deserts	500-4000	Ocotillo, Creosote bush, Salt bush	Collared lizard, Kangaroo rat
Dry Tropical*	1-6	Along Colorado River	below 500	Senita cactus, Organ pipe cactus	Gila monster, Sidewinder rattlesnake

* Considered as traditional deserts.

Mountain Deserts

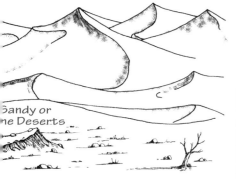

Rocky Mountain Plateau

MIRAGE

SUNLIGHT LIGHTING TRICKS

Atmospheric conditions and sunlight can cause tricks with your vision and interpretation of images that you see.

- A strong sun with low cloud density can combine to produce bright glaring light conditions during the day.
- Sometimes light allows unlimited visibility and your normal perception of distance can be totally distorted. In this case you will have a tendency to grossly underestimate distance. This is important if you are aiming at a target because you will shoot short.
- Visibility can be degraded by rising heat waves which cause mirages. This heat shimmer distortion is strongest when you look into the sun or through binoculars. Observation is best from a high point at dusk or dawn or on moonlit nights.

VW Thing

Sandy or Dune Deserts

Sage Sparrow
They live in sagebrush in the valleys of high deserts.

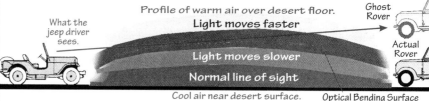

Mirage caused by the optical displacement of warm air over a cooler surface.

Profile of warm air over desert floor.
What the jeep driver sees.
Light moves faster
Ghost Rover
Actual Rover
Light moves slower
Normal line of sight
Cool air near desert surface.
Optical Bending Surface

HEAT WAVE MIRAGE

Image in green is the actual horizon. The brown shows the horizon through the diffraction of the rising heat waves. Your mind might project this image as being palm trees. What you think you are seeing (the palm trees) is a mirage.

Actual Horizon
The mirage you actually see.

 Because of rising heat waves, which cause distortions, it is difficult to use binoculars during the heat of the day.

REFRACTED LIGHT MIRAGE

A mirage of a distant image can be produced by refracted light that is reflected off air that is at a different temperature. In this example it occurs when you are looking down a slope
In the above case the air is cool, and dense, below the arrows show air (Black) that is hot coming from the sun heated ground. The distant image coming from "A" (can be clouds, mountains etc.) will be reflected by the unequal densities of the air and can appear as 'water' at "B". You can see this effect on highways that have a shimmering wet look on hot sunny days. In the case of the caravan in the Sahara the upside down mirage off a distant sea is caused by a double reflection in hot-cold layers causing an inversion of the distant sea.

Mirage seen by a caravan.

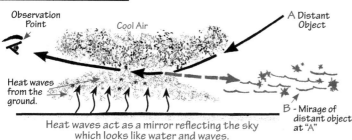

Observation Point
Cool Air
A Distant Object
Heat waves from the ground.
B - Mirage of distant object at "A"
Heat waves act as a mirror reflecting the sky which looks like water and waves.

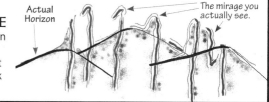

81

Desert Horned Lizard

They eat ants. Are well camouflaged. Love the sun. At night they dig themselves into the sand. Their nostrils have valves to keep out the sand.

Vulture

They hunt in the daytime looking for carrion. They use their excellent eyesight to find carcasses of animals which will usually are covered with sarcophagid flies.

Turkey Vulture

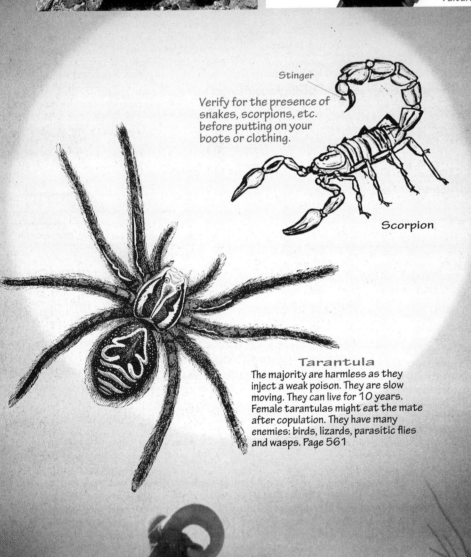

Stinger

Verify for the presence of snakes, scorpions, etc. before putting on your boots or clothing.

Scorpion

Tarantula

The majority are harmless as they inject a weak poison. They are slow moving. They can live for 10 years. Female tarantulas might eat the mate after copulation. They have many enemies: birds, lizards, parasitic flies and wasps. Page 561

Desert Bighorn

DESERT WILDLIFE
Invertebrates

Invertebrates such as spiders, scorpions and centipedes as well as insects of almost every type are found in the desert. Lice, mites, and flies are attracted by food or moisture or the presence of humans. These invertebrates are unpleasant and can carry diseases such as scrub typhus and dysentery. Scorpion stings, centipede and spider bites can be very painful but seldom fatal. Death can be caused by certain species of scorpion, black widow or recluse spiders.

Flies: are abundant throughout desert environments. Filth-borne disease is a major health problem posed by flies. Dirt or insects in the desert can cause infection in minor cuts and scratches.

Fleas: Avoid all dogs and rats which are the major carriers of fleas. Fleas are the primary carriers of plague and murine typhus.

Reptiles: are perhaps the most characteristic group of desert animals. Lizards and snakes occur in quantity. Lizards are normally harmless except for the gila monster.

Snakes: ranging from the totally harmless to the lethal, abound in the desert. A bite from a poisonous snake can easily become infected. Snakes seek shade (cool areas) under bushes, rocks, trees, and shrubs. These areas should be checked before sitting or resting. Always check your clothing and boots before putting them on. Vehicle operators should look for snakes before driving or performing maintenance. Look for snakes in and around suspension components and engine compartments as snakes may seek the warm areas on recently parked vehicles to avoid the cool night temperatures.

Mammals

The mammals that live in the desert have adapted to their environment. An example being small mammals such as rodents which conserve their moisture by burrowing underground and only come out during the night. The kangaroo rat does not require much water as its body synthesizes water from the elements of starchy foods or slow oxidation of fats and from the oxygen in the air. Man has not adapted to the desert environment and must carry his food and water with him.

White Tailed Ground Squirrel
Has stripes on the sides of the body.
Food: seeds, succulent herbs, grasshoppers, crickets, flies.

Peccary
Small wild pig 3' long and 15" high. The only native American wild pig. It has a black and white banding which has a salt and pepper grey color effect. This pig can eject an odorous liquid for protection or as a trail marker. It is found in roving bands. It lives in the wild brush country of low mountains. It can get aggressive if cornered. It has nocturnal feeding habits. Drinks water when necessary but the pulp of cacti will suffice. Enemies: mountain lions, jaguars and man.

Desert Bighorn
They live at higher elevation in a rocky habitat.
Male: 5' long from nose to tail.
Weight: 250-300 pounds.
Food: thistles, grass, annual flowers, leafy bushes. Will break open barrel cacti with their horns and eat the pulp inside.

Collared Lizard

SCORPIONS

Scorpions are prevalent in desert regions. particularly active at night. They prefer damp locations and are easily recognizable by their crab-like appearance, and by their long tail which ends in a sharp stinger. Adult scorpions vary from less than an inch to almost 8" in length. Colors range from nearly black to straw to striped. Scorpions hide in clothing, boots, or bedding, so hikers should routinely shake these items before using them. Their daytime dwelling is given away by a flat tunnel entrance that has been dug into the earth. The dirt entrails at the opening of the tunnel give away the location. Most are harmless and the sting being as bad as a bee or wasp sting. A small (2") scorpion found in Northern Mexico and the adjacent area in Arizona has a poisonous injection. Symptoms are: restlessness and increased flow of saliva. *See First Aid Chapter page 607.*

REPTILES

Lizards and snakes are common. Avoid the Gila Monster lizard. Desert snakes can be very dangerous. Generally a poisonous snake will present a danger to an adult only if it is over 2' long. It is dangerous to touch any snake because bites from harmless snakes can easily become infected. Snakes seek shade under bushes, rocks, trees, and shrubs. Verify for the presence of snakes, scorpions, etc. before putting on your boots or clothing. *For more information on rattlesnakes see the Chapters on First Aid and Reptile Chapters. Pages 608 & 501.*

Desert Whiptailed Lizard
They run at great speed and can dig their own burrows.

Kangaroo Rat
These are 2" high rodents that have affinity with the squirrel and chipmunk families. Their colors vary from pale to reddish. They have a habit of storing food. They eat plant stems, seeds, and fleshy fungi. Pouches in cheeks to transport food. They do not require much water as their bodies synthesize water from the elements of starchy foods or slow oxidation of fats and from the oxygen in the air. When surprised it will leap a foot or two into the air on its elongated hind feet and escape at 17 feet per second. The tail acts as a rudder. It can make a 90° turn while in flight. They are nocturnal. Predators: coyotes who will dig into their dens, desert kit fox also will hunt them on the ground. Snakes and hawks eat them to derive water from their flesh. They can be considered as the Desert Hamburger.

Desert Tortoise
They stay out of the sun by living in dens or hide under bushes. They eat green vegetation. When the wet season is over they subsist on dry grass and herbs. Their water source is eating plants and synthesis. They carry up to one pint of water in sacs just under their shell.

Millipedes
Small worms with a '1000' legs. They are harmless.

Catching a Lizard
To catch a lizard use a noose and pole. Distract the lizard with another object and gently slip the noose over its head. Lizards have a diet of insects, fruits, and eggs.

Hare's large ears serve as radiators by which it stays cool.

Gila Monster
This is the only poisonous lizard in North America. It is one of the largest being 20" long. It eats bird's eggs, nestlings, small rodents and other lizards. It bites and holds on and slowly chew while poison flows along grooves in the teeth. This lizard is slow and hard to provoke. It is rare and should not be harmed. Page 610

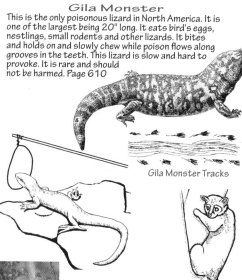

Gila Monster Tracks

Ringed Tail Cat
An excellent hunter of mice. Member of the raccoon family. They are nocturnal. Food: fruits, grasshoppers, insects, small mammals.

Desert Hare
Also called the desert jack rabbit or black tailed jack rabbit. Enemies: lynx, car accidents, large birds of prey, large snakes (gopher, bull snake, rattlesnake). They are nocturnal. Food: variety of green stuff and twigs.

Desert Kit Fox
Nose to tail 20" (51 cm) long. Its large ears serve as radiators by which the fox stays cool. Color: grizzled white with yellowish buff and black tipped over hair. It hunts at night Food: kangaroo rats, lizards, insects.

Mojave Rattlesnake

Collared Lizard

Giant Saguaro Cactus
Cacti store water in their pulpy flesh. The rib pattern on the outside of a cactus folds and unfolds depending on how much water is in the storage tissue.

Joshua-tree

Cougar

Rattlesnake

SNAKE BITE KIT

Barrel Cactus

Stinger

Scorpion

Desert Horned Lizard

Roadrunner

Desert Bat
There are different species of bats in the desert. They live in caves, crevasses, and mine tunnels all day. They leave to feed just before and after sunset. They fly in a zigzag pattern. Food: insects.

Cactus Wren
Largest of all wrens. Body 8" long. Nests are in the spines of the cholla cactus. Food: spiders, insects, larvae. Enemies are small owls, wood rats, wild mice, and ground squirrels eat their eggs.

Prickly Pear Cactus

Prickly Pear Cactus

Gambel's Quail

Giant Saguaro Cactus

California Quail

Northern Mexico Cactus Desert

Yucca

Joshua-tree

SOURCE OF FOOD

Food is hard to find in the desert. Food can be rationed as it is secondary to water. If a problem occurs start rationing immediately by stopping to eat immediately for twenty four hours to help you establish a new biorhythm.

NATURAL SOURCES

Animals: Animals are rare and hard to find in the desert. They are usually nocturnal and stay in cool areas, holes, shade, and your clothing! Rodents (mice, rats, prairie dogs, rabbits) and lizards caught near a water hole may be your only diet. Antelope or deer are hard to catch or kill without a gun. Other creatures that can be found are snakes, insects, snails, and birds.
Birds: Birds such as pelicans and grouse are found on the desert. Attract them by making a plucking sound by sucking the back of your hand. See *Trapping Chapter* on how to trap birds.
Finding Insects: Insects can be found in cool areas under rocks. While looking watch for snakes and scorpions.
Plants: Plants usually are found near a water source. These plants might look dry and unappetizing but they usually have soft parts that are edible. There might be fruits, seeds, young shoots and bark. These seeds or fruit can be beans that grow on bushes, the prickly pear of the cactus etc. Nearly all grass is edible. *See Edible Plants Chapter Page 566.*

COOKING & FIRE

Palm leaves and other growth near an oasis can be used as fuel. In the desert use any fuel you can find or build a solar stove. See Fire and Cooking Chapters for more information.

VEGETATION

The indigenous vegetation has physiologically adapted itself to desert conditions. Some plants, like the desert gourd, have vines which grow to 15 feet. Others have wide lateral roots just below the surface to take advantage of rain and dew, while still others grow deep roots to tap subsurface water.
• Palm trees indicate water within two to three feet from the surface.
• Salt Grass implies water within six feet.
• Cottonwood and willow trees imply water within 10 - 12 feet.
Other plants, e.g.. cacti, have no relationship to the water table because they store their water. Some drought resistant seeds lie dormant for years and only grow for a brief period after a rainstorm. In addition to indicating the presence of water, some plants are edible. The available vegetation is usually inadequate to provide much shade or shelter.

DESERT PLANT ROOT STRUCTURE

Root looks for water that can be deep in the ground. Plants that have this type of root structure indicate water at greater depths.

Vertical Root Structure

Horizontal Root Structure
This structure finds water just below the surface.

DESERT TEMPERATURE

The highest known ambient temperature recorded in a desert was 136°F. Lower temperatures than this produced internal car temperatures approaching 160°F in the Sahara Desert. Winter temperatures in Siberian deserts and in the Gobi –50°F. Low temperatures are aggravated by very strong winds producing high windchill factors. The cloudless sky of the desert permits the earth to heat during sunlit hours, yet cool to near freezing at night.

RAIN

There is a lack of water in all deserts. When it rains it might be as a single rainstorm, including hail, which will rapidly run off. Rain falling several hundred miles away can cause flash flooding in the local dry stream beds. This can be extremely hazardous so be alert to any sudden changes in the surrounding noise.

WATER

All life on the desert is based upon the availability of water. Permanent rivers do exist, e.g. Colorado, but they are fed by the drainage basin in wet areas outside of the desert area. Ground water in oasis or near surface wells comes from aquifers that might originate hundreds of miles away and the water might have fallen as rain 2000 years ago. Water in the desert should be given the highest respect and a natural source should never be disturbed or contaminated as it might take years for it to be potable again.

DESERT WINDS

Desert winds can achieve velocities of near hurricane force; dust and sand suspended within them make life intolerable and restrict visibility to a few meters. In all deserts, rapid temperature changes invariably follow strong winds. In the evening the wind normally settles down. In many deserts a prevailing wind blows steadily from one cardinal direction for most of the year, and eventually switches to another direction for the remaining months. Gales can raise huge sandstorms that rise to several thousand feet and may last for several days. Gales and sandstorms in the winter months can be bitterly cold.

DESERT WINDS & YOU

The wind can be as physically demanding as heat, as it burns the face, arms, and any exposed skin with blown sand. Sand gets into eyes, nose, mouth, throat, lungs, ears, and hair, and reaches every part of the body. Even speaking and listening can be difficult. Continual exposure to blown sand is exhausting and demoralizing. Spaces that are protected from dust and sand are likely to be very hot.

The combination of wind and dust or sand can cause extreme irritation to mucous membranes, chap the lips and other exposed skin surfaces, and can cause nosebleed. Cracked, chapped lips make eating difficult and cause communication problems. Irritative conjunctivitis, caused when fine particles enter the eyes, is a frequent complaint even when wearing goggles. Lip balm and skin and eye ointments should be available. Constant wind noise is tiresome.

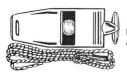

Emergency Whistle Used as signal to keep a group together.

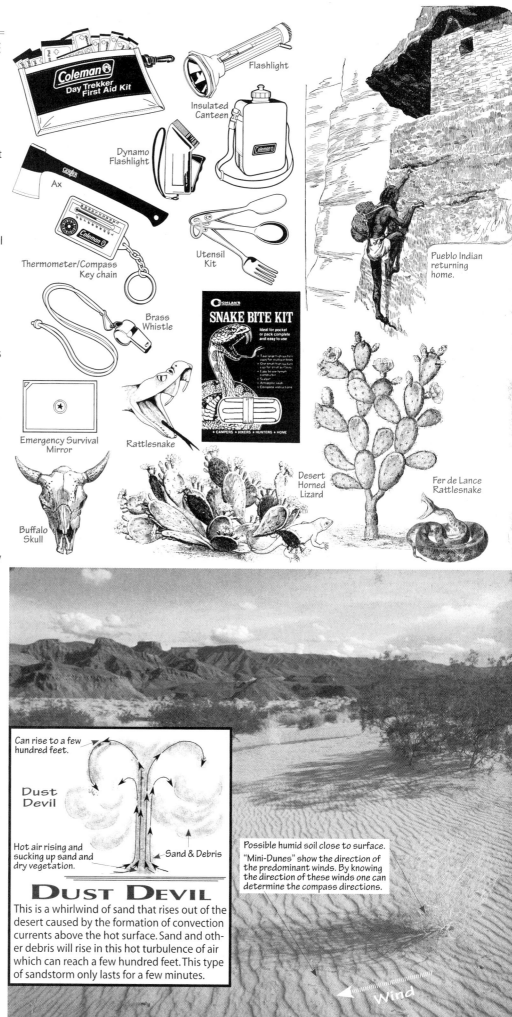

Flashlight

Coleman Day Trekker First Aid Kit

Insulated Canteen

Dynamo Flashlight

Ax

Thermometer/Compass Key chain

Utensil Kit

Brass Whistle

SNAKE BITE KIT
Ideal for pocket or pack complete and easy to use

Emergency Survival Mirror

Rattlesnake

Pueblo Indian returning home.

Desert Horned Lizard

Fer de Lance Rattlesnake

Buffalo Skull

Can rise to a few hundred feet.

Dust Devil

Hot air rising and sucking up sand and dry vegetation.

Sand & Debris

DUST DEVIL

This is a whirlwind of sand that rises out of the desert caused by the formation of convection currents above the hot surface. Sand and other debris will rise in this hot turbulence of air which can reach a few hundred feet. This type of sandstorm only lasts for a few minutes.

Possible humid soil close to surface. "Mini-Dunes" show the direction of the predominant winds. By knowing the direction of these winds one can determine the compass directions.

Wind

SAND DUNES

North American Sand Dunes

State	Sand Dune Park
Colorado	Great Sand Dunes
New Mexico	White Sands
California	Imperial Dunes
Utah	Coral Pink Sands
Idaho	St. Anthony Dunes
Idaho	Bruneau Sand Dunes
Oregon	Oregon Dunes
Michigan	Sleeping Bear Dunes
Indiana	Indiana Dunes
Wyoming	Killpecker Dunes

Sand dunes cover less than 1% of the deserts in North America. Sand dunes can move from less than one foot to up to 80 feet per year. This movement depends upon the strength of the wind (in a constant direction), the size of the dune, the shape of the dune, and the amount and height of the surrounding vegetation. Alaskan dunes are perched on the frozen ground.

SAND DUNE FORMATION

To have a sand dune you require:

Sand: A source which can be a dry riverbed.

Wind: A relatively constant prevailing wind.

Collection Obstacle: This is a protrusion which causes the wind to decelerate and it will drop the sand which will then build up. On a small scale this can be observed in a sandy area where there is a sand accumulation on the leeward side of a blade of grass protruding through the sand. In the winter you see snow drifts in sand dune type formations.

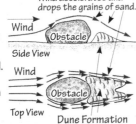

Wind decelerates and drops the grains of sand.

Side View — Wind — Obstacle

Top View — Wind — Obstacle — Dune Formation

SAND DUNE MIGRATION

Wind blowing at least at 15 mph picks up a grain of sand, depending upon the grain's weight, and carries it until the wind speed falls below 15 mph. Then the grain drops. Dunes advance as sand is driven up the shallow slope and tumble down the steeper (lee) slope. With time this pattern is repeated both in miniature as in large dunes. Note that the miniature dunes blown up a large dune (the ripples) are miniature copies of the large dune.

Wind : At least 15 mph. — Grain of Sand — Sand Dune — *Individual Grain of Sand Advancing*

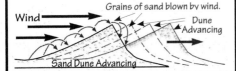

Wind — Grains of sand blown by wind. — Dune Advancing — *Sand Dune Advancing*

Traverse Dune
A variant of the crescent dune but it is more straight and usually found in the center of a dune field. They occur in areas of large quantities of sand and wind blowing from one constant direction.

Longitudinal Dune
They are parallel and form in the direction of the wind. They form where there is limited sand.

Star Dune
These are formed by winds blowing equally strong from different directions during the year. They occur in areas of much sand. Major examples of this type of dune are in the Sahara and Arabian deserts.

Parabolic Dune
These usually are stable dunes which are anchored by vegetation where the leeward tip can be creeping very slowly.

Crescent Shaped Dune (Barchan)
This is an active dune which moves up to eighty feet per year. The winds will usually blow from one direction all year and their tips point leeward. As this dune is always moving vegetation will not have time to establish a foot hold. These dunes usually are on the outside fringes of a dune field. They form in areas of limited sand.

Wind — Covered Person — Boulder or Vegetation — **Sandstorm Protection**

SANDSTORMS

The deserts of Iran are equally well known for the "wind of 120 days," with sand blowing almost constantly from the north at wind velocities of up to 75 mph. There is no danger of a traveler being buried alive by a sandstorm. Sandstorms are likely to form suddenly and stop just as suddenly. In a severe sandstorm, sand permeates everything making movement nearly impossible, not only because of limited visibility, but also because blowing sand damages moving parts of machinery, sandblasts windshields and camera lenses, etc. When visibility is reduced by sandstorms members should not be allowed to leave their group for any purpose unless secured by rope lines. During a storm always keep your nose covered and protect your eyes.

SANDSTORM & YOU

- Contact lenses are very difficult to maintain in the dry dusty environment of the desert.
- Mucous membranes can be protected by breathing through a wet face cloth, snuffing small amounts of water into nostrils or coating the nostrils with a small amount of petroleum jelly.
- Lips should be protected by lip balm.
- Scarves and bandannas can be used to protect the head, face, and prevent sand going down the collar.
- The face should be washed as often as possible
- The eyelids should be cleaned daily.

GI Can Opener

DESERT TRAVEL

DESERT CAMPING

If you want to camp in the desert have one twenty-four hour trial to see if you like it. It might not be fun. Animals in the desert only run around at night. The whole trial can be a great experience as you will be in direct exposure to the one thing that is hard to escape - HEAT. The extreme climate and environment of the desert can be a challenge as:

- The sunlight's effect on the landscape always changes and you might see mirages.
- The heat and intensity of the sun will affect your water intake and your diet.
- You will be adapting your daily schedule around the cooler hours.
- Build shelter against the heat of the sun, dust storms and the cold nights.

If you like the 24 hour trip then you might be ready for an extended camping trip and have a unique experience.

There are two types of deserts in North America. The low latitude sand deserts and the high altitude rocky, rugged, hilly terrain which has sand, stones and sometimes snow. Prepare yourself for the type of desert that you will visit.

Day Trip

The first day trip should be well-planned and possibly use a guide:

Planning Itinerary

Make a detailed plan as to where you are going and where you plan to stay. Leave a copy of the plan with someone and tell them when you will report back. If you do not report back in time they will report you "lost" to the authorities. When traveling do not leave the road or track because you will find that cacti and rocks all look the same if you are lost. If you have any problems en route or change your plan inform your contact.

BASIC DESERT TRAVEL KNOWLEDGE

When traveling in the desert you must know the type of terrain and the general environment you will encounter:

- Landmarks or significant permanent terrain features.
- Water sources, if any. • Prevailing winds.
- Possible rest or repair areas.

Food & Water

Have sufficient food with you as it is difficult to find food in the desert. Bring at least two or three days of water with 4 quarts per person per day and use the water sparingly. Use containers that help water keep its natural flavor. Get some hot weather water canteens. They are covered with canvas and you wet the canvas with water which gradually evaporates and cools the water in the container.

Clothing

Wear the right clothing and be prepared for cool nights.

Accessories

Bring sunscreen (use at least SPF 30), hats, bandana, and sunglasses. For tent anchors use "Ziploc" bags filled with sand. Place them inside self standing tents to hold them down. Pack your tent and retreat to the car during sand storms. Wood shrinks in a high-temperature, low-humidity environment. Equipment, such as axes carried can become safety hazards as heads are likely to fly off shrunken handles.

WALKING

Walking on sand is difficult as you have a tendency to slide back. The energy required for one mile on sand is equivalent to two miles on regular terrain. Wear boots and heavy socks as the sand is so hot that it can cause burns.

WINDS & TENTS

Desert winds, by their velocity alone, can be very destructive to large and relatively light materiel. Tents should be placed in protected areas and firmly picketed to the ground. If there are rocks available place them on the tent and possibly in the tent on the windward side. The door should be on the leeward side.

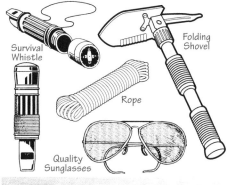

Survival Whistle

Folding Shovel

Rope

Quality Sunglasses

DESERT DRIVING

Roads and trails are rare in the open desert. Some trails have been used for centuries to connect trade centers. Some surfaces, such as lava beds or salt marshes, preclude routine vehicular travel, but generally foot travel is possible in all directions. Vehicle travel in mountainous desert country may be severely restricted. Driving can be difficult as hairpin turns are common on the edges of precipitous mountain gorges, and the higher passes may be blocked by snow in the winter.

DUSTY CONDITIONS

- Wear goggles if driving open vehicles regardless of visibility. Bandanas or surgical masks should be worn to avoid breathing heavy dust.
- Vehicles in a convoy should maintain a dust distance to allow time for the dust to dissipate. When driving on extremely dusty roads or trails a staggered formation can be used with vehicles alternately driving on the left and right side of the road. If the vehicles should become engulfed in dust move to the right side of the road and stop or slow to allow the dust to dissipate. Extreme caution must be observed for oncoming and following vehicles.

Land Rover

Emergency Candle
Used for heating of a
small shelter or car.

Emergency Candle
8 to 10 hours burn
time per candle.

Mess Kit

DRIVING: ROCKY AREAS

- Rock and boulder-strewn areas, including lava beds, may extend for many miles. Desert rocks, eroded and sharp-edged, vary in size and are so numerous that it is almost impossible to avoid any but the largest. The subsequent harsh jolting fatigues individuals and causes extreme wear on wheels, springs, and shock absorbers. Rocks and stones can become lodged between the tire threads on vehicles (these rocks might be launched as missiles when they detach) that can cause severe damage to tires and brake components.
- Vehicles can follow one another in this type of terrain but not to close to avoid any launched stones.
- Drivers should achieve a "rolling" effect as they cross large rocks by braking as the vehicle's wheels ride over a rock so the axle settles relatively gently on the far side.

DRIVING: WADIS

Wadis are dried water beds, vary from wide to barely perceptible depressions of soft sand, dotted with bushes, to deep, steep-sided ravines. There frequently is a passable route through the bottom of a dried wadi. The threat of flash floods after heavy rains poses a significant danger. Flooding may occur in these areas even if it is not raining in the immediate area.

DRIVING: SALT MARSHES

Salt marshes are normally impassable, the worst type being those with a dry crust of silt on top. Salt marshes develop at points where the water in the subsoil of the desert rose to the surface. Because of the constant evaporation in the desert, the salts carried by the water are deposited, and results in a hard, brittle crust.

- Many desert areas have salt marshes either in the center of a drainage basin or near the seacoast.
- Old trails or paths may cross the marsh, which are visible during the dry season but not in the wet season. In the wet season standing water indicates trails due to the crust being too hard or too thick for the water to penetrate. Vehicles may become severely mired if they break through the crust. Verify the crust strength before driving.

SANDY DESERTS

Sandy deserts may be relatively flat or interspersed with windblown dunes.

DRIVING ON SAND

- The best time to drive on sand is at night or early morning when the sand is damp and traction is better. However, this is not always the case especially with the newer type tires with closer tread design. Damp sand packs between the tread in the grooves of these tires resulting in virtually no surface traction.
- Vehicles may gain some traction by reducing the air pressure in the tires. Vehicles equipped with radial tires might not be affected by the lower tire pressure – at low speed.
- Vehicle loads must be evenly distributed. Rear-wheel drive should be used where possible to prevent the front wheels from digging into the sand and becoming mired.
- Switch to all-wheel drive or change gears before a vehicle bogs down in the sand.
- Before entering the sand select a gear that will allow the vehicle to maintain as much torque as possible without causing the wheels to spin. Minimize the changing of gears.
- Some sand areas will be covered by a surface crust. This is caused by chemicals in the ground cementing sand particles together.

DRIVING ON A CRUST

- As a general rule vehicles should not follow one behind the other on a crust.
- Ensure vehicles maintain a minimum speed below which they will break through the crust.
- Avoid sharp turns and abrupt starts or stops.
- Reconnoiter patches of the crust that are a different shade to ensure they are not softer than the surrounding crust.

CROSSING DUNES

- Crossing dunes requires careful reconnaissance. Normally, the upwind side (windward) of the dune will be covered with a crust and have a fairly gradual slope. The downwind side (leeward) will be steeper and have no crust.
- Prior to crossing a dune, the driver should climb it on foot checking crust thickness, the angle at the crest to ensure the vehicle will not become bellied at the top, and the degree of slope and softness of the downwind side. If satisfied that his vehicle can climb the dune, he should drive the vehicle straight up it at the best speed, crest it, and maintain a controlled descent on the other side.
- Little hills may be formed by the wind blowing sand around small shrubs. Do not drive through these areas.
- Cacti or thorn bushes will cause frequent flat tires.

Self inflating
sleeping mat.

Tarpaulin

Pneumatic
Mattress

Foot Air Pump

POSSIBLE VEHICLE PROBLEMS

Temperatures and dryness are major causes of equipment failure. Wind can spread sand and dust, clogging and jamming anything that has moving parts. Rubber components such as gaskets and seals become brittle, and oil leaks are more frequent.

Terrain: Terrain varies from nearly flat (easy to drive), to lava beds and salt marshes (very difficult to impossible). Drivers must be well trained in judging terrain over which they are driving so they can select the best method of overcoming the varying conditions they will encounter. The harsh environment requires a very high standard of maintenance. Operators must be fully trained in operating and maintaining their cars.

Heat: In temperature extremes, engines are apt to operate above optimum temperatures, leading to excessive wear, or leaking oil seals, and ultimately, engine failure.

- Check oil levels frequently to ensure proper levels are maintained (too high may be as bad as too low), that seals are not leaking, and that oil consumption is not higher than normal.
- Keep radiators and air flow areas around engines clean and free of debris and other obstructions.
- Fit water-cooled engines with condensers to avoid steam escaping through the overflow pipe. Cooling hoses must be kept tight.
- On jeeps do not remove hood side panels from engine compartments while the engine is running as this causes air turbulence and leads to ineffective cooling.
- Batteries do not hold their charge efficiently in intense heat. Check twice daily.
- Radiators require special attention. Proper cooling-system operation is critical in high-temperature environments. A mixture of 40% antifreeze and 60% water is usually acceptable.
- Air and all fluids expand and contract according to temperature. If tires are inflated to correct pressure during the cool of night, they may burst during the heat of day. If fuel tanks are filled to the brim at night, they will overflow at midday.

STATIC ELECTRICITY & EXPLOSIONS

Static electricity poses a danger in the desert. It is caused by atmospheric conditions coupled with an inability to ground out due to dryness of the sand. This is especially the case where vehicles having no conductor contact with the soil. When contact is made between two items an electrical discharge may occur and if flammable gases are present, they may explode and cause a fire. Establish a metal circuit between fuel source and car before and during refueling. Static electricity will also ruin circuit boards and other electronic equipment.

Static Electricity Kills

VW Thing
1973

DRIVING: DUST & SAND

Dust and sand are probably the greatest danger to the efficient functioning of a vehicle. It is almost impossible to avoid particles settling on moving parts and acting as an abrasive. Sand mixed with oil forms an abrasive paste.

- Oils must be of the correct viscosity for the temperature and kept to the recommended absolute minimum on exposed or semi exposed moving parts. Critical items should be checked frequently. Teflon bearings require constant inspection to ensure that the coating is not being eroded. Proper lubrication is crucial for success.
- Oil should be changed about twice as often under desert conditions, because grit accumulates in the oil pan.
- Keep your tools clean.

Dust and sand can easily cause failure of such items as radios, dashboards, and circuit breakers, and cause small electrical motors to burn out.

Towing: Sand Crust & Salt Marshes

Vehicles should carry the following items:

- Steel or aluminum channels. These are pierced to reduce weight and ribbed for strength.
- Sand mats made of canvas, preferably with lateral strips of metal to give strength and increase the traction of the wheels.
- Jacks and jack blocks. • Tow rope(s). • Shovels.

Mired: Once a vehicle becomes mired, remove the ground under the vehicle in a gradual slope towards the direction of recovery until no part of the underside is touching the ground. Channels and mats are laid under or against the wheels facing the direction of recovery. Tire pressure may be reduced to increase traction, but this also lowers the vehicle. It maybe necessary to lift the wheels with a jack if the vehicle is resting on its frame or axles.

Moves: When the vehicle begins to move, any slowing down will cause it to sink again. Once out, the driver must maintain speed until the vehicle has reached the nearest hard area. At this point the tires are reinflated, the vehicle inspected for any damage, and recovery equipment collected.

Winches: Vehicles equipped with winches can winch themselves out using ground anchors. The ground anchor may consist of a tarpaulin full of sand placed in a hole and the winch cable attached to it, or it may be one, or preferably two spare wheels well dug in.

If a vehicle breaks or bogs down in the desert, it might be better to stay with it. A vehicle is much easier to find than a lone man.

VEHICLE MAINTENANCE

Vehicles are subject to brake system component failures and power steering leaks on rocky deserts. Vehicles equipped with manual transmissions are prone to clutch failure caused by the driver slipping the clutch. Vehicles with automatic transmissions tend to overheat; therefore, stop frequently to allow the transmission to cool. Tire wear is very high, so all vehicles must carry one, or preferably two spare tires. Vehicles should be equipped with the following:

- Extra fan belts
- Extra radiator hoses
- Two spare tires
- Extra air & fuel filters
- Extra oil
- Jack stand support plate
- Heavy duty tape
- Siphoning hose & funnel
- Tow rope/cable
- Extra water cans
- Sand ladders (fabricated) & matting
- Jumper cables

GENERAL DESERT DRIVING TIPS

- Check drive belt adjustment frequently.
- Lubricate suspension items daily, and clean grease fittings.
- Reduce sand ingestion by stretching nylon stockings over air cleaners.
- Adjust battery specific gravity to the environment.
- Set voltage regulators at lower end of specifications.
- Have extra supplies of oils and lubricants.
- Use high-grade 20W-50 oil.
- Compensate for increased pressure due to severe heat in closed pressurized systems.
- Check transmissions for the correct viscosity of lubricants for higher temperatures.
- Keep lubrication to the absolute minimum on exposed moving parts
- Erect screens against blowing sand in rest areas.
- Cover the gap between the fuel nozzle and the fuel tank filler neck opening during refueling.
- Protect exposed electrical cables and wires with electrical tape.
- Keep optics covered; clean them with a soft clean paintbrush.
- Clean sand and dirt from vehicles
- Check tire pressure and fuel level at the midpoint of the temperature range during the day.
- Ground all refueling equipment.
  Static electricity kills
- Replenish radiators with potable water or radiator fluid whenever required.
- Consider draining fuel lines at night and in the morning due to condensation.

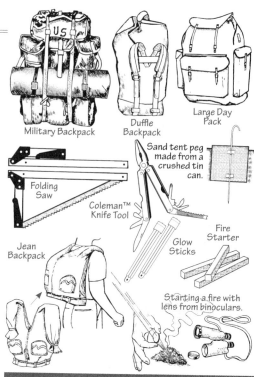

Military Backpack

Duffle Backpack

Large Day Pack

Folding Saw

Sand tent peg made from a crushed tin can.

Coleman™ Knife Tool

Jean Backpack

Glow Sticks

Fire Starter

Starting a fire with lens from binoculars.

Be prepared to walk...

Arizona Ghost Town
Notice the remains of sod homes.

DESERT NIGHTS & WINTERS

The desert can become dangerously cold. The dry air, wind, and clear sky can produce bone-chilling cold. The ability of the body to maintain body temperature within a narrow range is as important in the cold as in the heat. Loss of body heat to the environment can lead to cold injury; a general lowering of the body temperature can result in hypothermia, and local freezing of body tissues can lead to frostbite. Hypothermia is the major threat from the cold in the desert, but frostbite also occurs. Remember the Windchill factor. *See page 200*

DESERT HATS

Protecting the head and eyes is of prime importance. The hat should be of a two layer construction with a layer of air that can circulate between the head and the top outside layer. The old colonial pith helmets are ideal as they are not heavy and have a broad brim to cover the eyes and neck. The original helmets were called 'pith' helmets as the layer of material below the cloth was made of the white pulp from below the outside cover of an orange or other citrus fruit. Modern helmets usually have a Styrofoam core. This core is more fragile as it can be chemically unstable and can disintegrate in contact with petroleum products. You can chose a French Legionnaire style hat with a neck cover.

SUNGLASSES

Avoid scratching sunglasses with sand particles. If you have no glasses you can wear your scarf so that your eyes peer through a slit to reduce the reflected sunlight. A pair of Inuit slit sunglasses can be cut from a piece of wood, leather, plastic, or heavy cloth.

SUNBURN

Overexposure to the sun can cause sunburn. Persons with fair skin, freckled skin, ruddy complexions, or red hair are more susceptible to sunburn than others, but all personnel are susceptible to some degree.

People with darker complexions can also sunburn. This is difficult to monitor due to skin pigmentation, so one must be ever vigilant to watch for possible sunburn victims in the group. Sunburn is characterized by painful reddened skin, and can result in blistering and lead to other forms of heat illness.

You should acquire a suntan in gradual stages (preferably in the early morning or late afternoon) to gain some protection against sunburn. You should not expose bare skin to the sun for longer than five minutes on the first day, increasing exposure gradually at the rate of five minutes per day. You should be fully clothed in loose garments as this will reduce sweat loss and keep you cool.

Remember:

• The sun is as dangerous on cloudy days as it is on sunny days.
• Sunburn ointment is not designed to give complete protection against excessive exposure.
• Sunbathing or dozing in the desert sun can be fatal.

DESERT CLOTHING

In the desert the main purpose of clothing is to protect the body against the sun, the heat, insects, reptiles, and to regulate excessive sweat production. Follow the example of desert dwellers, cover the whole body, wear layers of light-colored clothing made of natural breathable materials such as cotton. This clothing should be loose fitting and in many layers so that it can gradually be removed during the day and reapplied in the evening. Wear long-sleeved shirts, and full-length trousers tucked into walking boots. A large woolen scarf can be draped to offer protection during the cold nights. A bandana can be worn loosely around the neck to protect it from the sun and to prevent sand from blowing down the collar. This bandana covers the face during a sand storm. In extremely hot and dry conditions a wet sweat rag worn loosely around the neck will assist in body cooling. Wash clothing if possible; if not, air it in the sun to kill bacteria or fungi growth. Do not expose your skin unless you are in the shade and even then reflected radiation can give you a sunburn.

Pants

US Army combat pants are ideal desert pants as they are 100% cotton and have a dense weave to make them wind proof. They are baggy, have numerous sealed pockets, and have an ankle drawstring to tighten around boots. Some models even have a lined seat and knees.

Inuit Slit Sunglasses
Whittled from wood.

Back

Cotton Shorts

Inuit Slit Sunglasses
These eye protectors can be made from a piece of cloth, , etc. The narrow slits reduce the amount of reflected light that reaches the eyes.

Cloth or Birch Bark Sunglasses

The 'Foreign Legion" hat offers the best protection as it covers the ears and neck. The high profile also creates an air space between the material and the head sot that with a few ventilation holes this area can keep the head cool.

Towel under a cap.

Pith Helmet

Poncho can be used as a ground sheet, tent from the sun, or cover for chilly nights.

Cotton Hat

90

DESERT FOOTWEAR

Your feet are the most sensitive part of the body. When they hurt or are injured they will impede travel.

The desert is very hard on boots. Leather should be treated with saddle soap or it will dry out and crack. Boots should be worn with heavy socks, to keep out the radiant heat of the ground. They should be well laced to keep out the sand. Sand will sift into the breather holes of military jungle boots. Cover the holes on military boots with glue or epoxies to prevent excessive sand from entering the boots. Boots will protect against snake and scorpion bites and help weak ankles. If the soles get worn reinforce them with a piece of cloth or other padding.

While resting in the shade remove your boots and socks. Be careful because your feet might swell. Before putting your boots back on always check for insects, snakes, and scorpions.

If your calves need covering make some puttees. Puttees were used by armies before high boots were commonly used. They are wound, above ankle boots, around the ankle up to below the knees. They are made from a stretchy (knit) strip of cloth 3 - 4" wide 4' long. They are wrapped in an overlapping spiral by starting at the knee to the ankle. They will keep out the sand and reduce the effect of the heat radiated from the sand.

- The sidewall of an old tire can be used to make the soles of a pair of sandals.
- Protect the tops of your feet from the sun because a sunburn in this location is extremely painful and you will not be able to wear boots.
- Do not walk barefoot because hot sand will blister your feet. If crossing barefoot on salt flats or mire you will receive alkali burns.
- Change socks when they become wet. Prolonged wear of wet socks can lead to foot injury. Although dry desert air promotes evaporation of water from exposed clothing and may actually promote cooling, sweat tends to accumulate in boots.

Travel Straps

Safari Hat

SHELTER IN THE DESERT

Shelter from sun, heat, wind and possible sandstorms (with access to water) is the most important factor for surviving in the desert.
- Material generally is not available to easily build a shelter.
- Covering your body with sand provides some basic protection from the heat and will reduce water loss from the skin.
- In sandy areas, dig a shallow depression or find a natural hollow and cover it with tarpaulin or parachute material. The edges can be anchored with sand.
- In rocky desert areas pile some stones to form a support for a parachute cover.
- Drape parachute material over desert growth and anchor with rocks and sand.
- Use natural desert features for shade or shelter: a tree, bushes, a rock pile, cave, slope of a sand dune, wall of dry stream bed (watch and listen for any signs of a flash flood which might be the result of a cloudburst many miles away).
- Use shelters that have been made by previous travelers.

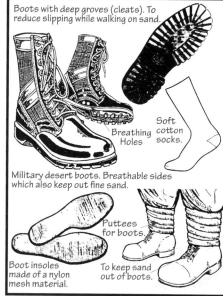

Boots with deep groves (cleats). To reduce slipping while walking on sand.

Breathing Holes

Soft cotton socks.

Military desert boots. Breathable sides which also keep out fine sand.

Boot insoles made of a nylon mesh material.

Puttees for boots.

To keep sand out of boots.

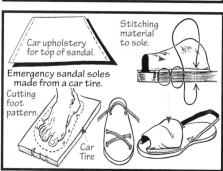

Car upholstery for top of sandal.

Stitching material to sole.

Emergency sandal soles made from a car tire.

Cutting foot pattern.

Car Tire

T-shirt arms.

Cotton T-shirt used for head protection.

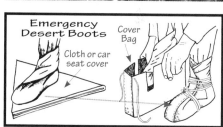

Emergency Desert Boots

Cover Bag

Cloth or car seat cover

DESERT SHELTER

Cover

Two layers of tarpaulin or parachute material. The layers should be at least 10" apart and will act as an insulation from the heat of the sun.

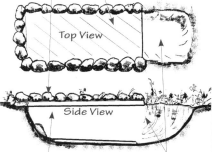

Top View

Side View

Trench

The trench should be 2'-3' deep and the entrance is oriented towards the north. Cover the ground in the trench to reduce ground humidity.

Entrance

Make the entrance very small or long so that the sun's rays do not reflect into the shelter.

DESERT SHELTER IN BLUFF

Wind - so that sand and hot air will not blow into shelter during a dust storm.

Use a shovel, knife or sharp flat stone to dig into the bluff.

Cover to keep out the heat. The temperature in the dug out hole will be cooler than on the surface.

At least 3 feet thick.

Great Horned Owl nesting on a Giant Saguaro Cactus

Humans and the desert are compatible as long as humans know what to expect, what to do and have the required equipment. Desert tribes and cultures have survived for centuries in the most difficult circumstances.

The desert is physically and emotionally fatiguing. Discipline and attention to detail are required. If you are not in an emergency situation you should have the luxury of approximately two weeks to acclimatize yourself in progressive degrees to both the heat and physical exertion in a hot area. Initially heavy labor should be limited to cooler times of the day with frequent rests. Shelter is lacking as there is minimal or no vegetation. You might have a phobia type of reaction - agoraphobia - fear of open spaces. This phobia normally disappears with acclimatization.

SUN'S RAYS & HEAT

The sun's rays and heat come from four directions...

- Directly from the sun.
- Sun reflected from the earth.
- Heat gain from the sand and rocks (radiant heat).
- Hot winds which might be sand laden.

The sun's rays, either direct or reflected, can cause eyestrain and temporary impaired vision. Too much exposure or lack of protection can cause sunburn especially to light-complexioned people. Do not expose skin for more than 5 minutes on the first day. Exposure can be increased by 5 minutes per day. Loose garments covering the body should be worn at all times following the example of the tribes of the desert.

You should never forget the high risk of getting skin cancer at a later stage of your life.

Cloudy days are as dangerous as sunny days. Sun tan lotion is not made to protect you against excessive exposure. Sleeping in the sun or too much sunbathing can be fatal.

Climatic stress can be caused by the heat's effect on the body, humidity, wind, and radiant heat. Consider the factors of lack of acclimatization, overweight, alcohol, lack of sleep, old age and poor health.

THE BODY

The human body has an internal thermometer that regulates the body heat at 98.6°F. This temperature is maintained by the body radiating heat, conduction, convection, and evaporation (sweat). Sweat is the most important, especially when the humidity is very low, because the evaporation of water from the skin causes the skin and body to cool. This is why dogs breath through wide open mouths with their tongue hanging out on hot days. If the relative humidity is very high this system of body air conditioning will not work.

US Army Acclimatization Schedule				
Schedule shows hours of work that may be performed in a minimum period of acclimatization.				
Day	Less <105°F (40.5°C)		More >105°F (40.5°C)	
	AM	PM	AM	PM
1	1 hr	1 hr	1 hr	1 hr
2	1.5	1.5	1.5	1.5
3	2	2	2	2
4	3	3	2.5	2.5
5	regular duty	3	3	
6	regular duty	regular duty		

HIGH ALTITUDE ROCKY DESERT TRAVEL

Desert mountains are high and rugged, with very steep slopes. Valleys running into a range become more and more narrow with the sides becoming gradually steeper. Valleys are usually the only routes for car travel. Water is nonexistent on hilltops and unusual in valleys except during flash floods after rains.

MOUNTAIN TREKKING ACCLIMATIZATION

Travelers in mountainous country must be in peak physical condition with high levels of stamina and energy.

Acclimatization to height varies much more among individuals than that for heat. Lack of oxygen at high altitudes can cause unacclimatized travelers to lose up to 50% of their normal physical efficiency in altitudes over 6,000 feet. Mountain sickness may occur at altitudes over 7,800 feet and is usually characterized by severe headache, loss of appetite, nausea and dizziness, and may last from 5 - 7 days. Acclimatize can occur by staging techniques. It may take several weeks to become completely acclimatized, depending on altitude and the individual's personal physical reactions.

SUNBURN

The risk of sunburn, particularly to the uncovered face, is greater in mountains than on the desert floor due to thinner atmosphere. Use anti sunburn ointment and keep the face in the shade around midday, using face nets or sweat rags.

HEAT ILLNESS

Recognition of heat illnesses in higher altitudes may not be as apparent as at lower altitudes because sweat evaporates very quickly. Measures to avoid dehydration and salt loss are extremely important.

TEMPERATURE VARIATIONS

Daily temperature variations may be considerable making it necessary to ensure you do not become chilled at night. Layering of clothing is essential. If you have been sweating heavily before the temperature starts to drop take your wet shirts off and place them over relatively dry shirts and sweaters. Add layers of clothing as it gets colder and remove them as needed.

HYGIENE

Hygiene is important in mountainous areas as in the sandy desert. Normal rocky ground will make it extremely difficult to dig any form of latrine so cover excrement with rocks in a specially marked area.

HEAT & BODY

Objects absorb heat from the sun and the air. In the desert, heat from these two sources is extreme. The clear, low-humidity air lets most of the sun's heat reach the ground.

ABSORBING HEAT

Direct Sun Heat: Heat absorbed from sunlight.
Indirect Air Heat: The ground, heated by the sun, in turn heats the air, often to temperatures well over 100°F. A person in the shade is heated by the air.
Body Heat: Heat produced by a human body. The more the human exerts energy the more heat is produced.

REDUCING HEAT

Radiation: Heat radiates from an object to a cooler object through a medium.
Conduction: Heat flows from a hot object to a cooler object through direct contact.
Convection: Heat flows from a hot object into a cooler surrounding medium like air.
Evaporation: Heat is absorbed in changing a liquid (like water) into a vapor.

The heat losses from radiation and conduction are relatively small. If the air is much cooler than the surface of an object, such as a vehicle radiator or a person's skin, convection can remove significant amounts of heat. As the two temperatures get closer, this loss becomes smaller. If the air is hotter than the object, as is often the case in the desert, heat is gained from the air. In hot, dry desert climates, the primary method of losing excess heat from the body is the evaporation of sweat. The rate of sweating depends on the amount of excess heat the body needs to lose. Hard work in hot climates can result in 1.5 - 2.5 quarts of sweat lost per hour.

Sleeping bag compression bag.

RESPONSE TO HEAT PROBLEMS

At the first evidence of heat illness, stop any strenuous activities, get into shade, and re hydrate. Early intervention is important.

ACCLIMATIZATION TO HEAT

Acclimatization to heat is necessary to permit the body to reach and maintain efficiency in its cooling process.
• *See US Army acclimatization chart.*
• Acclimatization does not provide total protection against the debilitating effects of heat.
• Acclimatization does not reduce, and may increase, water requirements.

CLIMATIC STRESS

Climatic stress in hot deserts can be caused by:
• air temperature   • humidity
• air movement   • radiant heat
The body is also adversely affected by:
• lack of acclimatization • dehydration,
• being overweight   • lack of sleep
• alcohol consumption   • old age & poor health
The body maintains its optimum temperature of 98.6°F by conduction/convection, radiation, and evaporation (sweat). The most important of these in the daytime is evaporation, as air temperature alone is probably already above skin temperature. If, however, relative humidity is high, air will not easily evaporate sweat and the cooling effect is reduced.

Sources of Heat in the Desert
A Reflected from ground.
B Hot winds - might include sand.
C Direct from sun.
D Radiant heat from sand & rocks.

A good hat is important.

RADIANT LIGHT

Radiant light comes from all directions. The sun's rays, either direct or reflected off the ground, affect the skin and can also produce eyestrain and temporarily impaired vision. Not only does glare damage the eyes but it is very tiring; therefore, dark glasses or goggles should be worn.

DESERT HEAT

The extreme heat of the desert can cause heat exhaustion and heatstroke. For optimum mental and physical performance, body temperatures must be maintained within narrow limits.

HOW BODY CONTROLS HEAT

Normally convection and evaporation assure transfer of excess body heat to the air. But when the air temperature is above the skin temperature (92°F+) the evaporation of sweat is the only cooling mechanism. When sweating, water must be consumed to replace the body's lost fluids. If the body fluid lost through sweating is not replaced, dehydration will follow. This will hamper heat dissipation and can lead to heat illness. *When the humidity is high, evaporation of sweat is inhibited and there is a greater risk of dehydration or heat stress.*

TO PREVENT DEHYDRATION

• Heat, wind, and dry air cause you to sweat and therefore you require more drinking water. Sweat rates can be high even when the skin looks and feels dry.
• Dehydration increases the susceptibility to heat injury, reduces the capacity to work, and decreases appetite and alertness. A lack of alertness can indicate early stages of dehydration.
• Thirst is not an adequate indicator of dehydration. You may not sense that you are dehydrated and will fail to replace lost body water, even when drinking water is available. Inexperienced travelers exhibit "voluntary dehydration" that is, they maintain their hydration status at about 2% of body weight (1.5 quarts) below their ideal hydration status without any sense of thirst.
• Chronic dehydration increases the incidence of several medical problems: constipation (already an issue in any outdoors situation), piles (hemorrhoids), kidney stones, and urinary infections. The likelihood of these problems occurring can be reduced by enforcing mandatory drinking schedules.
• Resting on hot sand will increase heat stress - the more a body surface is in contact with the sand, the greater the heat stress. Ground or sand in full sun is hot, usually 30°-45° hotter than the air, and may reach 150°F when the air temperature is 120°F. Cooler sand is just inches below the surface; a shaded trench will provide a cool resting spot.

DESERT WATER

HUMAN WATER REQUIREMENTS

Humans cannot perform to maximum efficiency on a decreased water intake. An acclimatized traveler will need as much (if not more) water as the non acclimatized one, as he sweats more readily. If the ration water is not sufficient, there is no alternative but to reduce physical activity or restrict it to the cooler parts of the day.

- In very hot conditions it is better to drink smaller quantities of water often rather than large quantities occasionally. Drinking large quantities causes excessive sweating and may induce heat cramps.
- Use of alcohol lessens resistance to heat due to its dehydrating effect.
- As activities increase or conditions become more severe, increase water intake accordingly.
- The optimum drinking water temperature is between 50°-60°F. Keep a wet cloth around canteens to help cool water.
- In very high temperatures and low humidity, sweating is not noticeable as it evaporates so fast the skin will appear dry.
- Remain covered is loose layers of light cotton to retain sweat on the skin to improve the cooling process or stay out of the sun.
- When you become thirsty you will be about a "quart and a half low".
- Carry as much water as possible when away from approved source. You can live longer without food than without water.
- Drink before you work; carry water in your belly, do not "save" it in your canteen. Learn to drink a quart or more of water at one time and drink frequently to replace sweat losses.
- Carbohydrate/electrolyte beverages (e.g., Gatorade) are not required, and if used, should not be the only source of water. They are too concentrated to be used alone. Many athletes prefer to dilute these 1:1 with water. Gaseous drinks, sodas, beer, and milk are not good substitutes for water because of their dehydrating effects.
- Diseases, especially diarrheal diseases, will complicate and often prevent maintenance of proper hydration.
- Salt, in correct proportions, is vital to the human body. The more you sweat, the more salt you lose and the more you have to replenish.
- If unacclimatized you need additional salt during their first few days of exposure and additional salt when sweating heavily. If the water demand to balance sweat loss rises, extra salt must be taken under medical direction. Salt, in excess of body requirements, may cause increased thirst and a feeling of sickness, and can be dangerous. Water must be tested before adding salt as some sources are already saline, especially those close to the sea.

POTABLE WATER: NUMBER ONE CONCERN

- Drinking water should be kept in distinctive containers that should not be contaminated by non-potable water.
- Drinking water should only be taken from a secure disease free location.
- Sufficient water to last until the next water hole is reached should always be on hand. Be prepared to back track if you cannot find your next source.
- Look for water before your supply is exhausted.
- Water canteens should be transported in such a way that they cannot be damaged or the seams split.
- To keep the water cool keep the containers in the shade or in a windy location.
- You can drink 3.5 pints of water at a time. The body sweats this amount in two hours.
- To maximize your water intake drink slowly and in sips. Drink as much as you can, rest and slowly drink again. Repeat this a few times until your body is saturated.
- Do not eat fats or proteins if you lack water. Food requires water for digestion especially for proteins and fats. Your tissues will supply the water if it is not otherwise available.
- We require a minimum of four quarts of water per day. Several gallons are required if you are doing strenuous activities on a hot day.
- To conserve water, do not travel in the heat of the day but only in the early morning, late evening or on a moonlit night. Set up a sheltered rest area for the day. A well built rest area might be 40°F cooler in the shade.
- The optimum drinking water temperature is between 50°-60°F. To cool water it can be wrapped in a wet cloth which will cause cooling when the water evaporates. The tribes people use animal stomachs as gourds. These gradually breathe water which evaporates and cools the gourd.

You cannot be trained to adjust permanently to a reduced water supply. If rations are insufficient then movement should be reduced to the cool times of the day or night. In very hot areas it is better to take smaller quantities more frequently. This will reduce the water lost by excessive sweating. Smoking increases the desire for water. Alcohol reduces the resistance to heat due to increased dehydration.

Water from barrel cactus.

Waiting

Filtering water from wet soil.

Insulated Canteens

Keep your canteen FULL.

DESERT WATER

WATER IN SAND DUNES

Sand dunes act as sponges and if there is any rainfall they will absorb the water. The top layer of sand acts as an insulator which will protect the moisture from evaporating. You can find moist sand a foot below the surface. Plants do not grow on this potentially ideal water source because the sand is continually shifting. Plants can be buried by the sand or their roots can be exposed by the shifting sand. The sand in the dunes does not provide the nutrients for plant growth. Desert areas with no dunes will usually lose any water from a rainstorm by runoff.

A Navajo shepherd has found water, between the sand dunes, for his flock of goats.

Water seeping into the sand

Find Water Here

Water Table

Find Water Here

Find Water Here

The lack of water is the most important single characteristic of the desert. Desert rainfall varies from one day in the year to intermittent showers throughout the winter. Severe thunderstorms bring heavy rain, and usually far too much rain falls far too quickly. The water soon soaks into the ground and may result in flash floods. Rainstorms tend to be localized, affecting only a few square kilometers at a time. Whenever possible, as storms approach, you should move to rocky areas or high ground to avoid flash floods. Permanent rivers such the Colorado is fed by heavy precipitation outside the desert so the river survives despite a high evaporation rate. Subsurface water may be so far below the surface, or so limited, that wells are normally inadequate to support any great number of people.

Of course if there are people they will have a green lawn by using this rare resource.

US Army Water Requirement Guidelines

Activity	Typical Duties	Quarts per person per day	
		less than 105°F	more than 105°F
Light	Desk work, Radio operating, Guard duty	6	10
Moderate	Route march on level ground	7	11
Heavy	Forced marches, Route march with heavy loads, Digging in.	9	13

WATER POCKETS IN DRY AREAS

After rainstorms or the melting of snow water will run off very rapidly especially in the Southwest of the United States where the bedrock is uplifted sandstone. This runoff erodes the sandstone and creates many ridges and valleys. Water pockets are hard to find due to the ruggedness of the area. Find a high point to look for some signs of vegetation, observe bird activity. Water is not always found in the lowest areas but inspect the sides of canyons, narrow valleys, etc. These areas are protected from the full impact of the sun. Some of these pools might last all summer.

POTABLE WATER

- Never drink water from a source that contains dead animals or animal remains. The animals might have died as the water has a high concentration, due to evaporation, of minerals that have been leached from the bed rock. These minerals might be chlorine, sulphur or arsenic.
- Animals and birds drinking the water does not mean that it is safe because water can have a bacterial or parasite content that cannot be neutralized by the human digestive tract.

POOLS OF WATER

Find natural deposits or accumulations in pools of water. These deposits can be found in gullies, behind large rocks, or under cliffs. These pools keep their water deposits because they are found on nonporous bedrock, on clay soil and are protected or partially protected from the sun.

WATER FROM PLANTS

If unsuccessful in your search for ground or run-off water, or if you do not have time to purify the questionable water, a water-yielding plant may be the best source. The clear sap from many plants is pure and is mostly water.

Plant Tissues: Many plants with fleshy leaves or stems store drinkable water.

- The barrel cactus of the southwestern United States is a possible source of water. Use it only as a last resort and only if you have the energy to cut through the tough, spine-studded outer rind. Cut off the top of the cactus and smash the pulp within the plant. Catch the liquid in a container. Chunks may be carried as an emergency water source. A barrel cactus 3-1/2 feet high will yield about a quart of milky juice and is an exception to the rule that milky or colored sap-bearing plants should not be eaten.

Cutting open a cactus.

Churning the inside of a cactus for water.

The large barrel cactus of American deserts contains considerable moisture which can be squeezed out of the pulp.

DESERT WATER INDICATORS

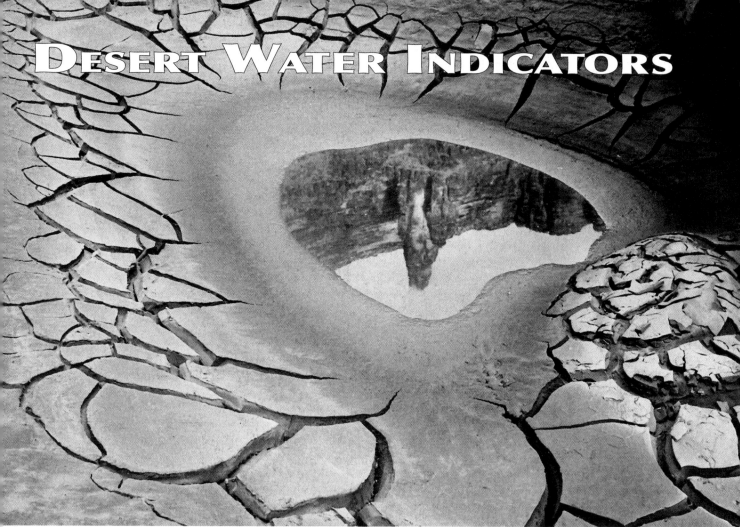

The rapid drying of the desert soil after a rainstorm.

WATER FROM PLANTS

Roots of desert plants: Desert plants often have their roots near the surface. Pry these roots out of the ground, cut them into 24-36 inch lengths, remove the bark, and suck the water.

Vines: Not all vines yield palatable water, but try any vine found. Use the following method for tapping a vine. It will work on any species:

- Cut a deep notch in the vine as high up as you can reach.
- Cut the vine off close to the ground and let the water drip from the upper part into your mouth or into a container.

Palms: Burl, coconut, sugar and nipa palms contain a drinkable sugary fluid. To start the flow in a coconut palm, bend the flower stalk downward and cut off the top. If a thin slice is cut off the stalk every 12 hours, you can renew the flow and collect up to a quart a day.

Coconut: Select green coconuts. They can be opened easily with a knife and they have more milk than ripe coconuts. The juice of a ripe coconut is extremely laxative; therefore, do not drink more than three or four cups a day. The milk of a coconut can be obtained by piercing two eyes of the coconut with a sharp object. To break off the outer fibrous covering of the coconut without a knife, slam the coconut forcefully on the point of a rock or protruding stump.

Light Weight Pup Tent

Prickly Pear Cactus

Clouds rise and lose their water as rain. By the time they cross the ridge of the mountain the clouds will have disappeared as they will be 'rained out'.

Rain on Windward Side

No rain on leeward side as winds have lost their moisture. Mountains cast a 'rain shadow'.

Dry Wind

Dry Wind

Dry Wind

Moist Wind

Impervious Layer

Impervious Layer

Natural Oasis

Pervious Layer - Water Bearing

Aquifer

Distance can be hundreds of miles from the source and water at oasis can have taken 1000's of years to travel from the source in the mountains. An aquifer is a geological structure of two impervious layers sandwiching a pervious layer (a layer that water can flow through).

AQUIFER

Humid air pushed up and over the mountains by the wind condenses and forms clouds. Clouds rise and lose their moisture as rain. By the time they cross the ridge they will have lost most of their moisture and become 'rained out'. The clouds will disappear and warm dry wind will blow down the leeward side of the mountain. If the geological structure of the mountain on the windward side is pervious (water can pass through) and impervious (water can not pass through) water can enter the pervious layer and flow to a distant oasis or well. This structure is called an aquifer.

Water found at base of cliff.

FINDING WATER

SURFACE CHARACTERISTICS

- Follow a dry river bed and because of the rock structure or composition, a stream might emerge. Dig a pit if the soil is moist.
- Look for springs and seepages. Limestone has more and larger springs than any other type of rock. Because limestone is easily dissolved, caverns are readily etched in it by ground water. Look in these caverns for springs.
- Lava rock is a good source of seeping ground water because it is porous. Look for springs along the walls of valleys that cross the lava flow. Look for seepage where a dry canyon cuts through a layer of porous sandstone.
- Desert natives often know of lingering surface pools in low places. They cover their surface pools, so look under brush heaps or in sheltered nooks, especially in semiarid and brush country.
- Follow the riverbed to the source. There might still be a trickle of water or humid soil.
- Find water at the leeward base (the steep side of the dune opposite the direction of the wind) of large dunes or at a very low spot between dunes.
- Watch for damp spots on the ground. This can be caused by a high water table.
- Old mines, ore dumps, and mining tailings might indicate the presence of water. Do not enter a mine because there is a danger of a mine collapsing. Water might be tainted by minerals that have been leached from the mining by-products.
- Water can be collected from dew deposits.

PLANTS

- Look for green leaf growth of plants and trees that require much water. These plants might be cattails, bulrush, elderberries, and reeds. Trees are cottonwood, poplars, greasewood, and willows. This growth indicates a high water table and might be located on a dry river bed. To get at the water dig into the ground for one to two feet. After a while water will accumulate in this pit. It will most likely be cloudy but will slowly settle; if it does not, it can be filtered through a tightly woven piece of cloth.
- At base of cliffs where there is vegetation.
- The pulp of some cacti (not the giant Saquarro) can be crushed to a watery mash. To do this burn off the needles or spines in a fire and peel the pieces of cacti. The pulp can be sucked to release a sweet jellylike liquid.

FINDING WATER

Page 351

Survival Mirror

DRY STREAM BEDS

Dry meandering stream beds might have water deposits just below the surface at outside bends. Dig in these bends for water.

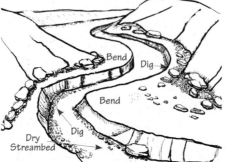

Bend
Dig
Bend
Dry Streambed
Dig

ANIMAL INDICATORS

- Animals are the best indicators of desert water. Places that are visibly damp, where animals have scratched, or where flies hover, indicate recent surface water.
- Watch insects (bees, hornets), birds and animals.
- Insects require water and live within flying range of water. You can watch the direction of their flight.
- Grazing animals will go towards water every morning and evening. Watch for animal trails which will usually be well-worn because animals will have followed these trails for many years.
- Doves have a habit of perching in trees or shrubs near desert water holes, especially in the evening.
- Birds will fly to and from water, they might circle water or congregate in large flocks. Birds of prey use their victims as a source of fluids and do not go to water as frequently. Parrots and pigeons must live within reach of water. The Bedouins of the Sahara desert, in North Africa, have a belief that birds flying to water fly low and directly to the water whereas birds flying from water are heavier and will have to rest frequently. A bird coming from water will be heavier and flaps louder.

WATER SUPPLY

Maintaining safe, clean, water supplies is critical. The best containers for small quantities of water (5 gallons) are plastic water cans or coolers. Water in plastic cans will be good for up to 72 hours; storage in metal containers is safe only for 24 hours.

Monitor Water Temperature

If the air temperature exceeds 100°F, the water temperature must be monitored. When the water temperature exceeds 92°F, the water should be changed, as bacteria will multiply and the water can become a source of sickness, such as diarrhea. Ice in containers can keep water cool.

POTABLE WATER

Potable drinking water is the single most important need in the desert. Ensure non-potable water is never mistaken for drinking water. Water that is not fit to drink but is not otherwise dangerous (it may be merely over salinated) may be used to aid cooling. It can be used to wet clothing, for example, so the body does not use too much of its internal store of water.

Carry enough water on a vehicle to last until the next planned resupply. It is wise to provide a small reserve. On vehicles carry water containers in the shade, in an air draft, and protected from puncture. Do not waste water. Water that has been used for washing socks, for example, is perfectly adequate for a vehicle cooling system.

DESERT DEW

Collect dew on clear nights by sponging it up with a handkerchief. During a heavy dew you should be able to collect about a pint an hour. When in snow fields, put snow in a water container and place it in the sun out of the wind.

Dew being sponged off of the trunk of a car.

Urine Indicator of Proper Hydration

If urine is more colored than diluted lemonade, or the last urination cannot be remembered, there is probably insufficient water intake. Collect urine samples in field expedient containers and spot check the color as a guide to ensuring proper hydration. Very dark urine warns of dehydration. You should observe your own urine, and use the buddy system to watch for signs of dehydration in others. *For more details see the First Aid Chapter Page 591 & 101.*

Water Loss

The body has a small reserve of water and can lose some without any effect. After a loss of about 2 quarts (which represents about 2.5 - 3.0% of body weight), effectiveness is impaired. You may begin to stumble, become fatigued and unable to concentrate clearly, and develop headaches. Thirst will be present but not overpowering. So unless well trained, or reminded or goaded to drink, you may not replace the water loss.

As dehydration continues, the effects will become more pronounced. The you will become less and less effective and more likely to become a heat casualty. Some will experience heat cramps, others will develop heat exhaustion or heatstroke. Heat cramps and heat exhaustion can be treated with prompt medical attention, heatstroke can be fatal.

Planning a Water Supply

Water planning is complicated because water is heavy (about 8.3 pounds per gallon) and may be considered perishable. Water stored in small containers gets hotter than water stored in large containers. As water gets hotter, it loses its disinfectant and becomes less desirable to drink. This makes it difficult to carry an adequate supply of water, and frequent resupply is often required. Before a desert trip estimate:
• How much water is needed?
• Where is it needed?
• When is it needed?

Water Uses etc.

• Water for radiators
  For food preparation or showers.
• Drinking water. Almost 2 gallons of water per person per day.
  When water is warmer than 75°- 80°F, it becomes difficult to drink. Bad tastes in water become more pronounced as water becomes warmer. Water tastes best, and it is easier to drink large quantities of it, if it is between 50°-70°F.

Walking & Water & Survival

Walking requires 1 gallon of water for every 20 miles covered at night, and 2 gallons for every 20 miles covered during the day. Without any water and walking only at night, you may be able to cover 20-25 miles before you collapse. If your chance of being rescued is not increased by walking 20 miles, you may be better off staying put and surviving one to three days longer. If you do not know where you are going, do not try to walk with a limited supply of water.

If you decide to walk to safety:
• **Take as much water as you have and can carry, and carry little or no food.**
• **Drink as much as you can comfortably hold before you set out.**
• **Walk only at night.**

Whether you decide to walk or not, you should conserve water in emergencies:
• Avoid the sun. Stay in shade as much as possible. If you are walking, rest in shade during the day. Use a tent, lie under vehicles, or dig holes in the ground.
• Cease activity. Do not perform any activities that do not contribute to survival.
• Remain clothed. It will reduce the water lost to evaporation.
• Shield yourself from excessive winds. Winds, though they feel good also increase the evaporation rate.
• Drink any potable water you have as you feel the urge. Saving it will not reduce your body's need for it or the rate at which you use it.
• Do not drink contaminated water from such sources as car radiators or urine. It will actually require more water to remove the waste material. Instead, in emergencies, use such water to soak your clothing to reduce sweating.
• Do not eat unless you have plenty of water.
• Do not count on finding water if you are stranded in the desert. Still, in certain cases, some water can be found. It does rain in the desert (although it may be 20 years between showers) and some water will remain under the surface. Signs of possible water are green plants or dry lake beds. Sometimes water can be obtained in these places by digging down until the soil becomes moist and then waiting for water to seep into the hole. Desert trails lead from one water point to another, but they may be further apart than you can travel without water. Almost all soils contain some moisture.

Desert Survival

Water is key to desert survival. Take all you can. If you have to leave some items behind keep things that provide shade, help reduce heat or water consumption. *See the First Aid Chapter regarding Heat Illnesses.*

• Travel only in the early morning or late evening. During the hot part of the day find shade or a low hollow and cover it with a piece of cloth and rest. Avoid expending energy and water in building a more elaborate shelter.
• Attempt to establish a direction towards a traveled route, water, or an inhabited area.
• Take the route that requires the least physical exertion. Do not attempt to take short-cuts over dunes or across loose sand or rugged terrain. Follow trails, the crests of sand dunes, or the low inter-dune area.
• Desert streams should not be followed, as they usually lead towards a temporary salty lake basin. In coastal areas desert streams and large rivers can lead to larger bodies of water.
• Dress properly to protect yourself against direct sunlight and excessive evaporation of sweat. Clothing is necessary for warmth in the desert because cool nights are common
• If you do not have sunglasses, make Inuit slit goggles.
• Care for your feet. Boots are needed for desert travel. You can cross sand dunes barefooted in cool weather, but during the summer the sand will burn your feet.
• Maps of desert regions are usually inaccurate. Check maps for accuracy by identifying obvious physical features.
• Take shelter, on the lee side of a dune, before a sandstorm arrives. It can be very disorienting so indicate the direction of travel before settling in, by scratching, placing a line of stones, position a stick, or clothing. Avoid traveling when visibility is bad. Cover your face, lie with your back to the wind. The blowing sand will not bury you.
• Due to the absence of distinctive features, your estimation of distances should be multiplied threefold.

Collapsible Water Container   Bota Bag

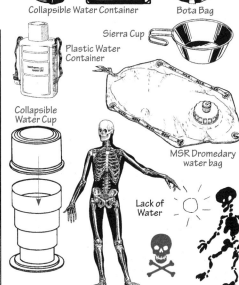

Sierra Cup

Plastic Water Container

Collapsible Water Cup

MSR Dromedary water bag

Lack of Water

Enameled Frying Pan

Nighttime reading.

Enameled Coffee Pot

HEAT INJURY PREVENTION

The temperature of the body is regulated within very narrow limits. Too little salt causes heat cramps; too little salt and insufficient water causes heat exhaustion. Heat exhaustion will cause a general collapse of the body's cooling mechanism. This condition is heatstroke, and is potentially fatal. To avoid these illnesses, you should maintain your physical fitness by eating adequately, drinking sufficient water, and consuming adequate salt. If you expend more calories than you take in, you will be more prone to heat illnesses. You may lose your desire for food in hot climates, you should eat, with the heavier meal of the day scheduled for the cooler hours. It is necessary to recognize heat stress symptoms quickly. When suffering from heatstroke, the most dangerous condition, there is a tendency for the victim to creep away from his group and attempt to hide in a shady and secluded spot; if not found and treated, he will die. When shade is required during the day, it can best be provided by tarpaulins preferably doubled to allow air circulation between layers and dampened with any surplus water. Approximately 75% of the human body is fluid. All chemical activities in the body occur in a water solution, which assists in the removal of toxic body wastes and plays a vital part in the maintenance of an even body temperature. A loss of 2 quarts of body fluid (2.5% of body weight) decreases efficiency by 25% and a loss of fluid equal to 15% of body weight is usually fatal. The following are some considerations when in a desert environment:

- Reduce heat injury by forcing water consumption.
- When possible, drink cool (50-55°F) water.
- Drink one quart of water in the morning, at each meal, and before strenuous work. In hot climates drink at least one quart of water each hour. At higher temperatures hourly water requirements increase to over two quarts.
- Take frequent drinks since they are more often effective than drinking the same amount all at once.
- Larger hikers need more water.
- Replace salt loss through eating meals.
- When possible, work loads and/or duration of physical activity should be less during the first days of exposure to heat, and then should gradually be increased to follow acclimatization.
- Modify activities when conditions that increase the risk of heat injury (fatigue/loss of sleep, previous heat exhaustion, taking medication) are present.
- Take frequent rest periods in the shade. Lower the activity rate as the heat condition increases.
- Limit activity to the cooler hours of the day such as early morning or late evening.

If VERY thirsty drink water in sips as a bird.

HEAT ILLNESS

The temperature of the body is auto-regulated within very narrow limits. Attention should be paid to anything that will possibly destabilize the system.

- Lack of salt may lead to heat cramps.
- Lack of salt and insufficient water may lead to heat exhaustion.
- General collapse of the body's cooling mechanism will lead to heat stroke which can be fatal.

If you expend more calories than you absorb you will become more prone to heat illness. You might lose your appetite due to the heat but you should eat your required ration with the major meal being during a cool period. Work in groups and learn to quickly recognize heat stress symptoms. When a person is suffering from heat stroke the tendency is for the victim to creep away from the group and attempt to hide in a shady and secluded spot. If he is not found and treated he will die.

DISEASE

Diseases found in the desert include: plague, typhus, malaria, dengue fever, dysentery, cholera, and typhoid. Some of these can be prevented with vaccines or prophylactic measures. High levels of field hygiene and sanitation should be observed at all times.

FUNGUS INFECTION & PRICKLY HEAT

Excessive sweating can aggravate prickly heat and some forms of fungus infections of the skin. The higher the humidity and if clothing is not cleaned or aired in the sun the greater the possibility of this happening.

RESPIRATORY DISEASE & COLD WEATHER INJURIES

The desert can be very hot during the day and cool to cold at night. You should gradually remove covering clothing in the morning and reapply the clothing in the evening. Never completely expose your skin. If traveling in the day do not discard clothing along the route as you will need it in the evening.

POLLUTED WATER INFECTION

Untested water should not be drunk or even used to wash your clothing, as it might cause skin diseases. Polluted water can be used for the vehicle cooling systems.

Stretch Cord

HYGIENE & SANITATION

Personal hygiene is absolutely critical to sustaining physical fitness. Take every opportunity to wash. Proper standards of personal hygiene must be maintained as a deterrent to disease. Cleaning the areas of the body that sweat heavily is especially important; change underwear and socks frequently, and use foot powder often. If sufficient water is not available, use sponge baths, solution-impregnated pads, a damp rag, or even a dry, clean cloth.

Waste Water: Dispose of waste water in a select area to prevent insect infestation. If sufficient water is not available for washing, a field expedient alternative is powder baths, that is, using talcum or baby powder to dry bathe.

Injury: Check for any sign of injury, no matter how slight, as dirt or insects can cause infection in minor cuts and scratches. Small quantities of disinfectant in washing water reduces the chance of infection.

Minor Sickness: Minor sickness can have serious effects in the desert. Prickly heat for example, upsets the sweating mechanism and diarrhea increases water loss, so you will become more prone to heat illnesses.

Intestinal Diseases: Intestinal diseases can easily increase in the desert. Site latrines well away and downwind. Flies are a perpetual source of irritation and carry infections. Only good sanitation can keep the fly problem to a minimum.

DESERT SICKNESS

Diseases common to the desert include: Plague, typhus, malaria, dengue fever, dysentery, cholera, and typhoid.

Diseases which adversely impact hydration: such as those which include nausea, vomiting, and diarrhea among their symptoms, can act to dramatically increase the risk of heat (and cold) illness or injury.

Infectious diseases:
Can result in a fever; this may make it difficult to diagnose heat illness.

Occurrences of heat illness to victims suffering from other diseases complicate recovery from both ailments.

Canteen on belt.

HEAT ILLNESSES

Illness	Cause	Symptoms	First Aid
Heat Exhaustion	Excessive loss of water and salt.	Cool moist skin, profuse sweating. Headache, dizziness, vomiting, weakness, rapid pulse and breathing. May be slight rise in temperature.	Heat cramps are relieved by replacing the salt lost from body. Place individual in cool outer clothing. Give all water slowly in the form of 0.1% saline solution. If cramps are very severe individual should be sent to a hospital.
Heat Cramps	Excessive loss of salt from body.	Severe cramps in limbs, back and/or abdomen, following exposure to heat. Body temperature remains normal.	Move patient to cool shaded place. Remove outer clothing. Elevate feet or message legs above the cramp area. Give all water that can be drunk in form of 0.1% saline solution. Get medical attention.
Heat Stroke	Collapse of body cooling mechanism.	Hot dry skin. Headache, mental confusion, and bizarre behavior, dizziness, weakness and rapid breathing and pulse. High temperature (106°F+). May be unconscious.	Medical emergency. Seek medical aid immediately. The lowering of the patient's body temperature as rapidly as possible is the most important objective in the treatment of heat stroke. Move individual to shaded area. Remove clothing. Sprinkle or bathe patient with cool water and fan to increase cooling effect. Massage trunk, arms, and legs. If evacuating to a hospital continue treatment on way.

Consult a Doctor for more information.

Heat Illnesses

Heat Cramps

Symptoms: Muscle cramps of arms, legs, and/or stomach. Heavy sweating (wet skin) and extreme thirst.

First Aid: Move victim to a shady area and loosen clothing. Slowly give large amounts of cool water. Watch the victim and continue to give him water, if he accepts it.
Get medical help if cramps continue.

Heat Exhaustion

Symptoms: Heavy sweating with pale, moist, cool skin; headache, weakness, dizziness, and/or loss of appetite; heat cramps, nausea (with or without vomiting), rapid breathing, confusion, and tingling of the hands and/or feet.

First Aid: Move the victim to a cool, shady area and loosen/remove clothing. Pour water on victim and fan him to increase the cooling effect. Have victim slowly drink at least one full canteen of water. Elevate the victims legs.
Get medical help.

Heatstroke

Symptoms: Sweating stops (red, flushed, hot dry skin).

First Aid: Get medical help immediately. Move victim to a cool, shady area and loosen or remove clothing. Start cooling him immediately. Immerse him in water and fan him. Massage his extremities and skin and elevate his legs. If conscious, have the victim slowly drink one full canteen of water.

Salt & You

- The more you sweat the more salt you lose.
- Too much salt will cause thirst, a sick feeling, and can be dangerous.
- Extra salt should be taken in proportion to the water available.
- Salt tablets should be dissolved before use.
- Water must be tested before adding salt as it might have a natural saline content that is sufficient for your needs.
- *See the First Aid Chapter on Heat Illness.*

Sun Safety & UV Radiation

Positive Effects: Positive effects of UV radiation include warmth, light, photosynthesis in plants, and vitamin D synthesis in the body. UV radiation gives a positive mood in people and kills bacterial and fungal growth. In the desert where washing is difficult it is good to air your clothing in the sun.

Negative Effects: Overexposure to UV radiation has adverse health effects. Overexposure to UV radiation is the primary environmental risk factor in the development of diseases of the eye, immune suppression, and skin cancers (Basal Cell, Squamous Cell Cancers, and Melanoma). Children are most at risk for overexposure to UV radiation.

Eye Damage: "Snow Blindness" a "burning" of the eye surface from extended exposure to bright sunlight. The effect usually disappear within a couple of days, but may lead to further complications later in life. Cataracts of the eye might also be caused by unprotected exposure to strong sunlight.

Photo Aging "Wrinkles": Chronic overexposure to the sun changes the texture and weakens the elastic properties of the skin. The epidermis, which is the outer layer of the skin, thickens, becomes leathery, and wrinkles as a result of sun skin exposure

Salt Requirements

US Army Salt Requirement Guidelines

Addition of table salt to produce 0.1% salt solution

Table Salt	Amount of Water
1/4 spoon (3.7 ml)	1 quart canteen (625 ml)
1 1/3 level mess kit spoons	5 gallon can (19 L)
9 level mess kit spoons (0.3 lb)	36 gallon bag (136 L)
1 lb (450 g)	100 gallon tank (379 L)
1 level canteen cup	250 gallons (946 L)

US Army Heat Illness Guideline

An individual who has already had a heat stroke or severe case of heat exhaustion is more likely to fall sick again than one who has not suffered from these illnesses. An individual who has already been affected should be subsequently exposed to potential heat stress with caution.

Symptoms to Distinguish Between Salt Depletion and Water Depletion

Symptoms	Salt Depletion	Water Depletion
Duration of symptoms	3-5 days	1 day
Thirst	seldom	prominent
Fatigue	prominent	seldom
Cramps	prominent	none
Vomiting	prominent	none
Weakness	progressive	acute

Dangers of Sun Exposure
Types of ultraviolet radiation

Type	Effect	Long Term Effects
UVA	No pain	Penetrates the deepest layers of the skin. Linked to skin cancer and photo aging. UV exposure is cumulative during your life.
UVB	Burns skin	The body protects itself by producing pigment melanin which produces a tan. Over exposure produces a burn which shows that the defence mechanism has been overwhelmed.
UVC		Filtered out by the ozone layer.

To reduce the chance of Desert Illness you must be... physically fit, thoroughly acclimatized, and drink sufficient water with the necessary salt.

11 RIVER TRAVEL

Ocean going Haida dugout canoe.

Inuit Kayak

Dogrib

Each canoe was designed for the environment where it was used.

Malecite

Montagnais

Slave

Ojibwa

Interior Salish

Algonquian

Chipewyan

Umiak of Alaska

TRADITIONAL CANOES

Indians using their blankets as sails.

RIVER TRAVEL

Each major continent has thousands of miles of navigable rivers. Some rivers, such as the Nile, Amazon, Mississippi, Lena, and Mackenzie, have hundreds of miles of navigable water with seldom a ripple. These navigable sections are generally found flowing through the flatlands, plains, tundras, and basins of the world. In these areas, only the temperatures of the water, and the plant and animal life may present hazards. In contrast, the headwaters of rivers like the Mackenzie, Yangtze, and Ganges are so rough that they would best be categorized as a threat to life. This would also be true of the Snake, Salmon, and Rogue Rivers of the northwestern United States. These rivers, although traveled by white water rafters, pose an unreasonable hazard for survival travel. In a survival situation one must take into account individual or group skills, injuries, type and severity of rapids, the temperature of the water, and direction the river flows in making the decision to travel. Even if a portage of several miles is required, the energy saved by floating on a river might warrant river travel. Rivers will most likely carry survivors past populated areas, where aid can be found. The group will most likely reach a lake shore or even the seacoast where, particularly the seacoast, one finds transition zones which are rich in food and other survival resources. It is much easier to spot signs of survivors along a shore, as opposed to the interior of a landmass.

EMERGENCY BOATS

An emergency boat can be made by stretching a tarpaulin or light, canvas cover over a shaped framework of willows and adding a keel of green wood, such as slender pieces of spruce. Gunwales (sides) of slender saplings are attached at both ends and the spreaders or thwarts are attached as in a canoe. Ribs of strong willows are tied to the keel. The ends of the ribs are bent upward and tied to the gunwales. The inside of the frame is closely covered with willows to form a deck upon which to stand. Such a boat is easy to handle and is buoyant, but lacks the strength necessary for long journeys. This boat can ferry a group across a broad, quiet stretch of river.

Rivers offer a safe means of travel and you can travel 20 to 25 miles in 5 hours. This is much faster and easier than the rate of travel on land.

Mandan Bull Boat

Bull Boat made from a buffalo hide - see tail.

BULL BOAT

Is a shallow-draft skin boat shaped like a tub and formerly used by American Indians (Mandan) in the Great Plains area. Construct an oval frame, similar to a canoe, of willow or other pliable materials and cover the framework with waterproof material such as a tarpaulin, poncho or a buffalo skin as used by the Indians in the illustration. See buffalo tail on front boat.

Wood Framework

Emergency or Bull Boat

Water Tight Cover

Digging out a canoe from a log.

These two images are from old Victorian books on the adventures of Robinson Crusoe by Daniel Defoe. This is how the Victorian England understood wilderness survival.

Dugout canoe with a sail.

Building a Dugout Canoe

A dugout canoe is good transportation but difficult to construct. One method is to build a long fire on the side to be dug out, and chop away the burned material when the fire is out. Repeat this procedure as often as necessary.

Fell Tree - having it fall on logs.

Cut groves with ax or saw.

Remove protruding wood.

Burn out the wood in the area to be dug out.

Dugout Canoe

CHOICE OF A CANOE

A canoe is a versatile watercraft as it might be paddled, poled, sailed, rowed, or motored. It must be light enough to be lifted, carried or portaged, yet stout enough to stand up to considerable abrasion and impact and able to transport 20 times it's weight or more. On top of all that, it should be fun and stimulating to paddle.

Canoe Performance: it is the interplay of the various elements that determines a canoe's performance and it is the art of the canoe designer to produce a craft for a specific function. What's best for a white water canoe is diametrically opposed to what's most desirable for a flat-water canoe. It's the designer's art and skill in reconciling all the aspects of canoe designs that determines the canoe's performance.

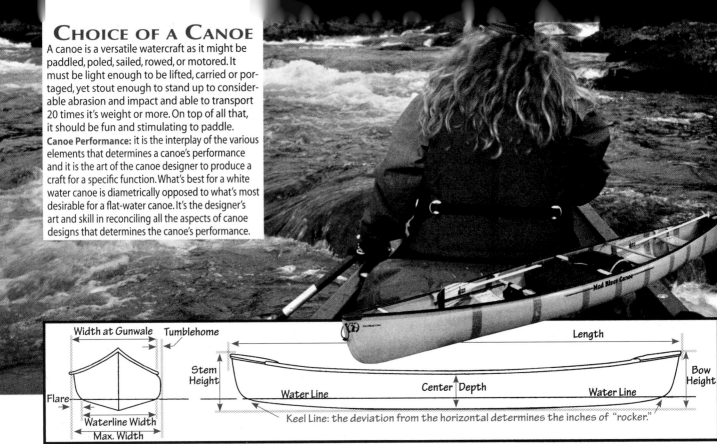

Width at Gunwale · Tumblehome · Length
Stem Height · Bow Height
Flare · Water Line · Center | Depth · Water Line
Waterline Width · Max. Width

Keel Line: the deviation from the horizontal determines the inches of "rocker."

LENGTH OF CANOE

Measured stem to stem and is the easiest measurement of canoe design.

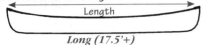

Length

Long (17.5'+)

Pros
· faster on open, flat water · increased capacity
· better carry or glide between strokes

Cons
· less maneuverable or nimble
· can have lower initial stability
· heavier than short canoe of same material

Medium (14.5-17')

Pros
· moderate speed and glide
· can be paddled tandem or solo
· moderate maneuverability

Cons
· slower than long canoes

Short (14.5' or less)

Pros
· increased maneuverability
· higher initial stability

Cons
· slower less glide or carry

In terms of versatility, canoes in and around 16' are preferred. Large enough to be paddled tandem with a load or soloed on occasion and fast enough for touring yet nimble enough to work their way down a twisty stream. Canoes with emphasis on cruising speed tend to be longer while white water canoes shorter with a premium on maneuverability.

KEEL LINE

A canoe's keel line is the profile of the hull bottom running from stem to stem, best seen by standing back and viewing the canoe from the side. The keel line can range from straight or level to highly arched or rockered (think of the runner on bottom of a rocking chair).

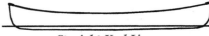

Straight Keel Line

Pros
· enhanced tracking, speed

Cons
· limited maneuverability

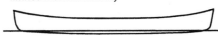

Straight Keel Line – with rockered ends

Pros
· good balance between maneuver ability and speed
· most versatile keel line

Cons
· reduced tracking than straight keel
· reduced speed than straight keel
· less maneuverable than rockered

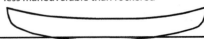

Highly Rockered Keel Line

Pros
· enhanced maneuverability

Cons
· poor tracking
· reduced forward speed

Approximate Rocker Classification

Slightly rockered: less than 2" of rocker as.
Moderately rockered: ranging from 2" to 3"
Extremely rockered: those with over 3"

HULL CROSS SECTION

Hull cross-section can impact canoe performance in a number of ways from stability to maneuverability to speed. Canoes usually feature one of three hull cross sections: *Flat, Shallow Arch, and Shallow Vee.*
Note that both Shallow Arch and Vee can vary in terms of degree or angle.

Flat Bottom

Pros
· high initial stability
· maneuverable

Cons
· poor final stability
· poor structural integrity
· slow unpredictable if leaned or in waves
· stability reduced as load increases
· tends to invert unless reinforced or heavily built

Shallow Arch

Pros
· paddling efficiency & speed in calm conditions
· higher final stability than flat bottom
· maneuverable when combined with moderate to extreme rocker

Cons
· performance degrades in rough waters
· lower final stability than shallow vee

Shallow Vee

Pros
· highest final stability
· better tracking
· most versatile hull cross section
· superior rough water performance
· superior rigidity for increased hull efficiency
· can be "tuned" (track: paddle straight up; maneuver: lean hull into turn)

Cons
· wear concentrated at point of Vee
· lower initial stability
· slower than shallow arch in calm conditions

SYMMETRY

Symmetry refers to the shape of the canoe viewed from overhead. Canoes can be symmetrical or asymmetrical. Asymmetrical canoes can be fish-form with widest point ahead of center or swede-form with widest point behind center.

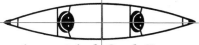

Asymmetrical - Swede Form

Pros
- enhanced forward speed
- enhanced glide

Cons
- can't be paddled backward without performance degrading
- can be wet when paddling into waves

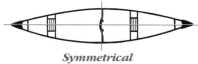

Symmetrical

Pros
- predictable handling
- can be paddled in reverse for better trim with adult/child paddlers or solo paddler

Cons
- slower than swede-form hull

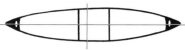

Asymmetrical - Fish Form

Pros
- improved buoyancy over drops

Cons
- slow   • decreased glide

SIDE PROFILE

Straight

Pros
- maintains final stability
- moderately dry vs. side waves

Cons
- in deep hulls makes for long reach to water
- subject to windage

Tumble Home

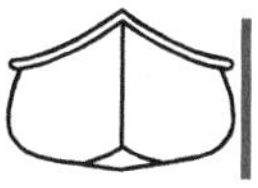

Pros
- allows more efficient paddle stroke
- preferable for flat/calm water solos

Cons
- reduces final stability
- wet vs side waves, as water will follow curve of hull up side

Tucked

Pros
- moderately dry
- maintains final stability
- protects gunwales from side impact or abrasion

Cons
- reduced paddling comfort and efficiency (farther reach to water)

Flared

Pros
- driest side hull profile
- increases final stability
- allows for narrower waterline for increased efficiency and speed

Cons
- reduced paddling comfort and efficiency (farther reach to water)

Based on information from Mad River Canoe.

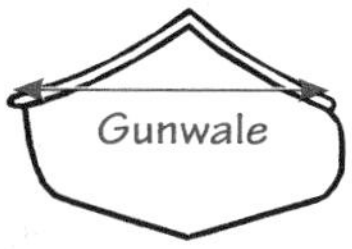

Waterproof Bag
1: Put articles in plastic bag. Press out the air.
2: Fold bag towards middle.
3: Continue folding by overlapping three or four times.
4: Secure with a rubber band.
5: Fold neck of bag
6: Fold end over end.
7: Tie folded end or use elastic bands.

BEAM
(Width at the Gunwale)

Measured at the widest point of the canoe and largely impacts stability and speed. The most common reference is width at the gunwales but an often more telling dimension is width at the waterline as this will determine the amount of effort required to move the boat through the water.

Narrow (33" or less)

Pros	**Cons**
• speed	• lower initial stability
• paddling efficiency	

Medium (34-37")

Pros
- good blend of speed, stability, and capacity
- versatility, can be paddled solo or tandem

Cons
- speed/glide falls below narrow canoe
- initial stability lower than wide canoe

Wide (38" or more)

Pros
- higher initial stability
- farther reach to water
- difficult to paddle solo

Cons
- slow • poor glide

Gunwale

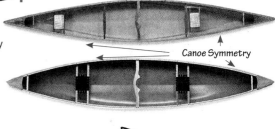

Canoe Symmetry

Inuit Kayak
These are ocean going kayaks that have "extreme rockers."

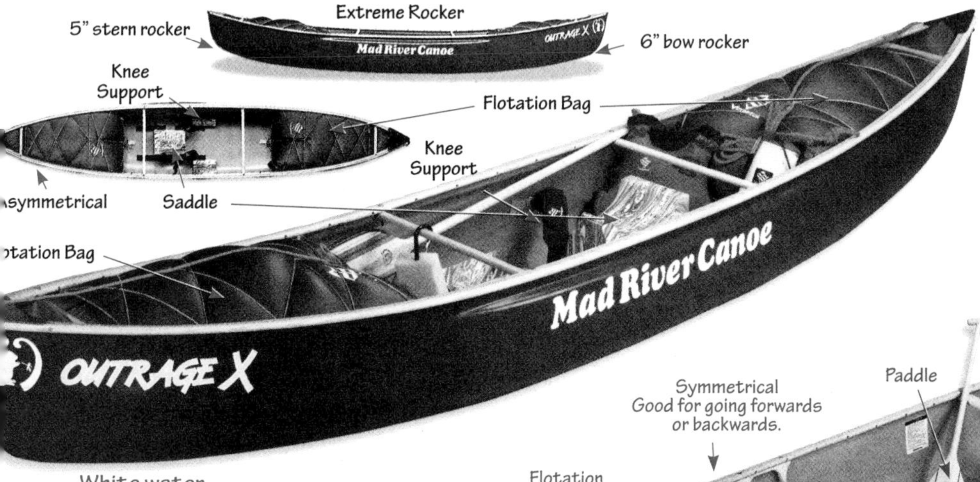

5" stern rocker   Extreme Rocker   6" bow rocker

Knee Support
Flotation Bag
Knee Support
Saddle
asymmetrical
otation Bag

White water Canoe

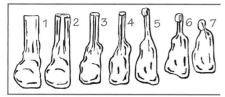

Mad River Canoe
OUTRAGE X

Storage
Storage Containers
Knee Pad
Life Jacket
Paddle
Flotation Bag
Symmetrical
Good for going forwards or backwards.
Flotation Bag
Rope
Mad River Canoe
Carrying Yoke
Shallow Draw

Well equipped canoe.

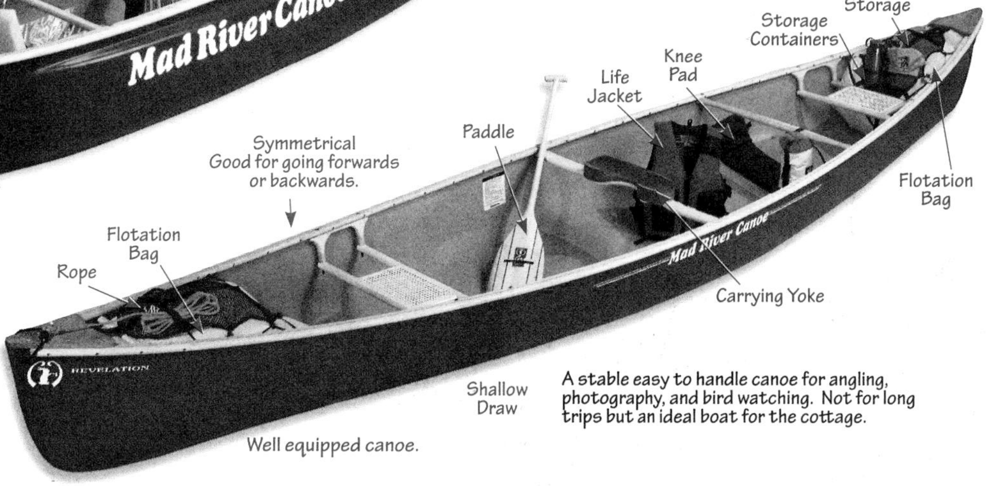

A stable easy to handle canoe for angling, photography, and bird watching. Not for long trips but an ideal boat for the cottage.

OBSTACLES IN THE WATER
Strainers

The most dangerous obstacles are strainers as they do not show themselves with a lot of white water to warn of their presence. A strainer is an obstacle through which water can pass but you or the boat would be wedged against by the current. The water pressure on you or a boat can be tremendous with little chance of escape. Strainers can be fallen trees, brush, boulders, or bridge pilings.

REACTION TO EMERGENCIES

- Evacuate the boat immediately if you feel that you are entering a strainer. A strainer is an obstacle through which water can pass but you or the boat would be wedged against by the current. Strainers can be fallen trees, brush, boulders, and bridge pilings.
- If you capsize recover by using the Eskimo roll.
- If you are swimming hold on to your boat as it is visible and has flotation. You might have to release your boat to reduce your risk if you are entering more difficult rapids or the water is very cold. You might have to swim to the nearest shore.
- Stay on the upstream side of a capsized boat. This will prevent the craft from crushing you against an obstacle.
- When being washed along, float with your feet downstream to push off rocks.
- Avoid getting caught in strainers, against rock cliffs or fissures, weirs, souse holes or water reversals.
- To escape, watch for eddies and slack spots which you should try to enter while gradually moving towards the shore.
- Always rescue boaters before considering the salvage of the equipment.
- The equipment should only be salvaged if it can be done with a minimum of risk.

BOATING - CANOE & KAYAK

- Do not boat in one boat but in a group of a minimum of three.
- Know how to swim.
- Boat in waters that are within your abilities and experience.
- Be in good physical condition.
- Know methods of artificial respiration and first aid. Practice frequently.
- Wear a life jacket with a buoyancy of at least 13 lb.
- If running complicated rivers have experience in the Eskimo roll and how to escape from a capsized craft.
- Wear a crash helmet and shoes to protect your feet during a bad trip.
- Boat should always be under control so that you can stop or reach shore in case of an emergency.
- Clothing should be chosen so that it will not get entangled with your boat, restrict you while swimming or get waterlogged.
- **Before entering a rapid:** Study the currents and topography to understand all possible hazards. Feel sure that you can safely swim the entire rapid if you capsize. Study a map of the run and take into account the level of the river, the changes in rapid profile and the flow rate of the water.
- File float plan with the authorities if you are going into the wilderness.

EQUIPMENT

- Make sure the boat is in good condition and remove any items which might cause a problem if the boat capsizes. Lash everything down.
- Carry a knife, compact first aid kit, and waterproof matches.
- Have float bags on the craft.
- Have 8 to 19 feet of rope attached to your craft to hold onto the boat in case of an upset.

DANGERS:
CANOEING & KAYAKING
Misjudging the High Water Level

To estimate the water volume of a river consider:
- Your angle of view. If you are very high the current and waves might look small.
- The effect of the volume of water when passing through a narrow channel.
- Water can rise suddenly because of:
  - *A distant rainstorm.*
  - *Melting snow raising the river in the afternoon.*
  - *A dam releasing water.*

Temperature of the Water

See the article on Hypothermia in the First Aid Chapter to fully appreciate the effect of cool water upon the body and your chances of survival. When water is less than 50°F (10°C) you will require a wet suit. Always carry dry clothing, matches and fire starter in a waterproof bag.

A Strainer

River Navigation

An individual in the group is designated to verify the progress on a river. Ideally, have an aerial photograph or a topographic map. A compass is helpful to corroborate the assumed position on the map. When navigating in a flat land area there might be many similar looking branches and tributaries which can easily confuse a navigator, especially if there are no prominent landmarks.

A member of the crew watches the water for obstacles, overhanging vegetation, and projections (tree trunks etc.) from the bank. If alone, be very observant for any telltale signs, such as unusual waves, that might indicate obstacles.

Safe River Travel

These are rules and guidelines that must be followed to reduce the dangers associated with river travel. The most important safety rule is personal preparation.

- Thoroughly scout the river. The conditions of the river will determine the intermittent stops. High banks along river provide needed visibility to plan each leg of travel. If there are numerous bends and no lookout points to view the river, stops are frequent.
- Sound judgment must be used when planning routes. Patience in planning each leg of travel helps prevent disaster. All members of the group must prepare, know the plans, and be able to handle the route safely, considering their skills and physical strength.
- Be aware of and avoid river hazards, and have alternate routes and communication signals in case flow conditions suddenly change, making the run more difficult.
- All rapids that cannot be seen clearly from the river should be scouted. The route should be discussed. The skills, knowledge, and abilities of the members must be considered, including swimming abilities and physical condition. Areas of high risk should not be attempted.
- Before reaching an area of suspected great difficulty, rafts should be beached and carried to the next point of travel; this is called portaging.

Entering a Boat

Embarking and debarking procedures.

- When launching, the crew should maintain a firm grip on the boat until they have embarked.
- When debarking, they should hold onto the boat until it is completely out of the water.
- Loading and unloading is done using the bow as the entrance and exit point.
- Keep a low center of gravity when entering and exiting the boat to avoid capsizing. Maintain 3 points of contact at all times. Two feet and one hand, or two hands and one foot.
- Beaching the boat is a method of debarking the entire crew at once into shallow water allowing the boat to be quickly carried out of the water.

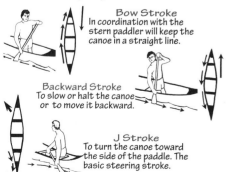

Bow Stroke In coordination with the stern paddler will keep the canoe in a straight line.

Backward Stroke To slow or halt the canoe or to move it backward.

J Stroke To turn the canoe toward the side of the paddle. The basic steering stroke.

Paddle Signals

STOP Following boats should not proceed until the 'Clear' signal is given.

EMERGENCY HELP Can also use a 3 blasts on a whistle to attract attention.

ALL CLEAR All clear in the direction that the paddle points. Never use the paddle to point as someone might misread the instructions.

Capsize

Inform all members of the crew of a potential capsize by crying "Prepare to capsize". This will alert the crew to raise their paddles above their heads, with the blades pointed outward. All loose articles should be stowed if possible.

Sweep Stroke Used to turn the canoe.

Push Over Stroke Moves the canoe away from the paddle side.

Draw Stroke To pull the paddler's end of the boat toward the side of his paddle.

River Boating Terminology

- A **bend** is a turn in the river course.
- A **reach** is a straight portion of river between two bends.
- A **slough** is a dead end branch from a river. They are normally quite deep and can be distinguished from the true river by their lack of current.
- **Dead water** is a part of the river, due to erosion and changes in the river course, has no current. Dead water is characterized by excessive snags and debris.
- An **island** is usually a pear-shaped mass of land in the main current of the river. Avoid the upstream portions of islands as they usually catch debris.
- The **current** in a narrow part of a reach is normally greater than in a wide portion.
- The **current** is greatest on the outside of a bend in the river; sandbars and shallow water are found on the inside of the bend.
- **Sandbars** are located at points where a tributary feeds into the main body of a river or stream. The main course of a river usually flows slower than the water in the tributary. This slower flow of the water lets suspended sediments drop onto the riverbed forming sandbars.

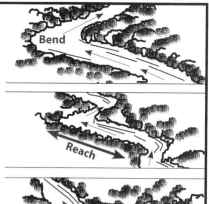
Bend / Reach

Slower Current / Slough

Dead Water / Current

Island / Slower Current / Main Current

Faster Current / Slower Current / Current

Sand Bars / Faster Current / Slower Current

Canoe Strokes

RIVER RAFTING

Rafting Logs Downstream
In the 1850's logs were transported to market by building a raft with the logs and driving them downstream.

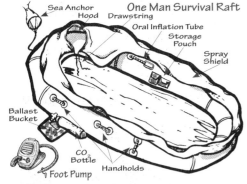

One Man Survival Raft

Sea Anchor Hood — Drawstring — Oral Inflation Tube — Storage Pouch — Spray Shield — Ballast Bucket — CO_2 Bottle — Handholds — Foot Pump

ONE MAN RAFT

When using a one-man raft for river travel, it may be advisable to tie or cut off the ballast bucket, fasten the spray shield in the opened position, and remove the sea anchor to prevent problems with swamping or entanglement with subsurface obstacles. Without the ballast bucket, the raft can be easily maneuvered by paddling with the backstroke, or for slight adjustment, with a front stroke.

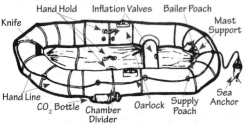

Hand Hold — Inflation Valves — Bailer Poach — Knife — Mast Support — Hand Line — CO_2 Bottle — Chamber Divider — Oarlock — Supply Poach — Sea Anchor

Seven Person Inflatable Raft

RAFTING & LIFE-PRESERVER

When using either the backstroke or the front stroke, you will find it easier if the two underarm cells of the life-preserver (LPU) are disconnected in front, and the cells placed behind the back. This gives you a full range of motion. When rough water is encountered, you should fasten the LPU and face downstream.

BEFORE ENTERING A RAFT

Don life preservers and suitable clothing for adequate protection. Equipment should be tested to ensure it is serviceable. Bulkiness is not advisable due to the possibility of the raft capsizing and being weighted down with water. The anti-exposure suit (if available) should be worn. Items that might absorb water should be packed in a waterproof container.

Check that:

- All medical supplies, a repair kit, and a survival kit are in the raft.
- Survival kit is checked and inventoried.
- Extra effort should be made to keep supplies and equipment in good condition.
- All items are secured to the raft to prevent loss and (or) injuries.
- Before use, the raft is checked for leaks and necessary repairs are made.

Safe River Rafting

- Scout ahead by climbing a large tree or hill and looking downstream. This will give you an overview of the surrounding land.
- Have a rudder to steer the raft when descending a river. Carry a long pole or paddle to maneuver around tight spots and to push the raft out of still water or off sand bars.
- Listen for any sounds of rushing water which might indicate rapids or waterfalls. Bad water does not always reveal itself until you are on top of it.
- Guide the raft over turbulent waters with ropes from the shore. If this is not possible, let the raft find its own course, down the rapids or over small falls, and attempt to retrieve it.
- On a raft, pack provisions in a waterproof bag and include a piece of light dry wood. This wood will give the bag buoyancy if it is lost overboard. Tie down everything securely to the raft.
- For steering down a slow moving river attach a pail or water-logged piece of wood to a short cord attached to the bottom of the raft. This cord is attached below the raft in the middle but forward of the longitudinal center of the raft. With this "sea anchor" your raft will automatically follow the main channel of the river and no steering is required. Throw some sawdust on the water to find the outlet of a slow flowing river (there will be many islands and much growth).

AVOIDING HAZARDS MULTIPLACE RAFT

The boarding ladder and sea anchor should be removed to prevent entanglement. If available, about 50 feet of line should be tied on the bow and stern of the raft to be used for tie-offs. An additional 200 feet of line should be coiled and tucked away for emergency and rescue work; one end is secured to the raft while the other end has a fixed loop. An improvised suspension-line rope may be used for this; for example, three-strand braid can support about 1,000 to 1,500 pounds of pressure, or a two-strand twist strengthens the line to support about 700 to 900 pounds of pressure.

Weight Distribution & Assignment on a Raft
Proper placement of equipment and travelers will equalize weight distribution to ensure stable control; overloading should be avoided. Assign crew positions and responsibilities in the raft; captain (person in charge), stern paddler (maneuvers raft), and side paddlers. Twilight and night rafting should be avoided, as poor visibility increases danger.

STEERING MULTIPLACE RAFT

Oar & Pole: To steer a raft by using sweeps (long oar) and poles. A pole is more efficient in fairly shallow water, but a sweep is preferable in deep water. Poles and sweeps from both ends of the raft are used. The person in the bow (front) can see any obstructions ahead, and the one in the stern (rear) can follow directions for steering. Poles are also useful for pushing a raft in quiet water.

STRAIGHT FORWARD PADDLE

Is used in calm and moderate waters where there is ample maneuvering time. Simply point the bow in the desired direction and follow the *forward-stroke* method of paddling. The back paddle is performed in the exact opposite manner of the forward paddle. Point the stern (back) in the desired direction and follow the *backstroke* method of paddling.

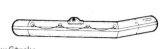

PADDLING A RAFT

When paddling, there are three possible body positions on a raft.

- The best way is to sit on the upper buoyancy tube with both legs angled to the inside of the raft. The body should be perpendicular to the sides of the raft, enabling the rafter to paddle.
- Sit cowboy style, straddling the upper buoyancy tube of the raft with one leg on either side, and folding at the knee with each leg back. However, the outside knee may collide with obstacles and cause injury.
- In calmer waters partially straddle the upper tube with legs comfortably extended.
- In a smaller raft sit down inside the raft and reach over the buoyancy tube.

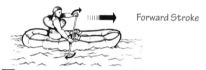

FORWARD STROKE

One of the easiest is the forward stroke, which is done with smooth continuous movements using these techniques:

A: Thrust the blade of the paddle forward using the outboard arm, then momentarily keeping the outboard arm stiff and away from the raft, push the grip. The inboard hand is then moved forward to cut the blade deeply into the water. Continue the stroke by pushing on the grip and pulling on the shaft, keeping the blade at a 90° angle to the raft. Stop the motion as the blade comes slightly past the hip, because a full follow-through provides little forward power and wastes valuable energy. Slide the blade out of the water by pushing down on the grip and swinging it toward the inboard hip, and turning the blade at a parallel angle to the water once it has cleared the water. By paralleling the blade, it cuts wind and wave resistance and saves time and energy. This cycle is repeated until the strokes are changed.

B: In mild water, there is no need to over reach or excessively twist the upper trunk of the body. When extra speed is needed, lean deeply into the strokes, which brings the entire body into play. Position the inboard hand across the tip of the paddle grip and the outboard hand halfway to three-fourths of the way down the shaft.

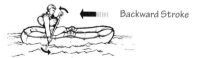

BACKWARD STROKE

The opposite of the forward stroke is the backward stroke. The blade is thrust into the water just behind the hip, and pressure applied by simultaneously pushing forward on the shaft and pulling back on the grip. End the stroke where the forward stroke would begin, and again angle the blade out of the water back to the beginning of the backward stroke.

SIDEWAY STROKES

The draw and pry strokes are opposite sideways strokes. These strokes are good for small sideways maneuvers and for turning the raft when used from the front or rear of the raft.

Draw Stroke: Reach out from the raft, dip the blade in parallel to the raft, and pull on the shaft while pushing on the grip. Pull the blade flat to the side of the raft. Pull the paddle out and repeat.

Pry Stroke: Dip the blade in close to the raft, and push out on the shaft while pulling in on the grip.

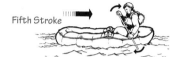

FIFTH STROKE
(Calm Water Crawl)

Is used alternately with the forward stroke when paddling through long calms. Sit cowboy fashion while facing the stern and hold the paddle diagonally in front with the shaft that is held by the outboard hand against the outboard hip, and the grip held by the inboard hand in front of the inboard shoulder. Extend the inboard arm to swing the blade behind, dip the blade in the water, and pull back on the grip, prying it forcefully, using the hip as a fulcrum (the point of support on which a lever works). Using the shoulder, hip, and hand for strength, the crawl is easy yet powerful.

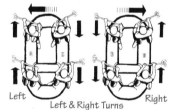

LEFT & RIGHT TURNS

To make a left turn, the left side of the raft will backpaddle, while the right side paddles forward. It's just the opposite to make the raft turn right. The right side on the raft backpaddles while the left side paddles forward - both performing the paddling maneuvers at the same time.

FERRY TO NAVIGATE BENDS

The ferry is a basic paddle-maneuvering technique used to navigate bends and to sidestep obstacles in swift currents. The ferry is essentially paddling upstream at an angle to move the raft sideways in the current. Paddle rafts can ferry either with the bow (front) angled upstream or downstream. The bow-upstream ferry is stronger because it uses the more powerful and easier forward stroke. It is carried out by placing the raft at a 45° angle to the current with the bow angled upstream and the side toward the desired direction. The bow-downstream ferry is weaker because it uses the less powerful backstroke, but it does offer certain advantages. It enables paddlers to look ahead without straining their necks, and makes it easy to put the bow into waves. It is carried out by backstroking with the stern (back) angled upstream at a 45° angle and the side facing the desired direction.

REVERSE FERRY

There may be times when the only way for a heavy raft to enter a small or violent eddy is with a reverse ferry. The following steps may be used for an oar or paddle raft, except the paddle raft approaches the eddy bow-first and finishes in a bow-upstream position:

1: Raft approaches sideways.

2: Raft turns around to angle its bow downstream.

3: With careful timing, the captain should have the crew begin to pull powerfully on the paddles. The angle of the raft to the current can be close to 90°, but is best at about 45°.

4: While aiming for the eddy, the crew should continue with the front stroke and to gain momentum.

5: With the crew still using the front stroke, the raft breaks through the eddy fence.

6: With the bow in the upstream eddy current and the stern still in the downstream current, the raft is spun into a normal ferry angle. The crew continues with the front stroke while making the necessary turn to bring the boat entirely into the eddy.

7: The raft rides easily in the eddy.

Note: The Reverse Ferry and Eddy Turns are not only used to enter eddies, but can also be used to dodge tight places. The Reverse Ferry (or sometimes an Extreme Ferry) moves the raft sideways, the Eddy Turn snaps the bow into a bow-downstream position, and the raft, rather than entering the eddy, rides the eddy fence past a major obstruction or hole.

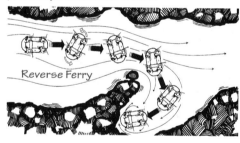

Reverse Ferry

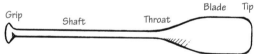

Grip   Shaft   Throat   Blade   Tip

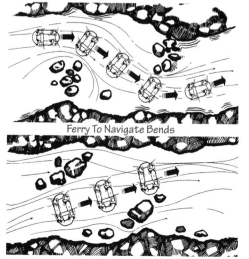

Ferry To Navigate Bends

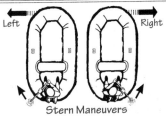

Stern Maneuvers

STERN MANEUVERS

Stern maneuvers are used to increase the maneuverability of the raft. The paddle used at the stern of the boat is basically a rudder, which controls direction. To turn right, the paddle blade is held to the right, square against the direction of the current. To turn left, the paddle is held to the left.

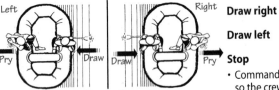

Pry & Draw Strokes
The pry and draw strokes are used to move the raft sideways.

FORWARD STROKE OR DRAW STROKE

Other strokes, such as a forward stroke or draw stroke, used at the stern of the raft, will cause it to turn or move faster. If stroking is done slightly to the side (either right or left) of the raft, it will help move the raft in the opposite direction.

✳ RAFT FLIPS ✳

When a raft is about to flip, there is little time to react to the situation. If the raft is diving into a big hole, the primary danger is being violently thrown forward into a solid object in the raft. *Rafters should protect themselves by dropping low and flattening themselves against the backside of the baggage or cross tube.* If the raft is being upset by a rock, fallen tree, or other obstacle, members should jump clear of the raft to prevent being crushed against the obstruction, or struck by the falling raft. If the raft is pinned flat against an obstruction, the members should stay with the raft and try to safely climb up the obstruction.

Attach line to an extremely sturdy D-ring (pull should be at right angles to the flat side of the D) or cut a small hole in the floor to pass a lie around the tube.

Attach line to frame or cross tube. Pull should be equal between the two tie-off points.

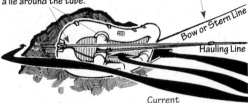

Bow or Stern Line

Hauling Line

Current

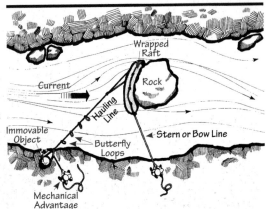

Wrapped Raft

Current

Rock

Hauling Line

Immovable Object

Butterfly Loops

Stern or Bow Line

Mechanical Advantage

RIVER TRAVEL & CAPTAIN'S COMMANDS

River travel requires fast, decisive action. Therefore, a paddle raft needs a captain to co-ordinate the crew's actions by the use of commands or signals. Communications between captain and crew are crucial; all members must agree on a set of short, clear commands. The following are suggested commands:

Captain's Commands & Crew Response

Forward	Crew paddles forward.
Backpaddle	Crew does backstroke.
Turn right	Left side paddles forward, right side does the backstroke.
Turn left	Right side paddles forward, left side does the backstroke.
Draw right	Right side uses draw stroke, left side uses pry stroke.
Draw left	Left side uses draw stroke, right side uses pry stroke.
Stop	Paddlers relax.

• Commands must be carried out immediately, so the crew should practice until they can snap through all the commands without hesitation. The captain controls both the direction and speed of the raft with a specific tone of voice and commands. This control, and the captain's ability to anticipate how the water ahead will affect the raft, will help avoid under compensation or over-compensation of maneuvers through obstacles. Good captains think well ahead and move with the river, issuing commands precisely and sparingly, working their crew as little as possible.

• When using commands and maneuvering the boat in harmony with the river's currents, paddling can be easy and effective, even fun. When instant action is necessary, the captain may say, "Paddle at will." When time permits, the captain should introduce commands with a preparatory statement, such as, "We're going to ferry to the right of that big rock. OK – (gives command)." This gives the crew time to prepare for the next response. If a command is not heard or understood, it should be repeated with zest until it is understood. If a raft member spots a better way through a rapid or channel, a fully extended arm is used to point it out. This signal, like the others agreed on, should be repeated until it is understood.

FREEING A WRAPPED RAFT

Sometimes the powerful force of swift water may pin and wrap a raft around a rock. *It is unusual for a raft to be equally balanced around the rock, so it will move more easily one way than it will in the other.* The part of the raft with more weight and bulk should be moved toward the flow of the current. Lines are attached to at least two points on the raft so, when pulled, the force is equally distributed. One of these points is on the far end of the raft, around the tube, and is called the hauling line.

NOTE and CAUTION: A small hole may need to be cut in the floor of the raft to pass the line through and around the tube if there is no ring to pass it through. The second tie-off point can be a cross tube. One person should hold the line attached to the stern of the raft. The raft should be moved over the rock into the pull of the current. Once it is freed, the person holding the stern line can move the raft to a safe position.

Did NOT jump!!

Crew did not quickly jump to the side of the raft nearest the rock. The raft got swamped and wrapped around rock.

Correct movement to avoid swamping.

ROCK COLLISION

Collisions with rocks above the surface of the water are common occurrences on a river. *If the collision is unavoidable, rafters should spin the raft powerfully just before contact, or hit the rock bow-on. If the rafter is able to spin the raft, it will usually turn the raft off and around the rock. If they hit the rock bow-on, it will stop the raft momentarily, giving time to manipulate a spin-off with a few turn strokes. When the bow-on method is used, occupants in the stern (aft) should move to the center of the tail before impact.* This allows the stern to raise and the rushing current to slide under the raft. If the stern is low, the water will pile against it, *causing the raft to be swamped. If rafters are colliding broadside with a rock, the entire crew must immediately jump to the side of the raft nearest the rock - always being on the raft's downstream side. This should be done before contact. If not, the river will flow over and suck down the raft's upstream tube. The raft will be flooded and the powerful force of the current will wrap it around the rock, possibly trapping some or all of the crew between the rock and the raft.* Once the water is removed, the broached (broad sided) raft on a rock is usually easily freed. If two people push with both feet on the rock in the direction of the current, the raft will swing or slide into the pull of the current. The rest of the crew should shift to the end that is swinging into the current. These methods rarely fail; however, if the raft refuses to budge, it can be freed using the enormous power of the current. Large gear bags or sea anchors are securely tied to a long rope and secured to the end of the raft expected to swing downstream. The sea anchors (gear bags) are then tossed downstream into the current. *A safety line should be used.*

BROADSIDE COLLISION WITH A ROCK

Just before a raft broadsides on a rock, the crew should jump to the side of the raft nearest the rock. This lifts the upstream tube and allows the current to easily slide under the raft If the crew is not quick enough to hop towards the rock side – swift flowing water will rapidly swamp the raft AND wrap it flat around the rock's upstream face.

ROCK COLLISION

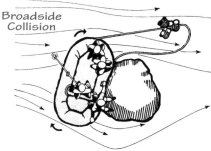

Broadside Collision

Handling a Broadside Collision with a Rock

Just before a raft broadsides on a rock, the crew should jump to the side of the raft nearest the rock. This lifts the upstream tube and allows the current to pass under the raft. If the crew is not quick to hop toward the rock, the fast moving water will swamp the raft and wrap it flat around the rock's upstream face.

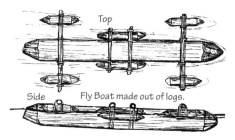

Top

Side — Fly Boat made out of logs.

Hardwood Spikes
Using hardwood spikes to fasten float logs when they are of a soft wood as Balsa.

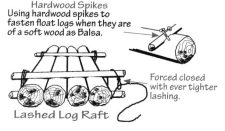

Forced closed with ever tighter lashing.

Lashed Log Raft

EMERGENCY RAFT

If you are lost consider rafting downstream.

Shape of a Raft

Build a long raft with three or four logs as it is easier to guide than a square raft which will have a tendency to spin. Build a raft of sound dry wood (spruce is the best) and if possible of dead trees that are still standing. Use roots, vines, handmade cordage or cut grooves to fasten the logs together. Rope is not too stable if the current is swift; use the groove system for better results.

Making a Raft

Assemble a raft by using three or four logs parallel to each other and put two or three cross pieces on top of the parallel logs. Mark where these logs cross and cut a dovetailed groove with an ax, knife, sharp rock, or burn with a burning stick. Place or wedge the three cross pieces into the grooves. Soak the assembled raft in the water to obtain a tight fit.

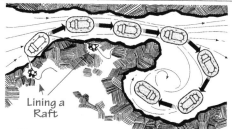

Lining a Raft

LINING A RAFT

Lining a raft through rapids is basically letting it run through rapids with a crew on shore controlling it by attached lines. The raft should be *moved slowly* by maintaining tight control of the lines attached to the bow and stern. If no strong eddies or steep, narrow chutes are present, one member should walk along the shore and control the raft with a strong, long line. The lines running to shore should be long enough to allow the raft full travel through the rapids.

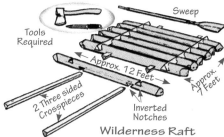

Tools Required

Sweep

Approx. 12 Feet

Approx. 7 Feet

2 Three sided Crosspieces

Inverted Notches

Wilderness Raft

RAFT CONSTRUCTION

A raft for three persons should be about 12 feet long and 6 feet wide, depending on the size of the logs used. The logs should be 12 to 14 inches in diameter and so well-matched in size that notches you make in them are level when crosspieces are driven into place.

- Build the raft on two skid logs placed so they slope downward to the bank. Smooth the logs with an axe so the raft logs lie evenly on them. Cut two sets of slightly offset, inverted notches, one in the top and bottom of both ends of each log. Make the notches broader at the base than at the outer edge of the log, as shown in the illustration. Use small poles with straight edges or a string pulled taut to make the notches. A three-sided wooden crosspiece about a foot longer than the total width of the raft is to be driven through each end of the four sets of notches.
- Complete the notches on all logs at the top of the logs. Turn the logs over and drive a 3 sided crosspiece through both sets of notches on the underside of the raft. Then complete the top set of notches, and drive through the two additional sets of crosspieces.
- You can lash together the overhanging ends of the two crosspieces at each end of the raft to give it added strength; however, *when the crosspieces are immersed in water they swell and tightly bind the raft logs together.*
- If the crosspieces fit too loosely, wedge them with thin, board like pieces of wood split *from a dead log.* When the raft is in water, the dry dead wood swells, and the crosspieces become very tight and strong.
- Make a deck of light poles on top of the raft to keep packs and other gear dry.

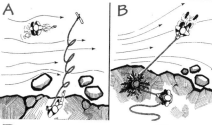

A

B

RESCUING FROM SHORE

The rescuer should carefully choose the right spot where the coil of rope thrown to the swimmer will not cross hazardous areas or obstacles, and yet be near a rock or tree that can be used for belaying (securing without being tied) the end of the line. The person throwing the line should make sure the line has a flotation device (life preserver or branch of wood) at the end before it is thrown to the swimmer. The rope should be coiled to allow it to flow smoothly, without entanglement, to full extension. One hand holds one-half to one-third of the coil while the other throws the remainder of the coil out. The weighted coil should be thrown to a spot where the swimmer will drift, which is usually downstream, in front of the swimmer. As the rope travels out, all of the line, except the last 10 or 12 feet, should be uncoiled. *The member pulling the swimmer should be braced, or have the line around a rock or tree to hold the swimmer once the line has reached him.*

REACTION TO RESCUE ATTEMPT

The swimmer should be aware of the rescuer's location and face downstream when waiting for the hauling line. When the line is thrown, the swimmer will usually be required to swim to reach it. Once holding the line, the swimmer should be prepared for a very strong pull from the current and line. The line should be held tightly, *but not wrapped around a wrist or hand.* Entanglement must be avoided. The swimmer should pull, hand over hand, until reaching shallow water, and then use the rope for steadiness while walking to shore.

Lining a Canoe

EMERGENCY RAFT

The Voyageurs: Donald Curley

RIVER HYDRAULICS

Side View - Mid Channel of River

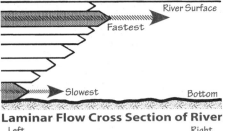

River Surface

Fastest

Slowest   Bottom

Laminar Flow Cross Section of River

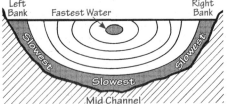

Left Bank   Fastest Water   Right Bank

Slowest

Slowest

Slowest

Mid Channel

MAIN CHANNEL DEEPEST PART OF RIVER

The main channel is the deepest part of the river and can wander from bank to bank. The turbulence caused by the wandering main current erodes wide curves into sharper, more defined bends, creating indirect courses.

RIVER HYDRAULICS & BOATING

An understanding of river hydraulics is important. Knowledge of the types of obstacles and why they should be avoided or overcome is necessary for a safe river journey.

LAMINAR FLOW

The drag produced when moving water flows over or past various types of objects and surfaces is called a *laminar flow*. The laminar-flow principle is that various layers or channels of water move at different speeds. The lower layer of the river moves more slowly than the top layer. This is due to the friction on the bottom and sides of the river, which is caused by soil, vegetation, or contours of the riverbank. The layers next to the bottom and sides are the slowest; each subsequent layer will increase in speed. The top layer of the river is affected only by the air. *The fastest part of the flow on smooth, straight stretches of water will be between 5-15% of the river depth below the surface.* Even straight-running riverbeds are not smooth; they have jutting and receding banks on the sides, which affect the laminar flow. The friction caused by the banks causes the sides of the flow to be slower than the midstream. The areas near the banks are shallower and have fewer layers. *When the river travels at 4-5 knots, turbulence begins to develop, which interferes with the regular flow of the current. When this rate of river flow is achieved, the friction between the layers of water will cause whirling and spinning actions that agitate the smooth flow of water, creating more resistance.*

This painting by Donald Curley, the outstanding Nova Scotia painter of the outdoors, shows the intensity and force of rapidly flowing waters.

FLOW IN SHARP TURNS

When the river makes sharp turns, the current is affected by *centrifugal force*, swinging it wide into the outside bank. The helical current diminishes, being smothered by the laminar flow, thereby increasing the corkscrew effect on the inside of the curve. The surface water is being whirled hard in the direction of the outside curve of the bank - the faster the water flow, the stronger the push. *Floating objects are forced, with the surface water, to the outside of the curve and into the banks, usually getting lodged against and onto the shore.*

- A powerful helical flow not only pushes the surface outward, but as it swirls up from the bottom it carries sediment with it. The sediment and other debris are deposited at the highest point of the inside bank of the bend. *The sediment is then dropped during high water, and when the water recedes, a point bar (made of sand and gravel) is revealed.* The point bar generally sticks out far enough to funnel floating objects into the swiftest part of the river during high waters, avoiding the sandbar.

- *Super-elevation* is a feature in which the water is being increased in volume, intensity, and height. When both the stream volume and movement are high, centrifugal force exerts another type of influence on flow characteristics. The river surface water tends to curve in a dish shape toward the outer bend, like a banked turn on a racetrack. *The dished inside curve is the easiest and safest route to travel.* If maneuvered correctly, the slight rise of water and the force of the current around the curve will cause the raft to slip gently off the wave and into the quiet pools of water below. *But if the raft was maneuvered across the line of the currents, the raft may either be sucked under by the dominant helical flow, or the power and force of the river on the outside of the dish on the curve could smash and pin any floating device against the outside bank.*

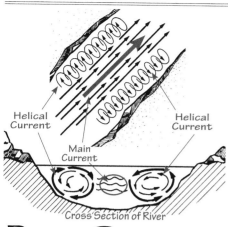

Cross Section of River

Helical Current • Main Current • Helical Current

RIVER CURRENTS
Reflex Current

When the current of a river is deflected by obstructions, the overall downward flow of a river will respond. These responses vary from mild to radical deflection, creating direction and speed changes of water flow. These changes are called reflex current. *The reflex current responds to an obstruction, such as bends or submerged rocks.*

Helical Current

One response to the laminar flow is a *spiraling, coil-springing flow called a helical current which corkscrews as a result of friction with the riverbank.* Going down river, on the left side of the supposed straight-line river, the helical flow turns *clockwise* to the main current, and on the right side the helical flow is *counterclockwise.* This results from friction and drag caused by shallow banks combined with the strong force of the main current flowing down. The helical flow and the mainstream create a circular, whirling secondary current that travels down along a line near the point of maximum flow. Helical current flow starts along the bottom of the river going out toward the riverbank, surfacing, and then spiraling back into the mainstream at a downward angle. *This flow causes floating objects around the edges to be pulled into the mainstream and held there. By understanding where the fast water is and how to observe the characteristics that show the current, you can maneuver the raft to take advantage of the faster water and increase the rate of travel.* Even at the quietest edge of a flow, particles are still drawn into the strongest part of the current. *Laminar and helical flows are always present in fast-flowing rivers.*

Wave crest falls back on itself

Sleeper
Breaking Hole
A small raft can be trapped here

BREAKING HOLES

Breaking holes occur where a large quantity of water flows over a sleeper, and the drop is not steep enough to create a suction hole. A wave of standing water, much like an ocean breaker, is found downstream. This wave is stationary and can vary from one to ten feet high, and even though it lacks the strong upriver flow of a suction hole, *it can be a trap for rafts too small to climb up and over the crest.* The size of the breaking hole and the rafter's seamanship must be considered before tackling this obstacle.

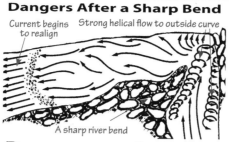

Dangers After a Sharp Bend

Current begins to realign • Strong helical flow to outside curve

A sharp river bend

DANGERS AFTER A SHARP BEND

Coming out of a sharp bend, the river currents are mixed, but the dangerous movement is still pulling. The result of the laminar flow shooting into a bank *creates a helical-flow effect immediately below the turn,* where the river is still trying to assume a natural "straight" flow. Being a liquid, water cannot resist stress, and it responds to a variety of obstacles (most common are submerged boulders).

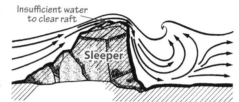

Insufficient water to clear raft

Sleeper

SLEEPERS & LARGE SLEEPERS

One type of hydraulic is the *surge,* which usually occurs when the current is slow and the water is deep. This hydraulic is formed downstream from an obstruction, with a surge in the water volume. When obstacles no longer have the ability to hold the water back, the pressure is released. Surges present few problems if the boulder or obstruction is covered with enough water flow to prevent contact when floating over the top. Rafters should be aware of obstructions (known as "sleepers") *if the water does not sufficiently cover them. Failing to recognize a sleeper can result in raft destruction and severe bodily injuries.* With large sleepers, the water flows over the top, creating a powerful current. This powerful, secondary current is trying to fill the vacuum created by the hydraulic downstream action.

DRIBBLING FALL

Another form of large sleeper is referred to as a dribbling fall. These are caused by minimal water flowing over submerged obstacles, with considerable drop below. This type of sleeper causes a bumpy ride, reducing speed, and can *capsize* the raft.

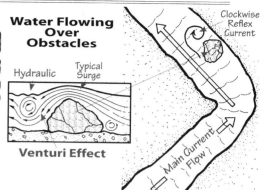

Water Flowing Over Obstacles

Clockwise Reflex Current

Hydraulic • Typical Surge

Venturi Effect

Main Current Flow

VENTURI EFFECT

When water flows over obstructions, such as submerged boulders, the character of the laminar flow is changed. As the water flows over the top of the rock, the layers of the laminar flow increase in speed. This is known as a venturi effect. *The hydraulic area is a type of "vacuum" formed as water flows around the rock.* Created directly below the obstruction are confused and disordered currents that accelerate the layers of the laminar flow.

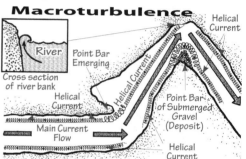

Macroturbulence

River

Cross section of river bank

Point Bar Emerging

Helical Current

Main Current Flow

Helical Current • Helical Current

Point Bar of Submerged Gravel (Deposit)

Helical Current

DANGERS OF MACROTURBULENCE

Macroturbulence is any extreme, unpredictable turbulence. It is an especially dangerous phenomenon, caused by a drop or decline in the river bottom. The phenomenon also occurs when the water comes in contact with the river bend or rocks. The extreme amounts of froth (air bubbles) created from the turbulence and the gravitational pull *cause rafts to spin.* Raft control is extremely limited because the *lack of water viscosity* causes resistance against paddles and a *lack of buoyancy,* making it difficult to float or maneuver. *This type of white water can be impassable, depending on how extreme the dip and amount of water flow.*

Two opposing three-dimensional eddies are formed by a true fall.

Two Reflex Currents

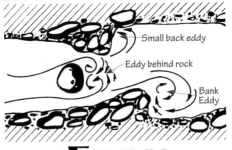

Small back eddy

Eddy behind rock

Bank Eddy

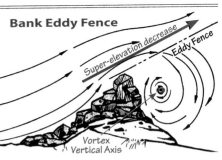

Bank Eddy Fence

Super-elevation decrease

Eddy Fence

Vortex Vertical Axis

WATERFALLS

In most falls, there are two reflex currents or suction holes forming, both whirling on crosscurrent axes into the falls. One current falls behind the crashing main stream of water while the other falls in front. *It's not too dangerous on a 2 or 3 foot drop, but when heights of 6 or more feet are present, it's a trap. The suction holes formed below these falls are inherently inescapable because of their power. The foam and froth formed at the bottom of falls can be dangerous. There might be hidden jagged boulders and other hazards.*

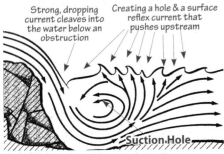

Strong, dropping current cleaves into the water below an obstruction

Creating a hole & a surface reflex current that pushes upstream

Suction Hole

SUCTION HOLE

☠ *The vacuum created by a suction hole is strong enough to pull a rafter wearing a life preserver beneath the surface. If pulled down into a suction hole, the survivor will normally be whirled to the surface down river and returned to the suction hole by the upriver flow, to be pushed under once again.* Objects too buoyant to sink usually *remain trapped.* It's often difficult to identify a suction hole because there is no frothing, no obvious curling water, and little noise. *Extreme caution should be used when a large bulge appears in the water.*

SURVIVING A SUCTION HOLE

There are three possible ways of surviving and avoiding serious injury in suction holes.

* One way is to find the layer of water below the surface that is moving in the desired direction.
* Second way is to reach down with a paddle or hand and feel for a current that is moving out of the hole. However, in a large suction hole the downstream flow will be too deep to reach. The rafter should attempt to cut across through the side of the eddy and into the water rushing by.
* The final and best solution is to scout ahead and try to identify the location of suction holes, and avoid them.

Pumping Air

EDDY

An eddy is a reaction to an obstruction. The type of eddy that occurs next to the bank is caused by parts of the main current being deflected and forced to flow back upriver, where it again joins the mainstream. These areas are usually associated with quiet and slow-flowing water. They are also associated with areas where the river widens, or just above or below a bend in the river.

BOILS

A boil may occur below a fall or sleeper, downstream of the curling or reverse-current suction. This appears as a dome or mound-shaped water formation. Boils are the result of layers of flows hitting bottom, aimed upward, and reaching the surface and parting into a flower-like flow. *The water billowing out in boils is super-oxygenated (many frothy bubbles), taking away the resistance needed to push with the paddles or to suspend a survivor in a life preserver.*

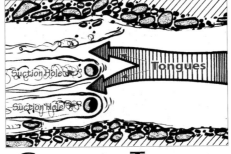

Suction Hole

Suction Hole

Tongues

CHUTE OR TONGUE

River chutes are good, logical travel routes, but they may harbor dangers. A chute (or tongue) is a swift-running, narrow passage between river obstructions caused by a damming effect. An example would be water forced between two large boulders. *Because the water flow is restricted, it accelerates and a powerful current rushes through. Because of the water velocity, there may be a suction hole on either side of the chute.*

SWEEPERS ☠

Sweepers can be the most dangerous obstructions on rivers. A sweeper is a large tree growing on a riverbank that has fallen over and is resting at or near the surface of the water. It may bounce up and down with the current. Rafters may be suddenly confronted with a sweeper that blocks the channel while rounding a bend in a river. Rafters are relatively helpless when they encounter sweepers in swift water. The only precautionary measure is to land above a bend in order to study the river ahead.

Many people have met disaster by hitting sweepers.

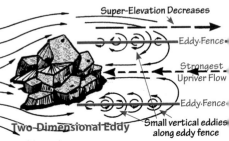

Super-Elevation Decreases

Eddy Fence

Strongest Upriver Flow

Eddy Fence

Two-Dimensional Eddy

Small vertical eddies along eddy fence

EDDY CURRENTS

An eddy has two distinct currents: the *upstream current* and the *downstream current.* The dividing line between the two is called an *eddy fence.* It is a line of small whirlpools spun off the upriver current by the power of the downstream current.

TWO-DIMENSIONAL EDDY & WHIRLPOOL

A two-dimensional eddy occurs when the tip of an obstruction is slightly above the water and causes a two-dimensional flow around the obstacle. Because of the speed and power of the current, the *water is super elevated* and is significantly higher than the level of water directly behind the obstacle. This creates a hole that is filled by the flow of water around the obstacle. *Two-dimensional eddies that occur in midstream will create two eddy fences, one on each side of the obstacle.* The water will enter the depression from both sides and will travel in a circular motion, clockwise from the right bank, counterclockwise from the left bank, and back upstream directly behind the obstacle. *If the projection is large enough and a strong circular motion is created, it becomes a whirlpool.* The outer reaches of the swirling water are super-elevated by centrifugal force and suction is created, similar to a drain in a bathtub. These vortexes are very rare and usually occur on huge rivers. Rafters may stop and rest where the eddies occur since there should be no strong swift currents in the eddy. *If the obstacle is huge, it may be impossible to paddle fast enough to cross the eddy fence without being spun around in a pin-wheeling manner.*

☠

LOGJAMS - STRAINERS

Logjams are extremely dangerous. They consist of logs, brush, and debris collected from high waters that become lodged across the current. They remain stationary while the river flows through them. If a craft should be swept up against the stationary logs, it will be pinned in place by the current. Should the craft be tipped and swamped it could be swept under the logjam. If the current is strong enough to do this, the occupants may also be pinned underneath the jam.

Back-ferry as you approach for a dry ride, if boat is large enough for wave.

Forward ferry after the bow has slapped water down to get over the top.

Keep aligned in trough.

Maintain steering forward ferry down off wave. Back-ferry or stay fast to meet next crest.

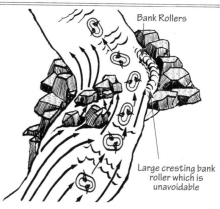

Bank Rollers

Large cresting bank roller which is unavoidable

ROLLERS

Another difficulty found when traveling on fast rivers are rollers. Rollers are large, cresting waves caused by a variety of situations. A wave seen below a breaking hole is one type of roller. *Velocity waves* are another type that occur on straight stretches of fast-dropping waters and are caused by the drag of sandy banks and submerged sandbars. They may be large enough to *overturn a raft* but are easily recognized, and are usually regular and easy to navigate by keeping the raft direction of travel in line with the crest of the wave.

TAIL WAVES

Tail waves are quiet waves that are a reflex from the current hitting small rocks along the bed of the river and deflecting the current toward the surface. They are usually so calm that going over them is not noticeable.

BANK ROLLERS

Bank rollers are similar in appearance to crested tail waves and occur when there is a sharp bend in the riverbed that turns so sharply the water can't readily turn in the bend. The water slams into the outside bank and super-elevates, falling back upon itself. *Small bank rollers cause few problems, but large ones cresting 5 feet or higher can capsize a raft.* There are three terms used to specify the severity or height of rollers - one of these is "washboard". *Washboard rollers* are a series of swells that gently ripple and are safe and easy to ride. The next stage of rollers is called *Standing-Water (cresting) Rollers*, in which the speed of contours on the bottom are such that the tops of the swells fall back onto themselves. The most dangerous and insurmountable rollers are referred to as *Haystacks, or Roosters.* They resemble haystacks of water coming down from every direction-giant, frothing bulges. *They may be so high a raft cannot go over them. It would be easy to become trapped in a deep trough (depression) and be buried under tons of frothing water. These troughs also hide dangers such as sharp rocks, which could tear a raft or break through the bottom of a boat.*

Dangerous Haystack

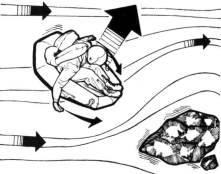

AVOIDING HAZARDS ONE MAN RAFT

One of the primary methods of avoiding hazards on the river is to slow the speed of the raft and move across the river to avoid a collision with an obstacle. A ferry position should be initiated early to avoid large rocks and reversals in the river. If obstacles are to be avoided, point the bow of the raft toward them and backstroke against the current to slow the speed of the raft's downstream progress and move it across the river. Usually, the best angle is about 45° to the current. The greater the angle, the quicker the movement across the river, but this also increases the downstream speed of the raft. Decreasing the angle will slow downstream speed, but movement across the width of the river will also be decreased. A raft is more maneuverable if it is well inflated. If the raft should pass over a rock, arch your back up to prevent injury to the buttocks or back.

Plastic Segmented Air Pockets

Closed Cell Foam Flotation

Horse Collar

Grass or sticks wrapped in waterproof material or plastic bags.

Plants which hold air pockets placed in a plastic bag.

Water Hyacinth

Two logs attached by ropes.

Two floating boxes lashed together with a rope.

The amount of air that cotton trousers will retain in water is enough to hold you afloat providing you remain calm. When the ends of the legs or drawstrings are tightly tied, each leg will hold a pocket of air.

Pant legs used as floaters.

Empty canteen mounted on a military belt.

LIFE JACKET INFORMATION
Page 19 & 134

Flotation Bag

Packing a Kayak

Flotation Bag

FLOTATION DEVICES

Vegetation Raft
A vegetation raft is built of small vegetation that will float, and is placed within clothing or plastic bag, to form a raft. Plants such as water hyacinth or cattail may be used.

Floating Logs
A good floating device can be fabricated by using two balsa logs or other lightweight wood. The logs should be placed about 2 feet apart and tied together. You sit on the lines and travels with the current.

Canteen Safety Belt
Attach at least 8 empty plastic canteens to a sturdy belt or rope. Make sure that the caps are screwed on tightly.

Poncho Life Belt
Roll Green vegetation tightly inside a poncho and fold over to make a watertight life belt. Roll up the life belt like a big sausage at least 8" in diameter and tie it. Wear it around the waist or across one shoulder and under the opposite arm like a bandoleer.

Water Wings
Two or more air-filled plastic bags, securely tied at the mouth, can be used as water wings. You can also use empty fuel or water cans.

Poncho Doughnut Raft
Can be used to transport equipment but not people. The raft is constructed by using saplings or pliable willows and a waterproof cover. A hoop-shaped framework of saplings or pliable willow is constructed within a circle of stakes. The hoop is tied with cordage or suspension line and removed from the circle of stakes and placed on the waterproof cover to which it will be attached. Clothing and equipment is placed in the raft, and then you swim, pushing the raft.

Poncho Doughnut Raft

BOATING SURVIVAL PLANNING

Have your personal Duffel Bag in which you store the items that might help you if there is a problem.

This bag should include...
- Your personal life jacket.
- A garment that will protect you from the sun, rain, and cold.
- basic personal items as sunglasses, sun screen, hat, first aid kit, and any personal medication that you require.
- If on the ocean - water.
- An Radio for weather information (even hearing the static caused by approaching storms is an indicator of a potential problem). It can also serve as a direction finder (by rotating the radio you can determine the direction of the strongest signal coming from the broadcast tower).
- One member of the group should include some tools and parts to make emergency repairs (spark plugs, sheer pins, even a spare propeller).
- If the boat is small include some oars.

TRAILERING BOAT

Choose the proper trailer for your boat. More damage can be done to a boat by the stresses of road travel than by normal operation. A boat hull is designed to be supported evenly by water. When transported on a trailer, your boat should be supported structurally as evenly across the hull as possible. This will allow for even distribution of the weight of the hull, engine and equipment. It should be long enough to support the whole length of the hull but short enough to allow the lower unit of the boats engine to extend freely.

Rollers & Bolsters
Rollers and bolsters must be kept in good condition to prevent scratching and gouging of the hull.

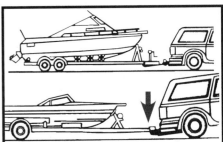

Too much weight on the hitch will cause the rear wheels of the tow vehicle to drag and may make steering more difficult.

Too much weight on the rear of the trailer will cause the trailer to "fishtail" and may reduce traction or even lift the rear wheels of the tow vehicle off the ground.

Securing Boat on Trailer
Tie-downs and lower unit supports must be adjusted properly to prevent the boat from bouncing on the trailer. The bow eye on the boat should be secured with either a rope, chain or turnbuckle in addition to the winch cable. Additional straps may be required across the beam of the boat.

Hitching a Trailer

Attaching Chain

Yes   No

Crisscross the chain under the coupler to the frame of the tow vehicle.

After a canoe spill!

CAPACITY OF TRAILER & VEHICLE

The capacity of the trailer should be greater than the combined weight of the boat, motor, and equipment. The tow vehicle must be capable of handling the weight of the trailer, boat, equipment, as well as the weight of the passengers and equipment which will be carried inside. This may require that the tow vehicle may need to be specially equipped with:

- Engine of adequate power.
- Transmission designed for towing.
- Larger cooling systems for the engine and transmission.
- Heavy duty brakes.
- Load bearing hitch attached to the frame, not the bumper. (Check your vehicle owner's manual for specific information.)

TOWING PRECAUTIONS

- Allow more time to brake, accelerate, pass, and stop.
- Remember the turning radius is also much greater. Curbs and roadside barriers must be given a wide berth when negotiating corners.
- Prior to operating on the open road, practice turning, backing up, etc. on a level uncongested parking area.

PRE-LAUNCH PREPARATIONS

- Prepare your boat for launching away from the ramp.
- Check the boat to ensure no damage was caused by the trip.
- Raise the lower unit (remove supports) to proper height for launching so it will not hit bottom.
- Remove tie-downs and make sure the winch is properly attached to the bow eye and locked in position.
- Put the drain plug in securely.
- Disconnect the trailer lights to prevent shorting of electrical system or burning out a bulb.
- Attach a line to the bow and the stern of the boat so the boat cannot drift away after launching and it can be easily maneuvered to docking area.
- Visually inspect the launch ramp for hazards such as a steep drop off, slippery area and sharp objects.
- When everything has been double checked, proceed slowly to the ramp remembering that your boat is just resting on the trailer and attached only at the bow. The ideal situation is to have one person in the boat and one observer at the water's edge to help guide the driver of the tow vehicle.

TO AVOID FALLING INTO THE WATER

- Never cross large bodies of water during rough weather.
- Stay with your boat if you capsize and can't get to shore.
- Avoid standing up or moving around in the boat. This includes your dog!
- Remain seated and be certain to store your equipment properly.
- If hunting NEVER move about your boat with a loaded gun or rifle.
- Don't overload your boat with passengers or equipment.
- Know the carrying capacity of your boat; use the capacity plate attached to the inside hull as guidance.

The boating section has information derived from the US Coast Guard & Metlife Publications.

LAUNCHING

- Keep the rear wheels of the tow vehicle out of the water. This will generally keep the exhaust pipes out of the water. If the exhaust pipes become immersed in the water, the engine may stall.
- Set the parking brake and place tire chocks behind rear wheels.
- Make sure someone else on shore is holding the lines attached to the boat.
- Lower the motor and prepare to start the engine (after running blowers and checking for fuel leaks).
- Start the boat motor and make sure water is passing through the engine cooling system.
- Release the winch and disconnect the winch line from the bow when the boat operator is ready.
- At this point, the boat should be able to be launched with a light shove or by backing off the trailer under power. Finish loading your boat at a sufficient distance from the ramp so others may use it.

RETRIEVAL

The steps for removing your boat from the water are basically the reverse of those taken to launch it. However, keep in mind certain conditions may exist during retrieval that did not exist during launching. As you approach the takeout ramp, take special care to note such factors as:

- Change in wind direction and/or velocity.
- Change in current and/or tide.
- Increase in boating traffic.
- Visibility, etc.

First, unload the boat at dock or mooring if possible. Next, maneuver the boat carefully to the submerged trailer and raise the lower unit of the engine. Then, winch the boat onto the trailer and secure it. Finally, drive the trailer with boat aboard carefully out of the ramp to a designated parking area for cleanup, reloading, and an equipment safety check. Practice will make launch and retrieval a simple procedure. The best advice is to retrieve your boat cautiously with safety as your main concern.

STORAGE OF BOAT

Since your boat may be sitting on its trailer for quite some time before it is used again, it is important to store it properly. To avoid damage from sun and weather, cover the boat with a tarp. To remove weight from the wheels, put cinder blocks or wood beams under the tongue and all four corners of the trailer frame.

KNOW YOUR PERSONAL LIMITATIONS
Fatigue

Hunting can be a physically demanding sport. Hours of sitting with exposure to wind, sun and glare can slow your reaction time.
Don't overextend your endurance by staying out on the water longer than you should.

Hypothermia

Hypothermia occurs when the body is subjected to prolonged cold temperatures. The most common cause of hypothermia is exposure to cold water, though long exposure to cold air can cause it as well. Immersion in cold water is the leading killer of boating hunters. A person immersed in cold water can lose body heat 25 times faster than in air at the same temperature. Each person is affected by the cold differently.

Dress appropriately for the environment you are in.

CHECK BEFORE HIGHWAY TRAVEL

- The tow ball and coupler are the same size and bolts with washers are tightly secured. The vibration of road travel can loosen them.
- The coupler is completely over the ball and the latching mechanism is locked.
- The trailer is loaded evenly from front to rear as well as side to side.
- Too much weight on the hitch will cause the rear wheels of the tow vehicle to drag and may make steering more difficult.
- Too much weight on the rear of the trailer will cause the trailer to "fishtail" and may reduce traction or even lift the rear wheels of the tow vehicle off the ground.
- The safety chains are attached crisscrossing under the coupler to the frame of the tow vehicle. If the ball were to break, the trailer would follow in a straight line and prevent the coupler from dragging on the road.
- The lights on the trailer function properly.
- Check the brakes. On a level parking area roll forward and apply the brakes several times at increasing speeds to determine a safe stopping distance.
- The side view mirrors are large enough to provide an unobstructed rear view on both sides of the vehicle.
- Check tires (including spare) and wheel bearings. Improper inflation may cause difficulty in steering. When trailer wheels are immersed in water (especially salt water), the bearings should be inspected and greased after each use.
- Make certain water from rain or cleaning has been removed from the boat. Water weighs approximately eight pounds per gallon and can add weight that will shift with the movement of the trailer.

HYPOTHERMIA SIGNALS

Shivering	Confusion
Numbness	Drowsiness
Impaired vision	Weakness
Impaired judgement	Dizziness

FIVE STAGES OF HYPOTHERMIA

- Shivering • Apathy
- Loss of consciousness
- Decreasing heart rate & breathing
- Death

Activity such as treading water only quickens heat loss. While awaiting rescue, the best thing to do is assume a Heat Escape Lessening Position (H.E.L.P.) that should reduce your body's heat loss by 50%. By using this position you will reduce direct exposure to the water of those body parts where heat is lost at a greater rate, such as armpits, ribs, groin and head. Your position will have to be adjusted depending on the PFD (personal flotation device) and clothing being worn.

STOP The spread of exotic weeds

AQUATIC NUISANCE SPECIES

ZEBRA MUSSELS

After the introduction of zebra mussels from Europe it rapidly spread due to its ability to attach to boats navigating lakes and rivers.

They get their name from the striped pattern of their shells. However, the pattern has been seen to vary greatly to where there are no stripes, only dark or light colored shells. Zebra mussels can grow to a maximum length of about 2 inches and live four to five years. They inhabit fresh water, usually at depths of 6 to 20 feet. Even though zebra mussels are freshwater animals, they have recently been found living in brackish water with higher salinity levels.

Effect of Zebra Mussels

Zebra mussels are notorious for their biofouling capabilities by colonizing water supply pipes of hydroelectric and nuclear power plants, public water supply plants, and industrial facilities. They colonize pipes constricting flow, therefore reducing the intake in heat exchangers, condensers, fire fighting equipment, and air conditioning and cooling systems.

Boating & Zebra Mussels

Boating can be affected by increased drag due to attached mussels. Small mussels can get into engine cooling systems causing overheating and damage. Navigational buoys have been sunk under the weight of attached zebra mussels. Fishing gear can be fouled if left in the water for long periods. Deterioration of dock pilings has increased when they are encrusted with zebra mussels. Continued attachment of zebra mussel can cause corrosion of steel and concrete affecting its structural integrity. Zebra Mussels have a similar effect on the food chain and water clarity as the quaggas mussel.

Zebra Mussel Quagga Mussel

"DE-MUSSEL" YOUR BOAT

Your active role in zebra mussel prevention and control is to "de-mussel" your boat before you leave an infested area.

Do the following away from the water.

- Draining the bilge, live wells and engine cooling system.
- Dumping any bait buckets.
- Inspecting the boat by checking the hull, trim plates, anchors, and the trailer.
- Washing down the boat with hot water (140°F), if mussels are found, and allowing the boat and trailer to sit for 2-5 days dry before going to another water location.

CAUTION!
This waterbody is infested with
Eurasian Watermilfoil

CAUTION!
This waterbody is infested with
Zebra Mussels

CAUTION!
This waterbody is infested with
Water Chestnut

EURASIAN WATERMILFOIL

Eurasian watermilfoil is a non-native aquatic plant. Once introduced to a lake (usually by boats) it grows and spreads very quickly, ultimately ruining valuable shore front property. Once Eurasian watermilfoil has infested a lake there is no known way to eradicate it.

Description

Stems grow to the water surface, usually extending 3' to 10'- but as much as 33' in length and frequently form dense mats. Stems of Eurasian milfoil are long, slender, branching, hairless, and become leafless toward the base. New plants may emerge from each node (joint) on a stem, and root upon contact with mud. The grayish-green leaves of Eurasian watermilfoil are finely divided and occur in whorls of three or four along the stem, with 12-16 pairs of fine, thin leaflets about 12 inches long and exhibits a reddish shoot near the surface. These leaflets give milfoil a feathery appearance that is a distinguishing feature of the plant.

Habitat: Fresh to brackish water of fish ponds, lakes, slow-moving streams, reservoirs, estuaries, and canals. Eurasian watermilfoil tends to invade disturbed areas where native plants cannot adapt to the alteration. It does not spread rapidly into undisturbed areas where native plants are well established. By altering waterways, humans have created a new and unnatural niche where milfoil thrives.

Distribution: Watermilfoil occurs in thirty-three states east of the Mississippi River and has recently been found in Colorado. It is abundant in the Chesapeake Bay, the tidal Potomac River, and several Tennessee Valley reservoirs.

Eurasian Watermilfoil, Variable Milfoil, & Fanwort

Commonly found in shallow bays and along the shoreline, these plants form dense beds that can seriously impair the recreational use of a lake, reduce the availability of fish spawning grounds, out compete beneficial native plants, and otherwise alter a lake's natural environment.

Ecological Threat: They can form large, floating mats of vegetation on the surface of lakes, rivers, and other water bodies, preventing light penetration for native aquatic plants and impeding water traffic. The plants thrive in areas that have been subjected to various kinds of natural and man made disturbance.

Travel: Can be introduced into a new water basin area by a "stowaway" fragment attached to a boat or trailer that was transported to a new lake. They can live out of water for many hours if it remains moist, like when they are wound around a wet carpeted bunk on a boat trailer. These displaced plants are usually first found near boat launch sites.

Reproduction & Dispersal: Most regeneration is from fragmented stems. Fragmentation can be caused by a propeller passing through the plants or a fish hook being pulled out of the water. The fragments drift away, sink, develop roots, and grow into new plants.

Fanwort   Eurasian Milfoil   Variable Milfoil

WATER CHESTNUT

Not the same species as the edible plant used in Asian cooking.

Water chestnut is a nuisance aquatic plant that limits boating, by creating nearly impenetrable mats, and fishing in infested areas. It can completely cover the surface of a water body and reduce oxygen levels which may increase fish kills. The plant spreads either by the rosettes detaching from their stems and floating to another area, or more often by the nuts being swept by currents or waves to other parts of the lake or river. The plant overwinters entirely by seed.

ZEBRA & QUAGGA MUSSELS

The quagga mussel closely resembles its cousin the zebra mussel.

Introduction into North America

They were most likely introduced into the Great Lakes and the St. Lawrence basin as the result of ballast water discharge from transoceanic ships that were carrying veligers, juveniles, or adult mussels. Their rapid dispersal throughout the Great Lakes and major river systems was due to the ability to attach to boats navigating these lakes and rivers. Attached mussels were scraped or fell off during routine navigation.

Overland Dispersal

Overland dispersal is also a possibility for aiding zebra mussel (zebra mussels arrived in NA before the quagga) range expansion. Many small lakes in proximity of the Great Lakes, unconnected by waterways but accessed by individuals trailering their boats from infested waters, have populations of zebra mussels living in them. Overland dispersal is by individuals trailering their boats from infested waters has rapidly spread the zebra mussel to small unconnected lakes. At least eight trailered boats crossing into California had zebra mussels attached to their hulls or in motor compartments; all were found during inspections at the agricultural inspection stations. Under cool, humid conditions, zebra mussels can stay alive for several days out of water.

Problems

They can clog water intake structures, such as pipes and screens. They can grow on docks, break walls, buoys, boats, and beaches.

QUAGGA MUSSELS

The spread of quagga mussels is a problem as they are prodigious water filterers, removing substantial amounts of food particles suspended in the water. They decrease the food source for other living creatures in the food chain. This feeding also increases the water transparency, decreases in the chlorophyll concentrations, and increases light penetration causing a proliferation of aquatic plants that can change species dominance in the entire ecosystem. A high concentration of quagga can cause an accumulation of organic pollutants that can be passed up the food chain into the wildlife. Quagga can have a negative impact on native freshwater mussels, invertebrates, and further up the fish food chain. Due to their limited time in North American it is not yet clear as to the full nature of there effect.

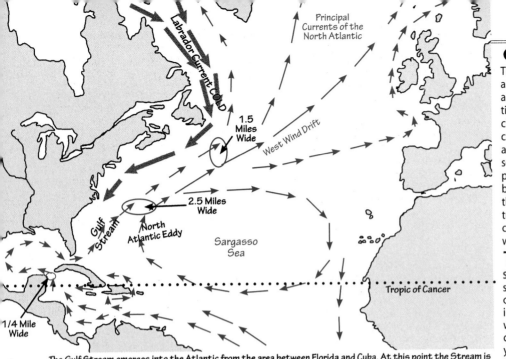

Principal Currents of the North Atlantic

Labrador Current COLD

1.5 Miles Wide

West Wind Drift

2.5 Miles Wide

Gulf Stream

North Atlantic Eddy

Sargasso Sea

Tropic of Cancer

1/4 Mile Wide

The Gulf Stream emerges into the Atlantic from the area between Florida and Cuba. At this point the Stream is 4-5 miles wide and it gets narrower as it proceeds further North. The Gulf Stream currents are not as clearly defined as in the illustration.

OCEAN CURRENTS

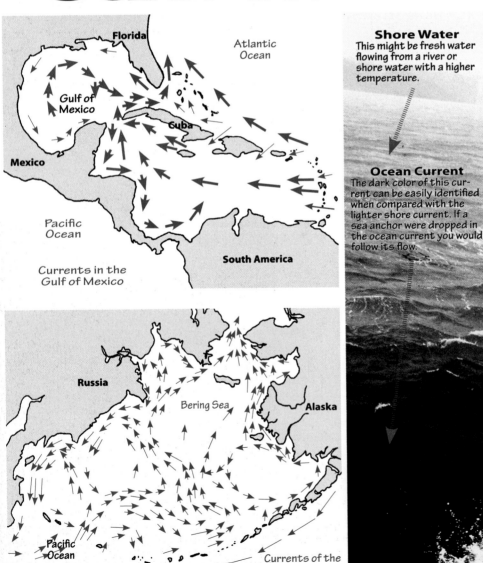

Florida

Atlantic Ocean

Gulf of Mexico

Cuba

Mexico

Pacific Ocean

South America

Currents in the Gulf of Mexico

Russia

Bering Sea

Alaska

Pacific Ocean

Currents of the Bering Sea

Shore Water
This might be fresh water flowing from a river or shore water with a higher temperature.

Ocean Current
The dark color of this current can be easily identified when compared with the lighter shore current. If a sea anchor were dropped in the ocean current you would follow its flow.

Drift of icebergs from West Greenland Glaciers to the Grand Banks of Newfoundland

Greenland

Baffin Island

Icebergs

East Greenland Current COLD

Icebergs

70°

Labrador Current COLD

Labrador

Icebergs

60°

50°

40°

Newfoundland

Atlantic

Icebergs

North Atlantic Current

Icebergs

OCEAN CURRENTS

These currents are like rivers in the ocean. They are immense flows of water much larger than any river on land. They flow in a clockwise direction in the Northern Hemisphere and counter-clockwise in the Southern Hemisphere. This is caused by three factors: the sun's heat, the winds, and the Earth's rotation (Coriolis effect). Most sea currents travel at speeds of less than 5 miles per hour. Using currents as a mode of travel can be done by putting out a sea anchor and letting the current pull the raft along. Use caution when traveling through areas where warm and cold currents meet. It could be a storm-forming area with dense fog and high winds and waves.

TYPES OF OCEAN CURRENTS

Surface Currents: The surface current is quite constant varying only with the seasons. The surface current is described by the *set:* the *direction* in which it flows, and the *drift,* the *velocity* at which it flows. These are indicated on nautical charts. You should know the surface currents in your path of travel.

Tidal Currents: These currents should be given consideration when approaching coastal waters. This current is caused by the rise and fall of the tide. Tidal currents do not exactly follow the rise and fall of the tide but depend upon the coastal features. Tidal currents are shown on Tidal Current Tables. There are four maximum currents for every tidal day period of 24 hours and 50 minutes.

Wind Driven Currents: Strong continuous winds can slightly affect the surface currents. The direction of the wind-driven currents is slightly to the right of the direction in which the wind is blowing in the northern hemisphere and slightly to the left in the southern hemisphere. This shift from the direction of the wind is due to the coriolis effect.

Deep Ocean Currents: Deep ocean currents do not affect boaters but they are involved with the overall movement of the oceans.

OCEAN TEMPERATURE

The surface layer of the ocean is warmed by the sun. In the polar regions the salt water freezes (28°-29°F – not 32°F as fresh water) and in the tropics the waters can reach 80° to 85°F. In enclosed areas as the Red Sea the water can reach 90° to 95°F. Ocean currents have a great influence on the ocean's temperature and help to equalize the surrounding temperature.

COLOR OF THE SEA

The blue color of the ocean is partially due to the reflection from the blue sky but it is mainly blue for the same reason that the sky is blue. Sunlight is made up of the rainbow spectrum of colors and when they enter water the sunlight is scattered but indigo and blue are reflected back – this gives us the blue color. In shallow waters there are more sediments and microscopic life and these cause the green color to be reflected so that the water is green.

Green: When the quantity of particles and organisms is high and when there is low salinity. Near shore or shallow water.

Blue: Organisms or particles low and salinity content high. Deeper water.

Current Colors: There can be strong adjacent color variations due to the different water temperatures - which would have different suspensions and plant growth.

• One could navigate by the knowledge of the coloration of the sea.
• In the tropics, coral reefs can be avoided by watching the change of color of the water (over coral it is usually yellowish-indigo).
• Colors cannot be accurately distinguished when the sun is low or if the weather is bad.

UNUSUAL OCEAN COLORS

Black Sea: Looks black because it has little oxygen and a high concentration of hydrogen sulfide.

Red Sea: Looks red because it contains seasonal blooms of algae that color the surface water red.

Yellow Sea: The Yellow Sea looks yellow because it contains a yellow mud carried into it by adjoining rivers.

Estimating Latitude By Polaris

Polaris 30° above the horizon means that you are at latitude 30°N. To estimate the angular distance that Polaris is above the horizon recall that directly overhead (the zenith) is 90°. Halfway to the horizon is 45° (as in the above example). Half of 45° would be 22.5°. If you do not have an instrument (sextant) to give you an exact reading the approximation of latitude is not too useful as a 1° error means that you are off by 60 miles (96 km) and a 10° error is 600 miles (960 km).

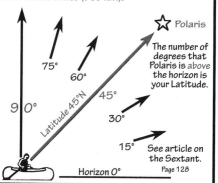

75°
60°
90°
45°
30°
Latitude 45°N
15°
☆ Polaris
The number of degrees that Polaris is above the horizon is your Latitude.
See article on the Sextant. Page 128
Horizon 0°

LOOKING FOR LAND

The lookout should watch carefully for signs of land. Some indications of land are:

• A fixed cumulus cloud in a clear sky, or in a sky where all other clouds are moving, often hovers over or slightly downwind from an island.
• In the tropics, a greenish tint in the sky is often caused by the reflection of sunlight from shallow lagoons or shelves of coral reefs.
• In the Arctic, ice fields or snow-covered land are often indicated by light-colored reflections on clouds, quite different from the darkish gray reflection caused by open water.
• Deep water is dark green or dark blue. Lighter color indicates shallow water, which may mean land is near.
• In fog, mist, rain, or at night, when drifting past a nearby shore, land may be detected by characteristic odors and sounds. The musty odor of mangrove swamps and mud flats and the smell of burning wood carries a long way.
• Roar of surf is heard long before the surf is seen.
• Continued cries of sea birds from one direction indicate their roosting place on nearby land.
• Birds are usually more abundant near land than over the open sea. The direction from which flocks fly at dawn and to which they fly at dusk may indicate the direction of land. During the day, birds are searching for food, and the direction of flight has less significance unless there is a storm approaching.

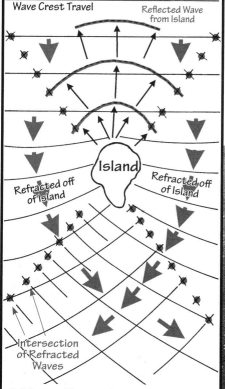

Wave Crest Travel
Reflected Wave from Island
Island
Refracted off of Island
Refracted off of Island
Intersection of Refracted Waves

WAVE PATTERNS & LAND

Land may be detected by the pattern of the waves, which are refracted as they approach land. The illustration shows the form the waves assume. Land can be located by observing this pattern and turning parallel to the slightly turbulent area (marked "X" on the illustration), and following its direction.

DIRECTION INDICATION FROM WAVES & SWELLS

A sea swell is formed by the prevailing wind. It takes a major wind to redirect a swell. Normally, the momentum of the swell does not change no matter what the weather.

Swells are not waves. The surface waves will assume the direction of the wind. The undulating swell will follow its normal direction.

Waves can sometimes indicate the presence of land as the wind might be deflected off the land mass. On the leeward side (wind shadow) of land the swell and waves will be smaller and if the wind is the prevailing wind the swells will also be reduced.

POLYNESIAN WAVE CHARTS

The Polynesians understood the movements of swells and waves. The Micronesians developed charts of the anatomy and topography of local water surfaces. These charts indicated the meeting points of the dominant swells around the islands. The charts were made of ribs of the coconut palms and tied together with coconut fiber. They showed the islands and used a sailing time scale not a distance scale.

These charts showed: the directional swells throughout the group of islands, the distance from land at which coconuts palms can be seen. Position and distance from the island of the meeting of the waters of the oncoming swell and the ebbing tide from an island or lagoon. These meeting places can be beyond the sight of land.

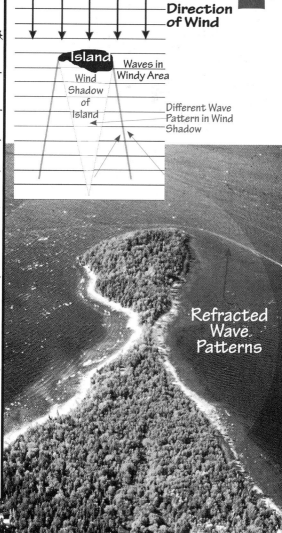

Direction of Wind
Island
Waves in Windy Area
Wind Shadow of Island
Different Wave Pattern in Wind Shadow
Refracted Wave Patterns

LAND INDICATORS

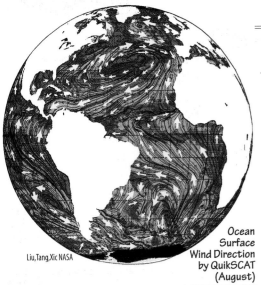

Ocean Surface Wind Direction by QuikSCAT (August)

Liu, Tang, Xic NASA

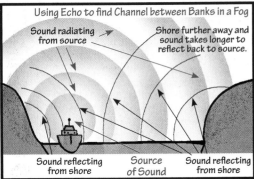

Using Echo to find Channel between Banks in a Fog

Sound radiating from source

Shore further away and sound takes longer to reflect back to source.

Sound reflecting from shore

Source of Sound

Sound reflecting from shore

WIND & DIRECTION

Winds are named for the direction from which they come:
North wind from the North

DOMINANT WIND

Each area has a predominant wind that dominates a season or all seasons.
In general, in regions of temperate climate, the wind usually blows from the west (both in the Northern and Southern hemispheres). In the tropics, the winds are between northeast and southeast; on the equator, usually from the east. If you have no compass, in the Northern hemisphere, a northerly wind is usually colder than a southerly wind.

- Winds from the desert are dry and carry dust.
- Winds from the ocean are moisture laden and might bring rain.
- The prevailing wind in all regions has its own personality of velocity, temperature, and humidity which varies with the seasons.
- On the ocean, the prevailing wind has its own characteristics and also its own accompaniment of clouds.
- In polar regions, the wind temperature, if warmer than the surroundings, will indicate the direction of water. A sudden drop in temperature, without change in direction, might indicate the presence of an iceberg.
- Wet your finger or throw ashes in the air to detect a light breeze.

ESTIMATING DISTANCE ON WATER

Objects look much nearer than they actually are when:
- The sun is shining, from behind you.
- Looking across water.
- Air is clear.

Objects look much farther away than they actually are when:
- Light is poor and there is low contrast or fog.
- Looking over larger regular waves especially when the waves are perpendicular to the observer.

Table to judge distance:

50 yds	Mouth & eyes can be clearly distinguished.
100 yds	Eyes appear as dots.
200 yds	General details of clothing can be distinguished.
300 yds	Faces can be seen.
500 yds	Colors of clothing can be distinguished.
800 yds	Man looks like a post. Canoes can be seen.
1 mi	Trunks of large trees can be seen.
2 1/2 mi	Chimneys & windows can be distinguished.
6 mi	Large houses, silos, & towers can be recognized.
9 mi	Average church steeple can be seen.

ECHOES & SOUND TO FIND DIRECTION

- The Inuits of Greenland use the sound of the male Snow Bunting's nesting area as a guide in the fog. Each male bird has a distinctive song and the Inuits know the song of the Snow Bunting at the head of their fjord. During a fog they will turn upon hearing the distinctive song and head home.
- When traveling rotate your head to "scan" for sounds. You will hear your environment. You might hear a heavy surf, nesting birds, boats, etc. When the sound of the breakers disappears, that indicates the presence of an inlet or harbor.
- In fog or at night a shout or whistle will echo from any promontory. If you hear an echo recall that sound takes 5 seconds to travel a mile so you can approximate the distance. This method is used on ships during a fog. They use bells, gunshots, siren blasts or shouting. Each second between blast and echo means a distance of about 560 feet from the reflecting surface.

Velocity of Sound
(In quiet open air)

Temp (F°)	Velocity (Ft/Sec)	1 Mile (seconds)
32°	1092	4.83
40°	1100	4.80
50°	1110	4.78
60°	1120	4.73
70°	**1130**	**4.68**
80°	1140	4.63
90°	1150	4.59
100°	1160	4.55
110°	1170	4.51
120°	1180	4.47

SENSE OF SMELL TO FIND LAND

The sense of smell is important, especially at sea.
- The Polynesians carried pigs on their 100 foot catamarans because pigs have a highly developed sense of smell and would get excited upon smelling land.
- The direction of the sea breeze and the smell give the direction of land.
- New smells are easier to distinguish at sea than on land as the smell of salt is more constant.

Marking Water Trail
During calm weather the Indians of British Columbia used cedar chips, dropped from the back of their dugout boats into the water, to mark their route in the fog.

Prevailing Wind on the Ocean
On the ocean, the prevailing wind has its own characteristics and also its own grouping of clouds.

STANDING CLOUDS & FINDING LAND

Standing clouds give the impression of staying in one spot while the surrounding clouds keep on moving. A standing cloud can even be the only one in the sky.
Standing clouds occur above islands. The island or hills on the island and cause humid air to rise and continuously form clouds which appear to be standing (staying) in one spot. The cloud is continually dissipating once the air has passed over the island. Due to their height, these clouds can be seen from many miles over the horizon. These clouds often have a woollier appearance than the normal trade-wind clouds.

In the tropics islands even produce distinctive reflections upon these clouds.
Coral islands though flat and low can produce standing clouds as the atoll reflects more heat than the surrounding water causing a temperature gradient along which clouds will form. These clouds usually are on the lee side of the island. They will reflect the bright turquoise lagoon of the atoll.

Clouds might even hover over dangerous shoals below the water.

The water in the wind condenses as it rises to a higher cooler elevation to form a cloud over the land. This forms a standing cloud that is nearly always present over the island.

The wind returns to a lower elevation after passing over the land, the air warms up and the cloud disappears.

Humid wind blows onto land mass and rises to a higher elevation

Wind   Island below the horizon   Horizon

Standing Cloud

Dominican Republic

Puerto Rico

Virgin Islands

Lightning & Finding Land
Lightning from one direction in the early hours of the morning (before sunrise) is usually a sign of land in the tropics.

DISTANCE AT SEA

Due to the curvature of the earth, the higher you are above sea level, the further you can see.

DISTANCE OF THE HORIZON

Take the square root of the height in feet of the observer's eye, above sea level, and multiply by 1.15. This will give you the distance of the horizon in miles.

e.g. Eye height above sea level 16 ft.
Square root of 16 ft. = 4
Multiply by 1.15   4 x 1.15= 4.6 miles
This tells you that any low object on the horizon will be approximately 4 1/2 miles away.

OBJECT BETWEEN YOU AND THE HORIZON

Estimate the proportionate distance between you and the object, object and horizon to give you the approximation of the distance.

OBJECT BELOW HORIZON (PARTIALLY VISIBLE)

If you can see a mast above the horizon but not the ship. From the mast you can recognize the type of ship and you can estimate the height of the ship above the waterline.

Boat Below the Horizon
From the type of mast we can assume that this type of boat is 49 feet high above sea level.

e.g. Part of mast of a sailboat above the horizon.
Assume a sailboat 49 ft. above the waterline.
Square root of 49 = 7.
Square root of height of observer 16 = 4.
Add 7 + 4 = 11 x 1.15 = approx.. 12 2/3 miles.
This means the sailboat is 12 2/3 miles away.
The same method can be used on objects where the height is known as a headland, church steeple, average tree height, palm tree.

FINGER METHOD OF JUDGING DISTANCE

This method is based upon the principle that the distance between the eyes is about 1/10 of the distance from the eye to the extended finger. When you know the width or height of a distant object e.g., the height of a person or building.

1 Extend your right arm and hold your forefinger upright and align it with one eye at the end of the object.

2 Do not move the finger and observe where it is when looking with the other eye. We actually look with one eye and judge depth with the second.

3 Estimate the displacement in feet along the length of the object.

4 The distance in feet of the object will be 10 times the displacement of the fingers.

This can also be done vertically but hold the head sideways. This might be easier because if you want to judge the distance of a building, we know the height of each floor is between 10 to 12 feet high. You can do this with your binoculars but measure the distance between the center of the eyepieces, when adjusted for your eyes, and multiply this distance by 10.

Tern: If you see one you are within 40 miles of land.

SEA BIRDS INDICATING THE PROXIMITY OF LAND

Bird	Time of Year	Birds at one time	Distance From Land
Albatross	Any month	Any number.	May be far from land.
	Breeding season	12+	Within 100 miles of breeding spot.
Petrel	Breeding season	6+	Within 75 miles of breeding spot.
	Other months	6 or less far from land.	
	Increasing numbers	Show proximity to land.	
	Direction of flight at dawn and dusk shows direction of land.		
Shearwater	Breeding Season	6 +	Within 100 miles of breeding spots.
	Direction of flight at dawn and dusk gives direction of land.		
	April-October	Any number	May be far from land.
Fulmar	Increasing numbers	Show proximity to land.	
Black Skimmer	Any month	1 +	Within 25 miles.
White Tern	Any month	1 +	Within 40 miles.
Atlantic Gannet	Any month	3 +	Up to 100 miles.
Brown Booby	Any month	3 +	75 miles
		6 or more	Usually within 30 miles.
Tropic-Bird	Any month	1 or 2	May be far from land.
		3 +	60-80 miles
Frigate-Bird	Any month	3 or more	100 miles
		6 or more	Within 75 miles.
	The direction of flight of even 1 bird at dusk usually points to land.		
	Do not sleep on the water.		
Cormorants	Any month	Any number	25 mile limit.
Pelicans	Any month	More than one	25 mile limit; usually much less.
		Increasing numbers.	Show approach to land.
Great Skua	Summer months	Increasing numbers	Show proximity to land.
	Winter months	Any number	May be far from land.
Gulls	Any month	3 or more depth off coasts).	50 miles (or within 100 fathom
		Increasing numbers	Show approach to land.
Common Guillemot	Any month	Increasing numbers.	Show proximity to land.

VISIBILITY OVER WATER

The daytime range that an unaided eye can see an unlighted object. On the water the distance of sight is affected by the amount of water vapor or water particles in the air. This can be fog, snow, or water mist.

International Code	Description	Visibility Range
0 - 2	Dense - moderate fog	0-500 yds (457 m)
3,4	Light to thin fog	500 yds-1 mi(1.67 km)
5	Haze	1-2 mi (3.2 km)
6	Light haze	2-5.5 mi (8.9 km)
7	Clear	5.5-11 mi (18 km)
8	Very clear	11-27 mi (43 km)
9	Exceptionally clear	over 27 mi (43 km)

Gulls: If you see 3 or more you are within 50 miles of land or within the 100 fathom depth off the coast. With an increase of gulls you are approaching land.

Horizon glass is attached perpendicular to the frame. The half of the horizon glass is transparent so that an object may be viewed through it, while the second half is a silvered mirror. These mirrors are set parallel to the vernier when it reads 0° on the arc.

Sun Filters: small colored glass filters of varying densities pivoted to the frame. These may be swung into position to protect the eye of the observer when sighting on the sun.

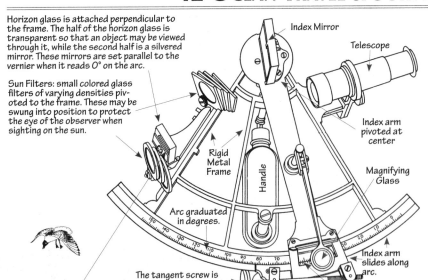

Index Mirror

Telescope

Index arm pivoted at center

Magnifying Glass

Rigid Metal Frame

Handle

Arc graduated in degrees.

Index arm slides along arc.

The tangent screw is used to precisely position the viewed image.

Index Arm Clamp

Vernier gauge is used to read precise measurement and is on the index arm.

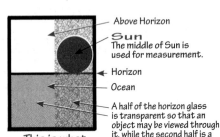

Above Horizon

Sun
The middle of Sun is used for measurement.

Horizon

Ocean

A half of the horizon glass is transparent so that an object may be viewed through it, while the second half is a silvered mirror.

This is what a sextant telescope sees.

SEXTANT

The sextant is a instrument for measuring the angle between two objects usually from a boat or ship. The angle is measured in the plane passing through the two objects and the instrument, therefore the angle is only horizontal or vertical when these three points are in a horizontal or vertical plane.

Using a sextant to measure the horizontal angle. An example would be the angle between a lighthouse and a point of land. By knowing the position of these two points on a map and the observed angle the navigator can determine the precise location of the boat. By making repeat timed observations he can calculate the speed of approach.

Using a sextant to measure the vertical angle. An example would be to find the Latitude of the boat. This could be determined by reading the angle of the Sun above the horizon - the navigator would have to know the precise time - and use charts to know the supposed location of the Sun at that time. At night the navigator could make an observation of the vertical angle off of Polaris.

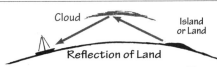

Cloud

Island or Land

Reflection of Land

REFLECTIONS IN THE SKY

Clouds can reflect features of the surface below.
- On land off an ice covered sea the clouds can reflect open water as there is less light reflected off dark water than the white frozen area. This reflection is a dark spot on the underside of the clouds. The dark spot would not indicate the size of the open water because a small area can affect a large area of cloud. This happens as open water in the Arctic gives off a vapor and this will affect the reflected light around the open area and increase the dark spot area. This is known as a "water sky".
- An ice flow or iceberg can be seen as an "ice blink" which is seen as a noticeable patch of brightness in a gray sky. A small area of ice can show a large "ice blink".
- Islands and other vegetation-covered areas, ice patches and small snow fields will reflect steel-blue on the under surface of the clouds.

Captive Bird Ocean Navigation

Density & Pressure of Sea Water
Sea water is heavier (has a greater density) than fresh water.

CAPTIVE BIRD OCEAN NAVIGATION

Sailors of antiquity would set sail with captive land birds. When looking for land a bird would be released. If the bird saw land it would fly in that direction. If not, it would return to the ship. This method was used by the ancient Babylonians, the Hindi of 500 BC, the Polynesians, the Vikings, Arabians in the Indian Ocean, etc.

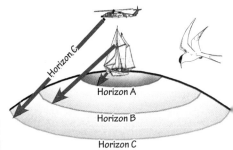

Horizon C

Horizon A

Horizon B

Horizon C

DISTANCE OF HORIZON

The distance of the horizon increases with the elevation above the Sea Level. This is due to the curvature of the earth's surface. The sailor on the deck of the boat has the nearest horizon (Horizon A) as the sailor is closest to the Sea. The person in the "crows nest" on the mast has a wider horizon (Horizon B). The Coast Guard helicopter has the widest horizon (Horizon C).

Marine Binoculars

Inflatable Raft

Four-fifths of the Earth's surface is covered by open water. Although accounts of sea survival incidents are often gloomy, successful survival is possible.

When using a raft you will find that you are at the mercy of the weather, currents, winds, and lack of water and food.

Polynesians traveling between islands in the Pacific.

EMBARKING & DEBARKING

- When launching, the crew should maintain a firm grip on the boat until they have embarked.
- When debarking, they should hold onto the boat until it is completely out of the water.
- Loading and unloading are done using the bow as the entrance and exit point.
- Keep a low center of gravity when entering and exiting the boat to avoid capsizing. Maintain 3 points of contact at all times. Two feet and one hand, or two hands and one foot.
- Beaching the boat is a method of debarking the entire crew at once into shallow water allowing the boat to be quickly carried out of the water.

"PREPARE TO CAPSIZE"

Inform all members of the crew of a potential capsize by crying "Prepare to capsize". This will alert the crew to raise their paddles above their heads, with the blades pointed outward. All loose articles should be stowed if possible.

OPEN SEA TRAVEL
Make Use of the Ocean Currents

- Deploy a sea anchor as in illustration.
- Sit low in the raft to minimize the effect of the wind.
- Keep the raft at low pressure to lower its profile in the water.

To Use the Winds

- Pull in the sea anchor.
- Inflate the raft so that it floats higher in the water.
- Sit up in the raft so your body catches more wind.
- Mount a sail or other item which will catch a breeze.

Fishing Off a Raft
Jigging

Jigging hooking, without bait, a fish from below. Jigging can be used to hook fish that are hiding in the shadow of your raft. Watch your hands!

Bait

After you have caught your first fish, examine the stomach and intestines and you will see what they are eating. You can use some of the remnants or parts of the fish to bait your hook.

Bare-handed Fishing

Takes patience but can be very successful. If you see a fish close to the side of the raft slowly submerge your hands and catch the fish from behind. Make sure that you know what you are catching! Watch for sea snakes, sharks, and moray eels.

Have an escape plan when using a boat, discuss the function of each member of the crew, and have frequent drills. Prior to abandoning a boat establish the geographic position and activate any locating device that is on board. Take the locating device with you.

NAVIGATION AIDS

Aids to Navigation are placed along coasts and navigable waters as guides to mark safe water and to assist mariners in determining their position in relation to land and hidden dangers.

Lateral Marks: Are buoys or beacons that indicate sides of a route to be followed. They follow the traditional 3R rule of "red, right, returning" when returning from seaward and proceeding toward the head of navigation.

Intracoastal Waterways employ markings that consist of a yellow square or triangle.

When following the conventional direction of buoyage:

YELLOW SQUARE - is kept on LEFT SIDE
YELLOW TRIANGLE - is kept on RIGHT SIDE

DO NOT rely on buoys alone to determine your position!

NON-PYROTECHNIC DEVICES

Orange Distress Flag: The distress flag is a day signal only. It must be at least 3 x 3 feet with a black square and ball on an orange background. It is most distinctive when attached and waved on a paddle, boathook or flown from a mast.

Electric Distress Light: The electric distress light is accepted for night use only and must automatically flash the international SOS distress signal (... --- ...).

A capsized boat, seen through a port-hole, with the crew sitting on the side of the boat. Note that the crew members have their personal life jackets.

PYROTECHNIC DEVICES

Pyrotechnic devices should be stored in a cool, dry location. A watertight container painted red or orange and prominently marked "Distress Signals" is recommended. Pyrotechnics are universally recognized as excellent distress signals. However, there is potential for injury and property damage if not properly handled. These devices produce a very hot flame and the residue can cause burns and ignite flammable material. Hand-held pyrotechnic devices, such as flares and smoke signals, may expel ash and slag as they burn. Even though these particles cool quickly, they can cause painful burns or ignite materials that burn easily. The flare itself is very hot and can start a fire if it is dropped. Therefore, these devices when burning should be held over the side and in such a way that hot slag can not drip on the hand.

Office of Boating Safety - Regulations & Publications - Metlife Publications

Red Flare
hand held
day & night

Orange
Smoke Signal
hand held / day only

Red Meteor
day & night

Floating
Orange
Smoke
day only

Parachute
Flare
day & night

Three Water Spouts

Coast Guard Rescue

Ring Buoy

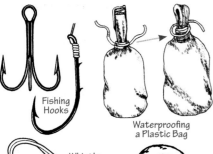

Boat's Compass

OCEAN WEATHER DANGERS

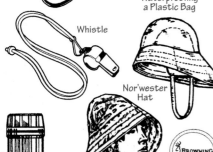

Fishing Hooks

Waterproofing a Plastic Bag

Whistle

Nor'wester Hat

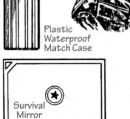

Plastic Waterproof Match Case

Fishing Line

Brass Whistle

Survival Mirror

WINDPROOF and Waterproof MATCHES

Plastic Water Bottle

Waterproof & Windproof Matches

LISTEN TO WEATHER FORECASTS

The best source of current weather information is the continuous National Weather Service broadcasts. The most common frequencies are 162.400, 162.475, and 162.550MHz). Taped information is re-played approximately every five minutes with broadcasts updated no less than every three to six hours. In the event of unusual or severe weather, the programming may be interrupted by live broadcasts. The Coast Guard also broadcasts special marine weather information, including small craft advisories, on VHF Channel 22.

STORM WARNINGS

Small Craft Advisory: Generally associated with sustained winds 18 to 33 knots, or waves hazardous to small boats.

Gale Warning: Sustained winds 34 to 47 knots.

Storm Warning: Sustained winds 48 knots or more.

Hurricane Warning: Sustained winds 64 knots or more associated with a hurricane.

Special Marine Warning: Winds of 35 knots or more lasting generally less than two hours. These are usually associated with an individual thunderstorm or an organized series of thunderstorms (squall line, cold front).

HURRICANE ARE DESTRUCTIVE

Hurricanes are among the most destructive phenomena of nature; their appearance is not to be taken lightly. Advance planning cannot guarantee that your boat will survive a hurricane safely or even survive at all. Planning can, however, improve survivability and is therefore certainly worth the time and money to do so.

BEFORE SETTING OUT

Obtain the latest available weather forecast for the boating area. Where they can be received, the NOAA Weather Radio continuous broadcasts (VHF-FM) are the best way to keep informed of expected weather and sea conditions. If you hear on the radio that warnings are in effect, don't venture out on the water unless confident your boat can be navigated safely under forecast conditions of wind and sea.

WHILE AFLOAT

- Keep an eye out for the approach of dark, threatening clouds which may foretell a squall or thunderstorm.
- Check radio weather broadcasts periodically for latest forecasts and warnings.
- Heavy static on your AM radio may be an indication of nearby thunderstorm activity.

THUNDERSTORM WHEN AFLOAT

- Put on a life jacket.
- Stay below deck if possible.
- Keep away from metal objects that are not grounded to the boat's lightning protection system.

PISTOL LAUNCHED DEVICES

Pistol launched and hand-held parachute flares and meteors have many characteristics of a firearm and must be handled with caution. In some states they are considered a firearm and prohibited from use. Whenever a pistol or hand-held rocket propelled distress signal is used, the wind must be taken into account. In calm winds keep your arm at approximately 60° above the horizon with the wind at your back when firing the device. As the wind increases, increase the angle of the arm up to but no more than about 80° to 85°. No pyrotechnic device should be fired straight up or in such a direction that it may land on your boat or another boat or on land and cause a fire. *US Coast Guard*

Lightning Rods for Boating

Grounding a Boat Against Lightning

Place a metal rod at the highest point of the boat and run a No. 4 copper wire to a thin copper plate either attached to the side of the hull below the water line or dangling in the water. Without a lightning rod the lightning will spark around the boat looking for a conducting path to the water. Without a proper ground passengers can be killed and the boat sunk.

LIGHTNING KILLS BOATERS

Lightning kills people on large and small boats - lightning as it looks for a high point is more likely to strike passengers of boats with no mast - even canoes. Sailboats and motorboats should be grounded.

Salt water is a better conductor than freshwater so it would require a one foot metal rod. A freshwater boat needs a long metal strip along the length of the hull. Also ground a wire to the propeller.

If you have a lightning rod make SURE that it is well grounded. When lightning strikes a rod and there is no escape route it will side flash and this can be extremely dangerous to passengers. Note that an antenna on a boat can attract lightning - and should be grounded.

Even with a grounded lightning rod there can still be substantial damage due to excessive voltage striking the rod.

A lightning strike will usually damage the electronics on a larger craft even items as radios, cell phones and your GPS. Basically anything with a microprocessor can be damaged. Windshield wipers have microprocessors!!

Water Spout

HURRICANE

Hurricanes are enormous cyclonic storm systems covering thousands of square miles which usually develop in the tropical or subtropical latitudes during the summer and fall. To be a hurricane, the system must be producing winds of 64 knots or more. Less intense storms are designated tropical depressions or tropical storms. Each hurricane is, essentially, an organized system made up of hundreds of individual thunderstorms. The core of the hurricane is called the eye, an area of relatively benign weather several miles across surrounded by turmoil. All of the severe weather conditions produced by individual thunderstorms (heavy rain, hail, lightning, tornadoes, down bursts, etc.) are produced and magnified within the hurricane. Working together, such storms generate tremendous tidal surges which can decimate coastal areas.

GET OFF THE WATER

If you know a hurricane is approaching your area, prepare for the worst. Get off the open water and as far away from the storm as possible. If this is impossible, keep in mind that the **right front quadrant** of a hurricane usually, but not always produces the most violent weather. You may have little more than 24 hours advance notice to get your boat secured against the storm's full force. If your boat is easily transported, store it ashore, far from the danger of high water.

Follow these tips:

- If you must move your boat, first inspect the trailer to ensure it is in proper operating condition. Check tires (including spare), wheel bearings, tow hitch and lights.
- If you can, put your boat and trailer in a garage. If they must be left out, secure them to strong trees or a "deadman" anchor. Strip off everything that could be torn loose by a strong wind.
- Increase the weight of your trailered outboard boat by filling it with fresh water and leaving in the drain plug (inboard boats must be drained to avoid motor damage). Insert wood blocks between the trailer frame and the springs for extra support with the added weight.

IF BOAT IN THE WATER

- Berth at a dock.
- Anchor your boat in a protected harbor.
- Hurricane Holes are ideal locations to moor your boat during a hurricane.

NEVER STAY WITH BOAT

Your boat should be stripped of anything that can become loose during the storm. This would include unstepping the mast in sailboats. Boat documents, radios and other valuables should be removed from the vessel prior to the storm.

Securing Boat Before Storm

Anchor your boat in a protected harbor where the bottom can allow a good anchor hold. An advantage to anchoring is that the boat can more easily respond to wind and water changes without striking docks or other boats than when moored. Heavy and extra anchors are needed for this option and enough line should be on hand to allow a scope of at least 10:1 for each anchor.

Wind — Protected Harbor

Wind — Hurricane Hole

The boating section has information derived from the US Coast Guard & Metlife Publications.

Hurricane Holes are ideal locations to moor your boat during a hurricane. These are deep, narrow coves or inlets that are surrounded by a number of sturdy trees which block the wind and provide a tie-off for anchor lines. The best location for a hurricane hole is one far enough inland to avoid the most severe winds and tides, yet close enough to reach under short notice.

Hurricane Diana

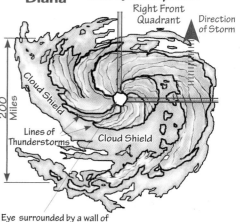

Usually the most violent weather in the right front quadrant.

Right Front Quadrant

Direction of Storm

200 Miles

Cloud Shield

Lines of Thunderstorms

Cloud Shield

Eye surrounded by a wall of thunderstorms (20 Miles Wide)

Securing Boat Before Storm

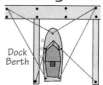

Dock Berth

Berth at a dock which has sturdy pilings and offers reasonable shelter from open water and storm surge. Double up all mooring lines but provide enough slack so your boat can rise with the higher tides. Cover all lines with chafe protectors (double neoprene garden hose cut along the side) at points where the line is likely to wear and put out extra fenders and fender boards (the more the better).

SUDDEN DOWNBURSTS

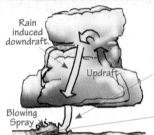

Rain induced downdraft.

Updraft

Evaporation enhanced downward speed.

Blowing Spray

Downbursts hit so rapidly that few signs may be available to alert boaters of their presence.

Blowing spray under or slightly ahead of a thunderstorm may be the only indicator.

Turn your craft with the bow facing into the wind, and "reef" your sails if you have them. These actions help minimize wind resistance.

No

Yes

REACTION TO DOWNBURST
- Turn your craft with the bow facing into the wind, and "reef" your sails if you have them. These actions help minimize wind resistance.
- Secure all loose objects and rigging on-deck, and make certain hatches or other openings are covered.
- Wear your life jacket, making sure it fits securely. Keep other lifesaving equipment readily accessible, including inflatable rafts and visual distress devices.

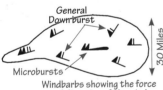

General Downburst

Microbursts

Windbarbs showing the force and direction of the wind.

After striking the ground, the microburst winds begin to spread out, eventually covering an area up to 30 - 40 miles across. Microbursts can still be embedded in the general down burst.

30 Miles

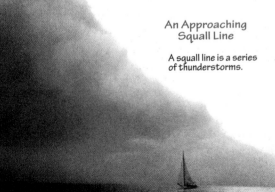

An Approaching Squall Line

A squall line is a series of thunderstorms.

DOWNBURSTS
- Winds may exceed 130 mph.
- Winds hit suddenly with little or no warning.
- Strongest winds affect a relatively small area.

FORMATION OF DOWNBURSTS
Down bursts can form within thunderstorms. Whenever a boater encounters a thunderstorm, a down burst is possible. This can be from an individual thunderstorm or a series of thunderstorms called a squall line. When a downburst first strikes the surface, it is often concentrated in an area less than three miles across. This is generally where the most extreme winds can be found. The term microburst is often used in describing this phase. After striking the ground, the winds begin to spread out, eventually covering an area up to 30 - 40 miles across. However, microbursts can still be embedded in the general down burst. Downbursts are usually short-lived high winds lasting only a few minutes. However, one thunderstorm can produce a series of these winds affecting a swath several miles long and lasting an hour or more.

Downbursts hit so rapidly that few signs may be available to alert boaters of their presence.

Blowing spray under or slightly ahead of a thunderstorm may be the only indicator. However, the best rule is to avoid all thunderstorms if possible. If not, expect and prepare for the worst whenever a thunderstorm is encountered.

CAUGHT IN A DOWNBURST
Boats caught on open water under these conditions can encounter a downburst without expecting it. Downbursts are generally short lived; lasting less than ten minutes. This fact makes predicting their occurrence almost an impossible task. The sudden loss of the sailing vessel "Pride of Baltimore" in the Atlantic near Puerto Rico in 1986 was attributed to a downburst wind. Witnesses claim that in less than two minutes, the ship was blown over, filled with water, and sank. Although this tragedy involved a larger sailing vessel on the open ocean, similar dangers have been experienced by vessels on inland or inshore waters. Thunderstorms can create several downbursts in succession, with varying degrees of intensity. A thunderstorm might even generate a combination of downbursts, water spouts, and tornados.

ABANDONING SHIP
- Prepare yourself to abandon the boat by: **Packing in a canvas duffel bag:** emergency flares, compass, emergency radio beacon, map of the area, water, and survival food. Tie the duffel bag with a rope to the raft or lifeboat.
  - Remain fully clothed and put on a life jacket. Clothing should include a wool sweater, heavy socks, and tie down hat.
  - Each person should attach a waterproof light or flare, knife, and whistle to his life jacket.
- *Do not launch the life raft unless there is imminent danger of sinking.* Do not inflate the life raft on the boat as it might get entangled with the deck gear or rigging. When the life raft is launched keep it tethered to the boat and climb into it. *Do not jump.* The first person in the raft should keep it away from the boat. Cut the tether only when everyone is aboard.
- If no life raft is available enter the water on the windward side of the boat. The untended boat can drift leeward endangering people in the water.
- Minimize movement in the water to keep body heat and assume the fetal position. *See First Aid Chapter: Drowning & Hypothermia.*

EMOTIONAL EFFECT
The panic reaction of members of the crew to abandoning ship can be totally unexpected and not in the character of the individual.
- A person may freeze, weep, scream for help, or fight for a place on the raft. He may become agitated, pale, tense, freeze up, or may stutter. Keep everyone busy and performing a function to avoid any irrational behavior.

ONCE ON THE RAFT
- A person may become delirious or behave dangerously to himself and others and might even suddenly attack other members.
- He might want to dive off the raft or "To go below for a cup of coffee."
- He might drink sea water or eat the rations on the raft. This person must be closely watched, talked to in a positive way or held in restraint if necessary.
- This initial reaction, to the stress, is a strained emotional attitude and speculation as to chances of survival. This problem can worsen into an intense preoccupation, moroseness, and withdrawal from the rest of the group with ideas of food and drink dominating thinking and dreaming.

SEA RESCUE
Remember that rescue at sea is a cooperative effort. Search-aircraft contact is limited by the visibility of survivors based on the availability of visual or electronic signaling devices. *Visual and electronic communications can be increased by using all available signaling devices (signal mirrors, radios, signal panels, dye marker, and other available devices) when an aircraft is in the area.*
A log should be maintained with a record of the navigator's last fix, time of ditching, names and physical condition of survivors, ration schedule, winds, weather, direction of swells, times of sunrise and sunset, and other navigation data.

DOWNBURST HAZARDS
- Extreme, sudden winds can tip a sailboat beyond its range of upright stability.
- Heavy seas that can capsize even powerboats.
- High winds that can blow equipment off the deck and cause persons on board to lose balance and fall overboard.

HOPELESSNESS IS DANGEROUS

It is important that the group help each other to maintain hope and a good group morale. Hopeless, once started, grows rapidly worse and harder to overcome. Treat any danger signs immediately by cheering up the group. Good humor can do much to lighten the tense grim moments which are certain to arise. Good morale reduces quarreling and potential pilferage of food and water. The group should have a leader, who is respected, as then they can follow orders.

DIVING UNDER A WAVE OR OIL SLICK

FUEL OIL CONTAMINATION

Swallowing fuel oil and salt water might produce vomiting and coughing from oil and water in the stomach and lungs. Eyes might be sore from the oil and salt water mixture. These problems will usually clear up. To clean the skin take a bath with a mild soap. Treat the eyes by applying some soft wax to the eyelids. Drink some warm milk with honey or sweet tea to help soothe the stomach. Get medical attention, especially if there are wounds.

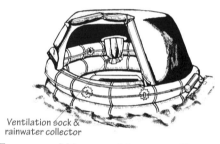

Ventilation sock & rainwater collector

TREADING WATER & HANGING FLOAT

Treading water and the hanging float are very important skills for water survival. They can be used while waiting for help to arrive and as resting positions when swimming to safety. The hanging float should not be used in cold water.

Sculling: Both the hanging float and treading water use sculling. This is a rhythmically controlled motion of the arms and hands to manipulate the water for upward thrust and keep the body vertically afloat. A common sculling action is the figure eight. With the fingers together and palms facing downward, draw a figure eight with each hand, pushing the water downward and outward during the motion. Keep the arms slightly bent in front of the chest. Use a minimum of effort to avoid excessive fatigue.

FLOAT STROKE (TREADING WATER)

Compared with the hanging float, treading water lets you maintain visibility and retain more body heat since your head is out of the water. However, it requires more physical exertion. To tread water, use the following procedure.

SWIMMING STROKE (HANGING FLOAT)

Once you master the hanging float, you will have control of yourself in the water. You will realize how buoyant you are with your lungs fully inflated and your body relaxed. To do the hanging float, use the following procedure.

ABANDONING SHIP

DROWN PROOFING

Every camper or boater should know and have practiced drown proofing. Swimming in a pool is quite different from choppy lake water where a hundred feet can feel like a major challenge. Be prepared psychologically to face the unknown element of open water.

FLOAT STROKE

Step 1
- Take a breath and immediately lay your head forward with chin on chest.
- Relax body with hands dangling
- Rest with back of your head protruding above the water.

Step 2
- Before air is needed gradually cross arms in front of head.
- Smoothly raise one knee toward chest while extending foot forward. At the same time extending the second foot behind you (Scissor movement). Remain vertical.

Step 3
- Raise head with chin in the water.
- Exhale though the nose while raising the head.

Step 4
- Complete exhaling.
- Open mouth to inhale while gently sweeping palms outward and stepping downwards in the water, bringing legs together. This helps keep mouth above the water while inhaling. A complete air change is not required.

Step 5
- Inhale completed, close mouth, and drop head forward toward the knees.
- Relax, and repeat Step 1.

All movements should be smooth.
Problems That Might Occur:

Sink a few feet below surface: Arms have not been dropped after head returned into water.
Chest feels tight under the water: Remaining under water between breaths too long or not exhaling enough.
Little water entering mouth, spurt it out under water between pursed lips.

A person who is relaxed, has lungs filled with air, and no food in the stomach will float on the water. If you do not panic, you cannot sink. Men will usually float vertically and women with a slight forward angle due to their heavier hips. You require some movement, as illustrated, as the tip of your head will only protrude above the water when floating and you will not be able to breathe.

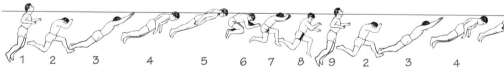

SWIMMING STROKE

Step 1
- Inhale and sink vertically.
- As head sinks, push down gently with your hands to stop any tendency to sink too deep.

Step 2
- Tilt head to a facedown position.
- Raise hands to forehead.
- Open-scissor legs raising the rear foot as high as possible.
- This movement will swing body into a horizontal position

Step 3
- Gradually raise arms, with hands together, forward toward the surface.
- When arms are fully extended make a scissors kick with legs.

Step 4
- While feet come together after kicking, slowly sweep arms outward and back reaching the thighs.

Step 5
- While floating forward and upward, keep hands extended to the thighs.
- All the while exhaling through the nose through Steps 5, 6, and 7.

Step 6
- To breathe, return to the vertical position by raising the back, bringing both knees toward chest, and lifting hands toward the head.

Step 7
- To reach the vertical, extend a leg in front while bringing the second foreword. At the same time raise arms in front of head with the forearms together and palms facing out.

Step 8
- Prepare to inhale.
- Open-scissor legs to propel body upward.
- Start raising head. Only raise head when body is vertical.

Step 9
- Open mouth to inhale while gently sweeping palms outward and stepping downwards in the water. This is done to help keep the mouth above the water while inhaling. Do not over-exert yourself as a complete air change is not required.

Source: Joseph P. Blank, "Nobody Needs to Drown" Everywoman's Family Circle, June 1960

133

HELP
Body Position

Huddling

HELP BODY POSITION

Remaining still and assuming the fetal position, or heat escape lessening posture; will increase the survival time. About 50% of body heat is lost from the head. It is therefore important to keep the head out of the water. Other areas of high heat loss are the neck, the sides, and the groin.

HUDDLING

If there are several survivors in the water, huddle close, side to side in a circle, and body heat will be preserved.

SURVIVAL TIMES

Situation No Flotation		Predicted Survival Time (Hours)
	Drown-proofing	1.5
	Treading Water	2.0
With Flotation		
	Swimming	2.0
	Holding Still	2.7
	HELP	4.0
Huddle		4.0

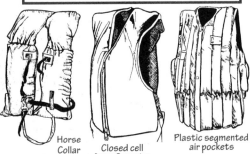

Horse Collar

Closed cell foam flotation

Plastic segmented air pockets

USING A LIFE PRESERVER

Swimming Without a Life Preserver

A survivor who knows how to relax in the water is in little danger of drowning, especially in saltwater, where the body is of lower density than the water. Trapped air in clothing will help buoy the survivor in the water.

If in the water for long periods, the survivor will have to rest from treading water. The survivor may best do this by floating on the back. If this is not possible, the following techniques should be used: Rest erect in the water and inhale; put the head face-down in the water and stroke with the arms; rest in this face-down position until there is a need to breathe again; raise the head and exhale; support the body by kicking arms and legs and inhaling; then repeat the cycle.

Swimming With a Life Preserver

The bulkiness of clothing, equipment, and (or) any personal injuries will require the immediate need for flotation.

- Proper inflation of the life preserver must be, preferably, done before entering the water. Limited swimming may be done with the life preserver inflated by cupping the hands and taking strong strokes deep into the water. The life preserver may be slightly deflated to permit better arm movement.
- The backstroke should be used to conserve energy when traveling long distances. If aiding an injured or unconscious person, the side-stroke may have to be used. When approaching an object, it is best to use the breaststroke. If a group must swim, they should try to have the strongest swimmer in the lead, with any injured persons intermingled within the group. It is best to swim in single file.

USING A RAFT

In an ocean disaster, rafts provide personal and psychological protection, mode of travel, and a limited protection against the elements.

One-Man Survival Raft

The one-man raft has a main cell inflation. If the CO_2 bottle should malfunction and not inflate the raft, or if the raft develops a leak, it can be inflated orally. The spray shield acts as a shelter from the cold, wind, and water. In some cases, this shield serves as insulation. The insulated bottom plays a significant role in the survivor's protection from hypothermia by limiting the conduction of the cold through the bottom of the raft.

- Travel is more effective made by deflating the raft to take advantage of the wind or current.
- The spray shield can be used as a sail, while the ballast buckets serve to increase raft drag in the water.
- A sea anchor may be used to control the speed and direction of the raft. *The primary purpose of the sea anchor is to stabilize the raft.*
- The raft may hit the water upside down, but may be righted by approaching the bottle side and flipping it over. The spray shield must be in the raft to expose the boarding handles.
- If the survivor has an arm injury, boarding is best done by turning the back to the small end of the raft, pushing the raft under the buttocks, and lying back. Another method of boarding is to push down on the small end until one knee is inside, and lie forward.
- In rough seas, it may be easier for the survivor to grasp the small end of the raft and, in a prone position, kick and pull into the raft. Once in and lying face down, the sea anchor should be deployed and adjusted. To sit upright in the raft, one side of the seat kit might have to be disconnected, and the survivor should roll to that side. The spray shield is then adjusted. The spray shield is designed to help keep the survivor dry and warm in cold oceans, and protect them from the sun in the hot climates.

1

2

Boarding a Raft

3

BUYING A LIFE JACKET

Life Jackets (PFD: Personal Flotation Devices) are the most important accessories worn on boating, fishing and water skiing trips.

- Life jackets are available in different US Coast Guard Approval Types, and not all life jackets are suitable for all activities. Make sure it's comfortable and the right type.
- Get a bright color - ORANGE.
- Make sure that it is for your weight and height.
- Everyone has their personal life jacket - with their name on it.
- Check the child jacket's fit by gently pulling up on the life jackets' shoulders. The child's chins and ears should not slip through the neck holes.

MAINTAINING LIFE JACKET

- Try life jacket at the start of every boating season. Never alter it to make it fit. Check its buoyancy in shallow water first before venturing far from shore.
- Check for rips, holes and tears and make sure straps and hardware are in place and secure.
- Do not keep a life jacket in the sun for long periods. Sunlight and heat can weaken some synthetic fabrics and can degrade the buoyancy material.
- If your boat is 16 feet or longer (excluding canoes and kayaks), you must also have a throwable flotation device.

1 Wind

2 Wind

3

4 Wind

Seven-Man Raft

A seven-man raft is found on some multiplace aircraft. It can also be in an air-carried survival drop kit. This type of raft may inflate upside down and may, therefore, require the survivor to right the raft before boarding. Always work from the bottle side to prevent injury if the raft turns over. Facing into the wind provides additional assistance in righting the raft. The handles on the bottom are pulled on to right the raft. The boarding ladder is used to board if someone assists in holding down the opposite side. If no assistance is available, the survivor should again work from the bottle side with the wind at the back to help hold down the raft. The survivor should separate the life preserver, grasp an oarlock and boarding handle, kick the legs to get the body prone on the water, and then kick and pull into the raft. If the survivor is weak or injured, the raft may be partially deflated to make boarding easier.

SURVIVAL RAFT

Adrift at Sea

Bottle side of raft.

Wind

Righting Upside-Down Raft

One- Man Raft Spray Shield Inflated

Plane Crash Survivors

First Consideration: Survivors should stay upwind and clear of the aircraft (out of fuel-covered waters), but in the vicinity of the crash until the aircraft sinks. A search for survivors is usually activated around the entire area of and near the crash site. Missing personnel may be unconscious and floating low in the water.

Rescuing Air Crew Members

The best technique for rescuing air crew members from the water is to *throw them a line with a life preserver attached*. The second is to send a swimmer (rescuer) from the raft with a line, using a flotation device that will support the weight of a rescuer. This will help to conserve energy while recovering the survivor. The *least acceptable technique* is to send an attached swimmer without floatable devices to retrieve a survivor. In all cases, the rescuer should wear a life preserver. The strength of a person in a state of panic in the water should not be underestimated. A careful approach can prevent injury to the rescuer. When the rescuer is approaching a survivor in trouble from behind, there is little danger of being kicked, scratched or grabbed. The rescuer should swim to a point directly behind the survivor and grasp the backstrap of the life preserver. A sidestroke may then be used to drag the survivor to the raft.

Someone Drowning?

- If the victim is within throwing distance, throw a floatable object to them. This includes a life jacket, kick board or even an empty gallon jug.
- If the victim is within reaching distance, assist them by extending something long, such as a rope, pole, ring buoy or a tree branch.
- If you must enter the water to assist someone, take a flotation device large enough to carry two adults to safety. Keep the device between you and the person in distress; even a child can put an adult at risk in deep water.

Signal & Navigation Equipment

Prepare all available signaling equipment for immediate use. Compasses, watches, matches, and lighters will become worthless unless they are kept dry.

Sun Protection

All areas of the body should be protected from the sun. Precautions should be taken to prevent sunburn on the eyelids, under the chin, and on the backs of the ears. Sunburn cream and Chapstick will protect these areas.

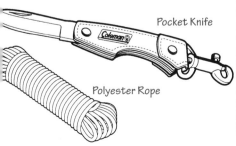

Pocket Knife

Polyester Rope

Life Raft Survival

- Secure gear, as any equipment not lashed down is liable to be lost.
- Dry clothing as soon as possible. If feet swell, remove your shoes but keep feet covered. A sunburn on top of the feet is very painful and can become infected.
- Rig a sail or covering against the sun's rays. Minimize direct exposure to the sun. Sunlight will reflect from the water during the day.
- Take inventory of provisions and store them where they will be safe. Keep the food cool if required. Immediately ration food and water. Avoid eating and minimize drinking during the first 24 hours.
- All movements should be slow and deliberate to conserve energy and to avoid perspiring.
- Save all clothing as the nights might be cold and clothing can be used to stay warm, if soaked.
- Prepare to signal any airplane or passing boat by having easy access to signal mirrors, marking dyes, flares, and smoke signals.

Adrift: Short Time

Survivors adrift in lifeboats or rafts need warmth, cover from the sun and ocean spray, dry clothing, water, and some food. Upon rescue, survivors who had been immersed for a short time in relatively warm water should be given a warm bath and dry clothing.

Adrift: Many Days

Upon rescue, if survivors experienced a shortage of food and water, they will be weak, demoralized, and at some stage of hypothermia. Treat for hypothermia if required (see First Aid Chapter). Give them warm drinks which they should not drink too fast as they might vomit. Food in the form of soup and bread should be given sparingly and should be easy to digest.

Seasickness

- A slight feeling of listlessness with a headache.
- A dry mouth.
- Sense of nausea in the stomach.
- Repeated vomiting due to the continual motion of a small boat. It might also have been caused by having swallowed oil or salt water. After severe vomiting lie down and keep warm.
- Feeling of wretchedness and mental depression.

Motion sickness is caused by the movement of the liquids in the inner ear that confuse the balance sensory devices producing a loss of balance and gastrointestinal disturbances. A victim should try to drink as much as possible (but not alcohol), and should eat a little at frequent intervals. See a doctor who can prescribe seasickness tablet and use them before it occurs.

Survival Planning

The leader should calmly analyze the situation and plan a course of action, to include duty assignments (watch duty, procuring and rationing food & water, etc.). Everyone, except those who are badly injured or completely exhausted, are expected to *perform watch duty, which should not exceed 2 hours*. The individual on watch should be looking for signs of land, passing vessels or aircraft, wreckage, seaweed, schools of fish, birds, and signs of chafing or leaking of the raft. Food and water should be conserved by saving energy. Remain calm. Maintaining a sense of humor will help keep morale high.

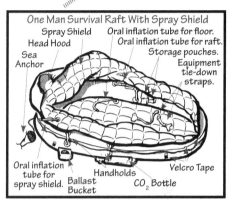

One Man Survival Raft With Spray Shield

Spray Shield
Head Hood
Sea Anchor
Oral inflation tube for floor.
Oral inflation tube for raft.
Storage pouches.
Equipment tie-down straps.
Oral inflation tube for spray shield.
Ballast Bucket
Handholds
CO_2 Bottle
Velcro Tape

Manual Inflation of Raft

Manual inflation can be done by using the pump to keep buoyancy chambers and cross-seat firm, but *the raft should not be over-inflated*. The buoyancy chambers and cross-seat should be rounded but not drum-tight. Hot air expands, so on hot days, some air may be released, while air may be added on cold days.

Raft Emergency Kit
Items placed in a duffel bag attached to the raft...

- First aid kit.
- Compass with cord.
- Waterproof matches in match case.
- Needle and thread and safety pins, razor blades.
- Cord (10 - 20 feet), fishing line hooks.
- Flares. Whistle with cord.
- Small stove.
- Tube tent for shelter, sail and catching water.
- Signal mirror with cord or sheet of shiny metal.
- Knife with cord (lanyard). • Waterproof plastic bags.
- High energy food. Tea bags, broth cubes.
- Purifying tablets and water filter.
- Water bottle.
- Emergency blanket (poncho).
- Small pot to catch water and drinking.

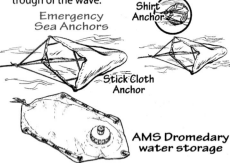

Crest — Direction of Raft → Crest

Trough

Sea Anchor

Sea Anchor Closed
When closed it will pull raft in the direction of the current.

Sea Anchor Open
When open the raft will remain stationary.

SEA ANCHOR

The sea anchor can be adjusted to either act as a drag by slowing down the rate of travel with the current, or as a means of traveling with the current. This is done by opening or closing the apex of the sea anchor.

Opened: The sea anchor will act as a drag, and one will stay in the general area.

Closed: When the sea anchor is closed, it will form a pocket for the current to strike and propel the raft in the direction of the current.

Adjust Cord Length: The sea anchor cord length should be adjusted so that when the raft is on the crest of a wave, the sea anchor is in the trough of the wave.

Emergency Sea Anchors

Shirt Anchor

Stick Cloth Anchor

AMS Dromedary water storage

THIRST

Dry mouth: A common problem which can be relieved by rinsing your mouth with drinking water. You can suck a button or a piece of metal such as a coin. You can chew gum or grease the inside of the mouth with butter or fat.

Urination problems: Urination will be dark and possibly thick as not much water is being consumed. If there is difficulty in passing urine, dangle your hand in the sea. This might be of some help.

LIFEBOAT & RAFT AILMENTS
Ailments can develop because of exposure to saltwater, wind, sun, heat and cold, and shortage of water.

SALT WATER PROBLEMS

Cracking skin: Skin gets covered with a fine layer of salt from salt water spray. To reduce this problem cover your skin with suntan lotion or soft paraffin wax. If exposed to direct sunlight do not use skin oils such as baby oil or butter as you might get a severe sunburn.

Salt water boils: Prolonged salt water spray exposure might lead to salt water boils. Do not squeeze or prick them. Do not remove excess liquid from boils that burst. Bad-looking boils should be covered with a dressing.

SUN & WIND EXPOSURE

Cracked and parched lips: These should be smeared with soft paraffin.

Cracked skin: Due to dryness from exposure to the sun, winds, salt water or washing in cold weather without adequate drying of the skin, will cause cracks on the backs of the hands, the feet, lips, or ears. There is often much irritation and pain. Can be helped by rubbing soft paraffin wax on the skin.

Eye inflammation: Caused by sunburn, wind, fuel oil contamination, or sun glare. Apply soft paraffin wax to the upper and lower eyelids.

Inuit sunglasses: Make some emergency slit sunglasses. These sunglasses will dramatically reduce the intensity of the sun's glare, the salt spray settling in the sensitive eye area, and reduce the drying action of the wind. Bandage eyes if painful and bloodshot.

OTHER PROBLEMS

Constipation: Bowel movements are limited because of the lack of food. Do not use laxatives.

Swollen legs: Swollen legs are common and will clear up after a few days on land.

Collecting drinking water from rain water.

DEBRIS & SALVAGE

All debris from the aircraft should be inspected and salvaged (rations, canteens, thermoses and other containers, parachutes, seat cushions, extra clothing, maps, etc.). Secure equipment to the raft to prevent loss. *Special precautions should be taken with flashlights and signaling equipment to keep them dry so they will function when needed.*

Check Raft

Rafts should be checked for inflation. Leaks and points of possible chafing should be repaired, as required. The raft repair plugs should be attached to the raft for easy access as soon as possible. All water should be removed from inside the raft. Care should be taken to avoid snagging the raft on shoes or sharp objects. *Placing the sea anchor out will slow the rate of drift.* If there is more than one raft, they should be connected with at least 25 feet of line. The lifeline attached to the outer periphery of the raft is to be used for the connection. Donning the anti-exposure suit is essential in cold climates. Erecting windbreaks, spray shields, and canopies will protect survivors from the elements. Survivors should huddle together and exercise regularly to maintain body heat.

Monitor Physical Condition

Monitoring the physical condition and administering first aid to survivors is essential. If available, seasickness pills will help prevent vomiting and the resulting dehydration.

DANGERS OF CORAL
Do not deploy a sea anchor when traveling through coral or near the coast.

Coral is normally found in warm waters along the shores. There are many different types of coral. They should be avoided since all can destroy a raft or severely injure you. It is best to stay in the raft when coral is encountered. If you must wade to shore, foot gear and pants should be worn for protection. Moving slowly and watching every step may prevent serious injuries. Coral does not exist where freshwater enters the sea.

DRINKING WATER

• Drinking sea water reduces survival time.

• The lack of drinking water causes dehydration which results in lassitude, loss of appetite (digestion requires water), drowsiness, nausea, and delirium. The senses, such as hearing and sight, are affected. A 25% loss of body fluids usually causes death. At a 15% loss of body fluids the victim will break down and drink salt water.

RED TIDE

A "red tide" occurs when either natural or human factors cause a rapid increase in the production of one-celled organisms (dinoflagellates), which ordinarily grow in water rich in nitrogen and phosphorus. These destructive red tides, often resulting in what is known as paralytic shellfish poisoning, have occurred since biblical times but are becoming much more prevalent today. Sewage effluent and runoff from farms and lawns contain nitrogen and phosphorus. The dinoflagellates consume the nitrogen and phosphorus, when added to the oceans, and then reproduce or "bloom" profusely. They spread across the water like a carpet, absorbing oxygen and shutting off sunlight from plants. When these organisms die and decay, they absorb more oxygen, literally suffocating marine life.

The insignificance of men on a raft during a storm at sea.

ENCOUNTERING SHIPS

Ships can be a welcome sight to a survivor, but they can also be a hazard. Since the raft is a small object in a very large sea, the survivor must constantly be aware that at night or during inclement weather, the raft will be difficult to see and could be struck by a large ship.

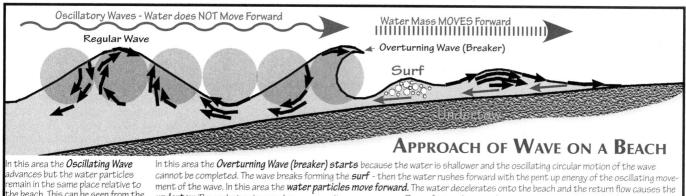

Oscillatory Waves - Water does NOT Move Forward

Regular Wave

Water Mass MOVES Forward

← Overturning Wave (Breaker)

Surf

Undertow

APPROACH OF WAVE ON A BEACH

In this area the *Oscillating Wave* advances but the water particles remain in the same place relative to the beach. This can be seen from the circular water particle movements.

In this area the *Overturning Wave (breaker) starts* because the water is shallower and the oscillating circular motion of the wave cannot be completed. The wave breaks forming the **surf** - then the water rushes forward with the pent up energy of the oscillating movement of the wave. In this area the **water particles move forward**. The water decelerates onto the beach and the return flow causes the **undertow**. The undertow is very dangerous as it can sweep you off your feet and you can be sweep out to sea. It is difficult to emerge from the undertow as the incoming water is coming in the opposite direction.

SAILING RAFT INTO THE WIND

Rafts are not equipped with keels, so they cannot be sailed into the wind. All rafts can be sailed downwind and multiplace rafts, due to the weight of the occupants, can be successfully sailed 10° off from the direction of the wind. *An attempt to sail the raft should not be made unless land is near.*

If the decision to sail is made and the wind is blowing toward a desired destination, fully inflate the raft, sit high, take in the sea anchor, rig a sail, and use an oar as a rudder, as shown in figure.

SAILING MULTIPLACE RAFT

In a multiplace raft, a square sail can be erected in the bow using oars, with their extensions as the mast and crossbar. A waterproof tarpaulin or parachute material can be used for the sail. If the raft has no regular mast socket and step, the mast can be erected by tying it securely to the front cross-seat, using braces. *The bottom of the mast must be padded to prevent it from chafing or punching a hole through the floor, whether or not a socket is provided.* The heel of a shoe, with the toe wedged under the seat, makes a good improvised mast step. *The corners of the lower edge of the sail should not be secured.* The lines attached to the corners are held with the hands so a gust of wind will not rip the sail, break the mast, or capsize the raft. Every precaution must be taken to prevent the raft from turning over. *In rough weather, the sea anchor is kept out and away from the bow. The passengers should sit low in the raft, with their weight distributed to hold the upwind side down. They should also avoid sitting on the sides of the raft or standing up to prevent falling out. Sudden movements (without warning the other passengers) should be avoided.* When the sea anchor is not in use, it should be tied to the raft and stowed in such a manner that it will hold immediately if the raft capsizes.

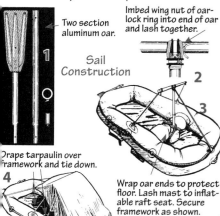

Two section aluminum oar.

Imbed wing nut of oar-lock ring into end of oar and lash together.

Sail Construction

1

2

3

Drape tarpaulin over framework and tie down.

4

Wrap oar ends to protect floor. Lash mast to inflatable raft seat. Secure framework as shown.

METHODS OF LANDING

SWIMMING ASHORE

This is a most difficult decision. It depends on many things. Some good swimmers have been able to swim 1500 yards in 50°F water before being overcome by hypothermia. Others have not been able to swim 100 yards. Furthermore, distances on the water are very deceptive. In most instances, staying with the raft is the best course of action. If the decision is made to swim, a life preserver or other flotation aid should be used. Shoes and at least one thickness of clothing should be worn. The side-stroke or breast-stroke will help conserve strength.

- If surf is moderate ride in on the back of a small wave by swimming forward with it, and making a shallow dive to end the ride just before the wave breaks. Stay in the trough between waves in high surf, facing the seaward wave and submerging when the wave approaches. After the wave passes you should work shoreward in the next trough.
- If caught in the undertow of a large wave, push off the bottom, swim to the surface, and proceed shoreward. A place where the waves rush up onto the rocks should be selected if it is necessary to land on rocky shores, but avoid places where the waves explode with a high, white spray. After selecting the landing point advance behind large wave into the breakers. Face shoreward and take a sitting position with the feet in front, 2 or 3 feet lower than the head, so that your knees are bent and the feet will absorb shocks when landing or striking submerged boulders or reefs. If the shore is not reached the first time, swim with hands and arms only. As the next wave approaches, the sitting position with the feet forward should be repeated until a landing is made.
- Water is quieter in the lee of a heavy growth of seaweed. This growth can be very helpful. Crawl over the top of the vegetation by grasping it with overhand movements.
- A rocky reef should be crossed in the same way as landing on a rocky shore. The feet should be close together with knees slightly bent in a relaxed sitting posture to cushion blows against coral.

REEF FISH

You will usually encounter reef fish during the landing process - *so you should avoid stepping on them*. They may also be caught while fishing. Watch your feet, and fingers in the water.

RAFTING ASHORE

In most cases, the one-man raft can be used to make a shore landing with no danger. Going ashore in strong surf is dangerous. The time should be taken to sail around and look for a sloping beach where the surf is gentle. The landing point should be carefully selected. Landing when the sun is low and straight in front of you is not recommended. Look for gaps in the surf line and head for them, while avoiding coral reefs and rocky cliffs. Reefs don't grow near the mouths of freshwater streams.

Avoid rip currents or strong tidal currents, which may carry the raft far out to sea.

When going through surf:

- Take down the mast.
- Don clothing and shoes to avoid injuries.
- Adjust and fasten life preserver.
- Stow equipment.
- Use paddles to maintain control.
- Ensure the sea anchor is deployed to help prevent the sea from throwing the stern of the raft around and capsizing it.

The sea anchor should not be deployed when traveling through coral.

- In medium surf with no wind, *keep the raft from passing over a wave so rapidly that it drops suddenly after topping the crest*. If the raft turns over in the surf, every effort should be made to grab hold of it.
- Ride the crest of a large wave as the raft nears the beach, staying inside until it has grounded. *If there is a choice, a night landing should not be attempted.* If people are seen, it might be advantageous to wait for assistance.

SEA ICE LANDINGS

Sea-ice landings should only be made on large, stable floes. *Icebergs, small floes, and disintegrating floes could cause serious problems.* The edge of the ice can cut, and the raft can become deflated. Use paddles and hands to keep the raft away from the sharp edges of the iceberg. The raft should be stored a considerable distance from the ice edge. It should be fully inflated and ready for use in case the floe breaks up. Make sure that it is well attached or it might be blown away.

Inuit umiaq skin covered sail boat.

DANGERS OF RIP CURRENTS

Water Height Difference

There is a difference of water height that occurs, when waves break over a sandbar, between the water accumulating behind the sandbar and the channel between the sandbars (where waves break nearer to the shore and water does not accumulate at the same time). So the higher level water behind the sand bar will flow to the lower level water in the narrow channel between the sandbars. This water flow is the rip current.

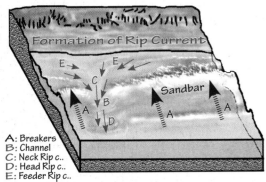

Formation of Rip Current

Sandbar

A: Breakers
B: Channel
C: Neck Rip c..
D: Head Rip c..
E: Feeder Rip c..

RIP CURRENTS NO SHORE OBSTRUCTION

Even when there are no near shore obstructions it is possible that rip currents can occur. Waves breaking on an unobstructed shore bring water to the shore, the accumulated water has to return to sea, and this might, under certain circumstances (possibly random), create a circulation pattern that forms a rip current along the shore.

Swim out of the current in a direction following the shoreline. When out of the current, swim towards shore.

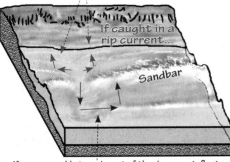

If caught in a rip current...

Sandbar

If you are unable to swim out of the rip current, float or calmly tread water. When out of the current, swim towards shore.

If caught in a rip current, remain calm to conserve energy and think clearly.

Don't fight the current. Swim out of the current in a direction following the shoreline. When out of the current, swim towards shore.

If you are unable to swim out of the rip current, float or calmly tread water. When out of the current, swim towards shore.

Lifeboat in the Surf

RIP CURRENTS

- Rip currents can be formed by the returning water of waves or tides when this returning water is channeled through a confined area. As a low area between sandbars, between coral reefs on an atoll, near jetties and piers, or between rock outcrops.
- The speed of rip currents is typically 1-2 feet per second but can be as high as 8 feet per second. Rip currents can sweep even the strongest swimmer out to sea. Usually rip currents are slow but can cause major problems with certain tide or/and storm conditions.
- Strong rip currents can occur and disappear within minutes.
- Strength and speed of a rip current usually increases as wave height increases and wave period becomes longer. This is due to the fact that increased wave height will let more water over the obstruction. With a longer wave period the water accumulated behind the barrier has more time to withdraw through the drainage path. A longer wave period also means that the trough of the wave will be lower and so the water behind the barrier will drain to a lower level.
- Size of rip currents. Shore width: 20-100 feet. Offshore length: 100's of feet. Outside of the surf zone they are usually on the surface.
- Rip current velocities, usually, increase as water levels (tide elevation) decrease. This is because, with lower water levels, the majority of returning water cannot flow over the obstruction but has to flow through the channel.
- People are not pulled under the water by rip currents – but pulled away from shore.
- People caught in a rip current drown because they cannot stay afloat to swim back to shore. They panic, get exhausted, and drown.
- Rip currents can occur at any beach with breaking waves – even on lakes. Minor rip currents occur on most beaches and some might become dangerous. This is why you should always be mentally prepared – especially if you see a change in wave patterns – even a change in wind direction (which might change the wave patterns).
- Water depths can increase, within minutes, in rip current channels. Waders can be surprised, by this, and swept off their feet and carried out to sea by a rip current.

Flotation Crates

TIDES

The forces that generate tides are a result of the gravitational attraction between the earth, the sun, and the moon and the centrifugal force due to the relative motions of the moon around the earth, and the earth around the sun.

There are two lunar and two solar high earth tides about each day. The period of the solar tide is exactly 12.00 hours, while the period of the lunar tide is slightly longer, 12.42 hours, due to the moon's revolution around the earth every 27 days. The inclination of the earth's spin axis to the plane of the moon's revolution about the earth and the earth's revolution about the sun creates in addition weaker tides with periods of roughly 1 day. One of the world's largest tides exists in the Bay of Fundy (maximum high tide 36-45 feet). The Bay of Fundy is next to the Bay of Main.

IDENTIFY RIP CURRENTS

Polarized sunglasses makes it easier to see a rip current.

Look for:
- Channel of churning, choppy water
- Area having a notable difference in color
- Line of foam, seaweed, or debris moving steadily seaward
- Break in the incoming wave pattern

Note: None, one, or more of these may indicate the presence of rip currents. Rip currents are often not readily or easily identifiable to the average beachgoer. For your safety, be aware of this major surf zone hazard.

AVOID & SURVIVE RIP CURRENTS
Learn how to swim!
- Never swim alone.
- Be cautious at all times, especially when swimming at unguarded beaches. Whenever possible, swim at a lifeguard protected beach.
- If caught in a rip current, remain calm to conserve energy and think clearly.
- Don't fight the current. Swim out of the current in a direction following the shoreline. When out of the current, swim towards shore.
- If you are unable to swim out of the rip current, float or calmly tread water. When out of the current, swim towards shore.
- If you are still unable to reach shore, draw attention to yourself: face the shore, wave your arms, and yell for help.
- If you see someone in trouble, get help from a lifeguard. Throw the rip current victim something that floats and yell instructions on how to escape. Remember, many people drown while trying to save someone else from a rip current.

Rip Tide
This is not a rip current. The rip tide is caused by the rise and fall of a tide when it moves through a constricted area as an inlet, the mouths of an estuary, or a harbor.

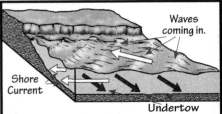

Waves coming in.

Shore Current

Undertow

UNDERTOW
This is the return flow of a wave along a sandy bottom. This water returns, from the beach, as a thin layer of water on the ocean bed but is pushed back onto the beach by the next incoming wave. Small children might be swept off their feet by an undertow but it does not pull you out to sea.

RAFTING: POLAR REGIONS

Iceberg that was hit by the Titanic.
Note scratch marks near the top of the iceberg.

FINDING WAY IN POLAR REGIONS

Use the following to confirm magnetic compass readings due to the proximity of the Magnetic North Pole. *See the Compass Chapter for the magnetic declinations etc.*

- Reflections in the sky.
- Direction of prevailing wind.
- Movement of clouds.
- Direction of sun and shadows.

LANDING ON ICE OR ICE FLOWS

Try to land on large stable ice slabs. If landing on small flows, icebergs and disintegrating flows, you might encounter serious problems:

- Ice can cut the raft. Use the paddle to keep it away from sharp edges.
- Store raft away from the ice's edge, keep it inflated and ready for use, and weigh it down as it might be blown away by the wind.

SEA ICE & NAVIGATION

- Bay ice is smooth, low, and flat, and can give you an indication as to the distance from a bay.
- Pieces of ice close together like a jigsaw puzzle indicate that land is near.
- The edges of the ice being sharp and fresh will indicate a closeness to shore. If the edges are rounded and the pieces far apart will indicate that the shore is at some distance.
- To get fresh water in an ice flow area, cut a piece of ice from the upper part of an older larger flow. The salt will have leached out.
- In polar regions, the wind temperature, if warmer than surroundings, will indicate the direction of water. A sudden drop in temperature, without a change in direction, might indicate the presence of an iceberg.

SEA ICE

Ice Type	Old Sea Ice	New Sea Ice
Color	Bluish or blackish	Milky or gray
Brittleness	Shatters easily	Does not break easily
Features	Rounded corners	Sharp corners
Taste	Relatively salt free	Tastes extremely salty

WATER SURVIVAL AT SEA

- Water temperatures below 68°F (20°C) can cause hypothermia if the body is not protected. Hypothermia will occur after 4 hours with limited clothing. It will occur in 8 hours if clothed. At 57°F (15°C) unclothed survival time is approximately 2 hours.
- If water is cold keep head out of the water and stay immobile to conserve heat. Drown proofing is dangerous in cold water. Drown proofing has a 50% higher cooling rate than treading water so drown proofing shortens survival time.
- Protect neck, sides of chest, and groin with insulation or wool clothing. These areas have high heat loss. Raise knees and wrap arms across the chest.

This painting "The Raft of the Medusa," by Gericault, records a shipwreck that at the time caused a wide-spread feeling of disgust and horror.

It shows the will of survival, in the most desperate situation, and the reaction and interaction of people in these circumstances.

A rafting sea survival drama.

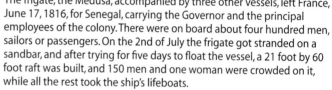

THE RAFT OF THE MEDUSA

The frigate, the Medusa, accompanied by three other vessels, left France, June 17, 1816, for Senegal, carrying the Governor and the principal employees of the colony. There were on board about four hundred men, sailors or passengers. On the 2nd of July the frigate got stranded on a sandbar, and after trying for five days to float the vessel, a 21 foot by 60 foot raft was built, and 150 men and one woman were crowded on it, while all the rest took the ship's lifeboats.

As supplies, all they had were 75 pounds of biscuits.

Soon after, the lifeboats cut the ropes by which they were towing the raft, and left it floating in the middle of the ocean. Then, hunger and thirst affected the abandoned people which lead to the settling of accounts, people being thrown overboard, and cannibalism. Finally, after thirteen days of agony, the Argus, one ship of the fleet, rescued the fifteen remaining starving and dehydrated men left on the raft.

M. Correard, who survived to write an account of the shipwreck, in the painting stands with his right arm stretched out, pointing to the Argus, and calling to the surgeon Savigny, who supports himself against the mast, and to the sailors who are near him, that help is at hand. Sailors, mounted on a barrel at the end of the raft, wave their handkerchiefs in sign of distress, while their companions, among whom is the naval cadet Condin, drag themselves toward them. At the left, an old man holds his dying son on his knees. Behind him a passenger, overcome with despair, tears his hair, while many dead bodies are lying on the raft.

COLD WATER EXPOSURE

Life-Expectancy Times

Temperature of Water	Time
70°- 60°	12 hours
60°- 50°	6 hours
50°- 40°	1 hour
40° - below	less than l hour

NOTE: These times may be increased with the wearing of an anti-exposure suit.

The best protection for a survivor against the effects of cold water is to get into the life raft, stay dry, and insulate the body from the cold surface of the bottom of the life raft. If this is not possible, wearing the anti-exposure suit will extend a survivor's life expectancy considerably. It's important to keep the head and neck out of the water and well insulated from the cold-water effects when the temperature is below 66°F. The wearing of life preservers increases the predicted survival time just as the body position in the water increases the probability of survival. The following table shows predicted survival times for an average person in 50°F water:

Other ailments of exposure are Heat exposure, Frostbite, Hypothermia, Trench Foot, etc.

PHYSICAL CONSIDERATIONS
Hypothermia

The greatest problem a survivor is faced with when submerged in cold water is death due to hypothermia. When a survivor is immersed in cold water, hypothermia occurs rapidly due to the decreased insulating quality of wet clothing and the fact that water displaces the layer of still air that normally surrounds the body.

Water causes a rate of heat exchange approximately 25 times greater than air at the same temperature.

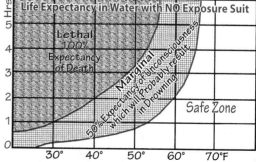

139

13 MOUNTAIN WEATHER & ROUTE PLANNING

MOUNTAIN TRAVEL

Mountainous regions present distinct challenges for travel by demanding increased perseverance, strength, will, and courage. Terrain characterized by steep slopes, great variations in local relief, natural obstacles, and lack of accessible routes restricts mobility, and drastically increases travel time. The weather, variable with the season and time of day, combined with the terrain, can greatly affect mobility and sleeping. Where there are no roads or trails, it is particularly important to have a full knowledge of the terrain to choose the most feasible route for cross-country movement. You should check all available data as topographic or photo maps, weather data, size, location and characteristics of land forms, drainage, nature and types of rock and soil, and the amount and distribution of vegetation.

MOUNTAIN TERRAIN

Mountains may rise abruptly from the plains to form a giant barrier or ascend gradually as a series of parallel ridges extending unbroken for great distances. They may consist of varying combinations of isolated peaks, rounded crests, eroded ridges, high plains cut by valleys, gorges, and deep ravines. Some mountains, such as those found in desert regions, are dry and barren, with temperatures ranging from extreme heat in the summer to extreme cold in the winter. In tropical regions, lush jungles with heavy seasonal rains and little temperature variation frequently cover mountains. High, rocky crags with glaciated peaks and year-round snow cover exist in mountain ranges at most latitudes along the western portion of the Americas and in Asia. No matter what form mountains take, their common denominator is rugged terrain.

CLASSIFICATION OF MOUNTAINS

There is no simple system available to classify mountain environments. Soil composition, surface configuration, elevation, latitude, and climatic patterns determine the specific characteristics of each major mountain range. When planning a trip you must carefully analyze each of these characteristics for the specific mountain region – and use the services of a guide.

LOCAL RELIEF

Mountains are commonly classified as low or high, depending on their local relief and, to some extent, elevation.

Low Mountains: have a local relief of 300 to 1,000 meters (1,000 to 3,000 feet) with summits usually below the timberline.

High Mountains: have a local relief usually exceeding 1,000 meters (3,000 feet) and are characterized by barren alpine zones above the timberline. Glaciers and perennial snow cover are common in high mountains.

MOUNTAINOUS REGIONS OF THE AMERICAS

Laurentians

Appalachians

Rocky
Mountain
Range

Andes

ROCKY MOUNTAIN RANGE

A broad mountainous region approximately 1,600 kilometers (1000 miles) wide dominates northwestern North America. It occupies much of Alaska, more than a quarter of Canada and the US, and all but a small portion of Mexico and Central America. The Rocky Mountain Range includes extensive high plains and basins. Numerous peaks in this belt rise above 30,000 meters (90,000 feet). Its climate varies from arctic cold to tropical heat, with the full range of seasonal and local extremes.

ANDES

Farther south, the Andes stretch as a continuous narrow band along the western region of South America. Narrower than its counterpart in the north, this range is less than 800 kilometers (500 miles) wide. However, it continuously exceeds an elevation of 3,000 meters (10,000 feet) for a distance of 3,200 kilometers (200 miles).

MOUNTAIN CHARACTERISTICS

Mountain slopes generally vary between 15°- 45°. Cliffs and other rocky precipices may be near vertical, or even overhanging. Aside from obvious rock formations and other local vegetation characteristics, actual slope surfaces are usually found as some type of relatively firm earth or grass. Grassy slopes may include grassy clumps known as tussocks, short alpine grasses, or tundra (the latter more common at higher elevations and latitudes).

TALUS & SCREE

Many slopes will be scattered with rocky debris deposited from the higher peaks and ridges. Extensive rock or boulder fields are known as talus. Slopes covered with smaller rocks, usually fist-sized or smaller, are called scree fields. Slopes covered in talus (individual stones can be stepped on) often prove to be a relatively easy ascent route. On the other hand, climbing a scree slope can be extremely difficult, as the small rocks tend to loosen easily and give way. However, this characteristic often makes scree fields excellent descent routes. Before attempting to descend scree slopes, carefully analyze the potential for creating dangerous rockfall and take necessary avoidance measures.

CLIMATE

Mountain climate has a very definite effect on the physiology and pathology of the individual because the human body is sensitive to weather changes, differing climates, and altitude.

MOUNTAIN AIR

Mountain air is relatively pure. The higher the elevation, the more nearly pure it becomes. Above 5,000 meters (15,000 feet) it is practically germ-free. The physical composition of the atmospheric air is considerably different at high altitudes from that found at sea level. Forests, especially those with coniferous trees, purify the air by lowering the percentage of carbon dioxide in the air. Falling snow purifies the air by capturing and holding many of the impurities remaining in the air.

High mountain air is dry, especially in the winter when the humidity in the air condenses into ice. The amount of water vapor in the air decreases as the altitude increases.

Atmospheric pressure drops as the altitude increases. The temperature drops and the air becomes more rarefied with altitude.

The sun's rays are either absorbed or reflected by the atmospheric haze which fills the air above low country, especially over cities. The rarefied dry air of the higher altitudes allows all the visible rays of the solar spectrum to pass. In pure atmosphere, the proportion of ultraviolet rays remains constant, regardless of the altitude. These conditions increase the possibility of sunburn especially when combined with the existing snow cover.

PRECIPITATION

The rapid rise of air masses over mountains creates distinct local weather patterns. Precipitation in mountains increases with elevation and occurs more often on the windward than on the leeward side of ranges. Maximum cloudiness and precipitation generally occur near 1,800 meters (6,000 feet) elevation in the middle latitudes and at lower levels in the higher latitudes. Usually, a heavily wooded belt marks the zone of maximum precipitation.

RAIN & SNOW

Both rain and snow are common in mountainous regions. Rain presents the same challenges as at lower elevations, but snow has a more significant influence on travel. Depending on the specific region, snow may occur at anytime during the year at elevations above 1,500 meters (5,000 feet). Heavy snowfall greatly increases avalanche hazards and can force changes to previously selected movement routes. In certain regions, the intensity of snowfall may delay easy travel for several months.

THUNDERSTORMS

Although thunderstorms are local and usually last only a short time, they can impede mountain travel. Interior ranges with continental climates are more conducive to thunderstorms than coastal ranges with maritime climates. In alpine zones, driving snow and sudden wind squalls often accompany thunderstorms. Ridges and peaks become focal points for lightning strikes, and the occurrence of lightning is greater in the summer than the winter. Although statistics do not show lightning to be a major mountaineering hazard, it should not be ignored take normal precautions, such as avoiding summits and ridges, water, and contact with metal objects.

TRAVELING STORMS

Storms resulting from widespread atmospheric disturbances involve strong winds and heavy precipitation and are the most severe weather condition that occurs in the mountains. If one encounters a traveling storm in alpine zones during winter, expect low temperatures, high winds, and blinding snow. These conditions may last several days longer than in the lowlands. Specific conditions vary depending on the path of the storm. However, when colder weather moves in, clearing at high elevations is usually slow.

MOUNTAIN FOG

The effects of fog in mountains are much the same as in other terrain. However, because of the topography, fog occurs more frequently in the mountains. The high incidence of fog makes it a significant planning consideration as it restricts visibility. Routes in areas with a high occurrence of fog may need to be marked and charted to facilitate passage.

WINTER AT HIGH ELEVATIONS

In winter, and at higher elevations throughout the year, snow may blanket slopes, creating an environment with its own distinct effects. Some snow conditions can aid travel by covering rough terrain with a consistent surface. Deep snow, however, greatly impedes movement and requires you to be well-trained in using snowshoes, skis, and over-snow vehicles. Steep snow-covered terrain presents the risk of snow avalanches as well. Snow can pose a serious threat if you are not properly trained and equipped for movement under such conditions. Avalanches have taken many lives and are the major terrain hazard in winter.

WIND IN MOUNTAIN AREAS

In high mountains, the ridges and passes are seldom calm; however, strong winds in protected valleys are rare. Normally, wind speed increases with altitude, since the earth's frictional drag is strongest near the ground, and this effect is accentuated by mountainous terrain. Winds are accelerated when they are forced over ridges and peaks or when they converge through mountain passes and canyons. Because of these funneling effects, wind may blast with great force on an exposed mountain side or summit. In most cases, the local wind direction is controlled by the area's topography and not the continental masses.

FORCE OF THE WIND

The force exerted by wind quadruples each time the wind speed doubles. Wind blowing at 40 knots pushes four times harder than does a 20 knot wind. With increasing wind strength, gusts become more important and may be 50% higher than the average wind speed. When wind strength increases to a hurricane force of 64 knots or more, you should hug the ground during gusts and push ahead during lulls. If a hurricane force wind blows where there is sand or snow, dense clouds fill the air, and rocky debris or chunks of snow crust are hurled along near the surface. Position yourself behind an obstruction. In general, the speed of the winds accompanying local storms is less than that of winds with traveling storms. There are two winds which result from the daily cycle of solar heating. During calm clear days in valleys that are subject to intense solar radiation, the heated air rises and flows gently up the valleys producing a wind called the valley or up-valley breeze. On clear nights the mountain sides lose heat rapidly and cool the surrounding air which settles down slope to produce the mountain or down-valley breeze. The down-valley breeze, by pouring cold air into a valley, aids in the creation of a temperature inversion. During the winter season or at extremely high altitudes, always be aware of the Windchill Factor and associated frostbite. Frostbite is a constant hazard when traveling at freezing temperatures, especially when the wind is strong.

During all seasons, exposed areas of the body are subject to windburn or extreme chapping. Although windburn is uncomfortable, it is seldom incapacitating.

PHYSICAL CONDITIONING

Hikers who have lived and hiked mostly at lower elevations tend to develop a sense of insecurity and fear about higher elevations - many are simply afraid of heights. With this in mind, your group must plan activities that accustom them to the effects of the mountain environment. Physical conditioning is important, since "new muscle" strain associated with balance and prolonged ascents/descents quickly exhausts even the most physically fit hiker. Even breathing becomes strenuous, given the thinner atmosphere at higher altitudes. Therefore, pre-training must emphasize exercises designed to strengthen leg muscles and build cardiovascular (aerobic) endurance.

Coleman™ Backpack

TRAVELING STORMS

After illnesses related to not being acclimatized, cold injuries, both freezing and nonfreezing, are generally the greatest threat. Temperature and humidity decrease with increasing altitude. Reviewing cold weather injury prevention, training in shelter construction, dressing in layers, and using the buddy system are critical and may preclude large numbers of debilitating injuries.

ALTITUDE SICKNESS & COLD INJURIES

Altitude sickness and cold injuries can occur simultaneously, with signs and symptoms being confused with each other. Coughing, stumbling individuals should be immediately evacuated to medical support at lower levels to determine their medical condition. Likewise, hikers in extreme pain from cold injuries who do not respond to normal pain medications, require evacuation. Without constant vigilance, cold injuries may significantly affect the viability of the traveling group. Usually with proper equipment, clothing, and training, all cold-weather injuries are preventable. *Page 156.*

ROUTE PLANNING
Simplicity of a Route Plan

When hiking and climbing on mountains the group is usually in file so that ongoing verbal communications are limited and possibly difficult. This is why a well planned route and the basic route strategy has to be discussed beforehand. A leader has to be chosen to help in carrying out the plan.

- Prepare clear, uncomplicated plans and clear, concise orders to ensure a thorough understanding.
- Plans and orders should be simple and direct. Simple plans and clear, concise orders reduce misunderstanding and confusion.
- Simple plans executed on time are better than detailed plans executed late.

ROUTE SELECTION

Plan an ascent or descent by noting each rock obstacle, the best approach, height, angle, type of rock, difficulty, distance between belay positions, amount of equipment, skill, condition, and number of individuals involved, the weather that might be encountered, and potential rock slides. Identify primary and alternate routes for ascents and descents. At least two vantage points should be used, so that a three-dimensional understanding of the climb can be attained. Use of early morning or late afternoon light, with its longer shadows, could be helpful.

HIKING & CLIMBING

Hikers in good condition can climb 1000 feet (300 meters) per hour. This varies with the type of terrain. On level ground the speed would be 2.5 to 4 miles per hour.

VISIBILITY WHILE TRAVELING

A sudden dust storm, squall, sleet or fog bank might envelope you. If you are not sure of your trail or are in hilly terrain it might be best to make a shelter and wait out the storm as to proceed might be very dangerous.

Upon lying down and covering yourself it is best to indicate your direction of travel with a line of stones or a stick. When the storm is over you might not recognize the surroundings and not know in which direction you were heading.

Avoid barriers (mountains, rivers, cliffs, etc.) and plan a route at the same elevation so that you avoid going up and down hills.

ROUTE DANGERS

- On long trips change in weather is an important consideration. Wet or icy rock can make an otherwise easy route almost impassable, cold may reduce climbing efficiency, and snow may cover holds. Obtain weather forecasts if possible.
- Smooth rock slabs are treacherous when wet or iced after a freezing rain. Ledges should be sought.
- Rocks overgrown with moss, lichens, or grass become treacherous when wet. Cleated boots will then be far better than composition soles.
- Tufts of grass and small bushes that appear firm may be growing on loosely packed and unanchored soil, all of which may give way if the grass or bush is pulled upon. Grass and bushes should be used only for balance by touch or as push holds, never as pull holds.
- Gently inclined but smooth slopes of rock may be covered with pebbles that will treacherously roll underfoot.
- Ridges may be free of loose rock, but may be topped with unstable blocks.
- Gullies provide the best defilade and often the easiest routes. Watch for flash floods and rocks.
- Climbing slopes of talus, moraine, or other loose rock is not only tiring to the individual but dangerous because of the hazard of rolling rocks on others in the party. Climbers should close up intervals when climbing.
- Lightning can endanger the climber on peaks, ridges, pinnacles, and lone trees should be avoided.

NAVIGATION

Navigation in the mountains is made more difficult because of inaccurate mapping, magnetic attraction that affects compass accuracy, and the irregular pace count while traveling. It is easy to mistake large terrain features that are very far away for features that are much closer. Limited-visibility restricts the use of normal terrain techniques as the primary means of determining and maintaining direction. Individuals must train to use a variety of equipment, such as a compass, an altimeter, global positioning system devices, and maps, as well as learn techniques pertaining to terrestrial navigation, terrain association, and dead reckoning.

"No plan...
extends with any degree of certainty beyond the first encounter with the main enemy force."

This is as true today as it was more than a century ago. Moltke's dictum, rather than condemning the value of planning, reminds leaders that any long route plan will encounter some unpredicted challenge - even a blister will change a plan. The purpose of any plan is to establish the conceptual basis of planned events. The plan provides a reasonably accurate forecast of execution. However, it remains a starting point, not the centerpiece of the trip.

German Field Marshal Helmuth von Moltke (victor in the Franco-Prussian war of 1870)

Main River

River Valleys

Mountains

Tributaries

Aerial photograph showing the difficulty in route selection when traveling through river basins.

RIVER DIVIDE TRAILS CROSS COUNTRY TRAVEL

A river is still considered as being man's natural highway. This is true where you have great rivers such as the Mississippi, Hudson, and St. Lawrence. Water travel is the only form of travel in the muskeg swamp country in Alaska and Northern Canada in the summer as land travel is impractical until everything freezes up.

In general the Indians did not use small rivers and streams but traveled along the ridges between streams or divides between two river basins. An exception to this was in the fur trade when heavy loads were carried by large canoes. These trading routes transported beaver pelts and merchandise along the river systems.

The advantage of a route traveled on a divide can be seen on the map. To travel from A or A' to B or B' it is easier to follow the divide and avoid fording all the rivers and streams. If the travelers had followed the bank of the river they would have had to ford streams and rivers, go through marshes, swamps, dense thickets and also have to face the 'friendly' mosquitoes and blood suckers. On ridges or divides, between two major river watersheds, the footing is usually better, vegetation is thinner, fallen trees are smaller, there is no mud or bog, and a better view of the surrounding area to help find your direction. In windblown areas there will hardly be any mosquitoes. If following a divide plan your trip, or take frequent sightings (climb a high tree), so that you do not end up in a dead end from which you have to descend to the lowlands.

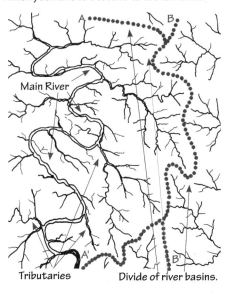

Main River

Tributaries   Divide of river basins.

MOUNTAIN SURVIVAL SHELTER

A two person mountain shelter is basically a hole 7 feet long, 3 1/2 feet wide, and 3 1/2 feet deep. The hole is covered with logs or walking poles to give the roof structural support. Then cover with tenting material or evergreen branches. Then top off with local material such as topsoil, leaves, snow, and twigs. The floor is usually covered with evergreen twigs, a tarpaulin, or other expedient material. Entrances can be provided at both ends or a fire pit is sometimes dug at one end for a small fire or stove.

A low earth parapet is built around the position to provide more height for the occupants. If you are on solid rock then pile stones to form an enclosure. Find insulating materials to fill the space between the stones and some form of roofing.

HIGH-ALTITUDE COOKING

High-altitude cooking requires special consideration:

- Low atmospheric pressure at high altitudes causes water to boil at:

  201°F at 5281 feet   93.8°C at 1600 m
  194°F at 10,000 feet   90°C at 3000 m
  212°F at sea level   100°C at sea level

- The lower boiling point of water, at high altitudes, means that it cannot get as hot before steaming and this cooler water will prolong cooking and baking time. At 2,000 meters (6000 feet) 3 minute eggs will take five minutes. Water steams off (evaporates) more rapidly, at 2,000 meters (6000 feet) twice as much water should be used in a cookie recipe.
- Add water to boiling water as it will rapidly boil away.
- A two pound fish that takes 15 minutes at sea level will take 20 minutes at 2,000 meters (6000 feet).
- Dehydrated foods should be soaked for a longer time and cooked at a low temperature.

MOUNTAIN LIVING

Successful mountain living requires that you adjust to special conditions, particularly terrain and weather. Mountain areas can be harsh, and training of your group should develop the field craft and psychological edge to operate effectively under mountainous conditions.

DISTANCE ESTIMATION IN MOUNTAINS

Range estimation is difficult In mountainous terrain. Depending upon the type of terrain in the mountains, distance can be either over or underestimated. Over smooth terrain, such as sand, water, or snow, you will generally underestimate distance. Looking downhill, the distance appears to be farther away and when looking uphill, they appear to be closer.

River photograph showing highlands.

GLACIERS

In arctic and sub arctic mountain regions, as well as the upper elevations of high mountains, you may be confronted with vast areas of glaciers. Valleys in these areas are frequently buried under massive glaciers and present special hazards, such as hidden crevices and ice and snow avalanches. The mountain slopes of these peaks are often glaciated and their surfaces are generally composed of varying combinations of rock, snow, and ice. Although glaciers have their own peculiar hazards requiring special training and equipment, movement over valley glaciers is often the safest route (usually you have no choice due to their size you cannot walk around them) through these areas. *See Glacier Chapter.*

WET-BULB TEMPERATURE

The evaporation of water from the thermometer with the bulb wrapped in wet cloth has a cooling effect. The temperature indicated by the wet bulb thermometer is less than the temperature indicated by a normal thermometer. The rate of evaporation from the wet-bulb thermometer depends on the humidity of the air-evaporation is slower when the air is already full of water vapor. *Page 425.*

TRAVELING ALONG A RIVER BASIN DIVIDE

On ridges or divides, between two major river watersheds, the footing is usually better, vegetation is thinner, fallen trees are smaller, there is no mud or bog, and there is a better view of the surrounding area to help find your direction.

Traveling along a ridge

Divide or Ridge Line →

Camping in the Alps in the 1880's

MEASURABLE WEATHER INDICATORS
Barometric pressure
Wind velocity
Wind direction
Temperature
Relative Humidity

MOUNTAIN WEATHER
Mountain weather is highly changeable and every effort must be made to anticipate the weather.
The safety or danger in almost all high mountain regions, especially in winter, depends upon a change of a few degrees of temperature above or below the freezing point. Ease and speed of travel are largely dependent on weather. Terrain that can be crossed swiftly and safely one day may become impassable or highly dangerous the next because of snowfall, rainfall, or a rise in temperature. The reverse can happen just as quickly. There is always a danger of avalanche or rockfalls.

INDICATORS OF CHANGING WEATHER
In the mountains, a portable aneroid barometer, thermometer, wind meter, and hygrometer are useful to obtain measurements that will assist in forecasting the weather. Marked or abnormal changes within a 12 hour period in the Indicators may suggest a potential change in the weather.

CLOUDS & WEATHER FORECAST
Clouds are good indicators of approaching weather conditions. By reading cloud shapes and patterns, observers can forecast weather even without additional equipment.
Shape and height are used to identify clouds. Shape provides information about the stability of the atmosphere, and height above ground level provides an indication of the distance of an approaching storm. Taken together, both indicate the likelihood of precipitation. The heights shown in the figure are an estimate and may vary, based on geographical location and season.

FORECASTING WEATHER IN THE MOUNTAINS
Weather at different elevations and areas, even within the same general region, may differ significantly due to variations in cloud height, temperature, winds, and barometric pressure. Therefore, general reports and forecasts must be used in conjunction with the locally observed weather conditions to produce reliable weather forecasts for a particular mountain area of operations. The use of the portable aneroid barometer, thermometer, and hygrometer can be of great assistance in making local weather forecasts. Reports from other localities and from any weather service are also of great value.

A typical afternoon mountain scene showing the diversity of the clouds. In the foreground there are some Cumulus and in the background (white) there are Cumulonimbus storm clouds building up.

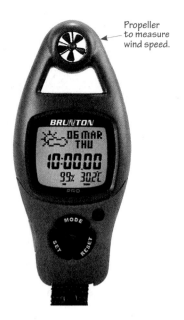

Propeller to measure wind speed.

PERSONAL WEATHER STATION
With this instrument you can obtain basic weather data. Information such as temperature, wind speed, barometric pressure, altitude, relative humidity, current time, daily alarm, chronograph and race timer. A log of historic data can be kept of the current wind speed, relative humidity, ambient temperature, barometric pressure, the altitude at the current location, the time and date, and the combined data for this exact time. In this way all the different bits of information can be used to make projections of future weather conditions.

Some interesting features are:
- A weather forecast display with the weather forecast symbol (sun, clouds, etc.).
- Calibrate the barometric pressure.
- Graph and numerical display of the barometric pressure for the last 24 hours.
- Storm Alarm: The alarm that alerts the user when the upcoming weather is stormy.
- A temperature graph for the last 24 hours.
- The current and minimum wind chill temperature: The wind effect on temperature.
- Alarm to alert the user when the current wind chill temperature is lower than the predefined limit.
- Current, average and maximum altitude air density and relative air density.
- Alarm sounds when the current altitude is higher than the predefined level. This is useful when you want to travel at a certain elevation to find and pass through a gap in the mountains.
- The characteristic of density altitude where the temperature, pressure and humidity have an effect on air density.
- Note that this instrument estimates altitude by air pressure. Hence, these altitude values may be changed if air pressure changes.
- Relative humidity includes four different readings; heat Index temperature, relative humidity, dew point temperature and wet-bulb temperature.

MEASURING WIND SPEED
This instrument is equipped with a propeller. When the propeller faces the wind, it rotates and the reading of the rotation per minute is converted it into wind speed. The screen will show the current, average and maximum wind-speed readings.

146

TYPES OF CLOUDS
Clouds Identified by Shape
Cumulus & Stratus

CUMULUS

Description: Cumulus clouds are often called "puffy" clouds, looking like tufts of cotton. Their thickness (bottom to top) is usually equal to or greater than their width. Cumulus clouds are primarily composed of water droplets that cause them to have sharp, distinct edges.

Indicator of: These clouds usually indicate instability at the altitude of the atmosphere where they are found. The stormy weather associated with cumulus clouds is usually violent with heavy rains or snow and strong, gusty winds. Precipitating cumulus clouds are called cumulonimbus.

Stratus Cloud Deck

STRATUS

Description: Stratus clouds are layered, often appearing flattened, with greater horizontal than vertical dimensions.

Indicator of: They usually indicate a stable atmosphere, but can indicate the approach of a storm. Stormy weather associated with stratus clouds usually does not normally include violent winds, and precipitation is usually light but steady, lasting up to 36 hours. Lightning is rarely associated with stratus clouds, however, sleet may occur. Fog is also associated with the appearance of stratus clouds. Precipitating stratus clouds are called nimbostratus, and clouds that cannot be determined as stratus or cumulus are referred to as stratocumulus. These latter types may be evolving from one type to another, indicating a change in atmospheric stability.

CLOUDS: BY HEIGHT

Clouds are also classified by the height of their base above ground level into three categories – low, middle, and high.

LOW CLOUDS

Height: below 6,500 feet. Low clouds may be identified by their height above nearby surrounding relief of known elevation.
Clouds: Cumulus or Stratus, or their precipitating counterparts.
Indicator of: Most precipitation originates from low clouds because rain and snow from higher clouds usually evaporates before reaching the ground. As such, low clouds usually indicate precipitation, especially if they are more than 3,000 feet thick. Clouds that appear dark at the base usually are at least that thick.

MIDDLE CLOUDS

Height: between 6,500 and 19,500 feet above the ground.
Clouds: have a prefix of "alto", and are called either Altostratus or Altocumulus. Middle clouds appear less distinct than low clouds because of their height. Warm "alto" clouds have sharper edges and are composed mainly of water droplets. Colder clouds, composed mainly of ice crystals, have distinct edges that grade gradually into the surrounding sky.
Indicator of: indicate potential storms, though usually hours away. Altocumulus clouds that are scattered in a blue sky are called "fair weather" cumulus and suggest the arrival of high pressure and clear skies. Lowering altostratus clouds with winds from the south indicate warm front conditions, decreasing air pressure, and an approaching storm system within 12 to 24 hours.

HIGH CLOUDS

Height: higher than 19,500 feet, are Cirrus, Cirrostratus, and Cirrocumulus. They are usually frozen clouds with a fibrous structure and blurred outlines. The sky is often covered with a thin veil of cirrus that partly obscures the sun or, at night, produces a ring of light around the moon.
Indicator of: The arrival of Cirrus indicates moisture aloft and the approach of a storm system. Precipitation is often 24 to 36 hours away. As the storm approaches, the Cirrus thickens and lowers becoming Altostratus and eventually Stratus. Temperatures warm, humidity rises, and winds approach from the south or southeast.

Altostratus

Altocumulus

Cirrus

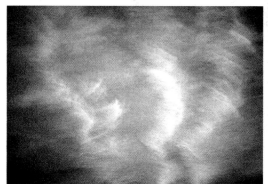

Cirrostratus

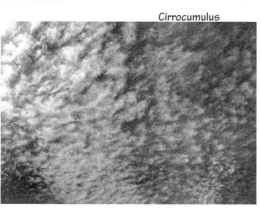

Cirrocumulus

Towering Cumulus cloud becoming a Cumulonimbus

Indications of local thunderstorms or squally weather:

- An increase in size and rapid thickening of scattered cumulus clouds during the afternoon.
- The approach of a line of large cumulus or cumulonimbus clouds with an "advance guard" of altocumulus clouds. At night, increasing lightning windward of the prevailing wind gives the same warning.
- Massive cumulus clouds hanging over a ridge or summit (day or night).

STRONG WINDS

Indications of approaching strong winds:

- Plumes of blowing snow from the crests of ridges and peaks or ragged shreds of cloud moving rapidly.
- Persistent lenticular clouds, a band of clouds over high peaks and ridges, or downwind from them.
- A turbulent and ragged banner cloud that hangs to the lee of a peak.

PRECIPITATION

When there is precipitation and the sky cannot be seen:

- Small snowflakes or ice crystals indicate that the clouds above are thin, and fair weather exists at high elevations.
- A steady fall of snowflakes or raindrops indicates that the precipitation has begun at high levels, and bad weather is likely to be encountered on ridges and peaks.

FAIR WEATHER

Continued fair weather associated with:

- A cloudless sky and shallow fog, or layers of haze at valley bottoms in early morning.
- A cloudless sky that is blue down to the horizon or down to where a haze layer forms a secondary horizon.
- Conditions under which small cumulus clouds appearing before noon do not increase, but instead decrease or vanish during the day.
- Clear skies except for a low cloud deck that does not rise or thicken during the day.

Signs of approaching fair weather:

- A gradual rising and diminishing of clouds.
- A decreasing halo around the sun or moon.
- Dew on the ground in the morning.
- Small snowflakes, ice crystals, or drizzle, which indicate that the clouds are thin and fair weather may exist at higher elevations.
- An increase in barometric pressure (registered as a loss in elevation on an altimeter).

Cloud Caps

Wave Clouds

OTHER CLOUDS
Serious Weather Ahead
TOWERING CUMULUS CLOUDS

Height: have bases below 6,500 feet and tops often over 19,500 feet.

Indicator of: They are the most dangerous of all types and usually do not occur when temperatures at the surface are below 32° F. Although exceptions can occur in some types of local temperature inversions. They indicate extreme instability in the atmosphere, with rapidly rising air currents caused by solar heating of the surface or air rising over a mountain barrier. Mature towering cumulus clouds often exhibit frozen stratus clouds at their tops, producing an "anvil head" appearance. Towering cumulus clouds may be local in nature, or they may be associated with the cold front of an approaching storm. The latter appears as an approaching line of thunderstorms or towering cumulus clouds. Towering cumulus clouds usually produce high, gusty winds, lightning, heavy showers, and occasionally hail and tornadoes (although tornadoes are rare in mountainous terrain). Such thunderstorms are usually short-lived and bring clear weather.

CLOUD CAPS & LENTICULAR CLOUDS

Cloud caps often form above pinnacle and peaks, and usually indicate higher winds aloft. Cloud caps with a lens shape (similar to a "flying saucer") are called lenticular and indicate very high winds (over 40 knots). Cloud caps should always be watched for changes. If they grow and descend, bad weather can be expected.

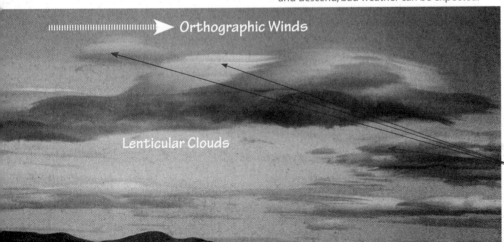

Orthographic Winds

Lenticular Clouds

Orographic Wave: A wind blowing over mountains produces a wavelike airflow pattern. If there is moisture in the wind then lenticular clouds will be formed.

Lenticular Cloud: A series of frequently stacked lens-shaped clouds that are formed on the lee side of a mountain range.

Characteristics of Mountain Weather

Mountain weather is erratic. Hurricane force winds and gentle breezes may occur just short distances apart. The weather in exposed places contrasts sharply with the weather in sheltered areas. Weather changes in a single day can be so variable that in the same locality one may experience hot sun and cool shade, high winds and calm, gusts of rain or snow, and then perhaps intense sunlight again. This variability results from the life cycle of a local storm or from the movement of traveling storms. In addition, the effects of storms are modified by the local influences:

- Variation in altitude.
- Differences in exposure to the sun and to prevailing winds.
- Distortion of storm movements and normal winds by irregular mountain topography. These local influences dominate summer storms.
- Local storms in the form of thunderstorms with or without showers.
- Traveling storms which may be accompanied by radical and severe weather changes over a broad area. Usually, each type of storm may be identified by the clouds associated with it. See Weather Chapter for cloud formations.
- Seasonal moisture-bearing winds of the monsoon type which bring consistently bad weather to some mountain ranges for weeks at a time.

Cloudiness & Precipitation

Cloudiness and precipitation increase with height until a zone of maximum precipitation is reached; above this zone they decrease. Maximum cloudiness and precipitation occur near 6000 feet (1800 m) elevation in middle latitudes and at lower levels as the poles are approached. Usually a dense forest marks the zone of maximum rainfall. Slopes facing the prevailing wind are cloudier, foggier, and receive heavier precipitation than those protected from the wind, especially when large bodies of water lie to the windward side. However, at night and in winter, valleys are likely to be colder and foggier than higher slopes. Heads of valleys often have more clouds and precipitation than adjacent ridges and the valley floor.

Indicators & Weather?

Weather forecasts are simply educated estimations or deductions based on general scientific weather principles and meteorological evidence. Forecasts based on past results may or may not be accurate. However, even limited experience in a particular mountainous region and season may provide local indications of impending weather patterns and increased accuracy. Native weather lore, although sometimes greatly colored and surrounded in mystique, should not be discounted when developing forecasts, as it is normally based on the local inhabitants' long-term experience in the region.

Temperature Inversion

Normally, a temperature fall off from 2°- 5°F per 1000 feet rise in altitude will be encountered. Frequently, on cold, clear, calm mornings when climbing is started from a valley, higher temperatures may be encountered as you rise in altitude. This reversal of the normal situation is called temperature inversion. This condition occurs when air cooled by ice, snow, and heat loss by radiation settles into valleys and low areas. The inversion will continue until the sun warms the surface of the earth or a moderate wind causes a mixing of the warm and cold air layers.

Aneroid Barometer
This is the traditional barometer used to obtain barometric pressure and help predict the weather. *See Weather Chapter.*

Bad Weather

Signs of approaching bad weather within 24 to 48 hours:

- A gradual lowering of the clouds. This may be the arrival or formation of new lower strata of clouds. It can also indicate the formation of a thunderhead.
- An increasing halo around the sun or the moon.
- An increase in humidity and temperature.
- Cirrus clouds.
- A decrease in barometric pressure (registered as a gain in elevation on an altimeter).

Storm Systems

Approach of a storm system:

- A thin veil of cirrus clouds spreads over the sky, thickening and lowering until altostratus clouds are formed. The same trend is shown at night when a halo forms around the moon and then darkens until only the glow of the moon is visible. When there is no moon, cirrus clouds only dim the stars, but altostratus clouds completely hide them.
- Low clouds, which have been persistent on lower slopes, begin to rise at the time upper clouds appear.
- Various layers of clouds move in at different heights and become abundant.
- Lenticular clouds accompanying strong winds lose their streamlined shape, and other cloud types appear in increasing amounts.
- A change in the direction of the wind is accompanied by a rapid rise in temperature not caused by solar radiation. This may also indicate a warm, damp period.
- A light green haze is observed shortly after sunrise in mountain regions above the timberline.

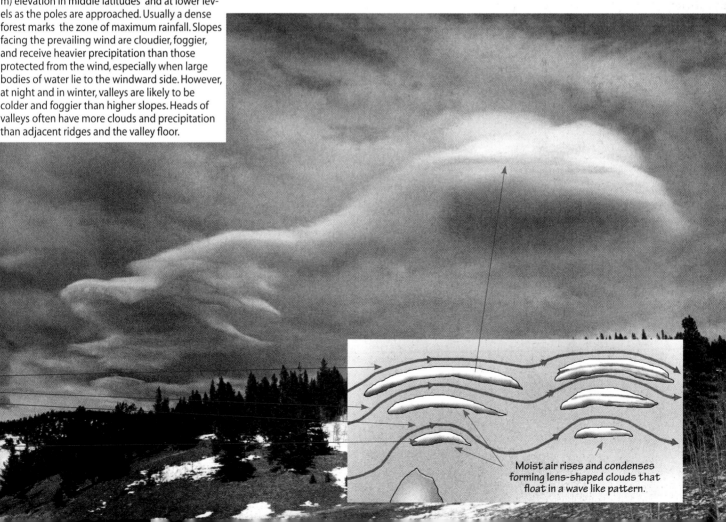

Moist air rises and condenses forming lens-shaped clouds that float in a wave like pattern.

A traveling storm in the mountains.

Stratocumulus

TRAVELING STORMS

The most severe storms involve strong winds and heavy precipitation and are the result of widespread atmospheric disturbances which generally travel in an easterly direction.

If a traveling storm is encountered in an alpine zone during winter, all your equipment and skill will be pitted against low temperatures, high winds, and blinding snow.

CAUSE OF TRAVELING STORMS

Traveling storms result from the interaction of cold and warm air. The center of the storm is a moving low pressure area where cyclonic winds are generally the strongest. Extending from this storm center is a warm front which marks the advancing thrust of warm air, and the cold front which precedes the onrushing cold and gusty winds. The sequence of weather events, with the approach and passing of a traveling storm depends on the state of the storm's development, and whether the location of its path is to the north or south of a given mountain area. Generally, scattered cirrus clouds merge into a continuous sheet which thickens and lowers gradually until it becomes altostratus. At high levels, this cloud layer appears to settle. Lower down, a stratus deck may form overhead.

A storm passing to the north may bring warm temperatures with southerly winds and partial clearing for a while before colder air with thundershowers or squally conditions moves in from the northwest. However, local cloudiness often obscures frontal passages in the mountains. The storm may go so far to the north that only the cold front phenomena of heavy clouds, squalls, thundershowers, and colder weather are experienced. The same storm passing to the south would be accompanied by a gradual wind shift from northeasterly to northwesterly, with a steady temperature fall and continuous precipitation. After colder weather moves in, the clearing at high altitudes is usually slower than the onset of cloudiness, and storm conditions may last several days longer than in the lowlands.

EFFECTS OF TRAVELING STORM

Rapidly changing weather conditions often create glaze, a coating of ice which forms on exposed objects. Glaze occurs under special storm conditions when light rain or drizzle falls through air below 32°F, and strikes a surface that also is below 32°F, freezing to the surface in the form of glaze. Glaze usually forms near the warm front of a storm and only persists if colder weather follows.

TRAVELING STORM INDICATORS

Approach of a traveling storm when:

- A thin veil of cirrus clouds spreads over the sky, thickening and lowering until altostratus clouds are formed. The same trend is shown at night when a halo forms around the moon and then darkens until only the glow of the moon is visible. When there is no moon, cirrus clouds only dim the stars while altostratus clouds hide them completely.
- Low clouds which have been persistent on lower slopes begin to rise at the time upper clouds appear.
- Various layers of clouds move in at different heights and become more abundant.
- Lens-shaped clouds accompanying strong winds lose their streamlined shape and other cloud types appear in increasing amounts.
- A change in the direction of the wind is accompanied by a rapid rise in temperature not caused by solar radiation. This may also indicate a warm damp period.
- A light green haze is observed shortly after sunrise in mountain regions above the timberline.

150

FOG IN MOUNTAINS

On windward slopes, persistent fog, as well as cloudiness and precipitation, frequently can last for days. They are caused by the local barrier effect of the mountain on prevailing winds. Any cloud bank appears as a fog from within. Fog limits visibility and causes whiteout conditions. If fog is accompanied by precipitation protection against the uncomfortable combination of cold and wetness is required. When traveling without landmarks it will be necessary to use a compass, altimeter and a topographic map to maintain direction.

Fog forming on glacier.

SOLAR HEATING

At high altitudes, solar heating is responsible for the greatest temperature contrasts. More sunshine and solar heat is received above than below the clouds. The important effect of altitude is that the sun's rays pass through less of the atmosphere and so more direct heat is received than at lower levels where solar radiation is absorbed and reflected by dust and water vapor.

There may be differences of 40°-50°F between the temperature in the sun and that in the shade. Special care must be taken to avoid sunburn and snow blindness which result from the combined action of intense sunlight and the reflected rays from snow fields or clouds. Besides permitting rapid heating, the clear air at high altitudes also favors rapid cooling at night. The temperature rises very fast after sunrise and drops quickly after sunset. Much of the chilled air drops downward, because of convention currents, so that the differences between day and night temperatures are greater in valleys than on slopes or higher elevations.

Glory of an Airplane

Warm Air

Cold Air

TRAPPER

An area where the cold air gets dammed gets trapped or pooled. If a valley area is called "Cold Hollow" it is a trapper. When the cold air builds up it might overflow the dam and let a bubble of cold wind flow to a lower elevation. If the trapper area is very large the overflow could be quite forceful.

Wind

Cornice

Banner Cloud

Indication of Avalanche

BANNER CLOUD

Cloud plume over the top and leeward side of mountain peaks produced by the condensation of rising air. These clouds can be present on cloudless days when they look like banners or flags draping on the peak.

Glory (Brocken Specter): This is an effect that can occasionally be seen by mountain climbers. It is where the climber is above a cloud deck and the sun is behind him. The sun will cast a shadow of the climber onto the cloud deck. The observed shadow will have an optical effect of concentric rings of color surrounding the shadow of an observer's head.

Day Time

Night Time

VALLEY BREEZE

In hilly areas the air flows up the slope in the daytime and down slopes at night. This happens because in the day the tops of the hills become warmer causing the air in the valley to rise. Hills cool off faster than the surrounding area at night and heavy cold air flows into the valleys.

CHINOOK

A foehn wind blowing down the eastern side of the Rocky Mountains and Sierra Nevada. The approach of a chinook is indicated by a bank of altostratus clouds east of the Rocky Mountains. The clouds have a unique appearance because they are formed by the condensation of the rising air and when observer from below or the east there is an arch of clear air between the cloud's leading edge and the mountains below. Note the Chinook wind originates in the west.

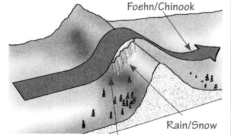

Foehn/Chinook

Rain/Snow

Rising cooling and condensing humid air dropping its moisture as snow or rain. The dry air then descends the slope and warms up.

Chinook

LIGHTNING & THUNDERSTORMS

Gap Winds: Gaps are openings in a mountain range. Winds on one side of the mountain range can pour through the gap. These strong winds can arrive suddenly and last a few days. These winds can have a major effect on climbers as they might be pinned down on steep slopes and have difficulty in advancing.

Clouds flowing through gap.

Mountain Wind System: Winds that form due to the daily heating and cooling by the sun. The wind flows are difficult to understand as they form over a complex topographic area. Climbers should understand the wind characteristics of the slopes they want to climb - even on an hour to hour basis.

Along-Valley Wind System: A valley wind whose lower stream blows up or down the length of the valley. The upper stream blowing in the opposite direction. This two direction thermal flow is a closed cycle. The upper or return stream is called the antiwind. This might cause localized thunderstorms, low valley clouds (fog).

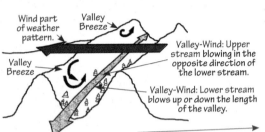

Wind part of weather pattern.
Valley Breeze
Valley Breeze
Valley-Wind: Upper stream blowing in the opposite direction of the lower stream.
Valley-Wind: Lower stream blows up or down the length of the valley.

THUNDERSTORMS

Although individual thunderstorms are normally local in nature and usually are of short duration, they can be part of a large weather system. In the alpine zone above timberline, thunderstorms may be accompanied by freezing precipitation and sudden squally winds. Ridges and peaks become focal points of concentrated electrical activity which is very dangerous. Thunderstorms occurring at night or in the early morning are associated with major changes in the weather conditions, which often results in a long period of foul weather before clearing on high summits. Thunderstorms occurring at these times may also be part of a general storm front and are followed by a prolonged period of cool, clear, and dry weather.

...treat lightning like a snake: if you see it or hear it take evasive measures...

LIGHTNING

Although statistics show that lightning is not one of the major hazards of mountaineering, enough casualties and near casualties are reported to make it a matter of concern. Mountain climbers often find themselves on prominent peaks and exposed ridges, which are particularly subject to lightning.

- Ridges help produce the vertical updrafts and the rain cloud conditions which generate lightning.
- Prominences serve to trigger lightning strokes. There are, however, precautionary measures that can be taken by the climber.
- Avoid being on exposed peaks or ridges, or in an unprotected flat area during an electrical storm.
- Do not climb if a storm is predicted. Lightning can strike in front of a storm.
- Avoid being under prominent or isolated trees.
- If caught in an exposed place, and you have some time before the storm reaches you, you should get as far down the mountain and away from exposed ridges as you can. Especially avoid ridges that dominate the skyline. If stuck the middle of a ridge is preferable to the edge of a ridge.
- If lightning seems imminent or is striking nearby, seek a place at once that will protect you from direct strokes and from ground currents. A flat shelf, a slope, or a slightly raised place dominated by a nearby high point would give protection from lightning.
- If there is any choice select a spot on dry, clean rock in preference to damp or lichen covered rock. A scree slope would be very good.
- Tie yourself in if you are where a severe shock might cause you to fall. The main thing to remember when caught in an electrical storm is to quickly take precautions.
- Kneel on a dry sleeping pad. Minimize the amount of body contact with the ground. Keep any metal objects at a distance (including your backpack).
- Keep your head low because it might be the highest protrusion in the vicinity.
- If possible find a depression surrounded by high trees. Do not stay under the tallest tree!
- Stay away from any water or other conductors of electricity.
- If you are a group spread out - at least 100 feet apart.

LIGHTNING

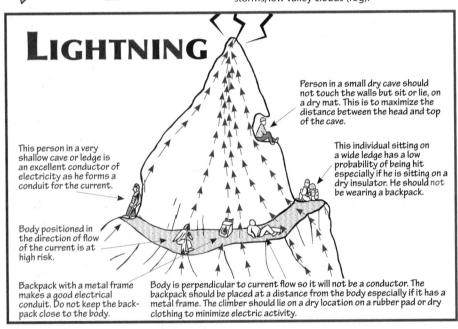

Person in a small dry cave should not touch the walls but sit or lie, on a dry mat. This is to maximize the distance between the head and top of the cave.

This individual sitting on a wide ledge has a low probability of being hit especially if he is sitting on a dry insulator. He should not be wearing a backpack.

This person in a very shallow cave or ledge is an excellent conductor of electricity as he forms a conduit for the current.

Body positioned in the direction of flow of the current is at high risk.

Backpack with a metal frame makes a good electrical conduit. Do not keep the backpack close to the body.

Body is perpendicular to current flow so it will not be a conductor. The backpack should be placed at a distance from the body especially if it has a metal frame. The climber should lie on a dry location on a rubber pad or dry clothing to minimize electric activity.

Electrical Fields During a Lightning Storm

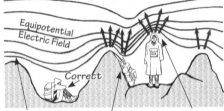

Equipotential Electric Field
Correct

Equipotential electric fields during a storm.
Metal on frame might attract lightning.
High probability of being hit as the head is the high point.

LOCAL WEATHER

Indications of local thunderstorm showers, or squally weather:

- An increase in size and rapid thickening of scattered cumulus clouds during the afternoon.
- The approach of a line of large cumulus or cumulonimbus clouds with an advance guard of altocumulus clouds. At night, increasing lightning windward of the prevailing wind gives the same warning.
- Massive cumulus clouds hanging over a ridge or summit at night or in the daytime.

Cumulus

Thunderstorm

Local Thunderstorms

Local thunderstorms develop from rising air columns resulting from the intense heating by the sun over a relatively small area. They occur most frequently in the middle or late afternoon. Scattered fair weather clouds (cumulus) often appear harmless, but when they continue to grow larger and reach a vertical depth of several thousand meters they may rapidly turn into thunderstorms.

"FLASH TO BANG" DISTANCE CALCULATION

If you see lightning, count the number of seconds until you hear thunder. Divide the number of seconds by five to get the distance the lightning is away from you. Note that this method of distance estimation has limits due to the difficulty of associating the proper thunder to the corresponding flash. In mountain areas the thunder can reverberate between the peaks. *If you see lightning and it takes 10 seconds before you hear the thunder, then the lightning is 2 miles away from you (10 ÷ 5 = 2 miles). Stay vigilant until 30 minutes after the last audible thunder.*

DISTANCE OF A THUNDERSTORM

If you are aware from an NOAA broadcast of a storm moving east at 30 mph (or 1/2 a mile per minute) towards your location, and the storm is 30 miles west of you. Then it will be upon you in approximately 10 minutes. This is the time you have to find shelter.

LIGHTNING & NO RAIN

Lightning can and occasionally does strike many miles away from the rain area of a thunderstorm. In fact, lightning strikes to the ground up to 20 miles away from thunderstorm rain. It is believed that quite a few people who are struck by lightning are struck by these rogue flashes, known as "bolts from the blue".

IF CAUGHT IN OPEN

The safest position to be in is crouched down on the balls of your feet. Do not allow your hands (or other body parts) to touch the ground, and keep your feet as close to one another as possible. Crouch on the balls of your feet because when lightning strikes an object, the electricity of the lightning discharge does not necessarily go down into the ground immediately. Quite often the electricity will travel along the surface of the ground where the flash makes contact with an object. Many people who are 'struck' by lightning are not hit directly by the flash, but are affected by this electricity of the lightning flash as it travels along the surface of the ground (this is especially true if the ground is wet).

By keeping the surface area of your body relative to the ground to a minimum (that is, keep your feet together and do not allow any other part of your body to contact the ground), you can reduce the threat of the electricity traveling across the ground from affecting you.

If the victim is not breathing, provide mouth to mouth resuscitation . If the victim has no pulse, (check for the pulse at the carotid [neck] or femoral [knee] artery for 20 -30 seconds). then start CPR. If the area is cold and wet, putting a dry article of clothing between the victim and the ground may decrease the threat of hypothermia that the victim suffers which can complicate the resuscitation. Page 593.

FIRST AID LIGHTNING STRIKE VICTIM

Most people struck by lightning are not struck directly, but are affected by the current running through the ground (also known as a "sideflash"). People who are adversely affected by a lightning flash, either directly or indirectly, need prompt medical attention:

• Call 911. Provide directions and information about the likely number of lightning strike victims; The first tenet of emergency care is "make no more casualties". Any rescuer must be aware of the continuation of danger that a lightning storm poses to the rescuers as well as to the victim(s). If the area is a high risk area (mountain top, open field, etc.), it may be better that the rescuers who are in a relatively safer area wait until the danger has passed before exposing themselves.

• It is relatively unusual for victims who survive a lightning strike to have major fractures that would cause paralysis or major bleeding complications unless they have suffered a fall or been thrown a distance. As a result, in an active lightning storm, if the rescuers choose to expose themselves to the lightning threat, it may be better to move the victim away from the area of risk (such as under a tree, etc.) rather than to give medical attention at the spot of the initial flash. Rescuers are reminded to stay as low as possible and provide as little area to the ground surface as possible.

MOUNTAIN THUNDERSTORMS

Mountain thunderstorms tend to form in the early to mid-afternoon. Hike to the high peaks early in the morning and you will be on your way down when the threat from thunderstorms is at its highest. Local conditions and passing fronts might cause unexpected storms so keep your eyes on the sky and be prepared to abandon your hiking plans.

RECOGNIZING THUNDERSTORM DEVELOPMENT

You should be able to recognize developing thunderstorms before they begin to produce lightning.

• Fair weather clouds (Cumulus) on a mountain may be puffy, are shallow and show little or no vertical development.

• When they begin to tower up and build into higher clouds with dark bases they are in the process of possibly becoming thunderstorms.

• A tall cloud flatten out at the top is a thunderstorm

SEVERE THUNDERSTORMS

Thunderstorms are considered severe whenever they produce one or more of the following: a tornado, hail that is 3/4 in or larger in diameter, or wind gusts (not associated with tornadoes) approaching 60 mph.

HAIL

Large hailstones occasionally can be dangerous, especially while climbing on an exposed mountain slope. A hailstone the diameter of a golf ball (roughly 1 3/4 inches) can produce an injury, especially if it strikes a person's head. A hailstone the diameter of a baseball (2 3/4 inches) falls at a speed comparable to that of a pitched baseball on the order of 100 mph. An injury from such a stone can be serious, or even fatal. *See page 445.*

Electric aureola round the head of traveler on a mountain peak. This is the source of the expression of "the hair standing on end." At high elevations before and during a storm the electrical charge from the high point tries to reach up to the charge in the clouds. This sometimes causes a aureola around the highest object which in this case is the head. The hair will also extend upwards and if you see this happen it is a good indicator of a possible lightning strike.

THUNDERSTORM WINDS

Strong winds, not associated with a tornado, can become very dangerous, especially if you are hiking or camping in a forest. Often the trees at high elevation have small root systems and are fairly easy for the wind to blow down. In some rare storms, many thousands of acres of trees have been mown down by the storm's wind gusts. Obviously, being in a forest during one of these "blowdowns" would be very perilous for campers. It's very hard just to look at an approaching storm and know how strong the winds are. The leading edge of the strong winds is often marked by a shelf cloud. In the mountains, a cloud marking the leading edge of the winds might be a lot more ragged as its structure can be affected by the high elevations. If you see one of these approaching, be prepared to seek shelter from the winds and the flying, falling debris the winds might cause. A thunderstorm can produce 30-50 mph winds, especially in the mountains. Since mountain air tends to be dry, evaporating rain from mountain storms produces cool air, which descends rapidly and spreads out in what are called "microbursts." Note that if you get wet in a mountain thunderstorm at high elevation, you are vulnerable to hypothermia, even if the storm isn't severe enough to cause you other problems. Having proper rain gear and using it can save your life in the mountains. In a few rare events, large hailstones combine with strong winds to produce a dangerous barrage of wind-driven hail and damaging winds. Such storms are rare, but certainly could be a serious threat to campers, who may not hear any warnings that normally reach people by radio and television. If such a storm develops, your only hope is to find shelter from the flying hail and debris.

HILLS

Rockfall

Mountain Walking

Uphill

Center of Gravity

Mountain walking is divided into four techniques dependent upon the general characteristics of the terrain;
- Walking on hard ground.
- Grassy slopes.
- Scree slopes.
- Talus slopes.

Scree Slope

Talus Slope

Traversing on Scree or Talus slope

Scree & Talus Slope

PROPER WALKING TECHNIQUE

This applies to all mountain travel.

Three Contact Points on Ground

- Weight centered over feet at all times.
- Maintain as much boot sole-to-ground surface contact as possible.
- Straighten the trail knee after each step to rest the leg muscles.
- Use all available hand and footholds.
- Keep a slow rhythmic pace, maintaining good balance, taking small steps.
- Normal progression as the slope steepens would be from walking straight up the slope, to a herring bone step (toes point out), and then to a traverse (zigzag pattern) on the steeper areas.
- On steep or slippery slopes, use a roped party climb to increase mutual safety.

WALKING ON HARD GROUND

Hard ground is firmly packed dirt that does not give way or crumble under the weight of your step.

Hard Ground

ASCENDING ON HARD GROUND

- Steep slopes are traversed at an angle rather than walked straight up.
- In traversing, the full sole (boot) principle is accomplished by rolling the ankle away from the hill on each step.
- For small stretches, the herring bone step may be used when ascending straight up with the toes pointed out. This can be very tiring.

DESCENDING ON HARD GROUND

- Walk straight down the slope without traversing.
- Keep the back straight and the knees bent.

Descent

- Keep the backpack securely attached, to keep it stable, but be ready to jettison.

GRASSY SLOPES

Grassy slopes are usually composed of small tufts of growth rather than continuous vegetation.

Grass Tufts

ASCENDING ON A GRASSY SLOPE

The upper side of each tuft is stepped on where the ground is more level.

DESCENDING ON A GRASSY SLOPE

It is best to traverse because of the uneven nature of the ground and the difficulty of aiming your foot onto the tuft of grass. If traversing, the uphill foot and the downhill foot point in the direction of travel or for more stability, especially with a heavy load, the downhill foot points about 45° downhill off the direction of travel.

SCREE SLOPES

Scree slopes consist of small rocks and gravel that vary in size from grains of sand to that the size of a fist. It may occur as a mixture of all sizes, but usually scree slopes consist of the same size particles. These particles tend to slide downhill and do not offer very stable support.

ASCENDING A SCREE SLOPE

- Ascending scree slopes is difficult, most tiring, and should be avoided whenever possible.
- Kick in with the toe of the upper foot so that a step is formed in the scree.
- Gradually transfer your weight from the lower to the upper foot, and repeat the process.
- Be careful not to dislodge any debris onto members of your group that are below you. If possible it is best to ascend in a traverse as any debris would roll freely down the hill.

DESCENDING A SCREE SLOPE

- Descend scree slopes by going straight down using a short shuffling step with the knees bent, back straight and feet pointed downhill.
- When several climbers descend a scree slope, together, they should be as close together as possible, one behind the other, to prevent injury from a dislodged rock.
- Avoid running down a scree slope as you might lose control.
- Use caution when the bottom of the route cannot be seen as there might be a cliff.

TALUS SLOPES

Talus slopes are formed by the accumulation of rock debris which is larger than a man's fist. When ascending or descending, always step on the top and on the uphill side of the rock. This prevents the rocks from tilting and rolling downhill. The rock is partially embedded and will distribute your weight to the rocks below it. Avoid dislodging rocks which may cause a rock slide. Climbers must stay in close columns while traversing.

BREATHING

If you find that you are breathing too fast, or gasping for breath, this means that you are traveling too fast.

REST

Rest 5 to 10 minutes every hour, but not for too long because your muscles will cool and stiffen.

FEET

Your feet have many nerves in them and when they hurt travel can be very painful. When you stop to rest change your socks and cool your feet. Never travel without bandages, change of socks, and other first aid items for your feet. Make sure that your new boots have been broken in before you leave on a major trip.

TRAVELING UPHILL

Do not walk straight up a slope but zigzag up the hill. You will find that on a long slope, by zigzagging, you will arrive at the top at more or less the same time but you will be less tired. When walking always plant each foot fully on the ground. Do not walk uphill on your toes. If the footing is not too secure gradually transfer your weight onto the advancing foot to see if the location is stable.

ROCK FALLS

A rock fall can be a single rock or a large rock slide covering a relatively large area. Rock falls occur on all steep slopes, particularly in gullies and chutes. Areas of frequent rock falls may be indicated by:
- Abundant fresh scars on the rock walls.
- Fine dust on the talus piles.
- Lines and grooves along the cliff.
- Rock strewn areas on snow beneath cliffs.
- Lack of trees or large vegetation along the slope.

Immediate action during a rock fall is to seek cover. If there is not enough time to avoid the rock fall, the climber should lean into the slope to minimize his exposure, cover his head, and not look up. Rock fall danger is minimized by careful climbing and by judgment in choice of route.

DANGERS OF ROCK FALLS

Rock falls are the most common mountaineering danger.
The most frequent causes of rock falls are:
- Other climbers.
- Great changes of temperature in high mountains that produce splitting action by intermittent freezing and thawing.
- Heavy rain.   • Grazing animals.

Indications of a rock fall are: a whistling sound, a grating, a thunderous crashing, or bright sparks where the rocks strike each other when they fall at night. Warning of a rock fall is the cry "ROCK!" or "Equipment!"

In Ascent:
Facing sideways: climbing will be easy to difficult.
Facing inward: climbing will be more difficult.

In Descent:
Facing out: climbing will be very easy when hill is not too steep.
Facing sideways: climbing will be easy to difficult.
Facing inward: climbing will be more difficult when hill is very steep.

STEEP SLOPES

You will have a tendency to "hug" the slope but this is not advisable as the angle at which your foot stands on the ground will be very flat and your footing might slip. Your hands can be used for balance but keep your body at least at arm's length from the slope. Test each hand hold and footing for each step before transferring your body's weight. Use the three secure point system to hold your body at dangerous spots on the slope, e.g. two handholds and one foot well placed before slowly shifting the second foot. When this foot is secure then you can shift one hand.

CLIMBING DOWN STEEP HILLS

This is more difficult than climbing uphill as your ankles, knees and legs tire faster as they have to absorb the weight for thousands of steps. Keep your backpack well attached, balance your weight, keep your knees bent to cushion your weight while shifting from leg to leg. Do not go too fast as you will have too much momentum and might sprain your ankle or fall because of insecure footing.

SAFETY ON SLOPES

The hiker on the upper part of the slope should be careful not to dislodge rocks that might fall on the column below. The column should advance at a slight angle up the slope so that any loose debris will fall without hurting anyone below. The lead climber can dislodge, with advance warning, any loose rocks that might affect his group. If you encounter areas of loose rocks or talus the group on the lower part of the hill can seek shelter behind a tree or boulder until the lead climbers pass the dangerous area.

FORDING STREAMS

Streams can range from small, ankle-deep brooks to large rivers. Mountain rivers are often so swift that you can hear boulders on the bottom being crashed together by the current. *If streams are of glacial origin, you should wait for them to decrease in strength during the night hours before attempting to ford.*

CROSSING STRATEGY

Careful study is required to find a place to safely ford a stream. If available, climb a high vantage point to observe the river. Finding a safe crossing area may be easy if the river breaks into a number of small channels. The area on the opposite bank should be surveyed to make sure travel will be easier after crossing. When possible, select a travel course that leads across the current at about a 45° angle downstream.
- Never attempt to ford a stream directly above, or close to, a deep or rapid waterfall or a deep channel. The stream should be crossed where the opposite side has a shallow bank or sandbars.

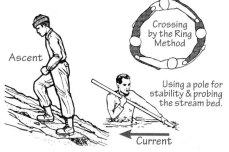

Ascent

Using a pole for stability & probing the stream bed

Current

STREAM CROSSING

Sudden rains or thaws can change placid streams into roaring torrents.
- The best time for crossing is in the early morning when the water is low. As glaciers, snow, or ice melt during the day, the rivers rise, reaching their maximum height between mid-afternoon and late evening, depending on the distance from the source.
- A crossing point should be chosen, if possible, at the widest point of the stream where the water is normally not as swift and usually not as deep or where it branches into several smaller streams. Wherever possible, select a point where there are few, if any, large stones on the river bed. Large stones increase the difficulty of maintaining an easy footing.
- Shoes should be worn to prevent foot injuries, but socks and insoles should be removed and kept dry.
- A shallow stream with a moderate current can be forded without the use of ropes or logs.
- The river should be crossed at an angle facing upstream.
- Legs should be dragged through the water, not lifted, so that the force of the current will not throw the individual off balance and drag him under.
- Feet should be set wide apart, kept flat with the bed of the stream, and should always be set down on the upper side of any obstruction in the stream bed.

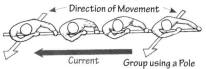

Direction of Movement

Current   Group using a Pole

Jumping: from boulder to boulder, jump from a crouching position pushing off simultaneously with both feet, and landing with both feet flat on the rock. Make sure that the rock is not wet, slimy or unstable.

Rope Crossing: each individual stays on the downstream side of the rope, as the current has a tendency to pull one under the rope.

Equipment Carried: always be ready to jettison it in case of an emergency. In order not to lose the equipment, attach it with a snaplink to the crossing rope before you start crossing.

Swift Current: To cross using the ring method, the group forms in a ring, locking hands with each other and placing the arms behind their backs. The body is bent well forward.

Swift Current: In the chain crossing, group forms in line, lock arms with each other, and then cross their own arms and lock their hands in front to give added support. The line then moves across diagonally downstream.

Moderate Current: If the current is moderate and the water less than knee deep, a staff or a walking stick may be used and worked ahead of the individual on the downstream side.

Fast Current: Where the current is fast, the water is more than knee deep, or when it has a shifting bottom crossing is facilitated by using a rope or balance pole that is at least head high. The balance pole is worked ahead of the individual, always on the upstream side. The weight of the body must be evenly distributed between the pole and the feet to maintain the necessary points of support. The pole is first moved forward and planted, and the feet are then moved ahead.

Water is normally turbulent over large stones, while it flows smoothly over small stones.

Crossing by the Ring Method

ROPES

ROPES

Ropes are the most important items of equipment for the rappeller. They provide access down an obstacle while ensuring individual safety.

TYPES OF ROPE

Two types of ropes are available to the rappeller:
- Static
- Dynamic

Static Rope: This rope allows for minimal stretch of the rope. The static rope stretches about 5 to 15% at the point of failure and about 2% under a working load.

Dynamic Rope: This rope allows for stretch within the fibers of the rope, which can be a disadvantage in rappelling, prusik climbing, and other applications. Dynamic ropes are more susceptible to abrasion and wear. They have about a 5 to 10% working stretch.

Two types of dynamic ropes are:
- Nylon-laid
- Kernmantle

Nylon-Laid Ropes: Synthetic fibers are the best climbing and rappelling material. Nylon has become the standard material for climbing ropes and has replaced manila, flax, hemp, and sisal. In mountaineering, critical application rope is constructed in a laid fashion with continuous multifilament-nylon fiber yarn twisted into strands. Three strands are twisted into a climbing rope of a specific diameter. Nylon-laid ropes are easy to inspect for serviceability by twisting the fibers. Laid ropes tend to untwist slightly when under a load, causing kinking and spinning. They are also susceptible to abrasion.

Kernmantle Ropes: These ropes are similar to their static counterparts in that they consist of an inner core and an outer sheath. The core is constructed of continuous twisted nylon filaments, which are laid or braided together and enclosed in a tightly braided outer sheath. These ropes are well suited for climbing on rock, snow, or ice where a brief elastic stretch of the rope occurs during a fall. They have a stretch of about 40% at the point of failure. The breaking strength is high, and there are no exposed strands for rock crystals to work between to damage the rope. There is less sliding friction through the snaplink and over other surfaces, since the outer sheath is smooth. Kernmantle ropes are available in many sizes, lengths, stretch factors, tensile strengths, and fall ratings.

Ropes are intended to provide security for climbers and equipment when there are steep ascents and descents. They are also used for establishing rope installations and hauling equipment.

Improvised Seat Harness

A: The tape is placed across the back so the midpoint (center) is on the hip opposite the hand that will be used for braking during belaying or rappelling. Keep the midpoint on the appropriate hip, cross the ends of the tape in front of the body, and tie half of a surgeon's knot (three or four overhand wraps) where the tapes cross.
B: The ends of the tape are brought between, the legs (front to rear), around the legs, and then secured with a jam hitch to tape around the waist on both sides. The tapes are tightened by pulling down on the running ends of the tape. This must be done to prevent the tape from crossing between the legs. Bring both ends around to the front and across the tape again.
C: Then bring the tape to the opposite side of the intended brake hand and tie a square knot with an overhand knot or two half-hitch safety knots on either side of the square knot. The safety knots should be passed around as much of the tape as possible.

IMPROVISED SEAT HARNESS

The seat harness is a safety sling which is used to attach the rope to the climber or rappeller. It must be tied correctly for safety and comfort reasons. An improvised seat harness can be made of 1-inch tubular nylon tape.

Once the seat harness has been properly tied, attach a single locking carabiner to the harness by clipping all of the web around the waist and the web of the half surgeon knot together. The gate of the carabiner should open on top and away from the climber.

Undamaged

Damaged

Inspect Rope Before Using

Rope suffers from abrasion when pulled over a rough surface.

Ropes when bent sharply, as around a snaplink, lose some of their strength at the bend and might even be permanently damaged.

Nylon-Laid Rope

Kernmantle Rope

SELECTING A ROPE

Rope can be chosen from various types, lengths, and diameters; and depending on its intended use (static or dynamic), environment (water-repellent), climate, hiking (lightweight ropes), and other factors. Static ropes should have minimal stretch; be smooth, flexible, and strong; resist abrasion and cutting; and have a low-impact force.

In Selection Consider...

- Laid rope is easier to inspect (by twisting the strands apart to observe the interior surfaces), has greater friction in holding knots, and is less expensive than kernmantle ropes. Its disadvantages include: much lower abrasion resistance, extremely high stretch factor for both static and dynamic loads, greater friction on rock, readiness to kink, tendency to spin a free-hanging rappeller, and greater absorption of water and dirt.
- Kernmantle rope is easy to work with, has less friction, does not kink easily, and has less susceptibility to abrasion. The outer sheath protects the internal fibers from dirt, abrasion, and ultraviolet radiation. Its disadvantages are that it is hard to determine damage to the core fibers, and it is more expensive than laid rope. Kernmantle rope is not readily identifiable as dynamic or static and must be marked accordingly.
- Manila rope 1.9 cm in diameter and larger is used in the construction of various types of installations as suspension and rope bridges because it has less of a stretch factor and are not affected by UV rays.
- Rope diameter and length vary with intended use. A standard diameter for many uses is 11 mm (7/16 inch). For stirrups, utility ropes, and hauling lines, 7 mm (5/16 inch), which can also be used in double strands, is adequate. Standards to remember are that the smaller the diameter, the less the tensile strength; but the larger the diameter, the heavier the rope. The standard lengths are 36 1/2 m (120 feet), 40 m (135 feet), 45 m (150 feet), and 50 m (165 feet). Normally, standard lengths should not be cut. If a nonstandard length is needed, the rope should be precut before the mission and clearly marked.
- A rope should be selected for a specific use. There are different types of ropes for various uses. A dynamic rope is designed for climbing, while a static rope is designed for rappelling, rescue operations, load hauling, and rope installations.
- Know the tensile strengths and characteristics and capabilities of the rope you select.

Using a rope for other than its intended use could result in personal injury or damage to equipment.

CARE OF ROPES

Because the rope is the rappeller's lifeline, it requires a great amount of care and maintenance.

- Inspect the ropes thoroughly before, during, and after use for cuts, excessive fraying, abrasions, mildew, soft and worn spots. If any of these defects are found, the rope is unserviceable. An unserviceable rope is destroyed by cutting it into usable parts. If no sections are usable, the rope is cut into smaller parts and discarded.
- Climbing rope should never be spliced, since it will be hard to manage at the splice.
- The rope must not come in contact with sharp edges. If this is likely, the areas must be padded or taped before rappelling.
- Keep the rope dry as much as possible. Dry it as soon as possible. Hang the rope to drip dry on a rounded peg, at room temperature (do not apply heat).
- Do not step on rope or unnecessarily drag it on the ground Small particles of dirt will be ground into the strands and will slowly cut them. This greatly reduces the tensile strength of the rope.
- Coil rope when not in use.
- New climbing rope should be marked, by whipping, in the middle. A mark at the middle of the rope, so that the exact center of the rope can quickly be found.
- New sling rope as well as any other rope that has been cut from a long piece should be whipped at the ends.
- New rope is stiff and should be worked.
- Avoid running rope over sharp or rough edges (pad if necessary) especially if under tension.
- Keep the rope away from oil, acids, and other corrosive substances.
- Avoid rubbing ropes together under tension (nylon to nylon friction will harm the rope).
- Do not leave rope knotted or tightly stretched longer than necessary.
- Clean in cool water, loosely coil and hang to dry (out of direct sunlight, since ultraviolet light rays will harm synthetic fibers). Store in a cool, dry, shaded area on a round wooden pegs.

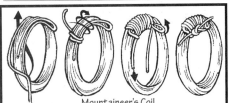

Mountaineer's Coil

A: Form a bight about 30 cm (12 inches) long with the starting end of the rope and lay it along the top of the coil.
B: Uncoil the last loop and use it to wrap around the coil and the bight.
C: Wrap toward the closed end of the bight, binding the final wrap across itself to lock it in place. Make 6 to 8 wraps to secure the coil. Push the end of the rope down through the closed end of the bight.

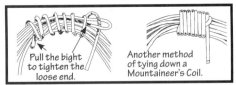

Pull the bight to tighten the loose end.

Another method of tying down a Mountaineer's Coil.

ROPE & KNOTS
See page 417

JUNGLE ROPES
See page 67

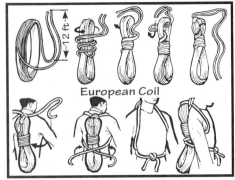

European Coil

ROPING TERMINOLOGY

Bight
Loop

Bight: is a simple bend of rope in which the rope does not cross itself.

Loop: is a bend of rope in which the rope does cross itself.

Half Hitch: is a loop that runs around an object and locks itself.

Running End: is the free end (working end) of the rope that can be used.

Standing Part: is the part that is static (anchored, coiled); the remaining part of the rope not being used (also called static end).

Lay: is the same as the twist of the rope.

Round Turn: is a single complete wrap of the rope around an object providing 360° contact. The running end leaves the completed circle in the same direction as the standing part. In a round turn, the rope is wrapped around an object 1 1/2 times.

Pigtail: is the short length of rope remaining at the end after tying a knot or coiling a rope.

Back Feeding: (or stacking) is taking off one wrap at a time from a coil, and letting it fall naturally to the ground.

Dress Down the Knot: is tightening down a knot to its functioning form.

Overhand: is a loop with the running end pulled through the loop.

COILING ROPE
MOUNTAINEER'S COIL

• To use the mountaineer's coil, grasp the rope about 3 feet from the end with the left hand. The right hand is then placed next to the left hand and runs along the rope until both arms are outstretched. Grasping the rope firmly, bring the hands together to form a loop, which is laid in the left hand. Repeat, forming uniform loops that run in a clockwise direction until the rope is completely coiled. If the rope tends to twist or form figure eights, give it a slight twist with the right hand when each loop is formed. Coil the rope in a clockwise direction to conform with the lay.

• To complete the coil, form a bight about 30 centimeters (12 inches) long with the starting end of the rope and lay it along the top of the coil. Uncoil the last loop and use it to wrap around the coil and the bight. Wrap toward the closed end of the bight, binding the final wrap across itself to lock it in place. Make six to eight wraps to secure the coil. Push the end of the rope down through the closed end of the bight. Carry the running end of the coil either in the pack (by forming a figure eight, doubling it, and placing it under the flap) or by placing it over the shoulder and under the opposite arm. If the rope to be coiled is anchored as in coiling a belay or rappel lane, start the coil near the end closest to the anchor so that the kinks work themselves out of the free end.

BUTTERFLY COIL

• The butterfly coil is easier and faster to coil than the mountaineer's coil. Establish the center of the rope either by locating its center mark or by grasping both ends of the rope and feeding them out until a bight comes up that is the center of the rope. Begin coiling with the doubled rope the same as the mountaineer's coil method. Leave about 4.6 meters (15 feet) of rope uncoiled. Then, squeeze the coils together and make four to six wraps around the middle of the coil, ensuring that the first wrap is held in place by the other wraps.

• Form a bight with the two running ends and place it through the bight formed by the top of the coil. Then, run the two running ends over the top of the coil and through the bight that is formed. Dress them in the center of the back of the carrier. Run the two ends over the shoulders to form shoulder straps. Then, bring them under the arms, cross them in the back over the coil, bring them around the body of the carrier, and tie them off with a square knot at the stomach.

EUROPEAN COIL

Starting in the center of the rope, coil the rope into 3 foot diameter loops until there is about 12 feet of rope tail left on the two ends. The ends are then wrapped three to four times around the coil, a bight is passed through the center of the coil, and the tails passed through the bight. This is then tightened down with two remaining tails of about 6 feet. The coil can now be carried by placing the coil on the back, passing one end over each shoulder, between the arm and the chest, and passing around the back to return to the front of the body. The two ends are now secured at waist level.

KNOTS

A knot is a fastening made by intertwining or tying pieces of string, cord, rope, or webbing.

Knots used by a rappeller are divided into four classes:

Class I   **Joining Knots**
Class II   **Anchor Knots**
Class III **Middle Rope Knots**
Class IV   **Special Knots**

These classes of knots are intended only as a general guide since some of the knots discussed may be appropriate in more than one class. The skill of knot tying may be lost if it is not used and practiced. With experience and practice, knot tying becomes instinctive and helps the soldier in many situations.

JOINING KNOTS: CLASS I

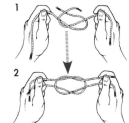

Square Knot
The square knot is used to tie the ends of two ropes of equal diameter.

Double Sheet Bend Knot
The double sheet bend knot is used to tie the ends of two or more ropes of equal or unequal diameter. When a single rope is tied to a multiple of ropes, the bight is formed with the multiple of ropes.

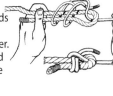

Fisherman's Knot
The fisherman's knot is used to tie two ropes of similar or dissimilar materials.

Double Fisherman's Knot
The double fisherman's knot (also called double English or grapevine) is used to tie two ropes of similar or dissimilar materials.

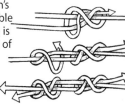

Water Knot
The water knot is used to attach two webbing ends. It is also called a ring bend, overhand retrace, or tape knot. It is used in

Water Knot

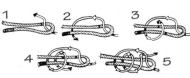

Double Sheet Knot

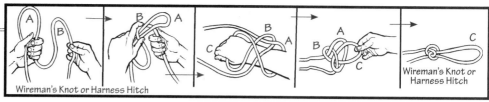
Wireman's Knot or Harness Hitch

ANCHOR KNOTS: CLASS II

Bowline Knot

The bowline knot is used to tie a single fixed loop in the end of a rope. It does not slip under strain and is easily untied. This knot is always used when there is alternating tension. It can also be used to tie the end of a rope to an anchor.

Round Turn & Two Half Hitches Knot

Is used to tie the end of a rope to an anchor and must have constant tension.

Figure-Eight Knot

Is also called a rerouted figure eight. Although it produces the same result as a figure-eight loop, by tying the knot in a retrace it can be used to fasten the rope to trees or to places where the loop cannot be used.

Clove Hitch Knot

The clove hitch knot can be used in the middle of the rope as well as at the end of the rope. The knot must have constant tension on it once tied to prevent slipping. It can be used as either an anchor or middle knot, depending on how it is tied.

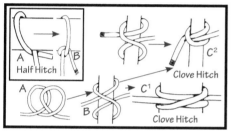
Half Hitch — Clove Hitch — Clove Hitch

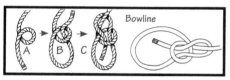
Bowline

Round Turn & Two Half Hitches Knot

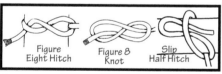
Figure Eight Hitch — Figure 8 Knot — Slip Half Hitch

IMPROVISED CHEST HARNESS

The Parisian bandolier or chest harness is a secondary safety sling used to attach to a safety sling at the top of climbs or for top belaying on high-angle rappels. A Parisian bandolier is made from a continuous loop of webbing. The loop should be 3 to 4 feet long. The knot connecting the two ends of tape together is a water knot with an overhand knot or half hitch as safeties. To don the bandolier, place one arm through the loop and bring the running end of the loop behind the back and under the opposite arm. A sheet bend is tied in the center of the chest by using the center of the tape which was passed under the climber's arm and inserted through the portion of bight formed by the tape that goes over the shoulder.

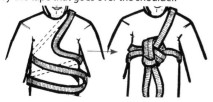

MIDDLE ROPE KNOTS: CLASS III

Wireman's Knot or Harness Hitch

A single, fixed loop in the middle of the rope.

Directional Figure-Eight Knot

Forms a single, fixed loop in the middle of the rope that lies back along the standing part of the rope.

Directional Figure-Eight Knot

Figure-Eight-on-a-Bight Knot

Is used to form two fixed loops in the middle of a rope.

Figure-Eight-on-a-Bight

Overhand Loop Knot

Forms a single loop in the middle of a rope. It should not be used in a transport tightening system.

Overhand Loop Knot

Sheet Bend — Double Sheet Bend

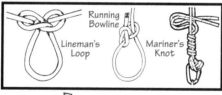
Lineman's Loop — Running Bowline — Mariner's Knot

Figure Eight Loop — Figure Eight Knot

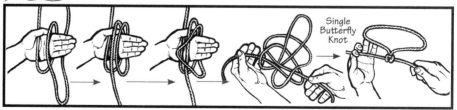
Single Butterfly Knot

SPECIAL KNOTS: CLASS IV

Single Butterfly Knot

Used to form a single, fixed loop in the middle of the rope without using the ends. The butterfly can be used for the middle man in a rope party as well as in a transport tightening system. The knot can be hard to untie when heavy weight has been placed on it for extended periods. *See below.*

Prusik Knot

Used to put a movable rope on a fixed rope such as a prusik ascent or a tightening system. This knot can be tied as a middle, finger, or end knot.

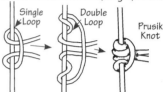
Single Loop — Double Loop — Prusik Knot

Three-Loop Bowline Knot

Used to form three fixed loops in the middle of a rope. It is used in a self-equalizing anchor system.

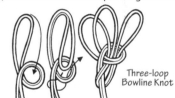
Three-loop Bowline Knot

Figure-Eight Slip Knot

It forms an adjustable bight in a rope.

Figure-Eight Slip Knot

Double Figure-Eight Knot

Used for temporarily joining Kernmantle or hard lay ropes (rappels, Tyrolean traverses). Carabiners should be placed between lines within the knot to prevent the knot from clinching down when loaded.

Double Figure-Eight Knot

CLIMBING HELMET

Climbers should wear a hard shell helmet which is designed to minimize injury during falls or when struck by a small object falling from above their position. The helmet consists of a hard shell which is held away from the head by a suspension system. The suspension system absorbs a portion of the blow to the top of the helmet. Helmet fit should be such that the side of the head is protected. A "Y" style strap system of lightweight webbing retains the helmet on the head better than a single strap. The headband is adjustable to allow donning over a wool cap in cold weather. The hard shell should not have cracks or breaks. The suspension system must be securely riveted in place. The straps must be free of cuts, frays, and securely fastened to the helmet.

NYLON WEBBING

Used for making runners, etriers (stirrups) and other general purpose slings. Flat or tubular nylon webbing is either 9/16 inch (1.43 cm) or 1 inch (2.5 cm) wide.

GLOVES

Gloves should be worn when belaying or rappelling. Since these techniques are performed frequently, the gloves should be attached to the climber (rescuer) at all times.

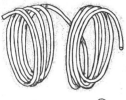

Divide rope coil in half. Throw first half and feed second half while the first half is in the air.

A stone or stick can be attached if throwing a short heavy rope into the wind or over a branch. A light guide rope, which is thrown, can be attached to a heavier rope which is then pulled over by the guide rope.

THROWING ROPE

Carefully coil the rope before throwing. In throwing the full rope, grasp the coil in the right hand and take the end of the rope nearest the fingertips and anchor it. Take five or six loops from the anchored end of the coil and hold it in the left hand while holding the remaining coil, which will be thrown first, in the right hand. A few preliminary swings will ensure a smooth throw with the arm nearly extended. The coil should be thrown out and up. A slight twist of the wrist so that the palm of the hand comes up as the rope is thrown will cause the coil to turn, the loops to spread, and the running end to fall free and away from the thrower. A smooth follow-through is essential. As soon as the coil is thrown and spreading, the loops held in the left hand should be tossed out. Where possible, the rope should be thrown with the wind so that the running end is to the leeward side. As soon as the rope starts to leave the hand, the thrower shouts the warning "ROPE" to alert anyone below his position.

CARE OF NYLON WEBBING

- Cut with a hot knife to fuse the ends to prevent fraying.
- Keep away from oil, acids and other corrosive substances.
- Inspect before, during and after use for fraying, cuts and excess dirt.
- Clean in cool water, air dry, and store in a cool dry area out of direct sunlight. Do not store on cement floors.
- Do not store in closed plastic bags.

INSPECTION OF EQUIPMENT

All equipment must be inspected before rappelling.

Carabiners: should be inspected daily before, during, and after use.

- The metal should be checked for cracks, grooves, burrs, rust, and flaws. The gate should open and close freely without binding. There should be no lateral movement when the gate is open. The gate spring action should snap shut when released. The locking notch should have a slant or slot so that the gate remains shut under the impact of a rappeller's fall. The gate pins should not work their way out of their holes and should not be shorter than their holes. If there is a locking mechanism, it should be inspected to ensure that threads are not stripped and that the sleeve tightly locks the gate.
- If burrs, grooves, or rough areas are identified, the carabiner should not be used. Rust should be removed with steel wool and the spot rubbed with oil or solvent. The spring should be lubricated as needed. The carabiner must be boiled in water for 20 to 30 seconds to remove the cleaning agents since solvents and oils cause dirt to cling to the carabiner and to rub off on the ropes. It is better to use a dry graphite-based lubricant on carabiners since such lubricants do not attract dirt.

Ropes: are inspected for serviceability. A rappel rope is unserviceable if it is saturated with petroleum products, is mildewed, shows excessive wear, has soft spots (internal damage), or if one strand is cut through more than one-half of its diameter. Ropes should be inspected daily - before, during, and after use. An applicable annotation should be made in a corresponding rope log.

CARABINERS

Carabiners are used to join equipment, rope, and people into a functioning system. When used properly, they are strong, versatile items. The carabiners used by climbers fall into two material designs-aluminum alloy and chrome vanadium steel. Both material designs may be either locking or non locking. They come in many sizes, shapes, and strengths (with and without locking gates). Alloy metals provide the maximum strength for adverse terrain work. As with ropes, carabiners are rated differently depending on the manufacturer. Aluminum alloy and chrome vanadium steel carabiners will be oval-shaped or D-shaped.

DESCRIPTION

Carabiners are available in many sizes and shapes to suit different needs. A locking snaplink is best for rappelling. Non locking snaplinks are easy to operate, but should be used only where they cannot be accidentally opened. Hollow carabiners should be avoided since their use is limited.

Alloy Standard Oval (non locking): is shaped in an oval with a gate to allow access into the center of the oval. The gate contains a locking pin which fits into the locking notch when the gate is closed. The alloy D-shape (non locking) is shaped in the fashion of a D which allows greater distribution of weight applied to the longer side. Features and operation are the same as the standard oval.

Alloy Locking D: or oval are both constructed the same as previously discussed but are machined with threads on the gate and a sleeve which, when screwed clockwise, will cover the locking notch and pin for a positive lock. The sleeve screws tightly over the gate opening end or hinge end to hold the gate closed. A reverse locking gate is needed to prevent a moving rope from unscrewing the sleeve. The locking sleeve and threads should be kept free of dirt and grit. If the sleeve is forced to close, it may strip the threads. The locking mechanism ages and weakens after repeated use and should be routinely inspected for wear.

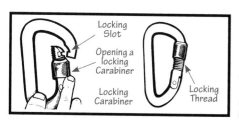

Locking Slot
Opening a locking Carabiner
Locking Carabiner
Locking Thread

CARABINERS

- Carabiners should not be dropped or used for other than the designed purpose since small fracture lines may develop and weaken the structure.
- Carabiners should not be used as a hammer nor loaded (stressed) beyond their maximum breaking strength.
- The moving parts, hinge and sleeve, of locking carabiners should be kept clean for free movement. If a carabiner "binds," do not oil it - discard it! The weakest part of a carabiner is the gate. The gate must be closed before applying a load. When the gate is open, carabiners should have little or no lateral movement of the gate.
- Carabiners should not be filed, stamped, or marked with an engraving tool. Colored tape or Teflon paint may be used to identify carabiners.
- All moving parts (gate, locking sleeve) should operate freely and the locking pin must properly align with the locking notch. Obvious fractures, regardless of size, are cause for condemning a carabiner. Locking pins should be checked to ensure that they are not loose, worn, or corroded.
- The metal should be checked for any cracks, grooves, burrs, flaws, or rust.
- The spring-loaded gate should automatically close securely from an open to a closed position with no gap between the locking pin and notch.
- If an engraver is used to mark snaplinks, it should be applied only to the gate, never to the load-bearing side.
- A carabiner should never be side-loaded (across the gate) since this reduces the overall strength to the point of gate failure.

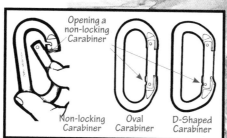

Opening a non-locking Carabiner

Non-locking Carabiner   Oval Carabiner   D-Shaped Carabiner

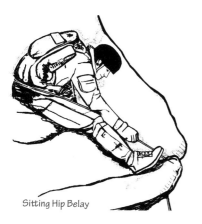

Sitting Hip Belay

PITONS, CARABINERS, & CHOCKS

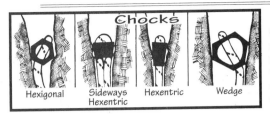

Hexigonal   Sideways   Hexentric   Wedge
             Hexentric

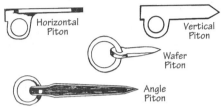

Horizontal Piton

Vertical Piton

Wafer Piton

Angle Piton

Types of Pitons

Vertical: For narrow (flush) vertical cracks.
Horizontal: For narrow horizontal cracks and for offset horizontal or vertical cracks.
Angle: For wide deep horizontal or vertical cracks. These must be placed with the wide or open side down in horizontal cracks and open side against either wall in vertical cracks.
Wafer: For small shallow vertical or horizontal cracks.

Second-Hand Pitons

Pitons that have been used, removed, bent, and straightened should be discarded. Pitons already in place should not be trusted, as they can be loosened by weathering. They should be tested and redrive until the climber is certain of their safety.

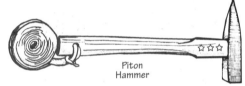

Piton Hammer

Piton Hammer

Always secure your piton hammer with a lanyard before starting the climb.
Piton hammers are used for:
• Driving and removing pitons.
  Do not use the point on the hammer.
• Testing rock (avoid hollow or rotten rock).
• Cleaning out cracks of dirt and debris.
• Chipping rock or ice.

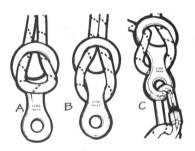

A   B   C

Figure-Eight Clog

A mechanical friction device used for belaying, rappelling, and breaking while lowering personnel and equipment. The device is formed in a figure-eight with two different size openings comprising the inner holes. The rope is passed through the larger hole of the "8" and over the connecting portion of the device. The smaller hole is attached to a carabiner.

Chocks

Chocks are metal alloy or copper shapes with unequal sides which are placed within cracks in rocks to serve as anchor points or parts of a protection system. A well placed chock is quicker and easier to place than pitons. Each type of chock is designed to fit within a variety of cracks in rocks. The various shapes with uneven sides allow one size to fit many rock openings. Carrying different sizes of chocks allows a person to choose the most suitable chock for the job. Chocks provide protection for a single direction of pull. Placing chocks in opposition gives additional security. Insert a proper size chock into the crack and rotate it so that at least two sides are wedged into the crack. Test by pulling up, down, sideways and out with increasing weight. Retrieve by pushing in and turning side to side or up and down. Well wedged chocks may require tapping out with a piton hammer.

Copperhead Chock

Cylindrical copper chocks have a relatively soft head that bites well into rock and has little rotation after placement. It is manufactured with a cable sling attached.

Hexentric Chock

A metal alloy chock constructed with six sides. Each side is a different length than the opposing side. The two ends are tapered, gradually getting smaller from the back to the front of the chock. The front of the hexentric chock is the narrowest of the faces. Small hexentric chocks are manufactured with wire slings and larger ones have two holes bored through the front to back for threading of a Kernmantle sling.

Wedge Chock

A solid alloy metal chock shaped in the form of a wedge. All four sides decrease in size from back to front. As with small hexentrics, small wedges are manufactured with wire slings while larger wedges require Kernmantle slings.

Cammed Chocks

Half moon shaped, wired and looped chocks come in a variety of sizes and are well suited for small to intermediate placements. Mechanical spring activated camming devices can be easily placed with one hand, and are easy to retrieve.

Maintenance of Chocks

All chocks should be treated the same as carabiners. However, chocks will take considerable abuse since they are wedged in rock, and at times, the leverage of a hammer may be required to remove them. Chocks manufactured with wire slings and wedges should be closely monitored for security. If there is doubt about the condition of a wedge, it must not be used. Rope or tape slings on chocks must meet inspection requirements. Cracks in any surface of the chock is cause to remove it from service. Small scratches or grooves on the outer surfaces are not cause for removal from service.

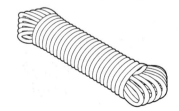

Pitons

Pitons are driven into cracks in the rock to increase the climber's safety. If well placed and tested they will limit his fall to twice the distance he is above the piton, plus the stretch factor of the rope. A well placed piton can withstand a force of several hundred pounds (wafer) to more than 2,000 pounds (900 kg) (angle). The advantage over chocks is that pitons provide support for an omnidirectional pull, and are well suited for anchors and rope installations. Pitons provide a secure point on the cliff to which the rope may be attached by means of a snaplink. If the leading climber falls he may be held, pulley-wise, by a man below him. It will also hold each following man. Successive pitons are driven as the climber moves upward this will secure points along the course of a fixed rope. The placement of pitons can be extended by attaching runners (utility ropes or nylon webbing). You can insert a snaplink through the eye of the piton.

In placing pitons the climber should study the rock. See that driving of a piton will not split or weaken it. Test rock for soundness by tapping with the hammer. In hard, solid rock select a crack which is wide enough to admit 1/3 to 1/2 of the piton shaft before driving the piton in. The driving of pitons in soft or rotten rock is not always practical. When this type of rock must be used, loose rock from the crack should be removed before driving the piton. In this type of rock it is not necessary to be able to insert the piton into the crack as far as in solid rock. Select the right piton; the one that the rock will support best and that the snaplink can be hooked into after the piton is driven in.

Piton Types

Pitons are metal alloy spikes of various shapes, widths, and lengths which are hammered into cracks in rock surfaces for anchor points or as part of a protection system.
Pitons are divided into two different categories: blades and angles.
Blades: The holding power results from being wedged into cracks. These pitons have flat surfaces and range in size from knife-blade thickness to one-half inch.
Angles: Hold by wedging and blade compression. These pitons have rounded or V-shaped blades and allow the sharp edges to cut into the edge of a crack. Sizes vary from a short "shallow angle" of one-half inch thick and 21/2 inches long to "bongs" (large angles of 4 inches in width). The leaper, a special Z-shaped angle, is designed to give greater holding power due to its cutting ability and blade compression.

Piton Strength & Damage

Pitons are made of chrome-molybdenum alloy metal which has a high strength versus weight ratio. Multiple holes further reduce the weight but do not compromise their strength. Pitons are virtually indestructible. However, they should only be used for the designed purpose. Damage may occur during the placement of a piton by ineffective or off-center hammering. Pitons must not have cracks or be bent from the shape of manufacture. Any piton which is suspected of cracks or bends should be removed from service.

DRIVING PITONS

While driving the piton, watch the rock to see that it is not being weakened by further cracking. The piton should go in smoothly and notice if the point hits a dead end. Listen to the piton's sound at each blow; good verticals and horizontals usually go in with a rising pitch, wafer and angle pitons will have no noticeable pitch as long as the ring is swinging free. Drive the piton with slow moderate strokes. The piton should always be attached to the hammer thong or to the sling rope by a snaplink. If the piton is knocked out of the crack while it is being driven it will not be lost. The greater the resistance overcome in driving the piton, the firmer it will be. An appropriately placed and well-driven piton into rock of average strength will withstand a force of from several hundred pounds (wafer) to more than 2,000 pounds (900 kg) (angle) exerted in the direction of pull.

Piton Placement: Basically, the use of pitons is a matter of locating a crack, selecting a piton which fits, driving the piton in, clipping a carabiner to the eye, and attaching the rope system to the carabiner.

- First look at the crack to decide the best position for driving the piton. The piton should be driven into the wider portion of the crack to reduce the likelihood of shifting or rotating under pressure. The crack must not widen or flare internally and not have a change in direction of more than 15 to 20 degrees.
- Before driving, the piton should fit one-half to two-thirds of the blade length into the crack. Drive until only the eye protrudes or the piton meets resistance. Do not attempt to overdrive the piton because it may fracture. Lightly tap the piton to test for movement or improper seating. If movement is noted, remove the piton and replace it with the next larger size or locate another anchor position. The proper placement of pitons in horizontal cracks is with the eye down. If the piton cannot be driven into the rock until only the eye protrudes, it may be tied off by placing a short sling around the piton with a girth or clove hitch as close to the rock as possible. In this case, the sling should be used as the attachment point and not the eye of the piton.

TESTING PITONS

Pull up approximately one meter of slack on the climbing rope, or use sling rope or the piton hammer thong; snap rope into a snaplink; grasp rope at least 1/2 meter from the snaplink. Make sure that you have secure footing, jerk vigorously outward, downward, and to each side, meanwhile observing the piton. Repeat if the test is questionable. Tap the piton. If the pitch has changed much, drive the piton in as far as possible; if the sound regains its original pitch the piton is good. If not, drive another piton into new location.

REMOVE PITONS

The climber should knock the pitons back and forth in the crack with the piton hammer, and when they are loosened, pull them out with a bight of the climbing rope or sling rope, or hammer thong, which has been hooked into a snaplink. Be well braced when pulling out pitons, as they sometimes tend to suddenly come out. Make sure that no one will be struck by the extracted piton.

ANCHORS

Anchors are secure points in the belay chain providing protection for the belayer and the climber. Anchor systems must be able to withstand high loads. The basis for any type of anchor is strong, secure points for attachment.

ANCHOR POINTS

Anchor systems may be simple and consist of a single anchor point, or complex and consist of multiple anchor points. Anchor points are divided into two classes-natural and artificial. Anchor systems may be constructed entirely of one class, or a combination of the two.

NATURAL ANCHOR POINTS

Spike: A spike is a vertical projection of rock. For use as an anchor point, a sling is placed around the spike.

Rock Bollard: A rock bollard is a large rock or portion of such a rock which has an angular surface enabling a sling or rope to be placed around it in such a manner that will not allow it to slip off. Care must be taken to ensure the bollard will not be pulled loose when subjected to a sudden load.

Chockstone: A natural chockstone is a securely wedged rock providing an anchor point for a sling. In most cases, the rock is wedged within a crack.

Tree: Trees often make very secure anchor points. A rope can be tied directly to the tree (or a sling doubled around the tree and connected by a carabiner). In loose or rocky soil, trees should be carefully watched and avoided if other anchor points are available.

ARTIFICIAL ANCHOR POINTS

Artificial anchor points are those constructed from equipment carried by the team. These are usually the chocks or pitons placed in cracks or bolts drilled in the rock.

Chock Placement: The basic principle is to wedge the selected chock into a crack so that a pull in the direction of fall will not pull the chock out. The proper method is to select a crack suitable for an anchor point and select a chock to fit that crack. The chock chosen should closely fit the widest portion of the crack. Work the chock into the crack until it is securely seated. It should be seated so that the load will come on the entire chock without rotating it out of position. When the chock is in place, jerk hard on the attached sling in the direction of fall to ensure it is well seated. (Ensure the chock cannot continue to work downward to a larger area of the crack and become dislodged). A chock may also be placed so that its pull is in one direction while the second chock has a pull in the opposing direction. One sling is passed through the loop of the other chock. A force exerted downward will pull the two chocks toward each other along the axis of the crack. In vertical cracks, the lower sling should be passed through the upper for best results. The two chocks should be placed far enough apart so neither sling will reach the other chock. (NOTE: Chocks are preferred over pitons and bolts since they do not deface the rock.)

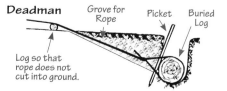

Deadman | Grove for Rope | Picket | Buried Log

Log so that rope does not cut into ground.

Good
Good
Good if bashed in
OK, better if eye is down
Poor

Poor: Crack widens
Good: Crack bottlenecks

Yes | No
Unsafe | Safer

Yes
No
Chromemoly
Poor: Piton grips only at end of crack
Good

Tree Anchor
Spike Anchor
Choke Stone
Rock Bollard

Anchors

Use slings to reduce the distance between the anchor and the equalizing system; this will minimize the amount of shift if an anchor fails.

Picket Holdfast

ANCHOR SYSTEM

The purpose of an anchor system is to unite weak anchor points into a strong anchor system. Systems are divided into two classes: equalizing and non equalizing.

Equalizing Systems: are constructed so that if there is a change in direction of the load, the stress will be equally distributed to all anchor points. One major problem with this system is that if one point fails, the remaining points will be shock loaded.

Non equalizing Systems: are constructed when a change of direction is not expected. The major advantage is the entire load is shared by the anchor points equally and would require the entire system to fail before coming loose. Any multipoint anchor system tied together so the attaching rope does not slip would be considered non equalizing.

CLIMBING LIST
Rock Climbing
- Helmet
- Chocks and nuts
- Piton hammer
- Hammer holster
- Pitons
- Carabiners
- Kletterschuhe (rock climbing shoes)
- Swami belt
- Rope (check each time before using)

Ice & Snow Climbing
- Helmet
- Cagoule (Balaclava)
- Extra socks
- Gaiters
- Mittens, Fingerless mittens
- Slings, rappel anchors, runners, seats, etc.
- Rock pitons
- Tubular ice screws
- Backpack
- Crampons
- Emergency shelter
- Boots
- Rope
- Carabiners
- Alpine Hammer
- Hammer holster
- Ice ax
- Down jacket

ROCK CLIMBING
Precautions while Climbing
- Margin of safety. Stay within individual abilities.
- Use roped party climbs as the slope steepens and the difficulty increases.
- Plan entire route this will prevent the group from getting "stuck".
- Avoid overstretching, i.e., "spread eagle" position.
- Avoid "hugging" the rock.
- Test loose rock before placing weight on it.
- Avoid using knees, elbows, and buttocks.
- Do not dislodge rocks intentionally. Yell "Rock" when causing rock to fall.
- Never climb alone.
- Do not jump or lunge to reach a hold.
- Avoid wet moss covered rock.
- Clean boot sole (cleats) before climbing.
- Do not use vegetation as foot or hand holds.
- Do not use snaplinks as hand holds.
- Avoid wearing gloves when climbing.
- Remove jewelry from the hands before climbing.
- When a climber falls, shout the warning "Falling" to signal the belay man and to warn climbers below.

THE SUCCESSFUL CLIMB
The successful accomplishment of a climb is based on the strict application of basic principles and techniques.

ROUTE SELECTION
Route selection can be the deciding factor in planning a climb. A direct line is seldom the proper route from a given point to the area of the survivor. Time spent at the beginning of the climbing operation in proper route selection may save a large amount of time once the operation has started. The entire route must be planned before it is carried out, with the safest route selected. Natural hazards present, retreat routes available, time involved to perform the climb, and logistics will be major influencing factors in selecting the route.

LEAD CLIMBER TECHNIQUES
The lead climber is responsible for following the pre planned route of climb and altering the route as necessary. If the route of climb must be altered, consideration must be given to the experience of the climber(s). Climbing moves which are considered easy for the leader may be difficult for the second climber. Additionally, lead climbers must provide for their own personal protection during climbs to minimize the distance of a possible fall. Each intermediate protection point placed must be secure and follow as direct a line as possible.

DANGERS TO AVOID
- On long routes, changing weather will be an important consideration. Wet or icy rock can make an otherwise easy route almost impassable; cold may reduce climbing efficiency; snow may cover holds. A weather forecast should be obtained if possible. Smooth rock slabs are treacherous, especially when wet or iced after freezing rain. Ledges should then be sought. Rocks overgrown with moss, lichens, or grass become treacherous when wet. Under these conditions, cleated boots are by far better than composition soles.
- Tufts of grass and small bushes that appear firm may be growing from loosely packed and unanchored soil, all of which may give way if the grass or bush is pulled upon. Grass and bushes should be used only for balance by touch or as push holds - never as pull holds. Gently inclined but smooth slopes of rock may be covered with pebbles that may roll treacherously underfoot.
- Ridges can be free of loose rock, but topped with unstable blocks. A route along the side of a ridge just below the top is usually best. Gullies provide the best protection and often the easiest routes, but are more subject to rockfalls. The side of the gully is relatively free from this danger. Climbing slopes of talus, moraines, or other loose rock are not only tiring to the individual but dangerous because of the hazards of rolling rocks to others in the party. Rescuers should close up intervals when climbing simultaneously. In electrical storms, lightning can endanger the climber. Peaks, ridges, pinnacles, and lone trees should be avoided.
- Rockfalls are the most common mountaineering danger. The most frequent causes of rockfalls are other climbers, heavy rain and extreme temperature changes in high mountains, and resultant splitting action caused by intermittent freezing and thawing. Warning of a rockfall may be the cry "ROCK," a whistling sound, a grating sound, a thunderous crashing, or sparks where the rocks strike at night. A rockfall can be a single rock or a rockslide covering a relatively large area. Rockfalls occur on all steep slopes, particularly in gullies and chutes. Areas of frequent rockfalls may be indicated by fresh scars on the rock walls, fine dust on the talus piles, or lines, grooves, and rock-strewn areas on snow beneath cliffs. Immediate action is to seek cover, if possible. If there is not enough time to avoid the rockfall, the climber should lean into the slope to minimize exposure. Danger from falling rock can be minimized by careful climbing and route selection. The route selected must be commensurate with the ability of the least experienced team member.
  NOTE: Yell "rock" when equipment is dropped.

LEADER BELAY

The length of the climbing rope or the length of the route climbed will determine when a belay will be established by the leader. If the route is longer than a rope length, a belay must be established by the leader to protect the first belayer's ascent to the leader's position.

The belay chain is established as shown above. The only alteration necessary to the belay chain would be if the second climber continued the climb as the leader once the belayer's (first leader's) position is reached. This leap frogging of the leader is referred to as "climbing through". The sequence for the climbing through method begins when the first leader reaches the end of the climbing rope length. The leader selects a suitable belay position when the belayer (second climber) states that approximately 20 feet of rope remain. With a suitable site selected, one that has anchor and an area for a standing or sitting belay, the lead climber belays. The second climber then climbs up to the lead climber. Once reaching the lead climber, the second climber assumes the lead climber's role and continues the climb.

- Terrain must be analyzed to find an efficient route of travel. The rescuer (climber) must make a detailed reconnaissance, noting each rock obstacle, the best approach, height, angle, type of rock, difficulty, distance between belay positions, amount of equipment, and number of trained rescuers needed to accomplish the mission on or beyond the rocks. If the strata dips toward the rescuer, holds will be difficult as the slope will be the wrong way. However, strata sloping away from the rescuer and toward the mountain mass provides natural stairs with good holds and ledges.
- At least two vantage points should be used so a three-dimensional understanding of the climb can be attained. Use of early morning or late afternoon light, with its longer shadows, is helpful in this respect. Actual ground reconnaissance should be made, if possible.

BELAYING

Belaying provides the safety factor or tension, which enables the party to climb with greater security. Without belaying skill, the use of rope in party climbing is a hazard. When climbing, a climber is belayed from above or below by another rescue team member.

The belayer must run the rope through the guiding hand, which is the hand on the rope running to the climber or rescuer, and around their body to the brake hand, making certain that it will slide readily. The belayer must ensure that the remainder of the rope is laid out so it will run freely through the braking hand.

EQUIPMENT FOR BELAY

Minimum equipment for a belay system is divided between rescue team and personal equipment. Rescue team equipment is comprised of the items necessary for the climbers to reach the objective. These are the climbing rope and climbing hardware, including chocks, pitons, slings, and carabiners. Individual equipment is comprised of items which allow each climber to perform belaying and climb. These equipment items are climbing helmet, seat harness, climbing boots, and gloves (worn while belaying or rappelling only).

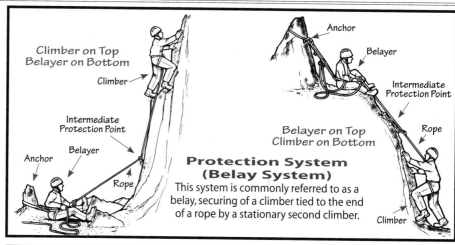

Climber on Top Belayer on Bottom

Climber — Intermediate Protection Point — Belayer — Anchor — Rope

Anchor — Belayer — Intermediate Protection Point — Rope — Climber

Belayer on Top Climber on Bottom

Protection System (Belay System)

This system is commonly referred to as a belay, securing of a climber tied to the end of a rope by a stationary second climber.

Sitting Belayer

Sitting Belayer is normally the most secure and preferred position.

Just below anchor (Correct)

Rope is too low on back and will pull under belayer.

Rope too high on back and rope will ride up into the belayer's armpits. Belayer is pulled forwards if the climber were to fall.

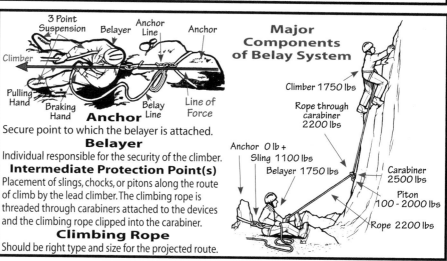

3 Point Suspension — Belayer — Anchor Line — Anchor — Climber — Pulling Hand — Braking Hand — Belay Line — Line of Force

Major Components of Belay System

Climber 1750 lbs
Rope through carabiner 2200 lbs
Anchor 0 lb + Sling 1100 lbs
Belayer 1750 lbs
Carabiner 2500 lbs
Piton 100 - 2000 lbs
Rope 2200 lbs

Anchor
Secure point to which the belayer is attached.
Belayer
Individual responsible for the security of the climber.
Intermediate Protection Point(s)
Placement of slings, chocks, or pitons along the route of climb by the lead climber. The climbing rope is threaded through carabiners attached to the devices and the climbing rope clipped into the carabiner.
Climbing Rope
Should be right type and size for the projected route.

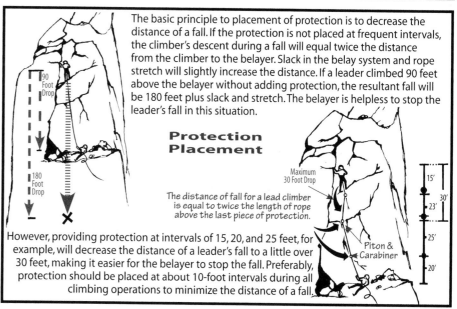

90 Foot Drop

180 Foot Drop

The basic principle to placement of protection is to decrease the distance of a fall. If the protection is not placed at frequent intervals, the climber's descent during a fall will equal twice the distance from the climber to the belayer. Slack in the belay system and rope stretch will slightly increase the distance. If a leader climbed 90 feet above the belayer without adding protection, the resultant fall will be 180 feet plus slack and stretch. The belayer is helpless to stop the leader's fall in this situation.

Protection Placement

Maximum 30 Foot Drop

The distance of fall for a lead climber is equal to twice the length of rope above the last piece of protection.

15'
30'
23'
25'
20'

Piton & Carabiner

However, providing protection at intervals of 15, 20, and 25 feet, for example, will decrease the distance of a leader's fall to a little over 30 feet, making it easier for the belayer to stop the fall. Preferably, protection should be placed at about 10-foot intervals during all climbing operations to minimize the distance of a fall.

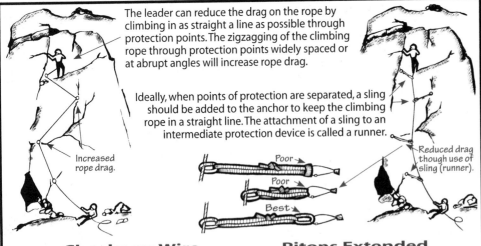

The leader can reduce the drag on the rope by climbing in as straight a line as possible through protection points. The zigzagging of the climbing rope through protection points widely spaced or at abrupt angles will increase rope drag.

Ideally, when points of protection are separated, a sling should be added to the anchor to keep the climbing rope in a straight line. The attachment of a sling to an intermediate protection device is called a runner.

Increased rope drag.

Poor
Poor
Best

Reduced drag though use of sling (runner).

Chocks on Wire

Chocks on wire should always have a runner placed on the wire. The runner reduces the direct rope movement of the wired chock, thereby reducing possible dislodgment. For all wired and roped chocks, runners should be clipped into a carabiner at the chock, and the climbing rope clipped into an additional carabiner.

Pitons Extended

Pitons may also be extended in a similar manner to that used for chocks. If sufficient runners are not available on long climbs, a chock sling may be used. The climbing leader must correctly thread the climbing rope through the carabiners attached to the piton. The carabiner should open either down and out or toward the belayer. Further, the rope running through the carabiner should run from the inside to the outside to prevent binding or the carabiner gate from opening.

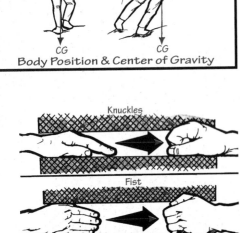

A — Distribution of Weight
B — Unstable Dangerous
Sliding
75 lbs — CG — 75 lbs
CG
150 lbs
C
CG: Center of Gravity of Body
CG
CG

Body Position & Center of Gravity

TYPES OF HOLDS

Push Holds: Push holds are desirable because they help the climber keep the arms low; however, they are more difficult to hold onto in case of a slip. A push hold is often used to advantage in combination with a pull hold.

Push Holds

Pull Holds: Pull holds are those that are pulled down upon and are the easiest holds to use. They are also the most likely to break out.

Pull Holds

Jam Holds: Jam holds involve jamming any part of the body or extremity into a crack. This is done by putting the hand into the crack and clenching it into a fist or by placing the arm into the crack and twisting the elbow against one side and the hand against the other side. When using the foot in a jam hold, care should be taken to ensure the boot is placed so it can be removed easily when climbing is continued.

Knuckles
Fist
Elbow Jam

Jam Holds

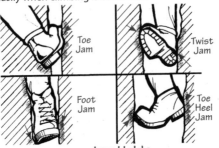

Toe Jam
Twist Jam
Foot Jam
Toe Heel Jam

Jam Holds

CLIMBING
BALANCE CLIMBING

Is the type of movement used to climb rock faces. It is a combination of the balance movement of a tightrope walker and the unbalanced climbing of a person ascending a tree or ladder. During the process of route selection, the climber should mentally climb the route to know what is expected. Climbers should not wear gloves when balance climbing.

BODY POSITION & CENTER OF GRAVITY

The climber must keep good balance when climbing (the weight placed over the feet during movement). The feet, not the hands, should carry the weight (except on the steepest cliffs). The hands are for balance. The feet do not provide proper traction when the climber leans in toward the rock. With the body in balance, the climber moves with a slow, rhythmic motion. Three points of support, such as two feet and one hand, are used when possible. The preferred handholds are waist to shoulder high. Resting is necessary when climbing because tense muscles tire quickly. When resting, the arms should be kept low where circulation is not impaired. Use of small intermediate holds is preferable to stretching and clinging to widely separated big holds. A spread-eagle position, where a climber stretches too far (and cannot let go), should be avoided.

FRICTION CLIMBING 1

A slab is a relatively smooth portion of rock lying at an angle. When traversing, the lower foot is pointed slightly downhill to increase balance and friction of the foot. All irregularities in the slope should be used for additional friction. On steep slabs, it may be necessary to squat with the body weight well over the feet with hands used alongside for added friction. This position may be used for ascending, traversing, or descending. A slip may result if the climber leans back or lets the buttocks down. Wet, icy, mossy, or a scree-covered slab is the most dangerous.

Friction Hold
Always maintain 3 points of contact with the rock. (I.e., 2 hands and 1 foot, or 2 feet and 1 hand).

FRICTION HOLDS

Friction holds depend solely on the friction of hands or feet against a relatively smooth surface with a shallow hold. They are difficult to use because they give a feeling of insecurity which the inexperienced climber tries to correct by leaning close to the rock, thereby increasing the insecurity. They often serve well as intermediate holds, giving needed support while the climber moves over them; however, they would not hold if the climber decided to stop.

FRICTION CLIMBING 2

Friction climbing is the type of movement used to climb rock faces. It is a combination of the balanced movement of a tightrope walker and the unbalanced climbing of a man ascending a tree or ladder. In balance and party climbing, the climber must study the route he is to travel in order to make sure he has selected the best route and has the necessary equipment. During the process of route selection, he should mentally climb the route so he will know what to expect. Climbers should not wear gloves when friction climbing. They should, however, wear gloves for all types of rappels to protect the palms from rope burns.

- Weight of body is centered over the feet.
- Feet and legs carry weight.
- Hands mainly for balance.
- As much boot sole as possible in contact with the rock.
- Keep handholds low, between waist and shoulder height. This helps keep the desired upright and balanced position while providing the maximum rest for the arms.
- Keep the body out and away from the rock surface. This will help you keep the weight and center of gravity on your feet. This posture will usually maximize the sole/ground contact.
- Three points of contact with the rock (i.e. 2 hands and 1 foot, or 2 feet and 1 hand).
- Use relaxed slow, rhythmic and deliberate motions.
- Be observant and plan your route two or three moves ahead.
- Use all available hand and footholds. Avoid over stretching and ending in a spread eagle position.

IN ASCENT

Facing sideways: climbing will be easy to difficult.
Facing inward: climbing will be more difficult.

IN DESCENT

Facing out: climbing will be very easy when the hill is not too steep.
Facing sideways: climbing will be easy to difficult.
Facing inward: climbing will be more difficult when the hill is very steep.

FOOTHOLDS

On steep slopes the body should be kept vertical, with use being made of small irregularities in the slope to aid friction. Footholds less than one inch can be sufficient for intermediate holds, even when they slope out.

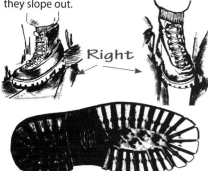

COMBINATION HOLDS

The holds previously mentioned are considered basic and from these any number of combinations and variations can be used. The number of these variations depends only on the limit of the individual's imagination. Following are a few of the more common ones:

Counterforce: The counterforce is attained by pinching a protruding part between the thumb and fingers and pulling outward or pressing inward with the arm.

Counterforce

Lay-Back: is done by leaning to one side of an offset crack with the hands pulling and the feet pushing against the offset side. Lay-backing is a classic form of force or counterforce where the hands and feet pull and push in opposite directions enabling the climber to move up in a series of shifting moves. It is very strenuous.

Lay-Back

Underclings: permit cross pressure between hands and feet.

Undercling

Mantleshelving: or mantling, takes advantage of down pressure exerted by one or both hands on a slab or shelf. By straightening and locking the arm, the body is raised, allowing a leg to be placed on a higher hold.

Mantle Shelving

Chimney Climb: This is a body-jam hold used in very wide cracks. The arms and legs are used to apply pressure against the opposite faces of the rock in a counterforce move. The outstretched hands hold the body while the legs are drawn as high as possible. The legs are flexed forcing the body up. This procedure is continued as necessary. Another method is to place the back against one wall and the legs and arms against the other and "worm" upward.

Chimney Climb

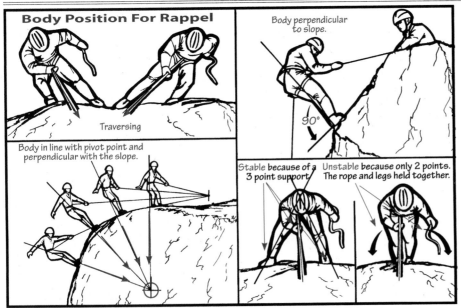

Body Position For Rappel

Traversing

Body in line with pivot point and perpendicular with the slope.

Body perpendicular to slope.

90°

Stable because of a 3 point support

Unstable because only 2 points. The rope and legs held together.

GROUND RAPPELLING

Ground rappelling is a technique that allows the climber to negotiate mountains and cliffs safely and rapidly. Before rappellers participate in mountain and cliff rappelling they should have completed the required training. To ensure the rappel is safely conducted consider several factors.

SELECT RAPPEL POINT

The selection of the rappel point depends on factors such as route, anchor points, and edge composition (loose or jagged rocks). The anchor point should be above the rappeller's departure point. Primary and secondary anchors must be solid and natural anchors are preferred. The rappeller should be sure that the rope reaches the bottom or a place from which he can further rappel or climb. Also, the rappel point should be carefully tested and inspected to ensure the rope will run freely and that the area is clear of obstacles that could be dislodged. If a sling or runner is used for a rappel point, it should be tied twice from two separate loops. Suitable loading and off-loading platforms should be available.

RAPPEL LANE

A rappel lane is the area and rope that a rappeller will use during his descent. It should have equal tension between all anchor points by establishing primary and secondary anchor points. If one anchor point fails, the rappel rope should not extend. All of the methods discussed below can be performed with a single or double rope. A double rope application should be used for safety.

CRAB WALK

A crab walk is facing away from the slope squatting over feet and hands when ascending, traversing, or descending slopes. The weight is evenly balanced over the hands and feet. This technique relies mainly on friction.

SHOULDER STAND

The shoulder stand or human ladder, is used to overcome a holdless lower section of a pitch in order to reach for easier climbing above. The lower man is anchored to the rock and belays the leader who uses his body as a ladder to overcome the difficult pitch.

ROPE TOO SHORT

Due to the length of the rappel, the rappel rope may not reach the anchor. If the rope is used to tie the knots, it may be too short to accomplish the rappel.

When using a natural anchor:
- Tie a sling rope, runner, or another rope around the anchor with a round turn anchor bowline.
- Tie a fixed loop (figure eight or butterfly) in one end of the rappel rope, which is attached to the round turn around the anchor through the two snaplinks (opposing gates).

When using an artificial anchor:
- Tie off a sling rope, runner, or another rope to form a loop.
- Put the loop through the snaplinks that are attached to the artificial anchor point.
- Bring the bottom of the loop up and connect it to the snaplinks that are between the artificial anchors (chocks, pitons, or bolts).
- Grasp the snaplinks that are between the chocks/pitons and pull them down and together.
- Tie a fixed loop (figure eight or butterfly) in the end of the rappel rope and connect this to the snaplinks that have been pulled together.

Rerouted figure-eight knots can be used instead of bowlines. Runners may be used from one or more anchor points.

THROWING ROPE

Backfeed (stack) the rope to ensure it does not snarl when thrown. Take off one wrap at a time and let it fall to the ground, ensuring that no kinks, knots, or twists occur that might hinder the rope from feeding out. When the rope is backfed, anchor off one end of the rope. The two methods used to throw the rope are underhand and overhand. Use the overhand method when trees or shrubs are on or near the rappel point.

ON A SLAB

On a smooth portion of rock, lie at an angle.
- Full sole-to-surface contact to increase balance and friction of the foot.
- Use all irregularities in the rock surface.
- Point lower foot downhill in claversing.
- Upper foot pointed in the direction of movement.
- Stand erect, maintain balance and control.
- Keep moving at a rhythmic pace.

RAPPEL LANE < 1/2 ROPE LENGTH

If a rappel lane is less than half the rope length, the rappeller may apply one of the following techniques:
- Double the rope and tie a three-loop bowline around the primary anchor to include the primary anchor inside two loops and enough rope in the third loop to run to the secondary anchor (another three-loop bowline secured with an overhand knot).
- Double the rope and tie it around a secure anchor point with a round turn anchor bowline secured with an overhand knot (or any appropriate anchor knot).
- Double the rope and establish a self-equalizing anchor system with a bowline-on-a-bight or figure-eight-on-a-bight knot. Tie off on the long standing and with a round turn anchor bowline.
- In an emergency, double the rope and place it behind or through a secure anchor point, or tie a runner around an anchor point with a snaplink inserted and place the rope through the snaplink. To preclude a rappeller from sliding off the end of the rappel lane, tie a double figure eight (square knot or double fisherman's knot) at the bottom end of the rope with both ends.

RAPPEL LANE > ROPE LENGTH

If a rappel lane is greater than half the rope length, the rappeller may apply one of the following techniques:
- Using two ropes, tie a round turn anchor bowline around a primary anchor point. Take the remaining rope (the tail from the primary anchor bowline) and tie another round turn anchor bowline to a secondary anchor point. The secondary anchor point should be in a direct line behind the primary anchor point. The anchor can be either natural or artificial. The ends of the rappel lane ropes should be offset by 15 cm (6 inches) so that the rope ends feed freely through the rappeller's snaplink.
- Using two ropes, establish a three-piton anchor system using a bowline-on-a-bight knot (or figure-eight-on-a-bight knot) and tie off on the long-standing end with a round turn anchor bowline.
- In an emergency, use two ropes and tie the two ends together with a joining knot. Place the joined ropes behind or through an anchor point, or tie a runner around an anchor point with a snaplink inserted and place the joined rope through the snaplink. Offset the joining knot to the left or right of the anchor. Tie off the bottom end of the rope with a joining knot to prevent a rappeller from sliding off the end of the rappel line.

MOVEMENT ON SLABS

A slab is a relatively smooth portion of rock lying at an angle. When traversing, the lower foot is pointed slightly downhill to increase your balance and friction of the foot. All irregularities in the slope should be utilized for additional friction. On steep slabs it may be necessary to squat with the body weight well over the feet and hands for added friction. This position may be used for ascending, traversing, or descending. A slip will result if you lean back or let the buttocks drag. Wet, icy, mossy, or scree-covered slabs are dangerous.

RETRIEVABLE RAPPEL POINT

Set up a retrievable rappel point by applying one of the following techniques:

- When the rappel is less than half the total length of the rope, double the rope. Place the rope around the primary anchor with the bight formed by the midpoint. Join the tails of the rappel rope and throw the rope over the cliff. Tie a clove hitch knot around a snaplink just below the anchor point ensuring the locking bar inside the snaplink points away from the gate opening end and faces uphill. Snap the opposite standing portion into the snaplink. Upon reaching the bottom of the cliff, pull on the part of the rope to which the snaplink is secured to allow the rope to slide around the anchor point.
- When the length of the rappel is greater than half the length of the rope used, join two ropes around the anchor point (double fisherman's knot or square knot). Adjust the joining knot so that it is away from the anchor. Tie a clove hitch knot around a snaplink just below the anchor point ensuring the locking bar inside the snaplink points away from the gate opening end and faces uphill. Snap the opposite standing portion into the snaplink. Upon completion of the rappel, pull the rope to which the snaplink is secured to allow the rope to slide around the anchor point.

When setting up a retrievable rappel using only a primary point, take care in selecting the point. Ensure climbers have a safety line when approaching the rappel point, with only the rappeller going near the edge.

DUTIES OF THE RAPPELLER

For safety each rappeller must know the duties of his job.

- Each rappeller down shouts, "Off rappel", untangles the ropes, and ensures the ropes run freely around their anchors. After the rope is cleared and the rappeller is off rappel, he acts as the belayer for the next rappeller.
- All rappellers should inspect the ropes for the next rappeller.
- The last rappeller to descend constructs a retrievable rappel point and rappels down. Then he gently pulls the rope to prevent the rising rope end from entangling with the other rope. Stand clear of the falling rope and any rocks that it may dislodge.

Wear gloves for protection from rope burns. Also, bounding rappels are discouraged since this stresses the anchor and causes undue wear and friction on the rope.

- Rappellers descend in a smooth, controlled manner. The body forms an L-shape with the feet shoulder-width apart, legs straight, and buttocks parallel to the ground. When carrying backpacks, a modified L-shape is used with the legs slightly lower than the buttocks to compensate for the added weight. The rappeller's back is straight. He looks over the brake shoulder. The guide hand is extended on the rope with the elbow extended and locked. The rope slides freely through the guide hand, which is used to adjust equipment and to assist balance during the descent. The rappeller grasps the rope firmly with the brake hand and places it in the small of his back. Releasing tension on the rope and moving the brake hand out to his rear at a 45° angle regulates the rate of descent. The rappeller never lets go of the rope with his brake hand until the rappel is completed.

TYPES OF RAPPELS
BODY RAPPEL

Face the anchor point and straddle the rope. Pull the rope from behind and run it around either hip, diagonally across the chest, and back over the opposite shoulder. Then, run the rope to the brake hand, which is on the same side of the hip that the rope crosses (for example, the right hip to the left shoulder to the right hand). Lead with the brake hand down and face slightly sideways. The foot corresponding to the brake hand precedes the guide hand at all times. Keep the guide hand on the rope above to guide - not to brake. Lean out at a sharp angle to the rock. Keep the legs spread well apart and relatively straight for lateral stability and the back straight to reduce friction. Turn the jacket collar up to prevent rope burns on the neck. Wear gloves, and use other clothing to pad the shoulders and buttocks. To brake, lean back and face directly toward the rock area so the feet are horizontal to the ground.

HASTY RAPPEL

Facing slightly sideways to the anchor, place the ropes horizontally across the back. The hand nearest to the anchor is the guide hand, and the other is the brake hand. Wear gloves to prevent rope burns. To stop, bring the brake hand across in front of the body locking the rope. At the same time, turn to face up toward the anchor point. Use this rappel only on moderate rock pitches. The hasty rappel's main advantage is that it is easier and faster than the other methods, especially when the rope is wet.

SEAT-SHOULDER RAPPEL

To hook up for the seat-shoulder method, face the rappel point. Snap into the rope that passes up through the carabiner. Bring the rope over one shoulder and back to the opposite hand (left shoulder to right hand). Use the same technique in the descent as in the body rappel. This method is faster than the body rappel, less frictional, and more efficient for rappellers with packs.

BELAYER FUNCTIONS

The belayer assumes a position at the base of the lane about one pace away from the rock area. He ensures that the rappel ropes are even with the ground. The belayer loosely holds the rappel ropes with both hands so as not to interfere with the rappeller but still able to stop the rappeller should he fall. If the rappeller shouts "Falling" or loses control of his brake hand or descent, the belayer immediately stops the rappeller by pulling downward on the rappel ropes. To ensure a firm grip on the rappelling rope, the belayer does not wear gloves. Because no friction exists between the belayer's hands and the rappelling rope, gloves are not required for safety. The belayer watches the rappeller at all times and maintains constant voice or visual contact with the rappeller. The belayer wears a helmet to prevent injuries from falling debris.

RAPPELLING PROCEDURES

Proper rappelling procedures must be followed for the safety of climbers.

- Ensure that the anchors are sound and the knots are properly tied.
- Ensure that loose rock and debris are cleared from the loading platform. *Standing Hip Belay*
- Only one rappeller on the loading point at a time.
- Ensure that each climber is properly prepared for the particular rappel: gloves on sleeves down, helmet with chin strap fastened, gear prepared properly, and rappel seat and knots correct (if required). The rappeller is correctly hooked up to the rope and is aware of the proper braking position.
- Use the proper signals.
- The rope should not run over sharp edges. Pad the rappelling surfaces as necessary to protect the rope. *Climber Descending*
- The rope should reach the bottom or is at a place where additional rappels can be made.

FIRST RAPPELLER DOWN

- Selects a smooth route for the rope that is clear of sharp rocks.
- Conducts a self-belay with a prusik sling tied from himself to the rappel rope.
- Clears the route and places loose rocks, which the rope may dislodge, far enough back on ledges to be out of the way.
- Ensures the rope reaches the bottom or is at a place from which additional rappels can be made.
- Ensures that the rope runs freely around the rappel point when pulled from below.
- Clears the rappel lane by straightening all twists and tangles from the ropes.
- Belays subsequent rappellers down the rope.
- Helps climbers as they arrive at the bottom.

A rappeller is always belayed from the bottom except for the first man down. The first man belays himself down the rope by using a safety line attached to his rappel seat that is hooked to the rappel rope with a prusik knot. As the first man rappels down the rope, he "walks" the prusik knot down with him.

PRUSIK CLIMBING

This is a method to climb using a fixed rope and does not require a belay. With two prusik slings, a chest prusik sling, and a carabiner, a person can climb the length of a fixed rope. The slings are attached with prusik knots that grip tightly when loaded yet slide when the load is removed. Prusiking is strenuous and requires the use of both hands and feet.

Prusik Climbing

Hasty Rappel

Body Rappel

Body Rappel

SINGLE FILE ASCENT

Travel in single file when ascending, permitting the leader to establish the route. The physical exertion of the lead climber is greater than that of any other member. The climbing leader must remain alert to safeguard other members, while choosing the best route of travel. The lead function should be changed frequently to prevent exhaustion of any one individual. Members following the leader should use the same leg-swing technique to establish foot positions, improving each step as they climb. Each foot must be firmly kicked into place, securely positioning the boot in the step. In compact snow, the kick should be somewhat low, shaving off snow during each step, thus enlarging the hole by deepening. In very soft snow, it is usually easier to bring the boot down from above, dragging a layer of snow into the step to strengthen and decrease its depth.

TRAVERSING SLOPE: NO ELEVATION CHANGE

When traversing a slope the heels rather than the toes form the step. During the stride the climber twists the leading leg so the boot heel strikes the slope first, carrying most of the weight into the step. The toe is pointed up and out. Similar to the plunge step, the heel makes the platform secure by compacting the snow more effectively than the toe.

DESCENDING SLOPE

Descending a slope uses a different strategy than the ascent. The type of route chosen may be different as climbing and descending have a different stepping process. Factor in snow conditions as; below surface icing, icy shadows and sun-softened snow. A good surface snow condition is ideal for descending rapidly since it yields comfortably underfoot.

The primary techniques for descending snow covered slopes are Plunge Stepping and Step-by-Step.

PLUNGE STEP DESCENT

The plunge step makes extensive use of the heels of the feet and is applicable on scree as well as snow. Ideally, the plunging route should be at an angle, one that is within the capabilities of the team and affords a safe descent. The angle at which the heel should enter the surface varies with the surface hardness. On soft snow slopes, almost any angle suffices; however, if the person leans too far forward, there is a risk of lodging the foot in a rut and being injured. On hard snow, the heel will not penetrate the surface unless it has sufficient force behind it. When roped, plunging requires coordination and awareness of all team members' progress. Speed of the team must be limited to the slowest member. Plunging is unsatisfactory when wearing crampons due to the snow compacting and sticking to them. Failure to firmly drive the heel into the snow can cause a slip and subsequent slide.

CHECKING OF A SLIP

The quickest way to check a slip is to shift the weight on to the other heel, making several short, stiff legged stomps. This technique is not intended to replace "the ice arrest" technique, which is usually more effective.

STEP-BY-STEP DESCENT

The technique of step-by-step descending is used when the terrain is extremely steep, snow significantly deep, or circumstances dictate a slower pace. On near vertical walls, it is necessary to face the slope and cautiously lower oneself step by step, thrusting the toe of the boot into the snow while maintaining an anchor or handhold with the ax. Once the new foothold withstands the body's full weight, the technique is repeated. On moderately angled terrain, the team can face away from the slope and descend by step kicking with the heels.

UPHILL CLIMBING ON SNOW

When climbing, less effort is exerted by traversing a slope. A zigzag or switchback route used to traverse a steep slope places body weight over the entire foot as opposed to the balls of the feet in a straight-line uphill climb. An additional advantage to zigzagging is alternating the stress and strain placed on the feet, ankles, legs, and arms when a change in direction is made.

CHANGING DIRECTION ON A SNOWY SLOPE

When a change in direction is made, the body is temporarily out of balance. Keeping your balance on a snow-covered slope can be difficult due to unstable footing. The proper method for turning on a steep slope is to pivot on the outside foot (the one away from the slope). With the upper slope on the right side, the left foot (pivot foot) is kicked directly into the slope. The body weight is transferred onto the left foot while pivoting toward the slope. The slope is then positioned on the left side and the right foot is on the outside.

SOFT SNOW ON STEEP SLOPES

In soft snow on steep slopes, pit steps must be stamped in for solid footing. On hard snow, the surface is solid but slippery, and level pit steps must be made. Steps are made by swinging the entire leg into the slope not by merely pushing the boot into the snow. In hard snow, when one or two blows do not suffice, crampons should be used. Space steps evenly and close together to facilitate ease of travel and balance. The lead climber must consider the other group members, especially those who have a shorter stride.

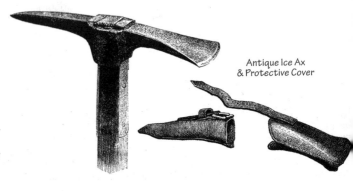

Antique Ice Ax
& Protective Cover

SNOW & ICE CLIMBING

Snow and ice climbing differs from rock climbing, yet many of the procedures and techniques are the same.

ICE AX TECHNIQUES

The ax is the most important tool a climber carries. It can be used for braking assistance when a climber begins sliding down a steep, snow covered incline. Practice the self-arrest technique before venturing on to steep grades. Since the ice ax arrest requires the use of the ice axe, the climber must hang on to it at all times. The ice axe, whether sharp or not, is a lethal weapon when flying about on the attached cord. Always hold the axe correctly. Mentally prepare by recognizing the importance of instantaneous application. A quick arrest, before the fall picks up speed, has a better chance of success than a slow arrest. Preparation for an ice ax arrest should be taken when traveling on terrain that could result in a fall.

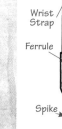

Head
Pick
Adze
Shaft
Glide Ring
Glide Ring Stop
Wrist Strap
Ferrule
Spike

TEAM ARREST

The team arrest is intermediate between self-arrest and belays. When there is doubt that a person could arrest a fall, such as on crevassed glaciers and steep snowfields, and conditions are not so extreme as to make belaying necessary, the party ropes up and travels in unison. If any member falls, arrest is made by two or three axes. The rope between the climbers must be fully extended, except for minimum slack carried by the second and subsequent persons to allow them to flip the rope out of the track (steps). This also allows easy compensation for pace variations. However, slack is minimized to bring the second and subsequent axes into action at the moment of need.

A roped climber who falls should immediately yell: "FALLING!" It is not advisable to delay the alarm to see how "self-arrest" will develop because team members may hear the signal only after they have been pulled into their own falls, decreasing their ability to help. When roped climber(s) hear the cry "falling" they immediately drop into self-arrest position.

USING CRAMPONS

If it is believed crampons may be needed, they must be carried. Conditions change rapidly; an east-facing slope may be mushy enough for step-kicking during the morning, but can become a sheet of smooth white ice in the afternoon shade. Furthermore, cramponing may contribute directly to the team's safety by enabling it to negotiate stretches of ice faster and with less fatigue than having to chop steps. The decision of whether or not to wear crampons is determine by the situation. Wearing crampons should not be considered mandatory because of venturing on to a glacier; neither should a team attempt to save time by never wearing crampons on steep, exposed icy patches just because they are fairly short. Another important guideline is to don crampons before they are needed to avoid donning them while teetering in ice steps. On mixed rock and ice climbs, constant donning and removing of crampons takes so much time that the objective may be lost.

Crampons should be worn throughout the entire climb if the terrain is 50% or more suitable for crampons (crampons may skid or be broken on rock surfaces). Crampons are not required if the snow or ice patches are fairly short, good belays are available, and rock predominates. Crampons should be taken off when the snow begins to ball up badly and no improvement in snow conditions is anticipated. On the ascent, it may be possible to clear away the soft surface snow and climb on the ice below, but this is usually impractical and futile on the descent. Occasionally the climber should kick the crampons free of accumulated snow. The timeworn practice of striking the ice-ax shaft against the crampons to knock out the snow is effective but hard on the axe and perhaps the ankle. In situations in which the crampons must be worn even though the snow balls up in them, shuffling the feet through the snow instead of stepping over the surface tends to force the accumulated snow through the back points. The normal kicking motion of the foot generally keeps the crampons snow-free on the ascent and while traversing.

Crampons

On the descent, with crampons, drive the toe of the boot under the surface of the snow ahead of the heel, walking on the ball of the foot. Keep the weight well forward and use short, skating steps, allowing the foot to slide forward and penetrate the harder sublayer.

The boot ax belay should be practiced until a sweep and jab of the ice ax can set up the stance within a couple of seconds. The ax provides an anchor to the slope, and the slope and the boot braces the ax.

BOOT AX BELAY

The boot ax belay can be set up rapidly and is used when a team is moving together, and belaying is only required at a few spots. The boot ax belay should be practiced until a sweep and jab of the ice axe can set up the stance within a couple of seconds. The ax provides an anchor to the slope, and the slope and the boot braces the ax. Both give a friction surface over which the run of rope is controlled.

- To prepare a boot ax belay, a firm platform, large enough for the axe and uphill boot, is stamped out in the snow. The ice axe shaft is jammed as deeply as possible, at a slight uphill angle (against the anticipated fall) into the snow at the rear of the platform. The pick is parallel to the fall line, pointing uphill, thus applying the strongest dimension of the shaft against the force of a fall. The length of the pick prevents the rope from escaping over the top of the shaft.
- The belayer stands below the ax, facing at a right angle to the fall line. The uphill boot is stamped into the slope against the downhill side of the shaft at a right angle to the fall line, bracing the shaft against downhill pull. The downhill boot is in a firmly compacted step below the uphill boot so the leg is straight, stiffly bracing the belayer. The uphill hand is on the axe head in arrest grasp, bracing the shaft against downhill and lateral stress. From below, the rope crosses the toe of the boot, preventing the rope from trenching into the snow. The rope bends around the uphill side of the shaft, then down across the instep of the bracing boot, and is controlled by the downhill hand. To apply braking through greater friction, the downhill, or braking, hand brings the rope uphill around the heel, forming an "S" bend.

CRAMPONS
ATTACHING CRAMPONS

When attaching the harness, the buckles should be positioned to cinch on the outward sides of the boots. Special care must be taken to strap the crampons tightly to the boots, running the strap through each attachment prong or ring. If crampons do not have heel loops, ankle straps should be long enough to be crossed behind the boot before being secured, to prevent boots from sliding backward out of the crampons. Many crampons have been lost because this precaution was not taken. When trimming new straps, allowance must be made for gaiters, which sometimes cover the instep of the boot. To attach lay each crampon on the snow or ice with all rings and straps outward, then place the boot on the crampon and tighten the straps. Straps should be checked from time to time to make sure they are tight, have not been cut, and are not trailing loop-strap ends, which could cause the wearer to trip.

175

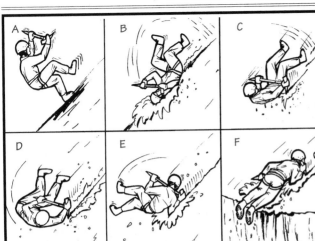

HOLDING AX FOR SELF-ARREST

The proper method of holding an ice ax for self-arrest is to place one hand on the head of the ax with the thumb under the adze and fingers over the pick. The other hand is placed on the shaft next to the spike. The pick is pressed into the slope just above the shoulder so the adze is near the angle formed by the neck and shoulders. The shaft should cross the chest diagonally with the spike held firmly close to the opposite hip. A short axe is held in the same position, although the spike will not reach the opposite hip. Chest and shoulders should press strongly on the shaft, and the spine should be arched slightly to distribute weight primarily to the shoulders and toes.

The legs should be stiff and spread apart, toes digging in (if wearing crampons, keep the toes off the surface until almost stopped) and hang on to the ax!

Plunging is unsatisfactory when wearing crampons due to the snow compacting and sticking to them. Failure to firmly drive the heel into the snow can cause a slip and subsequent slide.

Plunge Step Descent

FLAT FOOTING

Descending with Crampons

Flat footing involves a logical and natural progression of coordinated body and ice-ax positions to allow the climber to move steadily and in balance while keeping all vertical points of the crampons biting into the ice. The weight is carried directly over the feet, the crampon points stamped firmly into the ice with each step, with the ankles and knees flexed to allow boot soles to remain parallel to the slope.

- On gentle slopes, the climber walks straight up the hill. Normally, the feet are naturally flat to the slope and the axe is used as a cane. If pointing the toes uphill becomes awkward, they may be turned outward in duck fashion. As the slope gets steeper, the body is turned to face across the slope rather than up it. The feet may also point across the slope, but additional flexibility and greater security are gained by pointing the lower foot downhill. The ax is used only to maintain balance and may be carried in the cane position or the arrest grasp with either the pick or point touching the slope. (Movement is diagonal rather than straight upward, and the climber takes advantage of terrain irregularities and graded slopes. Changes in direction are done as in step-kicking on snow, by planting the downhill foot, turning the body toward the slope to face the opposite direction, and stepping off with the new downhill foot.)
- On gentler slopes, the flat-footed approach is used throughout, but it is more secure and easier on steeper slopes to initiate the turn by kicking the front points and briefly front-pointing through the turn. At some point in the turn, the grip on the axe must be reversed. The exact moment for this depends on the climber and the specific situation. However, the climber's stance must be secure when the third point of support, the ax, is temporarily relinquished.

ANCHORS

Snow and ice conditions require the use of special devices for establishing belay anchors or placement of intermediate protection during a climb.

SNOW PICKETS

Three to four foot lengths of aluminum "T" or tubular sections perform as long pitons and are suited for belaying. They must always be used in pairs or greater numbers, one anchoring the other.

SNOW FLUKE

A 12-inch piece of metal is buried with a runner coming to the surface; this can pull out if snow conditions are not just right. Better resistance to pull-out is gained with a large flat piece of metal driven into the snow surface at an angle, acting in the same manner as the fluke of an old-fashioned anchor. There is no danger of the runner being cut or weakened from wet conditions with the attachment of a wire cable. The softer the snow, the larger the plate should be. When using flukes, it is very important that the proper angle with the surface be maintained; otherwise, wire, instead of becoming stronger (going deeper) when pulled, will become weaker (surface). Additionally, the cable may act as a lever arm on hard snow, causing the fluke to pop out. This can be prevented by carefully cutting a channel in the snow for cables so that the pull comes directly at the plate. If attention is paid to placement, snow flukes will provide great security as belay and rappel anchors. A properly placed fluke is secure for a sitting or standing hop belay on snow.

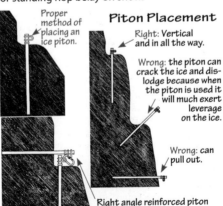

Proper method of placing an ice piton.

Piton Placement

Right: Vertical and in all the way.

Wrong: the piton can crack the ice and dislodge because when the piton is used it will much exert leverage on the ice.

Wrong: can pull out.

Right angle reinforced piton placement. The horizontal piton prevents the vertical piton from being dislodged.

STEEP SLOPES

On steep slopes, which approach the limit of practical use of this style of ascent, the climber relies on the ax for security of a hold as well as for balance. The ax is held in the arrest grasp with one hand on the head and the other on the shaft, above the point. The well sharpened pick is planted firmly in the ice at about shoulder height to provide one point of suspension while a foot moves forward and the crampons are stamped in.

DESCENT

Descent follows the same general progression of foot and ax positions; descend the fall line, gradually turning the toes out as the slope gets steeper. As the slope steepens, widen the stance, flex the knees, and lean forward to keep weight over the feet, and finally, face sideways and descend with the support of the ax in the arrest position. On very steep or hard ice, it may be necessary to face the slope and front-point downwards. When flat-footing downhill, all crampon points should be stamped firmly into the ice. It may be necessary to take small steps which allow the climber to maintain balance during moves; long steps require major weight shifts to adjust balance.

Snow Pickets
Maximize the amount of snow that retains the picket. The runner should be attached at the surface of the snow to minimize the leverage on the picket.

Cross section of cut steps

Steps cut in ice surface

Right

Wrong

Cross section of handholds

Wrong

CUTTING STEPS IN ICE

Steps are made with the pick end of an ice axe. Black ice is harder to cut and requires more blows. The blows should be made as close to right angle to the ice face as possible. This will reduce the danger of flaking off the outside layers. The step should slope inwards and downwards. In climbing, steps may be cut straight up or at a diagonal to the line of ascent. In descending, it is only practical to cut steps in a diagonal.

Placing Ice Anchors
See A

Stress breaks in the ice. See B

See C

Chipped ice removed.

Placement of Snow Fluke

40°

40°

Snow Fluke

el to Slope

ICE ANCHORS

Ice pitons and ice screws are used to establish anchor points. To implant a piton:

- Cut a horizontal recess in the ice and remove all the rotten ice.
- Drive the piton vertically all the way to the ring. The rope pull should be at right angles to the embedded piton.
- Test the piton: if it appears weak, pull it out and choose a new spot. For additional security use pitons in pairs with them driven at right angles to each other. This will prevent them from pulling out accidentally. **A**
- Placed pitons have a limited life span as they are heated by the sun and the exposed ice will gradually soften and crack. If placed pitons will be reused cover them with ice chips. Re-drive them if they look insecure. **B**

PLACEMENT OF ICE SCREWS

Note that the characteristics of ice vary as per: age of the ice, how the ice formed, what was the temperature life cycle, what time of day (temperature - in/out of sun) are you placing the ice screw at this location, how deep is the ice. etc. With all these variables the ice screw placement angles are difficult to determine. In general before placement of ice screws or pitons, any soft snow or loose ice should be scraped or chopped away until a hard and trustworthy surface is reached. A small starting hole punched out with the pick or spike of the axe or hammer facilitates a good grip for the starting threads or teeth. The screw is pressed firmly into the ice and twisted in at the same time, angled slightly uphill against the anticipated direction of pull. Ice pitons are, of course, driven straight in, but must also be angled against the pull that would result from a fall. If any spalling or splintering of the ice occurs **B**, the screw should be removed and another location tried 1 or 2 feet away. **C** Some glacier ice will spall near the surface but by continuing to place the screw and gently chopping out the shattered ice, a deep, safe placement may be obtained. As a general rule, short screws or pitons should be used in hard ice and long ones in softer ice. They should always be placed in the ice until the eye is flush with the surface. When removing ice hardware, take care not to bend it since this diminishes its effectiveness in future use.

ICE SCREWS
TUBULAR SCREWS

Tubular screws are very strong and are the most reliable. They are difficult to place in hard or water ice since they tend to clog and have a large cross section. Their main advantage is that they minimize "spalling" (a crater-like splintering of the ice around the shaft of the screw) by allowing the displaced ice to work itself out through the core of the screw. If the core of the ice remaining in the screw is frozen in place, it jams the screw in subsequent placements. The ice may be removed by pushing with a length of wire or by heating with a cigarette lighter. This type of screw requires both hands for placement; however, once it is started, the pick of an ice hammer or axe inserted in the eye allows the climber to gain the advantage of leverage. Removal is easy and melt-out is slow due to the large cross section.

Tubular Screw

COAT HANGER SCREWS

Heavier "coat hanger" type screws can be relied upon to stop a fall. They are easier to start in hard ice than tubular screws and can often be placed with one hand, although it may be necessary to tap them while twisting as they are started. Their holding power is less than tubular screws as they tend to fracture hard ice and, under heavy loads, tend to shear through the ice because of their small cross section.

Coat Hanger Screw

SOLID ICE SCREW

Developed as an attempt to make an easy-to-place and easy-to-remove screw, the solid screws are driven in like a piton and screwed out. They offer excellent protection in water ice but are less effective in other ice forms. Melt-out is sometimes rapid because of limited thread displacement and, under load, they tend to shear through the ice as do coat hanger screws.

Solid Ice Screw

Ice/Snow Bollard

ICE/SNOW BOLLARD

Although not a natural anchor in itself, an ice or snow bollard is easily made from natural materials. A semicircular trench is dug in the snow or ice. The trench should be 3 to 4 feet across and 6 to 12 inches deep. Allow a larger size for poor snow or ice conditions. The rope can be positioned in the trench to provide a downward belay.

Ice Ax

Using an Ice Ax as an anchor.

Traveling with picks and roped in.

FALLS ON SLOPES

Unforeseen falls are always a possibility when moving over ice or snow covered slopes. If the party is roped together, the person falling can usually be arrested by other members of the group.

UNROPED FALL DOWN A SLOPE

- If you are traveling unroped and you fall, immediately roll onto your stomach in the direction of the head of the ice ax.
- The ax should always be secured to the hand with the wrist strap.
- If you are wearing crampons, your legs should be spread apart and bent at the knee with the feet up in the air.

Emergency Mirror

Emergency Birch Bark Sunglasses

GLISSADING SAFETY

A glissade should be made only when there is a safe run out. Unless a view of the entire run can be obtained beforehand, the first person down the run must use extreme caution, stopping frequently to study the terrain ahead. Equipment must be adjusted before beginning the descent. Crampons and other hardware must be properly stowed. Never attempt to glissade while wearing crampons as it is extremely easy to snag a crampon and be thrown down the slope. Mittens or gloves are worn to protect the hands and to maintain control of the axe. Heavy waterproof pants provide protection to the buttocks. Gaiters are also helpful for all glissading. Glissades should never be attempted in terrain where the axe safety cord is required.

Never attempt to glissade while wearing crampons as it is extremely easy to snag a crampon and be thrown down the slope.
Mittens or gloves are worn to protect the hands and to maintain control of the ax.

Sunglasses

Coyote® Snow Pickets

GLISSADING

Glissading is a means of rapidly descending a slope. Consisting of two basic positions, glissading offers a speedy means of travel with less energy exerted than using the descending step-by-step or plunging techniques. Descend a slope by sliding and using your ice axe as a support and rudder. To slide keep your toes up but the weight of your body should be over the centre of the foot. The body should be bent forward. To stop, you slide into the slope of the hill. Do not glissade in an area where you cannot see the destination as you might go over a cliff.

SITTING GLISSADE

When snow conditions permit, the sitting glissade position is the easiest way to descend. The climber simply sits in the snow and slides down the slope while holding the axe in an arrest position. Any tendency of the body to pivot head downwards may be checked by running the spike of the axe rudder-like along the surface of the snow. Speed is increased by lying on the back to spread the body weight over a greater area and by lifting the feet in the air. Sitting back up and returning the feet to the snow surface reduces speed. On crusted or firmly consolidated snow, sit fairly erect with the heels drawn up against the buttocks and the boot soles skimming along the surface. Turns are nearly impossible in a sitting glissade; however, the spike, dragged as a rudder and assisted by body contortions, can effect a change in direction of several degrees.

OBSTRUCTIONS & GLISSADING

Obstructions on the slope are best avoided by rising into a standing glissade for the turn, and then returning to the sitting position. Speed is decreased by dragging the spike and increasing pressure on it. After the momentum has been checked by the spike, the heels are dug in for the final halt but not while sliding at a fast rate as the result is likely to be a somersault. Emergency stops at high speeds are made by arresting.

STANDING GLISSADE

The standing glissade is similar to skiing. Positioned in a semi crouch stance with the knees bent as if sitting in a chair, the legs are spread laterally for stability, and one foot is advanced slightly to anticipate bumps and ruts. For additional stability, the spike of the axe can be skimmed along the surface, the shaft held alongside the knee in the arrest grasp, with the pick pointing down or to the outside away from the body. Stability is increased by widening the spread of the legs, deepening the crouch, and putting more weight on the spike. A decrease in speed increases muscular strain and the technique becomes awkward and trying, although safe. Speed is increased by bringing the feet close together, reducing weight on the spike, and leaning forward until the boot soles are running flat along the surface like short skis. If the slide is too shallow, a long skating stride helps.

15 HIGH ELEVATION FIRST AID

HIGHER ELEVATION HEALTH FACTORS

- Air is colder.
- Air is thinner so there is less oxygen.
- Weather is more severe and can change rapidly.
- Above 14000 feet (4100 meters) our metabolism lacks oxygen to process and use fatty foods. Climbers can get bloated as they cannot digest fatty foods.
- Diet has to be changed to more carbohydrates (sugar, rice, wheat) and proteins (meat and dairy products).
- Air is dry. Sweating and deep breathing will rapidly dehydrate the body.

Medical Problems of Mountain Climbing

At **7000-8000 feet** (2000-2350 meters) mountain sickness can develop in some travelers.

At **12000+ feet** (3500+ meters) everyone can develop mountain sickness. *See Pulmonary Edema.*

Symptoms of Mountain Sickness

- General sense of weakness and lack of energy.
- Tiredness even when not exerting.
- Nausea and headaches.

Symptoms of Lack of Oxygen

- Lips and fingertips have a bluish cast.
- Face has a lack of color and looks greyish.

If Symptoms are Present

- Do not eat heavily as your system will require more oxygen to digest the food.
- Do not smoke.   • Do not drink alcohol.

Acclimatizing to Higher Elevations

Acclimatization requires the body to change by increasing the blood's capacity to absorb oxygen and the lungs to become more efficient. People have different acclimatization rates from 10 days to 5 or 6 weeks.

High Altitude Pulmonary Edema

Symptoms are similar as those of pneumonia. It is the accumulation of fluids in the lungs that reduces the their breathing capacity. Death can result from suffocation or heart failure. Pulmonary edema usually occurs above 9000 feet (2700 meters) but it varies from person to person. It depends upon the individual's capacity to become acclimatized to the elevation.

BODY'S RESPONSE TO HIGH ALTITUDE HYPOBARIC HYPOXIA

High altitude lowers the oxygen supply to the body, which in turn causes altitude illnesses and reduced physical and mental performance. It may also increase the likelihood of other environmental injuries (e.g., cold) or worsen pre-existing medical conditions. Altitude acclimatization allows you to achieve the maximum physical work performance possible for the altitude to which you are acclimatized. Once acquired, acclimatization is maintained as long as you remain at altitude, but is lost upon return to lower elevations. Exposure to higher altitudes requires further acclimatization. For most people at high to very high altitudes, 70-80% of respiratory component of acclimatization occurs in 7-10 days; 80-90% of overall acclimatization is generally accomplished by 21-30 days. Maximum acclimatization may take months to years. *There does not seem to be any way to speed acclimatization; some people acclimatize more rapidly than others, and few may not acclimatize at all.*

STAYING HEALTHY AT HIGH ELEVATIONS

High mountain environments are inherently dangerous. They can be unforgiving for those without adequate knowledge, training, and equipment. Adequate planning and preparedness for the trip can reduce or prevent adverse impacts. The ideal condition for travelers in high mountain terrain is to be well acclimatized. This will give you maximum physical and mental performance and minimize the incidence of altitude illness. *All members of the group should be aware of the threats associated with travel at high altitudes and take protective measures in order to minimize disease.*

ACCLIMATIZATION

Staged Ascent: Requires you to ascend (rise) to a moderate altitude and remain there for 3 days or more to acclimatize before ascending higher. When possible, make several stops for staging during the ascent to allow a greater degree of acclimatization.

Graded Ascent: Limits the daily altitude gain to allow partial acclimatization. The altitude at which you sleep is the critical element in this regard. Spend two nights at 9,000 ft and limit the sleeping altitude to no more than 1,000 ft per day above the previous night's sleeping altitude will significantly reduce the incidence of altitude illness. A combination of graded ascent and staging is the safest and most effective method for prevention of high altitude illnesses.

REACTION AT DIFFERENT ELEVATIONS

Altitude	Feet	Effects
Low Sea Level	5,000	None
Moderate	5,000 - 8,000	Mild, temporary altitude illness may occur.
High	8,000-14,000	Altitude illness and decreased performance is increasingly common.
Very High	14,000-18,000	Altitude illness and decreased performance is the rule.
Extreme	18,000+	With acclimatization, can function for short periods of time.

MEDICAL TERMINOLOGY

AMS: Acute mountain sickness.

Apnea: Temporary pause of breathing.

Edema: A local or general condition in which the body tissues contain an excessive amount of tissue fluid

HACE: High altitude cerebral edema (brain edema).

HAPE: High altitude pulmonary edema (lung edema).

Hypobaric Hypoxia: Decreased availability of oxygen in ambient (surrounding) air.

Hypoxia: Low oxygen content; decreased concentration of oxygen in inhaled air.

MOUNTAIN ALTITUDE

As one ascends in altitude, the proportion of oxygen in the air decreases. Without proper acclimatization, this decrease in oxygen saturation can cause altitude sickness and reduced physical and mental performance. One cannot maintain the same physical performance at high altitude as at low altitude, regardless of ones fitness level.

High Altitude Illness

The preferred step in treating any high altitude illness is to evacuate the person to a lower altitude.

Acute Mountain Sickness (AMS)

Caused by rapid ascent (altitude gain in 24 hours or less) to high altitudes. Symptoms include headache, nausea, vomiting, fatigue, irritability, and dizziness, and appear 3 to 24 hours after ascent. Everyone is susceptible. Staging, graded ascent, or movement to a lower altitude can prevent AMS.

- Consuming carbohydrates can reduce AMS symptoms (whole grains, vegetables, peas and beans, potatoes, fruits, honey, and refined sugar).
- AMS symptoms will normally subside in 3-7 days if you do not continue to ascend. Once symptoms are resolved, you can resume gradual ascent.
- If you continue to show signs of AMS you must be observed for development of HAPE or HACE, both of which are potentially fatal.

High Altitude Pulmonary Edema (HAPE)

Occurs when unacclimatized individuals rapidly ascend to high altitudes or when acclimatized people ascend rapidly from a high to a higher altitude. Untreated, HAPE can be rapidly fatal and is the most common cause of death among the altitude illnesses. If experiencing AMS and not treated and continue to ascend to higher altitudes are at significant risk for HAPE.

- HAPE usually begins within the first two to four days after rapid ascent to altitudes greater than 8,000 ft and generally appears during the second night of sleep at high altitude. Symptoms include coughing, noisy breathing, wheezing, gurgling in the airway, difficulty breathing, and deteriorated mental status (confusion, vivid hallucinations). **Ultimately coma and death will occur without treatment.**
- Countermeasures for HAPE include: proper acclimatization; sleeping at the lowest altitude possible; avoiding cold exposures; and avoiding strenuous exertion until acclimatized. Immediate descent is recommended as the best treatment for HAPE. People with AMS should be monitored carefully since AMS can rapidly evolve to HAPE.

Snow Blindness

Results from UV light absorption by the external parts of the eyes, such as the eyelids and cornea. There is no sensation, other than brightness, as a warning that eye damage is occurring with resulting sunburn-like damage occurring in a few hours. Sunglasses or goggles with UV protection will prevent snow blindness. Sunglasses with side protectors are recommended.

Terrain Injuries

You should be aware of the dangers of high altitude including avalanches and falls. Poor judgment at high altitude increases the risk of injury. The potential for being struck by lightning is also increased at higher altitudes, especially at areas above tree lines. Protective measures include taking shelter in solid-roofed structures or vehicles, staying low, and avoiding tall structures or large metal objects.

High Altitude Cerebral Edema (HACE)

The most severe illness associated with high altitudes. Individuals with HACE are frequently found to also have HAPE. As with other high altitude illnesses, HACE is caused by rapid ascent to high elevations without proper acclimatization. People with AMS who continue ascent are considered to be at high risk for development of HACE.

- HACE generally occurs later than AMS or HAPE. Untreated, HACE can progress to death over 1 to 3 days and, in some instances, in less than 12 hours. Symptoms often resemble AMS (severe headache, nausea, vomiting); however, **a more dramatic signal that HACE may be developing is a swaying upper body, especially when walking.** Early mental changes may include confusion, disorientation, and drowsiness. An affected person may appear to be withdrawn or demonstrate behavior generally associated with fatigue or anxiety.
- Countermeasures for HACE include: following countermeasures for AMS and HAPE (acclimatization, etc.) and immediate evacuation (descent) for individuals with HACE symptoms. If with AMS or HAPE they should be monitored carefully for signs of HACE. Under no circumstances should a person with severe AMS symptoms or suspected HAPE or HACE be allowed to continue ascent.

Subacute Mountain Sickness

Occurs in some individuals during prolonged living (weeks/months) at elevations above 12,000 ft.

- Symptoms include sleep disturbance, loss of appetite, weight loss, and fatigue. This condition reflects a failure to acclimatize adequately.
- Poor wound healing may occur at higher elevations resulting from lowered immune functions. Injuries resulting from burns, cuts, or other injuries may require descent for effective treatment and healing.

Cold Injuries

Once acclimatized to altitude, cold injuries are generally the greatest threat. Frequent winds in mountain areas cause extremely low wind-chill. Because hypoxia-induced psychological effects can result in poor judgment and decision-making, a higher incidence of cold injuries should be anticipated. Countermeasures for cold injuries include emphasis on: maintaining nutrition; drinking plenty of fluids; and dressing in layers.

Sunlight Injuries

The potential for solar radiation injuries, caused by sunlight, is significant at high altitudes due to increased ultraviolet (UV) radiation (resulting from thinner atmosphere), and reflection of light from snow and rock surfaces. Solar radiation injuries can be severe and occur with much shorter exposure at high altitude. Injuries include sunburn and snow blindness. Sunburn may be more likely to occur on partly cloudy or overcast days when you may not be aware of the threat and do not take appropriate precautions. Application of sun block (at least 15 SPF) to exposed skin, face, and neck will help prevent instances of sunburn.

Carbon Monoxide (CO) Poisoning

Is a frequent hazard and is caused by the inefficient fuel combustion resulting from the low oxygen content of air and higher usage of stoves, combustion heaters, and engines in enclosed, poorly ventilated spaces. Cigarette smoking is another source of CO.

To prevent CO poisoning do not:
... sleep in vehicles with engines running, or cook inside tents or sleep inside tents with working combustion heaters or stoves without adequate ventilation.

Other Injuries

- Hypoxia and cold can impair judgment and physical performance resulting in a greater risk of injury while traveling in rugged terrain.
- Heavy clothing worn for protection against the cold and specialized equipment can also restrict movement.
- Injuries can be prevented by carefully observing safety procedures.

Infectious Diseases

- Although there is generally a reduced threat of disease at higher elevations, take precautions to avoid diseases caused by insects, plants, animals, and diseases transmitted person to person.
- At moderate to high altitudes, insect-borne disease (from mosquitoes, ticks and flies) is common in most regions. At equatorial latitudes, malaria-bearing mosquitoes range as high as 6,000 ft.
- The threat of diseases transmitted from person to person is increased at higher, cold climates since hikers are more likely to gather together to keep warm.

High Mountain Activities

Reduced Physical Performance

- Hypobaric hypoxia causes a reduction in physical performance. You cannot maintain the same physical performance at high altitude that they can at low altitude, regardless of your fitness level.
- Countermeasures to prevent disease and injury include ensuring acclimatization; adjusting work rates and load carriage; planning frequent rests during work and exercise; and planning and performing physical training programs to altitude.

Physical Conditioning

If you have lived and trained mostly at lower elevations you may have developed a sense of insecurity and fear about higher elevations. Before undertaking a major climb you should train by making gradually higher climbs that will accustom you to the effects of the mountain environment. Initially you will find "new muscle" strain associated with balance and prolonged ascents/descents which will quickly exhaust you. Even breathing becomes strenuous, given the thinner atmosphere at higher altitudes. Therefore, training must emphasize exercises designed to strengthen leg muscles and build cardiovascular (aerobic) endurance. Frequent climbs will enhance conditioning and familiarize you to mountain walking techniques.

Psychological Effects

Altitude exposure may result in changes in senses (vision, taste, etc.), mood, and personality. These effects are directly related to altitude and are common at over 10,000 ft. Some effects occur early and are temporary while others may persist after acclimatization or even for a period of time after descent.

- Vision is generally the sense most affected by altitude exposure. Dark adaptation is significantly reduced, affecting people as low as 8,000 ft. and can potentially affect travel at high altitude.
- Mental effects most noticeable at very high and extreme altitudes include decreased perception, memory, judgment, and attention. To compensate for loss of functional ability, you should devise a strategy of a trade-off between speed and accuracy - allow for extra time to accomplish a task to minimize errors (and injuries).

Alterations in mood and personality traits are common during high-altitude exposures.

- Within hours of ascent, many hikers may experience euphoria (joy, excitement) that is likely to be accompanied by errors in judgment leading to mistakes and accidents. Use of the buddy system during this early exposure time helps to identify individuals who may be more severely affected.
- After a period of about 6-12 hours, euphoria decreases, often changing to varying degrees of depression. You may become irritable, or may appear listless.

Instilling a high morale and 'esprit de corps' before proceeding and reinforcing these frequently will help minimize the impact of negative mood changes.

Sleep Disturbances

High altitude has significant harmful effects on sleep. The most prominent effects are frequent periods of apnea (cessation of breathing) and fragmented sleep. Sleep disturbances may last for weeks at elevations less than 18,000 ft and may never stop at higher elevations. Reports of "not being able to sleep" and "awake half the night" are common and may also contribute to mood changes and daytime drowsiness. These effects have been reported at elevations as low as 5,000 feet and are very common at higher altitudes. *See a doctor as to possible medication.*

Hypoxia

Hypoxia occurs when there is a lack of oxygen. This occurs at high elevations.

Symptoms are...
- Breathing rate increases. • Dizziness.
- Warm sweating sensation. • Sleepiness.
- Skin, fingernails, and lips turning blue.
- Reduced field of vision. (Angle of vision)
- Problems of judgment and behavior. (Logic)
- Loss of consciousness.

Individuals who are not in good physical shape are more susceptible to be affected by hypoxia.

Other Altitude Factors

Other products that can seriously impact high altitude travel include tobacco, alcoholic beverages, and caffeine.

Tobacco: smoke interferes with oxygen delivery by reducing blood oxygen-carrying capacity; tobacco smoke in close, confined spaces increases the amounts of CO, and the irritant effect of tobacco smoke may produce a narrowing of airways interfering with optimal air movement. Smoking can effectively raise the "physiological altitude" as much as several thousand feet.

Alcohol: impairs judgment and perception, depresses respiration, causes dehydration, and increases susceptibility to cold injury.

Caffeine from coffee: and other sources may improve physical and mental performance; however, it also causes increased urination (leading to dehydration) and therefore should be consumed in moderation.

Dehydration

Is a very common condition in at high altitude. Causes include perspiration/sweating, vomiting, and hypoxia-induced diminishing of thirst sensation. Routine activities and chores performed at high altitudes require increased exertion. Even common activities, like walking, cause increased exertion, resulting in increased perspiration and contributing to hot or cold weather injuries. Refill water containers as often as possible. No matter how pure and clean mountain water may appear, water from natural sources should always be purified or chemically sterilized to prevent parasitical illnesses (giardiasis). Dehydration increases the likelihood of significant problems including cold injuries and decreased physical abilities. Note: Many symptoms of dehydration and HACE are similar.

You can prevent dehydration by consuming 3 to 4 quarts of water or other non-caffeinated fluids (or more) per day. Thirst is not an adequate warning of dehydration. Ensure that you drink enough fluids and do not become dehydrated as a result of diminished judgment or the desire to avoid latrines.

Nutrition

Caloric requirements increase in the mountains due to both the altitude and the cold. A diet high in fat and carbohydrates is important in helping the body fight the effects of these conditions. Fats provide long-term, slow caloric release, but are often unpalatable when at higher altitudes. Snacking on high-carbohydrate foods is often the best way to maintain the calories necessary to function. Poor nutrition contributes to illness or injury, decreased performance, poor morale, and susceptibility to cold injuries. Influences at high elevations that impact nutrition include a dulled taste sensation (making food undesirable), nausea, or lack of energy or motivation to prepare or eat meals. Poor eating habits may also lead to constipation or aggravation of hemorrhoids. You can reduce the effects of poor nutrition at high elevations by increasing the quantity eaten and eating all components of meals. High carbohydrate snacks are recommended since they are easily carried and require no preparation.

Night Vision Problems at High Elevation

At 5000 feet (1500 m) vision might become blurred, angle of vision is reduced, and night vision might be reduced.

At 8000 feet (2400 m) night vision might be reduced by 25%. This does not occur during the day time. With increased elevation and reduced oxygen other symptoms will occur.

Treat by increasing the supply of oxygen.

Hypothermia

High elevations have all the ingredients for hypothermia as being cold, wet, and windy. Low energy reserves due to the exertion involved in climbing and the probability of not eating properly will also be possible contributing factors.

Hyperventilation

Hyperventilation is excessive ventilation of the lungs from breathing too rapidly and too deeply. This results in the excessive loss of carbon dioxide from the body.

Excess ventilation can be caused by anxiety or possible fear of the unknown which can occur if lost.

The symptoms are...
- Dizziness and nausea. Shortness of breath.
- Muscle spasms and tingling of the fingers and toes.
- Body feels hot. Increase of the heart rate. Vision becomes blurred. Fainting and lose consciousness.

Help person to slow rapid breathing by giving reassurance and explaining why his fears are unfounded. Have him breath into a bag to increase the level of carbon dioxide in his system.

MOUNTAIN ILLNESSES & INJURIES

CHRONIC FATIGUE & ITS EFFECTS (ENERGY DEPLETION)

Cause
- Low blood sugar.
- Sources of energy are depleted.
- Insufficient caloric intake.

Prevention
- Provide adequate food (type and quantities).
- Monitor food intake & ensure you eat 4,500 calories or more per day.
- Eat small, frequent meals rather than large, infrequent meals.
- Snack lightly & often.
- Increase amounts of fat in diet.

Symptoms
- Difficulty sleeping.
- Fatigue, irritability, & headache.
- Difficulty thinking & acting coherently: impaired judgement.
- Victims begin to stumble & become clumsy & careless.

Treatment
- Proper diet & rest.
- Treat synergistic effects if required.

- Energy depletion resembles & aggravates hypothermia. The body does not have enough fuel to maintain proper body temperature. As a result inadequate sources of energy, coupled with cold, creats a compound or synergistic effect.

DEHYDRATION & ITS EFFECTS

Cause
- Loss of too much fluid, salt, & minerals due to poor hydration.

Contributing Factors:
- Water loss occurs through sweating, breathing, & urine output. In cold climates, sweat evaporates so rapidly or is absorbed so thoroughly by clothing layers that it is not readily apparent.
- In cold weather, drinking is inconvenient. Water is hard to resupply, heavy to carry, & freezes in colder climates.
- Lack of humidity in dry mountain air.
- Diminished thirst sensation induced by hypoxia.

Prevention
- Drink 3 to 4 quarts of water per day when static and up to 8 quarts during increased activity.
- Adequate rest.
- Avoid caffeine (coffee, tea, soda) & alcohol, as they compound dehydration.
- Use a buddy system to watch over each other.
- Keep canteens full.
- Use flavored powdered drink mixes to encourage water consumption.

Symptoms
- Generally tired & weak.
- Mouth, tongue, & throat become parched & dry, & swallowing becomes difficult.
- Darkening of urine.
- Constipation & painful urination.
- Loss of appetite.
- Rapid heartbeat.
- Headache, dizziness, & nausea with or without vomiting.
- Difficulty focusing eyes.
- Dehydration compounds the effects of cold & altitude.

Treatment
- Sufficient hydration to offset water loss.
- Rest.
- Severe cases may require medical attention.

GIARDIASIS & EFFECTS
(Parasitical Illness from Unpurified Water)

Cause
- Parasitical illness contracted from drinking unpurified water.

Prevention
- Drink only potable water.
- Boil water for 3 to 5 minutes.
- Use water purification tablets &/or filters.
- Keep water containers clean.

Symptoms
- Abdominal pain.
- Weakness & nausea.
- Frequent diarrhea & intestinal gas.
- Loss of appetite.

Treatment
- Proper hydration with potable water.
- Evacuation & prescribed medications.

HYPOXIA & EFFECTS

Cause
- Rapid ascent to high altitudes (above 3,000 to 4,000 meters or 10,000 to 13,000 feet).

Prevention
- Acclimatization.
- Slow ascent.
- Limited activities.
- Long rest periods.

Symptoms
- Impaired judgment, perception, & mental functions increasing with altitude.

Treatment
- Evacuation to lower altitude.

ACUTE MOUNTAIN SICKNESS (AMS) & EFFECTS

Cause
- Rapid ascent to high altitudes (2,400 m- 8,000 ft).

Prevention
- Acclimatization.
- Staged &/or graded ascent.
- During stops, no strenuous activity & only mild activity with frequent rest periods.
- Increased carbohydrate intake (whole grains, vegetables, peas & beans, potatoes, fruits, honey, & refined sugar).
- Possible medical prescription.

Symptoms
- Headache & fatigue.
- Insomnia, irritability, & depression.
- Coughing & shortness of breath.
- Loss of appetite, nausea, & vomiting.
- Dizziness.
- Swelling of the eyes & face.

Treatment
- Stop & rest.
- Symptoms will normally subside in 3-7 days if ascent not continued.
- Observe for the development of HAPE or HACE.
- If symptoms do not disappear, a rapid descent of 150-300 m (500-1,000ft) or more is necessary.
- Re-ascent should take place only after symptoms are resolved.

HIGH ALTITUDE PULMONARY EDEMA (HAPE) & EFFECTS

Cause
- Unacclimatized climbers rapidly ascending to high altitudes (2,400 meters or 8,000 feet)*.
- Acclimatized climbers ascending rapidly from a high to a higher altitude.
- Usually begins within first 2-4 days after rapid ascent & generally during the second night of sleep at high or higher altitudes.
- Fluid accumulation in the lungs.

Prevention
- Acclimatization.
- Staged &/or graded ascent.
- Sleeping at the lowest altitude possible.
- Slow assumption of physical activity.
- Protection from the cold.

*HAPE most often does not occur until above 3,500 m (12,000 ft).

Symptoms
- Wheezing & coughing (possibly with pink sputum).
- Gurgling sound in chest.
- Difficulty breathing.
- Coma.
- Death may occur if rapid descent is not initiated.

Treatment
- Rapid evacuation recommended.
- Observe for the development of HACE.
- Seek qualified medical assistance.

HIGH ALTITUDE CEREBRAL EDEMA (HACE) & EFFECTS

Cause
- Unacclimatized climbers rapidly ascending to high altitudes (2,400m/8,000 ft)*.
- Acclimatized climbers ascending rapidly from a high to a higher altitude.
- Excessive accumulation of fluid in the brain.

*HACE, like HAPE, most often does not occur until above 3,500 meters (12,000 feet).

Prevention
- Acclimatization.
- Staged &/or graded ascent.
- Slow assumption of physical activity.
- Protection from the cold.

Symptoms
- Most severe high altitude illness.
- Severe headache, nausea, & vomiting.
- Staggering walk/sway.
- Confusion, disorientation & drowsiness.
- Coma, usually followed by death.

Treatment
- Immediate evacuation; preferably by air.
- Seek qualified medical assistance.

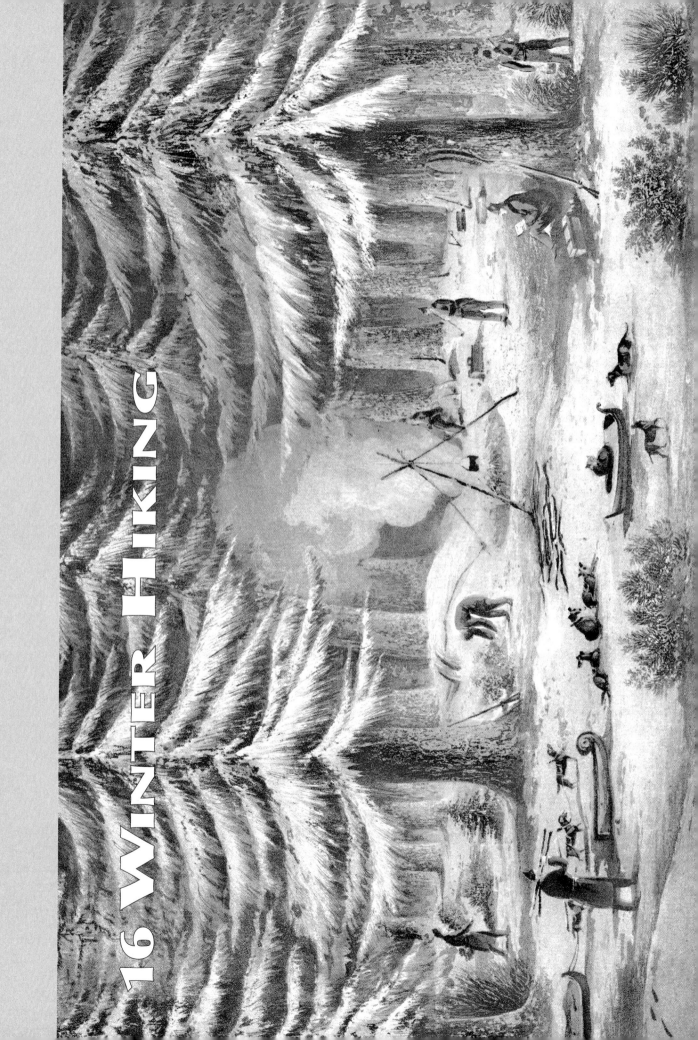

16 WINTER HIKING

What Makes a Winter Storm?

Cold Air: below freezing temperatures in the clouds and near the ground are necessary to make snow and/or ice.

Moisture: to form clouds and precipitation. Air blowing across a body of water, such as a large lake or the ocean, is an excellent source of moisture.

Lift: something to raise the moist air to form the clouds and cause precipitation. An example of lift is warm air colliding with cold air and being forced to rise over the cold dome. The boundary between the warm and cold air masses is called a front. Another example of lift is air flowing up a mountain side.

Winter Thunderstorms

Lightning and thunderstorms can occur when snow, sleet, or freezing rain fall. This can even occur when surface temperatures are near or below freezing. This occurrence is quite rare but occurs most often in the central United States during the winter and spring. There have been cases of this occurring around the Great Lakes during lake effect snowstorms.

Snow Types

Some forms of snow are of benefit to the winter traveler, while others are a source of great danger.

Snow is a substance that follows a life cycle starting as falling snow and terminating as water. An in-between step might even be ice.

Snow

Snow varies in moisture content and can be classified as...

Dry Snow

When it is squeezed together it will not become a clump.

Damp Snow

A snow which can be used to make a snowball.

Wet Snow

This snow will release water when squeezed.

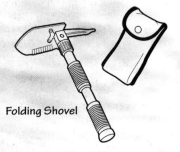

Folding Shovel

Snow Knife

Snow Saw

Impact of Winter Storms with Strong Winds

Sometimes winter storms are accompanied by strong winds creating blizzard conditions with blinding wind-driven snow, severe drifting, and dangerous wind chill. Strong winds with these intense storms and cold fronts can knock down trees, utility poles, and power lines. Storms near the coast can cause coastal flooding and beach erosion as well as sink ships at sea. In the West and Alaska, winds descending off the mountains can gust to 100 mph or more damaging roofs and other structures.

Extreme Cold

Extreme cold often accompanies a winter storm or is left in its wake. Prolonged exposure to the cold can cause frostbite or hypothermia and become life-threatening. Infants and elderly people are most susceptible. What constitutes extreme cold and its effect varies across different areas of North America. In areas unaccustomed to winter weather, near freezing temperatures are considered "extreme cold." Freezing temperatures can cause severe damage to citrus fruit crops and other vegetation. Pipes may freeze and burst in homes that are poorly insulated or without heat. In the north, below zero temperatures may be considered as "extreme cold." Long cold spells can cause rivers to freeze, disrupting shipping. Ice jams may form and lead to flooding.

Ice Storms

Heavy accumulations of ice can bring down trees, electrical wires, telephone poles and lines, and communication towers. Communications and power can be disrupted for days while utility companies work to repair the extensive damage. Even small accumulations of ice may cause extreme hazards to motorists and pedestrians.

Heavy Snow Storms

Heavy snow can immobilize a region and paralyze a city, stranding commuters, stopping the flow of supplies, and disrupting emergency and medical services. Accumulations of snow can collapse buildings and knock down trees and power lines. In rural areas, homes and farms may be isolated for days, and unprotected livestock may be lost. In the mountains, heavy snow can lead to avalanches. The cost of snow removal, repairing damages, and loss of business can have large economic impacts on cities and towns.

Winter Weather Terms

Winter Storm Warning: Issued when a combination of heavy snow, heavy freezing rain, or heavy sleet is expected. Winter Storm Warnings are usually issued six to 24 hours before the event is expected to begin.

Winter Storm Watch: The possibility of a blizzard, heavy snow, freezing rain, or heavy sleet. Winter Storm Watches are usually issued 12 to 36 hours before the beginning of a Winter Storm.

Winter Storm Outlook: Issued prior to a Winter Storm Watch. The Outlook is given when forecasters believe winter storm conditions are possible and are usually issued 48-60 hours in advance of a winter storm.

Blizzard Warning: Issued for sustained or gusty winds of 35 mph or more, and falling or blowing snow creating visibilities at or below 1/4 mile; these conditions should persist for at least three hours.

Lake Effect Snow Warning: Issued when lake effect snow is expected to occur. A Lake Effect Snow Advisory also cautions for the possibility of snow.

Wind Chill Warning: Issued when wind chill temperatures are expected to be less than 34°F below zero.

Wind Chill Advisory: Issued when wind chill temperatures are expected to be between 20° below and 34° below zero.

Winter Weather Advisories: Issued for accumulations of snow, freezing rain, freezing drizzle, and sleet which will cause significant inconvenience and moderately dangerous conditions.

Dense Fog Advisory: Issued when fog will reduce visibility to 1/8 mile or less over a widespread area.

Snow Flurries: Light snow falling for short durations. No accumulation, or light dusting is all that is expected.

Snow Showers: Snow falling at varying intensities for brief periods of time. Some accumulation is possible.

Snow Squalls: Brief, intense snow showers accompanied by strong, gusty winds. Accumulation may be significant. Snow squalls are best known in the Great Lakes region.

Blowing Snow: Wind-driven snow that reduces visibility and causes significant drifting. Blowing snow may be snow that is falling and/or loose snow on the ground picked up by the wind.

Blizzard: Winds over 35 mph with snow and blowing snow reducing visibility to near zero.

Sleet: Rain drops that freeze into ice pellets before reaching the ground. Sleet usually bounces when hitting a surface and does not stick to objects. However, it can accumulate like snow and cause a hazard to motorists.

Freezing Rain: Rain that falls onto a surface with a temperature below freezing. This causes it to freeze to surfaces, such as trees, cars, and roads forming a coating or glaze of ice. Even small accumulations of ice can cause a significant hazard.

WINTER WEATHER REGIONS

From the Mid-Atlantic Coast to New England... The classic storm is called a Nor'easter. A low pressure area off the Carolina coast strengthens and moves north. Wind-driven waves batter the coast from Virginia to Maine, causing flooding and severe beach erosion. The storm taps the Atlantic's moisture-supply and dumps heavy snow over a densely populated region. The snow and wind may combine into blizzard conditions and form deep drifts paralyzing the region. Ice storms are also a problem. Mountains, such as the Appalachians, act as a barrier to cold air trapping it in the valleys and adjacent low elevations. Warm air and moisture moves over the cold, trapped air. Rain falls from the warm layer onto a cold surface below becoming ice.

Along the Gulf Coast and Southeast... This region is generally unaccustomed to snow, ice, and freezing temperatures. Once in a while, cold air penetrates south across Texas and Florida, into the Gulf of Mexico. Temperatures fall below freezing killing tender vegetation, such as flowering plants and the citrus fruit crop. Wet snow and ice rapidly accumulate on trees with leaves, causing the branches to snap under the load. Motorists are generally unaccustomed to driving on slick roads and traffic accidents increase. Some buildings are poorly insulated or lack heat altogether. Local municipalities may not have available snow removal equipment or treatments, such as sand or salt, for icy roads.

In the Midwest and Plains... Storms tend to develop over southeast Colorado in the lee of the Rockies. These storms move east or northeast and use both the southward plunge of cold air from Canada and the northward flow of moisture from the Gulf of Mexico to produce heavy snow and sometimes blizzard conditions. Other storms affecting the Midwest and Plains intensify in the lee of the Canadian Rockies and move southeast. Arctic air is drawn from the north and moves south across the Plains and Great Lakes. Wind and cold sometimes combine to cause wind chill temperatures as low as 70°F below zero. The wind crosses the lakes, tapping its moisture and forming snow squalls and narrow heavy snow bands. This is called "lake-effect snow."

From the Rockies to the West Coast... Strong storms crossing the North Pacific sometimes slam into the coast from California to Washington. The vast Pacific provides an unlimited source of moisture for the storm. If cold enough, snow falls over Washington and Oregon and sometimes even in California. As the moisture rises into the mountains, heavy snow closes the mountain passes and can cause avalanches. The cold air from the north has to filter through mountain canyons into the basins and valleys to the south. If the cold air is deep enough, it can spill over the mountain ridge. As the air funnels through canyons and over ridges, wind speeds can reach 100 mph, damaging roofs and taking down power and telephone lines. Combining these winds with snow results in a blizzard.

In Alaska... Wind-driven waves from intense storms crossing the Bering Sea produce coastal flooding and can drive large chunks of sea ice inland destroying buildings near the shore. High winds, especially across Alaska's Arctic coast, can combine with loose snow to produce a blinding blizzard and wind chill temperatures to 90°F below zero! Extreme cold (-40°F to -60°F) and ice fog may last a week at a time. Heavy snow can impact the interior and is common along the southern coast. With only brief glimpses of the winter sun across the southern horizon, the snow accumulates through the winter months. In the mountains, it builds glaciers, but the heavy snow accumulations can also cause avalanches or collapse roofs of buildings. A quick thaw means certain flooding. Ice jams on rivers can also cause substantial flooding.

TYPES OF SNOW

New Fallen Snow: is very loose and light and the snow flakes still have their multiple branches. This snow is an excellent insulation. If new snow is dry, it is feathery; if damp, it quickly consolidates into a stage of settled snow.

In areas of extreme cold and at high altitudes, new snow is in two forms:

• Sand Snow falls at extremely low temperatures. It has a sandy sharp grandular texture like sandpaper. Skiing, sledding, and walking is difficult.

• Wild Snow is very dry new snow which falls during calm periods and at low temperatures. Extremely light and feathery and is easily blown by the wind. Wild snow can create dangerous whiteouts.

Powder Snow: is a loose snow but the flakes have lost their branches. Powder snow changes to some form of settling or settled snow.

Wind-Packed Snow: has been windblown, usually from one direction, and is compacted by the mechanical force of the wind. The blowing of the wind exerts pressure on the snow and causes a form of cold-heat hardening. In some areas of the snow surface it will be strong enough to carry your weight and you would have no problem staying on the surface with snowshoes. This is good snow to cut blocks for igloos or other snow structures.

Sun Crust: is snow that has had the upper layer melted by heat and subsequently refrozen. A layer of snow that is sun crusted and weathered throughout its thickness becomes corn snow. Sun crust commonly is a layer over powder snow. This snow type is not be very stable on a slope and can be dangerous.

Corn Snow: occurs after a period of thaw and a refreezing of the snow. The snow structure is grainy snow ice crystals. This usually occurs in the spring. This snow can be strong enough to carry weight but might indicate the presence of rotten snow which is very dangerous. Advanced corn snow or neve consists of closely associated grains of ice, separated by air spaces.

Rotten Snow: is caused by repeated melting and freezing and is found at lower levels of a snow field or on south sides of hills. The melting and freezing of the upper layer will cause water to seep to the lower layers. This water does not freeze during the cold because it is insulated from the weather by the covering snow layer. This rotten snow is strong enough to support the layers of snow above it. It can collapse if a heavy weight is placed on it. This snow type is dangerous because you might fall through it while walking on the surface. If it is 10" thick it would not be too dangerous but at 5 feet thick and over water it would be serious.

Slush Snow: has absorbed water from melting snow or rain. To recognize areas of slush, especially if on a river or lake, you will see a depression in the snow with some darker or bluish snow areas. These areas show holes in the ice or an accumulation of water on the surface of the ice.

Ice: can be frozen water or cold heat packed snow as in glaciers and icebergs that have broken off glaciers. If traveling on a snowmobile avoid river ice as the water currents can be eroding the ice from below.

Glacier Ice: is composed of crystals of advanced corn snow cemented by a film of ice. There is no air space between the grains and any air spaces present are within the grains themselves.

Lake Ice: for snowmobile travel requires at least 7" and for walking at least 3". Ice strength depends upon the conditions under which it was formed.

SNOW

Snowflakes are formed from water vapor, at or below 32°F, without passing through the liquid water state. Newly fallen snow undergoes many alterations on the ground. As the snow mass on the ground packs and becomes denser, the snowflakes consolidate and the entrapped air is expelled. These changes are caused by effects of temperature, humidity, sunlight and wind.

Temperature: In general, the lower the temperature, the drier the snow and the less consolidation. As the temperature rises, the snow tends to compact more readily. Temperatures above freezing cause wet snow conditions. Lowered night temperatures may refreeze wet snow and form an icy crust on the surface.

Sunlight: In the springtime, sunlight may melt the surface of the snow even though the air temperature is below freezing. When this occurs, dry powder snow is generally found in shaded areas and wet snow in sunlight areas. Movement from sunlit areas into shaded areas is difficult because the wet snow will freeze to skis and snowshoes. After sunset, however, wet snow usually refreezes and the ease of movement improves.

Wind: Wind packs snow solidly. Wind-packed snow may become so hard that skiing or even walking on it makes no appreciable impression on its surface. Warm wind followed by freezing temperatures may create an icy, unbreakable crust on the snow. Under such conditions, skiing and snowshoeing are very difficult. Another effect of wind is that of drifting the snow. The higher the wind velocity and the lighter the snow, the greater the tendency to drift. Movement is greatly affected by drifting snow and wind, the effect depending on the relative direction and velocity. In addition, as the wind, increases, the effect of extreme cold (windchill effect) on the body may slow down or temporarily stop travel and take shelter. The snowdrifts created by wind usually make the snow surface wavy, slowing down movement.

WINTER TRAVEL

If you weigh the odds of surviving in the Canadian north or in Alaska, in the summer or winter - winter might give you a better chance.

- In the winter there are no insects to drive you crazy.
- Frozen rivers and streams are excellent routes for travel. They are devoid of most obstacles except fallen trees and ice ridges (on the shores of larger bodies of water).
- Water has a special characteristic when it freezes. Upon cooling it contracts (as most materials) but when it starts to become ice it expands. Once it is ice and gets colder the ice starts contracting again and fissures in ice will occur. These fissures are filled with water that freezes. Now when the ice warms up and starts to expand it will not have enough space, and will explode upwards causing the buckles in the ice that are seen near the shoreline on lakes and rivers. These bucklings are called ridges.
- Snowshoes on deep snow cover can help you pass over brush and swamp which can be impenetrable in summer. This will let you shorten your travel time by many days.
- The dry cold air lets you see further and hear better. When it is very cold you might hear noise from an encampment 5 miles away. To determine the direction of the sound stand away from any obstructions (to avoid echoes), close your eyes, cup your ears and slowly rotate your head.
- If you have no snowshoes travel where loose snow is the thinnest, which would be on the windblown areas along stream beds, and in heavy evergreen groves.

SNOW & TRAVEL

Weight Carrying Capacity: Generally, when the snow is packed hard, carrying capacity is greater and movement is easier. Although the carrying capacity of ice crust may be excellent, movement generally is difficult because of its slippery surface.
Sliding Characteristics: All-important to the skier are the sliding characteristics of snow. They vary greatly in different types of snow and temperature variations and materially increase or decrease the movement of the skier, according to the conditions that exist.
Holding Capacity: The holding capacity of snow is its ability to act upon ski wax in such a way that backslapping of the skis is prevented without impairing the forward sliding capability. Holding capacity changes greatly with different types of snow, making it necessary to have a variety of ski waxes available.

DANGERS OF WINTER TRAVEL

The northern environment is a dynamic force. In recognizing and understanding its force one can make use of it; if disregarded or underestimated one is threatened with failure. In a northern winter the human element is all-important. The effectiveness of equipment is greatly reduced. Training, respect for the elements and experience are essential. The climate does not allow a margin of error for the individual or group. Travel must be carefully planned and executed - knowing it probably will be more difficult than expected. Because of the stresses imposed by the northern environment, equipment, food, shelter and clothing must be well chosen and maintained.

BEST WINTER TRAVEL TIME

- Early winter, after the formation of ice, as it lets you make short-cuts over streams and marshy areas.
- Best travel - midwinter to early spring before the breakup period. When the snow is "settled," for better mobility even in a roadless wilderness.

WINTER TRAVEL PROBLEMS

- The winter cold requires the use of special cold weather clothing and equipment.
- The blending of terrain features, lack of trails to follow, fog and blowing snow all combine to make land navigation exceedingly difficult.
- High winds, drifting snow, and the phenomenon of whiteouts can interfere with the best travel plans.
- High winds also combine with the cold to make moderately cold weather extremely uncomfortable.

ARCTIC, SUBARCTIC & HIGH ELEVATION REGIONS

They are characterized by deep snow, permafrost, seasonally frozen ground, frozen lakes and rivers, glaciers, and long periods of extremely cold temperatures. Cold regions are affected by wind and the possibility of thaw during warming periods. An unexpected thaw causes a severe drop in the soil strength which creates mud and water accumulation. Camp- sites near bodies of water, such as lakes or rivers, have to be well chosen to prevent flooding damage during the spring melt season. Sites protected from wind will greatly decrease the effects of the cold.

Good wind protection in:
- Densely wooded areas
- Small blocks of trees or shrubs
- Lee side of terrain elevations. (The protected zone extends horizontally up to three times the height of the terrain elevation). Watch for corniche overhangs and avalanche areas.
- Terrain depressions

WINTER HIKING

Winter cross-country travel is difficult but the challenge is satisfying. Of necessity, travel will be slower, but with the proper training, the proper enthusiastic leadership, and the will to reach a destination, nothing is impossible.

BASIC RULES

- Plot your route on a map and highlight the landmarks.
- Insure that all members participating are fully aware of the objective, route, and difficulties that might be encountered.
- Supplies are checked and loads evenly distributed.
- A trail breaking rotation established so that the lead person does not get too tired.
- You should travel in single file to limit the effort of trail breaking.
- Dress as lightly as possible consistent with the weather to reduce excessive perspiring and subsequent chilling. Consideration has to be given for any emergencies. Cold weather casualties result from too few clothes being available when a severe change in the weather occurs.
- The first halt should be made in approximately 15 minutes. This will allow adjustment of clothing and equipment. Subsequent halts should be frequent and of short duration to insure rest and to prevent chilling. Halts should, so far as possible, be made in sheltered places which will provide protection from the elements. Warm drinks should be provided during a halt if possible.
- The buddy system is mandatory in the North - watch your buddy carefully for early signs of frostbite. Individuals must not be allowed to fall out of the group, except in an extreme emergency. If this should occur, proper care must be taken to insure the individual does not become a cold weather casualty. The person at the rear of the column should not be forgotten.

EXTREME COLD & YOU

The effects of extreme cold must be considered in planning a trip. The proper use and care of clothing and equipment will largely overcome most difficulties; however, extremely low temperatures combined with wind can be very hazardous to you operating outside. The effect of these two elements occurring together is called windchill, which greatly increases the speed at which exposed flesh will freeze and the length of time you can operate in the open. The human body is continually producing or losing heat. Wind increases the loss of heat by reducing the thin layer of warm air next to the skin. This loss increases as the speed of wind increases. Any movement of air past the body has the same cooling effect as wind. Walking, running, skiing, or riding in an open vehicle may produce the chilling.

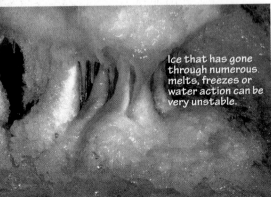

Ice that has gone through numerous melts, freezes or water action can be very unstable.

SUDDEN CHANGES IN WEATHER

These changes include extreme temperature changes, snowstorms, strong winds, and dense fog. Changes may be sudden and must, if possible, be anticipated as they might last a few days and a camp must be struck before they occur. The importance of local weather knowledge cannot be overemphasized.

WINTER DAYLIGHT & DARKNESS

The short winter day must be factored into any travel plans with special consideration on a possible overnight stay in an inhospitable environment.

LATE WINTER TRAVEL

Special consideration must be made for periods of seasonal transition. Climatic changes become more abrupt and the appearance of terrain features changes rapidly. A frozen river may one day present little problem and the next day be a major obstacle.

EXTREME COLD & EQUIPMENT

- In extreme cold, metal becomes brittle.
- Special care should be taken to avoid touching metal parts with exposed skin.
- Special light lubricants might be necessary on equipment or snowmobiles because of the effect of cold on normal lubricants.
- Avoid bringing metal (cameras – remove batteries, binoculars, etc.) into a warm shelter, condensation or the melting of accumulated snow may occur which will cause it to freeze when taken back into the outside cold temperatures.

CHOICE OF TRAIL

Follow along forest terrain with little or no underbrush. It provides protection against wind. Avoid thickets, and windfall forest areas.

TRAILS

HILLY & MOUNTAINOUS TERRAIN

Valleys and frozen rivers will most often provide the easiest route. If the valleys cannot be used, the trail may be broken on the lee side of the ridge line or hill mass that dominates the valley. Care must be exercised to detect avalanche snow conditions and bypass these areas as necessary. Use gentle inclines when climbing uphill or descending.

OBSTACLES

Since even minor obstacles retard a group, they should be bypassed whenever possible. If a wide obstacle is met, such as a ridge or a steep riverbank the challenge has to be met in crossing it.

WEATHER & SNOW CONDITIONS

In early winter there is more snow in open terrain than in dense forest; therefore, the trail should be broken close to the forest edge. In late winter the reverse is true. In early spring more snow can be found in ditches, ravines, and on the shadowy side of hills.

DARKNESS

Skiing and snowshoeing at night is slow and exhausting.

Sunglasses

FORESTED AREA

A great portion of the North is covered with vast coniferous forests, dense brush, swamps, and numerous lakes and rivers. Few trails exist through the forests and those that do exist are of poor construction, making progress difficult and slow. The numerous waterways, once they become frozen, will normally provide excellent routes for foot and some vehicle movement. Skiing and snowshoeing are relatively easy on frozen, snow-covered rivers, lakes, and swamps. In wooded areas greater skill is required in skiing to avoid trees and other obstacles. Woods retard the melting of snow in spring often allowing skiing after the open fields are clear of snow. In autumn, the situation is reversed; the deeper snow is generally found in the open fields allowing skiing earlier than in wooded areas.

MOUNTAINS

Mountains present special problems. Their varied and steep terrain place additional demands upon the skill of a skier and make movement on snowshoes or skis very difficult. Slopes which are easy to negotiate in summer often become difficult and dangerous to cross in winter because of deep snow cover which is prone to avalanche. Large drifts and snow cornices present other obstacles and dangers. Snow cover on glaciers obscures crevasses and makes their crossing hazardous.

Whistle

Avalanche Areas

Avalanche Areas

Loose Drifting Snow

Best travel route on windward side (harder packed snow) and through the tree area.

Deep Drift Snow

Wind Packed Snow is usually darker and looks icy.

Suspended
Ice

Suspended Ice

Layer of Air

Water

Air layer below ice because of
falling water during a cold spell.

SUSPENDED ICE

If the water level falls, which happens if it is very cold and no melting is occurring in the river drainage basin, the ice can be suspended in the air and become very fragile and the internal tension of the ice might not be stable. Walking on suspended ice can be very dangerous. If you fall through it you will have no grip to crawl out.

THICKNESS OF THE ICE

Less than 3" is dangerous

4" for ice fishing and skating.
7" for snowmobiles.
8" - 12" cars & ATVs.

These numbers are approximate because the type of ice has to be considered, how it was formed, how many snow layers are on the surface, and how many thaws there were.

DO NOT CAMP NEAR AN ICE RIDGE

Ice pressure ridges are formed by the contraction and expansion of ice which occurs with the change of temperature. The ice expands, upon getting warmer, it needs more space and might explode and buckle onto the shoreline. This might injure or drown you if you are camping in the area.

Ice Ridge

Exploding
Ice Ridge

FROZEN WATERWAY TRAVEL

Frozen lakes, rivers, and creeks offer the most suitable routes for the trails. They have an advantage in that they are relatively flat, usually have the snow blown off by the wind, and have a known destination. The only slopes found on such routes are at the entrance and exit to the waterway. The disadvantages are that a sudden temperature rise can make the route unusable. When traveling watch for thin spots. Areas of ice ridges should be approached with caution.

ICE ROUTE SELECTION

An experienced person should select the route over ice. One qualified to interpret ice characteristics to prevent the group from being needlessly endangered. The entire route over the ice is suspect as the ice can differ in many ways in a relatively short distance. Sometimes in winter, and especially in the spring, there may be water under the snow surface, on surfaces on the lakes and rivers, this will cause boots, snowshoes, or skis to freeze. Areas in which water is found under snow should be bypassed. Ice is never totally safe even when it is very cold. In rivers a swift current will continue to flow below the ice cover and these areas can be thin and dangerous but not visible above the surface.
Ice Strength: The thickness of the ice must be carefully checked before using any ice route. The minimum thickness of ice for skiers is 2" and for a group in single file on foot 4". Where there are water currents the ice will be much thinner than the surrounding areas. Warm water springs are prevalent in northern areas and can create a to travel. Many of these springs do not freeze, even in extremely low temperatures, and may cause streams to have little or no ice and some lakes to have only thin ice. Their presence in muskeg or tundra areas can cause weak spots in otherwise solid terrain.

Testing Ice: The strength of ice varies with its structure and temperature. A snow cover or a warm current will affect the ice temperature and generally will produce a thinner and weaker ice cover. If the ice depth and strength is unknown skiers, snowshoes, and ATV's drivers should make a detailed prior reconnaissance. Leaders of the party should be roped together. The lead trail breaker in a prone position drives an axe into the ice at arm's length; if the ice sounds solid he moves forward 5 yards and tests again.

Danger: Thin NEW Ice

Old Ice

Water

Danger Zone

If a pressure ridge has recently broken open, the ice forming on the newly exposed water will not have the time to freeze to the same thickness as the surrounding area. When traveling on an ATV or walking always be careful near pressure ridges.

FALLING THROUGH THE ICE

When traveling over water watch for areas of strong currents under the ice which can produce thin spots through which you can fall. Hypothermia might result in a few minutes after falling through ice.

- If you fall through ice, break off as much thin ice in the direction of escape as possible. When you are near ice that can support your weight, squirm up onto the surface. Slide and roll along the surface so that your weight is distributed and you do not break through a second time. Move towards shore, dry and warm up as soon as possible. Dry by rolling in the snow. Your weight will blot the water out of the clothing and the snow will absorb the water. The remaining water will freeze and make a shell around you. The ice will add additional weight and make you very uncomfortable. Your clothing will also lose most of its insulation capacity. Change your clothing and warm up as soon as possible or you might expose yourself to hypothermia.
- Another method is, while falling, to immediately stretch your arms so that they might find ice strong enough to support your weight. Keep your arms spread out and try to slide your legs onto the ice edge to crawl out.
- A sheath knife (or ice hook) can help you crawl out of icy water. Upon falling into the water, plunge your knife into the solid ice and roll yourself onto the solid surface.

ADDITIONAL ICE TRAVEL PRECAUTIONS

- Water can try to rise above the level of the ice and cause the ice surface to explode or be suddenly flooded.
- When traveling on ice carry a long light pole. This pole should be carried horizontally to help in case of falling through the ice. The pole can also be used to jab the ice surface to see how it rings. It might sound hollow, heavy, or muffled (might indicate a layer impregnated with air or water which might be 'candle ice').
- When traveling in a group make sure that you are in single file and well spread out. If you have a rope have it strung between you - but not tied to you.
- When the ice starts to melt, in the spring, it is dangerous because it is very fragile and unstable.
- **"Candle ice"** is extremely dangerous. Candle ice looks solid but is actually suspended vertical needles of ice that do not have a solid structure because they are not attached laterally. Stepping on candle ice is like stepping on slush. This ice is very dangerous because there is no solid rim to grab if you fall through it.

Helicopter landing between ice ridges.

Ice Ridges

Rotten Ice
"Candle Ice"

WINTER TRAVEL SHELTER

Carrying tents with stoves and fuel slows travel at low temperatures. When the day's stretch is completed, campsites must be prepared, tents erected, and stoves put into operation. During the cold season, shelters are not struck until the last possible moment prior to beginning the march, so as to provide heat and shelter as long as possible. Although considerable time is consumed in pitching and striking tents, experience has taught that it is still less time consuming to utilize this transportable type shelter than to construct improvised shelters. Under certain survival conditions small groups can utilize snow caves and snow houses for shelter. However, this means of shelter should be reverted to only as a last resort or when other shelter is unavailable.

Wind Break

CAMPING IN OPEN TERRAIN & ICE

Due to strong winds, and drifting snow, camping areas in the barren tundra must be carefully chosen.
Windbreaks: Tents should be pitched where they can be sheltered by natural windbreaks whenever possible. The windbreak may consist of depressions in the ground or pressure ridges on the ice. A visual inspection will indicate the degree of drifting, direction of the prevailing wind, and more suitable protected areas for locating the shelters. In areas where natural windfalls do not exist, snow walls may be constructed to provide protection from winds. In open areas with high winds, snow gathers rapidly on the lee side, making it necessary to clear the sides and tops of the tents periodically to prevent the weight of the drifting snow from collapsing the tent. The entrance to the shelter should face downwind from the prevailing wind. This will prevent the snow from blocking the exit and cutting off the ventilation.

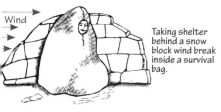

Taking shelter behind a snow block wind break inside a survival bag.

Tent on Ice: When the tent is pitched on ice, holes are chopped where the tent pins are normally set. "Deadmen" are inserted in the holes at right angles to the tent. The holes are then packed with snow or filled with water and left to freeze.

LATE SPRING TRAVEL

After the breakup season easy travel can be resumed only after the ground has dried sufficiently to allow cross-country movement. This is especially true when in the low areas with numerous streams and swamps. Poor drainage may cause low-lying country to become isolated from the surrounding terrain thus forcing major detours.

SPRING TRAVEL DIFFICULTIES

Travel in spring is possible if timed for the period when daytime thaw and nighttime freeze leave only a thin layer of mud on deeply frozen ground, and lake and stream ice is still firm. However, these travel plans may be interrupted by sudden breakup periods.

CAMPING ON MARSHY GROUND

In winter, when the ground is frozen, good camping sites may be found in areas which otherwise would not be usable. Some swampy areas may not freeze during the winter, because of warm water springs or gases. They provide poor facilities for a site. If it is necessary to camp on swampy ground some form of flooring must be constructed. If tree trunks are available, a "float" may be built under the shelter. In the absence of tree trunks, brush matting will serve the same purpose.
Long Term Occupancy: Areas to be used for extended periods of time require draining, clearing of existing creeks, digging of ditches around the shelter, or preparing a water trench inside the shelter.

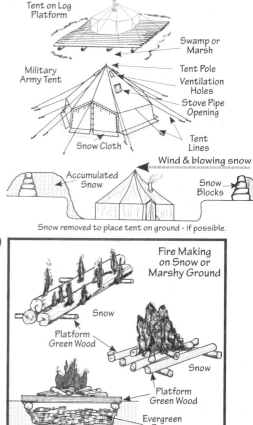

Tent on Log Platform

Swamp or Marsh

Military Army Tent

Tent Pole
Ventilation Holes
Stove Pipe Opening

Snow Cloth

Tent Lines

Wind & blowing snow

Accumulated Snow

Snow Blocks

Snow removed to place tent on ground - if possible.

FIREWOOD & SIGNALS

Boughs: Cutting boughs for bedding as well as for construction of improvised shelters is from a dense area of woods in which springy, unfrozen boughs are available.
Firewood: Dry, dead pine trees make the best firewood. If no dead trees are available, green birch trees may be chopped; they possess excellent burning qualities even when frozen.
The top parts of dead trees give off lighter colored smoke. The lower part of the trunk has more resin and tar, and burns better, and makes more and much darker smoke. *This dark smoke would be excellent for sending signals.*

Fire Making on Snow or Marshy Ground

Snow

Platform Green Wood

Snow

Platform Green Wood

Evergreen Bows

Snow

Collapsed Suspended Ice

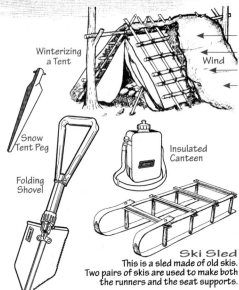

First Norwegian expedition to cross Greenland in the 1880's.

Winterizing a Tent

Wind

Snow Tent Peg

Folding Shovel

Insulated Canteen

Ski Sled
This is a sled made of old skis. Two pairs of skis are used to make both the runners and the seat supports.

SHOVELING SNOW

While shoveling snow can be good exercise, it can also be dangerous for optimistic shovelers who take on more than they can handle.

- Individuals over the age of 40, or those who are relatively inactive, should be especially careful.
- If you have a history of heart trouble, do not shovel without a doctor's permission.
- Do not shovel after eating or while smoking.
- Take it slow! Shoveling (like lifting weights) can raise your heart rate and blood pressure dramatically; so pace yourself. Be sure to stretch out and warm up before taking on the task.
- Shovel only fresh snow. Freshly fallen, powdery snow is easier to shovel than the wet, packed-down variety.
- Pushing snow is easier on your back than lifting the snow out of the way.
- Don't pick up too much at once.
- Use a small shovel.
- Lift with your legs bent, not your back. Keep your back straight. By bending and "sitting" into the movement, you'll keep your spine upright and less stressed. Your shoulders, torso and thighs can do the work for you.
- Do not work to the point of exhaustion. If you run out of breath, take a break. If you feel tightness in your chest, stop immediately.
- Dress warmly. Remember that extremities, such as the nose, ears, hands and feet, need extra attention during winter's cold. Wear a turtleneck sweater, cap, scarf, face protection, mittens, wool socks and waterproof boots.

CAMPING ON MOUNTAINS

Mountainous terrain is characterized by strong turbulent winds and cold. The wind overhead creates an extensive lee near the mountain. The overhead lee resembles the dry space behind waterfalls caused by water having such speed that it shoots over the edge of the cliff and descends in a curve. An inland wind blowing 50 mph may not strike the ground for several miles after passing the edge of a cliff or a very steep slope. While such a lee side is an attractive camping site from the standpoint of wind protection it should be noted that such a lee area is often an area of maximum snow deposit. The requirement to constantly dig out which may offset the wind-free advantages of a lee site during snowfall or snow blowing weather.

Before Storm   Wind

Note: the elevated area might cause drifting snow to settle in the wind shadow.

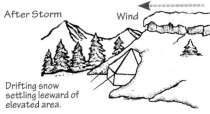

After Storm   Wind

Drifting snow settling leeward of elevated area.

COLD AIR IN VALLEYS

Cold air is heavier and frequently settles in valleys. The point where the temperature starts changing is low in summer and higher and more noticeable in winter. Therefore, in some instances it is better to establish a camp up the hillside above the valley floor and below the timberline. Avoid avalanche areas.

SNOW CONSTRUCTION

Dry snow is less suitable for construction than wet snow because it does not pack as well. Snow compacted by the wind, and after a brief thaw is even more suitable for shelters. A uniform snow cover with a minimum thickness of 10 inches is sufficient for shelter from the weather. Blocks of uniform size, typically 8 by 12 by 16 inches, depending upon degree of hardness and density, are cut from the snow pack with shovels, long snow knives, or snow saws. The best practices for constructing cold weather shelters are those adopted from natives of polar regions. The systematic overlapping block-over-seam method ensures stable construction. "Caulking" seams with loose snow ensures snug, draft-free structures. Igloo shelters in cold regions have been known to survive a whole winter. An igloo easily withstands above-freezing inside temperatures, thus providing comfortable protection against windchill and low temperatures. The entrance to the shelter, located on the side least exposed to the wind, is close to the ground and *slopes up into the shelter*. This upwards slope will help the higher pressure and lighter warm air keep out the heavier external cold air.

SNOW CONDITIONS

Travel time will vary from hour to hour. The best snow condition is one where the snow supports a person on or near the surface when wearing boots and the second best is a calf-deep snow condition. If possible, avoid traveling in thigh or waist deep snow. Snowshoes should be worn when conditions dictate.

- South and west slopes offer hard surfaces late in the day after exposure to the sun and the surface is refrozen. East and north slopes tend to remain soft and unstable. Walking on one side of a ridge, gully, clump of trees, or large boulders is often easier than the other side. Dirty snow absorbs more heat than clean snow; slopes darkened by rocks, dust, or uprooted vegetation usually provides more solid footing. Travel should be done in the early morning after a cold night to take advantage of stable snow conditions. Since sunlight affects the stability of snow, travel should in shaded areas where footing usually remains stable.
- Be cautious in areas covered by early seasonal snowfall when traveling between deep snow and clear ground. Snow on slopes tends to slip away from rocks on the downhill side, forming openings. These openings, called moats, are filled by subsequent snowfalls. During the snow season, moats below large rocks or cliffs may become extremely wide and deep, making it difficult to pass.

TRAVEL TIME ON SNOW

An overzealous drive to reach a destination may be too fast for the group. Fast starts in snowy terrain usually result in frequent stops for recuperation. Travel by starting with a steady pace and continue at that pace. Movement at reasonable speeds, with rest stops as required, will help prevent group "burnout." A steady pace helps maintain an even rate of breathing. After the initial period of travel, that is, one-half hour, a shakedown rest should be initiated to adjust boots, snowshoes, crampons, packs, etc., or to remove or add layers of clothing.

Winter Travel Time	Unbroken Trail	Broken Trail
On foot		
<1' of snow	1-2 mph	0.5-2 mph
>1' of snow	0.24-0.75 mph	1.25-2 mph
Snowshoeing	1-2 mph	2-2.5 mph
Skiing	1-3.5 mph	3-3.5 mph

Repairing Snowshoe

WINTER TRAVEL CONDITIONS

Snow travel is more complicated than summer travel and snow affects your mobility in a number of ways. Heavy snow cover impedes movement, either cross-country or on roads. Snow cover also blankets many terrain features, hiding obstacles to movement such as brush, stumps, rocks, ditches, small streams, fallen trees, and man made obstacles. There are no obvious trails, drifting snow can obstruct route markers and deep snow might leave markers at too low a level to be easily seen at a distance. Inherent dangers (avalanches, collapsing cornices, ice patches etc.) may necessitate an alternate route, or backtracking, entailing a longer trek. During all winter travel, safety, and not ease of travel, is the primary concern. Snow cover acts as a thermal insulator that retards the freezing or thawing of underlying ground. When snow melts, it saturates the ground and often makes it impassable. Snow or ice on roads, under certain conditions, makes driving difficult and dangerous.

The effect of snow cover on mobility varies greatly with both depth and physical characteristics of the snow at any particular time and location. On foot you cannot easily travel over flat terrain or roads when the depth of uncompacted snow exceeds 12" in depth. Frequently, movement across a snow-covered area impassable during the day may become passable during the night after a sharp drop in temperatures.

Skis: afford greater speed in moving, particularly over prepared trails and usually require less physical effort. Condition of snow (depth, trail broken, etc.) will affect this speed.

Snowshoes: Snowshoe movement, though slower than skis, are more practical in a confined area.

Snowshoes are excellent for over snow movement. Like skis, they provide flotation in snow and are useful for cross-country travel in snow-covered terrain. The snowshoe is an oval or elongated frame braced with two of three crosspieces and the inclosed space filled with a web lacing. A binding or harness attached to the webbing secures the wearer's foot to the snowshoe. Flotation is provided by the webbing, which is closely laced and prevents the snowshoe from sinking too deeply into the snow when weight is placed upon it. Depth and consistency of snow will determine the amount of support obtained on the snow cover and the rate of movement.

- Do not travel when there is an approaching storm. Avoid whiteouts because you can lose your sense of direction.
- When the weather is clear, distance is difficult to estimate and will usually be underestimated. This will cause you to go too far and be tired on your return trip or have to return in the dark.

SNOWSHOES: IDEAL WINTER TRAVEL AID

Snowshoes are particularly useful in confined areas because of their ease of maneuver. Transporting, carrying, and storing snowshoes is relatively easy due to their size and weight. Maintenance requirements are generally negligible and little skill is required to become proficient on snowshoes. However, the requirement for physical conditioning is as great, or greater, as that needed for skiing. The use of snowshoes when pulling and carrying heavy loads is particularly practical, as the hands and arms remain free.

SNOWSHOEING

USING SNOWSHOES

On steep slopes, however, the use of snowshoes is considerably limited because traction becomes negligible and the snowshoe will slide, causing loss of footing. Generally, the rate of movement in any type of terrain is slow because snowshoes will not glide over the snow. The gliding properties of the ski are not obtained with the snowshoes; this adversely affects the amount of time and energy spent in movement. In deep snow the trail breaker must be changed frequently. Especially when wet, snow tends to stick to the webbing, thereby adding weight to the snowshoe.

SNOWSHOE TYPES

Trail: The trail-type snowshoe is long, with a rather narrow body and upturned toes. The two ends of the frame connect and extend tail-like to the rear. The turned-up toe has a tendency to ride over the snow and other minor obstacles. The excellent flotation provided by its large surfaces makes the trail snowshoe best for cross-country travel, deep snow conditions, and trail breaking.

Bearpaw: This type of snowshoe is short, wide, and oval in shape, with no frame extension. The bearpaw snowshoe is preferable to the trail type in heavy brush, and in other confined areas. Carrying or storing is also easier.

Magnesium: The magnesium snowshoe is the lightest and most durable of the three types. The snowshoe has a magnesium frame with the center section made of steel, nylon-coated wire. The magnesium snowshoe is shorter than the standard wooden trail snowshoe but is wider giving it approximately the same flotation characteristics.

Aluminum: There are modern aluminum snowshoes that incorporate the different characteristics of the first three types.

SNOWSHOE MODELS

The US and Canadian armies use the Maine model shoe design. The advantage of the Maine model (quite similar to the Michigan model which is less upturned and the nose more rounded) is that it is good for travel on trails and in open wooded areas. The long tails help maintain their track in a straight line and if the harnesses are properly attached, they are tail heavy keeping them on course. The heavy tail will also keep the nose out of deep snow.

SELECTING SNOWSHOES

Size of Toe Hole: Front of boot should be able to move in and out of toe hole without rubbing the sides or the front crossbar.

Weight: Aim for the lightest snowshoe and harness. Do not buy an oversized snowshoe as it will be larger, weigh more and affect the width of your walk. One pound of weight on your foot is equal to five pounds on your back.

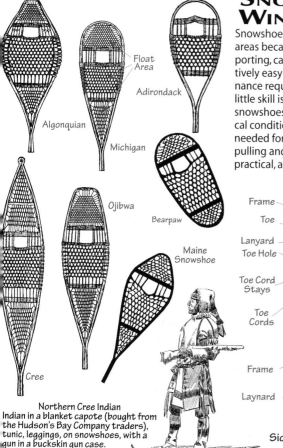

Float Area

Adirondack

Algonquian

Michigan

Ojibwa

Bearpaw

Maine Snowshoe

Cree

Northern Cree Indian
Indian in a blanket capote (bought from the Hudson's Bay Company traders), tunic, leggings, on snowshoes, with a gun in a buckskin gun case.

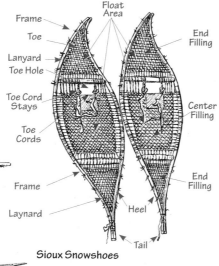

Frame
Toe
Lanyard
Toe Hole
Toe Cord Stays
Toe Cords
Frame
Laynard

Float Area

End Filling

Center Filling

End Filling

Heel

Tail

Sioux Snowshoes

Snowshoe Hare

December - Soft snow - Misery

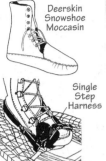

Deerskin Snowshoe Moccasin

Single Step Harness

Double Step Harness

Army nylon web harness on magnesium snowshoes.

March - On the crust - Pleasure

SNOWSHOE HARNESS

The type of harness depends upon the type of terrain on which the snowshoes will travel. The most popular traditional combination harness used in eastern Canada and the eastern United States are made of thick leather that can easily be, replaced or repaired at home. Current harnesses are a nylon webbing.

Aluminum Snowshoe

Aluminum Snowshoes

Modern snowshoe frames are made of high quality lightweight aluminum tubing. The frame is covered with a stretch resistant plastic compound. The shoe is attached with a harness that pivots on the balance cross bar. Some models have a crampon grip that pivots at the toe area which helps in crossing icy areas.

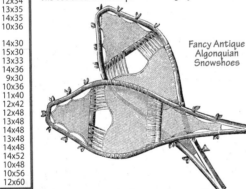

Fancy Antique Algonquian Snowshoes

Snowshoe Size Guide

	Weight (lbs)	Size (in)
Bearpaw "Westover"	125-150	12x34
	150-180	13x35
	180-210	14x35
Bearpaw "Green Mountain"	up to 200	10x36
Bearpaw (Standard)	150-175	14x30
	175-200	15x30
	175-200	13x33
	200-250	14x36
Maine	35-50	9x30
	50-60	10x36
	60-90	11x40
	100-125	12x42
	125-150	12x48
	150-175	13x48
	175-200	14x48
Michigan	150-175	13x48
	175-200	14x48
	200-250	14x52
Alaskan	125-150	10x48
	150-175	10x56
	175-200	12x60

SNOWSHOE TECHNIQUE

Striding Technique: is used for movement with snowshoes. In taking a stride, the toe of the snowshoe is lifted upward, to clear the snow, and thrust forward. Energy is conserved by lifting it no higher than is necessary to clear the snow and slide the tail over it. If the front of the snowshoe catches, the foot is pulled back to free it and then lifted before proceeding with the stride. The best and least fatiguing method in travel is a lose-kneed rocking gait in a normal rhythmic stride. Care is taken not to step on or catch the other snowshoe.

Stepping: On soft snow or semi compacted snow step forward firmly and let snowshoe sink into the snow to form a firm base for the next step. At each step give your body a slight lurch so that the snowshoe will get a firmer stand for the following step.

Gentle Slopes: ascent is made by climbing straight upward. Traction is generally very poor on hard-packed or crusty snow.

Steeper Terrain: is ascended by traversing and packing a trail similar to a shelf across it. When climbing, the snowshoe is placed as horizontally as possible in the snow. On hard snow, the snowshoe is placed flat on the surface with the toe of the upper one diagonally uphill to get more traction. In the event the snow is sufficiently hard-frozen to support the weight of a person, it is generally better to remove the snowshoes and proceed temporarily on foot.

Downhill Travel: Make sure that your binding is tight enough or your toes will slide under the crosspiece and you will fall forward. Study the hill to find the best path of decent. If it is steep you can descend in a zigzag or if snow is firm you can place one shoe behind the other and sit on the rear snowshoe to slide down the hill.

Turning: In turning around, the best method is to swing the leg up and turn in the new direction, as in making a kick turn on skis.

Turning Back: Use the kick turn by taking one leg and turning it 180° and firmly placing it and then moving the second foot 180°. Poles might help you maintain your balance especially if you are carrying a heavy backpack.

Obstacles: Obstacles such as logs, tree stumps, ditches and small streams should be stepped over. Care must be taken not to place too much strain on the snowshoe ends by bridging a gap, since the frame may break. In shallow snow there is danger of catching and tearing the webbing on tree stumps or snags which are only sightly covered.

Wet Snow: will frequently ball up under the feet, interfering with comfortable walking. This snow should be knocked off with a stick or pole as soon as possible.

Ski Poles: Although ski poles are generally not used in snowshoeing, one or two poles are desirable when carrying heavy loads, especially in mountainous terrain. Use a pole to help you climb a steep hill. Poles are useful if you have to back out of an area in heavy snow or between trees.

Binding: The bindings must not be fastened too tightly or circulation will be cut off, and frostbite may occur. During halts, bindings should be checked for fit and possible readjustment.

CARE & STORAGE OF SNOWSHOES

Care: The modern *aluminum snowshoes*. with neoprene or sheet webbing, are basically maintenance free but should be kept clean and you should follow the manufacturer's guidelines. Nylon webbing requires a heavy coating of finishing resin to keep it from wearing and breaking. *Wooden frames,* when dry, should be touched up with spar varnish when scratched. The finish waterproofs the snowshoes and keeps out the humidity. Frequent checks are necessary, particularly of webbing and binding, because individual strands may be ripped or worn out. Repairs must be made immediately, otherwise the webbing will loosen and start to unravel. The rawhide webbing should be coated with spar varnish, when dry, before use and ideally after every trip to stop stretching and rotting. If unvarnished, the rawhide webbing on wooden snowshoes will absorb moisture, stretch and turn white, particularly in wet snow. It should be dried out slowly, avoiding direct flames, and be revarnished at the first opportunity. Wooden frames may fray from hard wear and should be sanded and varnished. When snow cover is shallow, care must be taken not to step on small tree stumps, branches, or other obstacles, since the webbing may be broken or damaged. Stepping into water is to be avoided; the water will freeze and snow will stick to it. When not in use, snowshoes are placed in temporary racks, hung in trees, or placed upright in the snow.

Storage: In off-seasons, wooden snowshoes are stored in a dry, well-ventilated place so that the rawhide will not mildew or rot and the frames warp. Store snowshoes in a cool, dark, dry place especially if your snowshoes are laced with rawhide. Snowshoes should be protected against damage and from rodents. Magnesium snowshoes are cleaned and repainted if necessary. Webbing is examined and repaired or replaced if needed.

Canadian Army Emergency Snowshoes
For each snowshoe...
- Select 6 poles 6' long (height of traveler), poles 3/4" at base and 1/4" thick at the tip.
- Cut 6 sticks 3/4" thick and 10" long.
- Lash one stick to the float area and cut off the excess wood.
- Lash 3 sticks forward of the pivot center of the snowshoes.
- Lash 2 sticks where heel strikes the snowshoe.
- Lash the tips together.

Emergency Snowshoe

Harness
The harness (binding) is secured so that the snowshoe pivots on the foot while walking. The harness can be rawhide, parachute cord, cordage that you have made, etc.

Forest snowshoe travelers from the 1880's resting below an evergreen lean-to. They are heating water over a fire and making tea. One person is slicing bread and there is always someone watching - doing nothing!

EVERGREEN BOUGHS
Emergency snowshoes can be made of boughs of evergreen trees. Have the branch point forward. Attach the boughs to your feet with string, hide, cordage, rubber, etc..

GREEN SAPLINGS
If your path is through brush you want more compact and efficient shoes made in the shape of a bear's paw. The frame can be made by bending green saplings. If the saplings are frozen. thaw them over a small fire or in the sunlight. This will thaw the sap and the sapling will not break when bent. You can use strips of rawhide, cordage, parachute cord as webbing. To carry your body weight, place some green wood strips below your feet.

SIZE OF EMERGENCY SNOWSHOES
The size of the snowshoe required depends upon snow conditions, your weight, and your backpack's weight. Ideally they should be as small and light as possible. If the snow is deep and soft then the shoes might be up to five feet long and a foot wide.

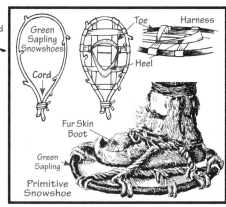

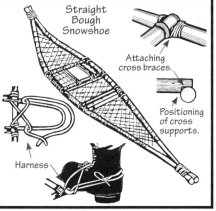

Watch for cornice overhangs.

A Cornice is formed by wind continuously blowing snow over an abrupt edge on a hill or mountain.

Snowshoe Harnesses

EMERGENCY SNOWSHOES

WINTER NAVIGATION

WINTER NAVIGATION

There is a lack of landmarks, large forested areas, periods of reduced visibility, difficulty of cross-country movement, and by large magnetic declinations in the northern areas.

AVOID GETTING LOST

Prior to traveling memorize details of the country to be traversed. Especially the winter characteristics of these landmarks. Routes should be plotted and as many landmarks located as possible to insure that you will not be without recognizable features for any appreciable length of time. If on barren terrain, all navigation instruments must be thoroughly checked and one of the most experienced of the group should be given the job of navigating and maintaining the "dead reckoning log." It is possible to become temporarily lost while hiking in a local area, especially in a unfamiliar white winter setting, as on a long trip. The main point to remember is to remain calm if you feel disoriented.

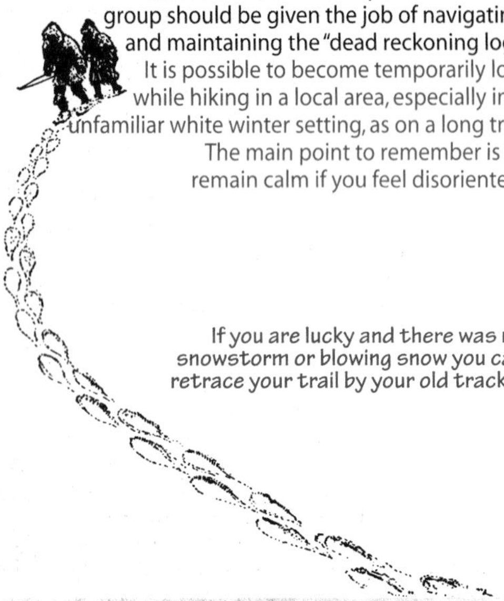

If you are lucky and there was no snowstorm or blowing snow you can retrace your trail by your old tracks.

South

LAND NAVIGATION

The normal methods of land navigation under cold weather conditions remain the same as anywhere else. Maps and aerial photos may be used alone during daylight in terrain which offers enough distinctive terrain features to serve as useful landmarks. They may also be used in conjunction with a compass, especially in terrain which contains insufficient landmarks or under circumstances when visibility is limited. However, in most instances, utilizing the map and compass together will provide for the surest land navigation in northern areas.

Additional Methods: Depending on various conditions, certain supplementary methods, such as position of the sun in daytime, North Star and Big Dipper at night may be used to aid in land navigation. Where possible, these methods should be employed in conjunction with the normal methods described above.

MELTED HALF CIRCLES INDICATING "SOUTH"

When a small, vertical, dark object (branch, leaf, etc.) is on the surface of the snow, on a sunny day, the object will absorb heat and melt a hole into the snow. The sun will continue shining into the hole and the sun's rays will raise the temperature melting the snow to create a hole up to a foot deep. The depth of the hole decreases when closer to the North Pole. The hole that is formed is in the shape of a half circle adjacent to the dark object. In the northern hemisphere, the straight side of the half (the diameter) is aligned east-west. The arc of the half circle is the south.

This action of the sun can also be seen in animal tracks in the snow .

North of the Arctic Circle, this method does not work because during the summer months the sun never sets but goes around the horizon and a practically round circle is formed.

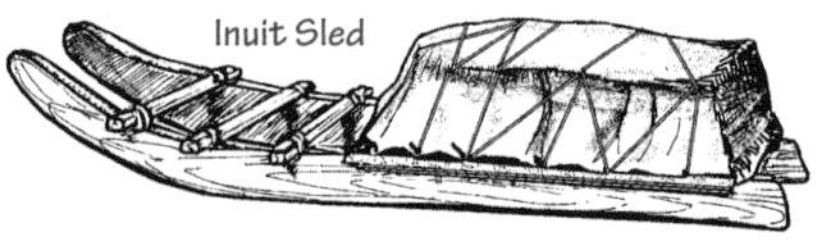

Inuit Sled

IMPORTANT
Be very careful if you are pulling a child on a sled. The child, in not moving the body, does not generate much heat and the child can freeze without you knowing it.

HAULING SLEDS

Man-hauled sleds can carry a load of 200 pounds over difficult terrain and are used for carrying tents, stoves, fuel, rations, and other necessary items. The ideal sled has a boat like shape, is easily maneuverable under a variety of snow and terrain conditions. It is superior to flat surfaced toboggans in maneuvering over difficult terrain, especially in deep snow and in heavily wooded areas. Distribute the load of the sled properly. Place heavy equipment on the bottom and slightly to the rear and lighter equipment toward the top, in order to prevent the loaded sled from being top heavy.

Canvas covers should be folded over the load. To keep snow from getting under the canvas and to keep the load from shifting, lash the load tightly. Place tools such as shovels, axes, and saws on top of the load outside the canvas.

Northern Winter Navigation

Basically, map reading, as well as navigation under cold weather conditions, follows the same principles as in the temperate zones. In addition to the normal procedures, every individual must be most familiar with certain conditions peculiar to the cold weather regions and the techniques applicable to navigation. Technical failure or human error may easily, and especially in the winter, be fatal; great care must be exercised when navigating in low temperatures.

Winter Navigation Problems

The following conditions, characteristic of the cold weather regions, will make accurate navigation very difficult:

· Lack of adequate large scale maps in the sparsely populated areas.

· Aerial photos of many areas will be difficult to read and interpret because of the absence of relief and contrast, and absence of man made works for use as reference points.

· Dense forests and wildernesses offer few landmarks and limit visibility. Also, barren, monotonous tundra areas north of the tree line are characterized by lack of landmarks as aids for navigation.

· In winter, short daylight, fogs, snowfall, blizzards, drifting snow, especially in the barren areas, drastically limit visibility. At times an overcast sky and snow-covered terrain create a phenomenon called whiteout which makes recognition of irregularities in terrain extremely difficult.

· Heavy snow may completely obliterate existing tracks, trails, outlines of small lakes, and similar landmarks. Because the appearance of the terrain is quite different in winter from that in summer, particular attention must be paid to identifying landmarks, both on the ground and in aerial photos.

· Magnetic disturbances are encountered, making magnetic compass readings difficult and sometimes unreliable.

· Magnetic declination in different localities varies considerably, and must be taken into consideration when transposing from a map to a compass.

· Handling maps, compass, and other navigation instruments in low temperatures with bare hands is difficult. Removing hand gear may often be possible for a very short period of time only.

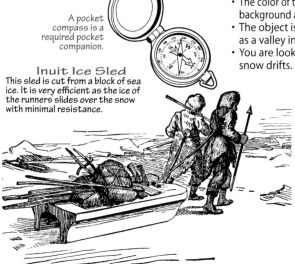

A pocket compass is a required pocket companion.

Inuit Ice Sled
This sled is cut from a block of sea ice. It is very efficient as the ice of the runners slides over the snow with minimal resistance.

Direction of Wind

Winds are named for the directions from which they come, i.e. North wind from the North. Each area has a predominant wind that dominates a season or all seasons. The dominant wind is nearly always the same as the prevailing wind which blows longer or more violently from a given direction. The dominant wind will affect the growth of trees, direction of snow drifts, direction of tall grass, etc. In northern snow covered areas the prevailing wind is usually from the northwest. To establish the direction find an open spot, where local landmarks do not deflect the wind, and look at wind features as snow drifts, wind packed or wind polished snow. Wind polished snow can be very hard and slippery. In the polar regions, the wind temperature, if warmer than the surroundings, indicates the direction of water. A sudden drop in temperature, without a change in the direction of the wind, might indicate the presence of an iceberg.

The sun and wind can leave signs which help in finding your direction.

· Erosion by frost is more evident on southern slopes of hills because there is a much larger temperature change from heating by day and cooling at night.

· On southern slopes, heat of the sun will leave "melted shadows" of trees, shrubs and stones in the accumulated snow. This is evident in the spring. There is less snow on the side of a hill facing south.

· The direction of the wind should be observed as a warm strong wind can melt snow faster than the sun. This might affect direction indicators.

Judging Distance on Snow Surfaces

Distance is underestimated when starting and overestimated at the end of the trip. An error in overestimation can also occur when a trip or route is difficult.

Objects look much nearer than they actually are when...
· Looking up or down hill.
· There is bright sunlight on the snow.
· Looking across water, or snow covered areas.
· The air is clear which is common in the winter.

Objects look much farther away than they actually are when...
· The light is poor during the latter part of a short winter day.
· The color of the destination blends in with the background as during a snowfall or blowing snow.
· The object is at the end of a long narrow area as a valley in the mountains.
· You are looking over undulating ground as snow drifts.

Navigation by Dead Reckoning

It is obvious that on vast barren grounds as well as in wide forests, navigation by dead reckoning often becomes the only practical method. Dead reckoning is the process by which position at any instant is found by applying to the last determined position the direction and distance of the course traveled. This method should also be used in areas where landmarks are very limited or totally non-existent. It is also useful when the landmarks are obliterated by the limited visibility.

Navigation by dead reckoning is outlined in the *Compass & Map Chapter Page 363*. Due to the peculiarities of the cold weather regions, the following hints should be observed when applicable:

· Responsibility for navigation is assigned to a member(s) thoroughly experienced in navigation techniques. This individual must be released from the carrying of individual heavy loads and trail breaking in order to perform his duties properly. In preference, use more than a single navigator because the method of pacing distances in deep snow has to be modified as described below.

· The navigator(s) have to take and record necessary data for precise location at all times and supply data to keep the group on course.

· Due to the sliding capacity of the skis, normal pacing system is very inaccurate or, in certain cases, such as on steep slopes, entirely useless. Pacing on snowshoes can be done in emergency. It must be borne in mind, however, that an individual mounted on snowshoes takes much shorter paces than on foot. The only recommended method for accurate ground measurements is a piece of line or field wire preferably 50 yds used by two navigators. The slope angle will have to be taken into consideration.

· Keeping a log is mandatory. The preparation of the log, as well as plotting the route from the log data on the face of the map or on a separate piece of paper at the same scale as the map, must be completed prior to the departure to minimize the use of instruments and equipment in low temperatures with bare hands.

· Of course there is the GPS. Make sure to keep the batteries charged and warm.

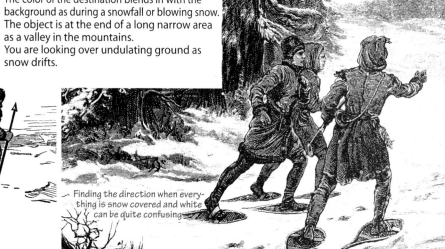

Finding the direction when everything is snow covered and white can be quite confusing.

FINDING WATER IN WINTER

Camping on an ice floe. Collecting water from puddles on the surface of the floe. The surrounding water would be salty.

DRINKING WATER

The problem of supplying water in the north in large quantities is very difficult. For instance, melting snow and ice on stoves, burners, or open fires in large quantities is impractical because a large amount of fuel is needed to obtain a small amount of water. Seventeen cubic inches of loose snow, when melted, yields only 1 cubic inch of water. Melting of snow is not recommended for supplying water in quantity except in an emergency.

FINDING WATER

When possible, water points on lakes and rivers are located on the leeward side where there is generally clearer water, less snow drifting, and more shelter from the wind. Sites on a lake are located as far from the shore as possible. To cut holes in ice at water points a hand ice auger can be used. Hand tools are generally inefficient if ice is over 24" thick. Ice is thinnest where the most snow covers it. At low temperatures, ice rapidly forming over the water in the hole can be kept clear by placing the suction strainer about a foot below the surface when pumping. *Note: water has to be treated.*

MELTING SNOW

If possible, water should be obtained from running streams or lakes rather than by melting ice or snow. Melting ice or snow to obtain water is a slow process and consumes large quantities of fuel, 17 cubic inches of uncompacted snow, when melted, yields only 1 cubic inch of water. If snow is used as a water source, it may be shoveled into a container and heated. When powdered or loosely packed snow is used for water, pack it tight in the container and tamp down or stir it frequently while melting to increase the moisture content and so increase its heat conductivity. Granular snow, usually obtainable near the ground, has higher water content than the lighter snow of the surface layers.

STERILIZATION IN COLD WEATHER

Chemical sterilization of water under freezing conditions requires a longer period because the disinfecting compounds act with retarded efficiency under such conditions. The time allotted for contact with purification tablets should be two to four times the normal period.

EATING SNOW

Eating ice or snow is unsatisfactory and may result in injury to lips or tongue. Contamination may also be a hazard. If no other water source is available, as in a survival situation, snow can be eaten but it must first be brought to the melting point by holding it in the bare hand. It may then be eaten slowly and in small amounts. This is best done during periods of temporary heat excess, as while walking, or while in the sleeping bag. The risk of frostbite to the hand must be considered and balanced against the need for fluids. Should some water be available in an uninsulated canteen during a survival situation, this should be warmed under the clothing or in the sleeping bag. Then snow may be added to the canteen after each drink to replace the water consumed. Body heat stored in the slightly warmed water will thus melt the snow with less risk of cold injury to hands or lips. A glass bottle or plastic bag can be used in place of an uninsulated canteen.

WATER IN WINTER

Water is plentiful in most cold regions in one form or another. Potential sources are streams, lakes and ponds, glaciers, fresh-water ice, and last year's sea ice. Freshly frozen sea ice is salty, but year-old sea ice has had the salt leached out. It is well to test freshly frozen ice when looking for water. In some areas, where tidal action and currents are small, there is a layer of fresh water lying on top of the ice; the lower layers still contain salt. In some cases, this layer of fresh water may be 20" to 40" in depth.

WATER HOLE IN ICE

In winter a hole may be cut through the ice of a stream or lake to get water; the hole is then covered with snow blocks placed over it. Loose snow is piled on top to provide insulation and prevent refreezing. In extremely cold weather, the waterhole should be broken open at frequent intervals. Water holes should be marked with a stick or other marker which will not be covered by drifting snow. Water is abundant during the summer in lakes, ponds, or rivers. The milky water of a glacial stream is not harmful. It should stand in a container until the coarser sediment settles.

WATER FROM SNOW TYPES OF ICE & SNOW

• When water is not available from other sources, it must be obtained by melting snow or ice. To conserve fuel, ice is preferable when available; if snow must be used, the most compact snow in the area should be obtained. Snow should be gathered only from areas that have not been contaminated by animals or humans.
• Ice sources are frozen lakes, rivers, ponds, glaciers, icebergs, or old sea ice. *Old sea ice is rounded* where broken and is likely to be pitted and to have pools on it. Its underwater part has a bluish appearance. *Fresh sea ice has a milky appearance and is angular in shape* when broken. Water obtained by melting snow or ice may be purified by use of water purification tablets.

MELTING SNOW & ICE

• Burning the bottom of a pot used for melting snow can be avoided by *"priming."* Place a small quantity of water in the pot and add snow gradually. If water is not available, the pot should be held near the source of heat and a small quantity of snow melted in the bottom before filling it with snow.
• The snow should be compacted in the melting pot and stirred occasionally to prevent burning the bottom of the pot.
• Pots of snow or ice should be left on the stove when not being used for cooking so as to have water available when needed.
• Snow or ice to be melted should be placed just outside the shelter and brought in as needed.
• In an emergency, an inflated air mattress can be used to obtain water. The mattress is placed in the sun at a slight inclined angle. The mattress, because of its dark color, will be warmed by the sun. Light, fluffy snow thrown on this warm surface will melt and run down the creases of the mattress where it may be caught in a container.

Inuit making a fire using dry moss, collected in the summer, as kindling.

Inuit Melting Snow — Snow — Piece of slate — Water Collected — Oil Fire

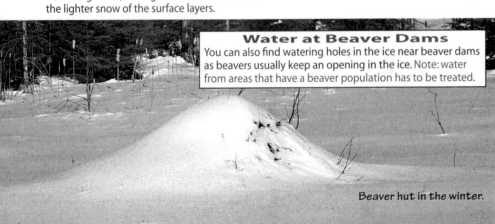

Water at Beaver Dams
You can also find watering holes in the ice near beaver dams as beavers usually keep an opening in the ice. Note: water from areas that have a beaver population has to be treated.

Beaver hut in the winter.

Metal — Insulated Cover — **Plastic or Metal Canteen** Carried in a heavy insulating fabric carrier or cover; however, this will not keep the liquid in the canteen from freezing in extreme cold.

Plastic Canteen Needs an insulated carrier.

Plastic lip for drinking. The drinkers lip will not freeze to the metal when it is very cold.

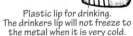

In winter or summer, water obtained from ponds, lakes and streams must be purified by chemical treatment, use of iodine tablets or in emergencies by boiling.

Cold Weather Canteens

Metal Canteen: This canteen is a *vacuum-insulated* canteen. The inner and outer stainless steel vessels are welded together at the top of the neck. A nonmetallic mouthpiece at the neck prevents lips from freezing to the metal neck. A plastic cap seals and protects the mouthpiece. A nesting type metal cup is provided for eating and drinking beverages. The canteen with cup is carried in a canvas cover.

Conventional Metal & Plastic Canteens: Carried in a heavy insulating fabric carrier; however, this will not keep the liquid in the canteen from freezing in extreme cold.

- When possible, the canteen should be carried in a pocket or wrapped in a woolen garment and packed in the rucksack.
- Warm or hot water should be placed in the canteen before setting out. During extreme cold the canteen should never be filled over two-thirds full. This will allow room for expansion if ice should form, and will prevent the canteen from rupturing.
- Insure that the gaskets are in the cap at all times. This is an important precaution and will prevent the liquid from leaking out and dampening the clothing in the rucksack.
- Conventional thermos bottles will keep liquids hot, or at least unfrozen for approximately 24 hours, depending on temperatures.
- If canteens or thermos bottles freeze, they should be thawed out carefully to prevent bursting. The top should be opened and the contents allowed to melt slowly.

Constipation & The Outdoors

During cold weather conditions there is a general tendency for individuals to allow themselves to become constipated. This condition is brought about by the desire to avoid the inconvenience and discomfort of relieving themselves under adverse conditions. This condition is also caused by changes in eating habits and failure to drink a sufficient amount of liquids. Constipation can usually be prevented by adjusting the normal eating and drinking habits to fit the activities in which engaged, and by not 'putting off' the normal, natural, processes of relieving the body of waste matter.

Inuit Whalebone Push Sleigh

Personal Hygiene

Because of the extremes in temperature and lack of bathing and sanitary facilities, keeping the body clean in cold weather will not be easy.

- The entire body should be washed at least weekly. If bathing facilities are not available, the entire body can be washed with the equivalent of two canteen cups of water, using half for soap and washing, and half for rinsing. If circumstances prevent use of water, a rubdown with a dry cloth will help. Care should be taken not to abrade the skin. The feet, crotch, and armpits should be cleaned daily.
- A temporary *sweat lodge* can be built in a large-size tent. Stones are piled up to form a furnace. The furnace is either heated inside the tent (ventilation flaps wide open) or in the open with the tent pitched over the furnace after the stones are heated. Wood is used for fuel. Seats and water buckets are taken into the tent after the stones are nearly red-hot and the fire has died down, so that they do not get sooty. The pouring and washing water is usually heated outside the tent. The water is thrown on the hot stones in small quantities. Thus it does not drop into the ashes and the temperature does not rise too fast. A naked person spends from 15 minutes to 1 hour in this steam bath. After thoroughly perspiring, the body is washed with tepid water.
- Beards should be shaved or clipped close. Hair should be combed daily and not allowed to grow too long. A beard or long hair adds very little in insulation value and soils clothing with the natural hair oils. In winter, a beard or a mustache is a nuisance since it serves as a base for the buildup of ice from moisture in the breath and will mask the presence of frostbite. Because shaving with a blade and soap removes the protective face oils, the individuals should shave, if possible several hours before exposing his face to the elements. This will reduce the danger of frostbite.
- Socks should be changed and the feet washed daily. If this is not possible, the boots and socks should be removed, and the feet massaged and dried. By sprinkling the feet liberally with foot powder and then rubbing the powder off, the feet can be efficiently dry cleaned.
- Sleeping bags should be kept clean. Wear the minimum clothing in the sleeping bag. Never wear damp socks or underwear in the sleeping bag. Dry underwear and socks should be put on before going to sleep and the other set hung up to dry. Perspiration will soil a sleeping bag, and cause it to become damp, therefore, the bag should be aired as frequently as possible. In the morning, the bag should be opened wide and air pumped in and out to remove the moist air within the bag.

Antique Toboggan

First Aid

In cold weather, the care of the body requires special emphasis. If you go without washing, fail to eat properly, do not get sufficient liquids or salt, efficiency will suffer. Lowered efficiency increases the possibility of cold injury.

Shock   *Page 592.*

Shock is brought about by a reduction of the circulating blood volume within the body. This can be caused by severe injuries, loss of blood, pain, emotional disturbances, or any of many factors. The normal reaction of the body to severe cold, reduction of the volume of blood circulating to extremities, is very similar to the reaction of the circulatory system to the condition of shock. Shock will usually develop more rapidly and progress more deeply in extreme cold than in normal temperature.

Signs of Shock: The signs of shock are apprehension, sweating, pallor, rapid, faint pulse, cold clammy skin, and thirst. *If the patient is not given good first aid treatment immediately the condition of shock may progress until the patient passes into unconsciousness and further into death.*

First Aid for Shock

The following is a general outline but immediate medical attention is required.

- The injured person should be made as comfortable as possible.
- Pain may be relieved by proper positioning, good bandaging and splinting.
- The litter should be positioned so that the patient is comfortable and not apt to inhale vomitus.
- The patient should be kept warm with blankets and sleeping bags.
- When the patient is conscious he should be given warm soup, chocolate, coffee, or tea.

The patient should receive medical attention as soon as possible.

Body Parasites

Body parasites are very common in more populated cold regions because of the crowded living conditions and shortage of bathing and cleaning facilities. When occupying shelters which have been used before, individuals must inspect clothing and body each night for parasites.

Means of Control: If clothing has become infested with lice, the following methods of removing them are recommended:

- While extreme cold does not kill lice, it paralyzes them. The garments should be hung in the cold; then beaten and brushed. This will help rid the garments of lice, but not of louse eggs.
- An appropriate insecticide powder can be used to free the body and clothing of body parasites.

Teeth: should be cleaned daily. If a toothbrush is not available, a clean piece of gauze or other cloth wrapped around the finger, or end of a twig chewed into a pulp may be used in lieu of a toothbrush.

Underwear & Shirts: should be changed at least twice weekly; however, if it is not possible to wash the clothing this often, the clothing should be crumpled, shaken out, and aired for about 2 hours.

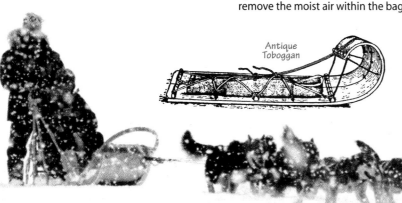

Dehydration & frostbite are a high risk in cold weather.

DEHYDRATION
Cause, Symptoms, Effects, Preventive Measures, & Treatment

- Dehydration results from failure to correct the body's "imbalance of liquids" through replacing liquid and salt which has been lost.
- The symptoms of cold weather dehydration are similar to those encountered in heat exhaustion. The mouth, tongue, and throat become parched and dry and swallowing becomes difficult. General nausea is felt and may be accompanied by spells of faintness, extreme dizziness and vomiting. A feeling of general tiredness and weakness sets in and muscle cramps may occur, especially in the legs. It becomes difficult to keep the eyes in focus and fainting or "blacking out" may occur.
- The effect of dehydration on the individual is to incapacitate him for a period of from a few hours to several days.
- Dehydration can be prevented during cold weather by following the same general preventive measures applicable to hot, dry areas. Salt and sufficient additional liquids are consumed to offset excessive body losses of these elements. The amount will vary according to the individual and the type of activities he is doing. Rest is equally important as a preventive measure. Each individual must realize that any strenuous activity done while bundled in several layers of clothing is extremely exhausting. This is especially true of any movement by foot, regardless of how short the distance.
- In treating a person who has become dehydrated, the individual should be kept warm but his clothes loosened sufficiently to allow proper circulation; liquids and salt should be fed gradually and, most important of all, he must have plenty of rest. When salt tablets are not available, common table salt may be used. Approximately one-half of a level spoon of salt mixed in one gallon of water makes a palatable solution.

The individual should receive prompt medical attention.

FROSTBITE

Frostbite is the freezing of some part of the body by exposure to temperatures below freezing. It is a constant hazard at freezing temperatures, especially when the wind is strong. Usually there is an uncomfortable sensation of coldness followed by numbness. There may be a tingling, stinging, or aching sensation, even a cramping pain. The skin initially turns red. Later it becomes pale gray or waxy white. For all practical purposes frostbite may be classified as superficial or deep. Treatment and management are based solely upon this classification.

Prevent: It is easier to prevent frostbite, or stop it in its very early stages, than to thaw and take care of badly frozen flesh. Clothing and equipment must be fitted and worn so as to avoid interference with circulation.

To prevent severe frostbite...
- Sufficient clothing must be worn for protection against cold and wind. The face must be protected in high wind.
- Every effort must be made to keep clothing and body as dry as possible. This includes avoidance of perspiring. For heavy work in the cold, remove outer layers as needed, and replace as soon as work is stopped. Socks should be changed as needed whenever the feet become moist, either from perspiration or other sources.
- Any interference with the circulation of the blood reduces the amount of heat delivered to the extremities. All clothing must be properly fitted and worn to avoid interference with the circulation. Tight fitting socks, shoes and hand wear are especially dangerous in very cold climates.
- Cold metal should not be touched with the bare skin in extreme-low temperatures. To do so could mean loss of the skin.
- Adequate clothing and shelter must be provided during periods of inactivity.
- The face, fingers, and toes should be exercised from time to time to keep them warm and to detect, any numb or hard areas. The ears should be massaged from time to time with the hands for the same purpose.
- The buddy system should always be used. Pair off and watch each other closely for signs of frostbite and for mutual aid if frostbite occurs. Any small frozen spots should be thawed immediately, using bare hands or other sources of body heat.

DEEP FROSTBITE

Some cases of frostbite may be superficial, involving the skin. But if freezing extends to a depth below the skin it constitutes a much more serious situation, demanding radically different treatment to avoid or minimize the loss of the part (fingers, toes, hands, feet). If a part of the body becomes frostbitten it appears yellowish or whitish gray. Frequently there is no pain, so keep watching one another's face and hands for signs. The face, hands, and feet are the parts most frequently frostbitten. The problem is to distinguish between superficial and deep frostbite. This can usually be told with respect to the face. The hands and feet are a different matter. A person may be able to judge by remembering how long the part has been without sensation. If the time was very short the frostbite is probably superficial. Otherwise assume the injury to be deep and therefore serious.

SUPERFICIAL FROSTBITE TREATMENT
For treatment of superficial frostbite in the field:
- Cover cheeks with warm hands until pain returns.
- Place uncovered superficially frost-bitten fingers under the opposite armpits, next to the skin.
- Place bared, superficially frostbitten feet under the clothing against the belly of a companion.
- Do not rewarm by such measures as massage, exposure to open fires, cold water soaks, rubbing with snow.
- Be prepared for pain when thawing occurs.

DEEP FROSTBITE TREATMENT
In treatment of deep frostbite (freezing injury) the following measures must be taken:
- If freezing is believed to be deep, do not attempt to treat it in the field.
- *Get to a hospital by the fastest means possible.*
- If transportation is available, avoid walking.
- Protect the frozen part from additional injury but do not attempt to thaw it out by rubbing, bending, massage.
- *Do not rub with snow; do not place in either cold or warm water; do not expose to hot air or open fires; do not use ointments or poultices.*
- Thawing in the field increases pain and invites infection, greater damage, and gangrene. There is less danger of walking on feet while frozen than after thawing. Thawing may occur spontaneously, however, during transportation to a medical facility. This cannot readily be avoided since the body in general must be kept warm.

COLD WEATHER DEHYDRATION

It is important to be aware that the danger of dehydration is as prevalent in cold regions as it is in hot, dry areas. The difference is that in hot weather the individual is conscious of the fact that the body is losing liquids and salt because he can see and feel the perspiration with its saline taste and "feel" it running down the face, getting in the eyes, and on the lips and tongue, and dripping from the body. In cold weather, it is extremely difficult for an individual who is bundled up in many layers of clothing to realize that this condition does exist. Under these conditions, perspiration is rapidly absorbed by the heavy clothing or evaporated by the air and is rarely visible on the skin.

The information in this chapter is provided to inform the reader to **get medical attention** as soon as possible if they encounter a similar situation. A First Aid course is strongly recommended. Some of the information in this chapter is based on US Army Data.

PERSONAL EMERGENCY KIT

It is recommended that *every* hiker carry an emergency kit for use in individual survival. With this kit, an individual can survive off the land by trapping and fishing and can procure the minimum amount of food necessary to maintain his strength for a short period of time.

- Emergency thong
- Safety pins
- Sharp pocketknife
- Fishing line
- Single-edge razor blades
- Salt tablets
- Waterproof matches
- Fire starters
- High protein candy bars
- Bouillon cubes

RECOGNIZING FROSTBITE

At the first signs of redness or pain in any skin area, get out of the cold or protect any exposed skin - frostbite may be beginning. Any of the following signs may indicate frostbite: a white or grayish-yellow skin area skin that feels unusually firm or waxy numbness. A victim is often unaware of frostbite until someone else points it out because the frozen tissues are numb.

WHAT TO DO?
Seek medical care!

If you detect symptoms of frostbite, *seek medical care.* Because frostbite and hypothermia both result from exposure, first determine whether the victim also shows signs of hypothermia, as described previously. Hypothermia is a more serious medical condition and requires emergency medical assistance.

If: frostbite but no sign of hypothermia *and* immediate medical care is not available, proceed as follows:

The following procedures are not substitutes for proper medical care.

- Get into a warm room as soon as possible.
- Unless absolutely necessary, do not walk on frost-bitten feet or toes - this increases the damage.
- Immerse the affected area in warm - not hot water (the temperature should be comfortable to the touch for unaffected parts of the body). Or, warm the affected area using body heat. For example, the heat of an armpit can be used to warm frostbitten fingers.
- Do not rub the frostbitten area with snow or massage it at all. This can cause more damage.
- Don't use a heating pad, heat lamp, or the heat of a stove, fireplace, or radiator for warming. Affected areas are numb and can be easily burned.

Hypothermia, a medical emergency, and frostbite should be evaluated by a health care provider. It is a good idea to take a first aid and emergency resuscitation (CPR) course to prepare for cold-weather health problems. Knowing what to do is an important part of protecting your health and the health of others.

Indians Hunting

Cree Indians returning from a caribou hunt. Caribou is being pulled on a tobagan.

HYPOTHERMIA

Hypothermia is a medical emergency
When exposed to cold temperatures, your body begins to lose heat faster than it can be produced. Prolonged exposure to cold will eventually use up your body's stored energy. The result is hypothermia, or abnormally low body temperature. Body temperature that is too low affects the brain, making the victim unable to think clearly or move well.

This makes hypothermia particularly dangerous because a person may not know it is happening and won't be able to do anything about it. Hypothermia is most likely at very cold temperatures, but can occur even at cool temperatures (above 40°F) if a person becomes chilled from rain, sweat, or submersion in cold water.

Victims of hypothermia are most often:
- elderly people with inadequate food, clothing, or heating.
- babies sleeping in cold bedrooms.
- people who remain outdoors for long periods - the homeless, hikers, hunters, etc.

Warnings Signs of Hypothermia
Adults:
- shivering / exhaustion · drowsiness
- confusion / fumbling hands
- memory loss / slurred speech
Infants:
- bright red, cold skin · very low energy

WHAT TO DO?

If you notice any of these signs, take the person's temperature. If it is below 95°F, the situation is an emergency:

Get medical attention immediately.
If medical care is not available, begin warming the person, as follows:
- Get the victim into a warm room or shelter.
- If the victim has on any wet clothing, remove it.
- Warm the center of the body first - chest, neck, head, and groin - using an electric blanket, if available. Or use skin-to-skin contact under loose, dry layers of blankets, clothing, towels, or sheets.
- Warm beverages can help increase the body temperature, but do not give alcoholic beverages. Do not try to give beverages to an unconscious person.
- After body temperature has increased, keep the person dry and wrapped in a warm blanket, including the head and neck.
- Get medical attention as soon as possible.

TOTAL IMMERSION

Immersion in near freezing water for but a few minutes, or exposure to severe dry cold while inadequately dressed will cause total body cooling, including a marked drop in the inner body (core) temperatures.

A person with severe hypothermia may be unconscious and may not seem to have a pulse or to be breathing. In this case, handle the victim gently, and get emergency assistance immediately.
Even if the victim appears dead, CPR should be provided.
CPR should continue while the victim is being warmed, until the victim responds or medical aid becomes available. In some cases, hypothermia victims who appear to be dead can be successfully resuscitated.

TRENCH FOOT

Trench foot is the thermal injury sustained as a result of exposure to cold, short of freezing, in a damp or wet environment. Arbitrarily, it is said to occur in the temperature range between 32°F and 50°F. Partial causes include immobility of the limbs (legs and feet down as in sitting or standing), insufficient clothing, and constriction of parts of the body by boots, socks, and other garments. This type of cold injury is almost identical with gradual frostbite, which might be expected, since the primary causes are the same except for differences in the degree of cold.

In the early stages of trench foot, feet and toes are pale and feel cold, numb, and stiff. Walking becomes difficult. If preventive action is not taken at this stage, the feet will swell and become painful. In extreme cases of trench foot the flesh dies and amputation of the foot or of the leg may be necessary.

Because the early stages are not painful, individuals must be constantly alert to prevent the development of trenchfoot. To prevent this condition:
- Feet should be kept dry by wearing waterproof foot gear and by keeping the floor of shelters dry.
- Socks and boots should be cleaned and dried at every opportunity, preferably daily.
- The feet should be dried as soon as possible after getting them wet. They may be warmed with the hands. Foot powder should be applied and dry socks put on.
- If it becomes necessary to wear wet boots and socks, the feet should be exercised continually by wriggling the toes and bending the ankles. Tight boots should never be worn.
- *In treating trenchfoot, the feet should be handled very gently.* They should not be rubbed or massaged. If necessary, they may be cleansed carefully with plain white soap and water, dried, elevated, and allowed to remain exposed. While it is desirable to warm the patient, the feet should always be kept at room temperature. The patient should be carried and not permitted to walk on damaged feet.

IMMERSION FOOT

Immersion foot is a form of injury which follows prolonged immersion of the feet in water not sufficiently cold to cause freezing or frostbite. It has also been observed after exposure in subtropical waters. Clinically and pathologically, it is indistinguishable from trenchfoot which would be expected, since its cause is essentially the same, lowering of the temperature of the part of the body involved. It is usually associated with dependency (legs and feet down as in sitting or standing) and immobility of the lower extremities and with constriction of the limbs by clothing and shoes. Other factors which play more or less important roles are-body cooling, as the result of wind; total immersion; and inadequate clothing (protection), sickness, and starvation. The incidence and severity of immersion foot however, is more directly influenced by the other factors listed. The treatment is the same as that given for trenchfoot.

COLD INJURY

WIND CHILL

The wind chill is based on the rate of heat loss from exposed skin caused by combined effects of wind and cold. As winds increase, heat is carried away from the body at a faster rate, driving down both the skin temperature and eventually the internal body temperature. Animals are also affected by wind chill. While exposure to low wind chills can be life threatening to both humans and animals alike, the only effect that wind chill has on inanimate objects, such as vehicles, is that it shortens the time that it takes the object to cool to the actual air temperature (it cannot cool the object down below that temperature).

Avoid Overexertion: such as shoveling heavy snow, pushing a car, or walking in deep snow. The strain from the cold and the hard labor may cause a heart attack. Sweating could lead to a chill and hypothermia.

WIND CHILL FACTOR

- To obtain the windchill factor take the actual temperature of your surroundings.
- Estimate the speed of the wind by looking at the characteristics outlined on the *Beaufort Wind Scale Page 430.* Take the temperature and apply both parameters to the Wind Chill Chart.

WIND CHILL & WINTER TRAVEL

30°F and below
Alert group to the potential for cold injuries.

25°F and below
Check that group has sufficiently warm winter clothing. Provide warm-up tents or areas and hot beverages.

0°F and below
Inspect the group for cold injuries. Discourage smoking.

-13°F and below
Initiate the buddy system by having members of the group check each other for cold injuries.

-25°F and below
Plan to curtail all but essential travel or outdoor activity especially in wind exposed areas.

READING WIND CHILL CHART

Look at the column headed with your actual "Temperature in Calm Air (°F)" and look at the horizontal line with your "Wind Speed MPH". The intersection of the column and line will indicate your "Windchill Factor".
For example, with a wind speed of 15 mph and the "temperature in calm air" of 10°F, the windchill factor temperature is -7°F.

SUNBURN

You may get sunburned when the temperature of the air is below freezing. On snow, ice, and water, the sun's rays reflect from all angles; in a valley the rays come from every direction. Sunlight reflected upward from the bright surfaces attacks where the skin is very sensitive-around the lips, nostrils, and eyelids. The exposure time which will result in a burn is reduced in the clear air of high altitudes. Sunburn cream and a chapstick should be carried in the pocket, and applied to those parts of the face that are exposed to direct or reflected light. In mild weather protection of the neck and ears can be improvised by draping a handkerchief over the back of the head which is held in place by the cap in the manner of a desert neckcloth. *Soap or shaving lotions with a high alcoholic content should not be used because they remove natural oils that protect the skin from the sun.* If blistered, get aid as soon as possible, as the blistered area, especially lips, may become badly infected.

SUNGLASSES

Sunglasses always should be worn on bright days when the ground is covered with snow. They are designed to protect the eyes against sun glare and blowing snow. If not used, snow blindness may result. They should be used when the sun is shining through fog or clouds, A bright, cloudy day is deceptive and can be as dangerous to the eyes as a day of brilliant sunshine. The sunglasses should be worn to shade the eyes from the rays of the sun that are reflected by the snow. Snow blindness is similar to sunburn, in that a deep burn may be received before discomfort is felt. To prevent *snow blindness,* sunglasses must be used from the start of exposure. Waiting for the appearance of discomfort is too late. When not being used, they should be carried in the protective case to avoid scratching or breaking the lens.

EMERGENCY SUNGLASSES

If sunglasses are lost or broken, a substitute can be improvised by cutting thin, one inch long slits through a scrap of wood or cardboard approximately six inches long and one inch wide. The improvised sunglasses can be held on the face with strips of cloth if a cord is not available.

Inuit emergency slit sun glasses made from whalebone

SNOW BLINDNESS

Snow blindness occurs when the sun is shining brightly on an expanse of snow, and is due to the reflection of ultraviolet rays. It is particularly likely to occur after a fall of new snow, even when the rays of the sun are partially obscured by a light mist or fog. The risk is also increased at high altitudes. In most cases, snow blindness is due to negligence or failure to use his sunglasses. Waiting for discomfort to develop before putting on glasses is folly. A deep burn of the eyes may already have occurred by the time any pain is felt. Putting on the glasses then is essential to prevent further injury but the damage has already been done.

The risk of snow blindness is increased at high mountain altitudes because the clear air allows more of the burning rays of sunlight to penetrate the atmosphere.

Symptoms: *of snow blindness are a sensation of grit in the eyes with pain in and over the eyes made worse by eyeball movement, watering, redness, headache, and increased pain on exposure to light.*
First aid measures consist of blindfolding, which stops the painful eye movement, or covering the eyes with a damp cloth, which accomplishes the same thing. Rest is desirable. If further exposure to light is unavoidable the eyes should be protected with dark bandages or the darkest available glasses. The condition heals in a few days once unprotected exposure to sunlight is stopped. This damage to the eyes might trigger some future problem.

Emergency Slit Sun Glasses
These glasses were developed by the Inuit. They can be made of birch bark, plastic, heavy cloth, bone, etc.

Avoid Snow Blindness

WIND CHILL CHART

Temperature (°F) in Calm Air

Frostbite Times	30 Minutes	10 Minutes	5 Minutes

Wind Speed (MPH)	40	35	30	25	20	15	10	5	0	-5	-10	-15	-20	-25	-30	-35	-40	-45
5	36	31	25	19	13	7	1	-5	-11	-16	-22	-28	-34	-40	-46	-52	-57	-63
10	34	27	21	15	9	3	-4	-10	-16	-22	-28	-35	-41	-47	-53	-59	-66	-72
15	32	25	19	13	6	0	-7	-13	-19	-26	-32	-39	-45	-51	-58	-64	-71	-77
20	30	24	17	11	4	-2	-9	-15	-22	-29	-35	-42	-48	-55	-61	-68	-74	-81
25	29	23	16	9	3	-4	-11	-17	-24	-31	-37	-44	-51	-58	-64	-71	-78	-84
30	28	22	15	8	1	-5	-12	-19	-26	-33	-39	-46	-53	-60	-67	-73	-80	-87
35	28	21	14	7	0	-7	-14	-21	-27	-34	-41	-48	-55	-62	-69	-76	-82	-89
40	27	20	13	6	-1	-8	-15	-22	-29	-36	-43	-50	-57	-64	-71	-78	-84	-91
45	26	19	12	5	-2	-9	-16	-23	-30	-37	-44	-51	-58	-65	-72	-79	-86	-93
50	26	19	12	4	-3	-10	-17	-24	-31	-38	-45	-52	-60	-67	-74	-81	-88	-95
55	25	18	11	4	-3	-11	-18	-25	-32	-39	-46	-54	-61	-68	-75	-82	-89	-97
60	25	17	10	3	-4	-11	-19	-26	-33	-40	-48	-55	-62	-69	-76	-84	-91	-98

CARBON MONOXIDE POISONING

CARBON MONOXIDE POISONING

Whenever a stove, fire, gasoline heater, or internal combustion engine is used indoors there is danger of carbon monoxide (CO) poisoning.
A steady supply of fresh air in living and working quarters is vital.

Deadly Gas: Carbon monoxide is a deadly gas, even in low concentration, and is particularly dangerous because it is odorless.

Symptoms: Generally there are no symptoms. With mild poisoning, however, these signs may be present: headache, dizziness, yawning, weariness, nausea, and ringing in the ears. Later on, the heart begins to flutter or throb. But the gas may hit without any warning whatsoever. A victim may not know anything is wrong until his knees buckle. When this happens, he may not be able to walk or crawl. Unconsciousness follows; then death. You may be fatally poisoned while you sleep.

Getting Help: *The following is an outline of providing help but it is important that you get medical attention.* In a case of carbon monoxide poisoning, the victim must be moved into the fresh air at once and must be kept warm. In the winter, fresh air means merely circulating air that is free from gases. Exposure to the outdoor cold might cause collapse. If the only fresh air is outdoors, the patient should be put into a sleeping bag for warmth. A carbon monoxide victim should never be exercised, because this will further increase his requirements for oxygen. If a gassed person stops breathing or breathes only in gasps, mouth-to-mouth resuscitation should be started immediately. In the latter case, the operator's movements must be carefully synchronized with the victim's gasps. Breathing pure oxygen removes carbon monoxide from the blood faster than does breathing air and greatly hastens recovery. Carbon monoxide is serious and a victim who survives it must be kept absolutely quiet and warm for at least a day. Hot water bottles and hot pads are helpful in maintaining body temperatures.

THINGS FOR YOUR POCKETS

There are several small items that should be carried in the pockets so they will be readily available for use.

- A quality sharp pocketknife is an essential item. It is useful for cutting branches, in shelter construction, in repairing ski bindings, and numerous other tasks.
- Waterproof matches should be carried and kept in the watertight matchbox and used only in an emergency. They should never be used when ordinary matches and lighters will function.
- Sunburn preventive cream will protect the skin from bright, direct sunshine, from sun rays reflected by the snow, and from strong winds.
- A chap stick will prevent lips from chapping or breaking due to cold weather or strong winds. The chap stick should be protected from freezing.
- An emergency thong has numerous uses, such as lashing packs, replacing broken bootlaces, and repairing ski and snowshoe bindings.

SHOVELING SNOW

While shoveling snow can be good exercise, it can also be dangerous for optimistic shovelers who take on more than they can handle.

- Individuals over the age of 40, or those who are relatively inactive, should be especially careful.
- If you have a history of heart trouble, do not shovel without a doctor's permission.
- Do not shovel after eating or while smoking.
- Take it slow! Shoveling (like lifting weights) can raise your heart rate and blood pressure dramatically; so pace yourself. Be sure to stretch out and warm up before taking on the task.
- Shovel only fresh snow. Freshly fallen, powdery snow is easier to shovel than the wet, packed-down variety.
- Pushing snow is easier on your back than lifting the snow out of the way.
- Don't pick up too much at once. Use a small shovel.
- Lift with your legs bent, not your back. Keep your back straight. By bending and "sitting" into the movement, you'll keep your spine upright and less stressed. Your shoulders, torso and thighs can do the work for you.
- Do not work to the point of exhaustion. If you run out of breath, take a break. If you feel tightness in your chest, stop immediately.
- Dress warmly. Remember that extremities, such as the nose, ears, hands and feet, need extra attention during winter's cold. Wear a turtleneck sweater, cap, scarf, face protection, mittens, wool socks and waterproof boots.

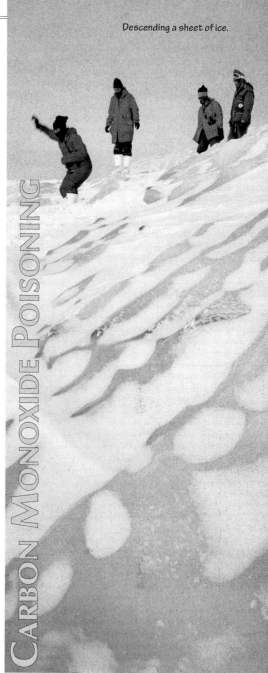

Descending a sheet of ice.

CARBON MONOXIDE POISONING

Inuit woman chewing sealskin waterproof boot to make it more flexible.

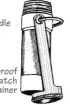

Survival Candle in metal tub.

Survival Candle in metal tub.

Waterproof Match Container

Emergency Candle

Survival Candle

Candle wax in a shoe wax type tin. There are three wicks. You can control the temperature, and the burning time, by the number of wicks that are lit. This is an important survival accessory. It provides light and heat for up to 36 hours. To be kept in a car or camper.

Survival Candle in metal tub.

17 Winter Clothing

Inuit Sealskin Parka
Female

Inuit Sealskin Parka - Female
The bottom of the parka is not straight as the men's parka. There is a front and rear flap as the women spend most of their time sitting and working. The men's parka has a straight bottom as they usually travel and hunt - the straight bottom offers more protection from the wind.

Inuit Kam-lay-kie, a waterproof shell garment. It is made of walrus intestines and worn while kayaking.

Inuit Sealskin Parka
Male

Cold Weather Conditions

The use of cold weather clothing is affected by two types of weather conditions: wet and dry. These conditions are amplified by humidity coupled with temperature and wind velocity; high humidity (wet conditions), low humidity (dry conditions).

Wet Conditions: Cold wet conditions occur when temperatures are near freezing and variations in day and night temperatures cause alternate freezing and thawing. This freezing and thawing is often accompanied by rain and wet snow, causing the ground to become muddy and slushy. During these periods wear clothing which consists of a water-repellent, wind-resistant outer layer and inner layers with sufficient insulation to provide ample protection in moderately cold weather (14°F+).

Dry Conditions: Cold dry conditions occur when average temperatures are lower than 14°F. The ground is usually frozen and snow is usually dry, in the form of fine crystals. Strong winds cause low temperatures to seem colder and increase the need for protection of the entire body (windchill). During these periods, you should have available additional insulating layers of clothing. This is particularly true when entering static situations form a period of strenuous exercise.

Emergency Bag

Wind Break

Emergency Bag

Similar to the emergency blanket but is in the shape of a body bag. It can be used as an emergency sleeping bag or over a regular sleeping bag. If used with a sleeping bag air the sleeping bag the next day as the emergency bag does not let the humidity pass through.

Emergency Blanket

Thermal blanket weighing 2 oz. but retains over 80% of radiated body heat to provide protection in cold or a crisis situation. Silver reflecting sides can be seen at a distance.

All-Weather Blanket

This reflective blanket retains over 80% of radiated body heat, even in subzero temperatures. Waterproof, windproof, light weight, and grommets on corners. In silver or orange.

Poncho
The most use full lightweight survival garment. It can be used as an actual poncho shell windbreak with layers of warming clothing below it. It can be used as a shell garment against the rain or wet snow - thus keeping the body clothing dry and warm. It can also serve as a ground blanket, small lean-to shelter, and the covering heat retaining shell for a sleeping bag.

Emergency Blanket
Compact and lightweight (1.5 ounces) aluminized polyethylene sheet that reflects the body's heat back to the body.

Cold Weather Clothing
Protection of Body Against the Elements

- If the body is to operate efficiently, it must maintain a normal temperature. The body attempts to adjust itself to the variable external conditions it encounters. These attempts are evidenced by the need for more food to produce additional heat during colder weather, by perspiration to increase removal of heat during hot weather, and by the gradual darkening of the skin as protection against extended exposure to the rays of the sun.
- Proper clothing, correctly worn, will assist the body in its adjustment to extreme climatic conditions. The clothing does this by holding in the body heat, thereby insulating the body against the cold outside air. The problem of protection becomes acute when freezing temperatures are involved. To understand this problem requires a knowledge of the methods by which the body resists the effects of climatic changes.

Balancing Heat Production & Heat Loss

The body loses heat at variable rates. This heat may flow from the body at a rate equal to or greater than the rate at which it is produced. When heat loss exceeds heat production, the body uses up the heat stored in its tissues, causing a rapid drop in body temperature. *Excessive heat loss can result in shivering.* Shivering uses body energy to produce heat which at least partially offsets the heat loss and slows the rate at which the body temperature will drop.

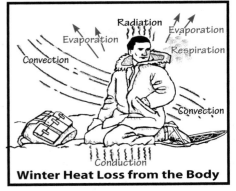

Winter Heat Loss from the Body

Shivering

Shivering is an important warning to start action to rewarm, either by adding more clothing, by exercising, by eating some food, or by entering a warm shelter, or by any combination of these actions. In freezing temperatures it is just as important to remove clothing and to prevent excessive overheating as it is to add clothing to prevent heat loss.

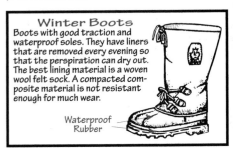

Winter Boots
Boots with good traction and waterproof soles. They have liners that are removed every evening so that the perspiration can dry out. The best lining material is a woven wool felt sock. A compacted composite material is not resistant enough for much wear.

Waterproof
Rubber

COLD WEATHER CLOTHING DESIGN

Certain principles are involved in the design of cold weather clothing: to control the loss of heat, to facilitate proper ventilation, and to protect the body.

INSULATION

Any material that resists the transfer of heat is known as an insulating material. Dry air is an excellent insulator. Woolen cloth contains thousands of tiny pockets within its fibers. These air pockets trap the air warmed by the body and hold it close to the skin. The principle of trapping air within the fibers or layers of clothing provides the most efficient method of insulating the body against heat loss.

LAYERS

- Several layers of medium-weight clothing provide more warmth than one heavy garment, even if the single heavy garment is as thick as the combined layers. This results from the layers of air which are trapped between the layers of clothing. These layers, as well as the minute air pockets within the fibers, retain the body heat.
- The layers of clothing are of different design. Winter underwear is most porous and has many air pockets. These air pockets trap and hold the air warmed by the body. To keep the cold outside air from reaching the still inside air that has been warmed by the body, the outer garments are made of windproof, water-repellent fabric.
- The layer principle allows maximum freedom of action and permits rapid adjustment of clothing through a wide range of temperatures and activities. The addition or removal of layers of clothing allows the body to maintain a proper body heat balance.

VENTILATION

Perspiration fills the airspaces of the clothing with moisture laden air and reduces their insulating qualities. As perspiration evaporates, it cools the body just as water evaporating from a wet canteen cover cools the water in the canteen. *To combat these effects, cold weather clothing is designed so that the neck, waist, hip, sleeve, and ankle fastenings can be opened or closed to provide ventilation.* To control the amount of circulation, the body should be regarded as a house and the openings in the clothing as windows of the house. Cool air enters next to the body through the openings in the clothing just as cool air comes into a house when the windows are open. If the windows are opened at opposite ends of a room, cross-draft ventilation results. In the same way, if clothing is opened at the waist and neck, there is a circulation of fresh air. If this gives too much ventilation, only the neck of the garment should be opened to allow warm air to escape without permitting complete circulation.

Crampons to Walk on Ice

These are attachments, with spikes, that are strapped onto boots and help you walk on ice.

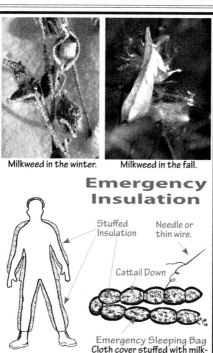

Milkweed in the winter.   Milkweed in the fall.

Emergency Insulation

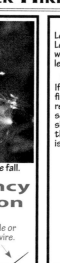

Stuffed Insulation

Needle or thin wire.

Cattail Down

Emergency Sleeping Bag
Cloth cover stuffed with milkweed, ripe cattail, dry moss, etc. The filling is stitched into pockets - this prevents the filling from shifting.

Ripe cattail or milkweed can be stuffed into clothing to act as insulation in cold weather. They can also be used to make comforters, sleeping bags or pillows.

Cattail

Leather Mitt Shell
Leather stays flexible even when it is very cold. Leather takes a long time to dry when it becomes wet. DO NOT dry next to a heat source as the leather will become hard and possibly crack.

Wool Glove Insert
If the ductility and fingers of a glove is required, as when setting a trap or shooting a gun, the leather shell is removed.

US Army Mitt

Army Very Cold Weather Mitt

Nose Wipe

Leather stays flexible in very cold weather.

Sheepskin drippy nose rubbing layer. The drippy nose is caused by condensation of the breath during very cold weather. You would not want to remove your hand from the mitt to wipe your nose every few minutes.

Rabbit Fur Mitts

Leather

Trigger Finger Wool Mitt

Winter Gloves

Have a high cuff to protect against snow. The palm is made of soft leather that will not get stiff when it is -30°F. The army mitt has a nose wipe cushion on top of the hand to remove condensation from the nose.

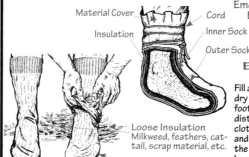

Material Cover

Insulation

Cord

Inner Sock

Outer Sock

Emergency Boot

Felt Insoles

Loose Insulation
Milkweed, feathers, cattail, scrap material, etc.

Sock

Emergency Insulated Sock or Boot

Fill a second sock with the fluff from a ripe cattail, dry grass or milkweed plant and pull it over your foot. Make sure that the insulation material is well distributed around your foot. Take a piece of square cloth or parachute material and lay it on the ground and place your foot flat on the surface and attach the corners of the material above your ankle. You will be able to walk with this sock or use it as a lining for a boot. It can be used as a boot for snowshoeing.

Wool Blanket

Inuit sealskin waterproof winter boot.

Inuit hunter waiting for a seal to come up to its breathing hole.

Seal Hole

Spear

Wind Break

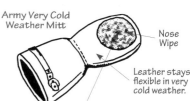

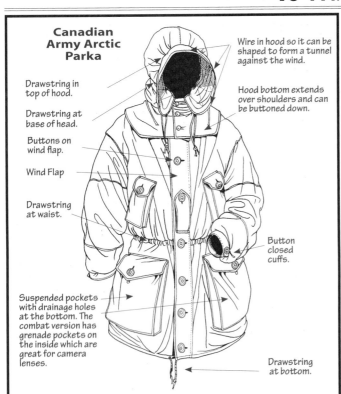

Canadian Army Arctic Parka

Drawstring in top of hood.

Drawstring at base of head.

Buttons on wind flap.

Wind Flap

Drawstring at waist.

Wire in hood so it can be shaped to form a tunnel against the wind.

Hood bottom extends over shoulders and can be buttoned down.

Button closed cuffs.

Suspended pockets with drainage holes at the bottom. The combat version has grenade pockets on the inside which are great for camera lenses.

Drawstring at bottom.

CANADIAN ARMY ARCTIC PARKA

This parka is designed for the Canadian Arctic which extends to the North Pole. It has many unique features that are made for cold weather survival.

Removable Lining: The lining can be removed to dry while you can still wear the shell. The filling is a suspended polyester which is like a web loft. There are drainage holes, for water, at the bottom of the lining to rapidly expel water.

Pockets: All pockets are suspended at the upper edges from the cover flaps so that if they are unbuttoned they will not fall open.

Buttons: Buttons are attached by pieces of ribbon. The buttons ride on these ribbons which do not wear out as fast as thread. Certain versions of the parka are made with survival buttons. These buttons are made of a protein plastic material that can be cooked in water to provide emergency food.

Hood: The hood, which can be unbuttoned and unzipped, is made with a wide bottom overlay that is buttoned onto the parka. This overlay protects from wind blowing into the zipper. The hood has a wire near the brim so that it can be shaped to make a tunnel for the face if there is a strong side wind. The hood has two drawstrings, one over the front of the face and the second over the scalp. This cups the head and does not let the hood fall over the eyes when the front cord is drawn.

Front Closure: The front zipper is made from heavy brass which is lubricated with wax or soap. To keep out the wind there are three overlapping wind flaps. The outside wind flap is buttoned down.

EFFECT OF COLD ON MATERIAL

Low temperatures change the strength, elasticity, and hardness of metals and generally reduce their impact resistance. Leather fabrics and rubber lose their pliability and tensile strength. Plastics, ceramics, and other synthetics are less ductile. Items composed of moving parts and of differing types of materials operate with reduced efficiency.

Rubber: rubber in warm weather, is flexible; during extreme cold it becomes stiff, and bending will cause it to break e.g., when a vehicle is parked for several hours during subzero weather, flattened-out areas develop in tires; these flattened-out areas have little resiliency until after the tires have warmed up.

Water Freezes & Expands: while it is expanding in a restricted space (as in an engine) it has tremendous power, enough to crack the toughest of iron.

Canvas: becomes stiff much the same as does rubber and it becomes difficult to fold or unfold without damaging it.

Glass: being a poor conductor of heat, will crack if it is exposed to any sudden increase in temperature. The windshield on a vehicle may break if intense defroster heat is suddenly applied.

Gasoline: will not freeze but becomes more difficult to vaporize. Since only vapor will burn, combustion of gasoline inside an engine is more difficult and unburned gasoline dilutes the oil in the crankcase contributing to the formation of sludge.

Oils: have a tendency to become thick, and consequently retard the flow through the oil pump to places where it is needed for lubrication. Thickened oils also increase the drag on the entire engine, thus making it more difficult to turn over.

Grease: which is a semisolid to begin with, becomes hard and loses a great amount of its lubrication properties.

Leather: cracks unless properly treated with neat's foot oil.

Paint: tends to crack very easily when exposed to extreme cold for any great length of time.

STATIC ELECTRICITY

Dry cold weather produces great amounts of static electricity in the layers of clothing worn and in liquids being transported. Extreme caution must be exercised when refueling vehicles, stoves, lanterns, etc., because the spontaneous discharge of static electricity may ignite these inflammable fuels. Static electricity should be "drained off" by grounding vehicles or fuel containers prior to starting refueling. You should ground themselves by touching a vehicle or container (away from vapor openings) with the hand.

A

B

C

D

Packed Snow Igloo
For construction information see the Survival Chapter

FACE PROTECTION

Vaseline should be applied on the face in cold weather. This coating provides protection again the biting wind. Wear a hat as most of the body heat is lost through the head. In very cold weather wear face protection.

Nose, Cheek Protectors & Masks

A protective face mask should be warm during severe windchill conditions. The mask must be removed at intervals to check for frostbite. The face and forehead can be covered with a long broad wool scarf. Adjust it, from time to time, by rotating the section opposite the mouth and nose because it becomes covered with frost. The frozen end should be left outside the parka. The scarf, like the mask, must be removed at intervals to check for frostbite.

Headgear: Headgear should be washed to remove perspiration, dirt, and hair oils. When drying, normal care must be exercised to avoid scorching or burning.

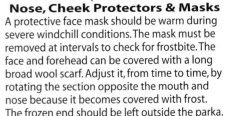

Cagoule or Balaclava

Tuque

Breath condensing as ice on hair, collar, hat, and hood.

FOOTWEAR

The feet are more vulnerable to cold than are other parts of the body. Cold attacks feet most often because they get wet easily (both externally and from perspiration) and because circulation is easily restricted. Foot gear is therefore one of the most important parts of cold weather clothing.

- The rule of wearing clothing loose and in layers also applies to foot gear. The layers are made up by the boot itself and by the socks. Socks are worn in graduated sizes. If blood circulation is restricted, the feet will be cold. Socks, worn too tightly, might easily mean freezing of the feet. For the same reason: Avoid lacing foot gear tightly.
- Since the feet perspire more readily than any other part of the body, the rules about avoiding overheating and keeping dry are difficult to follow. Foot gear is subjected to becoming wet more often than are other items of equipment. A change of dry socks should be carried at all times.

FEET GETTING WET

Whenever the feet get wet, dry as soon as possible and put on a pair of dry socks. The inside of the boots should be wiped as dry as possible.

- Foot gear should be kept clean. Socks should be changed when they become dirty. Socks and feet should be washed frequently. This washing will help keep feet and socks in good condition.
- The feet should be exercised. Stamping the feet, double-timings few steps back and forth, and flexing and wiggling toes inside the boots all require muscular action, produces heat, and will help keep the feet warm. The feet should be massaged when changing the socks.
- If boots are too tight, the circulation of blood is restricted and the feet will get cold.

Sock Washing: Should be washed daily, using lukewarm water to avoid excessive shrinkage. After washing, they should be wrung out and stretched to a natural shape before drying. Holes in socks should be repaired as soon as possible, taking special precautions to avoid bunching or roughness of the mended area. Proper repairs are important to avoid blisters.

Boots: Leather boots should be treated from time to time. The inside of the boots should be washed at least once a month with a mild soap, and rinsed with warm water.

HANDS & MITTS

Tight fitting sleeves should be avoided. They may cut down circulation and cause hands to become cold. When handling cold metals, the hands should be covered to prevent *cold burns* (immediate freezing of the flesh in contact with cold soaked metals). *To keep hands warm when wearing mitts, the fingers should be curled (inside the mitts) against the palm of the hand, thumb underneath the fingers, or flexed inside the mitten whenever possible to increase the blood circulation.* Hands may be exercised by swinging the arms in a vertical circle. Frostbitten hands can be warmed by placing them next to the skin under the armpits. Have an extra pair of mitten inserts on available.

Mittens & Gloves Maintenance: Holes should be mended promptly. Gloves or mitts should not be dried too near an open fire as a wool mitt would shrink and a leather will harden and might crack.

CLOTHING & KEEPING WARM

Keep Clothing Clean: This is always true from a standpoint of sanitation and comfort: in winter, in addition to these considerations, it is necessary for maximum warmth. If clothes are matted with dirt and grease, much of their insulation property is destroyed; the air pockets in the clothes are crushed or filled up and the heat can escape from the body more readily. Underwear requires the closest attention because it will become soiled sooner. If available, light cotton underwear may be worn beneath winter underwear to absorb body oils and lengthen the time interval between necessary washings of these more difficult to clean and dry garments. Winter underwear and cushion sole socks should be washed in lukewarm water. Hot water should not be used because it causes shrinkage of wool and cotton fibers. Synthetic detergents are more soluble than soap in cool water and also prevent hard-water scum. When outer clothing gets dirty it should be washed with soap and water. All the soap or detergent must be rinsed out of the clothes, since any left in the clothing will lessen the water-shedding quality of the clothing. In addition to destroying much of the normal insulation, grease will make the clothing more flammable. If washing is not possible for clothing that would normally be washed with soap and water, dry rubbing and airing will rid them of some dirt and accumulated body oils.

Avoid Overheating: In cold climates, overheating should be avoided whenever possible. Overheating causes perspiration which in turn, causes clothing to become damp. This dampness will lessen the insulating quality of the clothing. In addition, as the perspiration evaporates it will cool the body even more. When indoors, a minimum of clothing should be worn and the shelter should not be overheated. Outdoors, if the temperature rises suddenly or if hard work is being performed, clothing should be adjusted accordingly. This can be done by ventilating (by partially opening parka) or by removing an inner layer of clothing, or by removing heavy mittens or by throwing back parka hood or changing to lighter head cover. The head and hands, being richly supplied with blood, act as efficient heat dissipaters when overheated. In cold temperature it is better to be slightly chilly than to be excessively warm. This promotes maximum effectiveness of the body heat production processes.

Wear Clothing Loose and in Layers: Clothing and foot gear that are too tight restrict blood circulation and invite cold injury. Wearing of more socks than is correct for the type of foot gear being worn might cause the boot to fit too tightly. Similarly, a field jacket which fits snugly over a wool shirt would be too tight when a liner is also worn under the jacket. If the outer garment fits tightly, putting additional layers under it will restrict circulation. Additionally, tight garments lessen the volume of trapped air layers and thereby reduce the insulation and ventilation available.

Keep Clothing Dry

- Under winter conditions, moisture will soak into clothing from two directions-inside and outside. Dry snow and frost that collect on the uniform will be melted by the heat radiated by the body.
- Outer clothing is water-repellent and will shed most of the water collected from melting snow and frost. The surest way to keep dry, however, is to prevent snow from collecting. Before entering heated shelters, snow should be brushed or shaken from uniforms; it should not be rubbed off, because this will work it into the fabric.
- In spite of all precautions, there will be times when getting wet cannot be prevented and the drying of clothing may become a major problem. On the march, damp mittens and socks may be hung on the pack. Occasionally in freezing temperatures, wind and sun will help dry this clothing. Damp socks or mittens may be placed, unfolded near the body, where the body heat will dry them. In bivouac, damp clothing may be hung inside the tent near the top, using drying lines or improvised drying racks. It may even by necessary to dry each item, piece by piece, by holding before an open fire. Clothing and footwear should not be dried near a heat source. Leather articles, especially boots, must be dried slowly. If boots cannot be dried by any other method, it is recommended that they be placed between the sleeping bag and liner. Heat from the body will aid in drying the leather.

Descending a steep slope.

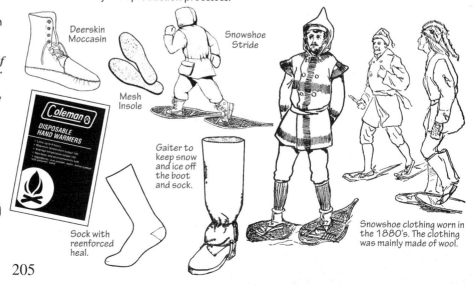

Deerskin Moccasin

Mesh Insole

Coleman
DISPOSABLE HAND WARMERS

Snowshoe Stride

Gaiter to keep snow and ice off the boot and sock.

Sock with reenforced heal.

Snowshoe clothing worn in the 1880's. The clothing was mainly made of wool.

Shaking the frost out of a sleeping bag after a nights sleep.

Removing snow from ground before setting up a sleeping area.

Down Mummy Sleeping Bag

Insulation Mat
Helps to insulate the sleeping bag from the cold ground and reduces the humidity from the ground.

WINTER SLEEPING BAG MAINTENANCE

- A sleeping bag for use in cold climates consists of three parts: a case, of water-repellent material; an inner bag (mountain type), of quilted tubular construction, filled with a mixture of down and feathers; and an outer bag (arctic bag), of the same material as the inner bag. In addition, an insulating air mattress and a waterproof bag into which the sleeping bags are packed.

- When temperatures are normally above 14°F, only one bag is used. When temperatures are below 14°F, both bags are used. The inner bag is placed inside the outer bag and secured at the foot with the loops and tie straps provided and the cover laced over the outer bag.

- When the bag is used, it is first fluffed up so that the down and feather insulation is evenly distributed in the channels, thus preventing matting. Since cold penetrates from below, and the insulation inherent in the bag is compressed by the weight of the body, additional insulation is placed under the bag whenever possible. Added ground insulation can be obtained by placing ponchos, extra clothing, backboards, or boughs between the sleeping bag and the ground.

- The insertion of a waterproof cover, such as a poncho, between the sleeping bag and air mattress will prevent the mattress and bag from freezing together at very cold temperatures. This is caused by condensation on the mattress due to the difference in temperatures between the lower side touching the ground and the upper side touching the relatively warm sleeping bag. Care must be taken to prevent puncturing the mattress or damaging sleeping bags. In general, the more insulation between the sleeping bag and the ground, the warmer the body.

- Avoid wearing too many clothes in the sleeping bag. When too many clothes are worn they tend to bunch up, especially at the shoulders, thereby restricting circulation and inducing cold. Too many clothes also increase the bulk and place tension upon the bag, thus decreasing the size of the insulating airspaces between layers and reducing the efficiency of the insulation. In addition, too many clothes may cause you to perspire and result in excessive moisture accumulating in the bag, a condition which will likewise reduce the bag's insulating qualities.

- A quality sleeping bag is equipped with a full length slide fastener which has a free running, non locking slider. In an emergency, the bag can be opened quickly by grasping both sides of the opening near the top of the slide fastener and pulling the fastener apart. As a safety precaution, bags should be tested at frequent intervals to insure that the slide fastener operates freely and will function properly.

- The sleeping bag should be kept clean and dry. It should be opened wide and ventilated after use to dry out the moisture that accumulates from the body. Whenever possible, it should be sunned or aired in the open.

- The bag should always be carried in the waterproof bag to prevent snow from getting on it. The warmth of the body could melt the snow during the night and cause extreme discomfort.

- Avoid breathing into the bag. If the face becomes too cold it should be covered with an item of clothing.

- Sleeping bags should be dry cleaned. As a safety precaution, bags should be thoroughly aired prior to use to prevent possible asphyxiation from entrapped dry cleaning solvent fumes.

WINTER ANIMAL TRACKS

Snowshoe Hare

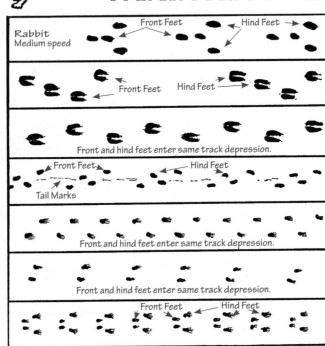

Rabbit Medium speed — Front Feet — Hind Feet

Deer High speed — Front Feet — Hind Feet

Deer Walking — Front and hind feet enter same track depression.

Muskrat or Skunk Slow lope — Front Feet — Hind Feet — Tail Marks

Muskrat or Skunk Walking — Front and hind feet enter same track depression.

Weasel, Mink, or Ermine Jumping — Front and hind feet enter same track depression.

Squirrel Medium speed — Front Feet — Hind Feet

Fox Running fast — Hind Feet — Front Feet

Raccoon Slow jumping gate — Tail Marks — Front Feet — Hind Feet

Raccoon Slow walk — Front and hind feet enter same track depression. — Tail Marks

Raccoon Fast trot — Tail Marks

Elk or Moose Jumping - high speed — Front Feet — Hind Feet

Elk or Moose Walking — Front and hind feet enter same track depression.

Fox Walking — Front and hind feet enter same track depression.

18 ARCTIC & SUBARCTIC SURVIVAL

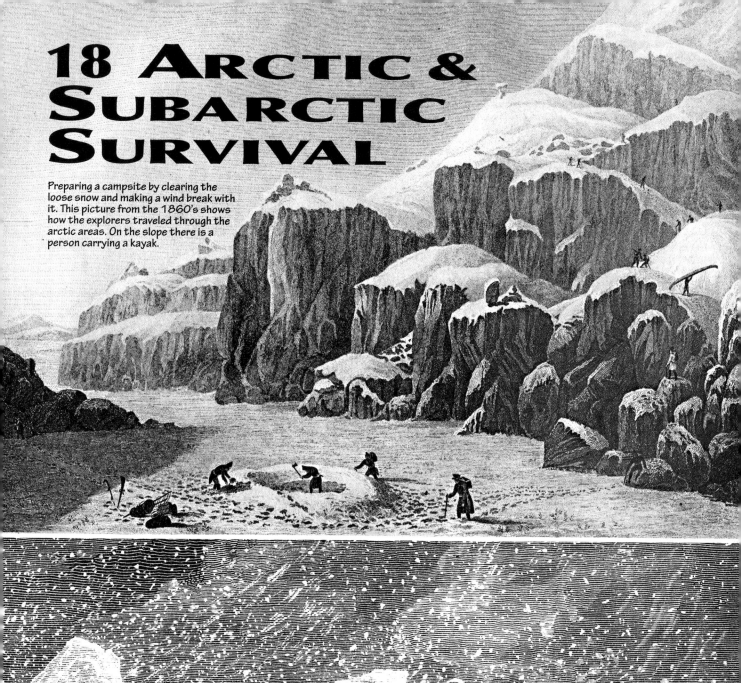

Preparing a campsite by clearing the loose snow and making a wind break with it. This picture from the 1860's shows how the explorers traveled through the arctic areas. On the slope there is a person carrying a kayak.

An arctic gale with a visibility of 10 to 20 feet.

SUMMER TRAVEL IN THE ARCTIC

Pulling a sea kayak over an ice flow in the arctic.

Dragging a kayak through a "puddle" of water on an ice flow.

Watching the icebergs.

Sleepingbag on shore of a frozen lake.

Kayaking on open water.

ARCTIC TUNDRA & SUBARCTIC PLATEAU

The arctic tundra and vast subarctic plateaus are similar. They are characterized by large plains and gently rolling terrain with scant vegetation where rocky ridges, scattered rock outcroppings, riverbanks, and scrubby brush still create obstacles to movement, when encountered. The shallow snow cover normally found in these areas, as a rule, is firmly packed by wind action and will usually support a man on foot. When the snow has not been wind packed and is still soft, mobility will be increased by the use of skis or snowshoes.

HUMANS IN THE ARCTIC

People of the polar regions have adapted themselves to harsh conditions such as 24 hour darkness, severe winter storms and temperatures, and unpredictable food sources. Many indigenous groups have lived in the Arctic for centuries, and still call it home.

ARCTIC ICE & SNOW COVERED AREAS

Travel north of the Tundra area, on ice and snow, is so different from other northern areas that different techniques and mind set are required. The absence of usable resources, except ice and snow, necessitates that every item required be transported into the area. Travelers have to be provided with protection from high winds and extreme cold. As a result, support requirements will be extremely high with construction of storage and maintenance shelters. Specialized vehicles for travel are required. The danger of polar bears has to be factored in.

Polar bear ready to swat a seal. The bear has blocked the escape route of the seal and while it is growling at the seal it swats the seal from behind.

ARCTIC CLIMATE

The arctic climate is extremely variable, and includes both polar maritime (influenced by the ocean) and continental (influenced by large land masses) climate subtypes. The main constant is that the climate in all arctic areas is affected by the sunlight conditions of high latitudes. The low sun angle (elevation of the sun above the horizon) means that even minor topographic features, such as low hills, can cause major differences in climate at the local level by shading.

Summer: Even though the Arctic receives a large amount of solar energy in summer, the high reflectivity of snow and ice surfaces keeps absorption of solar energy low. Therefore, the heat gained during the long summer days is small and highly dependent on surface properties. For instance, wet tundra and bare ground absorb more solar radiation than do ice sheets. Similarly, wet snow absorbs more radiation than dry snow. Solar effect is small or absent in winter. Although frost may occur in any month, long summer days usually provide three months with mean temperatures above 50° F, and at some stations in the continental interiors temperatures can exceed 86° F.

Winter: Maritime climate conditions prevail over the Arctic Ocean and coastal Alaska. In these areas, winters are cold and stormy. Summers are cloudy but mild with mean temperatures about 50° F. Annual precipitation is generally between 25 inches and 50 inches, with a cool season maximum (largely snowfall) and about six months of snow cover. In the interior, continental climates have much more severe winters, although precipitation amounts are less. In these regions, permafrost (permanently frozen ground) is widespread and often of great depth. In summer, only the top 3 - 6 feet of ground thaw. Since the water cannot readily drain away, this "active layer" often remains waterlogged. In winter, arctic weather is dominated by the frequent occurrence of inversions (when warm air lies above a colder air layer near the surface). The inversion layer decouples the surface wind from the stronger upper layer wind. For this reason, surface wind speeds tend to be lower in winter than one might expect. In summer, inversions are less frequent and weaker, and arctic weather patterns are dominated by the movement of low pressure systems (cyclones) across Siberia and into the Arctic Basin.

Fur clothing of the 1900's.

OBTAINING SUPPLIES

Supplies are brought in by boat during the short summer season. The short summer season usually is long enough to melt most of the ice and snow on the land areas and to break up the southernmost portions of the polar ice pack for several weeks. Poor visibility restricts observation, which is essential to picking a way through drift ice and the ice pack, and also hampers cargo discharge when vessels must anchor several miles from shore. The movement of the ice pack, which is governed by winds, tides, and currents, restricts navigation. Aerial observation by helicopter is essential for icebreakers because of the rapidly changing ice conditions. When the huge floes and chunks of ice are frozen together or packed solidly by the wind and currents, a powerful icebreaker is unable to force passage. Navigation is further hampered by the prevailing shallowness of the water off Arctic Ocean shores, and the numerous, migrating sandbars which prevent vessels from standing in close to shore to avoid heavy ice and to discharge cargo. A serious lack of adequate hydrographic data is an additional hazard.

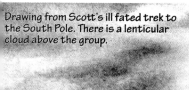

Drawing from Scott's ill fated trek to the South Pole. There is a lenticular cloud above the group.

"Had we lived, I should have a tale to tell of the hardihood, the endurance and the courage of my companions which would have stirred the hearts of every Englishman. These rough notes and our dead bodies must tell the story."

CPT Robert Scott in the Antarctic

Dog sleigh transporting supplies.

Arctic camping - note that boats are mounted on sleds to travel over ice floes. To reduce the friction between the ice and the sled tracks water is applied to the track which then forms ice. This method was learnt from the Inuits. In the distance fish are drying on the wood frames.

The Arctic is defined as...
The area north of the tree line (the northern limit of upright tree growth).
Locations in high latitudes where the average daily summer temperature does not rise above 10° Celsius.

Polar bears raiding a food cache.

Inuit collecting moss that will be used as bedding, insulation, and fire starter.

NORTHERN TRAVEL

The lack of roads, the soft, wet terrain prevalent in the summer, the snow and blizzards in winter, thick forests in mountains, and the innumerable waterways are some of the barriers to movement in most cold areas of the world. The ability to overcome the many obstacles to movement can be a challenge on any planned hiking trip.

SPRING BREAKUP & FALL FREEZEUP

The spring breakup and fall freezeup periods are by far the most difficult seasons in which to travel. The period of breakup may last from 3 - 6 weeks. The snow becomes slush and will support little weight. Winter roads break down, the ice in waterways melts, rivers are swollen and become torrents. Movement at this time of year poses many problems, however, but is still possible in cold areas at all times. Normally, at this time of year, temperatures drop at night, freezing the surface. During the day caution should be exercised in shady areas as they may contain ice and snow even though daytime temperatures are above freezing. The period of freezeup with rain and open or half-frozen waterways also presents barriers to movement. Complete freezeup may take up to 3 months. The early winter period when there is little snow and the ground and waterways are firmly frozen is the ideal time to travel.

WINTER

The low temperatures, snow, blustery winds, and bulky clothing make travel very difficult. By using skis, snowshoes, over snow vehicles, and aircraft, mobility is still possible. In the barren tundra or on icecaps the hard snow found in these areas will readily support an individual on foot as well as over snow vehicles. In the forested areas the snow will normally be deeper and the temperatures lower. The depth of the snow and the trees in these areas will prove to be the greatest obstacles to travel.

CLIMATE NORTHERN LATITUDES

Year: The northern year is divided into winter and summer. These periods are defined by thermometer readings rather than calendar dates. Winter occurs when the average daily temperature falls and remains below freezing, while summer occurs when this average temperature remains above freezing. Periods of transition with wide temperature variation precede each season.

After Summer Solstice: Winter progresses from north to south preceded by autumn freezeup and deep penetration of frost as the hours of sunlight decrease. The days begin to shorten with the summer solstice; however, since the daily change is about 6 minutes, the effect is not often noticed until passage of the autumnal equinox. As a result, the gradual descent of the long winter night appears to be sudden. During early autumn, the weather is relatively dry. As winter approaches, there is an increase in precipitation and muddy conditions. Snow and thin ice appear as early as late September and deep cold as early as October. In November, water courses freeze solidly and temperatures fall as low as -50°F in many areas. Snowfall varies but snow depths of 15" to 60" are common, and deep drifts in valleys and hollows change the appearance of the landscape.

After Winter Solstice: With passage of the winter solstice, the hours of daily sunlight increase. After the spring equinox, fluctuations in temperature cause daytime thaw and nighttime freeze. Continued melting conditions cause the spring breakup which, in addition to the spring rains, flooded lakes and streams, and turn the surrounding plains into a quagmire.

Arctic Fox

210

Northern Latitudes

Terrain: The terrain of northern latitudes consists of exposed bedrock, plains and plateaus covering this rock, and rugged mountains. Sedimentary deposits on slopes greater than 3° are constantly moving.

The Plains: have numerous shallow glacial depressions, sloughs, swamps, ponds, and lakes. These features range from 1' to 50' deep with banks from a few inches to hundreds of yards high.

The Plateaus: have relatively smooth uplands, many rolling hills, and broad sweeping valleys. Scattered rock outcropping are present. The elevations vary from hundreds to thousands of yards over distances of several hundred miles.

Mountain Elevations: range from 5,000' to more than 18,000' within a few miles. Weathering processes as well as mountain forming processes are found.

Streams: often have swift currents and extremely rocky bottoms. The many glacial rivers are silt-laden with numerous sandbars, shifting channels, and undercut banks.

Perennially Frozen Ground: or permafrost, is found in most of the subarctic and arctic. It varies in thickness from a few inches to several hundred yards in loosely defined continuous, discontinuous, and sporadic zones. The presence of permafrost affects drainage due to its impervious nature. When the permafrost thaws, the material changes to muck because of the large water content. Therefore, the presence or absence of permafrost can affect land travel.

Heavy Forests: with dense coniferous tree stands are found where little or no permafrost is present. Certain broad leaf trees will mix with narrow leaf types in zones of sporadic permafrost. As the area of permafrost becomes more continuous, vegetation growth becomes more stunted and is replaced by sedges, grasses, and mosses.

Boat frozen in by the arctic winter. The boat is surrounded by a snow block wind break. The boat is covered with a canvas tarpaulin tent and the animals (large bird and seals) from hunting are hung from a beam.

Inuit umiaq sailing in the arctic. The umiaq is made of walrus skins.

Inuit in a snow storm.

The danger of making camp on an ice floe is it might break up, leading to a potential disaster. In this old etching from the 1850's some members of the party have fallen into the water and might become victims of hypothermia.

Pulling a sled over a crevasse in the ice.

Ice Floe Boat

An ice floe can be used as a boat if a loose floe can be found and if the wind or current is going to your destination.

Loose Ice Floe   Current

Current

Destination

Arctic drifting snow is all invasive. The door to this camp is built perpendicular to the prevailing wind so that the passage does not get completely blocked. There are always sticks to indicate the location of the entrance and a shovel to dig to disengage it.

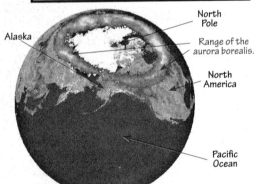

Salt Water

Collecting fresh water from puddles of melted ice on top of sheets of old sea ice. Old sea ice is relatively salt free. New sea ice tastes extremely salty.

Water & Sea Ice

Ice Type	Old Sea Ice	New Sea Ice
Color	bluish or blackish	milky or gray
Brittleness	shatters easily	doesn't break easily
Features	rounded corners	sharp corners
Taste	relatively salt free	tastes extremely salty

North Pole

Alaska

Range of the aurora borealis.

North America

Pacific Ocean

ARCTIC & SUBARCTIC PHENOMENA

The extreme weather conditions in arctic and subarctic regions are dramatic and can severely impact on visual observation and mobility. Specific weather phenomena:

NORTHERN ATMOSPHERE

Precipitation: varies from about 4" - 200" per year, depending upon the area. Snow may fall during any month, but does not always account for the major quantity of precipitation as the ratio in volume of snow to water can vary from 2 to 1 to 10 to 1. Although this area has very little atmospheric moisture, it has relatively high humidity due to the low temperatures.

Ground Level Temperatures: may vary from extremes of -95°F to +100°F. During the period of solar light, the extreme variation for one day might be as high as 100°F.

Visibility: In most areas, visibility is either very good or very poor with average visibility considered uncommon. Fog, blowing snow, and variation in air density can cause impaired visibility. In most areas, fog causes less problem in late winter. Periods, when blowing snow has reduced visibility below 1,000 yds range from 79 hours for an entire winter in one area to 265 consecutive hours in another.

Light & Mirages: is reflected at various angles in air of changing density producing mirages which confuse detail of the landscape. Often, flat terrain features are upended; objects far below the true horizon appear near at hand in sharp relief; and objects above the true horizon completely disappear. In unusual cases, terrain features are reflected in the sky.

Winter Darkness: During winter, long periods of darkness with heavy overcast are a problem. However, at many times, the quality of available light must also be considered. Most activities can be carried on in bright moonlight while light from the stars and the aurora is sufficient for many purposes.

Bright Sunlight: Sunlight, when reflected from snow and ice, becomes brighter. This light may be so intense that shadows are eliminated. This absence of contrast can make it impossible to distinguish outlines of terrain features or large objects, even at close range.

Whiteout: A milky atmospheric phenomena in which the observer appears to be engulfed in a uniformly white glow. Neither shadows, horizon, nor clouds are discernible making the horizon indistinguishable and eliminating the contrast between visible objects both near and far. Sense of depth and orientation is lost. The observer loses all sense of perspective, and aircraft and other operations become extremely hazardous. Only very dark nearby objects can be seen. Whiteouts occur over an unbroken snow cover and beneath a uniformly overcast sky. With the aid of the snowblink effect, the light from the sky is about equal to that of the snow surface. Whiteouts happen most frequently in spring and fall, when the sun is near the horizon. Further conditions necessary to the development of whiteouts are:
• uniform snow cover
• cirrostratus, altostratus or stratus overcast
The sky cover is the most important factor in the development of whiteout conditions and forecasters therefore use the cloud forecast to predict possible whiteout. Blowing snow can cause the same effect. The whiteout phenomena are experienced in the air as well as on the ground.

Greyout: This is similar to a whiteout except the horizon is distinguishable under greyout conditions. It is a phenomenon which occurs over a snow-covered surface during twilight conditions or when the sun is close to the horizon. There is an overall greyness to the surroundings, and when the sky is overcast with dense cloud there is an absence of shadows, resulting in a loss of "depth perception" which increases the hazard in landing an aircraft, driving a vehicle along a road, skiing or even when walking, with the effect greatest when a person is fatigued. Under certain greyout conditions, it has been found almost impossible when driving to distinguish the road from the ditch or from the snow banks along the roadside. The phenomenon is similar to whiteout except that the horizon is distinguishable under greyout conditions and not distinguishable during a whiteout.

Ice Fog: The phenomenon of ice-particle fogs is a very common occurrence around inhabited areas during cold winter weather. They are found most of the time when temperatures drop below 35°F. Their origin, in marked contrast to that of ordinary super-cooled fogs, lies in the copious local production of water vapor by human activities, coupled with an inability of the stagnant air at such low temperature to hold the water vapor. Such sources of water vapor may include the exhaust from vehicles and aircraft, the vents of steam from permanent type heating systems, the air ventilated from humid rooms, and the stovepipe from space heaters.

Ice fog obscures vision but can disclose an inhabited area to a person who is lost.
• Weather and terrain conditions cause disorientation; changing terrain and poor maps make self-location difficult.
• Bright sunlight reflecting off snow-covered landscape causes snow blindness.
• Amber filters on binoculars reduce the incidence of snow blindness.
• There is a lack of depth perception due to weather and terrain conditions.

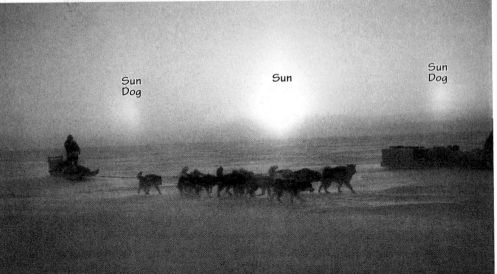

Sun Dog

Sun

Sun Dog

OPTICAL PHENOMENA

In the Arctic, people frequently see unique and beautiful optical phenomena. The atmospheric conditions that can lead to the development of these phenomena are the suspension of ice crystals in the atmosphere, the presence of strong surface inversions that refract light rays, the reflection of light by cloud bottoms, and interactions between the solar wind and gases in the upper atmosphere. Optical phenomena observed in the Arctic include the Aurora Borealis, Halos (sun dogs and fog bows), Coronas and Anticoronas, Water Sky and Ice Blink, Superior Mirages (looming, towering, fata morgana), and Optical Haze.

OPTICAL HAZE

Also called shimmer, optical haze occurs in a layer of air next to the ground where small-scale convective currents develop. In this layer warmer air ascends and colder air descends. The difference in how the warm and cold air refract light causes a blurring of objects seen though the layer. Optical haze occurs quite frequently in the Arctic in the same meteorological conditions as the inferior mirage, and often makes it difficult to identify details in the landscape.

HALOS

A halo occurs around the sun when light is refracted as it passes through ice crystals. When a thin uniform cirrostratus cloud deck containing ice crystals covers the sky, the halo may be in the form of a complete circle as seen below in the middle.

SUN DOGS

There are many types of halos. One of special note is the parhelion or "sun dog." Sun dogs are luminous spots on both sides of the sun that occasionally occur with a halo.

FOG BOW

A fog bow is caused by a process similar to that causing rainbows, but because of the very small size of the water droplets, the fog bow has no colors as there is no light diffraction that is visible.

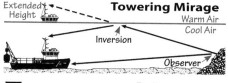

TOWERING MIRAGE

In looming, distant objects appear to float above the horizon, and objects that are below the horizon may come in to view. In towering, rays from the upper portion of an object are bent more than those from the lower portion. This results in the object appearing to be stretched as well as elevated.

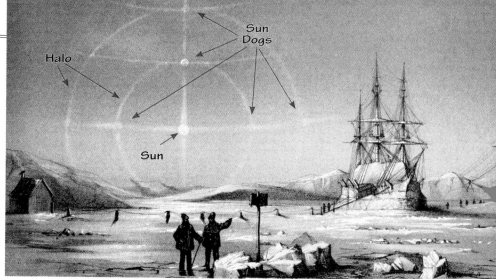

AURORA BOREALIS

Also called the Northern Lights, the spectacular color displays of the aurora borealis appear on clear, cold nights in the arctic sky during periods of solar activity. The aurora borealis is centered around the geomagnetic North Pole, but displays may be observed up to 4000 miles away. The height of the auroras is about 40 - 150 miles above the earth's surface. The amazing color displays and formations are produced by the solar wind, a stream of electrons and protons coming from the sun, as it collides with oxygen and nitrogen atoms in the upper atmosphere. High-altitude oxygen, about 150 miles up, produces rare, all-red auroras, while lower-altitude oxygen, about 40 miles up, is the source of the most common auroral color, a bright yellow-green. Blue light comes from ionized nitrogen molecules. The nitrogen also creates purplish-red and red colors in the aurora. The phenomena are called aurora borealis in the Northern Hemisphere and aurora australis in the Southern Hemisphere.

ARCTIC SUPERIOR MIRAGES

A superior mirage occurs when an image of an *object appears above the actual object*, due to the refraction or bending of light waves from the object down toward the eyes of the observer. Downward refraction occurs because air closer to the ground is colder, and therefore more dense, than air higher up. Superior mirages can take the form of looming, towering, and inversion, depending on the particular density structure of the air column.

FATA MORGANA

The fata morgana is a complex mirage in which distant objects are distorted as well as elongated vertically. For example, a relatively flat shoreline may appear to have tall cliffs, columns, and pedestals. The phenomenon occurs under much the same meteorological conditions as the superior mirage with inversion, and contains features of both towering and inversion.

ARCTIC HAZE

Fine dust or salt particles dispersed through a portion of the atmosphere. The particles are so small that they cannot be felt or individually seen with the naked eye, but they diminish horizontal visibility and give the atmosphere a characteristic opalescent appearance that subdues all colors. It may extend to a height of about 7 miles. It appears blue-grey when viewed away from the Sun, and reddish-brown toward it.

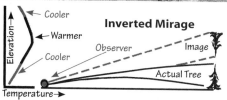

INVERTED IMAGE

In a superior mirage with an inverted image, the gradient in atmospheric density is so sharp that rays from the lower portion of an object are bent considerably more than rays from the upper portion of an object, causing a mirage of the object to appear inverted above the object. The object appears as it normally would at the same time, because some light continues to travel to the eye directly from the object.

The Sun in the center, a halo, and two bright sun dogs.

Sun halos from Scott's ill fated trip to the South Pole.

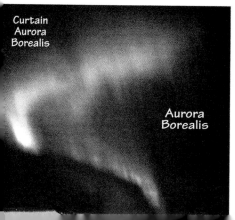

213

Traveling across an ice field between ice bergs.

ARCTIC WINDS

The Arctic winter is characterized by high winds with snowstorms between calm periods. With little to slow them, Arctic winds scour open areas, and deposit loads of snow in sheltered areas. Nevertheless, in the Arctic, winter surface wind speeds are often lower than in summer due to the frequent occurrence of inversions (when warm air tops a surface cold layer). The inversion layer decouples surface wind from stronger upper layer winds. Maximum wind speed occurs during periods of changing temperatures and prolonged velocities above 90 knots have been recorded. Snow and silt begin drifting with winds above 8 knots. With moderate winds, it is often difficult to determine whether snow is falling or being swirled up from the surface.

LARGE SCALE KATABATIC WINDS

Katabatic winds occur when cooled, dense air flows down slopes. Over extensive snow-covered plateaus or highlands large-scale katabatic drainage winds may develop. This is common over the Greenland ice sheet. In some places katabatic winds are channeled by mountain valleys, and the wind accelerates to potentially destructive speeds. Steep slopes can also accelerate the katabatic flow. Along the edge of the massive Greenland ice sheet, katabatic winds frequently exceed 65 miles per hour.

DIAMOND DUST

(ice needles, frost in the air, frost mist)

A type of precipitation composed of slowly falling, very small, unbranched crystals of ice which often seem to float in the air. It may fall from a high cloud or from a cloudless sky. It usually occurs under frosty weather conditions (under very low air temperatures).

PERMAFROST

Layer of soil or rock, at some depth beneath the surface, in which the temperature has been continuously below 0 °C for at least some years. It exists where summer heating fails to reach the base of the layer of frozen ground.

SUBLIMATION

The transition of a substance from the solid phase directly to the vapor phase, or vice versa, without passing through an intermediate liquid phase.

Hunting seal behind a white camouflage sheet that is mounted on a sled. The Inuit hunter gradually advances the sled when the seal looks in the other direction. The hunter is downwind from the seal.

REFLECTIONS IN THE SKY

Clouds can reflect certain surface features.

- On land, off an ice covered sea, clouds can reflect open water as there is less light reflected off dark open water than a white frozen snow area. This reflection is a dark spot on the underside of clouds. The dark spot does not indicate the size of the open water because a small area can affect a large area of cloud. This happens when open water in the Arctic gives off vapor which affects the reflected light around the open area and increases the dark spot area. This is known as a "water sky".
- An ice flow or iceberg can be seen as an "ice blink" which is a patch of brightness in a gray sky. A small area of ice can show a large "ice blink".
- In the arctic or snow mountain country, the whole anatomy of the land surface can be reflected on a high overcast sky. You will be able to see snow fields, open water areas, naked rock areas, new ice (which is blue green and will show as gray patches), patches of vegetation or the plants called "pink snow" will reflect pinkish. These contrasting areas will reflect on the lower sides of the clouds.
- In vegetation-covered areas, ice patches and small snow fields will reflect steel-blue on the under surface of the clouds.

SNOW BLINK (SNOW SKY)

A bright white glare on the underside of clouds, produced by the reflection of light from snow-covered surface. Snow blink is lighter than ice blink, and much lighter than land sky or water sky.

WATER SKY

The dark appearance of the underside of a cloud layer when it is over a surface of open water. It is darker than land sky, and much darker than ice blink or snow blink.

ICE BLINK

White glare on the underside of low clouds indicating presence of ice which may be beyond the range of vision.

ARCTIC NAVIGATION AIDS

When other means of reconnaissance are not available, water sky and ice blink can assist travelers in navigating the ice of the polar seas, since they give a rough idea of ice conditions at a distance.

LAND SKY

The relatively dark appearance of the underside of a cloud layer when it is over land that is not snow covered. This term is used largely in polar regions with reference to the sky map; land sky is brighter than water sky, but is much darker than ice blink or snow blink.

A polar bear entering a camp at night to visit the food cache in the tent on the left. The barking dogs raised the alarm and the travelers still in their pyjamas are protecting the cache.

ARCTIC CLOUDS

Cloud cover is extensive and wide, low clouds cause bleak and monotonous conditions. In general, much of the arctic sky is covered by low stratus and stratocumulus clouds. Total cloud cover is least extensive in December and January. Starting in May, cloudiness increases. Warm air over the water adjacent to ice, frequent temperature inversions, and fog, cause low level stratus clouds to form and persist through the entire warm period. In very high latitudes, overcast often persists for weeks and clear days are rare.

POLAR DAY

In polar regions, this is the portion of the year when the Sun is continuously in the sky. Its length changes from twenty hours at the Arctic/Antarctic Circle (latitude 66°33'N or S) to 186 days at the North/South Pole.

POLAR NIGHT

In polar regions, this is the portion of the year when the Sun does not rise above the horizon. Its length changes from twenty hours at the Arctic/Antarctic Circle (latitude 66°33'N or S) to 179 days at the North/South Pole.

VISIBILITY

The greatest distance that prominent objects can be seen and identified by unaided, normal eyes.

SOUND TRANSMISSION

People frequently report supernormal audibility in Arctic regions. As with optical phenomena, this phenomenon occurs when the vertical density structure of the air causes refraction, but instead of light being refracted, sound waves are refracted. The air near the surface tends to be colder and more dense than air higher up, causing sound waves to tend to bend down toward the surface rather than up away from the earth as they do in more temperate latitudes where air temperature on average decreases with height. The range at which sound can be heard depends on the temperature (and hence density) structure of the air, the speed and direction of the wind, and the rate at which sound energy is absorbed by the earth's surface. For instance, soft snow absorbs sound energy very efficiently, effectively muting the transmission of sound. In contrast, a hard-crusted snow surface absorbs little energy and a smooth ice surface is an almost ideal reflector of sound. Normal conversation has been carried on at a distance of 1.5 miles and shouted words have been heard at 2.5 miles. However, under other climatic conditions, the sound of an aircraft engine at full throttle has been inaudible at 0.5 mile.

Polar bear entering tent.

POLAR BEARS

Polar bears are silent plodders, fierce fighters, and very dangerous hunters. They can easily invade a campsite, and have no fear of humans. Their white coats act as camouflage. It uses stealth of moving between ice blocks while approaching its prey. Moves into the wind so that its prey does not smell it. It will even slide along the ice while pushing itself with its hind legs, like swimming. It is important that you see the bear before it sees you because it will go into stealth mode and be on top of you before you have time to defend yourself. A single unarmed human has a marginal chance of survival. Inuit usually have dogs near their dwellings to sound an alarm.

Polar bear caught sneaking up on an explorer's campsite. It uses stealth of moving between ice blocks or rock outcrops while approaching its prey. Moves into the wind so that its prey does not smell it. It is important that you see the bear before it sees you because it will go into stealth mode and be on top of you before you have time to defend yourself. A single unarmed human has a marginal chance of survival.

19 Avalanche

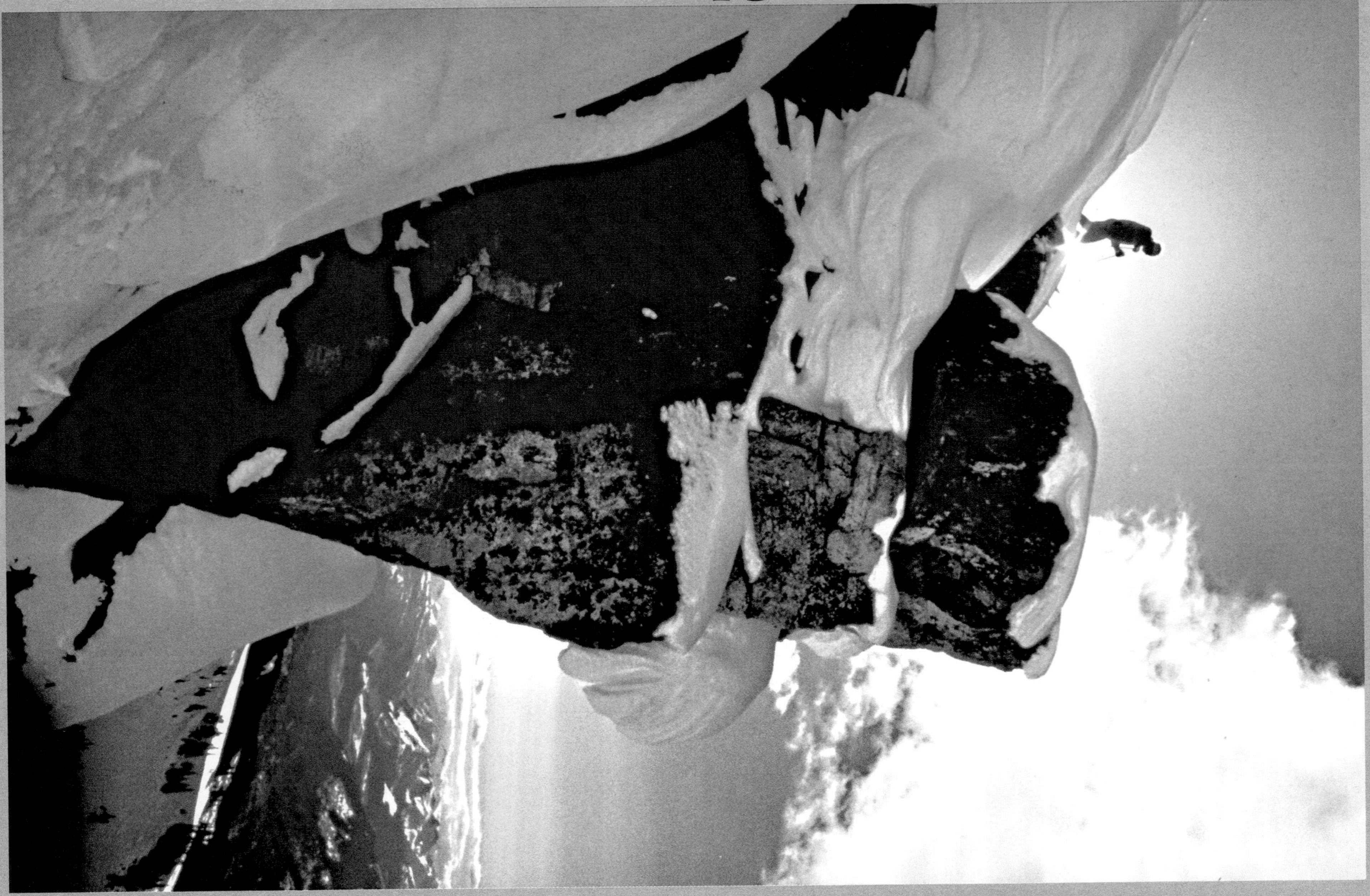

FREEZING NUCLEUS

Even with air temperature well below 0°C, a droplet will not automatically freeze unless it contains another type of impurity called a freezing nucleus. These are much rarer than condensation nuclei; a cubic centimeter of the atmosphere may contain only 10 freezing nuclei that are active at −10°C and above. However, the colder the air, the greater the probability of finding active freezing nuclei and hence frozen droplets. At −10°C, only about one in a million droplets freeze; at −30°C, one in a thousand; and at −40°C, all droplets freeze spontaneously. A rising parcel brought to saturation at air temperatures between 0° and −40°C, therefore, consists of a mixture of ice crystals and supercooled water droplets.

Air Masses & Avalanches

Most destructive avalanche cycles are caused by sustained heavy snowfall; other meteorological factors being secondary. Heavy and sustained snowfall in a mountain range occurs when the large-scale flow of the atmosphere assumes certain patterns with respect to a mountain range.

North America · Atlantic · Pacific · South America

The movement of air masses over the globe.

Plate Crystal
A precipitated snow crystal shaped like a hexagonal plate with major growth along the a-axis.

PACIFIC CYCLONE BELT

The primary moisture supply for the western United States is the Pacific Ocean. The greatest snowfall is in the Cascade Range of Washington and Oregon, where moisture-laden air carried from the Gulf of Alaska by the Pacific cyclone belt is lifted by a north-south chain of mountains. Substantial precipitation also falls in the Sierras, but there the moisture supply depends on storms that stray south of the main cyclone belt.

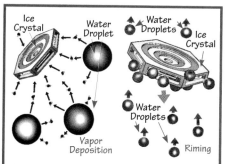

Two modes of growth of ice crystals at the expense of water droplets. In the vapor deposition mode, there is a net transfer of water molecules from the droplet to the air and then from the air to the crystal. In riming, water droplets collide with and freeze to the crystal.

Ice Crystal · Water Droplet · Water Droplets · Ice Crystal · Water Droplets · Vapor Deposition · Riming

ICE CRYSTAL FORMATION

Consider an ice particle suspended in the atmosphere. Again, the transfer of molecules between the ice surface and the air is controlled by temperature; the warmer the temperature, the higher the saturation vapor pressure over the ice surface. A fundamental law of snow physics is that for a given temperature below freezing less vapor can be retained over an ice surface than over water. In other words, the saturation vapor pressure is less with respect to ice than with respect to liquid water.

A: Water vapor deposits directly onto the crystal. As already noted, the vapor pressure over an ice crystal is less than over a water droplet; so, there is a net transfer of water molecules from droplets to the air and to the ice crystals. By this vapor process, ice crystals grow into a variety of hexagonal forms.

B: Ice crystals collide with the supercooled droplets, and the droplets freeze onto the crystals. The crystals become coated with a layer of frozen droplets, called rime. Vapor deposition and riming may occur simultaneously, although one process usually dominates in each atmospheric layer. Usually riming tends to obscure the hexagonal form of the parent crystal.

NEEDLE CRYSTAL

Usually precipitated snow crystal in the shape of a needle with a major growth along the c-axis. Some forms of surface hoar also have a needle shape.

SNOW CRYSTALS
Water Droplet Formation

A: Imagine a drop of water suspended in the atmosphere. Water molecules are exchanged constantly at the surface of the drop. The air is said to be saturated with respect to the drop's surface when the number of molecules leaving the drop, is equal to the number falling onto the drop.

B: Now, suppose the air temperature is lowered. The result is an increase in the number of molecules condensing onto the drop because the water vapor capacity of air decreases with a decreasing temperature. The transfer of molecules continues until a new balance is reached; that is, until saturation is reached for the new air temperature.

C: The amount of water vapor that the air can support over the drop is called the saturation vapor pressure with respect to the surface of the drop.

D: Next, consider a rising, moist air parcel that is cooled to saturation with respect to water. In this state, water molecules tend to condense onto water droplets, if droplets exist. Initial droplet condensation occurs on microscopic dust, salt, or soil particles that are lifted from the earth by wind. These are called condensation nuclei.

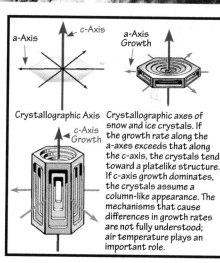

c-Axis · a-Axis · a-Axis Growth · Crystallographic Axis · c-Axis Growth

Crystallographic axes of snow and ice crystals. If the growth rate along the a-axes exceeds that along the c-axis, the crystals tend toward a platelike structure. If c-axis growth dominates, the crystals assume a column-like appearance. The mechanisms that cause differences in growth rates are not fully understood; air temperature plays an important role.

Water Droplets

When the number of water molecules condensing onto a droplet equals the number leaving the droplet, the air is said to be saturated with respect to the droplet. If the air and water-droplet temperatures are lowered, there will be a net flow of water molecules toward the droplet until a new balance is reached.

SNOW & ICE CRYSTAL FORMATION

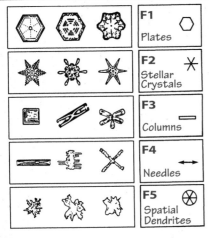

			F1 Plates	⬡
F2 Stellar Crystals	✳
F3 Columns	▬
F4 Needles	↔
F5 Spatial Dendrites	✳
F6 Capped Columns	⫤
F7 Irregular Particles	
F8 Graupel	⟁
F9 Sleet	△
F0 Hail	▲

Relative growth along the a- and c-axis is controlled mostly by air temperature and marginally by the abundance of water vapor in excess of saturation. The latter condition is called supersaturation; it is thought to control the complexity of the crystal. High supersaturation favors the development of intricate arms and branches, or dendritic growth, as in forms F2 and F5. The most peculiar feature of snow crystal formation is the extreme dependence of crystal form on small changes in temperature within a narrow range. As air temperature changes from 0°C to -25°C, the patterns change from a-axis growth to c-axis growth and back to a-axis growth. In the field, large crystals such as graupel and stellars are easily identified by the naked eye. Identification of medium and smaller specimens and their modifications requires 10-25X magnification. In making observations, one should be aware of classifying newly fallen snow solely on the basis of one or two very prominent symmetrical specimens. The life history of a snow crystal is complicated by a journey through different temperature, supersaturation, and wind layers, and the final product is rarely in the form of the textbook illustrations.

Snow Crystal Structure

The international classification of the basic forms of solid precipitation. The crystal structure of snow is described by four intrinsic axes, three a-axes and a c-axis. The a-axis lie in the base plane of the crystal; the c-axis is perpendicular to the base plane.

Depending on meteorological conditions, crystals grow either in the base plane or perpendicular to the base plane.
• Growth in the basal plane results in flat, plate crystals like forms F1 and F2.
• Growth along the c-axis results in column structures like forms F3, F4, and F6.

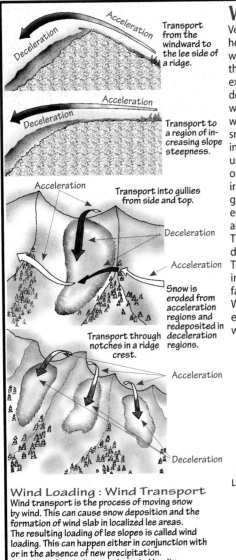

Transport from the windward to the lee side of a ridge.

Transport to a region of increasing slope steepness.

Transport into gullies from side and top.

Snow is eroded from acceleration regions and redeposited in deceleration regions.

Transport through notches in a ridge crest.

Wind Loading : Wind Transport
Wind transport is the process of moving snow by wind. This can cause snow deposition and the formation of wind slab in localized lee areas.
The resulting loading of lee slopes is called wind loading. This can happen either in conjunction with or in the absence of new precipitation.
A cornice often indicates that wind loading occurs on the slopes below it.

Wind Redistribution of Snow

Very light wind deflects snow crystals in the horizontal direction, plastering snow against the windward sides of obstacles, especially when the snow is wet. However, when windspeed exceeds a few meters per second, as it usually does during mountain storms, snow is picked up where windspeed is increasing and deposited where windspeed is decreasing. Transferred snow tends to accumulate in localized zones instead of spreading out evenly. These zones are usually terrain indentations, bounded by rock outcroppings, gully walls, tree groups, or other irregularities. The deepest accumulations are in gullies and bowls, where the snow may be several meters deep, but large accumulations can also form on flat or even convex slopes.
The amount of snow eroded by high winds depends on the "looseness" of the surface. The largest amounts are transferred during or immediately after storm periods, since newly fallen snow is especially susceptible to erosion. Wet snow is not as easily sheared loose. However, some snow can always be moved during winter if the wind is strong.

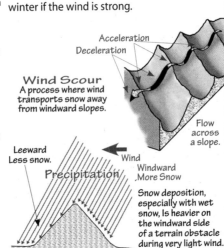

Wind Scour
A process where wind transports snow away from windward slopes.

Leeward Less snow.

Precipitation

Wind

Windward More Snow

Snow deposition, especially with wet snow, is heavier on the windward side of a terrain obstacle during very light wind.

Acceleration
Deceleration

Flow across a slope.

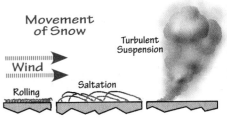

Movement of Snow

Wind

Rolling

Saltation

Turbulent Suspension

Movement of Snow

Rolling: is limited to a thin layer, no higher than 1/8 inch (5 mm) thick, on the surface of the pack. This is not thought to be important in loading avalanche slopes.

Saltation: involves bouncing particles. Each particle is kicked up into the airstream by the impact of another particle. Saltation may lift particles as high as 3 feet (1 m), but it is most effective a first few centimeters above the surface.

Turbulent Suspension: refers to particles suspended in the wind by aerodynamic forces. Heavy particles are suspended near the surface, light particles as high as 300 feet (100 m). The majority of snow is transported within 3 feet (1 m) of the ground.

Snow Eddies - Snow Devils

On steeper lee slopes, typical of many avalanche paths, the wind flow deceleration is sometimes strong enough to reverse airflow and so reverse shear. The reverse flows join the main stream to form circular swirls called vortexes or eddies. Each terrain feature induces a unique vortex pattern strongly dependent on the speed and direction of the main flow. Vortexes are generated in all sizes, from large "rolls," with dimensions on the order of the ridge height, to small eddies. Vortexes continuously build up and decay with new ones taking the place of dissipated ones. The passage of a vortex is observed as a gust or a sudden change in wind direction and by "snow devils."

SNOW ACCUMULATION

Accumulation

Accumulation

This accumulation of snow on tree branches might cause avalanches when some of the snow might fall and trigger a snow avalanche.

Blowing Wind

Snow Accumulation

Cornice

TRANSPORTED SNOW MORE DENSE

Due to pulverization, the average size of the blowing snow particles may be only 1/10 the size of those that fall undisturbed. Because of the small particle size, wind-deposited snow is two to four times denser than snow that falls in a sheltered area. Also, due to the small particle size and many inter-particle contacts, wind transported snow quickly takes on a firm, slab-like structure. In the right location these deposits can form cornices.

BAROMETRIC PRESSURE

Barometric pressure decreases with increase in elevation. In metric units, the barometric pressure at sea level is about 1000 millibars (mb). Pressure decreases with elevation at the rate of about 0.1 mb per meter or, in metric shorthand, 0.1 mb/m. Barometric pressure can be easily and accurately measured. Many instruments are available. With rare exceptions a barometer falling steadily below midrange is an omen of bad weather at high altitudes. The barometer rising steadily above midrange usually heralds a clearing trend.

WIND TRANSPORTED SNOW

CORNICE

Large amounts of snow accumulate in the form of cornices at sharp terrain bends. The most common cornice locations are on the lee side of ridge crests, sides of gullies, and other local slope angles which lie at or near right angles to the wind. The basic structure of a cornice consists of a root, roof, face, and scarp. Cornices grow as successive layers that are added during each period of snow transport. Each new layer adds to the roof that tends to extend out over the cornice face, supported as a cantilever sheet.

CORNICE WEAKNESS

After attachment to the roof, the layers are slowly deformed by gravity and bend towards the cornice face as a curved tongue that often encloses airspaces. The cavities caused by the deformed layers are major sources of structural weakness. The far end of the top layer is poorly attached to the old cornice surface. Throughout its life, the entire cornice steadily deforms outward over the slope, usually reaching a position of precarious balance. Overhanging cornices can be extremely massive. Cornices often extend as much as 45 feet (15 m) upward and outward from the ridge crest, with size and shape a function of ridge shape and lee-slope steepness. Falling blocks of snow are generally large enough to be dangerous. They may also release avalanches on the slopes below.

Close-up of a Cornice
Showing the individual deposit layers from different storms.

Root

Roof

Face

Scarp

The falling cornice can trigger an avalanche when it falls on this snow accumulation.

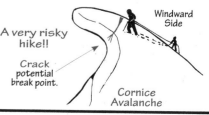

Wind

Cornice

Crack!!

A very risky hike!!

Windward Side

Crack potential break point.

Cornice Avalanche

SNOW SURFACE ENERGY BALANCE

Using the air temperature and some qualitative information about radiation, it is possible to guess the trends in the energy balance at the snow surface. For example, one may assume the following:

A: If the air temperature is rising, the snow temperature near the surface is also rising, at least up to 0° C. If the snow is wet and the air temperature rises above 0° C, then the snow will get wetter. This correspondence between snow and air temperature change is especially true when there is wind.

B: Similarly, falling air temperatures imply falling snow surface temperatures.

C: The important exception to (A) and (B) occurs in the evening, under clear skies, when terrestrial radiation loss from the surface is so strong that snow temperatures fall regardless of air temperature trends. The terrestrial loss is even strong enough to compete with warm winds.

D: During the daylight hours of winter, there may be some exceptions to (A) and (B), especially when winds are light. The air temperature may be observed to rise, but the snow could lose terrestrial radiation through clear skies, in which case, the snow temperature would be maintained at fairly constant levels. This exception is more likely on north-facing slopes.

SNOW DENSITY

High density snow correlates to warm air or high winds, and low density snow correlates to cold air or low winds.

For avalanche stability evaluation, manual measurements should include...
- Total depth of the snowpack
- 24-hour new snow and water equivalent
- Total snow and water equivalent of storm
- Snow and water equivalent for short intervals during storm.

PRECIPITATION MEASUREMENT

This is given in centimeters (cm) of snowfall or in millimeters (mm) of water equivalent. Typical measurements of precipitation are:

	Typical Value
Snowfall	10 cm
Water equivalent	10 mm
Snowfall rate	l cm/h
Water rate	l mm/h

SURFACE HOAR GROWTH

The growth of surface hoar offers another interesting example of surface energy exchanges. During the day, the relatively warm air layer above the snow may contain an appreciable amount of water vapor. Although the air is unsaturated at the daytime temperature, it may become saturated with respect to the snow surface at the colder evening temperature. Thus, at night the vapor condenses on the surface of the pack in the form of surface hoar, the solid equivalent of dew. Surface hoar layers are a few millimeters to several centimeters thick. They are extremely weak and cohesionless. Once buried in the snowpack, they represent a serious structural weakness.

A hoar crystal magnified. Black line is 1 mm.

STORM ANALYSIS

Indications of which slopes are being loaded.
- Windspeed and direction determine which slopes are being loaded.
- In the absence of ridge crest winds, or for very light winds, windward and lee slopes have an equal probability of being loaded.
- For moderate ridge crest winds, the loading is almost all on lee slopes or the lee sides of gullies.
- For very strong winds loading is on the lee side but snow tends to accumulate in relatively isolated, deep pockets rather than being spread over the entire lee slope. In general, the higher the wind, the more difficult it is to locate these pockets.
- Glaze, an ice layer resulting from freezing of supercooled water, tends to be deposited on windward exposures.
- Rain affects all slopes.

Indications of loading.
- The amount of loading is inferred from ridge crest winds and precipitation observed at a study plot.
- Heavy loading generally correlates with high precipitation intensity, as observed at a study plot.
- Regardless of the study-plot precipitation values, heavy loading correlates with sustained winds if the snow surface is dry and loose.

Indications of the rate of loading.
The rate of loading is inferred from the precipitation intensity and ridge crest wind information.

Standard Trend: initial storm temperatures are relatively high, and the temperature falls as the storm progresses.

Inverted Trend: the initial temperatures are relatively cold, and temperatures rise as the storm progresses.

For the mountain ranges of the western United States, the standard trend usually begins with southwesterly airflows that carry in warm, moist air masses. Eventually, the winds shift to the west and finally to the northwest. In the inverted trend, the initial surge of moisture is carried in on a northwesterly airflow. This is followed by a wind shift to the southwest and consequently warmer and usually more intense precipitation.

SOLAR & TERRESTRIAL RADIATION

Mid day in winter: (Dec.-Mar.) Small gain of radiant energy on south-facing slopes due to the excess of incoming solar radiation over outgoing terrestrial radiation. On steep, north-facing slopes, there is a continued loss of terrestrial radiation only partly offset by small amounts of incoming solar radiation.

Mid day in spring: Large gain of radiation on south-facing slopes and a small gain on north-facing slopes.

Evenings: All slopes radiate terrestrial energy into space. The amount that escapes mostly depends on humidity and cloud cover.

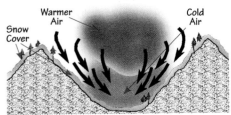

Temperature inversion in a mountain canyon. Inversions are the result of nocturnal cooling of the snow surface by radiation loss.

TEMPERATURE INVERSION

An example of the combined effects of exchange of energy at a snow surface. Consider a canyon bounded by two ridges. The terrain is snow-covered. On clear evenings, when the temperature of the snow surface drops due to terrestrial radiation loss, cold layers of air form over the snow surface. These cold layers, being denser and heavier than the warm air, drain down to the canyon floor. The warmer air that still retains some of its daytime heat energy is suspended in the canyon. On the upper slopes, the warm air mixes in with the cold surface layers, tending to produce warmer air and snow surface temperatures. This stratification of warm air over cold air is referred to as an inversion. During early morning hours, when the inversion is fully developed, air temperatures at the canyon floor may be 15° C colder than at mid slope.

FREE WATER CONTENT IN SNOW

Term	Remarks
Dry	Usually below 0° C, It can occur at any temperature up to and including 0° C. When its texture is broken down by crushing and the loose grains are lightly pressed together as in making a snowball, grains have little tendency to cling to each other.
Moist	T= 0° C. The water is not visible even with the aid of a magnifying glass. When lightly crushed, the snow has a distinct tendency to stick together.
Wet	T= 0° C. Water can be recognized by its meniscus between adjacent snow grains, but water cannot be pressed out by moderately squeezing the snow in the hands.
Very Wet	T= 0° C. The water can be pressed out by moderately squeezing the snow in the hands, but there still is an appreciable amount of air confined in the snow.
Slush	T= 0° C. Snow flooded with water: contains a relatively small amount of air.

SURFACE HOAR: HOARFROST

Ice crystals formed when water vapor from the atmosphere condenses directly into the solid phase onto a very cold surface. The process is the equivalent of dew. These crystals generally form during cold and clear conditions, particularly at night. Surface Hoar crystals grow in flat plates, and once they are buried they have very little shear strength. They also collapse into a very thin layer which can be difficult to identify and/or assess their strength.

Snow Crystal
A snow crystal can freeze and form an ice crystal.

TYPES OF SNOW

New Fallen Snow: is very loose and light and the snow flakes still have their multiple branches. This snow is an excellent insulation. If new snow is dry, it is feathery; if damp, it quickly consolidates into a stage of settled snow. In areas of extreme cold and at high altitudes, new snow is in two forms:
- *Sand Snow* falls at extremely low temperatures. It has a sandy sharp granular texture like sandpaper. Skiing, sledding, and walking are difficult.
- *Wild Snow* is very dry new snow which falls during calm periods and at low temperatures. Extremely light and feathery and is easily blown by the wind. Wild snow can create dangerous whiteouts.

Powder Snow: is a loose snow but the flakes have lost their branches. Powder snow changes to some form of settling or settled snow.

Wind-Packed Snow: has been windblown, usually from one direction, and is compacted by the mechanical force of the wind. The blowing of the wind exerts pressure on the snow and causes a form of cold-heat hardening. In some areas of the snow surface it will be strong enough to carry your weight and you would have no problem staying on the surface with snowshoes. This is good snow to cut blocks for igloos or other snow structures.

Sun Crust: is snow that has had the upper layer melted by heat and subsequently refrozen. A layer of snow that is sun crusted and weathered throughout its thickness becomes corn snow. Sun crust commonly is a layer over powder snow. This snow type is not very stable on a slope and can be dangerous.

Corn Snow: occurs after a period of thaw and a refreezing of the snow. The snow structure is grainy snow ice crystals. This usually occurs in the spring. This snow can be strong enough to carry weight but might indicate the presence of rotten snow which is very dangerous. Advanced corn snow or neve consists of closely associated grains of ice, separated by air spaces.

Rotten Snow: is caused by repeated melting and freezing and is found at lower levels of a snow field or on south sides of hills. The melting and freezing of the upper layer will cause water to seep to the lower layers. This water does not freeze during the cold because it is insulated from the weather by the covering snow layer. This rotten snow is strong enough to support the layers of snow above it. It can collapse if a heavy weight is placed on it. This snow type is dangerous because you might fall through it while walking on the surface. If it is 10" (25 cm) thick it would not be too dangerous but at 5 feet (2 m) thick and over water it would be serious. *See article on Candle Ice - page 189.*

Slush Snow: has absorbed water from melting snow or rain. To recognize areas of slush, especially if on a river or lake, you will see a depression in the snow with some darker or bluish snow areas. These areas show holes in the ice or an accumulation of water on the surface of the ice.

Ice: can be frozen water or cold heat-packed snow as in glaciers and icebergs that have broken off glaciers. If traveling on a snowmobile, avoid river ice as the water currents can be eroding the ice from below.

Glacier Ice: is composed of crystals of advanced corn snow cemented by a film of ice. There is no air space between the grains and any air spaces present are within the grains themselves.

SNOW PACK STRUCTURE

The top of a snow pack is called the snow surface; the bottom boundary, the ground surface. The level of the snow surface fluctuates up and down in response to snowfall, snow settlement, and the loss of mass due to melting, evaporation, erosion, and sublimation. At the ground surface, heat generally flows in one direction into the snow pack from the ground. Ground heat is energy stored in the surface soil during the summer. For this reason every snow pack contains some temperature variation. The variation in temperature is usually colder at the surface than at the ground surface.

SNOW PACK LAYERS

A snow pack consists of many separate layers, some relatively thick, others microscopically thin. The difference between layers can range from well defined to practically indistinguishable. Thick layers are deposited by steady and consistent snowfalls, by wind drift, or by prolonged periods of similar weather that obliterate the original differences in layers near the surface. Typically, thin layers consist of snow crystals deposited during special storm conditions, such as a thin graupel layer laid down during the passage of a front. Distinct thin layers also form at the snow surface between storms; for example, ice crusts formed by melting and refreezing, surface hoar, and wind crusts. Layers consist of a complex, randomly arranged skeleton of ice, broken snow crystals and much vacant space (pore space). Pores contain a mixture of air and water vapor. Liquid water may also be present if the temperature is warm.

SNOW METAMORPHISM

The instability of snow is revealed by the drastic changes or metamorphism (the slow change from snow to ice crystal - can also be called crystal growth) of crystal form that begin as soon as the snow is deposited. In snow hydrology, metamorphism refers to changes in snow texture caused by pressure and temperature conditions. The temperature of the layer determines the rate of metamorphism. After a few days it is normally impossible to identify the original form of the deposition.

DEPTH HOAR

Normally requires at least 2 weeks to form from newly fallen crystals or ET grains, but there are reports of depth hoar layers that formed within a week.

ET: *Crystal growth or metamorphism which occurs at a slow (near-equilibrium) rate in the absence of a large temperature gradient or other strong non-equilibrium factors. Grains become rounded and bonding between grains increases.*

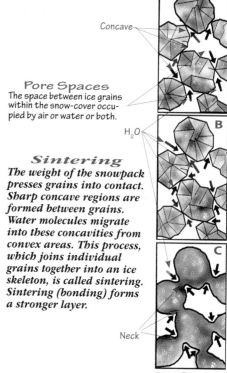

Concave

Pore Spaces
The space between ice grains within the snow-cover occupied by air or water or both.

H_2O

Sintering
The weight of the snowpack presses grains into contact. Sharp concave regions are formed between grains. Water molecules migrate into these concavities from convex areas. This process, which joins individual grains together into an ice skeleton, is called sintering. Sintering (bonding) forms a stronger layer.

Neck

Photograph of sintered snow.

FIRN SPIEGEL: FIRN MIRROR

An ice crust formed on the snow surface on sunny, cold days. The sun's heat penetrates the surface snow layers and causes melt around the grains beneath the surface but meltwater at the surface is refrozen forming a thin layer of ice. A highly reflective, mirror-like surface.

GRAUPEL

A form of precipitation which looks like round pellets. Graupel is subject to rolling and can collect in pockets. It can also form a layer with a great deal of pore space and poor bonding. The pellets themselves are snowflakes which accumulated rime ice as they fell through certain atmospheric layers.

METAMORPHISM

The process where deposited snow changes its form. Changes in the grain structure are caused by varying pressure and temperature conditions.

RIME

Supercooled water droplets which have frozen onto any surface (such as snow crystals, ski lift towers, rocks, trees,...). Or the process of freezing the droplets. Rime has a styrofoam appearance to it.

SLUSH

Water saturated snow.

SNOW PLUME

Snow being carried by the wind away from a peak or ridge into the air.

Below a snow crust over running water. Water condenses onto the ice/snow surface above the flowing stream.
Running Water

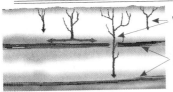

Lubrification
Free water penetrating the snowpack tends to spread out on top of hard layers and melts or erodes the attachment between the hard layer and the layer above.

Lubrification on Incline
Intensive lubrication of an ice layer in an inclined snowpack. Lubrication is also commonly observed above the ground surface.

LUBRIFICATION

A case of interest occurs when a cold snow layer of early winter is drenched by rain and then freezes. In such a layer, enlargement of grains by MF metamorphism is at a minimum, and the layer freezes into a very strong structure. The great changes in strength that result from melting and freezing have important implications in avalanche stability evaluation. A prime cause of spring avalanches is lubrication of the sliding surface. This is the result of free water percolating down to a hard surface such as an ice layer or the ground. If the water cannot penetrate the surface, it tends to spread out and melt or erode the bond between this surface and the snow above.

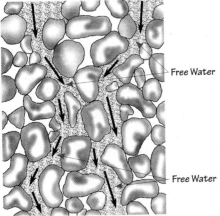

Water Percolation
In one mode of flow, free water percolates through the pore space, under the influence of capillarity action and gravity.

Spring Corn Snow

Rotten Snow
Snow which has lost its original bonding strength, usually by kinetic growth.

Spring Rotten Snow

SNOW DENSITY INCREASE : SETTLEMENT

Snow layers have the ability to sustain large, irreversible density changes. Higher densities are the result of metamorphism and the weight of the overlying snow pack. With a new snowfall the lower snow layer's density can increase by 50% in a day. As the density of the layer increases, so does its resistance to further densification. Evidence of densification is observed in a gradual settling of the snow surface. Settlement occurs at rates on the order of 1 cm/day and depends on snow cover depth and crystal types. Higher rates are observed during or immediately after heavy snowfalls. It is not uncommon for settlement to be on the order of 10 cm/day when new snow is being deposited at the rate of about 30 cm/day. Then, most of the settlement takes place in the top layers. During light snowfalls, the settlement rate of the older snow may exceed the new snowfall rate, in which case the total depth of the pack decreases, in spite of the incoming snow. The high compressibility of low-density snow is largely due to the flexibility of the ice skeleton. When load is applied, relatively high forces concentrate at the necks and other narrow regions of the skeleton into new positions, filling up vacant pore space. The necks then reform. This type of deformation is irreversible. The necks are easily distorted by the concentrated forces, and the grains are free to move; once the ice skeleton has been rearranged with new necks, it cannot spring back to its original shape.

SNOW PACK WATER CIRCULATION

Because of surface tension, small amounts of free water cling to melting grains. As melting accelerates, free water begins to flow into the pack. The rate of flow depends on the texture of the snow, the temperature of the ice skeleton, and the amount of water available. Some water flows by capillary motion through the pore spaces, and larger amounts flow in channels melted by the free water. Free water flows down until it either freezes on contact with a cold layer or is blocked by a hard layer. The water tends to spread out over a hard layer until a channel is eroded or melted. Free water flows very slowly, and the flow is referred to as percolation. When free water percolates into a cold region of tile pack, the water often freezes to form an ice lens. A buildup of a wet level will cause 'lubrification.'

SPRING SNOW & CORN OR ROTTEN SNOW

In spring, the entire snowpack reaches a temperature very close to 0° C. The snow temperature at the surface may vary widely between day and night extremes. These fluctuations originate at the snow surface and penetrate deeper into the pack where they cause melting and refreezing. This melt-freeze metamorphism builds clusters of large ice grains. After several melt-freeze cycles more large, coarse ice grains are produced. Depending on the number of cycles, the time of day, the depth of the layer, etc., corn snow or rotten snow result. This structure is then extremely weak and ductile and when the layer refreezes, it assumes enormous strength.

Spring Snow
This is snow which has accumulated through the winter. It usually consist of large, grains from melt-freeze cycles. Often the entire snowpack contains liquid water and snow layer boundaries are obscured.

FAST STRONG PRESSURE ON SNOW

If the applied force is strong and pushes fast on the sample, then the snow cannot respond by gradual collapse, and brittle fracture occurs. This is very important in avalanche stability evaluation, in that any snow mass, depending on its temperature and texture, has two limitations:
• it can store only a limited amount of elastic strain energy.
• it can dissipate the extra energy at a limited rate.

FRACTURE MECHANICS - SNOW

Studies have also been made of the lower density snow typical of alpine, seasonal snowpacks. Snow properties are so complex that it is difficult to predict with confidence how it will behave on the mountainside. When a compression is applied to a snow sample, the sample deforms considerably. The amount of deformation depends on the intensity of the force and the rate at which the force is applied. When the force is suddenly removed, the sample springs back slightly, but a large amount of permanent deformation remains in the sample. There are both a springy or elastic component and a permanent deformation component. The elastic component represents energy that is stored and recovered, and the permanent deformation component represents energy that is unrecoverable or has been dissipated. The snow skeleton is highly compressible and can sustain large amounts of permanent deformation. If the load is applied slowly enough that deformation is slow, then, in principle, the sample can be compressed to a mass of solid ice.

FRACTURE TOUGHNESS

The ability of a material to withstand catastrophic failure is called its fracture toughness. Hard, strong snow layers are as apt to propagate fractures as weak, soft snow.

BRITTLE FRACTURE PROPAGATION

During brittle fracture propagation, the energy of the system is quickly redistributed into fracture surfaces, kinetic motion, and heat. Fractures occur at flaws or localized regions of stress concentration. In the mountain snowpack, trees, rocks, ski tracks, etc. are regions of stress concentration and likely spots for fracture formation. This could trigger an avalanche.

TEMPERATURE & FRACTURE TOUGHNESS

Intuitively, one suspects that the colder the snow, the more brittle its behavior. On the other hand, laboratory tests indicate that snow gains strength as its temperature decreases. Snow exhibits brittle fractures at all temperatures up to 0° C, and sometimes even when an appreciable amount of free water is present.

HORIZONTAL SNOWPACK

In the horizontal snowpack the deformation of the snowpack is downward and each element of the snowpack is subject to a compressive stress component in the vertical direction, caused by the weight of the snow above. There is no component of shear stress acting in the horizontal snowpack.

Direction of gravity force and deformation - settlement of snow.

Horizontal Snowpack

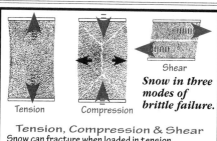

Snow in three modes of brittle failure.

Tension   Compression   Shear

Tension, Compression & Shear

Snow can fracture when loaded in tension, compression, or shear. Snow has substantial resistance to fracture in compression but is easily fractured in tension.

In compression, the potential fracture surfaces are pushed together so that the material gains strength from friction. In the case of snow, forcing the grains together by compression allows the material to gain strength by sintering.

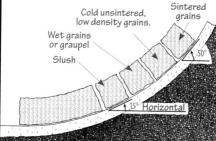

Loose Snow & Maximum Angle Before Sliding

Depending on its temperature, wetness, and texture, each snow type has a critical angle of repose - above which it will not cling to the snowpack. Loose snow avalanches result when this critical angle is exceeded.

Cold unsintered, low density grains.

Sintered grains.

Wet grains or graupel

Slush

50°

15° Horizontal

KEY TO SNOW & AVALANCHE TERMINOLOGY

Types of Metamorphism

Metamorphism refers to the change of texture of snow caused by pressure and temperature.

- Temperature of the layer determines the rate of metamorphism.
- Temperature gradient in the layer determines the type of metamorphism.
- Within a short time after a snowfall metamorphism starts and within a few days it is impossible to recognize the crystal structure of the original snowfall.
- Within two weeks the individual snow flakes will have been reduced to small ice grains - only one-fourth their original size.

Three Types of Metamorphism

TG Metamorphism: If the metamorphism is in response to a strong temperature gradient. *TG = temperature gradient.* Temperature gradient means that the temperature within a layer varies. An example would be that the upper part of a layer would be warmer during a sunny day and colder during a cold night or very cold spell.

ET Metamorphism: A process not driven by the temperature gradient, but instead by the tendency of snow to break up (e.g. crystals losing their arms) and form a tighter stronger texture. This would be good snow for the building of a snow cave or an igloo. *ET = equitemperature.*

MF Metamorphism: This takes place when the snowpack reaches 0° C and surface snow undergoes frequent melt-freeze cycles. Under these conditions, the smaller ice grains in the surface layers melt during the day and freeze during the night. Repeated freeze-thaw cycles produce large rounded clusters of ice grains. Corn snow would be an example of this metamorphism. *MF = Melt-Freeze.*

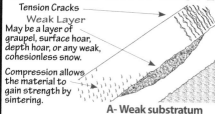

Inclined Snowpack

Gravity

Shear   Compression

Deformation by weight of snow/ice.

Angle of Slope

SOURCES OF TENSILE STRESS

Weak Substructure: A weak area below the snowpack (ill. A) will produce a similar stress as a slope curvature (ill. B).

Localized Curvature: Regions of tension and compression can develop wherever the inclined snowpack is curved. Tension regions develop over convex terrain features, and compression regions develop over concave terrain features (ill. B).

Snow Cushions: Another source of localized curvature is the nonuniform thickness of a snowpack deposited by strong winds. The pack may be shaped like a pillow or cushion. As shown in ill. C, a snow cushion has several regions of comparatively high stress.

Anchoring or Clamping: Top ends of snowpacks are often wedge shaped, as shown in ill. D. The top of the wedge tends to be anchored to the terrain. The snowpack pulls on the anchoring point, and a region of tension develops below the anchor. Trees, rocks, and other protrusions may also function as anchoring points and induce high local stresses.

SNOWPACK ON SLOPE

Shear Component: At angles typical of avalanche paths (30°- 50°) the vector forces have a shear component caused by gravity and this produces a down slope deformation. Failure occurs because the shear stress exceeds the shear strength at a certain depth.

Tensile Stress: In addition to the shear component another important factor to consider is tensile stress. Significant tensile stress can develop in an inclined snowpack.

Substratum Weakness : If an inclined snowpack rests on a locally weak substratum that cannot support its weight, then, in order for the snowpack to be in equilibrium, a tensile stress must develop in the snowpack up slope from the weak substratum, and a compressive stress must develop down slope. The redistribution of stress due to the weak substratum is shown in the illustration (ill. A). The weak substratum may be a layer of graupel, surface hoar, depth hoar, or any weak, cohesionless snow. This weak strata consists of faceted grains that are not well bonded together.

SOURCES OF TENSILE STRESS OF SNOW ON A SLOPE

Tension Cracks

Weak Layer
May be a layer of graupel, surface hoar, depth hoar, or any weak, cohesionless snow.

Compression allows the material to gain strength by sintering.

A- Weak substratum

Convexity causing tension cracks

Concavity

Compression allows the material to gain strength by sintering.

B- Slope curvature

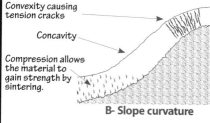

Snow Pillow
Snow Cushion

Tension Cracks

Snowdrift on a slope, often within the starting zone of an avalanche, which has the appearance of a cushion or pillow.

Compression

C- Inhomogeneity a snow cushion

Anchor Area

Tension Cracks

Snowpack pulls on the anchoring point, and a region of tension develops below the anchor.

D- Anchoring at the top boundary

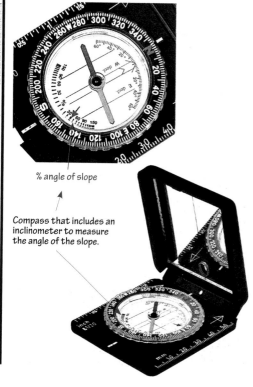

% angle of slope

Compass that includes an inclinometer to measure the angle of the slope.

AVALANCHE TYPES

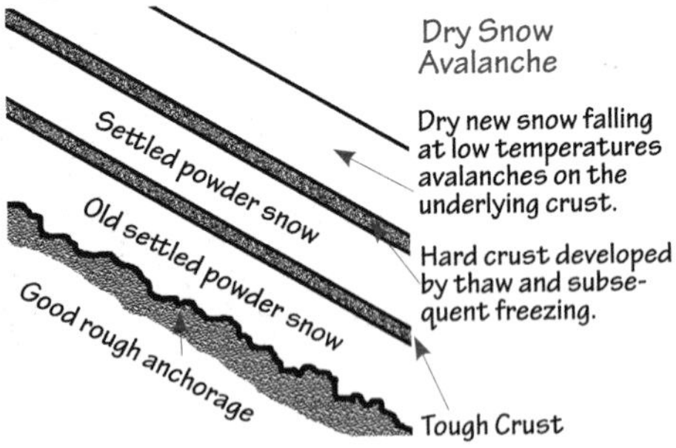
Dry Snow Avalanche
Dry new snow falling at low temperatures avalanches on the underlying crust.
Settled powder snow
Hard crust developed by thaw and subsequent freezing.
Old settled powder snow
Good rough anchorage
Tough Crust

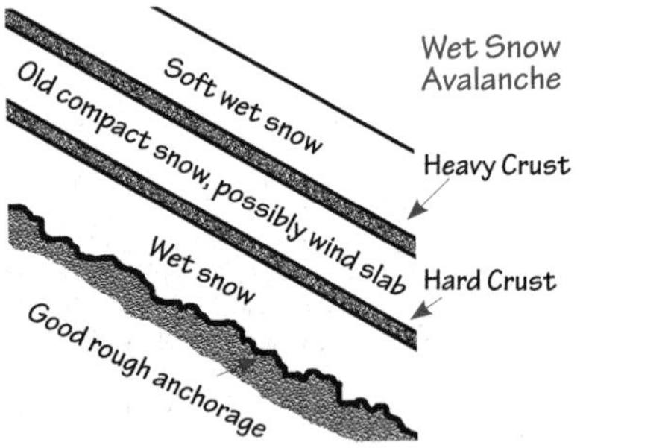
Wet Snow Avalanche
Soft wet snow
Heavy Crust
Old compact snow, possibly wind slab
Hard Crust
Wet snow
Good rough anchorage

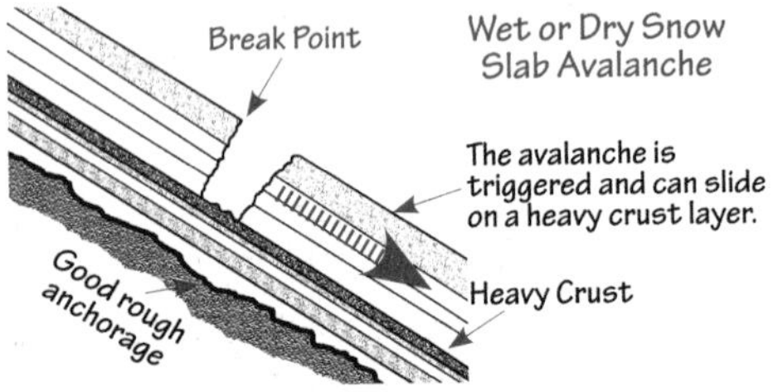
Break Point
Wet or Dry Snow Slab Avalanche
The avalanche is triggered and can slide on a heavy crust layer.
Heavy Crust
Good rough anchorage

Slab Avalanche
A snow mantle with a hard, frozen coating can be covered with a layer of snow that is composed of snow crystals, ice droplets, layers of refrozen snow. The layers and weather changes can cause loose cohesion and the top layer(s) of snow can slide off.

Avalanche Movement

Avalanche motion may be described as flowing, airborne powder, or mixed.

Flowing Motion: is the turbulent, tumbling action of snow moving mostly along the ground.

Airborne Powder Motion: most of the snow is swirling through the air. Pure powder motion seldom occurs except when the snow goes over a cliff.

Mixed Motion: in almost all avalanches; large blocks and particles tumble and bounce along the ground, and smaller particles are airborne.

Sunball
Balls of snow which roll down a steep slope after sun action. The trail they leave is sometimes called a "snow snake". If a sunball has a long path to roll down (it will get larger as it rolls) it could start a Loose Snow Avalanche.

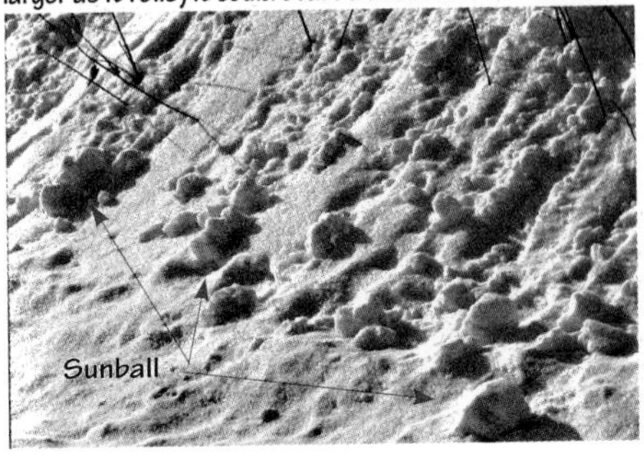
Sunball

Avalanche Types

Loose or Dry Snow Avalanche

Failure begins near the snow surface. A small amount of cohesionless snow slips out of place and starts down the slope. The initial mass may set an increasing amount of snow into motion if the snow in its path is also fairly cohesionless. When this process is observed from a distance, the avalanche seems to start at a point, and the sliding snow spreads down from the point, leaving an inverted V-shaped scar.

Damp or Wet Snow (Spring)

Resembles dry snow avalanches with the same arrowhead point of origin on the surface, gradually becoming wider. Their mass is much greater than that of a dry avalanche and they are much more destructive. They are heavier and stickier and so they develop more friction and travel at a slower pace. The principal hazard of damp and wet snow avalanches is to fixed installations.

Slab or Sheet Avalanche

Failure begins with brittle, catastrophic fracturing of cohesive snow that frees a slab-like area of the slope. The slab quickly breaks into smaller cohesive blocks, whose size varies with their cohesiveness and the roughness of the avalanche track. The initial slab may vary from about 100 to 10,000 m^2 in area and from about 0.1 to 10 m in thickness. Movement of larger slabs releases enormous amounts of energy. In contrast to loose-snow avalanches, slab avalanches depend on the propagation of fractures by stored energy in the relatively cohesive layers.

Windslab Avalanche

This is a sub variant of the Slab Avalanche. Windpacked snow, called windslab or snowslab is unquestionably the worst killer of all and equal to the Wet Spring Avalanche as a destroyer of property. Usually on slopes between 30° - 50°. Wind action can deposit snow 5-10 times faster than snow from a snow storm.

Hard Slab: Result of wind action on snow picked up from the surface.

Soft Slab: Result of wind action on falling snow.

A windslab avalanche combines great mass with high speed to produce enormous energy. It may originate either at the surface or through the collapse of a stratum deep within the snowpack.

In a packed-snow avalanche the main body of the slide reaches its maximum speed within seconds. Speeds of 63 mph (100 km) are not uncommon.

Combination Avalanche

Combination avalanches are composed of both loose and slab snow layers making it more difficult to determine which part of the combination acted as the trigger and which is the main charge of the avalanche.

Climax Avalanche

The climax avalanche is a special combination. The distinguishing characteristic of this type of avalanche is that it contains a large proportion of old snow and is caused by conditions which have developed over a considerable period of time - at least a month and possibly an entire season. Climax avalanches occur infrequently because they require an unusual combination of favorable factors.

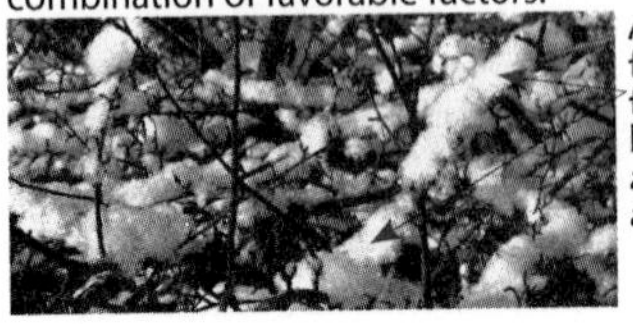

A fluff of new fallen snow falling from a branch can start a loose snow avalanche.

Natural & Artificial Avalanches

Natural Avalanches: Are not triggered directly by man or his equipment. A failing cornice, sluffing snow, stress change due to metamorphism, stress change due to weight of new snow, earth tremors, snow falling from trees, etc., can all trigger avalanches.

Artificial Avalanches: Are triggered by man or his equipment. A ski pass, a mountaineer's weight, an explosive blast, a sonic boom, etc., commonly precipitate artificial avalanches.

- There seems to be no difference in appearance between natural and artificial avalanches. The important fact is that artificial triggering leads to a far greater frequency of avalanches on a given path than if the path were left to avalanche naturally.

Loose Snow Avalanche

Slab avalanches are more dangerous than loose snow avalanches.

Loose-snow avalanches occur mostly because the steepness of the slope exceeds the angle of repose of certain types of weak snow. The exact critical angle of repose depends on the temperature, wetness, and shape of the snow grains. For example, wet, slushy snow has very little strength for its weight and can avalanche off slopes as gradual as 15°. Newly fallen snow has relatively low cohesion but generally has enough strength to cling to 40° to 50° slopes. However, if the new snowfall is cold enough, avalanches of cold, dry snow may occur on slopes of 30° to 40° because sintering cannot proceed fast enough at the cold temperatures to anchor the snow. Rounded graupel crystals generally will not cling to slopes steeper than 40° and often roll down steep slopes like ball bearings.

Loose Snow Avalanche Sequence

A: Layer is disturbed by any of several natural or artificial processes: overloading, from the added weight of newly fallen snow or a skier; vibration, from an earth tremor or explosive force; or, most important, internal changes such as the warming of the layer to a state of drastic loss of cohesion.

B: A small piece of the layer slips. The piece can be as small as a single grain but is typically the size of a large snowball.

C: The loose piece either comes to rest at a new angle of repose or imparts enough energy to the snow in its track to cause an avalanche.

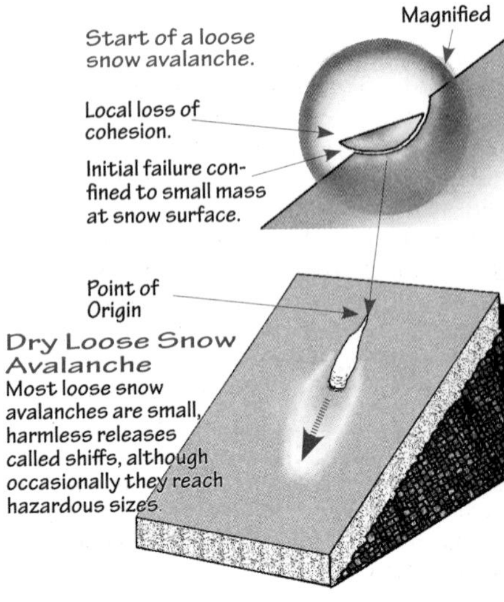
Magnified
Start of a loose snow avalanche.
Local loss of cohesion.
Initial failure confined to small mass at snow surface.
Point of Origin
Dry Loose Snow Avalanche
Most loose snow avalanches are small, harmless releases called shiffs, although occasionally they reach hazardous sizes.

AVALANCHE TYPES

LOOSE SNOW

DAMP OR WET SNOW (SPRING) AVALANCHE

Similar to dry Loose Snow Avalanches with the same arrowhead point of origin, gradually becoming wider. Their mass is much greater than that of a dry avalanche and they are much more destructive. They are heavier and stickier and so develop more friction with the slope, and travel at a slower pace. The principal hazard of damp and wet snow avalanches is to fixed installations. Their comparatively low speed causes them to stop rather suddenly when they lose momentum and to pile up in a towering mass. This is in contrast to the loose snow avalanche which tends to spread out like the splash of a wave. Damp and wet avalanches solidify immediately upon release from the pressure of motion. This adds to the difficulty of rescue or clearing operations. Wet slides have the distinctive characteristic of channelling. The moving snow constructs its own banks and flows between them like a river of slush, often in unexpected directions as it does not always choose the most direct downhill route. The damp snowslides of midwinter are generally shallow. But the wet avalanches of spring, caused by deep thawing either from rain or prolonged temperatures above freezing, often involve enormous masses of snow and debris and have tremendous destructive power.

LOOSE SNOW AVALANCHES

Hazard to Mountaineers & Skiers: Loose snow avalanches are generally small, but they are large enough to knock over a mountaineer. Small loose-snow avalanches have sent skiers on leg-breaking rides and have taken mountaineers over cliffs and into crevasses.

Hazard to Facilities: Occasionally, loose-snow avalanches are large enough to threaten moving or parked cars, fixed facilities, etc. Most of the notorious cases occurred either in spring or after continuous rain, when the snowpack became soaked and cohesionless to depths of a meter or more.

Stabilization of Steep Slopes: Loose-snow avalanches remove snow from steep slopes. During storms, sluffing occurs almost continuously where the slope angle is steeper than about 50°. Because of sluffing, dangerously thick layers rarely build on steep slopes. The exceptions to the 50° rule occur where snow is plastered against perpetual ice fields and snowfields, in narrow couloirs, or where snow conditions result in unusually steep angles of repose.

Stabilization of Lower Slopes: In terrain where high angle slopes empty down onto lower slopes, sluffing from the higher slopes may force the lower slopes gradually to shed small avalanches to become stable.

Loading of Lower Slopes: Sluffing transfers snow to the lower slopes, building up large deposits that may release as slab avalanches.

Triggering of Slab Avalanches: Loose-snow avalanches that would he harmless by themselves may spill onto lower slopes and trigger dangerous slab avalanches.

SLAB AVALANCHE

Slab Analysis

Slab avalanches begin with the fracturing of snow on a slope. Cracks usually propagate quickly and follow unique and complex paths that depend on slope geometry and slab anchorage. For a slab to detach completely from the slope, fractures must proceed around the entire slab boundary.

Slab Size

Slabs often contain large masses of snow and great amounts of potential energy. It is not uncommon for a slab to have an area the size of a football field and an average thickness of 1 m. When a slab breaks loose and slides down the mountainside, it may bring down 100 times the initially released amount of snow.

SLAB AVALANCHE PROPERTIES

Crown Thickness: This dimension can vary widely, from a few centimeters in the case of sluffs to several meters. Typically, slab avalanches become hazardous to skiers when the crown thickness exceeds 15 cm, the minimum thickness for extensive fracture propagation.

Slab Density: In almost all slabs, there is substantial variation in density between snow surface and bed surface. The density just above the bed surface is usually about twice the density at the snow surface.

SLAB FRACTURE TERMINOLOGY

Crown Surface: The top fracture surface of the slab, usually a smooth, clean cut, generally perpendicular to the slope. The snow that remains on the slope above the crown surface is called the crown.

Flank Surface: The side boundary of the slab, often saw toothed.

Bed Surface: The main sliding surface of the slab, generally smoothed and compacted by the sliding blocks.

Stauchwall: The downslope fracture surface of the slab, often difficult to identify since it is usually overridden and obliterated by the sliding blocks.

SLAB & TERRAIN SLOPE

Slab avalanches originate on a wide variety of terrain with the main requirement being steepness. *Dangerous slabs are most likely to start on slopes of 30° to 45°.*

- For slopes of less than about 30°, shear stress on the bed surface is not large enough to cause shear failure. Collapse and fracturing are often observed on slopes with inclinations of less than 30°, and even on horizontal surfaces, but in these cases vertical collapse is not followed by avalanching.
- The upper limit of about 45° probably indicates the tendency of snow to sluff gradually off steep slopes (45° to 60°).
- Isolated examples of slab avalanches are outside the 30° to 45° range. Certainly, mountaineers should not venture confidently onto 50° snow slopes. In cases where snow accumulates on steep terrain (45° to 60°), slab avalanches are a definite possibility.
- Slab fracture can propagate from high-angle slopes to slopes of less than 30°.
- Slope curvature can influence the stress distribution in a slab. However, the bed surfaces of almost all slabs are quite planar. Moreover, crown fractures usually form just below a terrain bend rather than directly on the bend due to the way snow is deposited and anchored.

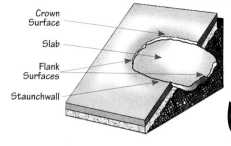

Crown Surface
Slab
Flank Surfaces
Staunchwall

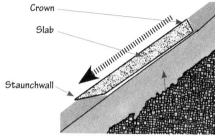

Crown
Slab
Staunchwall

Slab Substructure

Viewing the fracture pattern in ideal cross section, the bed surface and the crown surface typically intersect at approximately 90°; the slab has a wedge like shape at the stauchwall.

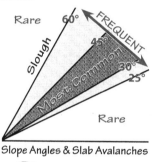

Rare   60°   FREQUENT
Slough   45°   Most Common   30°   25°
Rare

Slope Angles & Slab Avalanches

Clinometer

WET & DRY LOOSE SNOW AVALANCHES

Loose-snow avalanches occur throughout the snow season, from early fall to late spring. It is customary to distinguish between dry and wet loose snow avalanches, although there is no sharp dividing line. They occur in a variety of sizes. Most fall as small, innocuous masses called sluffs. Dangerous wet loose-snow avalanches are sometimes observed, especially in the Pacific Coastal ranges, where they have destroyed life and property. See: Damp or Wet Snow (Spring) Avalanche.

LARGE MIXED MOTION AVALANCHE

In large, mixed-motion avalanches the great majority of debris is transported close to the snow surface. Debris drops out continuously. The avalanche continues undiminished as long as the snow in the track feeds the moving mass and replaces the debris that drops out. This condition is fulfilled when the track snow is relatively unconsolidated or of soft slab texture. A moving avalanche is the result of successive failures connected by a common track. Under certain conditions, avalanches can run long distances over level terrain or up adverse grades.

SLAB AVALANCHE

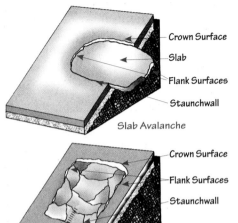

Slab Avalanche

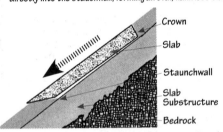

Slab Breaking Up

Crown Fracture

Although the first observed fractures are usually spectacular crown fractures, the crown may in fact be the last link to break. Crown fractures may extend considerable distances, jumping gullies and bowls and linking together several smaller slabs. Crown lengths of more than a kilometer have been recorded. A characteristic feature of the fracture boundary is that crown length usually exceeds flank length. In some cases, the crown surface blends directly into the staunchwall, forming an oval, flank less slab.

Viewing the fracture pattern in ideal cross section, the bed surface and the crown surface typically intersect at approximately 90°; the slab has a wedge- like shape at the staunchwall.

A skier triggering a slab avalanche.

The horizontal thrust of a large avalanche may cause impact pressures in the range of 5 - 50 tons/m². Vertical impact components are typically one-fourth to one-half the magnitude of the horizontal components. Airblast pressures are much smaller - perhaps no higher than one-half ton /m².

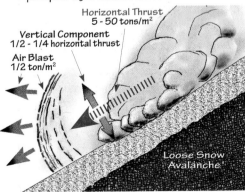

Horizontal Thrust 5 - 50 tons/m²
Vertical Component 1/2 - 1/4 horizontal thrust
Air Blast 1/2 ton/m²
Loose Snow Avalanche

SLAB TEMPERATURE RELEASE MECHANISM

Heavy snowfall, rain, thaw, and dynamic loads are important triggers of slab avalanches. Rapid changes in snow temperature are confined to the surface layers. Solar radiation is the most important variable in the short-time energy balance, yet most avalanches attributed to temperature release have been on north-facing slopes, where hourly radiation changes are minimal.

Temperature Release & Post Control Avalanches

- Temperature changes at the snow surface may cause failure and sliding in the surface layers. This, in turn, triggers deeper slab releases.
- Sudden temperature changes at the surface very likely do not cause deep slab instability in dry snowpacks.
- Explosives alone do not give an infallible test of snowpack stability and in some rare cases may weaken the slope.

Slab Temperature & Wetness

- Slab temperatures reflect the air temperatures of the mountain range. Avalanches have been observed in the cold environments of Mount McKinley. At the other extreme, slab avalanches have been observed when the snow was thoroughly drenched with free water.

To distinguish dry & wet slabs: Dry slab snow when squeezed in a gloved hand will not make a snowball, but liquid water can be squeezed from wet slab snow. This test should be made with snow from near the starting zone, not avalanche debris.

Slab Hardness: Hard Slab & Soft Slab

Hardness is based on subjective observations.

- For example, extreme hard slab snow cannot be penetrated by ski tracks and ski edges leave only a faint line. Excellent powder skiing is often possible through soft slab snow.
- On slopes of similar roughness, hard slab blocks can survive lengthy trips down the slope without disaggregation, while soft slab blocks break up very quickly into smaller lumps.
- There is no fundamental distinction between hard and soft slabs; slabs come in a wide range of hardness.
- Harder slabs pose special control problems in ski areas. Generally, hard slabs consist of high-density snow, either deposited by high winds or the result of aging and compaction.

BED SURFACE

Because the bed surface is altered by the sliding slab, definite information on its structure is rarely available. Studies on the extension of the bed surface into the crown reveal the following:

- In some cases it is possible to identify a distinct discontinuity, such as a transition from ET grains to TG grains, a graupel layer, the ground surface, an ice crust, or thin layers of surface hoar. *See page 223 for terminology.*
- In many cases it is not possible to identify any special discontinuity of snow stratigraphy at the bed surface extension, although snow at the bed surface is typically about 50 percent weaker than snow immediately above the bed surface.

TG Metamorphosed Grains

See page 223 for terminology. Weak TG grains are considered the most obvious clue that the snowpack is potentially unstable. Thick TG layers stand out from ET layers in the pitwalls and are easily identified. The importance of TG metamorphism in stability evaluation cannot be overemphasized. Instability is most apt to exist where metamorphism has advanced toward weak, large, depth-hoar grains. Attention is critical in a ski area or along a ski tour route where localized patches of TG grains produce small but dangerous slab avalanches. Stability can vary from season to season, depending on the weakness and extent of TG layers.

When weak TG layers have been identified, the following should be kept in mind:

- The probability of deep slab instability is many times greater on slopes that have depth hoar than on those that have an ET structure throughout.
- Although instability is most likely to be triggered during or immediately after storms, slopes with weak TG layers remain unstable for long periods between storms. Instability can be triggered at almost any time.
- The first storm that deposits snow on a TG layer may not produce avalanches. This should not give observers a false sense of security. Two or more storms may be required to build a slab on the TG substratum.
- Slopes with weak TG layers do not always respond immediately to explosive control. Instability is sometimes triggered several hours after avalanche control.
- If a slab is removed down to the TG substratum, TG metamorphism normally continues in the thinned snowpack, and instability reappears and sometimes intensifies.
- Instability remains until the TG grains are sintered under the pressure of a thick snowpack or until MF metamorphism dominates. Normally, TG instability is most acute during December and January and begins to diminish in February. Strengthening of the TG layers usually occurs by early March.
- After TG layers are strengthened, instability may reappear in spring because of melting of the bonds (thaw instability). Full-depth avalanches have run on layers of wet TG grains.

SLAB AVALANCHE

MECHANICS OF SLAB FAILURE

Possibility A: Shear stress / Shear strength.

Failure begins when shear stress exceeds shear strength at the bed surface. This may be the result of either an increase in the bed surface shear stress or a decrease in the bed surface shear strength, or a combination of the two. Such changes may be caused by:

- High-intensity snowfall or wind redistribution of older snow.
- Rapid application of shock load, explosive blast, cornice fall, etc.
- Load of one or more skiers traversing the slab.
- Weakening of the bed surface by TG metamorphism.
- Weakening of the bed surface due to slow straining.
- Weakening of the bed surface by melting.

The initial bed surface failure is always hidden from sight, so it is not obvious how rapidly failure progresses. There may be rather widespread shear fractures, or possibly slow, progressive straining. In any case, after shear failure begins, tensile stress begins to increase in the slab. Finally the slab fractures in tension, and the entire slab releases very rapidly as the shear support along the flanks and the compressive support at the stauchwall are overcome. This sequence could result in crown fractures propagating above a skier, trapping the skier in its descent.

In all three mechanisms, the necessary condition for failure is that a relatively stiff layer (the slab layer) rests on a relatively weak layer, that includes the bed surface. Tensile stress eventually develops in the slab layer, which stores elastic strain energy.

Possibility B: Collapse of thick, weak layer.

A second possible and related sequence of slab failure begins with the sudden collapse of a thick, weak layer of TG grains, or low-density snow. The collapse can be due to new snow load, weakening by metamorphism, or sudden shock. The sequence of events would be:

- Collapse of the substratum.
- High bending stress upslope from the collapsed area.
- Tension fracture in the region of high bending stress.
- Shear fracture at the bed surface.

It is known that substratum collapse is an important mechanism, since it explains the intense instability associated with thick TG layers. However, in many cases slabs have failed on hard substrata, where collapse was not possible.

Possibility C: Tension fracture.

Slab failure beginning with tension fracture, which in turn activates fracture at the bed surface. This requires a previous internal failure or straining in the snowpack to build up the necessary tensile stresses. Fracture could result from:

- Sudden ski traverse across crown, explosive blast, etc.
- Decrease in tensile strength due to warming of slab.
- Increase in tensile stress due to thermal contraction brought on by protracted cooling.
- Increase in tensile stress due to creep or glide.

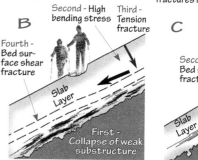

In one possible sequence, initial slab failure occurs in shear along the bed surface. High tensile stress develops upslope, ahead of the propagating shear failure. Finally, the slab layer fractures in tension.

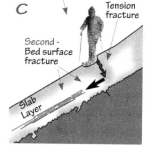

Initial failure may occur as a tension crack. The opening of the tension crack would induce shear fracture at the bed surface.

Initial failure may occur as collapse of a weak substratum. This would induce high bending stress, tension fracture, and finally shear fracture at the bed surface.

When the slab layer fractures, a sudden jolt is thrown onto the bed surface. This jolt reinforces any bed surface failure that began earlier. Finally, the shear fractures at the bed surface and the tension fractures at the crown reinforce one another, so that the slab rapidly breaks free on all boundaries.

This hill is *too steep to let snow accumulate for large avalanches. Sloughing will occur.*

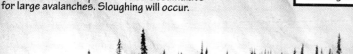

SLAB AVALANCHE MOTION

A slab avalanche usually passes quickly through several types of motion as it attains its maximum velocity.

- After breaking loose from the starting zone, a snow slab accelerates down the track and very quickly splits into smaller blocks.
- Within a short distance, the blocks begin tumbling and colliding. A stress wave of the avalanche advances in the snow slightly ahead of the avalanche front. As the avalanche passes over new snow, new mass is fed into the main body. An airblast sometimes precedes the avalanche.
- If the track is long and the motion continues, the blocks disaggregate into chunks and particles. The smallest particles are tossed into the air, forming a snow dust cloud. This results in mixed avalanche motion, with part of the snow flowing along the ground and part moving in a snow dust cloud.

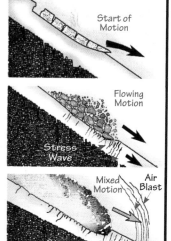

SNOW HARDNESS TEST (HAND TEST)

Hardness	Test
Fist hard	Gloved fist can penetrate at least 5 cm
Four-finger hard	Four gloved fingers can penetrate at least 5 cm
One-finger hard	One finger can penetrate at least 5 cm
Pencil hard	Pencil can penetrate at least 5 cm
Knife hard	Knife can penetrate at least 5 cm

SNOWPIT AVALANCHE TESTING

Snowpit

Layers of snow in a snowpit.

Slab Stratigraphy

The slab layers above the bed surface consist of a wide assortment of snow types.

The most frequently observed layers are:
• Newly deposited snow up to a few days old. Firm, wind-deposited layers are very common.
• Metamorphosed snow. Mostly ET grains and grains in the early stages of TG metamorphism. Quite often thin TG layers, crusts, graupel layers, and other special layers are sandwiched between thick ET layers.
• Wet layers and their water content.

Slab Substratum

In continental climates, the slab substratum beneath the bed surface consists of TG grains. In maritime climates, TG substrata are rare, and limited data indicate that most of the substrata consist of new snow, partly metamorphosed snow, or wet snow.

Different types of Strata that can be seen in a Snowpit

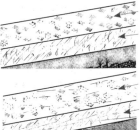

Slab
(warm, dense)

Weak Substratum
(cool, light)

Slab
Heavy to moderately rimed crystals

Weak Substratum
Tightly rimed crystals

Slab
Deposited by strong winds

Weak Substratum
Deposited by light winds

New snow instability is usually a result of a heavy, stiff layer deposited on a light, weak layer. This pattern may be caused by changes in temperature, snow-crystal form, and wind.

Diagnosis of Snowpack Structure

Weak layers correlated with instability are those that:
• Contain TG grains; loose, cold snow; surface hoar; graupel; radiation recrystallized grains; or wet snow.
• Instability is greatly intensified when any of these weak layers is immediately above or beneath a firm crust.
• Digging pits near the avalanche release points is the only reliable and efficient way to locate significant weak layers. The farther the pits are from the avalanche release points, the less reliable the pit information. Generally, one looks for both thick and thin weak layers. A thick, weak TG layer is the most obvious clue of potential structural instability. A thin, weak layer sandwiched between a stiff slab and a crust is also highly unstable, but this combination is difficult to detect.

Snow Pit Testing Kit

Required
Rucksack, Notebook & Pencils - Collapsible probe 3 m long - Aluminum shovel strong lightweight - Brush - Folding rule (3 m)
Optional
Ram penetrometer - Hand lens (and millimeter grid) Two thermometers (dial-stem preferred) Portable density kit - Any of a variety of strength measuring devices, such as a shear frame or Canadian hardness gage.

SNOWPIT TESTING

Snowpack observations are made by digging snowpits as close as possible to avalanche release points. Snowpits are relatively easy to dig on steep slopes. The dug snow is left on the slope. A pit much deeper than 2 m is usually not required due to the large variation in the thickness in the snowpack and the limited additional information obtained.

SNOWPIT INSPECTION

Several tests can be performed on the walls of the snowpit. However, if time is limited, the observer should concentrate on a qualitative investigation of the texture of the pitwall. The pitwall should be smoothed with the tip of the shovel, and then gently brushed with horizontal strokes of a soft brush, to bring out variations in hardness of the layers.

See page 223 for TG ET terminology.

First - look for major weak layers:
• In the deep snowpacks of maritime climates, these may be buried layers of cold, dry snow or thick layers of hard ice that may later be lubricated by melt water and act as avalanche bed surfaces.
• In more continental climates they are most likely layers of TG grains, usually just above the ground surface. The strength of TG metamorphism should be noted: beginning, intermediate, or advanced (depth hoar). The strength of the TG layer should be noted qualitatively as weak, medium, or strong. No guidelines can be stated for these strength categories, except that the observer learns quickly the great difference in strength between firm, well-sintered ET layers at one extreme and weak, cohesionless layers of depth hoar at the other.

Look next for more subtle weaknesses:
• The existence of any of the following may be worth noting: thin TG layers; weak layers above or below ice crusts; graupel layers; buried layers of surface hoar; or wet, cohesionless grains.
• To help locate crusts and thin layers, the tip of a small straightedge can be run down the pitwall. The pitwall texture can also be viewed through a magnifying glass.

Temperature measurements:
• Note the temperature variation in the snowpack. Temperature data give the observer a feel for whether TG metamorphism can be expected to intensify in the near future. They also can indicate how close the snowpack is to thaw (0° C throughout). The temperatures of the weak layers can indicate how rapidly they will gain strength through ET metamorphism and sintering.
• Temperature measurements should be taken in a north facing pitwall as soon as the pit is excavated. This is especially critical in spring, when pitwalls are likely to heat up rapidly.
• Because of their ruggedness, dial-stem thermometers are more suitable for pit work than breakable glass thermometers. (The 0° C point of each dial-stem thermometer should be checked by putting the stem in a well-stirred slush of clean snow and water.)
• To measure pitwall temperature first set the thermometer stem into the layer and allow a few minutes for the stem to come into equilibrium with the snow, then shift the stem horizontally to a fresh spot for the final reading. Working with several thermometers simultaneously saves time.

Ice Crusts
They are potential glide surfaces. The closer to the snow surface (where free water is produced) the greater the possibility that the free water can dissolve the bonds between ice and slab. Deeply buried ice crusts are usually not a problem.

Tensile Cracks
Slowly opening tensile cracks may sometimes be observed when a wet slab is gliding along a wet, lubricated surface. Most glide cracks that open early in the season (November - January) do not develop into dangerous slabs. Glide cracks later in the season are more likely to become unstable. The development is slow enough to provide ample warning.

Surface Hoar
Uncompressed layers of surface hoar are extremely weak. Widespread coverage of a slope by surface hoar leads to instability. Surface hoar layers can easily be detected while on the surface, before being buried and compressed. Once buried, they are difficult to identify. Surface hoar instability is relatively short-lived, lasting for only one or two storms.

Graupel

Graupel
Graupel is easily observed in snowpits. It is known to cause instability; however, graupel does not cause the intense instability that would be expected on the basis of its weak structure in snowpit walls. Graupel seems mainly to induce slab avalanches, of a one storm thickness. Few deep slab avalanches have released on graupel bed surfaces.

Loose & Cold Snow
If low temperatures remain for a long period after a storm and the surface snow is relatively loose and cohesionless, there is a good chance that any new snow may not bond well to the loose, cold surface. Potential instability is acute after air temperatures have remained below -15° C for several days and a new storm brings in a moderate amount of snow before the old snow surface has a chance to significantly warm up. Extreme instability can be expected when the old surface is a cold crust and the first few centimeters of new snow is of very cold, cohesionless grains.

Radiation Recrystallized Grains
These grains are caused by a rather peculiar radiation phenomenon. It occurs only rarely during the avalanche season and then only at high altitudes on south-facing slopes in late winter. On clear, dry days, an intense temperature gradient may be established between the snow surface (cooled by terrestrial radiation loss) and the sublayer (warmed by penetrating solar radiation). This produces a weak layer of recrystallized grains resembling depth hoar or an underlying ice crust.

Wet Snow
Wet snow instability is evaluated more from meteorological data than from snowpits. Snowpits are useful in determining when the temperature of a large part of the snowpack reaches 0° C and therefore approximately when the snowpack is susceptible to thaw. Snowpits are also useful in evaluating the amount of free water remaining in the pack after a rainstorm.

Avalanche runout zones shown by the lack of trees on parts of the mountain.

ROUTE SELECTION

It is not possible to give universal rules for route selection. Each tour has peculiarities that overrule idealization; the route is chosen to optimize efficiency, safety, and pleasure. Fortunately, the most efficient route and the safest route are very often the same. For example, since one can travel much faster on flat, windblown slopes than on steep, snow filled slopes, route selection generally favors ridges or low angle windward slopes rather than lee slopes. When instability is suspected, it is necessary to avoid avalanche paths completely. This may mean using a detour or inefficient route that gains or loses elevation, or it may mean traveling over difficult but avalanche-free terrain.

For example, to avoid open slopes and travel on forested slopes. As a simple rule, if trees are spaced within a few meters of one another, the protection they offer should be adequate. Generally, stay clear of slopes steeper than 30° during periods of potential instability. This is not overly restrictive, since downhill skiing can be enjoyed on slopes from 20° to 30° on most snow conditions, including deep powder. The more spectacular tours on steeper slopes must be saved for spring.

ROUTE SELECTION & ACCIDENTS

Back country safety is first of all a matter of controlling enthusiasm and exercising sound judgment. In the spirit of adventure, even the most experienced ski mountaineer may cause an accident by taking a "small" risk to reach an objective. This enthusiasm is reinforced by the feeling of group security that comes when several people push forward together. No member of the group likes to admit concern and turn the party around prematurely. Another important cause of accidents is the physical strain imposed by severe weather and terrain. Working under this strain, one may exhibit a carelessness that would be normally avoided. Professional mountain guides must set the highest safety standards and cannot habitually lead unknowing clients into areas of extreme avalanche danger.

Inspection of Vegetation
Inspection of vegetation in the runout zone is important. Vegetation gives clues to boundaries. The things to look for are:
• Destruction of trees and branches. The most convincing evidence of past avalanche activity is a patch of fallen trees, aligned in the same direction and sheared at about the same height above the ground. The common shear height can be assumed to be about the height of the snowpack at the time of the avalanche.
• At the boundary of the runout zone branches of upright trees may be damaged. Some of this damage may be caused by airblast or low-density snow dust. Branches are torn from the uphill sides of trees.

SEASON & ROUTE SELECTION

Early Season: *Usually November - February.*
Main problem is that the snowpack is unconsolidated. Touring is most hazardous during and immediately after storms, but instability persists between storms. North facing or shaded slopes are the most dangerous. They are most likely to have significant TG layers during the early part of the season. If enough time is allowed for new snow to stabilize, it may be possible to tour on south facing slopes.
Mid Season: *Transition period, usually from February - April.* The snowpack is consolidating, and deep slab instability tends to relax a few days after a storm. Touring must still be conducted with caution.
Late Season: *April - summer.*
Mountain snow compacts and becomes isothermal. Best time for alpine touring. With rare exception, slab avalanches are active the first few days of thaw after a new snowfall. Deep slab instability is rare; the thickness of the slab will be confined to the layer of new snow. After a few days of warm temperatures, the slab hazard will be essentially stabilized. The main threat will be loose, wet avalanches that run "on schedule" in the afternoon. These avalanches can be completely avoided by making an early morning start across the frozen pack and completing the tour as the snow surface turns to "corn" (when the skiing happens to be best). This usually means getting off all hazardous terrain before noon. Regardless of the lateness of the season, proper attention should be given to warning signs. Sudden collapse of the snow, fractures propagating out from skis, increasing wet snow instability, wind slab, persistent heavy snow, heavy rain, etc., are reasons to turn back or consider a safer route.

A   B   C

Graupel Formation

Inspection of Vegetation (cont'd)
• Change in species. Indication of past avalanche activity is a marked change in vegetation in the neighborhood of a suspected runout zone. A typical example might be a patch of slide alder, yellow cedar, or aspen surrounded by a closed forest of spruce and fir or other climax species. The explanation for these patches is that certain species of shrubs and fast-growing, light-tolerant trees invade disturbed sites more readily than climax plants. Trees of the climax species usually become established in the shade of the pioneer species and eventually crowd them out if given enough time without further disturbance.
• Differences in height of trees. Trees survive avalanches up to a height that varies with the strength and flexibility of the species and the thickness of the pack. Since avalanches ordinarily do not penetrate deeply under the pack in the runout zone, short trees may escape destruction. Thin, flexible trees up to about 3 m high may be bent by the moving snow and then recover. Certain rugged subalpine trees, such as thick limber pines, may be resistant to avalanches, and an occasional high tree is found in the middle of a path. In the great majority of cases, though, trees in the runout zone are shorter than trees outside the zone.

IDENTIFICATION OF AVALANCHE PATHS
• Avalanche paths can be studied by direct observation over a long period of time.
• Study indirect evidence: topography, climate, avalanche damage to vegetation, information from the local population. Path identification should be conducted throughout the year.
• Many avalanche paths are not active every winter but can run several times in winters when they are active.
• In winter, features are fracture lines and avalanche debris. Observations are made immediately after storms. Some fracture lines, and debris will be plainly visible, and some will be obscured by new snow and wind drifts.
• Avalanches that run early in the storm cycle may be obscured and quite difficult to identify.
• Spring avalanches are most active after storms followed by warming trends.
• Major avalanches may occur whenever the snowpack is thawed.
• Late in spring, and even in summer and fall, avalanche debris may he seen in gullies. The lumpy debris is dense, hard and often contains rocks, branches, mud, small animals, etc.
• In summer, detailed inspection can be made of the vegetation and topography of avalanche paths.
• In alpine and sub-alpine ski areas it can be assumed that all treeless slopes, gullies, and bowls steeper than about 30° are possible avalanche paths. People have been buried and killed by avalanches on paths only 10 m long.

LARGE AVALANCHE PATHS
• For large avalanche paths it is necessary to view the entire path. For very long paths, this may be impossible without using air reconnaissance or ascending the ridge across the valley from the suspected path. A view up from the valley floor often gives a distorted impression that may miss the starting zone. In some cases, large starting zones are hidden by cliff bands or other terrain features. The view down the path from the starting zone gives the best perspective of potential damage area.
• Large avalanches have enough power to destroy trees, and landscape scats provide important clues to avalanche activity. From far away, an active avalanche path below timberline normally appears as a treeless strip, often following a gully. Less active paths appear as strips of smaller trees, or strips of trees of a different species from those outside the path. From the air or from an opposing ridge, the runout zone may be outlined clearly by changes in vegetation.
• It is often impossible to enter large starting zones in the winter because of risk or inaccessibility. In those cases, the starting zone should be entered in summer to collect information not available from maps. Of particular interest are the slope angle and aspect.

Taking a break in South Dakota. One can see the potential avalanche zones on the distant slope.

Military
Avalanche Disasters
Large military disasters
occurred during World War I
when at least 40,000 men
died in avalanches in the Tyrol
and South Tyrol. It has been
estimated that during fighting
on the Austro-Italian front in
1916, as many as 9,000 to
10,000 troops were killed in a
single avalanche period of two
days duration.

ROUTE SELECTION

When planning a route under unknown circumstances ...

The problem is to grasp, in innumerable special cases, the actual situation which is covered by the mist of uncertainty, to appraise the facts correctly and to guess the unknown elements, to reach a decision quickly and then to carry it out forcefully and relentlessly.

Helmuth von Moltke, 1800–1891

CROSSING AN AVALANCHE PATH

If it is necessary to cross an avalanche path during a period of potential instability, it is better to move quickly across the runout zone rather than across the starting zone or track. This is because most avalanches are triggered by the victims.

If an emergency makes it necessary to cross a starting zone, improve your chances by the following strategies:

• While climbing to a ridge or saddle, enter the starting zone as high as possible. If the slab fractures, the chance are of ending up on the surface.

• When climbing or descending in a starting zone, try to keep to the flanks rather than the slab center. If the slab fractures, the flank snow tends to be deposited over the snow from the slab center. There is a better chance to escape by traversing out of the slab area.

• If there is a choice, favor starting zones that feed into flat, open runout zones, as opposed to gullies. There is a better chance for shallow burial on flat, open slopes.

• Avoid starting zones that feed into crevasses, cliffs, icefalls, and other terrain hazards.

• When TG instability is a possibility, choose a route that favors sun exposed areas over shaded areas.

• Avoid suspected areas of wind slab.

• Expect crown fractures to propagate between snowpack anchors such as rocks and trees; try to contour above the suspected fracture path.

Remove ski pole wrist straps...

Survival chances of a victim are improved if his hands are free. Wrist straps should be removed before entering an avalanche slope. Ski poles might be discarded when balance on skis becomes impossible. The removal of ski safety straps before entering a slope is debatable as first of all, the victim wants to keep his skis on long enough to get over to the flank. However, if the victim is carried down, the skis will flail against the body, compounding the injuries. There is also a chance that the skis will drag the victim under to a deeper burial. On the other hand, buried victims, have been found because part of a ski was on the surface or because a probe pole hit a buried ski.

BACK COUNTRY TRAVEL PRECAUTIONS

If a victim is completely buried there is statistically one chance in five of being found alive. The following information will try to improve a victim's chances:

Mountaineering Rope: A rope is often essential for crossing starting zones, especially where paths feed into gullies, crevasses, cliffs, etc. The rope may give protection against the forces of small powder avalanches but the dynamic forces of moderate to large avalanches far exceed the forces sustained in mountaineering falls. Avalanche forces are of much longer duration. To sustain these forces, the belay should be tied to a fixed anchor, such as a tree, rock, or rock pitons, rather than hand held. In an emergency, the belay may be supported by ice pitons, snow picket, or ice axe. A rope is especially useful in descending slopes where avalanches can be triggered to clear the descent route.

Probes & Shovels: Collapsible avalanche probes that fit into rucksacks can be purchased. As an alternative, some ski poles have removable baskets and can be attached together to make a probe about 3 m long. One or more strong, lightweight shovels should be taken on hazardous tours. Digging with skis and hands, it takes almost half an hour in typical avalanche debris to dig a hole 1.5 m deep and wide enough to give assistance to a buried victim. With a shovel it would take about 10 minutes.

Picking an Escape Route: Before starting across a slide path, study it and make a plan for escape should it fracture. When a slab fractures around and above a victim, the best chance is to escape to one side. If on skis, try to keep your balance and ski out the nearest flank exit. Keeping track of the escape route and react almost instantly when the slab fractures. The closer the victim gets to the flank, the better chance for a shallow burial. Very often the crown fracture occurs exactly along the victim's ski tracks, in which case an attempt should be made to hold a position above the moving slab.

Crossing Starting Zones: One person crosses at a time; the other members of the party watch from safe positions. When the first skier arrives at a safe location, he signals for the next to cross. Repeat the process until the entire party is at the safe location. Never assume that a slope is stable because one, two, three, or more people have crossed without triggering the slab. The first to cross may disturb the slab and initiate a relatively slow bed surface failure. The last to cross may trigger the final fractures.

Avalanche Beacon: A transceiver is a radio that can transmit and receive. It is the most effective safety device, and one should be carried by every avalanche worker and ski mountaineer. Before starting all members of the party should switch to transmit. If a member of the party is buried, the survivors switch to receive.

Avalanche Cord: Trailing out at least 15 m of brightly colored nylon cord. Avalanche cords are only partly reliable. Effectiveness of the avalanche cord is improved by attaching a small helium-filled balloon to the free end.

CURRENT & PAST AVALANCHES

Slopes with common aspect: Because loading is sensitive to wind direction, avalanches tend to occur on slopes that have a common aspect. For example, after a storm, it may be noticed that avalanche activity was most intense on southeast facing slopes. All southeast facing slopes that did not avalanche during the storm should then be suspected of instability.

Slopes with common elevation: Similarly, in an area that has a wide range of starting zone elevations, it may be observed that avalanche activity is confined to particular elevation zones. For example, the higher zones may be relatively inactive, but serious instability may exist at lower elevations. This phenomenon is usually caused by wind or temperature patterns.

Steepness: Most avalanches occur on slopes between 35°- 45°. Slopes below 30° seldom produce avalanches and slopes steeper than about 50° degrees frequently sluff so snow does not build up. Intermediate slopes produce most of the avalanches. A black diamond slope is usually around 35°.

Frequent and infrequent paths: This observation is most applicable to large avalanche paths that threaten highways and villages. Based on historical data, avalanche paths can be classified according to frequency. If frequent paths are moderately unstable, then instability can be expected on the infrequent paths. Conversely, if the frequent paths are stable, it is usually possible to evaluate as stable the infrequent paths.

Significant avalanches cannot occur until:
- Terrain irregularities such as boulders and brush are covered with snow.
- Additional snow is deposited on this smoothed foundation. For most paths, this requires about 1 m of snow in the starting zone and track. The exceptions are paths on permanent snowfields, smooth rock, dirt, grass, etc., where avalanches may run with perhaps 15 cm of coverage in the starting zone.

Thaw warnings: Small, wet avalanches of either the loose snow or slab type often give ample warning that free water is accumulating in the thawed snowpack. Wet avalanches of increasing size can be expected.

Repeaters: Once an avalanche path is activated, there is a good chance it will be reactivated later in the season. Many avalanche paths that are not active every avalanche season tend to run more than once in seasons when they are active. There is some evidence that the second avalanche on a path is usually larger than the first.

Sluffing: Visual observation may indicate that conditions were highly unstable during a storm and that small avalanches released to remove the instability. These avalanches may be obscured by additional snowfall.

VEGETATION & AVALANCHE FREQUENCY

Frequency - at least one avalanche in an interval of:

Frequency - at least one avalanche in an interval of:	Vegetation Clues
1-2 years	Bare patches, willows and shrubs, no trees higher than about 1 to 2 m. Broken timber.
2-10 years	Few trees higher than 1 to 2 m. Immature trees of disaster or pioneer species. Broken timber.
10-25 years	Predominantly pioneer species, young trees of the local climax species.
25-100 years	Mature trees of pioneer species, young trees of the local climax species.
100 years+	Increment core data.

TERRAIN & AVALANCHES

- There is a low avalanche probability if the ground surface is broken, serrated, or boulder strewn. This provides an anchor for the snowpack. Snow slides, breaking off at ground level, are unlikely.
- Smooth, even slopes of bare earth, solid rock, or shale favor massive ground level avalanches, typical of the high alpine zone.
- Contours of a mountain influence the avalanche. Terraces, talus, basins, and outcrops are effective barriers. They either divert the moving snow or give it room to spread out and lose its momentum.
- Gullies collect and channel the descending snow, making powerful slide paths which must be avoided.
- Ridges lying parallel to the slide path are relatively secure.
- On a concave surface, snow is under compression. The steepest part of the slope is generally near the top. The transition is more gradual and the anchorage at the toe is better than for a convex slope.
- The dimensions of the slope (length and width), are factors that determine the size of the snow slide and the possible destruction caused by it.
- The most important factor, of the terrain features, is the grade of the slope. The steeper the slope, the more likely it will cause a slide regardless of any other conditions. The minimum angle favorable to avalanches is 25°. Slopes from 25° to 35° may avalanche especially if disturbed by the cutting action of a skier or some other factor. The critical zone lies above 35°. From 35° to the angle where snow can no longer cling to the slope, except by wind packing, some form of snowslide is likely to occur with every storm.
- Vegetation of any kind, except grass, has a restraining effect on avalanches. The existence of heavy forest cover is an indication that slides in the location are rare or of minor importance. It is a mistake, however, to consider all forested areas as safe. Scattered timber is not a good deterrent. Slopes where the timber has been destroyed by fire or clear-cut has a good potential for slides.
- Slopes facing the sun favor avalanches produced by thawing.
- Loose snow avalanches are more common on slopes opposite the sun. North side of hills.
- Cornices form along ridges and crests lying at right angles to the prevailing wind.
- Lee slopes are the most probable locations for overloads of wind-driven snow and formation of a slab. Snow is blown from wind-beaten slopes and the remaining snow is packed and stabilized.

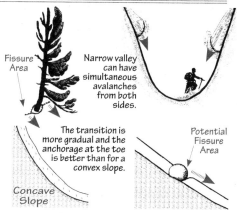

Narrow valley can have simultaneous avalanches from both sides.

The transition is more gradual and the anchorage at the toe is better than for a convex slope.

Concave Slope

Potential Fissure Area

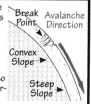

Avoid traveling on moraines as they are loose deposits, even large boulders can be unstable.

Potential avalanche slope. Do not travel in this area. Moraine

A convex slope is more likely to have avalanches because the snow layers are under tension. Avalanches usually fracture at the sharpest point on the curve, get up to full speed instantly, and pulverize rapidly. The steepest part of a convex slope is generally near the bottom, leading to a sudden transition and poor anchorage at the toe of the snow layer.

Break Point / Avalanche Direction / Convex Slope / Steep Slope

SNOWMOBILES & AVALANCHES

Snowmobilers should follow all the precautions of hikers and skiers while giving consideration for the speed of travel, weight, and vibration of the vehicle. The weight of the machine and driver leads to the following warnings:

- If a friend's snowmobile stalls do not "help" him by driving up to him as the weight of two machines will produce much stress on the snow layer. Only have one machine on a steep slope at a time.
- Do not drive up the center of a slope but follow the edge to escape a slab fracture.
- When traveling on ridges stay on the windward side. The snow will have been compacted by the wind and there will be less of an accumulation. Overhanging cornices can be a danger on the leeward side of a ridge.
- When cutting across a slope in the area of a possible start zone do not slow down because if a slide starts you will need your momentum to carry you off the moving snow.
- If high marking (high pointing) be very careful as you are attempting to climb a slope which is too steep for your snowmobile. This is also ideal terrain for avalanches. At the limit of your climb, when you are veering off making a near-stall turn, is when you exert the most static and vibration pressure on the snow. This is when you can trigger an avalanche. Your snowmobile also has a high probability of stalling.
- As the snowmobile is noisy you will not hear the possible airblast and downward rush of a slab avalanche overtaking you at 60 mph.

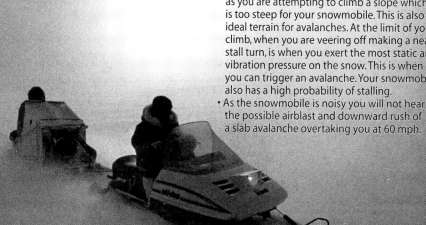

WEATHER — **AVALANCHE** (vertical side text)

LOCAL METEOROLOGICAL DATA

Field observations of snow buildup on or near avalanche release areas are often not feasible so it is necessary to rely on meteorological measurements. Indirect evidence of avalanche path loading can be inferred from precipitation measurements and ridge top wind measurements. The simplest way to use the numerical data furnished by instruments is to identify, for each path or group of paths, the following critical conditions:
• Wind directions that load the paths in question.
• Windspeed required for lee-slope loading (usually above 5 m/s)
• Critical precipitation intensity (e.g. 2 mm/h)
• Critical total water equivalent (e.g. 20 mm).

Each storm is monitored and analyzed. The slopes in question are evaluated as unstable when the four critical conditions are satisfied simultaneously. New data is incorporated continually to improve the choice of critical conditions.

For small paths, normally a threat in ski areas and on back-country tour routes, critical loading due to wind transport is always possible regardless of precipitation measurements. It is worthwhile to monitor ridge top windspeed and direction continually. Wind redistribution is greatest for a few days after a new snowfall, but transport may occur as long as the surface snow remains uncrusted.

AIR TEMPERATURE DURING STORM

Rising air temperature during a storm is considered an unstable trend, presumably because heavy snow is being deposited on lighter snow. Falling air temperature is considered a stable trend. In the north temperate zone, temperatures normally fall at the end of a storm, but when one storm follows on the tail of another, it is possible that some precipitation could fall at cold temperatures, and then the bulk of the precipitation could follow during the warmer temperatures of the next storm.

Snow Types

Some forms of snow are of benefit to the winter traveler, while others are a source of great danger.

Snow is a substance that follows a life cycle starting as falling snow and terminating as water. An in between step might even be ice.

OTHER METEOROLOGICAL FACTORS

Humidity: Controls how far a windblown snow grain can travel before sublimating. When relative humidity is high, wind transport of snow is more effective. When the air is dry, large amounts of blowing snow sublimate and never reach the lee slopes.

WET SNOW INSTABILITY

• Important variables to monitor, at least qualitatively, are rainfall, radiation, and air temperature. Heavy rain causes wet snow instability by adding weight, decreasing cohesion in the surface layers, and lubricating a potential bed surface. The amount of rain required for instability depends on the temperature of the top layers of the snowpack. If these layers are near 0° C before the rain, then relatively little rain can cause avalanches. Cold snowpacks have a high capacity for absorbing rain.
• Wet snow instability is most likely during the first warm-up (thaw) after a heavy snowfall. Wet snow instability should be expected after late spring and summer snowstorms. The delay between the end of the storm and the thaw can be estimated from the air temperature. If the air remained cold during the storm and then climbed slowly afterwards, instability may be delayed for several days. Air temperatures at high elevations can be estimated most of the time by subtracting 6°C per 1000 m of elevation above the elevation at which measurements are taken. Wet snow instability is most intense from mid afternoon, shortly after solar radiation reaches its peak. Melting is at first delayed, since the heat of fusion must be supplied. Once melting begins, the process accelerates because wet snow absorbs far more solar radiation than dry snow, and the onset of wet snow instability may seem to come rather rapidly. Similarly, wet snow instability may persist into late afternoon, until the melt water releases its heat of fusion.
• Usually, wet snow instability is confined to the most recently deposited layers, to a depth of about 1 m. Prolonged thawing occasionally triggers deeper or even full depth slabs. These deep, wet slabs may release almost any time during a prolonged thaw.

OLD SNOW SURFACE

A loose snow surface helps for good cohesion with a fresh fall but allows for a deeper avalanche if it starts. A crusted or wind packed surface means poor cohesion with the new snow, but restricts the avalanche to the new layer making for a shallower slide.

DEPTH OF NEW SNOW

10" (25 cm) of new snow is regarded as the minimum requirement to produce, by itself, an avalanche of dangerous proportions.

Types of new snow based upon free moisture content...

Very dry snow has low cohesion qualities and will readily avalanche so that it seldom builds up to a dangerous volume except under true blizzard conditions. The moisture in damp snow acts as a cement and improves cohesion. Wet snow is saturated with water that "lubricates" rather than cements Transition snow (on the dividing line between dry and damp) is especially susceptible to the formation of a slab under wind action. This is caused by the wind chill freezing the surface snow.

AVERAGE DENSITY & WATER CONTENT

The average density (water content per centimeter of snow) of dry snow varies from 0.06 -0.1" (0.15 - 0.25 cm) of water per 1" (2.5 cm) of new snow. Very dry snow, typical of the high alpine zones but found occasionally in other areas is much lighter with densities as low as 0.04" (0.10 cm). Damp and wet snow, in contrast, have a density as high as 0.14" (0.35 cm). These are normal densities and have little significance. When dry snow density exceeds 10%, its weight may be increasing faster than its cohesion strength and a slide may occur.

SNOWFALL INTENSITY

When the snow piles up at the rate of 1" (2.5 cm) or more per hour, the pack is growing faster than stabilizing forces, such as settlement, can take care of it. This sudden increase in load may fracture a lower slab and result in a slide.

PRECIPITATION INTENSITY

Based upon experience, a continuous precipitation intensity of 0.1" (0.25 cm) of water or more per hour with sufficient wind action, will cause the avalanche hazard to become critical when the total water precipitation reaches 1" (2.54 cm).

DEPTH & CONDITION OF BASE

A 24" (60 cm) depth is generally sufficient to cover ground obstructions and provide a smooth sliding base. Greater depths will obliterate such major natural barriers as terraces, gullies, outcrops, and clumps of small trees. If the bottom snow layer consists of granular snow (depth hoar), the slope is dangerous because the snow pack has no anchorage at its underside. This can be compared to the snow sitting on ball bearings. Depth hoar is usually at the bottom of the snowpack, and can be detected by reversed ski-pole probes, or digging vertical trenches.

Avalanche
Snow Shovel
Ortovox™

WEATHER & AVALANCHE HAZARDS

	Snowpack Change	Potential Avalanche Hazard
Rainfall	Impact of water absorption rate of snowpack.	Too much water can create a lubrification layer for avalanche.
Temperature change	Temperature increases during storm.	Destabilizing as heavy wet snow on light earlier snow.
Wind	Wind direction and intensity affects snow deposit.	Snow airborne: Dry Snow 10 mph. Looose Snow 25 mph. Eddies 35 mph.
Old snow inside	Snow structure visible by snow pit method. Can assess risk.	The old snow will include depth hoar which can cause structural instability.
Old snow surface	Usually hoar on surface.	How will new snow adhere to old weathered crystalline substructure.
Settlement	Weather condition impacts on compacting.	Slow settlement shows potential unstable snow layer structure.
Snowfall	Much snow adds to weight on substructure.	Destabilization of snowpack as it does not have time to settle.
New snowfall	Weight of new snow & slope overloading.	New tension points created by the weight of the new snow.
New snow type	Interaction of new snow layer with older snow.	Potential avalanche risk of new snow type and layer development.
New snow density	Instability created by the weight of the new snow.	Heavy snow on top of light snow leads to failure and avalanche.

SETTLEMENT OF SNOW

Snow settlement is continuous and with one exception it is always a stabilizing factor. The exception is shrinkage of a lower loose snow layer detaching it from a slab thus depriving it of support. In new snow a settlement ratio less than 15% indicates that little consolidation is taking place; above 30%, stabilization is proceeding rapidly. Over a long period ordinary snow layers shrink up to 90%, but slab layers may shrink no more than 60%. Abnormally low shrinkage in a layer indicates that a slab is forming.

WIND ACTION

Wind action is an important factor contributing to avalanches. It overloads certain slopes at the expense of others, it grinds snow crystals to simpler and less cohesive forms, it forms stable crusts and fragile slabs, often side by side. Warm wind ("Chinook" of North America and the "Foehn" of Europe) is an effective thawing agent, even more than sunlight. By sudden changes in direction and velocity, wind can act as a shearing trigger on a layer of snow it has just deposited. At 10 mph dry snow can be transported. At 25 mph snow is airborne and at 35 mph eddies can develop on the lee side of hills. This builds up avalanche hazards.

TEMPERATURE

Temperature directly influences the type of snow. Dry snow normally falls at 25°F (4°C) and below. Temperatures above 28° F (-2.2°C) promote rapid settlement and the metamorphosis of the snow is sometimes too rapid. A sudden rise of temperature causes a loss of cohesion fast enough to trigger an avalanche. A sudden drop increases tension.

NEW SNOW STABILITY

Humidity, Temperature, Crystal Form

It is possible to generalize the effects that humidity, temperature, and crystal form have on the stability of new snow. The unstable pattern seems to be a relatively heavy on strong layer over a relatively light or weak layer. This pattern might be generated by:

- Rising temperatures during a storm
- Lightly rimed or rime free crystals falling early in the storm, followed by a thick layer of heavily rimed crystals.
- Initial deposition during light winds, followed by rising winds toward the end of the storm.

Finally, it must be emphasized that humidity, temperature, wind, and the form of snow crystals are at best secondary compared to precipitation and its transport. Proof of this is that 90% of all avalanche activity occurs during or shortly after storms.

Potential avalanche start areas.

Emergency Snow Shelter

AVALANCHE PATHS

PATH OF AVALANCHE

Once set in motion, avalanches can move great distances. The larger avalanche paths in North America are about 3000 m long and have a vertical drop of about 1800 m. The average inclination for most avalanche paths that extend for a long distance is between 20°- 35°. Avalanche paths are divided into three sections: starting zone, track, and runout zone.

STARTING ZONE

It must be steeper than about 30° and receive large amounts of snow. Snow comes from:

- Wind direction if the slope is in the lee of a source of blowing snow or if the lee slope is an efficient collector of snow.
- Gullies and bowls are especially efficient collectors and make up a large proportion of the most active starting zones.
- Buttresses and flat, exposed faces are less efficient collectors and therefore less likely to contain active starting zones. However, when large amounts of snow are deposited with little or no wind, normally inactive and exposed starting zones may become active.
- The most active starting zones are gullies bounded at the top by horseshoe ridges or cliffs.
- Most starting zones are bare of trees, some have sparse timber, and a few contain stands of fairly dense timber. In the last case, slab fracture may spread into the timber from the clearing.

AVALANCHE TRACKS ZONE

The path between the starting zone at the top and the runout zone at the bottom. Avalanche tracks have an inclination of at least 15°; and more commonly, 20° - 25°.

Two categories:

Channeled Tracks: Gullies, couloirs, gulches, etc., with or without summer streams.

Unconfined Tracks: On slopes on open plains. Most of the longer avalanche tracks in the United States are channeled, because the confining action of the channel tends to concentrate the flow and propel the moving snow efficiently.

AVALANCHE TRACK: SEVERAL BRANCHES

Usually a main channeled track fed by several small tracks, each beginning at a separate starting zone. Multibranched tracks may have several avalanches in quick succession, as each branch empties into the main track. Fatal accidents have occurred when workers clearing the debris of a first avalanche were struck by a second that ran down the same track within hours of the first.

DRY AVALANCHES: FOLLOW STRAIGHT LINES

Where a gully makes an abrupt turn, the fast-moving "snow dust cloud" of a dry avalanche may jump the gully walls and continue on its straight line path.

WET AVALANCHES: FLOW

Wet avalanches flow more slowly and are easily channeled to follow curved gullies. Although starting zones must have the required steepness, avalanche tracks may include gentle slopes or even level terrain. The runout zone is usually the valley floor, but it may in extreme cases extend uphill.

AVALANCHE RUNOUT ZONE

The runout zone is the end boundary of the path. It is difficult to be certain of this boundary due to the great variation in weather from one winter to the next. It is possible that two large avalanches take the same path in fairly rapid succession. The second avalanche might exceed the known boundaries because it flows down a track and across a runout zone smoothed by the first avalanche, A series of avalanches may gradually force a path through a forest stand that previously stopped avalanches. Once most of the timber is destroyed, a major avalanche can break through and continue into a formerly protected area.

Avalanche Size Chart

Five Level Scale (US 1996)
Categories are relative to the width of the path which a slide could fill.

Scale	Name	Size
1	Sluff	any slide running < 50 meters
2	Small	relative to the path
3	Medium	relative to the path
4	Large	relative to the path
5	Major or Maximum	relative to the path

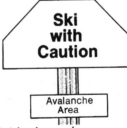

Ski with Caution

Avalanche Area

Individual members or a group traveling over a potential avalanche zone trigger 95% of avalanches in which they are caught.

LIMITS OF RUNOUT ZONE

In general runout zones on slopes of 5° - 10° can extend 300 to 500 m. To determine the limits of the runout zone, it is necessary to account for the airblast caused by the moving snow. Airblast zones may extend 100 m beyond the boundaries of a major avalanche path.

RUNOUT SNOW DEPOSIT

The snow deposited in the runout zone is about two or three times denser than the starting-zone snow, and it is much harder. While moving down the track, some of the snow is pulverized into fine particles. When the mass comes to rest, the fine particles and the larger pieces sinter (coagulate) rapidly to form a very firm aggregate. Wet avalanche debris is hard and ice-like, probably due to the refreezing of pressure-induced melt water. To dig into the debris of a large wet snow avalanche requires a pickax and shovel.

AVALANCHE VELOCITY

Many avalanches have been clocked, and typical speeds seem to be in the range of 25 - 75 m/s. Avalanches have reached speeds up to 125 m/s. These speeds are higher than would be expected on the basis of a balance between the pull of gravity and frictional drag resistance of the snow surface and the air. Large avalanches might adjust their shapes to minimize drag and that friction is minimized by an air-cushion effect. Speeds in excess of 30 m/s are observed only for large, dry avalanches with well-developed snow dust clouds. If an avalanche is very wet, it moves along the snow surface as a slurry with little or no snow dust cloud. The speed of wet-snow avalanches is typically in the range of 5 - 30 m/s; the higher limit is approached only by very large, wet avalanches.

AVALANCHE IMPACT PRESSURE

An avalanche moving at 50 m/s the maximum impact pressure at the snow surface is about 25 t/m²; impact pressure at the top of the snow dust cloud is about 2.5 t/m².

From the viewpoint of engineering design, avalanche impact pressures represent an extremely high external load; even concrete structures require substantial reinforcement.

AVALANCHE DAMAGE

Avalanches cause damage in several ways from the direct thrust of the avalanche impact pressure. In addition, avalanches may exert upward and downward forces. They have been known to lift up and move large locomotives, road graders, and buildings. The airblast of a fast-moving avalanche (speed in excess of 30 m/s) may exert pressures up to about 0.5 t/m². Airblasts can destroy doors, windows, and poorly designed roofs. There are also reports that an airblast has induced lung injuries. The strongest airblast effects are confined to within 100 m of the observed boundary of the snow dust cloud. As a very rough rule, the extension of the airblast is about equal to the height of the snow dust cloud. Slow-moving wet avalanches that cling to the snow surface have no airblast.

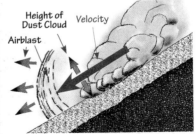

Height of Dust Cloud
Velocity
Airblast

19 Avalanche

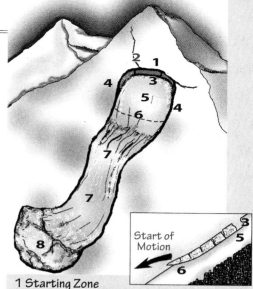

PROTECTIVE MEASURES

Areas which are considered hazardous may be placed "off limits". This may affect only a few narrow avalanche paths, or an entire valley, or several valleys depending upon the terrain and weather conditions.

SKIING STABILIZATION

Constant use of the hazardous slide path area prevents the snow from building up into avalanche conditions. The work is done by teams of expert skiers (2 and 3 on each team). Great care, coordination between teams, and supervision must be exercised because of the dangerous nature of the work.

EXPLOSIVES

Under extremely dangerous conditions it may be safer to stabilize the snow by using hand placed charges. Huge cornices are blasted by digging charges into the snow along the probable fracture line. Individuals digging holes and placing charges must be belayed (supported with rope) while working.

ARTILLERY, ROCKETS & INFANTRY WEAPONS

Artillery pieces can be used to trigger an avalanche. Due to the difficulty of moving artillery pieces off the road or over secondary mountain trails, recoilless rifles can be used. When aircraft are used the pilot selects suitable slopes and makes the snow slide by using guns, rockets or a sonic boom.

USE OF BARRIERS

Lines of communication and fixed installations, under avalanche threat, can be protected by the construction of avalanche barriers. Barriers can be formed by adding rocks and earth, concrete, or other similar materials to natural obstacles.

HIGHWAY ACCIDENTS

Largest number of accidents are suffered by highway maintenance crews. Avalanche hazard signs should be posted in danger areas and motorists should not stop in these zones.

Avalanche Hitting Buildings

Lodges and condominiums built in avalanche paths or runout zones can be destroyed.

Railroad Accidents

Avalanches can cover tracks in the Canadian Rockies.

Miscellaneous Accidents

Avalanches have struck snowmobilers, utility servicemen, hunters, and dam construction workers. Families have been buried while playing in the runout zones of avalanche paths.

SIGNS OF STRUCTURAL INSTABILITY

Propagation of Fractures: This is the most direct evidence of new snow instability. The deeper and more extensive the fracturing, the more unstable the new snow. Fracture propagation of one ski length or more generally indicates structural instability.

Collapse Noise: Sudden collapsing sounds in the snow cover might be clearly audible without fractures being observed, This effect can be observed on horizontal as well as inclined slopes. It indicates a weak structure and extreme instability. The exception is collapse noises from the fracture of very thin surface crusts in the spring which are usually harmless.

Hard Surfaces: It is necessary to distinguish between wind scoured slopes and deep, hard deposits in lee pockets. Wind scoured surfaces are identified by eroded features and are generally not an avalanche problem. Hard deposits in lee pockets may be quite unstable. When skis cannot penetrate a lee deposit, the tester should suspect hard slab instability, and should further investigate the structure by digging a pit to search for the combination of a hard slab over a weak substratum.

Very Unstable Thin Slabs: Occasionally, test skiing shows that the new snow is extremely unstable but that the instability is confined to a thin surface slab less than 15 cm thick. These thin slabs are comparatively harmless but avalanche activity can be expected when new deposits build on this weakness.

AVALANCHE ACCIDENT CATEGORIES

Back Country Accidents

These are the largest number of fatalities in North America. The victims are usually ski groups, helicopter skiers, or mountaineers. In almost all cases, the victims triggered their own avalanche while crossing the starting zone. In a few rare cases, the avalanche was triggered naturally and swept into the touring party lower down in the track or runout zone. In a few cases, the avalanche overran a camp area and buried victims in their tents. These accidents can be traced to a combination of inexperience, bad luck, and losing on a calculated risk.

Ski Area Accidents

Skiers skiing on a restricted trail could enter a dangerous area. Ski patrol accidents can occur as a result of carelessness or error. A patroller should have used explosives instead of skiing the slope. Or the patroller used explosives - the avalanche test proved negative but the avalanche released when the patroller skied down the slope.

1 Starting Zone
2 Trigger   6 Staunchwall obliterated by slide.
3 Crown   7 Track of Slide
4 Flanks   8 Runout Area & Debris
5 Bed Surface

UNITED STATES AVALANCHE SAFETY BASICS

- Avalanches don't happen by accident and most human involvement is a matter of choice, not chance.
- Most avalanche accidents are caused by slab avalanches which are triggered by the victim or a member of the victim's party.
- Any avalanche may cause injury or death and even small slides may be dangerous.
- Always practice safe route selection skills,
- Be aware of changing conditions and carry avalanche rescue gear.
- Learn to analyze snow stability evaluation techniques to help minimize your risk. Apply the required precautions.
- Remember that avalanche danger rating levels are only general guidelines.
- Changes in geographic areas, elevations, slope aspect, and slope angle might be transition zones between danger.
- No matter what the current avalanche danger, there are avalanche-safe areas in the mountains.

Five Level Canadian Avalanche Scale				
Size	Description	Mass	Length	Impact Pressure
1	Relatively harmless	<10 tons	10 meters	1 kPa
2	Bury, injure, or kill a person	100 tons	100 meters	10 kPa
3	Bury a car, destroy a small building, or break trees	1000 tons	1000 meters	100 kPa
4	Destroy a rail car	10,000 tons	2000 meters	500 kPa
5	Largest known	100,000 tons	3000 meters	1000 kPa

Outline of United States Avalanche Danger Indicators

Danger Level & Color	Probability & Avalanche Trigger	Types of Avalanche Danger	Recommended Activity
LOW (green)	Travel generally safe. Human trigger - unlikely	Natural trigger - very unlikely. Isolated areas of instability.	Generally stable snow. Normal caution.
MODERATE (yellow)	Natural trigger - unlikely. Human triggered-possible.	Unstable slabs possible on steep terrain.	Use caution in steeper terrain on certain aspects
MODERATE to HIGH (orange)	Natural trigger - possible. Human triggered - probable.	Unstable slabs probable on steep terrain.	Be increasingly cautious in steeper terrain.
HIGH (red)	Natural & human triggered avalanches likely.	Unstable slabs likely on a variety of aspects and slope angles.	Travel in avalanche terrain is not recommended. Safest travel on windward ridges of lower angle slopes without steeper terrain above.
EXTREME (black)	Widespread natural or human triggered avalanches certain.	Extremely unstable. Slabs certain on most aspects & slope angles. Large destructive avalanches possible.	Travel in avalanche terrain should be avoided and confined to low angle terrain well away from avalanche path run-outs.

Test Skiing

If the slope can be free tested, the standard procedure is for the tester to enter at one corner, under the watchful supervision of a second tester. The first tester skis diagonally down and across the crown region, bounding and thrusting his skis to add extra stress to the slope. The line of travel begins in a safe spot outside the starting zone, crosses the starting zone, and ends in a safe place. After the first tester arrives at the end of the diagonal, roles switch, and the first tester watches the second tester come across. The second tester traverses a slightly lower line. Testing may then continue diagonally down and back across the slope. A slope should not be judged absolutely stable on the basis of one or two ski traverses.

A good habit in skiing all avalanche paths, regardless of their apparent stability, is to end ski runs at the side of the path. Stopping to rest in the middle of the path should be avoided. In many cases skiers have been trapped because the crown fractured above them while they stood resting in the middle of the slope.

Limitations of Ski Tests

- Ski tests involve risk and require strict safety precautions. Should not be used where the skier may be exposed to the severe forces of large moving stabs.
- Although ski tests are the most reliable way to measure the stability of surface layers, they do not give a reliable measure of hard slab conditions nor of deep instability.
- Ski tests cannot practically be used on remote slopes.

Ski Testing Procedure & Safety Precautions

Performing and interpreting tests are skills that are developed by experience. Ski tests can be made "belayed" or "free." In belayed skiing, the tester is tied to a rope that is anchored to a secure point, such as a tree or lift tower. In free test skiing, the tester moves across the slope without the protection of a rope.

The following precautions apply:

- All test skiing on avalanche paths should be observed by a second person.
- Test skiing parties should carry transceivers and collapsible probes.
- Free test skiing should be strictly limited to those slopes where an avalanche ride could not have consequences.
- Test skiers should never enter a dangerous slope unbelayed on the assumption that they can ski across the slope fast enough to avoid being trapped.
- Before entering the slope, the tester should have his transceiver in the transmit position. The transceiver be turned on when the tester gathers his equipment in the morning and left on all day.
- For belayed test skiing, 11 mm mountaineering rope should be used. The tester should be tied around the waist with two or more loops knotted by a bowline knot on the coil; the rope must be anchored to a strong fixed point, such as a tree or lift tower. There should be as little slack as possible in the rope.
- Standard belays that are acceptable in rock climbing may not hold against the steady forces of snow pounding on a body. In any case, test skiing should not be performed where there is danger of such large forces against the tester's body.
- Test skiers should move as quickly as possible between safe points, and they should never stop in the middle of the slope.
- Test skiing should not be performed if there is any possible hazard to people in the track or runout zone.
- Regardless of precipitation amounts, test skiing should not be performed on large paths that have not been thoroughly ski packed before the new snow loading. No test should be done if not done safely.

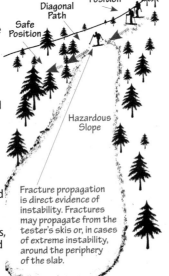

Safe Position
Diagonal Path
Safe Position
Hazardous Slope

Fracture propagation is direct evidence of instability. Fractures may propagate from the tester's skis or, in cases of extreme instability, around the periphery of the slab.

Limitations of Test Skiing

Limitations are: hazard to testers on large slopes, difficulty for evaluating deep slab instability, and difficulty for evaluating conditions on remote slopes.

Avalanche Survival Chances

There is a slight chance of survival if the avalanche carries you towards a clump of thick trees, deposits you in a deep gully, or carries you over a cliff. Survival chances are best if you are caught in a small avalanche path with a gentle sloping run-out path.

Small Avalanche Fatalities

Almost 50% of fatal accidents resulted from slides that ran less than 100 m. Small slides can kill as easily as large slides. The danger is determined not only by the length of the path but also by the terrain; a relatively small avalanche can produce a deep burial in gully terrain.

Partially Buried

Are avalanche victims covered by snow anywhere from the ankle to the neck when the avalanche stops.

Avalanche Shock Waves

Shock waves sometimes precede avalanches although destructive ones are not common. In certain slope environments airblasts occur more regularly. Airblasts may project its effect 100 yards (100 m) beyond the path of the slide. Airblasts rarely cause accidents.

Conditions Causing Avalanches

Mechanical and weather properties of snow that might cause avalanche are:

Terrain: Slope less than 30° : rare.
Slopes between 35°-45° and smooth slope with minor obstructions produce most avalanches. Slopes over 50° do not accumulate much snow because of sluffing.

Old Snow Depth: enough to cover ground obstructions which would retain the snow.

Surface Crusted: normally only new snow will slide.

Surface Loose: good cohesion between layers and both old and new snow may slide.

New Snow Depth: 10 inches (25 cm) or more.

Snowfall Intensity: 1" (2.5 cm) per hour or more is not uncommon. This can be assumed when snowfall is heavy enough to restrict visibility to 300-600 ft (100-200 m).

Precipitation Intensity: 0.01" (0.25 cm) or more per hour of water plus strong winds. This can be assumed if snowfall intensity is 1" (2.5 cm) per hour and snow is damp or noticeably heavy. Dry snow by comparison is of granular or pellet form. Rainfall may fall on the snow in coastal zones creating avalanche conditions.

Settlement: noticeably low. Watch the snow collars around the trees or posts.

Wind: an average of 15 knots or higher. This can be assumed if snow is blown parallel or almost parallel to the ground. Wind action during storms, in the mountains, is generally strong and its influence on snow is an important contributory factor for avalanches. It transports snow from one exposed area to another during storms and fair weather, this increases overloads on certain slopes. It also modifies the size and shape of snow particles.

Temperature: sudden changes up or down can cause avalanches, for example, a thawing temperature day and night for 36 hours and no overnight freezing. Temperature greatly affects the cohesion of snow; a rise in temperature slows settlement of the snow mass and increases the brittleness and tension of slab formation. Temperature fluctuates widely and rapidly in the mountains. Prolonged spells of extremely low temperatures occur and there might be occasional intrusions of warm air masses, usually in connection with a new storm.

Depth Hoar: Must be assumed on any avalanche slope in the high alpine zone.

Collapsing Snow: Air spaces in buried snow can collapse and give off a "whumph" sound. This sound indicates an unstable area and cracks might shoot out on the surface above this area. As the whumpf has a very low frequency sound it can be heard over a large distance - indicating potential trouble and extreme instability.

A skier triggering a slab avalanche.

Snow Saw

Avalanche Accidents

If Caught in an Avalanche

There are certain actions that can be taken which will greatly increase your chance of survival and recovery.

Shout: As you see or feel an avalanche starting. This will let the group know where you might be carried. Once an avalanche is moving it can be very noisy and drown out a call.

DON'T PANIC: Maintain self-control and attempt to stay on the surface and get out of the main slide path.

Do not outrun avalanche: If in the middle of the slope, do not try to outrun an avalanche but ski to the side. An avalanche can travel at 30 mph. Try to avoid the main mass of the slide.

Crumbling snow: If the snow crumbles below your feet, run uphill, grab a tree. You might reach a safe area above the avalanche area.

Lighten up: Get rid of your skis, ski poles, backpack if caught in an avalanche and unable to make a flank exit.

Stay on feet: As long as possible and if swept away, keep mouth shut and breath through your nose while "swimming" to the surface.

Swimming: Attempt to stay above the snow by swimming. The swimming motion should be as efficient as possible so that the victim is neither winded at the bottom nor choked by snow.

Thrust up hand: If snow starts to slow down and pile up on the victim at the end of the fall, thrust a hand up as high as possible before the snow settles in. A few victims owe their lives to having a hand above the snow. The other arm and hand should be in front of the chest and face to form an air pocket. It is important that you make these moves before the snow starts "to set" or harden.

Conserving oxygen: In order to conserve oxygen, the victim should relax and not fight the sensation of blackout.

Keep calm: Shout only if you hear members of your group

Survival Time

Statistics show that the victim's chance of survival diminishes rapidly with burial time and depth of burial.

- Statistically, after half an hour of burial, the victim's chance of surviving is about 50%.
- A victim often cannot survive a 15-minute burial in an unfavorable position (snow packed tightly around mouth and nose). After the stoppage of breath, a person loses consciousness in about 45 to 120 seconds.
- Brain damage occurs in about 4 minutes, and after 8 minutes, survival is unlikely even if it were possible to restore breathing and circulation.
- If the victim is buried in a favorable position, without snow packed tightly around mouth and nose, survival can last many hours.

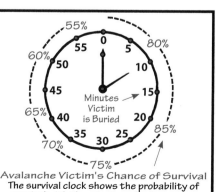

Avalanche Victim's Chance of Survival
The survival clock shows the probability of survival with the minutes of submersion.

Urgency in Finding Victim

If an individual is caught by an avalanche, prompt and organized rescue operations offer the only hope of getting the victim out alive.

The concept of probability is important to the design of search operations. The object is to optimize the victim's chance for survival. There is a double requirement for success. The victim must be found, and the victim must be found alive. A slow and thorough search could be organized which would almost guarantee finding the victim, but the chances of finding him alive would be remote. There are records of people who lived as long as 72 hours while buried. Ordinarily, the victims are either killed instantly by crushing, or die within a short time from exposure, shock, and suffocation.

One hour is the average survival time.

- Wait for avalanche to stop and the area is safe.
- Establish from witnesses where the victim was located just prior to the avalanche, then determine the point where the victim disappeared - the "last seen" point. Mark this position with a pole. Making use of this and any other information, establish a probable victim trajectory line leading to high priority search areas.

See section on Establishing Victim's Probable Location - Page 238.

Small Avalanche Fatalities

Almost 50% of fatal accidents resulted from slides that ran less than 100 m. Small slides can kill as easily as large slides. The danger is determined not only by the length of the path but also by the terrain; a relatively small avalanche can produce a deep burial in gully terrain.

Probable Location of Victim

In most cases the victim is carried by the moving avalanche to the places of greatest snow deposition, usually the toe of the slide. Occasionally he is snared by rocks, trees, or benches in the terrain. If the avalanche follows a wandering gully, all bends with snow deposits are likely burial places; again, the victim is likely to be where the greatest amount of snow is deposited. Finally, the victim may be thrown out of the slide. In a few cases, victims have been found dangling from trees.

Survival Chances

There is a slight chance of survival if the avalanche carries you towards a clump of thick trees, deposits you in a deep gully, or carries you over a cliff.

Survival chances are best if you are caught in a small avalanche path with a gentle sloping run-out path.

Rescue Action

A buried victim's chance for survival depends on what the surviving members of the party do in the first few minutes. If the survivors were standing in a safe place they could watch the victim's path. The survivors should search with whatever resources are available. If the victim is not wearing a beacon, the survivors must probe with skis, poles, collapsible avalanche probes, improvised probes made from tree branches, etc. Only if the touring party is large or if additional manpower is a few minutes away should a messenger be spared and sent for help. There are many instances of survivors leaving the scene in panic to seek help when a search of a few minutes would have uncovered the victim.

Two Ways Avalanche Victims Die

Suffocation: The majority of avalanche fatalities are due to suffocation. In a typical avalanche burial, little air is trapped in the space around the victim, and it is a matter of time before the victim loses consciousness and dies. Inhaling snow that blocks the airways, suffocating, can be caused by the hard setting of the snow when it stops moving. Wet snow might freeze and form heavy ice, restricting breathing by limiting the expansion of the chest. The victim is immobilized by the packed snow and must helplessly await his fate.

Traumatic Injuries: Physical injuries that occur during an avalanche - violent action of the snow: thrown against outcrops, trees, snow slabs: pushed over cliffs: If victim is still alive he will need immediate medical attention.

Killed by Moving Avalanche

Some victims are killed outright or severely injured by the moving avalanche. The victim may be dashed into a tree or building or hit by flying debris. Head injuries, abdominal injuries, and broken necks, backs, and legs are common. Possible lung injuries caused by avalanche pressure forces. Some victims die of hypothermia, exhaustion, or shock. Less than 20% of the victims buried with no trace showing are recovered alive.

Effort of the victim to extricate himself by vigorous motion and "swimming" will minimize the burial depth.

The closer the victim's trajectory is to the center of the slide, the greater will be the burial depth.

Ordinarily, the victim is either killed instantly by crushing, or dies within a short period from exposure, shock, and suffocation. One hour is the average survival time.

The concept of probability is important to the design of search operations. The victim must be found, and the victim must be found alive.

The victim may not be buried but may have been hurled away from the avalanche by the wind blast. In the case of a large and violent avalanche, a search of the surrounding terrain is advisable.

Avalanche victims who are rescued alive must be evacuated under the care of medical personnel by the most expeditious means available.

The likelihood of a victim being buried in a particular location or bend is proportional to the amount of debris deposited at that location. The more debris, the increased probability of the body being there.

Collapsible Avalanche Shovel

Survival Chances

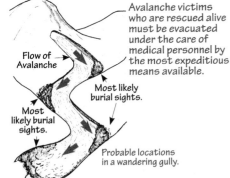

Last Sighting Point

Line of Flow

Probable Location of Victim

Location of victim established by the trajectory of the last points of sighting.

Effects of terrain on the location of a victim.

Most likely sites.

Bench or other obstacle that decelerates the flow of the snow. This can be a levelling off of the slope, trees, shrubs, rock moraine, buildings, or fences.

Avalanche victims who are rescued alive must be evacuated under the care of medical personnel by the most expeditious means available.

Flow of Avalanche

Most likely burial sights.

Most likely burial sights.

Probable locations in a wandering gully.

MOST PROBABLE LOCATIONS BASED ON TERRAIN

A moving avalanche can be compared to a fluid. A human body with a higher density can be expected to sink into the avalanche. But as a human body is bulky it might be thrown toward the surface or the sides. Many factors actually affect the location of the body. Turbulence, terrain shape, and the victim's effort to surface himself all interact to determine the final burial position.

Study of a large number of cases leads to the following conclusions.

- The majority of buried victims are carried to the place of greatest deposition, usually the toe of the slide.
- If two points of the victim's trajectory can be established, a high probability exists that the victim will be near the downhill flow line.
- Any terrain features that catch and hold avalanche debris are also apt to catch a victim.
- If an avalanche follows a wandering gully, all bends that show debris are likely burial spots. The likelihood of a victim being buried in a particular bend is proportional to the amount of debris deposited there.
- Vegetation, rocks and other obstacles act as snares. The victim tends to be retained above the obstacle. An obstacle may simply delay the victim's motion, leading to final burial down stream from the obstacle.
- Maximum speed of the flowing snow occurs at the avalanche's center. Friction reduces the flow's velocity along the edges. The closer the victim's trajectory is to the center of the slide, the greater will be the burial depth.
- Effort of the victim to extricate himself by vigorous motion and "swimming" minimizes burial depth. Conversely the limp body of an unconscious victim is likely to be buried deep.
- The victim may not be buried but may have been hurled away from the avalanche by the wind blast. In the case of a large and violent avalanche, a search of the surrounding terrain is advisable.
- If the victim is found and is unconscious artificial respiration must be administered at once.

NO BEACONS USED

Making use of any available information (see - Most Probable Location Based on Terrain), establish a probable victim trajectory line leading to high priority search areas. Make a rapid but systematic check of the avalanche debris surface and mark all clues. At signs of equipment, clothing or an avalanche cord, make an initial random probe of the high priority areas. A long pole or ski poles are used for probing. Rapidly make as many probe holes as possible as time is of essence. If there are no clues, make a coarse probe of all likely areas of burial. Repeat the coarse probe as long as a live rescue remains possible.

NO BEACON: BLIND PROBE FOR VICTIM

Compared to locating with a beacon, blind probing is a slow and tedious method of search. It is the only practical method if the victim is not carrying a beacon and if a search dog is not available.

FIRST STEPS IN PROBING FOR VICTIM

Making a speedy rescue may be hazardous to the rescuers. The avalanche proves there is instability on neighboring slopes. Precautions are taken to safeguard rescuers, including a lookout in a safe spot to watch for and warn probers of additional avalanches.

The search moves quickly and efficiently through the following steps:

- Wait for avalanche to stop and the area is safe.
- Establish from witnesses where the victim was located just prior to the avalanche, then determine the point where the victim disappeared - the "last seen" point. Mark this position with a pole. Making use of this and any other information, establish a probable victim trajectory line leading to high priority search areas.
- Determine the area where each victim disappeared, the "last-seen area."
- If the victim's disappearance was not seen, examine for clues as ski tracks, jettisoned clothing, etc.
- Using this information, establish probable trajectories for each victim.
- Determine the areas of highest priority search (usually a rough estimate).
- Make a rapid but systematic search of the avalanche debris surface in the regions of highest priority. Mark the location of all clues. Searching the surface is the first part of the probing operation, and it offers the greatest probability of a live rescue.

Avalanche Area

Most Likely Burial Areas

Victim's Last Sighting

Footprints: Victim might have walked out injured.

Possible Burial Area

Victim's Last Sighting

Possible Burial Area

Gully Sides

Victim's Last Sighting

Bench on Road

Possible Burial Area

Victim's Last Sighting

Victim Pined in Obstacles

Possible Burial Area

Victim Pined in Obstacles

WHERE TO PROBE

Since there is usually a shortage of manpower during the initial and critical phase of the probing operation, it is necessary to decide which areas have the highest priority for search and in what order these areas will be probed. The decision involves weighing the approximate probability that a victim is in a given area versus the relative time required to search that area. Normally, initial search is made of the main debris area, since this area can be searched most efficiently with the greatest chance of success. However, there may be clues that indicate a high probability that the victim was snared above the main debris or perhaps that the victim has escaped the slide. In such cases, manpower should be allocated to follow up the clues.

Avalanche Probe
Ortovox™

AVALANCHE PROBE

Assemble the probe segments by shaking with a throwing motion. Then pull strongly on the cord and put the knot into the fastener's slot. Secure the cord by tightening the nut.

ORGANIZING PROBERS

- Immediately after completing the surface search, rescuers should be organized into probe lines, using whatever probe equipment is available. Ideally, probe poles should consist of rigid steel or aluminum tubing, 3 - 4 m long. Longer poles are difficult to manage. The chance for making a live rescue of a victim buried deeper than 3 m is extremely small. The advantage to standardizing probe length, is to make it more obvious to the probe leader when one probe is stopped short of full probe depth by an obstacle.
- Probing is simple and requires very little practice. It is easy to feel the difference between striking a body and striking a snow layer; the real problem is discriminating between the ground surface and a deeply buried victim. Before starting to probe the avalanche debris, the probers should be briefed on their mission and given directions for evacuating quickly.
- Probe lines must be ordered and properly spaced for probing to be effective. About 20 probers per line is satisfactory, and 30 is an upper limit. If extra manpower is available, a person can be placed at each end of the line to hold a string for aligning the probers. The string should be marked to help properly space the probers.
- The probe line advances steadily upslope. Advancing uphill automatically helps set the proper pace and keeps order. Even so, proper spacing and discipline often become a problem after probing has continued for some time. Downhill probing is more difficult to control, although, if the rescue team approaches from above, the initial surface search can proceed downslope. Probing does not come to a halt when a possible strike is made. The probe line continues to advance, and a small crew falls out and shovels down to investigate the strike.

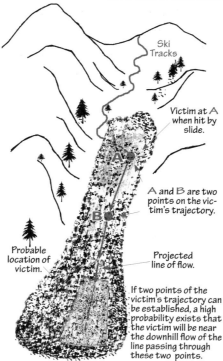

Ski Tracks

Victim at A when hit by slide.

A and B are two points on the victim's trajectory.

Probable location of victim.

Projected line of flow.

If two points of the victim's trajectory can be established, a high probability exists that the victim will be near the downhill flow of the line passing through these two points.

SAFETY & RESCUE SUFFOCATION OF VICTIM

The weight of the snow bears down on the victim's throat and chest further accelerating respiratory failure.

FINDING PROBABILITY WITH COARSE PROBE

The spacing of the probe holes is 75 by 70 cm, which is equivalent to 1.9 probes per M^2.

The chances for direct strike of victim are:
- Person on stomach or back 95%
- Person on side 75%
- Person in vertical position 20%
- Average position 70%

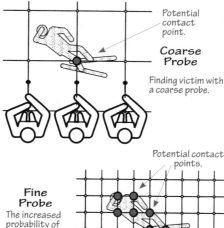

Potential contact point.

Coarse Probe

Finding victim with a coarse probe.

Fine Probe

The increased probability of finding victim with a fine probe.

Potential contact points.

COARSE PROBING

As long as there is any hope for a live rescue, probing is conducted at a vigorous pace according to a system known as "coarse probing." The idea behind coarse probing is to sacrifice some thoroughness to improve speed and thus maximize the chance of finding the victim alive. Coarse probing gives about a 70% chance of finding the victim; this may be compared with the alternative and more thorough method of probing known as "fine probing," which gives nearly a 100% chance of finding the victim. However, fine probing takes four or five times longer than coarse probing, and it is best to make several passes using coarse probing before resigning the operation to slow, thorough fine probing. Coarse probing does sacrifice some thoroughness because of the grid size, and it must be carried out precisely to keep the sacrifice to a minimum.

COARSE PROBING PROCEDURE

A: Probers are spaced along a line, 75 cm (center to center) apart. A distance of 50 cm is straddled, leaving 25 cm between the toes of adjacent probers.
B: The probe pole is inserted once at the center of the straddled span. (An alternative method, used where terrain is steep or there are only a few probers, is to stand "fingertip-to-fingertip." The prober then probes first on one side of his body, their on the other side. If done carefully, this gives the same probe spacing as the single-insertion system.)
C: On signal from the probe-line leader, the line advances one step (about 70 cm) and repeats step B. Usually one signal suffices for the complete sequence insertion of probe, retraction of probe, and advancement of line. The signals should be at a rhythm that enforces the maximum reasonable pace. Strict military discipline and firm, clear commands are essential for efficient probing. The probers should work silently. On the average, 20 men can search an area 100 x 100 m in 4 hours. Depth of probing is adjusted to depth of deposition, but should be no deeper than 3 m.

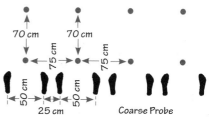

70 cm   70 cm
75 cm   75 cm
50 cm   50 cm
25 cm   Coarse Probe

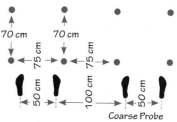

70 cm   70 cm
75 cm   75 cm
50 cm   100 cm   50 cm
Coarse Probe

Execution of coarse probe.

The coarse probe is used whenever live rescue is expected. The above spacing can be achieved by dressing the line "elbow-to-elbow" in a "hands-on-hips" position. One probe insertion is made, and the line advances one step. An alternative method, useful when the number of probers is limited or terrain is steep, is to have probers stand fingertip-to-fingertip. Probers then probe once to the left of their body and once to the right before the line advances.

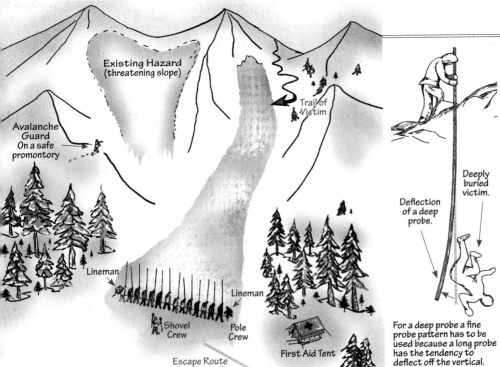

Existing Hazard (threatening slope)

Trail of Victim

Avalanche Guard On a safe promontory

Lineman

Lineman

Shovel Crew

Pole Crew

First Aid Tent

Escape Route known to all

First aid and support facilities are set up in a protected area. In this case an older growth of trees.
See article on vegetation indicators of past avalanches. An avalanche guard is posted, on a secure promontory, to warn for further avalanches.

Deeply buried victim.

Deflection of a deep probe.

For a deep probe a fine probe pattern has to be used because a long probe has the tendency to deflect off the vertical.

RESCUE USING A BEACON

- Turn beacon to the "Receive" position and look for clues (ski poles, clothing, backpack, etc.) while moving down the slide path. Listen for any signal from the beacon.
- Upon reception of signal establish a grid or tangential search pattern (see article).
- Upon finding the most probable location of the victim use a pole to probe for the exact location and start digging. You have a limited amount of time.

GRID SEARCH METHOD

- Based on perpendicular lines that are a structured method of making a search.
- The first sweep would be down in the direction of the slide. If there is a group the searchers would walk strung out perpendicular to the slope.
- If a member hears the signal the beacon would be angled for maximum reception. This angle would be maintained while continuing down the hill and the signal would get stronger and then will get weaker.
- Return to the point where the signal was the strongest. Turn perpendicular to the original search line and turn the volume to just being audible and proceed in the perpendicular direction. If the signal disappears you are going in the wrong direction. Turn around and proceed in the perpendicular line but in the opposite direction until the signal is strongest and walk until it weakens.

Go back to the strongest location.

- Repeat minimizing the volume and repeat the localized search but hold the receiver close to the snow and you will be on the final passes which should localize the possible location to two square feet.
- Probe for victim but do not push too hard as you might injure the victim.

TANGENTIAL SEARCH METHOD
(Field Line or Induction)

- Method is based upon the fact that the receiver is transmitting electromagnetic waves whose intensity varies inversely with the square of the distance ($I = 1/d^2$; I= intensity. d = distance).
- Upon hearing the strongest signal turn down the volume and reorient the direction of the beacon and you should detect a stronger signal which you follow to the maximum volume. Repeat this until by following an inward spiral you will find the victim. Use the same method as in the Grid Method to find the final location.

FINE PROBING

After repeating the coarse probe several times, it may be obvious that the objective is body recovery rather than live rescue. In order to preserve the strength and morale of the volunteers, the pace and discipline of the operation may relax to the more thorough and less vigorous fine probe technique:

A Volunteers are arranged the same as for the coarse probe.

B Each volunteer probes in front of his left foot, then in the center of his straddled position, and finally in front of his right foot.

C On signal, the line advances 30 cm and repeats the three probes.

The spacing of the probe holes is 25 by 30 cm, or 13 probes per m². This means that if the victim is in a favorable position, five direct strikes are likely to be made. If in an unfavorable position, one direct strike is likely. The overall probability of finding the victim is therefore 100%, providing the burial is not deeper than about 3-4 m. On the average, 20 men can fine probe an area 100 m² in 16 to 20 hours, depending on the depth of probing.

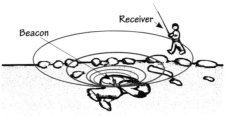

Receiver

Beacon

Avalanche Rescue Beacon

Signaling devices (beacons) used in avalanche areas. A person traversing an avalanche zone carries a transmitter / receiver which has 100 hours of transmission on 2 AA batteries. Replace the batteries at the start of a long trip. The beacons transmit on 457 kHz. Turn on the beacon -to transmit - before reaching the avalanche area. Check the transmission, reception and range of all beacons in the group before leaving. The latest beacons have two antenna and microprocessors which give a more accurate distance and better direction.
Search methods follow the "Tangential Search" or "Grid Search" patterns.

PROBE FOR VICTIM

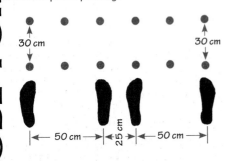

30 cm

30 cm

50 cm   25 cm   50 cm

Execution of fine probe.
The fine probe is used when live rescue is not anticipated. The setup is the same as in coarse probing. Three probe insertions are made, and the line advances about a half step.

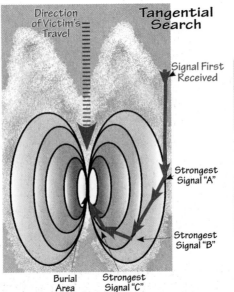

Direction of Victim's Travel

Tangential Search

Signal First Received

Strongest Signal "A"

Strongest Signal "B"

Burial Area

Strongest Signal "C"

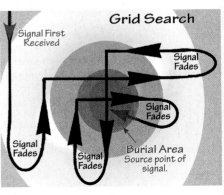

Grid Search

Signal First Received

Signal Fades

Signal Fades

Signal Fades

Signal Fades

Burial Area Source point of signal.

Victim with beacon.

Mark the opposite ends or fade points of the strongest signal - in one axis. Repeat the above at 90° to the midpoint of the original axis. Again mark a new line along the fade points of the strongest signal. The victim should be located at the intersection of the two axis.

Finding Victim with Transmitter

Approaching towards the transmitting signal - first the yellow then the red indicator lights will flash. Reduce the volume reception, on the receiver, and continue walking. Upon nearing the victim do not reduce the volume reception but start the pinpoint search.

Induction Line Line along which rescuer will be guided by receiver.

Green Visual indicator flashes at about 50m.

Acoustic range up to 80m.

Hearing the first audible signal.

Ortovox ™

Receiver

Max. 40 m wide

Walk through the anticipated search area. Search strips should be a maximum of 40m (40 yards) wide.

Victim's last ski track. Trigger
Crown
Flanks
Avalanche Gully (Track of slide)
Pole Crew
Linemen
Avalanche Deposit Runout area & debris

...as an avalanche shovel to find the victim.

Collapsible Avalanche Shovel

...for inspecting the snow pack.

...as a hoe when the shovel blade is bent.

...for doing the shovel shear test.

AVALANCHE SHOVEL

...for doing the compression test.

...for doing the snow pack stability test (Rutschblock).

Emergency Snow Shelter

...for building an igloo or a snow cave.

AVALANCHE SHOVEL

It is important to have a shovel if an avalanche rescue attempted. Example an Ortovox™ shovel.
- Lightweight and compact (fits in any backpack).
- Variable, ergonomic grip for right-handers and left-handers.   • Anatomical t-grip.
- Large volume of shovel blade.
- Telescopic arm made of aluminium.
- Unbreakable, torsion-free and abrasion-resistant shovel blades. High impact strength even at low temperatures
- An emergency sled can be assembled with the shovel parts.

Snow Saw

ORTOVOX

Hiking in a glacial valley. The glacier can be see flowing in the background. A "U" shaped valley contains the glacier.

Ellesmere Island, Canada

Glacier Areas of North America

GLACIER AREAS IN THE WORLD

Climatic and geographic conditions for glaciers to exist are in areas:
• Usually above the snow line.
• Areas of high snowfall in the winter.
• Cool summer temperatures to retain snow. In these conditions more snow will accumulate the winter than melt in the summer. Most glaciers are found in mountainous areas or the polar regions. The altitude is an important factor as the snow line in Africa is 15.000', Washington State is 4,500', and Antarctica at sea level. The amount of snowfall is important as in Siberia there is lack of snow so nearly no glaciation.

Regional Coverage by Glaciers (km²)

Antarctica	13,586,000	South America	26,000
Greenland	1,700,000	Iceland	12,000
Canada	200,000	Scandinavia	3,100
Central Asia	109,000	Alps	2,900
Russia	82,000	New Zealand	1,000
United States	75,000	New Guinea	15
China & Tibet	33,000	Africa	12

Total glacier coverage is over 15,800,000 km².

TYPES OF GLACIERS

• Ice Sheets
• Ice Shelves
• Ice Caps
• Ice Streams/Outlet Glaciers
• Mountain Glaciers
• Valley Glaciers
• Piedmont Glaciers
• Cirque Glaciers
• Hanging Glaciers
• Tidewater Glaciers

ICE SHEETS

Continental masses of glacial ice sheets in Antarctica and Greenland. The ice sheet on Antarctica is over 4 km thick in some areas.

ICE SHELVES

Occur when ice sheets extend over the sea, and float on the water. They may be a few hundred meters to over 1 km thick. They occur around most of the Antarctic continent.

ICE CAPS

Ice caps are miniature ice sheets, covering less than 50,000² km. They form primarily in polar and sub-polar regions that are relatively flat and high in elevation. To really see the difference between an ice cap and an ice sheet, compare Iceland and Greenland on a globe or world map. The much smaller mass of ice on Iceland is an ice cap.

ICE STREAMS & OUTLET GLACIERS

Ice streams are channelized glaciers that flow more rapidly than the surrounding body of ice. For instance, the Antarctic ice sheet has many ice streams flowing outward.

ICE FIELDS

Ice fields are similar to ice caps, except that their flow is influenced by the underlying topography. Kalstenius Ice Field, located on Ellesmere Island, Canada, shows vast stretches of ice. The ice field produces multiple outlet glaciers that flow into a larger valley glacier.

MOUNTAIN GLACIERS

These glaciers develop in high mountainous regions, often flowing out of ice fields that span several peaks or even a mountain range. The largest mountain glaciers are found in Arctic Canada, Alaska, the Andes in South America, the Himalayas in Asia, and on Antarctica.

VALLEY GLACIERS

Commonly originating from mountain glaciers or ice fields, these glaciers spill down valleys, looking much like giant tongues. Valley glaciers may be very long, often flowing down beyond the snow line, sometimes reaching sea level.

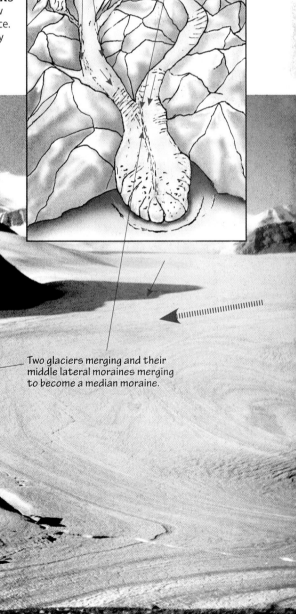

Lateral Moraine

Median Moraine

Two glaciers merging and their middle lateral moraines merging to become a median moraine.

Crossing an Ice Field in the summer - showing the many crevasses.

GROWTH OF GLACIERS

In regions where average temperatures hover below 32°F, glaciers grow with each snowstorm. Compressed by overlying snow, buried layers slowly grow together to form a thickened mass of ice. The pressure created from overlying snow squashes snow grains together. Individual grains eventually metamorphose, growing to the size of rock salt. If these enlarged crystals survive one melt season, they are considered firn. Most glaciers have accumulated and compressed so much snow that they are hundreds or even thousands of feet thick.

FIRN BECOMING ICE

Firn grains are generally four to 16 times the size of the original snow crystal and increase in size as the weight of the overlying snow increases. As the grains grow, they slowly snuff out pockets of existing air between the grains. Over time, individual firn grains are pressed together to form larger crystals, ultimately forming slabs of glacier ice.

GLACIAL MOVEMENT

Glacial movement is like an oozing plastic mass. Movement starts once the ice is around 18 yards thick, being so heavy that it begins to deform and move. The ice moves because of its immense weight responding to the force of gravity and will gradually flow downhill or over a relatively horizontal plain. Glacier ice flows down mountain valleys, fans across plains, and spreads into the sea.

The speed of movement will vary throughout the mass depending upon the friction of the rock on the ground and the sides of the valley. The movement of the ice is continuous - in advancing or retreating. The difference between an advance or retreat is the amount of snow being deposited at the head of the glacier. Glaciers usually move very slowly but sometimes can surge ahead several meters a day.

WERE DO GLACIERS FORM?

Glaciers require very specific geographical and climatic conditions. Most are found in regions of high snowfall in winter and cool temperatures in summer. These conditions assure that the snow accumulating in the winter remains throughout the summer. Such conditions typically prevail in the polar and high alpine regions.

GLACIAL EROSION

In areas of glacier growth, upon reaching a critical mass, the slabs of ice begin to flow and dramatically impact the surrounding environment. The great weight and slow movement causes glaciers to reshape the underlying and surrounding landscape. Acting as an enormous push broom, the ice erodes the land surface, carrying broken rocks and soil debris far from their place of origin. Glaciers slowly push earth and rock forward as they advance and leave these same materials behind in the form of moraines and other glacial deposition features as they retreat.

GLACIER RETREAT

Glacier retreat, melt, and ablation, result from increasing temperature, evaporation, and wind scouring. Ablation is a natural and seasonal part of glacier life. As long as snow accumulation equals or is greater than melt and ablation, glacier health is maintained.

Tidewater Glaciers
As the name implies, these are valley glaciers that flow far enough to reach out into the sea. Tidewater glaciers are responsible for calving numerous small icebergs, while not as imposing as Antarctic icebergs, can still pose problems for shipping lanes.

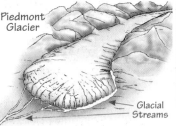

Piedmont Glacier

Glacial Streams

Piedmont Glaciers
Piedmont glaciers occur when steep valley glaciers spill into relatively flat plains, where they spread out into bulb-like lobes.

Calving Glacier

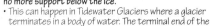
Cleavage point for next iceberg

Glacier

Calved Iceberg

Ocean

Calving Glacier

CALVING GLACIER

Refers to ice breaking off from the glacier's terminus. It happens when the glacier keeps on moving but there is no more support below the ice.

- This can happen in Tidewater Glaciers where a glacier terminates in a body of water. The terminal end of the glacier juts into the water, lacks support, and pieces fall off. In the ocean large chunks form icebergs. If a large piece falls off it can cause high sudden waves that can be dangerous to lighter water craft.

Calving Glacier

- On the land it applies to serac falls that form on slopes below hanging glaciers.

Dangerous to sail so close to a calving glacier - especially on a small boat. The jagged area is part of the Ablation Zone. The dark bands are Band Ogives.

Dangers of a Calving Glacier

DANGERS IN GLACIAL AREAS

Crevasses, icefalls, and ice avalanches are the principal dangers to movement in glacial areas. Snow-covered crevasses make movement on a glacier very treacherous. In winter, with poor visibility and snow cover, the difficulty of recognizing them is increased. Toward the end of the summer, crevasses are at their widest and are covered by the least amount of snow. Snow bridges constitute the biggest potential danger in movement over glaciers.

CREVASSES

When ice flows over an irregularity (a steep slope, a cliff) crevasses can appear on the down slope of the glacier. If the cliff is high the ice will break into ice blocks and towers which will be crisscrossed with crevasses. This jumbled cliff is known as an icefall (serac). Icefalls present a major obstacle for safe movement on glaciers. Ice avalanches are common in the vicinity of icefalls. The safest time to move through an icefall is early in the morning before sunrise.

THREAT OF ICEBERGS

Icebergs broken off, or calved, from ice shelves and tidewater glaciers pose a significant threat to sea lanes worldwide. One of the most famous examples is the Titanic, which in April 1912 carried 1,503 passengers to a watery grave after a collision with an iceberg that ripped a 90 meter hole in the ship. Shipping lanes along the coasts of Greenland and Newfoundland are historically iceberg-infested waters.

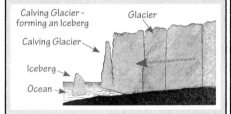

Calving Glacier - forming an Iceberg

Calving Glacier

Glacier

Iceberg

Ocean

FINDING COMPASS DIRECTION ON GLACIERS

"Glacier tables" form on glaciers with large boulders at their surface. A large rock protects the ice under it from melting and the rock will gradually protrude above the surface of the ice. With additional melting of the ice below the boulder it will gradually sit on a pedestal of ice two or three feet high. These pedestals can indicate the south because they usually tilt towards the south as the greatest amount of melting occurs on this side due to the sun's radiation. After a while, the boulder slips off and its original pedestal melts and the sun begins this process over again at the boulder's new position.

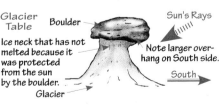

Glacier Table

Boulder

Ice neck that has not melted because it was protected from the sun by the boulder.

Sun's Rays

Note larger overhang on South side.

South

Glacier

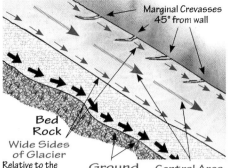

Marginal Crevasses 45° from wall

Bed Rock

Wide Sides of Glacier
Relative to the top center of the glacier the ice is moving slowly. Due to the friction with the walls and the faster flow of the center Marginal Crevasses are formed at a 45° angle up-stream from the wall.

Ground
Slow glacial movement as rocks are frozen into the bottom of the glacier and the rocks and ice gradually move down the slope while eroding the ground surface.

Central Area
This is the fastest part of the glacier as it moves as a viscous material and its movement is lubricated by the ice it is flowing on.

Based upon editorial by the National Snow and Ice Data Center of the University of Colorado affiliated with NOAA and NASA.

Direction of Glacier

Crevasse 45°

Crevasse 45°

Wall

MARGINAL CREVASSES

A crevasse forms where the glacier moves past the hard valley wall. They are formed by the difference of the glacier's advance caused by the friction with the valley wall. These crevasses point approximately 45° up-glacier from the valley wall. The yellow arrows are the best path near the wall side of glaciers.

FORMATION OF MARGINAL CREVASSES

Speed of different parts of a glacier. The center flows the fastest because it has the least resistance.

This line indicates the original location of the moving ice in this example.

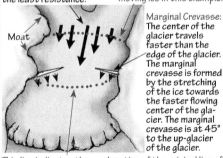

Moat

Marginal Crevasse: The center of the glacier travels faster than the edge of the glacier. The marginal crevasse is formed by the stretching of the ice towards the faster flowing center of the glacier. The marginal crevasse is at 45° to the up-glacier of the glacier.

This line indicates the new location of the original line of the moving ice in this example. Note that the Marginal Crevasse has formed on the wall sides of the glacier.

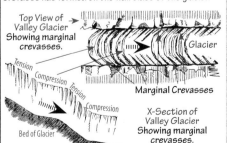

Top View of Valley Glacier Showing marginal crevasses.

Glacier

Tension

Compression

Tension

Compression

Marginal Crevasses

Bed of Glacier

X-Section of Valley Glacier Showing marginal crevasses.

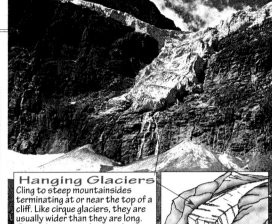

Hanging Glaciers

Cling to steep mountainsides terminating at or near the top of a cliff. Like cirque glaciers, they are usually wider than they are long. These glaciers can be very dangerous to travelers or campers on the downward slope. There can be deadly avalanches of ice and rock when a piece of glacier breaks off.

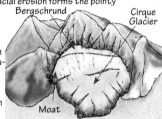

Cirque Glacier

Is a glacier in a basin or amphitheater found high on mountainsides. The geological shape formed by a cirque glacier is called a cirque. The cirque glacier has formed this bowl shaped enclosure by slowly gouging out the rock in the basin. This glacial erosion forms the pointy faces of mountains in glacial regions. Some mountain peaks have a sharp pyramid form created by the erosion from a few cirque glaciers situated on different sides. Most cirque glaciers have a circular shape, width slightly wider than the length.

Bergschrund

Cirque Glacier

Moat

Moulin/Glacier Mill

Flowing surface water entering a crevasse or point of weakness on a relatively flat section of the glacier and eroding a nearly vertical channel in the ice. Glacial mills are cut into the ice by the churning action of water. They vary in diameter. Glacial mills differ from crevasses not only in shape but also in origin, since they do not develop as a result of the tensions of moving ice. In places, the depth of a glacial mill may equal the thickness of the glacier.

Surface water enters.

Camping among the terminal moraines of a glacier.

U-shaped Glacial Valley

Probing...

Summit

Chimney

Gendarmes, Aiquilles, or Pinnacles

Saddle, Pass, or Col

Ridge or Arete

Rib

Rock Face

Gully or Couloir

Moat

Bergschrund

Moat

Ice Cliff

Ice Fall & Crevasses

Ice Fall/Serac
DANGER

Rib

Talus Slope

Glacier

Moat

Alpine Meadows

Moat

Marginal Crevasse

Medial Moraine

Medial Moraine

Rock Slide

Lateral Moraine

Medial Moraine

Glacial Cirque

Tarn (Lake)

Ravine

Ablation

Glacier Terminus

Moat

Timberline

Old Moraine

Ice Cave

Splays

Glacial Stream

VALLEY GLACIER

VALLEY GLACIERS

A valley glacier is essentially a river of ice and it flows at a rate of speed that depends largely on its mass, snowfall, temperature, and the slope of its bed. A glacier consists of two parts:
Lower Glacier: no snow on ice surface during the summer.
Upper Glacier: the ice is covered even in summer with layers of accumulated snow that changes into glacier ice.

MOVING & ANCHORED ICE

A large crevasse separates the glacier proper and defines the boundary between moving and anchored ice. This is very important in understanding where crevasses can appear.

CREVASSES: TRAVERSE & DIAGONAL

Ice is plastic-like near the surface but not smooth enough to prevent cracking as the ice moves forward over irregularities in its bed. Fractures in a glacier surface, called crevasses, vary in width and depth from only a few inches to many feet. Crevasses form at right angles to the direction of greatest tension, and due to a limited area tension is usually in the same direction. Crevasses in any given area tend to be roughly parallel to each other. Generally, crevasses develop across a slope. Therefore, when traveling up the middle of a glacier, people usually encounter only transverse crevasses (crossing at right angles to the main direction of the glacier). Near the margins or edges of a glacier, the ice moves more slowly than it does in midstream. This speed differential causes the formation of crevasses diagonally upstream and away from the margins or sides. While crevasses are almost certain to be encountered along the margins of a glacier and in areas where a steepening in slope occurs, the gentlest slopes may also contain crevasses.

GLACIAL STREAMS

On those portions of a glacier where melting occurs, runoff water cuts deep channels in the ice surface and forms surface streams. Channels can exceed 20 feet in depth and width. They usually have smooth sides and undercut banks. Many of these streams terminate at the margins of the glacier, where in summer they contribute to the torrent that constantly flows between the ice and the lateral moraine. Size increases greatly as the heat of the day moves to an end. The greatest caution must be taken in crossing a glacial surface stream since the bed and undercut banks are usually hard, smooth ice that offers no secure footing.

MORAINES

Lateral Moraines: As a glacier moves forward, debris from the valley slopes on either side is deposited on its surface. Shrinkage of the glacier from subsequent melting causes this debris to be deposited along the receding margins of the glacier.
Medial Moraine: Where two glaciers join and flow as a single river of ice, the debris on the adjoining lateral margins of the glaciers also unites and flows with the major ice stream, forming a medial moraine.
Terminal Moraine: is usually found where the frontage of the glacier has pushed forward as far as it can go, that is, to the point at which the rate of melting equals the speed of advance of the ice mass. This moraine may be formed of debris pushed forward by the advancing edge, or it may be formed by a combination of this and other processes.
Ground Moraine: continuous layer of debris underneath a glacier.

Ridge or Arete

Is a sharp, narrow ridge formed as a result of glacial erosion which occurs on both sides. This is especially evident when two or more cirque glaciers erode into each other.

Alpine Layers

As tree rings these are annual accumulations of snow and dust on a glacier that form distinctive layers. As with trees it is possible to date these layers by counting the layers. It is also possible to estimate the snowfall and contents of the dust (as pollen and volcanic eruptions) in the layers.

Annual Layers
X-Section of Glacier

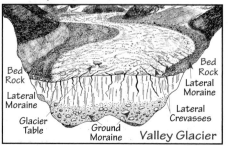

Bed Rock

Bed Rock

Lateral Moraine

Lateral Moraine

Lateral Crevasses

Glacier Table

Ground Moraine

Valley Glacier

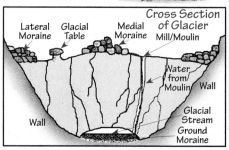

Lateral Moraine

Glacial Table

Medial Moraine

Cross Section of Glacier

Mill/Moulin

Water from Moulin

Wall

Wall

Glacial Stream

Ground Moraine

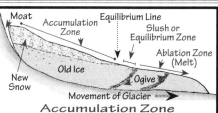

Accumulation Zone

Is the area on the glacier where some of the snow accumulation of the previous season remains to help the glacier grow. The snow in this area is usually clean and white.

Equilibrium Line

Is the balance line which divides the area on a glacier where on one side (higher elevation) some of the snow accumulation of the previous season remains (Accumulation Zone) and on the other side the seasonal snow disappears (Ablation Zone).

Slush or Equilibrium Zone

Occurs on a flat portion of the glacier just below the Equilibrium Line. It is a mixture of water and wet runny snow. It is very unpleasant to travel through these accumulations as it is hard to see the slippery areas below the slush and a fall might lead to hypothermia.

Ablation Zone

Is the area below the equilibrium zone where the ice that has flowed down the slope starts to melt on the surface. In this area the exposed ice (old ice) is darker or bluish. If the equilibrium line is in the same area year after year darker sedimentary lines called ogives appear.

Deep Ablation Zone

BAND OGIVES

Zebra-like bands of light and dark on a glacier. The dark color is from windblown dust deposited on the glacier and in the crevasses in the summer. Ogives are found on steeper locations (ice fall/serac) on a glacier and are formed by the summer and winter glacial flows and the ablation (melt or evaporation of ice/snow).
Wave Ogives that have a vertical aspect with the light bands on ridges and the dark in the hollows.
Sedimentary Ogives are bands at the firn line with the youngest at the higher elevation and the progressively darker bands at lower elevation.
A feature that might resemble ogives are called **False Ogives** which are light and dark layers formed by rock and gravel avalanches that fall on the glacier while it is advancing.

Summer Ogives Visible

Winter: snow protects ice. No band effect is visible. Winter

Snow Cover

Summer: dust settles on glacier and in the crevasses. The accumulation of sediment in the crevasses produces the ogives on the slope.

Top View
Shows how the band effect (ogives) would look on a glacier.

Bergschrund

Is a distinctive usually large crevasse that separates flowing ice from the stagnant ice at the head of a glacier. The stagnant ice is actually attached to the walls and ground below the glacier. The moving part of the glacier actually slides on this stagnant ice. The stagnant ice very slowly slips downwards and erodes the rock surface below it. This erosion will form cirques and aretes.

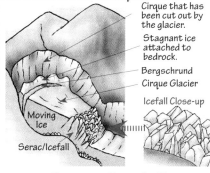

Cirque that has been cut out by the glacier.

Stagnant ice attached to bedrock.

Bergschrund

Cirque Glacier

Moving Ice

Serac/Icefall

Icefall Close-up

Serac/Icefall

An icefall forms when a glacier flowing on a mild slope goes down a steep area. Major stresses occur in the ice as the lower part has a shorter distance to travel while the upper area has to stretch and deep sharp crevasses appear. If the slope is very steep a jumble of jagged ice blocks will fall forming an icefall. This consists of no well defined crevasses. It is very difficult to travel through an icefall - and it can be dangerous as you might trigger an ice avalanche.

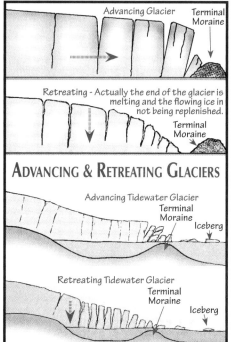

Advancing Glacier

Terminal Moraine

Retreating - Actually the end of the glacier is melting and the flowing ice in not being replenished.

Terminal Moraine

ADVANCING & RETREATING GLACIERS

Advancing Tidewater Glacier

Terminal Moraine

Iceberg

Retreating Tidewater Glacier

Terminal Moraine

Iceberg

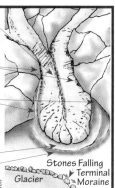

Dirt Cone Sequence

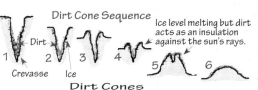

Ice level melting but dirt acts as an insulation against the sun's rays.

Dirt

1   2   3   4   5   6

Crevasse   Ice

Dirt Cones

Are cone-shaped deposits of ice that is covered by dirt. They are caused by the dirt deposit on their surfaces insulating the ice and causing the ice to melt slower than the surrounding area.

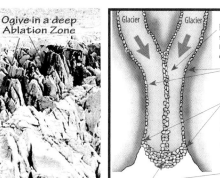

Ogive in a deep Ablation Zone

Medial Moraine
Formed by the merging of two glacial streams and consists of the eroded materials from the adjacent wall of each glacier.

Glacier   Glacier

Lateral Moraine
Deposits from the erosion of the valley walls.

Ground Moraine
Moraine formed along the edge and below of a glacier by rock falling off the ice or eroded below the glacier.

Two Merging Valley Glaciers

Terminal Moraine
A moraine found near the end of a glacier.

End & Push Moraine
A moraine at the glacier terminus. One that is still actively being pushed by the advancing glacier.

Stones Falling
Terminal Moraine
Glacier

Ground Moraine

Longitudinal X-Section

GLACIAL HIKING

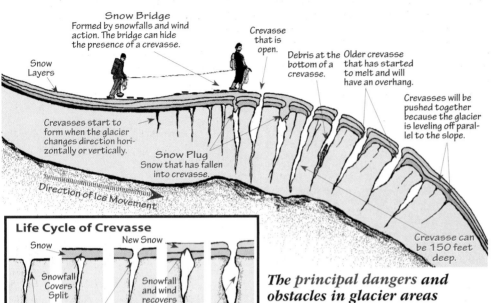

Snow Bridge
Formed by snowfalls and wind action. The bridge can hide the presence of a crevasse.

Crevasse that is open.

Snow Layers

Debris at the bottom of a crevasse.

Older crevasse that has started to melt and will have an overhang.

Crevasses start to form when the glacier changes direction horizontally or vertically.

Crevasses will be pushed together because the glacier is leveling off parallel to the slope.

Snow Plug
Snow that has fallen into crevasse.

Direction of Ice Movement

Crevasse can be 150 feet deep.

Life Cycle of Crevasse

Snow

New Snow

Snowfall Covers Split

Snowfall and wind recovers crevasse.

Small Opening

Split expands and snow cover opens.

Mature deep crevasse internal melting had caused the overhang inside the crevasse.

Fall into a crevasse.

The principal dangers and obstacles in glacier areas are crevasses and icefalls. Hidden crevasses present unique problems and situations since their presence is often difficult to detect. When one is detected, often it is due to a team member having fallen through the unstable surface cover.

GLACIER & MORAINE TRAVEL

Lateral and medial moraines may provide excellent avenues of travel. When the glacier is heavily crevassed, moraines may be the only practical routes. Ease of progress along moraines depends on the stability of the debris composition. If the material consists of small rocks, pebbles, and earth, the moraine is usually loose and unstable and the crest may break away at each footstep. If large blocks compose the moraine, they have probably settled into a compact mass and progress may be easy. In moraine travel, it is best either to proceed along the crest or, in the case of lateral moraines, to follow the trough that separates it from the mountainside. Since the slopes of moraines are usually unstable, there is a great risk of spraining an ankle. Medial moraines are usually less pronounced than lateral moraines because a large part of their material is transported within the ice. Travel on them is usually easy, but should not be relied on as routes for long distances since they may disappear beneath the glacier surface. Only rarely is it necessary for a party traveling along or across moraines to be roped together.

GLACIAL SUNBURN

Light and heat rays reflected from ice, snow, water, and rocks irritates and rapidly burns the skin. Sunburn can even occur on cloudy days. A strong wind will make the burn more severe. Sunburn cream should be applied frequently on all exposed skin. It is particularly dangerous to expose parts of the body which are not accustomed to the sun's rays. As soon as any part of the body becomes burned, it should be protected from further exposure. Bad cases of sunburn can lead to fever and possibly reduced muscle activity. It might take several days to recover.

PREPARATION FOR GLACIER TRAVEL

Hypothermia prevention should be of primary importance when traveling on glaciers. Sufficient clothing must be worn or carried to cover temperature variations. Climbers trapped in crevasses have died of hypothermia while their team members, helpless to assist from their position on the glacier surface above, were sweltering in the sunshine. Backpacks should be equipped with a lanyard consisting of a 6 foot piece of line with a figure-eight and non-locking carabiner at one end. The free end of the lanyard is attached to the pack and the unlocking carabiner is snapped into the buttock strap of the seat harness. If the climber falls into a crevasse and is suspended upside down by the weight of the pack, the pack can be released with the lanyard and the person can return to an upright position.

ROPING-IN

Rope-in during travel! Avoid crevasses! When stepping on to a glacier or on to a snowfield of unknown stability, whether crevasses are visible or not, ROPE-IN. An exception might be when avalanches present a greater hazard than the threat of crevasses. The most experienced climber in glacial travel should be the lead climber; however, if crevasses are completely masked, the lightest climber may lead. During moderate climbs, three climbers tied in to a 165 foot rope is ideal. During severe climbs requiring belay, a 120 foot rope with only two climbers is recommended. If a two-person climbing team falls, the team must be arrested by a single axe. If a three-person climbing team is roped in, the rope is usually so shortened that if one climber falls, the others are often dragged in before they have time to react.

HOW TO ROPE-IN

Climbers are roped together by constructing figure-eight knots at the ends and middle of the rope. The rope is attached by passing a locking carabiner through the figure eight and the crotch strap of the seat harness. Associated climbing equipment such as ice axes, slings, and packs are donned. When completely roped in and prepared for travel, there should not be less than 50 feet of rope between each of the climbers. The more rope between the climbers, the better the chance for a successful arrest.

SNOW BLINDNESS

Snow blindness occurs when strong sunlight shines on an expanse of snow. The injury is due to the reflection of ultraviolet rays. It is likely to occur after a new snowfall and even when the rays of the sun are partially obscured by a light mist or fog. In most cases, snow blindness is due to negligence or failure to use goggles. Symptoms of snow blindness are a sensation of grit in the eyes, pain in and over the eyes, watering, redness, headache and an avoidance of light. First aid includes blindfolding the eyes for a few days until the pain is gone.

Ice Crampon

Glacial Rivers

Glacial rivers are varied in type and present numerous crossing or navigation problems. Wherever mountains and highlands exist in the arctic regions, melting snows produce water pouring downward in a series of falls and swift chutes. Rivers flowing from icecaps, hanging piedmonts (lake-like), or serpentine (winding or valley) glaciers are all notoriously treacherous. Northern glaciers may be vast in size and the heat of the summer sun can release vast quantities of water.

Glacial Ice, Glacial Water & Fording

Glacier ice is extremely unpredictable. An ice field may look innocent from above, but countless sub-glacial streams and water reservoirs may be under its smooth surface. These reservoirs are either draining or temporarily blocked. Mile long lakes may lie under the upper snowfield, waiting only for a slight movement in the glacier to liberate them and send their waters into the valleys below. Because of variations in the amounts of water released by the sun's heat, all glacial rivers fluctuate in water level. The peak of the floodwater usually occurs in the afternoon as a result of the noonday heat of the sun on the ice. For some time after the peak has passed, rivers that drain glaciers may not be fordable or even navigable. However, by midnight or the following morning, the water may recede so fording is both safe and easy. When following a glacial river broken up into many shifting channels, choose routes next to the bank rather than taking a chance on getting caught between two dangerous channels.

Dangers of Flooding Glaciers

Glaciers from which torrents of water descend are called flooding glaciers. Two basic causes of such glaciers are the violent release of water that the glacier carried on its surface as lakes, or the violent release of large lakes that have been dammed up in tributary glaciers because of the blocking of the tributary valley by the main glacier. This release is caused by a crevasse or a break in the moving glacial dam, the water then roars down in an all-enveloping flood. Flooding glaciers can be recognized from above by the flood-swept character of the lower valleys. The influence of such glaciers is sometimes felt for many miles. Prospectors have lost their lives while rafting otherwise safe rivers because a sudden flood entered by a side tributary and descended as a wall of white, rushing water.

Katabatic Wind

Katabatic wind is caused by the air adjacent to the glacier cooling and thereby becoming heavier than the surrounding air and then rolling down the valley. In the summer when it is humid this wind might cause a rolling fog on the ice surface. A cold wind also blows out of glacial caves.

Glacial Cave

Streams of meltwater below a glacier can form a long cave in the glacial ice. These caves are usually in the glacial terminus. Melting, because of the warm air, will enlarge the cave entrance. This is most common in glaciers which do not show much movement. Cold glacial winds blow out of the caves. This is very evident in the summer.

Team Glacier Travel

Due to the difficulty of crevasse rescue, two or more rope teams are recommended for glacier travel since a single team is sometimes pinned down in the arrest position, and members are unable to free themselves to begin rescue. Rope teams must travel close together to lend assistance to one another, however, not so close as to fall into the same crevasse. During extended periods on a glacier, skis and snowshoes are often of great value. This foot gear will distribute the weight more widely than boots alone and place less strain on snow bridges. Neither skis nor snowshoes are substitutes for the rope, but may be used for easy travel.

Problems in Glacial Travel

Travel routes are limited by the limitations imposed by nature in glacial movement. Reaching the end portion of a glacier may be difficult due to abruptness of the ice and possible presence of crevasses. It is hard to climb onto a glacier because there may be swift glacial streams or abrupt mountain terrain bordering the glacier ice. These same obstacles have to be negotiated when leaving a glacial area. Further considerations to movement on a glacier are steep sections, heavily crevassed regions, and icefalls. The use of up-to-date aerial photographs, when available, with aerial reconnaissance is a valuable means of gathering advance information about a particular glacier.

Trail Wands

Trail wands are used to mark the route and crevasses. The wands, especially essential to safety during periods of adverse weather, are placed every 150 feet along the route and can be used during day or night.

Rest Stops & Camps on Glaciers

A climbing team should not cluster close together during rest stops. If areas of safety cannot be found, the rope must be kept extended during rests just as during travel. A party establishing camp on a snow-covered glacier similarly remains roped-in for as long a period as required to safely inspect the area by stomping and probing the surface thoroughly before placing trust in the site. Hidden crevasses should always be assumed to exist in the area.

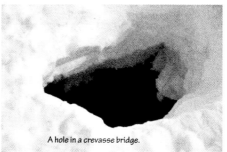

A hole in a crevasse bridge.

Jumping Over a Crevasse

Narrow cracks in a bridge can be stepped across, but wider crevasses require jumping. If the jump is so long that a run is required, the approach should be carefully packed. A running jump can carry the climber farther than a standing jump, although running jumps are often not practical. Most jumps are made with only two or three lead-up steps. In any case, care must be taken to locate the precise edge of the crevasse before any attempt is made to jump. Encumbering clothing and equipment must be removed before the jump, although the jumper must bear in mind the low temperature that often exists within crevasses.

Crossing a Bridge

Any bridge should be closely and completely examined before use. If overhanging snow obscures the bridge, the lead climber must explore at closer range by probing the depth and smashing at the sides while walking delicately, ready for an arrest or sudden drop. The second climber establishes a belay anchored by the third climber, who is also prepared to initiate rescue if the leader falls. An excessively narrow or weak bridge may be crossed by straddling or even slithering on the stomach to lower the center of gravity and distributing the weight over a broader area. When there is doubt about the integrity of a bridge, but it is the only possible route, the lightest climber in the team should be the first across, with the following climbers walking with light steps and taking care to step exactly in the same tracks.

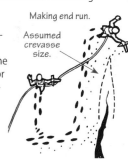

Crossing a Bridge

Trail Wand

Bridges vary in strength with changes in temperatures. In the cold of winter or early morning, the thinnest and most fragile of bridges may have incredible structural strength. However, when the ice crystals melt in the afternoon heat, even the largest bridge may suddenly collapse. Each bridge must be tested with care, being neither abandoned nor trusted until its worth is determined.

Single-File Travel & Crevasse Pinches

Normally a team will travel in single file, stepping in the leader's footsteps or in echelon formation. If a crevasse pinches out, an end run must be made, even if it involves traveling half a mile to gain a few dozen feet of forward progress. The time taken to walk around is generally much less than in forcing a direct crossing. Important to remember in an end run is the possible hidden extension of a visible crevasse. A frequent error is aiming at the visible end. Unless the true or subsurface end is clearly visible during the approach, it is best to make a wide swing around the end. In late summer, the visible end is often the true end due to surface snow and ice having melted. When end runs are impractical because of the distance involved or because the end of one crevasse is adjacent to another, snow bridges may provide a crossing point. One kind consists of remnant snow cover sagging over an inner open space. Another kind, with a foundation that extends downward into the body of the glacier, is less a bridge than a solid area between two crevasses.

Making end run.

Assumed crevasse size.

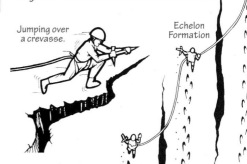

Jumping over a crevasse.

Echelon Formation

GLACIER RESCUE

Belay system for crevasse rescue.

Anchor Rope

End of Stirrup Rope

Variation of Belay

Support Bar

Stokes Litter

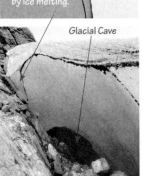

Snow Camouflaging Moat

Dark Stone Wall

Glacier

Moat created by ice melting.

In the summer the sun warms the dark-colored stone wall and melts the ice adjacent to the wall creating a deep moat. This can be a major danger when leaving or entering glacial surfaces because snow can be covering the moat.

Glacial Cave

CREVASSE RESCUE

Each climber must be able to effect a crevasse rescue if a team member falls into a crevasse. When a climber falls, the remaining team members must drop into a self-arrest position and stabilize their position. All climbers should never be dragged into the crevasse. If a climber falls, the remaining team members must support the weight until one of them can establish a reliable anchor point or until the second team arrives to help. A fallen climber might be able to climb out by using prusiks.

- A problem in crevasse rescue is the imbedding of the rope (caused by the fallen climber's weight) in the ice and snow. Unless the rope is buffered with an ice axe during the climb out, it will tend to entrench itself deeper in the ice, eventually creating a deep groove from which it will be extremely difficult to use or retrieve, or it will freeze in place, rendering it useless. Travel down along the rope, taking care not to drop debris on the climber, and free it from the ice. Another method is to drop a spare rope down to the climber, who shifts weight off the imbedded rope until it can be freed.

- If the climber is using prusiks to exit the crevasse, it will be extremely difficult to climb the few remaining feet as the rope is flush and exerts pressure on the ice edge. To overcome this is for the climber to tie in to the rope near the prusik. The climber then strikes the figure-eight knot from the harness and sends the end to the team above via a retrieving line. Once firmly anchored in peace, the rope affords a viable route of ascent. In most cases, the final few feet are overcome by brute strength.

- If a fallen climber is unable to help in the recovery, another climber may be required to enter the crevasse. Before the team member is lowered, all assurances must be made that the assistance will enhance the outcome of the operation and not compound it. The rescuer should administer medical treatment as needed, paying special attention to preventing or treating cold weather injuries, as the interior of the crevasse can become extremely cold. Warm protective clothing must be used if the medical situation does not permit immediate extraction.

Safety of Rescuers

The establishment of rescue systems must be thoroughly tested prior to use. One missed step in setting up a rescue system may result in further injury of the victim and (or) injury to the rescuers.

EVACUATION OF VICTIM

Evacuation of a victim from the position in a downhill direction is an easier task than establishing a mechanical leverage for pulling a victim to the top of a hill. The victim's medical condition will dictate the method of evacuation and equipment used. The primary litter used is the Stokes litter. This is a tubular-frame litter with a wire basket. The tubular main bar provides a very strong framework for mountain operations. The patient may be secured in the litter by means of several cross-body straps, or by the interlacing of slings. When an evacuation team arrives on the scene, there are two activities that should take place at the same time:

- The patient should be treated and prepared for transporting in the Stokes litter.

- An anchor and mechanical brake system must be established. Within obvious restraints of time and distance, low-angle evacuations are always preferable to high-angle evacuations. Low-angle work eliminates many hazards and requires a lesser degree of knowledge and skill. Using the Stokes litter eliminates the excessive knot tying and lashing essential with other litters.

EVACUATION & RESCUE

The performance of mountain rescue is not only physically demanding but also mentally challenging. There are no hard and fast procedures to fit all circumstances for mountain rescue. The team's ability to innovate will, in most instances, allow the adaptation of the basic principles, techniques, and procedures into a system suitable to effect the rescue. A normal rescue system will use anchors, belays, and various specialized systems. You will require a more specialized book and expert advice to preform a rescue.

Hidden Crevasse

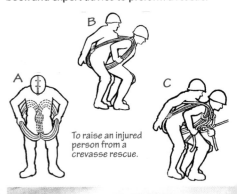

A   B   C

To raise an injured person from a crevasse rescue.

Two rope teams crossing a glacier.

Crevasse

Iroquois
Mask

Piegan Camp in
the Prairies

21 NATIVE SHELTERS

Camanchee
Warrior

Buffalo Hide Shield:
Northern Blackfoot

Prairie
Indians

NATIVE SHELTERS

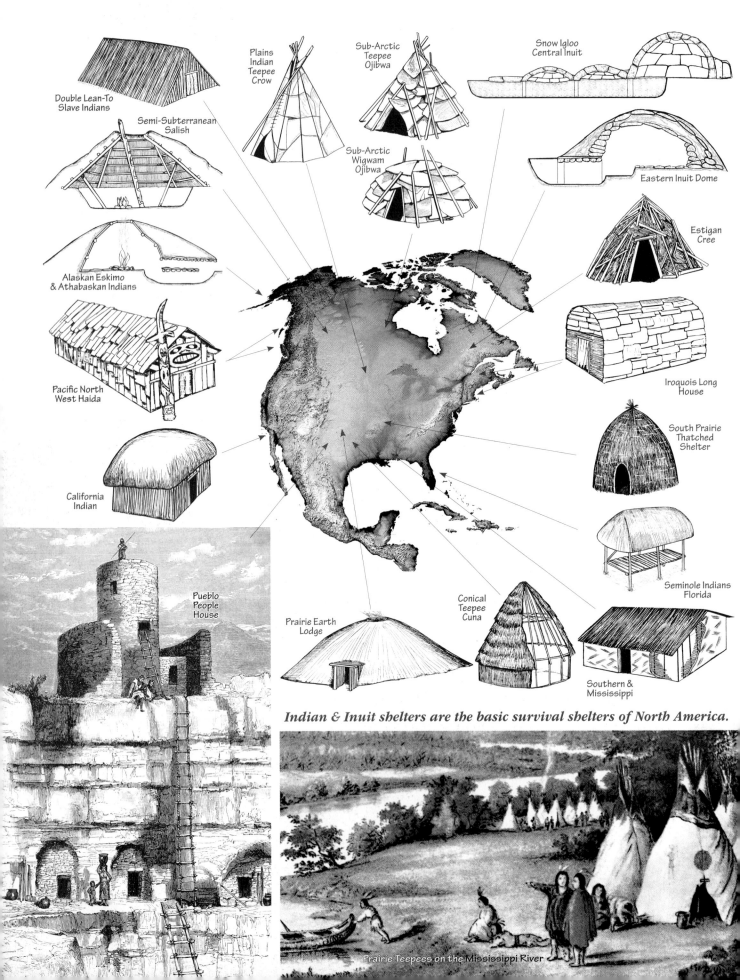

Double Lean-To
Slave Indians

Semi-Subterranean
Salish

Alaskan Eskimo
& Athabaskan Indians

Pacific North
West Haida

California
Indian

Plains
Indian
Teepee
Crow

Sub-Arctic
Teepee
Ojibwa

Sub-Arctic
Wigwam
Ojibwa

Snow Igloo
Central Inuit

Eastern Inuit Dome

Estigan
Cree

Iroquois Long
House

South Prairie
Thatched
Shelter

Seminole Indians
Florida

Pueblo
People
House

Prairie Earth
Lodge

Conical
Teepee
Cuna

Southern &
Mississippi

Indian & Inuit shelters are the basic survival shelters of North America.

Prairie Teepees on the Mississippi River

DOUBLE LEAN-TO: SLAVE INDIANS

The Slave Indians live in the western subarctic of North America. Double lean-tos are of similar construction as the survival lean-to, but larger. They have a wood frame and are covered with bark, hides, sod, and brush. The roof is low and the occupants crawl through the doorway. Usually made for a single family. A small fire can be made inside as the smoke goes through the overlapping material on the roof.

ALASKAN INUIT & ATHABASKAN INDIANS

This structure was built by the Alaskan Inuits and the adjacent Indian tribes. Built of a framework of horizontal logs. The roof was a rectangular pitched structure of logs. There was a center hole for smoke and lighting. The frame was covered with several feet of branches, earth, and sod. The doorway was the lower passage. The area above the passage was for storage. During cold weather the door was covered with layers of skin. The construction is similar to an igloo. The floor was covered with boughs and furs. The structure was usually large and occupied by a few families.

EASTERN INUIT DOME

Eastern Inuits used an off-round structure whose arched roof was made with whale ribs, drift wood or stone slabs. The frame was covered with sod or stone up to five feet (1.5 m) high. The entrance was a low-level vaulted tunnel similar to the igloos. This structure was reused every winter. The structure was common property and belonged to the first occupant of the season.

SNOW BLOCK IGLOO: CENTRAL INUIT

Used by the Central Inuits, the igloo was made to be a permanent winter residence and was used by one extended family. The feature of a permanent igloo is the extended entrance which was negotiated on hands and knees. This tunnel was a wind break, used for cold storage, and helped to keep heat in the igloo. Outer layer clothing made of untanned fur was stored in the cold tunnel. A double door of hide was suspended at the main lodging area. During severe cold and wind more hides could be hung along the tunnel.

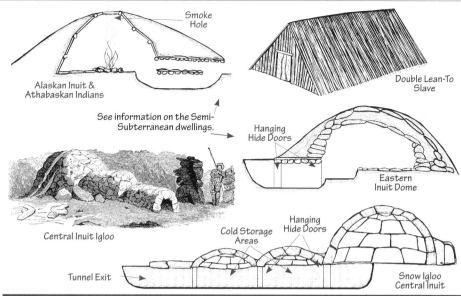

Smoke Hole

Alaskan Inuit & Athabaskan Indians

Double Lean-To Slave

See information on the Semi-Subterranean dwellings.

Central Inuit Igloo

Hanging Hide Doors

Eastern Inuit Dome

Cold Storage Areas

Hanging Hide Doors

Tunnel Exit

Snow Igloo Central Inuit

SEMI-SUBTERRANEAN: SALISH

Winter House in the Mackenzie River Region Similar to the Salish semi-subterranean but it also has a tunnel exit like the Alaskan Inuit & Athabaskan Indians.

Smoke Hole

Exit to Tunnel

Earth

Wood Floors

Tunnel Exit

The house was built over a pit dug two to three feet into the ground. The center pillar or pillars supported the roof. Teepee-type rafters were placed on the pillars and they were covered with small sticks which were then thatched with bark, sod, and covered with earth. The ventilation hole in the middle of the roof also served as a door. In the winter the hole was partially covered with a skin.

Inside a semi-subterranean Salish or Alaskan Inuit & Athabaskan Indians dwelling. Note how dark it is with fish being smoked on the ceiling rafters. The smoke hole in the roof serves with the fire as the source of light.

Semi-Subterranean Salish

Smoke Hole & Exit

Earth

Cree Estigan
A winter dwelling of the Cree. When traveling to seasonal hunting grounds the Crees lived in skin covered teepees.

Cree Summer Travel Teepee

ESKIGAN : CREE

Used by the Cree Indians who live in the James Bay area south of Hudson's Bay. The Cree live just south of the Inuits, and the Eskigan they build can be inhabited all year round, even in the freezing winter of -55°F (-48°C) with the wind chill factor. As there are trees in this semi-tundra area, logs are used to build a semi-conical structure similar to a teepee. Logs are placed side by side and the cracks are filled with mud, moss and pieces of bark. The door usually is a blanket or animal hide. In the cold of winter there might be two or three hides for better insulation. These might even be a vestibule. The fire is built in the middle of the floor with a small opening in the center of the roof. This is not a smoke hole but the logs are not sealed in the top. The floor is covered with spruce boughs covered with a blanket or hide.

SUB-ARCTIC INDIAN TEEPEE: OJIBWA

The Ojibwas built a teepee and covered it with bark and pieces of hide (not sewn together). This covering was held in place by additional outside poles. Smoke escaped through a smoke hole at the top.

WIGWAM: OJIBWA SUB-ARCTIC

These were used near the Western Great Lakes and called "Wigwam" in the Algonquian language. Similar in construction to the Subarctic teepee except that the poles were bent and tied together. The advantage over a teepee is that there is a lower wind profile and the more vertical walls give more headroom. They were covered by bark, hides, sewn or woven mats.

IROQUOIS LONG HOUSE

The Iroquois Indians lived in long houses that were up to 80 feet (24 m) long. Poles were set in the ground and supported by horizontal poles along the walls. The roof was made by bending a series of poles. The frame was covered by bark that was sewn in place and layered as shingles. Light poles were attached on the outside to hold down the shingles during a wind storm. Smoke from the cooking and heating fires passed through the loosely attached bark covering. Separate families occupied booths on both sides of a central hallway. The booths had a wood platform on the ground and platforms for sleeping. Fires were in the central hallway and shared by the two facing families.

PACIFIC NORTH WEST COAST

This multifamily house had a log frame covered with planks and bark. Some were over 60 feet (18m) long. Extended families, living in one lodge, cooperated in obtaining food and building long wood boats, but cooked at their individual fires. All west coast Indians built similar structures but the roof pitch varied depending upon the rainfall.

Sub-Arctic Wigwam Ojibwa

Ojibwa Sub-Arctic

Sub-Arctic Teepee Ojibwa

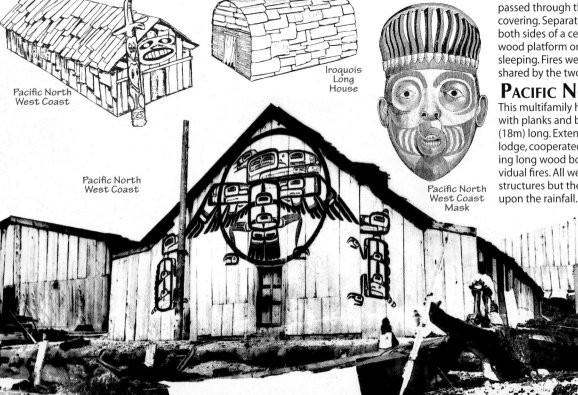

Pacific North West Coast

Iroquois Long House

Pacific North West Coast

Pacific North West Coast Mask

PRAIRIE EARTH LODGE

The frame was made of posts covered with smaller horizontal logs. These logs were covered with brush, sod, and then covered with earth. The floor, one to two feet below ground level, was covered with split logs. The inside of these multifamily lodges were up to 40 feet (13 m) in diameter.

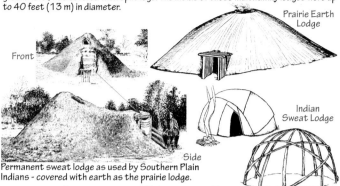

Front

Prairie Earth Lodge

Side

Indian Sweat Lodge

Permanent sweat lodge as used by Southern Plain Indians - covered with earth as the prairie lodge.

INDIAN SWEAT LODGE

A sweat lodge is a small domed structure of bent poles covered with hides, blankets and branches. A fire heats stones and the hot stones are carried into the lodge and water is poured over them. A hot dense cloud of steam is formed. Sweet grass and sage are placed on the rocks to perfume the steam. The bathers stay in the lodge as long as they can and then plunge into the river outside.

Plains Indians Traveling

Pole to open and close smoke flap. When the wind blew the flaps would be positioned so that the wind would not blow down the smokehole - because this would prevent the smoke from rising.

Omaha Tent

The tent was 10' to 12' high, 10' to 15' in diameter at the base, and 1 1/2' at the top. Ten to twelve dressed or tanned buffalo skins were used to cover the pole frame.

Smokehole

Tent skin cover fasted together with stickes or pieces of hide.

The entrance flap was usually opened into the opposite direction of the wind.

Bottom of tent secured to the ground by sticks.

PLAINS TEEPEE: CROW

The teepee was an ideal home on the prairies, as it was easy to transport. The cover was a sewn buffalo hide or, by the 1890's, denim, as most of the buffalo herds had disappeared. The cover was tailored for their poles. In winter, the floor was covered with buffalo hide which ran up the side to prevent drafts. Dogs dragged the poles with the buffalo hide when the settlement was following the buffalo herds. The poles were reused, as the plains are treeless.

Plains Indian Teepee: Crow

St. Lawrence & Great Lake Indian shelters in the primeval forest before civilization cut it down.

St. Lawrence Valley & Great Lake Indian Dwellings

Horse with a travois. The two poles of the travois are actually tent poles.

Conical Teepee Cuna

California Indian

South Prairie Thatched Shelter

Seminole Indians Florida

CONICAL TEEPEES: CUNA

Conical teepees were covered with bark, brush, and wood. Sand was piled around the structure as a windbreak. This structure had many variants as per: height of roof, domed roof, flat roof, rectangular, and different pitches depending upon the climate.

CALIFORNIA INDIAN

They built houses that had a thatched roof and walls. Sometimes the walls were covered with mud which dried and became a stucco-like surface. The roofs were domed or conical and sometimes covered with bark or thatched.

FLORIDA SEMINOLE INDIANS

The Seminole Indians built living areas above the swamps of the Everglades.

PUEBLO PEOPLE HOUSE

The Anasazi built large apartment structures that could house hundreds of people. The rectangular flat roof was supported by logs covered with mud and stones. The structures were multilevel, up to five stories, and accessible by ladders. Western Pueblo Indians built houses of stone which were covered with clay. The Indians of the Rio Grande built houses of clay mixed with grass.

SOUTHERN MISSISSIPPI & CENTRAL PLAIN

Houses similar to those of the Iroquois except the roof was sloping instead of round. The walls were woven sticks (like wicker) and covered with mud or thatched. The roof was covered with bark or thatched in layers to repel the rain. The fire was in the middle with the smoke passing through the roofing. Winter houses were semi-subterranean similar to the earth lodge of the Prairies. Towns of up to 30,000 inhabitants were built.

SOUTH PRAIRIE THATCHED SHELTER

These southern Prairie houses similar to the teepee except that the framing poles were bent to join at the center. Horizontal poles were attached at intervals and covered with grass. The grass was kept in place by outside pole binders. A fire was made in the middle with the smoke passing through the thatching.

Pueblo Dwelling

Walapi Dwelling

Southern & Mississippi

Native shelters vary as to...
- *climate*
- *raw materials that are available*
- *the season of the year*
- *how fast the shelter has to be built*
- *for how long the shelter will be used*
- *if raw materials are scarce the shelter has to be transported*

Navajo Dancing

Blackfoot raiding party - traveling light!

Sleeping Roll

Watching the wolves.

A-FRAME SHELTER

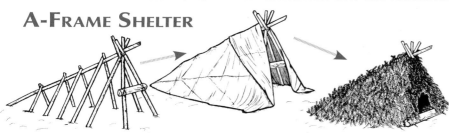

BEACH SHELTER

If roofing is strong add sand to cover branches and leaves.

Entrance pointing North to reduce exposure to the sun.

Extend sides to minimize angle of sun's penetration.

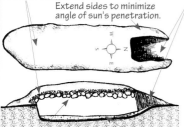

Drift wood roofing.

Make sure that the bedding keeps out the humidity.

- Sun, rain, heat, and wind protection.
- Build well above high-water mark.
- Entrance pointing north to reduce exposure to the sun.
- Long and wide enough to lie down.
- Collect drift wood to make the frame for the roof and to use as a digging tool.
- Dig or scrape to dig a trench. Pile mounds of sand on other 3 sides.
- Place drift wood across mounds to form a roof lattice. Cover with large leaves, palm branches, water plants, canvas, etc. If the roofing material is dense, and can carry additional weight, sand can be added as a final cover.
- For bedding use grass or leaves. Make sure that you are protected against humidity that will rise from the sand.

If building on a sand dune look for the direction of the wind from the shape of the dune. Make sure that you will not get buried during a sand storm.

Canvas or plastic roofing.

Two layers of roofing material with 18" (45 cm) of space in between will provide additional protection against the heat.

Cover entrance during sand storms.

Entrance pointing North to reduce exposure to the sun.

Rock and sand to anchor material.

Make sure that the bedding keeps out the humidity.

Desert Shelter

- Similar to the beach shade shelter.
- Time and effort important as there is limited water.

Above ground: A parachute, poncho, or aircraft material can easily build a shelter. Find a rock outcrop or make a pile of rocks that will be one side of the shelter. The pile of rocks should be on the south side of the shelter. A double roof can be made.

Below ground: A well-designed shelter will reduce mid-day temperature by 30°F (17°C). This shelter requires much energy to build. Build it during the night.
- Find a low spot or dig 18"-24" (45-60 cm) deep. Use a piece of wood or flat rock to dig.
- Pile sand on three sides to form a mound.
- Cover with material. If possible two layers of cover with an air space of 15" (40 cm), between the layers. This will give additional insulation against the heat. The cover can be anchored with sand and rocks.

Dig out area on lee side of dune.

Construct framework and use driftwood for roof and walls.

BEACH SHELTER

Cover with sand, This will help in insulating the structure from the heat of the sun.

Cover with a tarpaulin or plastic sheeting. Use a sheet for a door.

257

The hollow in the cliff looks like an ideal shelter - The only problem is that it is an hibernation spot for black bears.

The type of survival shelter to build depends upon the equipment and available material, the season of the year, and the length of the stay. With the proper use of available material, some sort of shelter can be built during any season and under any conditions.

Your comfort and ability to build a shelter will depend upon your initiative and skill at improvising a structure with the available materials.

This chapter and the next chapter, on Winter Shelters, outlines a wide range of shelters, with different levels of required skill, for any season of the year. Special emphasis has been made to show Indian, Inuit and pioneer shelters because these peoples were the original survivors in the vast diverse area of North America.

Do not just sit there do something...

WHY YOU NEED A SHELTER

If you are lost in the wilderness and have decided to stay put, at least for the night, your priority is to find or make a shelter.

Shelter is needed to:

Improve or boost morale: Help to give you a more positive morale and a good night's sleep.
Cool you off: A cooling shelter can be built in the sand on a beach or desert or be provided by a tree. Keep you warm: To get you out of the wind and rain. A shelter will help you retain your body heat, reduce the effect of wind and air currents and should be easy to heat. Body heat is not lost as fast by the body in still air.
Retard thirst: A shelter will reduce your need for water.
Protect from sun: This will reduce the water consumption and reduce the risk of heat illnesses.
Protect from rain or snow: Being wet will make you feel cold and can lead to hypothermia and feeling depressed.
Protect from animals: Even though animals normally are not dangerous ,you do not want them walking over you during your sleep.
Protect from insects: Mosquitoes and black flies, in large quantities, might drive you crazy.

NATURAL SHELTERS

Think of what type of shelters animals use: caves, ledges, hollow logs, boughs of trees, rock overhangs, crevasses, natural terraces. Watch an animal cross an open space in the winter. You will see it weave back and forth avoiding cold air currents that are invisible and undetectable to us. It is obvious that they are very sensitive to the environment and in the wilds - we should learn from them.
A natural shelter can be improved by adding a bedding of leaves, protective branches and other covering to retain heat or keep out moisture.

Tied saplings are covered.

Saplings are tied together.

Sapling Shelter
If you are in an area of young tree growth you can select two rows and cut the saplings that are in between. The chosen saplings are stripped of their branches and lashed together to form a dome. This dome is covered with material or it can be thatched.

Do not stay below tall trees during a thunderstorm especially if the tree is the highest object in the area.

When building a shelter always watch for the direction of the predominant wind. Make sure that the covering shelter faces into the wind.

An excellent shelter if tree does not fall.

TO AVOID IN BUILDING A SHELTER

- Dry gullies or river beds as there might be a flash flood from a distant storm.
- Building in thick woods as these shelters will be hard to dry due to the lack of wind and sun.
- Pebbly ground, it will be hard to sleep, dig or enter stakes.
- Areas with strong wind currents, as in the opening of a valley.
- Areas where branches or large pine cone might fall.
- Areas under high trees during a thunderstorm.
- Areas that might be a bear run or den.
- Ant nests, poisonous plants, bees, hornet dwellings and other pests.
- Dead trees or trees that might fall during a storm.
- Slow flowing woody river edges as they are humid and shelter mosquitoes.
- Slopes as it might be difficult to build. If you have no choice dig or scrape a drainage channel around the high part of shelter.
- Low valley areas where cold air pockets might be frosty at night.
- Avalanche areas; rock slides in the summer and snow avalanches in the winter. Summer avalanches or mud slides might be caused by a heavy rainfall. Summer avalanche areas can be recognized by the lack of vegetation on the slope.
- In the winter avoid snow cornices or ledges.

Lightning
When building a summer shelter below trees you are at the risk of being hit by lightning. When choosing a shelter support tree make sure that it is not the tallest in the area nor the only one. In summer a storm can blow up very fast and lightning can even strike in front of a storm.

Shelter built over fallen logs.

MAKING A SHELTER

The first consideration in building a shelter is how much time is left till nightfall and how much time do you expect to stay at this spot. If there are less than two hours before sunset, it is best to build a simple shelter for the first night. Examples are the Bough Shelter, Tree Bark Shelter, Root Shelter, or Poncho Shelter. *Study your surroundings to chose a spot to stay the night or for a longer term.* The area you are in will determine the type of shelter you can build by the choice of building materials available. In the summer your preoccupation is rain, sun, and insects which would usually require a simple shelter. Retaining heat is the principal factor for a shelter in the winter and this would need a more complex structure as an igloo, snow cave, or snow trench. *Winter shelters should be small, snug and windproof but with sufficient ventilation to avoid asphyxiation.* A winter shelter should be easy to build, and not require too much energy to build.

WHERE TO BUILD

The ideal location is near water, building materials, and fuel.

LAND FEATURES

- Site large and flat for comfortable bedding.
- Site elevated and well drained.
- Sheltered from wind. Choose south or east sides of hills, forests or other obstacles as the wind is usually from the west.
- Use natural windbreaks as cliffs, trees, fallen trees, caves, rock ledges, and sand dunes to minimize the building effort.
- If traveling in mountainous areas look for caves, crevices or rock ledges.
- If near large bodies of water avoid areas below the high water mark.
- Stay out of dry river gullies as a distant storm might flood the shelter.

WATER

- Is water available? Build a shelter at least 30 yards (27 m) from and down stream from your water source. This is to avoid polluting your water source.
- Do not build too close to stagnant or slow flowing water as there might be many insects.

BUILDING MATERIAL

- Location with building material and fuel.

INSECTS & ANIMALS

- Choose a breezy ridge or where there is an on-shore breeze to reduce the number of insects.
- Sites in forest near fast flowing streams are desirable as these streams do not breed mosquitoes.
- Avoid animal trails or watering holes.
- Watch for areas infested with ants.
- Check for bee and hornet nests.

OTHER FACTORS

- Visible - to signal for rescue if necessary.
- Make a small shelter as it requires less energy, needs less heating, and usually has a less complicated roof structure.
- Consider how long you will need the shelter and how long it will take to build.
- How much energy should you expend in building a shelter?
- In a temperate climate build with a southern exposure. The sun will give the longest and maximum heat and dry the shelter.
- Entrance should, if possible face east so that you will catch the first rays of sun. This will give you both a warm feeling and raise your morale.
- You might want to sleep in a hidden area to avoid any potential problems. A tent is more visible than using a natural shelter. Sleeping in a tent reduces your sensitivity to the environmental signals of danger (as abnormally chattering squirrels).
- The military requires concealment from enemy observation, good observation positions, and have a few camouflaged routes that can be used for escape.

Machete

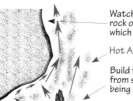

Watch for possible rock or mud slides which might bury area.

Hot Air Currents

Build fire far enough from shelter to avoid being smoked out.

Ledge & Crevice
Makes an excellent shelter especially in the summer. Watch for lightning and high during thunderstorms.

Curve drains water.

Bent Tree Shelter
Find a young sapling and slowly bend and attach it to a second tree or with a peg in the ground.
— Use a ground sheet.

Mosquito Bar
Netting should be dark mosquito netting. Commercial material or dyed cheesecloth can be used. Dark netting is used as it is easier to see through and dark colors attract fewer insects.

Make sure that the protective netting touches the ground.

Drip Cord
To divert rain water from running into the tent area.

Tube Tent
- One of the best camping and outdoor travel tents available.
- Light weight and easy to rig. No ground sheet required.
- Nine feet long. - eight foot (2.4 m) circumference for one man model. - twelve foot (3.7 m) circumference for two man model. Material should be 4 mil or thicker. Rope 24' (8 m) long.

Use soil as fill.

Toilet
A well placed toilet is very important for camping or in a survival situation. The toilet should be at least 150' (50 m) from the camp, inland and downstream. The water supply might not inadvertently become contaminated.

Fire can be made below the roots but be careful of your surroundings.
Wind
Shelter

Root Shelter
Can use protruding roots as a frame for a shelter. Dig into remaining root soil or add an additional wind break of branches to improve the shelter. The best is at a base of a fallen tree at right angles to the wind. Always be aware that a partially fallen tree might fall completely.

Roof structure built against a log. This can be covered with birch bark, canvas, branches, or sod.

Tree Bark & Fallen Tree Trunks
Large pieces of tree bark can be laid on a tree trunk. These pieces of bark should be overlapped so that rain will flow over the surface as roofing tiles.

Make sure to cut or add a drainage channel on uphill side.

Bark acting as a water channel.

Make sure to cut or add a drainage channel to control the flow of water.

Hold down with rocks logs, sand, or pegs.

Natural Hollow
Shallow depression in ground can be covered with branches, grass, turf and bark (placed as shingles) to deflect the rain.

Natural hollow in the ground.

Place cover on ground to protect against humidity.

Bough Shelter
Conifers are the best choice as they have the densest branch structure.

Branches can be added for more protection.

Make sure that the tree will not fall.

- Requires no construction if tree has fallen naturally. There might be a problem with the direction of the wind as it probably will blow into the shelter because the wind might have felled the tree
- Be careful how you make a camp. Watch for fire and tree falling.
- Is camouflaged if the tree has a natural fallen look.

Do not use a fire if the tree is dry.

Tree tied down.

PONCHO SHELTER

Poncho with hood with drawstring.

Transparent plastic poncho for rain.

Branches are placed on the trunk of a broken tree. See page 259.

Grommets & Snaps
When buying a poncho, buy two, as the snaps will match and they can be snapped together.

Backpack Poncho

Additional branches have been placed on the frame and branches have been added in front of the entrance.

The entrance is where the tree broke.

Poncho used as a sleeping cover and ground sheet.

Poncho
An excellent compact emergency garment that you should have whenever you are traveling, even in a car.

Excellent location in old growth forest: A lean-to shelter can be built on fallen trees, dry firewood is available, and the ground is dry. Note: Clear material that can burn from the fire area.

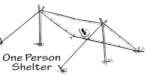

One Person Shelter

Use pole to avoid sag in middle.

Tie hood closed and use as a pocket.

Two Person Shelter

Forked Sticks

All that is left to be done is to add leafy branches or a tarpaulin on top of the branch frame. For cold weather one would place evergreen branches covered by sod or snow.

Poncho Lean-To (single poncho)
A poncho is one of the most versatile items for a trip or as a survival item for the car or boat. It can be used as a poncho, ground sheet, cover of lean-to or tent, sail on a raft, to catch rain water, etc.
• Fast installation. • Minimal equipment.
• 6'-12' (2-4 m) of rope. • Wood stakes.
• Check direction of wind.

Poncho Tent (two poncho)
• Avoid sag in middle by adding a pole support.
• Check the wind direction. • For two people.
• Snap fasteners will snap together to form a roof joint.

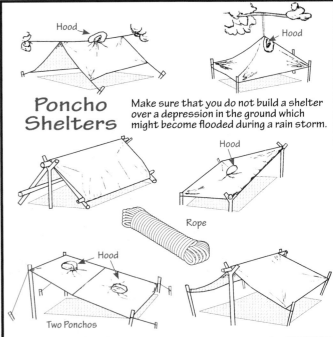

Hood

Hood

Poncho Shelters

Make sure that you do not build a shelter over a depression in the ground which might become flooded during a rain storm.

Hood

Rope

Hood

Two Ponchos

Camp Shower
Built with a teepee like frame. It is a luxury but it might make you feel at home.

Shower head with valve.

Poles are lashed together.

Water in bucket.

Camp Chair

Trowel to dig rain trenches around shelters.

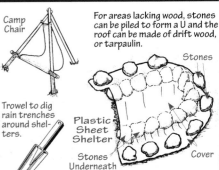

For areas lacking wood, stones can be piled to form a U and the roof can be made of drift wood, or tarpaulin.

Stones

Plastic Sheet Shelter

Stones Underneath

Cover

GROUND SHEET SHELTERS

TARPAULIN & WOVEN POLYETHYLENE

A tarpaulin is a very versatile camping and survival accessory. The original tarpaulins were made of heavy 8 oz. (227 g) cotton canvas that was impregnated with oils or wax. These are very resistant, long lasting and are hardly affected by the sun. They should be well dried, to avoid mildew, before being folded for storage. Modern 'tarpaulins' are made of woven ripstop polyethylene. This material is much cheaper and weighs less. It is affected by UV rays of the sun, can get worn by continuous wind movement, cannot be folded as well as canvas tarpaulins and is very noisy.

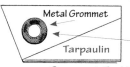

Metal Grommet

Tarpaulin

Grommet Tool Kit
Used to replace damaged grommets or to attach new ones.

Blanket on lashed poles used by Prairie Indians as a shelter from the wind and sun. Note how the survival food is stored in a pouch from the lashed part of the pole. The weight of this pouch helps to stabilize the tripod poles.

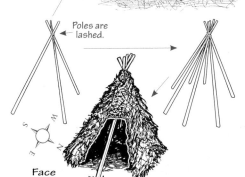

Tarpaulin
Sizes for Shelters
2 person   9' x 12'
4 person   11' x 14'

Folded Polyethylene Tarpaulin

Ground Sheet
Ground sheets should be smaller than the tent floor and never extend beyond the tent floor as it will accumulate water during a rainstorm.

Check for potential rock slides or avalanches.

Stone wall built at far side below tarpaulin.

Tarpaulin or Poncho

Tarpaulin Covering Cave
Entrance or ledge
Attach tarpaulin to the overhang by wedging it into cracks, use pegs weighed down with rocks, etc.

Make a fire against stone wall near the entrance.

Use a ground sheet or wood branches for bedding.

Tarpaulins can be used as covers. As they gather wind, make sure that they are fastened down. If you are covering a light object weigh it down or it might fly away. If you have a wide tarpaulin you can fold the bottom part to form a ground sheet. Attach it well because a shift in the wind's direction can cause your lean-to to balloon. Your ground sheet fold will not let the wind escape below the shelter.

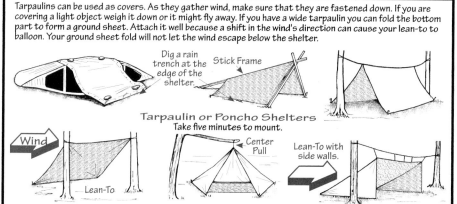

Dig a rain trench at the edge of the shelter.

Stick Frame

Tarpaulin or Poncho Shelters
Take five minutes to mount.

Wind

Lean-To

Center Pull

Lean-To with side walls.

WICKIUP

Used by the plains Indians, in areas where building material was scarce.

- Use three strong poles and lash them at the top using rope, if it is not available weave a braided rope out of straw or long grass. Lean some additional poles on the top.
- Fill in the sides with branches and cover with sagebrush, bush, or dry cacti. For additional protection and to keep out the rain, add denser roofing material such as sod, leather, or woven thatching. Make sure that the pitch of the roof is quite high so that rainwater can run off.
- The entrance to the house faces east so that you can catch the heat and light of the rising sun.

Poles are lashed.

Face East

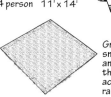

Tarpaulin

Smooth stone, ball, large button, coin, etc.

Place object below surface making sure that there are no sharp edges that might damage the material.

Tie cord tightly below the object and this will act as a grommet.

Tarpaulin or Rain Fly Garter
If tarp lacks sufficient grommets or ties then the garter system can be used. It is simple, economical and can be used in many situations. To act as a retainer a coin, pebble or ball can be used. Make sure that the retainer is not sharp as the material could be damaged.

WIND PROTECTING REFLECTORS

Reflector to retain the heat.

Wind

Reflector

Fire

Reflector

Fire

Birch Bark
Ideal covering material that has been used for thousands of years. It can be used for shelter, canoes, clothing, parchment, fire starter, torches, and water containers. To remove it from the tree incise the bark in two horizontal lines that are 18" (50 cm) apart. Make a vertical cut between these lines and peel off a layer of bark. Do not cut too deeply as you do not want to injure or kill the tree.

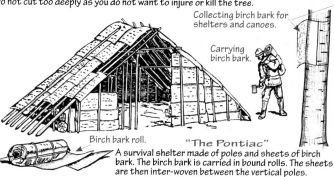

Collecting birch bark for shelters and canoes.

Carrying birch bark.

Birch bark roll.

"The Pontiac"
A survival shelter made of poles and sheets of birch bark. The birch bark is carried in bound rolls. The sheets are then inter-woven between the vertical poles.

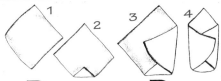

BLANKET BED

This sequence of folding a blanket can be used to make a sleeping bag replacement. A tarpaulin can be folded in the same way to give you a waterproof shelter. Your body in the bag will give it a form so that the water will flow off its surface.

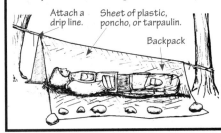

If you do not have a sleeping bag and no time to make better shelter you can use your backpack to cover your feet.

Place waterproof sheet on ground or use evergreen boughs.

BACK PACK BED/SHELTER

A shelter to use in emergencies where you cannot or do not have time to find or erect a more elaborate shelter and have no sleeping bag. Place a plastic sheet or bag on the ground below you to reduce the ground humidity.

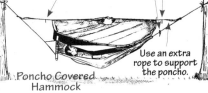

Attach a drip line.   Sheet of plastic, poncho, or tarpaulin.

Backpack

Attach a piece of cord or wood to prevent water from running down the rope into the sleeping area. This should be done on both sides.

Use an extra rope to support the poncho.

Poncho Covered Hammock

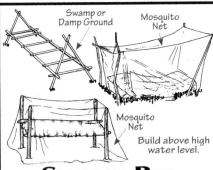

Swamp or Damp Ground   Mosquito Net

Mosquito Net

Build above high water level.

SWAMP BED

In damp areas you need protection from the wet ground. Find four well positioned trees or implant 4 poles, bamboo is preferred if available. This bed can be covered with a mosquito net or poncho.

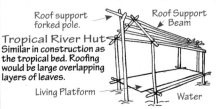

Roof support forked pole.   Roof Support Beam

Tropical River Huts
Similar in construction as the tropical bed. Roofing would be large overlapping layers of leaves.

Living Platform   Water

Jungle Shelter
Jungle shelters are used for protection from the harsh elements of the jungle. Shelters are necessary while sleeping and staying out of inclement weather.

Jungle Bed

• Choose high ground, away from swamps and dry river beds.
• Avoid game tracks and ant infested areas.

BAMBOO BED

Implant bamboo sticks in the mud. Cross ribbing and horizontals are bamboo which is attached with rope or vines. The size and strength depends upon your weight and height. The bedding is palm branches, long reeds, or bull rushes. With taller vertical supports the structure can be covered with a mosquito net.

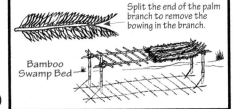

Split the end of the palm branch to remove the bowing in the branch.

Bamboo Swamp Bed

Nights can be dark... A shelter will make you feel more secure.

Importance of a Comfortable Bed
A good sleep in a well prepared bed will give you a positive morale, regenerate your energy, and avoid morning cramps. The features that are required: right size for your body, smooth and soft enough to carry your weight and to minimize the humidity rising from the ground.

Bedding
For bedding chose the driest fluffiest material as this will give the best loft (dry air space) and offer you dry warmth. Keep an extra pile within reach to stuff around your body and in your clothing if you get cold at night.

Before bedding down bury hot coals in the ground. Make sure that the coals do not burn the bedding.

BOUGH BED

Bed for the inside of a lean-to or other shelter. Place logs at the head and feet. Two horizontal poles are placed at the bottom of the log at the feet and on the log at the head. Cross-ribbing is attached to the two horizontal sticks and these are covered with leaves, grass or straw, pine boughs with ribbing at bottom, or ferns for bedding. The two horizontals at an angle create an air pocket below the upper part of the body. For cold weather the bed should be at least 16" (40 cm) thick. In the summer the bed should be 8" (20 cm) thick. The boughs will pack down after a few nights and they can be fluffed up or replaced.

Log at head acts as a support for bed poles. This inclines the bed and gives you a more relaxing sleep and creates an airspace with the ground to reduce the humidity.

Bed Pole

Log at feet acts as frame for bed poles.

Pegs have been driven into the ground. They keep the horizontal poles apart.

Cloth from which the two support poles can be removed for easy transportation.

TRAPPER'S BED

Made for comfortable sleep. If you have had a good sleep your attitude will be more positive, especially, if you are lost. Being rested will help you to be more observant of your environment and be able to respond faster to any situation. Made of a piece of cloth which has piping sewn on both sides. Poles are cut and passed through this piping and these poles, with 4 spacing pegs, rest on two logs.

Straw or heavy stick shaped (bull rushes) growth.

Wet rawhide binding.

Weaving with a Paling Hitch

The Indians used this system to form wall shelters, fences, etc. The best binding that can be used is wet rawhide as it shrinks upon drying, thereby producing a very tight binding.

Thatched Clothing
Make a form of thin young flexible branches. It can be woven or tied with cordage. This frame is then covered with straw and leaves in the same way as a shelter.

Rain Cape

THATCHED SHELTER & CLOTHING

This method of construction, especially for roofing, is still used in England and Ireland. It can last for many years if it has been well assembled and drained.

Thatching can also be used to make capes, blankets, bedding, door covers, and sails. In these cases the framing material is chosen for its flexibility and the layer of covering grass is of a finer quality and is tied in smaller bundles. It can be used on a roof, for a wind wall, and on a log cabin. First build a frame of poles. Thick strong poles for the vertical with thinner poles for the horizontal. The horizontal poles can be interwoven or lashed together with cord or hand made cordage (see Rope Chapter).

Material for Thatching: Long grass is preferable because it is good insulation, can easily be tied in packets, and offers good coverage against rain.

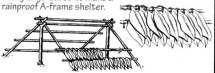

Layer 2
Layer 1

Straw bundles attached with cordage, then fastened to the horizontal ribbing, in overlapping layers, starting from the bottom.

The material used for thatching can be straw, bulrushes, strips if bark, paper from birch bark etc.

Using large leaves to make a rainproof A-frame shelter.

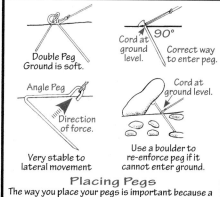

Double Peg Ground is soft.

Angle Peg

Direction of force.

Very stable to lateral movement

Cord at ground level.

Correct way to enter peg.

Cord at ground level.

Use a boulder to re-enforce peg if it cannot enter ground.

Placing Pegs

The way you place your pegs is important because a well placed peg will: Reduce tent flap in the wind and make sure that your tent will stay up in a storm.

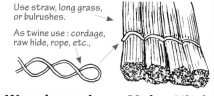

Woven straw can be used as roofing, clothing, floor matting, sail for a raft, or a raft.

Weaving Straw & Grass

Build a frame of poles, as in the illustration, and attach cord (A) between opposite poles. Attach a second set of cords from one set of poles to a horizontal stick (B). Raise the horizontal stick (B) and place a bundle of straw or rushes horizontally across the cord (A) and lower the stick (B) below the level of the cords (A). The first bundle of straw (X) will now have been attached. Continue ...

Use straw, long grass, or bulrushes.

As twine use : cordage, raw hide, rope, etc.,

Weaving using a Malay Hitch

This hitch is used in simple weaving. The strength and flexibility of the resulting matting, wall structure, poncho, depends upon the size, weight, and spacing of the material and binding cord that has been used. This is a very economical structure because upon leaving the campsite only the rope is taken with you and you can weave new matting at the next camping site.

Boat made of woven reeds.

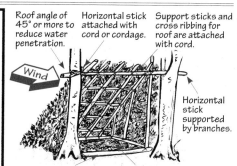

Roof angle of 45° or more to reduce water penetration.

Horizontal stick attached with cord or cordage.

Support sticks and cross ribbing for roof are attached with cord.

Wind

Horizontal stick supported by branches.

Frame for bedding. Bedding made of branches, grass, or leaves. Canvas or birch bark sheets can be used as a base to help reduce the humidity rising from the ground

BUILDING A LEAN-TO

Two vertical supports 6' to 8' (2-3 m) apart. These supports can be trees with branches, at approximately waist height, to hold the horizontal bar. The bar can be attached with a cord. The vertical supports can be a tripod of sticks (attached by rope or vines) or forked sticks which are stuck into the ground.

Covering of Roof & Sides

The covering can be logs that are cut to measure (if one requires a strong roof to support snow).
- To place the layers of roofing: Start at the bottom and the additional layers should overlap for waterproofing.
- Rotten log castings which can be placed, in an over-lapping fashion e.g., Spanish roof tiles.
- Tree boughs on a grid structure of branches.
- Grass sod on a grid structure of branches.
- Large leaves, palm branches on a matrix.
- Sheets of birch bark.

Lean-to that is heated by a fire built behind a reflector.

Reflector reflecting heat from fire.

A long lean-to used by Indians in the late 1880's.

Inuit family with a fur covered summer lean-to.

LEAN-TO

LEAN-TO

Lean-To

An easy to assemble shelter that can be built by using a support structure of two trees and some poles. The lean-to is one of the most practical and multipurpose shelters. It can be used as a temporary refuge on a travel circuit. This structure was called a Matchejin by the Indians. All that is required is a wooded area, a knife and some time. There are many variants and different materials can be used.

6'- 8' (2-3 m) Width

'Y' Sticks for support.

Waist Level High

Wind

Lean-To with a Reflector

Reflector for heat placed at 45° from the vertical.

Double Lean-to

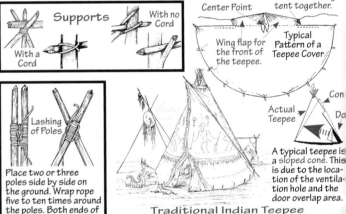

Note the direction of the wind and place the structure so that there is a cross wind to blow the smoke away ....

TEEPEE/WIGWAM

The teepee and its variants were developed by nomadic peoples. They were used on the American Plains, by the hordes of Genghis Khan and are still used on the steppes of Asia. The poles can be straight or curved as the yurts of Asia. The sloping poles can be covered with ponchos, parachute, woven material, branches, skins, birch bark, or modern materials. They are fast to assemble and can have an open fire in the interior. There is a ventilation hole at the top, for smoke, where the poles are lashed.

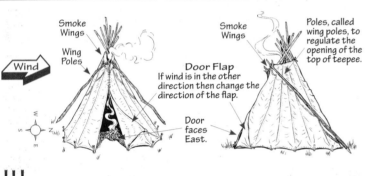

Smoke Wings

Wing Poles

Wind

Door Flap
If wind is in the other direction then change the direction of the flap.

Door faces East.

Smoke Wings

Poles, called wing poles, to regulate the opening of the top of teepee.

Supports

With a Cord

With no Cord

Holes for lacing tent together.

Center Point

Wing flap for the front of the teepee.

Typical Pattern of a Teepee Cover

Lashing of Poles

Place two or three poles side by side on the ground. Wrap rope five to ten times around the poles. Both ends of the rope are now tied lengthwise between the poles and a square knot is used to secure the rope. This might feel loose but when the structure is mounted the rope will tighten and keep the poles in place.

Actual Teepee

Con

Do

A typical teepee is a sloped cone. This is due to the location of the ventilation hole and the door overlap area.

Traditional Indian Teepee

The Plains Indians were nomads following the buffalo herds. They needed a transportable shelter that could comfortably accommodate a family and be strong enough to resist winter winds. The material used were buffalo hides that were stitched together to form a pattern as in the adjacent illustration. The Teepee was lined with buffalo hides in the winter. All Teepees had inside fires. The outside walls of the Teepees were decorated with records of war, bird and animal figures from visions.

TEEPEE

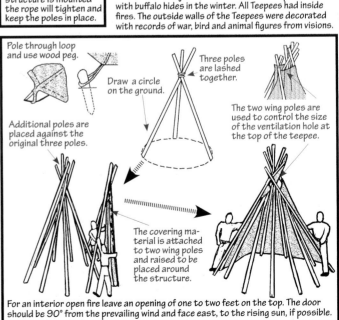

Pole through loop and use wood peg.

Draw a circle on the ground.

Three poles are lashed together.

Additional poles are placed against the original three poles.

The two wing poles are used to control the size of the ventilation hole at the top of the teepee.

The covering material is attached to two wing poles and raised to be placed around the structure.

For an interior open fire leave an opening of one to two feet on the top. The door should be 90° from the prevailing wind and face east, to the rising sun, if possible.

264

Donald Curley

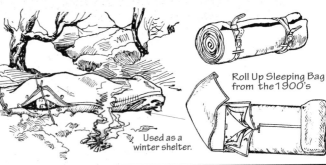

Roll Up Sleeping Bag from the 1900's

Used as a winter shelter.

Basic cold weather shelter... A blanket and a fire.

Making Bricks

Wood mold on four sides.

Mixture of mud and straw.

Let the "brick" dry in the sun and it can be used for building.

Mud-Straw Cement

Mud (the binding agent) and straw can be mixed together to form a mixture that can be plastered to fill cracks between rocks or logs. If you are in a very sunny hot climate you can make a brick-shaped mold out of wood. Place a mud-straw mixture in the mold, let it dry in the sun. After a few hours remove the brick from the mold and let it dry some more. This process can be repeated and the bricks can be assembled into a fireplace or small house etc. The bricks should be covered against falling rain as the mud binding will wash away. This is why old houses always had an overhanging roof in the direction of the falling rain.

To travel through the snow after a heavy snowfall you can follow deer feeding tracks which are usually well compacted. Later you can make some emergency snowshoes.

Winter Camp

The best location for a camp is in a thick forest, in a hollow, or a protected valley and out of the wind. Use as much natural insulation as possible. Dig into the snow, build wind breaks, and cover the shelter and shelter floors with boughs. Powder snow is a good insulation as there are many air pockets.

Winter Evergreen Bough Bed
Evergreen boughs keep the body off the ground, reduce the humidity from the ground, and add a layer of insulation for extra warmth.

Sod family house from the Prairies. The roof would be of wood and thatching.

Turf or sod is soil with the root structure of grass to hold it together.

Note: If in a rainy climate the roof should extend over the wall on the side of the predominant rain - otherwise the rainwater will erode the exposed side.

Dugout or buried houses that are built with a sod structure. These semi or permanent houses can be used year round. They are cool in the summer and warm in the winter.

Rolling Sod or Turf

Wall of Sod

Cutting of Sod

Sod turned over.

Debris or sod between parallel rows of sticks.

Wind Wall
Place debris between a parallel row of sticks. This structure can be expanded into a four walled house which can then be roofed over. This wall can also be used for hunting.

SOD SHELTER

These structures were used as houses by the settlers in the North American prairies during the turn of the century and even during the Great Depression. They are built in areas where there is a lack of trees. The tool required is a long heavy knife or ax. The method of construction is similar to placing bricks. The style of structure will depend upon how many people you have to house, how long you will stay, the climate (in the fall or winter you would consider having a fire or stove on the inside), and the material and tools available. You can build a simple lean-to, igloo, up to a small house. Cut pieces of turf 6"x 18" (15 x 46 cm).

Thickness of sod cover depends upon how cold it will become. It can be from two to four feet thick.

Keep angle steep to help water run off.

Door cover can be double layered canvas or a double thatched blanket.

Wind from side to keep the smoke of the fire out of the shelter.

A heat reflector can be built behind the fire to reflect heat into the shelter.

DEBRIS HUT

A variant of the lean-to but the covering provides more protection from the elements because it only has a small opening and a thick layer of insulation on the roof. The central roof pole is supported by a pile of rocks, tree stump, stick tripod etc. The roof ribbing is made of smaller sticks that lean on the roof pole. The ribbing is then covered with whatever is on hand: grass, moss, sticks, birch bark, pieces of dry turf, mud, etc. This covering should be from two to four feet thick, depending upon the temperature. Try to keep the covering steep to improve the protection against rain.

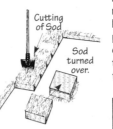

Trapper tarpaulin covered cold weather log cabin.

Fur trappers winter log cabin.

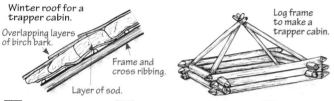

Winter roof for a trapper cabin.

Overlapping layers of birch bark.

Frame and cross ribbing.

Layer of sod.

Log frame to make a trapper cabin.

TRAPPER TARPAULIN CABIN

This can almost be considered as a permanent structure. It is hard work to build and difficult to displace if the wrong location is chosen. A location near water is ideal. A ridge or promontory is an excellent choice as with wind there will be less insects and the higher elevation provides less risk of flooding. A double layered (air-spaced) roof of canvas would improve the insulation and waterproofing. Requires straight logs of 4"-8" (10-20 cm) diameter.

Area around log cabin is clear-cut to provide logs for cabin's construction.

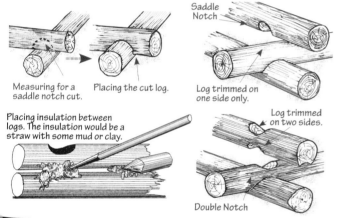

Measuring for a saddle notch cut.

Placing the cut log.

Saddle Notch

Log trimmed on one side only.

Placing insulation between logs. The insulation would be a straw with some mud or clay.

Log trimmed on two sides.

Double Notch

LOG CABIN

These shelters are built by forest dwellers in temperate climates from the Americas to Russia. Logs provide solid stable structures that are well insulated from the elements. Logs are placed as shown in the illustrations and mud/straw cement is placed between them as insulation. The design of the roof is important as it should extend over the wall that is exposed to the rain to prevent the rain from washing away the mud cement.

A low trapper log cabin that is easy to heat.

Sod home with a sod/grass roof.

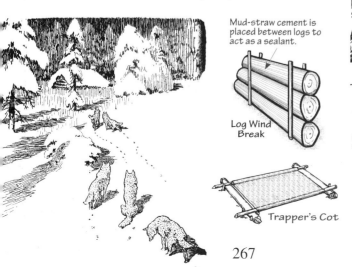

Mud-straw cement is placed between logs to act as a sealant.

Log Wind Break

Trapper's Cot

Winter visitors...
The whole pack !

267

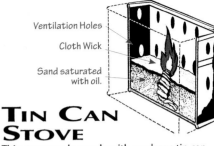

Animal skin covered cold weather shelter presently in use in the Yukon. This is a teepee type structure with skins covering the poles.

TIN CAN STOVE

This stove can be made with any large tin can. For ventilation pierce holes on the sides of the can. Partially fill the can with fine sand while holding a cloth wick in place. Saturate the sand with fuel or oil. Do not pour too much fuel and do not add fuel until the stove and sand are cold. This stove can be used for heating and cooking. Make sure that there is sufficient ventilation.

Lean-to winter shelter built of branches and boughs against a tree trunk.

HEATING WINTER SHELTERS

STOVE PIPE STOVE

This is an easy inexpensive stove. Place pipe stove on a dirt base. Stove is fed from the top.

Chimney Pipe Thimble

If you install a stove with a chimney in a tent you need a pipe thimble. The thimble creates a barrier between the tent material and the hot pipe. This thimble is made of two sheets of aluminum riveted together. Only use a stove in an approved fireproof tent.

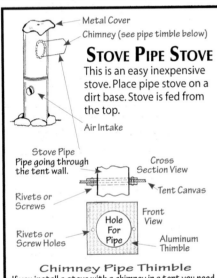

Indian Board Toboggan

Emergency Survival Candle

Tarpaulin and bark covered sod winter shelters. Firewood is stored in the covered piles next to the shelters.

HOT ROCK HEATING

To keep warm while sleeping on the ground, place large dry flat stones on the burning wood in the fire pit. Before going to sleep scrap the remaining burning wood to one side, removing all burning particles. Leave the hot stones in the pit and cover this warm area with a layer of sand. Place your ground cloth and sleeping bag over this spot and have a warm night.

No combustible material should be near the hot rocks as a fire could start up or you can be smoked out of your shelter.

Hot Stone

BUCKET HEATING

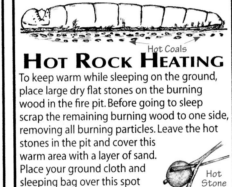

Air Holes

Small pail of embers for heating.

Hot Stones

Attention for CARBON MONOXIDE POISONING. ☠

Throw stones into a campfire. Once they are red hot place the hot stones into a metal bucket. Carry the bucket into the shelter and invert the bucket. This will warm the shelter. Do not invert the stones onto any flammable material.

Heating a Lean-to

Insulated Water Canteen
The insulation keeps the water from freezing.

KOOLIK

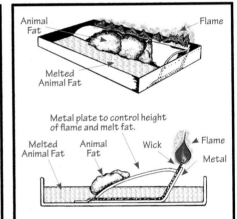

Animal Fat — Flame

Melted Animal Fat

Metal plate to control height of flame and melt fat.

Melted Animal Fat — Animal Fat — Wick — Flame — Metal

The Inuit have used the koolik for thousands of years. The Inuit koolik is carved from soapstone but it can be made out of any flat metal container. A piece of cloth, absorbent cotton, or dense moss can be used as a wick. The heat can be controlled by changing the length of the wick and by the metal or stone damper covering the wick. To avoid smoke, animal fats are used as fuel, in the case of the Inuit, seal oil or caribou fat. Lubricating oil can be burned but the wick will have to be frequently trimmed so that the flame will not smoke. Gasoline cannot be used as it is very explosive. Two or three drops of gasoline can be put on the wick to start the fire.

The koolik is used for heating, light and cooking. It is seated on sticks that have been pushed into the snow shelf. The cooking pot would be suspended from hooks pierced into the snow wall.

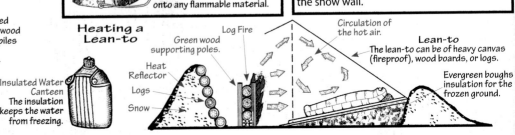

Log Fire
Green wood supporting poles.
Heat Reflector
Logs
Snow

Circulation of the hot air.

Lean-to
The lean-to can be of heavy canvas (fireproof), wood boards, or logs.

Evergreen boughs insulation for the frozen ground.

Snow Cornice

Military Sand & Snow Peg (very wide)

Do not camp below a snow cornice as it might collapse or cause an avalanche

Starting building a pole shelter.

Pole house shelter presently in use in the Yukon.

INSULATING A TENT

ent should be erected perpendicular to the prevailing wind to avoid snow accumulation in front of the entrance. Place a lattice frame over the tent and cover it with evergreen boughs. Slip branches of the boughs through the lattice to attach them. Throw a layer of snow over the boughs and add to the layer every few days as it will melt and get eroded by blowing snow. Powder snow is a good insulation as there are many air pockets.

Strong Tree

Snow

Snow

Wind

Evergreen boughs for bedding and insulation.

Pole Lattice

Evergreen Boughs

TENT SUPPORTS

During cold weather you have to plan the most efficient way to mount a tent. The taut-line and clove hitch are useful as they can be adjusted without being detached. The illustration also shows a deadman ground attachment. This deadman is made of a pole covered with evergreen boughs with snow being placed on the boughs to weigh them down.

Double Walled Tent
The two layers of tent are a few inches apart so as to provide additional wind break from the cold wind. The edge of the outside layer is covered by snow.

Clove Hitch
Permits variable adjustment as it can be raised or lowered and the pole can be moved in or out to remove wrinkles from the tent.

Taut-Line Hitch Permits variable adjustment of the ridge rope without having to untie it to adjust its length.

Winter Deadman
Branch buried in snow.

Outer wall of tent.

Inner Wall

Snow

Double Walled Winter Tent

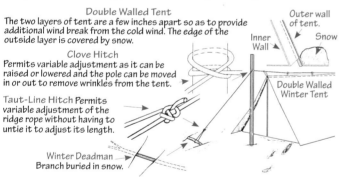

Winter Deadman
If no snow pegs are available, ground is frozen or will not retain pegs.

Ice — Water
Water will freeze.

Under rocks.

Ice or Hard Snow
Fill hole with water to freeze.

Buried in snow.

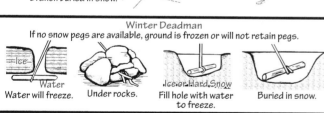

Snow Wall
Made with logs and snow.

Seeking shelter behind a snow wall in a reflective emergency blanket.

Snow Wall

Snow wall wind break built by Inuit for seal hunting.

SNOW WALL

In open areas a snow wall can be built as protection against strong winds and blowing snow. Make sure that you do not get covered by drifting snow on the lee side of the wall.

Snow is an excellent insulating material that keeps you warm, safe, and dry.

Tarpaulin Cover

Evergreen Boughs

Original snow wind depression which is built up by removal of the snow to enlarge the depression.

TREE SNOW SHELTER

Branches can be cut away from underside or you can tunnel into the snow drift below a large evergreen tree. The entrance should be at right angle to the wind. For insulation place a pile of evergreen boughs on the ground.

TREE-PIT

Select a large tree with thick lower branches and surrounded with deep snow. Below the tree you will find a pit with less snow. This area can be enlarged and you can dig deeper, even to ground level. As insulation you can collect tree branches from other trees and cover the bottom and walls. As roofing you can use a poncho or other material covered with snow. Position the entrance out of the wind's way. Make a small pit shelter to retain as much heat as possible.

Evergreens, with their large low branches, make a temporary shelter or hunting position.

Shake the frost out of a sleeping bag after use.

Scrape the loose snow off the ground before bedding down.

SEAM SEAL

A tarpaulin shelter built by hunters.

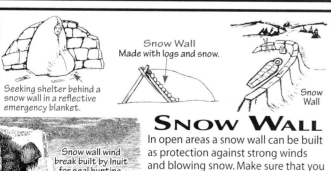

SNOW SHELTERS FACTS

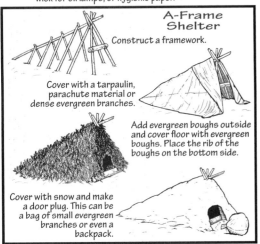

Inuits gathering moss that will be used as insulation, wick for oil lamps, or hygienic paper.

A-Frame Shelter

Construct a framework.

Cover with a tarpaulin, parachute material or dense evergreen branches.

Add evergreen boughs outside and cover floor with evergreen boughs. Place the rib of the boughs on the bottom side.

Cover with snow and make a door plug. This can be a bag of small evergreen branches or even a backpack.

Place insulating material as leaves, cattail fluff, milkweed, etc. below clothing to better retain your body heat.

Bulrush Sleeping Bag
Use bulrushes (cattail) as insulation to make an emergency sleeping bag. Collect the hair from ripe bulrushes, fluff it up, place it between two layers of material, and stitch the insulation in place. Ripe bulrushes can be found in humid areas or drainage ditches all winter.

Nylon or leather shell.

Cattail - Bullrush   Milkweed

Insulation can be a wool glove or other insulating materials - leaves, moss, feathers, cattail, milkweed.

Coleman
DISPOSABLE HAND WARMERS

Hand warmer
Activated by removing from packet and shaking. Warms in gloves or pockets for up to six hours.

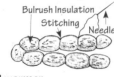

Bulrush Insulation
Stitching
Needle

Stuffing bird down and feathers inside socks for additional insulation. Can also stuff ripe cattail or milkweed fluff.

Wolf seeking shelter below an evergreen. This provides a wind break and insulation because the evergreen is snow covered

CARBON MONOXIDE (CO)
Carbon monoxide gas is colorless, tasteless & odorless.

Carbon monoxide gas is the highest risk of death in a well insulated environment.
It is produced by incomplete combustion when there is a lack of oxygen to turn the burnt product into carbon dioxide (CO_2). Hemoglobin in the blood will absorb carbon monoxide two hundred times faster than oxygen. It breaks down the hemoglobin's ability to absorb oxygen and the body will starve of oxygen. Carbon monoxide is cumulative and can accumulate over a number of days. You will not know that you are lacking oxygen as you will not be short of breath nor have a bluish discoloration of the fingernails, lips or the skin.

You cannot see it & You cannot smell it. It is an invisible killer.
The first signs of carbon monoxide poisoning are fainting and collapsing. Further effects are flu-like symptoms, watery eyes, headaches, dizziness, fatigue, heart flutter, vomiting, extreme sleepiness, shortness of breath, nausea, frontal headaches, and decreased mental capacity - and possibly DEATH. The brain requires a large supply of oxygen to function. To eliminate carbon monoxide from the system one requires four hours of fresh air to reduce the carbon monoxide by one half.

VENTILATION
Cross-ventilation is required to have a sufficient change of air in restricted quarters, especially when using interior oil, gas, or charcoal heaters. In cold regions carbon monoxide is a common cause of death because shelters are well insulated. Ventilation and awareness of potential carbon monoxide problems are extremely important in building a shelter.

If Carbon Monoxide poisoning is suspected...
· IMMEDIATELY get victim to fresh air.
· If victim is not breathing give mouth to mouth resuscitation.
· Get help!
· Administer oxygen to victim.

A snow shelter is an excellent way to stay warm and secure but the following should be observed...
· Watch for snow erosion on the outside walls. Blowing snow can be as abrasive as sandpaper and a whiteout can cause major damage. An inspection has to be made after every storm and additional snow should be piled up. If you are in a very windy area consider building a snow wall a few feet from the shelter.
· Remove some clothing, to reduce sweating, when doing physical work. Make sure your clothing is always dry as it should retain heat and also help avoid hypothermia.
· Clear snow accumulation from the entrance right after every storm. Build a snow wall if there is a problem of drifting.
· Do not overheat as the shelter will ice up and lose its insulation and breathing qualities. Overheating might also cause the roof to weaken and it might even collapse which could suffocate the occupants.
· Before entering, frost, ice, and snow must be brushed off your clothing.
· All gasoline stoves and lanterns must be filled outside. On the inside they must be placed in a location where they will not be knocked over.
· A smaller shelter is easier to heat.
· Drips can be stopped by placing snow on their source.
· Keep a digging tool in the shelter as you might have to dig yourself out.
· Check the ventilation holes frequently as they might be blocked with snow and the carbon monoxide and humidity cannot escape. At least two holes are required, one at the top, to let air escape, and one near the ground to let in fresh air.
· Make sure that you always have a supply of fuel and food in the shelter, stored at a low and cold level, as unexpected bad weather might set in and last for days.
· Clearly mark the entrance and remember the physical characteristics of your surroundings. This will help you find your shelter if a storm suddenly arises.
· Staying in a snow shelter can be boring. If there is a group, every person should be assigned a task that can be rotated. Tasks can be divided into: tending the fire at all times, gathering fuel, preparing food, gathering food, hunting in pairs, checking vent holes, checking structure, and watching for the possibility of signaling to a search party in a survival situation. These tasks should be viewed as entertainment especially when morale has to be raised.
· In the inside of a well built snow shelter the temperature will always be above 32°F (0°C). A survival candle will easily raise the temperature by 10°F (4°C). See article on the Inuit Koolik.

HOW TO BUILD FIRES ON A SNOW SURFACE

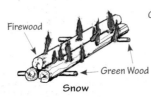

Firewood

Green Wood

Snow

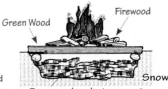

Firewood
Green Wood
Evergreen boughs to prevent snow from melting.
Snow

Firewood
Snow
Green Wood Base

SNOW CAVE

Remember cold weather construction takes much energy.

Consider ...

How long will you stay?

How many people in the group?

How much energy can you use up?

Make the shelter as small as possible to make it easy to heat but still have enough space for your group and space to scrape snow and ice off clothing.

DRIFT SNOW CAVE

Ventilation Hole

Elevated Sleeping Platform

1 Find a spot with well packed drift snow. Dig a chest high hole into the drift. Hole can be dug with a shovel, a wooden board, hands, snow saw, or snow knife.

2 Dig a horizontal rectangle at height of shoulders keeping the snow blocks that are removed.

3 Dig upward into the rectangular area. The objective is to make a platform for a sleeping area above the level of the ground. To help keep the hot air inside the cave. Extend the entrance at ground level for two feet and down for about one foot.

4 Cover the triangular opening with the snow blocks from the original digging. Fill any cracks with snow.

5 Make a ventilation hole in the roof of shelter. Block the entrance with a backpack.

LOCATION: SNOW CAVE

- Dig into a hard snow drift, or a slope with a firm crust. This is usually found on the lee side (the opposite side from which the wind is blowing) of a steep ridge or river bank. The snow drift should be at least 9' (3 m) deep. Snow that is newly fallen, powdery, or loose should be avoided.
- Before digging, test the depth of the snow and also its consistency by probing with sticks, ski pole, or skis.
- The entrance should be 45° downwind so that the wind will keep it free of snow.
- Make sure that the drift is not below a cornice or in an avalanche area.

LIVING: SNOW CAVE

- Heating with gas stove or candles. These should be extinguished when occupants are asleep. If weather is very cold one person will have to stay awake to watch the fire and the ventilation holes.
- The entrance should be small and can be blocked with a hard piece of snow or backpacks but leave a small crack, near the floor, for fresh air to enter.
- Ponchos, cardboard, and tree branches can be used for ground blankets.
- When you are cooking you might consider leaving the door open.
- Do not walk on the roof as it might collapse.
- Chores can be assigned to different individuals to ensure that everything is taken care of, to avoid any conflicts in a confined area, and to reduce boredom.

BUILDING: SNOW CAVE

- The shelter should be as small as possible so that minimum heating is required. A lit candle can raise the temperature to 40°F (4°C). It is better to build one large cave for numerous occupants than many small ones. It uses less fuel to heat and less energy to build. When a large cave is built it can be made to suit the physical constraints of the terrain and short side tunnels can be built for sleeping quarters, latrine, storage space, and kitchen.
- A small tunnel is burrowed, at the lowest level of the chamber, for one yard (one meter).
- A chamber is now dug at right angles to the tunnel entrance.
- The chamber should be high enough to provide comfortable sitting space.
- The sleeping and sitting platform should be above the level of the entrance. This will be the warmest area of the cave.
- The roof should be well arched, without sharp groves, to provide the maximum support. Groves would be weak spots as there could be a shearing in the packed snow. The arching would also prevent water from dripping on the floor as it would flow along the slope and ice up.
- The roof should be at least 18" (30 cm) thick.
- There should be a roof ventilation hole to allow carbon monoxide gases and smoke to escape and to prevent asphyxiation. There should also be a ventilation hole in the door to allow fresh air to enter. These should be checked every two to three hours.

SNOW CAVE SURVIVAL

- It is important to have an air vent 3 to 4 inches (7-10 cm) in diameter.
- Try to dig to ground level as the exposed ground has its own built-in heat supply.
- If there is a frosty coating on the ceiling after a cold night this indicates that the roof is too thin, add more snow on the roof.
- After a few days the ceiling can be ice. Scrape the ceiling because the roof should "breathe" to prevent the air from being stuffy and risking a buildup of carbon monoxide.
- If ceiling arches, there should be no problem with the ceiling collapsing.
- If the roof sags, scrape the inside to raise the ceiling's height. If possible cook outside.
- The snow cave is most comfortable during extreme cold. It will be humid and drippy when there is too much heat or it is warm outside.
- Take all your equipment into the snow cave as a snowstorm can bury everything.
- Sleeping bags should be turned inside out. Beat out the frost and fluff them up.
- Do not let candles or a stove burn all night as this might deplete the oxygen.
- Mark the entrance of the cave so that you will find it in the white wilderness. This is especially true if there are potential whiteouts or the land has no distinguishing features.

Survival Heating Candle

Waterproof Matches

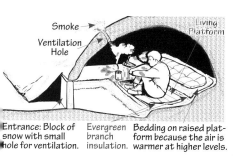

Smoke

Ventilation Hole

Living Platform

Entrance: Block of snow with small hole for ventilation.

Evergreen branch insulation.

Bedding on raised platform because the air is warmer at higher levels.

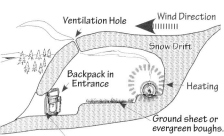

Ventilation Hole

Wind Direction

Snow Drift

Backpack in Entrance

Heating

Ground sheet or evergreen boughs.

Leave some space for air to come in from outside.

Entrance perpendicular to wind.

Emergency Candle 8 to 10 hours burn time. Can be used for light and heat.

Folding Shovel & Pick

Entrance perpendicular to wind. Note that the higher embankment is on the windward side in this way protecting the entrance.

PACKED SNOW IGLOO

1 Cover a pile of evergreen boughs or dry grass with material or plastic sheeting. Place snow on the pile and pack it down. Depending upon the humidity in the snow, the covering should be at least one foot thick and two feet at the base. Let the snow pile stand for one or two hours to let it harden. The entrance should be placed perpendicular to the wind.

2 Remove the evergreen boughs and the material cover.

3 Make an entrance stopper by packing some small boughs in a bag.

4 Place boughs of evergreens on the ground for bedding. Make a small ventilation hole in the top of the igloo.

Shovel to clear blowing snow.

Entrance

Wind

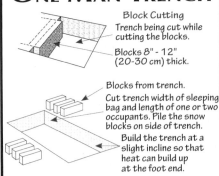

Digging a snow trench. Note pile of snow blocks.

Passage in large trench. This trench housed five or six people in side holes in the snow bed.

Entrance

Side holes for beds.

Inside a large snow trench.

Entrance

SNOW TRENCH

- A trench is easy and fast to build.
- **Tools:** Snow knife or snow saw.
- **Width:** width of sleeping bag.
- **Length:** height of one or two people.

Disadvantage: Very cramped. Not enough space to scrape snow and ice off clothing and sleeping bag. Will become damp when compared to an igloo. This should be considered as a temporary structure and an igloo built if a long stay is expected.

TWO MAN TRENCH

A two man trench has a central entrance below a square block construction. This is where baggage can be stored or a fire built.

Ventilation Hole

Wind

If snow piles up its weight will compact the snow until the bottom layer of snow will form ice.

ONE MAN TRENCH

Block Cutting
Trench being cut while cutting the blocks.

Blocks 8" - 12" (20-30 cm) thick.

Blocks from trench.
Cut trench width of sleeping bag and length of one or two occupants. Pile the snow blocks on side of trench.

Build the trench at a slight incline so that heat can build up at the foot end.

The trench should be oriented so that the wind blows from the foot (narrow) side as this would minimize snow erosion. A daily inspection should be made to avoid a collapse of the roof during a whiteout.

A triangular key block is placed vertically at the foot end of the trench. This will serve as the end support of the roof.

Key Block
Foot End
Notch

Cut a notch along the inside wall of trench. The size and width of this notch depends upon the condition of your snow.

Weak snow would require a larger notch.

The roof blocks are angle trimmed so that the tops meet at a point. The first roof block is a half block in width so that the joint lines of the other blocks do not meet as this would produce a weakness in the roof.

First block is half size.

Full size block.

First block is full size.

Use equipment as bedding to avoid direct contact with the snow.

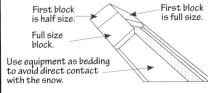

Fill spaces between snow blocks with snow.

Do not forget a ventilation hole in the roof.

Block doorway with a snow block or backpack.

Wind

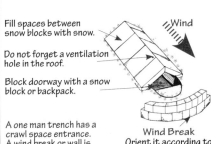

A one man trench has a crawl space entrance. A wind break or wall is built near the entrance.

Wind Break
Orient it according to predominant winds.

SNOW & LOCATION

Snow: Firmly packed snow usually in wind blown area with deep snow drifts. A cubic foot block of snow should support the weight of a man. The snow can be cut or sawed and easily split.

Location: Find a snow drift that is deep enough to cut blocks from the vertical face. Requires two feet of depth. Probe snow with a stick to find an area free of soft and hard layers. Snow should support your weight while leaving a slight mark of the boots. If not enough vertical snow is available, surface snow will have to be cut, but this is much more difficult.

Snow Home: If there is a lack of snow in one location, an above ground snow home can be built. A snow home is similar to a trench except the walls are vertical as the center section of a two man trench and the roof is usually flat. Snow is piled around the walls to reduce wall erosion by the wind blown snow.

SNOW KNIFE & SAW

The essential tools for arctic survival are the snow saw or snow knife. These are more important than a gun and should be included in any arctic travel package. These items are easy to make as they do not require any special tempering (tempering might make them too brittle for the cold) or fine honing.

The Inuit say that in the barren north you need a large knife or a miracle to survive.

Snow Knife
A knife with a 20" (50 cm) long and 2" (5 cm) wide blade, and a two-hands handle. The thick two hands handle provides a good grip while wearing a pair of arctic mitts.

Snow Saw
The blade is 20" (50 cm) long and 3 1/2" (9 cm) wide. The handle is made for two hands and is designed so that one saws vertically.

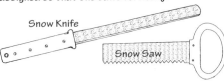

Snow Knife

Snow Saw

CUTTING SNOW BLOCKS

After having chosen the correct type of snow for an igloo start cutting two parallel lines to form the trench where the blocks will be cut.

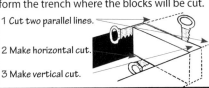

1 Cut two parallel lines.

2 Make horizontal cut.

3 Make vertical cut.

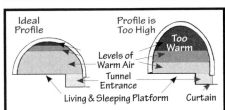

Ideal Profile

Profile is Too High

Too Warm

Levels of Warm Air

Tunnel Entrance

Living & Sleeping Platform

Curtain

IGLOO PROFILE

The profile of the dome of an igloo is very important. If it is too low it is hard to move in the igloo. If the dome is too high the igloo risks collapsing as to keep the living platform warm much more heat is required and as hot air rises the air in the top of the dome will be very warm making the snow warm, wet, heavy and soft.

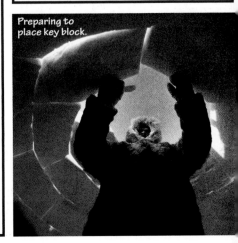

Preparing to place key block.

INUIT IGLOO CONSTRUCTION

INUIT IGLOO

This igloo was used by the Central Inuits as a permanent winter lodging for one or two families. The extended entrance was used for storage and to keep out the cold. The curtains between each igloo type tunnel were animal skins which were hung in two at a time to reduce heat loss.

IGLOO

- Solid, can be heated, can house a family, can be a relatively long-term shelter, and resists wind.
- Tools required: a snow saw or knife.

CHOICE OF A LOCATION

It is most important to find the correct snow. This snow should support a man's weight and leave only a slight imprint of the boot. This snow is usually found where drifts have been formed from windblown snow.

Size

Persons	1	2	3	4	5
Diameter (ft)	8	9	10	12	13
Diameter (m)	2.4	2.7	3	3.6	4

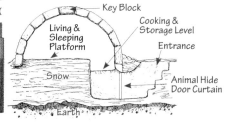

AGING OF IGLOOS

Heating causes igloos to ice up and lose their porous ventilating properties. Do not overheat. Shelters that have lost their ventilation and insulation properties are usually abandoned and new ones are built. The old houses can be reused by cutting out the top (2' - 3') and placing a tarpaulin top with a pipe thimble over the hole. An oil stove vent pipe can then be used in this shelter. Use water that freezes to 'glue' the canvas to the dome. To increase the insulation capacity of an old igloo pile snow around the outside walls.

TWO IGLOO TYPES

Flat Tier Model: Blocks are placed horizontally in layers as bricks.
Spiral Model: Blocks are inclined and gradually slope to the top. This method is easier for a beginner as the successive rows tie in better, reducing the chance of collapse. Below is a description of the spiral method.

SPIRAL MODEL
Layout of Floor

In an area where the snow is at least two feet deep, draw a circle with a diameter as per the occupant chart on the surface of the snow. This will be the inside diameter of the igloo. Layout the circle with the direction of the door perpendicular to the wind.
Lay a line A-B perpendicular to the door approximately 1/3 the diameter from the door. This moon-shaped floor area will produce some blocks and become the storage, cooking, and exit area.

Blocks Cut From Part of Floor Area

Blocks 40 x 40 x 80 cm (15 x 15 x 30 inches) are cut from the floor inside of the circle and placed outside of the circle. These blocks will then be split. See adjacent article.

Starting First Layer of Blocks

To start the first layer, place a full-sized block on the outside of the circle. Adjacent to it place a block with a slope cut into it. This will give the igloo its spiral form. The third and fourth blocks will also have a slope; then full blocks are used.

Second Layer & Other Layers

The blocks will start to tilt inwards and be trimmed for the contact points. To lay the layers of snow blocks, the person stays inside the igloo and then will dig himself out.

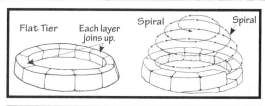

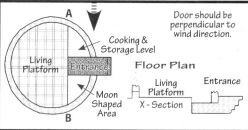

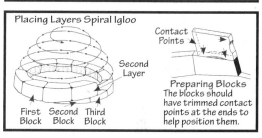

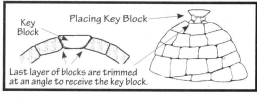

Splitting Igloo Blocks

The blocks from the floor area are split on the large flat side. To split cut a groove, with your saw, two inches wide at each end of the block six inches (15 cm) from the face. Then score a groove along the length of the block parallel to the surface joining the cut grooves.

Cut with a saw between the two inch grooves and the block will break apart. If using a snow knife deepen the groove by continuous scoring and then with a firm stroke the block will separate.

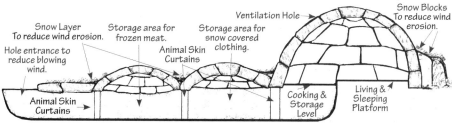

24 THE DONNER PARTY

One of the most famous survival tragedies in US history...

I was a child when we started to California, yet I remember and have cause to remember it, as a little band of emigrants who drove out of Springfield, Illinois that spring morning of 1846 have since been known in history as the "Ill-fated Donner party" of "Martyr Pioneers." My father, James F. Reed, was the originator of the party, and the Donner brothers, George and Jacob, who lived just a little way out of Springfield, decided to join him.

Our wagons, or the "Reed wagons," as they were called, were all made to order and I can say that nothing like our family wagon ever started across the plains. It was what might be called a two story wagon or "Pioneer palace car," attached to a regular immigrant train. The entrance was on the side, like that of an old fashioned stage coach, and one

The Donner Party was a group of emigrants traveling to California who in the winter of 1846-47 met with one of the most famous survival tragedies in US history. This was written by Virginia Reed the daughter of James F. Reed - the originator of the venture.

stepped into a small room, as it were, in the centre of the wagon. At the right and left were spring seats with comfortable high backs, where one could sit and ride with as much ease. In this little room was placed a tiny sheet iron stove, whose pipe, running through the top of the wagon, was prevented by a circle of tin from setting fire to the canvas cover. A board about a foot wide extended over the wheels on either side the full length of the wagon, thus forming the foundation for a large and roomy second story in which were placed our beds. Tinder the spring seats were compartments in which were stored many articles useful for the journey, such as a well filled work basket and a full assortment of medicines, with lint and bandages for dressing wounds. Our clothing was packed in strong canvas bags plainly marked. Strange to

say, we had to abandon this wagon, standing like a monument on the Salt Lake desert.

We had two wagons loaded with provisions. My father started with supplies enough to last us through the first winter in California, had we made the journey in the usual time of six months. We even took a cooking stove which never had a fire in it, and was destined never to have, as we cached it in the desert. Certainly no family ever started across the plains with more provisions or a better outfit for the journey; and yet we reached California almost destitute and nearly out of clothing.

The family wagon was drawn by four yoke (two oxen per yoke) of oxen. The other wagons were drawn by three yoke each. We had saddle horses and cows, and last but not least my pony. But a day came when I had no pony to ride, the poor little fellow gave out. He could not endure the hardships of ceaseless travel. When I was forced to part with him I cried until I was ill, and sat in the back of the wagon watching him become smaller and smaller as we drove on, until I could see him no more.

Never can I forget the morning when we bade farewell to kindred and friends. The Donners were there, having driven in the evening before with their families, so that we might get an early start. At last we were all in

The Reed pioneer palace car.

274

the wagons, the drivers cracked their whips, the oxen moved slowly forward and the long journey had begun.

That was the 4th day of April, 1846. Our party numbered thirty one, and consisted chiefly of three families,, the other members being young men, some of whom came as drivers. Milt Elliott, a knight of the whip, drove our family wagon. I soon found that Milt, with his "whoa," "haw," and "gee," could make the oxen do just as he pleased.

Nothing of much interest happened until we reached what is now Kansas. The first Indians we met were the Caws, who kept the ferry, had to take us over the Caw River. I watched them closely, hardly daring to draw my breath, and feeling sure they would sink the boat in the middle of the stream.

Every morning, when the wagons were ready to start, papa and I would jump on our horses, and go ahead to pick out a camping ground.

The daily progress went well until we came to the Big Blue River, which was so swollen that we could not cross. As the river remained high and there was no prospect of fording it, the men went to work cutting down trees, hollowing out logs and making rafts on which to take the wagons over. These logs, about twenty five feet in length, were united by cross timbers, forming rafts, which were firmly lashed to stakes driven into the bank. Ropes were attached to both ends, by which the rafts were pulled back and forth across the river. The banks of this stream being steep, our heavily laden wagons had to be let down carefully with ropes, so that the wheels might run into the hollowed logs. This was no easy task when you take into consideration that in these wagons were women and children, who could cross the rapid river in no other way. Finally the dangerous work was accomplished and we resumed our journey.

The road at first was rough and led through a timbered country, but after striking the great valley of the Platte the road was good and the country beautiful. Stretching out before us as far as the eye could reach was a valley as green as emerald, dotted here and there with flowers of every imaginable color, and through this valley flowed the grand old Platte, a wide, rapid, shallow stream. Our company now numbered about forty wagons.

Traveling up the smooth valley of the Platte, we passed Court House Rock, Chimney Rock and Scott's Bluff, and made from fifteen to twenty miles a day, shortening or lengthen-

Crossing Horseshoe Creek, a tributary of the Platte.

ing the distance in order to secure a good camping ground. At night when we drove into camp, our wagons were placed so as to form a circle or corral, into which our cattle were driven, after grazing, to prevent the Indians from stealing them, the camp fires and tents being on the outside. There were many expert riflemen in the party and we never lacked for game. The plains were alive with buffalo, and herds could be seen every day coming to the Platte to drink. The meat of the young buffalo is excellent and so is that of the antelope, but the antelope are so fleet of foot it is difficult to get a shot at one. I witnessed many a buffalo hunt and more than once was in the chase close beside my father. A buffalo will not attack one unless wounded. When he sees the hunter he raises his shaggy head, gazes at him for a moment, then turns and runs; but when he is wounded he will face his pursuer.

The only danger lay in a stampede, for nothing could withstand the onward rush of these massive creatures, whose tread seemed to shake the prairie.

Antelope and buffalo steaks were the main article on our bill of fare for weeks, and no tonic was needed to give zest for the food; our appetites were a marvel. We drove into the South Fork of the Platte and found no trouble in crossing, the only danger being in quicksand. The stream being wide, we had to stop the wagon now and then to give the oxen a few moments of rest. At Fort Laramie, two hundred miles farther on, we celebrated the fourth of July in fine style. Camp was pitched earlier than usual and we prepared a grand dinner. At Fort Laramie was a party of Sioux, who were on the war path going to fight the Crows or Blackfeet. The Sioux are fine looking Indians and I was not in the least afraid of them. They fell in love with my pony and set about bargaining to buy him. They brought buffalo robes and beautifully tanned buckskin, pretty beaded moccasins, and ropes made of grass, and placing these articles in a heap alongside several of their ponies, they made my father understand by signs that they would give them all for Billy and his rider (me!). Papa smiled and shook his head.

On the sixth of July we were again on the march. The Sioux were several days in passing our caravan, not on account of the length of our train, but because there were so many Sioux. Owing to the fact that our wagons were strung so far apart, they could have massacred our whole party without much loss to themselves. Some of our company became alarmed, and the rifles were cleaned out and loaded, to let the warriors see that we were prepared to fight; but the Sioux never showed any inclination to disturb us.

The Big Mistake... in route planning! The Unknown...

A new route had just been opened, called the "Hastings Cutoff," which passed along the southern shore of the Great Salt Lake rejoining the old "Fort Hall Emigrant" road on the Humboldt. It was said to shorten the distance three hundred miles. Much time was lost in debating which course to pursue; Bridger and Vasques, who were in charge of the fort, sounded the praises of the new road. My father was so eager to reach California that he was quick to take advantage of any means to shorten the distance, and we were assured by Hastings and his party that the only bad part was the forty mile drive through the desert by the shore of the lake.

None of our party knew then, as we learned afterwards, that these men had an interest in the road, being employed by Hastings. But for the advice of these parties we should have continued on the old Fort Hall road. Our company had increased in numbers all along the line, and was now composed of some of the very best people and some of the worst. The greater portion of our company went by the old road and reached California in safety. Eighty seven persons took the "Hastings Cutoff" and these are the unfortunates who have since been known as the "Donner Party."

The Bull Whacker
The bull whip was twenty to thirty feet long, which could be made to cut like a knife, at its full length.

On the morning of July 31 we parted with our traveling companions, some of whom had become very dear friends, and, without a suspicion of impending disaster, set off in high spirits on the "Hastings Cutoff"; but a few days showed us that the road was not as it had been represented. We were seven days in reaching Weber Canyon, and Hastings, who was guiding a party in advance of our train, left a note by the wayside warning us that the road through Weber Canyon was impassable and advising us to select a road over the mountains, the outline of which he attempted to give on paper. These directions were so vague that C. T. Stanton, William Pike, and my father rode on in advance and overtook Hastings and tried to induce him to return and guide our party. He refused, but came back over a portion of the road, and from a high mountain endeavored to point out the general course. Over this road my father traveled alone, taking notes, and blazing trees, to assist him in retracing his course, and reaching camp after an absence of four days. Learning of the hardships of the advance train, the party decided to cross towards the Great Salt Lake. Only those who have passed through this country on horseback can appreciate the situation. There was absolutely no road, not even a trail. The canyon wound around among the hills. Heavy underbrush had to be cut away and used for making a road bed. While cutting our way step by step through the" Hastings Cutoff," we were overtaken and joined by the Graves family. Finally we reached the end of the canyon where it looked as though our wagons would have to be abandoned.

It seemed impossible for the oxen to pull them up the steep hill and the bluffs beyond, but we doubled teams and the work was, at last, accomplished, almost every yoke in the train being required to pull up each wagon. While in this canyon Stanton and Pike came into camp; they had suffered greatly on account of the exhaustion of their horses and had come near perishing. Worn with travel and greatly discouraged we reached the shore of the Great Salt Lake. It had taken an entire month, instead of a week, and our cattle were not fit to cross the desert.

Crossing the Desert...
We were now encamped in a valley called "Twenty Wells." The water in these Wells was pure and cold, welcome enough after the alkaline pools from which we had been forced to drink. We prepared for the long drive across the desert and laid in, as we supposed, an ample supply of water and grass. This desert had been represented to us as only forty miles wide but we found it nearer eighty. It was a dreary, desolate, alkali waste; not a living thing could be seen; it seemed as though the hand of death had been laid upon the country. We started in the evening, traveled all that night, and the following day and night two nights and one day of suffering from thirst and heat by day and piercing cold by night. When the third night fell and we saw the barren waste stretching away apparently as boundless as when we started, my father determined to go ahead in search of water. Before starting he instructed the drivers, if the cattle showed signs of giving out to take them from the wagons and follow him. He had not been gone long before the oxen began to fall to the ground from thirst

and exhaustion. They were unhitched at once and driven ahead. My father coming back met the drivers with the cattle within ten miles of water and instructed them to return as soon as the animals had satisfied their thirst. He reached us about daylight. We waited all that day in the desert looking for the return of our drivers, the other wagons going on out of sight. Towards night the situation became desperate and we had only a few drops of water left; another night there meant death. We must set out on foot and try to reach some of the wagons. Can I ever forget that night in the desert, when we walked mile after mile in the darkness, every step seeming to be the very last we could take! Suddenly all fatigue was banished by fear; through the night came a swift rushing sound of one of the young steers crazed by thirst and apparently bent upon our destruction. My father, holding his youngest child in his arms and keeping us all close behind him, drew his pistol, but finally the maddened beast turned and dashed off into the darkness. Dragging ourselves along about ten miles, we reached the wagon of Jacob Donner. The family were all asleep, so we children lay down on the ground. A bitter wind swept over the desert, chilling us through and through. We crept closer together, and, when we complained of the cold, papa placed all five of our dogs around us, and only for the warmth of these faithful creatures we should doubtless have perished.

At daylight papa was off to learn the fate of his cattle, and was told that all were lost, except one cow and an ox. The stock, scenting the water, had rushed on ahead of the men, and had probably been stolen by the Indians, and driven into the mountains, where all traces of them were lost. A week was spent here on the edge of the desert in a fruitless search. Almost every man in the company turned out, hunting in all directions, but our eighteen head of cattle were never found. We had lost our best yoke of oxen before reaching Bridger's Fort from drinking poisoned water found standing in pools, and had bought at the fort two yoke of young steers, but now all were gone, and my father and his family were left in the desert, eight hundred miles from California, seemingly helpless. We realized that our wagons must be abandoned.

The company kindly let us have two yoke of oxen, so with our ox and cow yoked together we could bring one wagon. Some of the company went back with papa and assisted him in cacheing everything that could not be packed in one wagon. A cache was made by digging a hole in the ground, in which a box

Death of the oxen.

or the bed of a wagon was placed. Articles to be buried were packed into this box, covered with boards, and the earth thrown in upon them, and thus they were hidden from sight. Our provisions were divided among the company. Before leaving the desert camp, an inventory of provisions on hand was taken, and it was found that the supply was not sufficient to last us through to California, and as if to render the situation more terrible, a storm came on during the night and the hill tops became white with snow. Some one must go on to Sutter's Fort after provisions. A call was made for volunteers. C. T. Stanton and Wm. McClutchen bravely offered their services and started on bearing letters from the company to Captain Sutter asking for relief. We resumed our journey and soon reached Gravelly Ford on the Humboldt.

Hardship: Leadership and group stress...
On the 5th day of October, 1846, at Gravelly Ford, a tragedy was enacted which affected the subsequent lives and fortunes of more than one member of our company. At this point in our journey we were compelled to double our teams in order to ascend a steep, sandy hill. Milton Elliott, who was driving our wagon, and John Snyder, who was driving one of Mr. Graves's, became involved in a quarrel over the management of their oxen. Snyder was beating his cattle over the head with the butt end of his whip, when my father, returning on horse back from a hunting trip, arrived and, appreciating the great importance of saving the remainder of the oxen, remonstrated with Snyder, telling him that they were our main dependence, and at the same time offering the assistance of our team. Snyder having taken offense at something Elliott had said declared that his team could

pull up alone, and kept on using abusive language. Father tried to quiet the enraged man. Hard words followed. Then my father said: "We can settle this, John, when we get up the hill." "No," replied Snyder with an oath, "we will settle it now," and springing upon the tongue of a wagon, he struck my father a violent blow over the head with his heavy whip stock. One blow followed another. Father was stunned for a moment and blinded by the blood streaming from the gashes in his head. Another blow was descending when my mother ran in between the men. Father saw the uplifted whip, but had only time to cry: "John, John," when down came the stroke upon mother. Quick as a thought my father's hunting knife was out and Snyder fell, fatally wounded. He was caught in the arms of W. C. Graves, carried up the hill side, and laid on the ground. My father regretted the act, and dashing the blood from his eyes went quickly to the assistance of the dying man. I can see him now, as he knelt over Snyder, trying to stanch the wound, while the blood from the gashes in his own head, trickling down his face, mingled with that of the dying man. In a few moments Snyder expired. Camp was pitched immediately, our wagon being some distance from the others.

We then learned that trouble was brewing in the camp where Snyder's body lay. At the funeral my father stood sorrowfully by until the last clod was placed upon the grave. He and John Snyder had been good friends, and no one could have regretted the taking of that young life more than my father.

The members of the Donner party then held a council to decide upon the fate of my father, while we anxiously awaited the verdict. They refused to accept the plea of self defense and decided that my father should be banished from the company and sent into the wilderness alone. It was a cruel sentence. The feeling against my father at one time was so strong that lynching was proposed. He was no coward and he bared his neck, saying," Come on, gentlemen," but no one moved. It was thought more humane, perhaps, to send him into the wilderness to die of slow starvation or be murdered by the Indians; but my father did not die.

Cannibalism...
God took care of him and his family, and at Donner Lake we seemed especially favored by the Almighty as not one of our family perished, and we were the only family no one member of which was forced to eat of human flesh to keep body and soul together. When the sentence of banishment was communicated to my father, he refused to go, feeling that he was justified before God and man, as he had only acted in self defense.

Then came a sacrifice on the part of my mother. Knowing only too well what her life would be without him, yet fearful that if he remained he would meet with violence at the hands of his enemies, she implored him to go, but all to no avail until she urged him to remember the destitution of the company, saying that if he remained and escaped violence at their hands, he might nevertheless see his children starving and be helpless to aid them, while if he went on he could return and meet them with food. It was a fearful struggle; at last he consented, but not before he had secured a promise from the company to care for his wife and little ones.

Water!

My father was sent out into an unknown country without provisions or arms even his horse was at first denied him. When we learned of this decision, I followed him through the darkness, taking Elliott with me, and carried him his rifle, pistols, ammunition and some food. I had determined to stay with him, and begged him to let me stay, but he would listen to no argument, saying that it was impossible. Finally, unclasping my arms from around him, he placed me in charge of Elliott, who started back to camp with me and papa was left alone. I had cried until I had hardly strength to walk, but when we reached camp and I saw the distress of my mother, with the little ones clinging around her and no arm to lean upon, it seemed suddenly to make a woman of me. I realized that I must be strong and help mama bear her sorrows.

We traveled on, but all life seemed to have left the party, and the hours dragged slowly along. Every day we would search for some sign of papa, who would leave a letter by the way side in the top of a bush or in a split stick, and when he succeeded in killing geese or birds would scatter the feathers about so that we might know that he was not suffering for food. When possible, our fire would always he kindled on the spot where his had been. But a time came when we found no letter, and no trace of him. Had he starved by the way side, or been murdered by the Indians?

My mother's despair was pitiful. But life and energy were again aroused by the danger that her children would starve, it was apparent that the whole company would soon be put on a short allowance of food, and the snow capped mountains gave an ominous hint of the fate that really befell us in the Sierra.

Our wagon was found to be too heavy, and was abandoned with everything we could spare, and the remaining things were packed in part of another wagon. We had two horses left from the wreck, which could hardly drag themselves along, but they managed to carry my two little brothers. The rest of us had to walk, one going beside the horse to hold on my youngest brother who was only two and a half years of age.

The "11 Forlorn Hope"

On the 9th of October, while traveling along the Truckee, our hearts were gladdened by the return of Stanton, with seven mules loaded with provisions. Mr. McClutchen was ill and could not travel, but Captain Sutter had sent two of his Indian vaqueros (cowboys), Luis and Salvador with Stanton.

Hungry as we were, Stanton brought us something better than food news that my father was alive. Stanton had met him not far from Sutter's Fort; he had been three days without food, and his horse was not able to carry him. Stanton had given him a horse and some provisions and he had gone on. We now packed what little we had left on one mule and started with Stanton. My mother rode on a mule, carrying Tommy in her lap; Patty and Jim rode behind the two Indians, and I behind Mr. Stanton, and in this way we journeyed on through the rain, looking up with fear towards the mountains, where snow was already falling although it was only the last week in October. Winter had set in a month earlier than usual. All trails and roads were covered; and our only guide was the summit which it seemed we would never reach. Despair drove many nearly frantic. Each family tried to cross the mountains but found it impossible. When it was seen that the wagons

could not be dragged through the snow, their goods and provisions were packed on oxen and another start was made, men and women walking in the snow up to their waists, carrying their children in their arms and trying to drive their cattle. The Indians said they could find no road, so a halt was called, and Stanton went ahead with the guides, and came back and reported that we could get across if we kept right on, but that it would be impossible if snow fell. He was in favor of a forced march until the other side of the summit should be reached, but some of our party were so tired and exhausted with the day's labor that they declared they could not take another step; so the few who knew the danger that the night might bring yielded to the many, and we camped within three miles of the summit.

Dreaded Snow...
That night came the dreaded snow. Around the camp fires under the trees great feathery flakes came whirling down. The air was so full of them that one could see objects only a few feet away. The Indians knew we were doomed, and one of them wrapped his blanket about him and stood all night under a tree. We children slept soundly on our cold bed of snow with a soft white mantle falling over us so thickly that every few moments my mother

would have to shake the shawl our only covering to keep us from being buried alive.

In the morning the snow lay deep on mountain and valley. With heavy hearts we turned back to a cabin that had been built by an emigrant party two years before. We built more cabins and prepared as best we could for the winter. That camp, which proved the camp of death to many in our company, was made on the shore of a lake, since known as "Donner Lake." A family camped in Alder Creek Valley below the lake, and were, if possible, in a worse condition than ourselves. The snow came on so suddenly that they had no time to build cabins, but hastily put up brush sheds, covering them with pine boughs.

Three double cabins were built at Donner Lake, which were known as the " Breen Cabin," the "Murphy Cabin," and the "Reed Graves Cabin." The cattle were all killed, and the meat was placed in snow for preservation. My mother had no cattle to kill, but she made arrangements for some, promising to give two for one in California. Stanton and the Indians made their home in my mother's cabin.

Many attempts were made to cross the mountains, but all who tried were driven back by the pitiless storms. Finally a party was organized, since known as the "11 Forlorn Hope." They made snowshoes, and fifteen started, ten men and five women, but only seven lived to reach California; eight men perished. They were over a month on the way, and the horrors endured by that "Forlorn Hope" no pen can describe nor imagination conceive. The noble Stanton was one of the party, and perished the sixth day out, thus sacrificing his life for strangers. I can find no words in which to express a fitting tribute to the memory of Stanton.

The misery endured during those four months at Donner Lake in our little dark cabins under the snow would fill pages and make the coldest heart ache. Christmas was near, but to the starving its memory gave no comfort. It came and passed without observance, but my mother had determined weeks before that her children should have a treat on this one day. She had laid away a few dried apples, some beans, a bit of tripe, and a small piece of bacon. When this hoarded store was brought out, the delight of the little ones knew no bounds.

The storms would often last ten days at a time, and we would have to cut chips from the logs inside which formed our cabins, in order to start a fire. We could scarcely walk, and the men had hardly strength to procure wood. We would drag ourselves through the snow from one cabin to another, and some mornings snow would have to be shoveled out of the fireplace before a fire could be made. Poor little children were crying with hunger, and mothers were crying because they had so little to give their children. We seldom thought of bread, we had been without it so long. Four months of such suffering would fill the bravest hearts with despair.

Finding Gold...
During the closing days of December, 1846, gold was found in my mother's cabin at Donner Lake by John Denton. I remember the night well. The storm fiends were shrieking in their wild mirth, we were sitting about the fire in our little dark home, busy with our

thoughts. Denton with his cane kept knocking pieces off the large rocks used as fire irons on which to place the wood. Something bright attracted his attention, and picking up pieces of the rock he examined them closely; then turning to my mother he said, "Mrs. Reed, this is gold." My mother replied that she wished it were bread. Denton knocked more chips from the rocks, and he hunted in the ashes for the shining particles until he had gathered about a teaspoonful. This he tied in a small piece of buckskin an placed in his pocket, saying, "If we ever get away from here I am coming back for more." Denton started out with the first relief party but perished on the way, and no one thought of the gold in his pocket. Gold has never been found on the shore of the lake, but a few miles from there in the mountain canyons, from which this rock possibly came, rich mines have been discovered.

Time dragged slowly along till we were no longer on short allowance but were simply starving. My mother determined to make an effort to cross the mountains. She could not see her children die without trying to get them food. It was hard to leave them but she felt that it must be done. She told them she would bring them bread, so they were willing to stay, and with no guide but a compass we started my mother, Eliza, Milt Elliott and myself. Milt wore snow shoes and we followed in his tracks. We were five days in the mountains; Eliza gave out the first day and had to return, but we kept on and climbed one high mountain after another only to see others higher still ahead. Often I would have to crawl up the mountains, being too tired to walk. The nights were made hideous by the screams of wild beasts heard in the distance. Again, we would be lulled to sleep by the moan of the pine trees, which seemed to sympathize with our loneliness. One morning we awoke to find ourselves in a well of snow. During the night, while in the deep sleep of exhaustion, the heat of the fire had melted the snow and our little camp had gradually sunk many feet below the surface until we were literally buried in a well of snow. The danger was that any attempt to get out might bring an avalanche upon us, but finally steps were carefully made and we reached the surface. My foot was badly frozen, so we were compelled to return, and just in time, for that night a storm came on, the most fearful of the winter, and we should have perished had we not been in the cabins.

We now had nothing to eat but raw hides and they were on the roof of the cabin to keep out the snow; when prepared for cooking and boiled they were simply a pot of glue. When the hides were taken off our cabin and we were left without shelter Mr. Breen gave us a home with his family, and Mrs. Breen prolonged my life by slipping me little bits of meat now and then when she discovered that I could not eat the hide. Death had already claimed many in our party and it seemed as though relief never would reach us.

On his arrival at Sutter's Fort, my father made known the situation of the emigrants, and Captain Sutter offered at once to do everything possible for their relief. He furnished horses and provisions and my father and Mr. McCiutchen started for the mountains, coming as far as possible with horses and then with packs on their backs proceeding on foot; but they were finally compelled to return. Captain Sutter was not surprised at

their defeat. He stated that there were no able bodied men in that vicinity, all having gone down the country with Frémont to fight the Mexicans. He advised my father to go to Yerba Buena, now San Francisco, and make his case known to the naval officer in command. My father was in fact conducting parties there when the seven members of the Forlorn Hope arrived from across the mountains. Their famished faces told the story. Cattle were killed and men were up all night drying beef and making flour by hand mills, nearly 200 pounds being made in one night, and a party of seven, commanded by Captain Reasen P. Tucker, were sent to our relief by Captain Sutter and the magistrate, Mr. Sinclair.

On the evening of February 9th, 1847, they reached our cabins, where all were starving. They shouted to attract attention. Mr. Breen, clambered up the icy steps from our cabin, and soon he beard the blessed words, "Relief, thank God, relief! " There was joy at Donner Lake that night, for we did not know the fate of the "Forlorn Hope" and we were told that relief parties would come and go until all were across the mountains. But with the joy sorrow was strangely blended. There were tears in other eyes than those of children; strong men sat down and wept. For the dead were lying about on the snow, some even unburied, since the living had not had strength to bury their dead. When Milt Elliott died, our faithful friend, who seemed so like a brother, my mother and I dragged him up out of the cabin and covered him with snow. Commencing at his feet, I patted the pure white snow down softly until I reached his face. Poor Milt! it was hard to cover that face from sight forever, for with his death our best was gone.

On the 22d of February the first relief started with a party of twenty three men, women and children. My mother and her family were among the number. It was a bright sunny morning and we felt happy, but we had not gone far when Patty and Tommy gave out. They were not able to stand the fatigue and it was not thought safe to allow them to proceed, so Mr. Glover informed mama that they would have to be sent back to the cabins to await the next expedition. My mother said that she would go back with her children that we would all go back together. This the relief party would not permit, and Mr. Glover promised mama that as soon as they reached Bear Valley he himself would return for her children. It was a sad parting a fearful struggle. The men turned aside, not being able to hide their tears. Patty said, "I want to see papa, but I will take good care of Tommy and I do not want you to come back." Mr. Glover returned with the children and, providing them with food, left them in the care of Mr. Breen.

With sorrowful hearts we traveled on, walking through the snow in single file. The men wearing snow shoes broke the way and we followed in their tracks. At night we lay down on the snow to sleep, to awake to find our clothing all frozen, even to our shoe strings. At break of day we were again on the road, owing to the fact that we could make better time over the frozen snow. The sunshine, which it would seem would have been welcome, only added to our misery. The dazzling reflection of the snow was very trying to the eyes, while its heat melted our frozen clothing, making them cling to our bodies.

My brother was too small to step in the tracks made by the men, and in order to travel he had to place his knee on the little hill of snow after each step and climb over. Mother coaxed him along, telling him that every step he took he was getting nearer papa and nearer something to eat. He was the youngest child that walked over the Sierra Nevada… On our second day's journey John Denton gave out and declared it would be impossible for him to travel, he begged his companions to continue their journey. A fire was built and he was left lying on a bed of freshly cut pine boughs, peacefully smoking. He looked so comfortable that my little brother wanted to stay with him; but when the second relief party reached him poor Denton was past waking. His last thoughts seemed to have gone back to his childhood's home, as a little poem was found by his side, the pencil apparently just dropped from his hand.

Captain Tucker's party on their way to the cabins had lightened their packs of a sufficient quantity of provisions to supply the sufferers on their way out. But when we reached the place where the cache had been made by hanging the food on a tree, we were horrified to find that wild animals had destroyed it, and again starvation stared us in the face. But my father was hurrying over the mountains, and met us in our hour of need with his hands full of bread. He had expected to, meet us on this day, and had stayed up all night baking brad to give us. He brought with him fourteen men. Some of his party were ahead, and when they saw us coming they called out, "Is Mrs. Reed with you? If she is, tell her Mr. Reed is here."

When my father learned that two of his children were still at the cabins, he hurried on, so fearful was he that they might perish before he reached them. He seemed to fly over the snow, and made in two days the distance we had been five in traveling, and was overjoyed to find Patty and Tommy alive. He reached Donner Lake on the first of March, and what a sight met his gaze! The famished little children and the death like look of all made his heart ache. He filled Patty's apron with biscuits, which she carried around, giving one to each person. He had soup made for the infirm, and rendered every assistance possible to the sufferers. Leaving them with about seven days' provisions, he started out with a party of seventeen, all that were able to travel.. Three of his men were left at the cabins to procure wood and assist the helpless. My father's party (the second relief) had not traveled many miles when a storm broke upon them. With the snow came a perfect hurricane. The crying of half frozen children, the lamenting of the mothers, and the suffering of the whole party was heart rending; and above all could be heard the shrieking of the storm King. One who has never witnessed a blizzard in the Sierra can form no idea of the situation. All night my father and his men worked unceasingly through the raging storm, trying to erect shelter for the dying women and children.
At times the hurricane would burst forth with such violence that he felt alarmed on account of the tall timber surrounding the camp. The party were destitute of food, all supplies that could be spared having been left with those at the cabins. The relief party had cached provisions on their way over to the cabins, and my father had sent three of the men

forward for food before the storm set in; but they could not return. Thus, again, death stared all in the face. At one time the fire was nearly gone; had it been lost, all would have perished. Three days and nights they were exposed to the fury of the elements. Finally my father became snow blind and could do no more, and he would have died but for the exertions of William McClutchen and Hiram Miller, who worked over him all night. From this time forward, the toil and responsibility rested upon McClutchen and Miller.

The storm at last ceased, and these two determined to set out over the snow and send back relief to those not able to travel. Hiram Miller picked up Tommy and started. Patty thought she could walk, but gradually everything faded from her sight, and she too

seemed to be dying. All other sufferings were now forgotten, and everything was done to revive the child. My father found some crumbs in the thumb of his woolen mitten; warming and moistening them between his own lips, he gave them to her and thus saved her life, and afterward she was carried along by different ones in the company. Patty was not alone in her travels. Hidden away in her bosom was a tiny doll, which she had carried day and night through all of our trials. Sitting before a nice, bright fire at Woodworth's Camp, she took dolly out to have a talk, and told her of all her new happiness.

There was untold suffering at that "Starved Camp," as the place has since been called. When my father reached Woodworth's Camp, a third relief started in at once and rescued the living. A fourth relief went on to Donner Lake, as many were still there and many remain there still, including George Donner and wife, Jacob Donner and wife and four of their children. George Donner had met with an accident which rendered him unable to travel; and his wife would not leave him to die alone. It would take pages to tell of the heroic acts and noble deeds of those who lie sleeping about Donner Lake.

Most of the survivors, when brought in from the mountains, were taken by the different relief parties to Sutter's Fort, and the generous hearted captain did everything possible for the sufferers. Out of the eighty three persons who were snowed in at Donner Lake, forty-two perished, and of the thirty one emigrants who left Springfield, Illinois, that spring morning, only eighteen lived to reach California.

Great Desert to the west of Salt Lake.

Register Rock, Idaho, a landmark of western emigration.

Donner Lake

Chimney Rock, on the North Platte River.

An emigrant encampment.

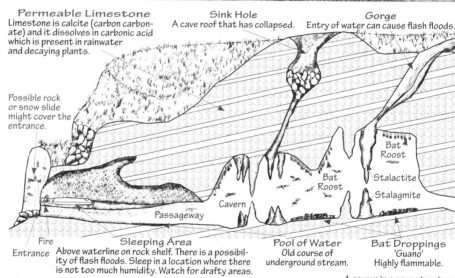

Indians seeking refuge in a cave.

CAVE AS A SHELTER

A cave is an ideal shelter as it offers a roof, fairly constant temperature and is secure.

FINDING A CAVE

- If there is one cave there is a high probability of finding more caves.
- To find caves watch from where bats are emerging at dusk or going to at dawn.
- Caves can be found by watching the disappearance and appearance of streams of water.
- Caves can be found along the coastline especially if the shore has risen. These caves will probably have been formed by wave action. Observe the level of the high water line or the cave entrance might be blocked during high tide.
- Limestone outcrops, in a rainy area, can indicate the possible presence of caves. Check every crack in limestone as it might be an access to a cave. Watch for cool air blowing from the crack. On cold days vapor might rise from the crack. In the winter the snow near a crack might have melted.
- The presence and direction of movement of camel crickets can show a cave opening or at least cracks leading to a cave.

FIRE IN A CAVE

Never light a fire inside a small cave. It uses up oxygen. It can cause an explosion of the bat guano. In the southwestern states be careful with fires at the mouths of caves as there might be an accumulation of tumbleweed and dry brush which are very flammable.

Permeable Limestone
Limestone is calcite (carbon carbonate) and it dissolves in carbonic acid which is present in rainwater and decaying plants.

Sink Hole
A cave roof that has collapsed.

Gorge
Entry of water can cause flash floods.

Possible rock or snow slide might cover the entrance.

Bat Roost

Bat Roost

Stalactite

Stalagmite

Cavern

Passageway

Fire Entrance

Sleeping Area
Above waterline on rock shelf. There is a possibility of flash floods. Sleep in a location where there is not too much humidity. Watch for drafty areas.

Pool of Water
Old course of underground stream.

Bat Droppings
'Guano'
Highly flammable.

A cavern in a cave structure.

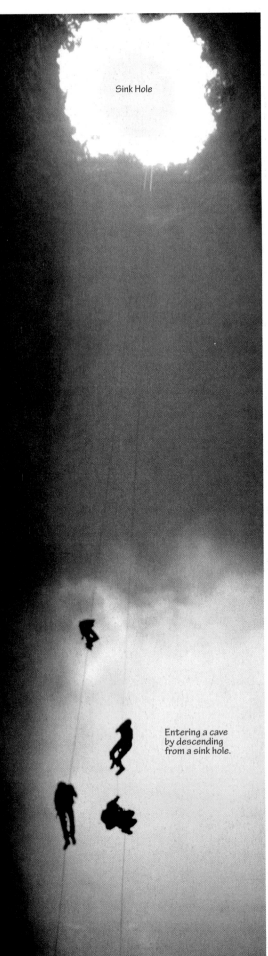

Sink Hole

Entering a cave
by descending
from a sink hole.

Cave Area Topography

Permeable Limestone
Limestone is calcite (carbon carbonate) and it dissolves in carbonic acid which is present in rainwater and decaying plants.

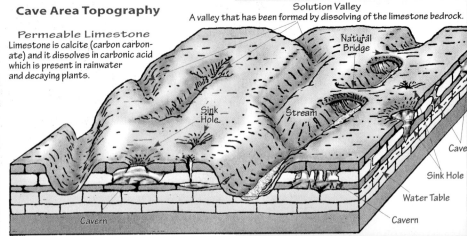

Solution Valley
A valley that has been formed by dissolving of the limestone bedrock.

Natural Bridge

Sink Hole

Stream

Cave

Sink Hole

Water Table

Cavern

Cavern

DANGERS IN A CAVE
- Beware of other occupants: rattlesnakes, bats.
- Do not venture too far into a cave as there might be crevasses, slippery slopes, rock falls, etc.
- Build a fire just outside entrance far enough not to be smoked out or use up the oxygen.
- Place leaves, grass and branches on ground for a bed. Try to make a thick branch base or waterproof sheeting as it will be less humid.
- Avoid air currents in cave.
- Watch for water as cave might be a water funnel and water can rush through after a distant rain storm.

CAVE FLOODING
If there has been a recent rain storm in the area be on the lookout for a potential flash flood in the cave. It is possible that the cave system serves as a drainage funnel and there could be flooding.
Be alert to: changes in air movement, rising water level, unusual noise from the stream's flow or increasing debris or mud in the water. If you notice any changes immediately leave the cave or climb to a higher level.

CAVE AIR
- If you are short of breath and do not know why, leave the cave immediately. You might have entered a pocket of bad air. This air might have been contaminated by rotting vegetation, and landfill seepage.
- Judging the quality of the air by the fact that there has been no effect on the flame of a carbide lamp is not a good standard. The human body has a lower danger point than a carbide flame.

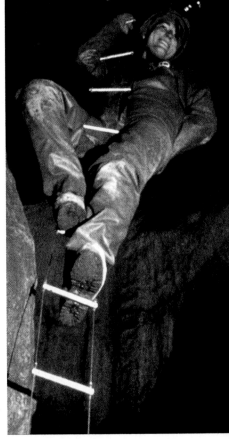

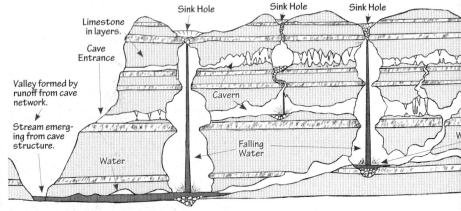

Sink Hole

Sink Hole

Sink Hole

Limestone in layers.

Cave Entrance

Cavern

Valley formed by runoff from cave network.

Stream emerging from cave structure.

Falling Water

Water

VISITING CAVES

- Watch for CO_2 as this shows an area lacking oxygen. To identify these areas watch a flame of a lantern or candle. If it starts to dim and seems to be trying to catch its breath leave the area immediately as there is a lack of oxygen.
- Wear a hard hat. You never know when you might bump your head or fall.
- A good lamp for caves is a carbide lamp. This is a lamp fueled by water drops dropping at regular intervals on calcium carbide this gives off acetylene gas which can be lit. Old cars had this system of lighting.
- A sudden downpour outside could cause a flash flood in the cave. Watch for indications of recent water flows in the cave. Make sure that entrance is not below high tide or waterline as your exit might become blocked.
- Do not venture too far into a cave as it might be dangerous. If an expedition is organized there should never be less than 3 people. If one gets injured then the other two can carry him out.

CAVE CONSERVATION RULES

- Do not leave anything behind.
- Do not take anything. Do not collect any plants or animals. Do not disturb the geological formations. Caves took thousands of years to form and can be destroyed in a few minutes.

Do Not Enter Old Mines
Danger of falling timber, bad air, vertical mine shafts, and collapsing passages.

Vampire Bat

Bat Skeleton

Little Brown Bat in hanging position.

Bat on Wall

Cave Bug

Cave Salamander

Cave Shrimp

Bats in a cave.

Cave Snail

Eyeless Cave Fish

Cave Dwellers
Caves have Two Zones

Twilight: Area used by rats, raccoons, porcupine, bears, skunks, and insects during part of the year. They use the twilight zone for protection from predators or the weather.

Total Darkness: Supports very specialized fauna. These consist of two categories: A group that only lives in caves (blind cave fish, cave salamander, shrimp, and snails) these commonly have no pigment and small eyes or no eyes at all. A group that can live in a cave or outside of the cave (salamanders, spiders, gnats, mosquitoes).

Bats

The most famous residents of caves are bats. They are the only flying mammals. There are two types of bats divided by the what they eat: insects or fruit.

Insect Eaters: Live in all temperate areas of in North America.

Fruit Eaters: Live in tropical climates. These are larger than the insect eaters. These are eaten as a delicacy on the Caribbean islands.

There might be two to a million bats in one cave. In the confined quarters of a cave, bats do not usually attack humans but might bump into you in a tight passage in a cave. If bitten, immediately wash the wound with hot soapy water for 15 minutes. See a doctor as soon as possible. Do not touch bats flapping on the ground as they might be sick. Bat droppings "guano" might fill the area below a large bat roost. Guano is highly flammable and explosive in large quantities. Do not disturb bats as they are part of the ecological system and eat large quantities of insects.

Vampire Bat

The most famous bats of them all are vampire bats. They have been made famous or infamous by the legends of the sucking of blood of humans. These bats are not monsters that fly in front of a full moon. Vampire bats are part of the insect eater family. They are smaller than fruit eaters and larger than insect eaters. These bats drink the blood of animals especially cattle and midsize animals. They have very sharp hollow teeth through which they can suck blood. The saliva forms an anti-coagulant, preventing the teeth from clogging up.

Humans are not necessarily their favorite meal. If they bite a sleeping human they usually bite the uncovered feet. The human will usually feel nothing as the teeth are very sharp. The only indication that you have been bitten is small holes in the skin. They are not dangerous but could be rabid. They live in South America and in the United States near the border of Mexico.

Long-Eared Bats

Mammoth Cave

Cave Crab

1849 Prospector

Digging a Claim

Bringing Gravel

Panning for Gold

ALLUVIAL MINING

Most of the important gold producing areas of the world were discovered because of placer operations. Among these may be mentioned California, Colorado, South Dakota, Idaho, Alaska, and the Yukon territory in America. South Africa and India are important foreign districts.

The early methods of extracting gold from the sands and gravels in which it occurred were confined to panning and the use of rather crude forms of rockers, the Long Tom, and the sluice.

ALLUVIAL DEPOSITS: THE PLACER

While the word "placer" usually causes one to think of gold, it must be remembered that many other substances may be found in placers. Of importance among these are platinum, gems, silver, tungsten, tin, and minerals containing the rare metals

Old River Bed   Present River Bed
Water
Bedrock
Gold Deposit   Crevasse in Bedrock

Larger nuggets may lodge in crevices and behind ledges; but if the slope is steep, everything loose is moved forward until it reaches a gentler descent, which is apt to be the mouth of a gully where it joins the main valley. There the gold is deposited on bed rock, or perhaps on a hard clayey bottom. The gold streaks would be found along the gulch and at the junction with the larger valley.

FORMATION OF PLACERS

Due to disintegrating (weathering) processes (change of temperature, wind, rain, earth movements, and chemical action) rock containing gold has been reduced to particles that are easily broken and the gold freed. Through the action of running water and of glaciers in some instances, the gold bearing rock is transported away from its source. The moving water causes the heavier gold particles to work slowly toward the bottom of the stream bed, On reaching bedrock, or hard pan (an impervious layer as clay), the gold moves slowly down stream until it lodges in crevices, cracks, or other irregular openings in the stream bed. Smaller particles will be mixed in with the gravel.

CLASSIFICATION OF PLACERS

Conditions in the formation of placers:
1 The occurrence of gold in bed rock to which erosion has access.
2 The separation of the gold from bedrock by weathering or abrasion.
3 The transportation, sorting, and deposition of the gold bearing material derived by erosion.

Gold placers can be characterized as:
  A Residual placers
  B Sorted placers
  • Hillside   • Creek and gulch
  • River sandbars   • Gravel wash-out plain
  • Bench   • High bench
  C Resorted placers
  • Creek and gulch   • Beach   • Elevated bench

New stream beds can cut through the deposits of old stream beds thus causing further concentration of the gold deposits. This can reoccur numerous times forming extraordinarily rich placers.

LOCATION: GOLD DEPOSITS

In general, the various sized particles of gold or other placer minerals will be found in the areas of the stream when the water has flowed continuously in one direction.
• The coarse gold will be deposited in the upper part of the stream.
• The finer gold will be deposited in the lower portions of the stream.
• The richest and coarsest gold will he deposited in the layers of comparative coarse gravel wash.
• The finer gold will be deposited in the finer sandy drifts,
• The best gold should occur in the layers of wash containing black sand and pebbles of magnetite or other heavy mineral.
• On a favorable bottom, gold will he ordinarily lodged on the down side of a bar of rock running across the bed of a stream.

GLACIER AREA PLACERS

In glaciated regions, placers may have been scattered by the ice action; or the placer may have been left undisturbed, but covered with glacial gravel. This covering can be so deep in some places that valuable placers long escaped discovery. The 10,000 years since the retreat of the glaciers has been too short for the formation of important placers by erosion. Some payable placers have been formed by the resorting of the gravels that have been scattered by the glaciers.

FINDING PLACER GOLD IN STREAMS

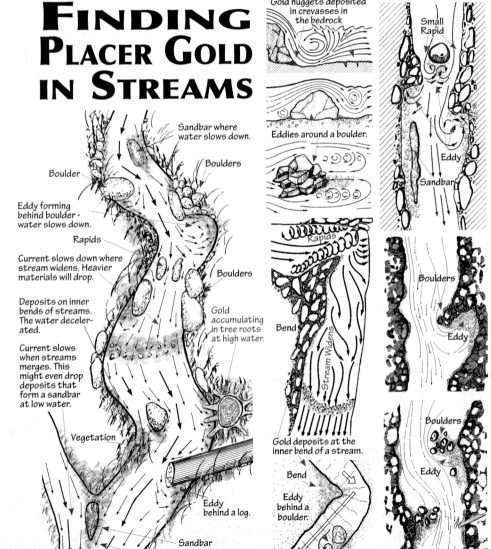

Sandbar where water slows down.

Boulders

Boulder

Eddy forming behind boulder - water slows down.

Rapids

Current slows down where stream widens. Heavier materials will drop.

Boulders

Deposits on inner bends of streams. The water decelerated.

Gold accumulating in tree roots at high water.

Current slows when streams merges. This might even drop deposits that form a sandbar at low water.

Vegetation

Eddy behind a log.

Sandbar

Gold Accumulation

Gold nuggets deposited in crevasses in the bedrock

Eddies around a boulder.

Small Rapid

Eddy

Sandbar

Rapids

Bend

Stream Widens

Gold deposits at the inner bend of a stream.

Bend

Eddy behind a boulder.

Boulders

Eddy

Boulders

Eddy

COMMON TYPES OF PLACERS

Residual Placers: These are placers in which the gold is accumulated in-place by the disintegration of the rock containing it. It is not transported from its original source.

Hillside Placers: These are very old deposits. occurring on the tops and sides of hills. They may have been left in this elevated position because of earth disturbances which lifted the area above the former stream bed, or the original stream which deposited them may have changed its course or have meandered to a new bed.

Creek Placers: *These are the best known and most productive placers* - The best deposits are usually on bedrock, though it sometimes is found an a clay layer (hard pan) which overlies the bedrock. Where no clay is present the gold is found not only on the bedrocks, but also in the joints and crevices. Streams are often found to have a layer of clay on bedrock, which gradually thins out up stream and finally disappears entirely. The presence of the clay on bed rock usually indicates that no gold will be found in the weathered rock below, as the impervious layers prevent the gold from working its way down. The entire width of the stream should be tested as the pay streaks are very irregular. *They usually run parallel to the direction in which the water is flowing.*

Gulch Placer: These are very similar to creek placers, except that there is now very little, it any, flowing water present. This can occur where there are intermittent streams as in dry areas.

Sandbar Placers: These are gold bearing sand or gravel that have been laid down by large streams or rivers. The gold is usually distributed throughout the bar. There is often more fine (flour) gold than coarse. The deposits are usually very low grade as compared to creek placers.

Bench Placers: These are more or less ancient placers, occurring in bench or terrace form, on sides of valleys or courses, of ancient streams, from 50 to 300 feet or more above the present stream level. The presence of well rounded gravel is indicative of material carried and sorted by water.

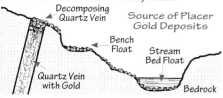

Source of Placer Gold Deposits

Placers can be found in active stream beds or streams may have worn down their beds, leaving the placers high up on benches (bench float).

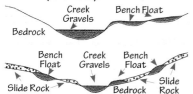

Beach Placers: Wave action has sometimes formed gold placers, such as the beach placers at Nome, Alaska. A good indicator of gold deposits is another heavy mineral, red garnet, (locally called "ruby") which will be found in heavy concentration with gold.

Core Drill Probe
To a depth of 390 feet.
A Gravel
B Gold bearing gravel.
C Impervious layer or false bottom - could be clay.
Probe Hole

GOLD LIKE???
Gold Au
- is soft, hardness 2.5 to 3
- is malleable: it can be beaten flat and easily bent.
- is very heavy, specific gravity is 19.3
- color is rich yellow but can be paler if much silver is present.
- Gold looks like metal. Pyrite looks like glass

Pyrite FeS_2 (Iron Sulfide)
- Common in gold regions.
- is much harder than gold, hardness 6 to 6.5
- is brittle and shatters when struck. If gold is struck it will flatten out.
- pieces can be little cubes as this is the basic crystal structure.
- is much lighter than gold, specific gravity is 5. As pyrite is relatively light it can often be found as gold specks on the surface of sand. Gold being much heavier would sink into the sand bed. Pyrite being light would be float off by panning.
- color is brassy – not yellow.
- becomes a black powder when finely ground.

Mica
- Common in gold regions.
- bright bronzy appearance which might give the impression of being gold.
- light weight & flat plate like cleavage.

Minerals that can be found with gold and have a high specific gravity.
Heavy hard minerals that concentrate with the gold are often a guide to finding placer deposits.
Platinum (Pt)
Silver (Ag)
Ilmenite (FeTiO₃): Iron-black mineral composed of iron, titanium, and oxygen.
Magnetite (Fe₃O₄): Magnetic iron oxide.
Hematite (Fe₂O₃): Non-magnetic iron oxide.
Marcasite (FeS₂): similar to pyrites but with a different crystalline structure. On fresh surfaces it is pale yellow to almost white and has a bright metallic luster. It tarnishes to a yellowish or brownish color and gives a black streak. It is a brittle material that cannot be scratched with a knife.
Rutile (TiO₂): titanium oxide
Wolframite (Fe,Mn)WO₄: Iron manganese tungstate with a brownish or grayish black luster
Scheelite (CaWO₄): Calcium tungstate
Zircon (ZrSiO₄): zirconium silicate
Cinnabar (HgS): mercury sulfide
Chromite (FeCr₂O₄): chromium and iron oxides
Tourmaline: aluminum and boron silicate.

Finding gold nugget in a chunk of quartz!

Fool's Gold
Is NOT gold but is usually discovered with great glee by new prospectors. It is a glitter that appears in rocks especially if they have not weathered. Fool's gold can be iron-stained mica or lead, but more often the "gold" is iron pyrite.

PLACER GOLD
The character of the gold found in placers is as different as the source of the placers. *Coarse gold* in nuggets is the easiest to recover, on account of its weight and shape. *Flake gold* is not so easy to save as nugget gold; however, its weight will make it sink as soon as it is cleaned. *Leaf gold* resembles flake gold, but is much thinner and lighter and consequently will sink with difficulty, muddy water seemingly having sufficient buoyancy to carry it away. *Flour gold* is very fine gold that it is very difficult to collect by the hydraulic methods practiced for nugget gold.

MINERAL INDICATORS OF POSSIBLE GOLD
In alluvial or placer areas are more or less *black sands*, prominent near the surface or coming to light in panning equipment. Their presence does not necessarily indicate gold or platinum; yet in general, where there is placer gold, there may be black sands, or conversely.
Another indicator is *pyrite*. This mineral is common almost from the outcrops of veins. It may or may not carry gold, but fine pyrite in quartz often does, especially at depths; likewise arsenopyrite.
Galena is a third indicator. The bluish mineral is unmistakable; and gold with it is good looking.

Lucky Shot! Finding a nugget after shooting a deer.

PANNING

Rocker   Panning   Gold Washing in California in 1849 - The Gold Rush!

SIZE OF GOLD PARTICLES/NUGGETS

Coarse Gold: that which remains on a 10 mesh screen (ten openings per linear inch).
Medium Gold: that which remains on a 20 mesh and passes a 10 mesh screen (about 2200 colors to 1oz.)
Fine Gold: that which passes a 20 mesh and remains on a 40 mesh screen (about 12,000 colors to 1oz.)
Very Fine Gold: that which passes a 40 mesh screen (about 40,000 colors to 1oz.)
Colors: are individual particles/specs of gold.

Wash & Remove Pebbles

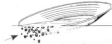

The pan is now raised until it is just covered with water. It is now given a slight oscillating, circular motion, with the result that the contents are shaken from side to side. This motion keeps the lighter material in suspension and washes it out of the pan. It also enables the gold and heavy minerals (black sand, magnetite, etc.) to work their way to the bottom of the mass.

Raise the pan to the surface and tilt the edge away from you with a slight jerk. This stirs the contents of the pan and the light sand and mud will flow off the far edge. Repeat a few times.

Light Particles

Tail of Heavy Materials (Gold etc.)

Put a small amount of water in a pan and add the concentrate. Tilt and rock the pan so that the water runs over the concentrate. The movement of the water will carry the lighter particles to the furthest end of the concentrate. Continue this until the lightest particles have been separated from the heavy particles, which will leave a distinct "tail."

Examine this tail with a loupe while gradually moving the pan. Any very heavy material like gold will move in a slow rolling motion.

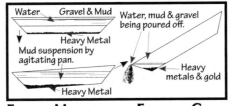

Water   Gravel & Mud   Water, mud & gravel being poured off.
Heavy Metal
Mud suspension by agitating pan.
Heavy metals & gold
Heavy Metal

EASIEST METHODS TO EXTRACT GOLD

In the order of simplicity, the construction of the apparatus, and operation of these three methods are the best for a beginner: *The Pan, The Rocker, and The Sluice.* These will be described in detail. The use of mercury (quicksilver) and arsenic will not be covered, in detail, as they can be very dangerous to an unqualified individual.

THE PAN

Panning is the prospector's method in searching for placers; it is an art requiring practice.

The object, in panning, is to separate the gold from the material with which it is associated. A gold pan varies from about 10 to 18 inches in diameter at the top. The depth is about three inches. It is easier for a beginner to handle a smaller pan. If the gold pan is made of stiff sheet iron. The inner surface of an iron pan must be kept clean and free of grease. Plastic pans are more common and they usually have riffles on one side. The riffles will be on the farthest side from you when used. As the pan is plastic a magnet can easily be used to remove the black sand. About 100 pans of dirt are the most that can be panned by an experienced miner in 10 hours.

PANNING

This is the simplest and least expensive way to extract gold from gold bearing concentrates. The object of panning is to separate and collect heavier materials by washing away the lighter materials.

Steps in Panning

A The pan is filled ¾ full with gravel.
B Pan is submerged in water, with both hands, and the larger pebbles are removed. While under water the contents are stirred or "kneaded" with both hands. This process is necessary to break up the lumps and to free the gold from clay like material. As the disintegration proceeds, the large stones and pebbles are first washed to remove any adhering dirt that may contain gold, after which they are thrown away. The light material will wash out of the pan into the current of the stream.
C When the material has been thoroughly broken up and the large rocks removed, the pan is taken in both hands for the panning operation. The position of the hands is slightly back of the middle of the pan. This permits the pan to be inclined down and away from the operator.
D While still under water shake the pan vigorously – this will allow the heavy gold to sink to the bottom. This will also allow some of the light material to float off into the stream. Remove the remaining pebbles towards you – this is to wash off any gold that might be clinging to the pebbles.
E The pan is now raised until it is just covered with water. It is now given a slight oscillating, circular motion, with the result that the contents are shaken from side to side. This motion keeps the lighter material in suspension and washes it out of the pan. It also enables the gold and heavy minerals (black sand, magnetite, etc.) to work their way to the bottom of the mass.
F Raise the pan to the surface and tilt the edge away from you with a slight jerk. This stirs the contents of the pan and the light sand and mud will flow off the far edge. Repeat a few times.
G Submerge the pan and repeat E and then F.
H The objective of this back-breaking work is that only the heavier materials will be left on the bottom. The materials can be black sand and if you are lucky some gold.
I In the residue there might be sulfite which looks like gold but is more glassy. To remove the sulfite, take a stone and run it around inside the pan and this will grind the sulfite into small particles that will wash away with the water.
J Now swirl the pan containing some water and the residue will take the shape of a shooting star along the bottom of the pan - the gold, with heavy metals, will show up at the tail end of the comet (as gold is the heaviest).
K If you are lucky and have found gold – if nuggets you can pick them with your fingers. Flakes can be picked up with the help of a matchstick or removed by touching your forefinger to your tongue and it will pick up the gold.
L Then dip your finger into a glass vial or bottle with water and the gold specks will drop to the bottom of the vial. All the particles are put in the vial.
M Place the remaining "flour gold" and other concentrate into a larger container. This concentrate will be treated later.
N The remaining concentrate is dried and the magnetite is removed with a magnet. *See page 290.*
O Other material, such as stream tin and heavy nonmagnetic minerals, are separated from the gold by amalgamating the gold with mercury.

My first impressions were not pleasant. The first miner I saw at his work was a rough, dirty looking man in a dry ravine. The banks were about as high as his shoulders. A double barreled shot gun lay on the edge of the bank within easy reach. He was picking up dry clay and gravel from the bottom of his claim, pulverizing it in his wooden pan with a stone, and then shaking it about till the lighter particles came to the top and were brushed over the rim. The pulverizing and shaking continued until a small quantity of dust and gold was left in the bottom. The dust was blown out with the breath. This process was called ***"dry washing."***

The Big Bar of the Mokelumne River lay in the gorge six or eight hundred feet below. The sight was not at all inspiring. ***What in mining parlance are called "bars" are deposits of sand, gravel, clay, and boulders made by rivers, usually opposite the angle of a bend.*** Sometimes these are small, and sometimes several acres in extent, and vary from a few inches to ten feet or more in depth to the bedrock. Our bar, as its name denotes, was a large one, of perhaps five or six acres, covered with boulders from a few pounds' weight to several tons. A few tall pines were scattered over it, and here and there were a number of tents. Though perhaps a hundred miners were at work, the river went merrily on unstained to the sea. Down the steep banks of the gorge we went, stirring up the red dust and covering ourselves with it from head to foot. The animals did not like so steep a trail, and would have their own way among the trees, loosening the packs; but we made the descent with average success. On the bar we found friends that we had made in Panama, who had preceded us a few days, long enough to speak the vernacular of mining and to pride themselves on being "old miners," assuming as such to know just where the gold would be found in the largest quantities, and where to expect the least.

And now my mining life began. It was as free from restraint as the air that came through the soughing pines. Only Mexican law (the US had just occupied California) could be said to exist, and in all the mining region there were no officers to enforce its feeble demands. Every man was a law unto himself, and it is little to say in behalf of the pioneers of California that they carried the laws of justice and humanity in their hearts to such a degree that no more orderly society was ever known on the face of the earth than in those early days.

Pioneer mining life - What was it? The miner must have an outfit of a pick, pan, shovel, rocker, dipper and bucket of wood, or of rawhide. A tent was good to have, but he could make shift during the dry season with a substitute of boughs, for there was no fear of rain from May to October. A blanket of rubber spread on a stratum of leaves, on which his woolen blankets were laid, sufficed for a bed. His culinary utensils were confined to a frying pan, a small iron pot, tin cups and plates, knife, fork, and spoon. His wardrobe consisted generally of a pair of serviceable shirts, a change of trousers, strong boots, and a slouch hat.

Gold was $16.00 an ounce in 1849.

Tweezer

Steel Mortar & Pestle

Iron Mortar & Pestle

The Hopper

The Rocker

Pan for panning concentrate.

Dipper

With these, and a supply of bacon, flour, salt, saleratus (bicarbonate of soda: a white soluble compound ($NaHCO_3$) used in effervescent drinks, in baking powders, and as an antacid), beans, a few candles, and occasionally fresh beef, the miner was ready for work. His luxuries were tea and raw sugar, with occasionally the addition of dried peaches from Chili. His bread was made by mixing flour, water, and saleratus in the ***tin or iron pan which did double duty in the kitchen and in gathering gold,*** and baking it about two inches thick, like a shortcake. But slapjacks, the legitimate successors of the Mexican tortillas, were also a standard article of diet. Tin teapots were sometimes carried, but the small iron pot with a hollow handle did duty for both tea and beans or frijoles. Beans were of a brown variety grown in Chili, and were prepared after the Mexican style with a piece of bacon or fresh beef and plenty of chili colorado, or red pepper. They were allowed to cook a long time, often standing in the hot embers over night to be ready for breakfast in the morning. The bill of fare did not vary much for breakfast, dinner, and supper.

The Rocker
The most expensive instrument of the early miner was ***the rocker,*** which, though simple in construction, cost in the mines from fifty to a hundred dollars. In general appearance it was not unlike a baby's cradle as used by our grandmothers and as still seen on the frontier. It consisted of a flat bottom with two sides that flared outward, and an end board at the head, while the foot was open save a riffle about an inch and a half high at the bottom to catch the gold that might pass another riffle across the bottom near the middle. At the head of the cradle was a hopper about eighteen inches square, with a perforated sheet iron bottom or wire screen. Under this was an apron, or board, sloping downward towards the head. Two substantial rockers under the whole completed the simple machine which gave to the world millions of dollars.

Using the Rocker
The modus operandi may be described as follows: ***Two sticks of wood hewn on the upper side were imbedded at the river's brink, one four inches lower than the other, on which the rockers were to rest, thus securing a grade in the machine to facilitate the outward flow of the water and sand. Two miners usually worked together as partners. One shoveled the earth into the rocker, while the other, seated on a boulder or block of wood, dipped the water from the river, and poured it upon the earth in the hopper with one hand, all the time rocking with the other.*** When the earth was thoroughly washed, he rose, lifted the hopper from its place, threw out the stones and gravel, replaced it, and thus the work went on. As the ground about the rocker became exhausted to the bedrock, the bucket was used, and the earth was carried sometimes 30 – 40 feet, making laborious work for the miner. To keep the rocker going a third person would be employed to carry earth, and each would carry two buckets at a time. Hard work of this kind foretold a need of improvements in mining methods. ***At noon the gold and black sand collected above the riffles were taken up on a scraper and thrown into the pan, which was carried to the river and carefully washed to remove as far as possible all but the gold.*** The yield of the forenoon was carried to the camp, dried over a blaze, the dry sand blown out, and the gold weighed in scales or guessed at, and poured into the partnership purse and deposited under the bed or anywhere else out of sight. Few miners thought of weighing themselves down with gold, and few taxed their resources much to find places of concealment. I was in many camps down to 1854, and in none did I ever know of a theft of gold, and I heard of but one, and that was punished by a cat o' nine tails, which was afterward nailed to the center post of a trader's tent, as a warning to evil doers.

Continued ...

Processing Concentrate

The heavy black sand, which is magnetite, is a large part of the remaining concentrate. To separate out the flour gold heat the black concentrate in a frying pan until dry. Cover a magnet with a dry cloth (or paper tissue) and pass it lightly over the dry black concentrate. The black particles that will cling to the magnet are magnetite. Remove the cloth (tissue) from the magnet and then the magnetic particles will fall off. Slightly shake the pan and repeat the above until all the black material is removed. *See below for details.* Examine the remaining material with a magnifying glass and you will see a rainbow of colors from red garnets, clear quartz crystals, pink quartz, and very small flakes and nuggets of yellow gold (!!!!).

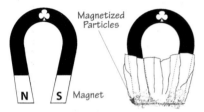

By using a bag on the magnet it is much quicker, to remove the magnetized particles, than placing the bare poles of the magnet against the black sand.

Magnets: Magnetic Separation

Care must be taken in making a magnetic separation of the magnetizable particles. If the magnet is too strong and rapidly swept through a large mass of black sand, the clusters of iron grains will almost always pick up and hold in suspension a certain number of gold particles.

• To minimize the loss of gold particles with a 5 pound horseshoe magnet cover the poles (ends) with a fine white closely woven material bag. By using a bag on the magnet it is much quicker, to remove the magnetized particles, than placing the bare poles of the magnet against the black sand.

• Spread out the black sand to the thickness of 1/16 inch on a piece of cardboard, and gently pass the covered magnet back and forth over the surface. The magnetizable grains will cluster on the outside of the bag.

• The covered magnet with its adhering particles is then placed in a glass bowl and the magnet withdrawn from the bag and the bag is shaken. Repeat this operation until all the magnetizable particles have been separated from the sample.

• The collected particles should again be spread out on a piece of cardboard and gone over a second time with the magnet; this time, however, the bag should be drawn tightly over the poles of the magnet. The magnet should be tapped gently while picking up the grains, so that any gold or platinum particles will be freed from the attached magnetized clusters and fall back on the cardboard because of its specific gravity.

Gold in Quartz

Gold frozen to quartz is frequently found when panning. This rock should be pulverized with a mortar and pestle and panned.

Mortar & Pestle Grinding
Gold in some heavier deposits is so locked up in pyrite and other minerals that it does not separate in the pan, a test sample should first be roasted (this can be done on a shovel, or in a tin can with a circle of holes near the bottom) and ground before being panned.

Treating for Sulfides

Panning and finding a large concentration of sulfides.
A The particles might be as heavy as gold and it might be difficult to remove the fine gold.
B Eliminate the sulfides by burning. Burning might also free fine gold particles that are locked up in larger sulfide pieces.
C *Do this outdoors!* Dry the concentrate obtained from panning. Place this dry concentrate on a tin lid or a very shallow tin can (or sardine can) and place it carefully on a fire. The sulfides will begin to burn – *note there will be sulfide and possibly arsenic fumed given off.*
D Remove the lid from the fire and let it cool.
E The remaining rusty looking pile should be put into a mortar and ground into a fine powder.
F Place the fine powder in a pan and repeat.
G If much sulfide is remaining repeat the above. If you have much sulfide in your concentrate and you want to accelerate the burning process you can mix potassium chlorate (KCIO$_3$) to the concentrate before burning. With heat potassium chlorate will decompose and provide additional oxygen (oxidizing agent) to accelerate the burning process.

Fine Gold Separation

Mercury Fumes are VERY Dangerous
Use in well ventilated area.
To separate the fine gold from the crystals, in a glass vial, add a few drops of mercury and shake the vial vigorously. Gold and mercury have an affinity so that they cling to each other while repulsing the other particles. this is called **amalgam.** When the gold particles have adhered to the mercury pour the mercury onto a piece of chamois (buckskin). Squeeze the mercury out of the chamois so that a small button of mercury and gold is left.

Removing Gold from Amalgam

A fresh and moist raw white potato can be used to recover the gold in up to an ounce of amalgam. More potatoes would be needed for additional amalgam.
A Cut the potato in half and scoop out the centre, of the larger half, the size of the amalgam.
B Wire the two halves together.
C *Note:* the fumes of mercury are very poisonous. In the OUTDOORS, with much air circulation, bake the wired potato until it is well done. On a campfire this might take an hour. To judge how well done the potato is – pick it up in a towel or other heat protective material and the potato should be soft on the inside.
D In the OUTDOORS build a good hardwood fire going and let it burn down in hot ashes – not glowing coals.
E Bury the potato in the ashes for an hour. The potato will be done when its skin is well blackened and a thin sharpened stick can be easily poked through it.
F Allow the potato to cool. Unwire the potato and remove the small gold button found in the interior. The mercury has evaporated into the potato.
G Place the baked halves on a dish and squeeze out the distilled mercury that will be reused. Do not reuse the dish for eating food, as there might be some contaminants remaining on the surface.
H Discard the remnants of the potatoes in a secure place, as they are now very poisonous.

California Gold Rush
The Diary of a '49er

Continued ...
The gold taken from the river bars was mostly in the form of scales resembling cucumber seeds, and of varying size. *It was most plentiful on the bedrock and in a few inches of soil above it, though sometimes three or four feet of earth would be washed.* Where the bedrock was hard the miner cleaned it, for a shovelful of dirt might contain a few dollars in small particles. *Where the bedrock was soft shale or slate on edge the miner picked away an inch or so and washed it, as frequently the scales were found to be driven quite thickly into the crevices.* When the ground was very rich the rocker was cleaned of gold every hour or two. When work was over, around the supper fire the events of the day were discussed, earnings compared, reports made of grizzly bears or deer being seen or killed, of better diggings of "coarse gold "discovered. This was the hour for speculations as to the origin of the gold in the rivers, and a strong opinion was entertained by many who were not well read that immense masses of the precious metal would some day be brought to light in the snow capped peaks towering to the east. "Coarse gold" was a charm to the ear of the ordinary miner. His claim might be paying him an ounce a day in fine gold, but he was always interested in some reported diggings far away there the product was in lumps, and not infrequently he left a good mine to seek some richer Eldorado.

Locating a Placer Gold Deposit
The characteristic and besetting fault of the early miner was unrest. He was forever seeking better fortune. Yet it was this passion for prospecting that resulted in the discovery of gold in an incredibly short time from he southern end of the San Joaquin Valley to the northern limits of the State. To "prospect" was to find a spot that looked favorable and make an examination of it. *The miner would take a pan of earth, shake and gyrate it under water, raising and tipping it frequently to run the dirt and water off, then plunge it again, and so continue until a small residue of black sand and gold remained.* A speck of gold was the *"color,"* several specks were *"several colors,"* and the number and size determined the judgment of the miner whether he should go to work or move on. I have seen ounces taken in this way in a single pan, but in the earlier days…

Gold $16.00 an Ounce
My observation was that the industrious miner rarely brought to his supper less than ten dollars, often an ounce, and sometimes six ounces, or even more. I myself took from the earth nearly one hundred and fifty ounces in seventeen successive working days. My largest clean up was $224. One day, in less than half an hour, I took with my knife from a crevice in the rocks six and a half ounces of gold. When the river went down after it had been swollen by the first rains and had swept over the bedrock of bars supposed to be worked out, hundreds of glittering scales were left exposed, affording pleasant picking for a day or two.

California Gold Rush
The Diary of a '49er

Continued ...

Camping & Weather

The nights in the mines were glorious for sleep. On hot days, I have known a thermometer hung on the north side of a pine tree to show 128°F at two o'clock, the nights were cool, requiring at least one good pair of blankets for comfort. Stretched on the ground under a tent or canopy of boughs, or with nothing but the purest air between him and the stars, the miner was lulled to rest by the murmur of the river or by a coyote, running his remarkable gamut. The great heat did not interfere with work, and there was not a case of sunstroke, nor was the atmosphere sultry or very oppressive. Eighty eight degrees in the moist climate of Panama made life vastly more uncomfortable.

Claim Size

At first, and until the blue skirted (denim) population became numerous, not much regard was had to the size of claims, the miner occupying about all the ground he desired. But a change soon came. The sense of justice of the first occupants of a locality, inspired, it may be, by the fact that the swarms of new immigrants would soon compel a division, allowed a mining statute limiting claims to a certain size. This varied in the different camps, and depended somewhat on the richness of the earth. Generally each miner was restricted to about fifteen feet front on the river, the claim extending across the bar to the hill, but where the bar was a wide one the length was shortened. In some cases a claim was from fifteen to eighteen feet square. ***Back from the river and near the foot of the mountain the bedrock was sometimes ten or twelve feet below the surface, and great labor was required to throw off the top earth to reach the auriferous stratum, and often such deep claims were very wet, calling for constant bailing.*** Of course such claims must be rich to pay, and some of them were, but it was not always so. I have known days and sometimes weeks of hard work to be spent in one of these pits, to find a smooth bed rock at last with very little gold on it. Now and then, after long and tedious toil and discouragements, the miner "struck his pile," but as often he found nothing but barren rock or gravel.

Re-Channeling Streams

The early miner soon observed in working by the river's shore that the pay dirt sometimes extended down under the water, and he was not slow in going after the yellow metal wherever it was to be found. Large prospects suggested turning the stream from its bed to work the bottom, and this was usually done by digging a canal across the bar, or by carrying the water in a wooden flume over the channel or across the bends. I have seen companies of men, filled with enthusiasm and confidence, at work for weeks until the river bed was laid bare, to find only a narrow strip of pay ground along the edge. But in some cases the reward was enormous.

One Sunday in September, 1849, I went on a pedestrian trip of observation down the river. The air of the morning was like champagne. The shaking of rockers or rattle of stones thrown from hoppers was little heard. Miners were washing their clothes by the side of the river. Campfires smoked everywhere, and many resting or sleeping men were stretched

BACKPACKING PROSPECTING KIT

- Small lightweight gold pan.
- Pick • Compass (GPS) • Folding saw
- Folding shovel • Ax • First Aid Kit
- Sheath knife for the belt & carborundum sharpening stone. • Source of light.
- Plastic sheeting for rain shelter. • Rope
- Compass and/or GPS • Waterproof matches
- Small tube tent • Sleeping bag • Toilet kit
- Mosquito bed net & hat • Insect repellent
- Water purification kit • Hat with a brim
- Fishing line & hooks • Rake
- Small glass vials with a secure tops.
- Small 10X folding pocket magnifying glass.
- Measuring tape of at least 50′ if you expect to stake a claim!!
- Plastic bags that seal to collect samples.
- 5 pound pull magnet to separate magnetic minerals from gold.
- Prospectors pick if you look for lode gold.

Additional Items

- Steel or iron mortar and pestle for the grinding of samples for panning. If this additional weight causes difficulties you can use a two inch pipe cap with your pick.
- For placer work add a screen (sieve) with a 60 to 80 holes/square inch (1/4"). This will reduce the material that you will have to pan. Do not throw away any nuggets

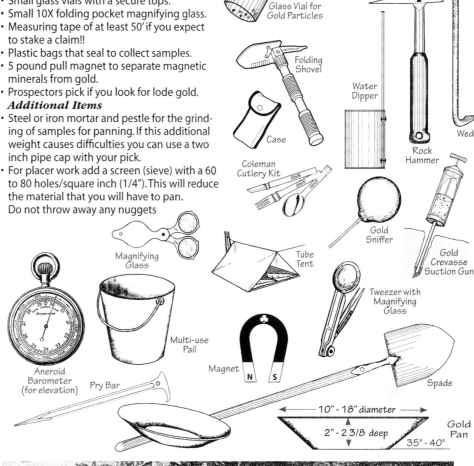

Lensatic Compass

Spoon

Plastic Gold Pan with Riffles

Iron Mortar & Pestle   Crevasse Tool

Glass Vial for Gold Particles

Folding Shovel

Water Dipper

Wedge

Rock Hammer

Case

Coleman Cutlery Kit

Gold Sniffer

Gold Crevasse Suction Gun

Magnifying Glass

Tube Tent

Tweezer with Magnifying Glass

Aneroid Barometer (for elevation)

Pry Bar

Multi-use Pail

Magnet   N   S

Spade

10" - 18" diameter

2" - 2 3/8 deep

35° - 40°

Gold Pan

Prospecting in California in 1851

PROSPECTING

THE ROCKER

Rockers are in many forms and sizes depending upon the available building materials and the gravel to be washed. They are rocked back and forth; one swing, however, is longer than the other, the object being to settle the heavy material. The motion of rocking is a quick jerk with a sudden stopping of the motion. In some cases the short swing is brought to an abrupt stop by a block, but more often the person manipulating the rocker decides on the length of swing from the fact that rocking like panning is not an entirely mechanical operation, but requires skill and judgment.

The rocker handles about three to five cubic yards of material per 10 hours, its capacity depending upon the size of the gold and amount of clay present. Large amounts of clay slow the operation down. It is necessary that all the clay be washed free of the gold, otherwise, the fine gold is washed away.

If water is scarce, the discharge can be caught in a small pool and rinsed. Good judgment must be exercised in the use of water. If too rapid a flow is used, the smaller gold particles will be washed over the riffles and lost with the discharge. At the same time, sufficient water must be used to completely disintegrate the gravel and remove the clay. An attempt should be made to keep a fairly steady stream flowing rather than an intermittent, surging supply. The amount of water must be sufficient to carry the tailings over the riffles. The heavy sands must not he permitted to build up back of the riffles. If this is allowed, the gold will wash over these sands and be lost.

TOO MUCH CLAY

Where there is much clay a good plan is to feed the material and water into a trough, and allow the dirt to be moved by the water along the trough and discharged into the rocker. The clay will be washed more thoroughly from the gold by this means, and the latter be given a better opportunity to form amalgam.

CLEAN-UP OF ROCKER

The canvas or blanket forming the apron is rinsed off in a tub of water two or three times a shift. The gold and sands back of the riffles are removed as often as thought necessary. The concentrates are dried and the gold removed in the same manner described under panning. The rocker is not very efficient. It permits the handling of more material than does the gold pan. When the over sized material is removed from the sieve box, it should be inspected for nuggets before being discarded.

California Gold Rush
The Diary of a '49er
Continued ...

on buffalo robes or blankets under trees and brush awnings. The trail was across rocky bars, stony points, and along the steep sides of the hills. I had sauntered for three or four miles when, on rounding a point, a busy and novel scene burst on my view. Files of Mexicans were coming and going, bearing earth in wooden baskets on their heads to make a dam in order to turn the stream. The work was being superintended by a stalwart American, the projector of the enterprise, in broad sombrero, and reclining on a serape spread on the bank, reminding one of a planter with his slaves. It proved to be Colonel James, who was afterwards a distinguished criminal lawyer of San Francisco. I learned from him that the dam, after weeks of labor, was nearly completed; an hour more and the river would be flowing in an old channel. My curiosity was excited, and I remained to see the result of his venture. *When the water was drawn off, the bed of the river presented the appearance of successive strata of hard slate, on edge, from three or four inches to a foot or more apart, the softer slate or shale between having been worn out and the depressions partly filled with sand and gravel. These strata on edge extended diagonally across the channel, forming an abundance of natural riffles to catch and retain the gold.* My recollection is that the bed of the river had been laid bare to an extent of 200 yards in length by 60 feet in width. The great moment of expectation had come. *By invitation I followed the colonel, who carried a pick, a pan, a shovel, and a small tin cup. It was plain there would be little gravel to wash, as the claim was on the slope of a "rapid," the grade being so great that most of the light material borne by the waters had been carried over. The shovel at once showed the wealth of one of the crevices, and I distinctly saw the colonel take his tin cup by the handle and scrape up from the bottom of the crevice a few handfuls that seemed to me to be half gold. I did not stay to see the gold washed, but I can safely say that I saw at least a thousand dollars go into the pan in half an hour.*

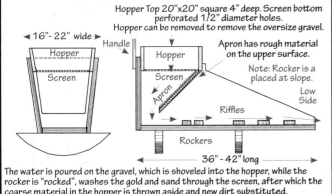

Hopper Top 20"x20" square 4" deep. Screen bottom perforated 1/2" diameter holes. Hopper can be removed to remove the oversize gravel.

◄ 16"- 22" wide ►
Handle
Hopper
Hopper
Screen
Screen
Apron
Apron has rough material on the upper surface.
Note: Rocker is a placed at slope.
Low Side
Riffles
Rockers
◄ 36" - 42" long ►

The water is poured on the gravel, which is shoveled into the hopper, while the rocker is "rocked", washes the gold and sand through the screen, after which the coarse material in the hopper is thrown aside and new dirt substituted. The rocker has pieces of plank (riffles) nailed transversely across the bottom, to catch the gold as the current transports the sand to the discharge end.

Magnifying Glass

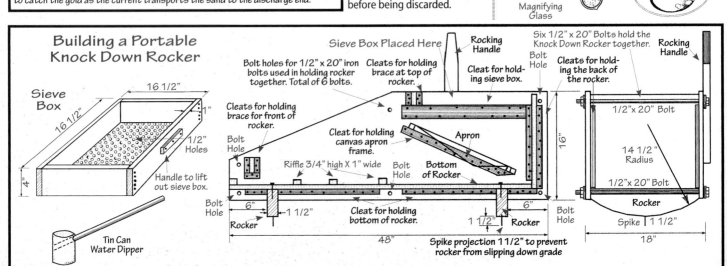

Building a Portable Knock Down Rocker

Sieve Box Placed Here
Rocking Handle
Six 1/2" x 20" Bolts hold the Knock Down Rocker together.
Rocking Handle
Bolt Hole
Bolt holes for 1/2" x 20" iron bolts used in holding rocker together. Total of 6 bolts.
Cleats for holding brace at top of rocker.
Cleat for holding sieve box.
Cleats for holding the back of the rocker.

Sieve Box
16 1/2"
16 1/2"
1"
1/2" Holes
Handle to lift out sieve box.
4"

Cleats for holding brace for front of rocker.
Bolt Hole
Cleat for holding canvas apron frame.
Apron
1/2"x 20" Bolt
16"
14 1/2" Radius
1/2"x 20" Bolt
Riffle 3/4" high X 1" wide
Bolt Hole
Bottom of Rocker
Rocker
Bolt Hole
6"
Rocker
1 1/2"
Cleat for holding bottom of rocker.
1 1/2"
Rocker
6"
Bolt Hole
Spike 1 1/2"
18"

Tin Can Water Dipper
Rocker
48"
Spike projection 11/2" to prevent rocker from slipping down grade

California Gold Rush
The Diary of a '49er
Continued ...

I had seen enough to make a rosy report, and soon was a member of a company to turn the river near our camp on the bar. We dammed the river, the bed rock of which was smooth and barren. It was no child's play, working in the water in the hot sun, sometimes up to our necks, laying boulders into a wall across the stream, and filling in above with the red clay of the mountain side. Miners would pass and re-pass, envy us our claim. Offers to sell were made but we were onto a "sure thing" so "no sale." Alas, the river claim proved a failure. Our earnings were nearly gone, and so we prepared to wander.

Dry Digging Old Stream Beds

The Rich Gulch was a good type of what were called "dry diggings" a long valley, dry in summer with a good stream running down it after a rain. Claims extended from bank to bank, and for sixteen feet in length. The brown and red soil from the hills had run down in the course of time and changed the channel of the stream in many places, and here the miners had to expend a good deal of labor on what they called "dead work," *removing this hill soil, sometimes twenty feet in depth, to get to the old gold bearing bed.* As cooperation in the way of drainage had at this time been little thought of, each claim had to get rid of its own water in any way without much consideration for neighbors below. The amount of bottom dirt washed was slight compared with the whole removed, but in most claims it was exceedingly rich. Many a man had reason to remember with pleasure those winter diggings for the fortune they gave him. *The gold was coarser and rougher than that of the rivers, not having been so much ground among the sand and gravel.*

Weighing Gold

In the evening we halted in front of a log house with a very steep roof made of tiles, and applied for supper. The hostess, a

tall, raw boned Missourian, on presenting our bill in the morning, to weigh the dust put a cube of lead in the scales that approximated the size of a hymn book, but the generosity and chivalry of the early miner and the rarity of women combined to make us ignore it.

1850

In the spring of 1850 I returned to San Francisco, and in May, with one companion and four animals, went around the bay to Sonoma and from thence began the exploration of that unknown region from Sonoma to Oregon. Wandering miners we knew had already gone over the mountains and found gold on the Trinity. Were there not other streams flowing into the Pacific north of San Francisco, and might not all be auriferous as well? It was a tedious, eventful, but fruitless journey of forty seven days, almost wholly over mountains trodden by Digger Indians and, what was more perilous, by ferocious grizzlies, of which we saw five at

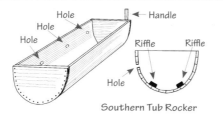

Southern Tub Rocker

SOUTHERN TUB ROCKER

In the South it was considered to be the best tool for washing dirt. Although it is a crude affair it is effective in the hands of one accustomed to its manipulation. The Southern placer gold is fine, most of it being mere colors, with some pieces the size of mustard seed and larger called nuggets. This rocker can treat from 2 to 2 1/2 cubic yards daily. The rocker has two longitudinal riffles. The riffles are about 4" in thickness and width, the object being to retain the black sands and gold between the two riffles.

• The dirt to be washed is shoveled into the tub until the bottom is covered. Water is next poured in and the apparatus rocked to clean the mud from the larger pieces of stone. The cradle is then tilted until the dirty water will run out of plug holes after which the larger pieces of rock are raked out over the side. This operation is repeated until the water poured in and agitated remains comparatively clear, and there are but a few small stones in the tub.

• Expert work now begins, the object being to wash the light sands over one riffle and leave the gold and heavy black sands between the two riffles. To accomplish this a quick jerk is given the rocker one way, and then as the water moves to one side it is allowed to come to rest slowly and flow back. The motion is similar to that given a pan when a pencil of black sand is being formed, except that the height of the wave movement is decreased gradually on one side of the tub and increased on the other until all the light sands are on the long wave side. When this is accomplished the heavy sands are between the riffles, and the gold is picked out. Expert manipulators of these cradles claim that they can save 90% of the gold.

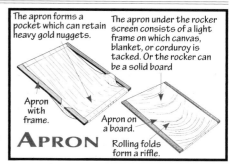

The apron forms a pocket which can retain heavy gold nuggets.

The apron under the rocker screen consists of a light frame on which canvas, blanket, or corduroy is tacked. Or the rocker can be a solid board

Apron with frame.

Apron on a board.

APRON

Rolling folds form a riffle.

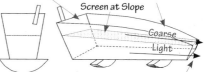

Water is poured on the upper end of the rocker, on the gravel; this water passes through the grating, carrying the finer material, sand and gold, with it into the box.

At each swing the coarser dirt which does not go through the screen is moved by the jar towards the discharge. The jar may not be sufficient to dispose of all the coarse material, in which case use the shovel.

Screen at Slope

Coarse

Light

The light sand is swept out by the current of water which passes through the screen.

Slant of Floor of Rocker

The floor of the rocker is given a slant, with the feed end about six inches higher than the discharge end. This inclination should depend upon the material to be washed and the amount of water available. Fine gold should be given less water and less inclination than coarse gold.

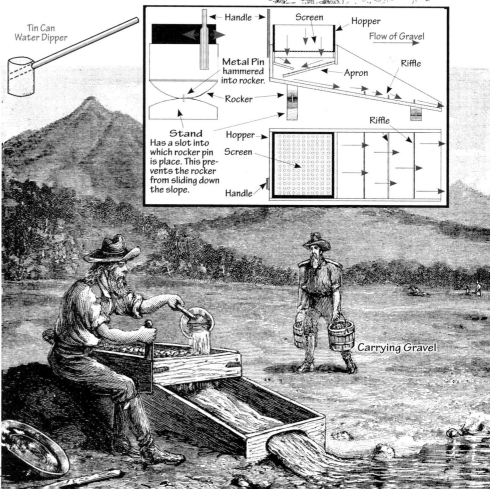

Tin Can Water Dipper

Handle — Screen — Hopper

Flow of Gravel

Metal Pin hammered into rocker.

Apron

Riffle

Rocker

Stand
Has a slot into which rocker pin is place. This prevents the rocker from sliding down the slope.

Hopper

Screen

Handle

Riffle

Carrying Gravel

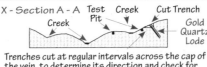

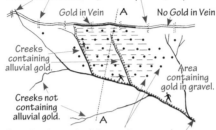

X - Section A - A Test Creek Cut Trench
Creek Pit Creek Gold Quartz Lode

Trenches cut at regular intervals across the cap of the vein, to determine its direction and check for gold inclusions. Samples are tested by crushing the stone and then washing the sample in a gold pan.

Gold in Vein A No Gold in Vein

Creeks containing alluvial gold.

Area containing gold in gravel.

Creeks not containing alluvial gold.

Original discovery of placer gold.

Test pits dug to check, by panning, for gold deposits. These pits are 3-4 feet in diameter and depth varies as to accuracy desired.

FINDING LODE GOLD

After finding a likely area for gold, one uses the pan to find the presence of "float" gold. Float gold is gold that has been displaced from its original deposit/bedrock area by water or glacier action. Finding the source after a glacier has passed through is very difficult as one has to study the striations the glacier has made on the bedrock to find the direction of travel. The last major iceage ended over 10,000 years ago. Upon finding float gold, by panning, one can study the stream, or if dry, the former stream system by assessing the contours of the land visually or with the aid of a typographic map. Then by traveling upstream - and panning samples upstream - until there is no more presence of gold. Again study the terrain - and go up any tributaries or depressions (which might have been streams), of the stream, that you might have crossed. Follow up streams that indicate the presence of gold - in each case until you come up empty. If, at this point, you have not crossed the gold bearing vein (usually quartz) you will have to start digging test pits, in a grid pattern, and pan test these samples. The above illustration shows the process to follow. Once the vein is found, it is necessary to determine its course of strike, and a series of trenches should then be cut across the outcrop every few feet to obtain samples. The samples should be tested systematically by crushing the stone and then washing the sample in a dish. The distribution of the gold, in the vein, will rarely prove to be even. The lode may frequently be found, but nine times out of ten it does not contain free gold in anything like the quantity or the size of grains that the placers would indicate. After all the placers are the gold concentration and accumulation of thousands of years of erosion.

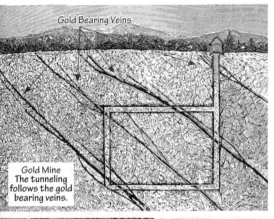

Gold Bearing Veins

Gold Mine
The tunneling follows the gold bearing veins.

Examining a quartz sample from a vein.

California Gold Rush
The Diary of a '49er
Continued ...

one time. No gold was found in any stream till we reached the Trinity, thirty six days from San Francisco, and there the diggings were not remarkably rich. The hardest toilers reported but from eight to ten dollars a day. *The style of mining did not differ from that which I have described, except that the pay dirt was carried a considerable distance in buckets from high and dry bars down to the river to be washed. Something better must be found, and a prospecting party was sent on an exploring expedition farther north.*

"I took ye for an Injun"

Mountain Men

3rd of July

On the 3rd of July two of our prospecting party returned and whispered the news that rich bars had been found on a stream full of salmon farther north, and the next morning we were off. The night of the fourth and fifth gave us the variety of a snowstorm, from which we took shelter under a roof of spruce boughs enclosed on three sides with the same material. After eleven days of exhausting climbing and descending steep and lofty mountains, tearing our clothes in the tangled chaparral, camping at night in the chilly air where the water from melting snows made green pastures for our mules, we reached the virgin diggings on Salmon River. There was no evidence that any white man had preceded us. The bars by the river were untouched; an interminable forest stretched all over the mountain sides and up and down the winding river, unmarked by the woodman's ax not dense, but relieved by glades and openings, and but for the steepness of the mountains easily traveled. Here was a newer scene and a more novel life. There were but eleven Americans of us all told, and a wide and rugged region lay between us and others of our race. Indians came in squads, shyly viewed us, made their comments, and passed on.

Long Tom

The miners of Nevada County originated or adopted most of the improved methods for facilitating washing and saving gold. *The Long Tom came into use early as the successor of the rocker. It was a trough of boards ten or twelve feet long, two feet wide on the bottom, with sides eight or ten inches high, and was furnished with a perforated sheet iron plate three feet long, which had the end part curved upward to stop the stones and gravel, while the water, sand, and small gravel dropped through into a riffle box below, set on an incline to allow the lighter matter to pass off with the water.*

California Gold Rush
The Diary of a '49er

Continued ...

The Long Tom was put on an easy grade and supplied with a constant stream of flowing water, enough to drive and wash all the earth thrown into it down upon the perforated screen. Two or more men shoveled the earth into the tom, and one threw out the stones from the screen with a fork or square pointed shovel, when they were sufficiently washed.

The Sluice

As the claim was worked back, the Long Tom was extended by means of *sluice boxes* until a dozen or more miners were shoveling dirt into them on both sides. *Afterward it was found that by putting riffles into the sluice boxes the Long Tom could be dispensed with, and miles of sluices of all sizes were seen, some supplied with a few inches of running water, a miners' measure, while others bore torrents of the muddy fluid.* The sluice requiring a rapid flow of water was set on a grade of say four inches to twelve feet in length. It is plain that in a short distance the pay dirt would have to be lifted higher than the miner's head. A descending bed rock added to the difficulty, and sometimes the earth was thrown by one set of miners up on a platform to be shoveled by another set into the sluice. *Numerous small boulders were kept in the sluice, around and over which the water boiled and leaped, dissolving the clay.* When the gold was fine and difficult to save, quicksilver was poured into the sluices to catch it, the riffles arresting the amalgam as it moved down.

River Channeling Method

As more experience was gained, water was made to do the labor of men. *Instead of carrying the dirt in buckets to the river to be washed, the river was carried to the dirt.* Ditches were dug at great expense and water from them was sold at a dollar an inch for ten hours' use, and often it was resold in its muddy state one, two, and three times at decreasing rates. The water belonged to the ditch owner as long as it could be used. The fact may here be noted that one of the first ditches constructed was that from Rock Creek to the hill diggings about Nevada City. It was nine miles long, and cost about ten thousand dollars, and so rich were the diggings and so active the demand for water that the enterprise paid for itself in six weeks.

Puddling Box

Water filled box used to dissolve possibly gold bearing gravel that is clumped up - Usually by the presence of clay or cemented gravel. The wooden box is usually 6'x6' and 18" deep. First fill the box with water and add the gravel in small quantities while using a rake to agitate the clumped material. When the clumps have been broken up the muddy water is drained by removing the corks on the sides of the box. The concentrate on the bottom of the box can then be panned for gold.

Water
Gravel
Rake
Removable cork for drainage.

Long Tom

The Tom is a six to twelve foot sluice box that is used in place of the rocker in suitable localities. The water is supplied by a continuous source as a stream or brought by a flue. One man shovels the gravel into the head box, others lift out boulders with a pitchforks (thus not disturbing the water flow) and break up the lumps of clay. It is capable of washing 6 yards of ordinary dirt, and from 3 to 4 yards of cemented dirt (mixed with clay) in 10 hours.

Working a Tom

Portable Tom or Built on Location

Top View
Feed Gravel
The Tom
Riffle Box
Water Source
Screen
Riffles

Slope 1 1/2" per foot
Logs for support and slope.
Elevation

The feed end of the Tom is about 20" wide, discharge end is about 30" wide, and terminates in a perforated iron screen. As the material enters it spreads out until it meets the screen which lets material finer than 1/2" in diameter fall with the water into the riffle box one end of which is underneath the screen. The coarse material is shoveled off the retaining screen, and the lumps of clay and dirt thrown up towards the head so that the water will have another chance to disintegrate them.

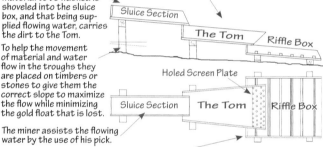

Material to be washed is shoveled into the sluice box, and that being supplied flowing water, carries the dirt to the Tom.

To help the movement of material and water flow in the troughs they are placed on timbers or stones to give them the correct slope to maximize the flow while minimizing the gold float that is lost.

The miner assists the flowing water by the use of his pick.

Sluice Section
The Tom
Riffle Box
Holed Screen Plate
Sluice Section
The Tom
Riffle Box

To catch fine gold another box can be added after the riffle box. On the floor of this box is a blanket or cow hide with the hair turned up stream to catch the fine gold. The blanket should be covered with a fine screen, be placed above the blanket, in order to prevent coarse sand and gravel from traveling over it and wearing it.

The Riffle Box has transverse riffles which collect the gold that moves with the stream of water. The constant movement of the water beneath the holed plate keeps the sand suspended and allows the gold to separate and sink by gravity to the floor of the riffle box. The inclination of the riffle box should be such that the bottom of the trough is covered with a thin coating of mud, and is not scoured by swiftly running water and sand.

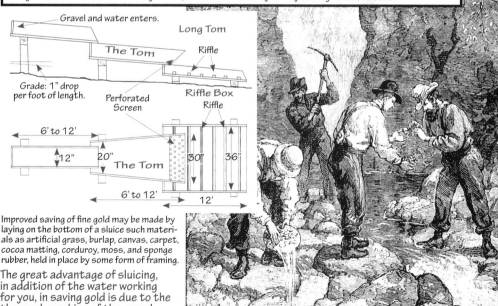

Gravel and water enters.
Long Tom
The Tom
Riffle
Grade: 1" drop per foot of length.
Perforated Screen
Riffle Box
Riffle
6' to 12'
12"
20"
The Tom
30"
36"
6' to 12'
12'

Improved saving of fine gold may be made by laying on the bottom of a sluice such materials as artificial grass, burlap, canvas, carpet, cocoa matting, corduroy, moss, and sponge rubber, held in place by some form of framing.

The great advantage of sluicing, in addition of the water working for you, in saving gold is due to the thorough washing of the gravel.

Prospector using a pick.

Sluicing

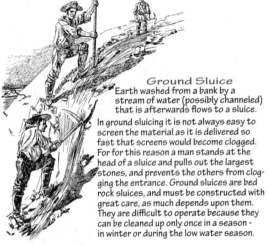

The partial damming of a stream so that water is channeled to go down this sluice. The amount of water channeled is sufficient to move the light mud and the stones but not too much so as to wash away the gold.

Ground Sluice

Earth washed from a bank by a stream of water (possibly channeled) that is afterwards flows to a sluice.

In ground sluicing it is not always easy to screen the material as it is delivered so fast that screens would become clogged. For this reason a man stands at the head of a sluice and pulls out the largest stones, and prevents the others from clogging the entrance. Ground sluices are bed rock sluices, and must be constructed with great care, as much depends upon them. They are difficult to operate because they can be cleaned up only once in a season - in winter or during the low water season.

Sluicing is the process of washing dirt through a channel by means of water. The controlled path through which the dirt is transported may be a wooden trough, or a ditch cut in bed rock (ground sluicing). If the sluice is not constructed properly there will be a loss of gold. The earth may be fed to the sluice by hand, or indirectly by machinery, or it may be washed from a bank by a stream of water that is afterwards led to the sluice - called ground sluicing. Sluices should be at least 240 feet long and set in as straight a line as possible, otherwise fine gold will be lost.

Material: The materiel from which the sluiced a made is rough finished lumber. There are some instances, such as in dredging and large scale hydraulics, where metal boxes might be used.

Dimensions: The sluice is made up in sections. The sections vary from 12 to 16 feet in length. Twelve foot sections are the most common. The width varies from one foot to five feet, but is usually between 12 and 15 inches. The depth is from eight to ten inches, The board, from which the boxes are made are about 1 1/2 inches thick. One end of each box should be narrower than the other. This permits the telescoping of the boxes. As the gravel bank recedes, boxes from the discharge end are brought to the head end. Thus, it is not necessary to move the entire sluice.

Head Box: The box in which the gravel is shoveled is the "head box." It is, equipped with a "grizzly" or bars to prevent the large boulders and rocks from entering the sluice. This is also where the water enters the sluice.

Grizzly: The grizzly is made of iron bars or heavy pipe. The spacing between the bars will depend upon the size of the gravel. If only medium sized gravel with very few large rocks to be encountered, a perforated sheet may be used.

Riffles: The riffles can be constructed of many different things: Wooden blocks, angle irons, sticks, cobblestones, boulders, etc, . They may run the length of the box or across it. If possible the riffles should not be permanently fastened in the sluice box as it is necessary to remove them for the clean up. They may be held in place by nailing the side boards of the box to the ends of the riffle. The nail should not be driven all the way in or they may be difficult to remove.

Sluice Size: Determined by the amount of gradient available, the character of the material, and the quantity of water which may be used.

Sluice Length: Depends upon the dumping ground and its distance from the workings; yet, were the dump close at hand the sluice must have sufficient length to thoroughly wash the alluviums, and break up the cemented gravel, and the clay.

Water Flow: The water in flowing through the sluice transports and washes the gold free from rocks to which it is adhering, and permits it to fall to the bottom of the sluice, where it is caught traps called "riffles." Large stones should be removed before entering a small sluice as they wear the boxes and require more water for their transportation. In many cases all material to be washed passes through "grizzlies" that prevent stones larger than 3" in diameter from entering the sluice.

Velocity of Water: In a sluice much of the success depends in the steadiness of flow, that is, the quantity of water passing and its velocity should be uniform to secure a maximum settling of the gold. The bulk of the gravel and boulders travel down the middle of a sluice, so its grade and depth are important. A swift current, while able to transport heavy material, will not let fine gold settle in the riffles.

Straight Line: Sluice boxes should be placed in a straight line, but if curving is necessary, the outer edge of the curve should have an elevation, to prevent the material from piling up and clogging the box when the direction of the flow changes. It may be necessary to give a slightly greater grade below the curve in order to obtain uniform flow of material and clear the curves.

Sluice Grade: Choice depends upon the character of the gravel; large, heavy stuff will require a steeper incline than lighter material. The amount of water available will influence, in a measure, the gradient, and the sectional area of the sluice must also depend upon it. Heavy material must be covered by water, and a steep enough grade given to have gravity give velocity to the water and exert some action upon the material. The grade is important otherwise there may be considerable loss of gold.

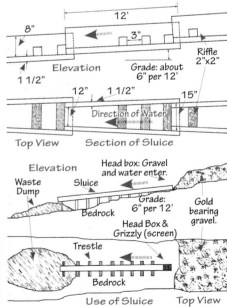

A hand sluice into which the miners shovel the gold bearing dirt, previously picking out the large stones and throwing them one side. Similar sluice boxes, although much larger and stronger, are used where mechanical apparatus is employed for excavating.

RIFFLES

Note: the use of mercury or arsenic will not be included in this article.

Riffles are traps intended to stop gold from moving along the sluice or rocker bottom. For coarse gold they are very effective, but for gold containing impurities, gold attached to rock, leaf gold, flour gold, or gold attached to black sands they are not satisfactory savers, unless aided by undercurrents. There are many kinds of riffles, consequently it is necessary to use judgment in their selection, as there would not be this number if it were possible to save all the gold in places.

Water Flow & Riffles in Sluicing

Sluicing is a purely mechanical operation, therefore one must know within reasonable limits what the physical condition of the gold is before attempting work and choosing a riffle pattern. *Coarse or nugget gold* will travel but a short distance even if there are no riffles, provided there is an uneven place for it to lodge, however a stone moving along will dislodge it and then it moves to the next uneven place. To prevent this riffles are needed as otherwise the gold will eventually reach the end of the sluice.

Flour gold is very fine and will be held in suspension in muddy water; *leaf gold* will float along the bottom of a sluice unless it can be stopped in some way, and gold attached to black sand, clay, or rock will be lost.

There are a variety of riffle patterns and materials to choose from, there objective being their ability to save gold. Every placer location has its own characteristics and the choice of a riffle type is based upon one's experience

Pole Riffles

Made of saplings split and nailed to the sluice box floor are the crudest of riffles, and yet they are useful when better riffles can not readily be obtained. The saplings are placed transversely or longitudinally to suit the ideas of the operator. Where there is much clay in the ground nails are driven in the poles so that they will project half an inch. This might break up the clay and thus free the gold.

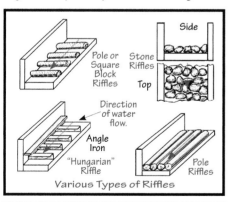

Various Types of Riffles

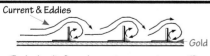

Current & Eddies

The hydraulic flow when water encounters a riffle. The gold will accumulate in the dead water in the corner below the eddy.

Water for Sluice

To operate a sluice, plenty of water must be available as a continuous flow through the system is required. If sufficient water a not at hand, it, is useless because the moving gravel will deposit in place and will dam if "restarted".

Placer Gold Vocabulary

Apron: A canvas covered frame used in a miner's rocker. The canvas will collect particles.

Aqua Regia: Mixture of 3 parts hydrochloric and 1 part nitric acid. Dissolves gold and platinum and precipitated from the liquor by mercury.

Arid Area: Very dry, barren, parched with heat.

Arroyo *(Spanish)*: A small stream: or deep, dry gully.

Black Sand: Heavy grains of magnetite, chromite, ilmenite, cassiterite, and tourmaline found in rivers, beaches, and sluice boxes. It sometimes carries gold and platinum.

Fissure: A crack or opening in rocks. Fissure veins are those formed by mineral matter being deposited in the cracks.

Float: The loose or scattered pieces of ore broken off from a vein outcrop. When prospecting is thoroughly done, the float may be traced to its source or outcrop. Also, leaf gold float in panning and other operations.

Float Gold: is either in thin scales or in such small light particles that it is termed flour gold. Float gold will be buoyed up by muddy water, particularly water containing much clay, or talc.

Flotation: A process of concentration when crushed ore is mixed with water and oil or chemicals, the minerals float while the worthless material sinks. Gold and silver ores are float able.

Floured: Mercury sometimes becomes broken up into very small globules and will not amalgamate with gold or join together, probably owing to some scum on the surface of the mercury.

Flume: A wood or sheet iron trough used for the conveyance of water. Flumes constitute part of a ditch for transporting water which will be uses in sluicing for gold.

Fluvial: Sand and gravel deposits laid down by rivers are of fluvial origin.

Grit: A sandstone composed of coarse, angular grains and very small pebbles.

Grizzly: An iron grating set on a slope for screening rock and ore. Usually made of spaced iron rods. Perforated screens have replaced the grizzly.

Gulch: A narrow ravine or small cañon. Also Gully.

Mother Lode: The mineralized formation that passes through any district, not rich enough to be worked as a whole but containing numerous workable veins.

Muck. A common term in Alaska for the surface soil and sand lying above placer deposits.

Native: A mineral that occurs in nature as a pure metal is termed native, as copper, gold, silver, platinum.

Sluice box: A trough, lined with riffles, through which gravel and water flows and in which gold is caught.

Sluicing: Moving gravel with the help of water.

Specific Gravity: The ratio of the weight of any substance to that of an equal volume of water. If a piece of quartz is weighed in air and then in water, its specific gravity is obtained by dividing its weight in air by its loss of weight when weighed in water.

Spongy Gold: is fine gold containing pores into which clay or other material has filtered to such an extent as to greatly decrease its specific gravity, and such gold will float over mercury.

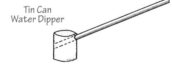

Tin Can
Water Dipper

TRANSPORTING POWER OF WATER

Water will carry dirt in suspension, it must however have a current, otherwise it will precipitate the dirt. If the current is swift and the water deep only the heavy particles will be precipitated. If the water is suddenly spread out and the current reduced the light particles will fall to the bottom. It is upon this principle that the sluice and undercurrent are constructed;

Sluice: intended to transport all dirt and water that is not too heavy.

Undercurrent: being for the purpose of recovering light particles of gold that are not sufficiently heavy to sink in a swift running current. The dirt when in suspension adds to the density of the liquid and hence to its transporting power.

How Water Transports: The right velocity, quantity (depth) of water, and slope will cause the coarse and heavy material to move along, not on the bottom of the sluice, *but above the bottom and below the water.* This combination will move rocks that aid by their movement to disintegrate and wash out the gold from the dirt that may hold it encased or in suspension, and also prevent sand from packing. Heavy rocks will not have the same velocity as lighter, *but their colliding has a grinding effect upon the material containing the gold.*

UNDERCURRENTS

are introduced in sluice lines to relieve the main sluice of coarse material and save fine gold. For this purpose a grizzly made up of iron bars, set on edge, one inch apart lengthwise of the sluice, is used for a sluice bottom.

The finer material passes through the bars, while the coarser material remains on the bars. Below the bars is a coarse iron screen which checks the momentum of the coarse material and affords any gold that passes over the bars an opportunity to reach the undercurrent. The undercurrent is a shallow wooden box, from four to ten times the width of the sluice and high enough to contain the material washed into it. It is paved with either wood or stone in such a manner as to stand wear and serve as riffles. The water and material that flows swiftly in the sluice is suddenly spread over a very much larger area and this gives the gold an opportunity to settle. After the material enters the undercurrent it is spread over the entire box width by the riffles, although the inclination of the undercurrent is considerably more than that of the sluice.

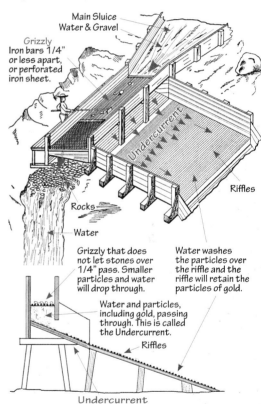

Main Sluice Water & Gravel

Grizzly Iron bars 1/4" or less apart, or perforated iron sheet.

Undercurrent

Riffles

Rocks

Water

Grizzly that does not let stones over 1/4" pass. Smaller particles and water will drop through.

Water washes the particles over the riffle and the riffle will retain the particles of gold.

Water and particles, including gold, passing through. This is called the Undercurrent.

Riffles

Undercurrent

SLUICE CLEAN UP

The frequency of the clean up depends upon the richness of the gravel being washed. It may vary from a few times a day to once the entire session. The first few riffles should be cleaned up at least once every two weeks.

To make the cleanup the gravel flow is discontinued and a stream of water, just large enough to wash the heavy sands, mercury, and amalgam, as permitted to flow down the incline. The riffles are taken up and the sand moved down the sluice and the contents are scraped with a spoon. All cracks and crevices are thoroughly cleaned. Blankets and burlap that may have been used are washed in a tub and burned. Any remaining gold is extracted from the ashes of the blankets.

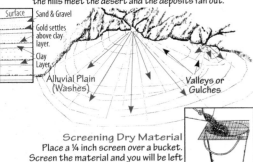

Nothing after digging this hole!

The best place for a higher concentration, of gold, is where the hills meet the desert and the deposits fan out.

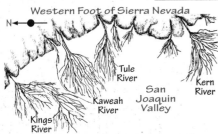

Surface — Sand & Gravel
Gold settles above clay layer.
Clay Layer.
Alluvial Plain (Washes)
Valleys or Gulches

Screening Dry Material
Place a ¼ inch screen over a bucket. Screen the material and you will be left with a higher concentration for panning.

Western Foot of Sierra Nevada
N
Tule River
Kern River
Kaweah River
San Joaquin Valley
Kings River

Map of southeastern margin of San Joaquin Valley showing fans built by streams which disappear after leaving their mountain canyons. The coalescing alluvial fans form in this manner an extensive bajada.

DRY BLOWER

1 Hopper/Upper Box
This box is rocked by the handle. The gravel is dropped into the higher end of this box. The gravel falls onto a 5 holes/inch screen. This box is rocked and the smaller particles fall through the screen onto an inclined board with riffles on it - with the gravel then falling into the Lower Box. The oversized gravel gets rocked along the sloped 5 holes/inch screen, depositing any attached gold particles through the screen, and then roll out, of the upper box, as coarse tailings.

2 Dry Blower / Lower Box
This box is attached to the bellows and is rocked while the bellows are pumped. The smaller particles from the Upper Box fall onto a 20 hole/inch screen (which has riffles on the surface - to catch larger gold pieces) the larger particles rolling down the screen as fine tailings. The particles that fell through the screen will fall onto a muslin cloth with riffles on its surface. Air from the bellows, blowing from below the muslin cloth, keeps the fine particles in motion and blows away some of the lighter dust.

Handle is pulled to rock the upper box and through the linkage pumps the bellows.

Tray with 5 holes / inch screen
Screen
Coarse Tailings
Upper Box
Tray with 60 holes / inch
Lower Box
Fine Tailings
Bellow

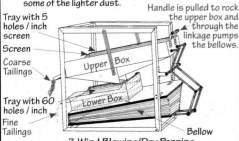

3 Wind Blowing/Dry Panning
Collect the concentrate, in a pan, from the riffles. Now pour the material from pan to pan allowing the wind to carry away the dust and fine sand as the material is dropped 6 feet from one pan to another.

RANDOM PANNING TEST
Based upon your initial analyses of your prospecting area. Run a few hoppers full of earth trough the dry washer. If you see some specks of gold keep on working the spot. If nothing move on.
A Use a fork pronged rake to remove the loose rocks, weeds, dry wood and branches – push them aside.
B With a pick break up the top soil, dig down, and remove up to the alluvial deposit zone – the hardened caliche.
C Using the fork pronged rake to loosen up the caliche and remove the stones. Place the worked caliche deposit into a five gallon plastic bucket.
D Pour the caliche from the bucket over the dry wash screen into the second bucket until the second bucket is full. Depending upon the screen mesh size the stones up to ½" will remain on the screen.
E Dry pan the contents of the second bucket.

Caliche
Thick, massive, rock-hard accumulations that cement gravel, sand, and fines of a sediment, producing a dense and impermeable layer that resembles fresh-water limestone. Such massive caliche layers (calcretes) are common in deserts at depths of a few inches to about 2 yards. The layers are a few inches to several yards thick. Some alluvial fans eventually become so plugged with caliche that surface runoff can no longer percolate into the gravel, producing short-lived but disastrous flooding in their terminal regions.

Weighing Gold - Troy Measure
Gold, silver, platinum are weighed by the Troy standard not the Avoirdupois standard used in daily weight standards.
Troy Weight   12 ounces = 1 pound
Avoirdupois Weight 16 ounces = 1 pound

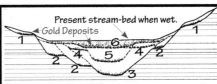

Present stream-bed when wet.
Gold Deposits

Cross-section of a gold-bearing desert stream valley showing the results of several periods of stream deposition from the oldest (1) to the youngest (6).

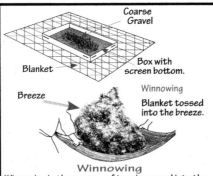

Coarse Gravel
Blanket
Box with screen bottom.
Breeze
Winnowing
Blanket tossed into the breeze.

Winnowing
Winnowing is the process of tossing gravel into the air to let the breeze remove the light airborne particles from the gold bearing gravel mixture. This gravel has to be dry and all clumps should be broken up.
The process:
• Place a tightly woven blanket flat on the ground and center a screening box (3'x3' and 8" high) on the blanket.
• Two people lift the screen box, with the coarse gravel, and agitate the box. The smaller particles will fall through a screen onto the blanket.
• The two people raise the ends of the slack blanket and toss the gravel concentrate into the air while stretching the blanket. This is the process of winnowing because the breeze carries away the light airborne particles letting the heavier gold fall to the blanket.
• Larger gold particles (nuggets) can be retrieved from the blanket's surface and when the blanket becomes worn it is burnt and the ashes are panned to remove the gold particles trapped in the weave of the blanket.

PLACER GOLD: NO WATER
The deserts of California, Arizona, New Mexico, and Nevada with their lack of flowing water require a different strategy of finding placer gold and extracting it. Usually placer gold is found by following a stream or river to find deposits and then the gold is extracted by using water. These dry area placers were formed by rivers, during old geological periods, which flowed southwest from the Rockies and south from the Sierra mountains. The ground in which the placers are found is not deep and is composed of sandy clay. The gold is found in clay that accompanies cement gravel and to disintegrate this material and free the gold without the aid of water is a problem.

FINDING GOLD: NO WATER
Deserts are vast and there are no obvious deposit streams as can be found along river beds.
• Check local government topographic or mining maps which might indicate the presence of minerals.
• Look for small canyons and washes where minerals can have been washed down during storms or the rainy season. Be aware of potential flash floods.
• Quartz outcrops on the sides of hills are indicators that gold nuggets might have eroded and washed down into the canyons and washes. If the canyons are very steep the water will travel faster and wash any potential gold further down the hill then it will be more difficult to find in a high concentration.
• Do not go into the hills, to find gold, because the gold is mixed with tons of dirt and stone material. The erosion of the rains will sift the sand and transport the gold to the alluvial plain (washes).

Gold Deposits in Alluvial Plain
• Efficiency of water working on your behalf is not available. Using the mechanical action of water in panning or sluicing is not available.
• The best place for a higher concentration, of gold, is where the hills meet the desert and the deposits fan out. In this area the gold will deposit first as it is the heaviest. This is the same principle as in using a sluice.
• If there is gold, it being so heavy, it settles to the very bottom of a wash – in the caliche bedrock (cement gravel).
• Gold will usually be found at the bottom of a layer of the sand and gravel on the top of clay layer because gold being heavy would have sunk through the gravel layer during any wet periods. This has happened for hundreds if not thousands of years and spreading the gold further and deeper onto the desert floor. The further you are from the hills the deeper you will have to dig for the gold.
• Difficulty in finding completely loose gravel. Dry clay with gravel form a cement like solid that can be hard to break down.
• Gravel used in dry washing must be completely dry and free of clumps. Below the surface the sand will be slightly damp and this will have to be dried before it can pass through a dry washer.
• If there is a very strong downpour its waters might wash through numerous layers of deposited gold - Thus displacing the gold into higher a concentration.

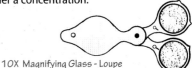

10X Magnifying Glass - Loupe

27 CAMOUFLAGE & TRACKING

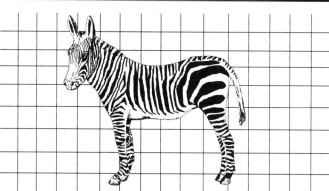

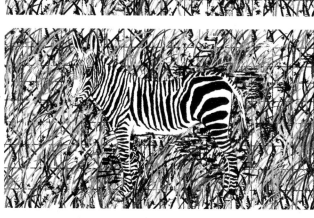

CAMOUFLAGE AGAINST DIFFERENT BACKGROUNDS

In our Zebra example one can see the zebra camouflage pattern against different backgrounds. The efficiency of the zebra pattern is shown when an example of a complete horizontal pattern is tried on a zebra body in a normal zebra background. The zebra pattern cuts across the body and legs so that the zebra body outline is bounded by a broken line and this hides the continuous outline of the body.

SEEING BODY SHAPE & CAMOUFLAGE

Shape is outline or form. A human body is also easily recognized because it is a known shape. Use camouflage and concealment to breakup shapes and blend them with their surroundings. Be careful not to overdo it.

199

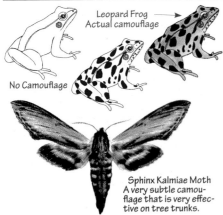

Leopard Frog
Actual camouflage

No Camouflage

Sphinx Kalmiae Moth
A very subtle camouflage that is very effective on tree trunks.

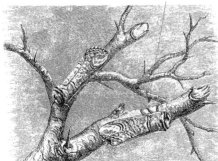

DECEPTION IN NATURE

Deception in animals are ways they mislead their victims/predator both for defensive and aggressive purposes.

Some of the most methods are...

Deceptive markings: These are markings on the body that will give a false impression to a victim or predator. This can be large eyes on the wings of a insect which appear to be to draw away the attention of an attacking enemy from the most vital part, the head. Most butterflies have eye spots near the edge of their wings - birds might be attracted to peck at this "head" and the butterfly can still escape - beak damage marking have been found at the fake eyes.

Deceptive behavior: Decoy movements, noises, and chirping by birds to draw away the enemy from their nests. A lizard, when attacked by a bird, detaches its tail and leaves it wriggling behind him while he takes up a new position and remains motionless. The bird is attracted by the movement of the tail and the lizard escapes further attention.

Mimicry: This is copying some item in the surroundings. Caterpillars can resemble a growing twig. Grasshoppers combines deceptive eye markings on its wings when it is flying with a realistic imitation of a leaf when it is at rest.

CONCEALMENT IN NATURE

Nature itself provides the basic principles of camouflage. Not only does it provide us with examples of concealment, but animals and their habits give us many ingenious ideas in the use of bluff and deception.

There are two ways of hiding an object...

• Hide it by placing it underneath something and completely hiding it.

• Leave it on the surface but make it resemble the background - so well that it is almost impossible to detect.

This applies to animals when they are in their natural environments. A polar bear is well concealed against a background of snow and ice, but will immediately become very conspicuous in a green field.

CAMOUFLAGE FACTORS IN NATURE

Resemblance in color: As animal to background.

Resemblance in texture: Most creatures that live on dry land avoid bright reflections from their skins by the use of fur, feathers or rough scales. Those that live in mud or water, on the contrary retain a smooth shiny appearance.

Obliterative shading: The back of any creature is darker than its belly. A fish has a darker back than belly - if looked at from the top it is as dark as the bottom of the pond. But when looked at a predator from below the light belly will blend in with the light sky.

Disruptive patterns: This is using a pattern that would be considered as being very visible. An excellent example of this would be the zebra with its black and white strips - which are very visible. In the case of the zebra the stripes are designed in such a way that the stripes cut across its body lines - vertical lines on the body - horizontal lines on the legs.

Concealment small vital points: An example is the eye of a frog or snake. In this case the concealment by a dark streak across the face which covers the eye and renders it much less conspicuous.

Eliminate cast shadows: Animals staying in a patch of shadow. Animals can also be shaped so that they do not cast an obvious shadow - moths lying flat on the bark of a tree.

Immobility: Movement is extremely difficult to hide. Sudden movement inevitably attracts the attention of the observer. Camouflaged animals often escape notice completely until they are seen to move. Many animals remain immobile in front of an advancing predator and bolt at the very last second.

Smoke screen: Escape camouflage screen or other decoy in nature. Example being the octopus, which escapes from its enemies by emitting a smoke screen of sepia.

Behavior: Animals choose tactics that help them survive. Brown birds will not have nests in green fields. Deer will rest in shaded areas from which they can observe the woods.

CAMOUFLAGE

Camouflage is the use of materials and techniques to hide, blend, disguise, decoy, or disrupt the appearance of a person, location or its background. Properly designed camouflage techniques take advantage of the immediate environment and natural and artificial materials.

CAMOUFLAGE TACTICS

Hiding: is screening a location. The location is undetected because a barrier hides it. When hiding all functions should be hidden – the access path, movement, etc

Blending: is trying to alter a location's appearance so that it becomes a part of the background. Generally, it is arranging or applying camouflage material on, over, and/or around a location to reduce its contrast with the background. Characteristics to consider when blending include the terrain patterns in the vicinity and the location's size, shape, texture, color, and background.

Disguising: is applying materials on a location to mislead the viewer as to its true identity. Disguising changes a location's appearance so that it resembles something else.

Disrupting: is altering or eliminating regular patterns and location characteristics. Disrupting techniques include pattern painting, deploying camouflage nets over selected portions of a position, and using shape disrupters (such as camouflage sails) to eliminate regular patterns.

Decoying: is deploying a false or simulated shape(s) within a location's scene or in a position where the viewer might conclude that it has found the correct location(s).

Background Selection: Select backgrounds that do not silhouette positions and obstacles or provide color contrast. Use shadows to hinder observation by staying under overhead cover, trees, or bushes or in any other dark area of the terrain. This technique prevents the disruption of terrain lines and hinders aerial detection. When using the terrain's natural concealment properties, avoid isolated features that can draw attention. Do not construct positions directly on or near other clearly defined terrain features (tree lines, hedge rows, hill crests). Offsetting positions into tree lines or below hill crests avoids silhouetting against the background.

MOVEMENT

Movement draws attention. When you walk, your movement can be seen by the naked eye at long ranges. Stay low and move only when necessary and move only on covered and on concealed routes. Avoid open areas. Outlines and shadows can be broken up with camouflage. When moving, stay in the shadows when possible.

The background against which an object is seen must dictate the kind of camouflage which is required.

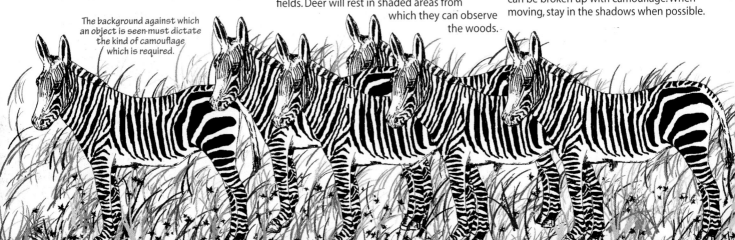

CAMOUFLAGE MATERIALS

Using natural conditions and materials is the first camouflage priority, but using man-made materials can greatly enhance camouflage efforts.

VEGETATION

Living Vegetation: can be readily obtained. Its color and texture make it a good blending agent. However, foliage requires careful maintenance to keep the material fresh and in good condition. If branches are not placed in their proper growing positions, they may reveal a location. Be careful when placing green vegetation since the underside of leaves are a lighter tone. Cutting large amounts of branches can point to the presence of a hidden spot, so cut all vegetation away from the hiding spot. As cut vegetation wilts, it loses color and its blending properties. Replace cut vegetation regularly because over time it becomes a detection cue rather than an effective concealment technique.

Dead Vegetation: Use dried grass, hay, straw, and branches for texturing. It provides good blending qualities if the surrounding background vegetation is also dead. Dead vegetation is usually readily available and requires little maintenance; however, it is flammable.

Foliage Selection: When selecting foliage for camouflage, consider the following:

- Coniferous vegetation is preferred to deciduous vegetation since it maintains its chlorophyll (green color) longer.
- Foliage cut during periods of high humidity (at night, during a rainstorm, or when there is fog or heavy dew) will wilt more slowly.
- Foliage with leaves that feel tough to the fingers and branches with large leaves are preferred because they stay fresher longer.
- Branches that grow in direct sunlight are tougher and will stay fresher longer.
- Branches that are free of disease and insects will not wilt as rapidly.

NATURAL MATERIALS

Before constructing a location, remove and save natural materials (turf, leaves, humus) for use in restoring the terrain's natural appearance for deception purposes. During excavation, collect spoil in carrying devices for careful disposal. Avoid disturbing the natural look of surroundings. Replace natural materials regularly or when they wilt or change color.

Man-made concealment must blend with its surroundings so that it cannot be detected.

CAMOUFLAGED FIRE

Making a fire that can be easily covered and its remains would be hard to see. Cut into the sod and roll it back. The exposed soil is humid and the fire can be set directly onto the soil. Do not make a fire that is too large or the root structure might start to smolder and burn. Spray the fire with water when finished and the rolled back sod can be placed over the fire's remains.

CAMOUFLAGE TERRAIN

The terrain generally dictates what camouflage techniques and materials are necessary. Different terrain types or background environments. Mountain, forest, plains, desert, or arctic require specific camouflage techniques. The weather and season are also critical factors.

Properly using terrain and weather is a first priority when employing camouflage. Cover can be provided by the terrain and by conditions of limited visibility. The effective use of natural conditions will minimize the use of resources and the time devoted to camouflage. The terrain's concealment properties are determined by the number and quality of natural screens, and terrain patterns.

Forests: generally provide the best type of natural screen, especially if the crowns of the trees are wide enough to prevent aerial observation of the ground. Forests with undergrowth also hinder ground observation. Deciduous (leafing) forests are not as effective during the months when trees are bare, while coniferous (evergreen) forests preserve their concealment properties all year. Movement should be made along roads and gaps that are covered by tree crowns. The broken areas of shade and light is excellent for concealment.

Open Terrain: Limited visibility is an especially important concealment tool in open terrain. When crossing open terrain during limited visibility, supplement movement with camouflage material as branches, follow natural land characteristics and shadows.

Dead Space: Areas where one is silhouetted against the sky is considered as dead space – to be avoided. Instead use reverse slopes of hills, ravines, embankments, and other terrain features as screens to avoid detection.

CAMOUFLAGE MATERIALS

Use earth, sand, and gravel to change or add color, provide a coarse texture, simulate the environment and create shapes and shadows. Mud makes is ideal for toning down bright, shiny objects. Add clay (in mud form) of various colors to make a paint-like goo. Use surface soils to mimic natural surface color and reflectivity.

WEATHER

Conditions of limited visibility (fog, rain, snowfall) are aids to unobserved movement. Dense fog and falling snow are excellent – as long as you know where you are going – and that you are sure that you are getting there.

UNEXPECTED EVIDENCE

When walking on a beach one compresses the beach sand. An incoming wave erodes the uncompressed sand leaving the compressed sand in the shape of the footprint. There are many other unintended signs of ones presence that are left...

- toilet remains
- scuff marks on been disturbed on tree trunks shelter or from make a fire.
- random rubbish

things that have as rope marks from building a breaking a stick to

EXPOSED SKIN

Exposed skin reflects light and even very dark skin, because of natural oils, will reflect light. Camouflage paint sticks cover these oils and help blend skin with the background. Avoid using oils or insect repellent to soften the paint stick because doing so makes skin shiny and defeats the purpose of the paint sticks. When applying camouflage paint work in pairs and help each other. Self-application may leave gaps, such as behind ears. Apply a two-color combination of camouflage stick in an irregular pattern.

Use the following technique:

- Paint high, shiny areas (forehead, cheekbones, nose, ears, chin) with a dark color.
- Paint low, shadow areas (around the eyes, under the nose, and under the chin) with a light color.
- Paint the exposed skin on the back of the neck, arms, and hands with an irregular pattern.
- Palms of hands are not normally camouflaged if arm-and-hand signals are to be used.
- Remove all jewelry to further reduce shine or reflection.
- When camouflage paint sticks are unavailable, use burnt cork, bark, charcoal, lampblack, or mud. Mud contains bacteria, some of which is harmful and may cause disease or infection, so consider mud as the last resource.
- Winter camouflage face paint, white and loam color combination, may be applied to exposed areas of the face and hands to blend effectively in with the snow cover.

Face Camouflage Blotch Pattern *Face Camouflage Splash Pattern*

Making Camouflage Materials

Paint Materials	Mixing	Color	Finish
Earth, soap, water, soot, paraffin.	Mix soot with paraffin (candle wax), add to solution of 8 gal water and 2 bars soap, and stir in earth.	Dark gray	Flat, lusterless
Oil, clay, water, gasoline, earth.	Mix 2 gal water and to gal clay, add earth, and thin with water.	Depends on earth colors	Glossy on metal, otherwise dull
Oil, clay, soap, water, earth.	Mix 1 bars soap with 3 gal water, stir in 1 gal clay, and add earth for color.	Depends on earth colors	Glossy on metal, otherwise dull

Use canned milk or powdered eggs to increase the binding properties of paints.

Disguise or distort body shapes with available materials to make it more difficult to recognize a body profile.

Looks like human body.

Casting a shadow with no camouflage. The body shape is evident.

Bear?

The body shape silhouette is broken up by attaching leafy branches to the body. The new silhouette is not identifiable as a human body but bear-like.

CAMOUFLAGE

DESERT CAMOUFLAGE

The color of desert terrain varies from pink to blue, depending on the minerals in the soil and the time of the day. No color or combination of colors matches all deserts. Patches of clothing color in the desert are usually 10 times larger than those in wooded areas. A neutral monotone tan is the best desert camouflage color.

Desert Topography: Desert terrain may appear featureless, but it is not completely flat. In some ways, desert terrain resembles unplowed fields; barren, rocky areas; grasslands; and steppes.

Desert Shadows: The lower the shelter is to the ground, the smaller its shadow; and a small shadow is easier to conceal. The best solution to the shadow problem in desert terrain is to dig in and use overhead concealment or cover. Otherwise, place items in a way that minimizes their broadside exposure to the sun – thus to cast the smallest shadow. Shadows are an important factor in a relatively barren area so that proper placement is important. Use gullies, washes, wadis, and ravines to reduce shadows and silhouettes and to take advantage of terrain masking. Move as the sun changes position to remain in the shadows.

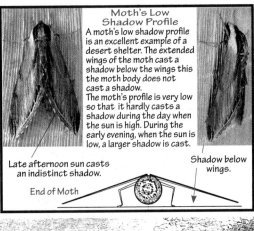

Moth's Low Shadow Profile

A moth's low shadow profile is an excellent example of a desert shelter. The extended wings of the moth cast a shadow below the wings this the moth body does not cast a shadow.

The moth's profile is very low so that it hardly casts a shadow during the day when the sun is high. During the early evening, when the sun is low, a larger shadow is cast.

Late afternoon sun casts an indistinct shadow.

Shadow below wings.

End of Moth

JUNGLE CAMOUFLAGE

Jungles are humid, tropic areas with a dense growth of trees and vegetation. Visibility is typically less than 100 feet, and areas are sparsely populated. Jungle vegetation provides excellent concealment. Adequate cover is available, if hiding places are located in natural ravines and gullies produced by erosion from the area's high annual rainfall. When shelters are constructed in jungles, primary consideration is given to drainage. Because of high amounts of rainfall and poor soil drainage, high water, shelters are built to allow for good, natural drainage. The platform is constructed of small branches or timber layered over cross-posts, thus distributing the floor load over a wider area.

SNOW CAMOUFLAGE

In winter the whiteness of the countryside emphasizes any item which may not blend in naturally with the surroundings. A blanket of snow often eliminates much of the ground pattern and makes blending difficult. Differences in texture and color disappear or become less marked. Snow-covered terrain, however, is rarely completely white. By taking advantage of dark features in the lines, stream-beds, evergreen trees, bushes, shadows of snowdrifts, folds in the ground, and the dark shadows of hillsides. Good route selection in snow-covered terrain is usually more important than any other camouflage measure. Every movement leaves tracks in the snow. Before every movement, consideration must be given to how these tracks can be kept to a minimum. Nature may assist by covering tracks with newly fallen snow or by providing a storm in which movement will be concealed. Because of the exposed tracks, skis and snowshoes are not used near the base area since their marks are more sharply defined than foot tracks. Note avoid shiny reflective items and any items that might be noisy as sound carries in cold weather.

SNOW CAMOUFLAGE *cont'd*

Materials: Natural camouflage includes defilade, grass, bushes, trees, and shadows.

Artificial camouflage: includes, white garments, camouflage nets, skin paint, and natural materials removed from their original positions. To be effective, artificial camouflage must blend with the natural background.

Vapor clouds: Breathing will, in extreme cold, cause local fog or vapor clouds which can be seen by an observer especially if the light falls in the correct direction.

Smoke from fires: hangs immediately above and will disclose the position if there is no wind to blow it away.

Sounds: The still, cold air of the North carries sound much farther than in temperate climates. All sounds must be kept to a minimum. Noise caused by motors, men coughing, and skiers breaking through snow crust can be heard at extreme distances.

Visibility: The long hours of daylight in the North during the summer allow for many more hours of travel but also more time to be observed and possible detection. As an example, during the period 15 December to 15 January at 68° N. Lat. the sun will never appear over the horizon. Daylight will consist of only twilight and will last for only 4 or 5 hours.

Tracks: Tracks made in a soft surface may become quite firm if the temperature drops during the night, and will remain indefinitely as indications of movement. Special consideration must be given to the tracks in camps. Number and size of trails must be kept to a minimum. Individuals may be forced to use only a certain trail. Tracks, even through wooded areas, appear like a white scar. Coniferous branches can be laid in a staggered pattern on each side of the track as well as on it.

Pay attention to shiny surfaces. A shiny object can be seen for miles. In this case the object is a watch.

California Indians Hunting

WINTER CAMOUFLAGE MATERIALS

- White is the predominant color in winter and snow is the most important camouflage material, By intelligent use of camouflage clothing and equipment together with what nature makes available, effective individual and group camouflage can be achieved.
- Improvised camouflage clothes can be made from sheeting, tape, whitewashed sacking, or painted canvas. White paper, when wet, can be applied and allowed to freeze on all kinds of surfaces. Snow thrown over the object helps to increase the camouflage effect.
- White paint has many uses in winter camouflage. Snowshoes, skis, and sleds can be effectively painted with white non-glossy paint.
- Winter camouflage clothing (over whites or shells) consists of white trousers and lightweight parka with hood. Mixed clothing white parka and dark trousers, or vice versa - is used against mottled backgrounds.
- Over whites, to keep their whiteness, should be washed or changed frequently. When changing, clothing should be checked to insure that it fits over the basic garments without restricting movement.
- Camouflage face paint, white and loam color combination, may be applied to exposed areas of the face and hands to blend effectively in with the snow cover.
- In fairly open forest areas during the winter, avoid wearing "whites" in the dark background of trees. In the same manner, if wearing dark clothing, stay under trees and avoid the open.
- In mixed surroundings frequent changes of camouflage clothing become necessary. The use of mixed clothing is often the most preferable.

Buffalo hunting with a wolf skin disguise. The buffalo are agitated but not scared of a wolf.

White camouflage sheet placed as a sail on a sled that is gradually advanced towards the seals. The white sail against the white background with the shadow cast behind the sails would make it quite invisible. The wind has to be blowing from the direction of the seals - otherwise the seals might get the sent of the man.

Small shadow cast when person crawls.

Shadow cast when person stands up to run. The risk of exposure of short time to run has to be evaluated with the longer crawl time.

TraTraTRACKING

TRACKING BASICS

With common sense and a degree of outdoors experience, you can track another person. *However, you must develop the following traits and qualities...*

- Be patient.
- Be able to move slowly and quietly, yet steadily, while detecting and interpreting signs. Avoid fast movement that may cause you to overlook signs and lose the trail.
- Be persistent and have the skill and desire to continue the mission even though signs are scarce or weather or terrain is unfavorable.
- Be determined and persistent when trying to find a trail that you have lost.
- Be observant and try to see things that are not obvious at first glance.
- Use your senses of smell and hearing to supplement your sight.
- Develop a feel for things that do not look right. It may help you regain a lost trail or discover additional signs.
- Know and learn the habits, equipment, and capability of the person being tracked.

ANIMAL TRACKS

The story of an animal passing through a meadow is left by its tracks. Tracks consist of bent blades of grass, gnawed bone, broken seeds, the dragged body or tail, and the foot print of the animal. All prints of an animal are not the same as they depend upon:

- The age of the animal.
- The movement of the animal - walking, running, bounding.
- The material it is walking on - sand, mud, clay, grass, or snow.
- The season - some animals have extra fur on their paws in the winter.
- The age of the track.

When you see a track:
- Choose a well defined area of the track.
- Study the track to determine the direction of travel, the forefoot and hind foot pattern.
- Are there any body rub points as a dragged tail, dragged foot, or dragged fur of the body?
- Is the animal running, hopping, walking, trotting, or just meandering?

OTHER TRACKING FACTORS

When tracking an animal or human, you should build a picture of the tracked in your mind. Ask yourself such questions as:

- How many persons am I following?
- Do they have evasion experience?
- How are they equipped?
- Are they healthy?
- How is their morale?
- Do they know they are being followed?

To find the answer to such questions, use all available signs. A sign can be anything that shows you that a certain act took place at a particular place and time. For instance, a footprint tells a tracker that at a certain time a person walked on that spot. The six fundamentals of tracking are:

- Displacement.
- Staining.
- Weathering.
- Littering (droppings).
- Camouflaging.
- Interpretation and/or immediate use of environmental evidence.

Any sign that you find can be identified as one or more of the first five fundamentals. In the sixth fundamental, you combine the first five and use all of them to form a picture of the tracked.

It happened one day, about noon, going towards my boat. I was exceedingly surprised with the print of a man's naked foot on the shore... Which was very plain to be seen in the sand... Robinson Crusoe

303

TRACKING (DISPLACEMENT)

An example is a footprint in soft, moist ground. The foot of the person that left the print displaced the soil, leaving an indentation in the ground. By studying the print, you can determine many facts. For example, a print that was left by a barefoot person or a person with worn or frayed foot gear indicates that he may have poor equipment.

ANALYZING FOOTPRINTS

Footprints show the following:

- The direction and rate of movement of a party.
- The number of persons in a party.
- Whether or not heavy loads are carried.
- The sex of the members of a party.
- Whether the members of a party know they are being followed.
- If the footprints are deep and the pace is long, the party is moving rapidly.
- Very long strides and deep prints, with toe prints deeper than heel prints, indicate that the party is running.
- If the prints are deep, short, and widely spaced, with signs of scuffing or shuffling, a heavy load is probably being carried.
- Determine a person's sex by studying the size and position of the footprints. Women generally tend to be pigeon-toed, while men usually walk with their feet pointed straight ahead or slightly to the outside. Women's prints are usually smaller than men's, and their strides are usually shorter.
- Party knows that it is being followed, it may attempt to hide its tracks.
- Persons walking backward have a short, irregular stride. The prints have an unusually deep toe. The soil will be kicked in the direction of movement.

AGE OF TRACK

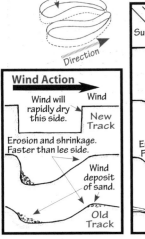

Floor of Track / Wall of Track / New track of a hoofed animal

Direction

Wind Action

Wind will rapidly dry this side. / Wind / New Track

Erosion and shrinkage. Faster than lee side.

Wind deposit of sand.

Old Track

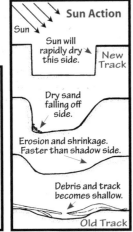

Sun Action

Sun / Sun will rapidly dry this side. / New Track

Dry sand falling off side.

Erosion and shrinkage. Faster than shadow side.

Debris and track becomes shallow.

Old Track

TRACKS & WEATHERING

Weather may either aid or hinder tracking. It affects signs in ways that help determine how old they are, but wind, snow, rain, and sunlight can also obliterate signs completely. By studying the effects of weather on signs, you can determine the age of the sign.

- When bloodstains are fresh, they may be bright red. Air and sunlight will change the appearance of blood first to a deep ruby-red color, and then to a dark brown crust when the moisture evaporates.
- Scuff marks on trees or bushes darken with time. Sap oozes from fresh cuts on trees but it hardens when exposed to the air.

FOOTPRINTS & WEATHERING

Footprints are greatly affected by weather.

Moisture: When a foot displaces soft, moist soil to form a print, the moisture holds the edges of the print intact and sharp. As sunlight and air dry the edges of the print, small particles that were held in place by the moisture fall into the print, making the edges appear rounded.

If particles are just beginning to fall into a print, it is probably fresh. If the edges of the print are dried and crusty, the prints are probably at least an hour old. The effects of weather will vary with the terrain, so this information is furnished as a guide only.

Rain: A light rain may round out the edges of a print. Try to remember when the last rain occurred in order to put prints into a proper time frame. A heavy rain may erase all signs.

Wind: Wind also affects prints. Besides drying out a print, the wind may blow litter, sticks, or leaves into it. Try to remember the wind activity in order to help determine the age of a print. For example, you may think, "It is calm now, but the wind blew hard an hour ago. These prints have litter blown into them, so they must be over an hour old." Make sure that the litter was blown into the prints, and was not crushed into them when the prints were made.

Streams: Trails leaving streams may appear to be weathered by rain because of water running into the footprints from wet clothing or equipment. This is particularly true if a party leaves a stream in a file. From this file formation, each person drips water into the prints. A wet trail slowly fading into a dry trail indicates that the trail is fresh.

> Tracks "age" due to the action of weather and other tracks being made over them. A track is made by the pressure of the weight of the animal on the ground and this pressure usually breaks the surface exposing humid soil or a lower layer of snow. As soon as a track is made the weather will start acting (aging) on the track. If frost crystals have formed on the track after a cold night, the track was made before the frost. If there is no frost, the track is recent. A fresh track in snow will have a crisp curl with snow particles kicked in the direction of movement. A track is old when evaporation or blown snow have dulled the crispness. Aging happens in a few hours as the sun dries the dew, frost, or humidity from a dirt track, and the edges start to crumble.

WIND, SOUND, ODORS

Wind affects sounds and odors. If the wind is blowing from the direction of a trail being followed, sounds and odors are carried to you. If the wind is blowing in the same direction as the trail you are following, you must be cautious as the wind will carry your sounds toward the party being followed. To find the wind direction, drop a handful of dry dirt or grass from shoulder height. To help you decide where a sound is coming from, cup your hands behind your ears and slowly turn. When the sound is loudest, you are probably facing the origin of sound. When moving, try to keep the wind in your face.

Sun: You must also consider the effects of the sun. It is hard to look or aim directly into the sun. If possible, keep the sun at your back.

LITTERING

Relaxed groups may leave trails of litter as they move. Gum or candy wrappers, cigarette butts, remains of fires, or human feces are unmistakable signs of recent movement. Weather affects litter. Rain may flatten or wash litter away, or turn paper into pulp. Winds may blow litter away from its original location. Use your memory to determine the age of litter. The last rain or strong wind can be the basis of a time frame.

CAMOUFLAGING OF TRACK

If a party knows that you are tracking it, it will probably use camouflage to conceal its movement and to slow and confuse you. Doing so, however, will slow it down. Walking backward, brushing out trails, and moving over rocky ground or through streams are examples of camouflage that can be used to confuse you. The party may move on hard surfaced, frequently traveled roads or try to merge with other hikers. Examine such routes with extreme care, because the party may try to avoid leaving a trail. Its members may wrap rags around their boots, or wear soft-soled shoes to make the edges of their footprints rounder and less distinct. The party may exit a stream in column or line to reduce the chance of leaving a well-defined exit. If the party walks backward to leave a confusing trail, the footprints will be deepened at the toe, and the soil will be scuffed or dragged in the direction of movement.

If a trail leads across rocky or hard ground, try to work around that ground to pick up the exit trail. This process works in streams as well. On rocky ground, moss or lichens growing on the stones could be displaced by even the most careful evader. If you lose the trail, return to the last visible sign. From there, head in the direction of the party's movement. Move in ever-widening circles until you find some signs to follow.

Ground Surface and Quality of Track	
Surface	**Track**
Dry sand	Walls rapidly collapse and there are not many details.
Very wet sand	Track fills with water and mud and disappears.
Dry sand surface	Ideal track when the surface is dry but humid below.
When humid below surface then:	
Humid sand	Good track. Track size will increase upon drying.
Humid clay	Can dry and preserve the track.
Humid snow	Good track.
Crusty snow	Track breaks crust but details lost in dry snow below.
Grass field	Track will be twisted and broken grass.

Sun, Wind & Rain Effect on a Track		
Weather	**Surface**	**Impact on Track**
Sun	Sand	Rapidly dry track and cause sides to fall.
	Snow	Melt snow, enlarge hole, and obliterate details.
	Rock	Wet footprint will dry it in a few minutes.
Rain	Sand	Wash out track.
	Snow	Obliterate track.
	Rock	No track will be made.
Wind	Sand	Dry track and cause sides to fall. Leave sand and other debris deposits in cavity.
	Snow	Drift snow across the track.
	Rock	Wet footprint will dry it in a few minutes.

BLOOD STAINING

A good example of staining is the mark left by blood from a bleeding wound. Bloodstains often will be in the form of drops left by a wounded animal. Blood signs are found on the ground and smeared on leaves or twigs.

You can determine the location of a wound on the animal being followed by studying the bloodstains. If the blood seems to be dripping steadily, it probably came from a wound on his trunk. A wound in the lungs will deposit bloodstains that are pink, bubbly, frothy. A bloodstain deposited from a head wound will appear heavy, wet, and slimy, like gelatin. Abdominal wounds often mix blood with digestive juices so that the deposit will have an odor. The stains will be light in color.

OTHER STAINS

- Staining can also occur when a person walks over grass, stones, and shrubs with muddy boots. Thus, staining and displacement together may give evidence of movement and indicate the direction taken.
- Crushed leaves may stain rocky ground that is too hard for footprints. Roots, stones, and vines may be stained by crushed leaves or berries when walked on.
- Yellow stains in snow may be urine marks left by personnel in the area.

DISPLACEMENT STAINS

In some cases, it may be hard to determine the difference between staining and displacement. Both terms can be applied to some signs.

- For example, water that has been muddied may indicate recent movement. The mud has been displaced and it is staining the water. Stones in streams may be stained by mud from boots. Algae can be displaced from stones in streams and can stain other stones or bark.
- Water in footprints in swampy ground may be muddy if the tracks are recent. In time, however, the mud will settle and the water will clear. The clarity of the water can be used to estimate the age of the prints. Normally, the mud will clear in 1 hour. That will vary with terrain.

OTHER TRACKING INDICATORS

Footprints are only one example of displacement. Displacement occurs when anything is moved from its original position.

- Foliage, moss, vines, sticks, or rocks that are moved from their original places; dew droplets brushed from leaves; stones and sticks that are turned over and show a different color underneath; and grass or other vegetation that is bent or broken in the direction of movement.
- Bits of cloth may be torn and left on thorns, snags, or the ground, and dirt from boots may make marks on the ground.
- Movement of wild animals and birds that are flushed from their natural habitats. You may hear the cries of birds that are excited by strange movements.
- Movement of tall grass or brush on a windless day indicates that some thing is moving the vegetation from its original position.
- Clearing a trail by either breaking or cutting through the heavy vegetation.
- Signs can be made while you stop to rest with heavy loads. The prints made by the equipment you carry can help to identify its type. When loads are set down at a rest halt or campsite, grass and twigs may be crushed. A sleeping man may also flatten the vegetation.
- Any changes in the normal life of insects may be a sign that someone has recently passed through the area. Bees that are stirred up, and holes that are covered by someone moving over them, or spider webs that are torn down are good clues.
- If a person uses a stream to cover his trail, algae and water plants may be displaced in slippery footing or in places where he walks carelessly. Rocks may be displaced from their original position, or turned over to show a lighter or darker color on their opposite side.
- A person entering or leaving a stream may create slide marks, wet banks, or footprints, or he may scuff bark off roots or sticks. Normally, a person or animal will seek the path of least resistance. Therefore, when you search a stream for exit signs, look for open places on the banks or other places where it would be easy to leave the stream.

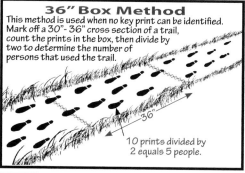

36" Box Method

This method is used when no key print can be identified. Mark off a 30"- 36" cross section of a trail, count the prints in the box, then divide by two to determine the number of persons that used the trail.

10 prints divided by 2 equals 5 people.

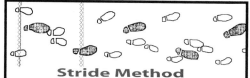

Stride Method

The stride as a unit of measure method is the most accurate of the two. Up to 18 persons can be counted using this method. Use it when the key print can be determined. To use this method, identify a key print on a trail and draw a line from its heel across the trail. Then move forward to the key print of the opposite foot and draw a line through its instep. This should form a box with the edges of the trail forming two sides, and the drawn lines forming the other two sides. Next, count every print or partial print inside the box to determine the number of persons. Any person walking normally would have stepped in the box at least one time. Count the key prints as one.

Last Person Followed

The last person walking in a group usually leaves the clearest footprints. Therefore, use his prints as the key set. Cut a stick the length of each key print and notch the stick to show the print width at the widest part of the sole. Study the angle of the key prints to determine the direction of march. Look for an identifying mark or feature on the prints, such as a worn or frayed part of the footwear. If the trail becomes vague or obliterated, or if the trail being followed merges with another, use the stick to help identify the key prints. That will help you stay on the trail of the group being followed.

Hind   Fore

Domestic Dog Track
Notice how it drags its toes when taking a step. This is especially visible in snow.

Deer hoof track that has partially dried. Note that the print is less distinct and the cleft mark of the hoof is hardly visible.

Crab Tracks
Yes they walk sideways.

Deer hoof track that is still humid. Note that the print is distinct and the cleft mark of the hooves is visible.

Domestic Dog Track

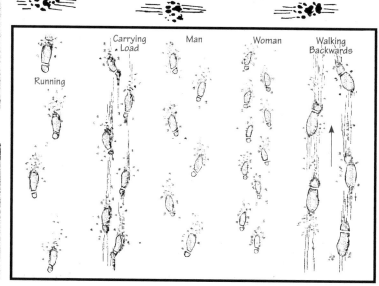

Running   Carrying Load   Man   Woman   Walking Backwards

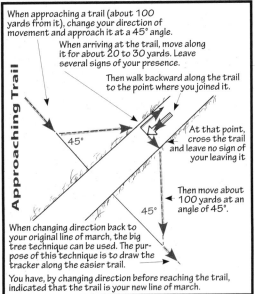

When approaching a trail (about 100 yards from it), change your direction of movement and approach it at a 45° angle.

When arriving at the trail, move along it for about 20 to 30 yards. Leave several signs of your presence.

Then walk backward along the trail to the point where you joined it.

At that point, cross the trail and leave no sign of your leaving it

Then move about 100 yards at an angle of 45°.

When changing direction back to your original line of march, the big tree technique can be used. The purpose of this technique is to draw the tracker along the easier trail.

You have, by changing direction before reaching the trail, indicated that the trail is your new line of march.

BEING TRACKED

False Trail: Trail or Stream

To leave a false trail and to get a tracker to look in the wrong direction, walk backward over soft ground. Continue this deception for about 20 to 30 yards or until you are on hard ground. Use this technique when leaving a stream. To further confuse the tracker, use this technique several times before actually leaving the stream.

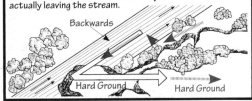

When moving toward a stream, change direction about 100 yards before reaching the stream and approach it at a 45° angle.

Enter the stream and proceed down it for at least 20 to 30 yards.

Then move back upstream and leave the stream in your initial direction.

Changing direction before entering the stream may confuse the tracker. When he enters the stream, he should follow the false trail until the trail is lost. He will waste a lot of time to re find your trail - if he does.

When your direction of movement parallels a stream, use the stream to deceive a tracker.

Stay in the stream for 100 to 200 yards. Stay in the center of the stream and in deep water. Watch for rocks or roots near the banks that are not covered with moss or vegetation and leave the stream at that point.

Walk out backward on soft ground.

Walk up a small, vegetation-covered tributary and exit from it.

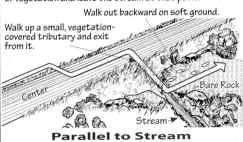

Parallel to Stream

HIDING TRACKS
Counter tracking techniques...

Move to open area: While moving from close terrain to open terrain, walk past a big tree (12" diameter or larger) toward the open area for three to five paces. Then walk backward to the forward side of the tree and make a 90° change of direction, passing the tree on its forward side. Step carefully and leave as little sign as possible. If this is not the direction that you want to go, change direction again about 50 yards away using the same technique.

The purpose of this is to draw the tracker into the open area where it is harder for him to track. That also exposes him and causes him to search the wrong area.

When being tracked by an experienced tracker, the best bet is to either try to outdistance him or to double back and encounter him.

Covering tracks with evergreen needles.

Animal path formed by grass being trodden. This path is from the feeding area to shelter in the woods.

Turning stones, breaking branches on trail, leaving boot prints.

Disturbed vegetation by treading on grass and breaking branches.

Slip marks in a muddy area.

HIDE TRACKS

Tracks of a Running Animal

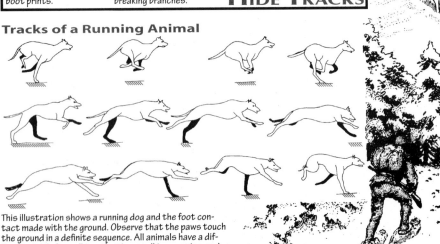

This illustration shows a running dog and the foot contact made with the ground. Observe that the paws touch the ground in a definite sequence. All animals have a different stride for walking, trotting, stalking, running, and just meandering. The track will also vary for each animal, sex of animal, age, and its physical condition.

Following a trail...

FIRE & SURVIVAL

Fire has a strong positive psychological impact upon an individual in a survival situation.

Fire is the most important survival tool after your personal wilderness knowledge, maintenance of calm and a positive attitude.

- Fire provides warmth which helps your mind have a positive approach.
- Fire makes you feel protected from all "those wild animals out there in the shadows".
- Fire lets you cook meals and use many edible plants that would otherwise be hard to prepare.
- Wet clothing can be dried in a fire. This can help you to avoid hypothermia.
- Water can be boiled for purification.
- Fire can be used to send smoke signals.
- Fire can be used to burn the end of a stick to make a pointed spear.
- Fire and smoke can repel insects.
- Fire can be used to burn trunks or large sticks so that they are more manageable to be used for construction of a shelter.
- Smoke can be used to smoke out wild bees to access their honey.
- Fire can be used to smoke small animals out of their burrows into traps.
- Fire torches, at night, can be used to blind fish in shallow streams making them easier to capture.

Building a fire, when needed, will increase your ability to survive in the wilderness. Build a fire as soon as you have a basic shelter. You can improve on your shelter, once you have a fire going, in the dark.

You should appreciate the importance of fire and know the different methods of starting a fire, transporting fire, and building a fire to fill your needs. Always keep a case of waterproof matches on you body.

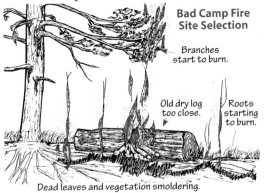

Clear any flammable material from the area of the fire.

Build a small fire as it requires less energy, burns wood at a slower rate, and is easier to control.
To maximize heat build a series of small fires, in a circle, around your encampment.

Bad Camp Fire Site Selection

Branches start to burn.

Old dry log too close.

Roots starting to burn.

Dead leaves and vegetation smoldering.

Building a small fire.

Wood

Starting a fire in a windy area.

High Wind

Low Wind

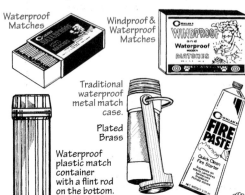

Waterproof Matches

Windproof & Waterproof Matches

WINDPROOF Waterproof MATCHES

Traditional waterproof metal match case.

Plated Brass

Waterproof plastic match container with a flint rod on the bottom.

FIRE PASTE
Quick Clean Fire Starter

Wax

Waterproofing of Matches
Bundle wood matches with an elastic band and dip heads at least one inch into melted paraffin wax. Make small bundles as the heads will stick together. Before using the match, scrape the wax off the head.

SITE FOR A FIRE

- Avoid windy areas as the fire can flare up and burn out of control. If required build a reflector or windbreak out of green wood, rocks, or dig a pit. The advantage of a reflector is that it concentrates the heat in the desired direction.
- Clear the camp ground of all inflammable material before starting a fire. Rake towards centre where you will burn all the dead leaves, pine needles, and other debris then clear a perimeter outwards from the fire area.
- Do not build a fire against an old log or tree trunk as it may smolder for days and burst into flame when fanned by a breeze.
- Do not build a fire below the boughs of a tree as they will be dried by the heat and might catch fire.
- Before decamping make sure that all sparks of the fire have been put out by thoroughly drenching or smothering it completely with wet earth or sand.
- If the ground is wet or snow covered build a platform of green or wet logs or stones.
Do not use wet or large humid rocks as they might explode when they are heated.

MATCHES

Matches are the easiest way to make a fire. Always carry matches on you. Carry matches in a waterproof container in you backpack, in your pant pockets and your jacket. Make sure the matches will not fall out of your pockets even when you fall out of a boat.

Lighting a Match in the Wind

Strike the tip of the match on a dry surface to light the match.
To light a match in the wind:
- Face the wind.
- Cup your hands against the wind.
- Hold the match with its head pointing down and towards the wind.
- Strike the match with the right hand and rapidly resume the former cupped position.
- Because of the wind the flame will run up the match stick having something to feed on.

Lighting a match in the wind.

Rotting Wood

Rotting wood decreases the potential energy in the wood. Dried rotten wood is flammable and will burn very fast but give off limited heat.
Rotten wood chips can be used as tinder.
Rotting is caused by fungi that require oxygen, humidity and temperatures between 60°F and 90°F. Wood in houses usually does not rot as it is too dry.

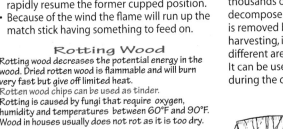

Splitting Wood
Split wood is better for a fire as it catches fire easier and burns more evenly.

Forgot matches at 40° below!

Green Wood
This wood has not been dried out or seasoned. All woods do not have to be seasoned to be used for fuel. Green wood can be used as reflectors for a fire and as a support for pots.

Green Wood

Seasoned Wood
Contraction cracks radiate from the center of logs. This does not necessarily mean that it is easier to split as it depends upon the characteristic of each wood.

Seasoned Wood

Cracks

SEASONING OF WOOD

When a live tree is cut into logs the wood is said to be "green" as there is sap in the cells of the wood. When the wood is dried it is called seasoned wood which usually produces a better fire.
Seasoning time depends upon the size of log, its age when cut (older trees have less sap), season of cutting, and climate. Medium sized logs of apple, oak, hickory will season in one year and, if exposed to the summer sun, in only a few months.

Why Does Wood Burn?... Pyrolysis!
The correct amount of oxygen, in the presence of a high enough temperature to ignite the different compounds in the wood, are required. If one of these elements is missing wood will not burn. The oxygen and temperature required vary with the type of the wood.
Pyrolysis is produced inside wood, in the absence of oxygen, by high temperatures that chemically break up the wood and release gases that burn further heating the wood thus releasing more gases...
Logs added to the fire, before burning, are heated to above 540°F (282°C), undergoing pyrolysis, giving off gases and burning. Gases need enough oxygen and a temperature of 1000°F (537°C) to burn. A flame ignites the gases.

PEAT MOSS

Peat moss is an accumulation of plant deposits that have collected in swamps and bogs over thousands of years. The plant debris did not decompose as it lacked oxygen. The peat moss is removed by slicing it like blocks of snow. On harvesting, it is dried before use. Peat is found in different areas of the United States and Canada. It can be used to make peat fires and was used during the colonist times.

Birch Bark Pouch

Birch Bark

Moss

Embers

Moss

Carrying Embers
It is easier to carry smoldering embers than to start a new fire with no matches. Containers that can be used: tin can, animal horn, birch bark pouch, hardwood box. Fill the bottom of the container with dry moss, place the embers on the moss and cover with moss. Check the embers from time to time and blow on them if they seem to be losing strength. Embers, if well taken care of, can be transported for a few days. The moss limits the air reaching the embers and retards their burning, but sufficient air has to reach the embers or they will go out.

SPACING OF WOOD

Wood Too Close
Lacks sufficient air to sustain a fire, the temperature drops, and it will go out. Blowing air into the cavity would keep the fire burning. If the pieces of wood were resting on green wood or a metal grate leaving an air space below the burning pieces, there might be an updraft to help the wood burn.

Correct Distance
Good balance of air and heat to let the fire burn. While the wood will burn very well the fact that it is burning will enlarge the spacing and you should stoke the fire so that the remaining wood will be pushed closer together or additional fuel added.

Too Far Apart
The heat is lost and the temperature is not high enough to sustain a fire. The fire will gradually go out.

Types of Wood
Hardwood
In general hardwoods make good, slow burning fires that yield long-lasting coals. These trees have broad leaves which most of them lose in the fall (deciduous). Hardwoods are not necessarily always harder than softwoods.

Softwood
Softwoods make a hot fast fire that is short-lived. These trees have needles (flat needles: cedars; round needles: pine) and cones. This is why they are called conifers. Most are evergreen (do not lose their needles) except larch, cypress, and tamarack.

Wood for a Fire
You have to know:
• The relative heating value of different woods.
• How well each wood burns in the green state.
• Which wood makes long lasting coals and which one dies down to ashes.
• Which wood pops when burning and casts embers that may burn holes in bedding, clothes, tents, and possibly cause a forest fire.
• Difficulty in splitting.
• Ease of lighting.

NATIVE FIRE MAKING
There were two methods of making fire that were in use by Native tribes in North America.
• Flint and pyrites (progenitor of flint and steel) was practiced by the Inuit and the Northern Indian tribes.
• Rubbing of wood on wood and igniting the ground of particles through heat generated by friction was widespread in America, where it was the most valued as well as the most effectual process known to the aborigines.

FIRE MAKING TOOLS
Fire Drill: The apparatus, in its simplest form, consists of a slender rod or drill and a lower piece or hearth, near the border of which the drill is worked by twisting between the palms, cutting a socket. From the socket a narrow canal is cut in the edge of the hearth, the function of which is to collect the powdered wood ground off by the friction of the drill, as within this wood meal the heat rises to the ignition point. This is the simplest and most widely diffused type of fire generating apparatus known to uncivilized man. Among the Inuit and some other tribes the simple two piece fire drill became a machine by the use of a hand or mouth rest containing a stone, bone, or wood socket for the upper end of the drill, and a cord with two handles or string on a bow for revolving the drill. By these inventions uniform and rapid motion and great pressure were effected, rendering it possible to make fire with inferior wood.
The four part drill consisted of two kinds:
Cord Drill: Requires the cooperation of two persons in its working.
Bow Drill: Enables one person to make a fire or to drill bone and ivory.
These drilling methods were used by the Inuit and their Indian neighbors.

Pump Drill: The pump drill has been employed for fire making only among the Onondaga of Canada, who used it in making sacred fire for the White dog feast; but the pump drill was little not used in fire making.

Fire Plow: The Onondaga also used the fire plow, like that of the Polynesians, in which a stick is held at an angle between the hands and rubbed back and forth along a plane surface, cutting a groove in which the wood meal produced by friction ignites. There is no other evidence that the fire plow ever existed in the western hemisphere.

NATIVE WOOD SELECTION
The wood selected for the fire drill varied in different localities, the proper kinds and qualities being a matter of acquired knowledge. Thus the weathered roots of the cottonwood were used by the Pueblos; the stems of the yucca by the Apache; the root of the willow by the Hupa and Klamath; cedar by the N. W. coast tribes; elm, maple, and buttonwood by the eastern Indians. In some instances sand was placed in the fire cavity to increase friction; often two men twirled the drill alternately for the purpose of saving labor or when the wood was difficult to use.

NATIVE TINDER SELECTION
The Inuit prized willow catkins; the Indians of the N. Vt. coast used frayed cedar bark; other tribes used fungi, softened bark, grass, or other ignitable material. Touchwood or punk for preserving fire was obtained from decayed trees, or some slowmatch (slow-burning wick or cord) was prepared from bark. From striking of a spark to the well-started campfire considerable skill and forethought were required. The glowing coal from the fire drill was usually made to fall into a small heap of easily ignitable material, where it was encouraged by fanning or blowing until the actual flame was produced; or the spark with the small kindling was gathered in a bunch of grass or a strip of bark and swung in the air.

TREES *Page 481*

MISCELLANEOUS CHARACTERISTICS OF WOOD
(Splitting, Embers, Green Wood)

Feature	Example	Special characteristics
Inflammable wood in green state (1)	Basswood, black ash, balsam, box elder, buckeye, cucumber, black or pitch pine, white pine, poplar, aspen, yellow poplar, tulip, sassafras, sour wood, sycamore, tamarack, sour gum, water oak.	Will scarcely burn in the green state. (1) These woods are good for backlogs, hand sticks, side logs on a cooking fire, pot supports.
	Butternut, chestnut, red oak, red maple, persimmon.	Burns very slowly in the green state.
Flammable when green	Yellow ash, white ash.	Burns better green than seasoned.
Dead logs only	Pine	Should be split, if not the outer shell catches fire but it chars and the fire goes out unless in proximity of tinder.
Green wood		Burns best in autumn and winter when the sap is low. Trees growing beside water is very hard to burn. Trees that grow on high, dry ground burn better than those of the same species that stand in moist soil.
	Chestnut	From summits of the Appalachians burns well even when green
Spitfire wood (Cause flying embers)	White cedar, chestnut box elder, red cedar, hemlock, sassafras, tulip, balsam, tamarack, spruce	Burns to dead coals that do not give off flame. Prone to pop - great crackling and snapping.
	Soft pines	Prone to pop.
	Sugar maple, beech, white oak, some hickory	Watch for embers after the fire is started as they shoot out, are long-lived and more dangerous that those of softwoods. *Excellent fuel.*
Stubborn wood (Hard to split)	Blue ash, box elder, buckeye, cherry, white elm, sugar maple, sycamore, winged elm, sour gum, hemlock (generally).	Hard to split.
	Hickory, beech, dogwood, sugar maple, birch, slippery elm	Easy to split when green.

CHOOSE THE CORRECT WOOD
Features of Different Trees to Consider in Choosing Firewood
Softwoods: Only when seasoned; good for kindling, quick cooking fire, split easily, shave readily, catch fire easily. Wood growing along streams is usually softwood, so driftwood is usually a bad choice of fuel unless available in large quantities.

Example	Special Characteristics
Balsam fir, basswood, white pines	Quick fires soon spent.
Gray (Labrador), pine (jack pine)	Considered good fuel in the north where hardwoods are scarce.
Tamarack	Good when seasoned.
Spruce	Poor fuel, being resinous it kindles easily & a good blaze for building up a fire.
Pitch pine	Most flammable of all woods when dry ('fat' with much resin). Will hardly burn in green state.
Yellow pine	Burns well as its sap is resinous instead of being watery as soft pines.
Red cedar	Hard to ignite and start with small pieces.

Hardwoods: Best fuel

Example	Special Characteristics
Northern: hickory, green or dry	Hot fire, lasts a long time, bed of hard coals that heats for hours.
South: oak & holly, chestnut oak, overcup, white, blackjack, post & basket oaks, pecan, ironwood.	
Magnolia, tulip, catalpa, willow	Poor fuels.
Dogwood, applewood	Burns to a characteristic white ash.
Black birch	Oil in the birch assists in combustion.
Birch: in order of black, yellow, red, paper, white	
Seasoned chestnut & yellow poplar	Hot fire, crackle, no coals.
Sugar maple (a favorite)	Ignites easily, clear steady flame, leaves good coals.
Locust, mulberry (excellent night wood)	Lasting fuel, easy to cut, splits well when green, thick bark takes fire readily, wood burns slowly, leaves good coals.
White ash (best of green woods)	Easy to cut and split, lighter to carry than most hardwoods, and is normally so dry that even green wood easily catches fire. Burns with a clear flame, and lasts.
Sycamore, buckeye	Good fuel when seasoned, will not split.
Northern poplar (large toothed aspen)	Dry: gives off intense heat with nearly no smoke, lasts well, does not blacken utensils. Favorite cooking fire.
Alder	Burns easily but does not last long.

Hardwood: Bad Fuels

Scarlet & willow oaks	Poorest of hardwoods for fuel.
White elm, slippery elm	Poor.

Making a Fire in the Rain

Find a fat pine log and split it open and light a fire from underneath. Dry fuel can be found under rock shelves, in a core of an old stump, the underside of a large fallen log, or look for a dead softwood tree that leans to the south as the wood and bark on the underside will be dry. If the rain is falling from a constant direction a tarpaulin can be used to protect the fire. The tarpaulin has to be placed far enough to accommodate the growing flames.

Fire genie not cooperating!

Tarpaulin placed far enough not to catch fire.

Trench

Campfire shielded from the rain.

Pitch Pine Tree

Pitch, Fat, or "Pine-Gum"

Is the resinous deposit found in old coniferous tree stumps or butt cuts on pine trees especially trees that died on the stump. The resin will have flowed down and collected at the bottom part of the tree. Old-timers and Indians swear by its use in fire making. A few shavings of pitch can start a fire at the touch of a match. Whenever you see some collect a few pieces for future use. Find pitch in the debris of rotting logs. It is yellowish in color and looks like a resin wood lamination on old stumps. Watch for old stumps that look yellowish as they might contain pitch. If the stump is gray it probably is rotten, old and soggy and contains no pitch.

Hudson's Bay Company Ax

Making a fire and cooking below snow laden boughs. The heat, from the fire, rises and melts the snow, on the branches, which falls onto the fire.

Tinder

Prepare some extremely dry tinder before attempting to start a fire without matches. Once prepared, shelter this tinder from wind and dampness.

Some tinder is:

- Birch bark, resin shavings, and pitch or fat from coniferous trees (described below). They burn even when wet.
- Punk (the dry insides of rotten trunks of trees), lint from cloth, rope or twine, dead palm frond, finely shredded dry bark, dry moss, powdered dry bat droppings, dry powdered wood, bird nests, shelf mushrooms growing on tree trunks, woolly material from plants (pussy willow, cat tail), dry grass, dry crushed leaves, and wood dust produced by insects and often found under the bark of dead trees.

Pine Needle Tinder

- These can be saturated with light oil, gasoline, or alcohol based insect repellents.

To prepare the tinder for use, break it, roll it in your hands, or cut it into small powdery pieces to minimize the surface area that the sparks or hot wood have to heat to ignite and smoke. To save tinder for future use, store it in a waterproof container.

Kindling

Kindling is material that also is used to start a fire. It is a step up from tinder, which is used to start a fire in very difficult situations i.e. having no matches or starter fire.

- Kindling can be small strips of dry wood, pine knots, bark, twigs, palm leaves, pine needles, dead upright grass, ground lichens, ferns, plant and bird down, and the dry, spongy threads of the giant puffball, which by the way are edible.
- Cut your dry wood into shaving before attempting to set it on fire.
- One of the best and most commonly found kindling materials is punk, as described under tinder. Dry punk can be found even in wet weather by knocking away the soggy outer portions with a knife, stick, or even your hands.
- Paper or gasoline may be used as tinder.
- Even when wet the resinous pitch (fat) in pine knots or dried stumps readily ignites.
- Loose bark of the birch tree also contains a resinous oil which ignites well.
- Arrange the kindling in a wigwam or log cabin pile to maximize the air flow.

Birch Bark Kindling
Bark of all species of birch, especially the Paper Birch, is excellent for kindling and torches. It is full of resinous oil which blazes up and will burn in the wind.

Birch Bark Kindling

Placing Fuzz Sticks

Fuzz Sticks
Cut a dry soft wood stick making sure that the shavings do not fall off the stick. These sticks can be piled into a teepee shape on some curls of birch bark. Light the fuzz and you will have a good blaze in a few minutes. Have heavier wood ready to add to the fire.

Cutting a Fuzz Stick

Earth

Wood

Charcoal

Charcoal makes a very hot fire, is smokeless, and has the least weight for a fuel. Wood burned with much air burns completely; if air is restricted, wood gives off gases and becomes charcoal. To produce charcoal, stack wood tightly together, cover it with earth, ignite in several places, and maintain a slow burn by admitting limited amounts of air. At 500°F (260°C) a chemical reaction occurs making the burning wood very hot which consumes the air and turns the wood into carbon (charcoal). The process can take a few days depending upon the quantity being produced. The charcoal should be left in the covered pit until it cools off or it will burst into flame when exposed to the air. The quality of charcoal depends upon the wood used.

Unusual Fuels

Any concentration of carbon, hydrogen, and methane can be used to make a fire. This can be dry peat moss, dry seaweed, animal dung in desert areas, bat droppings (use outdoors in small quantities as it is very flammable, even explosive), animal oils, dry leaves, coal, or oil that seeps to the surface or saturated as tar sands.

On polar ice, or in areas where other fuels are unavailable, blubber or animal fat is a source of fuel. If near the wreckage of an aircraft or a disabled snowmobile or car, use a mixture of gasoline and oil as fuel. Be careful as to how you ignite and feed the gasoline mixture.

You can use almost any plant for firewood, but do not burn the wood, leaves or branches of any plant that can poison on contact.

Coal or Wood?

Advantage of Wood

Easier to start a fire. Easier and cleaner to handle. Wood has a more pleasant and romantic country odor.

Advantage of Coal

Per heat value coal requires less space to store. A given quantity burns for a longer time. Gives off less heat so it is more comfortable for mild temperatures.

Inuit collecting moss. The moss would be used as insulation, bedding, fire starter, toilet paper, etc.

STEPS IN MAKING A FIRE

- Clean the surrounding area of any flammable material and watch for overhanging trees.
- A source of a flame, a spark, or other heat source. Start with a material that is easy to burn as grass, twigs, and other materials listed under tinder and kindling.
- Build a fire step by step, taking all the factors listed below into account, and you will succeed on your first try. Do not build a fire that is too large as it will be too hot to use for cooking and consume much fuel.

1 Tinder
Used to start a fire when no flame or matches are available.

Tinder

2 Kindling
Small sticks and leaves that will catch fire from the tinder or a match are placed in a teepee fashion. Leave one side open for the tinder and/or match.

Kindling stacked in the form of a teepee.

Match and/or tinder at the opening

3 Wood Fuel
Wood is gradually added, not too much to smother the fire. The first pieces should be finger thin and then, when the fire is hot enough, add larger pieces.

4 Fire Burning to Coals and Ashes
Once the fire is at the coal stage, it can be used for cooking, as the heat will be fairly constant. Two stones or greenwood supports can be added to each side of the fire to support a frying pan.

Star Shaped Fire for heating

Advance logs to increase size of fire.

5 Heavy Log Star Fire
If the cooking fire is to be used as a heating fire for the night, large logs can be butted together as a star. The log tips are gradually pushed into the fire. The advantage of this is that the logs do not have to be cut. A long heavy log can be placed across the fire and be burnt in half. Green wood can be used selectively to retard the burning.

Tin Can Heaters
Heat stones in a fire and place the hot stones into a tin can and put a few cans into your tent. This will provide excellent, safe, smokeless heat for your tent.

South Seas Fire Maker
This fire making method was developed by natives of the South Seas. The plunger is hit repeatedly with the palm of the hand. The air inside is so highly compressed that heat is generated igniting the tinder.

Dried moss is fastened by fibers to the end of the plunger.

Hard Wood Plunger

Bamboo Tube

Inside of cylinder is greased.

Plunger wrapped with fiber to make plunger tight fitting.

Bamboo Joint

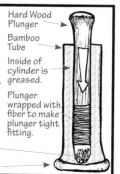

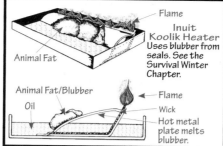

Flame

Inuit Koolik Heater
Uses blubber from seals. See the Survival Winter Chapter.

Animal Fat

Animal Fat/Blubber

Oil

Flame

Wick

Hot metal plate melts blubber.

Can Stove Using Gasoline and Sand

Breathing Holes

Sand impregnated with lubrication oil.

Any concentration of carbon, hydrogen, methane, etc. can be used to make a fire.

Cloth Wick

Spam™ Can Burner
Metal band around top of can. This is used to support the wick.

Bottom of Can

Cut

Cloth Wick

Lube Oil

Notches cut for air when a pot is placed on the can.

Tin Can Stove
Pour hot wax onto a wick in a tin can. The tin can should be notched or have holes near the top for air. Place the tin can on a flat surface before using. This tin can can be reused by adding wax. Animal blubber can also be used.

Wax   Cloth Wick

Bamboo Fire Saw

Sawing Motion

Rub Stick

Groove

Fireboard

Tinder

Preparing the Bamboo
On the inside of the fireboard pick and splinter some of the stringy fibers. On the outside opposite the fibers cut a narrow groove in which the sawing will be done.

FIRE SAW
The fire saw consists of two pieces of dry wood, one of which is rubbed vigorously against the other in a sawing motion. This method of starting fires is commonly used in the jungle. Use a split half piece of bamboo as the fireboard and soft wood as a rub stick. A good tinder is the fluffy brown covering of the apiang palm and the dry material found at the base of the coconut leaves.

Fire Thong

Thong

FIRE THONG
Use a strip of dry rattan (plant fibers), preferably about 1/4 inch (0.6 cm) in diameter and about two feet long; and a dry stick. Prop this stick off the ground by using a rock. Split the end of the stick. Hold it open with a small wedge. Place a small wad of tinder in the split, leaving enough room to insert the thong behind it. Secure the stick with your foot or knees, and work the thong back and forth.

FIRE PLOW
Method used by Iroquois Indians. A groove is cut in a soft baseboard. A hardwood shaft is pushed, under heavy pressure, up and down the groove more and more rapidly. This friction produces tinder which ignites.

Powder tinder collects at end of groove.

South Pacific islander using a fire plow to make a fire.

Tinder

Kindling

BOW & DRILL FIRE

Drill and Baseboard
Dry piece of balsam fir or in descending order:
• cedar • cypress • tamarack • basswood • cottonwood.

Starting a fire with a Bow & Drill action

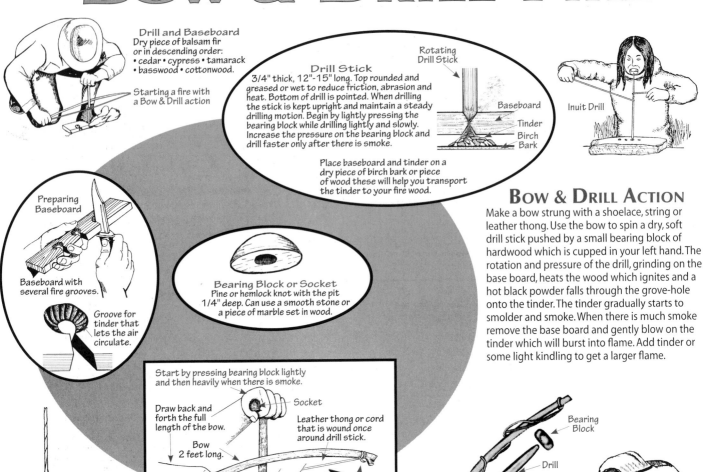

Drill Stick
3/4" thick, 12"-15" long. Top rounded and greased or wet to reduce friction, abrasion and heat. Bottom of drill is pointed. When drilling the stick is kept upright and maintain a steady drilling motion. Begin by lightly pressing the bearing block while drilling lightly and slowly. Increase the pressure on the bearing block and drill faster only after there is smoke.

Rotating Drill Stick

Baseboard
Tinder
Birch Bark

Place baseboard and tinder on a dry piece of birch bark or piece of wood these will help you transport the tinder to your fire wood.

Inuit Drill

Preparing Baseboard
Baseboard with several fire grooves.

Groove for tinder that lets the air circulate.

Bearing Block or Socket
Pine or hemlock knot with the pit 1/4" deep. Can use a smooth stone or a piece of marble set in wood.

BOW & DRILL ACTION
Make a bow strung with a shoelace, string or leather thong. Use the bow to spin a dry, soft drill stick pushed by a small bearing block of hardwood which is cupped in your left hand. The rotation and pressure of the drill, grinding on the base board, heats the wood which ignites and a hot black powder falls through the grove-hole onto the tinder. The tinder gradually starts to smolder and smoke. When there is much smoke remove the base board and gently blow on the tinder which will burst into flame. Add tinder or some light kindling to get a larger flame.

Start by pressing bearing block lightly and then heavily when there is smoke.

Socket

Draw back and forth the full length of the bow.

Leather thong or cord that is wound once around drill stick.

Bow 2 feet long.

Smoke

Thong slipped over bow. Thong should be tight.

Baseboard 2" x 8" 3/4" thick.

Tinder

Base board is held down with the foot, knee or wedged with a stone.

Deep brown powder from the friction of the drill and base will drop onto the tinder to ignite it.

California Indian Drill Disk

Bearing Block

Drill

Bow

Labrador Inuit Fire Drill Kit

Inuit Hand Drill
Drill stick is braced by a piece of wood, bone, or soapstone set in a piece of wood held in the mouth. The Inuit use a fire pan to hold the spark.

PUMP FIRE DRILL

Drill Stick

Leather Thong

Cross Bar

Direction of Motion

Hardwood Flywheel

Smoke

Baseboard

Tinder

Problems in Starting a Fire with a Fire Drill or Fire Pump

Problem	Reason or Action
Kindling gets covered with dark drilled powder.	Dust off the tinder.
Light brown	Wood is not under enough pressure or you are not drilling fast enough.
Black	Pushing too hard so that the powder burns before it lands on the tinder.
Spindle jumps out of bearing block	Hole in block not deep enough or too small for size of the drill stick.
Thong slips on drill stick	Thong loose, drill stick too smooth, too much pressure on bearing block.
Thong runs up and down drill stick	Thong should be in middle of drill stick and bow should be perpendicular to drill stick.
Bearing block smokes	Pushing too hard, wood too soft when compared to hardness of the drill stick add some lubrication (water, oil, grease).

PUMP FIRE DRILL
The Iroquois Indians had a fire drill that used the principal of the flywheel. The fly wheel was of hardwood with a hole at the centre through which the drill stick is forced and attached. The crossbar of hardwood is attached by a cord or leather thong and slides freely on the drill stick. The drill stick and fireboard use the same woods, dimensions, carved holes, and tinder as the fire drill.
The pump fire drill works by first winding up the flywheel which pulls up the cross bar. The cross bar is then pushed down and its momentum rewinds it in the opposite direction. The process is repeated until there is black powder and smoke.

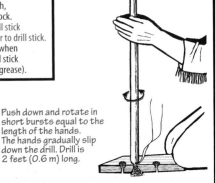

Push down and rotate in short bursts equal to the length of the hands. The hands gradually slip down the drill. Drill is 2 feet (0.6 m) long.

Navajo Hand Drill
This is a simpler method than the bow drill. Because of the lower rate of rotation, between the hands, it is used in hot dry climates where the wood is very dry. The wood usually used is yucca. Sun dried manure might be used as tinder. Indians carried their fire sticks in the quiver with their arrows.

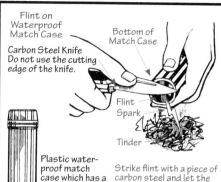

Flint on Waterproof Match Case

Carbon Steel Knife Do not use the cutting edge of the knife.

Bottom of Match Case

Flint Spark

Tinder

Plastic waterproof match case which has a flint in its base.

Strike flint with a piece of carbon steel and let the spark drop onto dry tinder.

Starting Fire: No Matches

This is the best method to light tinder if you do not have matches. Use the flint at the bottom of your waterproof match case. Hold the flint as near the tinder as possible and strike it with the back of knife blade or a small piece of carbon steel. Strike downward so that the sparks will hit in the center of the tinder. When the tinder begins to smolder, fan or blow it gently into a flame. These sparks are formed by tiny bits of metal from the steel that are superheated to the igniting point of the tinder. Gradually add kindling to your tinder, or transfer the burning tinder to the base of your firewood.

Potassium Permanganate

Flash Point

Pour a teaspoon of crystals of potassium permanganate (a mild antiseptic) from your first aid kit, onto a piece of paper, dry leaf, or piece of cloth. Add a few drops (too much fluid will retard heat production) of antifreeze from your radiator and tightly (to retain heat produced and raise temperature to 450°F (232°C) - average paper's flash point) roll the paper into a ball. Instantaneous combustion will cause the bundle to burst into flame in a few minutes. If for some reason this method is not successful, do not put the paper bundle in any flammable area as it might start burning at any time. Unwrap the package and bury any unsuccessful attempts in sand and pour water on the spot.

3 Fire Types
- A hot little fire that will quickly boil water and then burn down to embers that are not good for frying.
- A fire that produces a bed of long-lived coals that are smokeless and can produce heat for roasting, baking, and broiling.
- A fire that is made of big logs that will throw its heat forward on the ground towards a lean-to. This fire will last for a few hours without replenishing.

Maintaining a Fire
Bank your fire properly. Use green logs to keep your fire burning slowly. Keep the embers out of the wind. Cover them with ashes and put a thin layer of soil over them. Remember it takes less work to keep your fire going than to build another one.

Fire Buffalo Chips
Trees are sparse on the western plains. The Indians used dried buffalo dung for firewood. The smell was not too pleasant but it worked.

Hot Sand Bags
When you have no hot water bottle, heat sand in a frying pan. Pour sand into cloth bags and place these hot bags into your sleeping bag.

Ember Heaters
Punch holes into a large tin can. Scoop up embers and put them into the can and place the can on a few rocks in your tent. Note that the embers are still burning so you require ventilation.

Wood Storage
Place cut wood on two skid logs to keep it off the damp ground. Pile it neatly between two vertical supports. If wood is split, keep the bark side up. Cover the wood pile with long strips of bark or a piece of waterproof canvas.

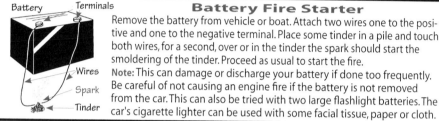

Battery   Terminals

Battery Fire Starter

Remove the battery from vehicle or boat. Attach two wires one to the positive and one to the negative terminal. Place some tinder in a pile and touch both wires, for a second, over or in the tinder the spark should start the smoldering of the tinder. Proceed as usual to start the fire.

Wires

Spark

Tinder

Note: This can damage or discharge your battery if done too frequently. Be careful of not causing an engine fire if the battery is not removed from the car. This can also be tried with two large flashlight batteries. The car's cigarette lighter can be used with some facial tissue, paper or cloth.

CARBON STEEL & FLINT

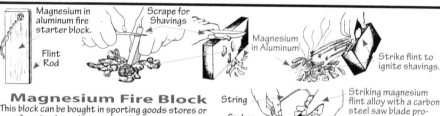

Magnesium in aluminum fire starter block.

Flint Rod

Scrape for Shavings

Magnesium in Aluminum

Strike flint to ignite shavings.

Magnesium Fire Block
This block can be bought in sporting goods stores or your favorite Army-Navy store. The block is in aluminium which contains magnesium. You cut or scratch, with a carbon steel knife, shavings off the block which are ignited by striking the blade on the flint rod embedded on the edge of the block.

String

Carbon Steel Saw Blade

Striking magnesium flint alloy with a carbon steel saw blade produces a large spark.

Magnesium Flint Alloy

Cotton Wool Tinder

FINDING FLINT & QUARTZ

Flint: Is jet black, very hard, and because of weathering, will look pitted and dull. Upon finding a rock, split it open by pounding it against another rock. If it is flint, it will crack as easily as glass and will have a smooth black sheen on the inside surface. Flint can be found on a river bed or on a hillside with loose rock deposits.

Quartz: Is white and looks like dull window glass but can be with or colored by other minerals. River beds, rocky slopes, and ridges are usually strewn with chunks of quartz. Mountain formations are streaked with white glassy quartz.

Carbon Steel Knife

Flint

Carbon Steel Knife

Tinder Cord

Sparks

Flint

Tinder

Carbon steel knife struck against any glassy stone as quartz, agate, jasper or flint will produce a spark that ignites the tinder. Blow on tinder when it starts to smoke.

Indians and the Inuit used iron pyrites, instead of iron or carbon steel, before the white man came to America. Indians carried the pyrites and flint in a pouch on the belt.

Wood Ash
Can be used as a fertilizer because of its potassium content. In wet regions, ashes can decrease the acidity of the soil. Potassium carbonate can be extracted from ash to make soap.

Indian Fire
Indians traditionally did not have good cutting tools so they developed efficient heating methods that can be used today to conserve fuel and save the forests. Cut hardwood saplings with a small hatchet. With tinder, build a hot fire and place saplings in a star shaped form radiating from the fire. While the fire is burning gradually advance the butts towards the centre and replenish with additional saplings as required. This fire saves much chopping, can be easily controlled, and economizes fuel. Build a windbreak behind you and lie close to the fire.

Using a Fire Drill

Camouflaged Fire

Making a fire that can be easily covered and its remains would be hard to see. Cut into the sod and roll it back. The exposed soil is humid and the fire can be set directly onto the soil. Do not make a fire that is too large or the root structure might start to smolder and burn. Spray the fire with water when finished and the rolled back sod can be placed over the fire's remains.

Platform fires built on humid wet, or snow covered ground.

Platform Fire

A platform of logs or rocks can be used to raise the level of fire above wet ground, snow, or mud.

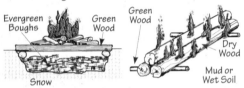

Tin Can Lantern

Useful if it is windy or you want to project the light in a specific direction. In a small tin the candle will burn slower as there is less air.

Signal Fire

A signal fire can be built as in the illustration. A small fire can be kept burning below the structure of green logs. When you want to signal, add dry wood to the fire and place green branches, rubber, plastic, or heavy oil on the structure. This will produce heavy black smoke.

Green Wood Structure   Small Fire

Automatic Fire

Dig a pit and line it with rocks. Make sure the rocks are dry as humid rocks can explode if heated. Start a small fire in the pit and place some semi-green logs vertically into the pit. These logs will gradually dry, burn, and slide down into the pit to dry and burn.

Logs   Fire Pit   Stones

Hunter's Fire

This is a fire for the colder part of the year. It can be a cooking fire and a heating fire.

Hunter's Fire

Cut two hardwood bed logs a foot thick and your height. Place the logs on level ground as an air draft, caused by the slope, will make the logs burn too fast. Place wood in a 'V' shaped position. Place green sticks across both logs and place a crisscrossed pile of dry wood on the sticks and light. The burning wood will burn to coals and fall between the logs which will start to slowly burn on the inner sides. The narrow part of the 'V' of the logs can be used for cooking. For an all night fire, place thick green logs across the bed logs and put night wood on them. The night wood will fall into the fire when the green logs are burnt. A more sophisticated fire construction is a caterpillar fire.

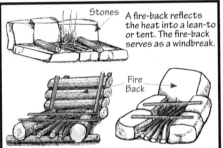

Stones   A fire-back reflects the heat into a lean-to or tent. The fire-back serves as a windbreak.

Fire Back

Winter Fire with Reflector

A fire-back can be big flat-faced rocks, green logs, or a ledge with the fire between the tent front and the fire-back. For better heating fill the space between the logs with mud. The face of the back logs should not be more than 5' (1.5 m) from the front of the tent. A well-tended small fire should not be over 4' (1.2 m) away. Choose wood that does not crack and send off too many embers.

Sun   Lens   Binoculars
Lens Focuses   Tinder   Lens Removed

Sun & Curved Glass

A camera lens, a convex lens (a convex lens is one that the centre bulges out and one that slopes in is concave) from a binocular, a lens from a telescopic sight, the bottom of an old pop bottle, a magnifying glass on a compass may be used to concentrate the rays of the sun on your tinder. Concave mirrors can also be used to make a fire but this method is difficult as a large reflector is required. This mirror can be from a shaving mirror, or car headlight.

Fire Starter

Stuff lint from your dryer or shredded cloth into the compartments of a paper egg carton. Melt candle wax and pour a thin layer over the lint or cloth and let it set. To use, break up the carton and light a section. The fire will burn from 5 to 15 minutes depending on the mixture of lint and wax.

Paper Egg Carton

Glass Bottle Lantern

Heat a clear glass bottle in a fire, then dip the bottom in cold water. This causes the bottom to crack and fall off. Place a candle inside the neck of the bottle and the neck is stuck in the ground.

Glass Bottle   Sand

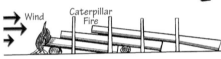

Wind   Caterpillar Fire

Caterpillar Fire

This type of fire should only be built when the wind direction is steady, the ground has been well cleaned and there are no overhanging trees. The logs are placed as in the illustration beginning the pile in the direction of the wind. The supports are in green wood. If there is little wind make the pile shorter by increasing the overlap of the pieces.

Birch Bark Torch

Birch Bark Torch

Take a thin strip of bark from a birch tree. Fold the bark lengthwise to form a narrow strip. Cut a yard (1m) long sapling and split it as in the illustration. Place the folded bark in the split. Light the end. The flame might last 15 minutes. Do not use this type of open torch when trees are dry as you might start a forest fire.

Hunter's Lamp

Stick a twisted rag or a piece of cotton through a hole in or wedged between two flat stones. This is placed in a clam shell or a tin can filled with oil or melted grease.

Oil   Shell   Stones   Wick

I remember lighting fires;
I remember sitting by them;
I remember seeing faces,
hearing voices through the smoke;
I remember they were fancy --
for I threw a stone to try 'em.
The Explorer - Rudyard Kipling

Fire: Starting

Candle Fire Starter

Place a lit candle below a tee-pee of kindling and it will start a fire. Remove and extinguish the candle for future use.

Cattail Torch

Cattail Torch

A cattail dipped in oil or animal fat can be used as a torch. The fuzz from a ripe cattail can be used as tinder to start a fire.

A traditional winter campfire.

This section on wilderness cooking outlines cooking fires, different methods of cooking such as clay baking, steaming, solar, and reflector cooking. It also includes methods of preparing fish, insects, oysters, and clams. Meat from animals has much more nutritional value per pound than food derived from plants. Animals are much harder to catch, as time has to be spent in stalking or trapping them, and this effort has to be factored in when evaluating the relative nutritional value. For more information about plant food and preparation, see the Chapter on Edible Plants. Food from fresh water lakes, ponds, streams, and rivers is an abundant and easy food source. You can easily find and catch water animals such as fish, frogs, snails, and crabs.

Camping mess kit by Coleman™

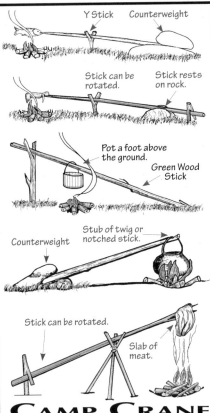

BAMBOO COOKING POT

Water or soups can be cooked in a bamboo pot. You can place a piece of metal from a tin can or aluminum foil on the bottom of the bamboo to dissipate the heat and to protect your "pot" from the flame.

Y Stick   Counterweight

Stick can be rotated.   Stick rests on rock.

Pot a foot above the ground.   Green Wood Stick

Counterweight   Stub of twig or notched stick.

Stick can be rotated.   Slab of meat.

CAMP CRANE

This is the best fire for hot water, soups, stews, coffee because the heat can be controlled by the length of the hook supporting the pot. A third vertical forked stake can be installed and then the horizontal support pole can be moved further from the heat to simmer. If forked stakes are not available, drive straight ones and split their tops. The cross ends of the stick can be trimmed to slide into the slots. The fire can be set on the flat ground or in a pit if there is too much wind or the surrounding ground has a fire hazard. The fire should not be too large or your food will burn. When cooking is finished, the hot coals can be used to start a log fire to heat your camping area. A fire built in a hole usually emits less smoke.

COOKING AT CAMP

- Cleanliness is of utmost importance. Leave no scraps lying around as they will attract animals. Cleanliness also includes leaving no dirty dishes or scraps, and keeping your clothing odor-free. If your clothing gets smoky from the odors of the food, place your dirty clothing at least 100 yards downwind from the campsite - DO NOT SLEEP IN THEM. Do not use scented deodorants, soaps or cosmetics. Bathe frequently to reduce sweaty body odors. These precautions are for your health and to avoid attracting bears.
- Cook at least 100 yards downwind from the sleeping area. Dump used dishwater at least 100 yards from the tents.
- Prepare food only for that meal - there should be no leftovers. Burn any scraps that may be remaining to minimize odors. Any noncombustible items should be carried out. This is to reduce pollution and prevent animals from digging up any items.
- Food should be stored in airtight containers and kept out of reach of animals. Suspend the food 100 yards from the camp (downwind if possible), at least 12 feet above the ground, and at least 8 feet from the rope supports.
- Read about bears - page 552.

FOOD SAFETY ON THE ROAD

Plan Ahead: Place food in a cooler with ice or freezer packs. When carrying drinks, consider packing them in a separate cooler so the food cooler is not opened frequently.

Pack Safely: Pack perishable foods directly from the refrigerator or freezer into the cooler. Meat and poultry may be packed while still frozen; in that way it stays colder longer. Also, a full cooler will maintain its cold temperatures longer than one that is partially filled. Be sure to keep raw meat and poultry wrapped separately from cooked foods, or foods meant to be eaten raw, such as fruits.

If the cooler is only partially filled, pack the remaining space with more ice or with fruit and some non-perishable foods. For long trips to the shore or the mountains, take along two coolers - one for the day's immediate food needs, such as lunch, drinks or snacks, and the other for perishable foods to be used later in the vacation. Keep the cooler in the air-conditioned passenger compartment of your car, rather than in a hot trunk. Limit the times the cooler is opened. *Open and close the lid quickly.*

When Camping: Keep the cooler in a shady spot. Keep it covered with a blanket, tarp or poncho, preferably one that is light in color to reflect heat. Bring along bottled water or other canned or bottled drinks. Always assume that streams and rivers are not safe for drinking. If camping in a remote area, bring along water purification tablets or equipment.

FOOD HANDLING SAFETY

Clean: Wash hands and surfaces often.

Separate: Do not cross-contaminate.

Cook: Cook to proper temperatures.

Chill: Refrigerate promptly.

STORING FOOD

Bacteria exist everywhere in nature. They are in the soil, air, water and the foods we eat. When they have nutrients (food), moisture, time and favorable temperatures, they grow rapidly, increasing in numbers to the point where some can cause illness. Therefore, understanding the important role temperature plays in keeping food safe is critical. If we know the temperature at which food has been handled, we can then answer the question, "Is it safe?".

THE DANGER ZONE (40°F-140°F)

Bacteria grow most rapidly in the range of temperatures between 40° and 140° F, doubling in number in as little as 20 minutes. This range of temperatures is often called the Danger Zone. That's why you should never leave food out of refrigeration for over two hours. If the temperature is above 90 °F, food should not be left out more than one hour.

If you are traveling with cold foods, bring a cooler with a cold source. If you are cooking, use a hot campfire or portable stove. It is difficult to keep foods hot without a heat source when traveling, so it's best to cook foods before leaving home, cool them, and transport them cold.

COOKING RAW MEAT & POULTRY

Raw meat and poultry should always be cooked to a safe internal temperature. Temperatures (160° to 212 °F) reached in baking, roasting, frying and boiling will destroy bacteria that can cause food-borne illness.

Cook ground meats (beef, veal, lamb, and pork) to an internal temperature of 160 °F, and ground poultry to 165 °F. Steaks and roasts cooked to an internal temperature of 145 °F are medium rare, 160 °F are medium, and 170 °F are well done. For doneness, poultry breast meat should be cooked to an internal temperature of 170 °F; 180 °F for whole birds. Use a meat thermometer to assure that meat and poultry have reached a safe internal temperature.

If raw meat and poultry have been handled safely, using the above preparation recommendations will make them safe to eat. If raw meats have been mishandled (left in the Danger Zone too long), bacteria may grow and produce toxins which can cause food-borne illness. Those toxins that are heat-resistant are not destroyed by cooking. Therefore, even though cooked, meat and poultry mishandled in the raw state may not be safe to eat even after proper preparation.

STORING LEFTOVERS

One of the most common causes of food-borne illness is improper cooling of cooked foods. Because bacteria are everywhere, even after food is cooked to a safe internal temperature they can be reintroduced to the food and then reproduce. For this reason leftovers must be put in shallow containers for quick cooling and refrigerated within two hours.

REHEATING

Foods should be reheated thoroughly to an internal temperature of 165 °F or until hot and steaming.

Avoid reheating if possible.

Beans, fish, potatoes...

COOKING HAMBURGER

When meat is ground, more of the meat is exposed to the harmful bacteria. Bacteria multiply rapidly in the "danger zone" - temperatures between 40° and 140 °F. To keep bacterial levels low, store ground beef at 40 °F or less and use within 2 days, or freeze. To destroy harmful bacteria, cook ground beef to 160 °F.

Illnesses caused by E. coli have been linked with the consumption of undercooked ground beef. Raw milk, apple cider, dry cured sausage, and undercooked roast beef have also been implicated.

- To avoid cross-contamination, wash your hands with soap and hot water before and after handling ground beef to make sure you don't spread bacteria.
- Don't reuse any packaging materials.
- Use soap and hot water to wash utensils and surfaces which have come into contact with the raw meat.
- Don't put cooked hamburgers on the same platter that held the raw patties.
- Never leave ground beef or any perishable food out at room temperature for more than 2 hours.
- Raw and undercooked meat may contain harmful bacteria. USDA recommends not eating or tasting raw or undercooked ground beef. To be sure all bacteria are destroyed, cook meat loaf, meatballs, casseroles, and hamburgers to 160 °F. Use a food thermometer to check that they have reached a safe internal temperature.
- The symptoms of food-borne illness - such as diarrhea or vomiting, which can cause dehydration - can be very serious.
- Do NOT partially cook ground beef to use later. Partial cooking of food ahead of time allows harmful bacteria to survive and multiply to the point that subsequent cooking cannot destroy them.

COOKING HOT DOGS

"Keep them Hot,
Keep them Cold,
Keep them Clean."

Although all hot dogs are fully cooked, you should reheat them and make sure they are steamy hot throughout. Never leave hot dogs at room temperature for more than 2 hours, or in the hot summer months when the temperature goes above 90 °F, no more than 1 hour.

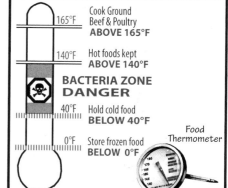

165°F	Cook Ground Beef & Poultry ABOVE 165°F
140°F	Hot foods kept ABOVE 140°F
	BACTERIA ZONE DANGER
40°F	Hold cold food BELOW 40°F
0°F	Store frozen food BELOW 0°F

Food Thermometer

COOKING TEMPERATURES

Most food-borne illnesses result from undercooked foods and improper food handling.
Meat: The inside of meat should reach 160°F for medium.
Poultry: Whole poultry should reach 180°F. Take the reading at the center or thickest part of cooked meat.

MEAT STORAGE

- Keep hot foods **HOT** - Cold foods **COLD**.
- When pre-cooking meat - make sure that the meat goes directly from oven to grill.
- Throw out leftover food (hot & cold) that has been left out for more than two hours.

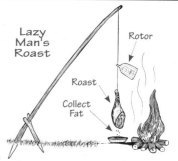

Lazy Man's Roast
Rotor
Roast
Collect Fat

Lazy Man's Roast

Using a green stick support structure, a wire and a fan paddle. Piece of wood, birch-bark, or large leaf. The paddle will be blown in the breeze and the food will rotate and be evenly cooked. A pan is placed below the meat to catch melted fat and juices which can be used for basting. The remaining fat can be used for lighting.

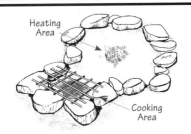

KEYHOLE FIRE

This dual purpose fire layout is ideal for both heating and cooking. First build a teepee style fire in the round part of the keyhole. When the fire has burnt down to coals scrape them into the narrow part of the keyhole and place a grill of green branches across the stones and you can cook. The main fire will continue burning and you can replenish the stove with additional coals when required.

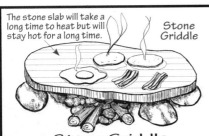

Stone Griddle

Find a flat stone, set it on a support, build a fire under it and then use the top as a frying area. Cover the food with a piece of wood or birch bark to reduce the cooking time.

The stone slab will take a long time to heat but will stay hot for a long time.

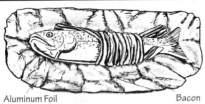

Aluminum Foil Cooking

Wrap food in foil. Place wrapped food on coals or place food in a hole in the coals and cover the food. By burying the food it is cooked more rapidly and space is left on the surface of the coals for other items. It will be difficult to check for how well done, if food is buried.

Broiling on a Stick

Impale a fish, bird or small animal on a green stick and sear the meat in the fire for a few seconds. This will keep the juice and flavor in the meat. To maximize the flavor place the food above coals, not the open flame, to cook very slowly.

Foil or Metal Sheet
This foil or sheet metal weighs less than a frying pan and can have a larger surface.

FIRE MAKING
Page 311

Egg Cooked in Onion

Cut open a large onion and remove the inside. Break an egg and pour it into the onion shell and place it on the coals. The egg and onion will be ready in a few minutes.

Cooking eggs and bacon in a frying pan made from aluminum foil.

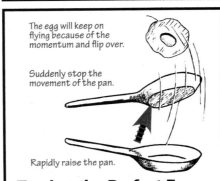

The egg will keep on flying because of the momentum and flip over.

Suddenly stop the movement of the pan.

Rapidly raise the pan.

Tossing the Perfect Egg
You can impress your friends by having the perfect toss. This can be used for fried eggs and pancakes.

Fresh Hard-Cooked Eggs - Hard to Peel
The fresher the egg, the more difficult it is to peel after hard cooking. That's because the air cell, found at the large end of the shell between the shell membranes, increases in size the longer the raw egg is stored. As the contents of the egg contracts and the air cell enlarges, the shell becomes easier to peel. For this reason, older eggs are better for hard cooking.

PICKLED EGGS
Pickled eggs are hard-cooked eggs marinated in vinegar and pickling spices, spicy cider, or juice from pickles or pickled beets. Studies done at the American Egg Board substantiate that unopened containers of brined eggs - marinated, hard-cooked eggs - keep for several months on the shelf. After opening, keep refrigerated.

EGGS
Eggs are among the most nutritious foods on earth. However, they are perishable just like raw meat, poultry, and fish. Unbroken, clean, fresh shell eggs may contain Salmonella Enteritis (SE) bacteria that can cause food-borne illness. While the number of eggs affected is quite small, there have been cases of food-borne illness in the last few years. To be safe, eggs must be properly handled, refrigerated, and cooked.

To prevent illness from bacteria: Keep eggs refrigerated, cook eggs until yolks are firm, and cook foods containing eggs thoroughly.

Hard-Cooked Eggs spoil faster than Fresh Eggs

When shell eggs are hard cooked, the mineral oil (applied by the processing plant) protective coating is washed away, leaving bare the pores in the shell for bacteria to enter and contaminate it. Hard-cooked eggs should be refrigerated within 2 hours of cooking and used within a week.

Don't wash eggs: That could remove the protective mineral oil coating and increase the potential for bacteria on the shell to enter the egg.

EGG AGING
A cloudy white (albumen) is a sign the egg is very fresh. A clear egg white is an indication the egg is aging. Pink or iridescent egg white (albumen) indicates spoilage due to Pseudomonas bacteria. Some of these microorganisms - which produce a greenish, fluorescent, water-soluble pigment - are harmful to humans.

Over time, the white and yolk of an egg lose quality. The yolk absorbs water from the white. Moisture and carbon dioxide in the white evaporate through the pores, allowing more air to penetrate the shell, and the air cell becomes larger. (The air cell is formed as a result of the different rates of contraction between the shell and its contents.) If broken open, the egg's contents would cover a wider area. The white would be thinner, losing some of its thickening and leavening powers. The yolk would be flatter, larger and more easily broken.

Old Eggs float in Water
An egg can float in water when its air cell has enlarged sufficiently to keep it buoyant. This means the egg is old, but it may be perfectly safe to use. Crack the egg into a bowl and examine it for an off-odor or unusable appearance before deciding to use or discard it. A spoiled egg will have an unpleasant odor when you break open the shell, either when raw or cooked.

EGG YOLK
The color of yolk varies in shades of yellow depending upon the diet of the hen. If she eats plenty of yellow-orange plant pigments, such as from marigold petals and yellow corn, the yolk will be a darker yellow than if she eats a colorless diet such as white cornmeal.

Green Ring - Hard-cooked Yolk
Is a result of overcooking, and is caused by sulfur and iron compounds in the egg reacting on the yolk's surface. The green color can also be caused by a high amount of iron in the cooking water. Scrambled eggs cooked at too high a temperature or held on a steam table too long can also develop a greenish cast. The green color is safe to consume.

QUICK MEAL FIRE

Collect dry hardwood twigs the thickness of a finger. Take no twigs that are lying flat on the ground as they will be damp. Set up tinder in the form of a wigwam. Leave air space between sticks as this will help the flow of oxygen. Start the fire and feed additional twigs and thicker sticks. Once the flame has burnt itself out you will have embers that will be used for frying. Place two 5" (12 cm) green logs or a pair of rocks to support the frying pan. It should take 20 minutes to assemble the fire and cook the meal.

TRENCH FIRE

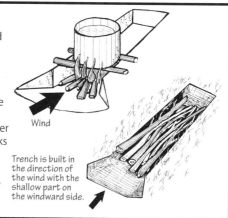

Wind

Use when there is danger of starting a ground fire, especially in times of drought, windy weather, or where the ground is strewn with dry leaves or pine needles. A trench is best if you are lacking fuel or have to use brushwood, as it will conserve heat. Dig in line of the prevailing wind as you will need a good draft. The windward side should be wider and deeper and slope it upwards on the far end. Place rocks on sides as they will retain heat and also keep up the walls which will have a tendency to crumble when the earth dries due to the heat. A small chimney of flat stones or sod at the leeward side will improve the draw of the fire.

Trench is built in the direction of the wind with the shallow part on the windward side.

COOKING IN PAPER

Cooking in paper has the advantage that no cleaning will be required because you will eat directly out of the paper bag or newspaper.
- Steam food wrapped in wet newspaper.
- Place food in paper bag and fry over some glowing coals.

Keep newspaper or bag wet and just above the coals. Dry paper burns. If paper gets dry spray with water. Cook on hot coals, not on an open flame.

Bacon & Eggs in Paper Bag
- Burn the fire down so that there are only glowing coals.
- Lightly wet a paper bag.
- Place strips of bacon on bottom of the bag and break the eggs on top of bacon.
- Fold the top of the bag and pierce a hole just below the fold of the bag for a support stick.
- Cook until the bacon stops sizzling. This will take approximately 10-15 minutes depending upon the surrounding temperature.
- If egg is not done to your taste keep on cooking.
- Wet down the bag if it starts to burn.

Hole for Stick

Paper Bag

Bacon

Eggs

Coals

1850's Cooking outside of a small log cabin.

To Clean Greasy Dishes or Pots
Use white ash and hot water to clean dishes and pots. The wood ash contains potash and soda which, when mixed with grease, makes a crude soap. The best white ash is made from hickory, beech or ash.

Baking Soda Substitute
Add white wood ash to flour and the dough will rise as well as with baking soda. White wood ash contains soda and potash. The best woods are hickory, beech, maple, dogwood and poplar. Do not use a resinous wood.

Testing Oven Temperature
Sprinkle a teaspoon of flour on a pan or heated surface. The color of the flour after five minutes indicates:

Temperature		Flour Turns
250-325°F	121-163°C	Delicate brown
325-400°F	163-204°C	Golden brown
400-450°F	204-232°C	Deep brown
450-500°F	232-260°C	Deep dark brown

Fork
A fork can be made from green wood.

Fire Starter
Stuff lint from your dryer or shredded cloth into the compartments of a paper egg carton. Melt candle wax and pour a thin layer over the lint or cloth and let it set. To use, break up the carton and light a section. The fire will burn from 5 to 15 minutes depending on the mixture of lint and wax.

Cooking a steak directly on slow burning coals.

Steak

Coals

Hot Stone Cooking

Place the hot rocks inside the cleaned fowl and adjacent to thick parts of the food. Cover the cooking food with leaves and bark to help retain the heat. Repeat this process if the food is not totally cooked.

BANNOCK... OUTDOORS TRAVEL FOOD

This is an outdoors staple for backpackers and canoeists. It travels light and is easy to prepare. Pack ingredients in Ziplock™ bags.

Two people Bannock Recipe

Fried or stick cooked.
2 Cups of flour*
2 tablespoons of baking powder
3 tablespoons of fatty material**
2 tablespoons of skim milk powder***
1/4 tablespoon of salt

* flour can be modern flour or from native materials as corn, ground roots, etc. See Edible Plants Chapter
** lard, margarine, butter, olive oil, or vegetable oil. For longer trips you might want to use lard as it has the highest calorie kick per weight. This fatty material will as flavor to the bannock.
*** optional

Before leaving on trip: Mix the dry material - flour, baking powder, skim milk powder, and salt and pour into a large Ziplock™ bag. Prepare individual bags for each meal. Keep the fatty material separate to blend in before use.
At camp add the fatty material to the bag. If lard is being used cut it into thin slices. Add a small amount of water to the bag and start kneading the water into the mix - add more water until the mixture forms a dough-like consistency - not to liquid and not to hard.

Branch Pothook

Trim a green limb but leaving a piece of one branch near the but to form a hook. Cut a few deep notches at the end of the stick to hang the handle of the kettle in the notch. The other end of the branch, with the hook, is hung over the horizontal stick of the stand.

Bannock Sticks

Saw Blade Knife

A very sharp knife blade can be made from a hack saw blade. The tip of the blade is broken off and the blade is sharpened on the non-saw edge. A handle is made by wrapping tape or a piece of leather around the non-sharpened end of the blade. Saw blades are carbon steel and they can rust.

No frying pan: Make a thicker dough by adding less water and roll or knead the dough into a ribbon one inch wide. Roll this ribbon around a preheated green hardwood stick where the bark has been removed. A green stick is cut from a live tree - it is still humid and not burn until dry. Cook about 8" above the coals remaining from the fire.

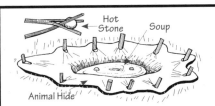

Hot Stone Water Heating

Collect stones 2 - 3 inches (5-7 cm) in diameter and place them between layers of wood in a log fire. By the time the fire burns down to coals the rocks will be very hot. Pick up the stones with green sticks and place them in a birch bark container or other water receptacle. A small amount of water can easily be brought to a boil.
A larger container can be made with a heavy plastic, rubber sheet, clay pot, or animal hide. Dig a depression in the ground and line it with the waterproof material. If the material is plastic or rubber, place a large stone in the container so that the hot rocks will not touch the plastic surface.

Bannock Cakes in Coleman™ frying pan

With frying pan: Grease the frying pan with the fatty material. Form the dough into 1/2" thick pancakes 3 to 5 inches in diameter. Dust the cakes with some flour so that they will keep their shape and not stick. Lay cakes in the warm frying pan and hold over the fire while rotating the pan. A bottom crust will form on the cakes and they can be flipped. Cooking will take over 10 minutes. Make sure the fire is not too hot.

Soup Hole

Hot stone water heating can be used to cook a soup. Add water and some wild onions or other greens and add small pieces of meat. Throw a few hot stones into the liquid and let them do the cooking.

Placing hot stones in soup.

Removing stones from soup.

Stones being heated on hot coals.
Earthware Pot

Stone

Mortar used by Florida Native peoples.

Iroquois Mortar for making of corn flour.

Cooking Out "Waiting"

Grinding grain for flour on a stone mortar with a stone pestle.

Sifting ground grains and flour.
Kneading dough for bread. Baking stove in background.

45 Gallon Can Stove

The surface area of this stove can be used to cook food. A chimney is required if you want to use this stove in a shelter. A door cover helps regulate the size of the flame.

Surface used for cooking.

Using GI can opener.

Stainless steel nesting utility set.

Dakota Hole Fire

This fire is used in prairie areas. The fire hole protects the fire from the constant wind. The hole also limits the loss of heat which is very important in areas that have limited amounts of wood. The fire can be controlled by limiting the air intake. This fire should not be used if there are wood deposits or tree roots in the ground.

Air Intake

Pocket Knife

Plank Cooking

For fish, steak, vegetable (squash, etc.) or fowl. Find a flat piece of green hardwood, place it at an angle 12 inches (30 cm) from the fire. Preheat the board by exposing it to the fire for a few minutes. When the board is hot, smear oil or animal fat on the surface. The food can be attached by using a wire or pegs or slivers in the hardwood. Fish will cook when heated on only one side, meat should be turned.

Wood Plank

Utensil Kit

Wire rim coffee cup.

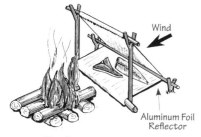

Wind

Aluminum Foil Reflector

Horn Cup

Cut the horn. Turn the handle by heating it in hot water and bending the horn.

Reflector Oven

You can buy a reflector oven or make one with a wide roll of aluminum foil.

• Build a fire in front of a rock or a green wood wall. This will help reflect additional heat into the reflector oven. The oven is placed on the opposite side of the flame from the rock.
• The pan area of the aluminum foil should be rolled on a flat surface of sand or rocks.
• The wind should be blowing from behind the oven or from the side of the oven. Avoid smoke blowing into the reflector as the contents will be smoked.
• Aluminum foil should be kept clean and bright.
• Do not put hand into oven area as it can be very hot.
• Keep the flames high to maintain a steady flow of heat.

Baking Corn

Attach top of husk with string or wire and place on coals. Use a fork or sharp stick to probe to see when the corn is soft.

Molding foil over trunk.

Aluminum Foil Pot Covers
Wrap foil around the outside of a pot before placing it on a fire. You will not have to clean the flame deposits off the pot. If pot is leaking line the inside with foil.

Roll edge of pot.

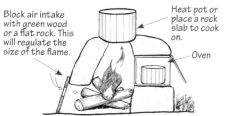

Block air intake with green wood or a flat rock. This will regulate the size of the flame.

Heat pot or place a rock slab to cook on.

Oven

Yukon Stove

This is a stove that you would build if you expect a long stay or will return to this camp site. This stove can be left unattended. Materials used are stones, mud, straw or tall grass, rocks, metal box, large dry flat rock for a griddle. This stove was used by the Hudson's Bay Company at its trading posts.

Aluminum Foil Pot
Make a pot by putting a sheet of foil over a stump. Mold the foil over the stump and fasten the edge by rolling the edge.

This is an illustration of a village encampment in the foothills, from 1896. By highlighting the cast iron stove and the cooking activity at the forefront it shows its importance at a campsite. One has to remember that the cast iron stove had to be transported hundreds of miles. From the chimneys on the tents - it means that they were ready for cold weather.

Lichen Yeast

Use liverwort or lungwort lichen (sticta pulmonaria). Steep the lichen overnight in warm water. Strain the liquid into some flour and blend it into the dough. Let this dough rise near a fire, take a piece and add it to the bread dough. Let the bread dough rise and bake the bread. The yeast dough can be stored in a cool place and used at every baking. You can even add flour and water to the yeast dough cultivation to replenish your stock.

Donald Curley, Painter of the outdoors.

321

Solar Oven

A solar oven works because the sun's light rays are of a short wavelength which can pass through glass. The short waves, upon hitting the objects below the glass change wavelength to long waves which cannot pass through glass. These long wavelengths bounce back and forth, dissipating their energy to heat inside the solar oven.

Hobo Stove

Use a metal drum. Pierce two rows of holes in the bottom for a sufficient air draft. The size of the fire can be controlled by blocking some of the holes. The logs can be fed by the top or by a side opening that can be cut into the metal. Food can be heated by placing it on metal skewers or green wood. Cuddle around the stove for heat. A smaller version of the hobo stove can be made out of a tin can. Holes are pierced on the sides and the top serves as a support for a pot. This stove is particularly suited to the Arctic.

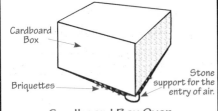

Cardboard Box Oven

Use a cardboard box lined with aluminum foil. Place hot charcoal briquettes near the edges, under the cardboard box. To calculate the temperature and heat that the briquettes will generate use the Fahrenheit degree formula of 40°F of heat per briquette. That's 400°F per 10 briquettes. Place the box over the food and place a pebble under one edge of the box to let fresh air enter so that the charcoal can burn. Baking time is the same as for a regular oven. Place new lit briquettes in the oven if the baking time is more than 45 minutes.

Fork
Fork for working in fire made out of a piece of wire or coat hanger

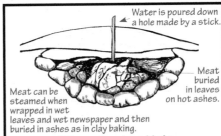

Steaming in a Hole

Dig a hole in the sand. Heat some stones. Roll the stones in the hole and place a thick layer of wet grass or seaweed over the hot stones. Place the food on the bed of grass and place some more grass on the food. Cover with a layer of sand. Pierce a hole in the sand hill and pour additional water into the hole. This water will seep onto the hot rocks and produce more steam. Pack the sand so that the steam will not escape. Let it steam for several hours. If you have used edible greens you can eat them with the meat.

Meat can be steamed when wrapped in wet leaves and wet newspaper and then buried in ashes as in clay baking.

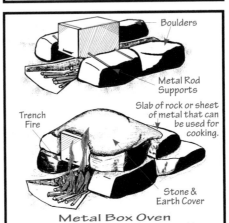

Metal Box Oven

This oven is quite permanent and can be used for baking and general cooking even in the rain. Position it so that the prevailing wind will blow into the fire pit. The metal box can be supported by two metal rods or by being placed on some stones. If the cover is very tight, leave it slightly open to avoid excess pressure. Cover the box with stones and a layer of earth. This will help to retain as much radiant heat as possible. A hole is left in the back of the oven for smoke. An empty army ammunition box is ideal as it is made of heavy gauge metal.

Steaming Food
This method uses hot steam to cook the food. The food is suspended by some means above the water and the pot is covered. On a good fire it takes approximately 5 minutes to have the water boil. Cooking time is from 5 to 15 minutes depending upon the density of the food.

Clay Bank Oven

If you are staying in an area for a long time you can find a clay bank and build a semi permanent oven.

• Hammer a 3 to 4 inch (7-10 cm) pointed stick, two feet from the edge of the bank, into the top of the bank. This hole will form the chimney.
• A foot below the top of the bank scoop out a stove into the bank. Give it the shape of a beehive with a small entrance. Dig as far as the stick. Smooth the inside by rubbing with wet hands. Remove the stick.
• Harden the inside walls of clay by making a small fire to cure the walls.
• To cook, make a fire in the stove to heat the inside. Remove the ashes and place leaves, a piece of stone or wood into the stove. Place the food on the layer. Block the door and the chimney. The food, depending upon size, should be cooked in half an hour or more.

Egg in Mud
Cover a whole egg with a coat of mud at least 1/2 inch (1.27 cm) thick. Place on the coals of a fire and let cook for 20 minutes. Break the mud shell and eggshell to eat the egg.

Cover egg with mud.

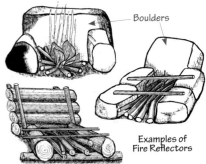

Examples of Fire Reflectors

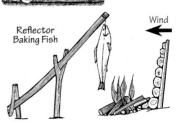

Reflector Baking or Back Log Fire
Build a strong fire, with a raised reflector to throw heat forward. Create a good bed of coals by using sticks 3 feet (1 m) long. To obtain coals in a hurry, use hardwood, either green or dry, and split these sticks into pieces of 2 inches (5 cm) thick. To prolong the life of the coals, cover them with ashes or bark which will limit the oxygen. In wet weather, cover ashes with large overlapping strips of green bark.

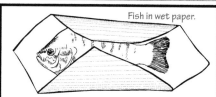

Wrap fish in three sheets of wet paper. The sheets should be applied individually taking care to seal the fish so that the steam will not escape. Spray the paper if it gets dry.

Fish, Clams, Corn Cooked in Paper
• Wet the paper.
• Wet the food and spice it.
• Wrap the food in three sheets of wet paper. Wrap it with a single sheet at a time so as to seal the steam inside.
• Place the paper bundles over the hot coals or in hot ashes and spray the paper if it gets dry.
Some items, as fish and corn, should be individually wrapped, and clams can be grouped to accommodate the size of the paper.

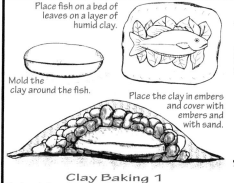

Clay Baking 1
Find some large leaves and wrap them around the fish. It is not necessary to remove the scales. Mould a thin layer of clay or mud around the wrapped fish; let it dry slightly. Wrap a thick layer of clay or mud around the package and place it in front of the fire to dry. When sufficiently dry, bury it in the hot coals and bake for 7 minutes per pound (0.5 kg). When cooked, break open the clay and peel back the skin. This same method can be used for birds. In the case of fowl do not pluck them but place the clay directly on the bird. When cooked, the feathers will come off as they will be stuck in the hard clay. This method is a variant of the adjacent method.

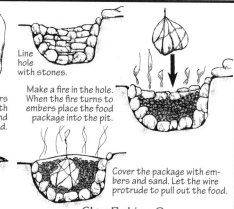

Line hole with stones.

Make a fire in the hole. When the fire turns to embers place the food package into the pit.

Cover the package with embers and sand. Let the wire protrude to pull out the food.

Clay Baking 2
Work some soft clay into a flat sheet with wet hands. Place the food on the clay and fold up the sides to seal in the food. Place the package on the hot ashes to cook. You do not have to scale, skin or pluck the animal but only remove the entrails. The scales, skin or feathers will be stuck to the hard clay and will come off when the clay is broken when the meal is cooked. The cooking time will be between half an hour to an hour. To accelerate the cooking, cover the clay bundle with hot ashes.

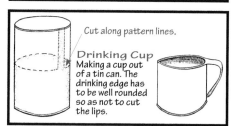

Drinking Cup
Making a cup out of a tin can. The drinking edge has to be well rounded so as not to cut the lips.

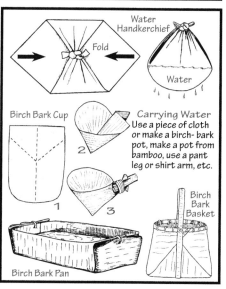

Water Handkerchief

Carrying Water
Use a piece of cloth or make a birch-bark pot, make a pot from bamboo, use a pant leg or shirt arm, etc.

Birch Bark Cup

Birch Bark Basket

Birch Bark Pan

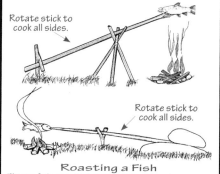

Rotate stick to cook all sides.

Rotate stick to cook all sides.

Roasting a Fish
Place a fish on a stick for roasting. Do not remove the skin as the fish will fall apart when it is cooked. You might want to baste the fish with oil or water while cooking. Rotate the stick every so often.

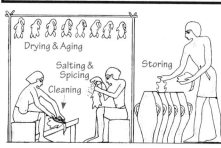

Drying & Aging

Salting & Spicing

Storing

Cleaning

Egyptians Storing Geese
The Egyptians cleaned the geese and then salted and spiced them and hung them up to partially dry. They were then placed in urns which were sealed with wax.

Keeping Soot Off Kettles
Before using a kettle on an open fire, cover the kettle or pan with a coating of heavy, soapy water. The soot of the fire will stick to the pasty surface and wash off with hot water.

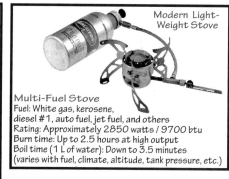

Modern Light-Weight Stove

Multi-Fuel Stove
Fuel: White gas, kerosene, diesel #1, auto fuel, jet fuel, and others
Rating: Approximately 2850 watts / 9700 btu
Burn time: Up to 2.5 hours at high output
Boil time (1 L of water): Down to 3.5 minutes
(varies with fuel, climate, altitude, tank pressure, etc.)

A Pueblo Stove

Hanging Fowl

Roasting Game

Roll of corrugated cardboard in can. Leave a small wick on top. This burner might burn for 20 to 30 minutes.

Tin Can

Camping Burner
A buddy burner is made of a strip of corrugated cardboard rolled with a wick into a low can (e.g. salmon, tuna). Make sure the cardboard is not tightly packed. Pour melted wax into the can and let it cool. This burner can be placed under the tin can stove.

Wind

Lighting a Match
To light a match when it is windy it is important to keep the head of the lit match down. The wind blows on the outside of the hand.

Pouring Hot Water

Sharpening Knife
See Knife Chapter

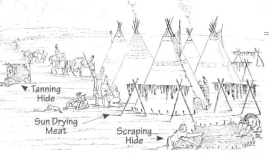

Tanning Hide ▲
Sun Drying Meat
Scraping Hide ►

Drying meat.

DRYING MEAT

Drying is the world's oldest and most common method of food preservation. The scientific principal of preserving food by drying is that by removing moisture, enzymes cannot efficiently contact or react with the food. Whether these enzymes are bacterial, fungal, or naturally occurring autolytic enzymes from the raw food, preventing this enzymatic action preserves the food from biological action.

Types of Food Drying

Two types of natural drying - sun drying and "adiabatic" (shade) drying - occur in open air. Adiabatic drying occurs without heat. Solar (sun) drying sometimes takes place in a special container that catches and captures the sun's heat. These types of drying are used mainly for fruits such as apricots, tomatoes, and grapes (to make raisins).

Hot Drying Meat

Hot Smoking Meat ►

Cold Smoking Fish

Inuit hanging fish to sun dry.

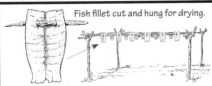

Fish fillet cut and hung for drying.

Inuit Sun Drying Meat
(moose, caribou, muskrats, seals, fish)
Cut up the meat/fish in slices 1 inch (2.5 cm) thick and hang over a pole. Be sure that the two halves do not touch. Keep turning it every day and keep a smoky fire burning to keep flies away.

Inuit drying seal meat.

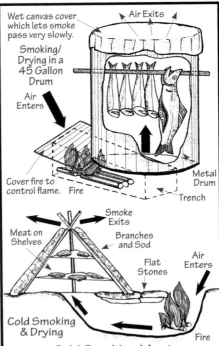

Wet canvas cover which lets smoke pass very slowly.

Air Exits

Smoking/ Drying in a 45 Gallon Drum

Air Enters

Cover fire to control flame. Fire

Metal Drum

Trench

Smoke Exits

Meat on Shelves

Branches and Sod

Flat Stones

Air Enters

Cold Smoking & Drying

Fire

Cold Smoking Meat
Smoking is the best way to conserve meat and fish. Choose a location with soft earth and dig a trench about 1 1/2' (0.45m) wide and 7' (2 m) long. Cover the trench with flat stones and earth. Place a teepee covered with branches and sod at the higher end of the trench. Leave an opening for smoke to escape. Shelves for thin slices of meat made of green wood are suspended in the teepee. Start a small intense fire 5 feet (1.5 m) up the tunnel to heat the walls to create an updraft. Build, at the end of the tunnel, and feed a small fire for about 10 hours. Store the smoked meat in a dry, well-aired, and shady area.

JERKY
Get health information before making homemade jerky.

Jerky is a staple of wilderness living and if well prepared can be kept for years without refrigeration. It is a nutrient-dense meat that has been made lightweight by drying. A pound of meat or poultry weighs about four ounces after being made into jerky. Once prepared, jerky can be eaten by slowly chewing it or using it as a base for a soup, meat drink, stew, or to make pemmican.

Temperature & Making Jerky
Illnesses due to *Salmonella* and *E. coli* from homemade jerky raise questions about the safety of traditional drying methods for making beef and venison jerky. The USDA Meat current recommendation for making jerky safely is to heat meat to 160 °F before the dehydrating process. This step assures that any bacteria present will be destroyed by wet heat. After heating to 160 °F, maintaining a constant dehydrator temperature of 130 to 140 °F during the drying process is important because:
• Process must be fast enough to dry food before it spoils.
• It must remove enough water that microorganisms are unable to grow.

MAKING JERKY

Cut red domestic or wild meat into 1"x2"x8" strips removing any fat, tendons, and gristle. Prepare seasoning of equal amounts of salt, pepper, chili pepper. Pound the meat and season heavily at the same time. Place the strips on a grill near coals and let cook until all the moisture has been removed. This will take approximately 6 hours. The finished jerky should be like dry leather and bend a little without breaking.

PEMMICAN

This is a high energy food developed by the North American Indian. Pemmican is a meal in a ball and it was the food used by the voyageurs to cross North America in canoes.

MAKING PEMMICAN

• Pound one pound (450 g) of dry jerky into a powder with a hammer or a clean stone.
• Melt small chunks of raw animal fat in a pan over a slow fire. Do not let it boil up and burn. When the fat has rendered, remove the tissue and pour liquid fat over the powdered jerky.
• Add dried chopped fruit (serviceberry, apples, nuts, raisins etc.).
• Mix the ingredients until it has the consistency of porridge and the fat will act as a bonding agent. Before the mixture cools shape it into golfball-sized balls. Store in a porous bag to reduce the humidity.

Pemmican does not keep as well as jerky because the fat will sour in warm weather. It keeps for approximately one month in cool weather. It is excellent for fall hunting, camping or hiking. It can be chewed on or used in soups or stews. The Indians used dried serviceberries (amelanchier) as the fruit ingredient. Supplement your diet with sources of Vitamin C. See Edible Plant Chapter.

Drying Meat while traveling.

FOOD STORAGE

In choosing a food storage method consider:

Animals: They will be attracted by the smells of your food, especially when they prowl around during the night.

Insects: Odors of food will attract unwelcome insect attention.

Spoilage: Foods that require a cool environment will rapidly spoil if they are too warm.

Suspend Food: Store food in plastic bags inserted into sturdy canvas bags and suspend them from trees. This will keep the food out of reach of animals. Suspend the food some distance from the camp and downwind if possible. You do not want an animal to stumble through your campsite while investigating those strange odors.

Cooling Food: Keep food cool by using plastic containers and placing these in a cool mountain stream. Do not forget to weigh the containers down with rocks or they might float away during a rainstorm. Make sure that the containers are well sealed.

High Altitude Storage: Food can be stored, in late spring or all year at high altitudes, in snow patches.

Cooling by Evaporation: Your forehead cools with the evaporation of sweat. This same principle can be used while camping or where you are surviving in the woods. Place the food in plastic bags into a cotton canvas bag which you suspend in a breezy shaded area. Keep the bag moist by dousing it with water. Evaporation of the water from the surface of the bag will keep the contents cool.

STORAGE OF EGGS

To store eggs for several months, coat them with a thin layer of lukewarm mineral oil, drain well and place them in a cool place.

Eggs: Limewater Storage

To prepare the limewater: Scald 2 pounds (0.9 kg) of hydrated lime in a little water and stir with 5 gallons (19 L) of previously boiled water. Allow to cool. Let settle and use the clear liquid. Place clean, fresh eggs in a clean jar and pour the liquid 2 inches (5 cm) above the eggs. Cover the jar and keep it in a cool dry place. To test eggs for freshness, put them in a bowl of cold water. If they are fresh they will sink to the bottom.

Food placed in canvas bags 12 feet (3.6 m) above the ground.

FOOD CACHE

To protect food from animals you can hang the food from a pole suspended between two trees. The height of the bags depends upon which visitors you are expecting. You will require 12 feet (3.6 m) for a bear. This storage area should be downwind from the camp as you do not want animals trudging through your camp on the way to your storage area. Place it at least 50 feet (15 m) from your shelter.

Hammock Storage

REVIVING STORED FOOD

- Fresh eggs will keep longer if dipped in a thin warmed mineral oil. Drain and store in a cool spot.
- Fresh potatoes can be frozen to be used all winter. Choose firm, clean potatoes and keep them frozen until ready to use. Put frozen potatoes in boiling salted water without peeling and cook until tender, then peel. Or defrost and cook in a microwave oven.
- Pour boiling water over stale walnuts.
- Break sprouts off stored potatoes, as soon as they appear, to prevent the potatoes from becoming soft.
- Freshen dried onion, red and green pepper or parsley flakes by soaking for 20 minutes in warm water. Drain and use as fresh vegetables.
- If cheese has started to mold, trim the mold, and wrap it in a cloth dipped in vinegar.
- Bake stale peanuts at 275°F (135°C) in an oven for one hour.
- To preserve butter store in a sealed pot in a cool dark place.
- Frozen fish can be cut with a saw or axe. Peel off the skin and cut into pieces Eat with salt and blubber. The blubber is to give you some fat to help you resist the cold as fish usually is quite lean, especially trout.
- Brown sugar can be kept soft by storing it in an airtight container with a slice of fresh bread.

FOOD SILO

Corn, carrots, apples etc. can be stored in a silo. Choose a dry spot and dig a hole in the ground. Line the hole with rocks, making sure that you leave breathing space between the rocks. Place the vegetables to be stored into the hole. Place some dry straw, twigs, grass, and flat stones over the food. Place a layer of sod on top. This silo will protect the food from animals, from drying too fast, and from frost.

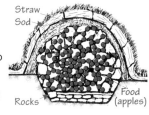

Straw
Sod
Rocks
Food (apples)

Boulders

Direction of Flow →

COOLING FOOD

Food can be stored in plastic jars or bags and placed in cool mountain brooks. Place boulders and stones as a retaining wall so that the food does not float away. Cover the containers with rocks to protect against animals.

GROUND STORAGE

Dig a hole and line it with large stones. Cover with heavy logs and rocks to protect food from animals.

Rocks

Logs

Ground Storage

NW Indian salmon cache.

West coast native storage.

West Inuit Subterranean shelter above ground storage.

Below ground shelter.

Entrance

Protection from Blow Flies

To protect meat from egg laying blow flies keep the meat in a dark cool dry location. Hang it 12 feet (3.6 m) above the ground. Keep it away from leaves. Suspend fresh meat above a small fire to smoke and sear the surface with a protective hardened dry covering around the meat.

Canoe trip cache.

Coyote eyeing the hind flank.

Sole fillets.

FILLETING FISH

EATING FISH

For fin fish: scale, gut and clean the fish as soon as they are caught. Wrap both whole and cleaned fish in water-tight plastic and store on ice. Keep 3-4 inches of ice on the bottom of the cooler. Alternate layers of fish and ice. Cook the fish in 1-2 days, or freeze and use it within 6 months. After cooking, eat within 3-4 days. Make sure the raw fish stays separate from cooked foods.

EATING CRABS & SHELLFISH

Crabs, lobsters and other shellfish must be kept alive until cooked. Store in a bushel or laundry basket under wet burlap. Crabs and lobsters are best eaten the day they are caught. Live oysters can keep 7-10 days; mussels and clams, 4-5 days. **Caution:** Be aware of the potential dangers of eating raw shellfish. This is especially true for persons with liver disorders or weakened immune systems. However, no one should do so! **At the Beach:** Take along only the amount of food that can be eaten, to avoid having leftovers. Partially bury the cooler in the sand, cover with blankets, and shade with a beach umbrella.

TROUT AS FOOD

One pound (0.5 kg) of rainbow trout has 200 calories. 5000 calories per day are required to survive in the wilderness, which would require over 25 trout per day. Salmon and other fatty fish are a better meal as they provide, on the average, four times the calories per pound (0.5 kg). If you do not supplement your diet with plants and animals, you will gradually starve.

SEAWEED

All seaweed is edible. Raw, simmered to make a soup, boiled with meat stew, or dry to store. The Edible Plant Chapter outlines some sea weeds.

SALT WATER CLAMS

Discard the dark portion of the meat between the end of April to the end of October. During this period there are possible dangerous concentrations of toxins.

CRABS & LOBSTERS

Cook them before eating. Salt water crabs can be eaten raw but do not take any risks.

SEA CUCUMBERS

These look like cucumbers but are actually animals. Remove its insides and scrape the slimy outside skin, keeping the fine long muscles. These muscles can be eaten boiled, fried, in a stew, or even raw.

SEA URCHIN

The insides are edible especially in temperate and arctic waters of North America. Collect sea urchins at low tide when they can be picked off emerged rocks.

ABALONE

The abalone is a mollusk that clings to rocks along the northern Pacific coast and is exposed during low tide. Use a knife or sharp stick to pry it loose. Pry with a sudden jerk or the abalone has time to attach itself more securely. Slice the white of the meat. Pound it with a rock so that it becomes tender. Cook as a chowder, or fried and boiled over an open fire. Be careful when detaching them as they might suddenly close and catch your hand or piece of garment. You will drown if you cannot release yourself before the next tide.

Filleting Fish illustrations

Cut behind the fin right down to the backbone.

Pass the knife along top side of backbone.

Push the knife through and cut the fillet free from the tail.

Cut flesh away from the bones.

Filleting Knife

Remove the fillet by cutting skin at stomach area.

FILLETING FISH

Field dress fish as soon as possible as the gills, guts and kidney will rapidly spoil in a dead fish. Wipe the slime off the fish to make it less slippery. ***Do not let any slime get into your eyes. See the First Aid Chapter on Fish Illnesses.*** Remove the gills by cutting the throat connection and pulling out the gills. Gut the fish but avoid cutting the gut and if you do, wash the fish. Do not use too much water as it softens the flesh. If the scales are very large remove the scales and skin before cooking.

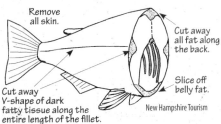

Remove all skin.

Cut away all fat along the back.

Slice off belly fat.

Cut away V-shape of dark fatty tissue along the entire length of the fillet.

New Hampshire Tourism

Use cooking methods that allow fat-laden juices to drip away.

Skinning a large catfish without a pair of pliers. First cut below the head, down the stomach, and around the fins.

CATFISH & BULLHEADS

Catfish are always skinned. The method varies with the size of the fish as they can weigh over 75 pounds (34 kg). Catfish under 12 inches (30 cm) are cooked whole after skinning and cleaning. Larger fish can be cut into fillets, flat cross section steaks, or chunks.

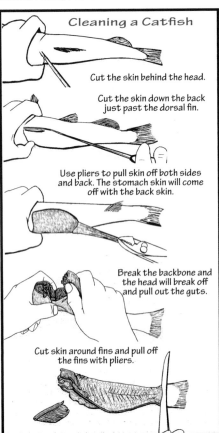

Cleaning a Catfish

Cut the skin behind the head.

Cut the skin down the back just past the dorsal fin.

Use pliers to pull skin off both sides and back. The stomach skin will come off with the back skin.

Break the backbone and the head will break off and pull out the guts.

Cut skin around fins and pull off the fins with pliers.

Opening an Oyster

Enter the blade of a dull knife or an oyster knife near the oyster's muscle. This muscle is found at the thick, more pointed end of the oyster. Twist the blade and the shell will open.

Do not eat fish if:
- Eyes look milky.
- Does not look fresh.
- Finger pressure points leave indentations.
- It does not look like a fish; it inflates, snout-like mouth, box-shaped, or stone. These are fish but usually are not good to eat and should not be touched.
- Never eat offal of a fish.

Sever gill covering from jawbone.

Ventral Cut

Gutting and removing gills of a large fish.

Fish should be gutted and washed when caught. The guts can be used as bait or else bury them in the ground as their odor will attract insects and scavengers. Keep the fish cool and cook as soon as possible.

Vegetation
Boiled Roots
Wash roots and boil until soft. Add to a pot of stew and eat with fatty meat or fish.

Inner Bark of Pine
The Lodge Pole Pine and other pines have an edible inner bark that can be eaten fresh or dried.

Pinon Nuts
Nuts from southern pines. They are soft and a delicacy. They can be eaten raw, roasted or used as a flour for bread.

Acorn Soup
Break shells of ripe acorns. Remove and crush the nuts. Pour warm water over the crushed nuts three or four times to remove the bitter taste. Indians buried acorns in swampy soil for a year to remove bitterness. Cook the acorn meal in hot water.

Birch Tree Spaghetti
The inner bark of the birch can be removed, cut into strips and added to soup or stew. The twigs and leaves can be cooked to make a tea.

Palmetto Cabbage
The Seminoles of Florida would cut off the new top of the palmetto and eat it raw or bake it.

Mushrooms
Avoid eating mushrooms as they have little food value and the risk of choosing the wrong one is very high. See Mushroom Chapter.

Arctic Vegetation
Arctic vegetation is nearly all edible except for some mushrooms. The best known food is rock tripe. It looks like a leathery dark lettuce leaf up to three inches wide attached to rocky surfaces. Rock tripe grows from the Arctic to the southern states. It can be eaten raw or in a soup or stew.

Indian Survival Food
Indians ate the contents of the stomachs of herbivorous (grass-eating) mammals, such as caribou, moose, and deer. The content consists of leaves, small branches, and water plants mixed in digestive acids. These acids have a sour taste as salad dressing.

Animal Blood
For additional iron take four tablespoons of animal blood which is equal to ten eggs.

Eating Rawhide
Rawhide, if it has not been treated with varnish, can be boiled or chewed raw.

Bone Marrow
Cook large bones to suck out the bone marrow.

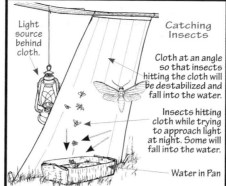

Light source behind cloth.

Catching Insects

Cloth at an angle so that insects hitting the cloth will be destabilized and fall into the water.

Insects hitting cloth while trying to approach light at night. Some will fall into the water.

Water in Pan

EATING INSECTS
Insects are excellent food as they are mainly protein and can provide more emergency energy than fish or meat. You can eat moths, mayflies and other insects. Attract them with a small light at night. If it's too cold for flying, look under rotten logs and stones. Ants can be a problem as they contain formic acid and have a bitter taste. Grasshoppers, termites, locusts and crickets can be eaten when the hard parts, such as wings and legs, are removed. An old method of catching insects and small animals was by setting fire to large tracts of grassland. Once the fire had passed, the roasted insects and animals could be collected. This method should not be used even in a survival situation as it is very destructive and the fire can get out of hand. People in different parts of the world consider grasshoppers, hairless caterpillars, wood boring beetle larvae and pupae, spider bodies, and termites as delicacies. Insects might actually be their only source of protein. There are different recipes in cooking, methods of finding, and raising insects. If you want to try eating insects or have to do so to survive, you will find them much more palatable if you cook them until they are dry or in a stew.

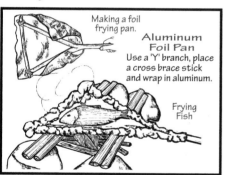

Making a foil frying pan.

Aluminum Foil Pan
Use a 'Y' branch, place a cross brace stick and wrap in aluminum.

Frying Fish

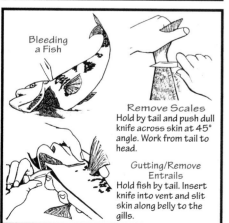

Bleeding a Fish

Remove Scales
Hold by tail and push dull knife across skin at 45° angle. Work from tail to head.

Gutting/Remove Entrails
Hold fish by tail. Insert knife into vent and slit skin along belly to the gills.

EATING FROGS
Skin frogs before eating as the skin of some frogs secretes an irritating and possibly poisonous liquid. Do not eat frogs with bright yellow or red marks.

While frog is watching wiggling fingers, gradually approach this hand to catch the frog. Make sure that this hand does not cast a shadow on or near the frog.

Wiggle fingers to attract the attention of the frog. Do not advance this hand.

Leopard Frog

Catching Frogs
Use a piece of cloth on a string. Let the cloth float on the water and yank the string when the frog takes the cloth into its mouth. Frogs can be speared. Frogs can be caught at night by holding a torch above the water. The frogs will watch the light and you can net them or even catch them from behind with your hands. The best part to eat is the hind legs, which can be cooked over hot coals.

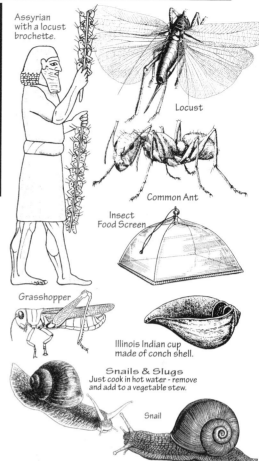

Assyrian with a locust brochette.

Locust

Common Ant

Insect Food Screen

Grasshopper

Illinois Indian cup made of conch shell.

Snails & Slugs
Just cook in hot water - remove and add to a vegetable stew.

Snail

Insect & Ant Protection
Perforate the bottoms of 4 tin cans. Slip them on the table legs. Use some sticky sap from a pine tree to mount and glue the cans upside down on the table legs. This will prevent ants from sharing in your meal.

Tin Cans

Tin Can

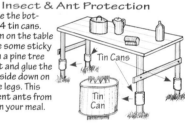

Lizards
Lizards are excellent to eat. The only poisonous lizards are the Gila monster of the Southwest and the beaded lizard of Mexico.

Lizard

Lizard Catching Loop
Make the loop of light wire and sway it slowly in front of the lizard. Gradually bring the loop closer and closer and then lasso the lizard. Skin the lizard and fry it. It tastes like chicken.

Boiling sap to make maple syrup. | Driving spigot into tree. | Maple sap from tree. | Maple sap collected.

MAPLE SYRUP

FISHING SPOTS

Fish are probably the most difficult water food to catch. If you have no previous fishing experience it may take hours or even days before you are successful. Fishing is possible with very crude equipment. Hooks can be improvised out of pins, bone, plant thorns, or hardwood. Line can be made by twisting bark or cloth fibers. With patience and trial and error you will find the right location, correct bait and the best time of day.

Large fish hunting small fish below lily pads.

Trout hiding under the weeds.

TIME TO FISH

The best time varies for each species and the environment the species lives in. In general fish feed just before dawn and just after dusk; before a storm as a cold front approaches; and at night when the moon is full or waning. Rising fish and jumping minnows may also be signs of feeding fish.

Large fish hiding in cool shadow of a large boulder.

Fish hiding between logs.

FINDING FISH

The place depends on the type of water available and the time of day.

During the Day: In fast running streams in the heat of the day, try deep pools that lie below the riffles. On lakes in the heat of the summer, fish deep because fish seek the coolness of deeper water.

Evening or Early Morning: Float the bait over the riffle, aiming for submerged logs, undercut banks, and overhanging bushes. On lakes, fish the edges as fish are more apt to feed in shallow water.

Spring and Late Fall: Fishing on a lake is more productive on the edge in shallow water because fish are either bedding or seeking warmer water. You can locate the beds of some species of fish by their strong, distinctively "fishy" odor.

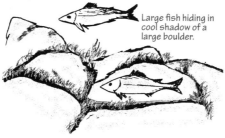

Birds gathering over a school of fish.

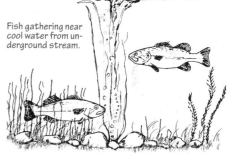

Fish gathering near cool water from underground stream.

Fish in shadow of rock.

Large fish in trunk of tree.

Breeze

Fish gathering on leeward side of island. The wind can blow insects into water.

Large fish chasing small fish.

Dorsal fin of a large fish.

Large predator fish in the shallows on moonlit nights.

Fish at stream's entry into lake. Stream's water has more oxygen and is cool.

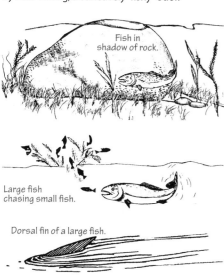

Small fish in the shallow slow water and weeds.

Medium Fish

Medium Fish

Larger fish in deep water and below the overhang.

Location of Fish in a Stream

1 Overhanging brush
2 Undercut from stream erosion
3 Pool from backwash - still water
4 Feeder stream - supplying oxygen, food, & cool water.
5 Behind rocks - calm water
6 Fallen tree - provides shelter & a predator can attack unsuspecting small fish.

329

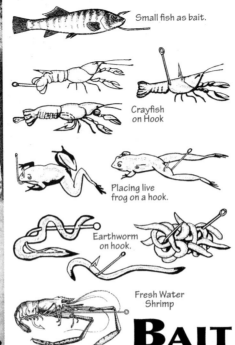

Small fish as bait.

Crayfish on Hook

Placing live frog on a hook.

Earthworm on hook.

Fresh Water Shrimp

BAIT

BAIT: NATIVE WATERS

In general, fish bite bait taken from their native water. Look for crabs, fish eggs, and minnows and on the banks for worms and insects. Inspect the stomach of a hooked fish to see what it has been eating and try to duplicate this food. Use the intestines and eyes of a caught fish for bait. If worms are used completely cover the hook. With minnows, pass the hook through the body of the fish under its backbone in the rear of the dorsal fin. Be sure you do not sever the minnow's backbone because you want it to keep active.

BEST FISH BAIT

The best way to know what bait fish will eat is to look at what is floating on the surface of the water and what items attract the curiosity of the fish. After you have caught your first fish, examine the stomach and intestines and you will see what they are biting. Could be: worms, minnows, fish eggs, crayfish, wood grubs or insects. You can use the intestines as bait for a larger fish.

FINDING BAIT: ROTTEN LOG

Rotten logs are an excellent source of bait for fishing. Look for a log that is on moist soil and roll it over to find worms, grubs, and larvae. You can then break open the log and find more tidbits of bait. Some of these insects might even add protein to your diet in case of an emergency.

Catching a Worm

CATCHING WORMS

Worms are the most tempting tidbit for fish including trout, bass, perch, eels, suckers, and bullheads. Collect them at night on a lawn, after a rainfall, or watering of the lawn. Use a flashlight and upon seeing a worm grasp it close to the end near the burrow and pull. The worm might look slow but he can return to his burrow in a flash. Store worms in a tin can on a bed of powdered peat moss covered with wet sphagnum moss. This should keep a worm for several days. Do not store the tin in the sun or in a closed car, or you will have some sorry looking cooked worms!

CRAYFISH

These are available in most of temperate North America. They look like a grayish green lobster but are all tail and from 3 - 6 inches (8-15cm) long. Look for them in waters from a few inches to a few feet (meters) deep. They are especially easy to catch in small ponds or backwash. You can catch them by grabbing them in shallow water by their back, to avoid their claws. In deeper waters they can be caught in (or they crawl into) a baited net or shirt.

That's it???

Young yellow perch hiding in weeds.

Northern pike below a log.

Fillet Knife and Case

Fishing with hooks attached to a dead branch.

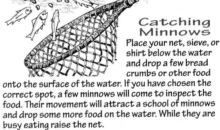

Catching Minnows

Place your net, sieve, or shirt below the water and drop a few bread crumbs or other food onto the surface of the water. If you have chosen the correct spot, a few minnows will come to inspect the food. Their movement will attract a school of minnows and drop some more food on the water. While they are busy eating raise the net.

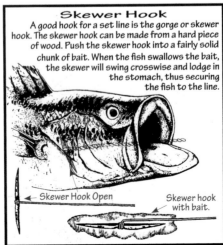

Skewer Hook

A good hook for a set line is the gorge or skewer hook. The skewer hook can be made from a hard piece of wood. Push the skewer hook into a fairly solid chunk of bait. When the fish swallows the bait, the skewer will swing crosswise and lodge in the stomach, thus securing the fish to the line.

← Skewer Hook Open

Skewer hook with bait.

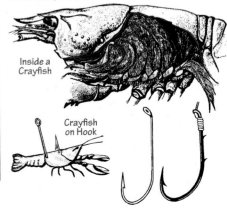

Inside a Crayfish

Crayfish on Hook

Stick Hooks

Hooks with wood slivers.

Barbed Hook

Hook with Nail

Hook with pins.

Hook with Thorn

Haida Dipnet

Alaska native halibut hook.

Hook with coin reflector bait.

Native Stone Sinker

Sinker

Wire hook with button spoon.

Safety Pin Hook

Pinch-on Sinker

Supreme Hook

Pliers to remove hooks.

Native Steatite Sinker

Hooks made from shells.

Native Granite Sinker

Aberdeen Hook

Hook with reflector.

Pinch-on Sinker

Simple Hitch Knot
The advantage of using this knot on hooks is that the harder to pull becomes the tighter it holds. It is also easy to untie this knot.

Tie Knot

Wire Fishing Noose
Wire in tube. Loop at the bottom. Pull handle at the top. Pull handle to catch fish.

Treble Hook

Snelled Hook

Minnow Hook

FISH HOOKS

A Jack-Beat

Fishing Bag

Florida native fish basket.

Chippeway Indians netting fish in birch bark canoes near Lake Superior 1850's.

Throat

Barb

Gap

Point

Shank

Eye

Jig Hook

FLY FISHING
ARTIFICIAL BAIT
Artificial bait can be made from pieces of brightly colored cloth, feathers, or bits of bright metal fashioned to duplicate insects, worms and minnows. Strive to make your artificial bait look natural by moving it slowly or copying the actions of natural fish food.

A Hy Watson picture of traditional fly fishing.

SPEARING FISH

Making Spear Point

Spear Point
A spear point can be cut from the 'Y' of a hardwood branch. Cut the point from a green branch. It will harden when it dries. Tie the point to the end of a straight stick.

Indian spearing salmon at night.

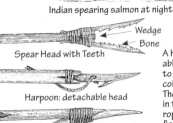

Wedge
Bone
Spear Head with Teeth

Harpoon: detachable head

Sharpened Antler

Harpoon
A harpoon has a detachable head that is attached to a rope that is kept coiled next to the hunter. The harpoon head will lodge in the large fish and the rope is used to pull in the fish. The harpoon spear is usually lost.

Fishing with a gaffing hook.

Indian Gaff Hook
Made in the same way as the fish spear except that the sharpened branch is longer and sharpened at the end.

Fishing torch from cattail.

Fishing torch from birch bark.

Fishing Torch
The Ojibway fished at night, in a boat or from the shore, while carrying a torch above the water. To make a torch, a stick, about 9 feet (2.7 m) long, was split at one end. A piece of tightly folded birch bark, soaked in some oil, was placed between the split of the stick and lit. Fish will drift towards the light and can be speared or netted.

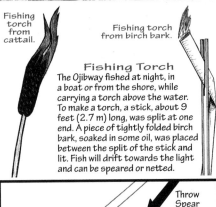

Water Surface
Throw Spear
Fish is "seen" here.
Fish is here.

WATER REFRACTION & THROWING SPEAR

If you aim directly at the fish you "see" you will miss it.

Fish is "seen" here.

Throw Spear

Fish is here.

To hit the fish you have to throw lower.

Difficulty of seeing fish in water.

SPEARING FISH
Spearing is difficult except when the stream is small and the fish are large and numerous as during spawning season or when the fish congregate in pools. Sharpen a stick, lash two long thorns on a stick, or fashion a bone spear point, and position yourself on a rock over a fish run, making sure that you do not cast a shadow. If you cast a shadow do not move. Wait for a large fish to swim by. Aiming can be tricky as water diffracts light so that the fish will not be where you think it is. The fish will be closer to you, so you have to aim low. To learn how to judge the fish's position, point your spear at a rock on the bed of the stream and push, without throwing, the spear into the water to touch the rock. You will not touch the rock because of diffraction but you will see the angle of your error.

HARDWOOD SAPLING SPEAR
Cut a straight young hardwood sapling just below a branch. The spear can be five feet long and about 3/4 (2 cm) of an inch thick. Remove all branches except the first branch. The first branch and the stick should be trimmed into a barbed spear head. Tie a leather thong or twine to the end of the stick to help you retrieve the stick. This spear can be used for fish or frogs.

BAMBOO SPEAR
A dry bamboo pole an inch thick and 5 feet (1.5 m) long can be used to make an effective spear. Cut two spear points opposite to each other on the heavier end of the bamboo stick. This point should be between the natural divisions in the bamboo. A bamboo spear can be very sharp because the point is cut in the direction of the grain and the wood is dry. This spear can be used for fish, frogs and small animals.

MUDDYING WATER

Small isolated pools caused by the receding waters of flooded streams are often abundant in fish. Muddy the bottom of the puddle by stamping or using a stick. Fish will seek clear water and rise to the surface. Catch and throw them onto the shore with your hands. You can catch the fish with your hands when the cloud gradually obscures the eyes of the fish.

TROLLING FOR FISH

Use a shiny object, such as a spoon blade, with a hook fastened to the end. Paddle slowly on a log or boat, creating as little disturbance as possible. Let out a lot of line so the troll is far from the boat. The darting about of the flashy spoon will attract some fish. You can also troll by attaching your line to a piece of driftwood. Attach the driftwood to a line and let it drift with the current. Place a floater on the line to see if a fish has bitten.

JIGGING

Jigging requires a wood pole, a hook, a piece of shiny metal shaped like a fishing spoon, a strip of white meat, pork rind or fish intestine, and a piece of short line about 10 inches (25 cm) long. Attach the hook just below the spoon on the end of the short line, and tie the line to the end of the pole. Submerge the hook just below the surface of the water near the edge of a lily pad or bed of weeds. From time to time slap the water with the tip of the pole to attract larger fish to the bait. This is effective at night when the moon is out or when using a flashlight or lantern. Jigging is a term also used for a fishing method in which an unbaited hook or hooks are moved up and down on the water in a school of fish to catch a fish by hooking a part of its body. This method is used to catch carp and suckers. This unbaited method is illegal in some areas as it lets many injured fish escape.

Automatic Fishing Rod

Set line with trigger.

Trigger

Hooks

SET LINES

Tie several hooks onto a line. Bait them and fasten the line to a low-hanging branch that will bend when a fish is hooked. Permanently keep the set line in the water checking it periodically to remove fish and re-bait the hooks. A good hook for a set line is the gorge or skewer hook. Push the skewer hook into a fairly solid chunk of bait. When the fish swallows the bait, the skewer will swing crosswise and lodge in the stomach thus securing the fish to the line.

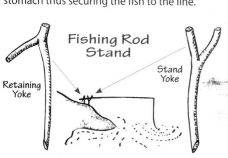

Fishing Rod Stand

Retaining Yoke

Stand Yoke

Salmon Scale

Bass Scale

Fish Age Scale Marking

Observe the scales. The scales will show you the summer (when fish grows faster) and winter (when fish grow slowly) markings. Fish scales grow as the rings of a tree grow. The first ring represents 2 years of growth in the fry stage. Each additional summer (wide line) and winter (dark narrow line) indicate the age of the fish.

Spoon

Movement Up & Down

Jigging

Baited Hook

Crayfish Trap

Wooden stick to float net.

Bait fastened in center of net

Net or porous cloth.

Gaffing a fish.

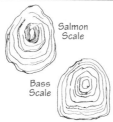

Supposed Indian methods of catching whales as seen by Europeans in 1500's

BARE-HANDED FISHING

This takes patience but can be very successful. This method is effective in small streams with undercut banks or in shallow ponds left by receding flood waters.

- Place your hands in the water and allow them to reach water temperature. Slowly reach under a river bank, keeping your hands close to the bottom. Slowly move your hands until you touch a fish. Work your hands gently along its belly until you reach its gills. Grasp the fish firmly just behind its gills otherwise it might slip away.

> **Bare-Handed Fishing**
> Place your hands in the water and allow them to reach water temperature. Slowly reach under a river bank, keeping your hands close to the bottom. Slowly move your hands until you touch a fish. Work your hands gently along its belly until you reach its gills. Grasp the fish firmly just behind its gills otherwise it might slip away.

- In faster water where there are boulders, feel into the nooks and crannies and you will possibly find trout and other fish that cannot escape. Do not do this in the ocean because you might be bitten by a moray eel.

Spearing a Barracuda

Speared barracuda pulling boat.

Ice fishing with a snow block windbreak.

Indians Ice Fishing

Ice fishing equipment all assembled on the sleigh.

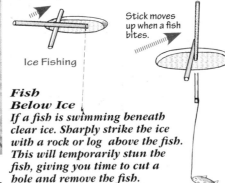

Ice Fishing

Stick moves up when a fish bites.

Fish Below Ice

If a fish is swimming beneath clear ice. Sharply strike the ice with a rock or log above the fish. This will temporarily stun the fish, giving you time to cut a hole and remove the fish.

This is a great catch. Notice the size if the hole relative to the size of the hand.

Automated fishing system. Flag, on a trigger, goes up when there is a fish on the line.

Ice Fishing

In the winter, fish can be caught by fishing through a hole in the ice. A spud bar or auger can be used to cut a hole up to 12" thick. Size of hole for yellow perch, sunfish is approximately 5" in diameter. Larger fish require an 8" hole. An 8" hole requires double the ice being removed over a 6" hole. Keep the hole open by covering it with brush and piling loose snow over the cover.

Fish, in winter, tend to gather in deep pools. Trout are frequently caught while cruising just a few feet under the ice. Cut the ice holes over the deepest part of the lake. Place a baited rig at several holes. If you tend the hole you can jig with a short fishing rig which can use an "automatic" tip-up when you are visiting the other holes. A jigging rod or hand line and a small jigging spoon or lure which uses a minnow as bait. The jig darts around when it is jerked by the angler. The flag moving to an upright position will signal a catch. The pole should be 3 feel long with a line long enough to reach the bottom. Make a small spoon-shaped spinner from a piece of bright metal. Attach a hook to the line with the spinner just above the hook. When fishing move the rod in an up and down motion in such a way that the bright metal object will vibrate. Try to fish close to where the shelf near the shore drops off to lake bottom, at the edge of the reeds, or close to a projecting rock formation.

Location: Most ponds and lakes can be ice fished: Large shallower lakes: chain pickerel, northern pike, yellow perch and sunfish. Deepwater lakes: northern pike, walleye, and trout.

Ice safety: Minimum of 3"-4" of clear, blue, hard ice on non-running waters is required for safety. Slush is 50% weaker, and ice on running water 20% weaker. Ice thickness strength depends upon many variables and your own judgement is essential - be careful.

Be especially careful over moving water.

ICE FISHING ICE FISHING ICE FISHING ICE FISHING ICE FISHING

Children netting minnows.

Adrien, one year and eight months, "catching" his first seaweed.

Netting

The edges and tributaries of lakes and streams are usually abundant with fish too small to hook or spear but large enough to net. Make a circular frame with a forked sapling. Tie your T-shirt or mosquito netting to the frame. Scoop upstream around rocks or in pools with this improvised net.

Crab & Lobster Trap

Entrance of trap for lobster.

Door to remove the lobsters.

CRAB & LOBSTER TRAPS

These traps are baited with smaller crabs or fish. Crabs and lobsters usually live on rocky beds near to the coast. To get at the bait the lobster or crab enters by tunnels at the ends of the trap. The bait might be enclosed in a protective cage so that it will be available to catch numerous lobsters in the same trap.

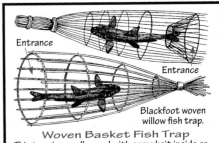

Entrance

Entrance

Blackfoot woven willow fish trap.

Woven Basket Fish Trap
This trap is usually used with some bait inside or with a dam to funnel the fish. Once the fish are inside they cannot leave.

Eel Traps
A long conical net trap is used to catch eel. These traps can be up to 50 feet long and the eel swims up the trap and cannot find its way out.

STREAM TRAPS

In small, shallow streams, make your fish trap with stakes, rocks, logs, fish net, earth, or branches set in the stream bottom so that the stream is blocked except for a small narrow opening into a stone or brush pen. Wade in and herd the fish into your trap. Dam the shallow area. Catch or club them when they get into the shallow water.

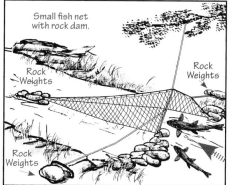

Small fish net with rock dam.
Rock Weights
Rock Weights
Rock Weights
Fish net placed across stream.

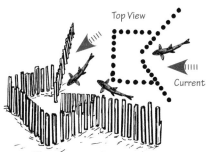

Top View
Current

Fence Fish Trap

A basic fish trap is an enclosure with a blind opening where two fence-like walls extend out like a funnel from the entrance. The effort you put into building a trap depends upon the length of time you plan to stay in one spot.

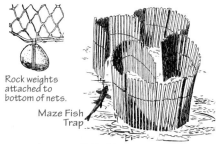

Rock weights attached to bottom of nets.
Maze Fish Trap

Fish Traps
These are usually a mesh-like permanent or removable structure that is submerged in the water. The fish enters the trap, but due to its design, cannot find its way out of the trap.

TRAPPING FISH

Shore Traps or Weirs

Traps can be used to catch fish, especially those moving in schools. In lakes or large streams, fish approach the banks and shallows in the morning and evening. Sea fish traveling in large schools regularly approach the shore with the incoming tide, often moving parallel to the shore and circumventing obstructions in the water. Sea fish schools can be located by watching the feeding water birds.

Tidal Shore Weir Trap

Natural Barrier Traps

If you are on a tidal sea, pick a trap location at high tide and build it at low tide. On rocky shores use natural rock pools. On coral islands use natural pools on the surface of reefs by blocking the openings as the tide recedes. On sandy shores, use sand bars and the ditches they enclose. Fish in the lee of offshore sandbars. Build your trap as a low stone wall extending out into the water forming an angle with the shore.

Tidal Pool
Shore
Sea
Rocks

CLAMS

To locate clams:

In the Water: Wade through the shallow salt water. When you feel a lump on the ocean bed quickly reach down and dig it out with the help of a short stick. This also applies to oysters and mussels.

On Seashore: Walk slowly a few feet above the waterline and hit the ground with a piece of driftwood. If you see small air holes these are from clams trying to reach the water. Place yourself between the water and the bubbles and start digging real fast because this clam is in a hurry and they are fast.

A healthy clam will close its shell very tightly. If you see that the shell is not tightly closed when you tap the clam throw it away. Do not eat clams that are found in industrial estuaries or inhabited sea shores.

RAZOR CLAM

Razor Clam

Dimple: a depression in the sand
Doughnut: has raised sides
Keyhole: is usually in drier sand areas and is shaped like an "hour-glass" or is a hole with very distinct sides. Clams might show at the edge of the surf line when you pound the beach with a shovel handle or your foot. They may squirt sand and water out of the hole where they are located. You need to be quick when digging in the surf as razor clams dig quite fast in the soft fluid sand.

1 Place the shovel blade 4 to 6 inches seaward of the clam show. The handle of the shovel should be pointed toward the sand dunes.
2 Use your body weight to push the shovel blade straight into the sand while you drop to one knee. In hard sand, gently rock the shovel handle from side to side for ease of entry. It is very important to keep the blade as vertical as possible to keep from breaking the clam shell.
3 Pull the handle back just enough to break the suction in the sand, still keeping the blade as straight as possible. The sand will crack as shown.
4 Remove sand by lifting the shovel upward and forward. Repeat this 2 to 3 times.
5 Succeeding scoops of sand expose the clam enough to reach down with your hand and grasp its shell. Razor clams move rapidly downward but not horizontally.

MOLLUSKS

These include fresh and salt water invertebrates such as snails, clams, mussels, bivalves, periwinkles, chitons, and sea urchins. Most members of this group are edible; however, be sure that you have a fresh mollusk and that you boil it. Do not eat it raw as you might introduce parasites into your body. To find them in fresh water look in the shallows, especially in water with a sandy or muddy bottom. Near the sea, wait for low tide and check in tidal pools or on and in the sand.

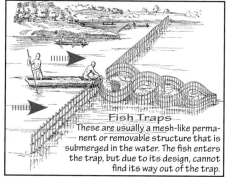

Pacific Geoduck Clam
Fresh Water Mussel
Water Out
Water In
Gaper Clam

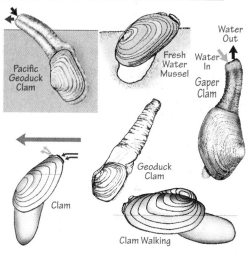

Clam
Geoduck Clam
Clam Walking
Clam Digging

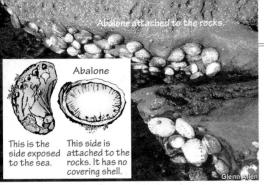

Abalone attached to the rocks.

Abalone

This is the side exposed to the sea.

This side is attached to the rocks. It has no covering shell.

Glenn Allen

ABALONE

To pry them loose use a tool as a strong stick, metal rod, screw driver. Work at low tide unless you are a strong swimmer. Do not use your hands to pry lose an abalone as its strong muscles might clamp your hand onto the rock and you might drown with the rising tide. This also applies to large clams.

FROGS

Hunt frogs at night when you can locate them by their croaking. Club them or snag the larger ones on a hook and line. Skin and eat the entire body.

NEWTS & SALAMANDERS

They are found under rotten logs or under rocks in areas where frogs are abundant.

CRUSTACEANS

These include fresh and salt water crabs, crayfish, lobsters, shrimps, and prawns. Most of them are edible, but they spoil rapidly and some harbor harmful parasites. Find them in moss beds under rocks or net them from tidal pools. Fresh water shrimp are abundant in tropical streams, especially in sluggish water where they cling to branches or vegetation.

Tarpon Forked Barb Hook

Catching a tarpon and taking it home.

REMOVING A FISH HOOK

Press hook down and pull out.

REMOVING HOOK

A

B

C

See a doctor as there might be an infection.

Fisherman's Conjunctivitis

This is a severe inflammatory condition of the eyes. It is caused by contact with the juices of marine animal growth that look like suet. These growths can be crushed and release juice which can accidentally enter the eye. This causes a very acute and painful inflammation of the conjunctiva or thin covering of the eye. Wash the slime off fish when they are caught and wash hands after handling caught fish. *See a doctor for treatment.*

FISHING FIRST AID
FISH POISONING (ERYSIPELOID)

This disease is more common during warmer months. It is a skin disease that usually occurs on the hands and forearms. It is caused by the skin being punctured by fins of fish, sharp bones, or fish hooks and the residue of fish slime or rotten fish enters these openings. A small red spot at the point of entry indicates the start of an infection. It will spread to adjacent areas. The infection will gradually become clear at the center with a reddish-purple color at the spreading margins. The affected parts will swell, itch, and have a burning sensation. First aid can be started with frequent hot bathing of the affected areas. *See a doctor for complete treatment.*

SALT WATER BOILS

Are very common with deep water fishermen. They are a collection of small boils around the wrists, back of the hands or forearms and occasionally around the neck. These are the areas that get rubbed by cracked, sodden and dirty oilskin jackets, and by the residue brought up from the sea bed. The friction causes minute cracks in the skin which become infected by organisms present in fish slime. Cleanliness will lessen the risk of infection from the slime. The condition, if neglected, becomes very painful and disabling. Keep your clothing clean especially at the abrasion points. *See a doctor for treatment.*

See First Aid Chapter for more details on fish injuries.

💀 DANGERS IN THE TROPICS 💀

Fishing in Tropical Waters

Warm tropical waters and special circumstances in temperate waters can trigger problems that make certain fish inedible.

The US Air Force Survival Manual indicates:
- Fish can be edible or inedible and this can vary from area to area due to their diet or special seasonal characteristics.
- Cooking will not eradicate the poison.
- Great sea eels: Avoid them.
- Never eat eggs or entrails of tropical fish.
- Avoid all fish with round or box like bodies with hard, shell-like skins covered with bony plates or spines. They can have parrot-like mouths, small gill openings, belly fins which are small or absent. They are named after their shape: puffer fish, file fish, globe fish, trigger fish, trunk fish.

Barracudas: Large fish can cause serious digestive illness. Barracudas under three feet can be eaten with safety.

Oilfish: Tasty, white flaky flesh but very poisonous.

Bare Feet

Coral reefs, dead or alive, can severely cut your feet.

Slide Feet When Walking

Slide your feet along muddy or sandy bottoms. This will help you to avoid stepping on sting rays or spined fish. A misplaced step on a stingray, pinning down its body, will give it leverage to throw up its tail and stab you with its stinging spine. The broken off spine (because of the barbs) can only be removed by cutting it out.

Hands

Do not probe in dark holes or around rocks as your fingers can look like supper.

Sponges & Sea Urchins

They can slip fine needles of lime or silica into your skin where they will break off and fester. Do not dig them out but use lime juice or other citric acid to dissolve them.

Camouflaged Stone Fish

Well camouflaged stone fish with thirteen poisoned spines can be stepped on with bare feet or light running shoes. The poison can cause great agony and death. This poison should be treated as a snakebite.

Cone Snails

These have poisonous teeth that can bite (as well as long, slender pointed terebra snails). Cone shells have smooth, colorful mottled shells with elongated, narrow openings. They live under rocks, in crevices of coral reefs, and along rocky shores of protected bays. They are shy and active at night. They have a long mouth and a snout which is used to jab or inject their teeth. These teeth are actually tiny hypodermic needles, with a tiny poison gland on the back end of each. The sting is swift and produces acute pain, swelling, paralysis, blindness, and possible death in four hours. Avoid handling all cone shells.

Big Conchs

Handle with caution as they have razor-sharp trap doors which might suddenly jab out, puncturing your skin.

Sharks, Barracudas & Moray Eel

When crossing deeper portions of a reef, check the reef edge shadows for sharks, barracudas, and moray eels.

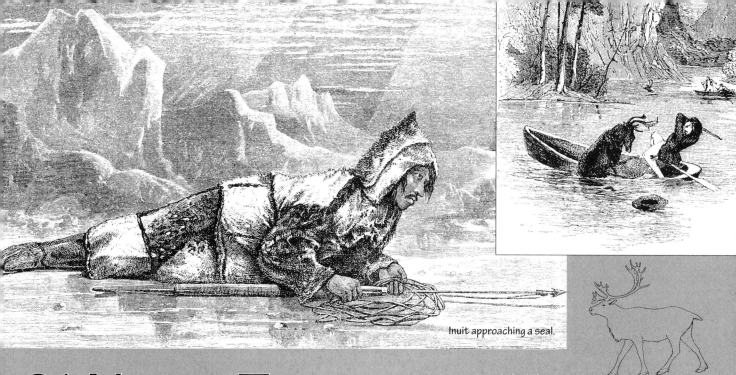

Inuit approaching a seal.

INDIAN & INUIT TRAPS

Traps are devices to trick animals into self imprisonment or possible death.

Indians had land, water, and air traps, and these acted by tension, ratchet (allowing motion in only one direction), gravity, spring, point, or blade. They were self set, ever set, victim set, or man set, and were released, when necessary, either by the hunter out of sight or by the victim. The following list shows the varieties of traps used by Indians north of Mexico and Inuit. These native peoples were very clever in making entrapment devices without the use of metal.

Enclosing Traps	Arresting Traps	Killing Traps
• pen	• meshes	• weights
• cage	• hooks	• piercer
• pit	• nooses	• knives
• door	• clutches	

Pen Traps: Were of the simplest kinds - darns (netting) placed in the water or stockades on land. Some of these were immense, covering many square miles. There were even pen structures that guided herds of buffalo over cliffs.

Cage: The cage was a pen (netting) for flying creatures.

Doors or gates: A whole class of traps were vertical shutters sliding between stakes and activated by some kind of latch or trigger.

Killing Traps: Usually work automatically after being triggered. The trigger mechanism usually consisted of a mechanism of setting and releasing. These mechanisms can be quite complex and the ideal mechanism is one that can be reused and easily transported.

Trapping methods compared to the actions of the human hand...

Arresting traps were all designed to take the place of the human hand.

Opened fingers: Meshes and netting
Bent forefinger: hooks
Encircling closed fingers: nooses
Grasping hand: the clutch (catch by grabbing)

Indians hunting by moonlight.

Deer Call

It is made from a piece of rhododendron leaf inserted into the split end of a twig. The sounds that you make can be varied by the amount of air pressure, by change in the angle of the lips upon the stick, and by cupping of the hands.

Deer Call

Leaf

Crow Caller

Study how crows call. The best way to attract them is to use the call they use when one of them has found a hawk or owl. Crows like to crowd one of these enemies and with the right call you will gather all the crows in the neighborhood.

Duck Hunting Blinds

Stick brush into the mud to form a dense screen. The inside of the screen should provide enough space for one or two hunters. The blind should shelter the hunters from high flying fowl. Decoys are planted in front of the blind.

Squirrel Scolding

A squirrel scolds when someone invades its territory. If you are quiet and a squirrel starts to scold you know that someone or something has entered their territory. This lets you know that an animal or human is approaching. Jays, crows, hawks, beavers, etc. have the same territorial characteristics.

Strike and rub two rocks together at an angle to attract squirrels.

Animals are Curious

Animals are curious especially when there is something new in their environment. Place a brightly colored handkerchief such as a flag on a stick. The flattering cloth will attract antelopes or deer who will walk right up to you. Make sure that the wind is blowing into your face. Small vermin are attracted to new noises as whistling or blowing on a blade of grass between the thumbs. They will come out of their burrows to see what's up.

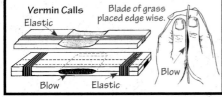

Vermin Calls
Elastic
Blade of grass placed edge wise.
Blow
Blow
Elastic

History of Traps

The use of traps is as old as human history. Traps serve the function of augmenting the food provider's ability to catch game while occupied somewhere else.

With ingenuity and understanding of an animal's habits the hunter was able to devise a mechanical system to catch animals and fish. Systems were developed by which the trapped animal would be transported out of reach of other predators. Hunters might have watched other predators, insect eating plants and their use of lures and liquid to drown the victim. The spider wove a net. The ermine going down rodent holes for their meals. Our ancestors also saw natural physical features as cliffs, quicksand, and depressions as areas to drive larger animals. "Modern" traps are all based on models of antiquity. A person who is attempting to survive in the wilderness will see many natural examples of traps and will also be able to choose from the examples of traps that are shown in this book.

It is important to remember that placing a trap is dangerous to animals and people. Traps should never be used in inhabited areas. Before setting any traps check the laws and regulations of the state or municipality.

Steel Traps

Steel traps are not described in this book. If used, you should follow the instructions enclosed with the trap and set under the supervision of an experienced trapper. The basic theory, of placing and baiting is the same as for the "primitive" traps discussed in this book.

Moose Calling Megaphone

Use canoe birch bark removed without injuring the tree. The horn can be the length of the forearm, the horn opening the width of the hand, and the mouth opening two fingers wide. This horn is only useful in the rutting season (end of September to October). The moose mating season.

The sounds that should be made are the love calls of the cow moose. The use of the moose call during the rutting season may attract a bull. Remember that he is cantankerous and dangerous.

Traditional moose calling megaphone.

The cow moose song is sung at three or four o'clock in the morning. The first call is for 1/2 minute. The megaphone is blown in a circle towards the ground. If a bull answers, the caller makes a second call and remains very still (remember the bull moose can move through the forest in total silence). Just before daybreak, make another call towards the forest terminating with the megaphone pointed towards the ground. At daybreak give a sequel but with the horn a foot from the ground. At this point, if you are lucky, you will hear a trampling of the undergrowth and a slashing of the antlers. If you imitate this sound the bull will get very mad and think that there is a second bull nearby. Make another cow call and then shuffle your feet through the leaves. The bull will think that another bull is on his way towards the cow.

Indian & Inuit Traps

The Inuit and Indian devices were of the simplest character, but very effective with unwary game. The victim was caught in a pound, deadfall, cage, hole, box, toil, noose, or jaw; or upon a hook, gorge, pale (upright wooden stake - impaled), knife, or the like.

The Indians placed an unstable prop, catch, or fastening, to be released in passing, curiously prying, gnawing, rubbing, or even in digesting. The Inuit used digesting by doubling up a skewer of baleen (whalebone), enclosed in frozen fat, and threw it in the snow for a bear to swallow. Once the frozen fat was swallowed by the bear the whalebone would pierce the internal organs and the bear would bleed to death.

Enclosing traps were common on land and in waters abounding with fish. Sir William Parry (1790-1855), the British arctic explorer, describes traps of ice with doors of the same material. The tribes of California and of the plains dug pits and covered them with brush on which a dead rabbit was tied. The hunter concealed beneath grasped a landing bird by its feet, dragged it below, and crushed it between the knees. Arresting traps were the most common, working by meshes, barbs, nooses, or by means of manual seizure. The natives were familiar with the gill net, trawl lines (wide-mouthed fishing net dragged by a boat(s) along the bottom), gorge hook, snares, springs, trawl snares, and birdlime (a sticky substance spread on twigs to trap small birds). Killing traps included ice, stone, and log deadfalls for crushing, impaling devices, and set knives for braining or for inciting mutual slaughter. The object of perhaps the most ingenious and efficient of Indian traps, consisting of a sharp blade enclosed in frozen fat, which was set up on a wolf path. When a wolf in licking the fat cut its tongue the smell of blood infuriated the whole pack (hungry especially in the winter) and drove them to destroy one another. In this way the Indians would eliminate the major competition for animal food in the winter.

Indians of North America

The Indians of North America used traps as:
· Deadfall traps made from logs and boulders.
· Snares made from horsehair (after the Europeans had imported the horse), from rawhide, and cordage made from plants.
· Pitfall traps for birds and animals.
· Woven baskets to catch fish and rodents.
· Toxic plants to paralyze fish so that they would float to the surface.
· Throwing sticks and bolas for birds.
· Animal drives: Indians were adept at erecting channeling barriers and then driving buffalo over cliffs. Indians would camouflage themselves in hides, stampede a herd, and guide them with beaters (Indians standing, waving and shouting) over a cliff or into a dead end valley.

String

Catching a bird with a baited skewer.

Animal path Into the woods.

FINDING ANIMALS

Many animals live at the meeting point of two different ecological areas. An example being between the forest and meadow (forest to hide, meadow to eat), water and land (land to eat or rest and water to escape). Find pathways that intersect these environments and these areas are prime areas for hunting. The photograph shows the forest meeting the meadow with an animal "highway" crossing the barrier.

GOOD TRAPPING AREAS

Chose your terrain and cover:
- Bushy woods bordering lakes, streams, hills, rocky canyons, springs, thickets, swamps, hollow logs, and arched roots.
- Abundance of food for animals.
- Identify dens, animal signs, tracks, trails, runways.
- Look for areas that are well drained by little, crooked, bush fringed streams that come down partly wooded hills.
- Places in thickets where a number of game trails cross.
- Overhang on river bank or stream is good for muskrat.

Use scent in small amounts as too much will arouse suspicion rather than attract the animal.

FOOD THAT ATTRACTS ANIMALS

Chose an animal's favorite food:
Muskrat: Carrots, parsnips, fish, flagroot, mussel meat.
Raccoon: Wild grapes, pokeberries, fish, small birds, frogs, mussel meat and persimmons.
Fox: Mice, rabbits, small birds, poultry, eggs, burnt cracklings, decayed fish.
Mink: Fish, small birds, muskrat, meat, poultry.
Skunk: Grubs, birds, roots, berries, and bird's eggs.
Weasel: Likes to kill its food, so you should use live rabbits, birds, poultry.

ANIMAL BAIT & LURES

- Animals have a strong reliance on scent in their daily lives. For this reason we use a scented bait for the specific animal and make sure that human scent does not contaminate the site.
- An ideal bait should contain an odor that is volatile (odor giving) and at the same time has a long time volatility. These are the same specifications as for a lady's perfume. The odors produced activate the saliva glands, or territorial instincts, in animal and make them think "food or an intruder". To avoid drying the bait or having it rot too fast, traps should be set in the shade. The required odor of the bait will vary from animal to animal.
- Some animals and birds having a keen sense of sight will require movement to be attracted to bait. That means you have to provide live bait which you would have to catch in some form of tilt platform pitfall trap.

ODORS THAT REPEL ANIMALS

- The most negative scent, to animals, is the human scent. Never handle traps with your bare hands or store them around the house.
- Any new smell that animals might encounter (even human if they have never smelled a human before). But a new scent might also attract their curiosity.
- Use smoke from a dry grass fire to remove human sent that might be present at a trap site or on a trap.
- Certain animals will avoid areas where they can smell the odor of their deadly enemies. Field mice will avoid areas where there is an ermine scent. Ermines are so audacious that they will enter into mouse holes, eat the occupants, and in cold climates line the former mouse den with the fur of their victims and move in.

CURIOSITY

Hang a piece of tin, aluminum, tinfoil in shape of a small fish one foot above the trap.

SCENTS

Use the scent of glands of beavers, muskrat, mink, fox, raccoon, or weasel. These scents can be blended in a fish oil base or used unblended. It is a complicated procedure to get the right mix without experience. Animal droppings and urine can be used but the secretions should be from the same kind of animal one is trapping. Fish oil makes an excellent lure for fish-eating animals.

THREE CATEGORIES OF SCENTS

Unusual & new scents: will be approached with caution.
Scent that means food: This scent is usually given off by the usual food of the animal.
Territorial odors: which are secreted by the animal and rubbed or urinated at the limits of its territory. This scent, depending upon the season, has sexual connotations. Using a scent of this type, in the right season, will cause the animal to lose many of its cautious ways. They will act in an aggressive manner which will help in trapping. The adjacent list of scents that when added to bait will produce the desired effect.

These scents might be of interest to wildlife photographers as they can mount their cameras and place the scented bait on a remote electronic shutter release.

Porcupine

ARTIFICIAL LURES
TRAPPING OR ANIMAL PHOTOGRAPHY

Do not confuse scents with bait. Bait is food that an animal likes to eat. Scents are lures appealing to the animal's sense of smell. These smells arouse the curiosity of the animal or its sexual impulse. The more wary the animal the less scent should be used. Scents will not mask human odor.

- Scents should be made in advance of the trapping season since, as a rule, they improve with time.
- To test the scent find a trail of the animal and put three drops ten feet from several trees or stumps. Check the next day to see if the animal's track deviates to inspect the scent. If it has the scent works.

Some Basic Ingredients

Fish Oil: For animals as raccoon, fox, wildcat, and coyote. Use any fish, trout, carp, and suckers are the most popular. Cut fish into small pieces and put them a glass jar which is stored in a warm spot. Do not seal the bottle but cover it to keep out insects. The oil from the fish will rise to the top. Fish oil can be used alone or mixed with other lures.

Fox Lures
- Chop one pound of muskrat meat and let it decompose as for the fish oil. Add some fox urine.
- Eel oil, 4 ozs; beaver castor, 1 oz; muskrat musk, 1 oz; skunk scent, 2 drops; tincture of asafetida, 4 drops. Age in a cool dark spot for 6 weeks.

Coyote Lures
- Trout oil, 4 ozs; beaver castor, 1 oz; asafetida, 1/4 oz; muskrat musk, 3 ozs; skunk scent, 5 drops. Age 2 months on a dark cool place.
- Coyote urine, 2 ozs; sun-rendered fish oil, 4 ozs; tincture of tonquin musk, 1 oz; valerian, 8 drops; beaver castor, 1/2 oz; skunk scent, 2 drops.

Mink Lures
- Sun-rendered trout oil, 4 ozs; tincture of muskrat musk, 1 oz; mink musk, 1/2 oz; beaver castor, 1/2 oz; oil of anise, 10 drops. Age 2 months.
- Commercial or homemade fish oil, 2 ozs; muskrat musk, 1/2 oz; tincture of tonquin musk, 8 drops; mink musk, 1 oz. A fairly efficient mixture.

Muskrat Lures
- Muskrat musk, 1 oz; mink musk, 1/2 oz; glycerin, 1/2 oz; oil of anise, 10 drops. Age 6 weeks.

Opossum Lures
- Fish oil, 4 ozs.; tincture of asafetida, 1 oz.; oil of lovage, 1/2 oz.; liquid camphor, 6 drops.

Raccoon Lures
- Honey, 4 ozs; beaver castor, 1/2 oz; muskrat musk, 1/2 oz; oil of anise, 20 drops.
- Fish oil, 1/2 pint; anise oil 12 drops; strained honey 1 oz. Age for 2 months in a dark cool place.
- Anise oil alone.

Skunk Lures
- Oil of skunk flesh, 4 ozs.; fish oil, 2 ozs.; muskrat musk, 2 ozs.; tincture of asafetida, 1/2 oz.

Weasel Lures
- Fish oil, 4 ozs; weasel musk, 2 ozs; beaver castor, 1/2 oz; rabbit blood, 2 ozs; oil of anise, 6 drops. Age in a cool dark spot for 6 weeks.

Wolverine

ANIMAL BAIT & LURES

STALKING

Stalking

Mountain Man

Inuit Netting Birds

STALKING

Study the wind and air currents as they can carry your scent to the animal's keen nose. *Always stalk against the wind.* When stalking in the mountains, early in the morning, remember that *air currents rise* in the morning because of the heat from the sun's rays. Always stalk from above. Animals' eyesight is usually not good but wear clothing that blends into the background. To confuse the animal, push a branch screen in front of you. Inuit usually push a white cloth screen fastened to runners. Turkey hunters in the south drape themselves with Spanish Moss.

STALKING CARIBOU

Walk towards the animal in a bent over position using a stick or rifle to simulate the front legs. Stop every so often as if browsing. If the wind is in your favor you should be able to approach the animal quite easily.

TWO-MAN STALK

Both hunters bend over. The second hunter rests his head on the front man's back holding on to his belt. Move forward like a four-legged animal. Make sure that the wind is blowing towards you.

DEER STALKING

Make sure the wind is towards you. Watch the deer while it is feeding. You will notice that the deer will feed with its head down and raise its head periodically to glance around. The white tail will twitch *just before it raises its head.* At this point you should freeze. The deer looks up and then lowers its head to feed again. At this point you can advance. With this method and some luck you can approach within ten feet the animal. Notice that the wind direction might be different close to the deer. To approach a branch screen might be helpful.

MOVEMENT OF DEER

· Deer move down to the water at dusk and before the sunrise. Air currents move uphill from the water at night. The deer will move into the night breeze.
· Deer move uphill when daylight comes. At the same time the wind shifts downhill towards the water. The deer are moving uphill into the morning breeze.
· Move into the breeze when approaching deer as they cannot smell your odor.

TRICKS TO APPROACH DEER

· Avoid light colored clothing, as it is more easily seen when you move. This is especially true where there are dark forests in the background.
· Camouflage your skin by growing a beard or using fire coals to mark your face.
· Remain motionless at a good location.
· Avoid scented soap, hair tonic, or body lotions as these odors might give you away.
· Rub old clothes with cedar oil or stand in fire smoke to camouflage your human scent.

INUIT BIRD SNARES

Inuit would place snares in shallow lakes to catch diving birds. These snares would be on lines over 20 feet long with each line having 50 to 60 snares.

Snare

Duck and Snare

BOLA

The Inuit use a bola to hunt flying birds and running animals. These bolas are made with cord or strips of hide approximately a yard (1m) long. The weights are carried inside leather pouches. The bola is thrown by holding the center and twirling it above the head. When flying the bola opens up while rotating towards the game. With practice it can be used very efficiently. A bola is used in South America where it is used on large animals to entangle their front feet.

Bola

SEA GULLS

To catch sea gulls tie a hook, sharp nail, wedge of wood, or sharpened bone to a string or fish line. Place some bait, piece of decomposing fish or meat, on the hook and tie the string to a sturdy branch or post. The sea gull will swallow the food and be caught.

Bait

MEXICAN GOURD TRICK

Float some empty plastic bottles or brush covered logs among a flock of geese or ducks on a pond. Once the flock is accustomed to their presence, place a plastic bottle over your head, leaving a slit for your eyes. Gradually swim towards the flock. When you reach a duck grab it by its feet and pull it under the water, twist its neck, and put it into a bag. If a plastic bottle is not available use some logs with weeds on them.

Plastic Bottle

THROWING STICK

This stick should be well balanced for your hand and approximately 2 feet (60 cm) long. Practice throwing it overhand and underhand

Throwing Stick

as targets at different heights. It is very effective at stunning animals or temporarily incapacitating them.

ANIMAL BURROW TRAPPING

To force an animal to leave its burrow one can place some burning leaves into the entrance or pour water down the hole. Traps would be set up at the exit holes.

Wood Rat

Rodent Skewer

This method was used by some Indians to catch small furry game in its burrow. Use a flexible

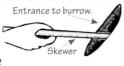

Entrance to burrow.
Skewer

branch from a willow tree with a fork at the end. If you see a rabbit or groundhog run down its burrow (there are a few burrows) flex the stick down the hole and upon feeling the softness of the animal quickly twist the fork of the stick into its fur. This will "tie" the animal to the stick which you will slowly withdraw form the hole.
If you feel that you are losing your "grip" give the animal a few gentle stabs while twisting.

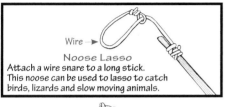

Wire

Noose Lasso
Attach a wire snare to a long stick. This noose can be used to lasso to catch birds, lizards and slow moving animals.

Least Chipmunk

Rabbit Stick

This stick was used to hunt groups of rabbits. A group of men would form a large circle and gradually tighten the circle while scaring rabbits into the center where they would throw rabbit sticks at the rabbits crowded into the restricted area. These sticks act as boomerangs but it does not return to the thrower.

Rabbit Stick

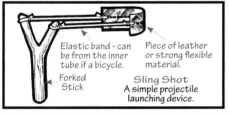

Elastic band - can be from the inner tube if a bicycle.

Piece of leather or strong flexible material.

Forked Stick

Sling Shot
A simple projectile launching device.

Barbs

Sticks in ground to guide bird into trap.

Turkey Trap

Grain Trail

Well embedded crossed sticks. The sticks are cut so that they are barbed to help retain the turkey's neck.

Quail: Use an inward spiraling stick fence in which you have dropped a path of seeds going to the center.
Geese: Lace a trail of wild grain that leads into a ditch or depression at least four feet deep. Rush the geese as they cannot escape because of the limited running range to start flying. They have difficulty spreading their wings.
Turkeys: Place a trail of seeds leading to a structure like a picket fence. The turkey will follow the bait below the picket and then will raise its head which will become trapped because of the direction of the feathers. Rush the turkey before it has time to untangle itself.

Trapping Birds
Using a Sticky Substance

This method catches birds by sticking them to the branch of a tree. The glue is made by boiling evergreen tree bark to extract the sap. This sap, when boiled, becomes a sticky gum that can be smeared on a branch on which a bird will alight. To help in attracting birds one adds seeds of grain or rice to the gum.

Deadfall Traps for Birds

These traps, which are similar to animal traps, are smaller and have a more sensitive triggering device. *See the Figure 4 Deadfall trap as an example.* Animals usually approach a trap because of the smell of the bait. Grain eating birds approach by seeing the bait so a *trail of grain* is required. As birds are not as strong as animals the weight of a dead fall trap can be less than that for an animal. A brick or flat pieces of wood can be used. If you want a live trap you can used a wire mesh cage instead of a weight. The birds that you will attract will be ground feeders as pheasant, quail, pigeons, partridges.
All birds are edible and are easy to catch with snares, baited hooks, noose at the end of a pole, deadfalls, and one way tunnels.

Grain Eating Birds

Large grain eating birds usually are ground birds. The grain can be laid down in a trail leading to a trigger. Some grain is placed below the trigger which is then disturbed by the bird, when it raises its head, and the trap falls. *See the Figure 4 Deadfall trap as an example.*

Carrion Eating Birds

Birds that eat carrion (crows, vultures, ravens) will be attracted by using meat as bait. The meat has to smell as they will be attracted by the odor, the same way as animals. If the weather is hot and dry the meat should be covered with fur or feathers as otherwise it will dry and lose its odor. Other bait can be killed animals (roadkill), eggs, porridge, etc.

Birds of Prey

Are attracted by live rabbits, birds or mice. If meat is used it has to be very fresh.

Noose & Snare Traps

These, as in the case of animals, are placed on trails used by ground running birds. Possible locations can be gaps in a fence, beside boulders. Birds and animals will pass close to them so that they will not be seen.

Snares close to boulder in a field.

Game Birds
Will be attracted by berries, wheat, sunflower seeds, and maize. These can be mixed together and scattered in an open sunny spot near the trap.

Pheasant

Entry Bird Traps
Pheasant & Partridge Traps

These are ground birds which usually hide by running through the undergrowth. Bait can be grain, berries, beans or peas. It is easy to trap these birds because they have stiff feathers that lay back in one direction and the feathers are difficult to bend.

Tunnel with Grain
Trail of Grain

Walk in Trap

Dig a near horizontal hole into the ground. Place a seed trail leading to the hole. The bird will follow the seeds into the hole (which gets narrower) and when it wants to back out its feathers will wedge against the walls of the hole. The bird will have difficulty to withdraw and can be caught.

Piece of wood with a hole.

Trail of Grain

Head Trap

A bottle or jar with a fairly large mouth is buried, mouth up, in the ground. Seed is placed leading up to the bottle and placed in the bottle. The feeding bird will place its head into the bottle but will not be able to withdraw it as its feathers will get wedged. This same method can be used with a flat piece of wood, which is weighed down, having a head sized hole cut in it.

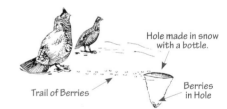

Hole made in snow with a bottle.

Trail of Berries
Berries in Hole

Soft Drink Bottle Trap

This trap can be used in the summer or winter. In the winter the bottle is pushed mouth down into the snow. If the bottle is too narrow it can be tilted back and forth to enlarge the hole. Remove the bottle. The snow should be fairly firm and coarse. Add some water to harden the snow. Fill the hole with some wild berries that you can find on bushes in the winter. The bird will eat the berries until its head gets stuck in the hole because of its feathers. A similar system can be used in the summer but the earth has to be firm.

Seagull

BEE HIVE TRAP

This trap is used for larger predators such as wolves, coyote, and fox. An igloo like structure is built with boulders. The sides slope inwards and the top remains open. The floor should be covered with boards or large flat rocks. This is to prevent

Bee Hive Trap

Entrance

trapped animals from digging themselves out. The trap is baited. The trap should be built using gloves and left unbaited for a few weeks so that the animals can get used to its presence.

BOTTLE TRAP

The bottle is buried in a field and a flat stone, supported by pebbles, is placed over the entrance. The flat stone will offer shelter to small animals. Walk in a spiral around the bottle while

Rock Cover

Entrance

Bottle Trap

Bottle

beating the grass and brush with a stick. Animals will be herded and take shelter under the rock. Use gloves when installing the bottle. The bottle should be aged for a few weeks to remove any trace of human scent.

BOX TRAP

This trap has a sliding door held open by a rod supported by a fulcrum. There is a peg trigger release. The trap is baited

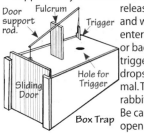

Door support rod.

Fulcrum

Trigger

Sliding Door

Hole for Trigger

Box Trap

and when the animal enters the trap its head or back disturbs the peg trigger and the door drops trapping the animal. This trap can catch rabbits, skunks, bobcats. Be careful when you open the door.

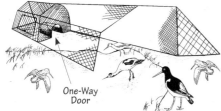

One-Way Door

WALK-IN BIRD TRAP

This trap is used for ground feeding birds. The trap is made of a fine wire or netting. The mesh should not be too dense as the birds might feel insecure if they cannot see through the 'wall'. Place seeds or other food on the ground and birds will walk into the one-way net. For wading birds place the trap when the tide goes out.

Entry traps are traps that are entered by the animal and from which they cannot escape. The animal will not be injured. This trap can be used to catch an animal or bird that will be transported to another site.

ENTRY TUBE TRAP

Can be made of stove piping or plastic plumbing tube. Bait is placed in the trap and the animal enters by the small tube but cannot leave because of the one-way funnel. The animal can be removed by removing the mesh.

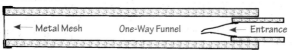

Metal Mesh   One-Way Funnel   Entrance

PITFALL TRAPS

The trap requires:
• The right depth and size for the animal.
• Camouflage to hide the presence of the trap.
• A retaining device.

This probably is the most primitive trap still being used. Humans must have gotten the idea for this trap after falling into a hole. Natural pitfall traps would be sinkholes that are formed in a limestone area were you would also find caves. It can be used to catch any animal except one living permanently in the water. A pitfall trap is made by digging a hole and camouflaging it. This trap relies upon surprise as it is built on the pathway of an animal. The second feature that is required is a way to retain the animal in the trap. This can be done by making the trap deep, lining its walls so that the animal can not climb out or burrowing animals cannot dig their way out. Sharp upright stakes can be embedded in the floor of the trap and the animal killed when it falls on the spikes. The pit could be lined with clay or other impervious material and filled with water so that the animal can drown. Modern pitfall traps can be used to catch live animals. In this case a revolving balanced lid (tilt trap) is placed on the trap and bait is put on the sensitive part of the lid. The predator jumps on the food and the lid rotates. The animal falls into the hole and the rotated lid levels off not letting it escape. Pitfall traps can be baited or unbaited. By choosing the bait one could partially predetermine what animal one will catch.

PLATFORM PITFALL

The Inuit use a tilting platform trap to catch Arctic Fox. This trap is dug in the snow and has steep walls. The top is covered with blocks of ice with an opening of 1 1/2 feet in diameter. Bait is *attached* to a tilting platform a foot below the entrance. The tilting platform is designed so that it will right itself with the bait always returning to the top. This trap can catch a few fox without being opened.
A similar trap can be used for rodents but the walls should be sheet metal or they will dig or gnaw their way out. A buried barrel could be used as the pitfall trap.

TILT PLATFORM TRAP

This trap is built over a box, basket, or pit. The bait is placed (glued or attached) on a board that is balanced over a central pivot. A bird landing on the board or walking on it will tilt the lid and fall into the box below. This type of trap can be used on the ground or in trees.

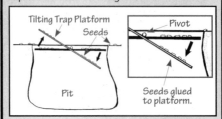

Tilting Trap Platform
Seeds

Pivot

Pit

Seeds glued to platform.

SNARE TRAPPING

This system of trapping uses a noose which is tied so that it will slide closed under tension. The material to use as a snare is rawhide, natural cordage, brass wire, sinews from animals or horsehair.

PASSIVE SNARE TRAP

These snares are successful with animals who have *regular pathways*. A passive snare trap does not use any bait to lure the animal. Snares can be neck snares or foot snares. Neck snares are usually used for smaller animals and birds. Foot snares would be used for deer, antelope, and bear.

ACTIVE SNARE TRAP

Baited traps are active traps because they attract the animal with the bait. The bait tempts the animal to pass its head through the noose. The noose can be activated by some trigger mechanism.

TRAPPING TRICKS

Narrow down a trail: Place a branch, chunk of wood, piece of bark beside the trail to narrow it to guide the animal into the set trap. Make sure that the material used fits into the environment and that there is no evidence of humans.
• Find natural traffic points; opening in a fence, wood or snowdrifts, edge of bushes, log piles and brush pits.
• Set traps at the opening of a den.
• Animals nearly always follow worn trails.
• Determine if animals are present by placing some bait at strategic spots and visit these locations the next morning.
• Set traps on a log spanning a waterway.
• Always make sure that the surroundings have not been disturbed after setting a trap (brush out your tracks, straighten broken weeds, replace earth and leaves).

SNARES

Are the most common traps as they can easy to transport, easy installation, and the choice of location is very simple. The snare trap is made of brass wire, string, plant cordage, roots, horsehair, rawhide, dried animal gut, emergency cable saw, etc. It has to be placed so that the loop stays open. When cord is used a few sticks might have to be used to keep the loop open. The best material is a brass wire as it keeps its round shape and is easily twisted to make the loop through which the moving part of the wire will slide.

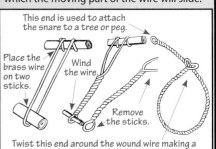

This end is used to attach the snare to a tree or peg.

Place the brass wire on two sticks.

Wind the wire.

Remove the sticks.

Twist this end around the wound wire making a slip loop that will slide closed under tension.

Winding a Brass Wire Snare

Eastern Mole

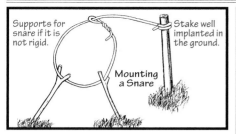

Supports for snare if it is not rigid.

Stake well implanted in the ground.

Mounting a Snare

Snares positioned around trunk of tree.

SQUIRREL TRAP

Arrange several small noose on an inclined trunk. The squirrel will pass its head through the noose and fall off the log. The dangling squirrel will not deter other squirrels from being caught.

Bough   Snare

DUCK BOUGH FENCE NOOSE TRAP

Ducks go ashore to sun themselves and for the night. They usually use small islands as protection from predators. Wooden boughs are planted in the ground. They are positioned so that they form a fence around the island overlapping each other by the width of a duck. Snares are suspended from the center of the boughs. The ducks, to get onto the island, have to pass through the hoops and are caught by the snares. Multiple catches can be made in one night.

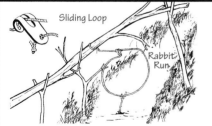

Sliding Loop

Rabbit Run

TRAPPING RABBITS OR COYOTES

Rabbits are not instinctively afraid or conscious of traps and they have regular "rabbit runs" which make them easy to trap. These regular and well warn runs show a trapper where to place his snares. Once the snares have been placed the hunter would approach the runways from a distance. Making as much noise as possible. All the rabbits in the area would head along the runways and some will be caught. This method can also be used for coyotes but heavier wires, stake, and sliding loops have to be used.

Bone   Fish

Barrier so that bear has to step into trap to approach the food.

Snare

Bear Foot Snare Trap
There is a covered pit below the snare.

Wooden Spike Trap
The spikes and pit are camouflaged.

FOOT TRAPS

These are similar to snares but are placed in an area where an animal is bound to pass. The animal enters its foot into the trap and a triggering mechanism or some form of friction causes the trap to close on the animal's foot. This method can be used to trap deer at a watering hole. Prepare a noose intertwined with grass in which sharp spokes of wood sticks have been hidden. The animal, wading into the water, seeing an empty area in the middle of this grass island places its foot in it and the wooden sticks hold the animal's foot and while it tries to withdraw the snare will tighten and the animal is caught. The snare is attached to a tree or stake.

Foot traps are very dangerous.

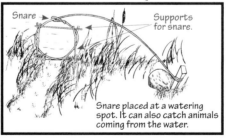

Snare   Supports for snare.

Snare placed at a watering spot. It can also catch animals coming from the water.

• • • • • • • • • • • • • •
DANGERS OF RABBIT FEVER

• The *Tularemia* germ can be fatal if it gets
• into an open scratch or wound. Wear gloves
• when cleaning a wild rabbit or work a heavy
• soap lather into your skin *before* opening
• the body. The soap film will protect your skin.
• Thoroughly wash your hands when finished.
• Do not hunt slow sluggish rabbits. Wait 2 or 3
• weeks *after a heavy frost* before hunting for
• rabbit. *Cook all rabbits until well done.* The rab-
• bit fever germ can be destroyed by intensive
• heat. Be very careful when trapping as you will
• not know the health of the rabbit. *Page 610.*
• • • • • • • • • • • • • •

NATURAL SPRING TRAPS

These are traps that use a spring. Either a flat spring or a coiled spring to release the trapping mechanism. Metal spring traps will not be discussed in this book. Natural springs can be made of young trees which are bent and will recoil when the triggering mechanism is activated. The tree spring trap is used, with a snare, when you want to *remove your catch from the reach of predators.* The quarry enters the snare, disengages the trigger and the spring (bent tree) flings the animal into the air, the noose tightens, and the quarry is out of reach of any predator. The same concept is used in an enclosure or box where the quarry enters and goes into the noose, activates the trigger and releases the spring. The catch will be protected from larger predators because it remains in the box.

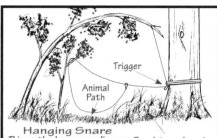

Trigger

Animal Path

Hanging Snare
This method used a sapling as the tension or spring device.

Brush to make animal stay on track.

Indian Sapling Spring Noose
This method used by the Indians and early settlers consisted of a sapling tied down to the ground with a salted rawhide string. The animal, attracted to the salt, eats the rawhide while standing on the snare. The eaten trigger (rawhide) releases the sapling and the snare catches the animal.

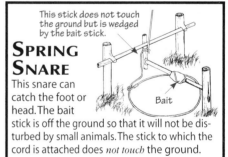

This stick does not touch the ground but is wedged by the bait stick.

SPRING SNARE

This snare can catch the foot or head. The bait stick is off the ground so that it will not be disturbed by small animals. The stick to which the cord is attached does *not touch* the ground.

Bait

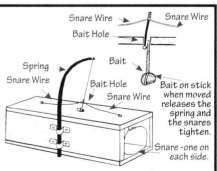

Snare Wire   Snare Wire

Bait Hole

Bait

Spring Snare Wire

Bait Hole

Snare Wire

Bait on stick when moved releases the spring and the snares tighten.

Snare -one on each side.

DOUBLE BOX SNARE

This box can be transported and used on trees (for squirrels) and on the ground. The bait is placed at the center so that the animal can approach from either side. The pulling on the bait will release the trigger which tightens the snare. As the animal will be caught in the box it will be protected from predators.

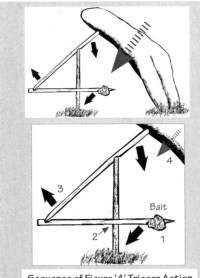

FIGURE '4' DEADFALL

This is the classic form of the Dead Fall Trap. One of the simplest methods of trapping. The rock, heavy plank, log or ice blocks is braced as in the illustrations. This method can catch animals from the size of a mouse to a bear the weight of the deadfall being the limiting factor.

Sequence of Figure '4' Trigger Action
1 Bait stick moved.
2 Bait stick disengaged from notch.
3 Angle stick loses its support.
4 Rock falls.

FIGURE '4' PORTABLE TRIGGER

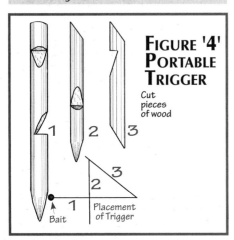

Cut pieces of wood

1 Bait
2
3 Placement of Trigger

PORTABLE SNARE TRIGGER BLOCK

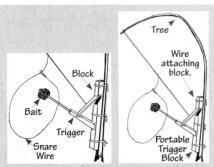

Bait
Block
Trigger
Snare Wire
Tree
Wire attaching block.
Portable Trigger Block

The snare trigger block is transportable and can be assembled in any location. It is very handy, especially in survival situations, as a well made sensitive block can be used while traveling. A trapper will not have to spend time looking for the material at each stop to make a trigger.

DEADFALL TRIGGER ACTIONS

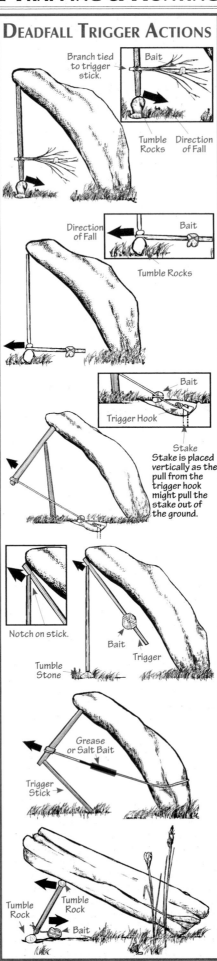

Branch tied to trigger stick.
Bait
Tumble Rocks
Direction of Fall

Direction of Fall
Bait
Tumble Rocks

Bait
Trigger Hook
Stake
Stake is placed vertically as the pull from the trigger hook might pull the stake out of the ground.

Notch on stick.
Tumble Stone
Bait
Trigger

Grease or Salt Bait
Trigger Stick

Tumble Rock
Tumble Rock
Bait

Winter Beaver Lodge Trap

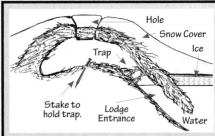

Hole
Snow Cover
Ice
Trap
Stake to hold trap.
Lodge Entrance
Water

This type of trap was used by the non-Indian trappers in the Rocky Mountains during the 1850's. It involves opening a beaver lodge from the top and installing a trap and closing the hole. Beavers were trapped in the winter for their heavy winter fur.

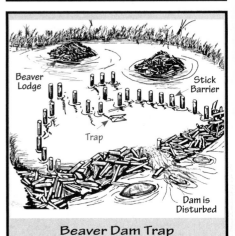

Beaver Lodge
Stick Barrier
Trap
Dam is Disturbed

Beaver Dam Trap

A wooden stick fence is erected between the beaver lodge and the beaver dam. A trap is placed in an opening of the fence. The dam is partially broken open to let water escape. The beavers will leave the security of their lodge to repair the dam and be trapped.

CATCHING INSECTS

Lantern
Sheet
Insects
Water Basin

Night Flying Insects

Night insects are attracted by light. Mount a light source behind a white sheet. The sheet should be hung at an angle. Place a flat basin with water below the blanket. Insects attracted to light will bump into the sheet and some will fall into the water. As they will be wet they will not be able to fly away.

INSECTS IN BUSHES

Place a sheet below a bush, plant or tree and shake the plant. Insects will fall onto the blanket. Pick them off the blanket and put them into a container. You can pick larger insects, as caterpillars, off plants. Pick up or break open logs to find termites, slugs and other high protein tidbits.

Termites, Caterpillars, Locusts, Grasshoppers, Earthworms

These are an excellent source of protein and can be fried and eaten. Remove legs, wings, burn the hair of caterpillars and fry.

DEADFALL TRAP

Deadfall trap triggered.

Deadfall Trap

Bait
Trigger
Weight

Vertical Trigger Stick

Vertical stick guides for deadfall log.
Additional weight for deadfall log.
Bait on horizontal trigger stick.

Deadfall Log

TREE DEADFALL

This trapping method drops a weight from a tree onto the unsuspecting animal. This trap is located on a well used animal path, on a favorite scratch tree, or on a baited tree. The triggering device is usually a trip wire or slip hook device. This trapping device is used for larger animals that use regular paths (deer, badgers). The weight should drop on the neck or back to immobilize the animal. The weight of the stone or log, the height it is placed above the ground, and the triggering device will depend upon the animal you want to catch.

Weight

Trigger

Bait

Brace or Dead Log

A fisher inspecting a deadfall trap.

These are traps that use a heavy object supported by a brace. The brace can be destabilized by a trigger mechanism which is baited. The animal is attracted to the bait, disturbs the trigger, which destabilizes the brace and the heavy object falls on the animal. In North America these traps were developed by the Indians and Inuit. The Indians used logs or rocks and the Inuit used blocks of ice. Unattended traps are dangerous.

NATIVE BOW & ARROW

The bow and arrow were the most useful and universal weapon and implement of the hunt possessed by the natives North of Mexico for striking or piercing distant objects.

ARROWS

An Indian arrow is made up of six parts: Head, shaft, foreshaft, shaftment, feathering, and nock. These differ in material, form, measurement, decoration, and assemblage, according to individuals, locality, and tribe.

Arrowheads have three parts: Body, tang, and barbs.

There are two kinds of arrowheads: Blunt and the sharp. Blunt heads are for stunning, being top shaped.

Sharp arrowheads are of two classes: The *lanceolate* (narrow oval shape tapering to a point at each side), which can be withdrawn, and the *sagittate*, intended for holding game or for rankling (to stay) in the wound. The former are used for hunting, the latter in war or retrieving arrows. In the SW a sharpened foreshaft of hard wood serves for the head. Arctic and NW coast arrows have heads of ivory, bone, wood, or copper, as well as of stone; elsewhere they are more generally of stone, chipped or polished. Many of the arrowheads from those two areas are either two pronged, three pronged, or harpoon shaped.

Attaching Head

The head is attached to the shaft or foreshaft by lashing with sinew, by riveting, or with gum. Among the Inuit the barbed head of bone is stuck loosely into a socket on the shaft, so that this will come out and the head rankle in the wound.

Barbed Head

The barbs of the ordinary chipped head are usually alike on both sides, but in examples from ivory, bone, or wood the barbing is either bilateral or unilateral, one barbed or many barbed, alike on the two sides or different.

Arrows in Ceremonies

In addition to their use in hunting and in war, arrows are commonly used in games and ceremonies. Among certain Hopi priesthoods arrowheads are tied to bandoleers as ornaments, and among the Zuñi they are frequently attached to fetishes.

Arrow Shafts

Arrow shafts of the simplest kind are reeds, canes, or stems of wood. In the Arctic region they are made of driftwood or are bits of hone lashed together, and are rather short, owing to the scarcity of material. The foreshaft is a piece of ivory, bone, or heavy wood. Among the Inuit foreshafts are of bone or ivory on wooden shafts; in California, of hard wood on shafts of pithy or other light wood; from California across the continent to Florida, of hard wood on cane shafts. The shaftments in most arrows are plain; but on the W coast they are painted with stripes for identification. The Plains Indians and the Jicarillas Apaches cut shallow grooves lengthwise down their arrow shafts, called "lightning marks," or "blood grooves," and are said by Indians to keep the shaft from warping or to direct the flight.

Feathering

The feathering is an important feature in the Indian arrow, differing in the species of birds, the kind and number of feathers and in their form, length, and manner of setting. As to the number of feathers, arrows are either without feathering, two feathered, or three feathered. As to form, feathers are whole, as among most of the Inuit and some SW tribes, or halved or notched on the edges. In length they vary from the very short feathering on SW arrows, with long reed shafts and heavy foreshafts, to the long feathering on Plains arrows, with their short shafts of hard wood. The feathers are set on the shaftment either flat or radiating; the ends are lashed with sinew, straight or doubled under, and the middles are either free or glued down. In some arrows there is a slight rifling, due perhaps to the twist needed to make a tight fit.

Nocks

The nocks of arrows, the part containing the notch for the string, are, in the Arctic, flat; in the south, where reed shafts were employed, cylindrical; and in localities where the shafts were cut, bulbous.

Other uses of Arrows

Besides its use as a piercing or striking projectile, special forms of the arrow were employed as a toy, in gaming, in divining, in rainmaking, in ceremony, in symbolism, and in miniature forms with prayer sticks. *The main factor in arrow making was the length each users arm. The manufacture of arrows was usually attended with much ceremony.*

Native Arrow Flight

The utmost flight, the certainty of aim, and the piercing power of original Indian arrows are not known, and stories about them are greatly exaggerated. The hunter or warrior got as near to his victim as possible. In shooting he drew his right hand to his ear. His bow register scarcely exceeded 60 pounds, yet arrows are said to have gone quite through the body of a buffalo.

BOW & ARROW

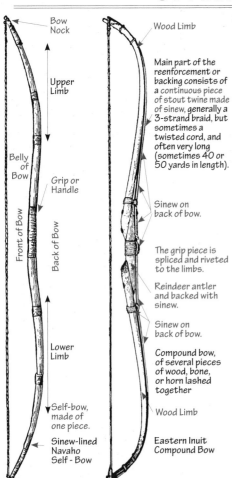

Bow Nock

Upper Limb

Belly of Bow

Grip or Handle

Front of Bow

Back of Bow

Lower Limb

Self-bow, made of one piece.

Sinew-lined Navaho Self - Bow

Wood Limb

Main part of the reenforcement or backing consists of a continuous piece of stout twine made of sinew, generally a 3-strand braid, but sometimes a twisted cord, and often very long (sometimes 40 or 50 yards in length).

Sinew on back of bow.

The grip piece is spliced and riveted to the limbs.

Reindeer antler and backed with sinew.

Sinew on back of bow.

Compound bow, of several pieces of wood, bone, or horn lashed together

Wood Limb

Eastern Inuit Compound Bow

The varieties of bows:
- Self-bow, made of one piece.
- Compound bow, of several pieces of wood, bone, or horn lashed together.
- Sinew backed bow, a bow of driftwood or other brittle wood, reinforced with cord of sinew wrapped many times about it lengthwise, from wing to wing.
- Sinew lined bow, a self bow, the back of which is further strengthened with sinew glued on. In some cases bows were decorated in colors.

BOWS

The varied environments and the materials available caused the development of different styles of bows. They are distinguished by the materials and the parts, which are known as back, belly, wings, grip, nocks, and string.

Regional varieties of bows:

1 Arctic Compound bows in the East are very clumsy, owing to scarcity of material; the grip may be of wood, the wings of whale's ribs or bits of wood from whalers. In the West excellent sinew-backed bows were made on bodies of driftwood. Asiatic influence is apparent in them.
2 Northern Athabaskan: Long, straight bows of willow or birch, with wooden wrist guards projecting from the belly.
3 St. Lawrence and East US: Self-bows of ash, second growth hickory, osage orange (small spiny NA deciduous tree that bears inedible green orange like fruit. Its durable yellowish-orange wood was formerly used by American Indians for bows and other weapons. Also called bowwood), oak, or other hard wood.
4 Gulf States: Long bows, rectangular in section, of walnut or other hard wood.
5 Rocky Mountains: a) Self-bow of osage orange or other hard wood; b) a compound bow of several strips of buffalo horn lashed together and strengthened.
6 North Pacific Coast: Bows with rounded grip and flat wings, usually made of yew or cedar.
7 Fraser-Columbian region: Similar to (6) but with wings much shorter and the necks curved sharply outward.
8 Interior Basin: A long slender stick of rude form; many are strengthened by means of a sinew lining on the back and cross wrappings.
9 California: Like (7) but neatly lined with sinew and often decorated.
10 Southwest: Like (8) but seldom sinew lined (Navaho). In the S part of this area long cotton-wood bows with cross lashing were employed by Yuman and Piman tribes. The Jicarilla Apache make a cupid's bow, strengthened with bands of sinew wrapping.
The bows of the Rockies have little distinction of parts, but the W Inuit and Pacific slope varieties have flat wings, and the former shows connection with Asia. The nocks are in some tribes alike, but among the Plains Indians the lower nock is cut in at one side only.

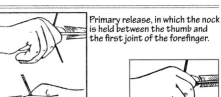

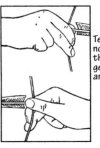

Primary release, in which the nock is held between the thumb and the first joint of the forefinger.

Secondary release, in which the middle and the ring fingers are laid inside of the string.

Tertiary release, in which the nock is held between the ends of the forefinger and the middle finger, while the first three fingers are hooked on the string.

Mediterranean method, confined to the Inuit, whose arrows have a flat nock, in which the string is drawn with the tips of the first, second, and third fingers, the neck being lightly held between the first and the second fingers.

ARROW RELEASE

Arrow release is the way of holding the nock and letting loose the arrow in shooting.
In general the NA tribes, the Navaho, Chippewa, Micmac, and Penobscot used the primary release; the Ottawa, Chippewa, and Zuñi the secondary; the Omaha, Arapaho, Cheyenne, Assiniboin, Comanche, Crows, Siksika, and some Navaho, the tertiary.

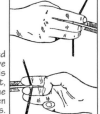

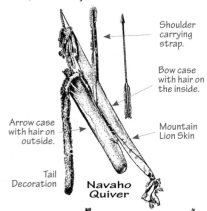

Shoulder carrying strap

Bow case with hair on the inside

Arrow case with hair on outside.

Tail Decoration

Mountain Lion Skin

Navaho Quiver

Bowstrings

Are of sinew cord tied at one end and looped at the other.

Wrist Guard

When the bowman's left arm was exposed he wore a wrist guard of hide or other suitable material to break the blow of the released string.

QUIVERS

The form of the quiver depended on the size of the bow and arrows; the materials, determined by the region, are skin or wood. Sealskin quivers are used in the Arctic region; beautifully decorated examples of deerskin are common in Canada, also E of the Rockies and in the Interior basin. On the Pacific coast cedar quivers are employed by the canoe using tribes, and others make them of skins of the otter, mountain lion, or coyote.

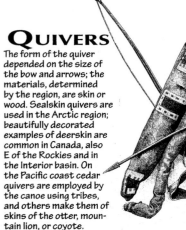

Bird Stunning Arrow

Feather — Sinew — Sinew — Bone tip or small stone in soft leather.

War & Large Game Arrow

White down tufts to help find arrow. — Sinew — Sinew — Trade metal tip.

War & Large Game Arrow

Colored wool strands. — Sinew — Steel Tip — Identification markings on arrow.

Bird & Small Game Arrow

Feather — Sinew — Hard Wood Tip — Identification markings on arrow.

Identification markings on arrow. — Sinew — Steel Tip — Feather — Blood grooves on length of arrow.

This long distance arrow has a lot of thrust and is good in the wind. Bleeding groves on the full length. These make the game bleed profusely and it is easier to track.

Game & War Arrow

INDIAN ARROWS

Identification markings on arrow. — Sinew — Hardwood

Nocked hardwood plug attached with sinew. — Sinew — Reed Section — Fine piece of flint, quartz, hardwood, or trade metal lashed with sinew.

Reed War Arrow

THROWING STICK

The end the spear is loosely attached to the stick in three ways:
1 by a shallow socket which fits on a spur,
2 by a socket at the end of the stick into which fits a conical projection on the spear shaft,
3 in Greenland, by pegs on the harpoon shaft that fit into holes in the throwing stick.

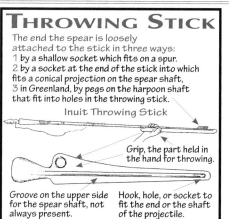

Inuit Throwing Stick

Grip, the part held in the hand for throwing.

Groove on the upper side for the spear shaft, not always present.

Hook, hole, or socket to fit the end or the shaft of the projectile.

THROWING STICK

This implement, also called throwing board, dart sling, and atlatl, is an apparatus for hurling a lance, spear, or harpoon at birds and aquatic animals. It measures from 16" - 20", with extremes from 8"- 30". This sling device was widely used on the shores of the Pacific. It was used by all the Inuit tribes, also in SE Alaska, the Interior Basin, California, and Florida.

The body may be a rod, a double cone, or a broad piece of wood. The grip may be the natural form of the stick, or this may also have holes, pockets, pegs, loops, or notches, alone or combined, to insure a firmer grasp, as was especially the case with the throwing sticks of the arctic region. The groove, when present, is either rounded or squared, and it serves as a rest for the shaft between the fingers and the butt end of the body. This device attained the highest perfection among the Mexicans and Peruvians whose atlatl were used as fighting weapon.

USE OF THROWING STICK

The throwing stick, the varieties of which are endless, added an extra joint to the arm and thus multiplied its efficiency and force in hurling; it could be used in places where the bow would be impracticable, as in a canoe or where only one hand would be available, also among marshy growth, and it propelled a missile many times heavier than an arrow. The thrower held the grip by his right hand, the thumb turned inward; fitted the butt end of the projectile to the hook socket, or hole in the outer end of the throwing stick; laid the shaft of the weapon in the groove, holding it down with three fingers, and placed the whole against the right shoulder, point forward, ready to drive the weapon at the game by a propulsive thrust. When the missile struck the animal it held the latter by means of a toggle or barbs, which retarded its progress and helped to bring it in, the whole apparatus being one of the most complicated and ingenious devices of the native peoples.

TO SHOT A BOW

- Stand relaxed with feet pointed apart.
- The shoulder of the hand holding the bow should be forward towards the target.
- Firmly hold the bow but be relaxed.
- Place the arrow on with the notch on the string.
- Grasp the string with the first 3 fingers with the end of the arrow being between the first and second finger. Hold the arrow lightly when you pull the string. An alternate method of holding the arrow is to hold it between the thumb and first finger. The arrow can slip when using this hold.
- When the arrow points at the target smoothly release the 3 fingers holding the string.

SAFETY RULES

- Never point your set bow at anyone.
- Never shoot an arrow straight up into the air.
- Make sure that you will not injure anyone *behind your target.*
- If target practicing shoot into a target that has a hill behind it. You will not injure anyone behind your target nor lose your arrows.

MAKING A BOW & ARROW

A bow and arrow is easy to make and does not require any specialized equipment:

Bow: Use a willow shaft or any straight flexible freshly cut sapling. No shaping will be required if the sapling is well chosen. The notches for the bowstring can be cut with a knife or by rubbing on a sharp rock. Eskimos made some of their bows with whale bones, they were riveted together.

Bowstring: A shoelace, dried sinew can be used, or cordage can be made from plants. The bowstring will carry the arrow around 15-20 yards (15-20 m) to hunt for small game and birds.

Arrows: Arrows have to be straight and a thin willow branch is a good choice. Peel off the bark, let the shaft dry while lying horizontally on a flat surface. Scrape the shaft if it has any small bumps. Arrow shafts can be made from reed with a hard wood insert as an arrowhead and string notch plug.

Fletching: Tie a feather to the shaft to give the arrow better stability. A piece of leaf or wing from a maple tree seed can be used.

Arrowhead: An arrow with a blunt point can be effective in stunning an animal. Use a small smooth rock attached to the arrowhead with a piece of cloth or some sticky pitch from a pine tree. Pieces of metal from a tin can can be wrapped around the tip of the arrow to make a sharp arrowhead. Make a selection of arrows with different heads for different game.

Digger Indians using a bow and arrow. Note that the quiver is an animal skin

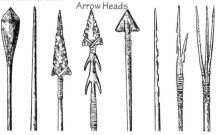

Arrow Heads

Seminole Indian hunting fowl in Florida. Note the quill.

Hercules

Inuit children learning how to use a bow.

Sling

Arrow

Fish

Persian gold coin from approximately 500 BC. The archer is holding a bow and a arrow, next to the bow, and he is throwing a stone with a sling (over his head).

Bone Arrowshaft Straightener

Bone Arrowshaft Rubber

Sandstone Arrowshaft Rubber

Waiting at a breathing hole to spear a seal or walrus. Note the skin rope that is attached to the spearhead which will detach, with the spearhead implanted, when the animal tries to escape.

Detachable Spearhead

Inuit Retrieving Harp Seal Spear

Inuit children learning how to spear "caribou".

Inuit Specialized Spears

Labrador Inuit killing lance 70" long

Labrador Inuit seal-hook 84" long.

Labrador Inuit bird spear 72" long.

Labrador Inuit bird dart with two sets of bone points 72" long.

LANCES - SPEARS

As an implement of hunting or of war the lance was widely used among the tribes of North America. Lances for hunting were used occasionally in war by the Inuit, but the Plains Indians, whenever possible, used two distinct varieties for war and for hunting, the hunting lance blade being shorter and heavier. *The lance appears to have originated through the need of striking animals from some distance in order to escape personal danger and to avoid the dangers of personal injury when using a stone knife or other implement at close quarters to an animal or enemy warrior.* The efficiency and range of the lance when thrown from the hand was increased by the throwing stick, and the original lance or spear developed into a number of varieties under the influences of environment, the habits of animals, acculturation of technologies, etc. The greatest number of lance forms sprang up among the Inuit, whose environment was characterized by a great variety of animal life and the dramatic changes of the seasons, while in most other regions a simple lance was used.

Plains Tribe Warfare

The Plains tribes, as a rule, living in a region conducive to warfare and aggression through its lack of physical boundaries, made more use of the lance in war than did coast, woodland, desert, or mountain tribes. These warfare and raiding party activities were greatly accelerated by the introduction of the horse. Elaborately decorated sheaths were made for lances, varying according to the society or office of the owner. At home the lance was leaned against the shield tripod, tied horizontally above the teepee door, or fastened lengthwise to an upright pole behind the teepee

Spearing a moose.

Buffalo

The range of the present type Bison was chiefly between the Rocky and Allegheny mountains. All the tribes within this range depended largely on the buffalo for food and clothing, and this dependence, with the influence of the habits of the animal, profoundly affected tribal customs and religions rites. This is more clearly seen in the tribes W of the Mississippi, where the Indians were in constant contact with the buffalo (during the summer and winter migrations of the great northern and southern herds. These great herds were composed on innumerable smaller ones of a few thousand each, for the buffalo was never solitary except by accident. This habit affected the manner of hunting and led to the organization of hunting parties under a leader and to the establishment of rules to insure an equal chance to every member of the party.

Hunting Buffalo

In the north pens were built of tree trunks lashed together and braced on the outside, into which the herds were driven and killed. Sometimes, as on the upper Mississippi, a hunter disguised in a buffalo skin acted as a decoy, leading the herd to a precipice where many were killed by the headlong plunge. Upon the plains of Kansas and Nebraska the hunters formed a circle around the herd and then, rushing in, shot the animals with arrows.

Buffalo Hunting Parties

The annual summer hunting party generally consisted of the entire tribe. As the main supply of meat and pelts was to be obtained, religious rites were observed throughout the time. "Single hunting" was forbidden under penalty of flogging, and if a man slipped away to hunt for himself, thereby scattering a herd and causing loss to the tribe, he was punished, sometimes even to death. These severe regulations were in force during the tribal or ceremonial hunt. This hunt occurred in June to August, when the animals were fat and the hair thin, the flesh being then in the best condition for food (drying in the hot sun) and the pelts easiest to dress on both sides for the making of clothing, shields, packs, bags, ropes, snowshoes, tent and boat covers. The meat was cut into thin sheets and strips and hung upon a framework of poles to dry in the sun. When fully "jerked" it was folded up and put into parfleche packs (a buffalo's hide, dried by being stretched on a frame after the hair has been removed) to keep for winter use. A cow was estimated to yield about 45 pounds of dried meat and 50 pounds of pemmican, besides the marrow, which was preserved in bladder skins, and the tallow, which was poured into skin bags. The sinew of the animal furnished bowstrings, thread for sewing, and fiber for ropes. The horns were made into spoons and drinking vessels, and the tips were used for cupping purposes; the buffalo horn was also worn as insignia of office. The hair of the buffalo was woven into belts, and personal ornaments. The dried droppings of the animal, known among plainsmen as "buffalo chips," were valuable as fuel.

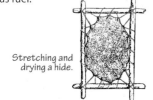

Stretching and drying a hide.

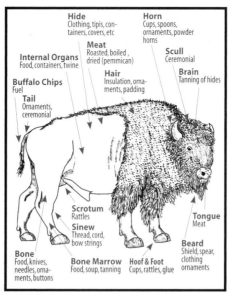

Hide Clothing, tipis, containers, covers, etc

Horn Cups, spoons, ornaments, powder horns

Meat Roasted, boiled, dried (pemmican)

Scull Ceremonial

Internal Organs Food, containers, twine

Hair Insulation, ornaments, padding

Brain Tanning of hides

Buffalo Chips Fuel

Tail Ornaments, ceremonial

Scrotum Rattles

Sinew Thread, cord, bow strings

Tongue Meat

Bone Food, knives, needles, ornaments, buttons

Bone Marrow Food, soup, tanning

Hoof & Foot Cups, rattles, glue

Beard Shield, spear, clothing ornaments

Tripod carrying warrior's shield, quiver, bow, and arrows.

Squaw scraping flesh from a buffalo hide.

Sioux Hide Scraper

Quartz Hide Scrapper

Accidents will happen.

Winter Buffalo Hunting

The buffalo was hunted in the winter by small, independent but organized parties, not subject to the ceremonial practices of the tribal hunt. The pelts secured at this time were for bedding and for garments of extra weight and warmth. The texture of the buffalo hide did not let itself to fine dressing, hence was used for coarse clothing, moccasins, tent covers, and other articles. The hide of the heifer killed in the fall or early winter made the finest robes.

FOOD CACHES

Metal or Plastic

Rope

Metal or Plastic

Inuit watching a walrus breathing hole.

Inuit repulsing a young polar bear.

Hudson's Bay Inuit bone skin scraper.

The horse changed the tactics in hunting the buffalo and also increased the territorial warfare among the tribes.

Retaining Ropes — *Spear Head*

Throwing Shaft — *First Shaft* — *3 Part Toggle - Head Inuit Harpoon*

SUMMARY

TRAPPING & HUNTING TACTICS

The pursuit of game may be divided into two sets of activities, which correspond to military type strategy (including a whole series of traps) and tactics (hunting weapons and processes). Beginning with the military type strategy, the following 9 categories embrace the principal hunting activities of the American Indians:

1 Taking animals with the hand without tile aid of any tools. Examples of this are picking up marine animals on the beach to eat on the spot, robbing birds' nests, and seizing birds on their roosts on dark nights. Such unskilled taking developed the utmost cunning, agility, and strength for pursuing, seizing, climbing, diving, stealing upon, and deceiving, and the same qualities were also useful in the pursuit with weapons. The highest level of this first category was the communal game drive, in which a whole band or tribe would surround a herd of animals and coax or force them into a gorge, a corral, or natural cul de sac.

2 Gathering with devices. To this class of activities belong substitutes for the fingers or palms of the hands, such as rakes for drawing or piling up sea food; a sharp stick for getting worms or animals by forcing them out of the ground; nets and scoops for taking animals from the water (fishing or nets); also reatas (lassoes type rope), and bolas for reaching out and grasping. The top of this category is reached when in a partnership or communal net, used by the Inuit and other tribes for taking seal and also small fish.

3 The employment of apparatus for striking, bruising, or breaking bones, including stones held in the hands, clubs with grips, and hard objects at the end of a line or handle, like a slung shot - a hard object, such as a stone or wood ball, attached by a strap or thong to the wrist and used as a weapon. The N. Pacific tribes took great pains with their clubs, carving on them their mystic symbolism.

4 Slashing or stabbing with sharp edged weapons. The Indians did not have many metals and used stone, bone, reeds, and wood for stabbing and slashing. Both chipped and ground weapons were used, either without a handle, with a grip, or at the end of a shaft (tomahawk). Every Inuit had a quiver of daggers for use at close quarters, and the Indian his side arms. Edged weapons, however, were not so common as the weapons of the next class.

5 Hunting with piercing weapons, the most common of all Indian methods of taking animals. The implements include the pointed stick or stone, the lance, the spear, the harpoon, and the arrow. Weapons of this class were held in the hand, thrust by the hand, shot from a bow or a blowgun, or slung from the throwing stick. Each of the varieties went through a multitude of transformations, depending on game, materials at hand, the skill of the maker, etc.

6 The use of traps, pits, and snares. The Tenan-kutchin of Alaska captured deer, moose, and caribou by means of a brush fence, extending many miles, in which at intervals snares were set; and the same custom was practiced by many other tribes in hunting larger game as buffalo. The plains tribes and the ancient Pueblos captured deer, antelope, and wolves by means of pitfalls.

7 Capturing game with the help of dogs. Indian tribes, with few exceptions, had no hunting dogs regularly trained to pursue game, but the common dog was very efficient in barking when encountering wild game. Fowls of the air, marine animals, and especially carnivorous animals, such as the coyote, by their noises and movements gave clues which aided the cunning and observant hunter to identify, locate, and follow his game.

8 Hunting by means of fire and smoke. The Indians used smoke to drive animals out of hiding, torches to dazzle the eyes of deer and to attract fish and birds to their canoes, and torches and prairie fires for game drives.

9 Taking animals by means of drugs and poisons. The bark of walnut root served to asphyxiate fish in fresh water pools in the Southern states; in other areas soap plant and buckeyes were used.

Inuit using a harpoon in hunting from a kayak.

RELATED HUNTING KNOWLEDGE

In addition to the hunting process there were activities in which the Indian had to know. There were foods to eat and foods that were traditionally not eaten, clothing and masks to wear, shelters and hiding places to build. The hunter must be familiar with calls, imitations, decoys, whistles, and the like. Also he must know the hunting songs, ceremonies, and fetishes, the time for the chase of the various animals, the laws for the division of game, and the clan names connected with hunting. Besides, there were numberless associated items needed in the hunt as how to make and maintain a canoe. In order to use the harpoon it was necessary to have a canoe or kayak. Every method of hunting required its related support items which taxed the ingenuity of the native as the identification of useful species, the best season for the species, and the construction and maintaining of fences or barriers. There were also certain activities which resulted from hunting such as preserving foods, transportation of food, and receptacles for food. A knowledge of anatomy was necessary in order to know where to strike and how to cut up game. All these gave excellent training in perception, skill, and the cooperative effort.

WATER POCKETS IN DRY AREAS

After rainstorms or the melting of snow, water will run off very rapidly especially in the Southwest where the bedrock is uplifted sandstone. This runoff erodes the sandstone and creates many ridges and valleys. Water pockets are hard to find due to the ruggedness of the area. Find a high point to look for some signs of vegetation, observe bird activity. Water is not always found in the lowest areas but inspect the sides of canyons, narrow valleys, etc. These areas are protected from the full impact of the sun. Some of these pools might last all summer. *See Desert Travel Chapter.*

Drinking water... before "civilization" arrived.

WATER & SURVIVAL

Nearly every survival account details the need survivors had for water. Many ingenious methods of locating, procuring, purifying, and storing water are included in the recorded experiences of downed air crew members. If survivors are located in temperate, tropic, or dry climates, water may be their first and most important need. The priority of finding water over that of obtaining food must be emphasized to potential survivors. An individual may be able to live for weeks without food, depending on the temperature and amount of energy being exerted. A person who has no water can be expected to die within days. Even in cold climate areas or places where water is abundant, survivors should attempt to keep their body fluids at a level that will maintain them in the best possible state of health. Even in relatively cold climates, the body needs 2 quarts of water per day to remain efficient.

32 FINDING WATER

DRINKING WATER

In areas with poor sanitation, only the following beverages may be safe to drink: boiled water, hot beverages (such as coffee or tea) made with boiled water, canned or bottled carbonated beverages, beer, and wine. Ice may be made from unsafe water and should be avoided. It is safer to drink from a can or bottle of beverage than to drink from a container that was not known to be clean and dry. However, water on the surface of a beverage can or bottle may also be contaminated. Therefore, the area of a can or bottle that will touch the mouth should be wiped clean and dry. In areas where water is contaminated, travelers should not brush their teeth with tap water.

The CDC makes no recommendation as to the use of any of the portable filters on the market due to lack of independently verified results of their efficacy.

WATER REQUIREMENTS

Normally, with atmospheric temperature of about 68°F, the average adult requires 2 to 3 quarts of water daily.
Water is necessary to replace that lost daily in the following ways:
Urine: About 1.4 qt. of water is lost in the urine.
Sweat: About 0.1 qt. of water is lost in the sweat.
Feces: Approximately 0.2 qt. of water is lost in the feces.

Water from the Soil
In a muddy or damp area dig a hole one to two feet (0.3-0.6 m) in the soil. Allow water to seep into the hole. This water can be purified and used. Wet sand can be put in a piece of cloth which is then pressed or wrung to force out the water. The water produced by the above methods will be cloudy and can be left to settle or filtered through a fine cloth. Purify the water.
See Summer Hiking Chapter.

LIQUID MUD FILTERING

Water can also be obtained from liquid mud. Mud can be filtered through a piece of cloth. Water taken by this method must be purified.

THE IMPORTANCE OF WATER

Water is the key to survival especially in the desert.
• The body is 75% water, by weight.
• The water lost by sweat, evaporation or body functions will have to be replaced.
• Water helps to maintain the body temperature. It is required to help in the digestion of food.
• Control sweating by wearing layers of cotton clothing and traveling in cool mornings, evenings and moonlit nights.
• You can travel 20 miles (32 km) with a gallon (5 L) of water but if you travel during the day you can only cover half that distance.
• A 2 quart (2.5 L) loss of body fluid (2.5% of body weight) reduces the body's efficiency by 25%.
• A fluid loss of 25% of body weight usually is fatal.

CONSERVING WATER

• Do not remove your clothing, even in the sun. Loose layers of clothing help to control sweating by keeping the humidity near the skin to maximize the cooling effect. You might feel cooler with no shirt. You feel cooler because your sweating has increased but you will also lose more water and get a sunburn.
• During the day stay in the shade, if possible off the ground, as sand usually is hotter than air.
• Move slowly to conserve water and energy.
• Do not use water to wash or cool yourself unless you have a sure supply. Spread out your clothing in the sun to kill any possible fungus growth.
• Drink in small sips. Do not gulp even if you have sufficient supply. Only moisten your lips if your water supply is critical.
• You require a certain level of salt but it should only be consumed with water. Remember that salt makes you require more water.
• To allay thirst: keep a small pebble or other item (grass, button etc.) in your mouth.
• To reduce water loss breathe through your nose and avoid talking.
• Lack of water invites dehydration which can cause major health problems.

WATER LOSS

Unawareness that water loss is actually occurring is referred to as insensible water loss.
It occurs by the following mechanisms:
Diffusion through the skin: Water loss through the skin occurs as a result of the actual diffusion of water molecules through the cells of the skin. The average loss of water in this manner is approximately 0.3-0.4 quart. Fortunately, loss of greater quantities of water by diffusion is prevented by the outermost layer of the skin, the epidermis, which acts as a barrier to this type of water loss.
Evaporation through the lungs: Inhaled air initially contains very little water vapor. However, as soon as it enters the respiratory passages, the air is exposed to the fluids covering the respiratory surfaces. By the time this air enters the lungs, it has become totally saturated with moisture from these surfaces. When the air is exhaled, it is still saturated with moisture and water is lost from the body.

WATER LOSS IS INCREASED BY...

Heat Exposure: When an individual is exposed to very high temperatures, water lost in the sweat can be increased to as much as 3.5 quarts an hour. Water loss at this increased rate can deplete the body fluids in a short time.
Exercise: Physical activity increases the loss of water in two ways, as follows:
• The increased respiration rate causes increased water loss by evaporation through the lungs.
• The increased body heat causes excessive sweating.
Cold Exposure: As the temperature decreases, the amount of water vapor in the air also decreases. Therefore, breathing cold air results in increased water loss by evaporation from the lungs.
High Altitude: At high altitudes, increased water loss by evaporation through the lungs occurs not only as a result of breathing cooler air but also as a result of the increased respiratory efforts required.
Burns: After extensive bums, the outermost layer of the skin is destroyed. When this layer is gone, there is no longer a barrier to water loss by diffusion, and the rate of water loss in this manner can increase up to 5 quarts each day.
Illness: Severe vomiting or prolonged diarrhea can lead to serious water depletion.

POTABLE WATER

• Never drink water from a source that contains dead animals or animal remains. The animals might have died as the water has a high concentration, due to evaporation, of minerals that have been leached from the bedrock. These minerals might be chlorine, sulphur or arsenic.
• Animals and birds drinking the water does not mean that it is safe because water can have a bacterial or parasite content that cannot be neutralized by the human digestive track.

DEHYDRATION

DEHYDRATION

Dehydration (body fluid depletion) can occur when required body fluids are not replaced.

Dehydration is accompanied by the following symptoms:

- Thirst
- Weakness
- Fatigue
- Dizziness
- Headache
- Fever
- Inelastic abdominal skin.
- Dry mucous membranes, that is, dry mouth and nasal passages.
- Infrequent urination and reduced volume. The urine is concentrated so that it is very dark in color. In severe cases, urination may be quite painful.

DEHYDRATION: *Watch for...*

The following behavioral changes in individuals suffering from dehydration:

- Loss of appetite
- Apathy
- Lagging pace
- Emotional instability
- Impatience
- Indistinct speech
- Sleepiness
- Mental confusion

Dehydration is a complication which causes decreased efficiency in the performance of even the simplest task. It also predisposes survivors to the development of severe shock following minor injuries. Constriction of blood vessels in the skin as a result of dehydration increases the danger of cold injury during cold exposure. Failure to replace body fluids ultimately results in death.

TREATMENT FOR DEHYDRATION

Replace lost body fluids: The oral intake of water is the most readily available means of correcting this deficiency. A severely dehydrated person will have little appetite. This person must be encouraged to drink small quantities of water at frequent intervals to replenish the body's fluid volume. Cold water should be warmed so the system will accept it easier.

US Army Water Requirement Guidelines			
Activity	Typical Duties	Quarts/person/day	
		less than 105°F (40.5°C)	more than 105°F (40.5°C)
Light	Desk work, Radio operating, Guard duty	6	10
Moderate	Route march on level ground	7	11
Heavy	Forced marches, Route march with heavy loads, Digging in.	9	13

PREVENT DEHYDRATION

Water loss must be replaced by periodic intake of small quantities of water throughout the day. As activities or conditions intensify, the water intake should be increased accordingly. Water intake should be sufficient to maintain a minimum urinary output of I pint every 24 hours. Thirst is not an adequate stimulus for water intake, and a person often dehydrates when water is available. Therefore, water intake should be encouraged when the person is not thirsty. Humans cannot adjust to decreased water intake for prolonged periods of time. When water is in short supply, any available water should be consumed sensibly. If sugar is available, it should be mixed with the water, and efforts should be made to find a local water source.

LIMITING DEHYDRATION

Until a suitable water source is located, individual water losses should be limited in the following ways:

Physical activity: should be limited to the absolute minimum required for survival activities. All tasks should be performed slowly and deliberately with minimal expenditure of energy. Frequent rest periods should be included in the daily schedule.

Hot climates: essential activity should be conducted at night or during the cooler part of the day.

Clothing: should be worn at all times, in hot climates, because it reduces the quantity of water loss by sweating. Sweat is absorbed into the clothing evaporated from its surface in the same manner it evaporates from the body.

This evaporation cools the air trapped between the clothing and the skin, causing a decrease in the activity of the sweat glands and a subsequent reduction in water loss.

Hot weather clothing: light-colored clothing should be worn rather than dark-colored clothing. Dark colored clothing absorbs the sun's light rays and converts them into heat. This heat causes an increase in body temperatures which activates the sweat glands and increases water loss through sweating. Light-colored clothing, however, reflects the sun's light rays, minimizing the increase in body temperature and subsequent water loss.

Relentless heat...

Axel is always coaxed to drink sufficient water during hot weather.

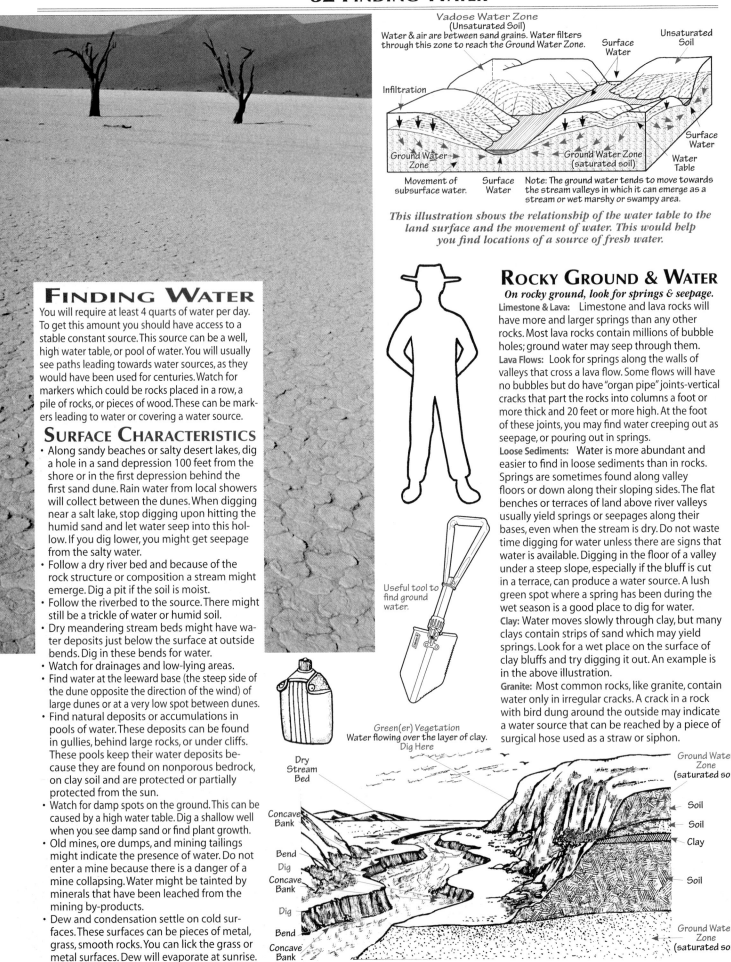

Vadose Water Zone
(Unsaturated Soil)
Water & air are between sand grains. Water filters through this zone to reach the Ground Water Zone.

Unsaturated Soil

Surface Water

Infiltration

Ground Water Zone

Surface Water

Movement of subsurface water.

Surface Water

Water Table

Ground Water Zone (saturated soil)

Note: The ground water tends to move towards the stream valleys in which it can emerge as a stream or wet marshy or swampy area.

This illustration shows the relationship of the water table to the land surface and the movement of water. This would help you find locations of a source of fresh water.

FINDING WATER

You will require at least 4 quarts of water per day. To get this amount you should have access to a stable constant source. This source can be a well, high water table, or pool of water. You will usually see paths leading towards water sources, as they would have been used for centuries. Watch for markers which could be rocks placed in a row, a pile of rocks, or pieces of wood. These can be markers leading to water or covering a water source.

SURFACE CHARACTERISTICS

- Along sandy beaches or salty desert lakes, dig a hole in a sand depression 100 feet from the shore or in the first depression behind the first sand dune. Rain water from local showers will collect between the dunes. When digging near a salt lake, stop digging upon hitting the humid sand and let water seep into this hollow. If you dig lower, you might get seepage from the salty water.
- Follow a dry river bed and because of the rock structure or composition a stream might emerge. Dig a pit if the soil is moist.
- Follow the riverbed to the source. There might still be a trickle of water or humid soil.
- Dry meandering stream beds might have water deposits just below the surface at outside bends. Dig in these bends for water.
- Watch for drainages and low-lying areas.
- Find water at the leeward base (the steep side of the dune opposite the direction of the wind) of large dunes or at a very low spot between dunes.
- Find natural deposits or accumulations in pools of water. These deposits can be found in gullies, behind large rocks, or under cliffs. These pools keep their water deposits because they are found on nonporous bedrock, on clay soil and are protected or partially protected from the sun.
- Watch for damp spots on the ground. This can be caused by a high water table. Dig a shallow well when you see damp sand or find plant growth.
- Old mines, ore dumps, and mining tailings might indicate the presence of water. Do not enter a mine because there is a danger of a mine collapsing. Water might be tainted by minerals that have been leached from the mining by-products.
- Dew and condensation settle on cold surfaces. These surfaces can be pieces of metal, grass, smooth rocks. You can lick the grass or metal surfaces. Dew will evaporate at sunrise.

Useful tool to find ground water.

Green(er) Vegetation
Water flowing over the layer of clay. Dig Here

Dry Stream Bed

Concave Bank

Bend
Dig
Concave Bank

Dig

Bend

Concave Bank

ROCKY GROUND & WATER

On rocky ground, look for springs & seepage.

Limestone & Lava: Limestone and lava rocks will have more and larger springs than any other rocks. Most lava rocks contain millions of bubble holes; ground water may seep through them.

Lava Flows: Look for springs along the walls of valleys that cross a lava flow. Some flows will have no bubbles but do have "organ pipe" joints-vertical cracks that part the rocks into columns a foot or more thick and 20 feet or more high. At the foot of these joints, you may find water creeping out as seepage, or pouring out in springs.

Loose Sediments: Water is more abundant and easier to find in loose sediments than in rocks. Springs are sometimes found along valley floors or down along their sloping sides. The flat benches or terraces of land above river valleys usually yield springs or seepages along their bases, even when the stream is dry. Do not waste time digging for water unless there are signs that water is available. Digging in the floor of a valley under a steep slope, especially if the bluff is cut in a terrace, can produce a water source. A lush green spot where a spring has been during the wet season is a good place to dig for water.

Clay: Water moves slowly through clay, but many clays contain strips of sand which may yield springs. Look for a wet place on the surface of clay bluffs and try digging it out. An example is in the above illustration.

Granite: Most common rocks, like granite, contain water only in irregular cracks. A crack in a rock with bird dung around the outside may indicate a water source that can be reached by a piece of surgical hose used as a straw or siphon.

Ground Water Zone (saturated so

Soil

Soil

Clay

Soil

Ground Water Zone (saturated so

GROUND WATER

Ground water is the part of precipitation that seeps down through the soil until it reaches impervious rock. If the water can not find any area to flow to it saturates the area above the rock with water. It then slowly moves underground, generally at a downward angle (because of gravity), and may eventually seep into streams, lakes, swampy areas, and oceans.

Above Water Table: The ground above the water table may be wet to a certain degree, but it does not stay saturated. The dirt and rock in this unsaturated zone contain air and some water and support the vegetation on the Earth.

Below Water Table: The ground is saturated with water below the water table. The saturated zone has water that fills the tiny spaces (pores) between rock particles and the cracks (fractures) of the rocks.

TYPES OF BEDROCK

The Earth's bedrock consists of many types of rock, such as sandstone, granite, and limestone. These rocks have different pore structures, void spaces, fractures, and other weathering characteristics - that hinder or permit the flow of water.

Conditions for travel of water:

Pervious (Porous): Bedrocks due to their structure or chemical composition let water pass through. e.g. certain layers of sandstone, limestone (chemical).

Impervious: These bedrocks or rock formations block the passage of water. e.g. granite, clay.

ROCK TYPES & CONDITIONS

Limestone: Is dissolved by water (chemical reaction) - which results in large cavities that fill with water. If there is major water corrosion large caves can be formed. Water can flow in these caves.

Clays: Once the clay is waterlogged, its small pores do not let water pass through.

Granite: Is usually (except if cracked) dense and does not let water penetrate.

Sedimentary Layers: If you look at a vertical cross-section of the earth you can see rock that is laid down in layers - these are called sedimentary layers. These layers are composed of different rock types. Some layers have rocks that are more porous than others, and here water moves more freely (in a horizontal manner) through the earth. These layers might form artesian formations.

SALT FRONT

When freshwater from rivers flows into the salty water of bays and estuaries, the waters mingle in a region that is neither freshwater nor saltwater, and is brackish. The boundary between freshwater and saltwater is not a distinct line, but is a region of water with a range in its salt content. The location of this region of brackish water, the salt front, will vary with changes in river flow and tides, as the opposing flows reach their balance points.

Springs emerge along lines of emergence of the water table that forms the marshy area.

Well B, too shallow to reach the water table, would usually be dry or contain some vadose water. The water table might rise during the wet season and some water might be in the well.

Well A, reaching below the water table, has a continuous water supply.

WELLS

Wells are dug to hopefully provide a reliable and ample supply of water.

TYPES OF WELLS

Dug Wells: Made with a pick and shovel if the ground is soft and the water table is shallow. They are often lined with stones to prevent them from collapsing. They cannot be dug much deeper than the water table because it keeps filling up with water. During the dry season or a drought the water table will fall and the depth of the well can be increased.

Driven Wells: are built by driving a small-diameter pipe into soft earth, such as sand or gravel. A screen is usually attached to the bottom of the pipe to filter out sand and other particles. They can only tap shallow water, and because the source of the water is so close to the surface, contamination from surface pollutants can occur.

Drilled Wells: Most modern wells are drilled. Drill rigs are often mounted on big trucks. They use rotary drill bits that chew away at the rock, percussion bits that smash the rock, or, if the ground is soft, large auger bits. Drilled wells can be drilled more than 1,000 feet deep. Often a pump is placed at the bottom to push water up to the surface.

WATER LEVELS IN WELLS

Seasonal variations in rainfall and the occasional drought affect the "height" of the underground water level. If a well is pumped at a faster rate than the aquifer around it, it is recharged by precipitation or other underground flow, then water levels around the well can be lowered. The water level in a well can also be lowered if other wells near it are withdrawing too much water. When water levels drop below the levels of the pump intakes, then wells will begin to pump air - they will "go dry."

These illustrations show the relationship of the water table to the land surface and the movement of water. This would help you find locations of a source of fresh water.

DESERT WATER

Page 94

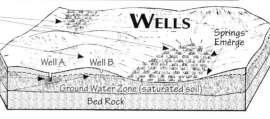

WELLS

Springs Emerge

Well A Well B

Water Table

Ground Water Zone (saturated soil)

Bed Rock

Water along the Coast

Along coasts, water may be found by digging beach wells. Locate the wells behind the first or second pressure ridge. Wells can be dug 3 to 5 feet deep and should be lined with driftwood to prevent sand from refilling the hole. Rocks should be used to line the bottom of the well to prevent stirring up sand when procuring the water. The average well may take as long as 2 hours to produce 4 to 5 gallons of water.

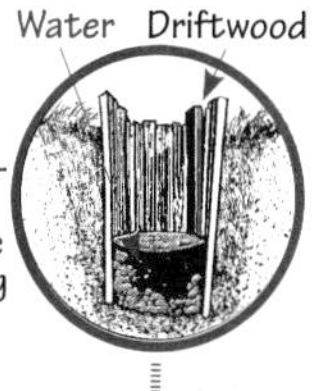

Water Driftwood

Ocean First Dune Dry Sand

Saturated Sand Movement of Water Dig for Water

Along sandy beaches or salty desert lakes, dig a hole in a sand depression 100 feet (30 m) from the shore. Filtered water will gradually seep into the hole.

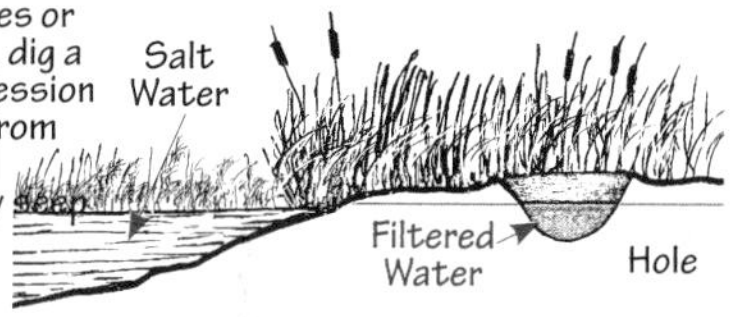

Salt Water

Filtered Water Hole

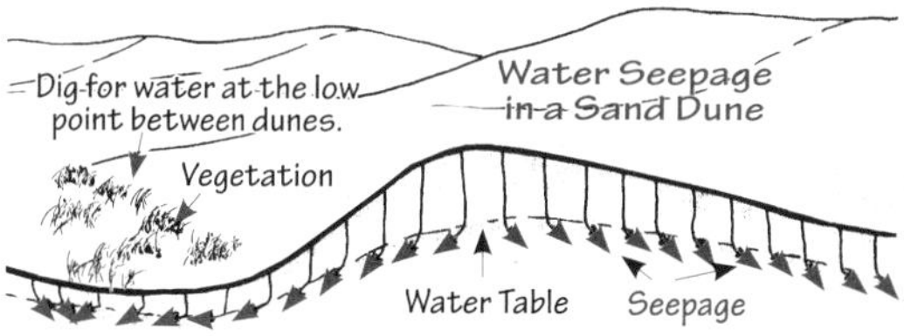

Dig for water at the low point between dunes.

Water Seepage in a Sand Dune

Vegetation

Water Table Seepage

Springs are fed by water that has seeps downward through the sandstone.

Springs emerge along the contact area of the pervious sandstone and underlying relatively impervious shale.

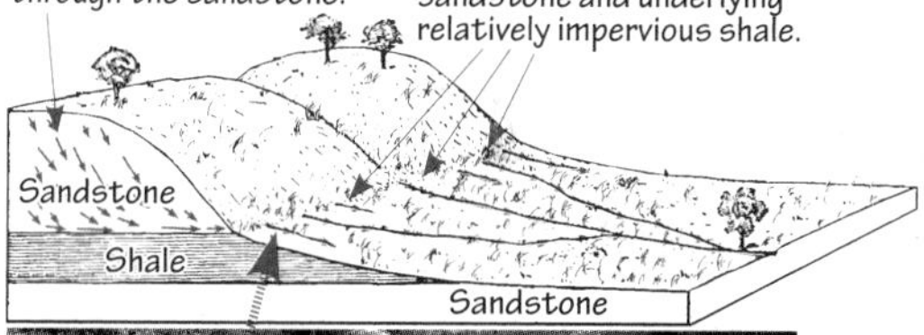

Sandstone

Shale

Sandstone

Spring water being transported from a spring that emerges along a impervious layer. Hollowed out tree trunks are used to "pipe" the water to a log trough.

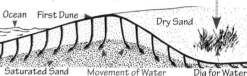

Note: Palm trees grow where the water table is closest to the surface.

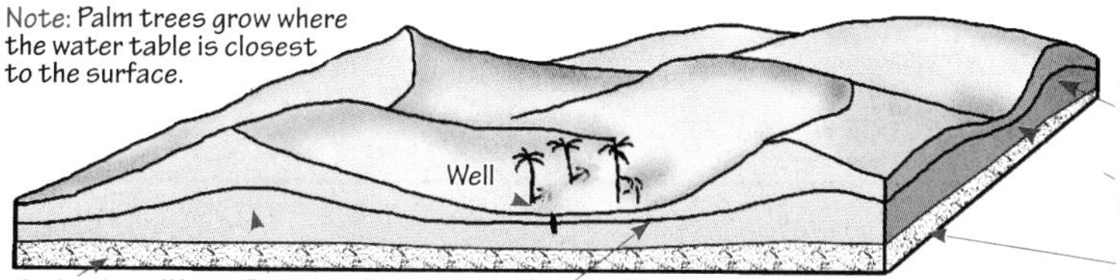

Well

Bedrock Water Saturated Zone Water Table

Water Table

Water table is closest to surface between dunes.

Bedrock

Movement of Underground Water

Once water enters the soil it starts to migrate towards the water table and gradually follow it towards a point at a lower level. If the water can not find a lower level where it can flow off it will super saturate the ground and form a swamp or bog and in extreme situations a temporary or permanent lake or pond.

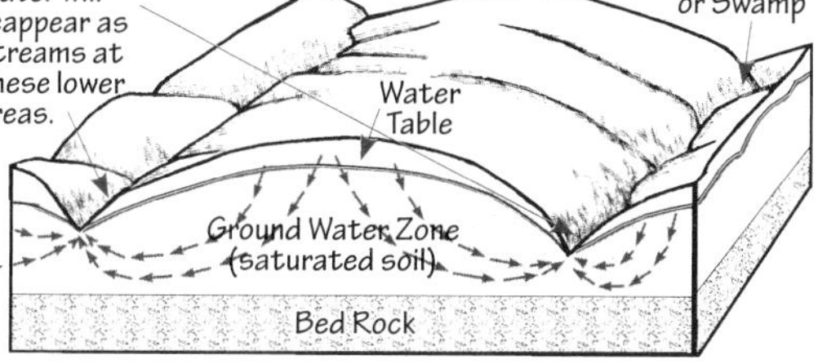

Water will reappear as streams at these lower areas.

Stream or Swamp

Water Table

Migration of Water

Ground Water Zone (saturated soil)

Bed Rock

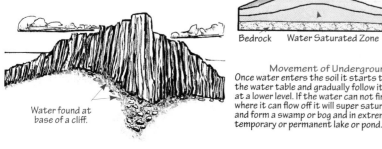

Water found at base of a cliff.

Vegetation showing possible water source between rocks.

Churning the inside of a cactus for water.

Cutting open a cactus.

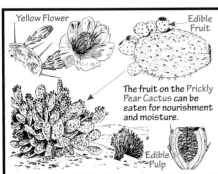

Yellow Flower

Edible Fruit

The fruit on the Prickly Pear Cactus can be eaten for nourishment and moisture.

Edible Pulp

WATER IN THE TROPICS

Depending on the time of the year and type of jungle, water in the tropical climates can be plentiful; however, it is necessary to know where to look and procure it. Surface water is normally available in the form of streams, ponds, rivers, and swamps. In the savannas during the dry season, it may be necessary for the survivor to resort to digging for water. Water obtained from these sources may need filtration and should be purified.

Plants: Many plants have hollow portions which can collect rainfall, dew, etc. Since there is no absolute way to tell whether this water is pure, it should be purified. The stems or the leaves of some plants have a hollow section where the stem meets the trunk. Look for water collected here. This includes any Y-shaped plants (palms or air plants). The branches of large trees often support air plants (relatives of the pineapple) whose overlapping, thickly growing leaves may hold a considerable amount of rainwater. Trees may also catch and store rainwater in natural receptacles such as cracks or hollows.

Collecting dew on a cloth while walking through tall grass in the morning.

Dromedary Bag

A collapsible water bag that is named after the one humped camel.

FINDING WATER PLANTS

- Look for green leaf growth of plants and trees that require much water. These plants might be cattails, bulrush, elderberries, and reeds. Trees such as cottonwood, poplars, greasewood, and willows. This growth indicates a high water table and might be located on a dry river bed. To get at the water, dig into the ground for one to two feet. After a while, water will accumulate in this pit. It will most likely be cloudy but will slowly settle; if it does not, it can be filtered through a tightly woven piece of cloth.
- Presence of abundant vegetation of a different variety, such as deciduous growth in a coniferous area.
- Large clumps of plush grass.
- At base of cliffs where there is vegetation.
- The pulp of some cacti (not the giant Saguaro) can be crushed to a watery mash. To do this burn off the needles or spines in a fire and peel the pieces of cacti. The pulp can be sucked to release a sweet jellylike liquid.
- The large barrel cactus of American deserts contains considerable moisture which can be squeezed out of the pulp. This is a difficult task and your best bet is a well or other source.

ANIMAL INDICATORS

- Animals are the best indicators of desert water.
- Watch insects (bees, hornets), birds and animals.
- Insects require water and live within flying range of water. You can watch the direction of their flight.
- Animal trails which may lead to water. The "V" formed by intersecting trails often points toward water sources.
- In damp places, animals may have scratched depressions into the ground to obtain water; insects may also hover over these areas.
- Grazing animals will go towards water every morning and evening. Watch for animal trails which will usually be well-worn because animals will have followed these trails for many years.
- Doves have a habit of perching in trees or shrubs near desert water holes, especially in the evening.
- Watch the flight of birds, particularly at sunset and dawn. Birds circle water holes in desert areas.
- Birds will fly to and from water, they might circle water or congregate in large flocks. Birds of prey use their victims as a source of fluids and do not go to water as frequently. The Bedouins of the Sahara desert, in North Africa, have a belief that birds flying to water fly low and directly to the water whereas birds flying from water are heavier and will have to rest frequently. A bird coming from water will be heavier and flaps louder.

Canteen on Military Belt

AQUIFER

Humid air pushed up and over the mountains by the wind, condenses, and forms clouds. Clouds rise and lose their moisture as rain. By the time they cross the ridge they will have lost most of their moisture and become 'rained out'. The clouds will disappear and warm dry wind will blow down the leeward side of the mountains. If the geological structure of the mountain on the windward side is pervious (water can pass through) and impervious (water can not pass through) water can enter the pervious layer and flow to a distant oasis or well. This structure is called an aquifer. Wells can be drilled into the aquifers and water can be pumped out. Precipitation eventually adds water (recharge) into the porous rock of the aquifer. The rate of recharge is not the same for all aquifers, though, and that must be considered when pumping water from a well. Pumping too much water too fast draws down the water in the aquifer and eventually causes a well to yield less and less water and even run dry.

Artesian Formation (Aquifer)

This is where a porous layer is sandwiched between two impervious layers. Water flowing in the porous layer will follow the direction of the porous layer and exit where the porous layer meets the surface. In this case, an oasis, it can even form the head of a stream. This might be hundreds of miles from where the water originally entered the porous rock.

CONFINED AQUIFER

This is the case in our illustration.

Sometimes the porous rock layers become tilted in the earth. There might be a confining layer of less porous rock (impervious layers) both above and below the porous layer. This is an example of a confined aquifer. In this case, the rocks surrounding the aquifer confines the pressure in the porous rock and its water. If a well is drilled into this "pressurized" aquifer, the internal pressure might (depending on the ability of the rock to transport water) be enough to push the water up the well and up to the surface without the aid of a pump, sometimes completely out of the well. This type of well is called an artesian well.

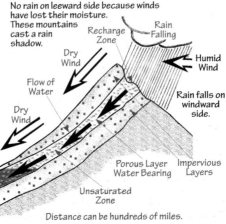

No rain on leeward side because winds have lost their moisture. These mountains cast a rain shadow.

Recharge Zone

Rain Falling

Humid Wind

Dry Wind

Flow of Water

Dry Wind

Rain falls on windward side.

Natural Oasis

Saturated with water.

Porous Layer Water Bearing

Impervious Layers

Unsaturated Zone

Distance can be hundreds of miles.

WATER TABLE INDICATED BY TREE GROWTH

Water Depth	Trees Growing on Surface
1 - 1.5 feet (0.3-0.45 m)	Balsam fir, white spruce, & to some extent, black ash, & red maple.
2 - 3 feet (0.6-0.9 m)	Rock maple, red maple, yellow birch, balsam fir, white spruce, & low quality sugar maple & basswood.
4 - 5 feet (1.2-1.5 m)	Flourishing sugar maple, basswood & white pine. For quality timber water table should be 4 feet or deeper.

Midwest forest trees at the edge of the prairie.

2 - 3 feet (0.6-0.9 m)	Bur oak, black oak, and scattered red oak, aspen, & box elder.
4 - 5+ feet (1.2-1.5 m+)	White oak, red oak, scattered black oak, walnut, hickory, white ash.

POTABLE WATER

Number one concern in a desert...

- Drinking water should be kept in distinctive containers that should not be contaminated by non-potable water.
- Drinking water should only be taken from a secure disease-free location.
- Sufficient water to last until the next water hole is reached should always be on hand. Be prepared to back track if you cannot find your next source.
- Look for water before your supply is exhausted.
- Water canteens should be transported in such a way that they cannot be damaged or the seams split.
- To keep the water cool keep the containers in the shade or in a windy location.
- You can drink 3.5 pints (2.1 L) of water at a time. The body sweats this amount in two hours.
- To maximize your water intake drink slowly and in sips. Drink as much as you can, rest and slowly drink again. Repeat this a few times until your body is saturated.
- Do not eat fats or proteins if you lack water. Food requires water for digestion especially for proteins and fats. Your tissues will supply the water if it is not otherwise available.
- We require a minimum of four quarts of water per day. Several gallons are required if you are doing strenuous activities on a hot day.
- To conserve water, do not travel in the heat of the day but only in the early morning, late evening or on a moonlit night. Set up a sheltered rest area for the day. A well built rest area might be 40°F cooler in the shade.
- The optimum drinking water temperature is between 50°-60°F (10°-15.5°C). To cool water, it can be wrapped in a wet cloth which will cause cooling when the water evaporates. The tribes people use animal stomachs as gourds. These gradually breathe water which evaporates and cools the gourd.

You cannot be conditioned to adjust permanently to a reduced water supply. If rations are insufficient then movement should be reduced to the cool times of the day or night. In very hot areas it is better to take smaller quantities more frequently. This will reduce the water lost by excessive sweating.

Smoking increases the desire for water. Alcohol reduces the resistance to heat due to increased dehydration.

Roadrunner

Vegetation Bag

This method involves cutting foliage from trees or herbaceous plants, sealing it in a large clear plastic bag, and allowing the heat of the sun to extract the fluids contained within. A large, heavy-duty clear plastic bag should be used. The bag should be filled with about 1 cubic yard of foliage, sealed, and exposed to the Sun. The average yield for one bag tested was 320 ml/bag 5-hour day. This method is simple to set up. The vegetation bag method of water procurement does have one primary drawback. The water produced is normally bitter to taste, caused by biological breakdown of the leaves as they lay in the water produced and super heated in the moist "hothouse" environment. Before the water produced by certain vegetation is consumed, it should undergo the taste test. This is to guard against ingestion of cyanide-producing substances and other harmful toxins, such as plant alkaloids.

Condensation
Cut Vegetation   Water

Collecting rainwater with split bamboo poles.

← Rain Water

Collecting Rainwater

Rainwater can be collected from a tree by wrapping a cloth around a slanted tree and arranging the bottom end of the cloth to drip into a container.

Finding water in plants after a rainfall.

Green Bamboo

Water may be trapped within sections of green bamboo. To determine if water is trapped within a section of bamboo, it should be shaken. If it contains water, a sloshing sound can be heard. An opening may be made in the section by making two 45° angle cuts, both on the same side of the section, and prying loose a piece of the section wall. The end of the section may be cut off and the water drunk or poured from the open end. The inside of the bamboo should be examined before consuming the water. If the inside walls are clean and white, the water will be safe to drink. If there are brown or black spots, fungus growth, or any discoloration, the water should be purified before consumption. Sometimes water can also be obtained by cutting the top off certain types of green bamboo, bending it over, and staking it to the ground A water container should be placed under it to catch the dripping water. This method has also proven effective on some vines and the rattan palm.

Bamboo joints contain water.

Rattan Palm & Spiny Bamboo

Water from the rattan palm and spiny bamboo may be obtained in the same manner as from vines. It is not necessary to test the water if positive identification of the plant can be made. The slender stem (runner) of the rattan palm is an excellent water source. The joints are overlapping in appearance, as if one section is fitted inside the next.

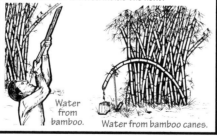

Water from bamboo.   Water from bamboo canes.

GETTING WATER

- Lay a piece of nonporous material such as a poncho, piece of canvas, plastic, or metal material on the ground. If rain or snow is being collected, it may be more efficient to create a bag or funnel shape with the material so the water can be easily gathered.
- Dew can be collected by wiping it up with a sponge or cloth first, and then wringing it into a container.
- Do not contaminate the water with the surfaces of the objects used to collect the precipitation.

Water Transpiration Bag

A large plastic bag is placed over a living limb of a medium-size tree or large shrub. The bag opening is sealed at the branch, and the limb is then tied down to allow collected water to flow to the corner of the bag. The amount of water yielded by this method will depend on the species of trees and shrubs available. During one test of this method, a transpiration bag produced approximately a gallon per day for 3 days with a plastic bag on the same limb, and

with no major deterioration of the branch. Transpired water has a variety of tastes depending on whether or not the vegetation species is allowed to contact the water. It only takes about 5 minutes' work and requires no special skills to instal the bag. The bag is removed to drink the water. The water transpiration bag method surpasses other methods (solar stills, vegetation bag, cutting roots, barrel cactus) in yield, ease of assembly, and in most cases, taste. In dry, semi-dry, or desert environments where low woodlands predominate. It can be used as a water transpirator; in scrubland, steppes, or treeless plains, as a vegetation bag; in sandy areas without vegetation, it can be cut up and improvised into solar stills. Up to three large, heavy-duty bags may be needed to sustain one survivor in certain situations.

Coconuts

Coconuts contain a refreshing fluid. Where coconuts are available, they may be used as a water source. The fluid from a mature coconut contains oil, which when consumed in excess can cause diarrhea. There is little problem if used in moderation or with a meal and not on an empty stomach. Green unripe coconuts about the size of a grapefruit are the best for use because the fluid can be taken in large quantities without harmful effects.

WATER IN DRY AREAS

Locating water in a dry environment can be a formidable task. Some of the ways to find water in this environment have been explored, such as locating a concave bend in a dry riverbed and digging for water. If there is any water within a few feet of the surface, the sand will become slightly damp. Dig until water is obtained.

Collecting Dew: Some deserts become humid at night. The humidity may be collected in the form of dew. This dew can be collected by digging a shallow basin in the ground about 3 feet in diameter and lining it with a piece of canvas, plastic, or other suitable material. A pyramid of stones taken from a minimum of one foot below the surface should then be built in this basin. Dew will collect on and between the stones and trickle down onto the lining material where it can be collected and placed in a container.

Roots: Plants and trees having roots near the surface may be a source of water in dry areas as their roots can run out 40 to 80 feet at a depth of 2 to 9 inches under the surface.

Cactus: Cactus-like or succulent plants may be sources of water, but remember that no plants should be used for water procurement which have a milky sap. The barrel cactus of the United States provides a water source. To obtain it, survivors should first cut off the top of the plant. The pulpy inside portions of the plant should then be mashed to form a watery pulp. Water may ooze out and collect in the bowl; if not, the pulp may be squeezed through a cloth directly into the mouth.

Solar Still: It uses both vegetation and ground moisture to produce water. A solar still can be made from a sheet of clear plastic stretched over a hole in the ground. The moisture in the soil and from plant parts (fleshy stems and leaves) will be extracted and collected by this emergency device. The still may also be used to purify polluted water.

Plant Condensation

Dig a shallow hole next to a plant with many leaves. Place a plastic bag over the plant and have its side slope to the lowest point which is in the hole. Tie or tighten the opening of the bag around the base of the plant. Water given off by the plant will condense on the inner surface of the bag and slowly flow towards the lowest part in the hole. The plant will continue collecting water with its root system. This installation should work for a few days as long as the plant in not too exposed to the sun as it will be killed by overheating in the bag.

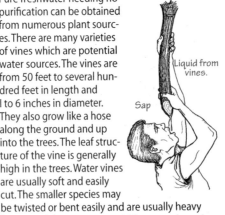

Plant Water Source

A banana or plantain trunk can be a source of water. Cut through the trunk 3" (7.6 cm) above the ground. Hollow out a bowl-like reservoir inside the trunk stub. Water from the roots will accumulate in the bowl. Water which first enters the bowl may contain a concentration of tannin (an astringent which has the same effect as alum). Remove cut chips. Scoop the water out until potable. A trunk can be used for approximately 4 days. Cover the bowl when not being used.

Cut out Bowl
Water in Bowl
Banana Plant
Cut Here
Water will fill bowl from the roots.

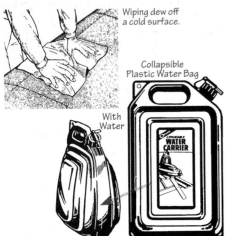

Wiping dew off a cold surface.

Collapsible Plastic Water Bag

With Water

LAND SOLAR STILLS

Produce varied amounts of water. This amount is directly proportionate to the amount of water available in the soil or placed into the still (vegetation, entrails, contaminated water, etc.), and the ambient temperature.

Top View
Plastic Sheet

The air under the plastic sheet heats up from the sun's rays. The warm air becomes saturated from the humidity in the soil. The saturated air touches the cooler plastic sheeting and the water condenses as droplets onto the plastic sheeting. The droplets gradually flow into the pail.

Earth weighing down the plastic sheet.
Stone to weigh down plastic sheet.
Cup or pail to catch water.

Side View
Condensation drops rolling down plastic sheet.

Solar Still
This is a system to extract water from the soil. Dig a hole in humid ground and set up as in the illustration.

WATER FROM VINES

Pure freshwater needing no purification can be obtained from numerous plant sources. There are many varieties of vines which are potential water sources. The vines are from 50 feet to several hundred feet in length and 1 to 6 inches in diameter. They also grow like a hose along the ground and up into the trees. The leaf structure of the vine is generally high in the trees. Water vines are usually soft and easily cut. The smaller species may be twisted or bent easily and are usually heavy because of the water content. The water from these vines should be tested for potability. The first step in testing the water from vines is to nick the vine and watch for sap running from the cut.

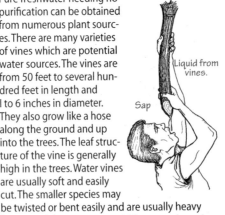

Liquid from vines.

Sap

Good for Drinking: Cut out a section of the vine, hold that piece vertically, and observe the liquid as it flows out. If it is clear and colorless, it may be a drinkable source. Let some of the liquid flow into the palm of the hand and observe it. If the liquid does not change color, you can now taste it. If it tastes like water or has a woody or sweet taste, it should be safe for drinking.

Do Not Drink: If cloudy or milky-colored sap is seen, the vine should be discarded. Liquid with a sour or bitter taste should be avoided.

How to Drink: Water trapped within a vine is easily obtained by cutting out a section of the vine. The vine should first be cut high above the ground and then near the ground. This will provide a long length of vine. When drinking from the vine, it should not touch the mouth as the bark may contain irritants which could affect the lips and mouth. The pores in the upper end of the section of vine may re-close, stopping the flow of water. If this occurs, cut off the end of the vine opposite the drinking end. This will reopen the pores allowing the water to flow.

Collecting water from a barrel cactus.

WATER IN SNOW & ICE AREAS

Due to the extreme cold of arctic areas, water requirements are greatly increased. Increased body metabolism, respiration of cold air, and extremely low humidity play important roles in reducing the body's water content. The processes of heat production and digestion in the body also increase the need for water in colder climates. The constructing of shelters and signals and the obtaining of firewood are extremely demanding tasks. Physical exertion and heat production in extreme cold place the water requirements at close to 5 or 6 quarts per day to maintain proper hydration levels. Your diet will often be dehydrated rations and high protein food sources. For the body to digest and use these food sources effectively, increased water intake is essential.

GLACIER-FED RIVERS

Water obtained from glacier-fed rivers and streams may contain high concentrations of dirt or silt. By letting the water stand for a period of time, most silt will settle to the bottom; the remaining water can be strained through porous material for further filtration.

ARCTIC WATER

Obtaining water need not be a serious problem in the arctic because an abundant supply of water is available from streams, lakes, ponds, snow, and ice. All surface water should be purified by some means. In the summer, surface water may be discolored but is drinkable when purified.

COLLECTING ARCTIC WATER

Porous Bag: Place snow on any porous material (such as parachute or cotton), gathering up the edges, and suspending the "bag" of snow from any support near the fire. Radiant heat will melt the snow and the water will drip from the lowest point on the bag. A container should be placed below this point to catch the water.

Body Heat: There may be little or no fuel supply with which to melt ice and snow for water. In this case, body heat can be used to do the job. The ice or snow can be placed in a waterproof container like a water bag and placed between clothing layers next to the body. This cold substance should not be placed directly next to the skin; it causes chilling and lowering of the body temperature.

Insulated Canteen

The first crossing of Greenland in 1888.

COLD SNOW & ICE CONSUMPTION

The ingesting of unmelted snow or ice is not recommended. Eating snow or ice lowers the body's temperature, induces dehydration, and causes minor cold injury to lips and mouth membranes. Water consumed in cold areas should be in the form of warm or hot fluids. The ingestion of cold fluids or foods increases the body's need for water and requires more body heat to warm the substance.

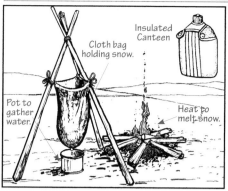

Cloth bag holding snow.
Insulated Canteen
Pot to gather water.
Heat to melt snow.

Fire from seal fat oil in a bowl made of soft stone.
Slab of Slate
Snow

Snow & Ice for Water

- Ice will yield more water per given volume than snow and requires less heat to do so. If the sun is shining, snow or ice may be placed on a dark surface to melt (dark surfaces absorb heat, whereas light surfaces reflect heat).
- If snow must be used, survivors should use snow closest to the ground. This snow is packed and will provide more water for the amount of snow than will the upper layers.

Melting Snow: When snow is to be melted for water, place a small amount of snow in the bottom of the container being used and place it over or near a fire. Snow can be added a little at a time. Allow water in the container bottom to become warm so that when more snow is added, the mixture remains slushy. This will prevent burning the bottom out of the container. Snow absorbs water, and if packed, forms an insulating airspace at the bottom of the container. When this happens, the bottom may bum out.

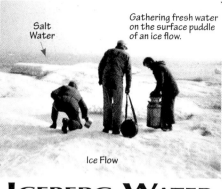

Salt Water
Gathering fresh water on the surface puddle of an ice flow.
Ice Flow

Iceberg Water

Since icebergs are composed of freshwater, they can be a readily available source of drinking water. Survivors should use extreme caution because even large icebergs can suddenly roll over and dump you into the frigid sea water. If sea ice is the primary source of water, survivors should recall that, like seawater itself, saltwater ice should never be ingested.

Old Sea Ice: To obtain water in polar regions or sea ice areas, select old sea ice, a bluish or blackish ice which shatters easily and generally has rounded comers. This ice will be almost salt free.

New Sea Ice: is milky or gray colored with sharp edges and angles. This type of ice will not shatter or break easily. Snow and ice may be saturated with salt from blowing spray; if it tastes salty, select different snow or ice sources.

Adrien

Water on the Open Sea

The lack of drinkable water could be a major problem on the open seas. Seawater should never be ingested in its natural state. It will cause an individual to become violently ill in a very short period of time. As in the desert, conserving sweat, not water, is the rule. Stay in the shade as much as possible and dampen clothing with seawater to keep cool. Never over exert but relax and sleep as much as possible.

Rain: Collect rainwater in available containers and store it for later use. Storage containers could be cans, plastic bags, or the bladder of a life preserver. Drinking as much rainwater as possible while it is raining is advisable. If the freshwater should become contaminated with small amounts of seawater or salt spray, it will remain safe for drinking. At night and on foggy days, collect dew for drinking water by using a sponge, chamois, handkerchief, etc.

Solar Stills: If available, a solar still will provide a drinkable source of water. Read the instructions immediately and set them up. Be sure to attach them to the raft.

Desalter Kits: If available, should probably be saved for the time when no other means of procuring drinking water is available. Instructions on how to use the desalter kit are on the container.

Collecting water from the rain on the ocean.

Consume Only Water

The so-called "water substitutes" do little for the survivor, and may do much more harm than not consuming any water at all. There is no substitute for water. Fish juices and other animal fluids are of doubtful value in preventing dehydration. Fish juices contain protein which requires large amounts of water to be digested and the waste products must be excreted in the urine which increases water loss. Survivors should never drink urine. Urine is body waste material and only serves to concentrate waste materials in the body and require more water to eliminate the additional waste.

PentaPur Travel Cup
The Travel Cup features:
Phase 1: Gravity filter.
Phase 2: Iodine resin.
Phase 3: Carbon filtration.
It provides micro biologically pure water from any water source. The carbon component removes unwanted chemicals and excess iodine from the treated water. The cup will treat a total of 100 gallons at 1/2 pint per minute. Weighs: 6 oz (170 g). Pentapur™

Filtration

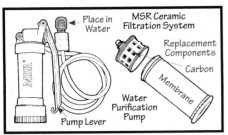

MSR Ceramic Filtration System
Place in Water
Replacement Components
Carbon
Membrane
Water Purification Pump
Pump Lever

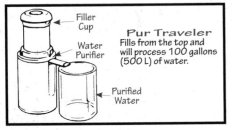

Filler Cup
Water Purifier
Pur Traveler
Fills from the top and will process 100 gallons (500 L) of water.
Purified Water

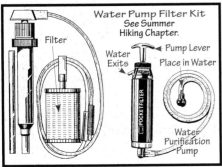

Water Pump Filter Kit
See Summer Hiking Chapter.
Filter
Water Exits
Pump Lever
Place in Water
Water Purification Pump

EMERGENCY PURIFICATION METHODS

Always follow instructions on the package.
Boil: Boil the water for at least 10 minutes.
Purification Tablets: Follow instructions on the bottle. In general: One tablet per quart of clear water; two tablets if water is cloudy. Let water stand for 5 minutes (allowing the tablet time to dissolve), then shake and allow to stand for 15 minutes. To clean the neck part of the canteen turn the canteen over and allow a small amount of water to seep out and cover the neck part.
Iodine: Eight drops of 2 1/2% iodine per quart. Stir or shake and let stand for at least 10 minutes.
Possible problems with water if...
- Strong odors, foam, or bubbles in the water.
- Discoloration or turbid (muddy with sediment).
- Water from lakes found in desert areas is sometimes salty because it has been without an outlet for extended periods of time. Magnesium or alkali salts may produce a laxative effect; if not too strong, it is drinkable.
- If the water gags you or causes gastric disturbances, drinking should be discontinued.
- The lack of healthy green plants growing around any water source.

TREATMENT OF WATER

Boiling is the most reliable method to make water safe to drink. Bring water to a vigorous boil, and then allow it to cool; do not add ice. At high altitudes, allow water to boil vigorously for a few minutes or use chemical disinfectants. Adding a pinch of salt or pouring water from one container to another will improve the taste.

Chemical disinfection can be achieved with either iodine or chlorine, with iodine providing greater disinfection in a wider set of circumstances. For disinfection with iodine, use either tincture of iodine or tetraglycine hydroperiodide tablets, such as Globaline® and Potable-Aqua®. These disinfectants can be found in sporting goods stores and pharmacies. Read and follow the manufacturer's instructions. If the water is cloudy, then strain it through a clean cloth and double the number of disinfectant tablets added. If the water is very cold, either warm it or allow increased time for disinfectant to work.

TREATMENT

Organism	Illness
Parasitic microorganism (protozoa)	Giardia cysts Lamblia "Beaver Fever"
Bacteria	Typhoid, diarrhea, etc.
Virus	Polio, hepatitis, etc.

Methods to Treat Water

Boiling: Kills nearly everything but is impractical as it requires time and much fuel.
Chemical Disinfectant: Is lightweight, inexpensive and effective. Iodine- based tablets are usually used but the water they produce is not tasty.
Filtration: Removes contaminants by passing the liquid through a fine filter.
Purification: Uses a filtration method combined with the chemical method.

WATER FILTER

With the "advance" of civilization, even the most remote water source has a high probability of being contaminated. The latest in water purification methods are filters that strain the water and remove microscopic contaminants.

The purity of the water depends upon the size of the pores in the filter. It takes a pore size of 0.4 microns to eliminate bacteria. Because of the large variety and similarity of products on the market a generic product is described.

This water purifier is usually self contained. You fill the bottle with water, you squeeze the bottle (or gravity pushes the water), and the treated water goes through the filter and comes out through a spout. In some models the bottle can be placed in the bottle attachment of your bicycle. One filter is good for approximately 100 gallons. With use, the filter clogs and it becomes more difficult to draw water. In some models you can clean the filter. Some models have a three-stage purification cartridge.

THREE STAGE PURIFICATION

Stage One: Removes the sediment and stops pathogenic cysts with a filter.
Stage Two: Using iodinated resin this stage kills and disables water borne microorganisms, including E. coli and Vibrio cholera bacteria, polio, hepatitis and other harmful viruses.
Stage Three: Is a coconut-based carbon which captures much of the water's unwanted flavors, odors and residual iodine (These flavors come from stage two).

WATER ILLNESSES

GIARDIASIS

Giardiasis is an illness caused by *Giardia lamblia*, a one-celled, microscopic parasite that lives in the intestines of people and animals. The parasite is passed in the bowel movement of an infected person or animal. During the past 15 years, Giardia lamblia has become recognized as one of the most common causes of waterborne disease in humans in the United States. This parasite is found in every region of the United States and throughout the world. Diarrhea, abdominal cramps, and nausea are the most common symptoms of giardiasis. They may lead to weight loss and dehydration. *Symptoms* usually appear 1-2 weeks after infection with the parasite. In healthy persons, symptoms may last 4-6 weeks. Occasionally, they last longer. However, not everyone infected has symptoms.
Get medical attention.
Giardia may be found in soil, food, water, or on surfaces. You can become infected by swallowing water contaminated with Giardia. A person can ingest a Giardia cyst, the infectious stage of the parasite, when swallowing water from swimming pools, lakes, rivers, springs, ponds, or streams contaminated with sewage or feces from humans or animals. Thoroughly wash with safe water all vegetables and fruits you plan to eat raw.

CRYPTOSPORIDIOSIS

You can get infected by "crypto" when swallowing water contaminated with crypto. Boil drinking water for 1 minute to kill the crypto parasite and make the water safe to drink.
A person can ingest a crypto oocyst, the infectious stage of the parasite, after...
(1) Swallowing water from swimming pools, lakes, rivers, springs, ponds, or streams contaminated with sewage or feces from humans or animals.
(2) Eating uncooked food contaminated with crypto. Thoroughly wash with water all vegetables and fruits you plan to eat raw.
Crypto is a microscopic parasite that can live in the intestines of humans and animals. The parasite is protected by an outer shell that allows it to survive outside the body for long periods of time and makes it very resistant to chlorine disinfection. *Symptoms* generally begin 2-10 days after being infected. Symptoms include diarrhea, loose or watery stool, stomach cramps, upset stomach, and a slight fever. Some people have no symptoms. Symptoms will last about 2 weeks; you may seem to get better, then worse. Once you feel better, you continue to pass Cryptosporidium in your stool for up to 2 months. During this 2 month period you may spread the infection to others.
Get medical assistance.

Birch bark water container.

BRASS JUGS & WATER TREATMENT

A recent study, by Rob Reed, a microbiologist, of brass jugs used in developing countries found that these might help combat many water-borne diseases. He followed an idea presented by "local wisdom" of the fact that "traditional brass water containers offer some protection against sickness." Reed followed up on this "folklore" and he found that "bacteria are indeed less likely to thrive in brass water pots than in earthenware or plastic ones." Reed, with P. Tandon and S. Chhibber, carried out research that tested this hypotheses with the Escherichia coli bacteria (E. coli). The test involved keeping a diluted culture of E. coli in brass and earthenware containers - the test was also made in India using naturally contaminated water.

In the brass vessels, the live E. coli levels fell and after 48 hours they were at undetectable levels.

Reed explains that the pots made of brass (alloy of copper and zinc) shed copper particles into the water that kill the bacteria. The levels of the metal that enter the water on a daily basis would be less than the daily recommended dose of copper or zinc. This is based upon a person drinking 10 liters per day.

Plastic water containers do not have these "disease-fighting properties" of inactivating the bacteria.

REVERSE OSMOSIS

Desalination: The process of removing salts from water using a membrane. With reverse osmosis, the product water passes through a fine membrane that the salts are unable to pass through, while the salt waste (brine) is removed and disposed. This process differs from electrodialysis, where the salts are extracted from the feedwater by using a membrane with an electrical current to separate the ions. The positive ions go through one membrane, while the negative ions flow through a different membrane, leaving the end product of freshwater.

Water Quality: An advanced method of water or wastewater treatment that relies on a semi-permeable membrane to separate waters from pollutants. An external force is used to reverse the normal osmotic process resulting in the solvent moving from a solution of higher concentration to one of lower concentration.

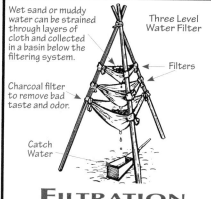

Wet sand or muddy water can be strained through layers of cloth and collected in a basin below the filtering system.

Three Level Water Filter

← Filters

Charcoal filter to remove bad taste and odor.

Catch Water

FILTRATION

Eliminating Odors & Improving Taste

Because of an aversion to water from natural sources, it should be rendered as potable as possible through filtration. Filtration only removes the solid particles from water - *it does not purify it.* One simple and quick way of filtering is to dig a sediment hole or seepage basin along a water source and allow the soil to filter the water. The seepage hole should be covered while not in use. Another way is to construct a filter-layers of material stretched across a tripod. Charcoal is used to eliminate bad odors and foreign materials from the water. Activated charcoal (obtained from freshly burned wood is used to filter the water). If a solid container is available for making a filter, use layers of fine-to-coarse sand and gravel along with charcoal and grass.

TREATMENT OF WATER - TINCTURE OF IODINE

Tincture of iodine	Drops* added / quart or liter	
	Clear water	Cold or cloudy water**
2%	5	10

*1 drop = 0.05 ml. Let stand for 30 minutes before water is safe to use.

**Very turbid or very cold water may require prolonged contact time; let stand up to several hours prior to use, if possible. To ensure that Cryptosporidium is killed, water must stand for 15 hours before drinking.

High Flow Ceramic Water Filter

A: Fill dry bag with water.
B: Gravity will pull the water through a ceramic filter that has an activated carbon core. Carbon core removes trace levels of pesticides, poor color and taste. Removes Giardia, Tapeworm, and Cryptosporidium Cysts. Outputs 15 liters per hour. Filters approximately 500 gallons per filter.
Stearns

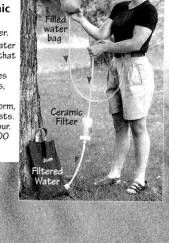

Filled water bag

Ceramic Filter

Filtered Water

You can survive!

WATER GLOSSARY

Acid: a substance that has a pH of less than 7 (7 is neutral). Specifically, an acid has more free hydrogen ions (H+) than hydroxyl ions (OH-).

Acre-foot (acre-ft): the volume of water required to cover 1 acre of land (43,560 sq ft) to a depth of 1 foot.

Alkaline: sometimes water or soils contain an amount of alkali (strongly basic) substances sufficient to raise the pH value above 7.0 and be harmful to the growth of crops.

Alluvium: deposits of clay, silt, sand, gravel, or other particulate material that has been deposited by a stream or other body of running water in a streambed, on a flood plain, on a delta, or at the base of a mountain.

Aqueduct: a pipe, conduit, or channel designed to transport water from a remote source, usually by gravity.

Aquifer: a geologic formation(s) that is water bearing. A geological formation or structure that stores and/or transmits water, such as to wells and springs.

Aquifer (confined): soil or rock below the land surface that is saturated with water. There are layers of impermeable material both above and below it and it is under pressure so that when the aquifer is penetrated by a well, the water will rise above the top of the aquifer.

Aquifer (unconfined): an aquifer whose upper water surface (water table) is at atmospheric pressure, and thus is able to rise and fall.

Artesian Water: ground water that is under pressure when tapped by a well and is able to rise above the level at which it is first encountered. It may or may not flow out at ground level. The pressure in such an aquifer commonly is called artesian pressure, and the formation containing artesian water is an artesian aquifer or confined aquifer.

Base: a substance that has a pH of more than 7 (7 is neutral). A base has less free hydrogen ions (H+) than hydroxyl ions (OH-).

Bedrock: the solid rock beneath the soil and superficial rock. A general term for solid rock that lies beneath soil, loose sediments, or other unconsolidated material.

Capillary Action: the means by which liquid moves through the porous spaces in a solid, such as soil, plant roots, and the capillary blood vessels in our bodies due to the forces of adhesion, cohesion, and surface tension. Capillary action is essential in carrying substances and nutrients from one place to another in plants and animals.

Condensation: the process of water vapor in the air turning into liquid water. Water drops on the outside of a cold glass of water are condensed water. Condensation is the opposite process of evaporation.

Cubic feet/second (cfs): a rate of the flow, in streams and rivers, for example. It is equal to a volume of water one foot high and one foot wide flowing a distance of one foot in one second. One "cfs" is equal to 7.48 gallons of water flowing each second.

Desalinization: the removal of salts from saline water to provide freshwater.

Discharge: the volume of water that passes a given location within a given period of time. Usually expressed in cubic feet per second.

Drainage Basin: land area where precipitation runs off into streams, rivers, lakes, and reservoirs. It is a land feature that can be identified by tracing a line along the highest elevations (ridge line) between two areas on a map, often a ridge. Also called a "watershed."

WATER GLOSSARY

Erosion: the process in which a material is worn away by a stream of liquid (water) or air, often due to the presence of abrasive particles in the stream.

Estuary: a place where fresh and salt water mix, such as a bay, salt marsh, or where a river enters an ocean.

Evaporation: process of liquid water becoming water vapor, including vaporization from water surfaces, land surfaces, and snow fields, but not from leaf surfaces. See transpiration

Evapotranspiration: the sum of evaporation and transpiration.

Freshwater: Water that contains less than 1,000 milligrams per liter (mg/L) of dissolved solids; generally, more than 500 mg/L of dissolved solids is undesirable for drinking.

Geyser: A geothermal feature of the Earth where there is an opening in the surface that contains superheated water that periodically erupts in a shower of water and steam.

Giardiasis: A disease that results from an infection by the protozoan parasite Giardia Intestinalis, caused by drinking water that is either not filtered or not chlorinated. The disorder is more prevalent in children than in adults and is characterized by abdominal discomfort, nausea, and alternating constipation and diarrhea.

Greywater: Wastewater from clothes washing machines, showers, bathtubs, hand washing, lavatories and sinks.

Ground Water: Water that flows or seeps downward and saturates soil or rock, supplying springs and wells. The upper surface of the saturate zone is called the water table.

Ground Water, confined: Ground water under pressure significantly greater than atmospheric pressure.

Ground-Water Recharge: Inflow of water to a ground-water reservoir from the surface. **Ground Water, unconfined:** Water in an aquifer that has a water table that is exposed to the atmosphere.

Hardness: Water-quality indication of the concentration of alkaline salts in water, mainly calcium and magnesium. If the water you use is "hard" then more soap, detergent or shampoo is necessary to raise a lather.

Headwater(s): (1) the source and upper reaches of a stream. (2) the water upstream from a structure or point on a stream. (3) the small streams that come together to form a river. Also may be thought of as any and all parts of a river basin except the mainstream river and main tributaries.

Hydrologic Cycle: Cyclic transfer of water vapor from the Earth's surface via evapotranspiration into the atmosphere, from the atmosphere via precipitation back to earth, and through runoff into streams, rivers, and lakes, and ultimately into the oceans.

Impermeable Layer: Layer of solid material, such as rock or clay, which does not allow water to pass through.

Infiltration: Flow of water from the land surface into the subsurface.

Leaching: Process by which soluble materials in the soil, such as salts, nutrients, pesticide chemicals or contaminants, are washed into a lower layer of soil or are dissolved and carried away by water.

Lentic Waters: Ponds or lakes (standing water).

Levee: Natural or man made earthen barrier along the edge of a stream, lake, or river. Land alongside rivers can be protected from flooding by levees.

Lotic Waters: Flowing waters, as in streams and rivers.

Nephelometric Turbidity Unit (NTU): Unit of measure for the turbidity of water. Essentially, a measure of the cloudiness of water.

Organic Matter: Plant and animal residues, or substances made by living organisms. All are based upon carbon compounds.

Osmosis: Movement of water molecule through a thin membrane. The osmosis process occurs in our bodies and is also one method of desalinizing saline water.

pH: Measure of the relative acidity or alkalinity of water. Water with a pH of 7 is neutral; lower pH levels indicate increasing acidity, while pH levels higher than 7 indicate increasingly basic solutions.

Particle Size: Diameter, in millimeters, of suspended sediment or bed material. Particle-size classifications are: • Clay - 0.00024-0.004 mm; • Silt - 0.004-0.062 mm; • Sand - 0.062-2.0 mm; and • Gravel - 2.0-64.0 mm.

Parts per Billion: Number of "parts" by weight of a substance per billion parts of water. Used to measure extremely small concentrations.

Parts per Million: Number of "parts" by weight of a substance per million parts of water. This unit is commonly used to represent pollutant concentrations.

Pathogen: Disease-producing agent; usually applied to a living organism. Generally, any viruses, bacteria, or fungi that cause disease.

Percolation: (1) The movement of water through the openings in rock or soil. (2) the entrance of a portion of the stream flow into the channel materials to contribute to ground water replenishment.

Permeability: Ability of a material to allow the passage of a liquid, such as water through rocks. Permeable materials, such as gravel and sand, allow water to move quickly through them, whereas impermeable material, such as clay, don't allow water to flow freely.

Porosity: Measure of the water-bearing capacity of subsurface rock. With respect to water movement, it is not just the total magnitude of porosity that is important, but the size of the voids and the extent to which they are interconnected, as the pores in a formation may be open, or interconnected, or closed and isolated. For example, clay may have a very high porosity with respect to potential water content, but it constitutes a poor medium as an aquifer because the pores are usually so small.

Potable Water: Water of a quality suitable for drinking.

Precipitation: Rain, snow, hail, sleet, dew, & frost.

Recharge: Water added to an aquifer. For instance, rainfall that seeps into the ground.

Runoff: That part of the precipitation, snow melt, or irrigation water that appears in uncontrolled surface streams, rivers, drains or sewers.

Saline Water: Water that contains significant amounts of dissolved solids. Parameters for saline water: Fresh water <1,000 parts per million (ppm); Slightly saline water - 1,000 to 3,000 ppm; Moderately saline water - 3,000 to 10,000 ppm; Highly saline water - 10,000 to 35,000 ppm.

Sediment: Usually applied to material in suspension in water or recently deposited from suspension.

Sedimentary Rock: Rock formed of sediment, and specifically: (1) sandstone and shale, formed of fragments of other rock transported from their sources and deposited in water; and (2) rocks formed by or from secretions of organisms, such as most limestone. Many sedimentary rocks show distinct layering, which is the result of different types of sediment being deposited in succession.

Seepage: (1) The slow movement of water through small cracks, pores, etc. (2) The loss of water by infiltration into the soil from a canal, ditches, watercourse, reservoir, or other body of water, or from a field.

Sinkhole: Depression in the Earth's surface caused by dissolving of underlying limestone, salt, or gypsum. Drainage is provided through underground channels that may be enlarged by the collapse of a cavern roof.

Stream: General term for a body of flowing water; natural water course containing water at least part of the year.

Surface Tension: Attraction of molecules to each other on a liquid's surface. Thus, a barrier is created between the air and the liquid.

Surface Water: Water that is on the Earth's surface, such as in a stream, river, lake, or reservoir.

Suspended Sediment: Very fine soil particles that remain in suspension in water for a considerable period of time without contact with the bottom. Such material remains in suspension due to the upward components of turbulence and currents and/or by suspension.

Transmissibility (ground water): the capacity of a rock to transmit water under pressure.

Transpiration: Process by which water that is absorbed by plants, usually through the roots, is evaporated into the atmosphere from the plant surface, such as leaf pores. See Evapotranspiration.

Tributary: Smaller river or stream that flows into a larger river or stream.

Turbidity: Amount of solid particles that are suspended in water and that cause light rays shining through the water to scatter. Thus, turbidity makes the water cloudy or even opaque in extreme cases.

Unsaturated Zone: Zone immediately below the land surface where the pores contain both water and air, but are not totally saturated with water.

Water Cycle: Circuit of water movement from the oceans to the atmosphere and to the Earth and return to the atmosphere through various stages or processes such as precipitation, interception, runoff, infiltration, percolation, storage, evaporation, and transportation.

Water Quality: Term used to describe the chemical, physical, and biological characteristics of water, usually in respect to its suitability for a particular purpose.

Water Table: Top of the water surface in the saturated part of an aquifer.

Watershed: Land area that drains water to a particular stream, river, or lake. It is a land feature that can be identified by tracing a line along the highest elevations between two areas on a map, often a ridge. Large watersheds, like the Mississippi River basin contain thousands of smaller watersheds.

Well (water): Artificial excavation put down by any method for the purposes of withdrawing water from the underground aquifers.

Based upon information from: the Nevada Division of Water Planning, the Water Quality Association, and the USGS.

An old print of surveyors crossing the Colorado Desert towards Signal Mountain. Notice that they are traveling in single file. A column of this type would usually have a "shepherd," at the end, to assist any stragglers - the column could not stop in the desert as the people and horses had a limited supply of water.

Signal Mountain

This irregular landscape shows you why you need to know how to use a compass. A GPS might give you your exact location and directions to your destintion but the knowledge of the use of a compass will give a greater insight as to your location ... and no batteries!

33 USING A COMPASS

THE GRAND CANYON

If you got lost in the Grand Canyon it would require all your survival knowledge and luck to find your way out. The ruggedness of the terrain and the fact that there is no easy line of sight in the valleys would be a challenge. This chapter will outline basic direction-finding techniques: by compass, stars, Moon, Sun, wind, smell, etc. The use of a GPS can be found in the manufacture's instructions. If you have a cell phone, and it has reception, you can always call for a helicopter to get you out.

The Grand Canyon is one of North America's most spectacular geologic features. Carved primarily by the Colorado River over the past six million years, the canyon sports vertical drops of 5,000 feet and spans a 445 kilometer long stretch of Arizona desert. The strata along the steep walls of the canyon form a record of geologic time from the Paleozoic Era (250 million years ago) to the Precambrian (1.7 billion years ago). This view was acquired by the Terra spacecraft. Visible and near infrared data were combined to form an image. **NASA**

Pin-on Compass

EARTH'S MAGNETIC FIELD

The Earth acts like a great spherical magnet, in that it is surrounded by a magnetic field. The Earth's magnetic field resembles, in general, the field generated by a dipole magnet (i.e., a straight magnet with a north and south pole) located at the center of the Earth.

The magnetic N-S axis is offset from the Earth's rotation axis (geographic N-S) by approximately 11.5°. This means that the N-S geographic poles and the N-S magnetic poles are not located in the same place. At any point, the Earth's magnetic field is characterized by a direction and intensity which can be measured. They are measured by the magnetic declination (**D**), the horizontal intensity (**H**), and the vertical intensity (**Z**).

MAGNETIC POLES

The magnetic poles are defined as the area where the dip on a compass is vertical. In reality, the surveyed magnetic pole is not a single point, but more likely an area where many 'magnetic poles' exist. The task of locating the principal magnetic pole is difficult for many reasons; the large area over which the dip or inclination (**I**) is nearly 90°, the pole areas are not fixed points, but move tens to hundreds of kilometers because of daily variations and magnetic storms, and finally, the polar areas are relatively inaccessible to survey crews.

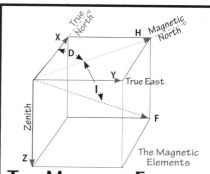

The Magnetic Elements

THE MAGNETIC ELEMENTS

To measure the Earth's magnetism in any place, we must measure the direction and intensity of the field. To describe the direction of the magnetic field:

D Magnetic Declination (in degrees (°)). The angle between magnetic north and True North. **D** is considered positive when the angle measured is East of True North and negative when West of True North.
I Magnetic Inclination (in degrees (°)). The angle between the horizontal plane and the total field vector (**F**).
F Intensity of the total field vector
H horizontal component of field
Z vertical component of field (Zenith)
X North component of the horizontal intensity
Y East component of the horizontal intensity

The Magnetic North

A compass will point along the magnetic North-South line and not along the geographic longitude. The Magnetic North is not at the North Pole but off Bathurst Island in northern Canada. The magnetic variations can be up to 30°W in Alaska and over 50°E in Greenland. There is no variation on the agonic line which divides the east and west magnetic variations. The agonic line passes along the western shore of Hudson Bay, through Lake Superior, western shore of Lake Michigan, off the west coast of Florida, and through Cuba.

Agonic Line: East of the line the variation is east and west of the line is west. This means that the compass reading has to be adjusted for the variation which depends upon your location.

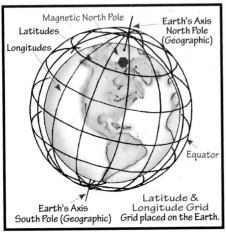

Use degrees to express direction and location.
**One degree (°) = 60 minutes (')
One minute (') = 60 seconds (")**

Magnetic North Pole
Latitudes
Longitudes
Earth's Axis North Pole (Geographic)
Equator
Earth's Axis South Pole (Geographic)
Latitude & Longitude Grid Grid placed on the Earth.

MAGNETIC FIELD

The magnetic field is different in different places on Earth. It is so irregular that it must be measured in many places to get a satisfactory picture of its distribution. At the magnetic equator the dip or inclination is zero. Unlike the Earth's geographic equator, the magnetic equator is not fixed, but slowly changes.

MAGNETIC EQUATOR

The magnetic equator is where the dip or inclination (**I**) is zero. There is no vertical (**Z**) component to the magnetic field. The magnetic equator is not fixed, but slowly changes. North of the magnetic equator, the north end of the needle dips below the horizontal, I and Z are positive. South of the magnetic equator, the south end dips below the horizontal, I and Z are measured negative. As you move away from the magnetic equator, I and Z increase.

COMPASS NEEDLE POINTING

The compass points in the direction of the horizontal component of the magnetic field *(along magnetic field lines)* where the compass is located, and not to any single point. Knowing the magnetic declination (angle between true north and the horizontal trace of the magnetic field) for your location allows you to correct your compass for the magnetic field in your area. A mile or two away, the magnetic declination may be considerably different, requiring a different correction.

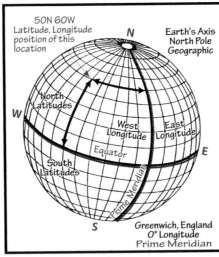

GEOGRAPHIC COORDINATES
LOCATING A PLACE ON EARTH

By drawing a set of east-west rings around the globe (parallel to the equator), and a set of north-south rings crossing the equator at right angles to the equator and converging at the poles, a network of reference lines is formed from which any point on the earth's surface can be located.

PARALLEL OF LATITUDE

The angular distance of a point north or south of the equator is known as its latitude. The rings around the earth parallel to the equator are called parallels of latitude or simply parallels.

MERIDIANS OF LONGITUDE

A second set of rings around the globe at right angles to lines of latitude and passing through the poles are known as meridians of longitude or simply meridians. One meridian is designated as the Prime Meridian (it is the 0° meridian and it passes through Greenwich, England. The distance east or west of the prime meridian to a point is known as its longitude.

GEOGRAPHIC COORDINATES

Geographic coordinates are expressed in angular measurement. Each circle is divided into 360°, each degree into 60 minutes, and each minute into 60 seconds.

Latitude: Starting with 0° at the Equator, the parallels of latitude are numbered to 90° both north and south. The extremities are the North Pole at 90° North latitude and the South Pole at 90° South latitude. Latitude can have the same numerical value north or south of the equator, so the direction N or S must always be given.

Longitude: Starting with 0° at the Prime Meridian, longitude is measured both East and West around the world. Lines east of the prime meridian are numbered to 180° and identified as East longitude; lines west of the prime meridian are numbered to 180° and identified as West longitude. The direction E or W must always be given. The line directly opposite the prime meridian, 180°, may be referred to as either east or west longitude.

All places on earth have a unique latitude & longitude which are represented as Latitude 32°15'00"N, Longitude 84°50'00"W.

Angular Distance on Surface of Earth

1° (degree) of latitude:
Approximately 111 kilometers (69 miles).

1' (second) of latitude:
Approximately 30 meters (100 feet).

1° (degree) of longitude:
At the equator is also approximately 111 kilometers (69 miles).

1° (degree) of longitude:
At the poles is zero as all longitudes meet at the poles.

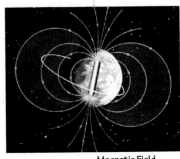

Magnetic Field around the Earth

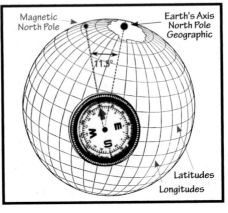

Expressing Direction

Directions are expressed in everyday life, as right, left, and straight ahead; but the question arises: "to the right of what?"

Angular Measure

Directions are expressed as units of angular measure, the most common being the unit of angular measure of degrees with its subdivisions of minutes and seconds.

Base Line

To measure anything, there must always be a starting point or zero measurement. The most common zero point is the magnetic north when working with the compass, or the true north when on a map.

True North

True north is a line from any position on the earth's surface to the north pole. All lines of longitude are true north lines. True north is usually symbolized by a star on a compass or map.

Magnetic North

Magnetic North points in the direction to the North Magnetic Pole, as indicated by the north-seeking needle of a magnetic compass. Magnetic north is usually symbolized by a half an arrowhead.

Azimuth & Back Azimuth

Azimuth

An azimuth is defined as a horizontal angle, measured in a clockwise manner from a north base line. When using an azimuth, the point from which the azimuth originates is imagined to be the center of the azimuth circle. Azimuths take their name from the base line from which they have been measured: true azimuths from the true north and magnetic azimuths from the magnetic north. Therefore, any one given direction can be expressed in two different ways: a magnetic azimuth if measured by a compass, or a true azimuth if measured from a meridian of longitude on a map.

Back Azimuth

A back azimuth is the reverse direction of an azimuth. It is comparable to doing an "about face." To obtain a back azimuth from an azimuth, add 180° if the azimuth is 180° or less, or subtract 180° if the azimuth is 180° or more. The back azimuth of 180° may be stated as either 0° or 360°.

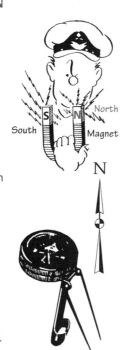

North

South   Magnet

N

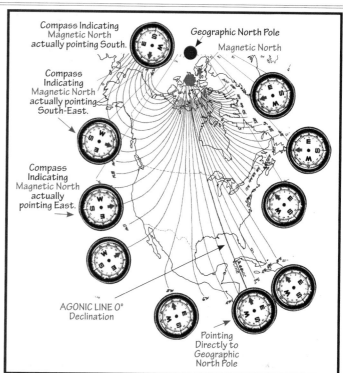

Compass Indicating Magnetic North actually pointing South.

Geographic North Pole

Magnetic North

Compass Indicating Magnetic North actually pointing South-East.

Compass Indicating Magnetic North actually pointing East.

AGONIC LINE 0° Declination

Pointing Directly to Geographic North Pole

Compass Bearing

A bearing expresses a direction as an angle measured East or West from the North or South reference line. Bearings cannot exceed 90° or a quarter circle. A quadrant is a quarter of a circle.

To give a bearing you require:
- The reference line (North or South).
- The amount of the angle.
- The direction in which the angle was measured (East or West).

Examples of Compass Bearing
- *A bearing of N 30° E means an angle of 30° measured from the North line in an eastward direction.*
- *A bearing NE would be N 45° E.*
- *A bearing of S 26° W means an angle of 26° measured from the South line in the westward direction.*

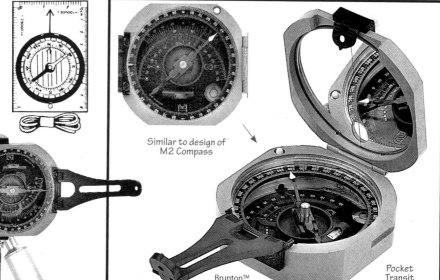

Similar to design of M2 Compass

Brunton™

Pocket Transit

At the Magnetic Pole the dip on a compass is vertical. This is a compass pointing directly at the ground.

Don't get discouraged: unlike poets, navigators are made and not born.

Pocket Transit

This compass is used by field geologists.

Special features are:
- Waterproof/dust proof body construction, needle lift mechanism, inclinometer, magnetic damping, gear-driven declination adjustment, and "international" needle balance. There are also non-waterproof versions and magnetic balance for any part of the world.

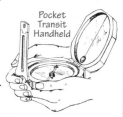

Pocket Transit Handheld

COMPASS READING

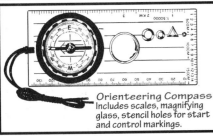

Orienteering Compass
Includes scales, magnifying glass, stencil holes for start and control markings.

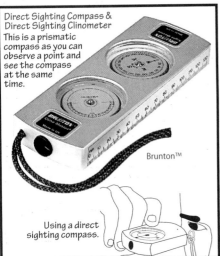

Direct Sighting Compass & Direct Sighting Clinometer
This is a prismatic compass as you can observe a point and see the compass at the same time.

Brunton™

Using a direct sighting compass.

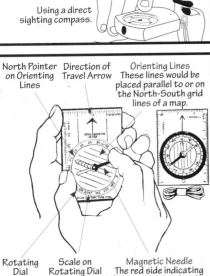

North Pointer on Orienting Lines **Direction of Travel Arrow** **Orienting Lines** These lines would be placed parallel to or on the North-South grid lines of a map.

Rotating Dial **Scale on Rotating Dial** **Magnetic Needle** The red side indicating North. The North side also has a luminous marker on it.

Fingers rotating the rotating dial.

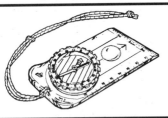

SILVA RANGER MODEL 15

Luminous points for night navigation. Red/black North-South lines. Accuracy within 1.0° from true course. Lid with large sighting mirror.
Graduation: 360°, 400 gon, 4 x 90° (each 2nd degree marked), 6300', 6400' (each 50th mil marked). Large numerals.
Scales: mm, inches and roamer scales 1:25 000 and 1:50,000.
Available also with built-in adjuster for magnetic variation, clinometer and a spirit level for accurate horizontal adjustment 1° accuracy.

Orienteering Compass

Variation Scale **Orienting Lines** **Rotating Dial** **Direction of Travel**

Magnetic Needle **Index Line** **Magnifying Lens**

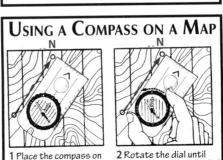

Orienteering Compass

USING A COMPASS ON A MAP

1 Place the compass on the map with the edge along the line of travel.

2 Rotate the dial until the N on the compass dial points to Magnetic North on the map. Make sure that the North-South lines are parallel with the map's meridians.

Silva

ORIENTEERING COMPASS

Using an orienteering compass, hold the compass horizontally in front of you and turn your body until the North of the compass needle is directly over the red part (North) of the North-South arrow. The direction of travel arrow now points precisely to your destination. Look up, sight on a landmark and walk to it. Silva

Direction of Travel Arrow

SIGHTING COMPASS

V-Sight

When using a sighting compass with mirrors, hold the compass, as per the picture, so you can see the compass housing in the mirror at the same time as a sighting is made through the v-sight. Silva

Product illustrations in this chapter courtesy of: Coghlan's, Outbound, Silva, World Famous of Canada, Brunton, US Army.

Features on a Compass **Sight**
Sighting Mirror
Sighting Line
Luminous North Sighting Needle
Clinometer
North-South Lines
Rotatable Compass Housing
Rubber Feet
Adjusting Pinion Screw
Map Scales

USING A COMPASS

Compasses are delicate instruments and should be cared for accordingly.

Inspection: A detailed inspection is required when first obtaining and using a compass. One of the most important parts to check is the floating dial, which contains the magnetic needle. The user must also make sure the sighting wire is straight, the glass and crystal parts are not broken, the numbers on the dial are readable, and most important, that the dial does not stick.

Effects of Metal & Electricity: Metal objects and electrical sources can affect the performance of a compass. However, nonmagnetic metals and alloys do not affect compass readings. The following separation distances are suggested to ensure proper functioning of a compass:

High-tension power lines	180 feet	55 m
Truck, car	55 feet	18 m
Telephone wires	30 feet	10 m
Heavy tripod	6 feet	2 m
Shovel, steel helmet	2 feet	0.5 m

Accuracy: A compass in good working condition is very accurate. However, a compass has to be checked periodically on a known line of direction. Compasses with more than 3°+ variation should not be used.

Protection: If traveling with the compass unfolded, make sure the rear sight is fully folded down onto the bezel ring. This will lock the floating dial and prevent vibration, as well as protect the crystal and rear sight from damage.

The magnetic compass is the most commonly used and simplest instrument for measuring directions and angles outdoors.

THE COMPASS ROSE

This is the traditional design of a compass dial. The outside scale is graduated in 360°. The cardinal points or directions, which are 90° apart, are North, South, East, and West.

For ease of use the compass is divided into quadrants:
Northeast (**NE**) 0°- 90°
Southeast (**SE**) 90°-180°
Southwest (**SW**) 180°- 270°
Northwest (**NW**) 270°- 360°

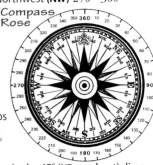

Compass Rose

The use of quadrants is important as they are the first indicator of your direction of travel. Knowing the quadrant helps you avoid the potential 180° error. If the compass points in the 45° (**NE** quadrant) direction but the map indicates the southwest direction (**SW** quadrant) you will know that you are facing 180° in the wrong direction. The classical compass has more subdivisions of the compass rose that are not frequently used. We now usually position ourselves in degrees (°).

LENSATIC COMPASS

The lensatic compass consists of three major parts: the cover, the base, and the lens.

Cover: The compass cover protects the floating dial. It contains the sighting wire (front sight) and two luminous sighting slots or dots used for night navigation.

Base: The body of the compass contains the following movable parts:

- The floating dial is mounted on a pivot so it can rotate freely when the compass is held level. Printed on the dial in luminous figures are an arrow and the letters E and W. The arrow always points to magnetic north and the letters fall at east (E) 90° and west (W) 270° on the dial. There are two scales: the outer scale denotes mils and the inner scale (normally in red) denotes degrees.
- Encasing the floating dial is a glass with a fixed black index line.
- The bezel ring is a ratchet device that clicks when turned. It contains 120 clicks when rotated fully; each click is equal to 3°. A short luminous line that is used in conjunction with the north-seeking arrow during navigation is contained in the glass face of the bezel ring.
- The thumb loop is attached to the base of the compass.

Lens: The lens is used to read the dial, and it contains the rear-sight slot used in conjunction with the front for sighting on objects. The rear sight also serves as a lock and clamps the dial when closed for its protection. The rear sight must be opened more than 45° to allow the dial to float freely.

GLASS BEZEL ON LENSATIC COMPASS

The glass bezel, on a lensatic compass, has two lines. One of the lines is long and one short, and they are at a 45° angle to each other.

- Turn your compass to face north.
- Rotate one of the lines on your glass bezel into the direction you want to walk. On better quality compasses one of the lines and the tip of the needle facing North is luminous so that the compass can be used at night.
- You can start walking in your chosen direction. You can verify your direction by pointing your compass to the magnetic North and checking the direction of your path with the line you have chosen on the glass of the bezel.

To set a desired azimuth in the dark, use the clicking feature on the bezel ring. Each click represents an interval of 3°. So 21° would be 7 clicks.

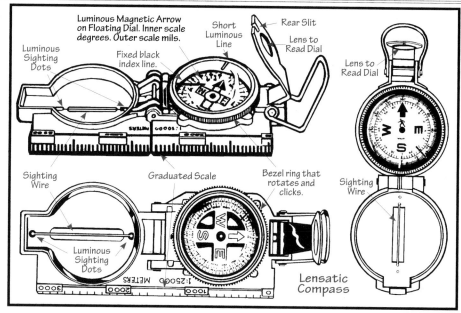

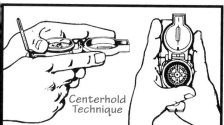
Centerhold Technique

USING A COMPASS

Magnetic azimuths are determined with the use of magnetic instruments, such as lensatic and M2 compasses. The techniques employed when using the lensatic compass are as follows:

Lensatic & Centerhold Technique
Hold the compass level.

- Open the compass to its fullest so that the cover forms a straightedge with the base. Move the lens (rear sight) to the rear most position, allowing the dial to float freely.
- Place your thumb through the thumb loop, form a steady base with your third and fourth fingers, and extend your index finger along the side of the compass.
- Place the thumb of the other hand between the lens (rear sight) and the bezel ring; extend the index finger along the remaining side of the compass, and the remaining fingers around the fingers of the other hand.
- Pull your elbows firmly into your sides; this will place the compass between your chin and your belt.

To measure an azimuth, simply turn your entire body toward the object, pointing the compass cover directly at the object. Once you are pointing at the object, look down and read the azimuth from beneath the fixed black index line. This preferred method offers the following advantages over the sighting technique:

- It is faster and easier to use.
- It can be used under all conditions of visibility.
- It can be used when navigating over any type of terrain.
- It can be used without removing eyeglasses.

Compass-to-Cheek Technique

- Fold the cover of the compass containing the sighting wire to a vertical position; then fold the rear sight slightly forward.
- Look through the rear-sight slot and align the front-sight hairline with the desired object in the distance.
- Then glance down at the dial through the eye lens to read the azimuth.

NOTE: The compass-to-cheek technique is used almost exclusively for sighting, and it is the best technique for this purpose.

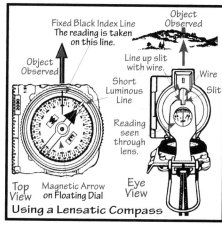
Using a Lensatic Compass

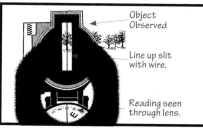

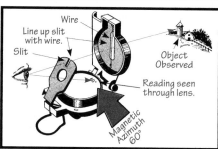

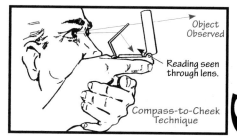
Compass-to-Cheek Technique

COMPASS READING

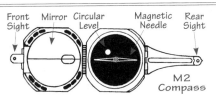

Front Sight | Mirror | Circular Level | Magnetic Needle | Rear Sight

M2 Compass

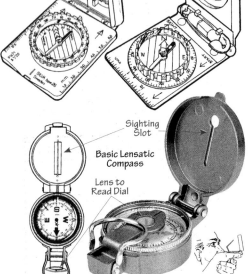

Degrees of Declination

Clinometer Compact Compass
Includes a clinometer to read the angle of a slope. For more details see the chapter on Avalanches.

Brunton™

Sighting Slot

Basic Lensatic Compass

Lens to Read Dial

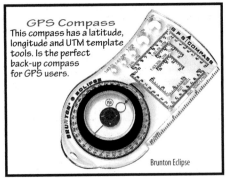

GPS Compass
This compass has a latitude, longitude and UTM template tools. Is the perfect back-up compass for GPS users.

Brunton Eclipse

Baseplate Compass
This compass has the basic N-S magnetic needle, three clinometer systems, and a round bubble level. It is declination adjustable and has a map magnifier. Between the compass and the rubber base there are field reference cards.

Brunton™

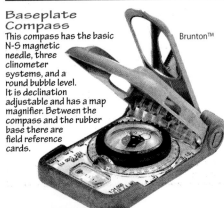

PRESETTING A COMPASS & FOLLOWING AN AZIMUTH

Although different models of the lensatic compass vary somewhat in the details of their use, the principles are the same.

During daylight hours or with a light source:

- Hold the compass level in the palm of the hand.
- Rotate it until the desired azimuth falls under the fixed black index line (for example, 320°), maintaining the azimuth as prescribed
- Turn the bezel ring until the luminous line is aligned with the north-seeking arrow. Once the alignment is obtained, the compass is preset.
- To follow an azimuth, assume the centerhold technique and turn your body until the north-seeking arrow is aligned with the luminous line. Then proceed forward in the direction of the front cover's sighting wire, which is aligned with the fixed black index line that contains the desired azimuth.

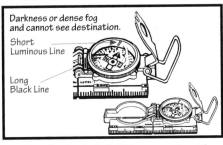

Darkness or dense fog and cannot see destination.

Short Luminous Line

Long Black Line

During limited visibility, an azimuth may be set on the compass by the click method. Remember that the bezel ring contains 3° intervals (clicks).

- Rotate the bezel ring until the luminous line is over the fixed black index line.
- Find the desired azimuth and divide it by three. The result is the number of clicks that you have to rotate the bezel ring.
- Count the desired number of clicks. If the desired azimuth is smaller than 180°, the number of clicks on the bezel ring should be counted in a counterclockwise direction. For example, the desired azimuth is 51°. Desired azimuth is 51° ÷ 3 = 17 clicks counterclockwise. If the desired azimuth is larger than 180°, subtract the number of degrees from 360° and divide by 3 to obtain the number of clicks. Count them in a clockwise direction. For example, the desired azimuth is 330°; 360° - 330° = 30 ÷ 3 = 10 clicks clockwise.
- With the compass preset as described above, assume a centerhold technique and rotate your body until the north-seeking arrow is aligned with the luminous line on the bezel. Then proceed forward in the direction of the front cover's luminous dots, which are aligned with the fixed black index line containing the azimuth.

When the compass is to be used in darkness, an initial azimuth should be set while light is still available. With the initial azimuth as a base, any other azimuth that is a multiple of three can be established through the use of the clicking feature of the bezel ring.

NOTE: Sometimes the desired azimuth is not exactly divisible by three, causing an option of rounding up or rounding down.
If the azimuth is rounded up, this causes an increase in the value of the azimuth, and the object is to be found on the left.
If the azimuth is rounded down, this causes a decrease in the value of the azimuth, and the object is to be found on the right.

M2 COMPASS (MILITARY)

The M2 compass is designed for accuracy. It is a rustproof and dust proof magnetic instrument that provides slope, angle of site, and azimuth readings. The compass is made of non-magnetic materials except for the magnetic needle. The needle is lifted from the pivot and held securely against the glass when the cover is closed. The M2 has a liquid circular level bubble used when measuring the azimuth. One of the most important features of the M2 compass is that it is graduated in mils and does not require a conversion from degrees to mils. It can be calibrated to provide a grid azimuth or it can be used uncalibrated to determine a magnetic azimuth. The artillery M2 compass is a special-purpose instrument designed for accuracy.

COMPASS MAGNETIC NEEDLE

Except for the magnetic needle and its pivot, the compass is made of non-magnetic materials. When the cover is closed, the magnetic needle is automatically lifted from its pivot and held firmly against the glass window. When the compass is open and leveled, the needle floats freely upon its pivot and points to magnetic north. Note that both ends of the needle are shaped like an arrow, and that one arrow is painted white and the other is black. It is the white end of the needle that points to magnetic north. Because the needle is magnetic, it will also be attracted to large iron or steel objects, to electrical power lines, and to operating generators. Magnetic compass readings measured near such objects are apt to be in error due to the magnetic attraction of these objects.

Modern Digital Navigation Units
Units of this type have many interesting features as compass bearings or direction readings and are declination adjustable. Some even have weather information, like altitude, temperature, and barometric pressure. There are time and date displays and some have two daily alarms.

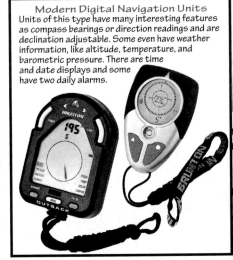

COMPASS TERMINOLOGY

Bearing: The direction between two points given as a reading in degrees. Example 20°W of the large maple tree.

Clinometer: A scale on a compass used to measure angles like the slope of a hill. It can also be used as a level to measure elevation.

Declination: Is the angle between the **true North** (geographic North Pole - the North on a map), and **magnetic North** (as read by a magnetic compass). The declination angle varies at different locations and has to be accounted for when following the directions on a map. Over the continental United States the declination varies by as much as 42°.

Magnifier: To read fine print on a map. Can also be used to start a fire.

Mirror: On compasses that make precise measurements. These compasses can make an in-line sighting and at the same time reflect upon the dial face of the compass where the etched line on the mirror will indicate a reading on the compass face.

Orienting Arrow: Fixed (not moving) red or black outlined arrow on the bottom of the compass or on the case. This is used with the red end (North) of the magnetic needle (this moves) to determine for the bearing or direction of travel.

Prismatic Compass: A compass with a mirror or prism so that the compass face and distant object can be seen at the same time.

Gun Type Sights or Rear Slit: These are on the M2 compass, the lensatic, and transit compasses to help in sighting and taking bearings.

Index Line: The mark on the front sight where you read a bearing on your compass.

Protractor: Can be used to make angular (bearing) readings on a map. Some compasses include protractors.

Sighting Line: Line you sight along to take a bearing.

Triangulation: A method of finding your location on a map by sighting on two visible land features. By plotting the two known bearings you can find your location at the point where the two lines intersect (see the compass instruction manual for a more complete definition and illustration).

Vial: The clear capsule which houses the magnetized needle and the clear fluid which dampens or slows the needle from spinning.

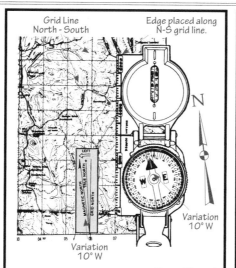

Grid Line North - South. Edge placed along N-S grid line.

Variation 10° W

Variation 10° W

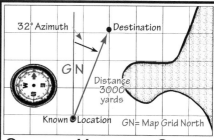

32° Azimuth   Destination

GN

Distance 3000 yards

Known Location   GN = Map Grid North

ORIENTING MAP WITH A COMPASS

Place the map on a flat surface. Place the compass edge along the grid line on the map. Rotate the map and compass so that the map's North matches the magnetic north of the compass. The compass needle will indicate north. Specialized maps will show the magnetic north and magnetic variation from the true north. Adjust the grid north on the map to compensate for the magnetic variation.

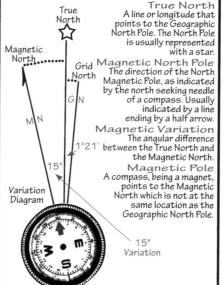

True North
Magnetic North
Grid North
G N
M N
1°21'
15°
Variation Diagram
15° Variation

True North
A line or longitude that points to the Geographic North Pole. The North Pole is usually represented with a star.

Magnetic North Pole
The direction of the North Magnetic Pole, as indicated by the north seeking needle of a compass. Usually indicated by a line ending by a half arrow.

Magnetic Variation
The angular difference between the True North and the Magnetic North.

Magnetic Pole
A compass, being a magnet, points to the Magnetic North which is not at the same location as the Geographic North Pole.

VARIATION DIAGRAM

- A variation diagram is placed on most large-scale maps to enable the user to orient the map properly. The diagram shows the interrelationship of magnetic north, grid north, and true north. On medium-scale maps variation information is shown by a note in the map margin.
- Variation is the angular difference between true north and either magnetic or grid north. There are two variations, a magnetic declination and a grid declination.
- The variation diagram contains three prongs representing magnetic north, grid north, and true north.

Polar Coordinates

A point on the map may be determined or plotted from a known point by giving a direction (in degrees) and a distance along that direction line. The reference direction is normally expressed as an azimuth and the distance in any convenient unit of measurement such as meters or yards. Polar coordinates are useful in the field because magnetic azimuth can be determined from the compass and the distance can be estimated.

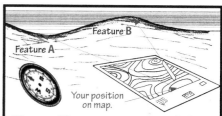

Feature B
Feature A
Your position on map.

FIND POSITION ON MAP WITH A COMPASS

Take two magnetic azimuth bearings (readings) on two prominent features that are visible on the terrain and on the map. Orient your map in the same position as the features on the terrain. Take the angle reading of feature **A**. Take a reading of feature **B**. Draw a line from feature **A** and from feature **B** with the readings that you have obtained. The point where the lines intersect is your present location.

Boat Compass

Boat Compass

Brunton™

Boat Compass

Kayak Compass

Estimating Distance

50 yds	46 m	Mouth & eyes of a person can be clearly distinguished.
100 yds	91 m	Eyes appear as dots.
200 yds	182 m	General details of clothing can be distinguished.
300 yds	247 m	Faces can be seen.
500 yds	457 m	Colors of clothing can be distinguished.
800 yds	752 m	A person looks like a post.
1 mile	1.6 km	Trunks of large trees can be seen.
2 1/2 mi	4 km	Chimneys and windows can be distinguished.
6 mi	10 km	Large houses, silos and towers can be recognized.
9 mi	14 km	Average church steeple can be seen.

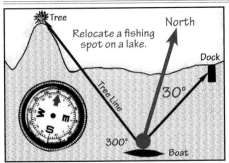

Relocate a fishing spot on a lake.

RELOCATE A FISHING SPOT ON A LAKE

Choose two prominent features - in this case a large tree and a boat dock. You will have to take cross-bearings. First, point the compass, with the direction of travel or wire on lensatic compass, towards the tree. Then rotate the compass until the north indicator points north. You will read 300°. Now point the compass towards the boat dock and obtain a reading of 30°.

So 300° to the tree and 30° to the boat dock. To find your spot next time; go towards the general area, set your compass at 300°, the reading of the tree, and continue towards the tree until the pointer points at the tree. This is one (tree line) of your coordinate lines for your fishing sight. Now look across the lake or behind the tree as a reference point for your "tree line". Then set your compass at 30° and point in the direction of the dock. If the pointer does not point at the dock, move up or down your "tree line" until you are at the right place.

Orientation
Before leaving your camp try to remember the point of departure and what you can see from this point: large trees, hills, mountains, roads, direction of sun, predominant wind, and in which direction does the water flow?

Establish bearing before descending into the hollow. You will not be able to see the tree on the hill when you are in the woods.

Cannot see tree on hill.

STAYING ON COURSE WHEN DESTINATION IS NOT ALWAYS VISIBLE

If the path to a location is not always visible because of woods or hollows then a compass can be used to give you the direction.

• At a point when the destination can be seen, use your compass to establish the bearing of your path. To establish the bearing, point the Direction of Travel Arrow at the destination.
• Turn the rotating dial so that the **N** on the rotating dial is lined up with the North end (the luminous end) of the magnetic compass needle.
• Read the bearing at the Direction of Travel Arrow line. This is the bearing of the destination. If you do not turn the rotating dial while you are traveling, use the Direction of Travel Arrow to indicate your direction when you can not see the destination; otherwise remember the reading.
• Check your reading whenever the destination can be seen.

The magnetic deviation does not have to be taken into consideration as all the readings are based upon the magnetic north.

DELIBERATE OFFSET OR INTENTIONAL ERROR

If you want to reach a spot which is located on a road, river bank, coast, or mountain range (base line), you might want to make an intentional error in your calculation of direction that will eliminate the need to decide "is it to the left or right?" when you get to the base line. Make your calculation as to the direction to take to reach the exact spot, whether by your compass, distant landmark, map, etc. Then choose a point to the left or right of your objective. Navigate to this chosen point. Upon reaching the base line you know that you have made an intentional error to the left or to the right. If you have made a left "error," then upon reaching the base line, turn right and you will walk towards your true destination. A deliberate offset by a known number of degrees in a known direction compensates for possible errors and ensures that upon reaching the linear feature, the user knows whether to go right or left to reach the objective. 10° is an adequate offset for most uses. Each degree offset moves the course about 54 feet (18 m) to the right or left for each 5/8 mile (1000 m) traveled.

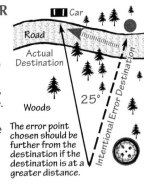

The error point chosen should be further from the destination and ensures that if the destination is at a greater distance.

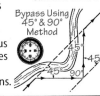

BYPASSING AN OBSTACLE

To bypass an obstacle and still stay oriented, detour around the obstacle by moving at right angles for specified distances.

• For example, while moving on an azimuth of 90° change your azimuth to 180° and travel for 100 yards. Change your azimuth to 90° and travel for 150 yards. Change your azimuth to 360° and travel for 100 yards. Then, change your azimuth to 90° and you are back on your original azimuth line.
• Bypassing an unexpected obstacle at night is a fairly simple matter. To make a 90° turn to the right, hold the compass in the centerhold technique; turn until the center of the luminous letter E is under the luminous line (do not move the bezel ring). To make a 90° turn to the left, turn until the center of the luminous letter W is under the luminous line. This does not require changing the compass setting (bezel ring), and it ensures accurate 90° turns.

Short Summary
Bypassing an Obstacle with a Compass

Use the 90° bypass method to bypass the swamp. In this case you are moving north (0° azimuth).

• Turn east (90° azimuth) walk 30 yards.
• Change your azimuth to 0° (north) walk 150 yards.
• Change your azimuth to 270° (west) walk 100 yards.
• Change your azimuth to 0° (north) and you should be back on your course.

At night you can use the 90° placing of the luminous line on the bezel. Do not move the bezel ring.

Change your azimuth to 0° (North).
Change your azimuth to 270° (West) walk 100 yards.
90° Bypass Method
Swamp
Turn East (90° azimuth) walk 100 yds.
Change your azimuth to 0° (North) walk 150 yds.

Bypass Using 45° & 90° Method

USING A PROTRACTOR

There are different types. The model shown is a half circle. They all divide the circle into units of angular measurement, and each has a scale around the outer edge and an index mark. A full circle has 360° and a half circle has 180° (as shown). When using a protractor on a map the base line is always oriented parallel to the North-South grid line.

To determine the grid azimuth:
1 Draw a line connecting point A and point B.
2 Place the index of the protractor at a point where the line A-B crosses a vertical (North-South) grid line.
3 Keeping the index of the protractor at the intersection point align the index line (the 0°- 180° line) of the protractor on the vertical grid line (North-South).
4 Read the value of the angle from the scale. This is the grid azimuth from point A to point B. Note that this reading is based on the grid North not the magnetic north.

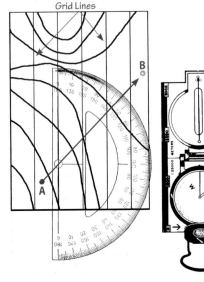

North-South Grid Lines

Razor Blade Compass

Suspended on a thread.

A blade is laminated of different metals and can be magnetized by carefully stroking it across the hand.

MAKING A MAGNETIC COMPASS

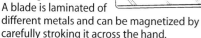

Needle Magnetized by a Battery

Needle

Magnetize a needle by winding insulated wire around the needle. Attach the wire to the terminals of the battery for a few minutes.

SEE MAPS

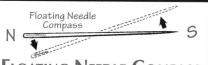

Floating Needle Compass

N   S

FLOATING NEEDLE COMPASS

To magnetize a needle stroke it in one direction with a piece of silk. By stroking it from the point to the eye you will make the point indicate north in the northern hemisphere. The needle can also be magnetized by running it on a small magnet or on your knife which might have become magnetized. Oil your needle by passing it through your hair. Place the needle gently on a stagnant water surface or dish with water in it. The oil on the needle will cause it to float on the water surface. The needle will gradually align itself in the North-South direction.

Sun

6 Fingers represent one hour.

Horizon

Hours to Sunset
Each finger represents 2.5° and the sun moves 15° per hour. That is 2.5°, one finger, represents 10 minutes.

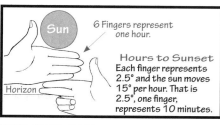

Boulder

Lake

Take a compass bearing on boulder.

BYPASS OBSTACLE WITH A COMPASS

You have approached a lake. Look at the other side and find a distinct feature, in this case the boulder; take a sighting on the boulder. The same method as "Staying on course when destination not always visible". Walk around the lake to the boulder; take a sighting from the boulder and continue on your route.

Sun Dial

Sun

Stick

SOUTH

EAST   WEST   0600
                                    0700
1800   0800
1700   Noon   0900
1600   1000
    1500 1400 1300 1200 1100
              NORTH

TIME WITH SUN DIAL

Use the East-West line as found above. Place a shadow stick vertically at intersection of the North-South line.

- The WEST side will be 0600 hours and the EAST side will be 1800 hours.
- The North-South line will indicate 1200 hours on the NORTH side. In the southern hemisphere it will be 1200 hours on the SOUTH side.
- Divide the arc into equal segments and this sun dial will give you the approximate time. The season is an important factor in the accuracy of the dial but it is fairly accurate around noon (1200).

NORTH: THE POLE STAR ☆

STAR METHOD

- Less than 60 of approximately 5,000 stars visible to the eye are used by navigators. The stars seen as we look up at the sky at night are not evenly scattered across the whole sky. Instead, they are in groups called constellations.
- The constellations that we see depend partly on where we are located on the earth, the time of the year, and the time of the night. The night changes with the seasons because of the journey of the earth around the sun, and it also changes from hour to hour because the turning of the earth makes some constellations seem to travel in a circle. But there is one star that is in almost exactly the same place in the sky all night long every night. It is the North Star, also known as the Polar Star or Polaris.
- The North Star is less than 1° off true north and does not move from its place because the axis of the earth is pointed towards it. The North Star is in the group of stars called the Little Dipper. It is the last star in the handle of the dipper. There are two stars in the Big Dipper, which are a big help when trying to find the North Star. They are called "the Pointers", and an imaginary line drawn through them five times their distance points to the North Star. There are many stars brighter than the North Star, but none is more important because of its location. However, the North Star can only be seen in the northern hemisphere so it cannot serve as a guide south of the equator. The farther one goes north, the higher the North Star is in the sky, and above latitude 70°, it is too high in the sky to be useful.
- Depending on the star selected for navigation, azimuth checks are necessary. A star near the north horizon serves for about half an hour. When moving south, azimuth checks should be made every 15 minutes. When traveling east or west, the difficulty of staying on azimuth is caused more by the likelihood of the star climbing too high in the sky or losing itself behind the western horizon than it is by the star changing direction angle. When this happens, it is necessary to change to another guide star. The Southern Cross is the main constellation used as a guide south of the equator, and the above general directions for using north and south stars are reversed. When navigating using the stars as guides, the user must know the different constellation shapes and their locations throughout the world.

Big Dipper   Cassiopeia

Polaris (Pole Star)

NORTH

FINDING THE POLE STAR
Locate the Pole Star to find the North.

- All other stars revolve around the Pole Star.
- The easiest way to locate the Pole Star is with the help of the constellation Ursa Major (Big Dipper). A straight line drawn between the two stars (pointers) at the end of the Big Dipper's bowl will point to the Pole Star. The distance to the Pole Star is about five times the distance between the point stars.
- Directly across from the Big Dipper is the constellation Cassiopeia. It is made up of five stars that resemble a lopsided "M" or "W". The Pole Star is straight out from the end star of Cassiopeia. It is almost equidistant between the Big Dipper and Cassiopeia.

> **No Compass**
> When a compass is not available, different techniques can be used to determine the four cardinal directions.

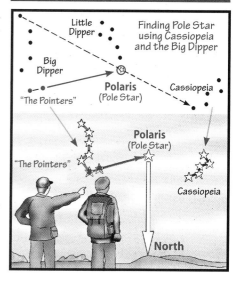

Little Dipper

Big Dipper

"The Pointers"

Polaris (Pole Star)

Cassiopeia

Finding Pole Star using Cassiopeia and the Big Dipper

Polaris (Pole Star)

"The Pointers"

Cassiopeia

North

NORTH: THE POLE STAR

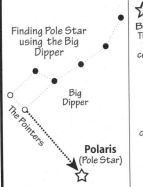

Finding Pole Star using the Big Dipper

Big Dipper

The Pointers

Polaris (Pole Star)

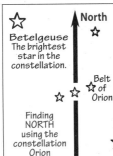

North

Betelgeuse The brightest star in the constellation.

Belt of Orion

Finding NORTH using the constellation Orion

Belt of Orion
The constellation of Orion consists of seven stars. The three stars that are close together are the belt of the constellation. The Orion constellation, when it can be seen, rises on the horizon due East and sets due West. At the Equator it will pass directly overhead, in the southern latitudes north of directly overhead, and in the north latitude south of directly overhead.

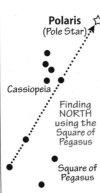

Polaris (Pole Star)

Cassiopeia

Finding NORTH using the Square of Pegasus

Square of Pegasus

Big Dipper

"The Pointers"

Finding the Pole Star using finger widths.

Polaris (Pole Star)

Cassiopeia

FINDING NORTH WITH THE SUN
Finding N-S Direction by E-W Line
Use the sun to find the approximate True North.
- This method can be used when the sun is bright enough for a stick to cast a shadow.
- Place a straight stick (shadow stick) upright, approximately 3 feet (one meter) long, in level ground so that it will cast a shadow.
- Mark the tip of the shadow with a stone.

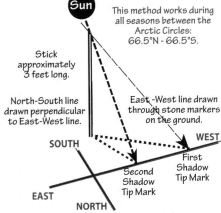

Sun

This method works during all seasons between the Arctic Circles: 66.5°N - 66.5°S.

Stick approximately 3 feet long.

North-South line drawn perpendicular to East-West line.

East-West line drawn through stone markers on the ground.

SOUTH | **WEST**

First Shadow Tip Mark

Second Shadow Tip Mark

EAST | **NORTH**

- Wait at least 10 minutes and mark the tip of the shadow with a second stone.
- Draw a straight line through the stone markers and this will give you an East-West line.
- The first shadow tip stone will be on the West side. This is true in the northern and southern hemispheres.
- A line perpendicular to the East-West line will be North-South. In the northern hemisphere the South side is the side where the shadow stick is located. In the southern hemisphere the shadow stick will be on the north side.
- If the shadow stick is kept up and the shadow points are marked all day, the shortest shadow will in the true north-south direction.

MOON NAVIGATION

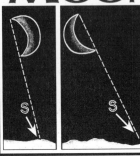

S   S

Finding the South Using the Moon
Drop a line along the points of the crescent of the Moon and project it to the horizon. The point on the horizon is in the direction South of your position.

Moon Compass
During a moonlit night, drive a stake into the ground. Mark the tip of the shadow with a stone. In ten minutes place a stone at the new tip of the shadow. A line drawn between the two points will indicate East-West. In the northern hemisphere the East side will be in the direction of the FIRST shadow point.

E   1   2   W

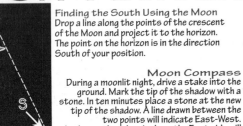

SOUTH: SOUTHERN CROSS

SOUTHERN CROSS
Polaris is not visible in the Southern Hemisphere and the Southern Cross is the most distinctive constellation.
An imaginary line drawn through the long axis of the Southern Cross or True Cross points toward the South Pole.
The True Cross should not be confused with the False Cross, a nearby larger cross known as the False Cross. In the False Cross, the stars are more widely spaced, are less bright and have a star in the center. *The False Cross has five stars while the True Cross has only four stars.* The stars on the southern and eastern arms are among the brightest stars in the heavens. Those on the northern and western arms, while bright, are smaller.
- When the lines are projected from the True Cross and between the two very bright stars east of the True Cross the intersection point is in an area devoid of any stars and very dark, known as the Dark Pocket.
- First extend an imaginary line along the long axis of the True Cross to the south. Join the two bright stars to the east of the True Cross with an imaginary line. Bisect this line with one at right angles. Where the two lines intersect is the South Pole. This South Pole Point can be used to estimate the latitude in the same way as with the North Pole Star.

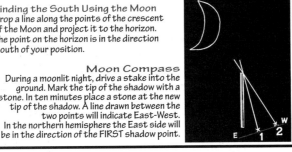

Pointer Stars

Southern Cross

Imaginary Point

South

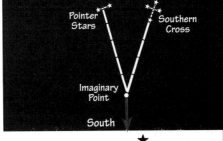

Pointer Stars

True Cross

False Cross

Finding SOUTH in the Southern Hemisphere

True Cross

Devoid Area

S

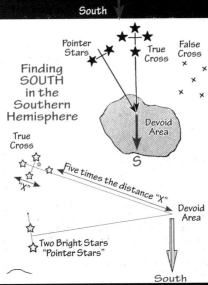

True Cross

"X"

Five times the distance "X"

Devoid Area

Two Bright Stars "Pointer Stars"

South

BYPASS METHOD
Using No Compass
This method requires two distinctive features that can be seen from each side of the obstacle. In this example there is a large tree behind you and a hill, in the distance, in front of you. At position **A** look at the tree behind you; turn 180°, and see the hill in front of you. Walk around the bend in the river until you reach a point where you will be between the hill and the tree. At this point **B** you will be on course and proceed towards the distant hill. Your destination is before you reach the hill.

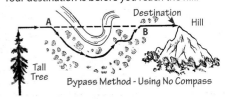

A

Destination

Hill

B

Tall Tree

Bypass Method - Using No Compass

Place Peg 1 in the ground where the tip of the shadow of the tree is cast. Due to the rotation of the sun this is always the west.

Wait 10 to 15 minutes until the tip moves and place peg 2 in the ground.

Draw a straight line through the two pegs to obtain an approximate east (Peg 2) - west (Peg 1) line. North will be perpendicular to this line.

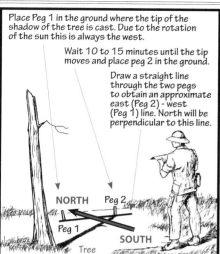

NORTH   Peg 2

Peg 1

SOUTH

Tree Stump Shadow

Place your left foot at peg 1 and your right foot in the direction of peg 2. North will be in front of you.

FINDING N-S DIRECTION BY E-W LINE

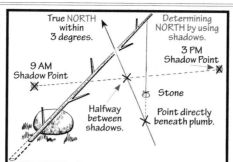

True NORTH within 3 degrees.

Determining NORTH by using shadows.

9 AM Shadow Point

3 PM Shadow Point

Stone

Halfway between shadows.

Point directly beneath plumb.

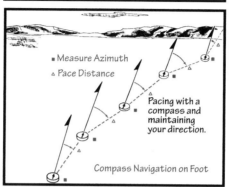

■ Measure Azimuth
△ Pace Distance

Pacing with a compass and maintaining your direction.

Compass Navigation on Foot

FINDING NORTH BY THE SHADOW-TIP

SHADOW-TIP METHOD

This simple and accurate method of finding direction by the sun consists of four basic steps.

- Place a stick or branch into the ground at a level spot where a distinctive shadow will be cast. Mark the shadow tip with a stone, twig, or other means. This first shadow mark is always the west direction.
- Wait 10 to 15 minutes until the shadow tip moves a few inches. Mark the new position of the shadow tip in the same way as the first.
- Draw a straight line through the two marks to obtain an approximate east-west line.
- Standing with the first mark (west) to your left, the other directions are simple: north is to the front, east is to the right, and south is behind you.
- A line drawn perpendicular to the east-west line at any point is the approximate north-south line. If you are uncertain which direction is east and which is west, observe this simple rule - the first shadow-tip mark is always in the west direction, everywhere on earth.

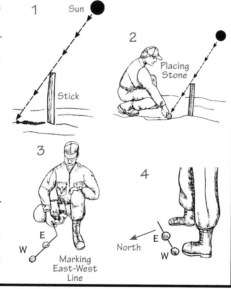

1   Sun

Stick

2   Placing Stone

3   E
W

Marking East-West Line

4   E   North   W

N-S: EQUAL SHADOW METHOD

This method is more accurate than the East-West Line method as it is used when the sun's shadow passes through noon. The disadvantage is that you have to wait to find your direction through the noon period.

- Place a stick vertically in flat sandy ground. This stick should be placed before noon and should cast a shadow at least a foot long.
- Place a stone or peg at the shadow tip.
- Draw an arc the radius of the shadow with the stick as the center.
- The sun's shadow becomes shorter at noon and then starts to get longer and it will cross the drawn arc.
- Mark the spot where the shadow crosses the arc.
- Draw a line straight line through the marks and this is the East-West line.
- Draw a line perpendicular to the line and it will indicate North-South.

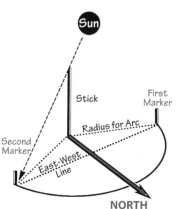

Sun

Stick   First Marker

Radius for Arc

Second Marker

East-West Line

NORTH

LOCATE POSITION ON A MAP
Without a Compass

- Go to a high point or climb a tree to see the surrounding area.
- Look for prominent features such as rivers, hills, valleys, cliffs, swamps, forests, ridge areas, or linear features such as roads, railroads, fence lines, power lines, etc.
- Find direction to place the map relative to your position and the surroundings.
- Find two prominent features and compare their relative location to each other and to you. Additional features will help you to be more precise or confirm your first estimate.
- Make sure that you have not aligned the map in reverse. A third feature would help you correct this potential error. Direction can also be verified by noting the position of the sun and the time of the day.
- From these observations you can approximate your position on the map.
- With the approximate position you can now use the map to establish a route while always keeping your prominent features as reference points.

LOCATE POSITION ON A MAP
Without a Compass (more precise)
This method is similar to the above.

- Orient the map on a flat surface using the above method.
- Choose at least two distant features and mark them on the map.
- Place a straightedge (ruler, edge of pad, etc.) on the map placing the edge on one of the feature marks that you have marked on the map. Align the straightedge with the distant feature and its mark on the map. Draw a line away from the feature mark on the map.
- Repeat the above with your second feature.
- The intersection point of the lines you have drawn is your location. You can determine your grid coordinates from your map grid.

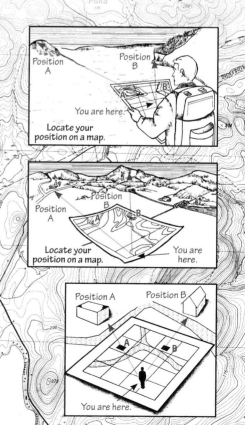

Position A   Position B

You are here.

Locate your position on a map.

Position A   Position B

Locate your position on a map.   You are here.

Position A   Position B

You are here.

DIRECTION WITH WATCH

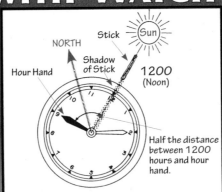

Half the distance between 1200 hours and hour hand.
SOUTH
Stick
1200 (Noon)
Shadow of Stick
Hour Hand
NORTH

NORTHERN TEMPERATE ZONE
23.5°N - 66.5°N
USING A WATCH TO FIND NORTH
- Point hour hand towards sun.
- The South is half way between the hour hand and 1200 hours (Noon). North is in the opposite direction.
  If watch is on Day Light Savings Time use 1300 hours instead of 1200 hours.

NORTH
Stick
Sun
Shadow of Stick
1200 (Noon)
Hour Hand
Half the distance between 1200 hours and hour hand.

SOUTHERN TEMPERATE ZONE
23.5°N - 66.5°N
USING A WATCH TO FIND SOUTH
- Point 1200 hours at sun.
- The North is half way between the 1200 hours on watch and the hour hand.

  If watch is on Day Light Savings Time use 1300 hours instead of 1200 hours.

Tree shaped by the wind.

DIRECTION: TREES & PLANTS
Each species of tree has its own distinct profile or silhouette. The wind and sun will affect a tree's normal profile and this is a clue to establish the North-South direction.
Wind Effects on Trees
- Trees can be windswept so sharing the direction of the dominant wind.
- Knowing the direction of the dominant wind, you can find the cardinal points by looking at a windswept tree.
- Wind can retard tree growth by damaging or desiccating young shoots on the windward side (the side from which the wind blows) of a tree.
- A tree used to determine the direction has to be in an exposed location and not sheltered by hills, trees, or buildings. Examine several trees in the vicinity. Make sure that these trees have not been pruned.
Sun Effects on Trees
While the wind effect usually retards the growth of trees, the sun enhances the growth of the leaves and branches.
- In the northern hemisphere, the arc of the sun is on the south side of the tree. The growth is more luxuriant on the south side. This is most evident on black and white poplars, beech, oak, plane tree, horse chestnut, Norway maple, and the black locust tree. These trees also show a slight declination towards the south. Make sure that these trees are sheltered from the predominant wind.
- Branches on the south of a tree are more horizontal and those on the north more vertical as if they were looking for the sun. Trees such as spruce, firs, and pyramid poplars remain straight.
- Flowering plumes of reeds grow away from the sun.
- Moss and lichen will grow on the side with the most shade. Still more important is where the moisture is retained the longest. In North America, as a general rule, there is less evaporation in the north and northeast sides of trees and rocks. Moss will have a brownish hue when growing in more sunlight and be greener or grayish-green in more shaded and humid spots.
- In the northern hemisphere, deciduous trees usually grow on the southern slope of a hill and evergreens are on the northern slope.
- In the Rocky mountains, the limber pines will be on the southern slope and the Engelmann spruce on the northern.
- The barrel cactus *(Ferocactus)* has a permanent lean to the south.
- In the northern temperate climate, flowers and plants have a tendency to face south or east.
- The pilot weed *(Silphium Lacinatum)* grows with its leaves pointing north-south when it is growing in the sunlight.

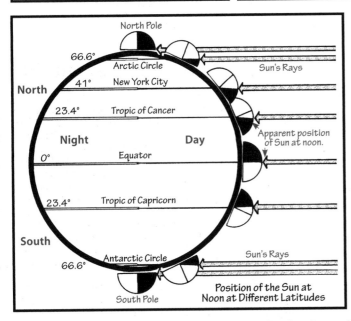
North Pole
66.6°
Arctic Circle
41° New York City
North
23.4° Tropic of Cancer
Night   Day
0° Equator
23.4° Tropic of Capricorn
South
66.6° Antarctic Circle
South Pole
Sun's Rays
Apparent position of Sun at noon.
Position of the Sun at Noon at Different Latitudes

ANIMALS & INSECTS
- Spider webs are not made against the wind. A broken and recently remade web might indicate that the current wind is not the prevailing wind.
- Most animals, birds and insects build their homes in protected areas out of the wind.
- In the high northern latitudes the east side of hills are more sheltered and one finds mice burrowing under dead logs, woodpecker nests, and open-nesting birds. This indicates the east, southeast or south directions.

Predominant Wind Direction
A solitary tree in an exposed area will adapt to the prevailing wind especially in temperate climates. In the winter the prevailing winds will blow hard snow and ice pellets on the tree, and break or sand off the young growth on the windward side. Tree branches get longer on the leeward side.

ANTHILL SIGNPOSTS
Some southern ants build their anthills on slopes facing southeast. This is to maximize the anthill's exposure to the rising sun in the fall and winter. When they build their mounds near trees or rocks, they are found on the south or southeast side. In the western part of the United States the harvester ant *(Pogonomyrmes occidentalis)*, the mound-building ant, builds the only entrance to the mound on the bottom of the southeastern side. The nest of the silver ant *(Formica argentata)* is oriented the same way in the Long Mountain areas of the State of Colorado.

SNOW FORMS & DIRECTION

The Polar regions have much in common with hot sand deserts.

- Snow dunes have the same shapes and properties of sand dunes but they are smaller and less stable.
- The most common snow dunes are similar to the longitudinal sand dune which is parallel to the prevailing wind. The "sastrugi" are a few inches high to three feet high and are always found close together. They are used for navigation on cloudy days. They are very useful near the magnetic pole where compasses do not work. Dig through newly fallen snow to see the direction of the sastrugi.
- The prevailing wind can polish compacted snow and ice.
- Erosion by frost is more evident on the southern slopes as there is more cooling at night and heating by day.
- On the southern slopes, the heat of the sun will leave "melted shadows" of trees, shrubs and stones in the accumulated snow. This is especially true in the spring.
- The direction of the wind is very important, as a warm strong wind can melt snow faster than the sun. This can be misleading when trying to determine your direction.

Sea Ice & Navigation

Bay ice, which is smooth, low and flat can give you an indication as to the distance from a bay. If the pieces of ice are close together like a jigsaw puzzle, you are not far from land. If the edges of the ice are sharp and fresh this will indicate a closeness to shore. If the edges are rounded and the pieces far apart, this indicates that the shore is at some distance.

Effects of Sun & Wind

- Erosion by frost is more evident on the south slope as there is more cooling at night and heating by day.
- In the warmer areas, the northern inclines of hills are smoother due to erosion.
- On the southern slopes, the heat of the sun will leave "melted shadows" of trees, shrubs and stones in the accumulated snow - especially in the spring.
- Note that the direction of the wind is very important as a warm strong wind can melt snow faster than the sun.

Snow melted on one side of tree indicating South.

Drifting light snow indicating predominant winds.

DIRECTION ON GLACIERS

Glaciers with large boulders at the surface form "glacier tables". These large rocks will protect the ice under them from melting and the rocks will gradually protrude above the surface of the ice. The boulder will

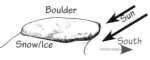

gradually sit on a pedestal of ice. These pedestals can indicate the south because they usually tilt towards the south as the greatest amount of melting occurs on this side due to the sun's radiation. After a while, the boulder slips off and its original pedestal melts and the sun begins this process over again on the boulder's new position.

DIRECTION BY ODORS

The sense of smell is useful in finding the direction.

- The Polynesians carried pigs on their 100 ft. (30 m) catamarans because pigs have a highly developed sense of smell and would get excited upon smelling land.
- The smell of the sea breeze can help give the direction of the land.
- New smells are easier to distinguish at sea than on land as the smell of salt is more constant.
- In the desert, any odor indicates human inhabitation. The best times are early morning and in the evening when the wind direction is predictable.
- Scent is nearly always stronger near the ground, if a ground object is emitting the smell.

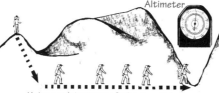

Using an altimeter to find a mountain pass. See Mountain Hiking Chapter.

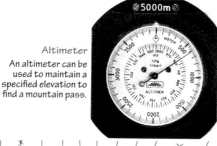

Altimeter

An altimeter can be used to maintain a specified elevation to find a mountain pass.

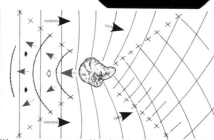

Wave patterns created by the island. See page 125.

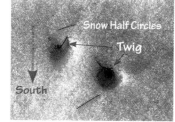

Snow Half Circles

Twig

South

DIRECTIONS FROM HILLS & RIVERS

By looking at maps, one can see an orderly arrangement of mountain ranges and rivers that originate in the mountains. Rivers only meander on flat plains.

HORSEBACK IN NORTH EAST

In the areas of New Brunswick, Nova Scotia to Maine and New Hampshire, one finds a group of low ridges (horsebacks) that run nearly parallel to the Appalachian chain (northeasterly southeastern direction). They are like ripples on water and are between fifteen and fifty feet high. On the southern side, the slopes are gradual. In the northerly side, they are steeper. Many lakes and ponds occur between the horsebacks. These areas were affected by glaciers.

The Rocky Mountains and the Pre-Cambrian Shield around Hudson's Bay are other examples. The ends

of the crescent on oxbow lakes or ponds always point towards the river that formed them.

New Hampshire: low ridges (horsebacks) that run nearly parallel to the Appalachian chain (northeasterly southeastern direction).

REFLECTIONS IN THE SKY

Clouds can reflect certain features off the land surface.

- On land near an ice covered sea the clouds can reflect open water as there is less light reflected off dark water than the white frozen area. This reflection is a dark spot on the underside of the clouds. The dark spot does not indicate the size of the open water because a small area can affect a large area of cloud. This might happen as open water in the Arctic will give off a vapor and this will affect the reflected light around the open area and increase the dark spot area. This is known as a "water sky".
- An ice flow or iceberg can be seen by an "ice blink" which can be seen as a noticeable patch of brightness in a gray sky. A small area of ice can show a large "ice blink".
- On land, clouds can show the light "pollution" of a city. A city which would be below the observable horizon can be seen at 30-50 miles (48-80 km).
- In the Arctic or snow mountain country, the whole anatomy of the land surface can be reflected in a high overcast sky. You will be able to see snow fields, open water areas, naked rock areas, new ice (blue green will show as gray patches), patches of vegetation or the plants called "pink snow" might reflect pinkish. These contrasting areas will reflect on the lower sides of the clouds.
- In vegetation-covered areas, ice patches and small snow fields will reflect steel-blue on the under surface of the clouds.
- In a cloudless desert there is a "desert blink", a shimmering caused by heat reflection. An oasis can produce a desert blink because of a lower reflecting power due to the vegetation.
- In the Sahara desert a camel rider is 10 feet (3 m) from the ground and the oasis is usually in depressions and may be surrounded by hills up to one thousand feet (305 m) high. The rider can see a special kind of haze produced by the sun's heat upon the green palmed oasis.

WALKING IN CIRCLES!

Why do we have a tendency to walk in circles?
Every human is lopsided usually caused by a difference in leg length. This "deformation" will cause the person to veer if he is walking normally. The Imperial German Army did research on the deviation factor of individual soldiers to help him correct his deviation in direction at certain intervals. The deviation is greater at a faster pace and is increased when the head is bent forward as when carrying a back pack. The full circle march time can vary from one to six hours.

Other causes of deviation from a straight line are:
- We all have a dominant eye. If you point at something, at a distance, with both eyes open, you will see that the finger has been aligned with only one eye.
- Wrong balance of items in a backpack or pack incorrectly adjusted on the back.
- Hikers tend to "edge away" from an obstacle such as the wind, rain, slope of a hill, snow, dust storm and strong sun in the face.
- Hikers approaching an obstacle might tend to always pass on the "right" side or up-slope and gradually veer off course. This has been shown to be the case in Swiss Army studies on mountain travel.

Straight Line Walking

"The shortest distance is between two points"
In open, treeless country pick a distant landmark and walk towards it or orient yourself by it.
- Find two landmarks ahead of you and line them up or find two prominent points behind you and line them up. Look back ever so often to make sure that you are still on course.
- If only one landmark is available place a second landmark (e.g. a flag on a stick which is lined up with a distant hill and walk forward). Make small fires along your path to help maintain your direction day or night. This would be useful on a flat surface as a plain or desert.
- Indian file: A group of hikers in a no landmark area can become landmarks themselves. The hikers are spaced so that the last individual is far enough back that he can watch the leader and the line. He lines up the leader with the people in the line. When he sees the leader deviate he can signal him to fall in line. This method can be used during snow storms (the group should be rope-linked). A dog team and sled which has a length of 50 feet (15 m) can be aligned to a distant landmark or with a definite angle to the direction of the snowdrifts (the drifts are formed by the predominant winds).
- In the dark or fog, shouts or a penetrating whistle can be used to keep direction.
- A distant noise can be chosen as the destination. To verify your direction cup your ears and rotate your head horizontally to get the direction of the highest sound intensity.

DIRECTION BY SOUND

Inuit of Greenland use the sound of the male snow-bunting nesting area as a guide in the fog. Each male bird has a distinctive song and the Inuit know the song of the snow-bunting at the head of their fjord. During a fog they will turn at this song and head home.
- When walking, rotate your head to "scan" for sounds. You will hear your environment - a brook, stream, highway traffic, wind down the valley, or heavy surf.

WIND DIRECTION

Winds are named for the directions from which they blow: i.e. North wind from the North.
Each area has a predominant wind that dominates a season or all seasons. The dominant wind is nearly always the same as the prevailing wind which blows the longest or most violently from a given direction. The dominant wind will affect the growth of trees, direction of snow drifts, or direction of tall grass.
- The prevailing wind in all regions has its own characteristics, such as velocity, temperature, and humidity. It might vary with the seasons.
- On the ocean, the prevailing wind has its own characteristics and also its own accompaniment of clouds.

Direction of Dominant Wind

Temperate Regions: The wind usually blows from the West both in the Northern and Southern hemispheres.
Tropics: Winds are between northeast and southeast.
Equator: Usually from the east.
Northern Hemisphere: Northerly wind is usually colder than a southerly wind.

Special Effects of the Wind

Desert Winds: Are dry and might carry dust.
Winds from Ocean: Are moisture-laden and might bring clouds and rain.
Polar Regions: Wind temperature, if warmer than the surroundings, will indicate the direction of water. A sudden drop in temperature, without change in direction, might indicate the presence of an iceberg.
On Land: A person can use the prevailing wind to find his direction and to keep moving in a straight line. The wind should keep blowing onto the same part of the body. Watch for any change in temperature, humidity and strength as this will indicate a shift in the wind direction.
In Forests: Watch the direction of the movement of clouds, especially the high clouds which are usually blown by the prevailing wind. Look at the tips of tall trees to see the direction of the wind.

Signs Used by the North American Indians

- Tips of some trees point south as they are attracted by the sun.
- Bark on some trees is more dull and dark on the northern side.
- Tree rings formed in the trunk of a tree are thicker on the side that faces north than the side that faces south.
- If a log is struck on the ground on the south side of a hill, the ground has a hollow ring. On the north side, the ground sounds heavy, as it is not as dry as the south side.

- In a fog or at night, in hilly country, a shout or whistle will echo from the hills. Sound takes 5 seconds to travel a mile (1.6 km) - you can determine your relative position by ear. This is used on ships during fog. They use bells, gunshots, siren blasts or shouting. Each second between a blast and the returning echo means a distance of about 560 feet (170 m) from the reflecting surface.
- Boaters can also listen to the sound of nesting seabirds, or the surf. When the sound of the breakers disappears, that indicates the presence of an inlet or harbor.
See the Ocean - Page 127.

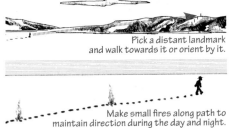

Pick a distant landmark and walk towards it or orient by it.

Make small fires along path to maintain direction during the day and night.

STEERING MARKS

Steering marks are well-defined objects in the direction of travel.

Steering Marks by Day

Objects such as lone trees, hills, and shapes on the horizon. A cloud formation or wind direction may be used if checked periodically by compass.

Steering Marks by Night

Stars are usually the single source of steering marks at night. It is important to find Polaris (the Pole Star) because of the rotation of the earth the positions of other stars are continually changing. Polaris is fixed in the sky and is less than 1° off true north, but above latitude 70° it is too high in the sky to be useful. A star near the north horizon serves for about a half hour. When moving south, azimuth checks should be made every 15 minutes to be safe. When traveling east or west, the difficulty of staying on azimuth is caused more by the likelihood of the star climbing too high in the sky or losing itself behind the western horizon than it is by the star changing direction angle. In all the above cases, it is necessary to change to another guide star.

Pace Count

A pace is the length of your natural step and is approximately 30" (76 cm). If you will be using this method you should determine your pace. Walk a pre-measured distance while maintaining your normal pace and count your footsteps. Divide the distance in inches or meters by the number of steps. If you have stopped growing, this is your pace for life.

Pace distance can change because of:
Slopes: Pace gets longer on a down slope and shortens on the upgrade. If you normally pace 120 paces per 100 meters (328 feet) on a slope, the number of paces can increase to 130, an 8.3% increase.
Winds: Head wind will shorten pace, a tail wind will increase the pace.
Surface: A rough surface of sand, mud, gravel, will shorten the pace.
Elements: Snow, rain, or ice cause the pace to shorten.
Clothing: Excess clothing and boots with poor traction tend to shorten the pace.
Visibility: Reduced visibility will shorten your pace because you do not feel secure. Your pace will also shorten if you are stalking or trying to be secretive.

SOUND BLOWN BY WIND

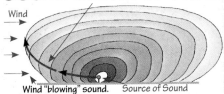

Wind

Wind "blowing" sound.   Source of Sound

Dead Reckoning

Dead reckoning is the process by which one's present location is determined by plotting the course and distance from the last known location.

With a Map

One's starting location and destination are known and if a map is available, are plotted, along with any known intermediate features along the route. These intermediate features, if clearly recognizable on the ground, serve as invaluable checkpoints. It is a matter of knowing one's position at all times through association of map features with the ground features.

With No Map

For many centuries, mariners have used dead reckoning to navigate their ships when they are out of sight of land or during bad weather, and it is just as applicable to navigation on land. If a map is not available, the plotting is done on a blank sheet of paper. A scale is selected such that the entire route will fit on one sheet. A north direction is clearly established. The starting point and destination are then plotted in accurate relationship to each other. The route of travel usually consists of several courses, with an azimuth established at the starting point for the first course to be followed. Distance measurement begins with the departure and continues through the first course until a change in direction is made. A new azimuth is established for the second course and the distance is measured until a second change of direction is made, and so on. Records of all data are kept and all positions are plotted.

Pacing Distance

A pace is approximately 30 inches. To measure distance, you count the number of paces in a given course and convert to the map unit. Paces are counted in hundreds, and the hundreds can be kept track of in many ways: count on your fingers, place small objects such as pebbles into an empty pocket, or tie knots in a string. It is important that each person who uses dead reckoning navigation establish the length of his average pace.

In the field, an average pace must be adjusted because of the following conditions:

Slopes: The pace lengthens on a downgrade and shortens on the upgrade.

Winds: A head wind shortens the pace while a tail wind increases it.

Surfaces: Sand, gravel, mud, and similar surface materials tend to shorten the pace.

Elements: Snow, rain, or ice cause the pace to be reduced in length.

Clothing: Excess weight of clothing shortens the pace while the type of shoes affects the pace length.

Fatigue: Tiredness affects the length of the pace.

Factors to Consider in Range Estimation

Distance is underestimated when starting & overestimated at the end of the trip.

Factors	Under Estimation	Over Estimation
Clear Outline & Detail	Clear outline & most of object exposed.	Only part can be seen, object is small in relationship to surroundings.
		The color of the object blends with the background.
Nature of Terrain	When looking across a depression mostly hidden from view.	When looking across a depression that is totally visible.
Position of Observer	When looking downward from high ground.	
	When looking down a straight open road or along a railroad.	When vision is narrowly confined, as in streets, draws, or forest trails.
	When looking over uniform surfaces like water, snow, desert, or grain fields.	When looking from low ground toward high ground.
		Looking over undulating ground.
Light & Atmosphere	In bright light or when the sun is shining from behind the observer.	In poor light, such as at dawn or dusk, in rain, snow, fog, or when the sun is in the observer's eyes.
	When the object is in sharp contrast with the background or is silhouetted because of its size, shape, or color.	When object blends into the background or terrain.
	When seen in the clear air of high altitudes.	

Rock Surface

Rock Slope

Grassy Slope

Downhill

Estimating Distance

Finger Method of Judging Distance

This method is based upon the principle that the distance between the eyes is about 1/10 of the distance from the eye to the extended finger.

To know the width or height of a distant object.

- Extend your right arm and hold your forefinger upright and align it with one eye at the end of the object.
- Do not move finger but observe where it is when looking with the other eye.
- Estimate the displacement in feet or meters along the length of the object.
- The distance from the object is 10 times the displacement of the fingers.
- With binoculars, measure the distance between the center of the eyepieces, when adjusted for your eyes, and multiply this distance by 10. Use this factor as above.

Rifle or Cannon Flash Method

This method uses the difference in time between seeing a flash of light (the speed of light can be considered instantaneous over distances of miles or kilometers) and hearing the sound.

When you see the flash, start counting the seconds. You can use a stopwatch or a steady count by saying one-thousand-one, one-thousand-two, ...

Multiply the number of seconds by 1085 feet (330 m) to get the approximate distance. Sound carries better in dry cold air.

Estimation of Distance

100 Yard Unit-of-Measure Method

You must visualize a distance of 100 yards on the ground. This can be done by having some scale as the "Judging Distance" table to estimate the distance. Then you can use other indicators to estimate longer distances by 50 or 100 yard increments. To verify your estimates, visualize the halfway points and see if they make sense as based upon the "Estimating Distance" table.

- When seen in the clear air of high altitudes.
- When object blends into the background or terrain.

Estimating Distance

Being able to judge distance is important in survival situations as it will help you maintain your bearings, judge height, and calculate time relative to the speed of walking.

Distance is underestimated when starting a trip and overestimated at the end of a trip.

Counting Paces *(a step being a pace)*

- An average person has a pace of 30" (76 cm) and will walk at three miles an hour over flat ground. You might want to calculate your average pace.
- To help you count your pace, count your right foot pace only and multiply by two when you reach 100 paces.
- To keep track of your counted paces put pebbles or nuts in one pocket and transfer one to the other pocket at each 100 paces.

Objects look much nearer when:

- Looking up a hill.
- There is a bright light on the object.
- Looking across water, snow or flat sand.
- The air is clear.
- When most of the object is visible and offers a clear outline.
- When looking across a depression that is mostly hidden from view.

Objects look much farther when:

- The light is poor.
- The object is at the end of a long avenue.
- You are looking over undulating ground.
- The color of the object blends with the background.
- When only a small part of the object can be seen or the object is small in relation to its surroundings.
- When looking downward from high ground.
- When looking down a straight, open road or along a railroad.
- In poor light, such as dawn and dusk; in rain, snow, fog; or when the sun is in the observer's eyes.

Other Factors effect estimation:

- In bright light or when the sun is shining from behind the observer.
- When looking across a depression that is totally visible.
- When vision is confined, as in streets, draws, or forest trails.
- Light and atmosphere When the object is in sharp contrast with the background or is silhouetted because of its size, shape, or color.

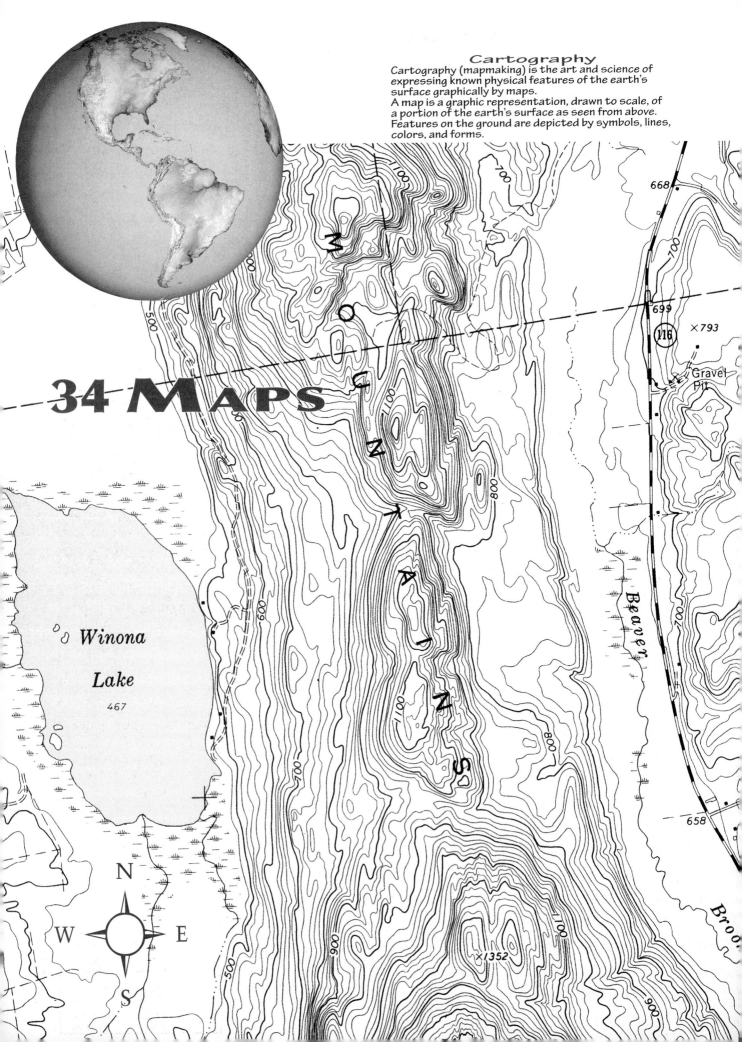

Cartography

Cartography (mapmaking) is the art and science of expressing known physical features of the earth's surface graphically by maps.

A map is a graphic representation, drawn to scale, of a portion of the earth's surface as seen from above. Features on the ground are depicted by symbols, lines, colors, and forms.

34 MAPS

MOUNTAINS

Winona

Lake

467

668

699

116

×793

Gravel
Pit

Beaver

658

×1352

Brook

MAP SCALE

All maps represent a portion of the earth's surface. The surface of the earth is represented on a much smaller scale on the map. All maps have a scale which represents the distance on the map to the distance on the ground. The scale of the map permits the determination of ground distance from the map.

The numerical scale of a map expresses the ratio of horizontal distance on the map to the corresponding horizontal distance on the ground. It usually is written as a fraction and is called the representative fraction (RF). It is independent of any unit of measure. An RF of 1/50,000 or 1:50,000 means that one (1) unit of measure on the map is equal to 50,000 of the same units of measure on the ground.

DIFFERENT MAP SCALES

Small Scale: Maps at scales of 1:600,000 and smaller are used for general military planning and for strategical studies. The standard small scale is 1:1,000,000.

Medium Scale: Maps at scales larger than 1:600,000 but smaller than 1:75,000. The standard medium scale is 1:250,000.

Large Scale: Maps at scales of 1:75,000 and larger. The standard large scale is 1:50,000.

SCALE 1:24 000   Scale 1 : 24,000

Scale 1:50,000   Scale 1 : 50,000

Primary highway, hard surface	
Secondary highway, hard surface	
Light-duty road, hard or improved surface	
Unimproved road; trail	
Route marker: Interstate; U. S.; State	
Railroad: standard gage; narrow gage	
Bridge; drawbridge	
Footbridge; overpass; underpass	
Built-up area: only selected landmark buildings shown	
House; barn; church; school; large structures	
Boundary:	
National, with monument	
State	
County, parish	
Civil township, precinct, district	
Incorporated city, village, town	
National or State reservation; small park	
Land grant with monument; found section corner	
U. S. public lands survey: range, township; section	
Range, township; section line: location approximate	
Fence or field line	
Power transmission line, located tower	
Dam; dam with lock	
Cemetery; grave	
Campground; picnic area; U. S. location monument	
Windmill; water well; spring	
Mine shaft; prospect; adit or cave	
Control: horizontal station; vertical station; spot elevation	
Contours: index; intermediate; supplementary; depression	
Distorted surface: strip mine, lava; sand	
Sounding; depth curve	
Perennial lake and stream; intermittent lake and stream	
Rapids, large and small; falls, large and small	
Swamp; marsh	
Submerged marsh; land subject to controlled inundation	
Woodland; scattered trees	
Scrub; mangrove	
Orchard; vineyard	

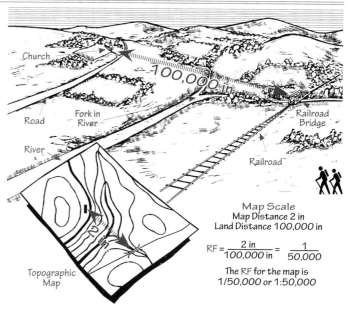

Church   Fork in River   Road   River   Railroad Bridge   Railroad   Topographic Map

Map Scale
Map Distance 2 in
Land Distance 100,000 in

$$RF = \frac{2\ in}{100,000\ in} = \frac{1}{50,000}$$

The RF for the map is
1/50,000 or 1:50,000

Contours showing elevation and the profile of the land can be deduced.

TOPOGRAPHIC MAP SYMBOLS

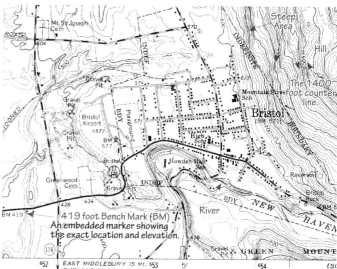

419 foot Bench Mark (BM)
An embedded marker showing
the exact location and elevation.

MAP TYPES

A map is a graphic representation of a portion of the earth's surface in a uniform and proportional relationship. The proportional relationship is known as the map scale. A map will show features that are present on the earth's surface or below the surface. Most maps are made for a specific purpose: street map, highway map, elevation map (topographic), geology of soil or rock formations below the surface, thermal maps showing the effluence of rivers, etc.

All maps have their own set of symbols by which the features they show are represented.

Ground Distance to Map Scale		
These are some of the standard scales used on maps:		
Map Scale	1 Inch Equals	1 Centimeter Equals
1:5,000	416.67 feet 127.00 meters	164.0 feet 50 meters
1:10,000	833.33 feet 254.00 meters	328.1 feet 100 meters
1:12,500	1,041.66 feet 317.00 meters	410.1 feet 125 meters
1:20,000	1,666.7 feet 508.00 meters	656.2 feet 200 meters
1:25,000	2,083.3 feet 635.00 meters	820.2 feet 250 meters
1:50,000	4,166.7 feet 1,270.0 meters	1640.4 feet 500 meters
1:63,360	5,280.0 feet (mile) 1,609.3 meters	2,078.7 feet 633.6 meters
1:100,000	8,333.3 feet 2,540.0 meters	3,280.8 feet 1,000 meters
1:250,000	20,833 feet 6,350.0 meters	8,202.0 feet 2,500 meters
1:500,000	41,667 feet 12,700 meters	16,404.0 feet 5,000 meters

N

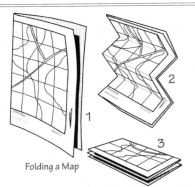

Folding a Map

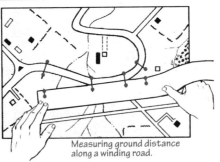

Measuring ground distance along a winding road.

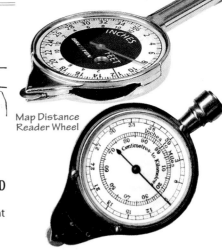

Map Distance Reader Wheel

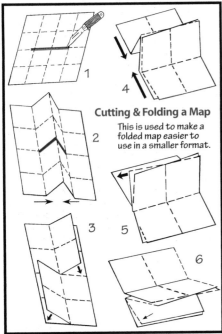

Cutting & Folding a Map

This is used to make a folded map easier to use in a smaller format.

Topographic Maps

Topographic maps portray terrain and land forms in a measurable form, as well as the horizontal positions of the features represented.

The vertical positions, or relief, are normally represented by contours. On maps showing relief, the elevations and contours are measured from mean sea level.

They describe the shape of the land and define and locate natural and man-made features like woodlands, waterways, important buildings, and bridges.

They show the distance between any two places, and they also show the direction from one point to another.

The topography of the land is shown by contours. These are imaginary lines that follow the ground surface at a constant elevation; they are usually printed in brown. Natural and man-made features are represented by colored areas and by a set of standard symbols on all U.S. Geological Survey (USGS) topographic maps. Some of the standard symbols are on page 379. The sample topographic maps are from the USGS series.

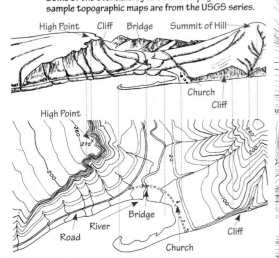

High Point   Cliff   Bridge   Summit of Hill

Church
Cliff

High Point

Bridge
River
Road   Cliff
Church

GROUND DISTANCE ALONG A WINDING ROAD

To measure distance along a winding road, stream or any other curved line, use the straight edge of a piece of paper. Make a tick mark at or near one end of the paper and place it at the point from which the curved line is to be measured. Align the edge of the paper along a straight portion, and make a tick mark on both map and paper at the end of the aligned portion. Keeping both tick marks together, place the point of the pencil on the paper's tick mark to hold it in place. Pivot the paper until another approximately straight portion is aligned and again make a tick mark on both map and paper. Continue in this manner until the measurement is complete. Then place the paper on the graphic scale and read the ground distance.

GROUND DISTANCE

The ground distance between two points is determined by measuring between the points on the map and multiplying the map measurement by the denominator of the RF.

STRAIGHT-LINE GROUND DISTANCE

To determine a straight-line ground distance between two points on a map, place a straight-edged piece of paper on the map so that the edge of the paper touches both points. Make a tick mark on the edge of the paper at each point. Move the paper down to the graphic scale and read the ground distance between the points.

CARE OF MAPS

Maps should be correctly folded.

Maps should be folded to make them small enough to be carried and still be available for use without having to unfold them entirely. After a map has been folded, it should be placed in a folder for protection. This will prevent the corners and edges of the map from wearing out and tearing easily when opened.

WATERPROOFING MAPS

Most maps are printed on paper and require protection from water, mud, and tearing. Whenever possible, a map should be carried in a waterproof packet to prolong its life. A liquid coating is available to protect paper maps. Some hiking trails have maps printed on non-tear-able waterproof plastic sheets.

MARKING A MAP

If it is necessary to mark a map, use light lines so that they may be erased without smearing or smudging. If the margins of the map must be trimmed, note any marginal information which may be needed, such as grid data, and magnetic declination data.

TOPOGRAPHIC MAPS

A knowledge of map symbols, grids, scale, and distance gives enough information to identify two points, locate them, measure between them, and determine how long it would take to travel between them. What happens if there is a 300 foot cliff between the two points? The map user reading a topographic map recognizes various landforms and irregularities of the earth's surface and will determine the elevation and relative differences in height of the terrain features.

Datum plane: This is a reference from which vertical measurements are taken. The datum plane for most maps is the average sea level.

Elevation: This is defined as the height (vertical distance) of an object above or below a datum plane.

Relief: Relief is the representation of the shape and height of landforms.

COLORS: MILITARY MAPS

Black: Indicates cultural (man-made) features (buildings, roads).

Reddish-Brown: Red and brown are combined to identify cultural features, all relief features, and elevation, such as contour lines on red-light readable maps.

Blue: Hydrography or water features such as lakes, swamps, rivers, and drainage.

Green: Vegetation with military significance, such as woods, orchards, and vineyards.

Red: Classifies cultural features, such as populated areas, main roads, and boundaries on older maps.

Other: Shows special information. These are indicated as marginal information.

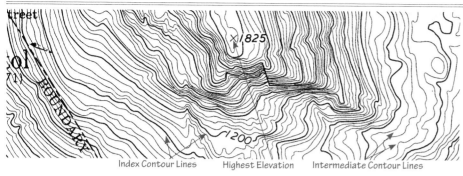

Index Contour Lines   Highest Elevation   Intermediate Contour Lines

A U.S. Geological Survey survey transit station on the Idaho Montana boundary.

CONTOUR LINES

There are several ways of indicating elevation and relief on maps. The most common way is by contour lines. A contour line is a line representing an imaginary line on the ground along which all points are at the same elevation. Contour lines indicate a vertical distance above or below a datum plane. Starting at sea level, normally the zero contour, each contour line represents an elevation above sea level.

The vertical distance between adjacent contour lines is known as the contour interval and the amount of the contour interval is given in the marginal information on the map.

• Contour lines are usually printed in brown.

Index Contour: Every fifth contour line is drawn with a heavier line and called an index contour. The elevation is indicated on these lines.

Intermediate Contours: The contour lines falling between index contours are called intermediate contours. They are drawn with a finer line than the index contours and usually do not have their elevations marked.

USING CONTOUR LINES

• Find the contour interval of the map from the marginal information.

• Find the numbered contour line (or other given elevation) nearest the point for which the elevation is being sought.

• Determine the direction of the slope from the numbered contour line to the point.

• Count the number of contour lines that must be crossed to go from the numbered contour line to the desired point and note the direction - up or down. The number of lines crossed multiplied by the contour interval is the distance above or below the starting value.

• To estimate the elevation of the top of an unmarked hill, add half the contour interval to the elevation of the highest contour line around the hill.

• To estimate the elevation of the bottom of a depression, subtract half the contour interval from the value of the lowest contour around the depression.

Pedometer

Pace adjusting gauge.

TOPOGRAPHIC MAP SYMBOLS & COLORS

The purpose of a map is to permit one to visualize an area of the earth's surface with pertinent features properly positioned. The map maker uses symbols to represent the natural and man-made features of the earth's surface.

TOPOGRAPHIC SYMBOLS

Topographic symbols are usually printed in different colors to facilitate the identification of features on the map. Each color identifies a class of features. The colors vary with different types of maps, but on a standard large-scale topographic map, the colors and features are:

Black: The majority of cultural or man-made features.
Blue: Water features such as lakes, rivers, and swamps.
Green: Vegetation such as woods and orchards.
Brown: Relief features such as contour lines.
Red: Main roads, built-up areas, and special features.

In the process of making a map, everything must be reduced from its actual size on the ground to the size at which it appears on the map. This requires, for purposes of clarity, that some of the symbols be exaggerated. They are positioned, however, in such a manner that the center of the symbol remains in its true location. An exception to this would be the position of a feature adjacent to a road. If the width of the road has been exaggerated, then the feature is moved from its true position to preserve its relation to the road.

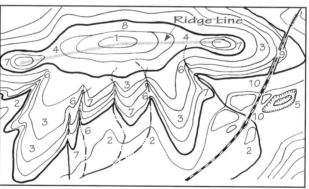

A terrain feature does not stand alone but is interrelated with its adjoining features. These maps show a top view of the terrain. They depict elevation by the use of contour lines. Contour lines are the graphic symbols that tie all the features together and tell their story.

Summit of Hill   1
Valley   2
To the south lies a valley. The valley slopes downward from east to west; note that the U of the contour line points to the east, indicating higher ground in that direction and lower ground to the west. Another look at the valley shows high ground to the north and south of the valley.

Ridge   3
There are four prominent ridges. A ridge is on each end of the ridge line and two ridges extend south from the ridge line. All of the ridges have lower ground in three directions and higher ground in one direction.

Saddle   4
The saddles have lower ground in two directions and higher ground in the opposite two directions. The contour lines of each saddle form half an hourglass shape. Because of the difference in size of the higher ground on the two opposite sides of a saddle, a full hourglass shape of a saddle may not be apparent.

Depression   5
Just east of the valley is a depression. Looking from the bottom of the depression, there is higher ground in all directions.

Draws   6
Between the ridges and spurs are draws. They, like valleys, have higher ground in three directions and lower ground in one direction. Their contour line U's and V's point toward higher ground.

Spurs   7
There are several spurs extending generally south from the ridge line. They, like ridges, have lower ground in three directions and higher ground in one direction. Their contour line U's point away from higher ground.

Cliff   8
Three contour lines on the north side of the center hill are touching or almost touching. They have ticks indicating a vertical or nearly vertical slope or a cliff.

Cut   9   Fill   10
The road cutting through the eastern ridge depicts cuts and fills. The breaks in the contour lines indicate cuts, and the ticks pointing away from the road bed on each side of the road indicate fills.

Ridge Line
Running east to west across the complex land mass is a ridge line. A ridge line is a line of high ground, usually with changes in elevation along its top and low ground on all sides. The changes in elevation are the three hilltops and two saddles along the ridge line. From the top of each hill, there is lower ground in all directions.

U's
The closed ends of the U's formed by the contour lines point away from higher ground.

TOPOGRAPHIC MAPS

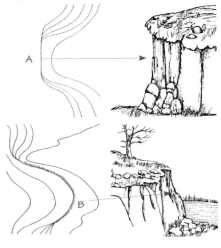

CLIFFS

Cliffs: Cliffs can be shown as in A where all contour lines merge or as in B where the lines merge and tick marks show the fall-off side of the cliff. These ticks are similar to the marks in a depression.

Interpretation of terrain features by interpreting contour lines.

WATER-CREATED FEATURES

Draw: A draw is a miniature valley that with time might develop into a valley. The contour lines look similar to a valley. There are usually many boulders on the stream bed of a draw.

Valley: A valley is usually created by erosion by a river or stream. A valley has rising slopes on two sides, a slight incline at the head of the water source (or where the water source was) and a decline to where the water flows. To find valleys on the map look for V-shaped or U-shaped contour lines. The water flows or flowed from the closed end of the V or U. A U-shaped valley might have been formed by glacial action.

Spur: These are juttings of land, usually areas between parallel valleys formed by streams or rivers. They usually will form off a ridge line. Spurs usually are in the shape of U's or V's.

Intermittent Streams

TYPES OF SLOPES

These examples show how contour lines represent different types of slopes.

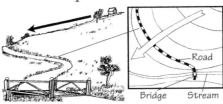

Gentle Slope: The contour lines are wide apart and evenly spaced.

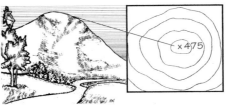

Hill: A hill is shown by relatively concentric contour lines. The highest area on the hill is shown by the smallest closed circle. The highest elevation can be shown by an "X" and a numeric height.

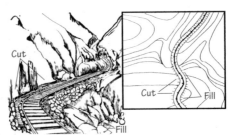

Cut & Fill: Cut and fill are man-made and are used when laying train tracks, making roads, terracing or building on slopes. The cut is where soil is removed from high ground. A fill is where soil is added to low land. The contour line extends along the length of the cut and fill with tick marks indicating a cut or fill. Cuts and fills are only shown if they are 10 feet or higher.

Steep Uniform Slope: The contour lines are close together and evenly spaced. The closer the contour lines the steeper the slope. When the lines are on top of each other this represents a cliff.

Concave Slope: The contour lines are closely spaced at the top of the hill, the middle has a relatively wider spacing, and the bottom is even wider. In the illustration, the contour lines near the road are closer as the road might have been cut into or filled on the slope.

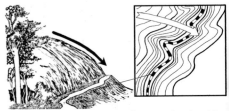

Convex Slope: The contour line spacing is wide at the top and close at the bottom. Note that the road has been cut into the slope and this creates the flat area on the slope.

382

Terminology

Bench: A strip of plain along a valley slope.

Bluff: A high, steep bank or low cliff.

Box Canyon: A canyon having practically vertical rock walls.

Brow: The point at which a gentle slope changes to an abrupt one.

Butte: An isolated hill or small mountain with steep precipitous sides. The top may be flat, rounded, or pointed. It might be the remains of some form of hard rock volcanic intrusion.

Canyon: A gorge or ravine of considerable dimensions; a channel cut by rapidly running water, the sides of which are a series of cliffs rising from the bed of the stream. A glacier would form a relative wide U-shaped valley.

Defile: Deep and narrow mountain pass.

Divide: The line of separation between drainage systems or basins.

Escarpment: High steep face of rock of considerable length.

Gorge: Very rugged and deep ravine.

Gulch: Shallow canyon with smoothly inclined slopes.

Hogback: Steep-sided ridge parallel to the adjoining mountains

Knob: Prominent mountain peak with a rounded summit.

Mesa: Flat-topped mountain bounded on at least one side by a steep cliff.

Mountain Gap: Opening between hills or in a ridge or mountain chain. See "notch."

Notch: A short defile or gap through a hill or mountain.

Pass: Depression in a mountain range through which a road may pass. See "mountain gap" and "notch."

Peak: Mountain area with a single conspicuous summit. This might even be as part of a mountain range.

Saddle: A shallow gap on a ridge.

Spur: Sharp projecting ridge from the side of a hill or mountain that might be the divide between two river basins.

Summit: Highest point of any undulating land or hills.

Water Gap: Gap through a mountain occupied by a stream. See "mountain gap."

Wind Gap: An elevated gap not occupied by a stream. See "mountain gap."

Wave Maps

- The Polynesians understood the movements of swells and waves but the Micronesians developed it into a science.
- The Micronesians developed charts of the anatomy and topography of local water surfaces. These charts were made from ribs of the coconut palms and tied together with coconut fiber.
- These chart maps were a framework of bent ribs tied in a net that accurately showed the meeting points of the dominant swells around the islands. The islands were small shells. These charts used a time scale and not distance scale. The representation of the islands was based upon their importance to the chart maker (cartographer).

These charts showed...

- the directional swells throughout the group of islands.
- Sticks would indicate the distance from land at which coconuts palms can be seen.
- Position and distance from the island of the meeting of the waters of the oncoming swell and the ebbing tide from an island or lagoon. These meeting places can be beyond the sight of land.

Major Terrain Features

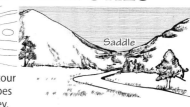

Saddle: A saddle is a low area between two higher areas. A saddle is important in traveling overland as it represents a pass and is the least difficult route to pass over through a high area or ridge. A saddle area usually looks like a figure-eight-shaped contour area. A saddle has two rising slopes and two declining slopes which are opposite each other. This is different from a valley.

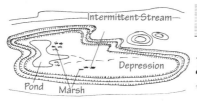

Depression: A depression is a low area surrounded by higher ground. A depression might indicate the presence of water. A sinkhole in limestone might indicate caves in the area.

Depressions that are deeper than a contour interval will be shown. Ticks on the contour line indicate a depression and they will slope into the depression.

Ridge: A ridge is a sloping line of high ground as shown in the illustration. When traveling on foot in a temperate climate, it might be easier to travel on the ridge as there will be less undergrowth, more wind to keep insects away, better observation, less of a slope to climb, no streams to cross, and no valleys to cross.

Ridge Line: All land features originate from a ridge line. It is the dividing line between drainage basins. Valleys, draws, and spurs originate in the slopes of the sides of the ridge line.

Wave patterns created by the island.

The coral reef can be seen.

Wave patterns created by an atoll.

Micronesian Wave Charts
These people of the Caroline and the Marshall Islands made wave and swell charts. These charts were based upon the fact that there were predominant winds in the area and that the islands and atolls would cause certain wave and swell patterns to occur.

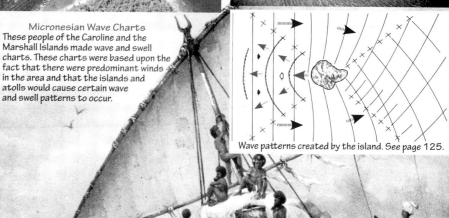

Wave patterns created by the island. See page 125.

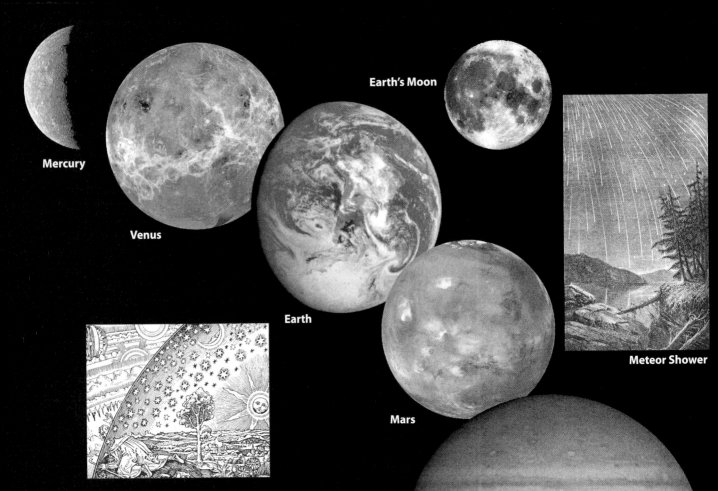

Mercury

Venus

Earth's Moon

Earth

Mars

Meteor Shower

35 ASTRONOMY

Jupiter

Saturn

Uranus

Neptune

SKY WATCHING
STAR IDENTIFICATION

With time and using a sky chart you can learn the approximate shape and location of 20 constellations and 10 to 15 of the brightest starts. The seasonal Sky Chart in this book is an excellent start.

STARS & STAR GROUPINGS

- Study the constellations. Look for Ursa Major and Minor, Cassiopeia, Draco, and Cepheus (these are the circumpolar constellations and are visible all night and rotate around the Pole (North) Star (Polaris)). Constellations are grouping of stars which have been given legendary or historical significance. These groups have been joined together with lines, outlining a figure or symbol, so that you can find them in the sky.
- Look for the Big Dipper in Ursa Major (the Great Bear). From the Big Dipper look at the pointer stars Dubhe and Merak to find the North Star (Polaris).
- Polaris is the star closest to the true north *(Note: the Pole Star was not always the Pole Star due to the movement of the earth. During time of the Egyptian pyramid building the pole star was Thuban in Draco).*
- Look for the constellations of the Zodiac: Aries, Taurus, Gemini, Cancer, Leo, Virgo, Libra, Scorpio, Sagittarius, Capricorn, Aquarius, and Pisces.
- Look at the inside of the Milky Way galaxy. The earth is part of it.
- Look for the five planets that you can see without a telescope, Mercury, Venus, Mars, Jupiter, and Saturn. Unlike the stars, the planets wander through the sky just like earth. The planets are seen because they reflect the light from the sun. Mercury and Venus, which are closer to the sun than earth, are seen as the evening or morning stars.
- Meteor showers can be seen with the best coming out of the Perseid constellation in August.
- Stars have colors examples are: blue white. Capella, yellow white, red etc.

STAR MAGNITUDE

The brightness of stars are categorized into magnitudes.
- The brightest are of 0 or 1st magnitude.
- The ones barely visible to the naked eye are of the 6th magnitude.

Some stars have variable magnitudes.

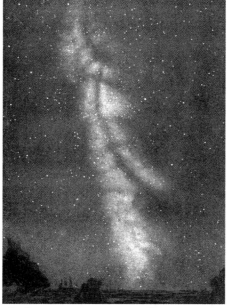

MILKY WAY GALAXY

Our Sun, all the planets around our Sun (including the planet Earth), are a part of the Milky Way galaxy. Galaxies are islands or clusters of many millions of stars in the universe. The Milky Way is only one of these galaxies. We see the Milky Way as a faint band of light crossing the sky. This spiraling band is made up of a vast number of faint stars (when seen from Earth) and we are in the Milky Way looking down the long axis of the Milky Way galaxy.

MOON PHASES

Best watching time is between the moon's last quarter and the first quarter. Three hours after sunset so that the sky is dark enough to see the low intensity stars.

You can see the phases of the moon on a calendar.

No Moon: Excellent for viewing the stars as there is no light from the moon.

First Quarter Moon: Is seen in the afternoon and evening. It will have gone down by midnight.

Full Moon: Difficult to see the stars as the sky is filled with glare.

Last Quarter Moon: Comes up after midnight and can be seen until noon.

The aurora in the northern hemisphere.

NORTHERN LIGHTS (AURORAS)

These lights can be seen in the northern latitudes. They are like moving curtains and can be whitish, yellow, green, pinkish. One theory is that they are caused by the sunlight hitting space gases at very high altitude. They have a neon light type reaction to the light. These Auroras usually occur a few days after the development of large sun spots.

Curtains of the Northern Lights (Aurora Borealis)

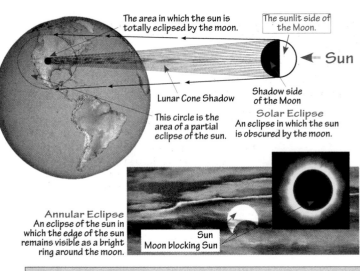

The area in which the sun is totally eclipsed by the moon.

The sunlit side of the Moon.

Sun

Lunar Cone Shadow

Shadow side of the Moon

This circle is the area of a partial eclipse of the sun.

Solar Eclipse
An eclipse in which the sun is obscured by the moon.

Star Magnitude
All stars are not shown on our sky map as it would be too crowded and you would not be able to learn the basic information which we are trying to convey. Stars are categorized by their brightness (called magnitude).

Annular Eclipse
An eclipse of the sun in which the edge of the sun remains visible as a bright ring around the moon.

Sun
Moon blocking Sun

DIRECTION OF THE EARTH'S ROTATION

You will notice that at the edge of the sky chart there is a rotation arrow. This arrows shows the stars come up (in the east) and going down in the west. Actually the stars are fixed and it is the earth rotating 15° per hour that give you the impression of the stars moving. This movement occurs around the Pole Star (Polaris). Our sky map shows the stars for 9:00 PM and if you are watching the stars at 10:00 PM (one hour after the 9:00 PM chart time) the stars will have "moved" 15° in the direction of the arrow.

WHAT IS A SKY CHART?

This is a map of the sky above your head at a certain time and place (Latitude). The map is round because when you look up the horizon is all around you and forms a near circle.

LATITUDE

Our sky maps are for 40° North Latitude and can be used for most of the Northern Hemisphere (United States, Southern Canada & Europe). If you are in Northern Canada or Alaska then stars on the southern edge of our sky maps will disappear but additional stars will be seen to the North. At the North Pole the Polaris star will be at the middle of the sky *(above your head)* and you will see all of the Northern Hemisphere sky. If you are further south you will see more of the southern sky and the Polaris star will be closer to the Northern edge of the sky chart.

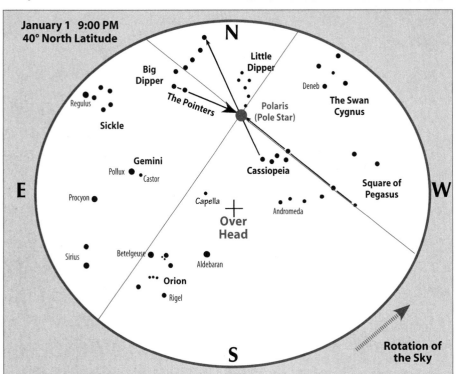

January 1 9:00 PM
40° North Latitude

N

Big Dipper

Little Dipper

Deneb

The Swan Cygnus

The Pointers

Polaris (Pole Star)

Regulus

Sickle

Gemini

Pollux   Castor

Cassiopeia

Square of Pegasus

E

Procyon

Capella

Over Head

Andromeda

W

Sirius   Betelgeuse

Aldebaran

Orion

Rigel

S

Rotation of the Sky

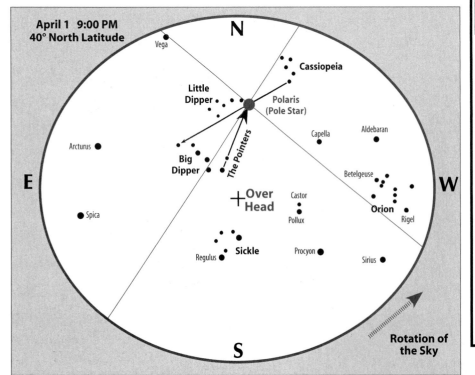

April 1 9:00 PM
40° North Latitude

N

Vega

Cassiopeia

Little Dipper

Polaris (Pole Star)

The Pointers

Arcturus

Big Dipper

Capella

Aldebaran

E

Spica

Over Head

Betelgeuse

Castor

Pollux

Orion

Rigel

W

Sickle

Regulus

Procyon

Sirius

S

Rotation of the Sky

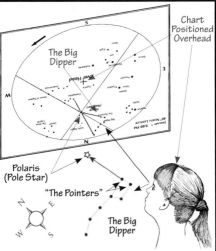

Chart Positioned Overhead

The Big Dipper

Polaris (Pole Star)

"The Pointers"

The Big Dipper

USING A SKY CHART

Locate the north by using a compass or by finding the Big Dipper and following "The Pointers" to find Polaris (North Star). Place the chart above your head with the "N" on the chart pointing North.

You will have noticed that the East and West printed on the sky map are on the opposite side of the East and West of an Earth map. The reason for this is that when the sky chart is held above your head the East and West markings will be the same as the terrestrial (earth) East and West.

To read the sky chart, in the dark, use a flash light with a red filter so that your eyes will not have to readjust to the dark sky.

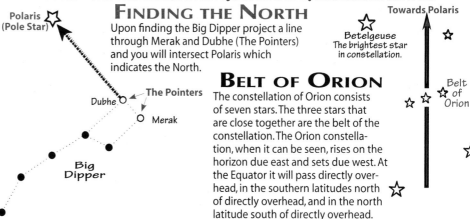

The Pointers

Big Dipper

Finding Pole Star using Cassiopeia and the Big Dipper

Little Dipper

Polaris (Pole Star)

Polaris (Pole Star)

Cassiopeia

Cassiopeia

Finding Pole Star using Cassiopeia and the Square of Pegasus

Square of Pegasus

FINDING THE NORTH

Upon finding the Big Dipper project a line through Merak and Dubhe (The Pointers) and you will intersect Polaris which indicates the North.

Polaris (Pole Star)

Dubhe — The Pointers

Merak

Big Dipper

BELT OF ORION

The constellation of Orion consists of seven stars. The three stars that are close together are the belt of the constellation. The Orion constellation, when it can be seen, rises on the horizon due east and sets due west. At the Equator it will pass directly overhead, in the southern latitudes north of directly overhead, and in the north latitude south of directly overhead.

Towards Polaris

Betelgeuse
The brightest star in constellation.

Belt of Orion

To locate the Pole Star...

• All stars seem to revolve around the Pole Star.
• The Pole Star is the last star in the handle of the constellation Ursa Minor (Little Dipper), but the complete Little Dipper is often difficult to see.
• The easiest way to locate the Pole Star is by using the constellation Ursa Major (Big Dipper). A straight line drawn between the two stars (pointers) at the end of the Big Dipper's bowl will point to the North Star. The distance to the Pole Star is about five times the distance between the points.
• Directly across from the Big Dipper is the constellation Cassiopeia. It is made up of five stars and resembles a lopsided "M" or "W" depending on its position in the sky. The Pole Star is straight out from the side star of Cassiopeia. It is almost equidistant between the Big Dipper and Cassiopeia.

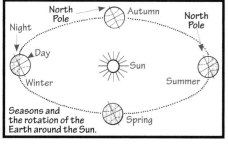

Seasons and the rotation of the Earth around the Sun.

North Pole — Autumn
North Pole
Night
Day
Winter
Sun
Summer
Spring

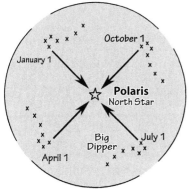

October 1
January 1
Polaris North Star
July 1
April 1
Big Dipper

Movement of Earth in its Orbit

This illustration shows how the Big Dipper will appear from earth at different times of the year. This displacement is due to the movement of earth in its orbit around the sun. The sky charts show the same phenomenon for the sky.

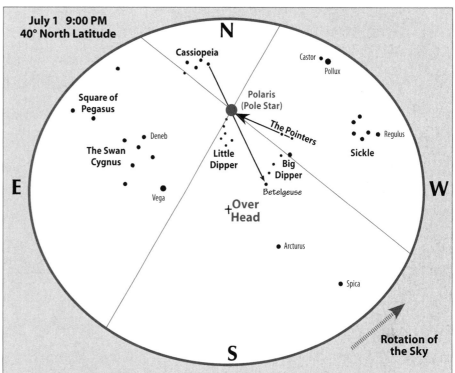

July 1   9:00 PM
40° North Latitude

N

Cassiopeia
Castor
Pollux
Square of Pegasus
Polaris (Pole Star)
The Pointers
Deneb
Regulus
The Swan Cygnus
Little Dipper
Big Dipper
Sickle
Vega
Betelgeuse
E   W
+Over Head
Arcturus
Spica
S
Rotation of the Sky

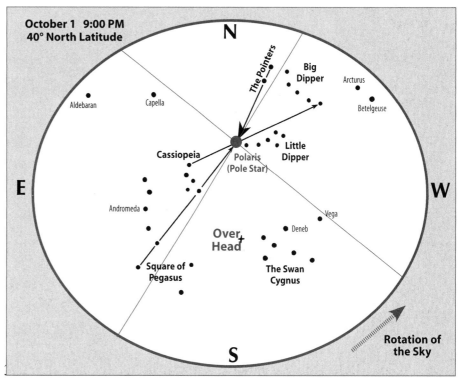

October 1   9:00 PM
40° North Latitude

N

The Pointers
Big Dipper
Aldebaran
Capella
Arcturus
Betelgeuse
Cassiopeia
Little Dipper
Polaris (Pole Star)
E   W
Andromeda
Vega
Over+ Head
Deneb
Square of Pegasus
The Swan Cygnus
S
Rotation of the Sky

Southern Cross

Milky Way (the light milky looking area) and the Southern Cross (Crux)

False Cross

Devoid Area The Coalsack dark cloud of dust

South

SOUTHERN CROSS (CRUX)

Polaris is not visible in the Southern Hemisphere and the Southern Cross is the most distinctive constellation. An imaginary line drawn through the long axis of the Southern Cross or True Cross points toward the South Pole. The True Cross should not be confused with the False Cross a larger cross nearby known as the False Cross. In the False Cross the stars are more widely spaced, is less bright and has a star in the center. The False Cross has five stars while the True Cross has only four stars. The stars on the southern and eastern arms are among the brightest stars in the heavens. Those on the northern and western arms, white bright, are smaller.

- When the lines are projected from the True Cross and between the two very bright stars east of the True Cross the intersection point is in an area devoid of any stars and very dark known as the Dark Pocket or Devoid Area.
- First extend an imaginary line along the long axis of the True Cross to the south. Join the two bright stars to the east of the True Cross with an imaginary line. Bisect this line with one at right angles. Where the two lines intersect is the South Pole. This South Pole Point can be used to estimate the latitude in the same way as with the North Pole Star.

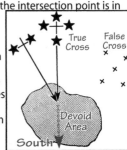

True Cross False Cross

Devoid Area

South

TIDES

High tidal waters may occur at very different hours at ports within a hundred or two miles of one another. These differences occur because the progress of the tidal waves is interfered with by masses of land, round or between which it has to make its way. Highest tides do not occur at new and full moon, but one, two, three, or more days later, according to locality.

HEIGHT OF TIDAL WAVES

Tidal waves of the open ocean are but swellings a few feet high and hundreds of miles wide moving at a terrific pace, but quite imperceptible by a boat passing over them.

When a tide approaches shore the shallowing of water causes the wave to travel more slowly, and therefore to gain height; and if, in addition, the width of the passage or estuary decreases, the tidal wave, being more and more cooped in, becomes a moving mass of water which may attain an extraordinary depth. The highest tide being in the Bay of Fundy, to the south of the isthmus joining Nova Scotia to New Brunswick. Here the tidal wave, after its sweep across the Atlantic, is trapped in a gradually shallowing and narrowing gulf 150 miles long, and at times rushes up it with a force which piles the water to a depth of 70 feet above land exposed at low spring tides. Yet in the open bay to the north of the same isthmus the maximum rise is only 7 or 8 feet.

TIDES & WINDS

The height to which any tide rises may be affected by the wind. If a strong gale is blowing on shore or up an estuary, it may raise the level several feet at both high and low water; while an offshore gale will have the contrary effect. Should a spring tide be assisted by a gale, the effects on low lying lands may be very disastrous, sea walls being overtopped and washed away. The "range" of a tide is the vertical distance between low water and high water levels.

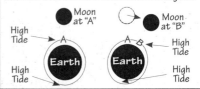

The revolution of the moon round the earth causes a high tide, at a specific location, to be more than 12 hours apart. The moon's rotation around the earth and its effect upon the movement upon the high tide from location A to B is shown in the diagram.

Moon at "A"

Moon at "B"

High Tide A High Tide

High Tide Earth High Tide

A B

High Tide Earth High Tide

UT UNIVERSAL TIME

This time standard is used in astronomy and shortwave radio transmission. UT is the time at 0° longitude (Greenwich, England) and is divided into 24 time zones around the world. To convert North American Time zones into UT.

EST (Eastern Standard Time winter) subtract 5 hours.
EDT (Eastern Daylight Time summer) subtract 4 hours.
PST (Pacific Standard Time winter) subtract 8 hours.
AST (Atlantic Standard Time winter) subtract 4 hours.
PST (Prairie Standard Time winter) subtract 6 hours.
MST (Mountain Standard Time winter) subtract 7 hours.

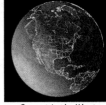

Sunrise in the East   Sunset in the West

Attraction of the Moon

Earth High Tide Moon

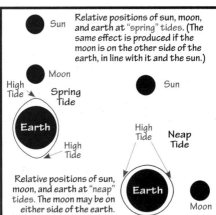

Sun

Relative positions of sun, moon, and earth at "spring" tides. (The same effect is produced if the moon is on the other side of the earth, in line with it and the sun.)

Moon

High Tide Spring Tide

Earth

High Tide

Sun

High Tide Neap Tide

Earth

Moon

Relative positions of sun, moon, and earth at "neap" tides. The moon may be on either side of the earth.

SUN & MOON TIDE EFFECTS

When the moon is directly between the earth and the sun, or the earth directly between the moon and sun, there are the highest tides, called the spring tides. Half way between the "springs" come the "neap" tides, when lines joining the centres of the sun and moon with the centre of the earth contain a right angle. At these times the crests of the tides formed by the sun called "solar waves" fill in the hollows between the lunar tide waves. "Springs" occur at new moon and full moon; "neaps" when the moon is half full and half waned (at the ends of the first and second quarters). As new moon or full moon approaches, the tides will rise higher and higher, and as gradually diminish towards the "neaps."

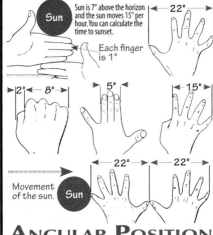

Sun is 7° above the horizon and the sun moves 15° per hour. You can calculate the time to sunset.

Sun

22°

Each finger is 1°

2° 8° 5° 15°

Movement of the sun. Sun

22° 22°

ANGULAR POSITION

To help you find the angular distance on a sky chart. Extend your arm and you can determine angular degrees with your hands and fingers.

- The width of your little finger is 1°.
- The three center fingers are 5°.
- The four fingers spread out 15°.
- Knuckles of your closed hand are 8° plus 2° for the closed thumb totaling 10°.

This will help you find stars and also explain to your friend which star you are looking at. This method of calculation can also be used to find the location of a star from a sky chart which is made for a different hour.

An example of this is our sky charts are made for 9:00 PM. If it is 10:00 PM the stars will have "rotated" 15° in the direction of the arrow on the outside of the chart. The stars "rotate" 15° per hour but we know that the stars are fixed and it is actually the earth that has rotated.

36 BINOCULARS & TELESCOPES

Warning: Never look directly at the sun.

Marine Binoculars

Water Resistant Binoculars

Binocular Support

Binocular Monopod

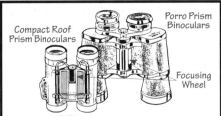

Compact Roof Prism Binoculars

Porro Prism Binoculars

Focusing Wheel

PRISMS

The prisms make binoculars more compact. Prisms of higher quality glass and a better coating will transmit a brighter and sharper image. As the prisms are a critical feature, it is important that they are well aligned and do not go out of alignment with rough use. There are two prism systems that are used in better quality binoculars- the Roof Prism and the Porro Prism. The roof prism has a higher loss of light transmission than the porro prism binoculars.

ROOF PRISM BINOCULARS

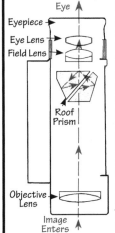

Eye

Eyepiece

Eye Lens

Field Lens

Roof Prism

Objective Lens

Image Enters

Binoculars with roof prisms usually have straight barrels. They usually are more compact and the objective lens is smaller when compared to the magnification.

Prisms reduce the length of binoculars. The light path is folded backwards and forwards to expand the focal length.
Prisms correct or rectify the image to be the right side up. If no prisms were used, the observed object would appear upside down and reversed horizontally (left to right).

FIELD OF VIEW

This is the angle of view or the area you will see through the binoculars at 1,000 yards. The recommended range is 300 to 450 feet across. This is important when viewing fast moving objects because if the angle (feet across) is too small the object will be hard to find and easily leave the field of view.

EYE RELIEF

This is the distance that the eye should be from the viewing lens to properly see the image. Most binoculars are made to have correct relief for normal eyes. Eyeglass wearers require a longer eye relief of an average of 16-20 mm. Many binoculars are now made with rubber eye cups that fold down to accommodate eyeglasses. This places the eyes at the correct distance.

NEAR FOCUS

Near focus is the closest distance to which a pair of binoculars will focus (provide a sharp image). For watching birds you will require a near focus of 15 feet or closer to allow close-up viewing.

FIT AND FEEL

How do the binoculars fit to your face and eyes? Do they have an eye space adjustment to accommodate the distance between your eyes? How well or comfortably can they be held? Do they feel stable in your hands? These are factors in your choice of binoculars.

CHEMICAL COATINGS

These are applied to lenses to reduce light scattering which will give an impression of higher contrast and improved sharpness. Manufacturers designation of "coated" means at least one surface of the lens is coated. "Multi-coated" indicates that all air-to-glass surfaces have received more than one coating.

ARMOR SHIELDING OR COATING

This provides a better grip, might be waterproofed, and reduces wear and tear. This coating increases the weight.

EYEGLASS WEARERS

You will need a "long eye relief" of 16-20 mm. If you have this you can look through your binoculars without removing your glasses. Modern binoculars have a rubber cap on each eye ring which can be folded back to accommodate glasses.

AUTO FOCUS BINOCULARS

These binoculars use averages to establish a focus and usually are not as bright because they use a large "f number". Photography buffs would understand this and also "depth of field". Avoid this "special" feature of some models of binoculars.

ZOOM BINOCULARS

These binoculars work in a similar fashion as zoom lenses for cameras. In general it is difficult enough for the manufacturer to align the lens without including the zoom feature. Each barrel has to be aligned and focused for all distances and magnifications. These binoculars are more sensitive to abuse. Avoid them if you want a half-decent optic.

CAUTION

Viewing the sun can cause permanent eye damage. Do not directly view the sun with binoculars, telescopes, or the naked eye.

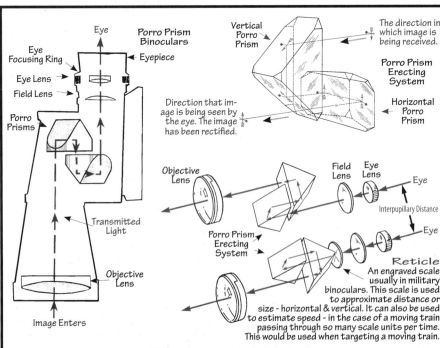

Eye

Eye Focusing Ring

Eye Lens

Field Lens

Porro Prisms

Transmitted Light

Objective Lens

Image Enters

Porro Prism Binoculars

Eyepiece

Vertical Porro Prism

The direction in which image is being received.

Porro Prism Erecting System

Horizontal Porro Prism

Direction that image is being seen by the eye. The image has been rectified.

Objective Lens

Field Lens

Eye Lens

Eye

Interpupillary Distance

Eye

Porro Prism Erecting System

Reticle
An engraved scale usually in military binoculars. This scale is used to approximate distance or size - horizontal & vertical. It can also be used to estimate speed - in the case of a moving train passing through so many scale units per time. This would be used when targeting a moving train.

PORRO PRISM BINOCULARS

Binoculars with these prisms look offset when looking between the eyepiece and the objective lens. The glass used to make the prisms can be a borosilicate glass (BK-7) or a barium crown glass (BK-4). The barium crown glass has a higher density glass which controls light-scattering and produces a sharper image.

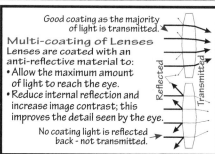
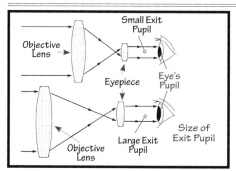

EXIT PUPIL (EP)

The size of the EP of a pair of binoculars lets you know how much light they transmit. This is very important as this is the maximum amount of light that is available for your eye to use. To measure the EP hold a pair of binoculars at arm's length with the objective lens pointing to a light source. At the eyepiece you will see a small circle of light - this is the exit pupil. The size of the EP is measured in mm and is calculated by dividing the diameter of the objective lens by the magnification.

7x50 binoculars have a 7.14 mm exit pupil (50 ÷ 7=7.14)

LIGHT REQUIRED BY EYE

Daytime: In normal light the eye's pupil is small and opens 2.5 mm to 3 mm in diameter.
Evening: The eye's pupil opens from 3 mm to 4.5 mm to obtain more light.
Dark: The eye's pupil expands to 5 mm+ to maximize the transmission of light.

To maximize the visibility and details seen through binoculars the exit pupil should equal or exceed the human eye's pupil size.

RELATIVE BRIGHTNESS

Relative brightness is the exit pupil's diameter, squared. As stated above, the EP is calculated by the mm diameter of the objective lens divided by the magnification. This means that the major factor for a high brightness is the diameter of the objective lens - the more the better.

7x50 EP of 7.14 mm and a relative brightness of 51 (note the objective lens is 50 mm).
7x35 EP of 5 mm and a relative brightness of 25 (objective lens is only 35 mm).
7x42 EP of 6 mm and a relative brightness of 36 (objective lens is only 42 mm).

TWILIGHT FACTOR (TF)

This indicates how well the binocular performs under low light, in the shadows, or at dusk. It is different from relative brightness as magnification is also considered.

It is calculated by taking the square root of magnification x objective lens in mm.
7x50 = 350, square root = 18.7 TF
7x35 = 245, square root = 15.7 TF
7x42 = 294, square root = 17.2 TF

BINOCULAR RESOLUTION

The resolution of a binocular is how it is able to resolve fine details - that you want to see. This is measured by observing a special chart. High quality lenses, prisms, coatings, alignment, and binocular construction will greatly affect the quality of resolution.

TO FOCUS BINOCULARS

· Close your right eye and sight an object with your left eye. Focus the binocular by rotating the center focus wheel until the image in the left eye is sharp and clear.
· Now close your left eye. Rotate the right eyepiece until the object sighted is sharp and clear. Note the setting on the diopter scale on the right eyepiece. This will be the adjustment for your eyes. Both sides of the binoculars are now in focus and you only use the center focus wheel to focus them.

Viewing with Glasses
Fold down the rubber rim on the binoculars if you are wearing eyeglasses.

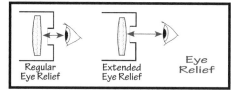

EYE RELIEF

Eye relief of a pair of binoculars is obtained by pointing a binocular at the sky (NOT THE SUN) and projecting the eyepiece side onto a piece of wax paper. When by looking through the translucent wax paper the image is clear and reaches its smallest diameter - this is the eye relief distance. In general, the longer the distance (called extended) the better. In actual usage this distance is the point where your eye can see the full field of view. Eyeglass wearers need an extended eye relief to see the full field of view, otherwise the field of view is restricted and he will have "tunnel vision."

MAGNIFICATION

Binoculars and monoculars are described by two numbers: Magnification x front (objective) lens diameter (in mm). Example 7 x 50.
Magnification (Power): The number of times the object looked at is enlarged. The larger the number the greater the magnification. A magnification of greater than 10 is not practical without a tripod, as your hand would shake. Usual magnifications will read 6 x 30, 7 x 35, 7 x 50, 10 x 50. In the 7 x 50 the image would appear 7 x closer or 7 x larger than to the naked eye.
Lens (Objective) Size: This is the diameter of the front lens. The larger the front lens the more light is admitted and the image will be brighter. This is important in choosing a pair of binoculars because at dusk or in a forest the larger lens size will be more important than the power. Usual lens size will read 6 x 30, 7 x 35, 7 x 50, 10 x 50. The larger the objective lens the wider the field of view. This means that you will be able to see more of the landscape at one time. This is important if you are watching an active sport or wildlife which might fly out of view.

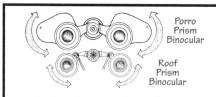
Good coating as the majority of light is transmitted.
Multi-coating of Lenses
Lenses are coated with an anti-reflective material to:
· Allow the maximum amount of light to reach the eye.
· Reduce internal reflection and increase image contrast; this improves the detail seen by the eye.
No coating light is reflected back - not transmitted.

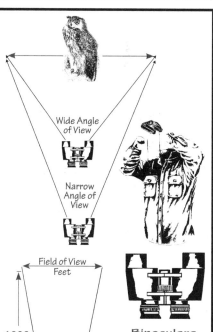
Porro Prism Binocular
Roof Prism Binocular

Adjusting Interpupillary Distance
To set the Interpupillary Distance, look through the binoculars while grasping them and gradually bending until you see one circle of view. If they do not merge, the binoculars are the wrong size or the prisms are out of alignment.

FIELD OF VIEW

The "field of view" is the width of the viewing area that can be seen through a binocular. It may be expressed in feet at a 1000 yards, meters at a 1000 meters or degrees of angle.
Note that the field of view can be compared to a telephoto lens (narrow angle) and a wide angle lens. If a field of view is narrow (and probably of high magnification) it is difficult to find your target especially if it is moving - in the case of bird watching.

Degree of Angle = Feet?
Multiply the degrees of angle by 52.36 feet - there are 52.36 feet per degree of angle at 1000 yards.
e.g. 6.7° = 350 feet at 1000 yards

BUYING BINOCULARS
FOCUS TEST

Focus on a distant object. Remove your eyes from the binoculars, wait a minute, cover one lens (do not refocus) look at the same object. Do the same with your second eye. If your eye is not immediately in focus when you look through the eyepiece the optics are of bad quality and your eye is compensating for the lens errors. Do not buy these binoculars or others of the same brand.

ALIGNMENT TEST

After the binoculars have been adjusted for your eyes, focus, with both eyes, on a distant object e.g. a flagpole. Look through the binoculars and both eyes should, in your mind, merge this flagpole as one. If they do not coincide, the alignment is off. Try this while holding the binoculars at 45° and vertically. If this problem occurs at any angle try another pair of binoculars (even the same brand).

PINCUSHION & ASTIGMATISM

When the binoculars have been adjusted for your vision you can check for distortion produced by the binoculars. Go outside and look at a tall building with long parallel vertical lines. Focus on the lines. Do they stay parallel and vertical? You will see a slight divergence which will vary from binocular to binocular but will nearly be eliminated on very expensive binoculars. Choose a pair that you can live with.

FLARE

Look at a shiny surface or a burning light bulb. Are there many reflections? Can you see past the light bulb or is it all "burnt out". The amount of flare that a pair of binoculars can eliminate depends upon the quality of the binoculars. Choose what you can accept depending upon your use. For night vision you would want less flare.

BINOCULARS AND THE SKY

Binoculars are ideal for a beginner stargazer. They are more compact, easier to use, have a wider angle of vision and are less expensive than a telescope. For star watching, the objective lens of a binocular should be as large as possible as it gathers more starlight. If the binoculars are too large they will be heavy and difficult to hold. In general the ideal binocular for astronomy is the 7 x 50. If the binoculars are of a larger magnification you will need a special clamp and tripod to keep it stable.

MAINTAINING BINOCULARS
or Other Optical Instruments

- Keep the lens covered when binocular, camera, or telescope is not in use.
- When wiping the lens, use the lens cloth that comes with the binocular, camera lens tissue, or a soft lint-less cloth. Before wiping, blow any grit or sand off the lens or the grit might scratch the lens while you are wiping.
- To remove any remaining dirt or smudges, add one or two drops of isopropyl alcohol to the cloth.
- Store your optical instruments in a moisture-free area. Do not store in a sealed plastic bag.
- Never attempt to clean the inside of your binocular or take it apart as you might disturb the alignment of the optics and prisms.

Difference of Intensity: Foreign matter or misfocused.

Lateral & Vertical Misalignment

This is an example of a misaligned pair of binoculars, as the individual images of both telescopes are merged in the mind's eye. Extended use of these binoculars will produce eye strain and a headache. The binoculars in this case have three problems: Lateral alignment, vertical alignment, and the possibility that one telescope has foreign matter (possible fungus) on some glass surfaces (or misfocus of one telescope). The possibility of foreign matter can be seen as both images do not have the same intensity. This lack of the same intensity might also be caused by a misfocused telescope.

DOUBLE VISION

- Hold the binoculars in the hands, and focus both telescopes on a distant object. Close either eye for a minute or so. Then open the eye quickly. If any double vision exists it can be detected at once. The target will appear to blur apart and then together again quickly, as the eye corrects for the defect. To use this method, use a sharply outlined target such as a telephone pole or a smokestack.
- An alternate method of checking for double vision is as follows: Sight into a telescope and observe an object on the edge of the field of view of one telescope, and see that it is exactly in the same position in the other telescope. Check on an object at the side of the field of view and also at the top. It should be noted that, as the eyepiece is focused in and out, the size of the field of view changes. It is also true that many eyepieces are not optically centered and the collimation will change slightly as the eyepiece is focused. For these reasons it is best to set the binoculars on a solid surface while making the check, and carefully focus both eyepieces with the same eye.

Left ___ Right

Merged image as seen in the mind's eye.

Left Telescope / Right Telescope

An example of lateral misalignment.

Perfect alignment when observing an object at INFINITY - beyond 600 feet.

Vertical misalignment.

Angular misalignment.

Left Telescope / Right Telescope

CHECKING OPTICAL ELEMENTS

Sight into the objective end and check the objective lens and porro prisms for cleanliness, or presence of moisture, grease, dirt, chipped lens, and for deterioration of the cementing agent between compound elements. Inspect the eye lens and field lens by sighting into the eyepiece.

OPERATION OF MOVABLE PARTS

- Check the eyepiece cell assembly to make sure it turns smoothly under a moderate pressure.
- Check movement of the hinge. The hinge should maintain any interpupillary setting for all normal handling, but should not be tight enough to cause binding.

CHECK INFINITY FOCUS

Rotate the center focus until distant objects (beyond 600 ft. is considered as being INFINITY) in the field of view appear sharp and clear. The extreme of this rotation should focus at infinity. In case the right scope has a calibration system the INFINITY focus should be with the left scope.

PARALLAX OF RETICLE (MILITARY BINOCULARS)

Checking for parallax is as follows: Place the instrument on a solid surface, and observe a distant target (beyond 600 ft.) through the binoculars. Move the head, and watch for movement of the reticle at its nearest point of center in relation to the distant target in the field of view. Any apparent movement is parallax. There must be no movement.

TILT: FIELD OF VIEW

Pronounced cases of tilt can be detected by looking through the objective end of each telescope separately, observing a straight line. Hold the instrument about a foot from the eyes and look through and around the telescope simultaneously. The part of the line visible in the field of view of the telescope should not be tipped in relation to the actual line.

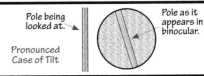

Pole being looked at.

Pronounced Case of Tilt

Pole as it appears in binocular.

Testing Binoculars for Sharpness
Focus the binoculars at a point source of light. By moving the binoculars, the point should remain in sharp focus to at least 2/3 the way to the edge of the viewing area.

Additional Features for Telescopes
Eyepieces
Eyepieces are interchangeable on telescopes so you can increase or decrease the magnification.

Camera Adapters
The telescope can be used for astrophotography or, if low-powered, for distant nature photography.

Filters
These help increase contrast or enhance astrophotography.

Image-Erecting Prisms
These are for terrestrial viewing as these prisms will make the image right-side up.

Equatorial Mount
This mount inclines the axis of the celestial sphere. You will only have to move the telescope in one direction to follow a star.

Barlow Lenses
These expand the performance of the eyepieces.

Spotting Scopes
As the name indicates, this is a sight on a high powered telescope. It is of lower magnification and helps you position your telescope on a star or object. If an erecting prism is placed on a spotting scope it can be used to watch birds or animals.

Kellner Eyepiece
An all purpose eyepiece.

Huygens Eyepiece
Works well with long focus refractors, but image distortion by spherical aberration occurs with short focal ratios. As it does not used cemented lenses, it is recommended for solar projection.

Orthoscopic Eyepiece
All purpose lens well suited for short focal length telescopes. It gives a high quality image and good eye relief.

Plossl Eyepiece
A high quality image over a wide field of view with good eye relief. Works well on a telescope with a short focal length.

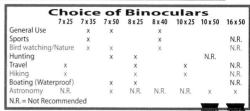

Choice of Binoculars

	7 x 25	7 x 35	7 x 50	8 x 25	8 x 40	10 x 25	10 x 50	16 x 50
General Use	x	x			x			
Sports			x		x			N.R.
Bird watching/Nature	x	x			x			N.R.
Hunting			x	x			N.R.	
Travel	x			x		x		N.R.
Hiking	x			x		x		N.R.
Boating (Waterproof)		x	x					N.R.
Astronomy	N.R.		x	N.R.	N.R.	N.R.	x	x

N.R. = Not Recommended

BUYING A TELESCOPE
In buying a telescope the most important factor is the aperture (the diameter of the lens or mirror). The larger the aperture the more light can be gathered and the brighter the object viewed.

Spotting Scope

Compact Spotting Scope

Antique Refracting Telescope

METEOR SHOWER DATES

Date	Source Constellation	From
Jan 4	Quadrans	North East
Apr 21	Lyra	North East
July 27-29	Aquarius	South East
Aug 12	Perseids	North East
Oct 20	Orion	East
Nov 16	Leo	East
Dec 13	Gemini	East

Short Eared Owl

Warning: Never look directly at the sun.

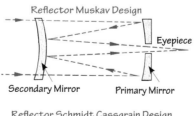

Objective Lens

Refracting Telescope
No Mirrors

Eyepiece

REFRACTING TELESCOPE
This is the type of telescope used by Galileo. It is a tube with an objective lens that collects the light, and an eyepiece which can be changed to have different powers. These telescopes are fairly inexpensive in small sizes and are of good value for a beginner. In the case of telescopes bigger is usually better because they accumulate more light and can be of higher magnification. Refractors have a good resolution of fine line detail especially when used for planetary observation. It is physically more stable than the reflector.

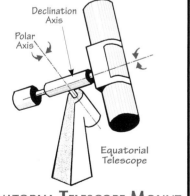

Declination Axis
Polar Axis
Equatorial Telescope

EQUATORIAL TELESCOPE MOUNT
Is a telescope mount which rotates about the polar axis and the declination axis. The advantage of an equatorial mount is that it only has to be moved around the polar axis to compensate for the Earth's rotation. A Second type of mounting system is the Altazimuth mount which allows you to move the telescope up and down (altitude) and to the left and right (azimuth) to help you track celestial bodies.

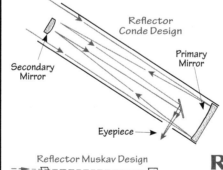

Reflector Conde Design
Secondary Mirror
Primary Mirror
Eyepiece

Reflector Muskav Design
Secondary Mirror
Primary Mirror
Eyepiece

Reflector Schmidt Cassgrain Design
Secondary Mirror
Primary Mirror
Eyepiece

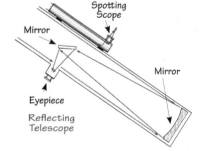

Spotting Scope
Mirror
Mirror
Eyepiece
Reflecting Telescope

REFLECTING TELESCOPE
This telescope uses a concave mirror as the main optical element (primary mirror). The mirror, which acts as a lens, is at the bottom of the tube. The light goes down the tube to the primary mirror, is focused, and reflected back to a mirror which reflects into the eyepiece. Sir Isaac Newton used this type of telescope in 1668. The advantage of this type of telescope is that the image is captured and focused in a relatively short tube. These telescopes are lighter, easier to mount, and stabilize than a refractor. Reflecting telescopes are more sensitive to misalignment than the refracting telescope. A catadioptric telescope is a hybrid, with mirrors and lenses that achieve the widest aperture for the shortest possible barrel.

The Scout

37 SIGNALS

SURVIVAL & SIGNALING

The person who is lost has to know the techniques of signaling to aid rescue teams to help in being found. This knowledge and the ability to use it can make the difference between life and death.

HOW TO ASSIST IN RECOVERY

- If, on departure, a route plan and instructions have been left as to when there is a "lost situation", the authorities will be notified and a search begun. This time frame will let the lost hiker know that a search is possibly beginning and give him time to install a "lost" signal.
- The lost hiker has to know how to use items in the survival kit and when to put each item into use. They should also be able to improvise signals to improve their chances of being sighted.
- It is not easy to spot one individual or a group especially when visibility is limited. Emergency signaling methods help make it easier to find a person.
- You should visualize how emergencies might develop, recognize them, and, at the appropriate time, use the best signaling method you know to attract attention. The length of time before being rescued often depends on the effectiveness of emergency signals and the speed with which they can be used.
- Signal sites should be carefully selected. These sites should enhance the signal and have natural or manufactured materials readily available for immediate use.
- Survivors should avoid using pyrotechnic signals wastefully as they may be needed to enhance rescue efforts. Signals used correctly can hasten recovery and eliminate the possibility of a long, hard survival episode.

INDIAN SIGN LANGUAGE

Indians, to communicate with different tribes, developed a common sign language. Some examples of this non-vocal method of communication are shown.

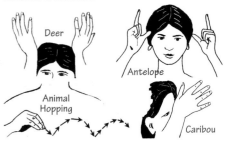

Warbling Whistle   Boy Scout or Sailor's Whistle

WHISTLE

The Hudson's Bay Company issues a whistle in all its survival kits. This whistle is used to maintain contact with other members of a party. A shrill high pitched whistle's sound carries better in the wilderness than a shout. The direction of a high pitched sound is also easier to ascertain than that from a low frequency shout.

DISTRESS SIGNALS

All major distress signals are in units of three.

- 3 gun shots
- 3 whistle blasts
- 3 car honks
- 3 fires
- 3 smoke puffs
- 3 blazes on a tree, etc.

Important Warning!

Grass

SIGNAL TRANSMISSION
Sight
Where a message is seen, e.g. the use of blazes, flags, hand signals when boating, or hand signals as in Indian sign language.
Sound
By using the voice, whistles, horns, or guns.
Light
By using flares, lights, or mirrors.
Radio Transmission
Using citizen band, GPS, cell phone or amateur radio transmission.

The first three methods of signaling have been used for thousands of years and radio transmission for the last 100 years. Marconi's radio transmission established its importance with the sinking of the Titanic.

Native Indians Using Signals

A signal method is used to transmit information over a long distance where a detail of facial expression, hand symbols or sound is not possible. Signals may be executed by...

- Exclusively by bodily action
- Action of the person in connection with objects, such as a blanket, or a lance, or the directional movements of a horse
- Various devices, such as smoke, fire or dust, when the individual sending the signal is not visible or too small

Native Signal Usage

The Body

Question: ... Do not know you. Who are you?
Answer: The advancing party halts and ... raises right hand, palm in front and slowly moved to the right and left. In this illustration signal is made by giving the tribal sign for the Paui.

Q: ... To inquire if advancing party is peaceful.
A: Raise both hands, grasped in the manner of shaking hands, or by locking the two forefingers firmly while the hands are held up. If friendly they will respond with the same signal.

Objects & Body

Buffalo Discovered: When the Ponkas or Omahas discover buffalo the watcher stands erect on the hill, with his face toward the camp, holding his blanket with an end in each hand, his arms being stretched out (right and left) on a line with shoulders.

Camp! When it is intended to encamp, a blanket is elevated upon a pole so as to be visible to all the individuals of a moving party.

Come! To beckon a person. Hold on to the lower edge of a robe or blanket, then wave it in to the legs.

Come Back! Gather or grasp the left side of the unbuttoned coat (or blanket) with the right hand, and, sitting in position so the signal can be seen, wave it to the left and right as may be necessary for the sign to be recognized. When made in a standing position the person should not move his body.

Danger!

... Horsemen at a distance, galloping, passing and re-passing, and crossing each other -- enemy comes! But upon seeing a herd of buffalo, they gallop back and forward abreast AND do not crossing each other.

... Riding rapidly round in a circle, "Danger! Get together as quickly as possible."

... Point the right index in the direction of the danger, and then throw the arm over the front of the body diagonally, so that the hand rests near the left shoulder, back outward. If the person to be notified of the danger should be in the rear precede the above signal with that for "Attention."

... Passing and re-passing one another, either on foot or mounted, is used as a war signal

Discovery: The discovery of enemies, game, or anything else, is announced by riding rapidly to and fro, or in a circle. Parties away from their regular encampment are generally in search of some special object, such as game, or of another party, either friendly or hostile, which is generally understood, and when that object is found, the announcement is made to their companions in either of the above ways.

Riding Side to Side: The reason that a horseman may ride from side to side is, that the party to whom he desires to communicate may be at a particular locality, and his movement - at right angles to the direction to the party - would be perfectly clear. Should the party be separated into smaller bands, or have flankers or scouts at various points, the only way in which the rider's signal could be recognized as a motion from side to side, by all the persons to whom the signal was directed, would be for him to ride in a circle.

Question: ... Do not know you. Who are you?
Answer: The advancing party halts and ... raises right hand, palm in front and slowly moved to the right and left. In this illustration signal is made by giving the tribal sign for the Paui.
Q: ... To inquire if advancing party is peaceful.
A: Raise both hands, grasped in the manner of shaking hands, or by locking the two forefingers firmly while the hands are held up. If friendly they will respond with the same signal.

Signal Maker Not Visible
Smoke, Fire, Arrow or Dust Signals
Smoke Signals

Some comments from settlers as to smoke signals... "Their systems of telegraphs are very peculiar, and though they might seem impracticable at first, yet so well are they understood by the natives that it's usage is frequently of immense tactical advantage. The most is by raising smoke, by which many important facts are communicated at a considerable distance and can be "read" by the manner, size, number, or repetition of the smoke, which are commonly raised by firing spots of dry grass."

The highest land is selected as stations from which signals with smoke are made. These can be seen at a distance of from twenty to fifty miles. By varying the number of columns of smoke different meanings are conveyed. The most simple as well as the most varied mode, and resembling the telegraphic alphabet, is arranged by building a small fire, which is not allowed to blaze; then by placing an armful of partially green grass or weeds over the fire, as if to smother it, a dense white smoke is created, which ordinarily will ascend in a continuous vertical column for hundreds of feet. Having established a current of smoke, the Indian simply takes his blanket and by spreading it over the small pile of weeds or grass from which the

smoke takes its source, and properly controlling the edges and corners of the blanket, he confines the smoke, and in this way is able to retain it for several moments. Waiting a few moments until the smoke was beginning to escape from beneath, the blanket was suddenly thrown aside, when a beautiful balloon-shaped column puffed upward like a white cloud. Again casting the blanket on the pile of grass, the column was interrupted as before, and again in due time released, so that a succession of elongated, egg-shaped puffs of smoke kept ascending toward the sky. This bead-like column of smoke, considering the height from which it began to ascend, was visible from points on the level plain fifty miles distance.

Other comments made by settlers...

"Columns of smoke rose over the country at scattered intervals—signals by which the Indians here, as elsewhere, communicate to each other that enemies are in the country,"

"While we were speaking, a smoke rose suddenly from the cottonwood grove below, which plainly told us what had befallen him. It was raised to inform the surrounding Indians that a blow had been struck, and to tell them to be on their guard."

Hunting Party

A hunting party in advancing takes the same precautions as a war party, so as not to be surprised by an enemy. If a scout ascends on a prominent elevation and discovers no game, the blanket is grasped and waved horizontally from side to side at the height of the shoulders or head; and if game is discovered the Indian rides back and forth (from left, to right) a short distance so that the distant observers can see the movement. If a large herd of buffalo is found the extent traveled over in going to and fro increases in proportion to the size of the herd. A quicker gait is traveled when the herd is very large or haste on the part of the hunters is desired.

Success of a War Party
Whenever a war party, consisting of either Pima or Papago Indians, returned from an expedition into the Apache country, their success was announced from the first and most distant elevation visible from their settlements. The number of scalps secured was shown by a corresponding number of columns of smoke, arranged in a horizontal line, side by side, so as to be distinguishable by the observers. When the returning party was unsuccessful, no such signals were made.

Camanchee Warrior

Smoke Signals cont'd
Gathering at Safe Planned Spot
This is made by sending upward one column of smoke from a fire partially smothered by green grass. This is only used by previous agreement, and if seen by friends of the party, the signal is answered in the same manner. But should either party discover the presence of enemies, no signal would be made, but a runner would communicate the knowledge of potential danger.

Smoke Signals of the Apaches
The materials used in making smoke of sufficient density and color consist of pine or cedar boughs, leaves and grass, which can nearly always be obtained in the regions occupied by the Apaches of Northern New Mexico. They employ but three kinds of signals, each of which consists of columns of smoke, numbering from one to three or more.

Alarm Smoke Signal
This signal is made by having three or more columns of smoke to ascend, and signifies danger or the approach of an enemy. These signals are communicated from one camp to another, and the most distant bands are guided by their location. The greater the urgency - the larger the number of columns of smoke are made. These are often so hastily made that they may resemble puffs of smoke, and are caused by throwing heaps of grass and leaves upon the embers again and again.

Attention! Smoke Signal
This signal is generally made by producing one continuous column, and signifies attention for several purposes, as… when a band has become tired of one locality, or the grass may have been consumed by the ponies, or some other cause necessitates changing location, or should an enemy be reported, which would require further watching before a decision as to future action would be made. The intention or knowledge of anything unusual would be communicated to neighboring bands by causing one column of smoke to ascend.

Establishing a Campsite Smoke Signal
When a move of a camp has been made, after the signal for *"attention"* has been given, and the party have selected a place where they propose to remain until there may be a necessity or desire for another move, two columns of smoke are made, to inform their friends that they propose to remain at that place. Two columns are made at other times during a long continued residence, to inform the neighboring bands that a camp still exists, and that all is OK and quiet.

Fire Arrows – at night
Travelers on the prairie have often seen the Indians shooting burning arrows up as signal lights at night, and have wondered how it was done…
The Indians take off the head of the arrow and dip the shaft in gunpowder mixed with a gluey substance (pine resin, etc.). The gunpowder/glue adheres to the wood, and coats it three or four inches from its end and up to of one-fourth of an inch thick. Chewed bark mixed with dry gunpowder is then fastened to the stick, and the arrow is ready for use. When it is to be fired, a warrior places it on his bowstring and draws his bow ready to let it fly; the point of the arrow is then lowered, another warrior lights the dry bark, and it is shot high in the air. When it has gone up a little distance, it bursts out into a flame, and burns brightly until it falls to the ground.
Various meanings are attached to these fire-arrow signals.
One arrow meant, among the Santees, 'The enemy are about'.
Two arrows from the same point, 'Danger'; three, 'Great danger'.
Many 'They are too strong, or we are falling back'.
Two arrows sent up at the same moment 'We will attack'; three, 'Soon'.
Four arrows 'Now'.
Shot diagonally 'In that direction.'
These signals are constantly changed, and are always agreed upon when the party goes out or before it separates. The Indians sent their signals very intelligently, and seldom make mistakes in telegraphing each other by these silent monitors. The amount of information they can communicate by fires and burning arrows was amazing. Every war party carries with it bundles of signal arrows.

Use of Gunpowder
The use of gunpowder was an influence from the settlers but before they came the native people used burning arrows with pine pitch, birch bark, etc. attached to burn enemy fortifications. They frequently used arrows, to which flaming material was attached, to set fire to the wooden houses of the early colonists.
The Caribs (Indians from the Caribbean Islands) were acquainted with these same methods of destruction as appears by the following quotation from early settlers…
"Their arrows were commonly poisoned, except when they made their military excursions by night; on these occasions they converted their arrows by arming the points with balls of cotton dipped in oil, and set on fire, they fired them on their enemy villages. They could destroy whole villages from a safe distance."

Buffalo Discovered
When the Ponkas or Omahas discover buffalo the watcher stands erect on the hill, with his face toward the camp, holding his blanket with an end in each hand, his arms being stretched out (right and left) on a line with shoulders.

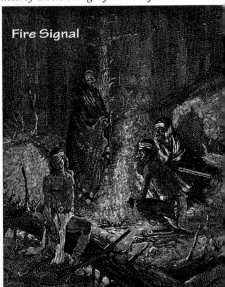

Fire Signal

DUST SIGNALS

When an enemy, game, or any special object of search is discovered, handfuls of dust are thrown into the air to announce that discovery. This signal has the same general signification as when riding to and fro, or, in a circle, on an elevated portion of ground, or a bluff. When any game or any enemy is discovered, and should the sentinel be without a blanket, he throws a handful of dust up into the air.

DIRECTION & TIME

When a war party encamps for a night or a day or more, a piece of wood is stuck into the ground, pointing in the direction traveled, with a number of cuts, notches, or marks corresponding to the number of days which the party spent after leaving the last, camp until leaving the present camp. This is to show any following parties the direction to follow and how much time has been spent at this location.

MIRRORS SIGNALS

Indians also use mirrors and reflective objects to signal from one elevation to another.

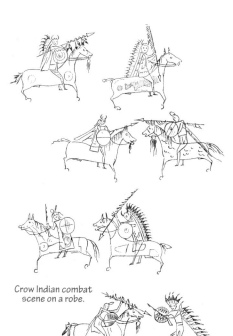

Crow Indian combat scene on a robe.

Danger!

... Horsemen at a distance, galloping, passing and re-passing, and crossing each other -- enemy comes! But upon seeing a herd of buffalo, they gallop back and forward abreast AND do not crossing each other.
... Riding rapidly round in a circle,
"Danger! Get together as quickly as possible."
... Passing and re-passing one another, either on foot or mounted, is used as a war signal

General Custer being spotted: This "discovery signaling" action was noticed by Dr. Hoffman in 1873, on the Yellowstone River, while attached to the Stanley Expedition. The Indians had again concentrated after their first repulse by General Custer, and taken possession of the woods and bluffs on the opposite side of the river. As the column came up, one Indian was seen upon a high bluff to ride rapidly round in a circle, occasionally firing off his revolver.

The signal announced the discovery of Custer's advancing force, which had been expected, and the signaling rider could be distinctly seen from the surrounding region. As many of the Indians were still scattered over the area, some of them would not have been able to recognize this signal had he ridden to and from an observer, but the circle produced a lateral movement visible from any point.

General Custer being spotted.

ADVANCING CHEYENNE WAR PARTY STRATEGY

The main objective of a war party is to have the advantage of surprise over the enemy. Some Indian Chiefs, from the Indian Territory, outlined the following strategy in the 1880's...

A party of Indians going on the war-path leave camp, announcing their project to the remaining individuals and informing neighboring friends by sending runners. A party is not organized until several days away from its gathering point, unless circumstances should require immediate action. The pipe-bearers are appointed, who precede the party while on the march, carrying the pipes, and no one is allowed to cross ahead of these individuals, or to join the party by riding up before the head of the column, as it could endanger the success of the expedition. All new arrivals fall in from either side or at the rear. *Upon coming in sight of any elevations of land likely to give a good view of the surrounding country the warriors come to a halt and secrete themselves as much us possible.* Scouts who have already been selected, advance just before daybreak to within a moderate distance of the elevation to ascertain if any of the enemy has preceded them or is on the lookout protecting their territory. *This is discovered by carefully watching the summit to see if any objects are in motion; if not, the flight of birds is observed, and if any should alight upon the hill or butte it would indicate the absence of anything that might ordinarily scare them away. Should a large bird, as a raven, crow, or eagle, fly toward the hilltop and make a sudden swerve to either side and disappear, it would indicate the presence of something/someone to require further examination.* When it is learned that there is reason to suspect an enemy the scout, who has all the time been closely watched by the his war party in the rear, makes a signal for them to be still, signifying danger or caution. With the right hand and waving it earthward from a position in front of and as high as the shoulder. (This is the same signal for 'remain quiet')

Should the hill, however, be clear of anyone, the Indian scout will ascend the hill. If there is no one to be seen, the blanket is grasped and waved horizontally from right to left and back again repeatedly, showing a clear surface. If the enemy is discovered, the scout will give the alarm by running down the hill, in a zigzag manner, upon a side visible to the watchers. Should any expedition or advance be attempted at night, the same signals as are made with the blanket are made with a firebrand, which is constructed of a bunch of grass tied to a short pole.

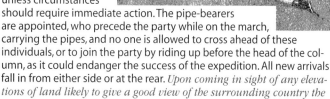

The watchers being watched!

LIGHT SIGNALS

At night, a lost hiker should use any type of light to attract attention. A signal with a flashlight, or a light or fire in a parachute shelter, can be seen from a long distance.

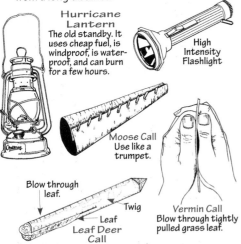

Hurricane Lantern
The old standby. It uses cheap fuel, is windproof, is waterproof, and can burn for a few hours.

High Intensity Flashlight

Moose Call
Use like a trumpet.

Vermin Call
Blow through tightly pulled grass leaf.

Blow through leaf.

Twig
Leaf

Leaf Deer Call

Vermin Call
Blow through elastic band between the two pieces of wood.

A - Flat Elastic Band — Groove
B - Elastic bands holding the pieces of wood together.

Canoe Signals

Stop

Help Emergency

All Clear

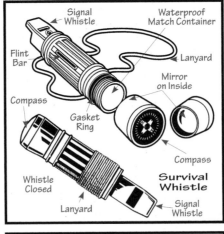

Signal Whistle
Flint Bar
Compass
Gasket Ring
Waterproof Match Container
Lanyard
Mirror on Inside
Compass
Whistle Closed
Lanyard
Survival Whistle
Signal Whistle

VELOCITY OF SOUND

In quiet open air

Temperature F°	Velocity Ft./Sec	1 Mile Seconds
-30°	1030	5.13
-20°	1040	5.08
-10°	1050	5.03
-0°	1060	4.98
10°	1070	4.93
20°	1080	4.88
32°	1092	4.83
40°	1100	4.80
50°	1110	4.78
60°	1120	4.73
70°	1130	4.68
80°	1140	4.63
90°	1150	4.59
100°	1160	4.55
110°	1170	4.51
120°	1180	4.47

The velocity of sound can be used to determine distance. If a rifle shot flash is seen on a distant hill the distance can be calculated by counting the number of seconds it takes the sound of the shot to be heard.

AUDIO SIGNALS

Sounds carry far over water under ideal conditions; however, they are easily distorted and deadened by the wind, rain, or snow. On land, heavy foliage cuts down on the distance sound will travel. Shouting and whistling signals have been effective at short ranges for summoning rescuers. Most contacts using these methods were made at less than 200 yards, although a few reports claim success at ranges of up to a mile. A weapon can be used to attract attention by firing shots in a series of three. Survivors have used a multitude of devices to produce sound. Some examples are: striking two poles together, striking one pole against a hollow tree or log, and improvising whistles out of wood, metal, and grass.

WOOD WHISTLE

Wood Used: Green sycamore or willow.
Step 1: Select a piece of wood 4-5 inches (10-12 cm) long with a smooth bark and as round as possible. Cut a slanting piece off one end. This will be for the mouth.
Step 2: Make a notch on the top side. Cut a ring in the bark, 3 inches (8 cm) from the mouth side, around the stick. Gently tap on the bark, on the mouth side, with the knife to loosen the bark.
Step 3: The bark will detach from the wood and slide off in the direction of the mouth. Wipe the sap from the wood and enlarge the notch. Then cut a sliver along the top from the notch to the mouthpiece. This sliver area is to blow air into the whistle.
Step 4: Replace the bark on the stick and the whistle should work.
Possible Problems: The notch is not long enough or the sliver cut is not deep enough.

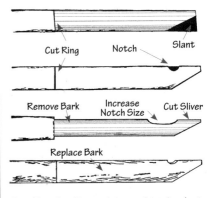

Cut Ring — Notch — Slant
Remove Bark — Increase Notch Size — Cut Sliver
Replace Bark

Flute: To make a flute make several notches (as in Step 2) and cut the sliver to join all the notches as in Step 3. The stick for a flute should be 9 inches (22 cm) long.

Surveyor's Line
Spot Trail

BLAZES

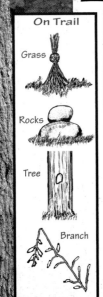

An old overgrown blaze.

On Trail	Turn Right	Turn Left	Important Warning
Grass			
Rocks			
Tree			
Branch			

MARKING BLAZES

On a thin barked tree, a blaze is made by a single downward stroke, the ax being held almost parallel to the trunk. Do not swing too hard as you might injure yourself.

The blaze stays at the original height above the ground. To check the age of the blaze chop a billet of the wood, adjacent to the blaze and containing the mark and count the annular rings that have grown from the bottom of the scar outwards. There will be one annular growth per year. Blazes on the bark of chestnut, tulip poplar, young white oak, many locusts, and some other trees are not permanent because these trees shed their bark.

FOLLOWING A BLAZED TRAIL

Most trails are spotted (marked) coming and going so that they can be seen from both directions of travel. Professional woodsmen usually mark a blaze on the trail side of the tree and only mark one blaze per tree. Make sure that you are following a blaze and not an abrasion on a tree caused by a falling branch or gnawed by an animal such as a moose, beaver or bear.

Man-made blazes will usually have a mechanical feature such as a straight cut. When there is not much light you might have to check a blaze by touching it. If a path seems to have stopped (if you see no more blazes) mark your spot and return to the last blaze and check to see that it is a valid blaze. If yes, try to line yourself in the direction of the path. It is possible that a tree with the next blaze has fallen. If you feel unsure of yourself and it is late in the day, pitch camp and proceed in the light of day.

Old blazes on spruce or pine trees are the easiest to follow because the resin deposits of the oozing sap leave a very noticeable and durable mark. Blazes are made at breast height. When a blazed line turns abruptly, so that you might miss the turn, a long slash is made on the side of the tree facing the new direction. If it snows, the blowing snow might be stuck to the tree and make them hard to find.

BLAZED TRAIL - WHERE TO?

Hiking Trail: The blazes and the trail have a point of origin and have a destination. The trail might circle back to the point of origin or merge with the main trail.

Trapper's Line: Trail leads from one stream to another, the blazes would usually not be too visible, the trail meanders, every eight to ten miles there is bound to be a small shelter that will contain some supplies.

Woodcutter's Line: This would mark the easiest route toward some select timber and towards a river to float the timber.

Surveyor's Line: This trail would be nearly absolutely straight. When it reaches a cliff or swamp there would be right angle turns. The blazes would be well placed and usually cut square.

FIRE & SMOKE SIGNALS

Fire and smoke can be used to attract the attention of recovery forces. Three evenly spaced fires, 100 feet apart, arranged in a triangle or in a straight line, serve as an international distress signal. One signal fire will usually work for a survivor. During the night, the flames should be as bright as possible, and during the day, as much smoke as possible should be produced.

SMOKE SIGNAL

Smoke signals are most effective on clear and calm days. They have been sighted from up to 50 miles away. High winds, rain, or snow tend to disperse the smoke and lessen the chances of it being seen. Smoke signals are not dependable when used in heavily wooded areas.

The smoke produced should contrast with its background. Against snow, dark smoke is most effective. Likewise, against a dark background, white smoke is best. Smoke can be darkened by rags soaked in oil, pieces of rubber, matting, or plastic being added to the fire. Green leaves, moss, ferns, or water produce white smoke.

SIGNAL FIRE

If you are lost and people are searching for you, prepare a signal fire. The fire should ignite quickly, generate a lot of smoke and at night have a high exposed flame. The fire wood should be kept dry until lit. To ignite quickly, have good tinder, adequate ventilation, wood and branches containing much pitch. To produce a heavy smoke, burn green branches, rubber, plastic, and heavy oil. Emergency signals are usually grouped in 3's, so if possible, have three fires in line. If you have one fire you can use a wet blanket to temporarily cut off the fire to send smoke signals in puffs of three. In the winter drain the engine oil before it congeals.

SMOKE FIRES

Raised Platform

- Build a raised platform above wet ground or snow.
- Place highly combustible materials on the platform.
- Then place smoke-producing materials over the platform and light when search aircraft is in the immediate vicinity.

Log Cabin-Type Fire

- Build a large log cabin fire configuration on the ground. This provides good ventilation and supports the green boughs used for producing smoke.
- Place smoke-producing materials over the fire lay; ignite when a search aircraft is in the immediate vicinity.

Tree Torch Smoke Signal

- Locate a tree in a clearing to prevent a forest fire hazard.
- Add additional smoke-producing materials.
- Add igniter. Light when a search aircraft is in the immediate vicinity.

Framework for an emergency fire.

Evergreen Boughs They burn fast and give off a darker smoke.

Wood shavings, kindlings, twigs...
Raised Platform

Small opening for lighting fire. Once you hear or see a potential rescue group light the fire.

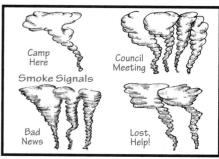

Camp Here

Council Meeting

Smoke Signals

Bad News

Lost, Help!

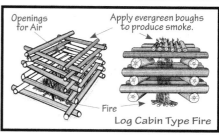

Openings for Air

Apply evergreen boughs to produce smoke.

Fire

Log Cabin Type Fire

Tree Torch Smoke Signal

Daytime

Nighttime Tree Torch

Camp to Right

Trap to Right

Trap to Left

Camp to Left

A smoke signal from a distance of five miles.

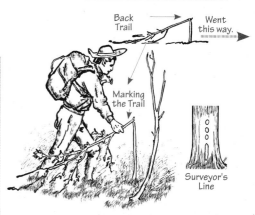

Back Trail

Went this way.

Marking the Trail

Surveyor's Line

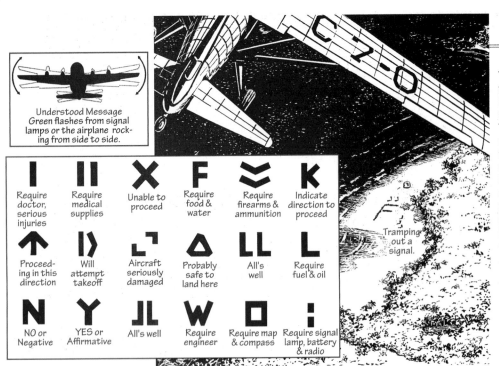

Tramping out a signal.

Ground to Aircraft Signals

I	**II**	**X**	**F**	**⋙**	**K**
Require doctor, serious injuries	Require medical supplies	Unable to proceed	Require food & water	Require firearms & ammunition	Indicate direction to proceed
↑	**I>**	**⌐**	**△**	**LL**	**L**
Proceeding in this direction	Will attempt takeoff	Aircraft seriously damaged	Probably safe to land here	All's well	Require fuel & oil
N	**Y**	**⊔**	**W**	**▢**	**⋮**
NO or Negative	YES or Affirmative	All's well	Require engineer	Require map & compass	Require signal lamp, battery & radio

Understood Message
Green flashes from signal lamps or the airplane rocking from side to side.

Ground to Aircraft Signals
These markings are recognized internationally. They can be made on a beach with stones, driftwood, salvage, stamping in the sand, on a snowfield, field with a uniform vegetation growth that can be stamped. The markings should contrast with the background and high contrast shadows should be used.

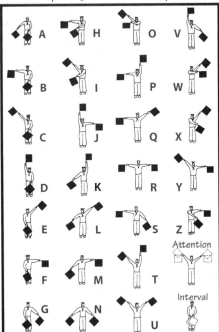

Did not understand
Red flashes of signal lamps; Complete right hand circuit of airplane.

Pointing Arrow
Shows the direction in which you intend to go or have gone.
K: asks the pilot to indicate the direction you should go. The pilot will waggle his wings in confirmation of your question, and fly in the direction that you should follow.

Semaphore
These are messages sent by flags. They can be seen over a long distance especially if the receiver has a telescope or binoculars and the sender is well contrasted against the background.
Semaphore uses two hand flags employed to form characters. The arms holding the flags are placed at an exact position for each letter, a distinct pause is made before the next letter. The arms are moved from one position to the next by the shortest possible motion. Numbers are spelled out to avoid errors.
Semaphore is also called "wigwagging."

Body Aircraft Signals

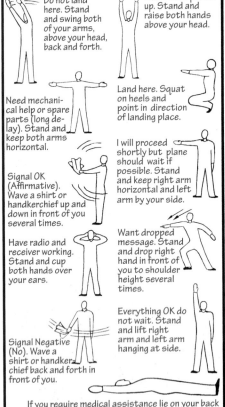

Do not land here. Stand and swing both of your arms, above your head, back and forth.

Want to be picked up. Stand and raise both hands above your head.

Need mechanical help or spare parts (long delay). Stand and keep both arms horizontal.

Land here. Squat on heels and point in direction of landing place.

Signal OK (Affirmative). Wave a shirt or handkerchief up and down in front of you several times.

I will proceed shortly but plane should wait if possible. Stand and keep right arm horizontal and left arm by your side.

Have radio and receiver working. Stand and cup both hands over your ears.

Want dropped message. Stand and drop right hand in front of you to shoulder height several times.

Everything OK do not wait. Stand and lift right arm and left arm hanging at side.

Signal Negative (No). Wave a shirt or handkerchief back and forth in front of you.

If you require medical assistance lie on your back with your arms stretched above your head.

These signals are used by aircraft crew members. Position yourself in a location where you are well contrasted from the background and wear bright clothing. Exaggerate your movements so that they will give the correct message. An airplane will respond Affirmative by dipping up and down (the same way you would nod your head); Negative - slight zig zag the same as shaking your head.

PATTERN SIGNALS
The construction and use of pattern signals must take many factors into account. Size, ratio, angularity, contrast, location, and meaning are each important if the hiker's signals are to be effective. The type of signal constructed will depend on the material available. Remember that the signals have to be seen from a distance or from an aircraft.
Size: The signal should be as large as possible. To be most effective, the signal should have "lines" no less than 3 feet wide and 18 feet long.
Ratio: Proper proportion should also be remembered. For example, if the baseline of an "L" is 18 feet long, then the vertical line of the "L" must be longer (27 feet). Keep the letter in proper proportion.
Angularity: Straight lines and square corners are not found in nature. For this reason, make all pattern signals with straight lines and square corners.
Contrast: The signal should stand out sharply against the background. The idea is to make the signal look "larger." The survivor should do everything possible to disturb the natural look of the ground. In grass and scrubland, the grass should be stamped down or turned over to allow the signal to be easily seen from the air. A burned grass pattern is also effective. When in snow, a trampled out signal is very effective. Survivors should use only one path to and from the signal to avoid disrupting the signal pattern. Consider the shadow cast by the sun and trample the snow that it maximizes the shadow in the foot markings.
Location: The signal should be located so it can be seen from all directions. Make sure the signal is located away from shadows and overhangs. A large high open area is preferable. It can serve a dual function: one for signaling and the other for rescue aircraft to land.
Meaning: If possible, the signal should tell the rescuers something pertaining to the situation. For example: "require medical assistance," as shown using the internationally accepted symbols.

SHADOW SIGNALS
If no other means are available, lost individuals may have to construct mounds which will use the Sun to cast shadows. These mounds should be constructed in one of the international distress patterns. Brush, foliage, rocks, or snowblocks may be used to cast shadows. To be effective, these shadow signals must be oriented to the Sun to produce the best shadow. In areas close to the Equator, a north-south line gives a shadow at any time except noon. Areas farther north or south, require the use of an east-west line or some point of the compass in between to give the best results.

IN THE SNOW
Walk back and forth on snow to write your message. Position the message north and south to maximize the shadow that will fall in the packed snow area. You can also add evergreen boughs to the trench to increase the contrast.

FIELD OR ROCKY AREA
Make rock piles, trample grass, lay strips of cloth. Attempt to maximize the contrast of colors or shadows. The symbols should be large with the letters or lines 10 feet wide and if possible 40 to 100 feet long. The markings should be deep or high and positioned so that the shadows cast by the sun are the longest. You could use the simple signal of S O S or build three smoky fires if you can not remember the ground to aircraft codes.

SIGNAL MIRROR

The signal mirror is probably the most underrated signaling device. It is the most valuable daytime means of visual signaling. A mirror flash has been visible up to 100 miles under ideal conditions, but its value is significantly decreased unless it is used correctly. It also works on overcast days. Practice is the key to effective use of the signal mirror. Whether the mirror is factory manufactured or improvised, aim it so the beam of light reflected from its surface hits the searching aircraft.

USING A SIGNAL MIRROR

- Reflect sunlight from the mirror onto a nearby surface-raft, hand, etc.
- Slowly bring the mirror up to eye-level and look through the sighting hole where a bright spot of light will be seen. This is the aim indicator.
- Hold mirror near the eye and slowly turn and manipulate it so the bright spot of light is on the target.
- Sweep the horizon even though no aircraft or ships are in sight.

IMPROVISED SIGNAL MIRROR

Improvised signal mirrors can be made from metal tins, parts from an aircraft, polished aluminum, glass, or aluminum foil. However, the mirror must be accurately aimed if the reflection of the Sun in the mirror is to be seen by the pilot of a passing aircraft or the crew of a ship.

AIMING IMPROVISED MIRRORS

A: The simple way to aim an improvised mirror is to place one hand out in front of the mirror at arm's length and form a "V" with two fingers. With the target in the "V" the mirror can be manipulated so that the majority of light reflected passes through the "V". This method can be used with all mirrors.

B: Another method is to use an aiming stake. Any object 4 to 5 feet high can serve as the point of reference. The hiker should hold the mirror so they can sight along its upper edge. Changing their position until the top of the stick and target line up, they should adjust the angle of the mirror until the beam of reflected light hits the top of the stick. If stick and target are then kept in the sighting line, the reflection will be visible to the rescue vehicle.

Double-faced Mirror

With a survival double-faced mirror or improvised double-faced mirror (shiny on both sides). A sighting hole can be made in the center of the mirror.

Greeks using their polished shields to send messages in the morning sun.

HELIOGRAPHY

Heliography is the use of the sun's light to transmit messages. Mirrors or polished combat shields were used by the Greeks and Romans. The US Army troops in the 1880's used mirrors to communicate over long distances from mountain range to mountain range in the west.

Pocket survival mirrors, which can be aimed, can reflect light and be seen at distances exceeding ten miles and up to 100 miles under ideal conditions.

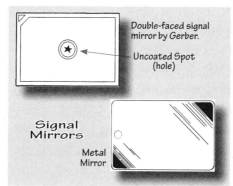

Double-faced signal mirror by Gerber.

Uncoated Spot (hole)

Signal Mirrors

Metal Mirror

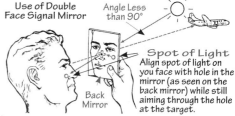

Use of Double Face Signal Mirror — Angle Less than 90°

Spot of Light
Align spot of light on you face with hole in the mirror (as seen on the back mirror) while still aiming through the hole at the target.

Back Mirror

Angle of Sun to Target is Less than 90°
Hold mirror 3" to 6" (7-14 cm) from the face and sight the target through the hole in the mirror. The sun shines a spot of light through the hole, in the mirror, onto your face. To aim the mirror, at the target, align the reflected spot of light on your face with the hole in the mirror while still aiming your eye, through the hole, at the target. Note that the mirror is coated on the front and back sides so that you can see the spot of light on your face's reflection on the back coating. The front of the mirror will be aiming the reflected light, of the sun, at your target.

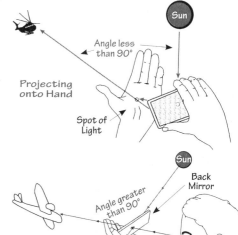

Sun — Angle less than 90°

Projecting onto Hand

Spot of Light

Sun — Back Mirror — Angle greater than 90°

Spot of Light
Align spot of light on your hand with hole in the mirror (as seen on the back mirror) while still aiming through the hole at the target.

Angle between Sun & Target is Greater than 90°
Use this method when the target is almost on the horizon and the sun on the opposite horizon (180° apart). See above illustration. Sight the target through hole. The spot of light coming through the hole in the mirror, will appear on your hand. Move the mirror (while still sighting your target through the hole) so that the reflection of the light spot (as seen on the back mirror) coincides with the hole in the center of the mirror and disappears (into the hole).

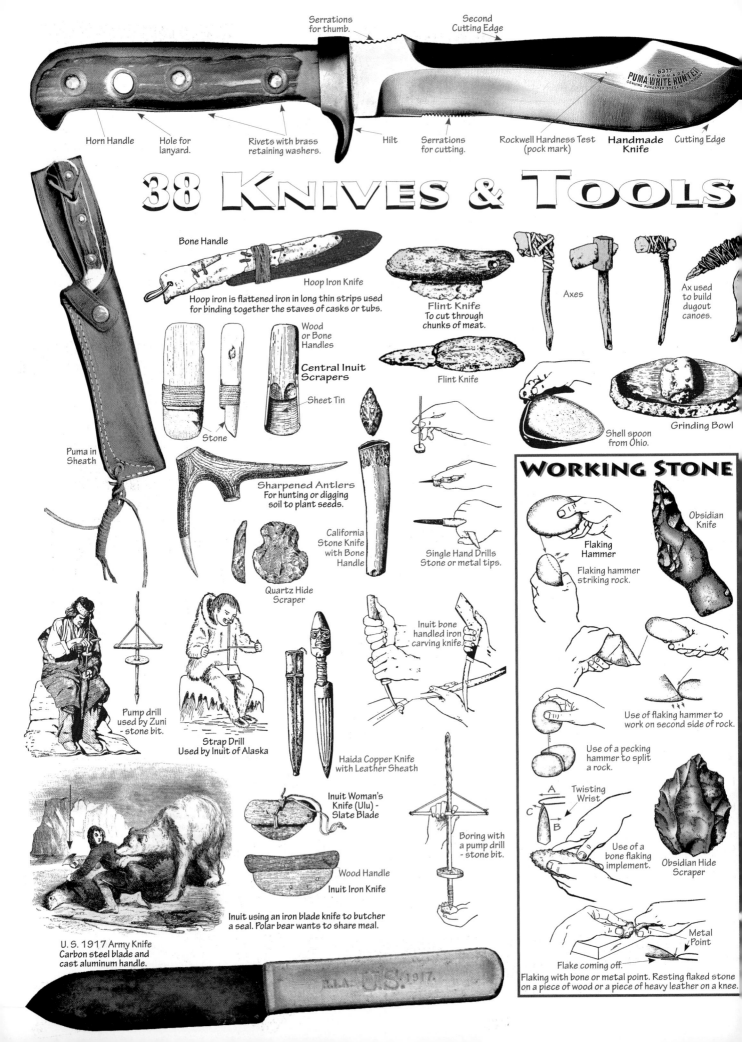

38 KNIVES & TOOLS

Serrations for thumb.

Second Cutting Edge

PUMA WHITE HUNTER
GENUINE PUMASTER STEEL W. GERMANY
6377

Horn Handle

Hole for lanyard.

Rivets with brass retaining washers.

Hilt

Serrations for cutting.

Rockwell Hardness Test (pock mark)

Handmade Knife

Cutting Edge

Puma in Sheath

Bone Handle

Hoop Iron Knife

Hoop iron is flattened iron in long thin strips used for binding together the staves of casks or tubs.

Wood or Bone Handles

Central Inuit Scrapers

Sheet Tin

Stone

Sharpened Antlers
For hunting or digging soil to plant seeds.

California Stone Knife with Bone Handle

Quartz Hide Scraper

Single Hand Drills
Stone or metal tips.

Flint Knife
To cut through chunks of meat.

Flint Knife

Axes

Ax used to build dugout canoes.

Shell spoon from Ohio.

Grinding Bowl

WORKING STONE

Obsidian Knife

Flaking Hammer

Flaking hammer striking rock.

Use of flaking hammer to work on second side of rock.

Use of a pecking hammer to split a rock.

Twisting Wrist
A
C
B

Use of a bone flaking implement.

Obsidian Hide Scraper

Pump drill used by Zuni - stone bit.

Strap Drill
Used by Inuit of Alaska

Inuit bone handled iron carving knife.

Haida Copper Knife with Leather Sheath

Inuit Woman's Knife (Ulu) - Slate Blade

Wood Handle

Inuit Iron Knife

Boring with a pump drill - stone bit.

Inuit using an iron blade knife to butcher a seal. Polar bear wants to share meal.

U. S. 1917 Army Knife
Carbon steel blade and cast aluminum handle.

U.S. 1917

Metal Point

Flake coming off.

Flaking with bone or metal point. Resting flaked stone on a piece of wood or a piece of heavy leather on a knee.

CHOOSING A GOOD POCKETKNIFE

BODY

A well-made back spring keeps the blade of the knife either open or closed. A low quality spring can only handle two blades, one on each side of the spring, never parallel.

SPACERS OF BRASS

The spacers between the blades prevent the blades from sticking to each other.

SIDE PLATES

The side plates sandwich the blades and spring together. The knife and side plates are held together by a pair of end rivets which also act as the pivots for the blades. To protect the pivots, good knives have two solid metal bolsters, one on each side of the knife. The bolsters reinforce the pivot action of a pocket knife and hold the decorative plates in place. A quality knife should have well fitted parts and the blades should have a solid-sounding return when released.

BLADES

The blades should feel comfortable in your hands and should have a rest area when half opened to prevent it from snapping closed on your fingers. Blades should be easy to open. With blades open, check the alignment of all moving parts and the body. The blades should move parallel to the body. Blades should not feel loose and move from side to side when open.

CARBON STEEL OR STAINLESS STEEL BLADES?

Carbon Steel: Carbon steel will accept a very fine edge but is subject to rust and staining. It will discolor if in contact with acids, as from peeling an orange. Quality carbon steel is very brittle and should not be used as a screw-driver. If it is stored wet in an area where it cannot dry, carbon steel will rust.

Stainless Steel: As it says, it does not "stain" or rust. It cannot be honed as well as carbon steel as it is much harder than carbon steel.

Stainless or Carbon Steel? Use carbon steel if you will require a continuous sharp blade, as for cutting wood, leather, etc. Carbon steel is softer than stainless steel so is easier to sharpen. Use stainless steel if you don't like the "stain" on carbon blades. Use a stainless blade in saltwater, for fishing or basic outdoor activities.

HARDNESS OF STEEL

The standard of measuring hardness is the Rockwell Hardness Test, and for a knife the hardness should be from 20-68, and most blades specify 55-65. The Rockwell hardness of 65 is not necessarily the ideal as it is too hard to sharpen and the blade might be brittle. A quality knife blade will be tested for temper and hardness. You can see the test point as a small pock mark on the side of a quality blade.

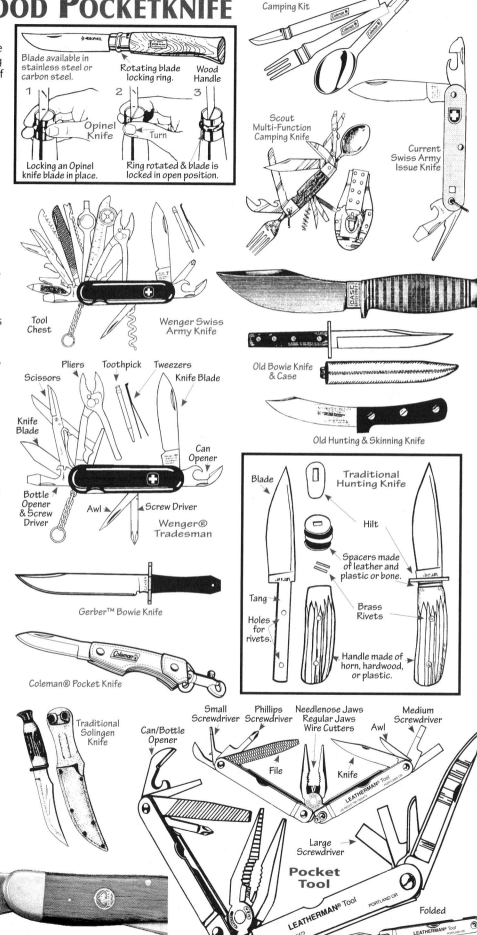

Blade available in stainless steel or carbon steel.

Rotating blade locking ring.

Wood Handle

Opinel Knife

Turn

1 Locking an Opinel knife blade in place.

2 Ring rotated & blade is locked in open position.

3

Camping Kit

Scout Multi-Function Camping Knife

Current Swiss Army Issue Knife

Tool Chest

Wenger Swiss Army Knife

Scissors

Pliers

Toothpick

Tweezers

Knife Blade

Knife Blade

Can Opener

Bottle Opener & Screw Driver

Awl

Screw Driver

Wenger® Tradesman

Gerber™ Bowie Knife

Coleman® Pocket Knife

Old Bowie Knife & Case

Old Hunting & Skinning Knife

Traditional Hunting Knife

Blade

Hilt

Spacers made of leather and plastic or bone.

Tang

Brass Rivets

Holes for rivets.

Handle made of horn, hardwood, or plastic.

Traditional Solingen Knife

Small Screwdriver

Phillips Screwdriver

Needlenose Jaws Regular Jaws Wire Cutters

Medium Screwdriver

Awl

Can/Bottle Opener

File

Knife

Large Screwdriver

Pocket Tool

LEATHERMAN® Tool

Folded

Rockwell Hardness Test (pock mark)

572 PUMA – SENIOR

Handmade Pocket Knife

KNIFE SHARPENING

SHARPEN KNIFE ON OILSTONE

A Slide blade away from you while applying an easy pressure on stone.

Hold Blade Tip

B While sliding make a sideward movement to hone the entire length of the blade. During the stroke keep the angle of the blade at about 15° to the stone.

C Flip the blade over at the end of the stroke.

D Slide the knife back towards you reversing the side motion that at the end of the stroke you will be sharpening near the handle.

Knife is Sharp when...

Knife is sharp when a feather edge appears. It can be felt by sliding your hand over the flat of the blade to over the newly sharpened edge. If the feather can not be felt or not felt over the length of the blade keep on sharpening.
When the feather can be felt on the whole edge pass the blade over the fine side of the stone to remove the feather.
For a razor sharp edge give the edge a few strokes on a leather strop. A strop is strip of top grain belting leather used to give the final touch in sharpening a straight razor.

Feather Edge
Highly Magnified

SHARPENING & STRENGTH OF BLADE

The narrow sharp edge is thin and would be fragile and if very tempered it would be brittle when used in a sideways movement.

This sharp edge would be stronger as it gains strength from the thick metal base of the blade. This blade will not retain its sharpness as the sharp edge is not very deep.

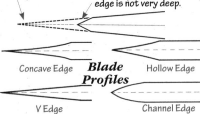

Concave Edge   **Blade Profiles**   Hollow Edge

V Edge   Channel Edge

Angle of Blade
Stone

POCKETKNIFE SHARPENING

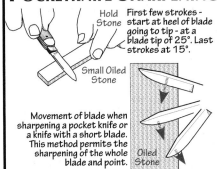

Hold Stone

First few strokes - start at heel of blade going to tip - at a blade tip of 25°. Last strokes at 15°.

Small Oiled Stone

Movement of blade when sharpening a pocket knife or a knife with a short blade. This method permits the sharpening of the whole blade and point.

Oiled Stone

HONING A FINE EDGE

Buy a quality sharpening stone and apply a lubricant as specified for the stone. Immerse the stone in oil for a day before using. The oil prevents the grit from clogging the holes in the stone. Sharpen the knife as soon as you feel it's getting dull. For minor touch ups, place the blade on the stone and pull it toward you with the cutting edge at a 10° angle on your side. Repeat this on both sides an equal number of times. First pull the blade over the coarse side of the stone and then hone with the fine stone.

Angle of Blade & Stone

Type of Edge		Angle
Very sharp edge	10° or less	Very sharp
General purpose	15°	General work
Tough edge	20°	Rugged work

USING A STEEL

A steel is used to maintain a fine edge, not to produce one. The same angle should be used on the steel but the blade should be pulled from the cutting edge and not as in the case of the stone, where it is pushed towards the edge.

Knife Blade Preserver

To keep a carbon steel from staining and for polishing a stained blade, use wood ash. Wood ash rubbed on a stained blade will remove the stains without scratching the blade. Leave some ash on the blade to prevent future staining. Wipe off the ash before using.

Two Sided Honing Stone

Sharpening Tool
The blade is lightly pulled through the 'V' notch.

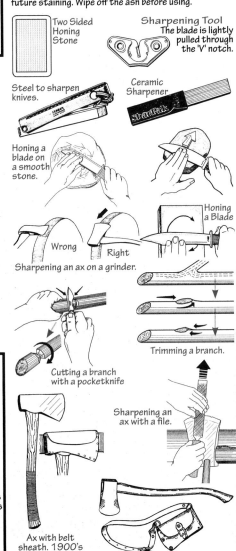

Steel to sharpen knives.

Ceramic Sharpener

Honing a blade on a smooth stone.

Wrong   Right
Sharpening an ax on a grinder.

Honing a Blade

Cutting a branch with a pocketknife.

Trimming a branch.

Sharpening an ax with a file.

Ax with belt sheath. 1900's

Follow the backbone, with a filleting knife, and slice toward the tail while cutting the flesh away from the bone.

To remove the skin - hold the tail skin - side down on a flat surface and cut forward with a slight saw motion.

Filleting Knife

This knife is very sharp and should be kept in its case.

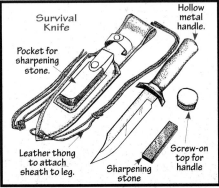

Gerber® Folding Saw

Survival Knife

Hollow metal handle.

Pocket for sharpening stone.

Leather thong to attach sheath to leg.

Sharpening stone

Screw-on top for handle

Gerber™ Ax

Machete & Sheath
18" hardened steal blade. Coleman™

Handmade Machete
Used in the jungles of South America.

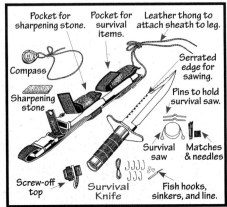

Pocket for sharpening stone.

Pocket for survival items.

Leather thong to attach sheath to leg.

Compass

Sharpening stone

Serrated edge for sawing.

Pins to hold survival saw.

Survival saw

Matches & needles

Screw-off top

Survival Knife

Fish hooks, sinkers, and line.

KNIFE SHARPENING OVERVIEW

- A file and sharpening stone are often packed in a survival kit. The file is normally used for axes, and the stone is normally used for knives.
"A sharp cutting tool is a safe cutting tool"
- Control of a cutting tool is easier to maintain if it is sharp, and the possibility of accidental injury is reduced.
- One of the most valuable item when lost, is a knife, since it has a large number of uses. Unless the knife is kept sharp, however, it falls short of its potential.
- A knife should be sharpened only with a sharpening stone as repeated use of a file rapidly removes steel from the blade. In some cases, it may be necessary to use a file to remove plating, if plated, from the blade before using the stone.

Sharpening: One of two methods should be used to sharpen a knife. One method is to push the blade down the stone in a slicing motion. Then turn the blade over and draw the blade towards you. The other method is to use a circular motion the entire length of the blade turn the blade over and repeat the process. What is done to one side of the cutting edge should also be done to the other to maintain an even cutting edge.

Whetstones: Usual sharpening stones available in survival kits would be a whetstone. Water or light oil should be applied to these stones. The water will help to float away the metal removed by sharpening and make cleaning of the stone easier. If a commercial whetstone is not available, a natural whetstone can be used. Any sandstone will sharpen tools, but a gray, clay like sandstone gives better results. Quartzite should be avoided. Quartzite instantly scratches the knife blade as the quartz crystals will bite into steel. If no sandstone is available, granite or crystalline rock can be used. If granite is used, first, two pieces of the stone should be rubbed together to smooth the surface before use.

Too Thick   Correct   Too Thin
X-Section of Ax Blade

USING AN AX

- As with a knife, a sharp ax will save time and energy and be much safer.
- A file should be used on an ax or hatchet. File away from the cutting edge to prevent injury if the file should slip. The file should be worked from one end of the cutting edge to the other. The opposite side should be worked to the same degree. This will ensure that the cutting edge is even. After using a file, the stone may be used to hone the ax blade. The blade will then be very sharp and would have to be handled with care.
- When using an ax, don't try to cut through a tree with one blow. Rhythm and aim are more important than force. Too much power behind a swing interferes with aim. When the axe is swung properly, its weight provides all the power needed.

File to Sharpen Ax
File the flat surface of the blade. File 1/2" away from edge of blade. Keep the file at right angles to edge of the blade. Always file away from edge.
You want a 3" fan shaped effect after the filing in 'A'.
File the edge making rounded strokes away from edge.
3"

Sharpening Ax: File & Whetstone
Ideally you need a metal file and a whetstone. The file is used to remove any burrs on the cutting edge, and the whetstone to sharpen the blade. The file is pushed onto the blade. The whetstone is moved in a circular motion. When sharpening the blade try to maintain the original angle of the cutting edge. A blade that is sharpened too narrow can easily be damaged due to the temper in the metal.
Whetstone

39 WOOD CUTTING

Platform
Double Bit (two blades) Axes
Two Man Cross-Cut Saw

Coleman™ Camp Ax
Drop forged carbon steel ax head with forged steel handle. Non slip handle.

Never let the sharp edge of the ax touch the ground as even a pebble can chip it.

Modern Camping Ax Gerber™

Ax with belt sheath. 1900's

Ax handle should be straight.

Warming a Cold Blade
Do not overheat. You should be able to touch the blade.

Grinder to Sharpen Ax
Use grinding wheel only when the ax is badly damaged. Use the same procedure as when sharpening with a file. Keep the stone wet. You can damage the temper on a quality ax blade by exposing it to heat. If ax is sharpened by grinding keep the blade cool with oil or water. Filing and honing the blade will give the best result.

Wrong   Right

Head   Shoulder
Eye
Face   Back   Belly
Front
Blade   Heel
Toe   Bit
Hudson's Bay Co. Ax 1860's
Fawn Foot
Knob

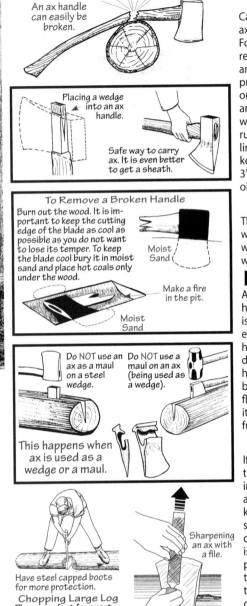

An ax handle can easily be broken.

Placing a wedge into an ax handle.

Safe way to carry ax. It is even better to get a sheath.

To Remove a Broken Handle
Burn out the wood. It is important to keep the cutting edge of the blade as cool as possible as you do not want to lose its temper. To keep the blade cool bury it in moist sand and place hot coals only under the wood.

Moist Sand

Make a fire in the pit.

Moist Sand

Do NOT use an ax as a maul on a steel wedge.   Do NOT use a maul on an ax (being used as a wedge).

This happens when ax is used as a wedge or a maul.

Have steel capped boots for more protection.
Chopping Large Log
Place your feet far apart and swing with a 45° angle on the side of the log farthest away from you.

Sharpening an ax with a file.

CHOPPING ANGLE

Angle should be 45° to maximize the chopping efficiency. Angles lower than 45° can deflect off the tree. This can be very dangerous. At higher than 45° the ax will be ineffective.

Best Angle 45°   Too Steep

Too Low CAN DEFLECT

Trimming Branches
Always trim on the far side of feet. Never straddle a tree. Always trim branches from the bottom of each branch.

CARE OF AX HANDLE

Carving a new ax handle and mounting the ax head takes a great deal of time and effort. For this reason avoid actions which would require the handle to be changed. Using aim and paying attention to where the ax falls will prevent misses which could result in a cracked or broken handle. Do not use an ax as a pry bar and avoid leaving the ax out in cold weather where the handle may become brittle. To avoid rusting, put a few drops of oil on the blade. Rub linseed oil on handle to keep it waterproof. To keep handle well-oiled drill a 1/4" diameter hole 3" into the butt of the handle, fill it with linseed oil and plug the hole with a wood stopper.

COLD WEATHER

The steel ax head becomes very brittle in cold weather. A lightweight ax blade should be slightly warmed before use. The friction of continuous use will keep it warm after the initial strike.

REMOVING AX HANDLE

A broken handle is difficult to remove from the head of the ax. Usually the most convenient way is to burn it out. For a single bit ax (one cutting edge), bury the bit in the ground up to the handle, and build a fire over it. For a double bit dig a small trench and lay the middle of the ax head over it, cover both "bits" with earth, and build the fire. The covering of earth keeps the flame from the cutting edge of the ax and saves its temper. A little water added to the earth will further ensure this protection against the heat.

MAKING AX HANDLE

If improvising a new handle, in the wild, save time and trouble by making a straight handle instead of a curved one like the original. Use a young, straight piece of hardwood without knots. The wood should be whittled roughly into shape and finished by shaving. A slot should be cut into the ax head end of the handle. After it is fitted, a thin, dry wooden wedge can then be pounded into the slot. Use the ax awhile, pound the wedge in again, then trim it off flush with the ax. If the head still becomes loose the head can be submerged in water to let the wedge and handle swell. The handle must be smoothed to remove splinters. To smooth, a smooth rock can be used if no sandpaper is available. The new handle can be seasoned to prevent shrinkage by "scorching" it in the fire.

Cutting Sapling
To make cutting of a sapling easier, bend it over with one hand, straining grain. A slanting blow close to the ground will cut the sapling.
Make sure that the blade does not deflect to hit leg.

Splitting Branch   **Removing Branches**
Note: Trim on far side of legs.

To prevent damage to the ax head and possible physical injury, any splitting of wood should be done on a log. The log can also be used for cutting sticks and poles.

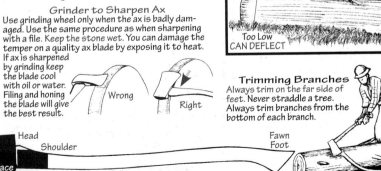

Clear underbrush in swing area.

Clear the area around the tree from underbrush and overhanging branches to prevent injury by hitting the underbrush and deflecting the ax.

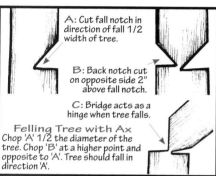

Make two cuts. The first cut should be on the leaning side of the tree and close to the ground and the second cut on the opposite side and a little higher than the first cut.

A: Cut fall notch in direction of fall 1/2 width of tree.

B: Back notch cut on opposite side 2" above fall notch.

C: Bridge acts as a hinge when tree falls.

Felling Tree with Ax
Chop 'A' 1/2 the diameter of the tree. Chop 'B' at a higher point and opposite to 'A'. Tree should fall in direction 'A'.

Escape Route

Before starting make sure that you have planned an escape route. Check for other trees and branches that might be affected by your cutting or the falling tree. Watch for dead branches that might be dislodged and fall. Do not forget hornet's or wasp's nest.

Avoid balsam and hemlock knots. They are extremely hard and will break an ax blade. Cut around knots if possible.

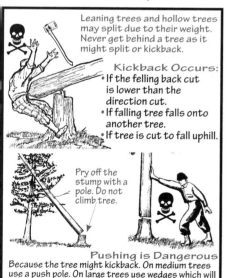

Leaning trees and hollow trees may split due to their weight. Never get behind a tree as it might split or kickback.

Kickback Occurs:
- If the felling back cut is lower than the direction cut.
- If falling tree falls onto another tree.
- If tree is cut to fall uphill.

Pry off the stump with a pole. Do not climb tree.

Pushing is Dangerous
Because the tree might kickback. On medium trees use a push pole. On large trees use wedges which will be inserted on opposite side of direction of fall.

Good Fall   Dangerous   Dangerous

FELLING A TREE
- Ax should be sharp, well-balanced and the correct size for you and the job being done.
- Secure footing. Build a level platform if you are cutting a very large tree.
- Your clothing should not obstruct your movement.
- Swing with short, smooth strokes as this will keep you on target.
- The most efficient cut is at a 45° angle. This cut will cut 5 times deeper than a perpendicular cut. It will easily eject the wood chips.
- First determine the direction in which the tree is to fall. It is best to fell the tree in the direction in which it is leaning. The lean of the tree can be found by using the ax as a plumb line. Then clear the area around the tree from underbrush and overhanging branches to prevent injury by hitting the underbrush and deflecting the ax.
- Before starting make sure that you have planned an escape route. Check for other trees and branches that might be affected by your cutting or the falling tree. Watch for dead branches that might be dislodged and fall. Do not forget hornet's or wasp's nest.
- Make two cuts. The first cut should be on the leaning side of the tree and close to the ground and the second cut on the opposite side and a little higher than the first cut.
- Falling trees often kick back and can cause serious injury, ensure that you have a clear escape route. When removing branches from a fallen tree, start at the base of the tree and cut toward the top. This procedure will allow for easier limb removal and results in a smoother cut. For safety, stand on one side of the trunk with the limb on the other.

- *If possible drop the tree in a clearing.*
- *If possible drop in direction of lean.*
- *Drop it in the direction of the wind.*
- *Drop it in the direction that you want to move the log.*
- *Heavy limb in direction of fall can cause the trunk to break. This can also happen if tree falls on a stump or a large boulder.*

How to Hold an Ax
Use both hands.

Checking the direction of lean of a tree.

DIRECTION OF FALL
- Make small notch 'B' on the opposite side of the tree from the direction of fall. This notch will reduce the possibility of the trunk splitting.
- Make notch 'A', at a lower level than notch 'B', on the side that the tree should fall. This notch will be larger. Once it passes through more than half of the tree place a few ax strokes at notch 'B' and the tree will fall.
- These two notches create a fulcrum (bridge) over which the tree falls.
- When the tree falls, and other people are present, yell 't-i-m-b-e-r' and move to a safe spot.

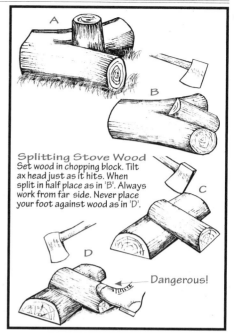

Splitting Stove Wood
Set wood in chopping block. Tilt ax head just as it hits. When split in half place as in 'B'. Always work from far side. Never place your foot against wood as in 'D'.

Dangerous!

Splitting Log
When ax hits the log give your wrist a slight twist and this will help split the log.

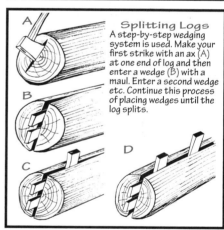

Splitting Logs
A step-by-step wedging system is used. Make your first strike with an ax (A) at one end of log and then enter a wedge (B) with a maul. Enter a second wedge etc. Continue this process of placing wedges until the log splits.

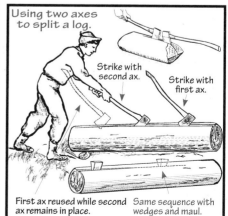

Using two axes to split a log.

Strike with second ax.

Strike with first ax.

First ax reused while second ax remains in place.   Same sequence with wedges and maul.

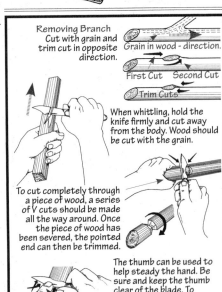

Removing Branch
Cut with grain and trim cut in opposite direction.

Grain in wood - direction.

First Cut   Second Cut

Trim Cuts

When whittling, hold the knife firmly and cut away from the body. Wood should be cut with the grain.

To cut completely through a piece of wood, a series of V cuts should be made all the way around. Once the piece of wood has been severed, the pointed end can then be trimmed.

The thumb can be used to help steady the hand. Be sure and keep the thumb clear of the blade. To maintain good control of the knife, the right hand is steadied with the right thumb while the left thumb pushes the blade forward. This method is very good for trimming.

WHITTLING

Whittle means to cut, trim, or shape (a stick or piece of wood) by taking off bits with a knife. Campers should be able to use the techniques of whittling to help save time, energy, and materials as well as to prevent injuries. They will find that whittling is a necessity in constructing triggers for traps and snares, shuttles and spacers, and other improvised equipment. Branches should be trimmed before working a piece of wood..

Light-Weight Bow Saw

CUTTING A LOG

Place the log on a support. This will prevent the saw from getting pinched by the log as the weight of the cut end will open the cut.

FELLING TREE WITH SAW

A
Undercut

B
Felling Cut

C Bridge is the falling hinge.

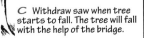

Height 1/4 diameter of tree.

A Chop undercut. The tree should fall in this direction. Notch has height of 1/4 diameter of the tree.

B Saw on opposite side of tree from the notch, one or two inches above the lower surface of the notch. This is very important because if sawn below the notch the tree can kick back, pinch the blade, and might go out of control. Saw should be level to the ground. Keep saw straight to avoid pinching. Insert a wedge, in the sawed groove behind the saw blade, to keep the sawed groove from pinching the blade when sawing a large tree.

C Withdraw saw when tree starts to fall. The tree will fall with the help of the bridge.

Taking a break in a logging camp.

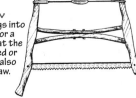

Folded Saw

15" Bow Saw Coleman™

Bucksaw

Used to cut small logs into the required length for a stove. Make sure that the blade is well tightened or it might buckle. This also applies to the bow saw.

CARE OF SAW

Avoid nails, rocks, soil, or pinching the blade. Pinching occurs when the log, which is partially cut, seizes (binds) the blade. This might cause the blade to overheat and you lose the correct temper or a few saw teeth. Use a log support because the log cut will open as you are cutting. When sawing a tree you can use metal or wood wedges. Use kerosene to remove the tree sap or pitch from the blade. Oil the blade before storing.

TWO MAN CROSS-CUT SAW

This saw can be in lengths of 5' to 14' but usually is 5 1/2'. Make sure that the log does not pinch the blade. When sawing you pull blade towards you and then on the return the second person pulls. Do not push blade or the blade might buckle. Lubricate the blade with kerosine while sawing. Keep the saw straight to avoid pinching the blade. If blade pinches, drive a wedge into the cut to widen it. Make short strokes at end of sawing.

Two poles used to force the split log open.

Sawing a log to make planks.

Spacers

Planks laid to dry

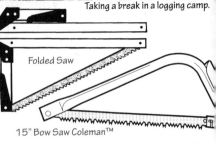

Folding Saw Gerber™

Folding Sierra Saw

SURVIVAL SAW

This saw is included in most survival kits. The saw is sold in two grades. Buy the top grade because the saw will have a better temper and not be as fragile. In using the saw avoid sawing in a way that the blade assumes a sharp angle or kink. Place the log so that it will not pinch the blade. If a large log is being cut rest the log on a support and saw from the bottom up.

A Survival saw held between thumbs of two people.
B Survival saw stretched between the extremities of a bent branch.
C Survival saw used as a trapping noose for animals.
D A saw used by one person.

Two Persons Cutting a Log
Wrap your finger to avoid blisters.

Survival Saw to Cut a Branch
Two cords tied to a survival saw. This can be used to saw a branch that cannot be reached.

Survival Knife

Handles for survival saw.

Survival Saw

A

B

Pocket Commando Survival Saw

C

D

Skidding Log
Using the leverage of a tree.

Removing Stump

Cut Roots

Place a rolling log as close to the stump as possible. Cut any exposed roots and dig into ground around stump if it is very large.

Stump being removed.

Rope anchored by clove hitch.

Bark removed from lever log.

6' long turning pole. Two men are needed to turn pole.

2' deep hole where pole rotates.

STUMP-PULLER WINCH

Use a 6" thick 8' long lever log as a log puller. Apply force very slowly as much rope tension is developed. Make sure that the rope is strong enough. Stop turning when the stump starts to turn over as the tension in the rope might finish the job. Reapply tension very slowly if required. This can be very dangerous. Cut large surface roots before starting.

Removing Stump

Rope attached to cut root.

Pull

Cut Root

Clearing the land.

Putting out spot fires.

HOW FIRES START IN NATURE

Lightning: During a single lightning storm there might be thousands of strikes, of which 1% might start fires. The percentage can be higher and depends upon drought conditions, availability of fuel, and the quantity of rain during the storm.

Humans: Deliberately setting a fire or by simple carelessness.

Spontaneous Combustion: This is when rags, paper or other flammable material has been soaked in a solvent, paint or other petrochemical product, reaches a temperature in the presence of oxygen, at which point it starts burning on its own.

SPEED OF SPREADING

Depends upon the wind, the humidity of the fuel, the topography and the actual size of the fire:

• Grass fires will advance at 2 to 4 miles an hour. This fire can easily be out-walked.

• Crown fires can spread at over 5 miles per hour. A strong wind can cause the fire to spread much more rapidly but then the fire front will only burn the crowns of the trees. The remaining forest will burn more slowly.

• A ground fire can smolder for months.

How a Wildfire Starts
Wind
Tail of Fire
Flank of Fire
Origin of Fire
Flank of Fire
Head of Fire

HOW FIRES SPREAD

A fire starts at a point and gradually spreads out from the point, ideally in a circle. In real life there is wind, the slope of the land, and obstacles that will misshape the circle, usually into an eclipse. The center, being the source of the fire, will be burnt out and the factor for misshaping the circle (wind, slope) will cause the fire to burn in a certain direction. The direction of travel is called the head, the sides are the flank, and the end is the tail.

• The wind affects the fire by blowing the heat (which dries the adjacent fuel) and flames in a certain direction causing that part of the circle to expand more rapidly. This misshaped circle usually has the form of an ellipse.

• The slope affects a fire by the fact that the heat of the fire rises up the slope. This dries the fuel higher up so that it can ignite more easily. Even if there is no wind the fire is pulled uphill by the rising heat (updraft) which causes wind in the form of convection currents.

• The fire soon breaks out of this ideal circle structure and adapts to the wind, updraft, and topography of the land. The fire advances in a line or front.

WILDFIRE SEASONS

The fire season varies in different parts of the country. Regional drought conditions can be an additional factor. Weather that increase the possibility of wildfires:

• The number of consecutive hot and dry days.
• Very low humidity for an extended period.
• High temperatures.
• Strong winds.
• Unstable air masses that produce dry thunderstorms in which strong downdrafts produce lightning and not much rain.
• Strong dry foehn winds dry out the vegetation which becomes easily flammable.
• Low level jet stream produces a windy dry cold front.

FUEL OXYGEN HEAT
Components needed for a Fire

Parts of this chapter are based on information from the: U.S. Department of Agriculture: Forestry Service, Department of the Interior, National Park Service, Bureau of Land Management, US Fish & Wildlife Service.

Temperatures at Stages of a Fire		
400°-700°F	200°-370°C	Wood glows
800°F	426°C	Burst into flames.
2300°F	1230°C	Temperature of a fire.

LIFE CYCLE OF A FIRE

A fire starts in a location that has all the required conditions: fuel, oxygen, and heat.

For fire to spread:

• It heats the potential adjacent fuel and dries it out.
• The heat then chemically breaks down the potential fuel so that it gives off flammable gases which ignite, causing it to burn and spread.
• To stop the fire you have to remove one of the three ingredients of a fire (fuel, oxygen or heat).

WILDFIRE PSYCHOLOGY

Each fire has its own personality and, as in a human, it is not totally predictable.

The factors that affect a wildfire are:

Humidity: How wet is the fuel and the ground.

Fuel to burn: Ground deposits (deadwood), type of trees, grass, etc.

Spread of the fire: Height of trees and winds for a crown fire to be high enough so that embers can be blown over natural firebreaks or roads to start a fire on the other side.

Weather: If it is raining, humid, or very dry.

Wind: Feeds oxygen to a fire and spreads embers.

Topography: The features on the land.

TOPOGRAPHY AFFECTING FIRES

Slopes: Fires travel uphill faster than downhill because the hot air currents rise and dry out and preheat the fuel on the uphill side of a fire. The hot air currents help a fire move up the slope. The slope on the south and west sides has more sun so is dryer, has a tendency to have more, larger and hotter fires.

Barriers: As roads, rivers, previously burned areas, fire trenches, etc. will slow down or stop a fire.

TYPES OF FIRES

Surface: These fires burn the shrubs, grass, ground debris and small trees.
- **Marsh Fires:** These occur in the spring or fall when the vegetation of reeds and cattails are dry. Never have the wind blowing towards you when you are fighting a fire, as it can easily flare up.
- **Grass Fires:** These fires, which are used to burn dry grass, can get out of control and cause extensive damage.

Ground Fire: After much sun and periods of drought, the layers of debris of rotten dry leaves, needles, peat moss, and other vegetation can easily catch fire. The fire can be easily started by lightning. A ground fire burns the organic deposits below the surface. This fire does not burn with a flame, as there is a lack of oxygen, but glows. A fire can start and smolder for many days betrayed by only a few wisps of smoke. If more oxygen becomes available the fuel can burst into flame. This can happen if you remove the covering soil. This fire is bad for wildlife because it kills the root structure of the plants deep in the ground. It is difficult to fight this fire because it is hard to reach. A heavy downpour would be of great help in controlling this type of fire. Ground fires can occur in coal mines and they can burn for a hundred years.

Forest Floor Fires: These burn swiftly through the underbrush and kill the seedlings and young growth, scar the trunks of larger trees and damage their roots. This fire burns the humus that nourishes the forest.

Crown Fires: These spread rapidly and burn only the tops (crowns) of trees and shrubs. These fires are usually carried by high winds. This is the most dangerous of fires because it can travel at high speeds when blown by the wind and can rapidly engulf complete mountain-sides.

CONFLAGRATION

These are crown fires that are spreading quickly, are very large, and have a tendency to throw their embers (spotting) over long distances ahead of the fire (because of the wind) that start spot fires. These spot fires can occur two to three miles ahead of the fire.

Winds and updrafts (convection) generated by a large fire might...
- Make fire front suddenly advance at great speed causing firestorms.
- Sudden intense burning might make flames shoot into the sky. This produces a large amount of heat, strong updrafts, and long distance spotting.
- Strong winds might cause a rapid spread of crown fires and produce tornado-like fire whirls.

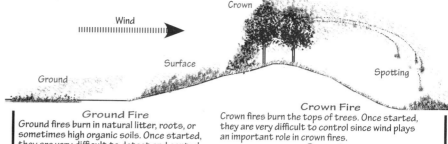

Ground ... Surface ... Spotting ... Wind ... Crown

Ground Fire
Ground fires burn in natural litter, roots, or sometimes high organic soils. Once started, they are very difficult to detect and control.

Surface Fire
Surface fires burn in grasses and low shrubs or the lower branches of trees. Surface fires may move rapidly if it is windy.

Crown Fire
Crown fires burn the tops of trees. Once started, they are very difficult to control since wind plays an important role in crown fires.

Spotting
Spotting can be produced by crown fires as well as wind and topographic conditions. Large burning embers are thrown ahead of the main fire. Once spotting begins, the fire will be very difficult to control.

WIND & WILDFIRES

Wind is an important factor in forest fires:
- Wind has both speed and direction and this will determine the speed at which the fire advances and the direction of travel.
- A large fire produces much heat. Hot air rises as it is lighter than the surrounding cooler air. This upward moving column, convection column or updraft, of air carries smoke and embers. As the column of hot air rises it pulls cool air into the fire which brings in additional oxygen to increase the size of the fire which can become a fire whirl which acts more like a small tornado. These winds can carry the flames and embers up to 300 feet (90 m).
- Wind increases the size of the fire as it increases the supply of oxygen to the fire.
- Wind will blow embers from the fire in advance of the fire and this will ignite spot fires. These spot fires will partially dry its area of contact which will burst into large flames when the fire front actually arrives.
- The extreme form of a convection column is a fire storm. A fire storm throws a shower of embers onto the surrounding area.
- Wind will blow hot air in front of it and this will dry out the timber and preheat the fuel in front of the fire.
- A strong wind will push the flames so fast that they will have less time to burn the fuel. This in effect might cause less damage to an area.
- Wind will also blow the smoke in front of it so that it is difficult to see the front of the fire. This is especially dangerous for fire fighters.

Fire Whirl
Spinning vortex column of ascending hot air and gases rising from a fire and carrying aloft smoke, debris, and flame. Fire whirls range in size from less than one foot to over 500 feet in diameter. Large fire whirls have the intensity of a small tornado.

Putting out spot fires.

FIRE FIGHTING

HEIGHT OF THE FLAMES

Under 4 feet (1.2 m) can be fought with traditional hand tools to remove fuel or oxygen supply. To remove the oxygen, to fight a small fire, use wet brush, burlap bags, sand, or blankets. Remove branches and other flammable objects from the direction of travel of the fire and it might burn out. This method can be supplemented by digging a fire trench. This is usually successful if there is no strong wind. Fight a small fire from the direction it is moving in.

Above 4 feet (1.2 m) it is more difficult because of the heat the fire radiates and it is hard to approach it without insulated clothing. Fight these fires from the sides of their direction of travel. Pay close attention to any possible changes in the direction or intensity of the wind. Use water, wet sand, drop water-soaked burlap bags along the edge of the fire. Try to guide the front of the fire towards a natural break such as a road, stream, or lake. Never set a back fire unless there are experienced fire fighters present, because the fire can easily get out of hand.

Above 12 feet (3.3 m) a fire is considered as being a crown fire and it can travel very fast, if driven by strong winds, across large areas. Never be in front of a crown fire but stay on its flank. Watch for shifts of wind which can change the direction of the fire.

Wait for water drops from a helicopter.

Spring after a fire.

Smoke from Fire

The deposits of fire smoke line the lungs in a similar fashion as cigarette smoke. The smoke is made up of different chemicals that come from the burning resins and oils of the trees and particles of charcoal and ash.

Fighting a prairie fire.

FIRE FIGHTING HEAT DISORDERS

Heat stress disorders include heat cramps, heat exhaustion & heat stroke.

Heat Cramps: are involuntary muscle contractions caused by failure to replace fluids or electrolytes, such as sodium and potassium. Cramps can be relieved with stretching and by replacing fluids and electrolytes.

Heat Exhaustion: is characterized by weakness, extreme fatigue, nausea, headaches, and a wet, clammy skin. Heat exhaustion is caused by inadequate fluid intake. It should be treated by resting in a cool environment and replacing fluids and electrolytes.

Heat Stroke: is a medical emergency caused by failure of the body's heat controls. Sweating stops and the body temperature rises precipitously. Heat stroke is characterized by hot dry skin, a body temperature above 105.8°F (41°C) mental confusion, loss of consciousness, convulsions, or even coma. Seek medical help at once and begin rapid cooling with ice or cold water, fanning the victim to promote evaporation. Treat for shock if necessary. For rapid cooling, partially submerge the victim's body in cool water.

PROFESSIONAL FIRE SHELTER

Training is required as to how, when, and where to deploy the shelter.
The fire shelter saves lives by:

Reflecting Radiant Heat: The foil reflects 95% of the flame front's radiant heat.

Trapping Air: There's a supply of more breatheable air inside the shelter. The shelter also protects the lungs and airways from flames and hot gases (Two leading killers in an entrapment).

NOT Fail-safe: Direct flame contact can destroy the shelter's protective properties. Avoid areas where flame contact is likely.

LEAVE IF POSSIBLE: If entrapment seems likely, attempt proven escape procedures first.

If Entrapped: Take your shelter out of the case, pull the red tab, and remove the plastic bag. If time is critical, leave your gear and run with the shelter in your hands. If escape plans fail or become impossible to execute, then use your shelter.

Fire Coming! You will hear its deafening roar, smell the smoke, hear the wind howling, feel the earth shake as you are deploying your shelter.

WATER: Water in your body is vital in an entrapment, so always keep well hydrated when fighting fire. Being adequately hydrated promotes sweating - which is the body's primary means of cooling. If entrapped, continue to sip water to replace lost fluids. If your body stops sweating, a feeling of panic will follow, so stay well hydrated. Always take canteens into the shelter if time permits, but leave your pack outside and well away from the shelter.

DO NOT WET YOURSELF DOWN: If you anticipate entrapment or escape, never wet yourself down. In a fire shelter, wet clothing is doubly hazardous. Wet clothing conducts heat to the skin five times faster than dry clothing, making burns likely, and it increases humidity. At equivalent temperatures, breathing moist hot air will damage airways and lungs sooner than breathing dry hot air.

Helicopter dropping water and retardent.

FUNCTION OF A FIRE SHELTER

- Because the fire shelter protects primarily by reflecting radiant heat, deploy the shelter as far as possible from fuel concentrations.
- The shelter is aluminum foil bonded to fiberglass cloth with a nontoxic high-temperature adhesive. These are the best lightweight materials available for maintaining structural integrity in extreme heat and high wind.
- The pup tent shape allows you to lie flat against the ground. This exposes less of your body to radiant heat and more to ground cooling. With your face pressed to the ground, you're in the best position to breathe cooler, cleaner air. The shelter's low profile exposes it to less turbulence and flame contact, while providing better cooling. Death is almost certain if you get caught off the ground in a flame front.
- It is absolutely necessary for the fire shelter to be held down on the ground before the flame front arrives. The shelter is quickly damaged if flames or radiant heat contact the inner surface.
- When the shelter is deployed correctly, the flame front rides a cushion of air over the top of the shelter and normally does little damage.
- The foil reflects 95% of the flame front's radiant heat. The remaining 5% is absorbed. This gradually makes it hotter inside the shelter. With prolonged exposure, temperatures can reach over 150°F. You can survive such temperatures (dry saunas often reach 190°F).
- Breathe through your mouth, stay calm, and stay in your shelter. Stay completely under the shelter even if you get burned or the shelter starts to fail.
- The foil/cloth laminate may emit some smoke during prolonged exposure to heat, but it will be minimal, and it is nontoxic. Don't panic. The shelter will still protect you.
- The shelter hold-down straps and perimeter skirt make it unlikely that the shelter can be blown away if buffeted by high winds. The skirt also helps keep out smoke and heat.

Temperature in a Fire Shelter

Peak temperatures can range from 150° to 200°F. Studies indicate that by taking short, shallow breaths through the mouth, air as hot as 400°F can be inhaled at very low humidity for a brief time - so it's important to keep humidity low.
- Never get your clothing wet or wear a wet bandanna or moisten your face. Instead, you should drink water so you can continue to sweat, which aids body cooling.
- High temperatures can induce panic. Panic can cause people to leave their shelters and make a run for it - a far more hazardous gamble than staying put.

DEPLOYING A FIRE SHELTER

- While preparing a site, keep an arm or leg through a shelter strap, or you may lose your shelter in the high winds generated by the flame front.
- Take your canteens into the shelter with you. To prevent dehydration, continue sipping water when you're in the shelter.
- Place your shelter so your feet are toward the oncoming flames. The end facing the advancing fire will become the hottest part of the shelter and is easier to hold down with your feet than with your elbows and hands.
- The optimal survival zone is within a foot of the ground with or without a fire shelter.
- Once you've prepared your spot, get into your shelter (wearing gloves, hardhat, and shroud) and stay there.
- Keep firmly in mind that you must protect your airways and lungs from the fire's hot gases. *Turbulence can lift a shelter edge, letting in hot gases. Flame fronts can generate winds of 50 mph or more, so you must hold the shelter down firmly. Gloves are critical: without them you may burn your hands and be unable to hold down the shelter.*
- Keep the shelter volume as large as possible so the shelter surface does not contact your body. Even small air gaps offer excellent insulation.
- Keep your nose pressed to the ground as much as possible. There's usually about a 6 inch layer of cooler cleaner air right at ground level. To help reduce the heat and smoke you inhale, breathe through a dry bandanna.
- During entrapment, talk to other trapped firefighters by radio, or shout back and forth. If someone yells at you, try to let them know you're okay. If someone doesn't respond to your shouts, do not leave your shelter. Fire entrapment can induce panic, and some people may not answer until after the danger has passed. At a fire's peak, the noise can be deafening, and you may be unable to hear anyone. Keep calm. As soon as the noise subsides, resume talking to each other.
- During very turbulent conditions, it will take all your effort to hold down the shelter.
- The fire shelter has pinholes and may have cracks along its folds. Entrapped firefighters say that firelight entering these openings looks like hot coals or embers on clothing. These openings do not reduce your protection. No matter how big a hole or tear your shelter may have, you are still better off inside the shelter.

SUPERHEATED GASES

Be alert for signs of superheated gases; there may be little smoke or color in hot gases. Your only warning may be a rise in air temperature or movement, or embers blowing past. If it gets hot enough to cause burns, it is time to get under your fire shelter. Be especially careful to hold down the shelter edges to keep the cooler air under the shelter. When considering escape, remember that you can hold your breath for only about 15 seconds while running through flames or superheated air. Before passing through superheated gases, try to close the front of your shroud. You can take your shelter out of the plastic bag and use it for a heat shield to pass quickly through a hot area. If you use the shelter in this way, don't drop it or allow it to snag on brush. And remember, your lungs are still vulnerable.

Fire shelter works best...

- In an area with no fuels, or in light fuels such as grass, where the flame front passes quickly. Scrape away ground fuels. A clean area minimizes flame contact with the shelter - and the chance of fuels smoldering nearby or underneath the shelter. Never deploy immediately above a large concentration of fuel.
- Pick natural firebreaks - meadows, dry creek beds, rockslides, the lee side of ridgetops and knobs, and depressions in the ground. Low spots will have less heat and smoke. Wide firelines like bulldozer lines, drainage ditches on the uphill side of roads, and burned-over areas normally make good deployment sites.
- When moving up steep hills or ridges, look for benches to deploy on. On ridgelines, look for the widest areas.
- Avoid heavy brush, trees with low branches, and logs and snags.
- Avoid gasoline cans, supply boxes, packs, and other firefighting gear.
- Keep away from narrow draws, chutes, and chimneys. They tend to funnel smoke, flames, and hot gases. Avoid saddles on ridgetops; they also funnel smoke and heat.

How long do you stay in shelter?

There is no fixed time to stay under your shelter. Don't move until the flame front has passed. A drop in noise, wind, and heat - and a change in color - are usually tip-offs that it's safe to leave the shelter. But play it safe - stay put until you notice temperatures have cooled significantly or until a supervisor tells you it's safe to come out. Leaving a shelter too soon can expose your lungs to superheated air or dense smoke. Firefighters have died when they came out too soon, so extra caution is essential.

FIRE FIGHTING PROTECTION

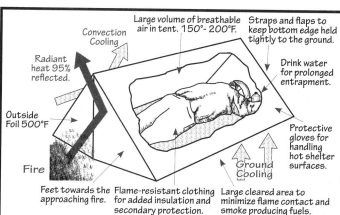

Convection Cooling

Large volume of breathable air in tent. 150°- 200°F.

Radiant heat 95% reflected.

Straps and flaps to keep bottom edge held tightly to the ground.

Drink water for prolonged entrapment.

Outside Foil 500°F

Protective gloves for handling hot shelter surfaces.

Fire

Ground Cooling

Feet towards the approaching fire.

Flame-resistant clothing for added insulation and secondary protection.

Large cleared area to minimize flame contact and smoke producing fuels.

Fire Shelter

Looks very much like an aluminum foil pup tent, the fire shelter is carried by each firefighter. If trapped by a fire, firefighters find an area clear of burnable vegetation, or clear an area themselves. Then they place their hands and feet in straps at each corner of the shelter and lie on the ground on their stomachs with their feet towards the advancing fire. The tent traps air over them which is maintained at a cooler temperature than the surrounding fire by the reflective material contained in the shelter's fabric. This trapped cool air protects the firefighters' lungs from the hot air of the fire and the shelter shields them from the flames themselves. Firefighters remain in the shelters until they are completely confident that they are no longer in danger from the fire.

WILDFIRE GLOSSARY

Aspect: The direction towards which a slope faces.

Backfire: A fire suppression technique of creating a fire break by burning all fuel between the existing fire line and the oncoming fire. It can also be used to change the direction and force of the fire convection column.

Blowup: Sudden increase in intensity or rate of spread of fire. Often accompanied by violent convection that resembles or may have characteristics of a fire storm. This can occur when atmospheric temperature and wind increases and humidity decreases.

Break Over/Slop Over: A fire edge that crosses a line intended to control the fire.

Burning Conditions: The environmental factors that affect fire.

Burn Out: This is a process of igniting a fire between the control line and the wildland fire. Its purpose is to burn any fuel remaining in a controlled way so that the wildland fire will have nothing further to consume and will die out.

Canopy: The foliage and branches making up the "roof" of the forest.

Cat Line: A fire line constructed by a bulldozer or caterpillar.

Crown Fire: A fire that runs from top to top of trees or shrubs. This kind of fire can be extremely difficult to stop.

Crown Out: Where a fire has a "ladder" of fuels to climb (grass to shrubs to small trees to large trees), it may rise from ground level to canopy level and begin advancing from tree top to tree top.

Drift Smoke: Smoke that has drifted from its point of origin and has lost its original "billow" form. Drift smoke sometimes gives the false impression of a fire in the general area to which it has drifted.

Dry Lightning: Lightning storm with only trace precipitation.

Duff: The partly decomposed organic material of the forest floor beneath the litter of freshly fallen twigs, needles and leaves.

Extreme Fire Behavior: Winds, steep slopes, and highly combustible vegetation can combine to produce a fire with the potential to spread rapidly and unpredictably. These fires are potentially very dangerous.

Entrapment: A situation in which personnel are unexpectedly caught in fire behavior-related, life threatening positions where planned escape routes or safety zones are absent, inadequate, or compromised. An entrapment may or may not include deployment of a fire shelter for its intended purpose.

Fine Fuel Moisture: The moisture content of fast drying fuels such as grass, leaves, ferns, tree moss, draped pine needles and small twigs.

Fire Retardant: A substance that uses chemical or physical action to reduce flammability of fuels and slow the rate of their combustion.

Fire Break: A natural or constructed barrier used to stop or check fires.

Fire Line: Also often called a "control line," this includes line constructed by firefighters as well as natural barriers to fire such as rock outcroppings, roads, and streams or other water bodies. Crews construct fire lines by using shovels, pulaskis, rakes and chain saws to clear the line of vegetation so that the fire will have nothing to burn when it arrives at that point.

Flame Height: The average maximum vertical extension of flames at the leading edge of the fire front. Occasional

flashes that rise above the flames are not considered. This distance is less than the flame length if flames are tilted due to wind or slope.

Flaming Front: That zone of a flaming fire where the combustion is primarily flaming. Behind this flaming zone, combustion is primarily glowing or burning out of larger fuels (greater than about 3 inches in diameter).

Flanking: Attacking a fire by working along its edges. Flanking fire lines move towards the fire front where they are linked to stop the fire.

Flash/Fine Fuels: Grass, leaves, pine needles, and other fuels which ignite easily and burn rapidly when dry.

Foam: A chemical fire-extinguishing mixture. It adheres to fuels, cooling and moistening them. It also excludes oxygen from them, eliminating one of the items fire needs to burn.

Ground Fire: A fire that consumes the organic material on or beneath the surface litter of the forest floor.

Head of Fire: The most rapidly spreading portion of a fire's perimeter.

Heavy Fuels: Fuels of large diameter such as snags, logs, and large limbwood, which ignite and are consumed more slowly than flash fuels. Also called coarse fuels.

Holdover Fire: A fire that remains dormant for a day or two before flaring up. Dry lightning storms often cause holdover fires.

Indirect Attack: A method of suppressing fires by building lines along natural firebreaks and using topography while staying some distance from the head of the fire.

Jump Spot: A landing spot selected for smokejumpers.

Ladder Fuels: Fuels which provide vertical continuity between strata, thereby allowing fire to carry from surface fuels into the crowns of trees or shrubs with relative ease. They help initiate and assure the continuation of crowning.

Prescribed Burning: Prescribed fires allow us to incorporate fire in the ecosystem under controlled circumstances. Fire managers ignite them when weather conditions enhance our ability to confine them to predetermined areas and after crews have developed fire breaks or lines. These fires typically burn in a mosaic pattern, leaving unburned areas within their boundaries. Prescribed fires are used to improve forage and habitat for wildlife and livestock, to improve watershed, or to reduce hazardous build up of fire fuels.

Reburn: A fire may sometimes pass through an area without burning all materials there. These remaining materials, dried by the first fire pass, can reignite and the area may "reburn."

Retardant: A substance dropped on fires from air tankers to reduce flammability of fuels.

Slash: Debris left after logging, pruning, thinning or brush cutting. It includes logs, limbs and understory trees or brush.

Slurry: Another name for retardant.

Smokejumper: Specially trained firefighter who parachutes to fire sites.

Snag: A standing dead tree or part of a dead tree from which at least the leaves and smaller branches have fallen.

Spot Fire: Fire ignited outside the perimeter of the main fire by a firebrand.

Trenching: Digging trenches on a side slope to catch any burning or other materials which might roll across control lines. (Based on data by the NIFC)

Firefighting helicopter hovering over a lake. Heavy air tankers work on hot spots.

Smokejumper

Airplane dropping fire retardant.

Fighting smoldering forest fire on the trunk of a tree.

Making a backfire: A backfire is a fire suppression technique of creating a fire break by burning all fuel between the existing fire line and the oncoming fire. It can also be used to change the direction and force of the fire convection column.

Fire crew setting fire back bur

ROPE TERMINOLOGY

Bight: Rope doubled over and usually is between the end and the standing part.

Bitter End: is the very end of the rope.

Clockwise: Placing the rope from left to right around a fixed object (counter clockwise is the opposite).

Cow's Tail: Rope end that is frayed or unraveling.

End: Either extremity of the rope. Usually one end is worked with to tie a knot.

Eye: Loop usually at the end of a rope.

Grommet: Ring made of metal, stitched, or rope. Used to attach a tarpaulin, etc.

Hawser: Thick rope over 6" in circumference. Rope can be specified in diameter or circumference - sailors use circumference.

Hitch: Method to attach ropes together or to attach a rope to a fixed object. (e.g.. horse hitch)

Knot: Tying the rope onto itself by using a loop. Knot in a rope will reduce its carrying strength.

Lash: Tie down or attach objects together so that they will not move.

Loop: Rope that is curved and usually an end will be passed through.

Messenger: Light rope that is used to pull a heavier rope. This is usually used to pull a heavier rope onto a ship.

Overhand Loop: End brought over the standing part.

Painter: Short rope used to tie a small boat to a mooring post.

Rope: Cord over one inch in circumference.

Round Turn: Rope looped twice around a fixed object.

Seize: Use cord to tie two rope ends together.

Snugged: To tighten.

Splice: Join two rope ends together by interweaving the unraveled end strands. This is different than "Seizing."

Standing Part: Part of the rope that is not actually being used in tying the knot.

Toggle: Piece of smooth hard wood that is pushed into a knot to either tighten the knot or used to undo a knot.

Turn: Rope looped once around a fixed object.

Underhand Loop: End brought under the standing part.

Whip: Winding of cord around the end of a rope to stop the rope from fraying.

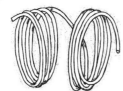

Preparing rope for throwing. See adjacent article on 'Throwing Rope'

A stone or stick can be attached if throwing a short heavy rope into the wind or over a branch. A light guide rope, which is thrown, can be attached to a heavier rope which is then pulled over by the guide rope.

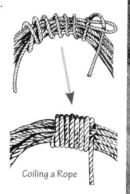

Coiling a Rope

JUNGLE ROPES
Page 67

THROWING ROPE

Carefully coil the rope before throwing. In throwing the full rope, grasp the coil in the right hand and take the end of the rope nearest the fingertips and anchor it. Take five or six loops from the anchored end of the coil and hold it in the left hand while holding the remaining coil, which will be thrown first, in the right hand. A few preliminary swings will ensure a smooth throw with the arm nearly extended. The coil should be thrown out and up. A slight twist of the wrist so that the palm of the hand comes up as the rope is thrown will cause the coil to turn, the loops to spread, and the running end to fall free and away from the thrower. A smooth follow-through is essential. As soon as the coil is thrown and spreading, the loops held in the left hand should be tossed out. Where possible, the rope should be thrown with the wind so that the running end is to the leeward side. As soon as the rope starts to leave the hand, the thrower shouts the warning "ROPE" to alert anyone below his position.

41 ROPE & KNOTS

Qualities of a Good Knot
Should be easy to tie.
Should not jam or be hard to untie.
Should not slip when under tension.

ROPE SAFETY

Knots weaken rope and the reef knot (or square knot) is the most destructive. Avoid sharp bends in a rope and if using a pulley, use the largest pulley possible. If rope is under tension and has a risk of breaking, hang a blanket, heavy coat, or rug, on the rope to absorb the tensile energy if the rope snaps. After and before usage, inspect your rope for damage so that you will avoid any surprises. Have the right rope for the job. The safe static load of a rope is usually 10 to 20% of the breaking strength.

Storage of Rope
Store rope in a dry, cool, clean, well ventilated area and away from sunlight and extreme heat. Examine the rope for frays and powdery internal fibers. Do not store it wet or with acids or alkaline.

Plain Laid Rope

Strands: Twisted Yarns

Yarns: Twisted Fibers

Fibers

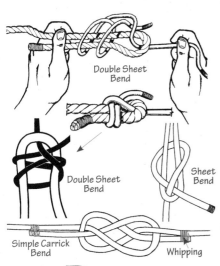

Double Sheet Bend

Double Sheet Bend

Sheet Bend

Simple Carrick Bend

Whipping

BENDS
Used to join ropes.

Sheet Bend (Weaver's Knot)
Join two ropes of unequal size. Can also be used for ropes of equal size. This is probably the best knot to use to join two ropes. It is made by forming a bight in one of the ropes, bringing up the other rope end through the bight, twisting it over and under the bight, and then bringing it under itself.

Double Sheet Bend
The end of the bending line is passed twice around the standing line and through its own part, giving added security.

Slippery Sheet Bend
Tie two ropes together that might have to be detached rapidly. Use when tying up the flaps on a tent when expecting a storm.

Heaving Line Bend
To joint two ropes of different sizes. This knot will hold without seizing.

Carrick Bend
This knot is made by first crossing the end of one rope and then passing the end of the other down through the bight, under the standing part, over the end and down through the bight again. The ends are seized to their own parts. The bend is used for joining two ropes. Is very bulky but one of the strongest bends especially if it is whipped.

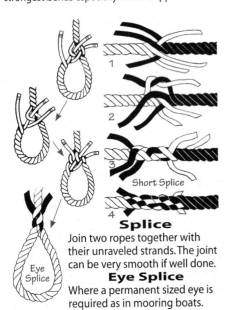

1
2
3
Short Splice
4

Splice
Join two ropes together with their unraveled strands. The joint can be very smooth if well done.

Eye Splice
Where a permanent sized eye is required as in mooring boats.

Eye Splice

Making Cordage from Thistle
Collect the stalks of thistle, preferably in the fall and winter when they are dry. If they are wet, dry them in the sun or over a fire. Crush the stalk with a round smooth rock to expose the pith (sponge-like substance) at the center. Break the pith into small sections by bending the nettle stalk and peel out the pith with your fingers. You will now have a long strip of fibers that are rubbed between your hands or slowly pulled while rotating, over a round smooth piece of wood. The fiber strip will become soft and pliable.

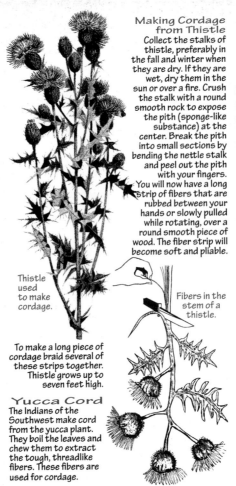

Thistle used to make cordage.

Fibers in the stem of a thistle.

To make a long piece of cordage braid several of these strips together. Thistle grows up to seven feet high.

Yucca Cord
The Indians of the Southwest make cord from the yucca plant. They boil the leaves and chew them to extract the tough, threadlike fibers. These fibers are used for cordage.

STOPPER KNOTS
Used to make a knot at the end of a rope.

Overhand Knot (Thumb Knot)
Stopper knot at the end of a rope, to stop a rope from passing through a hole or end knot to stop a cord from fraying.

Figure of Eight Knot
This knot resembles the figure eight, and is used to prevent the end of the rope from unreeving when rove through blocks. The end of the rope is passed around the bight over its own part and through the loop. Stopper knot is larger than the Overhand Knot.

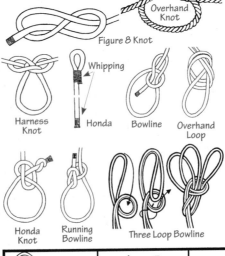

Overhand Knot

Figure 8 Knot

Whipping

Harness Knot

Honda

Bowline

Overhand Loop

Honda Knot

Running Bowline

Three Loop Bowline

ROPE MAKING MATERIAL
NYLON
Nylon is the material of choice as it has the maximum breaking strength to the least weight. It resists most chemicals, rot, mildew, abrasion, and has minimum loss of strength upon exposure to sunlight. Nylon has elasticity, depending upon construction, and will stretch approximately 10% at normal working loads and up to 40% to 70% at breaking loads. Nylon is used as a dynamic rope in mountain climbing as it will absorb the energy of a fall. It is easier to tie a knot in nylon than stiff polypropylene. Three strand nylon has a more bumpy surface which makes knots more stable.

POLYESTER
Has a low elasticity and is used as a static rope in mountain climbing. Used both for repelling and rescue work. Polyester has a slightly lower breaking point than nylon. When new, polyester is the least inclined to slip when making a knot.

POLYPROPYLENE
Floats on water and does not absorb water so it will not freeze in the winter. Only has 2/3 the strength of an equivalent nylon rope. It is sensitive to ultraviolet rays which cause it to degenerate and it can lose 50% of its strength at 150°F (65°C).

HEMP
Hemp was the traditional rope of choice. It is a natural fiber but on a per weight per strength basis the synthetic ropes are a better buy. It should be kept humid as it loses its strength when dry. The best current use for hemp ropes is as a fire rope because it is easier to grasp due to its rough texture.

LOOP KNOTS
Used to fasten a rope to something.

Bowline Knot 'King of Knots'
One of the most common and useful knots forms an eye which may be of any length and cannot slip. It is used for lowering individuals, for forming an eye in the end of a line to be thrown over a bollard, and for a great variety of similar purposes. A bowline is made by forming a bight in the line with the end part on top; bringing the end part up through the bight; then passing it under the standing part above the bight, and back through the bight. Very stable from untieing and can be used for different sized ropes. The bowline is used to form a loop which will not slip.

Overhand Loop
To make a loop in the middle of a rope. Both ends of the rope are still unused.

Honda Knot
One of the oldest knots that was used on bowstrings by primitive people. Some variants can be made by whipping an end with cord.

Harness Knot (Fisherman's Loop)
To put a loop in the middle of a rope. This is handy when several people are pulling on a rope.

Running Bowline
A Bowline Knot made into a noose. This is formed by making a bowline and pulling the standing part through the eye.

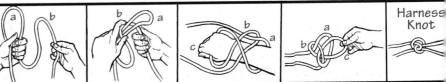

a b
b a
b a c
a b c
Harness Knot

SPECIAL KNOTS

Taut Line Hitch
For tent line hitches as it will only slide one way. It is better than the clove hitch on slippery poles.

Fisherman's Figure of Eight Bend
This is formed by passing the end twice around the ring and under the turns, and seizing the end back. This bend is used for securing a rope to a buoy or a hawser to the ring of an anchor. To attach fish hooks. Hooks will hang in the same direction as the line. As Figure 8 Knot.

Fisherman's Knot (Smooth Knot)
To attach nylon leaders.

Square Lashing
To attach two poles at right angles to each other. This form of attaching poles can be very rigid if using rawhide or rope that shrinks when it dries.

Prusik Knot
Used by climbers to climb a vertical rope.

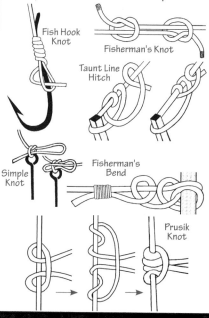

Fish Hook Knot

Fisherman's Knot

Taunt Line Hitch

Simple Knot

Fisherman's Bend

Prusik Knot

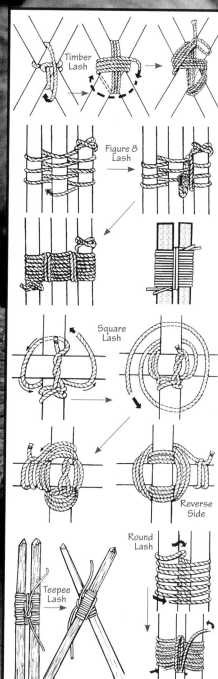

Timber Lash

Figure 8 Lash

Square Lash

Reverse Side

Teepee Lash

Round Lash

Different Lashings

CARE OF ROPES

- Inspect the ropes thoroughly before, during, and after use for cuts, excessive fraying, abrasions, mildew, soft and worn spots. If any of these defects are found, the rope is unserviceable. An unserviceable rope is destroyed by cutting it into usable parts. If no sections are usable, the rope is cut into smaller parts and discarded.
- Climbing rope should never be spliced, since it will be hard to manage at the splice.
- The rope must not come in contact with sharp edges. If this is likely, the areas must be padded or taped before rappelling.
- Keep the rope dry as much as possible. Dry it as soon as possible. Hang the rope to drip dry on a rounded peg, at room temperature (do not apply heat).
- Do not step on rope or unnecessarily drag it on the ground Small particles of dirt will be ground into the strands and will slowly cut them. This greatly reduces the tensile strength of the rope.
- Coil rope when not in use.
- New rope is stiff and should be worked.
- Avoid running rope over sharp or rough edges (pad if necessary) especially if under tension.
- Keep the rope away from oil, acids, and other corrosive substances.
- Avoid rubbing ropes together under tension (nylon to nylon friction will harm the rope).
- Do not leave rope knotted or tightly stretched longer than necessary.
- Clean in cool water, loosely coil and hang to dry (out of direct sunlight, since ultraviolet light rays will harm synthetic fibers). Store in a cool, dry, shaded area on a round wooden pegs.

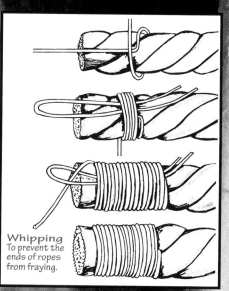

Whipping
To prevent the ends of ropes from fraying.

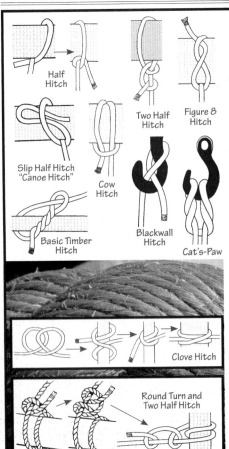

Half Hitch

Two Half Hitch

Figure 8 Hitch

Slip Half Hitch "Canoe Hitch"

Cow Hitch

Blackwall Hitch

Basic Timber Hitch

Cat's-Paw

HITCH

Attach a rope to something.

Half Hitch

Easy to tie but not secure as it might slip without the end being seized.

Two Half Hitch

More secure than the half hitch but seize the end. This knot is used to moor boats to posts or rings. Formed by leading the end over an under and up through the standing part and repeating process: this is another method of bending a rope's end to a bollard or ring.

Round Turn and Two Half Hitches

To moor a boat. The advantage over the two half hitch is that the additional turn around the pole will lessen the wear on the rope. You should seize the end. This is formed by encircling a bollard, spar, or other rope twice; passing the running end over and under the standing end and through the space between the bollard and crossover. Repeat crossover with running end and pass through space between both crossovers to make second hitch.

Canoe Hitch (Slipped Half Hitch)

Easy knot to tie and untie especially if fingers are cold or oily.

Figure-8 Hitch

If the post to which the rope is hitched is of a small diameter this hitch is better than the Half Hitch.

Clove Hitch

Holds well, nearly non-slipping. Best used on a vertical pole. Leave the end part long if you fear slippage. This is a great knot for tying down a tent or attaching a hammock. It can be used to secure the middle of a rope without using the ends. The end is passed around the spar, crossing the standing part, then around the spar again, bringing the end through between the end part, and standing part under its own part.

Cow Hitch (Lanyard Hitch)

Attach an animal to a post or horizontal bar. To attach an object which has a looped rope on it. Hitch a horse onto a post where the rope can be passed over the post end. To attach baggage hang tags.

Timber Hitch

Easily tied and will not undo if the rope is not under tension. Useful when towing something. This hitch is formed by passing the end around the item being towed and its own standing part; then passing several turns around its own part.

Cat's-Paw

A convenient, secure, double loop is, formed by twisting two bights of a rope and passing the hook of a tackle through them.

Blackwall Hitch

A hitch, either single or double, around the back of a hook, with the bitter end on one side of the hook and the standing part on top of the other side of the hook.

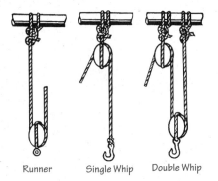

Clove Hitch

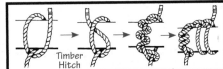

Timber Hitch

Round Turn and Two Half Hitch

PULLEYS & TACKLE

Runner

Single Whip

Double Whip

Block

Pulling

Traveling Block

Single Luff Tackle

3 Supporting Lines

In this case there are 3 supporting lines. This means that the pulling action of one pound can lift three pounds. This is called the theoretical mechanic advantage of 3:1. This is theoretical as there will be friction in the pulleys and rope. The fact that the rope is not pulled vertically means that less downward pull is actually applied.

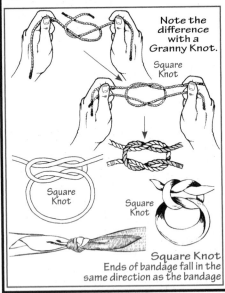

Note the difference with a Granny Knot.

Square Knot

Square Knot

Square Knot

Square Knot
Ends of bandage fall in the same direction as the bandage

BINDING KNOTS

Knots used to tie packages or bandages.

Square Knot (Reef Knot)

Very reliable and serves many purposes. It ties and unties very easily. It is used to tie bandages. It can be used to join two ropes of the same size. This knot will not slip or jam. When tying be careful that you do not tie a granny knot. A granny knot slips and jams.

Granny Knot

Made similarly to a square knot, the granny knot should be carefully distinguished from the square knot. It should not be used because it will slip and fail to hold. This knot is unstable under tension as it might slip. It is a miss-tied square knot. (Note: A granny knot will not lie flat when it is pulled tight).

Bow Knot (Shoelace Knot)

Name is obvious. It is useful as it is easy to tie. The rope has to remain under tension to keep this knot stable.

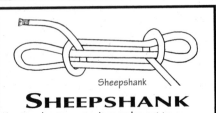

Sheepshank

SHEEPSHANK

Knot to shorten rope. It can also act to strengthen rope at a specific location. The bight of the rope is laid in three parts, and each part half hitched around the bight of the other two parts.

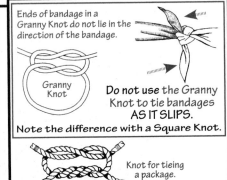

Ends of bandage in a Granny Knot do not lie in the direction of the bandage.

Granny Knot

Do not use the Granny Knot to tie bandages AS IT SLIPS.

Note the difference with a Square Knot.

Knot for tieing a package.

WEATHER FORECASTING & SURVIVAL

Weather forecasting enables survivors to make plans based on probable changes in the weather. Forecasts help survivors decide what clothes to wear and type of shelter to build. While accurate weather prediction or forecasting normally requires special instruments, an awareness of changing weather patterns and attention to existing conditions can help a survivor prepare for and, when appropriate, use changing weather conditions to enhance their survivability. The following are some elementary weather indicators that could help predict the weather and help save lives.

This chapter explains weather with the great outdoors in mind. In the wilderness you can see the horizon all around you, you see the movement of the different cloud formations, and you will gradually recognize cloud patterns, wind, animal movements, trees, insects which precede certain weather conditions. In the city you just see wisps of clouds between buildings and even then they might be hidden by the smog.

The origins of our weather are highlighted with illustrations and numerous photographs. These will help you "see" the weather around you.

PIONEER WEATHER INDICATORS

GENERAL WEATHER PREDICTORS

• A red sun has water in his eye. (It will rain)
• When walls are unusually damp rain is expected.
• Doors and windows are hard to shut in damp weather.
• Sailors note the tightening of the cordage on ships as a sign of coming rain.
• Tobacco becomes moist preceding rain.
• When rheumatic people complain of more than ordinary pains it will probably rain.
• When the locks turn damp in the scalp house (human scalps) it will rain. American Indians.
• If corns, wounds, and sores itch or ache more than usual rain is likely to fall shortly.
• When matting on the floor is shrinking, dry weather may be expected. When matting expands, expect wet weather.
• Ropes shorten with an increase of humidity.
• Ropes being difficult to untwist indicate rain.
• Quarries of stone and slate indicate rain by a moist discharge from the stones
• Salt increases in weight before rain.
• If metal plates and dishes sweat it is a sign of bad weather.
• When the perfume of flowers is unusually perceptible rain may be expected.
• In dry weather, when creeks and springs that have gone dry become moist, or, as we may say, begin to sweat, it indicates approaching rain. Many springs that have gone dry will give a good flow of water just before rain. Kansas.
• Drains, ditches, and dunghills are more offensive (smell) before rain.
• Guitar strings shorten before rain.
• Human hair (red) curls and kinks at the approach of a storm, and straightens after the storm.
• Lamp wicks crackle, candles burn dim, soot falls down, smoke descends, walls and pavements are damp, and disagreeable odors arise from ditches and gutters before rain.
• Soap covered with moisture indicates bad weather.
• Smoke falls to the ground preceding rain.
• People work better, eat more, and sleep sounder when the barometer is high.
• Campfire smoke stays near the ground before a storm, and rises upon improving weather.
• People say "when sounds are clear, rain is near," because sound travels farther before storms.
• As humidity increases, the rocks in high mountain areas will "sweat" and provide an indication of forthcoming rain.
• Smoke, rising from a fire then sinking low to the ground, can indicate that a storm front is approaching.

ANIMAL & PLANT WEATHER PREDICTORS

The changes in temperature before, during, and after storms also have an effect on animal and plant life, and many proverbs are based upon observations of these effects. As, however, changes, in temperature are direct results of wind directions, sayings regarding temperature are almost invariably associated with those relating to the wind.

INSECTS WEATHER PREDICTORS

• Bees will not swarm before a nearby storm.
• When bees remain in their hives or fly but a short distance, expect rain.
• Flies sting and are more troublesome than usual when the humidity increases before rain.
• Spiders spin long webs on hot dry days but when wet weather is coming, the webs will be short or none at all.

FISH WEATHER PREDICTORS

• Fish bite better before a rainfall.
• Fish swim near the surface when rain is expected.
• At high temperatures, fish will stay in cooler, deeper water and will not bite.

PLANTS WEATHER PREDICTORS

• Sunflower raising its head indicates rain.
• When the mountain moss is soft and limpid expect rain. When mountain moss is dry and brittle expect clear weather.
• Sensitive plants contract their leaves and blossoms when the humidity increases.
• A piece of seaweed hung up will become damp before it rains.
• Many acorns, bad weather.
• Thick corn husk, bad weather.
• Thick onion skins, light winter.
• Stormy weather will probably follow within hours when flowers seem to be much more fragrant.
• Alders & cottonwood show the bottoms of their leaves before bad weather.
• The flowers of many plants, like the dandelion, will close as humidity increases and rain is on the horizon.

Kelp: This seaweed is very sensitive to humidity. When the weather is fine, it will be all shriveled up; but if the humidity increases, and rain is coming, it will swell and feel damp. This seaweed has been used for centuries along the seashore to be a forecaster of the weather. Weather plays an important role in fishing villages because when the fishermen go to sea they can easily risk their lives if a storm blows up.

ANIMAL WEATHER PREDICTORS

• Cats have the reputation of being weather wise, an old notion which has given rise to a most extensive folklore. It is almost universally believed that good weather may be expected when the cat washes herself, but bad when she licks her coat against the grain, or washes her face over her ears, or sits with her tail to the fire.
• Dogs making holes in the ground, eating grass in the morning, or refusing meat are said to indicate coming rain.
• All shepherds agree in saying that before a storm comes sheep become frisky, leap, and butt or "box" each other.
• When horses and cattle stretch out their necks and sniff the air it will rain.
• Horses, as well as other domestic animals, foretell the coming of rain by starting more than ordinary and appearing in other respects restless and uneasy.
• Hogs crying and running up and down with hay or litter in their mouths foreshadow a storm to be near at hand.
• When oxen or sheep collect together as if they were seeking shelter a storm may be expected. Apache Indians.
• Snakes expose themselves on the approach of rain.
• Horses sweating in the stable is a sign of rain.
• Squirrels have heavy coat, bad winter.
• Field mice enter houses early, then there will be a bad winter.
• Rabbits will be out at unusual times before a storm.
• Toads and frogs moving towards water mean rain.

AIR PRESSURE WEATHER PREDICTORS

"The farther the sight, the nearer the rain," is a seaman's chant. When bad weather is near, the air pressure goes down and the atmosphere becomes clearer. High atmospheric pressure with stable and dusty air means fair weather.

SOME WEATHER PHOBIAS

Astraphobia: Fear of being struck by lightning.
Brontophobia: Fear of thunder and thunderstorms.
Frigophobia: The fear of the cold and cold things.
Heliophobia: The fear of the sun.
Lilapsophobia: The fear of tornadoes and hurricanes.
Lygophobia: The fear of darkness.
Nebulaphobia: The fear of fog.
Pluviophobia: The fear of rain or of being rained on.
Psychorophobia: The fear of the cold.

Pioneer Weather Predictor
• Cows, when they assemble at one end of a field with their tails to windward, often indicate rain or wind.
• When cattle go out to pasture and lie down early in the day it indicates early rain.

BIRD WEATHER PREDICTORS

- Birds can help predict the weather. Water birds fly low across the water when a storm is approaching. Birds will huddle close together before a storm.
- Migratory birds fly south from cold and north from warm weather. When a severe cyclone is near, they become puzzled and fly in circles and dart in the air. (North Carolina.)
- When birds cease to sing, rain and thunder will probably occur.
- Birds and fowls oiling feathers indicate rain.
- If fowls roll in the dust and sand, rain is at hand.
- If cocks crow late and early, clapping their wings occasionally, rain is expected. If the cock goes crowing to bed, He'll certainly rise with a watery head.
- When chimney swallows circle and call, they speak of rain. Zuni Indians
- When cranes make a great noise or scream, expect rain.
- One crow flying alone is a sign of foul weather, but if crows fly in pairs expect fine weather.
- If the wild geese gang out to sea, Good weather there will surely be.
- If crows make much noise and fly round and round, expect rain.
- Wild geese flying past large bodies of water indicate change of weather. Going south, cold; going north, warm.
- Gulls will soar aloft, and, circling around, utter shrill cries before a storm.
- When grouse drum at night, Indians predict a deep fall of snow.
- When herons fly up and down as in doubt where to rest, expect rain.
- When swallows in evenings fly high and chirp, fair weather follows; when low, rain follows.
- Cranes soaring aloft and quietly in the air foreshows fair weather, but if they make much noise, as if consulting which way to go, it foreshadows a storm that's near at hand.
- Martins fly low before and during rainy weather.
- Geese fly low before the arrival of bad weather.
- Birds and bats fly at a lower level as the insects they eat stay closer to the ground before bad weather.
- Woodpeckers will call before rain falls.
- Screeching owls announce rain.

The shiny underside of the leaves can be seen on some trees before a storm.

Jet Stream
Canada
Weather movement slowed by Rocky Mountains.
United States
Mexico

Developed Cyclone Possible hurricane over Atlantic Ocean

Weather movement slowed by Andes Mountains.

South America

Cloud cover of the Earth, from 23.000 miles, showing the Americas. A cyclone is present in the mid Atlantic Ocean. The Jet Stream can be seen in central to eastern Canada.

THE ATMOSPHERE

The atmosphere is like an ocean of air that surrounds the surface of the Earth. It is a mixture of water and gases. The atmosphere extends from the surface of the Earth to about 1,200 miles in space gradually thinning as it approaches its upper limit. Gravity holds the atmosphere in place. The atmosphere exhibits few physical characteristics; however, it shields the inhabitants of the Earth from ultraviolet radiation and other hazards in space. Without the atmosphere, the Earth would be as barren as the moon.

Near the Earth's surface, the air is relatively warm due to contact with the Earth. As altitude increases, the temperature decreases by about 3.5°F for every 1,000 feet until air temperature reaches about 67°F below zero at 7 miles above the Earth.

STRUCTURE OF THE ATMOSPHERE

The atmosphere consists of several concentric layers, each displaying its own unique characteristics. Each layer is known as a sphere. Thermal variances within the atmosphere help define these spheres, offering aviation personnel an insight into atmospheric conditions within each area. Between each of the spheres is an imaginary boundary, known as a pause. To understand where the weather patterns originate, a brief familiarization of the "layers" or structure of the atmosphere is needed. The atmosphere is divided into four layers. The lowest layer (first) is the "troposphere" where the temperature changes. Nearly all weather occurs in this lower layer that begins at the Earth's surface and extends upwards for 6 to 10 miles. The second layer is the "stratosphere" where the temperature remains constant.

COMPOSITION OF THE ATMOSPHERE

The atmosphere of the Earth is a mixture of gases. Although the atmosphere contains many gases, few are essential to human survival. Those gases required for human life are nitrogen, oxygen, and carbon dioxide.

Nitrogen

The atmosphere of the Earth consists mainly of nitrogen. Although a vital ingredient in the chain of life, nitrogen is not readily used by the human body. However, nitrogen saturates body fluids and tissues as a result of respiration. Air crews must be aware of possible evolved-gas disorders because of the decreased solubility of nitrogen at higher altitudes.

Oxygen

Oxygen is the second most plentiful gas in the atmosphere. The process of respiration unites oxygen and sugars to meet the energy requirements of the body. The lack of oxygen in the body at high altitudes will cause drastic physiological changes that can result in death.

Carbon Dioxide

Carbon dioxide is the product of cellular respiration in most life forms. Although not present in large amounts, the CO_2 in the atmosphere plays a vital role in maintaining the oxygen supply of the Earth. Through photosynthesis, plant life uses CO_2 to create energy and releases O_2 as a by-product. As a result of animal metabolism and photosynthesis, CO_2 and O_2 supplies in the atmosphere remain constant.

Other Gases

Other gases such as argon, xenon, and helium are present in trace amounts in the atmosphere. They are not as critical to human survival as are nitrogen, oxygen, and carbon dioxide.

Summer Temperature
To find the temperature in °F in the summer count the number of cricket chirps in 15 seconds and add 40. This will give you the °F. As the cricket is cold blooded it slows down when it is cold.

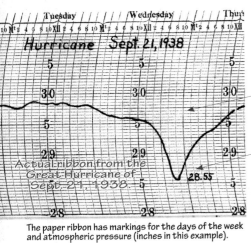

Actual ribbon from the Great Hurricane of Sept. 21, 1938.

28.55

The paper ribbon has markings for the days of the week and atmospheric pressure (inches in this example).

There is a clock movement in the cylinder that makes it rotate.

The paper ribbon is mounted on the cylinder and records the pressure for a week.

Low Pressure

Key to wind clock mechanism.

Plotter Pen

Ink Container

These levers magnify the change of size of the chambers and transmit this displacement (up or down) to the plotter (pen) which marks a line on the paper ribbon

Aneroid Barograph

The vacuum chambers (aneroid) are squeezed by the increase of atmospheric pressure (it is heavier). When the atmospheric pressure decreases the chambers expand.

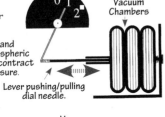

Barometer Vacuum Chamber
Chambers expand with low atmospheric pressure and contract with high pressure.

Vacuum Chambers

Lever pushing/pulling dial needle.

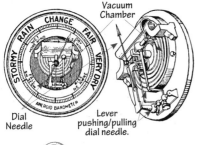

Vacuum Chamber

Dial Needle

Lever pushing/pulling dial needle.

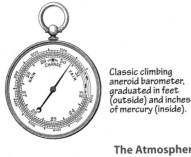

Satellite

Aurora

70 miles

Spacecraft

60 — Meteor Trails

Thermosphere

50 —

40 —

Mesosphere

30 —

Stratosphere

20 —

Troposphere

10 —

Mount Everest

Sea Level

Classic climbing aneroid barometer, graduated in feet (outside) and inches of mercury (inside).

The Atmosphere is divided into:
• Troposphere
• Stratosphere
• Mesosphere
• Thermosphere

This is where our weather occurs.

TROPOSPHERE

Extends from sea level to about 26,405 feet over the poles to nearly 52,810 feet above the equator. It is distinguished by a relatively uniform decrease in temperature and the presence of water vapor, along with extensive weather phenomena. Temperature changes in the troposphere can be accurately predicted using a mean-temperature lapse rate of -1.98°C per 1,000 feet. Temperatures continue to decrease until the rising air mass achieves an altitude where temperature is in equilibrium with the surrounding atmosphere.

STRATOSPHERE

Extends from the tropopause to about 158,430 feet (30 miles). The stratosphere can be subdivided based on thermal characteristics found in different regions. Although these regions differ thermally, the water-vapor content of both regions is virtually nonexistent.

Isothermal Layer: The first subdivision of the stratosphere. In the isothermal layer, temperature is constant at −55°C (-67°F). Turbulence, traditionally associated with the stratosphere, is attributed to the presence of fast-moving jet streams, both here and in the upper regions of the troposphere.

Ozonosphere: The second subdivision, it is characterized by rising temperatures. The ozonosphere serves as a double-sided barrier that absorbs harmful solar ultraviolet radiation while allowing solar heat to pass through unaffected. In addition, the ozonosphere reflects heat from rising air masses back toward the surface of the Earth, keeping the lower regions of the atmosphere warm, even at night during the absence of significant solar activity.

THERMOSPHERE

Extends from 264,050 feet (50 miles) to about 435 miles above the Earth. The uppermost atmospheric region, the thermosphere is generally characterized by increasing temperatures; however, the temperature increase is in direct relation to solar activity. Temperatures in the thermosphere can range from −113°C at the mesopause to 1,500°C during periods of extreme solar activity. Another characteristic of the thermosphere is the presence of charged ionic particles. These particles are the result of high-speed subatomic particles emanating from the sun. These particles collide with gas atoms in the atmosphere and split them apart, resulting in a large number of charged particles (ions).

ATMOSPHERIC PRESSURE & ANIMALS

A change of 1 inch in the mercurial column of the barometer means a change in pressure of about 70 pounds to every square foot of surface. Changes in atmospheric pressure exert a marked influence upon the body and its functions. A change in the barometer of 1 inch in twenty four hours is not uncommon in many parts of North America, and this change in the barometer causes a change of about one half ton in the weight of the atmosphere that is sustained by the average human body. It is not difficult, therefore, to imagine that the physical organism of animals may be sensitive to these changes, and that it has become an inherited instinct to associate the sensations experienced under different atmospheric pressures with the kinds of weather they indicate. Human bodies, and of many animals can be extremely sensitive to atmospheric changes, and aches, pains, and nervousness in humans, and restless behavior on the part of animals, birds, and insects may, in a measure, be attributed to low, rapidly decreasing atmospheric pressure that precedes and during stormy periods.

BAROMETRIC PRESSURE & BIRDS

• Birds fly high when the barometer is high and fly low when the barometer is low. The explanation of this fact is that when the barometer is high the air is heavier and denser and has more sustaining capacity, and birds are therefore able to fly or soar high with less effort than would be required at times when the barometer is low and the air less dense.
• Everything is lovely and the goose honks high. Wild geese fly high in pleasant weather and low in bad weather.
• The low flight of crows indicates rain.
• When the cuckoo is heard in lowlands, it indicates rain; when on high lands, fair weather.

MESOPHERE

Extends from the stratopause to an altitude of 264,050 feet (50 miles). Temperatures decline from a high of −3°C at the stratopause to nearly −113°C at the mesopause. Noctilucent clouds are another characteristic of this atmospheric layer. Made of meteor dust/water vapor and shining only at night, these cloud formations are probably due to solar reflection.

ATMOSPHERIC PRESSURE

Standard atmospheric pressure, or barometric pressure, is the force (that is, weight) exerted by the atmosphere at any given point. An observable characteristic, atmospheric pressure can be expressed in different forms, depending on the method of measurement. Atmospheric pressure decreases with increasing altitude, making barometric pressure of great concern to air crews because oxygen diffusion in the body depends on total barometric pressure.

BAROMETRIC PRESSURE
Barometer

The barometer was invented by Torricelli (1608-1647) a pupil of Galileo. He said that we live submerged in the bottom of an ocean of air which, by experiment, undoubtedly has weight and is the most dense near the surface of the earth. This led to mercury barometers being developed to measure air pressure and make rudimentary projections of weather.

Aneroid Barometer

Is a barometer which contains no liquid. It has a small metal container from which most of the air has been removed. The rise and fall of the atmospheric pressure causes the metal container to contract and expand. The surface movement is amplified and transmitted by gears to a pointer that indicates the pressure in millibars or inches. Aneroid barometers are not as accurate as mercury barometers but can be adjusted by a set screw and an elevation indicator.

Barometric Pressure

At sea level, the air pressure is 14 pounds per square inch. This is equal to the weight of a column of mercury, 29.92 inches or 760 mm of height*. Barometers indicate the air pressure in inches or millibars of mercury. Weather stations use the unit millibars and 29.92 inches of mercury is equal to 1,013.2 millibars. Each 3.4 millibars of fluctuation is equal to 1/10 of an inch of mercury. *reduced to sea level.

INDICATORS OF CHANGING WEATHER
Measurable Indicators

- Barometric Pressure
- Wind Velocity
- Wind Direction
- Temperature
- Moisture Content of the Air

In the mountains, a portable aneroid barometer, thermometer, wind meter, and hygrometer are useful to obtain measurements that will assist in forecasting the weather. Marked or abnormal changes within a 12-hour period may suggest a potential change in the weather.

Weather Forecasting
The use of the portable aneroid barometer, thermometer, and hygrometer can be of great assistance in making local weather forecasts.

BAROMETER WEATHER PREDICTORS

A sky covered with clouds need not cause apprehension, if the latter are high, and of no great density, and the air is still, the barometer at the same time being high. Rain falling under such circumstances is generally light, or of not long continuance.

CHANGE OF BAROMETRIC PRESSURE
Note that these are North American indicators.

- Rapid changes in the barometer indicate early and marked changes in the weather.
- A sudden rise in the barometer is very nearly as dangerous as a sudden fall, because it shows that the level is unsteady. In an ordinary gale the wind often blows hardest when the barometer is just beginning to rise, directly after having been very low.
- Should the barometer continue low when the sky becomes clear, expect more rain within twenty four hours.
- If the barometer falls gradually for several days during continuing fine weather, much wet weather will probably ensue in the end. In like manner, if it keep rising while the wet continues, the weather, after a day or two, is likely to set in fair for some time.
- A very low barometric reading usually occurs during stormy weather, with wind and rain at intervals, but the rain is not necessarily in any great quantity. If the weather during a very low pressure, is fine and calm, a change may come on very suddenly.
- If the barometer and thermometer both rise together, It is a very sure sign of coming fine weather.
- If the barometer falls two or three tenths of an inch in four hours, expect a gale.
- If you observe that the surface of the mercury in the barometer vibrates upon the approach of a storm, you may expect the gale to be severe.
- In summer, when the barometer falls suddenly, expect a thunderstorm; and if it does not rise again when the storm ceases, there will be several days of unsettled weather.
- A summer thunderstorm which does not much depress the barometer will be very local and of slight consequence.
- When the barometer falls considerably without any particular change of weather, you may be certain that a violent storm is raging at a distance.
- In winter heavy rain is indicated by a decrease of pressure and an increase in temperature.
- The barometer falls lower for high winds than for heavy rain.

WET & DRY BULB THERMOMETERS

Greater the difference between the readings of the wet and dry bulb thermometers the greater will be the probability of fine weather, and vice versa.

BAROMETER

An instrument used for measuring air pressure. The two most common types are the mercury barometer and the aneroid barometer. It is based on the principle that the pressure exerted by the ambient air is sufficient to hold up a column of mercury. The height to which this column is held varies directly with the air pressure. The aneroid barometer operates on the principle that the volume of gas in a flexible, enclosed space will increase when the pressure on it decreases; for example, during ascent to altitude.
Barometric Pressure: The actual pressure value indicated by a pressure sensor. For example, at 18,000 ft in the altitude chamber, the barometric pressure should be 380 mm/Hg.
Barometric Tendency: The amount and direction of change in barometer readings over a three-hour period. In this way the rise and fall of the barometer can be determined - thus predicting a change of the weather.

Chief Boatswain Strydr Nutting slings the psychrometer to get wet and dry bulb temperatures. NOAA

Wet & dry-bulb thermometers (psychrometer) to measure the relative humidity.

Dry Bulb   Water   Wet Bulb

WET-BULB TEMPERATURE

The evaporation of water from the thermometer with the bulb wrapped in wet cloth has a cooling effect. The temperature indicated by the wet bulb thermometer is less than the temperature indicated by a normal thermometer. The rate of evaporation from the wet-bulb thermometer depends on the humidity of the air-evaporation and is slower when the air is already full of water vapor.

MEASURING HUMIDITY

Some instruments used to measure humidity are: the psychrometer, the wet-bulb thermometer, the hair hygrometer, and the dew-point hygrometer. The psychrometer consists of one dry-bulb thermometer and one wet-bulb thermometer mounted side by side with a fan to force air past the thermometers. The dry-bulb thermometer measures the ambient air temperature. Air streaming past the wet-bulb thermometer vaporizes water from the wet muslin wick wrapped around the bulb, and causes evaporative cooling. The drier the air, the greater the evaporation, and the lower the reading will be on the wet-bulb thermometer compared with the dry-bulb reading. The temperature difference between the two thermometers, called the "wet-bulb depression," is calibrated in terms of percent relative humidity on a psychrometric table. When the temperature is below freezing, the muslin wick is removed and the wet bulb thermometer is used with a thinly coated ice bulb. Sometimes, the dry and wet bulb thermometers are mounted in an instrument shelter without aspiration; appropriate tables to determine dew-point temperature and relative humidity are available in either case. The hair hygrometer measures changes in humidity using the fact that human hair lengthens slightly as the relative humidity increases and shrinks slightly as the relative humidity drops. A dew-point hygrometer detects when condensation or crystallization first occur on a cooled surface to give the dew-point or frost-point temperature.

Propeller to measure wind speed.

PERSONAL WEATHER STATION

With this instrument you can obtain basic weather data. Information such as temperature, wind speed, barometric pressure, altitude, relative humidity, current time, daily alarm, chronograph and race timer. A log of historic data can be kept of the current wind speed, relative humidity, ambient temperature, barometric pressure, the altitude at the current location, the time and date, and the combined data for this exact time. In this way all the different bits of information can be used to make projections of future weather conditions.

How Wind Speed is Measured

This instrument is equipped with a propeller. When the propeller faces the wind, it rotates and the reading of the rotation per minute is converted it into wind speed. The screen will show the current, average and maximum wind-speed readings.

Table of Relative Humidity
System for measuring the moisture content of air.

Difference Between Wet-bulb	Temperature of Air, Dry-Bulb Thermometer & Dry-Bulb Readings							
	30°F	40°F	50°F	60°F	70°F	80°F	90°F	100°F
1	90%	92%	93%	94%	95%	96%	96%	97%
2	79	84	87	89	90	92	92	93
3	68	76	80	84	86	87	88	90
4	58	68	74	78	81	83	85	86
6	38	52	61	68	72	75	78	80
8	18	37	49	58	64	68	71	71
10		22	37	48	55	61	65	68
12		8	26	39	48	54	59	62
14			16	30	40	47	53	57
16			5	21	33	41	47	51
18				13	26	35	41	47
20				5	19	29	36	42
22					12	23	32	37
24					6	18	26	33

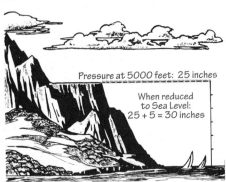

Pressure at 5000 feet: 25 inches

When reduced to Sea Level:
25 + 5 = 30 inches

Altimeter   Elevation
Uses the atmospheric pressure to measure elevation.

HUMIDITY

Humidity is a measure of the amount of water vapor in the air. It can be expressed in several ways. "Specific humidity" is the mass of water vapor per unit mass of combined dry air and water vapor, generally expressed in grams per kilogram. The specific humidity of an air parcel does not change with temperature. "Absolute humidity" is the density of water vapor, expressed as grams per cubic meter of air. "Relative humidity" is discussed below. Related terms are "saturation," which describes the condition where water vapor is at a maximum concentration for the air temperature (warm air can hold more moisture than cold); "dew point temperature," the temperature at which saturation occurs if air is cooled at constant pressure without addition or removal of water vapor; and "vapor pressure," which in meteorology is that part of the total atmospheric pressure due to water vapor content.

RELATIVE HUMIDITY

Relative Humidity: A dimensionless ratio, expressed in percent, of the amount of atmospheric moisture present relative to the amount that would be present if the air were saturated. Since the latter amount is dependent on temperature, relative humidity is a function of both moisture content and temperature. As such, relative humidity by itself does not directly indicate the actual amount of atmospheric moisture present. Relative humidity is the most familiar way to describe the air's moisture content. When "humidity" is used alone, generally relative humidity is meant. Relative humidity compares the actual concentration of water vapor in the air with the concentration of water vapor that the atmosphere could hold (if the atmosphere were at saturation). Relative humidity is usually expressed as a percentage. When the actual concentration of water vapor in air is equal to the water vapor concentration at saturation, the relative humidity is 100%. The relative humidity will vary with the air temperature. Generally, the relative humidity varies inversely with air temperature such that the relative humidity is highest when the temperature is lowest, and vice versa. After sunrise, as the air warms, the relative humidity drops. The relative humidity of air also increases when water vapor is added to the air. As relative humidity increases, clouds may begin to form. When the air temperature and dew point temperature are equal the relative humidity is 100%.

HUMIDITY IN THE ARCTIC

In the Arctic, the prevalent air mass is characterized by low temperatures and low moisture content. The continental air of the subarctic in winter is significantly colder and dryer than arctic marine air. Steam fog which occurs when cold air moves out over a warm water surface, causing moisture to evaporate into the air near the surface, is common in arctic regions. A typical value of relative humidity at the surface is 50-60%. The most important characteristic of clouds in the Arctic is the summer stratus. From about mid-June to mid-September, the ocean area covered by sea ice is 80-90% covered with this cloud type. Summer stratus has important effects on the radiation balance of the surface.

ELEMENTS AFFECTING WEATHER

Weather conditions in the troposphere and on the Earth are affected by four elements:
- Temperature
- Wind
- Air pressure
- Moisture

TEMPERATURE

Temperature is the measure of the warmth or coldness of an object or substance and, for this discussion, the various parts of the atmosphere. The sunlight entering the atmosphere reaches the Earth's surface and warms both the ground and the seas. Heat from the ground and the sea then warms the atmosphere. The atmosphere absorbs the heat and prevents it from escaping into space. This process is called the greenhouse effect because it resembles the way a greenhouse works. Once the sun sets, the ground cools more slowly than the air because it is a better conductor of heat. At night the ground is warmer than the air, especially under a clear dry sky. The ground cools more slowly than the humid nights. Temperature changes near the ground for other reasons. Dark surfaces are warmer than light colored surfaces. Evening air settles in low areas and valleys creating spots colder than higher elevations. Seas, lakes, and ponds retain heat and create warmer temperatures at night near shore. The opposite is true during the day, especially in the spring when lakes are cold. On the beach, daytime temperatures will be cooler than the temperatures on land further from shore. Knowing this will help a survivor determine where to build a shelter.

LAPSE RATE

The rate of change of an atmospheric variable, usually temperature, with height. A steep lapse rate implies a rapid decrease in temperature with height (a sign of instability) and a steepening lapse rate implies that destabilization is occurring. The global average rate of temperature change with height in the atmosphere is 6.5°C/km. The adiabatic lapse rate (or dry adiabatic lapse rate) is the normal rate of change (9.8°C/km) for a dry parcel of air that is moved up or down and cools or warms as the pressure changes. The wet (moist) adiabatic lapse rate (4.9°C/km) is the rate at which saturated air cools as it ascends.

AIR PRESSURE

Air pressure is the force of the atmosphere pushing on the Earth. The air pressure is greatly affected by temperature. Cool air weighs more than warm air. As a result, warm air puts less pressure on the Earth than cool air. A low-pressure area is formed by warm air whereas cool air forms a high-pressure area.

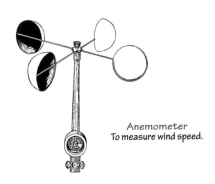

Anemometer
To measure wind speed.

WIND

Wind is the movement of air from a high-pressure area to a low-pressure area. The larger the difference in pressure, the stronger the wind. On a global scale, the air around the Equator is replaced by the colder air around the poles.

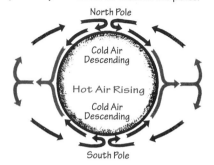

This same convection of air on a smaller scale causes valley winds to blow up slope during the day and down the mountainside at night. Cool air blows in from the ocean during the day due to the heating and rising of the air above the land and reverses at night. This movement of air creates winds throughout the world. When cool air moves into a low-pressure area, it forces the air that was already there to move upward.
The rising air expands and cools.

MOISTURE

Moisture enters the atmosphere in the form of water vapor. Great quantities of water evaporate each day from the land and oceans causing vapor in the air called humidity. The higher the humidity, the higher the moisture content in the air. Air holding as much moisture as possible is saturated. The temperature at which the air becomes saturated is called the dew point. When the temperature falls below the dew point, moisture in the air condenses into drops of water. Low clouds called fog may develop when warm, moist air near the ground is cooled to its dew point. A cooling of the air may also cause moisture to fall to the Earth as precipitation (rain, snow, sleet, or hail).

CIRCULATION OF THE ATMOSPHERE

If the Earth did not rotate, wind would move directly from the high-pressure areas of the poles to the low-pressure areas of the Equator. The movement of air between the poles and the Equator would go on constantly. The rotation of the Earth prevents winds from the poles and the Equator from moving directly north or south. The Earth rotates from west to east, and as a result, winds moving toward the Equator seem to curve toward the west. Winds moving away from the Equator seem to curve toward the east. This is known as the "Coriolis effect". This effect results in winds circling the Earth in wide bands. These prevailing winds are divided into six belts which are known as the:
• Trade winds
• Prevailing westerlies
• Polar easterlies
All three are found in both the Northern and Southern Hemispheres. This totals six prevailing winds.

WIND

Air pressure gradient, or the *difference between regions of high and low air pressure*, impels air in the direction of lowest pressure, creating wind. The larger the air pressure gradient, the greater the wind speed. Several other factors interact to affect wind speed and direction. The most important of these are the Coriolis effect and friction.

CORIOLIS EFFECT

The earth's rotation creates an apparent force ("Coriolis force") that deflects moving air to the right of its initial direction in the Northern Hemisphere and to the left of its initial direction in the Southern Hemisphere. The magnitude of the deflection, or "Coriolis effect," varies significantly with latitude. The Coriolis effect is zero at the equator and increases to a maximum at the poles. The effect is proportional to wind speed; that is, deflection increases as wind strengthens. The resultant balance between the pressure force and the Coriolis force is such that, in the absence of surface friction, air moves parallel to *isobars* (lines of equal pressure). This is the geostrophic wind.

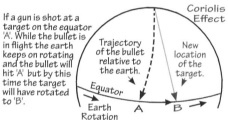

If a gun is shot at a target on the equator 'A'. While the bullet is in flight the earth keeps on rotating and the bullet will hit 'A' but by this time the target will have rotated to 'B'.

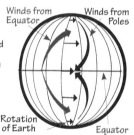

The Coriolis effect explains why winds circulate around high and low pressure systems as opposed to blowing in the direction of the pressure gradient. This figure shows how wind is deflected in each hemisphere.

WIND WEATHER PREDICTORS

• In Texas and the Southwest when the wind shifts, with strength, during a drought, expect rain.
• In the West and Southwest when brisk winds from the south continue for a day or more, expect a "norther."
• Over a great part of the United States a steady and strong south to east wind will bring rain within thirty six hours.
• Easterly winds are proverbially bringers of rain, and when they blow from the northeast quadrant in winter heavy snow is likely to be followed by severe cold.
• When, during a storm, the wind shifts from the east to the west quadrants, clearing weather will soon follow.
• When the wind is from points between west and north and the temperature falls to 40° or below, frost will probably occur.
• The strength of the wind and the severity of storms depends upon barometric conditions.
• Westerly winds (southwest to northwest) are fair weather winds.
• The warmth of the south wind causes one to feel drained of energy or vitality.
• The cold of the north wind is fresh and invigorating.
• The chill of the east wind is conducive to aches and pains.

FRICTION

Air moving over the earth's surface creates friction, which affects the lowest one kilometer of the atmosphere. Friction can interact with other forces to change the wind direction. Above the so-called Atmospheric Boundary Layer where friction is negligible, the pressure gradient force and the Coriolis force are in balance and the wind blows parallel to the isobars. This is called the geostrophic wind. At lower elevations where friction can not be neglected, the wind has a component pointing toward the lower pressure (and away from the higher pressure).

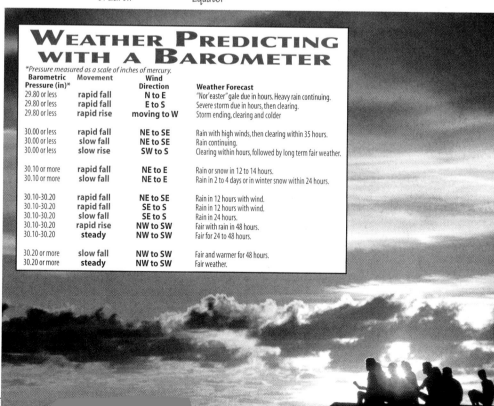

WEATHER PREDICTING WITH A BAROMETER

Pressure measured as a scale of inches of mercury.

Barometric Pressure (in)*	Movement	Wind Direction	Weather Forecast
29.80 or less	rapid fall	N to E	"Nor'easter" gale due in hours. Heavy rain continuing.
29.80 or less	rapid fall	E to S	Severe storm due in hours, then clearing.
29.80 or less	rapid rise	moving to W	Storm ending, clearing and colder.
30.00 or less	rapid fall	NE to SE	Rain with high winds, then clearing within 35 hours.
30.00 or less	slow fall	NE to SE	Rain continuing.
30.00 or less	slow rise	SW to S	Clearing within hours, followed by long term fair weather.
30.10 or more	rapid fall	NE to E	Rain or snow in 12 to 14 hours.
30.10 or more	slow fall	NE to E	Rain in 2 to 4 days or in winter snow within 24 hours.
30.10-30.20	rapid fall	NE to SE	Rain in 12 hours with wind.
30.10-30.20	rapid fall	SE to S	Rain in 12 hours with wind.
30.10-30.20	slow fall	SE to S	Rain in 24 hours.
30.10-30.20	rapid rise	NW to SW	Fair with rain in 48 hours.
30.10-30.20	steady	NW to SW	Fair for 24 to 48 hours.
30.20 or more	slow fall	NW to SW	Fair and warmer for 48 hours.
30.20 or more	steady	NW to SW	Fair weather.

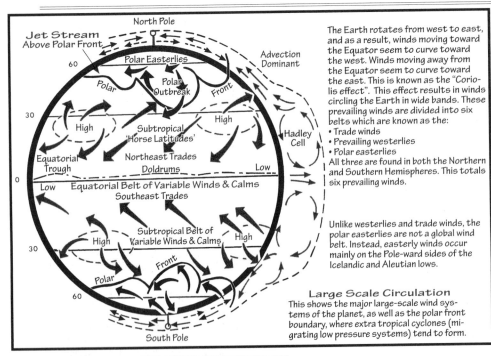

The Earth rotates from west to east, and as a result, winds moving toward the Equator seem to curve toward the west. Winds moving away from the Equator seem to curve toward the east. This is known as the "Coriolis effect". This effect results in winds circling the Earth in wide bands. These prevailing winds are divided into six belts which are known as the:
• Trade winds
• Prevailing westerlies
• Polar easterlies
All three are found in both the Northern and Southern Hemispheres. This totals six prevailing winds.

Unlike westerlies and trade winds, the polar easterlies are not a global wind belt. Instead, easterly winds occur mainly on the Pole-ward sides of the Icelandic and Aleutian lows.

Large Scale Circulation
This shows the major large-scale wind systems of the planet, as well as the polar front boundary, where extra tropical cyclones (migrating low pressure systems) tend to form.

TRADE WINDS
The winds blowing toward the Equator are known as the trade winds. The air above the Equator is so hot it is always rising. The north and south trade winds move in to take the place of the rising air. The Coriolis effect makes the trade winds appear to move from the east. The weather in the region of the trade winds moves from east to west because of the Earth's rotation. The doldrums is the region where the trade winds from the north and south meet near the Equator. The doldrums is usually calm, but it is quite rainy and may have periods of gusty winds.

PREVAILING WESTERLIES
The prevailing westerlies blow away from the Equator. They occur north of the trade winds in the Northern Hemisphere and south of the trade winds in the Southern Hemisphere. The prevailing westerlies seem to move from the west because of the Coriolis effect. The weather in the region of these winds blows from west to east. The prevailing westerlies move across most of the United States and Canada, and are divided from the trade winds in a region called the Horse Latitudes. The air in the Horse Latitudes blows downward to fill the space that was left between the prevailing westerlies and the trade winds. The winds are very light in the Horse Latitudes.

POLAR EASTERLIES
The winds from the North and South Poles are known as the polar easterlies. Because the air is so cold, making it heavy, the air above the poles sinks downward. The air spreads out when it reaches the ground and moves toward the Equator. The weather in the region of the polar easterlies moves from east to west with the Coriolis effect making the winds seem to blow from the east. The polar front is the meeting place of the polar easterlies and the prevailing westerlies and is a cloudy, rainy region.

WINDS

Winds are caused by differences in the atmospheric pressure.

Midlatitude Jet Stream (Summer)

Subtropical Jet Stream (Summer)

Smoke from fires in the Yucatan Peninsula.

Smoke from fires on the west coast of Mexico.

Midlatitude Jet Stream (Winter) 125 Km/h

Midlatitude Jet Stream (Summer) 60 Km/h

JET STREAM
Above the Polar Front is a band of west winds called the jet stream. These are high altitude air flows which circulate as high speed (up to 200 mph) streams at 6-8 miles (10-13 km) above the earth. They are located between the cold and warm air streams (of the north and south). Storms form along this junction area.

White Ash Wind Direction Indicator
White ashes wrapped in a porous cloth will filter out minute particles of ash that float in the air. By shaking the pouch you can determine the slightest movement of the air.

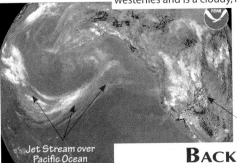

Jet Stream over Pacific Ocean

North America

BACKING
It is the counterclockwise turning of the wind direction as we move up through the atmosphere. For example, the wind direction would change from the north at the ground to the northwest. This is indicative of the airmass cooling.

BACKING WINDS
Winds which shift in a counterclockwise direction with time at a given location (e.g. from south to southeast), or change direction in a counterclockwise sense with height (example: west wind at the surface but becoming more southerly aloft). The opposite of veering winds. In storm spotting, a backing wind usually refers to the turning of a south or southwest surface wind with time to a more east or southeasterly direction. Backing of the surface wind can increase the potential for tornado development by increasing the directional shear at low levels.

Direction of Low

Your Face

Direction of Wind

DIRECTION OF STORMS
Low: The wind blowing at your face, the Low will be to your right. This is the direction of the upcoming storm.
High: The wind blowing from behind you in the northern hemisphere. Rotate your body by 45° right. The high pressure area will be to your right and low pressure area to your left.

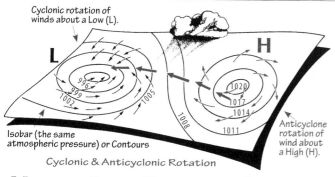

Cyclonic rotation of winds about a Low (L).

Anticyclone rotation of wind about a High (H).

Isobar (the same atmospheric pressure) or Contours

Cyclonic & Anticyclonic Rotation

Local Winds

Local winds result from thermal differences that generate a local pressure gradient.

Warm Land Day

Sea Breeze: Warm land has lower pressure due to heating allowing cooler moist air to flow onshore from adjacent water areas.

HIGH & LOW PRESSURE SYSTEMS

Pressure systems are highs or lows covering areas as big as I million square miles. Most pressure systems found in the United States and Canada develop along the polar front. There, the cold winds of the polar easterlies and the warmer winds of the prevailing westerlies move past one another and create swirling winds called eddies. These eddies are carried eastward across the United States and Canada by the prevailing westerlies. *There are two kinds of eddies: cyclones and anticyclones.*

CYCLONE FLOW TOWARDS LOW PRESSURE

Cyclones formed by eddies are not the same as the storms known as cyclones. The winds of eddies create cyclones that swirl inward toward a center of low pressure. A low-pressure system is formed by the cyclone and its low-pressure region. Because of the rotation of the Earth, cyclones that build north of the Equator blow in a counterclockwise direction. Cyclones that form south of the Equator move in a clockwise direction. Cyclones in North America generally approach on brisk winds, bringing cloudy skies and usually rain or snow.

ANTICYCLONES BLOW FROM HIGH PRESSURE

Anticyclones swirl outward around a center of high pressure, forming a high-pressure system. Anticyclones move in a clockwise direction north of the Equator and counterclockwise south of the Equator. Anticyclones come after cyclones, bringing dry, clearing weather and light winds.

AIR MASSES

Air masses depend largely on the temperature and moisture of the areas in which they originate. Air masses may cover 5 million square miles. As they move away from their source regions and pass over land and sea, the air masses are constantly being modified through heating or cooling from below, lifting or subsiding, absorbing or losing moisture. In general, however, they retain some of their original characteristics and can be recognized and identified.

Cooler Land Night

SEA BREEZES

Sea breezes form during the day as the sun heats the land. The warm air rises and cool air from the ocean blows in and under the rising air. At night, the land cools faster than the ocean and the wind direction reverses to blow offshore.

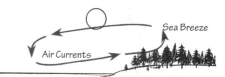

Sea Breeze

Air Currents

SEA BREEZE

Occurs in the daytime because air on the sea is cooler and heavier than the air on the land. The air on the land will rise and be replaced by the cooler air from the sea.

Land Breeze

LAND BREEZE

At night the land cools off faster than the water. The warmer air on the water rises and the heavier cool air from the land flows onto the sea to replace the hot air that has risen. The land breeze is less intense than the sea breeze.

N W E S

Mountain valley breeze: Night Time

Mountain valley breeze: Day Time

MOUNTAIN & VALLEY WINDS

Mountain and valley winds are part of the localized air circulation that develops along mountain slopes heated by solar radiation after winter snows have melted. Differences in air density as air is heated by day and cooled by night lead to an up-valley wind by day and a down-valley wind by night.

By day, the air in contact with the bare valley walls facing the sun is heated and, as it rises, neighboring cooler and denser air flows in an adiabatic wind. At night, the mountain slopes cool rapidly and the air in contact with the slopes is chilled. The now cold, dense air flows downslope as a katabatic wind. These winds are generally shallow (100-300 yards in altitude) with speeds of about 2 to 4 yards per second.

LARGE SCALE KATABATIC WINDS

Katabatic winds occur when cooled, dense air flows down slopes. Over extensive snow-covered plateaus or highlands large-scale katabatic drainage winds may develop. This is common over the Greenland ice sheet. In some places katabatic winds are channeled by mountain valleys, and the wind accelerates to potentially destructive speeds. Steep slopes can also accelerate the katabatic flow. Along the edge of the massive Greenland ice sheet, katabatic winds frequently exceed 75 mph.

WIND SPEED CONVERSION TABLES — WIND SPEED

mph	m/s	km/in	knots
1	0.4	1.6	0.9
2	0.9	3.2	1.7
3	1.3	4.8	2.6
4	1.8	6.4	3.5
5	2.2	8.0	4.3
6	2.7	9.7	5.2
7	3.1	11.3	6.1
8	3.6	12.9	6.9
9	4.0	14.5	7.8
10	4.5	16.1	8.7
12	5.4	19.3	10.4
14	6.3	22.5	12.2
16	7.2	25.7	13.9
18	8.0	29.0	15.6
20	8.9	32.2	17.4
30	13.4	48.3	26.1
40	17.9	64.4	34.7
50	22.4	80.5	43.4
60	26.8	96.6	52.1
100	44.7	160.9	86.8
150	67.1	241.4	130.3
200	89.4	321.9	173.7

Currents affecting North America

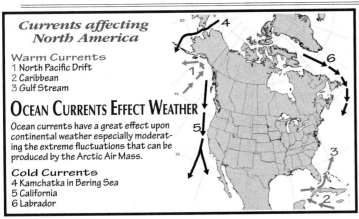

Warm Currents
1 North Pacific Drift
2 Caribbean
3 Gulf Stream

OCEAN CURRENTS EFFECT WEATHER

Ocean currents have a great effect upon continental weather especially moderating the extreme fluctuations that can be produced by the Arctic Air Mass.

Cold Currents
4 Kamchatka in Bering Sea
5 California
6 Labrador

BEAUFORT LAND WIND SCALE

Speed mph	Beaufort Scale		Air Indicators Movement
0-1	0	Calm	Smoke and steam rise vertically.
2-3	1	Light air	Wind affects direction of smoke but not waves.
4-7	2	Slight breeze	You feel wind on face, leaves rustle, fresh snow swirls in eddies.
8-12	3	Gentle breeze	Leaves and twigs move continuously. Flags fly.
13-18	4	Moderate breeze	Small branches move continuously, dust & snow stir.
19-24	5	Fresh breeze	Small deciduous trees sway, tents flap.
25-31	6	Strong breeze	Large branches wave, whitecaps on most waves. Difficult to use umbrella.
32-38	7	Moderate gale	Whole large trees sway. Difficult to walk.
39-46	8	Fresh gale	Twigs break off trees, you lean into the wind in order to walk.
47-54	9	Strong gale	Whole branches break off, high waves. Slight damage to roofs.
55-63	10	Full gale	Poorly rooted trees topple, branches fly.
64-75	11	Storm	Extensive wind damage of all types can occur.
75+	12	Hurricane	Devastation.

Sir Francis Beaufort (1774-1857) Developed the Beaufort Wind Scale.

An anemometer is used to measure the wind speed.

Wind direction is always reported as the direction the wind is coming from. For example, a wind out of the west is reported as a west wind, or wind direction 270°. Interestingly, this convention is the opposite of that used by oceanographers for ocean currents.

MEASURING WIND SPEED

Meteorologists usually report wind speed in meters per second (m/s). Ship observations may be reported in knots (one knot is one nautical mile per hour or about 1.15 miles per hour, approximately 0.5 meters per second). *The Beaufort scale, named after Admiral Sir Francis Beaufort (1774-1857), allows observers on ships to judge wind strength by the ocean's appearance.* For example, Beaufort Force 9, also known as a "strong gale," is indicated by dense foam blowing from the tops of breaking waves. Force 9 compares to a wind speed of 21 m/s to 24 m/s.

WINDS IN THE ARCTIC

The Arctic winter is characterized by high winds with snowstorms between calm periods. With little to slow them, Arctic winds scour open areas, and deposit loads of snow in sheltered areas. Nevertheless, in the Arctic, winter surface wind speeds are often lower than in summer due to the frequent occurrence of inversions (when warm air tops a surface cold layer). The inversion layer decouples surface wind from stronger upper layer winds.

BEAUFORT SEA WIND SCALE

Beaufort Scale	Descriptive Term	Speed mph	Appearance of the Sea
0	Calm	-	Like a mirror (no ripples).
1	Light air	1-3	Ripples with the appearance of scales; no foam crests.
2	Light breeze	4-7	Small wavelets; crests of glassy appearance, no breaking waves.
3	Gentle breeze	8-12	Large wavelets; crests begin to break; scattered whitecaps.
4	Moderate breeze	13-18	Small waves that are becoming longer; numerous whitecaps.
5	Fresh breeze	19-24	Moderate waves, longer form; many whitecaps; some spray.
6	Strong breeze	25-31	Large waves beginning to form; whitecaps everywhere; more spray.
7	Near gale	32-38	Sea forms heaps. White foam from breaking waves begins to be blown in streaks.
8	Gale	39-46	Moderately high waves of greater length; edges of crests begin to break into spin drift; foam is blown in well-marked streaks.
9	Strong gale	47-54	High waves; dense streaks of foam and sea begins to roll; spray may affect visibility.
10	Storm	55-63	Very high waves with overhanging crests; foam is blown in dense white streaks, sea appears white; rolling of the sea becomes heavy; visibility reduced.
11	Violent storm	64-72	Exceptionally high waves (small and medium-sized ships might be temporarily lost to view in the troughs of the waves); the sea is covered with white patches of foam; everywhere the edges of the wave crests are blown into froth; visibility further reduced.
12	Hurricane	73-82	The air is filled with foam and spray; sea completely white with driving spray; visibility greatly reduced.

Fighting an arctic gale.

The water in the wind condenses as it rises to a higher cooler elevation to form a cloud over the land. This forms a standing cloud that is nearly always present over the island.

Humid wind blows onto land mass and rises to a higher elevation

The wind returns to a lower elevation after passing over the land, the air warms up and the cloud disappears.

BANNER CLOUDS

Similar to Mountain Clouds but they occur over islands at sea. These clouds are also called standing clouds as they remain over the island. The cloud will dissipate once it has passed over the island but a new cloud is always forming. This special cloud is used by mariners to find land and is discussed in the *Ocean Travel Chapter.*

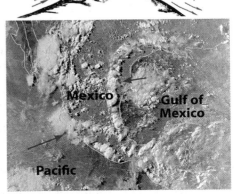

Banner clouds forming over the coast line's of Mexico.

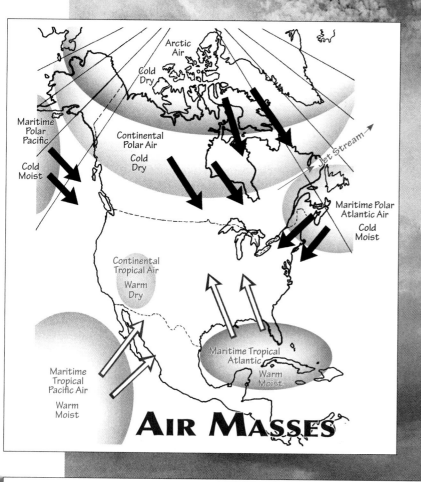

AIR MASSES

Major North American Air Masses

Air Mass	Typical Weather	Origin
Marine Tropical	Cloudy with rain or drizzle. Fog.	Pacific high on west coast.
Marine Polar (Marine Arctic)	Showers and bright periods. Good visibility.	Polar high.
Returning Marine Polar	Cool but fair, good visibility.	Same as Marine Polar but changed by ocean passage.
Continental Polar	Intense cold can also have cloudy sky in winter.	North Canadian (Arctic) high.
Continental Tropic	Very warm and usually cloudless.	Southern USA.

Air Masses

This is the movement of large bodies of air, in the atmosphere, which cause the changes in our weather. In North America we have seven air masses that are continually pushing each other for predominance in their area of action.

Arctic

Very cold and dry air. It is too cold to retain much humidity. This air mass occupies the northern parts of Alaska and northern Canada. It creates the cold winters in Canada with temperatures down to -60° F (-50° C) and with a very high wind-chill factor caused by the blowing wind.

Continental Polar (cP)

This cold air mass can penetrate into the United States especially in the winter when it will stay for a week at a time. This mass develops the snow storms off the Great Lakes.

Maritime Polar Pacific (mP)

This air comes from Siberia and collects moisture over the Pacific. The moisture is dropped, because of the mountains, as rain or snow over the Pacific Coast west of the Rocky Mountains right down to California.

Maritime Polar Atlantic

This comes from the Northern Atlantic Ocean and brings devastating snow storms to Newfoundland and Nova Scotia. In the early summer it brings the banks of fog over the Grand Banks and the "east wind" of New England.

Maritime Tropical Atlantic (mT)

This air mass originates in the Gulf of Mexico and adjacent Atlantic Ocean. It is hot and moving north over the ocean makes it very humid. It causes steady showers that can reach southern Canada and up to the Rocky Mountains. The heavy snowfalls in the winter, in Nova Scotia and along the United States Atlantic coast, are caused by this air mass when it meets the Arctic air.

Maritime Tropical Pacific (mT)

This mass originates in the equatorial Pacific. It causes the heavy rainfalls in California and the southwestern states.

Continental Tropic (cT)

This is the very dry air originating in the desert southwest of the United States. This air is very hot and causes the drought conditions across the plains.

AIR MASSES OF NORTH AMERICA

A squall blowing through.

AIR PRESSURE & FRONTAL SYSTEMS IN THE ARCTIC

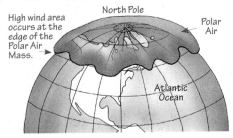

High wind area occurs at the edge of the Polar Air Mass.

North Pole

Polar Air

Atlantic Ocean

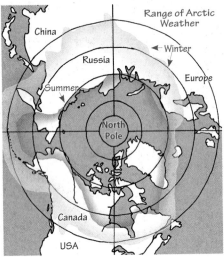

Range of Arctic Weather

China

Winter

Russia

Europe

Summer

North Pole

Canada

USA

FRONTS

A boundary or transition zone between two air masses of different density, and thus (usually) of different temperature. A moving front is named according to the advancing air mass, e.g., cold front if colder air is advancing.

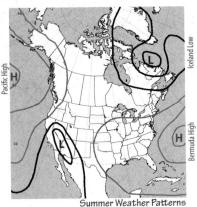

Summer Weather Patterns

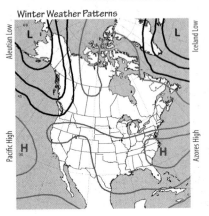

Winter Weather Patterns

Polar Front: Several fronts and semipermanent high and low pressure systems characterize the Arctic. The "polar front" marks the boundary between cold polar air masses and warm tropical air masses. The polar front is intermittent rather than continuous around the globe. The strength of the polar front depends on the magnitude of the horizontal temperature gradient across the front. *Where the temperature gradient is steep, the front is strong and is a potential site for cyclone or low pressure system development. Where temperature contrast is small, the polar front is weak.*

Arctic Front: Like the polar front, the "arctic front" is discontinuous and depends on the temperature contrast between two air masses. The arctic front is the boundary between polar and arctic air masses and lies to the north of the polar front. The arctic front can be as strong as the polar front. It is particularly prominent during summer in northern Eurasia. Semipermanent high and low pressure systems ("highs" and "lows") are identified with particular regions and have seasonal characteristics. In winter, the *Icelandic Low* extends from near Iceland north into the Barents Sea, and is associated with frequent cyclone activity. The *Aleutian Low* is present in the Gulf of Alaska. The Beaufort-Chukchi Sea region is dominated by a ridge of high pressure linking the *Siberian High* and high pressure over the Yukon of Canada. In April and May arctic pressure gradients decrease.

The Icelandic and Aleutian lows weaken. The Siberian High disappears, and is replaced by a wide but shallow low. The *Arctic High* is centered over the Canadian Arctic Archipelago. In summer, pressure gradients are generally weak. Intermittently, however, cyclones enter the Arctic from northern Eurasia and the north Atlantic, and tend to persist over the Canadian Basin. By October the pattern has almost returned to the winter configuration. The Icelandic and Aleutian lows strengthen, as does the Siberian High.

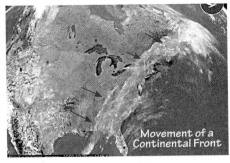

Movement of a Continental Front

WEATHER FRONT MOVEMENTS

Understanding the movement of fronts (boundary between two differing air masses) and their related clouds helps you predict future weather conditions – which can be crucial for your survival. Clouds are good indicators of approaching weather conditions. By reading cloud shapes and patterns, observers can forecast weather even without additional equipment. Shape and height are used to identify clouds. Shape provides information about the stability of the atmosphere, and height above ground level provides an indication of the distance of an approaching storm. Taken together, both indicate the likelihood of precipitation.

DRYLINE: GREAT PLAINS

A boundary separating moist and dry air masses and an important factor in severe weather frequency in the Great Plains. It typically lies north-south across the central and southern high Plains states during the spring and early summer, where it separates moist air from the Gulf of Mexico (to the east) and dry desert air from the southwestern states (to the west). The dry line typically advances eastward during the afternoon and retreats westward at night. However, a strong storm system can sweep the dry line eastward into the Mississippi Valley, or even further east, regardless of the time of day. A typical dry line passage results in a sharp drop in humidity (hence the name), clearing skies, and a wind shift from south or southeasterly to west or southwesterly. (Blowing dust and rising temperatures also may follow, especially if the dry line passes during the daytime; see dry punch). The dry line's eastward movement at the surface is often not as fast as it is aloft. Dry air at about 1000 feet can overrun the moist air, creating what is called a capping inversion. Hot air over warm air acts like a lid that keeps heated air from rising. On some days this lid is very thick preventing the blossoming of storms. But on other days, the lid holds the unstable air down for only so long before it breaks through the inversion and clouds explode into thunderstorms. Storms may grow to 50,000 feet or higher in minutes as moist air rockets skyward at 100 mph, creating large hail, torrential rain, deadly lightning and strong winds. And with low-level winds changing speed and direction with height, from south to southwest then to west, storms are likely to rotate, which can lead to powerful tornadoes. ***The thunderstorms most likely to produce tornadoes are called supercells and are often a product of the severe weather trigger known as the dry line.*** When the dry line retreats westward at night, the dew points will rise rapidly and the wind will shift from the west or southwest to the south or southeast.

FRONTAL CLOUD PATTERNS

Often typical or "classic" weather patterns precede and follow fronts as they move through an area. Approaching warm fronts are often preceded with an orderly procession of high clouds, middle clouds, and finally the extensive lower clouds. Weather typically associated with particular fronts may vary according to geographic location.

Temperature Change: Is an indicator of a front's arrival and the rate of change shows the intensity.

Wind: Front's passage is evidenced by a marked change in wind direction and speed. Wind speed is often variable and usually higher and gustier behind a cold front. Other times, the wind speed may be low until the actual frontal surface passes through your location. Steady southeasterly, southerly, or southwesterly winds precede cold frontal passage with the strongest pre-frontal winds observed just before cold frontal passage. Cold fronts are accompanied with gusty westerly, northwesterly, to northerly winds.

Barometric Pressure: A front lies in a pressure trough, an area of lowest surface barometric pressure, with the pressure higher on either side of the trough. Thus, the pressure usually decreases when a front approaches and rises after the front moves through. The rate of barometric pressure change often accelerates as a front moves through.

WEATHER FRONT MOVEMENTS

WEATHER FORECASTING

Weather forecasts are simply educated estimations or deductions based on general scientific weather principles and meteorological evidence. Forecasts based on past results may or may not be accurate. However, even limited experience in a particular region and season may provide local indications of impending weather patterns and increased accuracy. Native weather lore, although sometimes greatly colored and surrounded in mystique, should not be discounted when developing forecasts, as it is normally based on the local inhabitants' long-term experience in the region.

BAD WEATHER

Signs of approaching bad weather (within 24 to 48 hours).

- A gradual lowering of the clouds. This may be the arrival or formation of new lower strata of clouds. It can also indicate the formation of a thunderhead.
- An increasing halo around the sun or the moon.
- An increase in humidity and temperature.
- Cirrus clouds.
- A decrease in barometric pressure (registered as a gain in elevation on an altimeter).

FAIR WEATHER

Continued fair weather...

- A cloudless sky and shallow fog, or layers of haze at valley bottoms in early morning.
- A cloudless sky that is blue down to the horizon or down to where a haze layer forms a secondary horizon.
- Conditions under which small cumulus clouds appearing before noon do not increase, but instead decrease or vanish during the day.
- Clear skies except for a low cloud deck that does not rise or thicken during the day.

Signs of approaching fair weather...

- A gradual rising and diminishing of clouds.
- A decreasing halo around the sun or moon.
- Dew on the ground in the morning.
- Small snowflakes, ice crystals, or drizzle, which indicate that the clouds are thin and fair weather may exist at higher elevations.
- An increase in barometric pressure (registered as a loss in elevation on an altimeter).

STORM SYSTEMS - FRONTS

The approach of a storm system is indicated when...

A thin veil of cirrus clouds spreads over the sky, thickening and lowering until altostratus clouds are formed. The same trend is shown at night when a halo forms around the moon and then darkens until only the glow of the moon is visible. When there is no moon, cirrus clouds only dim the stars, but altostratus clouds completely hide them.

- Low clouds, which have been persistent on lower slopes, begin to rise at the time upper clouds appear.
- Various layers of clouds move in at different heights and become abundant.
- Lenticular clouds accompanying strong winds lose their streamlined shape, and other cloud types appear in increasing amounts.
- A change in the direction of the wind is accompanied by a rapid rise in temperature not caused by solar radiation. This may also indicate a warm, damp period.
- A light green haze is observed shortly after sunrise in mountain regions above the timberline.

Cold Front advancing... there was a major storm the next day.

THUNDERSTORMS

Indications of local thunderstorms or squally weather are...

- An increase in size and rapid thickening of scattered cumulus clouds during the afternoon.
- The approach of a line of large cumulus or cumulonimbus clouds with an "advance guard" of altocumulus clouds. At night, increasing lightning windward of the prevailing wind gives the same warning.
- Massive cumulus clouds hanging over a ridge or summit (day or night).

STRONG WINDS

Indications of approaching strong winds...

- Plumes of blowing snow from the crests of ridges and peaks or ragged shreds of cloud moving rapidly.
- Persistent lenticular clouds, a band of clouds over high peaks and ridges, or downwind from them.
- A turbulent and ragged banner cloud that hangs to the lee of a peak.

PRECIPITATION

When there is precipitation and the sky cannot be seen...

- Small snowflakes or ice crystals indicate that the clouds above are thin, and fair weather exists at high elevations.
- A steady fall of snowflakes or raindrops indicates that the precipitation has begun at high levels, and bad weather is likely to be encountered on ridges and peaks.

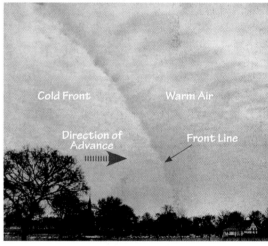

Cold Front   Warm Air

Direction of Advance   Front Line

WEATHER FORECASTING

The use of the portable aneroid barometer, thermometer, and hygrometer can be of great assistance in making local weather forecasts. Reports from other localities and from any weather service are also of great value.

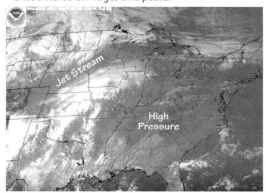

Jet Stream

High Pressure

Antique Portable Barometer

The High deflects this northern cold air and prevents it from going further south east (towards the High).

AIR PRESSURE - AIR MASSES - FRONTS

An air mass is a large volume of air that is relatively uniform (horizontally) in temperature and water vapor concentration over hundreds of miles. Air masses are generally identified with the regions over which they develop. Two examples are continental polar and maritime tropical air masses. While air masses can persist over their formative regions for a considerable length of time, they often move across regions. As air masses move from one region to another, the air mass characteristics are modified by the underlying surface. For instance, as cold, dry "arctic air" moves over an ocean surface it gains heat and moisture.

MEETING OF AIR MASSES

When two different air masses meet, they do not ordinarily mix (unless their temperatures, pressures, and relative humilities happen to be very similar). Instead, they set up boundaries called frontal zones, or "fronts." The colder air mass moves under the warmer air mass in the form of a wedge. If the boundary is not moving, it is termed a stationary front. Usually, however, the boundary moves along the Earth's surface, and as one air mass withdraws from a given area, it is replaced by another air mass. This action creates a moving front. If warmer air is replacing colder air, the front is called "warm;" if colder air is replacing warmer air, the front is called "cold." Most changes in the weather occur along fronts. The movement of fronts depends on the formation of pressure systems. Cyclones push fronts along at speeds of 20 to 30 miles per hour. Anticyclones blow into an area after a front has passed.

Cirrus clouds indicating the approach of a warm front.

FOUR MAIN FRONTAL TYPES

Cold Front: occurs when a cold air mass advances and replaces a warm air mass. Advancing cold fronts force warm moist air to rise sharply, producing showers and thunderstorms during the warm season, and snow during the cold season. As a cold front passes, temperature and humidity drops and air pressure rises.

Warm Front: occurs when a cold air mass retreats and is replaced by a warmer, generally more humid air mass. As a warm front passes, temperature and humidity rise. The passage of a warm front often implies that a cyclone is approaching and pressures may fall.

Stationary Front: occurs when a cold air mass and warm air mass meet, but neither moves much in any direction. Cloudiness and light to moderate precipitation may persist for days on the cold side of a stationary front as the warm air gradually rises over the cold air.

Occluded Front: occurs as a cold front overtakes a warm front, and forces the warm air to rise. The cool air mass remains at the surface. Low clouds and light precipitation usually accompany the passing of an occluded front.

COLD FRONT

Colder air overtakes and wedges underneath the warmer air forcing the warmer air aloft. Surface friction slows the air in contact with the surface, creating a bulge in the frontal slope. This tends to give the front a steep slope near its leading edge. Cold fronts may be accompanied by dramatic weather changes.

Fast Moving Cold Fronts: Rapidly moving cold fronts force the air upward in the area ahead of the front's surface position. Therefore, most of the thick cumuliform cloudiness and showery precipitation is located just ahead of the front where the opposing air currents meet. The severity of weather is determined by the instability of the warm air ahead of the cold front and clashing air mass differences. If the preceding warm air has high humidity and strong southerly winds, the potential exists for severe weather. Sometimes if the cold front has a steep slope and is quickly moving, a squall line may form.

Slow Moving Cold Fronts: When a cold front moves slowly, there is an up-gliding of warm air over the frontal surface. This results in a rather broad cloud pattern in the warm air, with clouds extending well behind the front's surface position - warm, stable air creating stratiform clouds. Slow cold fronts can affect local weather for 12 to 18 hours with slow improvement. In the summer, cumuliform clouds and garden-variety thunderstorms develop, if the warm air is moist and unstable.

Cold Front/Squall Line Weather Hazards: Under certain atmospheric conditions, a squall line composed of thunderstorms may develop 50 to 200 miles ahead of and parallel to a fast moving cold front. If a squall line does develop, little activity usually occurs at the cold front. Thunderstorms along a squall line are frequently similar to those along a cold front, but may be more violent. The cloud bases are often lower and the tops higher than with most other thunderstorms. The most severe conditions (large hail, damaging winds, tornadoes) are generally associated with squall line thunderstorms. Squall lines are usually most intense during the late afternoon and early evening hours, just after maximum daytime heating.

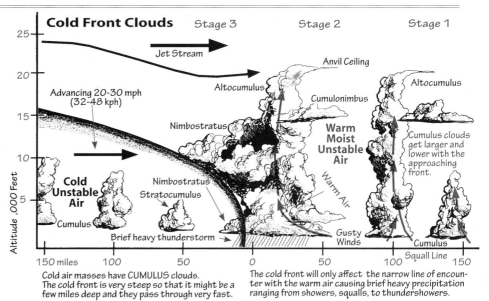

Cold Front Clouds — Stage 3 — Stage 2 — Stage 1

Altitude, 000 Feet

Jet Stream

Advancing 20-30 mph (32-48 kph)

Anvil Ceiling

Altocumulus

Cumulonimbus

Nimbostratus

Warm Moist Unstable Air

Altocumulus

Cumulus clouds get larger and lower with the approaching front.

Cold Unstable Air

Warm Air

Nimbostratus

Stratocumulus

Cumulus

Brief heavy thunderstorm

Gusty Winds

Cumulus

Squall Line

150 miles — 100 — 50 — 0 — 50 — 100 — 150

Cold air masses have CUMULUS clouds. The cold front is very steep so that it might be a few miles deep and they pass through very fast.

The cold front will only affect the narrow line of encounter with the warm air causing brief heavy precipitation ranging from showers, squalls, to thundershowers.

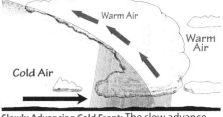

Jet Stream — Anvil

Nimbostratus

Warm Air

Cumulonimbus

Warm Air

Cold Air

Lightning

Warm Air

Warm Air

Cold Air

Rapidly Advancing Cold Front: If the cold front arrives very fast the angle of the wedge is usually steeper therefore rapidly raising the warm air and causing thunderstorms and violent winds.

Slowly Advancing Cold Front: The slow advance will result in a lower angled wedge causing the warm air not to rise as fast and the resulting rain will not be as severe but might last longer.

FRONTS

A change in air pressure signals the advance or passage of a front. Fronts are the narrow transition zone boundaries separating two air masses of contrasting properties (temperature and humidity). Low pressure systems often develop along frontal boundaries and cloud cover and precipitation often occurs in the vicinity of fronts.

Arrival of a Cold Front

In this 180° composite photograph a Cold Front is approaching from the West.

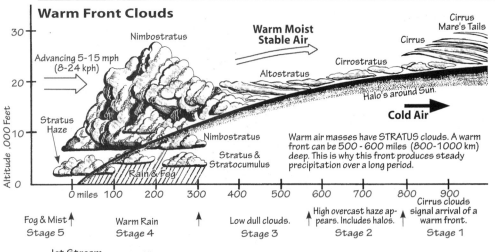

Warm Front Clouds

Advancing 5-15 mph (8-24 kph)

Stratus Haze

Nimbostratus

Nimbostratus

Stratus & Stratocumulus

Rain & Fog

Warm Moist Stable Air

Cirrus Mare's Tails

Cirrus

Cirrostratus

Altostratus

Halo's around Sun.

Cold Air

Warm air masses have STRATUS clouds. A warm front can be 500 - 600 miles (800-1000 km) deep. This is why this front produces steady precipitation over a long period.

Altitude , 000 Feet

0 miles 100 200 300 400 500 600 700 800 900

Fog & Mist Stage 5 | Warm Rain Stage 4 | Low dull clouds. Stage 3 | High overcast haze appears. Includes halos. Stage 2 | Cirrus clouds signal arrival of a warm front. Stage 1

Jet Stream

Anvil

Cumulonimbus

Warm Air

Warm Air

Rain

Cold Air

Moist and Unstable Warm Front Overrunning Cold Air
The warm front being unstable will cause cumulonimbus clouds to form with very heavy precipitation under the cloud. The rain from the cumulonimbus cloud can be heavy and brief at a specific location but the rain from the front will last for some time.

Clouds forming in cold air.

Warm Air

Cold Air

Moist and Stable Warm Front Overrunning Cold Air
A warm front rolling over a retreating cold mass of air. The warm air rising will cause precipitation and where some warm air mixes with the cold air, clouds will form in the cold air.

WARM FRONT

Since cold air is denser than warm air, the cold air is slow to retreat in advance of the overriding warm air. This produces a warm frontal slope that extends ahead of the surface front, and has a more gradual slope.

Warm Front Moist & Stable: If the advancing warm air is moist and stable, stratiform clouds develop. Precipitation increases gradually with the approach of this type of warm front and usually continues until it passes.

Warm Front Moist & Unstable: If the advancing warm air is moist and unstable, altocumulus and cumulonimbus are embedded in the cloud masses normally accompanying the front. Precipitation in advance of the front is usually showery with periods of steady light rain

Classic Warm Front Advance: At first, the sun or moon will be seen dimly through the thin leading edge of the altostratus deck of clouds, but as the cloud deck thickens and the cloud base lowers, celestial bodies will disappear from sight. From the thick altostratus clouds, intermittent light precipitation may be encountered. If the altostratus deck is still quite high, this precipitation may not reach the ground. The altostratus/altocumulus deck will lower and the precipitation will increase in intensity. Passage of the warm air front will be indicated by a rise in temperature and a wind shift.

Low Stratus & Fog: The widespread precipitation ahead of a warm front is often accompanied by low stratus and fog. In this case, the precipitation raises the moisture content of the cold air until saturation is reached. This stratus/fog area can cover thousands of square miles. When rain begins to fall from warmer air above the front into the colder air below the frontal surface, ragged clouds (stratus fractus) form in the cold air. Steady precipitation will provide a constant source of moisture allowing the low stratus clouds to continuously form. Ceilings are often in the 300 to 900 foot range during steady, warm frontal rain situation. Just before the warm front passes, ceilings and visibilities can drop to zero with drizzle and fog.

TYPES OF WEATHER FRONTS

Cold Front
Cold air is denser and heavier than warm air. The warm air is pushed upward.

Warm Front
A warm front is warm air moving towards a cold air mass. It will squeeze the cold air mass away from the area at the surface. This occurs when the warm air mass is stronger than the cold air front.

Stationary Front
This occurs when two touching air masses do not move.

Occluded Front
Occurs when a cold front rapidly overtakes a warm front and meets another cold or cool front. This causes the warm air to be lifted or 'pinched' by the two cooler fronts. There are three types of occluded fronts:

Cold Occluded: Precipitation falls close to and behind the front.

Warm Occluded: Produces precipitation ahead of the front.

Neutral: Precipitation falls along the front line.

MOVEMENT OF FRONTS
Fronts can move 30 to 50 miles per hour (48-80 km/h).

Frontal Slope
Cold air mass displacing a warm mass. The cold air mass slides under the warm mass which is pushed upward. The cold air mass has a downward slope.

Warm mass displacing a cold mass. The slope is upward when the warmer air pushes on a colder air mass.

Two major air masses in North America.
• Polar   • Tropical

Cold

Warm

Stationary   **Front**

Cold

Warm

STATIONARY FRONTS
Stationary fronts are another type of front that occurs when air masses meet but move very slowly. It may remain over an area for several days bringing moderate weather.

STATIONARY FRONTS
Sometimes, opposing forces exerted by adjacent air masses are such that the frontal surface between them shows little or no movement. In such cases, surface winds tend to blow parallel to the front rather than against or away from it. This is called a stationary front, since it does not move and neither air mass replaces the other.

Classic Stationary Front: Although there is no movement of the surface position of the stationary front, there still is movement of air towards the front from either side of it. Warmer air will move towards it, generally from the South, while colder air from the North will also move towards the front. The clash of the two air masses will cause an active weather band to develop. The stronger air mass controls the angle of the air flow in relation to the front's surface position, the strength of the upgliding wind, and determines the inclination of the frontal slope.

Stationary Fronts Weather Conditions: Weather conditions occurring with stationary fronts are similar to those found with warm fronts, but are usually less intense. Stationary fronts can cause heavy precipitation with resulting local flooding.

Occluded Front

Occlusion Weather: Since occlusions result from one frontal system overtaking another, occlusions combine the weather of both warm and cold fronts into one extensive system. A line of showers and thunderstorms typical of cold fronts merges with the warm front's low ceilings. Precipitation and low visibilities are widespread on either side of the occlusion's surface position. In addition, strong winds occur around an intense low pressure center at the occlusion's northern end.

There are two types of occluded fronts; *warm and cold occlusions.* The portion of the occluded front which intersects the earth's surface determines whether the occlusion is a cold or warm occluded front.

Cold Front Occlusion: travels about twice as fast as warm fronts. As a result, cold fronts often catch up to warm fronts. When a cold front reaches a warm front, an occluded front develops. In a cold-front occlusion, the air behind the cold front is colder than the air ahead of the warm front. The weather of a cold-front occlusion resembles that of a cold front.

Warm Front Occlusion: When the air behind the cold front is warmer than the air ahead of the warm front, it is known as a warm-front occlusion. Warm front occlusion weather is similar to a warm front. These fronts produce milder weather than do cold or warm fronts.

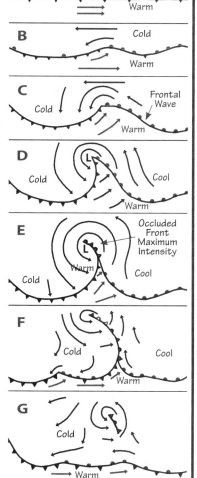

Cold Front Occlusion

Cumulonimbus — Warm Air — Altocumulus — Cirrus — Altostratus — Nimbostratus — Warm Frontal Surface — Cold Frontal Surface — Cold Air — Cool Air — Stratocumulus — Stratocumulus — Rain

Altitude ,OOO Feet — 30, 20, 10, 0 — 250 miles 200 150 100 50 0 50 100 150

Warm Front Occlusion

Cumulonimbus — Warm Air — Altocumulus — Cirrus — Altostratus — Cool Air — Nimbostratus — Cold Air — Stratocumulus or Stratus — Stratocumulus — Rain

Altitude ,OOO Feet — 30, 20, 10, 0 — 0 miles 50 100 150 200 250

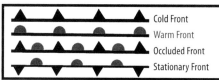

Cold Front
Warm Front
Occluded Front
Stationary Front

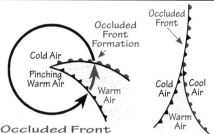

Occluded Front Formation — Occluded Front — Cold Air — Pinching Warm Air — Warm Air — Cold Air — Cool Air — Warm Air

Occluded Front
An occluded front occurs when a warm air mass and a cold air mass are stalled. This results in a mixture of warm front and cold front weather that might last for days.
Trough
Part of the stalled front might include a trough which is a warm front pinched between two cold fronts or one cold front that has or is encircling the warm front as shown in the illustrations.

Front Development & Occlusion

Frontal Waves are primarily the result of the interaction of two air masses; they usually form on slow-moving cold fronts or stationary fronts. During stage (**A**), the winds on both sides of the front blow parallel to the front. Small disturbances in the wind pattern, as well as uneven local heating and irregular terrain, may start a wave-like bend in the front (**B**). If this tendency persists and the wave increases in size, a counter-clockwise (cyclonic) circulation starts to form.

Circulation Centers Develop: One section of the front begins moving as a warm front, while the section next to it begins moving as a cold front (**C**). This deformation area is a frontal wave. As the pressure at the peak of the frontal wave falls, a low-pressure center forms. The cyclonic circulation strengthens, and the winds begin moving the fronts. The cold front moves faster than the warm front (**D**).

Occlusion Process: When the cold front catches up with the warm front, the two of them occlude (close together). The result is called an occlusion (**E**). This is the time of maximum intensity for the wave cyclone. The occluded front exhibits characteristics from both the cold front and warm front. That is why the weather symbol depicting an occlusion is a combination of the symbols and colors of warm and cold fronts. As the occlusion continues to grow in length, the low pressure area weakens and the frontal movement slows (**F**). At this point, a new frontal wave may begin to form on the long westward trailing portion of the cold front. In the final stage, the two fronts are a single stationary front again. The low center with its remnant of the occlusion is disappearing (**G**).

A — Cold — Warm
B — Cold — Warm
C — Cold — Frontal Wave — Warm
D — L — Cold — Cool — Warm
E — Occluded Front Maximum Intensity — L — Cold — Warm — Cool
F — Cold — Cool — Warm
G — Cold — Warm

Forecasting the Weather with Warm & Cold Fronts

Advancing Warm Front

	Before Arrival	During Passage	After Passage
Pressure	Falls steadily.	Fall stops.	Little or no change.
Wind	Backs and increases.	Veers and decreases.	Remains steady in direction.
Temperature	Slow rise.	Rise continues.	Little change.
Cloud	Cirrus well ahead, then lower cloud.	Low cloud, mainly nimbus.	Higher clouds. Stratus or stratocumulus.
Weather	Continuous rain or snow as front is approached.	Rain or snow stops.	Fair, with some drizzle or intermittent showers.
Visibility	Good before the rain	Poor	Poor (mist or fog rising from the wet ground).

Advancing Cold Front

	Before Arrival	During Passage	After Passage
Pressure	Falls.	Rises rapidly.	Rises slowly.
Wind	Backs and increases, becoming squally.	Sudden veer, often with heavy squall.	Backs a little, then steady and veers in later squalls.
Temperature	Fairly steady.	Sudden fall.	Little change.
Cloud	Patchy, then continuous, heavy towering cloud near front.	Low dense cloud.	Cloud lifts rapidly.
Weather	Rain and perhaps thunder.	Heavy rain, perhaps thunder and hail.	Heavy rain for short period, fair with occasional showers.
Visibility	Poor	Poor	Good

TYPES OF CLOUDS

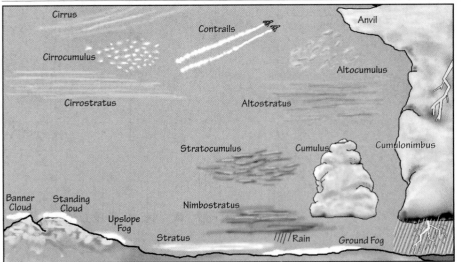

Cirrus
Contrails
Anvil
Cirrocumulus
Altocumulus
Cirrostratus
Altostratus
Stratocumulus
Cumulus
Cumulonimbus
Banner Cloud
Standing Cloud
Nimbostratus
Upslope Fog
Stratus
Rain
Ground Fog

TYPES OF CLOUDS
CLOUDS BY SHAPE

Clouds may be classified by shape as cumulus or stratus.

CUMULUS

Cumulus clouds are often called "puffy" clouds, looking like tufts of cotton. Their thickness (bottom to top) is usually equal to or greater than their width. *Cumulus clouds are primarily composed of water droplets that cause them to have sharp, distinct edges.* These clouds usually indicate instability at the altitude of the atmosphere where they are found. The stormy weather associated with cumulus clouds is usually violent with heavy rains or snow and strong, gusty winds. Precipitating cumulus clouds are called *cumulonimbus.*

STRATUS

Stratus clouds are layered, often appearing flattened, with greater horizontal than vertical dimensions. They usually indicate a stable atmosphere, but can indicate the approach of a storm. Stormy weather associated with stratus clouds usually does not normally include violent winds, and precipitation is usually light but steady, lasting up to 36 hours. Lightning is rarely associated with stratus clouds, however, sleet may occur. Fog is also associated with the appearance of stratus clouds. Precipitating stratus clouds are called *nimbostratus,* and clouds that cannot be determined as stratus or cumulus are referred to as *stratocumulus.* These latter types may be evolving from one type to another, indicating a change in atmospheric stability.

Clouds

Clouds display a wealth of information about present and future weather. They provide visible evidence of atmospheric motions, water content and instability. Clouds are also classified by the height of their base above ground level into three categories – low, middle, and high. There is also a group of potential storm clouds that have a vertical structure.

CREATION OF CLOUDS

Clouds are factors in climate that influence the radiation budget and therefore temperature. Clouds reflect a large fraction of solar radiation, resulting in surface cooling. On the other hand, clouds inhibit longwave radiation loss from the surface, which can lead to higher surface temperatures. The dominant process depends on many factors including cloud type and thickness, the magnitude of the solar radiation, and the albedo of the underlying surface. Clouds are composed of minute water droplets, ice crystals or a combination of the two that have condensed on such atmospheric particles as airborne dust, smoke, sea salt, chemical compounds, and meteoric fragments. Condensation on nuclei occurs at relative humidities near 100%. Many condensation nuclei such as salts are hygroscopic, that is, they have a special chemical affinity for water molecules and promote condensation at relative humidities under 100%.

CHANGING WEATHER

After fine, clear weather the first signs in the sky of a coming change are usually light streaks, curls, wisps, or mottled patches of white distant clouds, which increase and are followed by an overcast of murky vapor that grows into cloudiness. Usually the higher and more distant such clouds seem to be, the more gradual but general the coming change of weather will be.

Haze before cold front.

CLOUDS & UPCOMING WEATHER

High Altitude 16,500 to 45,000 feet
(Cirrus, Cirrostratus, Cirrocumulus)

Cloud: High Cirrus *p 442*
Indicates: Fair weather.
Followed by: Cirrostratus.
Indicates: Rain within 18 to 36 hours.
Cloud: Lower Cirrus - mare's hair *p 443*
Indicates: Bad weather.
Followed by: Cirrostratus.
Indicates: 80% chance of rain next 24 hours.
Followed by: Altostratus.
Indicates: Rain or snow in 6 to 12 hours.
Cloud: Cirrocumulus *p 442*
Indicates: Fair weather.

Middle Altitude 6,500 to 25,000 feet
(Altostratus and Altocumulus)

Cloud: Cirrus or Cirrostratus *p 441*
Then: Altostratus.
Indicates: 90% rain in 6 to 12 hours.
Cloud: Altostratus (low) *p 441*
Followed by: Towering Cumulus.
Indicates: Rain.

Low Altitude surface fog to 6,500 feet
(Stratocumulus, Stratus, Nimbostratus)

Cloud: Stratocumulus *p 439*
Indicates: In winter, short period of rain or snow.
Cloud: Stratocumulus
Indicates: Clearing in evening and cooler.
Cloud: Stratus *p 439*
Indicates: Drizzle.
Cloud: Nimbostratus *p 440*
Indicates: Long period of steady snow or rain.

Clouds below 50 feet and extending to the surface are classified as Fog.

Vertical Clouds 1,600 feet and up
(Cumulus, Cumulonimbus)

Cloud: Cumulus (warm weather) *p 454*
Indicates: High possibility of forming of cumulonimbus clouds.
Weather: Heavy thunder showers.

CUMULUS and CUMULONIMBUS are clouds with vertical development. Their bases are usually below 6,500 feet and the tops can sometimes exceed 60,000 feet.

CLASSIFICATION OF CLOUDS

	High Clouds	Middle Clouds	Low Clouds	Vertical Clouds
Group	16,500 feet to 45,000 feet 5-13 km	6,500 feet to 25,000 feet 2-8 km	Surface fog to 6,500 feet 0-2 km	1,600 feet and up 488 meters +
Cloud Type	Cirrus (Cu) Cirrostratus (Cist) Cirrocumulus (Cicu)	Altostratus (Ast) Altocumulus (Acu) Altocumulus (Acu)	Stratus (St) Nimbostratus (Nbst) Stratocumulus (Stcu)	Cumulus (Cu) Heavy Cumulus Cumulonimbus (Cunb)

CLOUDS THAT PREDICT RAIN

Cloud Type	Form of Precipitation
Stratus and Stratocumulus	Drizzle, freezing drizzle, snow grains
Thick Altostratus and Nimbostratus	Snow (continuous), rain (continuous)
Thick Altostratus and Stratocumulus	Snow (intermittent), rain (intermittent)
Altocumulus, Heavy Cumulus, Cumulonimbus	Snow showers, rain showers
Cumulonimbus	Snow pellets and/or hail, showers of ice pellets
Any cloud that will give rain	Hail
(Non-showery precipitation in the form of hail is usually the result of the rain drops freezing)	
No Cloud Necessary	Ice prisms deposit at night on cold surfaces

LOW CLOUDS

Low clouds, below 2,000 meters (6,500 feet), are either *cumulus or stratus,* or their precipitating counterparts. Low clouds may be identified by their height above nearby surrounding relief of known elevation. Most precipitation originates from low clouds because rain and snow from higher clouds usually evaporates before reaching the ground. As such, low clouds usually indicate precipitation, especially if they are more than 1,000 meters (3,000 feet) thick (clouds that appear dark at the base usually are at least that thick).

Stratus: Is a low, uniform, sheet-like cloud. When associated with fog or heavier precipitation, stratus clouds often become mixed with nimbostratus clouds. A slowly lifting fog layer often becomes a stratus cloud before dissipation. Fog formed over water bodies and driven inland by onshore winds, becomes stratus.
Composed of: Minute water droplets and if temperatures are low, ice crystals.
Shape: Gray with a uniform structure less base. A low hanging cloud that covers coasts or hills. Stratus clouds are similar to altostratus, but are much lower.
Weather: Precipitation is not usually associated with this cloud as it comes into existence by the lifting of lower layers of a fog bank. This may happen in a fog layer in which the bottom portion has evaporated, or where up-slope winds are blowing. These up-slope winds will cause the humidity in the air to condense forming stratus clouds. This often occurs as standing or banner clouds over islands in the ocean. Another form is called the 'stratus fractus' which brings unpleasant weather.

Stratocumulus: Appear as large, globular masses or rolls which look like dirty gray cotton balls. They often result from a layer of stable air lifted and mixed by wind blowing over rough terrain. Stratocumulus also form from the breaking up of a stratus layer and from the spreading out of cumulus clouds.
Composed of: Small water droplets, sometimes including large ones, soft hail and rarely snow flakes.
Shape: Gray or whitish and are rounded heap rolls broken or covering the sky.
Weather: These clouds usually indicate that there is no change in weather. Wind is normally light to moderate and can gradually shift direction.

Cumulus: Form as warmed "blobs" of air rise and visibly condense. They can also form as a cold air mass warms as it passes over a warmer surface. Relatively flat bases, dome-shaped tops, and a cauliflower appearance characterize cumulus. Fair weather cumulus indicate a shallow layer of instability. If cumulus clouds continue to vertically develop, they become towering cumulus and can eventually become cumulonimbus clouds.
Composed of: Suspended water droplets (which are sometimes super cooled) and by falling raindrops or snow flakes.
Shape: Dark gray in color and cover a large area across the sky. They are very thick and blot out the sun. A lower layer of clouds can form below them called 'facto cumulus' clouds. These clouds are formed by the heavy precipitation of Nimbostratus.
Weather: These clouds are not always seen due to the continuous precipitation they produce. Nimbostratus rarely produce lightning, thunder, or hail. They can be confused as a thick

Stratus

Stratus

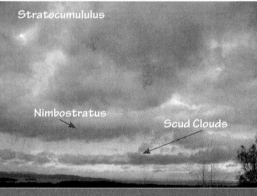
Vigra
Stratocumulus Vigra

Cumulus Humilis

Cumulus Humilis Fractus

Stratocumululus
Nimbostratus
Scud Clouds
Stratocumulus Undulatus

LOW CLOUDS

Cumulus Mediocris

Nimbostratus: Gray or dark, extensive cloud layer accompanied by continuous precipitation. They appear as dense threatening clouds, and often produce nearly continuous periods of precipitation. When precipitation becomes heavy, the bases of nimbostratus clouds become obscured. Ragged cloud shreds underneath nimbostratus clouds are called stratus fractus.

Composed of: Suspended water droplets (which are sometimes super cooled) and by falling raindrops or snow flakes.

Shape: Dark gray in color and cover a large area across the sky. They are very thick and blot out the sun. A lower layer of clouds can form below them called 'facto cumulus' clouds (scuds). These clouds are formed by the heavy precipitation of nimbostratus.

Weather: These clouds are not always seen due to the continuous precipitation they produce. Nimbostratus rarely produce lightning, thunder, or hail. They can be confused as a thick altostratus.

- General squalls are preceded, accompanied, or followed by clouds; but the dangerous white squall of the West Indies is indicated only by a rushing sound and by white wave crests to windward.
- A small, fast growing black cloud in violent motion, seen in the Tropics, is called the "bull's eye," and precedes the most terrible hurricanes.
- A horizontal streak or band of clouds immediately in front of the mountains on the east side of Salt Lake Valley is an indication of rain within one or two days. When black clouds cover the western horizon, rain will follow soon, and extend to the eastward over the valley.
- When you observe greenish tinted masses of composite cloud collect in the southeast and remain there for several hours, expect a succession of heavy rains and gales.
- When the clouds rise in terraces of white, soon will the country of the corn priests be pierced with the arrows of rain. Zuñi Indians
- When the cumulus clouds are smaller at sunset than they were at noon, expect fair weather.
- When cumulus clouds become heaped up to leeward during a strong wind at sunset, thunder may be expected during the night
- When Lookout Mountain (Tennessee) has its cap on, it will rain in six hours.
- Soft billowing cumulus clouds, in the afternoon, forecast fair weather (if they grow to cumulus nimbus, in the late afternoon, they indicate a fast and heavy rainstorm).
- Clouds, which move higher, are good signs of fair

PIONEER WEATHER PREDICTING

Cumulus Mediocris

Cumulus Humilis

Cumulus Congestus

- When on clear days isolated clouds drive over the zenith from the rain wind side, rain or snow will follow within twenty four hours - more likely within a few hours.
- Clouds flying against the wind indicate rain.
- It will not rain much as long as the sky is clear before the wind; but when clouds fall in against the wind, rain will soon follow.
- When a heavy cloud comes up in the southwest, and seems to settle back again, look out for a storm.
- If clouds at the same height drive up with the wind, and gradually become thinner and descend, expect fine weather.
- If the upper current of clouds come from the northwest in the morning, a fine day will follow.
- It never clouds up in a June night for a rain.
- If two strata of clouds appear in hot weather to move in different directions, they indicate thunder.
- If clouds float at different heights and rates, but generally in opposite directions, expect heavy rains.
- Clouds upon hills, if rising, do not bring rain; if falling, rain follows.

weather. Lower clouds indicate an increase in humidity, which in all probability means precipitation.
- "Low-hanging" clouds over mountains mean a weather change. If they get larger during the daytime, bad weather will arrive shortly. Diminishing clouds mean dry weather is on its way. High thin cirrus clouds arriving from the west often precede storms. When these thicken and are obscured by lower clouds, the chances increase for the arrival of rain or snow.
- Well defined cumulus clouds forming a few hours after sunrise, increasing toward the middle of the day, and decreasing toward evening are indicative of settled weather; if instead of subsiding in the evening and leaving the sky clear they keep increasing, they are indicative of wet weather.

MIDDLE CLOUDS

Middle clouds, between 2,000 and 6,000 meters (6,500 and 19,500 feet) above ground, have a prefix of "alto", and are called either *altostratus* or *altocumulus*. Middle clouds appear less distinct than low clouds because of their height. Warm "alto" clouds have sharper edges and are composed mainly of water droplets. Colder clouds, composed mainly of ice crystals, have distinct edges that grade gradually into the surrounding sky. *Middle clouds indicate potential storms, though usually hours away.* Altocumulus clouds that are scattered in a blue sky are called "fair weather" cumulus and suggest the arrival of high pressure and clear skies.

Lowering altostratus clouds with winds from the south indicate warm front conditions, decreasing air pressure, and an approaching storm system within 12 to 24 hours.

Altostratus: Relatively uniform gray to blue sheets covering the entire sky. They will signal the arrival of a warm front or approaching storm by appearing as a thinly veiled, whitish-gray sheet. The sunlight dimly shines through this higher altostratus cloud deck as though shining through frosted glass. The altostratus usually becomes thicker or lowers until the sun gradually disappears and assumes a grayer, uniform appearance. Light precipitation usually will form in lower altostratus clouds.

Composed of: Super cooled water droplets and ice crystals.

Shape: Gray or bluish cloud cover, thin and smooth that might blanket the whole sky. They look dark and opaque when the sun or moon tries to shine through.

Nickname: "A watery sun".

Weather: Can produce a light continuous precipitation.

Altocumulus: White or gray patches of solid cloud. They can be composed of both water and ice crystals of varying compositions. These clouds are associated with many types of approaching frontal systems and often signal a change in the weather in the next few hours. Altocumulus develops from dissolving altostratus or lifted cumulus. Altocumulus clouds can appear as layered cells and also be at differing altitudes.

Composed of: Small water droplets that can be super cooled.

Shape: They are level heap clouds that can be in a checkerboard pattern of white and gray layers seldom covering the whole sky. They can be lenticular (lens-shaped) and castellanus (looking like small towers) and floccus (chaotic clouds of thunder skies).

Nickname: "Mackerel Sky" (see Cirrocumulus)

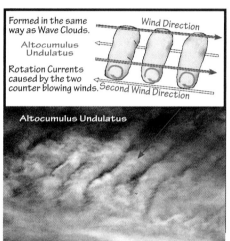

Formed in the same way as Wave Clouds.

Altocumulus Undulatus

Rotation Currents caused by the two counter blowing winds.

Wind Direction

Second Wind Direction

Altocumulus Undulatus

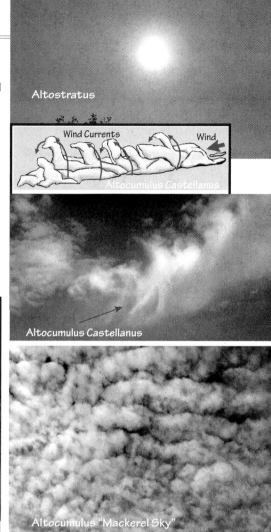

Altostratus

Wind Currents

Wind

Altocumulus Castellanus

Altocumulus Castellanus

Altocumulus "Mackerel Sky"

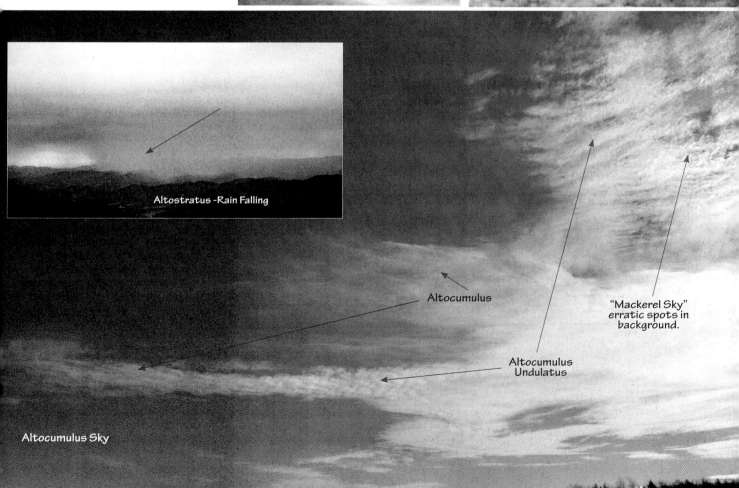

Altostratus - Rain Falling

Altocumulus

Altocumulus Undulatus

"Mackerel Sky" erratic spots in background.

Altocumulus Sky

Cirrus at Sunset

Cirrus Mare's Tails

Cirrus Fibratus

Cirrus Intortus

HIGH CLOUDS

High clouds, higher than 6,000 meters (19,500 feet), are cirrus, cirrostratus, and cirrocumulus. They are usually frozen clouds with a fibrous structure and blurred outlines. The sky is often covered with a thin veil of cirrus that partly obscures the sun or, at night, produces a ring of light around the moon. The arrival of cirrus indicates moisture aloft and the approach of a storm system. Precipitation is often 24 to 36 hours away. As the storm approaches, the cirrus thickens and lowers becoming altostratus and eventually stratus. Temperatures warm, humidity rises, and winds approach from the south or southeast.

Cirrus: Thin, feathery clouds in patches or narrow bands. Clouds arranged in bands or connected with cirrostratus or altostratus, may be a sign of approaching bad weather. Wispy cirrus appearing to have trailing tails or looking like "mares' tails" indicate upper level wind direction. Cirrus clouds herald incoming bad weather or indicate that stormy weather is still several hundreds of miles away. These clouds are traveling at 100 mph (160 km/h).

Composed of: Ice particles or crystals.

Shape: Slightly dense veil from which narrow bands of tenuous filaments emerge which produce hooks and banner like forms.

Nickname: "Mare's Tails"

Weather Prediction: There is a strong cyclonic weather system upwind and there might be strong winds within the next 8-15 hours especially at sea in the winter. Temperature will become cooler and if windy it can become bitter in winter.

Cirrostratus: Thin, whitish cloud layers appearing as a sheet or veil. The ice crystals composing cirrostratus may produce halos. Sun will appear slightly dimmed through cirrostratus clouds. Gradually thickening cirrostratus will eventually transition into high level altostratus clouds. They usually signal the approach of a warm front by 12 to 24 hours.

Composed of: Ice crystals

Shape: High, thin, whitish, smooth and transparent. Can be seen by the halos they form around the sun or moon. These halos are caused by the reflection of light in ice crystals.

Cirrocumulus: Thin, closely-spaced, individual elements, appearing as small cotton balls. Large layers of cirrocumulus are called "mackerel sky." They signal upper level instability and can precede thunderstorms by up to 12 hours.

Composed of: Small ice crystals super cooled water or mixture of both.

Shape: High sheets of white balls or puffs with distinct outlines having a rippled regular appearance. They can be confused with altocumulus which are at a lower elevation.

Cirrus Fibratus

Cirrus Radiatus

Cirrostratus Nebulosus with halo

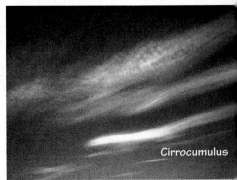

Cirrocumulus

Cirrostratus Fibratus : Sunset

Cirrus clouds as seen from an airplane.

PIONEER WEATHER INDICATORS
CIRRUS

- When cirrus merge into cirro stratus, and when cumulus increase toward evening and become lower, expect wet weather.
- When cirro cumulus clouds appear in winter, expect warm and wet weather. When threads of cirrus clouds are brushed back from a westerly direction, expect rain and wind.
- If cirrus clouds dissolve and appear to vanish, it is an indication of fine weather.
- The longer the dry weather has lasted, the less is rain likely to follow the cloudiness of cirrus.
- If cirrus clouds form in fine weather with a falling barometer, it is almost sure to rain.
- Cirrus clouds announce the east wind. If their streaks point upward, they indicate rain; if downward, wind and dry weather.
- When cloud streamers point upward, the clouds are falling, or descending, and rain is indicated; when cloud streamers point downward, the clouds are ascending, and dry weather is indicated.

MACKEREL SKY & MARE'S TAILS

- Mackerel scales and mare's tails make lofty ships carry low sails. (It will be windy)
- Mackerel clouds in sky, expect more wet than dry.
- A mackerel sky, not twenty four hours dry.
- The mackerel clouds always indicate storm if they first appear about 15° north of west. (Kansas)

Halo Effect

Cirrostratus Nebulosus

Cirrocumulus Undulatus

HIGH CLOUDS

Cirrus Uncinus "Mare's Tails"

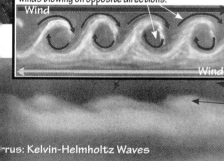

Rotational currents produced by winds blowing on opposite directions.

Wind

Wind

...rus: Kelvin-Helmholtz Waves

Cirrus: Kelvin-Helmholtz Waves

Cirrostratus Nebulosus

Contrail being dissipated by high altitude winds

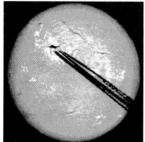

Contrails in front of the Sun.

Contrails

Contrails are formed by the water vapor added to the air from the exhaust processes in aircraft engines. If sufficient water vapor is released into a clear, cold and air mass, a cloud of crystals will form behind the engine in a linear fashion.

Contrails

Cirrocumulus Undulatus

ICE STORM

It is usually used to describe occasions when damaging accumulations of ice are expected during freezing rain situations. Significant accumulations of ice pull down trees and utility lines resulting in the loss of power and communications. These accumulations of ice make walking and driving extremely dangerous. Significant ice accumulation are accumulations of 1/4" or greater.

Freezing Rain

PRECIPITATION

1 The process where water vapor condenses in the atmosphere to form water droplets that fall to the Earth as rain, sleet, snow, hail, etc.

2 As used in hydrology, precipitation is the discharge of water, in a liquid or solid state, out of the atmosphere, generally onto a land or water surface. It is the common process by which atmospheric water becomes surface, or subsurface water.

The term "precipitation" is also commonly used to designate the quantity of water that is precipitated. Precipitation includes rainfall, snow, hail, and sleet, and is therefore a more general term than rainfall.

FREEZING RAIN & ICE STORMS

Ice storms cause a yearly average of 10 fatalities, 600 injuries, and 100's of millions of dollars in damage. Ice storms occur most frequently during the months of December and January. Freezing rain occurrences increase rapidly from October through December and decrease at a slower rate from February through April. Freezing rain is frequently found in a narrow band on the cold side of a warm front.

Hoar frost on a plant leaf.

Hoar frost on a plant leaf.

FROST WEATHER PREDICTORS

- Hoar frost indicates rain.
- Heavy frosts bring heavy rain; no frosts, no rain. (California.)
- Dew on grass indicates there will be no rain as the dew (moisture) is deposited out of the air onto the colder vegetation.

MIST

A visible aggregate of minute water particles suspended in the atmosphere that reduces visibility to less than 7 miles, but greater than or equal to 5/8 miles.

DRIZZLE

Fairly uniform precipitation composed exclusively of fine drops with diameters less than 0.02" (0.5 mm) which are very close together. Drizzle appears to float while following air currents, although unlike fog droplets, it falls to the ground. The intensity of drizzle is based solely on visibility. Drizzle intensity versus visibility is measured as: Light you can see >1/2 mile; Moderate 1/4 to 1/2; Heavy <1/2 mile.

FREEZING RAIN

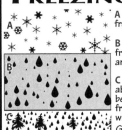

A - Temperature below freezing. Snow is falling.

B - Warm layer above freezing and snow melts and falls as rain.

C - Cold layer of air just above the ground. Rain becomes supercool and freezes upon impact with any cold surface. Ground

Freezing rain forms as falling snow falls (**A**) through a layer of warm air (**B**) were the snow can *completely melt* and become rain. This falling rain passes through a layer of cold air - below freezing - (**C**) just above the ground and cools to a temperature below freezing. The rain drops do not freeze, but are *supercooled*. Upon striking any cold surface the supercooled drops *instantly* freeze, forming a thin film of ice which is called *freezing rain*. The layers of thin ice film can build up and their weight can down power lines and branches of trees.

RIME ICE

It is a rough, milky, opaque ice formed by the instantaneous freezing of small supercooled droplets as they strike a cold surface. The fact that droplets maintain their nearly spherical shape upon freezing and thus trap air between them gives the ice its opaque appearance and makes it porous and brittle

FROST

The formation of ice crystals on the ground or other surfaces in the form of scales, needles, feathers, or fans. Frost develops under conditions similar to dew, except the temperatures of the Earth's surface and earthbound objects fall below 32°F. As with the term "freeze", this condition is primarily significant during the growing season. If a frost period is sufficiently severe to end the growing season or delay its beginning, it is commonly referred to as a "killing frost". Because frost is primarily an event that occurs as the result of radiational cooling, it frequently occurs with a temperature reading in the mid 30's. Frost may also form on aircraft in flight during descent from subfreezing into a warmer, moist layer below. This may cause considerable consternation if the windshield glazes over or the windows frost over.

A street after a hail storm.

FORMATION OF HAIL

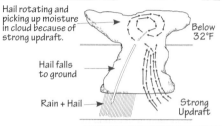

Frozen drops become larger due to added moisture

Drop Freezes

Rain Drops

Picks Up Moisture

Hail picked up by updraft.

Temperature below 32°F

Hail falls to ground.

Hail rotating and picking up moisture in cloud because of strong updraft.

Below 32°F

Hail falls to ground

Rain + Hail

Strong Updraft

HAIL

Precipitation in the form of balls or lumps usually consisting of concentric layers of ice. A thunderstorm is classified as severe when it produces hail 3/4″ or larger in diameter. Individual hailstones are an accumulation of frozen raindrops and snow produced by intense thunderstorms. There formation occurs in the central updraft where snowflakes and liquid water form ice pellets. These pellets will continue to grow as more and more water droplets and snowflakes accumulate around the initial pellet. When the pellet reaches the bottom of the cloud and it is too heavy to be lifted back into the cloud by the updraft - it will fall to the ground. If the pellet were smaller or the updraft very strong the pellet would be carried back into the cloud and it will accumulate more ice and grow larger. The hailstone will reach the ground as ice as it will not be in the warm air below the thunderstorm long enough to melt. Hail size is usually reported by the size of familiar circular or spherical objects (e.g., various coins or balls) as dime, nickel and quarter (coin) size hail, golfball size hail and baseball size hail. The following table shows hail size estimates:

The accumulation of numerous smaller hail stones is shown in this large hail stone.

Layers in a hail stone showing the hail stone's numerous up and down rotation caused by the strong updraft.

Baseball sized hail approximately four inches in diameter.

An accumulation of hail stones next to a one inch ruler.

Pea	0.25″	Golf ball	1.75″
Marble/Mothball	0.50″	Hen Egg	2.00″
Penny	0.75″	Tennis Ball	2.50″
Nickel	0.88″	Baseball	2.75″
Quarter	1.00″	Tea Cup	3.00″
Half Dollar	1.25″	Grapefruit	4.00″
Walnut/Ping Pong Ball	1.50″	Softball	4.50″

DEW

Dew is a collection of water droplets on a colder surface than the surrounding air. It is condensation which occurs when the temperature of a surface is low enough to allow the moisture in the warmer air, above the surface to condense.

Conditions
• Forms on still clear nights. Clear nights let the ground radiate the heat absorbed from the sun during the day causing it to get colder than the surrounding air. If the adjacent air is humid, condensation can occur as dew.
• If this humid air layer is thick, radiation fog and dew can form.
• Low humidity in the air at higher levels.

Characteristics
• Usually evaporates by mid-morning.

Special Information
• Can cause roads to become slippery.
• Can cause logs and bridges on hiking paths to be very slippery.

Dew on grass in the morning.

Dew on a spider web in the morning.

DEW

Large crystal frost pattern on a window.

Frost pattern on a window.

A western snowstorm in the 1930's.

FROST

Frost is formed by condensation of moisture from humid air on a surface below 32°F (0°C).

Conditions

- Its formation is similar to the formation of dew or radiation fog. It usually forms on still clear nights.

FROST TYPES

Hoar Frost: forms when a thin layer of humid air forms ice crystals on a below freezing cold surface. These crystals go directly from being water vapor to crystals without passing through the liquid water stage (dew).

Window Frost: are large crystals that form on scratches, deposits or other nuclei on the insides of windows. They form when the window pane is extremely cold outside and there is relatively high humidity in the room. This is not really a frost but actually ice and is similar to ice forming on freezing water.

Special Information

- Frost can form on cold roads and on bridges. This ice is so thin and hard to see that it is called 'black ice'.

SNOW

Precipitation of snow crystals, mostly branched in the form of six-pointed stars. It usually falls steadily for several hours or more. Qualifiers, such as occasional or intermittent, are used when a steady, prolonged (for several hours or more) fall is not expected. Like drizzle, its intensity is based on visibility.

The amount of snow that falls is highly dependent upon temperature. For example, at 10°F, one inch of precipitation will produce 30" of snow. At 20°F, one inch of precipitation will produce 20" of snow. At 30°F, one inch of precipitation produces 10" of snow. At freezing, one inch precipitation will produce approximately 6" of snow.

Blizzard: A winter storm which produces the following conditions for at least 3 hours: Sustained winds or frequent gusts to 35 miles per hour or greater, and considerable falling and/or blowing snow reducing visibility to less than 1/4 mile.

Snowing limit in the Winter.

Snowing limit in the Summer.

Russia

Canada USA

Winter snow cover & sea ice extent.

A rain shaft falling in a bay.

Rain below a altostratus cloud.

RAIN

Rain develops when growing cloud droplets become too heavy to remain in the cloud and as a result, fall toward the surface as rain. Rain can also begin as ice crystals that collect each other to form large snowflakes. As the falling snow passes through the freezing level into warmer air, the flakes melt and collapse into rain drops.

Snow Crystal

A local rainstorm seen in the distance.

Fog

A visible aggregate of minute water particle (droplets) which are based at the Earth's surface and reduces horizontal visibility to less than 5/8 statue mile, and unlike drizzle, it does not fall to the ground. It occurs most frequently in coastal regions because of the great water vapor content of the air. However, it can occur anywhere. The rapidity with which fog can form makes it especially hazardous. It forms by any atmospheric process that does one of the following: Cools the air to its dew point, or Raises the dew point to the air temperature. Names given to fog types identify their methods of formation. The principle types are radiation fog, ice fog, advection fog, upslope fog, rain induced fog, and steam fog. These types of fog are called "dense" when the surface visibility is equal to or less than 1/4 miles.

Fog Weather Predictors

- Three foggy or misty mornings indicate rain. (Oregon.)
- A rising fog indicates fair weather; if the fog settles down expect rain.
- Fog from seaward, fair weather; fog from landward, rain. (New England.)

Advection

The horizontal movement of an air mass that causes changes in the physical properties of the air such as temperature and moisture. Commonly used with temperatures, i.e., "warm air advection", or moisture, i.e., "moisture advection".

Low Stratus Clouds
Stratus Fog

Advection Fog

ADVECTION FOG

Fog that forms as warmer, moist air moves over a cold ground. The air is cooled to saturation by the loss of heat to the cold ground. Unlike radiation fog, advection fog may form under cloudy skies and with moderate to strong winds. Initial stability is relatively unimportant since low level cooling makes the air unstable near the ground.

Advection fog blown by the wind up onto the land.

Fog

Lake

Cold Land

ADVECTION FOG

Advection fog on Golden Gate Bridge

ADVECTION FOG

A fog formed by condensation as radiation fog. The difference is that advection fog is caused by moist air moving over a colder surface. Movement of air is called advection. Radiation forms during still nights.

Conditions For Advection Fog
- Forms when humid air moves over a colder surface.

Characteristics
- Is a low-level cloud that can form over land or sea.
- Can often be recognized by its horizontal movement. Radiation fog forms during still clear nights.
- Radiation fog forms during the night so that a fog forming during the day will probably be advection fog.

Variants of Advection Fog
Sea Fog: is a fog that forms when moist air above a warm current moves over a colder current. Under certain weather sea fog can move over adjacent land.

Steam Fog: Occurs when cold air passes over warm water.

Special Information
- Limits visibility on land and sea.
- Foggiest spot is Cape Disappointment WA with an average of over 100 days of fog every year.

Valley Fog

Valley Fog

Valley Fog: in Alaska

Valley Fog

Advection Fog

Valley Fog: note sign

FOG AREA

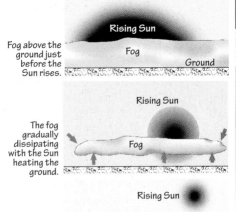

Rising Sun

Fog

Ground

Fog above the ground just before the Sun rises.

Rising Sun

Fog

The fog gradually dissipating with the Sun heating the ground.

Rising Sun

With more heating the fog just disappears.

Fog

STRATUS FOG VALLEY FOG

Is a very low thin cloud or bank of fog that covers a large area.

Conditions
- The formation of fog stratus is the sun's effect on radiation fog.
- The sun first heats the ground adjacent to radiation fog causing its perimeter to get smaller. At the same time the rays start to heat the ground below the radiation fog causing the bottom of the radiation fog to evaporate. This results in a layer of fog stratus which does not touch the ground.
- There is usually no wind and the fog stratus seems to lift off the ground. It does not lift but the base evaporates.
- The fog usually evaporates and disappears by mid-morning.

Characteristics
- If there is a slight breeze the fog might migrate horizontally while it gradually disappears.
- A mist or slight drizzle might occur below a thick layer of fog stratus.

Special Information
- Fog stratus can cover extensive areas and might limit visibility in elevated areas.

UPSLOPE FOG

Upslope Fog

Upslope Fog

UPSLOPE FOG

It forms as air is cooled adiabatically by blowing up sloping terrain. The upslope cooling may form clouds concurrently with the fog. As is the case with advection fog, upslope fog can form with moderate to strong winds under cloudy skies. In stable air, upslope fog will form as soon as the air is cooled to the surface dew point. Temperature and dew point close at about 4°F for each 1,000 feet rise in altitude. When air is unstable, convective clouds may form; fog forms at the surface where the ground level is at or above the condensation level.

Is a cloud formed by air blown up a slope.

Conditions
- Upslope fog is a cloud formed by moist air being blown up a slope of a hill or mountain.
- It moves on or close to the ground.
- Air currents forming the upslope fog are very weak.

Characteristics
- Is very common in hilly areas especially in areas not far from bodies of water.
- Can occur in the summer after a humid rainstorm.

SIMILAR CLOUDS

The upslope fog can be confused with orographic stratus as they are similar except that the air currents in orographic stratus are relatively strong. Orographic stratus clouds nearly always form near the top of a peak or above a peak. Upslope fog usually forms closer to the base of a slope - especially on mountains.

Special Information
- Can be hazardous to small aircraft.

RADIATION FOG

This is the most common cause of fog and it is actually a cloud on the ground. The fog produced results from the air near the ground being cooled to saturation by contact with the cold ground. The cooling of the ground results from night time loss of heat from the Earth to space (terrestrial radiation). Favorable conditions for radiation fog are clear sky, little or no wind, and high relative humidity. It occurs in stable air and is primarily a night time or early morning phenomenon. As the Earth and the lower layers of the atmosphere warm during the day, air that was stable during the early morning hours may become unstable - at least in the lower levels. For this reason visibility usually improves as the temperature rises during the day. Mixing in the lower levels disperses the fog into a thicker layer, and eventually it evaporates into the warmer air. When cloud layers form aloft over a radiation fog and retard heating from the sun, visibility improvement is very slow. Similar to Ground Fog and Valley Fog.

Conditions for Radiation Fog

The radiation cooling of the ground produces condensation in the warmer humid layer of air above the surface. A thin layer of humid air will produce a coating of dew and a thick layer of air will produce radiation fog.

Characteristics

- A fog that is always found at ground level as it is a cloud on the ground.
- Forms on clear and still nights.
- It can be 3 feet (1m) to 1000 feet (300 m) thick.
- Depending on its thickness it gradually disperses at sunrise.

Special Information

- As the fog limits visibility (possibly to 3 feet) it can be dangerous when driving.
- A clear day usually follows a night that produced radiation fog.

RADIATION FOG

Radiation Fog

Radiation Fog

Radiation Fog on snow.

STEAM FOG

It forms as cold air moves over warm water. Water evaporates from the warm water surface and immediately condenses in the cold air above. Heat from the water warms the lower levels of the air creating a shallow layer of instability. It rises like smoke from the warm surface. The low level convection can become quite turbulent. Steam fog is most common in Arctic regions where it is called "Arctic Sea Smoke", but it can and does occur occasionally at all latitudes.

OTHER CLOUDS

ORTHOGRAPHIC

Orthographic Cloud

Valley Fog

OROGRAPHIC STRATUS

Elevation: 0-1,000 ft (0-300m)
Composed of: Small water droplets, sometimes including large ones, soft hail and possibly snow flakes.
Formation: Humid air blown by wind up the slope of a mountain. As it becomes colder at higher elevations condensation occurs. When the cloud descends on the other side of the landform it dissipates. The cloud seems to stand on top of the mountain but it actually is in continual formation and dissipation.
Shape: The shape and size of the cloud depends upon the amount of humidity in the air mass, the height and shape of the mountain, the strength of the wind, and the angle at which the wind hits the obstacle.
Weather: These clouds are created by an obstacle and not a weather system.

Orthographic Cloud

Wind

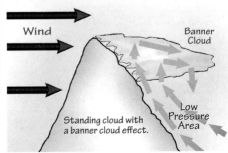

Standing Cloud

Banner Cloud

Wind

Upslope flow occurs when air is forced to rise and cool due to terrain features such as hills or mountains. If the cooling is sufficient, water vapor condenses into clouds. Additional cooling results in rain or snow. It can cause extensive cloudiness and increased amounts of precipitation in higher terrain.

Wind

Banner Cloud

Low Pressure Area

Standing cloud with a banner cloud effect.

BANNER CLOUD (OROGRAPHIC STRATUS)

Formation: Differs from a normal orographic cloud in that the wind strikes the hill top horizontally causing a low pressure area on the lee side of the peak. Low pressure and less wind will let condensation form a banner cloud.
Shape: The shape of a banner on the lee side of the peak.

VIRGA

Virga
Thin mist of rain falling which evaporates before it reaches the ground.

Rain Virga

Nimbostratus with Virga

Virga in the winter.

Ice Crystal Virga

Altocumulus Glaciations
Altocumulus cloud gradually disintegrating & producing streamers of ice crystals.

LENTICULAR CLOUDS

They are lens-shaped because they are formed by the movement of air flowing over mountain ranges. The ups and downs between the ranges causes a frequency vibration in the wind pattern that is maintained for a certain distance after passing over the mountains.
The lowest level of wind forms a Cap Cloud and this will form a Rotor Cloud that has a round possibly sausage shape.

Lenticular Cloud

Lenticular Cloud

Lenticular Cloud or possibly a Rotor Cloud

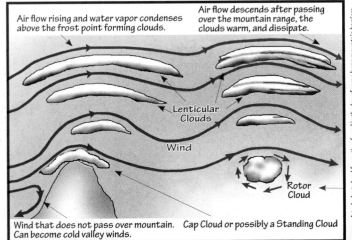

Air flow rising and water vapor condenses above the frost point forming clouds.

Air flow descends after passing over the mountain range, the clouds warm, and dissipate.

Lenticular Clouds

Wind

Rotor Cloud

Wind that does not pass over mountain. Can become cold valley winds.

Cap Cloud or possibly a Standing Cloud

Cloud Streets: Rows of cumulus or cumulus-type clouds aligned parallel to the low-level flow. Cloud streets sometimes can be seen from the ground, but are seen best on satellite photographs.

REEF CUMULUS CLOUDS

Hot air, from the Sun warmed ground, rises and condenses in the cool air at higher elevations. This can cause evening storms and lightning.

Hot Moist Air

Wind Direction

Second Wind Direction

Rotation currents caused by the two counter blowing winds.

WAVE CLOUDS

GRAVITY WAVES RIPPLE

Over marine stratocumulus clouds. Similar to the ripples that occur when a pebble is thrown into a still pond, such "gravity waves" sometimes appear when the relatively stable and stratified air masses associated with stratocumulus cloud layers are disturbed by a vertical trigger from the underlying terrain, or by a thunderstorm updraft or some other vertical wind shear. The stratocumulus cellular clouds that underlie the wave feature are associated with sinking air that is strongly cooled at the level of the cloud-tops. Such clouds are common over mid-latitude oceans when the air is unperturbed by cyclonic or frontal activity.

ATMOSPHERIC VORTICES

This is a turbulent atmospheric flow pattern known as the von Karman vortex street. The alternating double row of vortices can form in the wake of an obstacle, in this instance the eastern Pacific island of Guadalupe. The vortex pattern is made visible by the marine stratocumulus clouds around the island. The areas within the vortex centers (going around the mountain on the island) tend to be clear because the rotating motions induce a vertical wind component that can break up the cloud deck.

SWIRILS OF LACE

The turbulent atmospheric eddies (von Karman Vortex Streets) form in the wake of an obstacle, in this instance the 1050-meter-high summit on the island of Socorro, Mexico. The surrounding clouds make the vortex patterns visible. To the northeast, much subtler disturbances are associated with the tiny Isla San Benedicto.
NASA/GSFC/LaRC/JPL, MISR Team

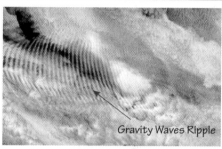

Gravity Waves Ripple

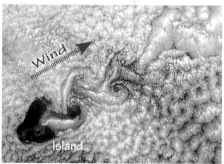

Wind

Island

Guadaloupe Eddy ; von Karman Vortex Street

Swirils of Lace

Wind

Island

LAKE EFFECT

LAKE EFFECT IN THIS **NOAA** IMAGE

Lake effect snow in the Great Lake region. This is the region in North America that has frequent lake effect storms and is called the "snow belt". As the wind moves over the relatively warm surface of the lakes, clouds form downstream producing occasionally heavy snow in a rather narrow area. Note the snow cover, especially visible in the lower peninsula of Michigan where lake effect snow has fallen.

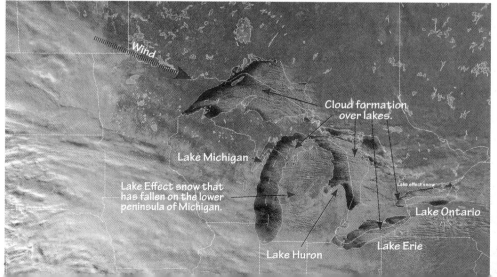

Wind

Cloud formation over lakes.

Lake Michigan

Lake Effect snow that has fallen on the lower peninsula of Michigan.

Lake effect snow

Lake Ontario

Lake Erie

Lake Huron

MOUNTAIN WEATHER INDICATORS

Inclement weather sitting behind the mountains.

APPROACHING TRAVELING STORMS

- A thin veil of cirrus clouds spreads over the sky, thickening and lowering until altostratus clouds are formed. The same trend is shown at night, when a halo forms around the moon and then darkens until only the glow of the moon is visible. When there is no moon, cirrus clouds only dim the stars while altostratus clouds hide them completely.
- Low clouds which have been persistent on lower slopes begin to rise at the time upper clouds appear.
- Various layers of clouds move in at different heights and become more abundant.
- Lens-shaped clouds accompanying strong winds lose their streamlined shape, and other cloud types appear in increasing amounts.
- A change in the direction of the wind is accompanied by a rapid rise in temperature not caused by solar radiation. This may also indicate a warm damp period.
- A light green haze is observed shortly after sunrise in mountain regions above timberline.

FORECASTING WEATHER IN THE MOUNTAINS

Weather at different elevations and areas, even within the same general region, may differ significantly due to variations in cloud height, temperature, winds, and barometric pressure. Therefore, general reports and forecasts must be used in conjunction with the locally observed weather conditions to produce reliable weather forecasts for a particular mountain area.

Traveling storm in the mountains.

LOCAL DISTURBANCES

Indications of local thunderstorm showers, or squally weather are:

- An increase in size and rapid thickening of scattered cumulus clouds during the afternoon.
- The approach of a line of large cumulus or cumulonimbus clouds with an advance guard of altocumulus clouds. At night, increasing lightning windward of the prevailing wind gives the same warning.
- Massive cumulus clouds hanging over a ridge or summit, at night or in the daytime.

STRONG WINDS

Indications of strong winds seen at a distance may be:

- Plumes of blowing snow from the crests of ridges and peaks or ragged shreds of cloud moving rapidly.
- Persistent lens-shaped clouds, or a band of clouds, over high peaks and ridges or downwind from them.
- A turbulent and ragged banner cloud which hangs to the lee side of a peak.

FAIR WEATHER

Fair weather may be associated with:

- A cloudless sky and shallow fog or layers of smoke or haze at valley bottoms in the early morning; or from a vantage point of high elevation, a cloudless sky that is quite blue down to the horizon, or down to where a level haze layer forms a secondary horizon.
- Conditions under which small cumulus clouds appearing in the forenoon do not increase, but decrease or vanish during the day.
- Clear skies, except for a low cloud deck which does not rise or thicken during the day.

DURING PRECIPITATION

When there is precipitation and the sky cannot be seen:

- Very small snowflakes or ice crystals indicate that the clouds above are thin and there is fair weather at high altitudes.
- A steady fall of snowflakes or raindrops indicates that the precipitation has begun at high levels, and that bad weather is likely to be encountered on ridges and peaks.

Stratocumulus in the mountains.

A wall cloud of a thunderstorm passing through a mountain valley.

DOWNSLOPE/UPSLOPE FLOW

Air that descends down a mountain chain or over sloping terrain (pressurized air moving from high pressure to low pressure), resulting in subsequent drying, and in some cases, dramatic warming of air that can quickly melt a snowcover. Local names for downslope winds or "foehn winds" in the western United States are Chinook Winds, East Winds, North Winds and Mono Winds. Usually associated with little or no clouds. On the other hand, the upslope flow is representative of air being lifted by rising terrain and is normally associated with extensive clouds and/or precipitation.

Bad Weather in Mountain Areas

Most of the bad weather experienced in mountain regions is a result of...

- Local storms in the form of thunderstorms with or without showers.
- Traveling storms which may be accompanied by radical and severe weather changes over a broad area. Usually, each type of storm may be identified by the clouds associated with it.
- Seasonal moisture-bearing winds of the monsoon type which bring consistently bad weather to some mountain ranges for weeks at a time.

Characteristics of Mountain Weather

Mountain weather is erratic. Hurricane force winds and gentle breezes may occur just short distances apart. The weather in exposed places contrasts sharply with the weather in sheltered areas. Weather changes in a single day can be so variable that in the same locality one may experience hot sun and cool shade, high winds and calm, gusts of rain or snow, and then perhaps intense sunlight again.

This variability results from the life cycle of a local storm or from the movement of traveling storms. In addition, the effects of storms are modified by the following local influences:

- Variation in altitude.
- Differences in exposure to the sun and to prevailing winds.
- Distortion of storm movements and the normal winds by irregular mountain topography.

These local influences dominate summer storms.

Cloudiness & Precipitation in Mountain Areas

Cloudiness and precipitation increase with height until a zone of maximum precipitation is reached; above this zone they decrease. Maximum cloudiness and precipitation occurs near the 5900 feet (1800 m) elevation in middle latitudes and at lower levels as the Poles are approached. Usually a dense forest marks the zone of maximum rainfall.

Slopes facing the prevailing wind are cloudier, foggier, and receive heavier precipitation than those protected from the wind, especially when large bodies of water lie to the windward side. However, at night and in winter, valleys are likely to be colder and foggier than higher slopes. Heads of valleys often have more clouds and precipitation than adjacent ridges and the valley floor.

Fog in Mountains

On windward slopes, persistent fog, as well as cloudiness and precipitation, frequently can last for days. They are caused by the local barrier effect of the mountain on prevailing winds. Any cloud bank appears as a fog from within. Fog limits visibility and causes whiteout conditions.

High Mountain Clouds

These clouds are formed by the wind blowing across water and rising when moving over mountains. The humidity in the air condenses and forms mountain clouds. The loss of temperature is approximately $5 1/2°F$ ($3°C$) per 1000 feet (304 m). Rain has fallen on the windward side and the wind pushes over the hill and upon descending the slope the air will warm up and the relative humidity will become very dry as it has lost its humidity on the windward side. This phenomenon causes the Chinook of the North America plains, the Santa Ana of Southern California.

Traveling Storms

The most severe storms involve strong winds and heavy precipitation, and are the result of widespread atmospheric disturbances which generally travel in an easterly direction. Traveling storms result from the interaction of cold and warm air. The center of the storm is a moving low pressure area where cyclonic winds are generally the strongest. Extending from this storm center is a warm front which marks the advancing thrust of warm air, and the cold front which precedes the onrushing cold and gusty winds. The sequence of weather events, with the approach and passing of a traveling storm, depends on the stage of the storm's development, and whether the location of its path is to the north or south of a given mountain area. Generally, scattered cirrus clouds merge into a continuous sheet which thickens and lowers gradually until it becomes altostratus. At high levels, this cloud layer appears to settle. Lower down, a Stratus deck may form overhead. A storm passing to the north may bring warm temperatures with southerly winds and partial clearing for a while before colder air with thundershowers or squally conditions moves in from the northwest. However, local cloudiness often obscures frontal passages in the mountains. The storm may go so far to the north that only the cold front phenomena of heavy clouds, squalls, thundershowers, and colder weather are experienced. The same storm passing to the south would be accompanied by a gradual wind shift from northeasterly to northwesterly, with a steady temperature fall and continuous precipitation. After colder weather moves in, the clearing at high altitudes is usually slower than the onset of cloudiness, and storm conditions may last several days longer than in the lowlands.

Alberta Clipper

A fast moving low pressure system that moves southeast out of Canadian Province of Alberta (southwest Canada) through the Plains, Midwest, and Great Lakes region usually during the winter. This low pressure area is usually accompanied by light snow, strong winds, and colder temperatures. Another variation of the same system is called a "Saskatchewan Screamer".

Frequently the mountains will be in the clouds.

Clouds and weather finding their way through mountain passes.

The build up an afternoon storm.

Cloud patterns formed by air flowing over mountains.

Chinook Wind

A warm, dry wind that descends the eastern slope of the Rocky Mountains. The warmth and dryness of this wind can quickly melt and evaporate snow cover. Another name for this type of wind is "foehn".

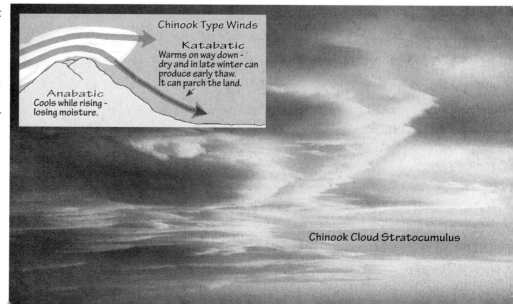

Chinook Type Winds

Katabatic
Warms on way down - dry and in late winter can produce early thaw. It can parch the land.

Anabatic
Cools while rising - losing moisture.

Chinook Cloud Stratocumulus

VERTICAL CLOUDS

Cumulus building up in the afternoon.

Simple afternoon Cumulus clouds can grow into violent Cumulonimbus clouds.

VERTICAL CLOUDS

CUMULUS (CU)

Composed of: Close packed, small water droplets usually super cooled. Larger droplets usually fall from the base of the cumulus cloud as rain. Ice crystals can form in the upper parts of a large cumulus cloud.

Shape: The cumulus clouds are formed by the vertical movement of air currents. They are dense in appearance and have a clearly defined outline (with the exception of the cumulus-strato cumulus combination). These clouds form over land in the afternoon and over water at night.

CUMULONIMBUS (CB)

Composed of: In upper portion of ice crystals and super cooled water droplets.

Shape: This is a billowing cloud of great height rising up to the high cloud range. The upper portion of this cloud is frequently classed as a cirrus variety because of their great height. The high portion nearly always assumes a distinctive anvil shape which is caused by the strong horizontal winds (jet stream) that flatten the towering rounded heads. This cloud causes lightening, thunder and often torrential rain and hail.

Weather: These clouds are summer clouds producing violent thunderstorms and possibly tornadoes.

Some vertical clouds indicate serious weather ahead...

Towering Cumulus clouds have bases below 2,000 meters (6,500 feet) and tops often over 6,000 meters (19,500 feet). They are the most dangerous of all types and usually do not occur when temperatures at the surface are below 32° F. They indicate extreme instability in the atmosphere, with rapidly rising air currents caused by solar heating of the surface or air rising over a mountain barrier. Mature towering cumulus clouds often exhibit frozen stratus clouds at their tops, producing an *"anvil head"* appearance. Towering cumulus clouds may be local in nature, or they may be associated with the cold front of an approaching storm. *The latter appears as an approaching line of thunderstorms or towering cumulus clouds. Towering cumulus clouds usually produce high, gusty winds, lightning, heavy showers, and occasionally hail and tornadoes (although tornadoes are rare in mountainous terrain). Such thunderstorms are usually short-lived and bring clear weather.* Cloud caps often form above pinnacles and peaks, and usually indicate higher winds aloft. Cloud caps with a lens shape (similar to a "flying saucer") are called lenticular and indicate very high winds (over 40 knots). Cloud caps should always be watched for changes. If they grow and descend, bad weather can be expected.

Towering Cumulus: A transition cloud between the fair weather cumulus and the eventual cumulonimbus cloud. Not all towering cumulus clouds become cumulonimbus, but towering cumulus do indicate the potential for further vertical development. Towering cumulus clouds signal changes in atmospheric stability from stable to unstable. When rapidly growing, they indicate an unstable atmosphere with probable thunderstorms within minutes.

Cumulonimbus / Thunderstorms: Large, dense, towering clouds with cauliflower-like tops. The mature cumulonimbus top portion is often flattened into the classic anvil shape or consists of a cirrus formation. Water droplets form the major portion of cumulonimbus, but ice crystals appear in the upper portions. Cumulonimbus and thunderstorm are synonymous terms. Cumulonimbus result in strong winds, lightning, and potentially heavy rains. A well developed cumulonimbus can spawn hail and tornadoes.

Cumulonimbus tower as seen from an airplane.

Afternoon Cumulonimbus

454

TYPES OF THUNDERSTORMS

WARM FRONT THUNDERSTORM

Usually takes place when warm moist air overruns a retreating mass of cold air. The warm air becomes very unstable.

COLD FRONT THUNDERSTORM

This occurs in the warm air near the frontal zone where cold air is pushing against the warmer air. This type of storm usually occurs in the afternoon, in the summer, and is more violent than a warm front thunderstorm.

COLD FRONT ADVANCE

A cold front advances 20 mph (33 km), faster during the winter months. This is the speed of approach of possible thunderstorms and lightning as cold fronts, in the summer, are the major source lightning.

AIR MASS THUNDERSTORMS

These storms are formed within a warm moist air mass and are scattered over a large area.

CONVECTIVE THUNDERSTORM

In temperate zones during the summer months. They develop over land and water during the afternoon hours when cool, moist air from the water is heated as it travels towards the warmer land surfaces. They can form over the water at night as cool land air moves out over the warmer water, then rises to form clouds. Convective thunderstorms usually start as cumulus clouds which are fed by rising currents of warm air to become large menacing thunderheads.

OROGRAPHIC THUNDERSTORM

This occurs when unstable air is forced upwards by an obstacle as a mountain barrier. These storms can form quickly and spread over a large area. They can stay stationary on the windward side, and rumble for hours. These storms are a major threat to mountain climbers. See Mountain Travel.

NOCTURNAL THUNDERSTORM

These occur late at night or in the early morning usually at the end of spring and in the summer. They are common on the Central Plains from the Mississippi westward.

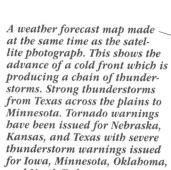

A mid-west perfect storm.

THUNDERSTORMS

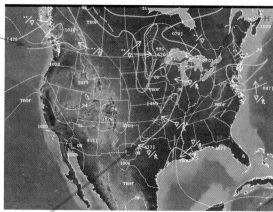

A weather forecast map made at the same time as the satellite photograph. This shows the advance of a cold front which is producing a chain of thunderstorms. Strong thunderstorms from Texas across the plains to Minnesota. Tornado warnings have been issued for Nebraska, Kansas, and Texas with severe thunderstorm warnings issued for Iowa, Minnesota, Oklahoma, and North Dakota.

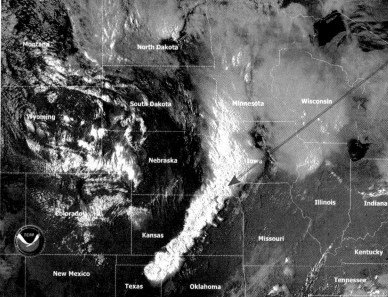

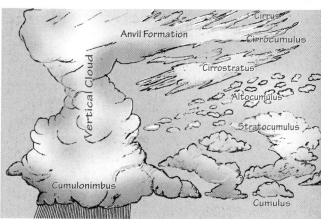

Tops of Thunderstorms.

Flanking line of sloping towering cumuli. Tornadoes could be at the ends.

Thunderstorms and towering cumulus clouds as seen from the air.

THUNDERSTORM FORMATION

For a thunderstorm we need:

Moisture: The basic fuel is moisture (water vapor) in the lowest levels of the atmosphere.

Upper Level Cold Air: The air above the lowest levels has to cool off rapidly with height, so that 2-3 miles above the ground, it is very cold.

Humid Air to Rise: The moist air near the ground has to be pushed to a higher elevation to cool off. This can happen when warm air encounters a cold front and the cold front (being heavier) pushes the lighter warm air up its sloping front to a higher elevation where condensation starts. It can also happen when warm air encounters a hill or mountain. The warm air activity is actually more complicated as once the warm air meets the front (or mountain) it starts to rise as a hot air blob. It rises and cools off and after a while, some of the water vapor turns into liquid drops (that we see as clouds). This condensation into droplets warms up the rest of the air in the blob so that it doesn't cool off as fast as it would if the air was dry. When that blob of air gets to the part of the atmosphere where it is very cold, it will be warmer and less dense than the air around it. Since it is less dense, it will start to rise faster without being pushed, just like a balloon filled with helium. Then more water vapor turns into liquid in the blob and the blob warms up more and rises even faster until all of water vapor is gone. The blob eventually reaches a part of the atmosphere where it isn't warmer than the environment (typically 5-10 miles) and it dissipates as it is not held together by the surrounding cold air. A continuous rising of warm air can cause a major updraft and lead to a violent thunderstorm.

DETECTION OF THUNDERSTORMS

We can see thunderstorms with a variety of tools. Radar lets us see where rain and hail are located in the storm. Doppler radars also let us see how the wind is blowing within and near the storm. Some features of thunderstorms, such as the anvil that spreads out at the top of the storm, can be seen from the ground or satellites.

SQUALL LINE

A squall line is defined as any line or narrow band of active thunderstorms. In its most organized form, it has a significantly different structure from the tornadic storm. The associated precipitation distribution is shown in this schematic as magenta, green, and red, the gust front is shown by the blue line with teeth, and the cloud anvil in light blue (edge marked). Updrafts form a nearly continuous curtain along the edge of the precipitation, above the gust front. Downdrafts are located in the precipitation region of the squall line, to the rear (usually west or north)

of the leading updrafts. Hail is usually smaller than that occurring in tornadic storms, so considerably fewer significant tornadoes result. Very strong low-level straight-line winds are common with severe squall lines. Strongest winds generally occur a few minutes after gust front passage, sometimes during heavy rain and hail. Tornadoes, if they occur, are usually weak, short-lived, and are found along the gust front. The most distinctive cloud associated with the squall line is the shelf cloud. It is found along, above, or immediately trailing the gust front and is indicated here by the black band. The

shelf cloud is wedge-shaped and smooth as it approaches and sometimes appears layered or terraced. Although the shelf cloud can accompany the gust front associated with tornadic storms as well, it is much more frequent with squall lines. Squall lines most often occur with or ahead of cold fronts or other large-scale wind shift lines. They usually move perpendicular to their length. For example, this line would probably be moving southeast from 15 to 60 mph. The strongest winds and severe weather often, but not always, accompany the faster moving lines. When moving rapidly and producing very strong winds, they often bow outward. Regions of heavy rain and hail, associated with individual storms within the line, often move along (parallel to) the line. So these storms would probably be moving northeast a is the line moves southeast. When squall lines move slowly or become stationary, the individual storms generally move along the line. In that case, a given location can record a number of thunderstorms. Prolonged heavy rains have occurred under those conditions and resulted in flash flooding.

NSSL Storm Spotter's Guide

The Perfect Squall Line

Squall Line

Thunderstorms forming a solid line of storms is called a "squall." With a squall line, the warm air feeds the storm ahead of it, so that the updraft on the front portion of the storm dominates.

Occasionally, a storm of the severe tornadic type will develop in association with a squall line. Those storms are usually on the south end of the line.

CROSS-SECTION OF SQUALL LINE

This diagram shows that large quantities of air from low levels are lifted high into the atmosphere in the leading updrafts while air from the middle levels is brought down to replace it in the trailing downdrafts. The atmosphere is then "stabilized," leading to pleasant weather in the wake of the storm. Let's consider what an observer typically sees and experiences as a strong squall line approaches from the west or north. This squall line is moving from left to right at about 30 mph. The day is typically relatively warm and humid with cumulus or towering cumulus clouds and strong gusty winds blowing from a southerly direction. Once the squall line has formed, an extensive anvil cloud, marking the strong outflow aloft from the main updrafts, can spread up to 100 miles or more in advance of the line. The leading edge of the anvil passes the observer and its base gradually lowers and becomes a darker gray. Within a few miles of the passage of the gust front itself, there are often 2 or 3 distinct layers or decks of clouds visible. These are associated with the more organized stronger updrafts. The underside of these clouds is rain-free and often appears distinctly darker, with a rippled appearance. The shelf cloud is generally seen as the lowest layer of cloud, and marks strong updraft along the leading edge of the gust front. It is attached to the cloud layer above and is characterized by strong upward motion. As we shall see, shelf clouds often change rapidly and have many variations in appearance. At the surface, the strong gusty southerly winds generally decrease, sometimes becoming nearly calm, as the leading edge of the gust front and shelf cloud approach. A wind shift to the west or northwest then occurs, followed by an increase in wind speed and gustiness and a rapid drop in temperature. The often abrupt beginning of heavy rain and hail may then be experienced with strong, sometimes damaging winds. Frequent lightning usually accompanies the precipitation. A gradual decrease in wind and rainfall follows, with skies eventually clearing.

NSSL Storm Spotter's Guide

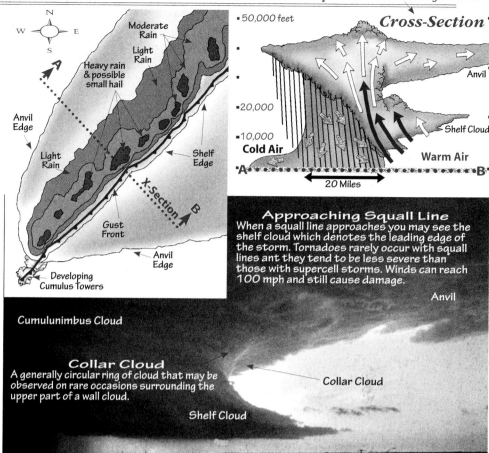

Approaching Squall Line

When a squall line approaches you may see the shelf cloud which denotes the leading edge of the storm. Tornadoes rarely occur with squall lines ant they tend to be less severe than those with supercell storms. Winds can reach 100 mph and still cause damage.

Cumulunimbus Cloud

Collar Cloud
A generally circular ring of cloud that may be observed on rare occasions surrounding the upper part of a wall cloud.

Shelf Cloud

Collar Cloud

Anvil

YOUNG THUNDERSTORM

All thunderstorms grow from cumulus clouds. They are composed of air in the form of large "bubbles" or columns which rise because they are warmer than the surrounding atmosphere. The air is made visible by tiny water droplets which form as the rising air cools and the water vapor in the air condenses. As the cumulus clouds grow taller and larger, they develop a dense nonfibrous appearance with distinct outlines, much like a rising mound, dome, or cauliflower. The tops of such towering cumulus clouds, or TCU, grow (as shown here) to higher levels as the updrafts (the red arrows) may be as strong as 40 mph. In fact, the average updraft transports upward over 8000 tons of air per second, which is drawn from miles around. Cloud droplets grow rapidly within the cloud and precipitation begins to develop, but is held aloft during this phase of development.

LIFE OF A THUNDERSTORM

MATURE THUNDERSTORM

When thunderstorms form, winds near the surface of the earth usually blow from a southerly direction, while at higher levels they are somewhat stronger and often from the southwest or west. It is with the average wind through the depth of the cumulonimbus (CB) cloud that the thunderstorm moves and not with the wind at the ground. Since the thunderstorm usually moves more slowly than the winds around it, the updraft and its visible signature, the cumulonimbus, often tilt somewhat downwind as shown here. The updraft is strongest in the area indicated by the red arrows. Above that, the updraft slows and spreads out very rapidly forming the anvil cloud. In the ordinary storm it is normally fibrous and smooth in appearance. Near the time that the anvil cloud begins to form, precipitation begins to fall from the northeast section of the cloud. Here, in the rain area, lightning is most frequent. As the precipitation forms and falls to the ground, the dryer air mixed into the cloud from the surroundings, cools by evaporating some of the precipitation. The cool heavy air sinks and a downdraft results. Cloud and precipitation within the descending air continue to evaporate, keeping the air cooler than its surroundings. This precipitation and downdraft, extending from below the anvil to the ground, usually sunlit, cumulonimbus cloud with its remaining rain-free base. Some small hail and heavy rain may occur in the precipitation area of stronger storms. A large active thunderstorm may contain as much as 500,000 to 1,000,000 tons of condensed water while producing more energy than an atomic bomb (the equivalent of about 100 million kilowatt hours of electricity).

DISSIPATING

The precipitation and downdraft generally spread through the remaining portion of the storms, choking off the life blood of the storm, its updraft. As a result, the cumulonimbus cloud becomes increasingly indistinct and fuzzy updrafts within weaken. The base of the cloud where updrafts originate will dissipate and be replaced by rain. This leaves only the upper portion of the cloud or light blue area. This cloud is called an "orphan anvil." The only updrafts remaining are weak and contained in this anvil, while downdraft predominates throughout the gradually decreasing precipitation. Finally, even that precipitation stops and the anvil dissipates. Most thunderstorms are composed of several up and down drafts, each at different stages of the life cycle we have described. So while a thunderstorm, composed of only one major updraft and resulting downdraft, might last only 30 minutes, one composed of several such "cells" would last perhaps 2 hours or more.

Source: The NSSL Storm Spotter's Guide.

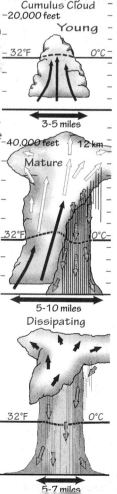

SUPERCELL THUNDERSTORM

A thunderstorm with a persistent rotating updraft. Supercells are rare, but are responsible for a remarkably high percentage of severe weather events - especially tornadoes, extremely large hail and damaging straight-line winds. They frequently travel to the right of the main environmental winds (i.e., they are right movers). Visual characteristics often include a rain-free base (with or without a wall cloud), tail cloud, flanking line, over-shooting top, and back-sheared anvil, all of which normally are observed in or near the right rear or southwest part of the storm. Storms exhibiting these characteristics often are called classic supercells.

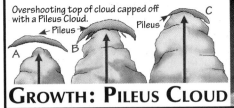

Overshooting top of cloud capped off with a Pileus Cloud.

GROWTH: PILEUS CLOUD

Pileus Cloud

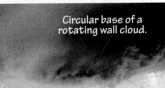

Supercell

Shelf Cloud

Rain-free base.

Overshooting top of cloud capped off with a Pileus Cloud

Mammatus clouds on the underside of an anvil.

Main Storm Tower

Flanking Line Tower

South West

Rain-free base.

Collar

Tail

Tornado

Rotating Wall Cloud Area from which tornadoes are generated.

Mammatus Clouds
Rounded, smooth, sack-like protrusions hanging from the underside of a cloud (usually a thunderstorm anvil). Mammatus clouds often accompany severe thunder-storms, but do not produce severe weather; they may accompany non-severe storms as well.

Anvil

Anvil

Cumulonimbus

Virga and/ or Rain

North East

Shelf Cloud

Precipitation

Overshooting Top
A dome-like protrusion above a thunderstorm anvil, representing a very strong updraft and hence a higher potential for severe weather with that storm. A persistent and/or large over-shooting top (anvil dome) often is present on a supercell. A short-lived overshooting top, or one that forms and dissipates in cycles, may indicate the presence of a pulse storm or a cyclic storm.

Anvil
The flat, spreading top of a Cumulonimbus Cloud. Thunderstorm anvils may spread hundreds of miles downwind from the thunder-storm itself, and sometimes may spread upwind.

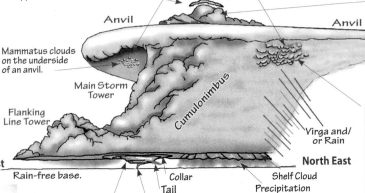

Mammatus Cloud
The mammatus clouds hang from the underside of the anvil. This mammatus was seen at some 10-15 miles from beneath the anvil. While mammatus often accompany severe thunderstorms, they are not severe in themselves and are not always associated with severe thunderstorms.

Tail Cloud

Circular base of a rotating wall cloud.

Rotating Wall Cloud
A rotating wall cloud is the single most important visual precursor of a developing tornado. Not all wall clouds produce tornadoes, and some tornadoes develop directly from the rain-free base. However, most tornadoes develop from a rotating wall cloud. As with tornadoes, rotation will most often be counter-clockwise.

Squall Line

Shelf Cloud

Approaching thunderstorm with a lead gust front. Rain-cooled air from the storm moves out ahead of the storm It ploughs under the warm moist air forming a flat "shelf cloud"

Anvil

Anvil

Mammatus

The updraft slows and spreads out very rapidly forming the anvil cloud. In the ordinary storm it is normally fibrous and smooth in appearance. Near the time that the anvil cloud begins to form, precipitation begins to fall from the northeast section of the cloud.

Collar Cloud
A generally circular ring of cloud that may be observed on rare occasions surrounding the upper part of a wall cloud.

Shelf Cloud
A low, horizontal wedge-shaped arcus cloud, associated with a thunderstorm gust front (or occasionally with a cold front, even in the absence of thunderstorms). Unlike the roll cloud, the shelf cloud is attached to the base of the parent cloud above it (usually a thunderstorm). Rising cloud motion often can be seen in the leading (outer) part of the shelf cloud, while the under-side often appears turbulent, boiling, and wind-torn. It is accompanied by gusty, straight-line winds and is followed by precipitation.

Shelf Cloud

Shelf Cloud

SUPERCELL / TORNADIC THUNDERSTORM

Here we see a representation of a tornadic storm as might be seen when east of the tornadic storm looking west. This storm is different from a non-severe storm in that the updraft and downdraft remain separated. Strong winds aloft, which usually accompany severe storms, are blowing from southwest to northeast or generally from left to right in this diagram. Precipitation near the top of the main storm tower is blown from left to right, and falls to earth (with a downdraft) to the northeast of the rain-free base. The continued separation of the updraft and downdraft and the energetic, large scale weather patterns in these situations may combine to allow updraft speeds to exceed 100 mph. Such an intense updraft is usually sufficient for large hail and sometimes tornado production. We will briefly consider each cloud structure here but will examine them in more detail later.

The core of the updraft, which rises within the main storm tower, is located at the cloud base by the wall cloud. As often occurs and is depicted here, tornadoes may descend from the wall cloud. The tail cloud, when it is present, usually extends out from the wall cloud toward the precipitation area. Motion in the tail cloud is often rapid and toward the wall cloud. It is a horizontal cloud and not a tornado. Between the wall cloud and the visible precipitation, very large hail often falls. However, these hailstones usually do not fall in dense curtains but, instead, are more widely scattered and are not usually visible. The collar cloud, sometimes

incorrectly used as a synonym for the wall cloud, is actually a ring of cloud located around the upper portion of the wall cloud. True collar clouds are seen only rarely. Often the upper (top) and right (north and northeast) sides of the main CB or storm tower are obscured as in the non-severe storm by the gray, indistinct area of precipitation descending from the anvil, shown here by vertical lines. Those structural features always present are: anvil, main storm tower, and rain-free base. A flanking line of towering cumulus clouds frequently extends southwestward from the main storm tower. This cloud line has roughly a stair step appearance, with higher cloud tops closer to the main storm tower. Tornadoes can develop directly from the rain-free base. However, the wall cloud frequently precedes tornadoes and is otherwise a very good indicator of an intense updraft and potentially severe storm. Remember, most tornadoes develop as pendants from wall clouds and form adjacent to and usually on the southwest side of the precipitation. The NSSL Storm Spotter's Guide.

Supercell Top View

These storms are basically a prolonged and intense version of the mature stage of an ordinary thunderstorm but with some differences. They are called "supercells" to distinguish them from ordinary thunderstorms. The intense updraft, which is rising, is located within the main storm tower and shown by the scalloped lines in a semicircle A. Beneath the storm tower is the rain-free base and the wall cloud B. The strong updraft allows the main storm tower to stand almost erect, despite the strong southwest to northeast winds aloft. Imagine this updraft as a water fountain on a windy day. Where does the water fall to the ground? It falls downwind. The fountain of water is analogous to the updraft and the water to the rain and hail formed in the updraft. Large hailstones, which fall most rapidly, reach the ground adjacent to the updraft C. Heavy rain and smaller hail fall more slowly and are carried further northeast before they reach the ground D. Precipitation, usually light rain, is on the extreme north and east sides of the storm. The air within the strong winds aloft is very dry and is cooled by evaporation when it flows into the precipitation region. This air then sinks, developing a downdraft in the heavy rain area, similar to the ordinary thunderstorm E. A second downdraft forms just southwest of the updraft. In contrast with ordinary thunderstorms these up and downdrafts remain separate for long periods forming an "efficient machine". At the ground, both of the cool downdrafts combine to form the windshift line known as the gust front F. A 5 to 10 mile diameter swirling motion sometimes forms between the updraft and the southwest downdraft. This vortex causes a bend or wave in the gust front similar in shape to a developing low pressure system seen on the daily weather map. It is here, between the updraft and southwest downdraft, that the tornado vortex may form about 4 miles above the earth and descend to the ground G. The flanking line is usually located along the gust front extending south from the storm. Occasionally, the southwest edge of the anvil extends beyond the end of the flanking line H. Most supercell storms move eastward or northeastward at average speeds of 20 to 40 mph. However, some supercells move at speeds up to 75 mph.
The NSSL Storm Spotter's Guide.

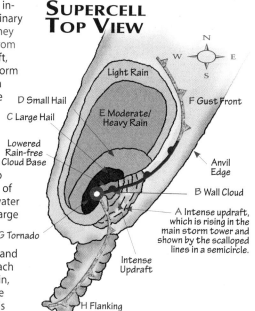

Supercell Top View

- Light Rain
- D Small Hail
- C Large Hail
- Lowered Rain-free Cloud Base
- E Moderate/ Heavy Rain
- F Gust Front
- Anvil Edge
- B Wall Cloud
- A Intense updraft, which is rising in the main storm tower and shown by the scalloped lines in a semicircle.
- G Tornado
- Intense Updraft
- H Flanking Line

Rain-Free Base

A dark, horizontal cloud base with no visible precipitation beneath it. It typically marks the location of the thunderstorm updraft. Tornadoes may develop from wall clouds attached to the rain-free base, or from the rain-free base itself - especially when the rain-free base is on the south or southwest side of the main precipitation area. Note that the rain-free base may not actually be rain free; hail or large rain drops may be falling.

Air Mass Thunderstorm

Generally, a thunderstorm not associated with a front or other type of synoptic-scale forcing mechanism. Air mass thunderstorms typically are associated with warm, humid air in the summer months; they develop during the afternoon in response to insolation, and dissipate rather quickly after sunset. They generally are less likely to be severe than other types of thunderstorms, but they still are capable of producing downbursts, brief heavy rain, and (in extreme cases) hail over 3/4" in diameter.

Severe thunderstorm with a clear slot near main updraft core. Typically a tornado, if present, will form in this area out of the wall cloud. (As the air goes up in the thunderstorm's updraft, it creates an area of low pressure under the updraft that acts to pull air in from around the thunderstorm. This low pressure region is also typically a few millibars lower than the environment of the storm. At the top of the storm the pressure is high compared to places far away from the storm and air is blown out and forms the anvil.)

Squall arriving - this is very dangerous for boating.

Wall cloud below a towering cumulus with rain-free base. A wall cloud, a lowering of the cloud base underneath main storm updraft, forms in this thunderstorm. Tornadoes can form out of the wall clouds.

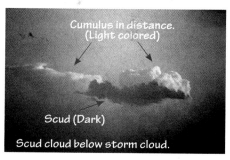

Cumulus in distance. (Light colored)
Scud (Dark)
Scud cloud below storm cloud.

Severe Thunderstorm Warning

This is issued when either a severe thunderstorm is indicated by radar or a spotter reports a thunderstorm producing hail 3/4" or larger in diameter and/or winds equal or exceed 50 kts (58 mph); therefore, people in the affected area should seek safe shelter immediately. Severe thunderstorms can produce tornadoes with little or no advance warning. Lightning frequency is not a criteria for issuing a severe thunderstorm warning. They are usually issued for a duration of one hour. Severe Thunderstorm Warnings include where the storm was located, what towns will be affected by the severe thunderstorm, and the primary threat associated with the severe thunderstorm warning. If the severe thunderstorm is also causing torrential rains, this warning may also be combined with a Flash Flood Warning. After it has been issued, the affected National Weather Forecast Office will followed it up periodically with Severe Weather Statements. These statements will contain updated information on the severe thunderstorm and they will also let you know when warning is no longer in effect.

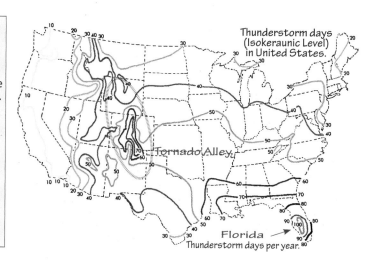

Thunderstorm days (Isokeraunic Level) in United States.
Tornado Alley
Florida Thunderstorm days per year.

THUNDERSTORMS & CAMPING

Shadow of Airplane

THINGS TO WATCH
BEFORE & DURING A THUNDERSTORM

- A thunderstorm can arrive very fast and lightning can strike in front of the storm.
- A lightning bolt can be 4 or 5 miles long.
- Calculate the speed of the approaching storm from the time between the flash and the thunderclap.
- Make sure that you are not the tallest high point in the area (in a field, on a beach, in the water), that you are not next to a prominent high point (next to an isolated tree, steeple, flagpole).
- Avoid being in a boat on a lake during a storm. Ground the boat.
- Make sure that you are not in a location where the electric current from the ground would pass through you. Examples are: in small, humid caves, on the ledge of a mountain or in a small mountain canyon, as your body might act as a conductor for the current that wants to pass across the canyon.
- Avoid damp area as a damp cave or ledge below a high point.
- Canyons are dangerous because there can be a flash flood caused by a storm. Because of the thunder you will not be able to hear the noise of the water descending the canyon.
- Walk fast but do not run as your rapid movement can cause air currents that might attract an electrical strike.
- Avoid a humid hollow in which there is lichen growing as it would be a good conductor.
- If in the open, crouch very low and try to insulate yourself from the ground by standing on a backpack (with no metal), raincoat, jacket, sleeping bag. The importance of this insulation is that the ground charge cannot rise through your body to attempt to reach the lightning discharge.
- Keep your hands off the ground, especially if it is humid.
- Stay away from any metal such as tent poles, metal backpack frames, metal walking poles, etc. You might even abandon these items, in a flat field, as they might create a better potential impact point than yourself.
- Do not lean against a stone wall as it might be a conductor.
- Make sure that the storm has completely passed and that you do not attract the last lightning strike.
- If hiding next to a wall, stay 6 to 12 feet from the wall which should be 5 to 6 times your height. Make sure that this wall is not the most prominent location on a flat field.
- Do not group together during a storm. A flash of lightning killed 504 sheep that had huddled together during a storm.

SIGN OF THUNDERSTORMS

Some thunderstorms can be seen approaching (on flat land), while others hit without warning (especially in mountains). It is important to learn and recognize the danger signs and to plan ahead.

Thunderstorm Danger Signs

The presence of a thunderstorm is shown by a thick column(s) of dark, fleecy cumulus clouds that rise to the height of twenty thousand feet or more.

You will see:

- Wisps of cloud that swirl both up and down. These show the powerful wind currents that are present.
- Dark, towering or threatening clouds
- A flattened top of the cloud projects horizontally, in one direction, in the shape of a blacksmith's anvil. This flattened top occurs because the top of this massive cloud is being moved by the jet stream.
- Distant lightning and thunder.

FLASH FLOODS

Flash floods are the second most dangerous thunderstorm hazard.

THUNDERSTORMS

Although individual thunderstorms are normally local in nature and usually of short duration, they can be part of a large weather system. In the alpine zone above timberline, thunderstorms may be accompanied by freezing precipitation and sudden squally winds. Ridges and peaks become focal points of concentrated electrical activity which is highly dangerous. Thunderstorms occurring at night or in the early morning are associated with major changes in the weather conditions, which often results in a long period of foul weather before clearing on high mountain summits. Thunderstorms occurring at these times may also be part of a general storm front and are followed by a prolonged period of cool, dry weather.

LOCAL THUNDERSTORMS

Local thunderstorms develop from rising air columns resulting from the intense heating by the sun of a relatively small area. They occur most frequently in the middle or late afternoon. Scattered fair weather clouds (cumulus) often appear harmless, but when they continue to grow larger and reach a vertical depth of several thousand feet they may rapidly turn into thunderstorms.

WINDS, FLASH FLOODS & LIGHTNING

Many hazardous weather events are associated with thunderstorms. Fortunately, the area affected by any one of them is fairly small and, most of the time, the damage is fairly light. Lightning is responsible for many fires around the world each year, as well as causing deaths when people are struck. Under the right conditions, rainfall from thunderstorms causes flash flooding, which can change small creeks into raging torrents in a matter of minutes, washing away large boulders and most man-made structures. Hail up to the size of softballs damages cars and windows, and kills wildlife caught out in the open. Strong (up to more than 120 mph) straight-line winds associated with thunderstorms knock down trees and power lines. In one storm in Canada in 1991, an area of forest approximately 10 miles wide and 50 miles long was "blowdowns." Tornados (with winds up to about 300 mph) can destroy all but the best-built man-made structures.

Thunderstorm rainshaft and the precipitation free area on the right side.

Rain-Free Area

Rain Virga not reaching ground

LIGHTNING

Lightning is a major threat during a thunderstorm. In the United States, between 75 and 100 people are killed each year by lightning. If you are caught outdoors, avoid natural lightning rods such as tall, isolated trees in an open area or on the top of a hill, and metal objects such as wire fences, golf clubs, and metal tools. It is a myth that lightning never strikes the same place twice. In fact, lightning will strike several times in the same place in the course of one discharge. While thunderstorms and lightning can be found throughout the United States, they are most likely to occur in the central and southern states. The state with the highest number of thunderstorm days is Florida.

LIGHTNING: ELECTRICAL DISCHARGE

Lightning is an electrical discharge that results from the buildup of positive and negative charges within a thunderstorm. When the buildup becomes strong enough, lightning appears as a "bolt." This flash of light usually occurs between the clouds and the ground. A bolt of lightning reaches a temperature approaching 50,000° F in a split second.

The rapid heating and cooling of air near the lightning cause thunder.

FLORIDA LIGHTNING

The corridor from Tampa Bay, FL to Lakeland, FL receives the most lightning in the United States. Furthermore, about 90% of the lightning in this area occurs from May through September, between the hours of noon and midnight, when most people are awake. During this time of day and year, people in this region who spend a large portion of their lives outdoors are much more likely to be struck than anytime or anywhere else in the country.

LIGHTNING

Wall cloud with lightning.

IF IN THE OPEN

If you are in the open during a storm, stay away from tall, exposed objects (even if they offer shelter from the rain) or away from open areas (such as lakes, beaches, etc.). History has shown that many people who are struck by lightning were near water, in an exposed location, or under/near trees.

CROUCH DOWN ON THE BALLS OF YOUR FEET

If you are caught in the open and lightning is nearby, the safest position to be in is crouched down on the balls of your feet. Do not allow your hands (or other body parts) to touch the ground, and keep your feet as close to one another as possible.

Why? When lightning strikes an object, the electricity of the lightning discharge does not necessarily go down into the ground immediately. Quite often the electricity will travel along the surface of the ground where the flash makes contact with an object. Many people who are 'struck" by lightning are not hit directly by the flash, but are affected by this electricity of the lightning flash as it travels along the surface of the ground (this is especially true if the ground is wet). By keeping the surface area of your body relative to the ground to a minimum (that is, keep your feet together and do not allow any other part of your body to contact the ground), you can reduce the threat of the electricity traveling across the ground from affecting you.

"FLASH TO BANG"

If you see lightning, count the number of seconds until you hear thunder. Divide the number of seconds by five (5) to get the distance the lightning is away from you.

Example: If you see lightning and it takes 10 seconds before you hear the thunder, then the lightning is 2 miles away from you (10 divided by 5 = 2 miles), which is too close!

Lightning & Boating
Mariners who get caught out in a storm in a boat which does not have an enclosed cabin should get as low as possible in the center of the boat. If the boat does have an enclosed cabin, get into the center of the cabin away from electrical equipment and all metal objects. Do not use electronic equipment (except in an emergency). Stay away from tall objects (masts, etc.). All boats should be properly grounded. People in small boats, such as rafts, and especially metal canoes, should head immediately for shore at the first signs of a lightning activity. Remember, be alert for lightning storms developing overhead, the first lightning flash from the storm might hit you!

Lightning Rod
Usually is a copper rod placed on the highest point of a structure. The rod is connected to the ground (is grounded) by a low-resistance heavy gauge wire. The wire is grounded by burying it in humid soil or by connecting it to a water pipe that goes into the ground. The lightning rod protects a building from lightning by diverting the current from the building and provides a conductive path to enter the ground. An individual lightning rod protects the area below it that is approximately equal in radius to the height of the rod above the ground.

Lightning Damage
Cloud-to-ground lightning can kill or injure people by direct or indirect means. The lightning current can branch off to a person from a tree, fence, pole, or other tall object. It is not known if all people are killed who are directly struck by the flash itself. In addition, flashes may conduct their current through the ground to a person after the flash strikes a nearby tree, antenna, or other tall object. The current also may travel through power or telephone lines, or plumbing pipes to a person who is in contact with an electric appliance, telephone, or plumbing fixture. Similarly, objects can be directly struck and this impact may result in an explosion, burn, or total destruction. Or, the damage may be indirect when the current passes through or near it. Sometimes, current may enter a building and transfer through wires or plumbing and damage everything in its path. Similarly, in urban areas, it may strike a pole or tree and the current then travels to several nearby houses and other structures and enter them through wiring or plumbing.

Lightning: A sudden visible flash of energy and light caused by an electrical discharges from thunderstorms.

Lightning Flash: The total luminous phenomenon accompanying a lightning discharge. It may be composed of one to a few tens of strokes that use essentially the same channel to ground.

LIGHTNING TYPES

CLOUD-TO-AIR

CLOUD-TO-CLOUD

CLOUD-TO-GROUND

Cloud-to-Cloud

Cloud-to-Ground

Lightning Channel: The irregular path through the air along which a lightning discharge occurs. A typical discharge of flash between the ground and the cloud is actually a composite flash which is composed of several sequential lightning strokes, each of which is initiated by a leader and terminated by a return streamer.

ABOUT LIGHTNING

Definition: Lightning is a transient discharge of static electricity that serves to re-establish electrostatic equilibrium within a storm environment.
Summary of NOAA article: by Holle and Lopez

Cloud Electricity & Lightning

• Thunderstorms have strong updrafts and down drafts, even within small thunderstorms.
• The updrafts transport water droplets up into the cloud, while ice particles descend from the frozen upper regions of the cloud. As they do, they bump and collide with each other. Through this process, electrons shear off of the ascending water droplets and collect on the descending ice particles. (A similar effect occurs when you rub your feet across a carpet before touching a door knob.)
• This generates an electric field within the cloud, with the top having a positive charge, and the bottom having a negative charge.
• An electric field is also generated between the bottom of the cloud and the surface of the earth, though not nearly as strong as the field within the cloud. As a result, most lightning (~75-80%) occurs within the cloud itself.
• Opposite (positive & negative) charges attract each other - they are separated by insulators - in this case - air acts as an insulator.
• In a thunderstorm: the top of the cloud is (+) charge and the bottom (-) charge and there is an electric attraction (i.e. electric field) between them.
• By the continuous agitation within the cloud the electric charges increase. The greater the magnitude (strength of charges) of separation, the stronger the field, and the stronger the attraction between the positively charged top and the negatively charged bottom.
• The atmosphere is a very good insulator, so a TREMENDOUS amount of charge has to build up before lightning can occur.
• When that threshold is reached, the strength of the electric field overpowers the atmosphere's insulating properties, and lightning results.

LIGHTNING & MOUNTAINEERING

Statistically, lightning is not one of the major hazards of mountaineering. Casualties and near casualties are reported, making it a matter of concern. Mountain climbers often find themselves on prominent peaks and exposed ridges which are particularly subject to lightning. There are two reasons for this:
• Ridges help produce the vertical updrafts and the rain cloud conditions which generate lightning.
• Prominences serve to trigger lightning activity.
The weather in the mountains can change rapidly, especially in the afternoons when most storms occur. Watch for changes in the wind, cloud movement, animals and insects becoming excited (bees might make noise in their hives). Sometimes, the storm arrives so fast that you can see the cumulus clouds become cumulonimbus clouds in front of your eyes and engulf the mountain. The air bristles with energy and there might be unusual odors.
Lightning might strike before the actual storm arrives. There are, however, precautionary measures that can be taken by the climber. The most obvious way of avoiding lightning in the mountains is not to be on exposed peaks or ridges, or in an unprotected flat area during an electrical storm. Do not climb if a storm is predicted. Avoid being under prominent or isolated trees. If you are caught in an exposed place, and you have some time before the storm reaches you, you should get as far down the mountain as you can and away from the exposed ridges. Especially avoid ridges that dominate the skyline. It is better being stuck in the middle of a ridge than being at the end of a ridge. If lightning seems imminent or is striking nearby, immediately seek a place that will protect you from direct strikes and from ground currents. A flat shelf, a slope, or a slightly raised place dominated by a nearby high point would give protection from lightning. If there is a choice, select a spot on dry, clean rock in preference to damp or lichen covered rock. A scree slope would be very good. If on a slope, tie yourself down. If lightning hits, you will be in severe shock and you might fall. The main thing to remember, when caught in an electrical storm, is to quickly take precautions.

Heat Lightning
Illuminates the lower sky at night. Not a form of lightning but regular lightning flashes that might be active below the horizon.
Forked Lightning
Lightning bolts that have numerous leaders. These leaders can shoot between the clouds with some hitting the ground.
Single Streak Lightning
The most common form of lightning. It can flash between clouds or hit the ground.

Ground Shock
Is the fusion of electrical voltage through the ground. Ground shock is where ground electrical currents try to join up with a lightning strike. It will be strongest near where lightning will hit. To protect against ground shock, lie on a dry surface or place some dry insulation between you and the ground. This insulation can be sleeping bags, bed roll, clothing - but not metal. A 4" thick dry insulation should be enough.

LIGHTNING IN MOUNTAINS

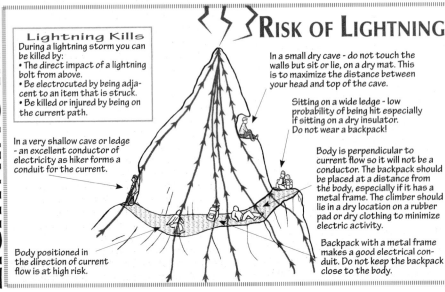

RISK OF LIGHTNING

Lightning Kills
During a lightning storm you can be killed by:
• The direct impact of a lightning bolt from above.
• Be electrocuted by being adjacent to an item that is struck.
• Be killed or injured by being on the current path.

In a small dry cave - do not touch the walls but sit or lie, on a dry mat. This is to maximize the distance between your head and top of the cave.

Sitting on a wide ledge - low probability of being hit especially if sitting on a dry insulator. Do not wear a backpack!

In a very shallow cave or ledge - an excellent conductor of electricity as hiker forms a conduit for the current.

Body is perpendicular to current flow so it will not be a conductor. The backpack should be placed at a distance from the body, especially if it has a metal frame. The climber should lie in a dry location on a rubber pad or dry clothing to minimize electric activity.

Body positioned in the direction of current flow is at high risk.

Backpack with a metal frame makes a good electrical conduit. Do not keep the backpack close to the body.

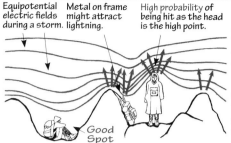

Equipotential electric fields during a storm.

Metal on frame might attract lightning.

High probability of being hit as the head is the high point.

Good Spot

ELECTRICAL EQUIPOTENTIAL LINES

All objects during a storm have electrical force lines around them. The lines of equal force (similar to contour lines on a map) are called electrical equipotential lines. The major electrical equipotential lines are between the storm cloud and the land profile. The probability of lightning striking are the highest where the equipotential lines are the closest together and the closest to the negative charge of the lower clouds. At a certain point, the insulation offered by the air breaks down and lightning strikes.

Recognize Electrical Equipotential critical areas...
- Watch for hair standing on end. This is the (+) charge of the ground trying to reach the (-) charge of the lower clouds.
- There can be a bluish halo around objects (St-Elmo's Fire).
- There can be a high frequency "zinging" sound.

These signs might indicate an imminent lightning strike.

LIGHTNING STROKE

Any of a series of repeated electrical discharges comprising a single lightning discharge (strike). Specifically, in the case of a cloud-to-ground discharge, a leader plus its subsequent return streamer.

LIGHTNING SAFETY GUIDELINES

Plan Ahead! Make sure you get the weather forecast before going out.
- Carry a NOAA weather radio or a portable radio with you on your travels, especially if you will be away from sturdy shelter (such as boating, camping, etc.). This way you will always be able to get the latest forecast.
- If thunderstorms are expected, have a lightning safety plan of action in case thunderstorms threaten. How far away are you from a safe enclosed structure (or enclosed vehicle)? How long will it take you to get to this safe location if storms threaten?
- If the time delay between you observing a flash of lightning and the rumble of thunders is 30 seconds or less, or if thunderheads are building overhead, Implement your lightning safety plan of action.
- It is recommended that you be sheltered and/or alert for after 30 minutes after the last audible thunder.

Important Caveat: lightning can and occasionally does strike many miles away from the rain area of a thunderstorm. In fact, lightning strikes to the ground up to 20 miles away from thunderstorm rain areas have been documented in Florida. It is believed that quite a few people who are struck by lightning are struck by these rogue flashes, known as "bolts from the blue". **"Sideflash:"** Most people struck by lightning are not struck directly, but are affected by the current running through the ground known as a "sideflash."

THUNDER

Summary of NOAA article: by Holle and Lopez.
Thunder is the acoustic shock wave caused by the extreme heat generated by a lightning flash. When a lightning bolt occurs, the air surrounding its channel is instantaneously heated to as much as 50,000° F (~28,000°C), a temperature that is five times the surface of the sun. Like all gases, when air molecules are heated, they expand. The faster they are heated, the faster their rate of expansion. But when air is heated to 50,000°F in a fraction of a second, its expansion rate exceeds the speed of sound, and a sonic boom (thunder) results.
In short, the air literally explodes.
When lightning strikes very close by, the thunder will sound like a loud bang, crack or snap, and its duration will be very short. As the shock wave (thunder) propagates away from the strike center, it stretches and becomes elongated. At large distances from the center, the shock wave (thunder) is often many miles across. As it passes through different points, a continuous rumble results that may last for several seconds, depending on your distance from the strike. Thunder can typically be heard up to 10 miles (16 km) away. During heavy rain and wind this distance will be less, but on cool, calm, and quiet nights when a storm is many miles away, thunder can be heard beyond 10 miles.

LIGHTNING SAFETY

Lightning kills more people in Florida than all other meteorological phenomena combined. Because of the capricious nature of thunderstorms, no one can guarantee an individual or group absolute protection from lightning strikes. Following proven lightning safety guidelines can greatly reduce the risk of injury or death.

LIGHTNING VICTIMS IN FLORIDA

It was found that most of the people were struck either prior to the storm (rain) reaching their location, or after the storm (rain) had ended. Most of the people struck were either near water or near/under trees. Results of this study indicate that people do not seek safe shelter early enough, or resume outdoor activities too soon after the storm (rain) has ended.
Lightning Safety Plan of Action
1) how far away is group from a safe location?
2) how long will it take the group to get to the safe location?
These questions need to be answered before thunderstorms threaten. By knowing the answer to the above questions will greatly increase your chances of not becoming a lightning strike victim.

LIGHTNING & CARS

A lightning current flows on the outside - the *metal surface* of a *hard topped* car. This is called the skin effect. For this reason a person in a metal hard topped car is not affected by a lightning strike. A person in a convertible or fiberglass car is not protected from lightning. When in a hardtop metal roofed car during a lightning storm do not tough any metal surface or object that might be connected to the outside shell of the car. This includes the stick shift, radio knob, door handle, steering wheal, etc. It is best to safely pull to the side of the road, turn on the emergency flashers, shut off the engine, and put your hands in your lap.

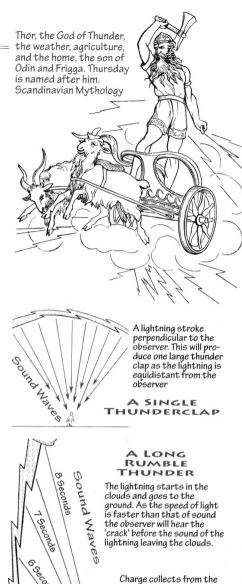

Thor, the God of Thunder, the weather, agriculture, and the home, the son of Odin and Frigga. Thursday is named after him.
Scandinavian Mythology

A lightning stroke perpendicular to the observer. This will produce one large thunder clap as the lightning is equidistant from the observer

A SINGLE THUNDERCLAP

A LONG RUMBLE THUNDER

The lightning starts in the clouds and goes to the ground. As the speed of light is faster than that of sound the observer will hear the 'crack' before the sound of the lightning leaving the clouds.

Charge collects from the ground and/or objects on the ground. When this positive charge collects into a high enough concentration, they form bolts of Ground-to-Air lightning known as streamers. These streamers connect with the Cloud-to-Ground lightning.

Sound Waves
8 Seconds
7 Seconds
6 Seconds
5 Seconds
CRACK

SAFE LOCATIONS DURING A LIGHTNING STORM

No place is absolutely safe from lightning. However, some places are much safer than others.
Safe: Large enclosed structures which are occupied by people on a permanent bases, such as a shopping center, schools, office buildings or a private residence. Once in a sturdy building, stay away from metal objects (faucets, showers, pipes) and phones, unless it is an emergency (cordless phones and battery operated cell phones are safe). Computers may also be dangerous - as phone lines are often connected to them.
Not Safe: Even if they are "grounded." These include beach shacks, small metal sheds, picnic shelters, baseball dugouts etc. In general, buildings which are NOT safe have exposed openings.
Safe Vehicles: Automobiles, vans, school buses, etc. offer excellent protection from lightning.
Not Safe Vehicles: Convertibles offer no safety from lightning, even if the top is "up". Other vehicles which are not safe during lighting storms are vehicles which have "open" cabs, such as golf carts, open cab tractors/construction equipment, etc.

PROMPT MEDICAL ATTENTION
People affected by a lightning flash, either directly or indirectly, need prompt medical attention:

- Call 911.
- "Make no more casualties". Any rescuer must be aware of the continuation of danger that a lightning storm poses to the rescuers as well as to the victim(s). If the area is a high risk area (mountain top, open field, etc.), it may be better that the rescuers who are in a relatively safer area wait until the danger has passed before exposing themselves.
- It is relatively unusual for victims who survive a lightning strike to have major fractures that would cause paralysis or major bleeding complications unless they have suffered a fall or been thrown a distance. As a result, in an active lightning storm, if the rescuers choose to expose themselves to the lightning threat, it may be better to move the victim away from the area of risk (such as under a tree, etc.) rather than to give medical attention at the spot of the initial flash. Rescuers are reminded to stay as low as possible and provide as little area to the ground surface as possible.
- If the victim is not breathing, provide mouth to mouth resuscitation . If the victim has no pulse, (check for the pulse at the carotid (neck) or femoral (knee) artery for 20 -30 seconds) then start CPR. If the area is cold and wet, putting a dry article of clothing between the victim and the ground may decrease the threat of hypothermia that the victim suffers which can complicate the resuscitation.

A lightning strike scar on this tree. Trees can be blown up by a lightning strike. Heat of the lightning strike generates steam in the tree and the steam pressure causes it to blow up or expand and scar as this tree.

A burn mark on the ground that was hit by lightning.

Lightning coming down the wet rope of a church bell.

30/30
LIGHTNING SAFETY RULE
Two things to remember about lightning safety.

- How close should you let the lightning get to you before implementing your lightning safety plan of action? Estimate distance.
- How much time should elapse before resuming outdoor activities?

ESTIMATING DISTANCE
To estimate the distance between you and a lightning flash, use the "Flash to Bang" method: *If you observe lightning, count the number of seconds until you hear thunder. Divide the number of seconds by five (5) to get the distance (in miles) the lightning is away from you.*
Example: If you see lightning and it takes 10 seconds before you hear the thunder, then the lightning is 2 miles away from you.
(10 divided by 5 = 2 miles)

If Thunder is heard... Seconds after a Flash	The Lightning is... Miles Away
5	1 miles away
10	2 miles away
15	3 miles away
20	4 miles away
25	5 miles away
30	6 miles away
35	7 miles away
40	8 miles away

It is recommended that you should begin to seek shelter if the time between the lightning flash and the rumble of thunder is 30 seconds or less.

RESUME OUTDOOR ACTIVITIES
You should not resume activities until 30 minutes after the last audible thunder.
The combination of the above is known as the "30/30 Lightning Rule".

One thing to remember: Sometimes lightning storms can develop overhead. This means that the first lightning strike from the cloud might be in your immediate location. It is recommended that you should be alert for developing thunderclouds overhead when outdoors.
If you see thunderclouds developing, you should implement your lightning safety plan of action.

An Aureola - showing strong electrical fields.

Ball Lightning
A relatively rare form of lightning consisting of a luminous ball, often reddish in color, which moves rapidly along solid objects or remains floating in mid-air. It may suddenly explode. Also known as globe lightning.

St-Elmo's Fire
Is the flickering discharge or glow on the yardarms of sailing ships, the wind shields of aircraft or tall buildings. This might show an area of electrical differential.

THE FUJITA TORNADO SCALE

Max Wind Speeds	Typical Effects
F0 Category 40-72 mph	**Gale Tornado.** Light Damage: Some damage to chimneys; breaks twigs & branches off trees; pushes over shallow rooted trees; some windows broken; **hurricane wind speed begins at 73 mph.**
F1 Category 73-112 mph	**Moderate Tornado.** Moderate damage: Peels surfaces off roofs; mobile homes pushed off foundations or overturned; moving autos pushed off the roads; trees snapped or broken.
F2 Category 113-157 mph	**Significant Tornado.** Considerable damage: Roofs torn off frame houses; mobile homes demolished; frame houses with weak foundations lifted & moved; large trees snapped or uprooted; light object missiles generated.
F3 Category 158-206 mph	**Severe Tornado.** Severe damage: Roofs & some walls torn off quality houses; trains overturned; most trees in forests uprooted; heavy cars lifted off the ground and thrown; weak pavement blown off roads.
F4 Category 207-260 mph	**Devastating Tornado.** Devastating damage: Well constructed homes leveled; structures with weak foundations blown off some distance; cars thrown & disintegrated; large missiles generated; trees in forest uprooted & carried some distance away.
F5 Category 261-318 mph	**Incredible Tornado.** Incredible damage: Strong frame houses lifted off foundations & carried considerable distance to disintegrate: automobile-sized missiles fly through the air in excess of 300 ft; trees debarked; incredible phenomena will occur.
F6-F12 Category > 319 mph	The maximum wind speeds of tornadoes are not expected to reach the F6 wind speeds. Hard to measure!!

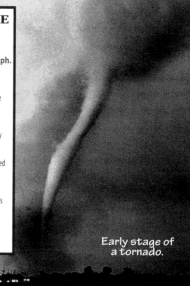

Early stage of a tornado.

TORNADOES

Tornadoes are one of nature's most violent storms. In an average year, about 1,000 tornadoes are reported across the United States, resulting in 80 deaths and over 1,500 injuries. A tornado is a violently rotating column of air extending from a thunderstorm to the ground. The most violent tornadoes are capable of tremendous destruction with wind speeds of 250 mph or more. Damage paths can be in excess of one mile wide and 50 miles long. Tornadoes come in all shapes and sizes and can occur anywhere in the US at any time of the year.

ORIGIN OF TORNADOES

Thunderstorms develop in warm, moist air in advance of eastward-moving cold fronts. These thunderstorms often produce large hail, strong winds, and tornadoes. Tornadoes in the winter and early spring are often associated with strong, frontal systems that form in the Central States and move east. Tornadoes come from the energy released in a thunderstorm. As powerful as they are, tornadoes account for only a tiny fraction of the energy in a thunderstorm. What makes them dangerous is that their energy is concentrated in a small area, perhaps only a hundred yards across (funnel). Not all tornadoes are the same, of course, and science does not yet completely understand how part of a thunderstorm's energy sometimes gets focused into something as small as a tornado.

TORNADO SPEED

Movement can range from virtually stationary to more than 60 miles per hour... what is typical is roughly 10-20 miles per hour.

TORNADO DAMAGE

The damage from tornadoes comes from the strong winds they contain. It is generally believed that tornadic wind speeds can be as high as 300 mph in the most violent tornadoes. Wind speeds that high can cause automobiles to become airborne, rip ordinary homes to shreds, and turn broken glass and other debris into lethal missiles. The biggest threat to living creatures (including humans) from tornadoes is from flying debris and from being tossed about in the wind. It used to be believed that the low pressure in a tornado contributed to the damage by making buildings "explode" but this is no longer believed to be true.

TORNADOES... WHERE, WHEN?

Tornadoes can occur at any time of the year. Whenever and wherever conditions are right, tornadoes are possible, but they are most common in the central plains of North America, east of the Rocky Mountains and west of the Appalachian Mountains. During the spring in the Central Plains, thunderstorms frequently develop along a "dryline," which separates very warm, moist air to the east from hot, dry air to the west. Tornado-producing thunderstorms may form as the dryline moves east during the afternoon hours. Along the front range of the Rocky Mountains, in the Texas panhandle, and in the southern High Plains, thunderstorms frequently form as air near the ground flows "upslope" toward higher terrain. If other favorable conditions exist, these thunderstorms can produce tornadoes. Tornadoes occur mostly during the spring and summer; the tornado season comes early in the south and later in the north because spring comes later in the year as one moves northward. Tornadoes are most likely to occur between 3 and 9 p.m. but have been known to occur at all hours of the day or night. The average tornado moves from southwest to northeast, but tornadoes have been known to move in any direction. The average forward speed is 30 mph but may vary from nearly stationary to 70 mph. They have been known to occur in every state in the United States, on any day of the year, and at any hour.

Signs of Approaching Tornado
- Approaching or developing thunderstorm.
- Strong & persistent rotation in the cloud base.
- Whirling dust or debris on the ground under a cloud base - tornadoes sometimes have no funnel.
- Hail or heavy rain followed by either dead calm or a fast, intense wind shift. Many tornadoes can't be seen because of heavy rain.

Day or Night: Loud, continuous roar or rumble, which doesn't fade in a few seconds like thunder.

Night: Small, bright, blue-green to white flashes at ground level near a thunderstorm (as opposed to silvery lightning up in the clouds). These mean power lines are being snapped by very strong wind, maybe a tornado.

Night: Persistent lowering from the cloud base, illuminated or silhouetted by lightning - especially if it is on the ground or there is a blue-green-white power flash underneath.

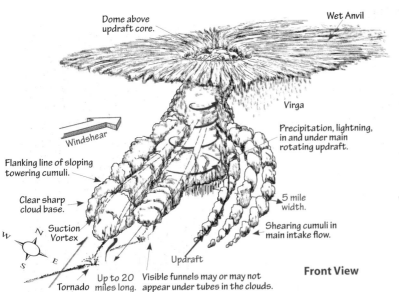

Dome above updraft core.

Wet Anvil

Windshear

Virga

Precipitation, lightning, in and under main rotating updraft.

Flanking line of sloping towering cumuli.

Clear sharp cloud base.

Suction Vortex

5 mile width.

Shearing cumuli in main intake flow.

Up to 20 Tornado miles long.

Visible funnels may or may not appear under tubes in the clouds.

Updraft

Front View

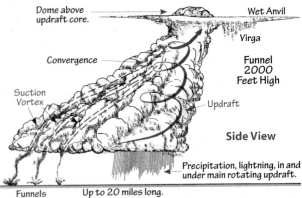

Dome above updraft core.

Wet Anvil

Virga

Convergence

Funnel 2000 Feet High

Suction Vortex

Updraft

Side View

Precipitation, lightning, in and under main rotating updraft.

Funnels

Up to 20 miles long.

TORNADO FORMATION

1..Before thunderstorms develop, a change in wind direction and an increase in wind speed with increasing height creates an invisible, horizontal spinning effect in the lower atmosphere.

2..Rising air within the thunderstorm updraft tilts the rotating air (wall cloud) from horizontal to vertical.

3..An area of rotation, 2-6 miles wide, now extends through much of the storm. Most strong and violent tornadoes form within this area of strong rotation.

4..The area of rotation intensifies (rotating wall cloud). This area is often nearly rain-free.

5..Moments later a strong tornado develops in this area. Softball-size hail and damaging "straight-line" winds also occurred during the storm.

Canadian Tornado Alleys

Tornado Alley

TORNADO ALLEY

Is a nickname for an area of relatively high tornado occurrence in the central states.

TORNADOES IN CANADA

- Average of 80 tornadoes per year. More unreported tornadoes occur in unpopulated areas.
- May to September are the tornado months with June to early July is the peak period. They are rare in winter.

WEAK TORNADOES

- 69% of all tornadoes
- Less than 5% of tornado deaths
- Lifetime 1-10+ minutes
- Winds less than 110 mph

STRONG TORNADOES

- 29% of all tornadoes
- Nearly 30% of all tornado deaths
- May last 20 minutes or longer
- Winds 110-205 mph

VIOLENT TORNADOES

- Only 2% of all tornadoes
- 70% of all tornado deaths
- Lifetime can exceed 1 hour
- Winds greater than 205 mph

TORNADO FEATURES

- Rapid cloud-base rotation.
- Concentrated, whirling debris or dust cloud at ground level under the thunderstorm base.

COLOR OF TORNADOES

Dark: When looking southwest through northwest in the afternoon as they are often silhouetted in front of a light source, such as brighter skies west of the thunderstorm.

Dark Gray, Blue, or White: If there is heavy precipitation behind the tornado. The color varies depending on where most of the daylight is coming from. This happens when looking north or east at a tornado.

Gray Shades on Gray: Tornadoes wrapped in rain and if they are visible at all.

Color of Debris: Lower parts of tornadoes can assume the color of the dust, debris, or soil.

Colorless: Tornadoes may appear nearly transparent until dust and debris are picked up.

"WEDGE" TORNADO

Appear to be at least as wide as they are tall (from ground to ambient cloud base).

"ROPE" TORNADO

"Rope" tornadoes are very narrow, often sinuous or snake-like in form. Tornadoes often (but not always) assume the "rope" shape in their last stage of life. Again, tornado shape and size does not signal strength! Some rope tornadoes can still do violent damage of F4 or F5.

GUSTNADO

Is a small and usually weak whirlwind which forms as an eddy in thunderstorm outflows. They do not connect with any cloud-base rotation and are not tornadoes. They typically appear as a swirl of dust or debris along the "gust front" of a thunderstorm and can form a considerable distance away from the storm. Strong, straight line winds can follow behind the gustnadoes, these can cause more damage than the gustnadoes. Gustnadoes can do minor damage (e.g., break windows and tree limbs, overturn trash cans and toss lawn furniture), and should be avoided.

LAND SPOUT

Are weak small sized tornadoes when compared to the most intense tornadoes. They have a narrow, rope like condensation funnel extending from the cloud base to the ground, and are seen under small storms or large, growing cumulus clouds. They are usually weak and short-lived. They are capable of doing significant damage and killing people.

TORNADO OR FUNNEL CLOUD?

The definition of a tornado means that the vortex of rapidly rotating air must be in contact with the ground. This means that to be a tornado, the swirling winds must be at the surface, capable of doing damage. If you see debris (dust and other objects swirling in the winds), it is definitely a tornado, even if there is no visible funnel cloud. If you can't see debris with a funnel cloud, then it might be a tornado but you can not be certain that it is (or is not). A tornado can move over a surface with few objects to be picked up and swirled about, or you may not be able to see all the way to the surface beneath a funnel cloud because of intervening hills, trees, or buildings. All funnel clouds should be treated as if they are tornadoes, unless you can be certain that they will not touch down, and being certain about such things is difficult. Even if the funnel is not in contact with the surface when you first see it, that situation can change quite rapidly!

MULTIVORTEX (FUNNEL) TORNADO

Multivortex (multi-funnel) tornadoes contain two or more small, intense funnels orbiting the center of the larger tornado circulation. These funnels can appear and disappear in a few seconds.

SOUND OF A TORNADO

- Most common sound: continuous rumble, like a close by train.
- Sometimes a loud whooshing sound, like that of a waterfall or of open car windows while driving very fast.
- Tornado tearing through densely populated areas may be producing all kinds of loud noises at once, which collectively may make a tremendous roar.

TORNADO... DISSIPATION (ENDING)

At one point in a tornado's life the active thunderstorm robs this particular tornado of force creating an instability - and the tornado "falls apart" or dies. It is still possible that another tornado will spawn.

TORNADO ROTATION

Most tornadoes rotate cyclonically (due to the Corriolis Effect), which is counterclockwise in the northern hemisphere and clockwise south of the equator. Anticyclonic tornadoes (clockwise-spinning in the northern hemisphere) have been observed.

Hurricanes & Tropical Storms Might Produce Tornadoes

Tornadoes occasionally accompany tropical storms and hurricanes that move over land. Tornadoes are most common to the right and ahead of the path of the storm center as it comes onshore. Some land falling hurricanes in the U.S. fail to produce any known tornadoes, while others cause major outbreaks.

TORNADO DETECTION

Development of Doppler radar has made it possible, under certain circumstances, to detect a tornado's winds with a radar. The National Weather Service has strategically located Doppler radars across the country which can detect air movement toward or away from the radar. Early detection of increasing rotation aloft within a thunderstorm can allow life-saving warnings to be issued before the tornado forms. However, human beings remain an important part of the system to detect tornadoes, because not all tornadoes occur in situations where the radar can "see" them. Ordinary citizen volunteers make up what is called the SKYWARN network of storm spotters, who work with their local communities to watch out for approaching tornadoes, so that those communities can take appropriate action in the event of a tornado.

TORNADO PREDICTION

Although the process by which tornadoes form is not completely understood, scientific research has revealed that tornadoes usually form under certain types of atmospheric conditions. Those conditions can be predicted, but not perfectly. When forecasters see those conditions, they can predict that tornadoes are likely to occur. However, it is not yet possible to predict in advance exactly when and where they will develop, how strong they will be, or precisely what path they will follow. There are some "surprises" every year, when tornadoes form in situations that do not look like the right conditions in advance, but these are becoming less frequent.

TORNADO SIZE

The easiest way to estimate the size of a tornado is by the size of the damage path. The typical tornado damage path is about one or two miles, with a width of about 50 yards. The largest tornado path widths can exceed one mile, and the smallest widths can be less than 10 yards. Widths can vary considerably during a single tornado, because the size of the tornado can change considerably during its lifetime. Path lengths can vary from what is basically a single point to more than 100 miles. Note that tornado intensity (the peak wind speeds is not necessarily related to the tornado size ... bigger is not necessarily stronger!

Time Tornado is on Ground

The time can range from an instant to several hours... typically 5 minutes or so.

SKIPPING TORNADOES

A tornado must be in contact with the ground to be considered to be a tornado. When the vortex is not in contact it is not a tornado. If the same funnel again contacts the ground it is a separate tornado.

OUT RUNNING... TORNADO

The standard advice is to leave your car and find appropriate shelter.
If you are caught during highway travel to or from camp, it may be possible simply to drive away from a tornado. Vehicles are notorious as death traps in tornadoes, because they are easily tossed and destroyed. Either leave the vehicle for sturdy shelter or drive out of the tornado's path.

Traffic Jam: Traffic jammed or the tornado is bearing down on you at close range, your only option may be to park safely, get out and find a sturdy building for shelter or lie flat in a low spot, as far from the road as possible (to avoid flying vehicles).

Open Country: Watch the tornado closely for a few seconds compared to a fixed object in the foreground (such as a tree, pole, or other landmark). If you are in open country and your road options let you drive at right angles to the direction the tornado is moving, the best strategy is to head off to the right of the tornado's movement: if it's moving east, drive south away from it, and so on. This strategy requires you to be able to assess accurately the direction of tornado movement... *sometimes tornadoes change direction and speed of movement, so be prepared to adjust your tactics!* If the tornado appears to stay in the same place, growing larger or getting closer - but not moving either right or left - it is headed right at you. You must take shelter away from the car or get out of its way fast!

- It is *nearly* always possible to outrun a tornado in a motor vehicle as long as the road and traffic permit free movement. Tornadoes occasionally move at 60+ miles per hour, but most of them don't go nearly that fast. If you are on a road that permits you to drive safely at speeds of 60 mph or faster, you *probably* can outrun a tornado... *however, only do so until you reach a road that allows you to travel at right angles to the tornado's path.* You get out of danger from a tornado most quickly (in just seconds, usually) by moving directly out of its path.
- If your road options don't permit such maneuvers, *abandon your vehicle and seek the best shelter nearby you can find.* Most injuries in tornadoes come from being struck by flying debris. Therefore, you want to get low and out of the wind. Vehicles are often picked up and tumbled, sometimes being smashed into something that looks like a "carball" such that no one would survive inside the vehicle.
- When camping or hiking, outrunning an approaching tornado may not be an option. Given that many tornadoes develop from thunderstorms that are already severe in terms of ordinary wind and large hail, you should already be taking steps to protect yourself from a truly severe thunderstorm.

1: Tornado at an early stage with the middle part of the funnel nearly being transparent. The point where the funnel touches the ground produces a very visible dust cloud.

2: The dust cloud rises up the funnel making it more visible.

3: The tornado starts to decay. Tornadoes often (but not always) assume the "rope" shape in their last stage of life.

4: At one point in a tornado's life the active thunderstorm robs this particular tornado of force creating an instability - and the tornado "falls apart" or dies. It is still possible that another tornado will spawn.

Tornado Forming

Funnel Cloud: Not a tornado as it did not reach the ground.

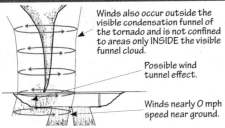

Winds also occur outside the visible condensation funnel of the tornado and is not confined to areas only INSIDE the visible funnel cloud.

Possible wind tunnel effect.

Winds nearly 0 mph speed near ground.

Seeking shelter under a highway overpass is to become a stationary target for flying debris, with a substantial risk of being blown out and carried by the tornado winds.

HIGHWAY OVERPASSES
Not Good Shelters

Tornado winds interacting with an overpass depend on many factors including (but not limited to):
- The strength of the tornado circulation.
- Tornado's "angle of attack" on the overpass.
- Overpass location relative to the path of the center of the tornado circulation.
- Construction of the overpass (particularly underneath).
- Amount and type of debris that has been entrained into the circulation.

Highway overpasses, in general, are inadequate tornado sheltering locations because...

Debris: All tornadoes have some amount of debris within their near-surface flow. In the case of a strong or violent tornado, much more debris would be present, traveling at much higher speeds, especially debris from man-made structures. In strong and violent tornadoes, typically harmless everyday items such as shingles, boards, pop cans, dishes (or pieces thereof) become dangerous missiles and are responsible for most tornado casualties.

Higher speed winds: Under an overpass, people will be exposed to higher wind speeds and more flying debris.

Increase of wind speed: The narrow passage underneath an overpass might cause an increase in the wind speed under the bridge. The extent to which this is true, and the circumstances under which it could happen are not known, but this is at least a possibility.

Direct hit: Most modern overpasses don't have girders or support beams for handholds or small ledges into which to crawl. If an overpass is directly in the path of a tornado, the wind will change direction nearly 180° as the vortex passes. If one side of the overpass was protected from the highest wind speeds as the tornado approached, that same side of the bridge will be completely exposed to the wind and flying debris as the tornado moves away and vice-versa.

TORNADO GROUND WINDS

The tornadic wind has a very strong horizontal component. In most cases the strongest horizontal and vertical components of the wind can be found not far above the ground surface. In almost all tornadoes, the very strong wind extends outside the diameter of the visible funnel – and in many cases, a considerable distance outside the visible funnel. Not all tornadoes exhibit a visible funnel cloud. The only evidence that the tornado circulation exists at ground level is usually a dirt or debris cloud at the surface underneath a funnel cloud aloft, giving the illusion that the tornado is not 'on the ground.'

Tornadic Airflow Underneath Overpass

Based on current knowledge of airflow through and around obstacles, such as buildings and other man-made structures, it is possible to indicate the outcome of an interaction between a tornado and an overpass with a fairly high degree of confidence. In general, the wind speed decreases at the ground surface, becoming zero right at the ground. This is why one of the first and foremost rules in general tornado safety is to get as low as possible, because that is where the wind speed is the lowest. By climbing up underneath the overpass, people are moving into a place where the wind speeds typically will be higher. In addition, under an overpass, it is possible in some situations that when air is forced through the narrow passage underneath the bridge, this might cause an increase in the wind speeds. Further, under different circumstances, the area beneath and just downstream of an overpass might become a debris deposition zone, where piles of debris accumulate.

TORNADO MYTHS

Areas near rivers, lakes, & mountains are safe from tornadoes.
FACT: No place is safe from tornadoes. In the late 1980's, a tornado swept through Yellowstone National Park leaving a path of destruction up and down a 10,000 ft. mountain.

The low pressure with a tornado causes buildings to "explode" as the tornado passes overhead.
FACT: Violent winds and debris slamming into buildings cause most structural damage.

Windows should be opened before a tornado approaches to equalize pressure and minimize damage.
FACT: Opening windows allows damaging winds to enter the structure. Leave the windows alone; instead, immediately go to a safe place.

Tornadoes are always visible from a great distance.
FACT: Tornadoes can be hidden in heavy rainfall or nearby low hanging clouds.

In Weather Broadcasts Listen for...

TORNADO WATCH: Tornadoes are possible in your area. Remain alert for approaching storms.
TORNADO WARNING: A tornado has been sighted or indicated by weather radar. If a tornado warning is issued for your area and the sky becomes threatening, move to your pre-designated place of safety.
SEVERE THUNDERSTORM WATCH: Severe thunderstorms are possible in your area.
SEVERE THUNDERSTORM WARNING: Severe thunderstorms are occurring.

TORNADOES & CAMPING

Generally speaking, tornadoes are rare, even in the places where they occur most often. Many of the mountainous regions favored for outdoor wilderness camping are much less likely to experience tornadoes even than that. Tornadoes have been reported in every state in the United States, and at every hour of the day and night. There certainly have been tornadoes in mountainous regions all over the west, including a large and violent tornado in the Grand Teton Wilderness of Wyoming, so just being in the high country does not mean you can ignore completely any threat of tornadoes. Tornadoes are most common on the Great and High Plains regions of the United States, in the early to late spring.

CAMPING... TORNADO

Find the best shelter from flying debris you can. Ditches, caves, and so on will work. Don't count on some flimsy outbuilding or mountain cabin to protect you ... a tornado can disintegrate flimsy buildings and turn the pieces into high-speed missiles. *Obviously, a tent is virtually the same as no shelter at all.* You are best to **get low** and out of the wind. The majority of tornado casualties are from being struck by flying objects, so the idea is to get out of harm's way.

- Cover your head with your hands (or some better protection if you have it) to give yourself the best protection from flying debris.
- Find something *to hang onto* if your shelter from the wind is not complete. Becoming airborne is a distinct possibility, so you don't want the wind to get under you and lift you into the air.
- Learn how to recognize a tornado. Not all tornadoes look the same. A tornado's funnel-shaped cloud, if it has one, does not have to touch the ground for it to be a true tornado. The tornado is the wind, not the cloud... if there is debris beneath a funnel cloud, it is a tornado... Some tornadoes appear as a dark, boiling mass of clouds on the ground. A tornado in the mountains might look very much like a dust devil... except that the dust and debris at the surface is beneath a dark thunderstorm base, not occurring on a sunny, nearly cloudless afternoon.
- Don't depend on hearing a tornado... not all tornadoes make a lot of noise until they are very close to you. Keep your eyes open in the wilderness, especially if there are thunderstorms.

Tornado near end of life. Notice the rope-like appearance.

Early Stage

Tornado Damage

TORNADO DISASTER KIT

- A 3 day supply of water (one gallon per person per day) and food that won't spoil.
- Change of clothing and footwear per person.
- One blanket or sleeping bag per person.
- First-aid kit, including prescription medicines.
- Emergency tools, including a battery-powered NOAA Weather Radio and a portable radio, flashlight, and plenty of extra batteries.
- Extra set of car keys and a credit card or cash.
- Special items for infant, elderly, or disabled family members.

TORNADO FIRST AID KIT

Store your first aid supplies in a tool box or fishing tackle box so they will be easy to carry and be protected from water. Inspect your kit regularly and keep it freshly stocked.

- Drugs and Medications   • Eye drops
- Hydrogen peroxide to wash & disinfect wounds
- Antibiotic ointment   • Diarrhea medicine
- Individually wrapped alcohol swabs
- Aspirin & non-aspirin tablets
- Prescriptions and any long-term medications

NOTE: Important medical information and most prescriptions can be stored in the refrigerator, which provides excellent protection from fires.

- Dressings, band-aids & rolled gauze
- Clean sheets torn into strips
- Elastic bandages for sprains
- Cotton-tipped swabs   • Splinting materials
- Adhesive tape roll   • Needle & thread
- First aid book   • Writing materials
- Scissors & Tweezers   • Thermometer
- Bar soap & Tissues   • Sunscreen
- Paper cups & Plastic bags
- Instant cold packs   • Safety pins
- Sanitary napkins   • Pocket knife

TORNADO SAFETY

Before the Storm:
- Develop a plan for you and your family for home, work, school and when outdoors.
- Have frequent drills.
- Know the area in which you live, and keep a highway map nearby to follow storm movement from weather bulletins.
- Have a NOAA Weather Radio with a warning alarm tone and battery back-up to receive warnings.
- Listen to radio and television for information.
- If planning a trip outdoors, listen to the latest forecasts and take necessary action if threatening weather is possible.

Warning issued & threatening weather...
- In a home or building, move to a pre-designated shelter, such as a basement.
- If an underground shelter is not available, move to an interior room or hallway on the lowest floor. Get under a sturdy piece of furniture.
- Stay away from windows.
- Get out of car. Do not try to outrun a tornado in your car; instead, leave it immediately.
- Mobile homes, even if tied down, offer little protection from tornadoes and should be abandoned.
- Occasionally, tornadoes develop so rapidly that advance warning is not possible. Remain alert for signs of an approaching tornado. Flying debris from tornadoes causes most deaths and injuries.
- Observe threatening skies, YOU must make the decision to seek shelter before the storm arrives. It could be the most important decision you will ever make.

TORNADO! WHAT TO DO...

House with a basement: Avoid windows. Get in the basement and under a heavy table or work bench, or cover yourself with a mattress or sleeping bag. Know where very heavy objects rest on the floor above (pianos, refrigerators, waterbeds, etc.) and do not go under them. They may fall down through a weakened floor and crush you.

House with no basement, a dorm, or an apartment: Avoid windows. Go to the lowest floor, small center room (like a bathroom or closet), under a stairwell, or in an interior hallway with no windows. Crouch as low as possible to the floor, facing down; and cover your head with your hands. A bath tub may offer a shell of partial protection. Even in an interior room, you should cover yourself with some sort of thick padding (mattress, blankets, etc.).

Office building, hospital, nursing home or skyscraper: Go directly to an enclosed, windowless area in the center of the building - away from glass. Then, crouch down and cover your head. Interior stairwells are usually good places to take shelter, and if not crowded, allow you to get to a lower level quickly. Stay off the elevators; you could be trapped in them if the power is lost.

Mobile home: Get out! Even if your home is tied down, you are probably safer outside, even if the only alternative is to seek shelter out in the open. Most tornadoes can destroy even tied-down mobile homes. If there is a sturdy permanent building within easy running distance, seek shelter there. Otherwise, lie flat on low ground away from your home, protecting your head. If possible, use open ground away from trees and cars, which can be blown onto you.

School: Follow the drill! Go to the interior hall or room in an orderly way as you are told. Crouch low, head down, and protect the back of your head with your arms. Stay away from windows and large open rooms like gyms and auditoriums.

Car or truck: Vehicles are extremely dangerous in a tornado. If the tornado is visible, far away, and the traffic is light, you may be able to drive out of its path by moving at right angles to the tornado. Otherwise, park the car as quickly and safely as possible - out of the traffic lanes. Get out and seek shelter in a sturdy building. If in the open country, run to low ground away from any cars. Lie flat and face-down, protecting the back of your head with your arms. Avoid seeking shelter under bridges, which can create deadly traffic hazards while offering little protection against flying debris.

Open outdoors: If possible, seek shelter in a sturdy building. If not, lie flat and face-down on low ground, protecting the back of your head with your arms. Get as far away from trees and cars as you can; they may be blown onto you in a tornado.

Shopping mall or large store: Do not panic. Watch for others. Move as quickly as possible to an interior bathroom, storage room or other small enclosed area, away from windows.

Church or theater: Do not panic. If possible, move quickly but orderly to an interior bathroom or hallway, away from windows. Crouch face-down and protect your head with your arms. If there is no time to do that, get under the seats or pews, protecting your head with your arms or hands.

Summary: NOAA Roger Edward

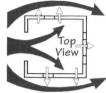

Wind Pressure on Roof
Internal pressure adds to roof uplift.

Wind Pressure on Walls
Internal pressure adds to wall suction.

Top View

Decaying or Dissipating Tornado: At this stage a "rope" tornado might form just before the break-up.

AFTER THE TORNADO...

Keep your family together and wait for emergency personnel to arrive. Carefully render aid to those who are injured. Stay away from power lines and puddles with wires in them; they may still be carrying electricity. Watch your step to avoid broken glass, nails, and other sharp objects. Stay out of any heavily damaged houses or buildings; they could collapse at any time. Do not use matches or lighters, in case of leaking natural gas pipes or fuel tanks nearby. Remain calm and alert, and listen for information and instructions from emergency crews or local officials.

Summary: NOAA Roger Edwards.

Tree's branches stripped by a tornado.

WATERSPOUTS

Sailors, 1830's, firing a canon to divert a waterspout.

Notice the rotation of the water below the waterspout.

Water Spray

WATERSPOUTS

- A violently rotating column of air, usually hanging downward from a cumulus or cumulonimbus cloud, over a body of water with its rotation reaching the water.
- In the summer and spring, these phenomena are usually considered as "tornadoes over water" that have been generated by thunderstorms.
- In the fall months, these most often begin as cold air funnels, being generated by a cold air mass passing over much warmer waters. Such waterspouts are generally much less intense than tornadoes and usually dissipate upon approaching shore.
- Waterspouts are most common along the Gulf Coast and southeastern states. In the western United States, they occur with cold late fall or late winter storms, during a time when you least expect tornado development.
- They can happen over seas, bays and lakes.
- Waterspouts occasionally move inland becoming tornadoes causing damage and injuries.
- They don't officially count in tornado records unless they hit land.
- Waterspouts can overturn small boats, damage ships, do significant damage when hitting land, and kill people.

TORNADIC WATERSPOUT

This is when a tornado passes over a stretch of water. It is just as dangerous as a tornado is over land.

MICROBURST

A great variety of environments can produce microbursts. The two principal ones are:

Dry convection: In the extremely dry environment, where moist convection is just barely possible, cumulus clouds with very high bases form in an environment that is nearly saturated at about 3 km (9800 ft) above the surface; below this high-based cloud layer there is a deep, dry layer. An instability might release a sudden downdraft of rain or virga.

Wet convection: The wet microburst environment is marked by a deep, nearly saturated layer with a nearly moist later that is topped by an elevated dry layer. This might cause an unstable situation where a severe downdraft might suddenly sink to the ground.

WARNING OF A MICROBURST

- Most microbursts are short-lived (~5 min), but some might last 20 - 30 minutes.
- Precipitation (or dust) curl that is carried by the wind back up toward cloud base.
- Horizontal bulging near the surface in a rain shaft, forming a foot-shaped prominence.
- Increase rather than a decrease in wind speed as the microburst expands out over the ground.
- Abrupt surface wind gusts followed by a rapid dissipation.
- A concentrated rain shaft or virga shaft might indicate the origin of a microburst.
- Sometimes it is very difficult to recognize the presence of microbursts. For example, narrow rain shafts look normal below a cloud, but on closer inspection you can see upward curls near the surface. Upward curls on the edges of narrow rain shafts may be indicating embedded microbursts with vortex circulations that carry a spray of raindrops back up toward the cloud.

DANGERS OF MICROBURSTS

- Passenger jets crash on attempted takeoffs and landings.
- Small sailboats can be capsized by sudden-shifting, strong winds.
- Forest fire fighters can be suddenly engulfed in a fire storm fanned up in an unexpected wind direction caused by a microburst.

MESOCYCLONE

A storm-scale region of rotation, typically around 2-6 miles in diameter and often found in the right rear flank of a supercell. The circulation of a mesocyclone covers an area much larger than the tornado that may develop within it. Properly used, mesocyclone is a radar term; it is defined as a rotation signature appearing on Doppler radar that meets specific criteria for magnitude, vertical depth, and duration. It will appear as a yellow solid circle on the Doppler velocity products. Therefore, a mesocyclone should not be considered a visually observable phenomenon (although visual evidence of rotation, such as curved inflow bands, may imply the presence of a mesocyclone).

Downburst: A strong down draft, initiated by a thunderstorm, that induces an outburst of damaging straight line winds on or near the ground. Downburst winds can produce damage similar to a strong tornado. The damage from aloft often looks like a star with debris spreading out from the center in straight lines. Although usually associated with thunderstorms, downbursts can occur with showers too weak to produce thunder. Downbursts come in the following 2 categories: microburst and macroburst.

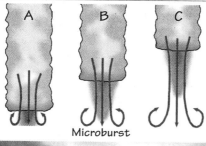

Microburst

Microburst

DRY MICROBURST

A microburst with little or no precipitation reaching the ground; most common in semi-arid regions. They may or may not produce lightning. Dry microbursts may develop in an otherwise fair-weather pattern; visible signs may include a cumulus cloud or small cumulonimbus with a high base and high-level virga, or perhaps only an orphan anvil from a dying rain shower. At the ground, the only visible sign might be a dust plume or a ring of blowing dust beneath a local area of virga.

Anti-cyclonic circulation was observed in this tornado.
Anti-cyclonic Circulation
High altitude air suddenly sinks to the ground. This can be very dangerous to aircraft

DUST PLUME

A non-rotating "cloud" of dust raised by straight-line winds. Often seen in a microburst or behind a gust front. If rotation is observed, then the term dust whirl or debris cloud should be used.

DUST STORM

Severe weather conditions marked by strong winds and dust filled air over an extensive area. Visibility is reduced to 1/2 mile or less.

DUST WHIRL

A rotating column of air rendered visible by dust. Similar to debris cloud.

WHIRLWIND

A small, rotating column of air; may be visible as a dust devil.

MACROBURST

One of 2 categories of downbursts (the other category is called a microburst). This downburst has an affected outflow area of at least 2.5 miles wide and peak winds lasting between 5 and 20 minutes. Intense macrobursts may cause tornado-force damage up to F-3.

MICROBURST SEQUENCE

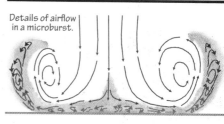

This is a sequence of a typical dry microburst that is just beginning to spread out over the surface. The microburst is rendered visible by an expanding ring of dust under a virga shaft descending from a high-based cumulonimbus. The precipitation largely evaporates before reaching the surface, so the surface rainfall is probably no more than a trace.

Details of airflow in a microburst.

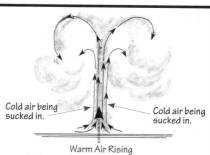

Cold air being sucked in.   Cold air being sucked in.

Warm Air Rising

DUST DEVIL

A small, vigorous whirlwind, usually of short duration, rendered visible by dust, sand, and debris picked up from the ground. They form on sunny, and dry days. They range from 10 feet to greater than 100 feet in diameter, and can extend up to 1000 feet above the ground. They are caused by intense surface heating. This heating causes the air to rapidly rise and thus, a mini low pressure system is formed. They are only seen on fair usually cloudless days - because they require the sun's heat to form the hot air columns. They are usually found in desert or dry climatic regions where dust and dirt can be easily lifted. Only rarely do they cause any damage. Wind speeds can reach 30 to 60 mph. Strong dust devils can displace lawn furniture and items weighing a few hundred pounds. If you observe a dust devil while driving - remember that a car might be hard to handle if you "hit" one.

SUDDEN BURSTS OF AIR

Hurricane Katrina

Hurricane Katrina over Florida.

Hurricanes

HURRICANE STRUCTURE

The main parts of a hurricane are the rainbands on its outer edges, the eye, and the eyewall. Air spirals in toward the center in a counter-clockwise pattern, and out the top in the opposite direction. In the very center of the storm, air sinks, forming the cloud-free eye.

Eye: The "eye" is a roughly circular area of comparatively light winds and fair weather found at the center of a severe tropical cyclone. Although the winds are calm at the axis of rotation, strong winds may extend well into the eye. There is little or no precipitation and sometimes blue sky or stars can be seen. The eye is the region of lowest surface pressure and warmest temperatures aloft. People in the midst of a hurricane are often amazed at how the incredibly fierce winds and rain can suddenly stop and the sky clear when the eye comes over them. Then, just as quickly, the winds and rain begin again, but this time from the opposite direction. The calm eye of the tropical cyclone shares many characteristics with other vortical systems such as tornadoes, waterspouts, dust devils and whirlpools. Eyes range in size from 5 mi (8 km) to over 120 mi (200 km) across, but most are approximately 20-40 mi (30-60 km) in diameter.

Eyewall: Is the dense wall of thunderstorms forming a roughly circular area of deep convection and is the area of highest surface winds in the tropical cyclone. The eye is composed of air that is slowly sinking and the eyewall has a net upward flow as a result of many moderate - occasionally strong - updrafts and downdrafts. Changes in the structure of the eye and eyewall can cause changes in the wind speed, which is an indicator of the storm's intensity. The eye can grow or shrink in size, and double (concentric) eyewalls can form.

Spiral Rainbands: Convection in tropical cyclones is organized into long, narrow rainbands which are oriented in the same direction as the horizontal wind. A direct circulation develops in which warm, moist air converges at the surface, ascends through these bands, diverges aloft, and descends on both sides of the bands. The storm's outer rainbands (often with hurricane or tropical storm-force winds) can extend a few hundred miles from the center. Hurricane Andrew's (1992) rainbands reached only 100 miles out from the eye, while those in Hurricane Gilbert (1988) stretched over 500 miles. These dense bands of thunderstorms, which spiral slowly counterclockwise, range in width from a few miles to tens of miles and are 50 to 300 miles long. Sometimes the bands and the eye are obscured by higher level clouds, making it difficult for forecasters to use satellite imagery to monitor the storm.

As a general rule of thumb, the hurricane's right side (relative to the direction it is travelling) is the most dangerous part of the storm because of the additive effect of the hurricane wind speed and speed of the larger atmospheric flow (the steering winds). The increased winds on the right side increase the storm surge and tornadoes are also more common.

Right Side (Front Quadrant) of the Storm

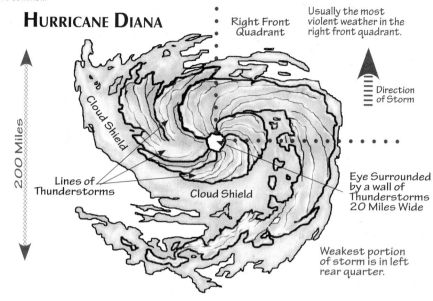

HURRICANE DIANA

Right Front Quadrant

Usually the most violent weather in the right front quadrant.

Direction of Storm

200 Miles

Lines of Thunderstorms

Cloud Shield

Cloud Shield

Eye Surrounded by a wall of Thunderstorms 20 Miles Wide

Weakest portion of storm is in left rear quarter.

With all of the intense thunderstorm activity in a tropical cyclone, large amounts of high-level cirrus clouds are generated in the upper regions of a tropical system. Sometimes these high-level clouds actually obscure the surface center on satellite imagery making it difficult for forecasters to monitor a storm's position and development.

Hurricane-force winds can extend 40 - 100 miles (64 -161km) from the eye.

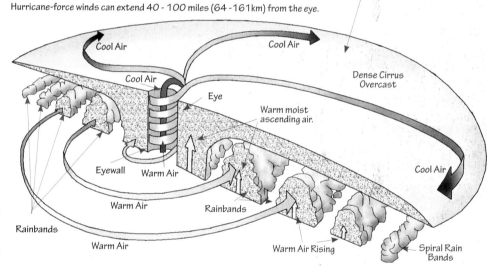

Cool Air

Cool Air

Cool Air

Eye

Warm moist ascending air.

Dense Cirrus Overcast

Cool Air

Eyewall

Warm Air

Warm Air

Rainbands

Rainbands

Warm Air

Warm Air Rising

Spiral Rain Bands

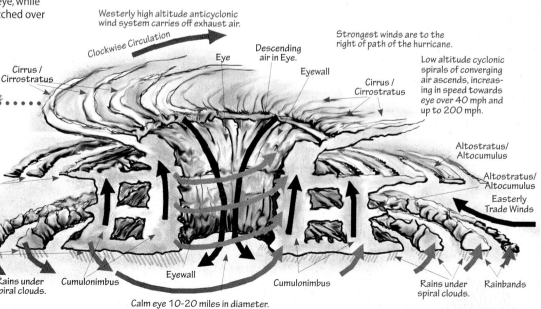

Westerly high altitude anticyclonic wind system carries off exhaust air.

Clockwise Circulation

Eye

Descending air in Eye.

Eyewall

Strongest winds are to the right of path of the hurricane.

Cirrus / Cirrostratus

Cirrus / Cirrostratus

Low altitude cyclonic spirals of converging air ascends, increasing in speed towards eye over 40 mph and up to 200 mph.

40,000 feet

Altostratus/ Altocumulus

Altostratus/ Altocumulus

Altostratus/ Altocumulus

Easterly Trade Winds

10,000-15,000 feet

Rainbands

Rains under spiral clouds.

Cumulonimbus

Eyewall

Cumulonimbus

Rains under spiral clouds.

Rainbands

Calm eye 10-20 miles in diameter.

Hurricane Katrina

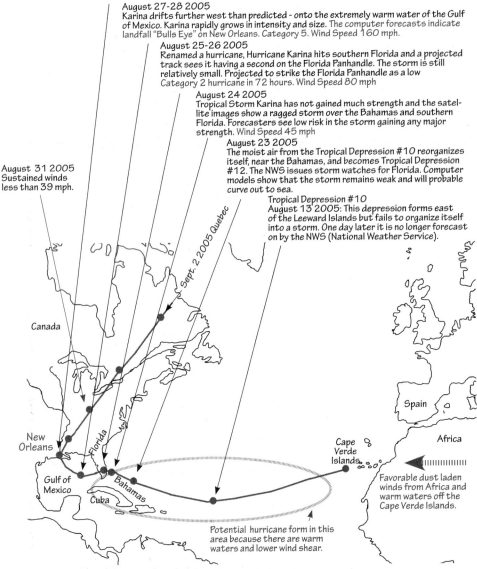

August 29 2005 LANDFALL
Katrina's center strikes slightly to the east of New Orleans. Katrina made an easterly turn just before landfall - New Orleans did not have a direct hit. It also makes landfall in the costal area of Louisiana and Mississippi. The estimated storm surge is as high as 29 feet in some areas. Category 4. Wind Speed 145mph.

August 27-28 2005
Karina drifts further west than predicted - onto the extremely warm water of the Gulf of Mexico. Karina rapidly grows in intensity and size. The computer forecasts indicate landfall "Bulls Eye" on New Orleans. Category 5. Wind Speed 160 mph.

August 25-26 2005
Renamed a hurricane, Hurricane Karina hits southern Florida and a projected track sees it having a second on the Florida Panhandle. The storm is still relatively small. Projected to strike the Florida Panhandle as a low Category 2 hurricane in 72 hours. Wind Speed 80 mph.

August 24 2005
Tropical Storm Karina has not gained much strength and the satellite images show a ragged storm over the Bahamas and southern Florida. Forecasters see low risk in the storm gaining any major strength. Wind Speed 45 mph.

August 23 2005
The moist air from the Tropical Depression #10 reorganizes itself, near the Bahamas, and becomes Tropical Depression #12. The NWS issues storm watches for Florida. Computer models show that the storm remains weak and will probable curve out to sea.

Tropical Depression #10
August 13 2005: This depression forms east of the Leeward Islands but fails to organize itself into a storm. One day later it is no longer forecast on by the NWS (National Weather Service).

August 31 2005
Sustained winds less than 39 mph.

Sept. 2 2005 Quebec

Canada

New Orleans

Florida

Gulf of Mexico

Cuba

Bahamas

Cape Verde Islands

Spain

Africa

Favorable dust laden winds from Africa and warm waters off the Cape Verde Islands.

Potential hurricane form in this area because there are warm waters and lower wind shear.

The hurricane's force will increase the longer it stays over warm water - like the Gulf of Mexico.

For a hurricane to form ocean water has to be over 80°F (27°C) to a depth of approximately 150ft (46m).

Hurricanes

There are no other storms on earth like hurricanes. Views of hurricanes from satellites located thousands of miles above the earth show how unique these powerful, tightly coiled weather systems are.

A hurricane is a type of tropical cyclone, the general term for all circulating weather systems (counterclockwise in the Northern Hemisphere) over tropical waters.

Tropical cyclones are classified as follows:

Tropical Depression: An organized system of clouds and thunderstorms with a defined circulation and maximum sustained winds of 38 mph (33 knots) or less.

Tropical Storm: An organized system of strong thunderstorms with a defined circulation and maximum sustained winds of 39 to 73 mph (34-63 knots).

Hurricane: An intense tropical weather system with a well defined circulation and maximum sustained winds of 74 mph (64 knots) or higher. In the western Pacific, hurricanes are called "typhoons," and similar storms in the Indian Ocean are called "cyclones."

Hurricanes Formation

Hurricanes are products of the tropical ocean and atmosphere. Powered by heat from the sea, they are steered by the easterly trade winds and the temperate westerlies as well as by their own ferocious energy. Around their core, winds grow with great velocity, generating violent seas.

"Cape Verde" Hurricanes: Cape Verde-type hurricanes are those Atlantic basin tropical cyclones that develop into tropical storms fairly close 600 miles off the Cape Verde Islands and then become hurricanes before reaching the Caribbean. Typically, this may occur in August and September, but in rare years there may be some in late July and/or early October.

Easterly Waves: Lower tropospheric (from the ocean surface to about 3 mi (5 km) elevation) westward traveling disturbances often serve as the "seedling" circulations for a large proportion of tropical cyclones over the North Atlantic Ocean. These African easterly waves, have their origins over North Africa. The waves move generally toward the west in the lower tropospheric tradewind flow across the Atlantic Ocean. They are first seen usually in April or May and continue until October or November. The majority of hurricanes have their origins as easterly waves. Moving ashore, they sweep the ocean inward while spawning tornadoes and producing torrential rains and floods.

Hurricane Size

Typical hurricanes are about 300 miles wide although they can vary considerably. Hurricane-force winds can extend outward to about 25 miles from the storm center of a small hurricane and to more than 150 miles for a large one.

The area over which tropical storm-force winds occur is even greater, ranging as far out as almost 300 miles from the eye of a large hurricane.

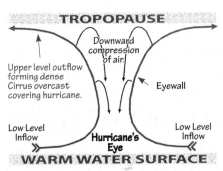

TROPOPAUSE

Downward compression of air.

Upper level outflow forming dense Cirrus overcast covering hurricane.

Eyewall

Low Level Inflow

Hurricane's Eye

Low Level Inflow

WARM WATER SURFACE

Side view of a simplified model hurricane. Air in the lowest levels of the system flows cyclonically inward toward the eyewall where it rapidly turns upward toward the tropopause. Greater atmospheric stability above the tropopause forces the air to flow outward. However some of this air is pushed in toward the cyclone center and downward helping to form and maintain the eye.

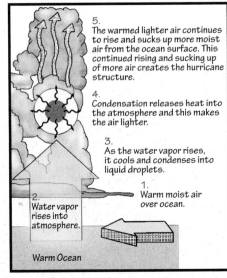

5. The warmed lighter air continues to rise and sucks up more moist air from the ocean surface. This continued rising and sucking up of more air creates the hurricane structure.

4. Condensation releases heat into the atmosphere and this makes the air lighter.

3. As the water vapor rises, it cools and condenses into liquid droplets.

2. Water vapor rises into atmosphere.

1. Warm moist air over ocean.

Warm Ocean

HURRICANES & HEAVY RAINS

Widespread rainfall of 6 to 12 inches or more is common during landfall, frequently producing deadly and destructive floods. Such floods have been the primary cause for tropical cyclone-related fatalities. The risk from flooding depends on a number of factors: the speed of the storm, its interactions with other weather systems, the terrain it encounters, and ground saturation. Even storms with relatively light winds can be very damaging. Rains are generally heaviest with slower moving storms (less than 10 mph). To estimate the total rainfall in inches, one rule of thumb is to divide 100 by the forward speed of the hurricane in miles per hour (100/forward speed = estimated inches of rain). The heaviest rain usually occurs near or along the cyclone track in the period 6 hours before and 6 hours after landfall. However, storms can last for days. Occasionally hurricanes produce little rain where it is expected. Strong winds can blow salt spray many miles inland, causing severe damage to vegetation from salt accumulation.

FLASH FLOODS

Large amounts of rain can occur more than 100 miles inland where flash floods are typically the major threat along with mudslides in mountainous regions. Tornadoes and high winds generally become less of a threat the farther inland a hurricane moves (although there have been several exceptions), but the heavy rains frequently continue and even intensify as the dying, but still powerful, hurricane is forced up higher terrain or merges with other storm systems in the area.

HIGH WINDS

The intensity of a landfalling hurricane is expressed in terms of categories that relate wind speeds and potential damage.
Tropical storm-force winds are strong enough to be dangerous to those caught in them. Hurricane-force winds can easily destroy poorly constructed buildings and mobile homes. Debris such as signs, roofing material, and small items left outside become flying missiles in hurricanes. Extensive damage to trees, towers, water and underground utility lines (from uprooted trees), and fallen poles cause considerable disruption. High-rise buildings are also vulnerable to hurricane-force winds, particularly at the higher levels since wind speed tends to increase with height. It is not uncommon for high-rise buildings to suffer a great deal of damage due to windows being blown out.

THE SAFFIR/SIMPSON HURRICANE SCALE

Hurricanes can be fickle beasts with the observed or potential damage ranging from relatively minimal to catastrophic. The damage is dependent upon several factors. Not only is the intensity of the storm important, but geophysical factors such as the size of the storm and it's associated windfield, surrounding weather situation, coastal geological features, and the astronomical tide situation play an important part.

Following numerous on-site investigations of hurricane damage, especially that from Hurricane Camille, Herbert Saffir devised a five-category damage scale in the early 1970's. The scale had the advantage of relating ranges of sustained winds to effects on vegetation and structures. Robert Simpson added additional reference to expected storm surge (the rise of a body of water above astronomical tide due to a tropical cyclone). The Tropical Prediction Center adopted the Saffir/Simpson Hurricane Scale to relate hurricane intensity and damage potential. This scale uses the storm surge, central pressure, and/or the maximum sustained winds to classify Atlantic hurricanes into one of five categories.

THE SAFFIR / SIMPSON HURRICANE INTENSITY CATEGORIES

Wind Speed / Storm Surge	Equivalent Fujita Scale* / Central Pressure	Typical Effects
		Category One Hurricane -- Weak
74-95 mph (64-82kt)	F1.0 - F1.4	Minimal Damage: Damage is primarily to shrubbery, trees, foliage, and unanchored mobile homes. No real damage occurs in building structures. Some damage is done to poorly constructed signs.
4-5 ft (1.2-1.5m)	Greater than 980 mb (28.94 in)	Low-lying coastal roads are inundated, minor pier damage occurs, some small craft in exposed anchorages torn from moorings.
		Category Two Hurricane -- Moderate
96-110 mph (83-95kt)	F1.5 - F1.9	Moderate Damage: Considerable damage is done to shrubbery and tree foliage, some trees are blown down. Major structural damage occurs to exposed mobile homes. Extensive damage occurs to poorly constructed signs. Some damage is done to roofing materials, windows, and doors; no major damage occurs to the building integrity of structures.
6-8 ft (1.8-2.4m)	965-979 mb (28.50-28.91 in)	Coastal roads and low-lying escape routes inland may be cut by rising water 2-4 hours BEFORE the hurricane center arrives. Considerable pier damage occurs, marinas are flooded. Small craft in unprotected anchorages torn from moorings. Evacuation of some shoreline residences and low-lying island areas is required.
		Category Three Hurricane -- Strong
111-130 mph (96-113kt)	F2.0 - F2.4	Extensive damage: Foliage torn from trees and shrubbery; large trees blown down. Practically all poorly constructed signs are blown down. Some damage to roofing materials of buildings occurs, with some window and door damage. Some structural damage occurs to small buildings, residences and utility buildings. Mobile homes are destroyed. There is a minor amount of failure of curtain walls (in framed buildings).
9-12 ft (2.7-3.7m)	945-964mb (27.91-28.47in)	Serious flooding occurs at the coast with many smaller structures near the coast destroyed. Larger structures near the coast are damaged by battering waves and floating debris. Low-lying escape routes inland may be cut by rising water 3-5 hours BEFORE the hurricane center arrives. Flat terrain 5 feet (1.5 m) or less above sea level flooded inland 8 miles or more. Evacuation of low-lying residences within several blocks of shoreline may be required.
		Category Four Hurricane -- Very Strong
131-155 mph (114-135kt)	F2.5 - F2.9	Extreme Damage: Shrubs and trees are blown down; all signs are down. Extensive roofing material and window and door damage occurs. Complete failure of roofs on many small residences occurs, and there is complete destruction of mobile homes. Some curtain walls experience failure.
13-18 ft (3.9-5.5m)	920-944mb (27.17-27.88in)	Flat terrain 10 feet (3 m) or less above sea level flooded inland as far as 6 miles (9.7 km). Major damage to lower floors of structures near the shore due to flooding and battering by waves and floating debris. Low-lying escape routes inland may be cut by rising water 3-5 hours BEFORE the hurricane center arrives. Major erosion of beaches occurs. Massive evacuation of ALL residences within 500 yards (457 m) of the shoreline may be required, and of single-story residences on low ground within 2 miles (3.2 km) of the shoreline.
		Category Five Hurricane -- Devastating
Greater than 155 mph (135kt)	F3.0+	Catastrophic Damage: Shrubs and trees are blown down; all signs are down. Considerable damage to roofs of buildings. Very severe and extensive window and door damage occurs. Complete failure of roof structures occurs on many residences and industrial buildings, and extensive shattering of glass in windows and doors occurs. Some complete buildings fail. Small buildings are overturned or blown away. Complete destruction of mobile homes occurs.
Greater than 18 ft (5.5m)	<920mb (<27.17IN)	Major damage occurs to lower floors of all structures located less than 15 ft (4.6 m) above sea level and within 500 yards (457 m) of the shoreline. Low-lying escape routes inland are cut by rising water 3-5 hours BEFORE the hurricane center arrives. Major erosion of beaches occurs. Massive evacuation of residential areas on low ground within 5 to 10 MILES (8-16 km) of the shoreline may be required!

* The Fujita Tornado Scale is a six-category wind speed classification scale used to classify tornado intensities. The values range from F0 to F5 and cover wind speeds up to 318 mph. The strongest SUSTAINED hurricane wind speeds correspond to a strong F3 (Severe Tornado) or possibly a weak F4 (Devastating Tornado) value.

Wreck of the City of Savannah

Widespread torrential rains often in excess of 6 inches can produce deadly and destructive floods. This is the major threat to areas well inland.

STORM SURGE

A storm surge is the greatest potential threat to life and property associated with hurricanes. It is the rise in the level of the ocean that results from the effects of wind and the drop in atmospheric pressure associated with hurricanes and other storms. It is a large dome of water often 50 to 100 miles wide that sweeps across the coastline near where a hurricane makes landfall. The surge of high water topped by waves is devastating. The stronger the hurricane and the shallower the offshore water, the higher the surge will be. Along the immediate coast, storm surge is the greatest threat to life and property.

STORM TIDE

If the storm surge arrives at the same time as the high tide, the water height will be even greater. The storm tide is the combination of the storm surge and the normal astronomical tide. The hurricane moves ashore. This mound of water, topped by battering waves, moves ashore along an area of the coastline as much as 100 miles wide. The combination of the storm surge, battering waves, and high winds is deadly. Because much of the United States' densely populated Atlantic and Gulf Coast coastlines lie less than 10 feet above mean sea level, the danger from storm tides is tremendous.

The level of surge in a particular area is also determined by the slope of the continental shelf. A shallow slope off the coast will allow a greater surge to inundate coastal communities. Communities with a steeper continental shelf will not see as much surge inundation, although large breaking waves can still present major problems. Storm tides, waves, and currents in confined harbors severely damage ships, marinas, and pleasure boats.

Storm surge also affects rivers and inland lakes, potentially increasing the area that must be evacuated. Obviously, the more intense the storm, and the closer you are to its right-front quadrant, the larger the area you will have to evacuate. Wave and current action associated with the tide also causes extensive damage. Water weighs approximately 1,700 pounds per cubic yard; extended pounding by frequent waves can demolish any structure not specifically designed to withstand such forces.

The currents created by the tide combine with the action of the waves to severely erode beaches and coastal highways. Many buildings withstand hurricane force winds until their foundations, undermined by erosion, are weakened and fail. In estuaries and bayous, intrusions of salt water endanger the public health and send animals, such as snakes, fleeing from flooded areas.

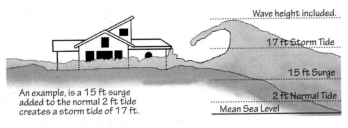

Wave height included.

17 ft Storm Tide

15 ft Surge

2 ft Normal Tide

Mean Sea Level

An example, is a 15 ft surge added to the normal 2 ft tide creates a storm tide of 17 ft.

A 20 ft storm surge is quite impressive.

6 ft

A sudden storm surge.

HURRICANES & TORNADOES

Almost all tropical cyclones making landfall in the United States spawn at least one tornado. Most of the tornadoes form in outer rainbands some 50-200 miles from the tropical cyclone center (eye). Tropical cyclones may spawn tornadoes up to three days after landfall. In general, it appears that tropical cyclone tornadoes are somewhat weaker and briefer than mid latitude tornadoes. Hurricane Beulah spawned a reported 141 tornadoes in southeast Texas during the first several days after its landfall in September 1967. In 1992, Hurricane Andrew spawned 62 tornadoes. Hurricane tornadoes are often spawned by unusually small storm cells that may not appear particularly dangerous on weather radars, especially if the cells are located more than about 60 miles from the radar. In addition, these small storms often tend to produce little or no lightning or thunder, and may not look very threatening visually to the average person. Furthermore, the tornadoes are often obscured by rain, and the storm cells spawning them may move rapidly, leaving little time to take evasive action once the threat has been perceived.

Hurricane lantern swaying in the breeze.

Tropical Storm Watch: Tropical Storm conditions are possible in the specified area of the Watch, usually within 36 hours.

Tropical Storm Warning: Tropical Storm conditions are expected in the specified area of the Warning, usually within 24 hours.

Hurricane Watch: Hurricane conditions are possible in the specified area of the Watch, usually within 36 hours. During a Hurricane Watch, prepare to take immediate action to protect your family and property in case a *Hurricane Warning* is issued.

Hurricane Warning: Hurricane conditions are expected in the specified area of the Warning, usually within 24 hours. Complete all storm preparations and evacuate if directed by local officials.

Short Term Watches & Warnings: These provide detailed information on specific hurricane threats, such as tornadoes, floods, and high winds.

A 2x4 implanted in the trunk of a palm tree after a hurricane.

AREAS AT RISK

Coastal Areas & Barrier Islands

All Atlantic and Gulf coastal areas are subject to hurricanes or tropical storms. Although rarely struck by hurricanes, parts of the Southwest United States and Pacific Coast suffer heavy rains and floods each year from the remnants of hurricanes spawned off Mexico. Due to the limited number of evacuation routes, barrier islands are especially vulnerable to hurricanes. People on barrier islands and in vulnerable coastal areas may be asked by local officials to evacuate well in advance of a hurricane landfall. If you are asked to evacuate, do so IMMEDIATELY!

Inland Areas

Hurricanes affect inland areas with high winds, floods, and tornadoes. Listen carefully to local authorities to determine what threats you can expect and take the necessary precautions to protect yourself, your family, and your property.

HURRICANE SEASON

The portion of the year having a relatively high incidence of hurricanes. The hurricane season in the Atlantic, Caribbean, and Gulf of Mexico runs from June 1 to November 30. The hurricane season in the Eastern Pacific basin runs from May 15 to November 30. The hurricane season in the Central Pacific basin runs from June 1 to November 30.

HURRICANE WARNING

A warning that sustained winds 64 kt (74 mph or 119 kph) or higher associated with a hurricane are expected in a specified coastal area in 24 hours or less. A hurricane warning can remain in effect when dangerously high water or a combination of dangerously high water and exceptionally high waves continue, even though winds may be less than hurricane force.

HURRICANE WATCH

An announcement of specific coastal areas that a hurricane or an incipient hurricane condition poses a possible threat, generally within 36 hours.

PRE-HURRICANE SQUALL LINE

It is often the first serious indication that a hurricane is approaching. It is a generally a straight line and resembles a squall-line that occurs with a mid-latitude cold front. It is as much as 50 miles or even more before the first ragged rain echoes of the hurricane's bands and is usually about 100 to 200 miles ahead of the eye, but it has been observed to be as much as 500 miles ahead of the eye in monstrous size hurricanes.

ATLANTIC & GULF COAST

They typically have low-lying shorelines subject to storms and erosion can change dramatically over time.

These illustrations show the destructive erosion sequence.
A: a typical pre-storm profile is shown of the coastline several hundred feet deep.
B: the same area during a hurricane, with the ocean waves inundating and damaging several houses.
C: the storm eroded the coastline destroying the house that was closest to the ocean. The remaining houses are now closer to the ocean.
D: decades later, a second hurricane hits the area.
D differs in two important ways from B.
- Because the coastline has eroded (50 to 100 ft over 30 years is fairly common for the Atlantic and Gulf coasts), storm wave heights at each house now are somewhat further inland and higher than they were before and, therefore, are capable of causing greater damage.
- Some of the houses that were not previously within the high-hazard now are located there. Now, because of erosion, these houses are subject to the bigger and higher velocity waves that they were not designed to withstand.

HOUSES ON ERODING BLUFF

Houses built on high bluffs above the oceans (as often occurs along parts of New England and the West Coast) or high cliffs along the Great Lakes. Flood damage in the house is not a problem; the water never gets as high as the bluff. However, the bluff beneath the house can erode, and when the foundation is reached, the house will be lost or damaged sufficiently to become uninhabitable. Regardless, in an eroding area, the land and house will sooner or later be lost.

SEQUENCE OF BLUFF EROSION

A: stable bluff from the water's edge to several hundred feet inland.
B: the same bluff during a storm or higher than average lake levels. The base (or toe) of the bluff is being eroded away by waves. The top of the bluff eventually becomes unstable as erosion undercuts the bluff.
C: new bluff profile after the bluff stabilizes, with the edge of the bluff further inland than before and a lost house.

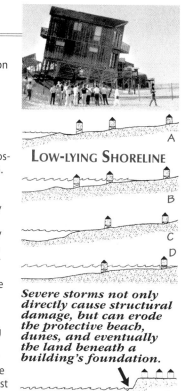

LOW-LYING SHORELINE

Severe storms not only directly cause structural damage, but can erode the protective beach, dunes, and eventually the land beneath a building's foundation.

BLUFF EROSION

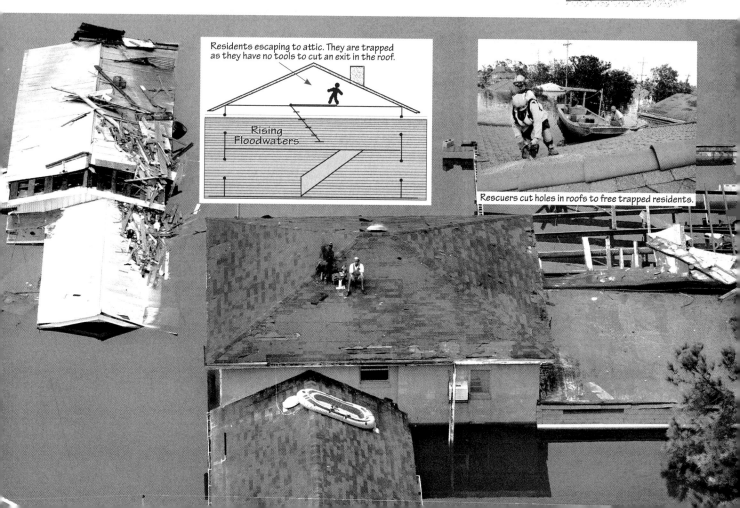

Residents escaping to attic. They are trapped as they have no tools to cut an exit in the roof.

Rising Floodwaters

Rescuers cut holes in roofs to free trapped residents.

OPTICAL ATMOSPHERIC PHENOMENA

Lunar Halo with Moon Dogs

Sun Dog
Sun

Arc Reflex
Halo
Sun
Sun Dog

Arc Reflex
22° Halo
Sun
Sun Dog

ARCS

These are arcs formed by refracted light - there are two arcs - one above and one below (if seen) the Sun. These arcs appear 22° or more above and below the Sun. The Arc Reflex, if seen, would intersect the 22° Halo.

22° Halo around the Moon

Sun Dogs
Sun
22° Halo

Sun, Sun Dog and Haloes

PARHELIA (SUN DOGS, MOCK SUNS)

The scientific name for sun dogs. Either of two colored luminous spots that appear at roughly 22° on both sides of the sun at the same elevation. They are caused by the refraction of sunlight passing through ice crystals. They are most commonly seen during winter in the middle latitudes and are exclusively associated with cirriform clouds. They are also known as mock suns.

Lunar Corona - As drawn on Scott's expedition to the South Pole.

CORONA

A white or colored circle or set of concentric circles of light of small radius seen around a luminous body, especially around the sun or moon. The color varies from blue inside to red outside and the phenomenon is attributed to diffraction of light by thin clouds or mist (distinguished from halo).

STRANGE WEATHER PREDICTORS

Refractions of light of any remarkable kind frequently forebode rain, sometimes storms; at sea the knowledge of this is very useful. Circles around the sun and moon, mock suns, and other phenomena of this kind, together with the unusual elevation of distant coasts, masts of ships, etc., particularly when the refracted images are inverted, are known to be frequent foreboders of stormy weather.

HALO WEATHER PREDICTOR

- The Moon, Sun, and stars are all weather indicators. A ring around the Moon or Sun means rain. The ring is created when tiny ice particles in fine cirrus clouds scatter the light of the Moon and the Sun in different directions. When stars appear to twinkle, it indicates that strong winds are not far off, and will become strong surface winds within a few hours. Also, a large number of stars in the heavens show clear visibility with a good chance of frost or dew.
- The larger the halo about the moon the nearer the rain clouds and the sooner the rain may be expected.
- Evening red and morning gray will set the traveler on his way; But evening gray and morning red will bring down rain upon his head.
- Ring(s) around the moon means rain (the ring is due to high ice clouds). With the barometer falling at the same time, the probability of being correct is 75%.

478

Sky Glossary

Astronomical Dawn
The time at which the sun is 18° below the horizon in the morning. Astronomical dawn is that point in time at which the sun starts lightening the sky. Prior to this time during the morning, the sky is completely dark.

Astronomical Dusk
This is the time at which the sun is 18° below the horizon in the evening. At this time the sun no longer illuminates the sky.

Civil Dawn
The time of morning at which the sun is 6° below the horizon. At this time, there is enough light for objects to be distinguishable and that outdoor activities can commence.

Civil Dusk
The time at which the sun is 6° below the horizon in the evening. At this time objects are distinguishable but there is no longer enough light to perform any outdoor activities.

Diamond Dust
A fall of non-branched (snow crystals are branched) ice crystals in the form of needles, columns, or plates. These ice crystals while still in the sky reflect and refract sun or moon light and produce the optical phenomena of haloes, sun pillars, sun dogs, etc.

Fallstreak
Same as Virga; streaks or wisps of precipitation falling from a cloud but evaporating before reaching the ground. In certain cases, shafts of virga may precede a microburst.

Nautical Dawn
The time at which the sun is 12° below the horizon in the morning. Nautical dawn is defined as that time at which there is just enough sunlight for objects to be distinguishable.

Nautical Dusk
The time at which the sun is 12° below the horizon in the evening. At this time, objects are no longer distinguishable.

Nautical Twilight
The time after civil twilight, when the brighter stars used for celestial navigation have appeared and the horizon may still be seen. It ends when the center of the sun is 12° below the horizon, and it is too difficult to perceive the horizon, preventing accurate sighting of stars.

Sunrise
Phenomenon of the sun's daily appearance on the eastern horizon as a result of the earth's rotation. The word is often used to refer to the time at which the first part of the sun becomes visible in the morning at a given location.

Sunset
Phenomenon of the sun's daily disappearance below the western horizon. The word is often used to refer to the time at which the last part of the sun disappears below the horizon in the evening at a given location.

Undersun
An optical effect seen by an observer above a cloud deck when looking toward the sun, as sunlight is reflected upwards off the faces of ice crystals in the cloud deck.

Mirage off Greenland 1822. See page 81 & 212

Partial Halo

Sun Pillar

22° Halo

Sun Dogs

Sun Pillar

Sun Pillar
Bright column above or below the sun produced by the reflection of sunlight from ice crystals.

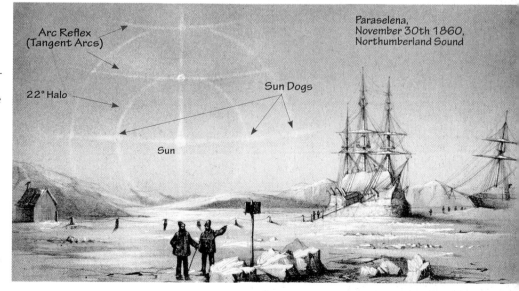

Arc Reflex (Tangent Arcs)

22° Halo

Sun

Sun Dogs

Paraselena, November 30th 1860, Northumberland Sound

Brocken Specter

An optical phenomenon sometimes occurring at high altitudes when the image of an observer placed between the sun and a cloud is projected on the cloud as a greatly magnified shadow. The shadow's head is surrounded by rings of color, called a glory.

GLORY

An optical effect characterized by concentric rings of color (red outermost and violet innermost) surrounding the shadow of an observer's head when the shadow is cast onto a cloud deck below the observer's elevation (see Brocken Specter).

Sun is behind the airplane. Airplane shadow is cast upon the cloud.

CREPUSCULAR RAYS

The alternating bands of light and dark (rays and shadows of the clouds) seen at the earth's surface when the sun shines through clouds.

Crepuscular Rays: Formed by shadc cast by distant clouds or mountain

RAINBOW WEATHER PREDICTORS

- Rainbow in morning, shepherds take warning; Rainbow at night, shepherds' delight.
- Rainbow at night, sailors' delight; Rainbow in morning, sailors' warning.
- Rainbow in morning shows that shower is west of us and that we will probably get it. Rainbow in the evening shows that shower is east of us and is passing off.
- A morning rainbow is often followed by a squall. Afternoon rainbow means unsettled weather, while an evening rainbow marks a passing storm. A faint rainbow around the Sun precedes colder weather.

RAINBOW

A rainbow is formed by sunlight diffracting inside individual raindrops. This diffraction separates the sunlight (considered as white) into the colors of the spectrum (as seen in the visual spectrum on the right). This usually happens when a summer storm rapidly passes through an area and then the sun reemerges. The sun has to be low in the sky and behind the observer. Because of this rainbows are seen early in the mornings or in the late afternoon. The upper side of a rainbow is red and the lower side is blue-violet. Raindrops only have a diameter of 0.05 inch.

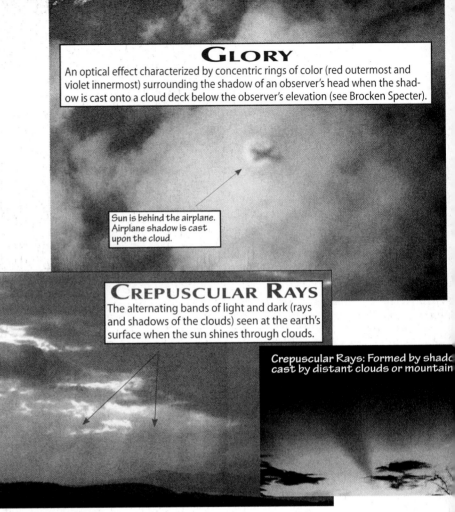

Sun's Rays

Rain Cloud

Each color emerges from the raindrop at a different angle.

Red

Violet

Raindrop Magnified

Observer

Rainbow: An arc that exhibits in concentric bands the colors of the spectrum and is formed opposite the sun by refraction and reflection of the sun's rays in rain drops.

Secondary Rainbow
It forms when light is reflected twice inside a raindrop. This rainbow is lighter as there is less light reflected twice. The colors are opposite to the primary rainbow. It forms at 51°.

Alexander's Dark Band
A band of 9° between the two rainbows.

Primary Rainbow
Has red on the outside (top) and violet on the inside (bottom). It forms at 42°.

White Light (Sunlight)
Sunlight integrated over the visible portion of the spectrum (4000 - 7000 angstroms - wavelength measurement) so that all colors are blended to appear white to the eye.

Violet

51°

42°

Raindrops

Violet

Sun's Rays

Observer

Raindrops act like a prism which splits sunlight (considered as white) into its component colors as shown in this band.

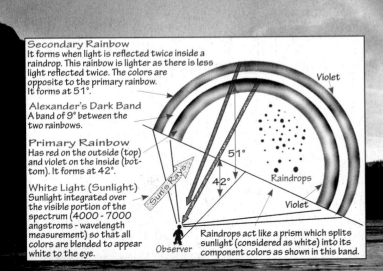

43 Trees

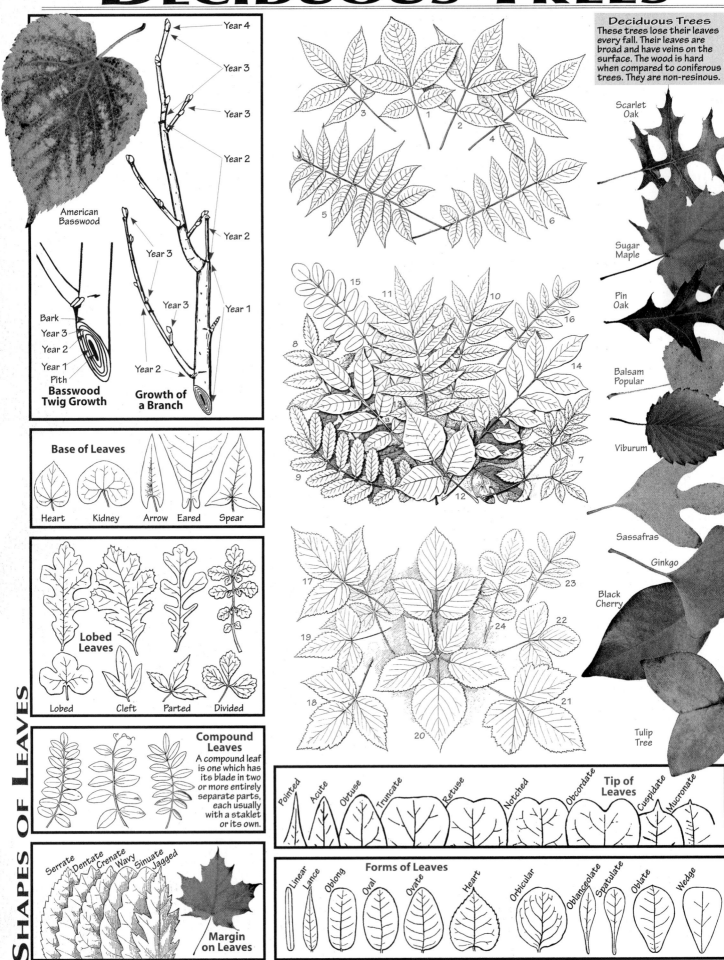

American Basswood

Year 4
Year 3
Year 3
Year 2
Year 2
Year 3
Year 3
Year 2
Year 1
Year 2

Basswood Twig Growth

Bark
Year 3
Year 2
Year 1
Pith

Growth of a Branch

Deciduous Trees
These trees lose their leaves every fall. Their leaves are broad and have veins on the surface. The wood is hard when compared to coniferous trees. They are non-resinous.

Scarlet Oak
Sugar Maple
Pin Oak
Balsam Popular
Viburum
Sassafras
Ginkgo
Black Cherry
Tulip Tree

Base of Leaves

Heart   Kidney   Arrow   Eared   Spear

Lobed Leaves

Lobed   Cleft   Parted   Divided

Compound Leaves

A compound leaf is one which has its blade in two or more entirely separate parts, each usually with a staklet or its own.

SHAPES OF LEAVES

Serrate   Dentate   Crenate   Wavy   Sinuate   Jagged

Margin on Leaves

Pointed   Acute   Obtuse   Truncate   Retuse   Notched   Obcordate   Cuspidate   Mucronate

Tip of Leaves

Forms of Leaves

Linear   Lance   Oblong   Oval   Ovate   Heart   Orbicular   Oblangeolate   Spatulate   Oblate   Wedge

1 **Shagbark** *Tree* 80 ft. Shaggy bark, best of the nuts to eat, husk separate in 4 parts, nut pointed.

2 **Pignut** *Tree* 70 ft. Bark light blue-gray, finely cracked, fruit pear shaped, kernel bitter; nuts from some trees are edible.

3 **Walnut** *Tree* 70 ft. Bark ash-gray, rough furrowed, kernel sweet, leaves strong scented, nut round oval.

4 **Bitternut** *Tree* 70 ft. Light-gray bark, less rough, fruit round, smooth, nut shell thin, kernel very bitter.

5 **Black Walnut** *Tree* 70 ft. Bark dark gray, rough, fruit short stemmed, round, smooth, husk spongy, kernel oily, rich.

6 **Butternut** *Tree* 40 ft. Bark gray, rough furrowed, fruit long stemmed, egg shaped, leathery husk, kernel oily but sweet.

7 **Wild Sarsaparilla** *Shrub like* 2 ft. The aromatic, spicy rootstock only woody, the shoots herb-like, black berries in a bunch. There are several kinds.

8 **American Mountain Ash** *Shrub or slender tree* 20 ft. White blossoms berries bright orange-red.

9 **European Mountain Ash** *Tree* 40 ft. Has larger fruits.

10 **Staghorn Sumach** *Tree* 20 ft. Fruit scarlet, flowers yellowish-green; young shoots covered with wool.

11 **Smooth Sumach** *Shrub* 10 ft. Yellowish-green scenting flowers, fruit velvety crimson, shoots smooth.

12 **Poison Ivy** *Creeping & climbing*; flowers yellowish-white; poisonous to touch.

13 **Shining Dwarf Sumach** *Shrub* 6 ft. Branches and footstalks brown dotted, berries crimson.

14 **Poison Dogwood** *Shrub* 15 ft. Stem gray, young shoots purplish. Our most poisonous plant.

15 **Locust** *Tree* 30 ft. Flowers yellowish-white, beautifully scented, fruit a bean.

16 **Prickly Ash** *Shrub* 5 ft. Stem gray, shoots brown, wood yellow, bark bitter.

17 **Raspberry** *Shrub* 4 ft. Flowers white, berries light red and finely flavored.

18 **Thimbleberry (Rasberry)** *Shrub* 3 ft. Flowers white, berries purplish-black and good.

19 **Dwarf Raspberry** *Shrub* 1 ft. Fruit a few red grains.

20 **High Blackberry** *Shrub* 6 ft. Berries black, large and late. There is a smooth and smaller trailing variety.

21 **Low Blackberry** *Trailing* Berries black, large, and sweet; early.

22 **Swamp Blackberry** *Trailing* Berries of a few grains, red or purple, sour.

23 **Virginia Rose** *Shrub* 2 ft. Flower rose color, fruit smooth.

24 **Carolina Rose** *Shrub* 7 ft. Flower rose color, fruit bristly.

25 **Virgin's Bower** *Climbing* Flowers white, fruit feathery.

26 **Bladdernut** *Shrub* 10 ft. Fruit a large, skinny pouch containing seeds; grows in wood swamps.

27 **Red Elder** *Shrub* 6 ft. Flowers white, berries red.

28 **Black Elder** *Shrub* 10 ft. Flowers white, fruit purplish-black, pleasant.

29 **Black Ash** *Tree* 70 ft. Slender, dark granite-gray bark; shoots yellowish with lighter dots.

30 **Red Ash** *Tree* 50 ft. Dark ashy-gray bark.

31 **White Ash** *Tree* 70 ft. Whitish bark; shoots gray-green, dotted gray.

32 **Buttonwood (Sycamore)** *Tree* 100 ft. Bark gray, peeling off, showing light under bark.

33 **Sweetgum Tree** *Tree* 40 ft. Gray bark, with corky ridges on the branches; leaves fragrant when bruised.

34 **Swamp Gooseberry** *Shrub* Berries small, dark purple, and bristly.

35 **Roundleafed Gooseberry** *Shrub* Berries small, purple, smooth, and sweet.

36 **Smooth Wild Gooseberry** *Shrub* 3 ft. Berries small, purple, sweet, and

37 **Prickly Wild Gooseberry** *Shrub* 3 ft. Berries large, covered with long prickles.

38 **Red-Flowering Raspberry** *Shrub* 5 ft. Flowers large, purple-rose color; berries of few reddish grains.

39 **Black Currant** *Shrub* 4 ft. Flowers large, berries black.

40 **Red Currant** *Shrub* 3 ft., Straggling; fruit red and smooth.

41 **Red Swamp Currant** *Stem low, straggling* berries red and bristly, smelling skunky.

42 **Moonseed** *Climbing vine* Flowers white; fruit grape-like; black berries.

43 **Silver Maple** *Tree* 60 ft. Stem gray; shoots light green-yellow, with brown dots or stripes.

44 **Sugar Maple** *Tree* 80 ft. Stem blue-gray. From the sap of this maple sugar is made.

45 **Red Maple** *Tree* 40 ft. Stem gray; shoots crimson, dotted with brown.

46 **Mountain Maple** *Shrub* 10 ft. Light gray, with olive stripes; shoots light fresh green; when older, light purple dotted or striped green.

47 **Striped Maple** *Tree* 20 ft. Stem brown striped; shoots green, white striped.

48 **Virginian Creeper** *Vine* Berries upright, dark blue.

49 **Fox Grape** *Vine* Grapes dark purple, black, or white, in close bunches; Berries large, some pleasant. Early and late varieties.

50 **Summer Grape** *Vine* Grapes dark blue, loose in the bunch; agreeable; ripe in October.

51 **Chicken Grape** *Vine* Grape dark purple, almost black; as large as a pea; acid, but good; ripens late.

52 **Post Oak** *Tree* 30 ft. Acorns on very short stems; small and sweet.

53 **Bur Oak** *Tree* 40 ft. Acorns 1 in. long, deep in a mossy, fringed cup.

54 **White Oak** *Tree* 60 ft. Acorns 1 in. long; eatable, particularly when roasted.

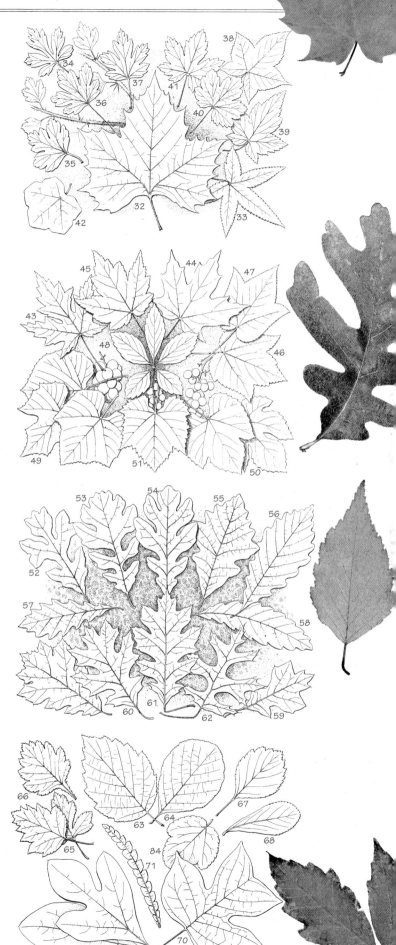

483

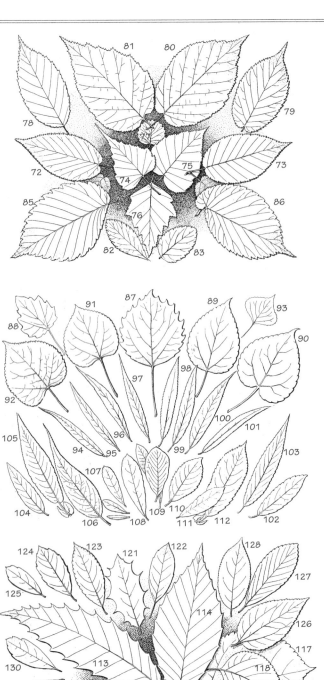

55 **Swamp Oak** *Tree* 60 ft. Whitish shaggy bark, peeling off in shreds; many horizontal branches; acorns sweet.
56 **Chestnut Oak** *Tree* 50 ft. Acorn 1 in. long, sweet; bark reddish-gray.
57 **Dwarf Chinquapin Oak** *Shrub* 4 ft. Our smallest oak. Acorns sweet, many on a limb; bark bitter.
58 **Chinquapin Oak** *Tree* 30 ft.- Bark whitish, wood very yellow; acorns 3/4 in. long, sweet, and edible.
59 **Scrub Oak** *Shrub* 8 ft. Bark greenish-black, dotted with gray; acorns 1/2 in. long, bitter.
60 **Black Oak** *Tree* 90 ft. Under bark yellow, wood reddish; acorns 1/2 in. long, very bitter, kernel yellow.
61 **Red Oak** *Tree* 75 ft. Bark dark green-gray, smooth; acorns 1 in. long, kernel white & bitter.
62 **Scarlet Oak** *Tree* 70 ft. Bark reddish-gray, under bark reddish;. acorns 1/2 in. long, kernel white and bitter.
63 **Speckled Alder** *Shrub or tree* 20 ft. Bark reddish or dark green, with light gray dots.
64 **Common Alder** *Shrub* 15 ft. Bark gray, with horizontal, oblong, gray-orange dots.
65 **Scarlet Hawthorn** *Tree* 20 ft. Flowers white, rosy tinted; berries bright scarlet-red.
66 **Pear Hawthorn** *Tree* 15 ft. Berries crimson or orange colored; roundish pear shaped; edible.
67 **Dotted Hawthorn** *Tree or shrub* 15 ft. Berries dull red, yellowish with white dots.
68 **Cockspur Hawthorn** *Tree* 20 ft. Berry bright red; slender, long thorns.
69 **Sassafras** *Tree* 30 ft., Young shoots, bright green; oval, dark blue berries, on red stems.
70 **Tulip Tree** *Tree* 100 ft. Flowers, 2 in. wide, greenish-yellow, marked with orange.
71 **Sweetfern** *Shrub* 2 ft. A round-headed bush; leaves fragrant.
72 **Sweet Birch** *Tree* 80 ft. Bark dark purplish, smooth; leaves aromatic, spicy.
73 **Yellow Birch** *Tree* 80 ft. Bark dirty yellowish-gray, with silvery luster, peeling off and shaggy.
74 **Gray Birch** *Tree* 40 ft. Bark chalky white, with black spots.
75 **Canoe Birch** *Tree* 100 ft. Bark white, with pearly shine.
76 **Red Birch** *Tree* 50 ft. Bark reddish-chocolate color, ragged and broken.
77 **Dwarf Birch** *Shrub* 2 ft. Bark brownish, dotted with warty specks.
78 **Hornbeam** *Tree* 20 ft. Stem ridged; bark bluish-gray, smooth; nuts 8 sided, taste like chestnuts; white, hard wood.
79 **Iron or Leverwood** *Tree* 40 ft. Bark brownish, finely furrowed; very hard, white wood, nut small and smooth.
80 **Common Hazel Nut** *Shrub* 8 ft. Fruit cover leafy.
81 **Beaked Hazel Nut** *Shrub* 6 ft. Fruit cover long-beaked and bristly.
82 **Meadow-Sweet** *Shrub* 6 ft. Flowers white; stem red-copper color.
83 **Hardhack** *Shrub* 5 ft. Flowers purple-rose color; stem dark bronze.
84 **Ninebark** *Shrub* 7 ft. Flowers white, with rosy tinge.
85 **American Elm** *Tree* 120 ft. Branches often cover 100 ft.
86 **Slippery Elm** *Tree* 50 ft. Inner bark edible.
87 **Large Toothed Poplar** *Tree* 50 ft. Bark light greenish-gray, smooth, leathery.
88 **Silver Poplar** *Tree* 70 ft. Light gray bark and white foliage.
89 **Balsam Poplar** *Tree* 80 ft. Bark light gray, smooth, leather-like.
90 **Balm of Gilead** *Tree* 100 ft. Bark light gray, and large, sticky leaf buds.

91 **Quaking Aspen** *Tree* 40 ft. Bark white clay-colored, smooth, and leathery; dark brown, triangular blotches under the limbs.
92 **Cottonwood** *Tree* 80 ft. Bark dark gray; fruit with large, white, cotton tufts.
93 **Lombardy Poplar** *Tree* 70 ft. Bark brown-gray; branches not spreading, shape like a shut umbrella.
94 **Basket Osier** *Small tree* 15 ft. Best willow for basket work; grows in wet meadows.
95 **Hoary Willow** *Shrub* 5 ft. Twigs reddish; a whitish-looking bush.
96 **Longleaf Willow** *Tree* 20 ft. Stems & branches often laying on the ground, taking root.
97 **Weeping Willow** *Tree* 25 ft. Branches and leaves drooping.
98 **Silkyleaf Willow** *Shrub* 10 ft. Of grayish appearance, on sandy river banks.
99 **Stalked Willow** *Shrub* 10 ft.
100 **Brittle Willow** *Tree* 40 ft. Bark very rough; young shoots, smooth, polished green.
101 **Black Willow** *Tree* 25 ft. Rough bark.
102 **Silky-Headed Willow** *Shrub or small tree* 15 ft. Fruit long, silky.
103 **White Willow** *Tree* 80 ft. Young shoots bright yellow or reddish.
104 **Pussy Willow** *Shrub* 15 ft. Grows in low meadows.
105 **Heart-Shaped Willow** *Shrub or small tree* 15 ft.
106 **Shining Willow** *Shrub or tree* 15 ft. Glossy.
107 **Dwarf Pussy Willow** *Shrub* 1 1/2 ft.
108 **Low Bush Willow** *Shrub* 8 ft.
109 **Bog Willow** *Shrub* 3 ft.
110 **Long-Beaked Willow** *Small tree* 15 ft.
111 **Purple Willow** *Small tree* 15 ft. Polished olive-colored branches.
112 **Silky Willow** *Shrub* 15 ft.
113 **Chestnut** *Tree* 100 ft. 3 sweet nuts in a burr, bark, dark lead-gray.
114 **Beach** *Tree* 70 ft. 2 triangular nuts in each cup; bark light gray, smooth.
115 **Basswood** *Tree* 40 ft. Yellowish-white fragrant flowers.
116 **Witch Hazel** *Shrub* 20 ft. Yellow flowers; late in autumn when leaves have fallen.
117 **Red Mullberry** *Tree* 30 ft. Dark purple, blackberry-like berries.
118 **Hackberry Nettletree** *Tree* 40 ft. Sweet cherry-like berries.
119 **Buckthorn Common** *Small tree* 20 ft. Black, purging berries in clusters.
120 **Alder Buckthorn** *Shrub* 3 ft. Black pear shaped berries with 3 kernels.
121 **Holly** *Tree* 20 ft. Flowers white, bright scarlet-red berries.
122 **Canadian Holly** *Shrub* 10 ft. Beautiful pale crimson berries on long red stems.
123 **Winterberry** *Shrub* 10 ft. Bright red berries on short stems, scattered on branches.
124 **Singleberry Holly** *Shrub* 10 ft. Orange-red berries on very short stems.
125 **Inkberry** *Shrub* 6 ft. Evergreen white flowers and black berries.
126 **New Jersey Tea** *Shrub* 3 ft. White flowers, in clusters; white flower stems.
127 **Sweet Pepperbush** *Shrub* 6 ft. White fragrant flowers, late in August.
128 **Bittersweet** *Vine* orange-red berries, in clusters.
129 **Sweet Gale** *Shrub* 4 ft. A dark bush, growing in patches in swamps.
130 **Bayberry (Wax Myrtle)** *Shrub* 7 ft. Leaves and berries with balsamic odor.
131 **Common Barberry** *Shrub* 6 ft. Flowers yellow, long oval, orange berries in clusters, thorny, wood yellow.
132 *Previous Page* **Shadbush** *Shrub or small tree* 15 ft. Pear shaped purplish berries, sweet.
133 **Chokeberry** *Shrub* 5 ft. Reddish-purple, dry puckery berry.

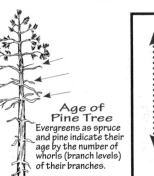

Age of Pine Tree
Evergreens as spruce and pine indicate their age by the number of whorls (branch levels) of their branches.

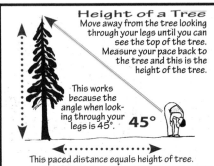

Height of a Tree
Move away from the tree looking through your legs until you can see the top of the tree. Measure your pace back to the tree and this is the height of the tree.

This works because the angle when looking through your legs is 45°.

45°

This paced distance equals height of tree.

134 Yellow Plum *Tree* 115 ft. Reddish-orange, puckery plum.

135 Beach Plum *Shrub* 4 ft. Plum roundish, purple.

136 Bullace Tree *Tree* 15 ft. Plum round, black, with yellowish bloom.

137 Wild Red Cherry *Tree* 15 ft. Small, sour, red cherries.

138 Sand Cherry *Trailing* 1 ft. Dark red cherries; edible.

139 Black, or Rum Cherry *Tree*, 40 ft. Black-purplish, aromatic cherries.

140 Choke Cherry *Tree* 10 ft. Dark red, pleasant, but puckery cherries.

141 Withe Rod *Shrub* 10 ft. Berries dark blue

142 Nannyberry Viburnum *Shrub* 15 ft. Berries dark scarlet color.

143 Arrowwood *Shrub* 10 ft. Berries dark blue-lead color.

144 Mapleleaf Arrow Wood *Shrub* 6 ft. Berries blue-black.

145 Cranberrybush Tree *Shrub* 10 ft. Berries red, pleasant acid.

146 Wayfaringtree (Hobblebush) *Shrub* 20 ft. Berries egg shaped, dark red.

147 Honeysucle Bush *Shrub* 4 ft. Flowers yellow.

148 Greenbriar *Thorny vine* green stem, blue-black berries.

149 Carrion Flower Greenbriar *Vine* not thorny, flowers stink.

150 Persimmon *Tree* 30 ft. Plumlike, fruit edible after frost.

151 Tupelo, Pepperidge *Tree* 30 ft. Horizontal branches, blue berries.

152 Spicebush *Shrub* 10 ft. Flowers yellow, berries red, leaves fragrant.

153 Rhodora *Shrub* 5 ft. Flower purple rose color.

154 White Azalea (Swamp Pink) *Shrub* 8 ft. White fragrant flowers.

155 Pink Azalea *Shrub* 5 ft. Dark red flower, fragrant before leaves.

156 Leatherwood *Shrub* 5 ft. Bark very tough, stem looks jointed.

157 Staggerbush *Shrub* 6 ft. White flower, cylindrical bell shaped.

158 Maleberry *Shrub* 8 ft. White flower, round, globular bell shaped.

159 Highbush Blueberry *Shrub* 8 ft.
(a) Leaves and edge smooth.
(b) Leaves and edge bristly, hairy.
(c) Leaves woolly below, berries black.

160 Pinweeds *Heath-like bushes* 1 ft. Purple-brown flowers.

161 Sunrose 1 ft. *Flower* yellow.

162 Medium Blueberry *Shrub* 2 ft. Late blueberry.

163 Low Blueberry *Shrub* 1 ft. Earliest blueberry; also a black variety.

164 Huckleberry *Shrub* 2 ft. Berries shining black, sweet; leaves dotted below.

165 Dangleberry *Shrub* 5 ft. Berries large, blue on slender stem; acid.

166 Canada Huckleberry *Shrub* 2 ft. Berries large, black, tasteless

167 Deerberry *Shrub* 3 ft. Berries greenish-white. Not edible.

168 Beechheathers *Heath-like sand plants* 6 in., of gray aspect; flowers yellow.

169 Rhododendron (Rose Bay) *Shrub* 7 ft. Flowers pale rose color

170 Magnolia *Shrub* 8 ft. Flowers large, white.

171 Laurel *Shrub* 8 ft. Flowers white, and pinkish-white.

172 Sheep's Laurel *Shrub* 2 ft. Flowers deep rose-red; leaves in 3's

173 Dwarf Laurel *Shrub* 1 ft. Flowers pale lilac-purple, leaves opposite.

174 Labrador Tea *Shrub* 3 ft. Flowers white, leaves rusty-woolly below.

175 Cranberry *Shrub* 2 ft. Berries large, bright scarlet-red.

176 Dwarf Cranberry *Plant* 1/2 ft. Berries red, small.

177 Leatherleaf *Shrub* 3 ft. Flowers white, grows in patches in meadows.

178 Crowberry *Shrub* 2 ft. Flowers purple, heath-like plant.

179 Bog Rosemary *Shrub* 1 ft. Flowers snow-white or flesh color.

180 Cowberry *Shrub* 6 in. Creeping; berries dark red, bitter.

181 Wintergreen *Plant* 6 in. Flower flesh color.

182 Wintergreen *Plant* 4 in. Leaves spotted with white.

183 Teaberry *Plant* 4 in. Berries red, & leaves spicy.

184 Pyrola *Low-creeping evergreens* Flower stems, 8 in. Flowers pale greenish-white.

185 Bearberry *Trailing plant on rocks* Leaves thick, berries red.

186 Snowberry *Creeping plant* White berries. Edible.

187 Mayflower *Creeping* Flowers rose color, or pearly white, fragrant.

188 Bunchberry *Plant* 6 in. Flowers white, berries red, in bunches.

189 Flowering Dogwood *Tree* 10 to 30 ft. Flowers white, berries bright scarlet.

190 Roundleaf Cornel *Shrub* 6 to 10 ft. Flowers white, berries blue, turning whitish.

191 Red Osier Dogwood *Shrub* 3 to 6 ft. Blood red stems, fruit white, or lead color.

192 Paniceld Dogwood *Shrub* 4 to 8 ft. Flowers white, berries round, pale white.

193 Alternate Leaf Dogwood *Shrub* 8 - 20 ft. Flowers pale yellowish-white, berries blue-black.

194 Silky Dogwood (Kinnikinnik) *Shrub* 3 - 10 ft. Flowers white inside, yellow outside.

195 Privet, Prim, *Shrub* 8 ft. Flowers white, berries shining black.

196 Buttonbush *Shrub* 10 ft. Flowers in yellowish-white balls.

197 Fly Honeysuckle *Shrub* 5 ft. Pale greenish-yellow flowers in two, to one red berry.

198 Hairy Fly Honeysuckle *Shrub* 3 ft. Flowers yellow, berries blue.

199 Horsegentian *Shrub* 3 ft. Flowers purple, in clusters, berries orange.

200 Small Honeysuckle *Vine* Yellow tinged purple flowers, berries orange..

201 Hairy Honeysuckle *Vine Flowers* pale yellow outside, rich orange inside, berries orange.

202 Twinflower *Creeping* Flowers in 2's, white and rose-tinted ; fruit dry.

203 Partridge Berry *Creeping* Flowers in 2's, white or rose color, fragrant, scarlet berries.

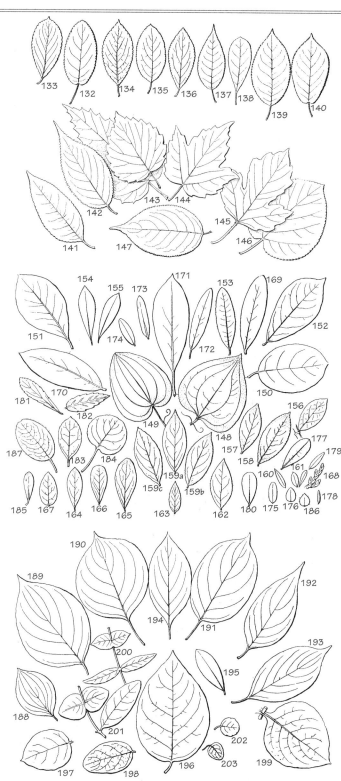

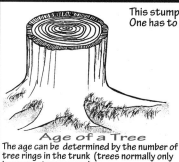

Age of a Tree

The age can be determined by the number of tree rings in the trunk (trees normally only have one ring per year).

This stump has 24 annual rings so the tree was 28-30 years old when cut. One has to allow for 4-6 years, of a seedling to show its first growth rings.

This stump has some special characteristics:

Young: When the tree was young (near the middle) it has very wide growth rings - this showing that the tree was growing very fast. This can be from good rain and the fact that the area was sunny as all neighboring trees might have been small.

Next Stage: After the initial rapid growth - for the following 11 years the growth was slow. This might have been due to the lack of rain or the fact that the surrounding trees have grown and are competing for water and might be casting a shadow this tree.

Before Cutting: In the last 6 years, before the cutting, the tree grew increasingly fast. This must have happened because the surrounding taller trees were cut.

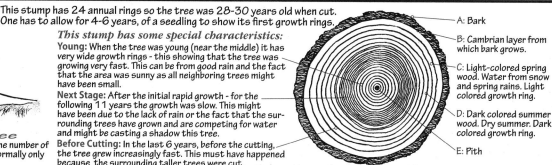

A: Bark

B: Cambrian layer from which bark grows.

C: Light-colored spring wood. Water from snow and spring rains. Light colored growth ring.

D: Dark colored summer wood. Dry summer. Dark colored growth ring.

E: Pith

DECIDUOUS TREES

TREES

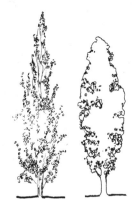

Round Globe Shaped
Arnold Crab-apple • Japanese Maple
Mulberry • Green Ash • Pistachio
Hawthorne Sycamore

Columnar Tree
Dawyck Beech • Siberian Crab tree
Enflish Oak • Poplar • Sargent Cherry
Sentry Ginkgo • Lombard Poplar
Pyramidal European Birch
Linden

Broad Oval Tree
Bradford Pear
Sugar Maple • Laburnum
European Mountain Ash

Fan Shaped
Horizontal Branching
Flowering Dogwood
Silk Tree • Redbud
Amur Maple

Conical Tree or Triangle
American Sweetgum
Pin Oak

SHRUBS

Low 1.5 - 5 Feet
February Daphne
Bush Cinquefoil
Anthony Waterer Spirea
Japanese Barberry

Medium 5 - 12 Feet
Snowball • Forsythia • English Privet

Tall 12 - 18 Feet
Crapemyrtle • Spindle Tree
Russian Olive • Lilac

LOW GROUND COVER OR VINES

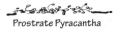

Prostrate Pyracantha

Lantana

Ground Cover 6 - 18 Inches
Cranberry Cotoneaster
Carpet Bugle • Memorial Rose
Aaronsbeard St. Johnswort

Vines
Wisteria • Passionflower
Bittersweet • Virginia Creeper
Clematis • Grapes

CONIFER TREES

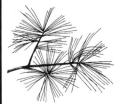

Pine
• Leaves needle-like.
• Leaves in bundles or tufts.
• Bundles of two to six needles with sheath at base.

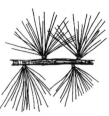

Larch
Many needles arranged in tufts without sheaths at base and shed in the winter. In the fall the trees are a bright yellow.

Fir
• Leaves set singly and scattered along the branch.
• Leaves are flat, blunt at tip, pale underneath, and cones stand erect.

Hemlock
Cones droop and leaves are with little stalks.

Spruce
Four-sided leaves (in cross section), sharp at tip, not pale underneath.

White Cedar
Foliage small scale like or spiny and close pressed to the twig. Fruit very small cones.

Juniper
Foliage spiny or scale like or both. Fruit a blue berry.

Eastern Red Cedar   Rocky Mountain Juniper

Key to Conifers

Spruce or Fir?
Take a needle between your fingers and roll it:
Spruces will spin as needles are nearly round.
Firs have a flat cross-section and will slide.

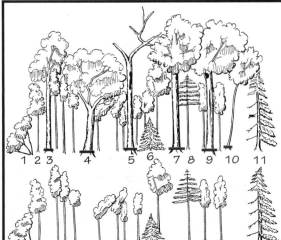

Maintaining a Woodlot
The trees that should be cut have a cut mark on them.
1 Shrub should be left to protect the interior of lot.
2, 6, & 8 Are fine straight trees of medium size that should not be cut, but they will grow betterif the trees shading them are removed.
3 & 7Are sound mature trees that should be cut and used for boards and the scrap for firewood.
4 Should be cut because its wide spreading crown is retarding the growth of the quality trees beneath it.
5 Dead tree.
9 Defective tree.
10 Crooked tree.
11 Tree should be left to protect the interior of lot.
Province of Ontario Guideline

CONIFERS EVERGREENS

Medium
Pfitzer Juniper

Round
Globe Arbor-vitae
Norway Spruce
(Dwarf Varieties)

Tall
10-20 Feet
(Junipers)
Canada Yew

Tall
Over 20 Feet
(Italian Cypress)
Lawson Cypress
Japanese Yew

Round
Pones • Cedars

Wind Swept or Trained
Picturesque or Exotic
Japanese Black Pine
Scots Pine • True Cedars
Eastern White Pine

Low or Ground Cover
Spreading or Creeping Juniper
Waukegan Creeping Juniper
Bar Harbor Creeping Juniper

Triangle
Nordmann Fir • Pines
Spruce • Hemlock

BROADLEAF EVERGREENS

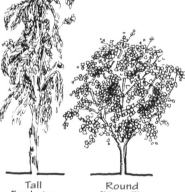

Medium
Pittosporum • Cotoneaster
Bayberry • Barberry
Rhododendrons

Tall 12-20 Feet
Pyracantha • Bottlebrush
California Laurel
Holly • Privet

Tall
Eucalyptus
Palmetto Palm

Round
Chinese Elm
Carob • Citrus • Live Oak
Southern Magnolia • Pepper Tree

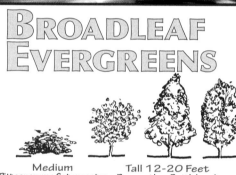

Ivy
Climbing Fig
Bougainvillea

Ice Plant

Low Ground Cover or Vines
Cotoneaster • Bearberry
Vinca Minor

Dwarf Mahonia • Azaleas
Boxwood • Natal Plum
David Viburnum

NEEDLES ON TREES

Needles growing in bunches.

2 in each bunch	#205
3 in each bunch	#206
5 in each bunch	#207

Many in a bunch, not evergreen #204

Needles growing single all round the stem.

Needles flat, point blunt	#208
Needles four edged, sharp pointed	#209

Needles growing on top and sides only.

Needles flat, blunt, upper one smaller	#210
Needles flat, pointed	#215
Needles sharp, prickly, in 3's of equal size	#214

Needles of 2 kinds. Scales on young shoots.

Young shoots, 4 edged	#213
Branches flat, slender, bluish green	#212
Compact, broad, dark green	#211

204 Larch (Tamarack) *Tree* 70 ft. Cones 1/2 in. long; bark bluish-gray.
205 Red Pine *Tree* 70 ft. Bark reddish, rather smooth; cones 2 in. long, in clusters, not prickly.
206 Pitch Pine *Tree* 60 ft. Very rough, dark bark; very pitchy cones, 2 in. long, prickly.
207 White Pine *Tree* 150 ft. Bark smooth; cones 5 in. long, not prickly; brittle, soft, white wood.
208 Balsam Fir *Tree* 40 ft. Cones 3 in. long, standing upward on the limbs.
209 Black Spruce *Tree* 50 ft. Cones 1 in. long, hanging downwards from limb.
210 Hemlock Spruce *Tree* 70 ft. Cones 1/2 in. long; most graceful tree when young; poor wood, very knotty, hard; bark smooth.
211 Northern White Cedar *Tree* 40 ft. Cones small, 1/2 in. long.
212 Atlantic White Cedar *Tree* 60 ft. Cones as large as peas. In swamps.
213 Red Cedar *Tree* 30 ft. Wood red, fragrant; berries blue.
214 Juniper Spreading *Shrub* 2 ft. Dark purple berries.
215 Canada Yew *Low struggling bush* Red berries.

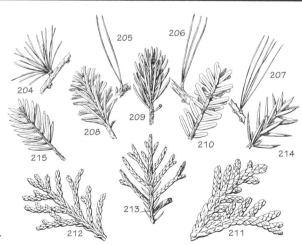

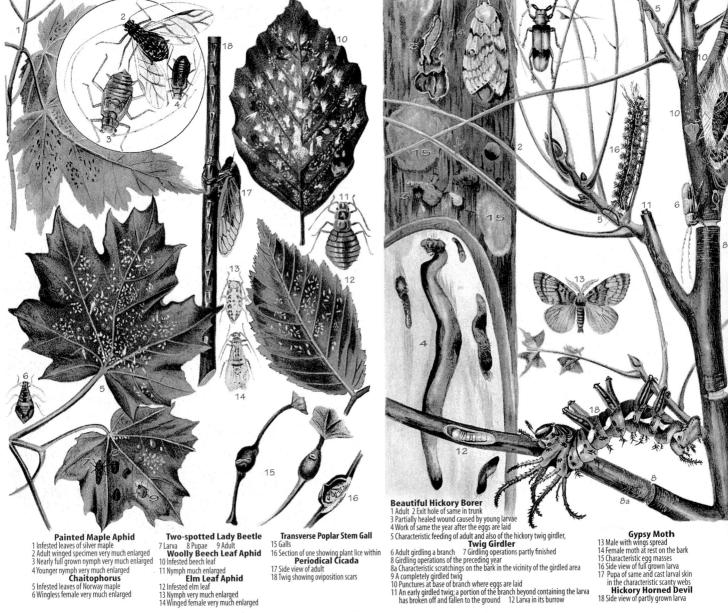

Painted Maple Aphid
1 Infested leaves of silver maple
2 Adult winged specimen very much enlarged
3 Nearly full grown nymph very much enlarged
4 Younger nymph very much enlarged
Chaitophorus
5 Infested leaves of Norway maple
6 Wingless female very much enlarged

Two-spotted Lady Beetle
7 Larva   8 Pupae   9 Adult
Woolly Beech Leaf Aphid
10 Infested beech leaf
11 Nymph much enlarged
Elm Leaf Aphid
12 Infested elm leaf
13 Nymph very much enlarged
14 Winged female very much enlarged

Transverse Poplar Stem Gall
15 Galls
16 Section of one showing plant lice within
Periodical Cicada
17 Side view of adult
18 Twig showing oviposition scars

Beautiful Hickory Borer
1 Adult 2 Exit hole of same in trunk
3 Partially healed wound caused by young larvae
4 Work of same the year after the eggs are laid
5 Characteristic feeding of adult and also of the hickory twig girdler,
Twig Girdler
6 Adult girdling a branch   7 Girdling operations partly finished
8 Girdling operations of the preceding year
8a Characteristic scratchings on the bark in the vicinity of the girdled area
9 A completely girdled twig
10 Punctures at base of branch where eggs are laid
11 An early girdled twig; a portion of the branch beyond containing the larva
   has broken off and fallen to the ground   12 Larva in its burrow

Gypsy Moth
13 Male with wings spread
14 Female moth at rest on the bark
15 Characteristic egg masses
16 Side view of full grown larva
17 Pupa of same and cast larval skin
   in the characteristic scanty webs
Hickory Horned Devil
18 Side view of partly grown larva

TREE INSECTS

Fall Web Worm
1 Cluster of eggs, natural size.
2 Dorsal views of full and partly grown larvae
   and also a side view of a full grown caterpillar
3 Pupa, natural size 4 Pupa, more enlarged
5 White form of moth in resting position, natural size
6 Spotted form of moth with wings expanded,
natural size
Figures 2, 5 and 6 are on a small web showing within
the partly skeletonized, discolored leaves and the
excrement of the caterpillars.

Spiny Elm Caterpillar
7 Cluster of eggs on a leaf stem, natural size
8 One egg, much enlarged
9 Caterpillar feeding, natural size
10 Chrysalis hanging from a leaf stem, natural size
11 Butterfly with wings spread, natural size
The figures of the egg and caterpillar are on a twig
of elm representing the characteristic work of the
caterpillar.

Black Walnut Caterpillar
1 Bunch of cast skins
2 Side and dorsal views of full grown larvae
3 Silk spun by larvae on molting place
4 Parent moth

Hickory Tussock Moth
5 Side view of full grown larva
6 Parent moth with expanded wings

Painted Hickory Borer
7 Piece of hickory showing work
8 Larval galleries in sapwood
9 Pupal chamber containing pupa
10 Adult
11 Sawdust stopping exit from pupal chamber
12 Exit hole. This pierces the bark in nature.

Locust Borer
1 Pupa in its cell
2 Plug of wood fibers closing the free end of the pupal cell
3 Beetle at rest
10 Eggs deposited in crevices of the bark

Carpenter Worm
4 Female at rest on the bark
4 Dark colored eggs deposited loosely in the crevices
5 Pupal case partially projecting from the burrow
6 Pupa within its cell
7 Full grown larva with its head protruding from a burrow
8 Young larva at work in a small twig
9 Irregular borings of the full grown caterpillars

TREE INSECTS

Sugar Maple Borer
1 Place where egg was laid.
1a Another more than normally discolored and showing excrement or borings thrown out by borer
2 Borer or grub in September from egg laid the same season
3 Nearly full grown borer
4 Adult or beetle
5 Hole through which the beetle escaped from the trunk
6 Sawdust or borings packed in burrow

Maple & Oak Twig Pruner
7 Grub or borer in its burrow, a portion of the twig being cut away to show its work.
7a Small twig with only a thin shell of bark, the wood being nearly all eaten
8 Pupa in burrow. The base of both twigs represented has been nearly eaten off by the larva
9 Adult or beetle

Cottony Maple Scale
10 Active or recently hatched young
11 Adult females, many eggs can be found in the woolly masses
12 Leaf with many young scales on its underside

Maple Phenacoccus
1 Clusters of male cocoons on sugar maple bark
2 Females and young on underside of leaf

Black-banded Lecaniurn
3 Badly infested soft maple twigs
4 Young along sides of leaf veins 10 Male very much enlarged
11 Full grown female scales showing characteristic markings
   much enlarged   12 Young very much enlarged

Golden Oak Scale
5 Infested oak twig

Tulip Tree Scale
6 Badly infested tulip branch
8 Recently hatched young very much enlarged
9 Young scales very much enlarged

White Flower Cricket
7 Oviposition scars

Poplar Tent Maker
1 Larva on its nest   2 Moth of same

Elm Sawfly
4 Larva   5 Adult of same   6 Cocoon

Mottled Willow Borer
7 Portion of willow branch cut to show work
8 Adult, dorsal aspect
9 Shrunken, discolored area over larval galleries

Puss Moth
10 Side view of larva   11 Eggs
12 Cocoon from which moth has emerged

Sesia Albicornis
13 Pupal cases

Cottonwood Leaf Beetle
14 Eggs   15 Full grown larva
16 Group of larvae   17 Young larvae
18 Beetles or "hard shells" showing variation in marking
19 Pupa or "hanger"
20 Badly eaten leaves showing characteristic method of feeding

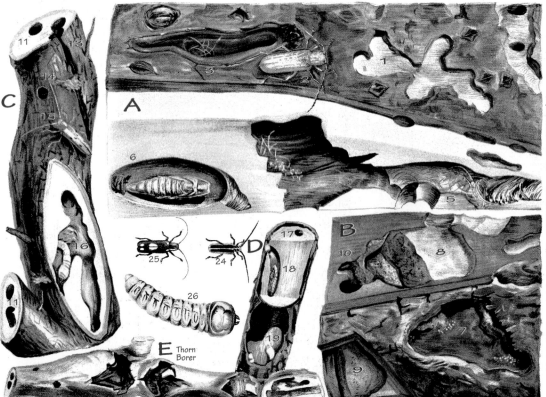

TREE INSECTS

Poplar Borer
A Piece of poplar showing work of this insect
1 Work of young larva
2 Adult
3 Orifice in bark through which borings are expelled
4 Gallery leading to orifice shown at 3
5 Peculiar excelsior like borings made by larva
6 Pupa in its chamber with one end stopped by excelsior like borings
26 Full grown larva

Linden Borer
B Portion of base of linden showing the work of this species
7 Expanded gallery tinder bark made by larva
8 Gallery in wood extending tinder bark to 7
9 Sawdust packed in the larval gallery
10 Gallery leading into heart of the tree

C A piece of linden root with portion cut away to show work of the grub
11 Larval galleries - cross section
12 Circular exit hole of beetle
13 Wound made by borer
14 Frass ejected by larva
15 Adult beetle on the bark
16 Bark cut away showing the borer in its gallery

Woodbine Borer
D Piece of woodbine showing work of this species
17 Larval gallery
18 Pupa in chamber showing orifice
19 Larva and its work tinder the bark
24 Adult beetle

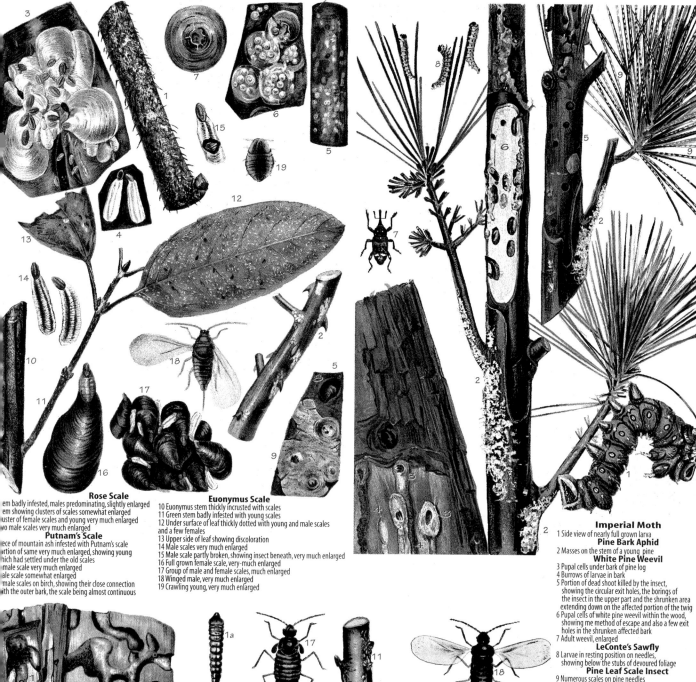

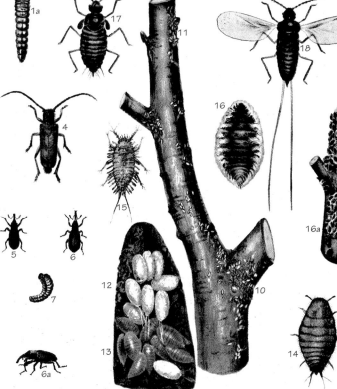

Rose Scale
...em badly infested, males predominating, slightly enlarged
...em showing clusters of scales somewhat enlarged
...uster of female scales and young very much enlarged
...wo male scales very much enlarged

Putnam's Scale
...ece of mountain ash infested with Putnam's scale
...rtion of same very much enlarged, showing young
...hich had settled under the old scales
...male scale very much enlarged
...ale scale somewhat enlarged
...male scales on birch, showing their close connection
...ith the outer bark, the scale being almost continuous

Euonymus Scale
10 Euonymus stem thickly incrusted with scales
11 Green stem badly infested with young scales
12 Under surface of leaf thickly dotted with young and male scales and a few females
13 Upper side of leaf showing discoloration
14 Male scales very much enlarged
15 Male scale partly broken, showing insect beneath, very much enlarged
16 Full grown female scale, very-much enlarged
17 Group of male and female scales, much enlarged
18 Winged male, very much enlarged
19 Crawling young, very much enlarged

Imperial Moth
1 Side view of nearly full grown larva

Pine Bark Aphid
2 Masses on the stem of a young pine

White Pine Weevil
3 Pupal cells under bark of pine log
4 Burrows of larvae in bark
5 Portion of dead shoot killed by the insect, showing the circular exit holes, the borings of the insect in the upper part and the shrunken area extending down on the affected portion of the twig
6 Pupal cells of white pine weevil within the wood, showing me method of escape and also a few exit holes in the shrunken affected bark
7 Adult weevil, enlarged

LeConte's Sawfly
8 Larvae in resting position on needles, showing below the stubs of devoured foliage

Pine Leaf Scale Insect
9 Numerous scales on pine needles

Tree Insects

Elm Borer
1 Larva or grub within its burrow just under the bark
1a Larva or grub extended
2 Pupa within its cell just under the bark
3 Burrows of the grub as exposed after removal of the bark
4 Adult beetle

Elm Snout Beetles
5 Adult 6 Adult 6a Side view 7 Larva side view
8 Pupa within its oval cell just beneath the bark
8a Empty pupal cell
9 Burrows as exposed after removal of the bark
9a Holes in the bark through which the beetles escape
9b Showing how bark is loosened by the burrows insect

Elm Bark Louse
10 Group of partly grown bark lice as they appear in early spring
11 Group of male cocoons
12 Group of male cocoons, much enlarged
13 Group of virgin females, much enlarged
14 A female, much more enlarged
15 Recently hatched young, very much enlarged
16 Mature female, much enlarged
16a Matured females on a twig, enlarged
17 Wingless male, much enlarged
18 Winged male, much enlarged, note also the long, white, anal filaments

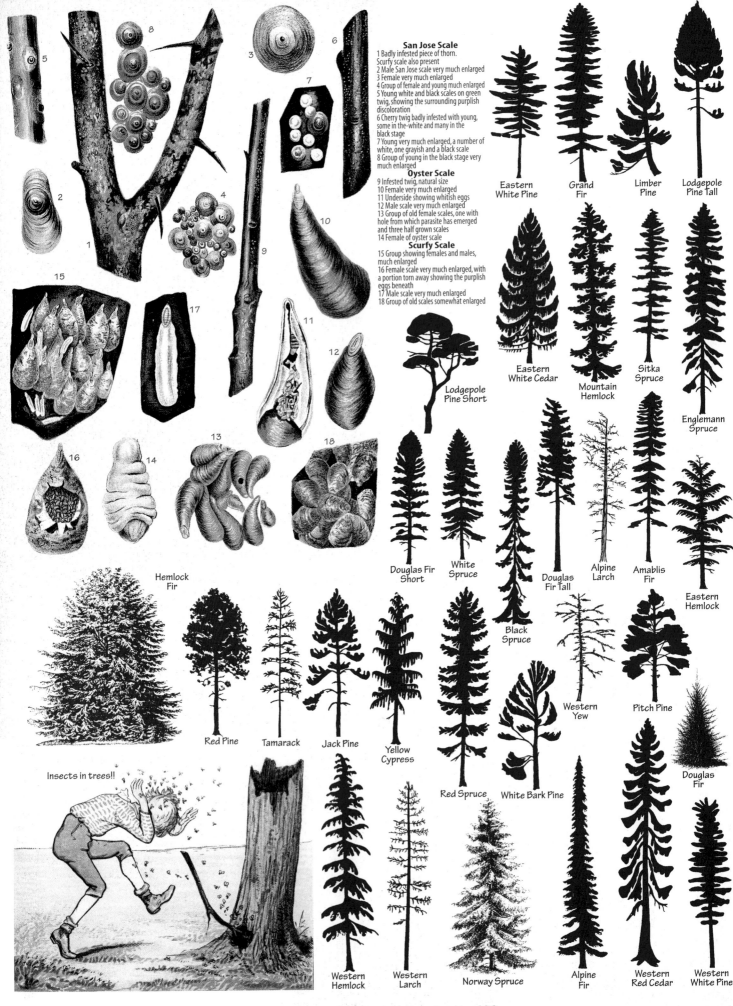

San Jose Scale

1 Badly infested piece of thorn. Scurfy scale also present
2 Male San Jose scale very much enlarged
3 Female very much enlarged
4 Group of female and young much enlarged
5 Young white and black scales on green twig, showing the surrounding purplish discoloration
6 Cherry twig badly infested with young, some in the-white and many in the black stage
7 Young very much enlarged, a number of white, one grayish and a black scale
8 Group of young in the black stage very much enlarged

Oyster Scale

9 Infested twig, natural size
10 Female very much enlarged
11 Underside showing whitish eggs
12 Male scale very much enlarged
13 Group of old female scales, one with hole from which parasite has emerged and three half grown scales
14 Female of oyster scale

Scurfy Scale

15 Group showing females and males, much enlarged
16 Female scale very much enlarged, with a portion torn away showing the purplish eggs beneath
17 Male scale very much enlarged
18 Group of old scales somewhat enlarged

Eastern White Pine

Grand Fir

Limber Pine

Lodgepole Pine Tall

Eastern White Cedar

Mountain Hemlock

Sitka Spruce

Englemann Spruce

Lodgepole Pine Short

Douglas Fir Short

White Spruce

Douglas Fir Tall

Alpine Larch

Amablis Fir

Eastern Hemlock

Black Spruce

Western Yew

Pitch Pine

Hemlock Fir

Red Pine

Tamarack

Jack Pine

Yellow Cypress

Red Spruce

White Bark Pine

Douglas Fir

Insects in trees!!

Western Hemlock

Western Larch

Norway Spruce

Alpine Fir

Western Red Cedar

Western White Pine

492

CORAL REEF

A coral reef is formed by living hard coral polyps which are tiny animals living in colonies. When hard coral polyps die they form a deposit of limestone on which new coral polyps will grow. Corals are carnivores that eat zooplankton. Food is caught by using poisonous stingers on their tentacles that surround their mouth. Corals reefs are important for many tropical fish, crabs, mollusks, etc. as they offer shelter and a source of food. Coral reefs are under threat because of water pollution and temperature changes.

Coral Types
Hard Corals: have hard, limestone skeletons. These form the deposits in coral reefs.
Soft Corals: have soft do not build coral reefs.

Types of Coral Reefs
Fringing Reefs: form in shallow water along a coastline.
Barrier Reefs: grow parallel to shorelines and are separated from the land by a deep lagoon. They can be dangerous hidden obstacles when boating or rafting near the shore.
Coral Atolls: See illustration.

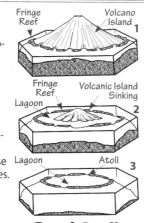

Fringe Reef — Volcano Island — 1

Fringe Reef — Volcanic Island Sinking — Lagoon — 2

Lagoon — Atoll — 3

Coral Atoll
1 A fringe reef grows around an island formed by a volcano.
2 A barrier reef grows upwards from the fringing reef. This occurs because the ocean level is rising or the volcanic island is sinking. The water in the reef is called a lagoon.
3 If the island relative to the sea level sinks an atoll will form.

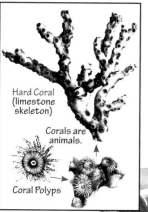

Hard Coral (limestone skeleton)

Corals are animals.

Coral Polyps

Coral atoll from the air.

Children playing in tidal pool. This can be very dangerous as a rogue wave or the tide can come in.

Joe Heath

Caribbean Corals & Fish

SURVIVAL FOOD FROM INTERTIDAL ZONES TIDE POOLS

The tide pools that are formed by a receding tide can be an interesting experience because many creatures and plants from the ocean floor will be trapped in these water filled depressions. Commonly you will find slugs, snails, crabs, sea stars, shrimp, lobsters (after storms), anemones, numerous fish, urchins, etc.

When exploring a tide pool always be aware that the tide will be returning and avoid becoming trapped on an elevated area and being cut off from shore.

SURVIVAL FOOD FROM INTERTIDAL ZONES

High Tide Zone ←

Tide Pool

← Mid Tide Zone

Tide Pool

← Low Tide Zone

Tide Pool

High Tide

SUB-TIDE ZONE

Low Tide

SPRAY ZONE

HIGH TIDE ZONE

This area is flooded during high tides. The highest tides occur every two weeks when the moon and sun are in line with earth. At the same time this alignment will produce the lowest tide at the other side of the earth.
• Life includes: barnacles, wrack seaweeds, barnacles, anemones, brittle sea stars, crabs, mussels, sea stars, snails, and whelks.

SPRAY ZONE

This area is dry most of the time but is sprayed by waves during high tides and during storms. It might be partially covered during extreme high tides and major storms blowing towards the shore.
• Plants and animals in this zone have to be adapted to salted conditions and growth is sparse consisting of some vegetation, lichens, lice, periwinkles, barnacles, sea-snails, and some welks at the lower levels.

MIDDLE TIDE ZONE

This area is covered and uncovered twice a day.
• Life includes: barnacles, larger kelp seaweeds, sea lettuce, sponges, barnacles, anemones, brittle sea stars, crabs, mussels, sea stars, snails, whelks, and abalone at the lower areas.

LOW TIDE ZONE

This area is usually covered with water and is exposed only at extreme low tides - even during this exposed period waves will usually still break onto the low tide zone. The lowest tides occur every two weeks when the moon and sun are in line at the other side of the earth. Life in this area is not adapted to long periods of dryness and might die if there is an extended drop in water level. If possible this is a very interesting zone to explore - because you are seeing an underwater environment.
• Life includes: abalone, anemones, larger kelp seaweed, green algae, sea lettuce, sea palms, chitons, crabs, hydroids, nudibranchs, isopods, limpets, mussels, sculpin, sea cucumber, sea stars, sea urchins, shrimp, small octopus, snails, sponges, surf grass, tube worms, and whelks.

SUB-TIDE ZONE

Is the area always underwater - there might be brief exposure at low tide when there are large receding waves.
• Life in this area is an extension of the Low Tide Zone.

INTERTIDAL ZONE
Page 46

Intertidal Zone

Overlap the characteristics of the saltwater marshes (see page 47) but are areas between the high and low tide. Travel is difficult due to the tides and constantly changing landscape. If entering this area, special consideration has to be given to the turbulent movement of the water when the tide comes in and goes out. In the zone you have to know when the tide comes in and also where the high ground is because what you consider high ground might be covered or wave swept during high tide.

DANGERS in Intertidal Zones

• Know where the high water mark is. What's wet, what's not.
• Direction of the tide. What is the extreme high and low of the day?
• How the incoming tide changes affect the shoreline. You might be stranded (thinking it is sufficiently elevated) on an elevated area that will be flooded at high tide.
• Watch the wave patterns if you are near the water. Observe how large and how close together the waves are within a set of waves. Watch the interval (or lulls) between sets of waves. There might be a wave surge coming in if you see the water withdraw in an unusual way. Watch the swell. As the swell increases in size, the dynamics of the ocean become stronger resulting in strong currents, riptides and sometimes undertow. Learn about the characteristics of these currents - they can easily kill you.
• Always keep in mind that you have to be prepared to swim to shore.

Nancy Sefton

Anemones

SEA ANEMONE

Sea Anemone live attached to firm objects - they do not root but can slowly slide on the surface. They are predatory animals by using their poisonous stinging tentacles to stun their food. Their mouth is at the centre of the flower shaped array of tentacles.

Handle with gloves If stung wash wound with alcohol or ammonia. Recovery might take from minutes to hours.

Sea Cucumbers

Cylinder-shaped animals that can vary in shape but have a distinct front and rear. The front usually has tentacles and a mouth and the rear the anus. They live on the ocean floor, in tropical waters to deep sea trenches. They have tube feet with which they crawl. Usually they are relatively small but some are up to a few feet long. These usually are edible.

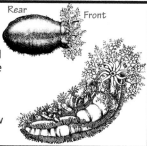

Rear   Front

MOLLUSKS

Mollusks are soft-bodied invertebrate animals. All mollusks do not have a hard external shell. They can live in the salty seas, fresh water, and on land.

The mollusk groups are...

Bivalves (freshwater & saltwater: clams, mussels)
Cephalopods (octopi & squid)
Aplacophorans (worm-like mollusks)
Gastropods (freshwater & saltwater: snails, slugs, periwinkles, sea urchins)

FINDING MOLLUSKS

Fresh Water: River snails or freshwater periwinkles can be found in rivers, streams, and lakes. Mussels can be found, in colonies, in the shallows, especially in water with a sandy or muddy bottom. Look for the narrow trails in the mud or for the dark slits of their open valves.

Tidal Pools: These are pools of water that are left standing in depressions when the tide recedes. These pools will have easily accessible mollusks and even fish that have been trapped. Snails will cling to rocks awaiting the return of the tide.

DO NOT eat shellfish that are not covered during high tide as without water they will be dead or dying.

Bivalves

Bivalves are soft-bodied animals that are protected by *two* hard shells that are attached by a muscular hinge. They are in the mollusk family.

Siphon — Foot
Clam "Walking"

Siphons — Littleneck Clam

Siphons — Razor Clam — Foot

Soft-shell, Gaper, Long-neck, or Steamer Clam

Current — Siphons — Feeding — Clam Feeding — Foot

CLAMS

Clam Digging

Out — In — Siphons
Geoduck Clam

Geoduck

The geoduck is the biggest clam caught and eaten in North America. Clam caught in the inter tide area of the Northwest Pacific waters, weighs an average three pounds and yields over a pound of flavorful meat. Great for cutlets and chowders.

Nudibranchs

Gold-line Sea Goddess

Are sea slugs with no hard shells. On their back they have ornamented tubercles. They have two tentacles on their head (in front) and a flower-like group at the rear. They are carnivores.

Sea Lemon Nudibranch

Nudibranch

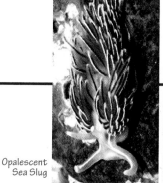

Opalescent Sea Slug

Worm-like Animals & Slugs

Blood Worm

Clam Shell Growth

A thin tissue that adheres to the inner surfaces of the shell, called the mantle, and a thickened rim of muscular tissue at the mantle edge deposit new shell material at the shell edge.

Rings on the shell indicate the age of a clam.

OTHER CLAMS

CLAMS

Horse Clam

Quahog Clam

Siphons — Siphons

Soft Shell Clams
The retractable siphons are in a single long tube.

Common Washington Clam

Puget Sound Clam

Clam Harvesting

Hitting ground with stick and watching for bubbles that will indicate the presence of clams.

CLAMS
Clams are bivalved animals.
CLAMS ATTACHING THEMSELVES
Certain kinds of clams, in early stages of life possess a gland that produces a thread-like material (byssus) that serves to anchor them to grains of sand or rocks. Other types of clams lack a byssal gland and use the foot to burrow into the seabed. As the clam grows, its wedge-shaped foot, which expands and contracts as it moves, becomes more important as a burrowing tool.

Clam Squirts Water Through Siphon
The siphon serves three main purposes: breathing, obtaining food, and eliminating waste products. Since clams are relatively immobile and movement is usually limited to burrowing in the sand, their double-tubed siphon which operates much like a snorkel is their lifeline. In flowing water is pumped through the siphon, passed over the gills, and strained to remove food particles. After receiving carbon dioxide from the gills and other waste products from the digestive tract, the water is expelled through the outgoing siphon. Constant circulation of the water is maintained by the beating of a multitude of microscopic hairs (called cilia) located inside the tube and in the gill chamber.

Oyster Months
Fresh oysters properly refrigerated are wholesome and nutritious throughout the year. They spoil rapidly at high temperatures, however. The belief that oysters were unsafe to eat in May through August arose in earlier days when refrigeration was less prevalent than it is today.

Oyster Borers
An oyster borer, or drill, is an aquatic snail that preys on oysters, especially thin-shelled young oysters. Using a band of scraping teeth (a radula) and a shell-dissolving secretion, the gastropod drills a hole in the oyster shell and eats the creature within.

Oyster

Pacific Oyster

Thorny Oyster

Barnacle on Oyster

OYSTERS
Oysters are bivalved animals. Oysters remain at one location and so not move. Clams can move - see note. The shape of the oysters shell is formed by the place it is attached and how crowded it is by the adjacent oysters.

OYSTERS & CLAMS
Oysters and clams are filter feeders and eat plankton. By pumping water through their bodies, the mollusks strain the microscopic organisms through their gills, which act as sieves.

OYSTERS & PEARLS
Pearls begin with the presence of a foreign substance, such as a grain of sand, that lodges in the oyster shell. The oyster's body reacts by depositing layers of nacreous (pearl-like) material around the foreign body to wall it off and reduce irritation. Many oysters - as well as some clams and mussels - manufacture material like the pearl - producing substance. True pearl-producing oysters, however, inhabit waters of the Indo Pacific.

SHUCKED OYSTERS & CLAMS
A reddish color in the liquor is sometimes present when oysters and clams are shucked. This is due to the red algae they sometimes consume, often composed of the microscopic one-celled dinoflagellates which appear in planktonic mass.

SCALLOPS
Scallops are bivalves. Scallops have a primitive eye system and can detect light and shadows. When something moves it will cause the change of lighting and the background contrast. The scallop will take evasive action with its jet propulsion.

Movement of a Scallop
It compresses the valves of its shell and forces water backward in jets near the shell hinge. The force drives the scallop in the direction of the shell opening. The bivalve appears to be clapping the two sides of its shell together.

Note: Mussels and other shellfish can be poisonous during some summer hot spells - especially in the tropics.

Eyes

Dann Blackwood

EATING MOLLUSKS
These include fresh and salt water invertebrates such as snails, clams, mussels, bivalves, periwinkles, chitons, and sea urchins. Most members of this group are edible; however, be sure that you have a fresh mollusk and that you boil it. Do not eat it raw as you might introduce parasites into your body. To find them in fresh water, look in the shallows, especially in water with a sandy or muddy bottom. Near the sea, wait for low tide and check in tidal pools or on, and in the sand.

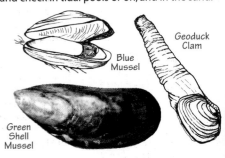

Geoduck Clam

Blue Mussel

Green Shell Mussel

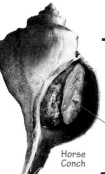

CONCH

Are found in warm shallow waters in grass beds of the Caribbean Sea.

Operculum acts like a trapdoor protecting the conch. It can also be used as a claw.

Horse Conch

Periwinkle

Channeled Whelk

Apple Shell

Dollum Shell

King Helmet Shell

Miter Shell

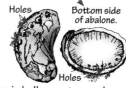

Abalone Shell Holes
Internal gills discharge water through the holes along the edge of an abalone shell. This is part of an abalone's respiratory process.

This side is attached to the rocks. Notice that it has no covering shell.

Holes

Bottom side of abalone.

Holes

Abalone exposed at low tide.

ABALONE

Abalone live in shallow or semi-shallow waters and can often be seen attached to rocks when the tide goes out. To pry them loose use a tool as a strong stick, metal rod, screw driver. Work at low tide unless you are a strong swimmer. Do not use your hands to pry lose an abalone as its strong muscles might clamp your hand onto the rock and you might drown with the rising tide. This also applies to large clams.

CONE SHELLS
Snails that Bite
A bite can cause: acute pain, swelling, paralysis, blindness, and possible death in a few hours.

- Cone-shaped shells with a smooth surface.
- Live in crevices along rocky shores and coral reefs.
- A bite injects a very poisonous venom through a holes in their tiny teeth.

Do not handle any cone shells.

Terebra Shell

Cone Shell

Cone Shell

Terebra
Are found in both temperate and tropical waters. They have small sharp teeth that can inject a poisonous venom - not as strong as that of the cone shell.

Tentacle   Siphon   Shell   Extended Mantle

Proboscis

Foot

Eye

Atlantic Deer Cowrie

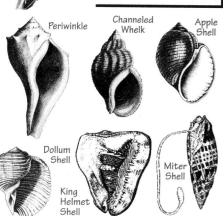

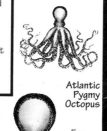
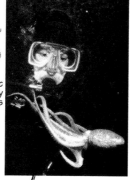

Atlantic Pygmy Octopus

White-Spotted or Grass Octopus

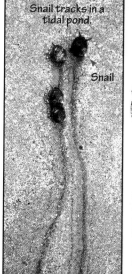

Snail tracks in a tidal pond.

Snail

Eye   Eye

OCTOPUS

Octopuses, a mollusk, have eight arms and live on the ocean floor. The Common Pacific Octopus has up to a 32 ft arm span and weighing up to 500 pounds. They have a soft body and two rows of suction cups on the underside of each arm. Severed arms will regrow. The arms and suction cups help in catching prey. The octopus then bites the victim with its sharp beak while paralyzing the it with a nerve poison. The nerve poison acts as a digestive juice which helps decompose the flesh of the victim. When attacked an octopus will squirt ink into the water to act as a "smoke cloud" while it escapes. They live in dens under large rocks. These protective dens can be dug by the octopus and it will even pile rocks in the entrance to limit access.

A special characteristic of octopuses is that they can change their color to camouflage into the environment. An octopus has very good sight with the two eyes on the sides of the head.

Snail tracks in a tidal pond.

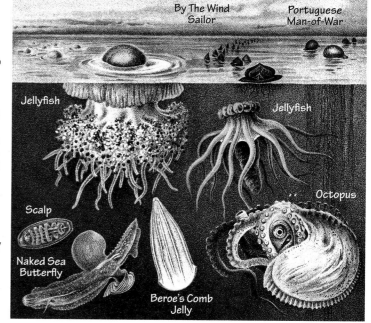

By The Wind Sailor

Portuguese Man-of-War

Jellyfish

Jellyfish

Scalp

Octopus

Naked Sea Butterfly

Beroe's Comb Jelly

497

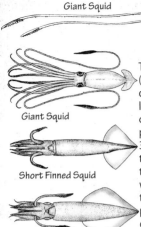

SQUID

They have eight arms (with suckers), a long cylindrical body, and two long tentacles. They are closely related to the octopus. They can swim up to 30 mph - using this speed to catch fish with their tentacles, hold the victim with their arms, and tear the flesh with their sharp parrot-like beaks. They can change color and squirt ink like an octopus.

Giant Squid

Giant Squid

Short Finned Squid

Long Finned Squid

Lion's Mane Jellyfish

This is the largest jellyfish and some have been found that are 8' wide. The tentacles are HIGHLY TOXIC and can produce blistering and severe burns.

JELLYFISH

They have soft jelly-like bodies with long poisonous tentacles. Fish getting entangled in the tentacles are poisoned by the venom in the stinging cells. The largest jellyfish is the lion's mane whose body can be over 96" wide.

Jellyfish & Portuguese Man-of-War

Toxins are injected by the tentacles. These toxins are used to catch fish and other food. Upon brushing your skin, their stinging cells pierce your skin and release the poison. Avoid touching a jellyfish, but if you come in contact with the tentacles:

- Do not move the affected area as the muscle action will increase the amount of toxin that enters the bloodstream.
- Rinse immediately with salt water (not fresh water); neutralize the poison with alcohol, vinegar, ammonia or meat tenderizer.
- The toxin reacts very rapidly and immediate attention should be given. The victim's physical condition and age might be a factor causing a critical reaction.
- Remove all tentacles that are attached to the skin.

Float: is gas-filled, deflatable, blue to pink with a translucent body. 12" long & 6" high. The float acts like a sail moving the animal throughout the tropics and if it catches the Gulf stream - all the way to Europe.

Tentacles: up to 60 feet long which can be regenerated. The tentacles have poisonous stingers that paralyzes the prey. See article on Jellyfish & Portuguese Man-of-War poisoning.

Portuguese Man-of-War

It resembles a jellyfish but is actually a colony of sea animals. It is called a Portuguese Man-of-War because it looks like a old Portuguese battleship under sail. In the 1500's Portugal was a major marine military power having far flung colonies.

Jellyfish Stings

To remove attached tentacles, do not use bare hands. Wrap hands in a towel or plastic sheet and whip away attached tentacles. Apply sand and sea water and scrape off with a knife or piece of wood.

Treatment

- Apply baking soda as a paste on jellyfish stings.
- Apply vinegar for man-of-war stings.
- Relieve itchy area with antihistamines.
- Take a pain reliever if pain persists.
- Make sure that your tetanus shot is up to date.

JELLYLIKE ANIMALS

Hood

Tentacles

Mouth

Oral Arms

Sea Nettle

1 Planula Larva: This larva develops after the free floating egg and sperm of the adults meets in the water.
2-3 Floating Polyp.
4 Polyp anchors and develops during the winter on a hard surface.
9-10 Polyp hydroid colony: This structure is a linkage of feeding tubes for the units that will become individual jellyfish.
11 The polyp in the spring season breaks off as tiny jellyfish.
12-14 Jellyfish at its adult cycle.

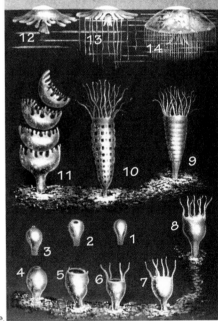

12   13   14

11   10   9

3   2   1   8

4   5   6   7

LIFE CYCLE OF JELLYFISH

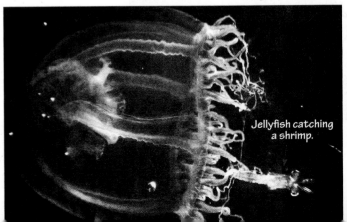

Jellyfish catching a shrimp.

Mouth on underside.

SEA URCHIN

Is a spiny, globular, hard-shelled animal that lives on the rocky sea floor. The spines that radiate from the body are used for protection, for moving slowly along the seabed, and for trapping drifting algae. The mouth is a set of claw-like plates and is on the underside. Many sea urchins have venomous spines.

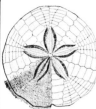

Keyhole Urchin

Sand Dollar

Sand Dollars are disk-shaped spiny-skinned sea bed animals and have the shape of an old silver dollar. Their mouth is on the bottom and the holes on the upper surface are to release the eggs and sperm. They also have small gill like feet on the bottom surface.

FISHING IN TROPIC WATERS

Warm tropical waters and special circumstances in temperate waters can trigger problems that make certain fish inedible.

The US Air Force Survival Manual indicates:

- Fish can be edible or inedible and this can vary from area to area due to their diet or special seasonal characteristics.
- Cooking will not eradicate the poison.
- Barracudas: Large fish can cause serious digestive illness. Barracudas under three feet can be safely eaten.
- Oilfish: Tasty, white flaky flesh but very poisonous.
- Great sea eels: Avoid them.
- Never eat eggs or entrails of tropical fish.
- Avoid all fish with round or box like bodies with hard, shell-like skins covered with bony plates or spines. They can have parrot-like mouths, small gill openings, belly fins which are small or absent. They are named after their shape: pufferfish, file fish, globe fish, trigger fish, trunk fish.

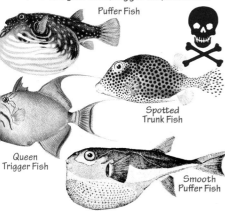

Puffer Fish

Spotted Trunk Fish

Queen Trigger Fish

Smooth Puffer Fish

Red Starfish

Northern Sea Star

Sea Stars

Sea Stars are spiny, hard-skinned animals found on sandy bottoms, turtle grass beds, under rocks, or corals. They eat shellfish.

DANGERS

WALKING WITH BARE FEET

Coral reefs, dead or alive, can severely cut your feet.

SLIDE FEET WHEN WALKING

Slide your feet along muddy or sandy bottoms. This will help you to avoid stepping on sting rays or spined fish. A misplaced step on a sting ray, pinning down its body, will give it leverage to throw up its tail and stab you with its stinging spine. The broken off spine (because of the barbs) can only be removed by cutting it out.

SPONGES & SEA URCHINS

They can slip fine needles of lime or silica into your skin where they will break off and fester. Do not dig them out, but use lime juice or other citric acid to dissolve them.

CAMOUFLAGED STONE FISH

Well camouflaged stone fish with thirteen poisoned spines can be stepped on with bare feet or light running shoes. The poison can cause great agony and death. This poison should be treated as a snake bite.

HANDS

Do not probe in dark holes or around rocks as your fingers can look like supper.

CONE SNAILS

These have poison teeth that can bite (as well as long, slender pointed terebra snails). Cone shells have smooth, colorful mottled shells with elongated, narrow openings. They live under rocks, in crevices of coral reefs, and along rocky shores of protected bays. They are shy and active at night. They have a long mouth and a snout which is used to jab or inject their teeth. These teeth are actually tiny hypodermic needles, with a tiny poison gland on the back end of each. The sting is swift and produces acute pain, swelling, paralysis, blindness, and possible death within four hours. Avoid handling all cone shells.

BIG CONCHS

Handle with caution as they have razor sharp trap doors which might suddenly jab out puncturing your skin.

SHARKS, BARRACUDAS & MORAY EEL

When crossing deeper portions of a reef, check the reef edge shadows for sharks, barracudas, and moray eels.

SALT WATER BOILS

Are very common with deep water fishermen. These small boils are found around the wrists, back of the hands or forearms and occasionally around the neck. These are areas of friction from cracked, wet and dirty oilskin clothing. The friction causes minute cracks in the skin which in turn is infected by organisms present in fish slime. A clean environment is important to reduce the risk of infection from the slime. If neglected, it can be very painful.
See a doctor for treatment.

FISHERMAN'S CONJUNCTIVITIS
(Pink Eye)

Fisherman's conjunctivitis is a severe inflammatory condition of the eyes. It is caused by contact with the juices of marine animal growth that look like dumplings. These growths when crushed release the juice which may accidentally enter the eye. This juice in the eye causes a very acute and painful inflammation of the conjunctiva or thin covering of the eye. Avoid rubbing your eyes when handling fish.
See a doctor for treatment.

FISH POISONING
(Erysipeloid)

This disease is usually more common during the warmer months. It is a skin disease that usually occurs on the hands and forearms. It is caused by the skin being punctured by fins of fish, sharp bones, or fish hooks. The residue of fish slime or rotten fish enter these openings in the skin. A small red spot on the skin indicates the start of an infection. This infection will spread to the adjacent area. The infection will gradually become clear in the middle with a reddish purple color at the spreading margins. The affected parts will swell, itch, and have a burning sensation. First aid can be started with frequent hot bathing of the affected areas. *See a doctor for complete treatment.*

Yellow Bellied Sea Snake

CRUSTACEANS

Crustaceans are animals that have a hard skeleton, jointed legs, and a segmented body.
- A hard skeleton made of calcium - no internal skeleton.
- The head has two compound eyes, two pairs of sensory antennae, and three pairs of mouthparts.
- A pair of green glands excrete wastes near the base of antennae.
- The abdominal segments have swimming legs.
- The tail is fan-shaped.
- There is no heart.
- Most live in water, but some live on land.

LOBSTER

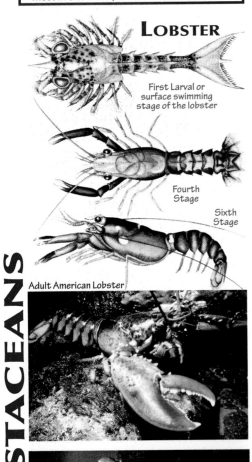

First Larval or surface swimming stage of the lobster

Fourth Stage

Sixth Stage

Adult American Lobster

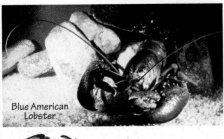

Blue American Lobster

LOBSTER

Two kinds of lobster-like crustaceans exist in United States waters. The "true" American lobster and the spiny lobster. The two, from different families, display two differences:

AMERICAN LOBSTER

The true lobster has claws on the first four legs, lacking in the spiny lobster; the spiny lobster has a pair of horns above the eyes, lacking in the true lobster. To avoid confusion over common names, it is best to call the true lobster the "American lobster," and the spiny lobster just that. The item marketed as "lobster tail" usually is a spiny lobster. The spiny lobster is found in warm waters off Florida, in the West Indies, and off southern California. Record weight for the American lobster is 45 pounds.

Growth of a Lobster

Lobsters grow by molting. This is the process in which they struggle out of their old shells while simultaneously absorbing water which expands their body size. This molting, or shell-shedding, occurs about 25 times in the first 5-7 years of life. Following this cycle, the lobster will weigh approximately one pound and reach minimum legal size. A lobster at minimum legal size may then only molt once per year and increase about 15% in length and 40% in weight. The maximum age of a lobster may approach 100 years. They can grow to be 3 feet or more in overall body length.

Distance Lobster Travels

Inshore lobsters tend to stay in one place, seldom moving more than a mile or so, but deepwater lobsters farther out on the Continental Shelf follow a seasonal migratory pattern shoreward in summer, returning to the Shelf again in the autumn. The record travel so far is 225 miles covered by a lobster tagged off the Continental Shelf and recovered at Port Jefferson, Long Island, NY.

COOKING LOBSTER

When plunged into boiling water, a live lobster curls its tail under and you know the lobster was alive. It remains in that position until it dies. Upon death the tail loses its elasticity and ability to curl under the body and the lobster is cooked. Lobsters are not poisonous if they die before cooking, but cooking should not be delayed. Many lobsters sold commercially are killed and frozen before cooking. Lobsters and other crustaceans do spoil rapidly after death, which is why many buyers insist on receiving them alive. If the lobster is "headed" before or soon after death, the body meat will keep fresh longer. This is because the so-called head includes the thorax, the site of most of the viscera and gills, which spoil much more rapidly than claw or tail meat. Freezing slows deteriorative changes and harmful chemical actions that follow death.

Cooked Lobster Turn Red

The red pigment is the most stable component of the coloring in a lobster shell. The greens and browns which darken the shell in a live lobster are destroyed by cooking so the lobster turns red.

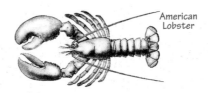

American Lobster

California Rock Lobster (Spiny)

Lobster's Blood Color

Is colorless and when exposed to oxygen, it develops a bluish color.

Tomalley

Tomalley is the lobster's liver. It turns green when cooked and is considered a delicacy.

Lobster Eggs

The coral colored material often seen in a lobster are the egg mass of a female lobster. Cooking colors the tiny eggs a deep coral or red.

Prawns, Crayfish & Shrimp

As so often happens, common names are used loosely and inconsistently in the shrimp family. The "prawn" of Great Britain and other countries is essentially the same animal as the shrimp of the United States, the only biological difference being that prawns have their second abdominal flap (counting from the head towards the tail) overlapping the first and the third. In this country, the term "shrimp" applies to all crustaceans of the Natantia group, regardless of size. "Crayfish" or "crawfish" are names given to both a common freshwater crustacean and to the saltwater spiny lobster.

Freshwater Crayfish

Crayfish live in freshwater streams and ponds and are similar to lobsters - but much smaller.

Shrimp

Are animals where species live in salt water or freshwater.

Pink Shrimp

Crayfish

Mantis Shrimp

Salt Water Shrimp

Coon Stripped Shrimp

Common Shore Shrimp Side

Common Shrimp Top

Deep Water Shrimp

Common Shrimp

Spotted Shrimp

CRUSTACEANS

CRABS

There are over 4500 species of true crabs (ones with a hard carapace) and 500 hermit crabs (crabs with a relatively soft shell and 'borrow' other animals' old shells (snails, etc.) for protection. Most crabs live in the water. Most crabs are omnivores (plants and meat), while some specialize in plants or meat. Marine crabs breathe using gills under the carapace. Land crabs have lung-like cavities to breathe air.

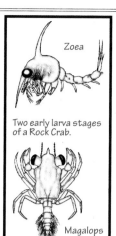

Zoea

Two early larva stages of a Rock Crab.

Magalops

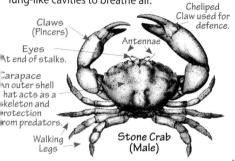

Cheliped
Claw used for defence.

Claws (Pincers)

Antennae

Eyes
At end of stalks.

Carapace
An outer shell that acts as a skeleton and protection from predators.

Walking Legs

Stone Crab (Male)

Soft & Hard Shell Crabs

Soft and hard shell crabs are the same species. A soft-shell crab is one that has just discarded its shell. Crabs which have just shed their shell hide in rocks or bury themselves in sand and mud to escape predators. They emerge after the new shell hardens, a quick process.

Crabs Movement

Most crabs "walk" or run across the ocean bottom. Some, such as the blue crab of the Atlantic coast (a member of the one family of "swimming crabs") can swim. Their rear most pair of legs is modified for swimming and legs are paddle-shaped.

Blue Crab

Crab walks sideways.

Crab Tracks

Hermit Crab

Hermit Crab

It does not have a very hard shell and uses the discarded shells of other animal for protection. The crab will find larger shells to inhabit as it grows. A favorite shell is the whelk shell.

Horseshoe Crab
(King Crab)

It lives in warm, shallow coastal waters. It is not a true crab and is closely related to spiders and scorpions.

Tail
Not dangerous but is used as a rudder.

Horseshoe Crab

Top

California Rock Crab

Flat Mud Crab

Dungeness Crab

Atlantic Rock Crab

Spider Crab

Snow Crab

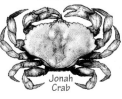

Jonah Crab

Oyster Crab
A very small crab that lives inside an oyster. It helps in household chores!

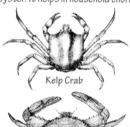

Kelp Crab

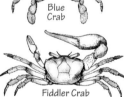

Blue Crab

Fiddler Crab

Green Crab

Lady Crab

Flame Streaked Box Crab

Red Crab

Eye

Eyestalk

Ghost Crab

Crabs Shedding Shell

Crabs grow by shedding their outgrown shell. The rigid shell imprisons the crab and limits growth. Once the shell is shed, the crab can absorb water and expand into its new grown shell.

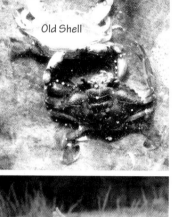

Old Shell

Horseshoe Crab

Sea Turtles

Sea Turtles spend most of their lives in shallow coastal waters of warm and temperate seas. The female returns to its birth beach to lay eggs. They are cold blooded. They are carnivores except for the Green Turtle which is a herbivore.

Green Turtle

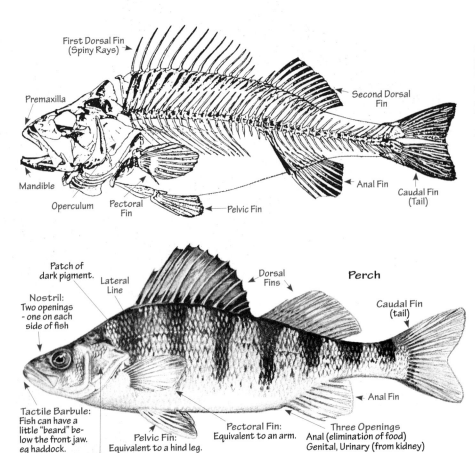

First Dorsal Fin (Spiny Rays)

Second Dorsal Fin

Premaxilla

Mandible

Operculum

Pectoral Fin

Pelvic Fin

Anal Fin

Caudal Fin (Tail)

Patch of dark pigment.

Lateral Line

Nostril: Two openings - one on each side of fish

Dorsal Fins

Perch

Caudal Fin (tail)

Tactile Barbule: Fish can have a little "beard" below the front jaw. eg haddock.

Pelvic Fin: Equivalent to a hind leg.

Pectoral Fin: Equivalent to an arm.

Anal Fin

Three Openings Anal (elimination of food) Genital, Urinary (from kidney)

Gills: Protected by a cover (operculum) supported by four bones. Behind the gills is a flexible membrane supported by bony rays.

45 FRESH WATER FISH

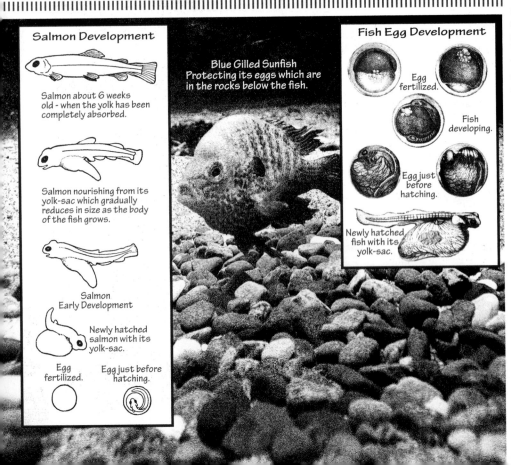

Salmon Development

Salmon about 6 weeks old - when the yolk has been completely absorbed.

Salmon nourishing from its yolk-sac which gradually reduces in size as the body of the fish grows.

Salmon Early Development

Newly hatched salmon with its yolk-sac.

Egg fertilized.

Egg just before hatching.

Blue Gilled Sunfish Protecting its eggs which are in the rocks below the fish.

Fish Egg Development

Egg fertilized.

Fish developing.

Egg just before hatching.

Newly hatched fish with its yolk-sac.

SCIENTIFIC NAMES OF FISH

Common or colloquial names of fish vary from place to place (menhaden, for example, are known by at least three different names, and striped bass are called "stripers" in New England and "rockfish" in Chesapeake Bay), scientists would have no way of differentiating among species without a uniform naming system. The system used to name the 20,000 odd fishes known to science is called "the binomial system of nomenclature." It usually consists of a scientific name in two parts, the generic and specific names, or three parts for subspecies. The words of the names are latinized regardless of the language or alphabet of the study and are frequently descriptive of a significant feature of the organism. The name generally applies to several species showing basic characteristics while a specific (species) name is based on a few characteristics applying to one species, separate and distinct from all others. (Example: The generic name Morone applies to white perch, white bass, and striped bass; the species names for those three fishes are Morone americanus, M. chrysops, and M. saxatilis.)

HOW FISH EAT

Fish do not chew their food in the human manner. Carnivorous fish like sharks use their sharp teeth to seize and hold prey (while shaking it to tear the meat) while swallowing it whole or in large pieces. Bottom dwellers such as rays are equipped with large flat teeth that crush the shellfish they consume. Herbivorous fish (grazers) often lack jaw teeth, but have tooth-like grinding mills in their throats, called pharyngeal teeth. Fish would suffocate if they tried to chew, for chewing would interfere with the passage of water over the gills, necessary for obtaining oxygen.

AGE OF A FISH

Growth "rings" on scales, and/or ringlike structures found in otoliths (small bones of the inner ear), are examined and counted. The rings correspond to seasonal changes in the environment and can be compared to the annual rings of tree trunks. A series of fine rings are laid down in scales for each year of life in summer, the rings grow faster and have relatively wide separations; in winter, slower growth is indicated by narrow separations between rings. Each pair of rings indicates one year. Because scale rings are sometimes influenced by other factors, scientists often use otoliths, whose ringlike structures also indicate years of life.

LIFE SPAN OF FISH

Fish live from a few weeks or months (some of the small reef fishes) to 50 years or more (sturgeons). Longevity information is still sparse, but scientists have learned that species live 10 to 20 years in temperate waters.

Some Fish Give Birth to Living Young

These are called viviparous fishes. The sea perches of the Pacific coast, for example, give birth to living young of considerable size, sometimes one-fifth the size of the mother. Several kind of sharks produce living young.

Salmon Growth Rings

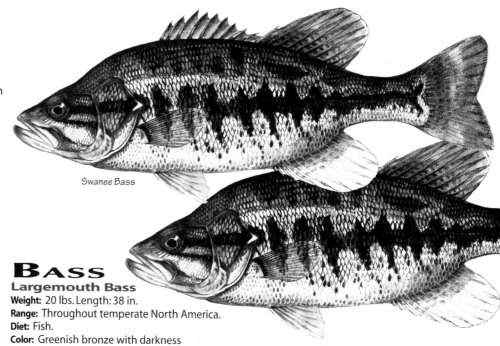

Swanee Bass

Fish Seeing Color

Most fish are color blind, despite the opinion of many sport fishermen. Fish can see color shadings, reflected light, shape, and movement, which probably accounts for the acceptance or rejection of artificial lures used by fishermen.

Fish Breathe Air

Fish breathe air (actually oxygen not air - as humans) but not directly into the lungs as mammals do (except for some tropical fish). As water passes over a system of extremely fine gill membranes, fish absorb the water's oxygen content. Gills contain a network of fine blood vessels (capillaries) that take up the oxygen and diffuse it through the membranes.

Edibility of Fish

Most kinds encountered by anglers are edible. The organs of some species are always poisonous to man; other fish can become toxic because of elements in their diets. The latter are most often from tropical regions of both the Atlantic and Pacific Oceans. Scientific literature has pinpointed danger areas in which the disease called "ciguatera" may occur in tropical and subtropical fish.

Identifying Poisonous Fish

There is no easy way to know if an individual fish is poisonous as certain types of fish are poisonous under certain conditions. Frequently local customs can be relied upon as an indicator as to if a certain fish might be "in or out of season".

Food Fish & Strong Odor

For most species, truly fresh fish is almost odorless. Fish begin to smell "fishy" when deterioration sets in. This can be caused by incorrect storage practices that bring about the release of oxidized fats and acids through bacterial and enzymatic action.

Blood-Like Fluid in Fish

The kidney is the blood-like material found along the backbone in the body cavity of most fishes. It is usually removed when the fish is cleaned.

How Fish Swim

Fish swim primarily by contracting bands of muscles in sequence on alternate sides of the body so that the tail is whipped very rapidly from side to side in a sculling motion. Vertical fins are used mainly for stabilization. Paired pectoral and pelvic fins are used primarily for stability when a fish hovers, but sometimes may be used to aid rapid forward motion.

Swimming Speed

Tunas and tuna-like fish, billfish, and certain sharks are the speed champions, reaching 50 mph in short bursts. Sustained swimming speeds generally range from about 5 to 10 mph among strong swimmers.

EXOTIC FISH

Is a fish not native to an area, but introduced either by accident or design. Some such species can cause problems. Often their natural predators are absent from the new area, permitting more rapid reproduction rates than those of natural inhabitants, sometimes at the expense of more desirable native fish. The "walking catfish" in Florida is an example. Thought to have escaped from a private aquarium, the catfish have shown a remarkable ability to avoid eradication efforts by man. An aggressive and voracious fish, it poses a threat to other forms of aquatic life. Population is now estimated in the millions.

BASS

Largemouth Bass
Weight: 20 lbs. **Length:** 38 in.
Range: Throughout temperate North America.
Diet: Fish.
Color: Greenish bronze with darkness depending upon water.
To differentiate from Smallmouth Bass: Mouth on Largemouth extends past area below the eye and fins on back are separated. Morning and evening enter shallow water. During hot hours they enter deep water holes.

Rock Bass
Weight: 1 lb.
Range: East of the Allegheny Mountains - Gulf of Mexico to Canada.
Color: Back; dark green marked with black. Sides: golden brown with dark markings.
Head: mottled with dark brown. Special characteristic; black spot on gill cover and red eyes. Swim in schools and can be found in places where they can find cover as weeds, lily pads, logs, brush, rocky shores. Eat anything.

Smallmouth Bass
Weight: 11 lbs. **Length:** 27 in.
Range: Throughout temperate North America.
Diet: Insect larvae, fish, crayfish.
Color: Body; bronze green with light gray or yellowish belly.
Back: darker with vertical descending markings.
See Largemouth characteristics. Smallmouth also has scales on the base of dorsal fin. There are none on those of the Largemouth.
Diet: Will eat anything. In lakes look for rock formations and in streams for shallow water or deep pools.

Striped Bass
Weight: 70 lbs. **Length:** 50 in.
Range: Gulf of St. Lawrence to North Florida. Gulf of Mexico to Louisiana
Diet: Fish.

Swannee Bass
Weight: 3-4 lbs. **Length:** 14 in.
Range: Swannee River basin, Florida and Georgia.
Diet: Crayfish, fish, shrimp.

White Bass
Related to the Stripped Bass.
Weight: 3-4 lbs. **Length:** 18 in.
Range: Mississippi Valley, Great Lakes, deep lakes as far south as Texas, up to eastern Canada.
Diet: Minnows and small invertebrates.
Body: Silvery with darker horizontal stripes. Feed at night in large schools.

White Perch
Weight: 3-4 lbs. **Length:** 12 in.
Range: Atlantic Coast - Nova Scotia to Georgia.
Diet: Small fish and invertebrates.

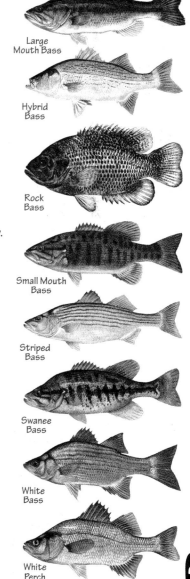

Large Mouth Bass

Hybrid Bass

Rock Bass

Small Mouth Bass

Striped Bass

Swanee Bass

White Bass

White Perch

BASS

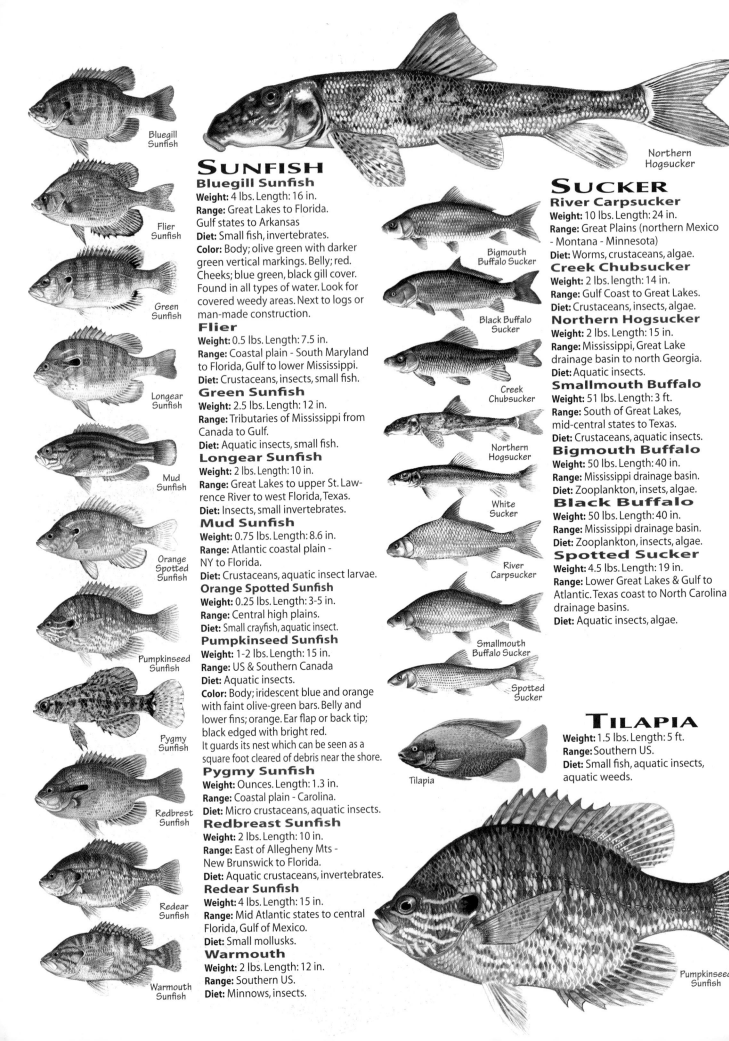

SUNFISH

Bluegill Sunfish
Weight: 4 lbs. **Length:** 16 in.
Range: Great Lakes to Florida. Gulf states to Arkansas
Diet: Small fish, invertebrates.
Color: Body; olive green with darker green vertical markings. Belly; red. Cheeks; blue green, black gill cover. Found in all types of water. Look for covered weedy areas. Next to logs or man-made construction.

Flier
Weight: 0.5 lbs. **Length:** 7.5 in.
Range: Coastal plain - South Maryland to Florida, Gulf to lower Mississippi.
Diet: Crustaceans, insects, small fish.

Green Sunfish
Weight: 2.5 lbs. **Length:** 12 in.
Range: Tributaries of Mississippi from Canada to Gulf.
Diet: Aquatic insects, small fish.

Longear Sunfish
Weight: 2 lbs. **Length:** 10 in.
Range: Great Lakes to upper St. Lawrence River to west Florida, Texas.
Diet: Insects, small invertebrates.

Mud Sunfish
Weight: 0.75 lbs. **Length:** 8.6 in.
Range: Atlantic coastal plain - NY to Florida.
Diet: Crustaceans, aquatic insect larvae.

Orange Spotted Sunfish
Weight: 0.25 lbs. **Length:** 3-5 in.
Range: Central high plains.
Diet: Small crayfish, aquatic insect.

Pumpkinseed Sunfish
Weight: 1-2 lbs. **Length:** 15 in.
Range: US & Southern Canada
Diet: Aquatic insects.
Color: Body; iridescent blue and orange with faint olive-green bars. Belly and lower fins; orange. Ear flap or back tip; black edged with bright red. It guards its nest which can be seen as a square foot cleared of debris near the shore.

Pygmy Sunfish
Weight: Ounces. **Length:** 1.3 in.
Range: Coastal plain - Carolina.
Diet: Micro crustaceans, aquatic insects.

Redbreast Sunfish
Weight: 2 lbs. **Length:** 10 in.
Range: East of Allegheny Mts - New Brunswick to Florida.
Diet: Aquatic crustaceans, invertebrates.

Redear Sunfish
Weight: 4 lbs. **Length:** 15 in.
Range: Mid Atlantic states to central Florida, Gulf of Mexico.
Diet: Small mollusks.

Warmouth
Weight: 2 lbs. **Length:** 12 in.
Range: Southern US.
Diet: Minnows, insects.

SUCKER

River Carpsucker
Weight: 10 lbs. **Length:** 24 in.
Range: Great Plains (northern Mexico - Montana - Minnesota)
Diet: Worms, crustaceans, algae.

Creek Chubsucker
Weight: 2 lbs. **length:** 14 in.
Range: Gulf Coast to Great Lakes.
Diet: Crustaceans, insects, algae.

Northern Hogsucker
Weight: 2 lbs. **Length:** 15 in.
Range: Mississippi, Great Lake drainage basin to north Georgia.
Diet: Aquatic insects.

Smallmouth Buffalo
Weight: 51 lbs. **Length:** 3 ft.
Range: South of Great Lakes, mid-central states to Texas.
Diet: Crustaceans, aquatic insects.

Bigmouth Buffalo
Weight: 50 lbs. **Length:** 40 in.
Range: Mississippi drainage basin.
Diet: Zooplankton, insets, algae.

Black Buffalo
Weight: 50 lbs. **Length:** 40 in.
Range: Mississippi drainage basin.
Diet: Zooplankton, insects, algae.

Spotted Sucker
Weight: 4.5 lbs. **Length:** 19 in.
Range: Lower Great Lakes & Gulf to Atlantic. Texas coast to North Carolina drainage basins.
Diet: Aquatic insects, algae.

TILAPIA
Weight: 1.5 lbs. **Length:** 5 ft.
Range: Southern US.
Diet: Small fish, aquatic insects, aquatic weeds.

Bluegill Sunfish

Flier Sunfish

Green Sunfish

Longear Sunfish

Mud Sunfish

Orange Spotted Sunfish

Pumpkinseed Sunfish

Pygmy Sunfish

Redbrest Sunfish

Redear Sunfish

Warmouth Sunfish

Northern Hogsucker

Bigmouth Buffalo Sucker

Black Buffalo Sucker

Creek Chubsucker

Northern Hogsucker

White Sucker

River Carpsucker

Smallmouth Buffalo Sucker

Spotted Sucker

Tilapia

Pumpkinseed Sunfish

TROUT

Brook Trout
Weight: 3 lbs. **Length:** 21 in.
Range: All North America and South America.
Diet: Aquatic insects, invertebrates.
Color: Body; depends upon type of water and food eaten, usually back is black mottled with lighter tones. Sides; red or pink spots. Belly; almost white. Lower fins; red with white edges. Likes deep cold water. Look for deep shade and other cover. Look scaleless but have minute scales embedded in the skin.

Brown Trout
Weight: 35 lbs. **Length:** 3 ft. 4 in.
Range: From Europe found NE and west US and Canada.
Diet: Small fish, insects, invertebrates.
Color: Body; brownish with large scales. Back; almost black. Belly; almost white. Fins; bottom have white edges. Sides; red and black spots surrounded with lighter rings. Feed from the surface at night. In warmer waters than the Brook Trout.

Golden Trout High Sierra
Weight: 1 lb.
Range: Over 10,000 feet. Native of cold waters of High Sierra Nevada Mountains and have been introduced to other mountain systems.
Color: Body; golden yellow. Side; red stripe with dark splotches. Dorsal fin, tail; red markings. Pectoral fins, lower half of gill plates; red. Lower fins; tipped red.

Lake Trout
Weight: 5 lbs.
Range: Cold water fish found in Northern States, Canada & Alaska.
Color: Body; gray with yellowish spots. Has teeth on base of tongue and roof of mouth. In the summer only found in deep water. In the Spring and Fall they can be caught in shallow water.

Rainbow Trout
Weight: 30 lbs. **Length:** 3 ft. 9 in.
Range: US and Canada to Alaska.
Diet: Small fish, invertebrates.
Body & fins: are spotted with black. Broad horizontal red or purplish-red band running the full length of body. Lower fins edged with white. Roof of mouth has zigzag rows of teeth. If they enter the ocean they change coloration and become silvery and be considered a sea-run trout and called Steelheads.

Cutthroat Trout
Weight: 2 lbs.
Range: Western fish native to waters in the Rocky Mountains from California to Alaska.
Color: Body; yellowish with black spots. Under lower jaw; bright red marking. Live in the sea and ascend rivers to spawn. In the Spring they are in the estuaries and have a light blue or green back. When they ascend a stream they will change colors to having sides that are rosy pink and black spots will appear.

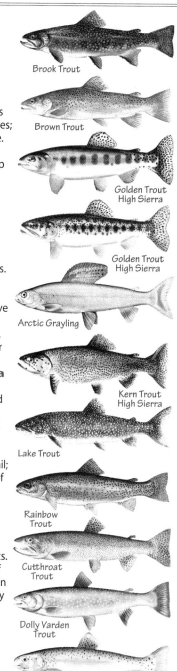

Brook Trout

Brown Trout

Golden Trout High Sierra

Golden Trout High Sierra

Arctic Grayling

Kern Trout High Sierra

Lake Trout

Rainbow Trout

Cutthroat Trout

Dolly Varden Trout

Rainbow Trout Alaska

New Zealand biologists have found that the rainbow trout navigates by having *"a magnetic compass in their noses,"* reports New Scientist magazine. In trout, researchers at the University of Auckland discovered a nerve fiber in the fish's face that fires when exposed to a magnetic field. Tracing the fiber led them back to the fish's nose, where they found nerve cells that contain magnetite

PERCH

Yellow Perch
Related to the walleye.
Weight: 0.25-0.75 lbs. **Length:** 24 in.
Range: Great Lakes, eastern Canada, US east coast. Mississippi, west Florida.
Diet: Small fish, invertebrates.
Color: Body: yellow marked with broad dark vertical stripes.
Belly: almost white.
Lower fins: vivid orange or red. Dorsal fins are separated. Found in lakes, ponds and streams. They swim in schools. Look under cover as logs, rock formations, docks, weeds. They might school with walleyed pike.

Sauger
Weight: 4 lbs. **Length:** 18 in.
Range: Central North America.
Diet: Fish, crayfish.

Walleye
Weight: 5 lbs. **Length:** 36 in.
Range: Lakes & rivers east of Mississippi - Gulf of Mexico to Canada
Diet: Fish.
Color: brassy brown color, flecked with yellow, marked with dark brown bars. Eyes; are filmy with milky appearance.
Fins: Have two separate dorsal fins. Feed at night. Stay in deep water during the day preferring clear water, with clean gravel or rock bottoms.

American Eel

AMERICAN EEL
Weight: 16 lbs. **Length:** 54 in.
Range: Newfoundland, Atlantic and Gulf coasts, Caribbean to Brazil.
Diet: Omnivorous.

Mosquitofish

MOSQUITOFISH
Weight: Ounces. **Length:** 2.6 in.
Range: Mid Atlantic, Delaware to Florida.
Diet: Surface insects, larvae, small crustaceans, algae, its own young.

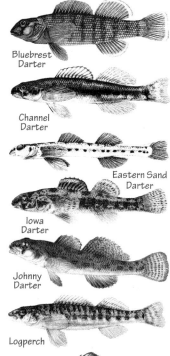

Bluebrest Darter

Channel Darter

Eastern Sand Darter

Iowa Darter

Johnny Darter

Logperch

Pirate Perch

Rainbow Darter

Spotted Darter

Trout-Perch

Variagate Darter

Sauger

Walleye

Yellow Perch

Trout Head

Perch

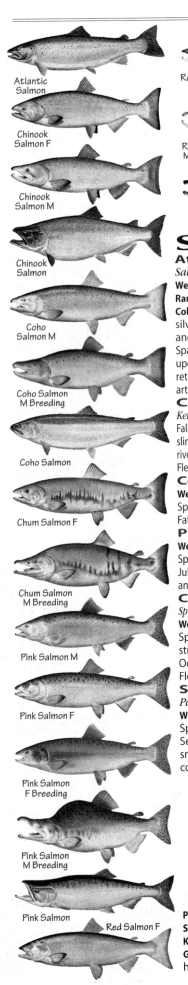

Atlantic Salmon

Chinook Salmon F

Chinook Salmon M

Chinook Salmon

Coho Salmon M

Coho Salmon M Breeding

Coho Salmon

Chum Salmon F

Chum Salmon M Breeding

Pink Salmon M

Pink Salmon F

Pink Salmon F Breeding

Pink Salmon M Breeding

Pink Salmon

Red Salmon F

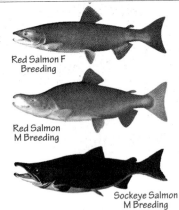

Red Salmon F Breeding

Red Salmon M Breeding

Sockeye Salmon M Breeding

SALMON

Atlantic Salmon
Salmon, Kennebec Salmon
Weigh: 15 lbs.
Range: Maine to Labrador.
Color: body; blue and silver. Sides; silvery sprinkled with red, orange and black spots.
Spawns several times. (Pacific salmon dies upon spawning). Salmon do not eat upon returning to fresh water but will rise to artificial flies.

Chum Salmon
Keta Salmon, Dog Salmon, Qualler, Calico
Fall Salmon. Similar to Sockeye but has slimmer "waist" above tail. Spawns in Pacific rivers and streams in October and November. Flesh pale to light pink.

Coho Salmon
Weight: 4-10 lbs.
Spawns mid-June to November.
Fat fish, fine textured flesh, pink or red.

Pink Salmon
Weight: 3-5 lbs.
Spawns in Pacific rivers and streams from July to September. Firm flesh, fine texture and small flakes.

Chinook Salmon
Spring Salmon, King Salmon, Chub Salmon.
Weight: 10-50 pounds.
Spawn in Pacific Coast rivers and streams. Fishing season from March to October. Fattest of all Pacific Salmon. Flesh is large, flaked and rich in oil.

Sockeye Salmon
Pacific Salmon
Weight: 5 lbs.
Spawning in Pacific from June to September. Fat fish, firm flesh of small flake and deep orange or red coloration.

STAGES OF SALMON'S LIFE
Parr: Lives in a stream.
Smolt: Upon entering salt water.
Kelt: After spawning.
Grisle: If salmon do not reach adulthood but return to fresh water.

Difference Between Atlantic & Pacific Salmon
The Atlantic Salmon is actually a member of the genus Salmo, or trout family, not a salmon, which is placed in the genus Oncorhynchus. The misnomer is so widely accepted that it would only cause confusion to rename the species. The main biological difference between the Atlantic and Pacific "salmons" is that salmon may spawn more than once, and Oncorhynchus die soon after one spawn.

Pacific Salmon Species
There are seven: Chinook, coho, pink, sockeye, chum, steelhead, and masu. The masu occurs only on the Asiatic coast of the North Pacific. Based on DNA and behavior, the steelhead was re-classified as the seventh species of Pacific Salmon.

Steelhead: Salmon or Trout?
The steelhead is a rainbow trout that migrates to sea as a juvenile and returns to fresh water as an adult to spawn. Unlike the Pacific salmon, the steelhead trout does not always die following spawning and may spawn more than once and return to the sea after each spawning.

Salmon Eggs
Salmon generally have from 2,500 to 7,000 eggs depending on species and size of fish. The chinook salmon generally produces the most and largest eggs.

Salmon Spawning
Salmon almost always return to spawn in freshwater areas where they were born. Some straying has been documented, but it is minor. Most spawning salmon return to the precise stream of their birth, sometimes overcoming great distances and hazardous river conditions to reach home.

Kokanee, or Silver Trout
It is the landlocked subspecies of a sockeye salmon. The kokanee spends its entire life in fresh water and usually does not attain the size of its sea-migrating cousin.

Landlocked Pacific Salmon
Landlocked Pacific salmon die after spawning. This phase of their life history is the same as their seagoing relatives.

Salmon Size
Atlantic Salmon: Weights of over 100 pounds have been reported from European countries.
Chinook: the record for the largest of the Pacific species is 126 pounds.

Salmon by Different Names
Chinook salmon: (Oncorhynchus tshawytscha) King salmon, black mouths, springers
Coho salmon: (O. kisutch) silver salmon
Pink salmon: (O. gorbuscha) humpback salmon
Sockeye salmon: (O. nerka) blueback, red salmon
Steelhead: (O. mykiss) a seagoing rainbow trout

Steelhead

ANADROMOUS FISH
An anadromous fish, born in fresh water, spends most of its life in the sea and returns to fresh water to spawn. Salmon, smelt, shad, striped bass, and sturgeon are common examples.

CATADROMOUS FISH
A catadromous fish does the opposite - lives in fresh water and enters salt water to spawn. Most of the eels are catadromous.

Salmon in the Ocean
Contrary to earlier beliefs, many salmon from North American rivers roam far at sea in the North Pacific Ocean and the Bering Sea.

The oceanic distribution of the salmon is dependent upon the species and point of origin. Sockeye and chinook salmon from northwest Alaska, for example, may migrate across the Bering Sea to areas close to Kamchatka, Russia, and south of the Aleutian Islands into the North Pacific Ocean; the sockeye also migrate eastward to the Gulf of Alaska.

Salmon such as the pink, chum, and coho from central and southeast Alaska, British Columbia, and Washington State, migrate out into the northeastern Pacific and Gulf of Alaska.

Many steelhead trout from Washington and Oregon are known to migrate far at sea to areas off the Alaskan Peninsula.

Some salmon migrate several thousand miles from the time they leave the rivers as juveniles until they return as adults.

A chinook salmon tagged in the central Aleutian Islands and recovered a year later in the Salmon River, Idaho, had traveled about 3,500 miles.

A steelhead trout tagged south of Kiska Island (western Aleutians) was recovered about six months and 2,200 miles later in the Wynoochee River, Washington.

Fish Ladder
A fish ladder, or fish way, often used in salmon country, is constructed to provide for up-stream passage of fish over a dam or a natural barrier that might prevent or impede progress to spawning grounds.

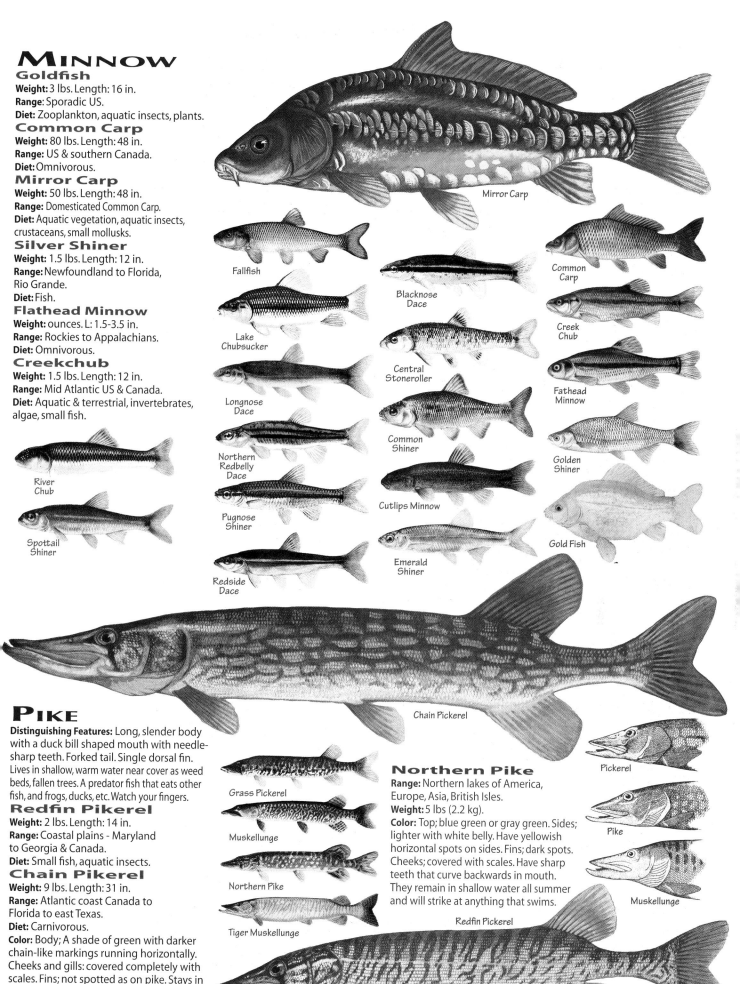

Minnow

Goldfish
Weight: 3 lbs. **Length:** 16 in.
Range: Sporadic US.
Diet: Zooplankton, aquatic insects, plants.

Common Carp
Weight: 80 lbs. **Length:** 48 in.
Range: US & southern Canada.
Diet: Omnivorous.

Mirror Carp
Weight: 50 lbs. **Length:** 48 in.
Range: Domesticated Common Carp.
Diet: Aquatic vegetation, aquatic insects, crustaceans, small mollusks.

Silver Shiner
Weight: 1.5 lbs. **Length:** 12 in.
Range: Newfoundland to Florida, Rio Grande.
Diet: Fish.

Flathead Minnow
Weight: ounces. **L:** 1.5-3.5 in.
Range: Rockies to Appalachians.
Diet: Omnivorous.

Creekchub
Weight: 1.5 lbs. **Length:** 12 in.
Range: Mid Atlantic US & Canada.
Diet: Aquatic & terrestrial, invertebrates, algae, small fish.

Mirror Carp

Fallfish

Blacknose Dace

Common Carp

Lake Chubsucker

Central Stoneroller

Creek Chub

Longnose Dace

Common Shiner

Fathead Minnow

Northern Redbelly Dace

Cutlips Minnow

Golden Shiner

Pugnose Shiner

River Chub

Spottail Shiner

Emerald Shiner

Gold Fish

Redside Dace

Pike

Distinguishing Features: Long, slender body with a duck bill shaped mouth with needle-sharp teeth. Forked tail. Single dorsal fin. Lives in shallow, warm water near cover as weed beds, fallen trees. A predator fish that eats other fish, and frogs, ducks, etc. Watch your fingers.

Redfin Pikerel
Weight: 2 lbs. **Length:** 14 in.
Range: Coastal plains - Maryland to Georgia & Canada.
Diet: Small fish, aquatic insects.

Chain Pikerel
Weight: 9 lbs. **Length:** 31 in.
Range: Atlantic coast Canada to Florida to east Texas.
Diet: Carnivorous.
Color: Body; A shade of green with darker chain-like markings running horizontally. Cheeks and gills: covered completely with scales. Fins; not spotted as on pike. Stays in shallow water where it feeds on everything.

Chain Pickerel

Grass Pickerel

Muskellunge

Northern Pike

Tiger Muskellunge

Northern Pike
Range: Northern lakes of America, Europe, Asia, British Isles.
Weight: 5 lbs (2.2 kg).
Color: Top; blue green or gray green. Sides; lighter with white belly. Have yellowish horizontal spots on sides. Fins; dark spots. Cheeks; covered with scales. Have sharp teeth that curve backwards in mouth. They remain in shallow water all summer and will strike at anything that swims.

Redfin Pickerel

Pickerel

Pike

Muskellunge

507

CATFISH

Environment: catfish are adaptable bottom feeders that can live in inhospitable muddy, low oxygen, environments.
Distinctive Features: No scales, eight barbels (whiskers), sharp spines at the front of some fins (these can easily injure an unsuspecting fisherman), broad flat head.
General: Are very tasty. Active at night using their barbels help locate food.

Channel Catfish

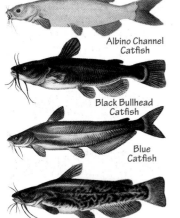

Albino Channel Catfish

Black Bullhead Catfish

Blue Catfish

Brown Bullhead Catfish

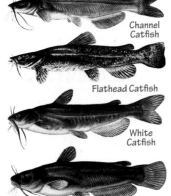

Channel Catfish

Flathead Catfish

White Catfish

Yellow Bullhead Catfish

Channel Catfish
Weight: 60 lbs. **Length:** 4 ft.
Range: US & southern Canada.
Diet: Insects, crayfish, fish.

Albino Channel Catfish
Genetic variation of Channel Catfish
Weight: 60 lbs. **Length:** 4 ft.
Range: US & southern Canada.
Diet: Insects, crayfish, fish.

Flathead Catfish
Weight: 90 lbs. **Length:** 5 ft.
Range: Rio Grande, Pecos, Gila watersheds.
Diet: Crustaceans, insect larvae, fish.

Blue Catfish
Weight: 60 lbs. **Length:** 4 ft.
Range: Mississippi & Gulf drainage.
Diet: Detritus insects, crayfish, worms, mollusks, fish.

White Catfish
Weight: 15 lbs. **Length:** 24 lbs.
Range: Coast, New York to Florida.
Diet: Aquatic plants, insects, fish.

Black Bullhead
Weight: 2 lbs. **Length:** 12 in.
Range: Central US & Canada.
Diet: Insects, crustaceans.

Yellow Bullhead
Weight: 2 lbs. **Length:** 12 in.
Range: Eastern US & Canada.
Diet: Detritus plant matter, crayfish, insects, mollusks, fish.

Brown Bullhead
Weight: 5 lbs. **Length:** 20 in.
Range: Eastern US & Canada.
Diet: Crustaceans, insects, worms, mollusks, fish.

DRUM

Freshwater Drum
Weight: 54 lbs. **Length:** 35 in.
Range: Great Lakes, Canada, Mississippi basin, Alabama, east Mexico.
Diet: Invertebrates.

Spotted Sea Trout
Weight: 16 lbs. **Length:** 36 in.
Range: NY to Florida, Gulf of Mexico.
Diet: Shrimp, fish.

Red Drum
Weight: 90 lbs. **Length:** 61 in.
Range: NY to Texas coast.
Diet: Crustaceans, mollusks.

Freshwater Drum

Red Drum

Spotted Seatrout

GAR

Alligator Gar
Weight: 150-300 lb. **L:** 7-9.5 ft.
Range: Gulf Coast rivers.
Diet: Fish.

Spotted Gar
Weight: 28 lbs. **Length:** 3 ft.
Range: Coastal plains - Texas, Louisiana, Missouri.
Diet: Fish.

Longnose Gar
Weight: 15 lbs. **Length:** 40 in.
Range: Eastern US river ways.
Diet: Fish.

Shortnose Gar
Weight: 3.5 lbs. **Length:** 2 ft.
Range: Mississippi, Missouri, Ohio Rivers basins.
Diet: Fish, crayfish, insects.

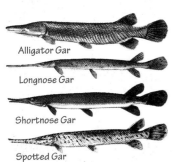

Alligator Gar

Longnose Gar

Shortnose Gar

Spotted Gar

CRAPPIE

Black Crappie
Weight: 5 lbs. **Length:** 16 in.
Range: Southern Canada, Great Lakes to east Texas.
Diet: Small fish.
Color: Body; olive green, top; black sides; speckled with black, Fins and tail; spotted black. Slow to take bait and set the hook carefully. Active all year and can be taken while ice fishing.

White Crappie
Weight: 5 lbs. **Length:** 16 in.
Range: Great Lakes, Texas, Louisiana, east coast.
Diet: Small fish.

Black Crappie

White Crappie

BROOK STICKLEBACK
Length: 3.5 in.
Range: Great Lakes, Mississippi River, Atlantic & Arctic drainage basin.

Brook Stickleback

SHEEPSHEAD
Weight: 20 lbs. **Length:** 3 ft.
Range: Nova Scotia to Gulf of Mexico

Sheepshead

BOWFIN
Weight: 20 lbs. **Length:** 3 ft.
Range: Southern Canada to Florida.
Diet: Fish, invertebrates.

Bowfin

BANDED KILLIFISH
Length: 5 in.
Range: Atlantic drainage - Newfoundland to S. Carolina.

Banded Killifish

Alligator Gar

Paddlefish

PADDLEFISH
Weight: 160 lbs. **Length:** 5 ft.
Range: Mississippi & Missouri River basins.
Diet: Plankton.

BLUEFISH
Weight: 45 lbs. **Length:** 48 in.
Range: East coast US.
Diet: Fish.

Bluefish

MOONEYE
Weight: 3 lbs. **Length:** 18 in.
Range: St. Lawrence, Great Lakes,
Mississippi River, Hudson Bay.
Lives in deep pools.

Mooneye

RAINBOW SMELT
Length: 13 in.
Range: Great Lakes, Mississippi River,
Arctic & Pacific drainage. Cool clear lakes.

Rainbow Smelt

SLIMY SCULPIN
Length: 4 in.
Range: St. Lawrence, Great Lakes,
Atlantic, Arctic, & Pacific basins -
mainland Canada and Alaska.

Slimy Sculpin

CENTRAL MUDMINNOW
Length: 5 in.
Range: St. Lawence - Great Lakes,
Hudson's Bay, New York State.

Central Mudmonnow

ROUND WHITEFISH
Weight: 23 lbs. **Length:** 20 in.
Range: Northern drainage basins
(east, west, arctic),
Great Lakes. Cold water fish.
Diet: Small mollusks, aquatic insect
larvae, plankton, crustaceans.

Round Whitefish

STURGEON
Shortnose Sturgeon
Weight: 20 lbs. **Length:** 43 in.
Range: East coast rivers & coastal waters.
Diet: Invertebrates, mollusks, small fish.
Atlantic Sturgeon
Weight: 1,100 lbs. **Length:** 14 ft.
Range: East coast rivers & coastal waters.
Diet: Invertebrates, mollusks, small fish.

Atlantic Sturgeon

Lake Sturgeon

Shortnose Sturgeon

BROOK SILVERSIDE
Length: 5 in.
Range: St. Lawrence, Great Lakes,
Mississippi River, and related areas.

Brook Silverside

BURBOT
Weight: 18 lbs. **Length:** 33 in.
Range: Northern US, Canada, Alaska.
Diet: Fish.

Burbot

Seal chasing
Salmon

HERRING
Blueback Herring
Weight: 3 lbs. **Length:** 15 in.
Range: East coast US & Canada.
Diet: Insects, shrimp, worms & fish.
Alabama Shad
Weight: 3 lbs. **Length:** 18 in.
Range: Alabama, Georgia, Florida,
Missouri, Mississippi, Illinois.
Diet: Small fish, aquatic insects.
Skipjack Herring
Weight: 3.5 lbs. **Length:** 21 in.
Range: Mississippi, Ohio, Missouri.
Diet: Small fish.
Alewife
River Herring, Kyak, Glut Herring.
Weight: 1 lb. L: Freshwater 5-17 in.,
Saltwater 14 in.
Range: East coast, Great Lakes,
northern lakes.
Diet: Zooplankton.
American Shad
Related to Alewife. Has more than
4 lateral spots, Alewife has only one.
Weight: 4 lbs. **Length:** 30 in.
Range: Coastal waters Newfoundland -
Florida. Introduced into west coast.
Diet: Fish & invertebrates.

Alabama
Shad

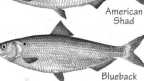
Alewife

American
Shad

Blueback
Herring

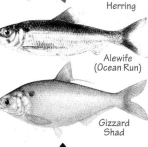
Alewife
(Ocean Run)

Gizzard
Shad

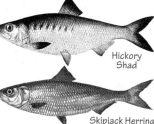
Hickory
Shad

Skipjack Herring

Atlantic Sturgeon

509

46 SALT WATER FISH

WHY THE OCEAN IS SALTY?

The ocean is salty because of the gradual concentration of dissolved chemicals eroded from the Earth's crust and washed into the sea. Solid and gaseous ejections from volcanoes, suspended particles swept to the ocean and by onshore winds, and materials dissolved from sediments deposited on the ocean floor have also contributed. Salinity is increased by evaporation or by freezing of sea ice and it is decreased as a result of rainfall, runoff, or the melting of ice. Salinities are much less than average in coastal waters, in the polar seas, and near the mouths of large rivers.

WHAT IS SEA WATER?

Sea water has been defined as a weak solution of almost everything. Ocean water is indeed a complex solution of mineral salts and of decayed biologic matter that results from the teeming life in the seas. Most of the ocean's salts were derived from gradual processes such the breaking up of the cooled igneous rocks of the Earth's crust by weathering and erosion, the wearing down of mountains, and the dissolving action of rains and streams which transported their mineral washings to the sea. Some of the ocean's salts have been dissolved from rocks and sediments below its floor. Other sources of salts include the solid and gaseous materials that escaped from the Earth's crust through volcanic vents or that originated in the atmosphere.

SALINITY OF THE OCEANS

The salinity (total salt content) of ocean water varies. It is affected by such factors as melting of ice, inflow of river water, evaporation, rain, snowfall, wind, wave motion, and ocean currents that cause horizontal and vertical mixing of the saltwater.

Saltiest Water: occurs in the Red Sea and the Persian Gulf, where rates of evaporation are very high. Of the major oceans, the North Atlantic is the saltiest. Within the North Atlantic, the saltiest part is the Sargasso Sea, an area of about 2 million square miles, located about 2,000 miles west of the Canary Islands. The Sargasso Sea is set apart from the open ocean by floating brown seaweed "sargassum" from which the sea gets its name. The saltiness of this sea is due in part to the high water temperature (up to 83° F) causing a high rate of evaporation and in part to its remoteness from land; because it is so far from land, it receives no fresh-water inflow. Eels mate in the Sargasso Sea and then swim back to there native waters.

Low Salinities: occur in polar seas where the salt water is diluted by melting ice and continued precipitation. Partly landlocked seas or coastal inlets that receive substantial runoff from precipitation falling on the land also may have low salinities. Salinity of sea water along the coastal areas of the conterminous United States varies with the month of the year as well as with geographic location. The water off the coast of Miami Beach has a high salt content because it is undiluted sea water. Off the coast of Astoria, however, the sea water is less saline because it is mixed with the fresh water of the mighty Columbia.

Other Chemical Effects in the Ocean

Sea water is not simply a solution of salts and dissolved gases unaffected by living organisms in the sea. Mollusks (oysters, clams, and mussels, for example) extract calcium from the sea to build their shells and skeletons. Foraminifers (very small one-celled sea animals) and crustaceans (such as crabs, shrimp, lobsters, and barnacles) likewise take out large amounts of calcium salts to build their bodies. Coral reefs, common in warm tropical seas, consist mostly of limestone (calcium carbonate) formed over millions of years from the skeletons of billions of small corals and other sea animals. Plankton (tiny floating animal and plant life) also exerts control on the composition of sea water. Diatoms, members of the plankton community, require silica to form their shells and they draw heavily on the ocean's silica for this purpose.

• Some marine organisms concentrate or secrete chemical elements that are present in such minute amounts in sea water as to be almost undetectable: Lobsters concentrate copper and cobalt; snails secrete lead; the sea cucumber extracts vanadium; and sponges and certain seaweeds remove iodine from the sea.

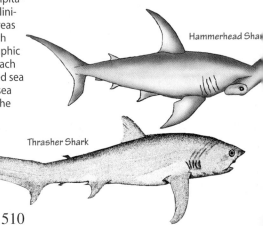

Hammerhead Shark

Thrasher Shark

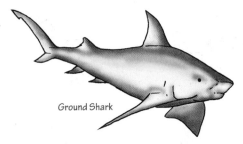

Ground Shark

SHARK STIMULANTS

Considerable research has been devoted to finding out what stimuli attract sharks and incite them to attack. Results are mostly inconclusive, but some general principles have been advanced: Certain types of irregular sounds - like those made by a swimmer in trouble or a damaged fish - seem to attract sharks from great distances. Sound, rather than sight or smell, seems to be a shark's primary cue for moving into an area. Some scientific experiments indicate that sharks can distinguish light colors from dark, and that they may even be able to distinguish colors. Yellow, white, and silver seem to attract sharks. Many divers maintain that clothing, fins, and tanks should be painted in dull colors to avoid shark attacks.

SHARK SENSES

Sharks have 8 unique senses. They are hearing, smell, lateral line, pit organs, vision, Lorenzini, touch, and taste. The shark shares many sense that humans do such as taste and smell, but it has three senses that we do not have. The lateral line, pit organs and Lorenzini are senses that have been discovered over the past 10 to 20 years, and play an important role in how the shark functions when swimming around.

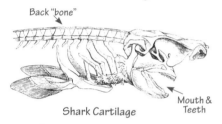

Back "bone"

Shark Cartilage

Mouth & Teeth

Sharks: No Bones!

Sharks do not have bones. Sharks are made up of cartilage, and are called Elasmobranchs, which translates into fish made of catilaginous tissues. Why it has been so hard for scientists and shark researches to study sharks of the past, is because of the material they are made of. Cartilage does not fossilize, and therefore the only clue as to sharks from the past are teeth.

Shark Meat for Humans

Shark meat is palatable and nutritious if properly prepared. In some countries shark meat is marketed under its common name, in others it is marketed under various names. The fish in England's "fish and chips" is often dogfish or school shark. The prejudice against shark meat arises from a distaste for the scavenging habits people attribute to sharks, and to the fact that the meat spoils quickly. The meat of certain species is apt to be strongly flavored, a characteristic that may be reduced by icing for 24 hours, then soaking for two hours in brine. Dry salted shark has become a staple food in some countries where salt cod was formerly popular.

Shark liver should never be eaten because the high concentration of vitamins can cause illness in humans.

The Great White Shark has a poisonous liver. In general AVOID eating the livers of untested wild animals or the offal of fish in general.

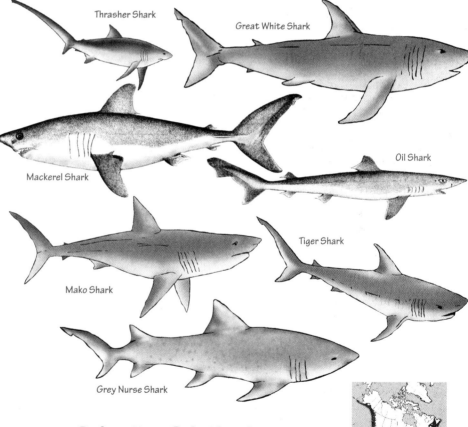

Thrasher Shark

Great White Shark

Mackerel Shark

Oil Shark

Mako Shark

Tiger Shark

Grey Nurse Shark

Spiny Dogfish Shark

The Dogfish has spines on the dorsal fin. These spines have venom glands which break when they enter the flesh. The infection is painful and might be fatal. Dogfish should be handled with care when caught in a net or on a hook. Dogfish are found in shallow waters in protected bays.

Range of Dogfish

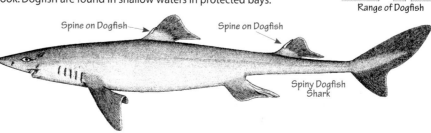

Spine on Dogfish

Spine on Dogfish

Spiny Dogfish Shark

Sharks Are Fish

Sharks are fish. They live in water, and use their gills to filter oxygen from the water. Sharks are a special type of fish known because their body is made out of cartilage instead of bones like other fish. The name, or classification of this type of fish is called "Elasmobranchs." This category also includes Rays, Sawfish, and Skates.

Sharks Eat Anything

Sharks are omnivorous, which means they eat both meat and vegetation. Sharks will eat anything, and if there is not an abundant supply of meat in the area, they will resort to eating sea vegetation. The largest shark of them all, the Whale Shark is mainly a plankton feeder.

Shark Eyesight

Sharks do have very good eyesight. In fact, sharks can see extremely well in darkly lit areas, have fantastic night vision, and can see colors. Avoid wearing bright colors in the water, such as oranges and yellows, as sharks can indeed see them.

SHARKS

SHARKS

Sharks are the perfect swimming and hunting machine and should be feared by humans when swimming or in a boating accident.

SHARK ATTACK

Most attacks occur just offshore, areas where there is food for sharks. This food is usually between the shore and the coastal sandbars. The sharks while feeding get trapped when the tide recedes and might become aggressive. Fish congregate at coastal drop-offs and they also attract sharks.

Shore   Sandbar   Shore Falloff

TYPE OF ATTACK

Hit and Run: These attacks, that seem to be random tests, are the most common. Usually the victim does not see the shark but the passing shark, for some reason - the victim's similarity to a regular food, a shiny object as jewelry, water turbulence that distorts the silhouette of the victim, territorial threat, etc. - makes a fast attack and rapidly releases the victim and leaves. The injury is usually minor lacerations below the knee (the part hanging below a surfboard or the randomly moving part of the body) which are minor lacerations.

Sneak Attack: The shark will strike without initially circling the victim but will attack and keep on attacking. Injuries are usually severe and fatal.

Bump and Bite: In these attacks the shark will circle the intended victim, come in and bump the victim - as if testing the victim, and then come in for the attack. This type of attack usually results in death.

Shark attacks usually between May & October - can vary year to year depending upon the warmth of the water.

Sharks active ALL year.

DANGEROUS SHARKS

All large sharks are dangerous.

Though blood itself may not attract sharks, its presence in combination with other unusual factors will excite the animals and make them more prone to attack. The most dangerous species in order of documented attack records are: the great white shark, bull shark, tiger shark, grey nurse shark, lemon shark, blue shark, sand tiger, several species of hammerheads, and the mako. Some species such as the nurse shark are extremely sluggish and have poorly developed teeth, but even these have been known to attack man when excited or disturbed. Small sharks can also be dangerous because they swim in schools and can swarm a victim. If injured by a shark the priority is to stop the bleeding and leave the water. The presence of blood will cause sharks to go into a feeding frenzy. If swimming in a group form a tight circle around the victim while he leaves the water.

DANGEROUS SEA CREATURES

Other dangerous sea animals can be...
The barracuda (though divers claim its ferocious reputation is undeserved), moray eels, octopuses, and sharp-spined sea urchins can be dangerous to swimmers. The Portuguese man-of-war has tentacles up to 50 feet long with specialized cells that produce painful stings and welts on contact by swimmers. Sting rays, toadfish, catfish, and jellyfish can inflict damage on swimmers and waders. Certain coral-reef organisms are to be avoided by divers.

Sharks that Attack Humans
Bull Shark - Great White Shark -
Mako Shark - Tiger Shark -
Hammerhead Shark - Gray Nurse Shark

*All sharks will attack
if threatened or molested*

Reduce Shark Attack Risk

- Do NOT swim while bleeding.
- Stay in groups - do not swim alone. Do not swim in isolated areas as it will be more difficult getting help. Do not swim in the evening or night. Shark might be following their food towards shore. Shark will be difficult to see.
- Avoid commercial fishing areas as sharks might be attracted to the targeted fish, to the bait, or the remnants of the dressed fish being thrown overboard. Flocks of diving birds indicate the presence of fish - and possibly sharks.
- Avoid shiny and reflective objects or bright contrasty clothing.
- Stay out of murky water - you or the shark can not see too well. In general avoid splashing as a shark might think that there is an injured potential victim.
- Do not bring your dog into the water as its running and splashing might attract sharks.
- Do NOT enter water when sharks are present.

STINGRAYS

They have a long whiplike tail that has one or more spines on the upper surface. There is one sac of venom attached to each side of the spine. These sacs can rupture when the spine is aggressively thrashed about and the venom will enter the wound made by the sharp spine. The spine has barbs and can break off and remain in the cut - removing the spine can cause much damage. The venom is not too poisonous but very painful and it might lead to an infection if not treated. Stingrays that have their spines located in an area on their tail that can cause major injury to humans include the Stingray and the Yellow Stingray. The California Bat Ray and the Spotted Eagle Ray has the sting near the base of the tail - but can still be dangerous if you happen to walk on it.

Prevention: Shuffle your feet on the ground while walking as the stingrays lie buried in the sand with their eyes only protruding. If you step on a stingray you will pin down its body giving it the leverage to forcefully strike with its tail. Use a walking stick to jab the water in front of you.

Getting stung by a sting ray.

Dart

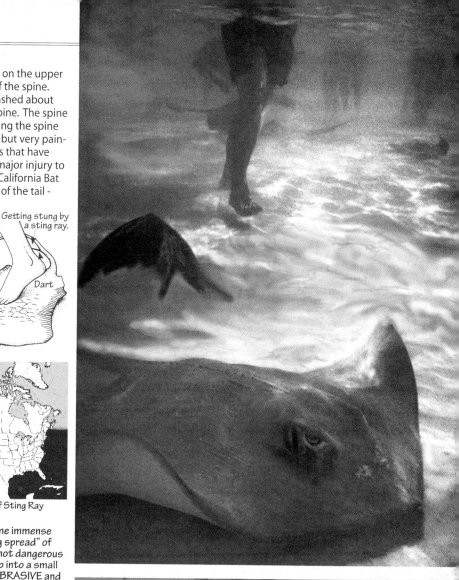

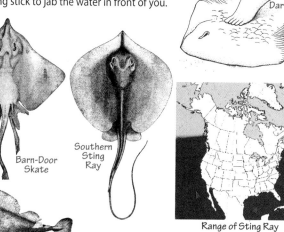

Barn-Door Skate

Southern Sting Ray

Range of Sting Ray

Torpedo Ray

Torpedo Rays
These rays can give a 200 volt electric discharge.

Manta Ray

The Manta Ray or Devil Ray can become immense weighing 3500 lbs, and having a "wing spread" of more than 20 feet. The manta ray is not dangerous but it might, because of its size, bump into a small boat or a swimmer. Its skin is VERY ABRASIVE and can cause a major abrasion when it brushes against a diver. This abrasion might become infected.

Manta Ray

Manta Ray 20 ft "wingspan"

Manta Ray sunning itself on the surface.

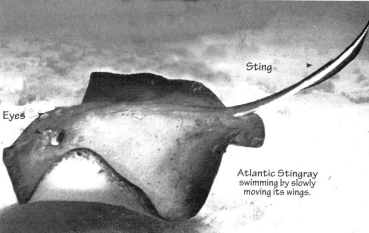

Sting

Eyes

Atlantic Stingray swimming by slowly moving its wings.

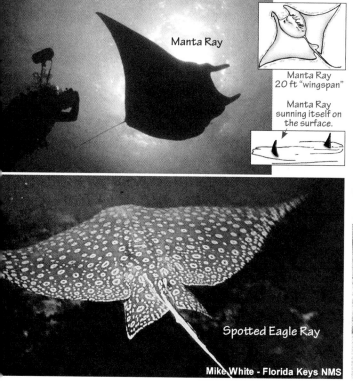

Spotted Eagle Ray

Mike White - Florida Keys NMS

Venomous barbed spine in tail.

Atlantic Stingray

513

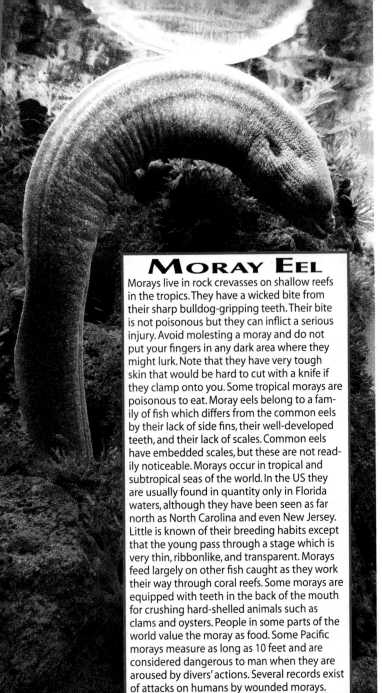

MORAY EEL

Morays live in rock crevasses on shallow reefs in the tropics. They have a wicked bite from their sharp bulldog-gripping teeth. Their bite is not poisonous but they can inflict a serious injury. Avoid molesting a moray and do not put your fingers in any dark area where they might lurk. Note that they have very tough skin that would be hard to cut with a knife if they clamp onto you. Some tropical morays are poisonous to eat. Moray eels belong to a family of fish which differs from the common eels by their lack of side fins, their well-developed teeth, and their lack of scales. Common eels have embedded scales, but these are not readily noticeable. Morays occur in tropical and subtropical seas of the world. In the US they are usually found in quantity only in Florida waters, although they have been seen as far north as North Carolina and even New Jersey. Little is known of their breeding habits except that the young pass through a stage which is very thin, ribbonlike, and transparent. Morays feed largely on other fish caught as they work their way through coral reefs. Some morays are equipped with teeth in the back of the mouth for crushing hard-shelled animals such as clams and oysters. People in some parts of the world value the moray as food. Some Pacific morays measure as long as 10 feet and are considered dangerous to man when they are aroused by divers' actions. Several records exist of attacks on humans by wounded morays.

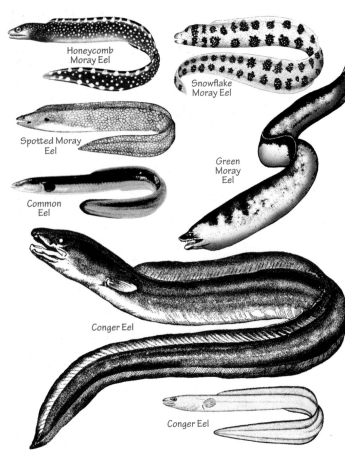

Honeycomb Moray Eel

Snowflake Moray Eel

Spotted Moray Eel

Green Moray Eel

Common Eel

Conger Eel

Conger Eel

Sea Snakes

Live in shallow waters around the continental shelf. Can remain underwater for two hours. The yellow Bellied Sea Snake is very poisonous. The venom in fang and one drop can kill over 2 adult men. The effect is very slow - a poisonous snack uses poison to help in digestion(!). It might bite when it has become entangled in a fishing net or enter a low sided raft.

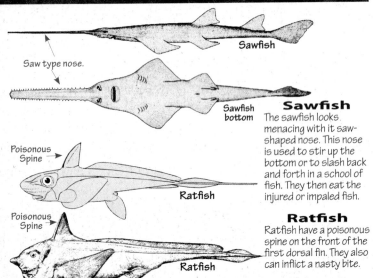

Sawfish

Saw type nose.

Sawfish bottom

Poisonous Spine

Ratfish

Poisonous Spine

Ratfish

Sawfish

The sawfish looks menacing with it saw-shaped nose. This nose is used to stir up the bottom or to slash back and forth in a school of fish. They then eat the injured or impaled fish.

Ratfish

Ratfish have a poisonous spine on the front of the first dorsal fin. They also can inflict a nasty bite.

Northern Porgy

Sea Bream

Porgies are excellent for food.

Jolthead Porgy

Goathead Porgy

PORGY FAMILY

Southern Scup

Sheephead Porgy

514

PUFFER FISH

Puffers have the ability to inflate and deflate themselves very rapidly. All puffer-like fish inflate by pumping water into special sacs when in their natural environment. Out of water, a puffer fills the sacs with air instead, and takes on a ballon-like appearance. This inflation is used as a form of protection.

Their liver, muscles, skin & ovarie contain a deadly paralyzing poiso

Puffers are
EXTREMELY POISONOUS
but some of them are considered a delicacy by the Japanese.
Special preparation of the meat is required.

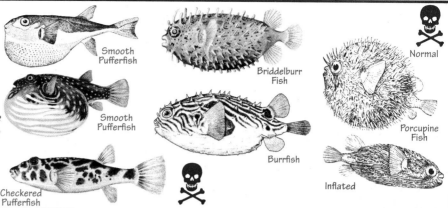

Smooth Pufferfish

Briddelburr Fish

Smooth Pufferfish

Burrfish

Checkered Pufferfish

Normal

Porcupine Fish

Inflated

BOXFISH / TRUNKFISH

These fish have a triangular bony box type structure. They swim slowly and stay close to the bottom. These fish are poisonous to eat.

Spotted Trunkfish

Honeycomb Cowfish

Scorpionfish

This is a large family which includes some that have venomous spines. They are well camouflaged so they might be stepped on or touched by accident.

Lionfish/Turkeyfish

These members of the family have venomous darts under the lacy fins - The Stonefish is the most deadly.

Turkeyfish

Zebra Lionfish

Scorpionfish

SCORPIONFISH

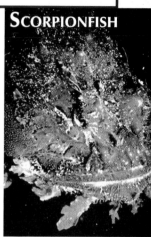

Lamprey

Lamprey Mouth
A lampray fish attaches itself to fish and rips hunks of flesh from the victim fish (usually herring or salmon).

Cutlass Fish

Atlantic Hagfish

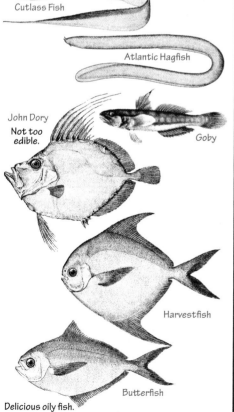

John Dory
Not too edible.

Goby

Harvestfish

Butterfish
Delicious oily fish.

Red Rockfish

Canary Rockfish

Tiger Rockfish

Quillback Rockfish

Rockfish are related to the Scorpionfish but most of then do not have poisonous spines. Rockfish are very popular with anglers in California.

ROCKFISH

Black & Yellow Rockfish

TUNA / MACKEREL

Great game fish.

Skipjack Tuna

Very important food fish.

Atlantic Mackerel

Cero

Little Tunny

Chub Mackerel

Alalonga (Long Finned Tuna)

Spotted Cero

Atlantic Bonito

Frigate Mackerel

Spanish Mackerel

Tuna is the most powerful fish.

TUNA

There are seven commercial and sport-caught tunas, as well as several related species, all of which are members of what is called the scombrid family. Commercially caught tunas consist of albacore, bigeye, blackfin, bluefin, bonito, skipjack, and yellowfin. Yellowfin, taken in the eastern Pacific and tropical Atlantic, makes up the biggest U.S. commercial catch. Albacore, caught in the eastern Pacific, is the true "white-meat" tuna; skipjack, caught throughout the world in tropical and subtropical waters, makes up the second largest U.S. commercial catch; bigeye is caught mostly in tropical waters; blackfin is caught commercially only in the Caribbean and off South America; the very large bluefin (rod-and-reel record, 1,040 pounds) is a highly prized sport catch in the Atlantic and Pacific; and the widely distributed bonito is used largely as pet food.

Dog Snapper

Gray Snapper

Lane Snapper

Mangrove Snapper

SNAPPER

Mutton Snapper

Pensacola Snapper

Red Snapper

Schoolmaster Snapper

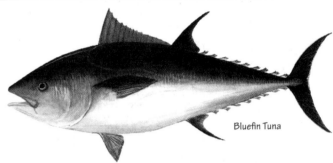

Bluefin Tuna

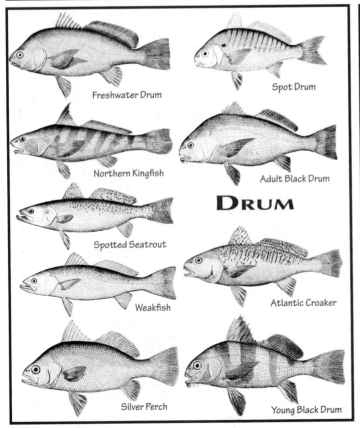

Freshwater Drum

Spot Drum

Northern Kingfish

Adult Black Drum

Spotted Seatrout

DRUM

Weakfish

Atlantic Croaker

Silver Perch

Young Black Drum

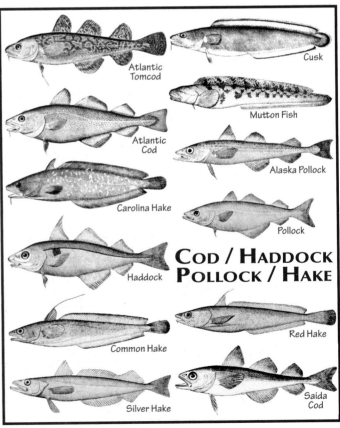

Atlantic Tomcod

Cusk

Atlantic Cod

Mutton Fish

Carolina Hake

Alaska Pollock

Pollock

Haddock

COD / HADDOCK POLLOCK / HAKE

Common Hake

Red Hake

Silver Hake

Saida Cod

Atlantic Spadefish

Banded Butterfly Fish

Spadefish

Butterfly Fish

Blue Angelfish

Blue Tang Angelfish

ANGELFISH & BUTTERFLYFISH

Diver with Red Hind Grouper

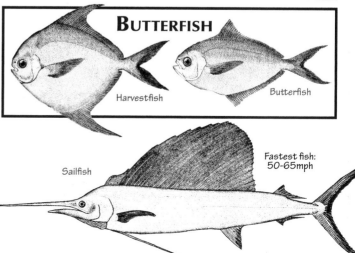

Red Grouper

Nassau Grouper

Red Hind Grouper

Red Hind Seabass

Seabass

Indies Seabass

SEA BASS FAMILY
This is a large family including
- basses, groupers and hamlets.
They live in the sub tropics and the
tropics. They are an excellent food fish.

Warsaw Grouper

GOATFISH

Red Goatfish

Yellow Goatfish

Great food!
Goatfish can rapidly change color.

Male

Female

Great game fish.

DOLPHIN FISH

MULLET

Stripped Mullet

White Mullet

Swordfish

White Marlin

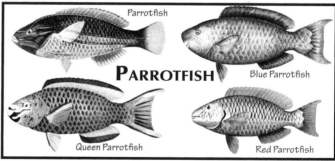

Parrotfish

Blue Parrotfish

PARROTFISH

Queen Parrotfish

Red Parrotfish

BUTTERFISH

Harvestfish

Butterfish

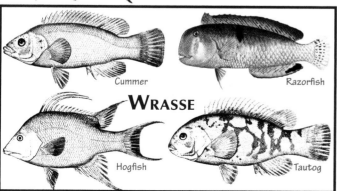

Cummer

Razorfish

WRASSE

Hogfish

Tautog

Sailfish

Fastest fish:
50-65mph

FLATFISH

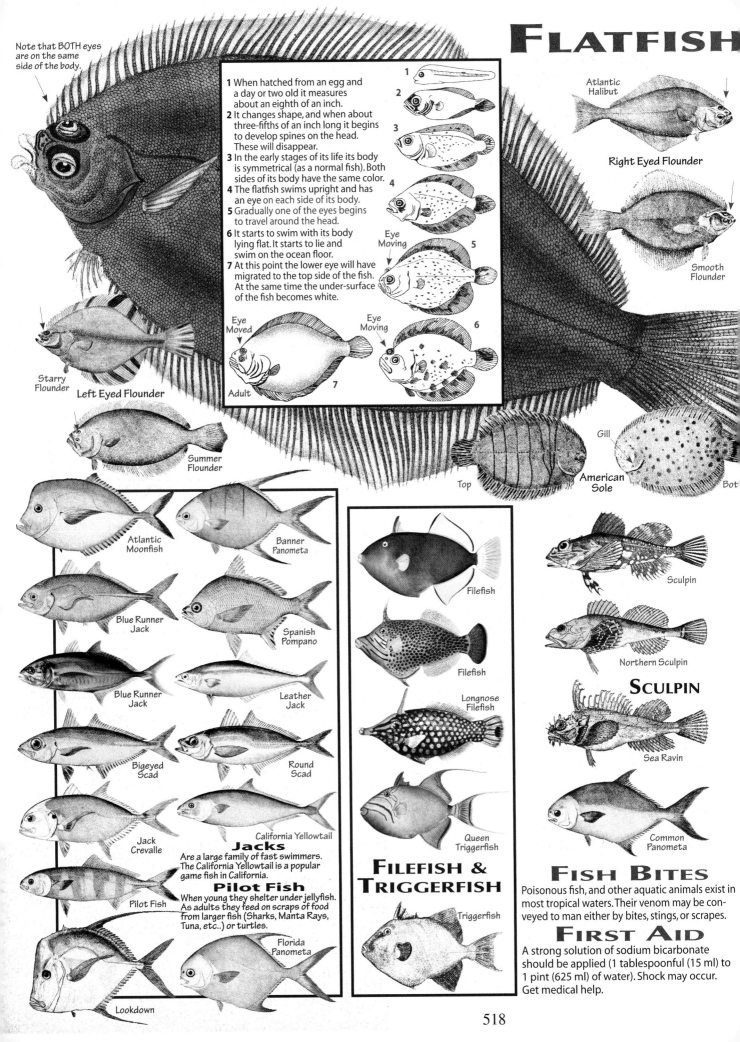

Note that BOTH eyes are on the same side of the body.

1 When hatched from an egg and a day or two old it measures about an eighth of an inch.
2 It changes shape, and when about three-fifths of an inch long it begins to develop spines on the head. These will disappear.
3 In the early stages of its life its body is symmetrical (as a normal fish). Both sides of its body have the same color.
4 The flatfish swims upright and has an eye on each side of its body.
5 Gradually one of the eyes begins to travel around the head.
6 It starts to swim with its body lying flat. It starts to lie and swim on the ocean floor.
7 At this point the lower eye will have migrated to the top side of the fish. At the same time the under-surface of the fish becomes white.

Eye Moving

Eye Moved

Eye Moving

Adult

Atlantic Halibut

Right Eyed Flounder

Smooth Flounder

Starry Flounder

Left Eyed Flounder

Summer Flounder

Gill

American Sole

Top

Bot

Atlantic Moonfish

Banner Panometa

Blue Runner Jack

Spanish Pompano

Blue Runner Jack

Leather Jack

Bigeyed Scad

Round Scad

Jack Crevalle

California Yellowtail

Jacks
Are a large family of fast swimmers. The California Yellowtail is a popular game fish in California.

Pilot Fish

Pilot Fish
When young they shelter under jellyfish. As adults they feed on scraps of food from larger fish (Sharks, Manta Rays, Tuna, etc..) or turtles.

Lookdown

Florida Panometa

Filefish

Filefish

Longnose Filefish

Queen Triggerfish

FILEFISH & TRIGGERFISH

Triggerfish

Sculpin

Northern Sculpin

SCULPIN

Sea Raven

Common Panometa

FISH BITES
Poisonous fish, and other aquatic animals exist in most tropical waters. Their venom may be conveyed to man either by bites, stings, or scrapes.

FIRST AID
A strong solution of sodium bicarbonate should be applied (1 tablespoonful (15 ml) to 1 pint (625 ml) of water). Shock may occur. Get medical help.

518

CIGUATERA

The exact origin of ciguatera contamination is not known but it is assumed to be from fish eating things in its food chain that contain a toxic form of blue-green algae. A carnivorous fish (Barracuda) might eat a herbivorous fish and accumulate the ciguatera contamination. As the ciguatera contamination does not affect the contaminated fish there is no way of knowing that this fish is toxic- until you have cooked it and tried it!

Symptoms:
Can appear up to 30 hours after eating fish.
- Tingling lips, throat, & tongue.
- Vomiting & diarrhea.
- Difficulty in walking.
- Temporary blindness.

Ciguatera is most prevalent in subtropical and tropical areas and usually with shore fish.

Fish that might be contaminated:
NOTE: *the ciguatera contamination is not in all of these fish - but only in those individuals that have consumed the toxin.*
Barracuda, Moray Eel, Surgeonfish, some Jacks, Parrotfish, Bonito Tuna (in tropics), Seabass (in tropics), Porgy.

SALT WATER BOILS
Are very common with deep water fishermen. These small boils are found around the wrists, back of the hands or forearms and occasionally around the neck. These are areas of friction from cracked, wet and dirty oilskin clothing. The friction causes minute cracks in the skin which in turn is infected by organisms present in fish slime.
A clean environment is important to reduce the risk of infection from the slime. If neglected it can be very painful. See a doctor for treatment.

ERYSIPELOID
This disease is usually more common during the warmer months. It is a skin disease that usually occurs on the hands and forearms. It is caused by the skin being punctured by fins of fish, sharp bones, or fish hooks. The residue of fish slime or rotten fish enter these openings in the skin. A small red spot on the skin indicates the start of an infection. This infection will spread to the adjacent area. The infection will gradually become clear in the middle with a reddish purple color at the spreading margins. The affected parts will swell, itch, and have a burning sensation. First aid can be started with frequent hot bathing of the affected areas.
See a doctor for complete treatment.

SCOMBROID FISH POISONING
If Tuna, Mackerel, Skipjack, etc.. are not properly preserved a bacteria might produce a poison in the body of the fish. The fact that the preserved fish is toxic can be detected by a - sharp peppery taste.

FISHERMAN'S CONJUNCTIVITIS
(Pink Eye)
Fisherman's conjunctivitis is a severe inflammatory condition of the eyes. It is caused by contact with the juices of marine animal growth that look like dumplings. These growths when crushed release the juice which may accidentally enter the eye. This juice in the eye causes a very acute and painful inflammation of the conjunctiva or thin covering of the eye. Avoid rubbing your eyes when handling fish.
See a doctor for treatment.

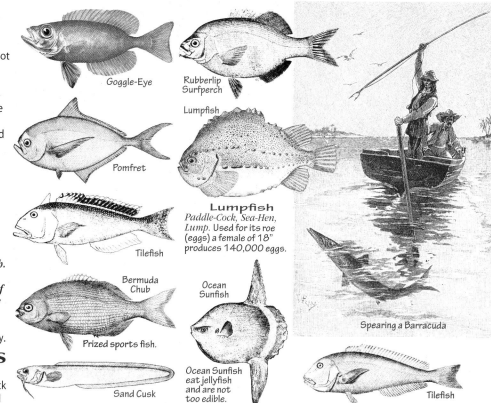

Goggle-Eye

Rubberlip Surfperch

Lumpfish

Pomfret

Lumpfish
Paddle-Cock, Sea-Hen, Lump. Used for its roe (eggs) a female of 18" produces 140,000 eggs.

Tilefish

Bermuda Chub
Prized sports fish.

Ocean Sunfish

Ocean Sunfish eat jellyfish and are not too edible.

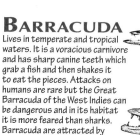
Sand Cusk

Spearing a Barracuda

Tilefish

MARINE ANIMALS THAT PUNCTURE THE SKIN WITH STINGS ON TENTACLES

Injury Caused by	Treatment	Possible Problems
Portuguese man-of-war*, Jellyfish*, Anemones* *Handle with gloves.	Wash with ammonia or alcohol. Meat tenderizer might help with jellyfish stings. Dry affected skin with talcum powder and remove the embedded stings.	Depends upon victim's reaction and species: Welt like allergic reactions, painful stings, respiratory arrest, stomach cramps, dizziness, numbness, infections.

MARINE ANIMALS THAT BITE

Injury Caused by	Treatment	Possible Problems
Shark, Barracuda, Alligator, Sea Bass	Stop bleeding and prevent shock. If required give life support. Splint the injury and get medical help.	Infection and shock.
Turtle, Moray Eel, Billfish, Needlefish Sea Lions	Clean wound and splint the injury. Can bite when provoked especially during breeding season	Infection and shock. Infection and shock.

MISCELLANEOUS MARINE LIFE INJURIES

Marine Life	Injury	Treatment	Possible Reaction
Electric fish*	Shocks	Electric shock is temporary.	Shock may cause a panic reaction.
Marine parasites	Skin rashes	Usually clear up with time.	
Corals	Abrasions on body	Treat abrasions.	Infections are possible if not well cleaned.
Sea Snakes	Possibly fatal bite	Apply a tourniquet.	Pain may occur from 20 min. to hours.
*Electric Eels are the most common.		Get medical attention.	

BARRACUDA
Lives in temperate and tropical waters. It is a voracious carnivore and has sharp canine teeth which grab a fish and then shakes it to eat the pieces. Attacks on humans are rare but the Great Barracuda of the West Indies can be dangerous and in its habitat it is more feared than sharks. Barracuda are attracted by bright-colored objects.

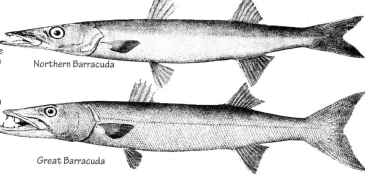

Northern Barracuda

Great Barracuda

It is might be dangerous to eat Barracuda flesh as it might be carrying Ciguatera a poison it might ingest from the fish it eats.

Teeth on a Barracuda

BIRD FLIGHT

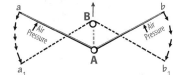

Raising effect of a bird on the downstroke of its wings. With the downward action of the wings they are pressing downward upon the air as levers which causes the bird's body to rise from **A** to **B**.

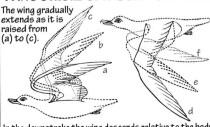

A: Position of bird at the beginning of the downstroke of its expanded wing. Its wing tips are at left side (a) and right side (b).

B: At the end of the downstroke the wings have moved down and are now at left side (a_1) and right side (b_1).

WING STROKE OF A GULL - SIDE VIEW

The wing gradually extends as it is raised from (a) to (c).

In the downstroke the wing descends relative to the body. Note that at the termination of the downstroke the wing is pulled in in preparation of the upstroke (d) to (f).

WING STROKE OF A GULL - FRONT VIEW

Body Falls

Position of wings during upstroke. The body falls during the upstroke.

Body Rises

Position of wings during the downstroke. The body rises during the downstroke.

HEAD OF BIRD

Eyebrow Stripe
Would be a color marking that would start at the eye and go to the back of the head.

- Forehead
- Nostril
- Lores
- Crown
- Upper Mandible
- Lower Mandible
- Throat
- Malar Region
- Auricular (cheeks)
- Eye Ring
- Nape

Yellow-Bellied Woodpecker
(Male- top)

47 BIRDS

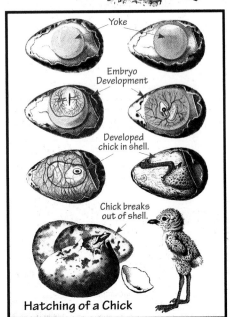

- Yoke
- Embryo Development
- Developed chick in shell.
- Chick breaks out of shell.

Hatching of a Chick

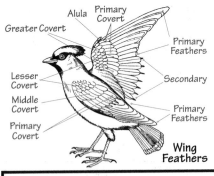

- Alula
- Primary Covert
- Greater Covert
- Primary Feathers
- Lesser Covert
- Secondary
- Middle Covert
- Primary Feathers
- Primary Covert

Wing Feathers

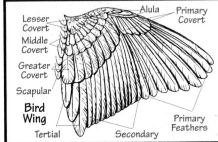

- Lesser Covert
- Middle Covert
- Greater Covert
- Scapular
- Alula
- Primary Covert
- Primary Feathers
- Secondary
- Tertial

Bird Wing

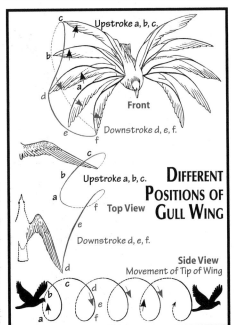

- Upstroke a, b, c.
- **Front**
- Downstroke d, e, f.
- Upstroke a, b, c.
- **Top View**
- Downstroke d, e, f.

DIFFERENT POSITIONS OF GULL WING

Side View
Movement of Tip of Wing

520

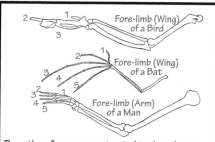

Fore-limb (Wing) of a Bird

Fore-limb (Wing) of a Bat

Fore-limb (Arm) of a Man

These three figures are contrasted to show the two widely different ways in which an original five-finger fore-leg has been transformed to fulfil the purposes of flight and the holding/grasping action in man. The 1,2,3,4,5 are the fingers. In the bird the thumb (digit 1) and the third finger (digit 3) have been greatly reduced.

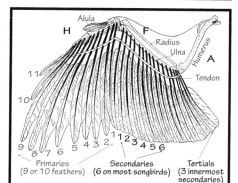

Alula
H   F
Radius
Ulna
Humerus
A
Tendon

Primaries (9 or 10 feathers)   Secondaries (6 on most songbirds)   Tertials (3 innermost secondaries)

Upper surface of a bird's wing, showing the relationship of the large "quill" or the flight feathers to the skeleton.

"A" the arm, of which the humerus forms the support. "F" forearm; consisting of the radius and ulna (both acting as supporting rods). The ulna supports the great flight or quill feathers known as the secondaries - 1, 2, 3, 4, 5, 6.

"H" the hand; consists of the bones representing the thumb and the 2nd and 3rd fingers. The thumb bears three small stiff, quill-like feathers known as the Alula. The 2nd and 3rd fingers support the flight-feathers of the hand (1-4). Of these 1-6 rest upon the bases of digit fingers 2 and 3, feather 7 rests upon the tiny remenant of digit finger 3. Feathers 8, 9, 10, and 11 rest upon the penultimate bone and the ultimate point of digit finger 2. The narrow band through which the bases of the quills pass is a band of tendon helping to keep the feathers in position.

SKELETON OF A BIRD

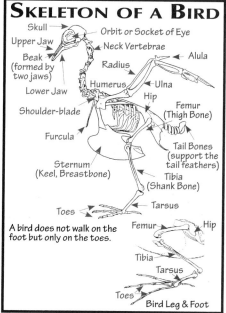

Skull
Upper Jaw
Beak (formed by two jaws)
Lower Jaw
Shoulder-blade
Furcula
Sternum (Keel, Breastbone)
Toes
Orbit or Socket of Eye
Neck Vertebrae
Radius
Alula
Humerus
Ulna
Hip
Femur (Thigh Bone)
Tail Bones (support the tail feathers)
Tibia (Shank Bone)
Tarsus

A bird does not walk on the foot but only on the toes.

Femur   Hip
Tibia
Tarsus
Toes
Bird Leg & Foot

HOW TO MEASURE A BIRD

Length: Distance in a straight line from the end of the bill to the tip of the longest tail feather.

Bill: The distance in a straight line from where the bill (upper mandible) Joins the skin of the forehead "A" to the tip "B"

Wing: Distance from the carpal joint "C" (bend in wing) to the tip of the longest primary feather "D."

A
B
C
D

Tarsus: Distance in front of the leg from what appears to be the knee joint (end of tibia) to the root of the middle toe.

Tail: Distance from the tip of the longest tail feather to its base (the point where it enters the body).

PARTS OF A PIGEON

Cere Area of bare skin found on Pigeons, Hawks, Eagles, & Parrots.

Forehead
Crown
Nape
Neck
Scapulars
Wing Coverts
Back
Greater Coverts
Secondaries
Primaries
Tail
Beak
Throat
Base of Neck
Breast
Abdomen

DISSECTED MODEL OF A PIGEON

DISTRIBUTION OF FEATHERS

Note: the featherless spaces (apteria). Feathered areas are called "pterylae." These tracks vary greatly in different species of birds.

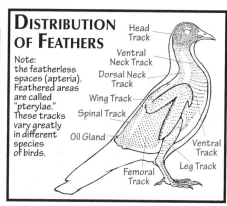

Head Track
Ventral Neck Track
Dorsal Neck Track
Wing Track
Spinal Track
Oil Gland
Ventral Track
Leg Track
Femoral Track

SKELETON OF PIGEON

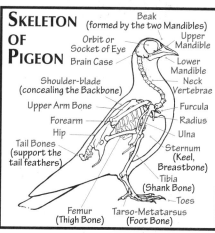

Beak (formed by the two Mandibles)
Orbit or Socket of Eye
Brain Case
Shoulder-blade (concealing the Backbone)
Upper Arm Bone
Forearm
Hip
Tail Bones (support the tail feathers)
Femur (Thigh Bone)
Upper Mandible
Lower Mandible
Neck Vertebrae
Furcula
Radius
Ulna
Sternum (Keel, Breastbone)
Tibia (Shank Bone)
Toes
Tarso-Metatarsus (Foot Bone)

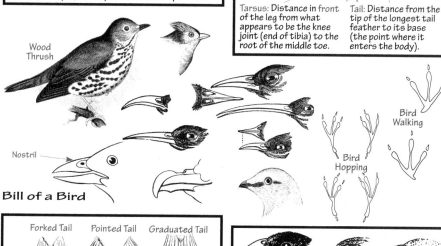

Wood Thrush

Nostril

Bill of a Bird

Bird Walking
Bird Hopping

INTERNAL ORGANS OF A PIGEON

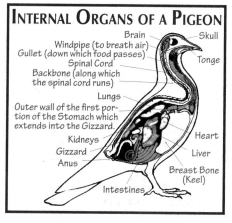

Brain
Windpipe (to breath air)
Gullet (down which food passes)
Spinal Cord
Backbone (along which the spinal cord runs)
Outer wall of the first portion of the Stomach which extends into the Gizzard.
Kidneys
Gizzard
Anus
Skull
Tonge
Lungs
Heart
Liver
Breast Bone (Keel)
Intestines

Bird Tails

Forked Tail   Pointed Tail   Graduated Tail

Marginated Tail   Rounded Tail   Square Tail

Rose-breasted Grosbeak   Song Sparrow   Crossbill

Types of Bills

There are four types of bills.
1. Upper mandible longer than lower. The tip hooked over lower mandible.
2. Lower mandible longer than upper.
3. Both mandibles equal length.
4. Mandibles crossed.

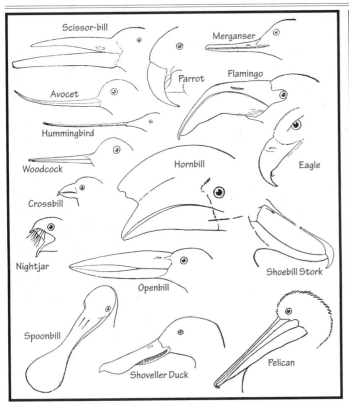

Scissor-bill, Merganser, Parrot, Flamingo, Avocet, Hummingbird, Woodcock, Hornbill, Eagle, Crossbill, Nightjar, Openbill, Shoebill Stork, Spoonbill, Shoveller Duck, Pelican

Parts of a Feather

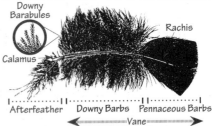

Downy Barabules, Calamus, Rachis

Afterfeather — Downy Barbs — Pennaceous Barbs
Vane

Rachis: is the central shaft of the feather.
Calamus: inserts into the skin of the bird.
Down barbs: are found at the base of the feather, and are insulation.
Pennaceous barbs: at the tip of the feather. These are the most visible part of a bird and provide protection to the bird as a barrier and/or camouflage coloration.

Feather Morphology
Birds are the only animals with feathers. Although shape, color, texture, and size of feathers vary with species, and with position on the body, each feather has one or more of the parts of a typical body feather.

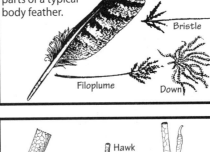
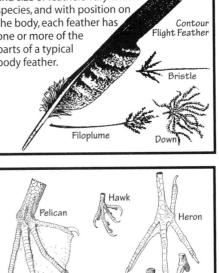

Contour Flight Feather, Bristle, Filoplume, Down

Types of Feathers
Feathers have different functions as: insulation, flight, protection and display.

Contour Body Feather

Contour feathers: create the outline of the bird, and include flight feathers of the wings and tail, as well as coverts of the body, wings or tail.

Down

Down feathers: (or plumes) are completely constructed of down, with little or no rachis.

Semiplume

Semiplumes: are similarly constructed completely of down, but have a distinct rachis.

Filoplume

Filoplumes: have only a rachis with a few barbs at the tip, while bristles have a few barbs at the base of an otherwise bare rachis.

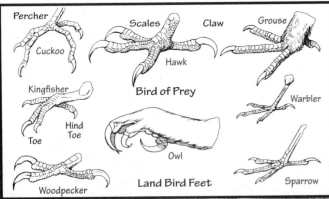

Water Bird Feet — Loon, Skuas, Web, Grebe, Lobe, Cormorants, Duck, Sea Duck, Godwit, Avocet, Phalarope, Stilt, Sandpiper, Bittern

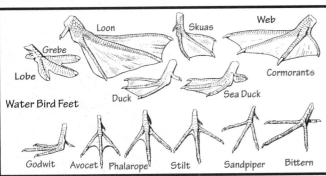

Land Bird Feet — Percher, Cuckoo, Scales, Claw, Grouse, Hawk, Bird of Prey, Kingfisher, Warbler, Hind Toe, Toe, Owl, Woodpecker, Sparrow

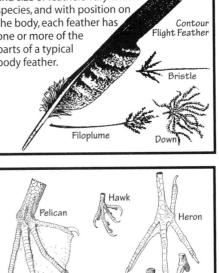

Pelican, Hawk, Heron, Kingfisher, Heron - middle toe, Black Grause, Parrot, Ostrich, Grebe, Duck

Owl Feather

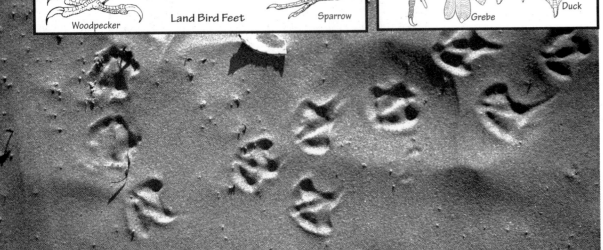

THE PASSENGER PIGEON
EXTINCT

Condensed from a British book from 1884 with reference to writings by Alexander Wilson, the father of American ornithology, and Audubon, the great bird artist.

…Flights of locusts are often seen passing through the air, like vast clouds, obscuring the sky. The passenger pigeon of America appears in almost equal numbers. The accounts of their vast flights would be incredible, were they not thoroughly well authenticated.

…The female hatches only one bird at a time. Upwards of one hundred nests have been found in one tree, with a single egg in each of them. In a short time the young become very plump, and so fat, that they are occasionally melted down for the sake of their fat alone. Passenger pigeons choose particular places for roosting - generally amid a grove of the oldest and largest trees in the neighborhood.

…Wilson, Audubon, and other naturalists, give us vivid a description of the enormous flights of these birds with some flocks taking a week to pass. (Wilson estimated that one flock he saw was two hundred and forty miles long and a mile wide). One flock that Audubon saw, in Louisville, Ky, in the autumn of 1813 obscured the noonday sun as if it were an eclipse. This flock took three days to pass. The flock, flying low over the Ohio River, were shot in great numbers and served as food for a week.

…Audubon describes the flight of one of these almost solid masses of birds pursued by a hawk; now darting compactly in undulating and angular lines, now descending close to the earth, and with inconceivable velocity mounting perpendicularly, so as to resemble a vast column, and then wheeling and twisting within their continued lines, resembling the coils of a gigantic serpent.

…We will now hurry on towards their breeding area, in a forest on the banks of the Green River in Kentucky, fully forty miles in length, and more than three in width… Here, in wait, are assembled a large number of persons, with horses, wagons, guns, and ammunition; and a farmer has brought three hundred hogs to be fattened on the refuse of the pigeons.

…As the vast flight arrives at the spot - men with long poles knock down thousands. The birds continue to pour in. The pigeons arrive by the thousands, alighting everywhere, one above another, until solid masses, are formed on the branches all around. Here and there the perches give way with a crash, and fall to the ground, destroying hundreds of birds on the loaded branches beneath. The pigeons continue to come, and it is past midnight before there is any sign of a decrease in their numbers. The ground in all directions is strewed with branches broken by the weight of the perched birds.

…By sunrise, the enormous multitude have departed, while wolves, foxes, and other animals, who had assembled to feast on the bodies of the slain, are seen sneaking off. The hunters had taken their toll.

Now extinct, the last living specimen died in the Cincinnati Zoological Garden, September 1, 1914. Before its extinction it was perhaps the most numerous of all birds in North America. It inhabited practically the whole forested area of North America – from the Hudson Bay to Guatemala. Some were accidentally blown to the British Isles and Europe.

One flock that Audubon saw, in Louisville, Ky, in the autumn of 1813 obscured the noonday sun as if it were an eclipse. This flock took three days to pass.

The pigeons arrive by the thousands, alighting everywhere, one above another, until solid masses, are formed on the branches all around. Here and there the perches give way with a crash, and fall to the ground, destroying hundreds of birds on the loaded branches beneath.

Mourning Dove

Rock Pigeon

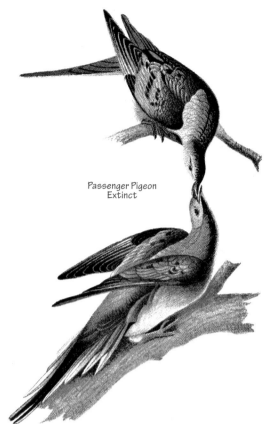

Passenger Pigeon
Extinct

Mourning Dove

LAND BIRDS

Chimney Swift

Tail feather
with extended spine which gives added support when perching.

Whip-poor-will

Whip-poor-will Mouth

Nighthawk

Calliope Hummingbird

Belted Kingfisher

Northeast Horned Lark (M)

Desert Lark

South Texas Horned Lark (M)

Greater Roadrunner

Horned Lark

Downey Woodpecker

Woodpecker Drilling
The woodpecker draws its head back as far as possible - then strikes with all its force - sending its strong beak into the wood. To withstand the shock the beak is springy and to avoid a concussion of brain it has a shock absorbing membrane around the brain. The tongue system coiling around the brain also acts as a shock absorber.

Feeding: When the woodpecker has drilled the hole, to the burrow of a boring beetle, it can open its beak slightly, thrust the tongue forwards, with its strong muscles, and spear the insect with the tip of the tongue.

Bone of Tongue: (hyoid) This bone gives the tongue its strength. Having two parts they are enclosed in a sheaths and they fit into a grove on the top of the scull. This lets the Hairy Woodpecker extend its tounge 1 1/2 inches past the end of its bill.

Side View

Bill: Shaped like a stout chisel. It strikes out small chips - so it gradually drills its way into a tree trunk.

Tongue

Tongue

Bottom View

Spear like tongue-tip of the Downy Woodpecker. It is as hard as horn.

Tongue: A woodpecker's tongue is extremely specialized. The tongue lies in a depression in the lower mandible (lower part of bill). It is slender, nearly round, and its upper surface is covered with very minute spines, directed backwards; the tip is as hard as horn, with many small barbs, like a fishing spear. It is power full muscles and it can be thrust out when feeding. When feeding the tongue is coated with a very sticky juice. Formed by two glands on the side of the head.

Hard Tip

Tongue Extended

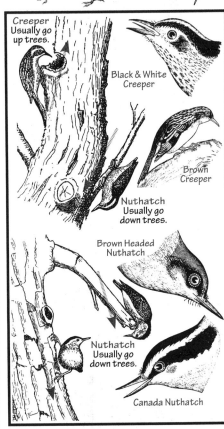

Creeper Usually go up trees.

Black & White Creeper

Brown Creeper

Nuthatch Usually go down trees.

Brown Headed Nuthatch

Nuthatch Usually go down trees.

Canada Nuthatch

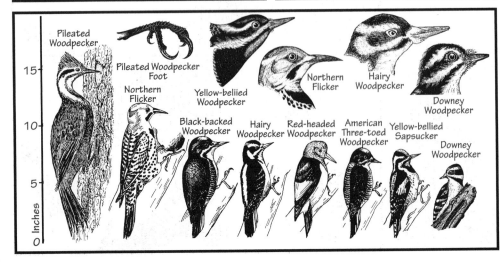

Pileated Woodpecker

Pileated Woodpecker Foot

Northern Flicker

Yellow-beliied Woodpecker

Northern Flicker

Hairy Woodpecker

Downey Woodpecker

Black-backed Woodpecker

Hairy Woodpecker

Red-headed Woodpecker

American Three-toed Woodpecker

Yellow-bellied Sapsucker

Downey Woodpecker

15
10
5
0
Inches

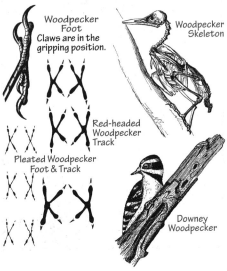

Woodpecker Foot
Claws are in the gripping position.

Woodpecker Skeleton

Red-headed Woodpecker Track

Pleated Woodpecker Foot & Track

Downey Woodpecker

LAND BIRDS

Derby Flycatcher

Kingbird

Flycatcher

Golden-Crowned Kinglet

Tree Swallow

Barn Swallow

Cliff Swallow

Cliff Swallow

Tree Swallow

Barn Swallow Nest

Mockingbird

Mockingbird

Gnatcatcher

Yellow-Breasted Chat

Meadow Starling

Starling Tracks

Raven Skull

Raven

Red Headed Grossbeak Head

Pine Grossbeak

Crow Foot

Crow Track

Crow

Crossbill

White Winged Crossbill

Robin

Robin

Robin

Varied Thrush

Water Thrush

Wood Thrush

Grey Cheeked Thrush

Water Thrush

Wood Thrush

Wood Thrush Tracks

Wilson's Thrush

Water Thrush

Hermit Thrush

Olive Thrush

Mountain Chickadee

Boreal Chickadee

Black Capped Chickadee

Black Capped Chickadee

Short-billed Wren

Rock Wren

Long-billed Marsh Wren

Marsh Wren

House Wren Eggs

525

LAND BIRDS

Eastern Bluebird

Bobolink

Towbee

Baltimore Oriole

American Goldfinch

Ovenbird

Northern Oriole

Black Throated Bunting

Snowflake Bunting

Snow Bunting

Black Throated Bunting

Red Eyed Vireo

Cowbird

Indigo Bunting

Black & White Warbler

Warblers feeding on caterpillars of the Gypsy Moth.

Yellow Headed Blackbird

Louisiana Tanager

Scarlet Tanager

Yellow Warbler

Cerulean Warbler

Blackburnian Warbler

Western Tanager

Cardinal

Black - Throated Blue Warbler

Prairie Warbler

American Pipet

Bohemian Waxwing

Black - Throated Green Warbler

Parula Warbler

Nashville Warbler

Yellow Wagtail

Wilson's Warbler

Chestnut - Sided Warbler

Catbird

St. Lucas Thrasher

Brown Thrasher

Thrasher

Arizona Thrasher

526

Meadowlark

Meadowlark

Strikes Bills

Blue Jay

UPLAND BIRDS

Fox Sparrow

Swamp Sparrow

Chipping Sparrow

Henslow's Sparrow

Sparrow Tracks

Field Sparrow

Lincoln's Sparrow

Clay Colored Sparrow

Pine Woods Sparrow

White Crowned Sparrow

White Throated Sparrow

Vesper Sparrow

Savanna Sparrow

Lark Sparrow

Song Sparrow

House Sparrow

Song Sparrow

California Quail with Nest (Male: Left)

Montezuma Quail

Morning call of a "bob" - "white."

Mountain Quail

Bobwhite Quail Tracks

Northern Bobwhite Quail

Gimbel's Quail

California Quail

UPLAND BIRDS

Ruffed Grouse

Ruffed Grouse

Ruffed Grouse

Ruffed Grouse Tracks

Ruffed Grouse

Northern Sharp-tailed Grouse

Short-tailed Grouse

Western Ruffed Grouse

Canada Grouse

Spruce Grouse

Grouse Leg

Ptarmigan Track Summer

Ptarmigan Track Winter

Ptarmigan Track Summer

Rock Ptarmigan Summer & Winter

Willow Ptarmigan Winter

Greater Prairie Chicken

Ruffed Grouse in Winter

Thanksgiving Meal

Tail Feathers

Major Caruncles Large & fleshy growth on throat area.

Ear Opening

Head Crown

Back & Body Feathers

Eye

Tail Coverts

Snood

Major Caruncles

Breast Feathers

Primary Wing Feathers

Beard on Jake

Foot

Male Turkey "Jake"

Spur
They are on a Jake (male turkey).

Eastern Wild Turkey + Nest (insert)

Photographs: NWTF
(National Wild Turkey Federation)

Gray Partridge

Partridge

Red Necked Pheasant Hen

Red Necked Pheasant

Pheasant Track

RAPTORS & OWLS

Bald Eagle Taraus

Bald Eagle

Bald Eagle in Flight

Golden Eagle in Flight

Rough-legged Buzzard

Eagle Skeleton

Bald Eagle Taraus in flight

Bald Eagle trying to steal an Osprey's fish.

Golden Eagle Taraus

White Tailed Sea Eagle

Buzzard Egg

California Condor

Golden Eagle

Turkey Vulture

Turkey Vulture in Flight

Vulture Skeleton

Scull

Neck

Furcula

Coracoid

Back

Scapola

Humerus

Ulna

Ribs

Tail

Alula

Metacarpus

Phalanges

Femur

Pelvis

Breast Bone

Tibia

Metatarsus

Toes

Hawks

Osprey

Peregrine Falcon

Prairie Falcon

Peregrine Falcon

Osprey

Osprey

Kestrel

Osprey

White Phase Gyrfalcon

Hawk Prints

Goshawk in Flight

Swainson's Hawk

Marsh Hawk

Marsh Hawk

Rough-legged Hawk

Swallow Hawk

Marsh Hawk

Fereu Rough-legged Hawk

Marsh Hawk

California Goshawk

Red Tailed Hawk

Sharp Shinned Hawk Immature Female

Cooper's Hawk Male

Cooper's Hawk Female

Sparrow Hawk

Sharp Shinned Hawk

White-tailed Kite

Pigeon Hawk

Sharp Shinned Hawk Male

Hawk Skeleton

Merlin Hawk

OWLS

During the daytime crows will harass perched owls.

Short Eared Owl

Great Grey Owl

Screech Owl

Barred Owl

Northern Hawk Owl

Short Eared Owl

Richardson's Owl

Saw-whet Owl

Great Horned Owl

Horned Owl

Great Eagle Owl

Snowy Owl

Spotted Owl

WATER BIRDS

Loon Foot

Loon Tracks

Yellow-Billed Loon

LOONS

They are excellent swimmers and can swim long distances under water. They can change their specific gravity (with grebes) so they can sink into the water without diving. Because of the construction of their feet they can hardly walk on land. Loons have to take a long taxiing run to get airborne. It is a northern bird. It has a very special melancholic cry.

Black Footed Albatross

Laysan Albatross

ALBATROSS

This oceangoing bird needs the wind to stay aloft as it glides through the sky.

STORM-PETRELS

Leach's Storm-Petrel

Storm-Petrel

Black Storm-Petrel

Storm-Petrel Leg

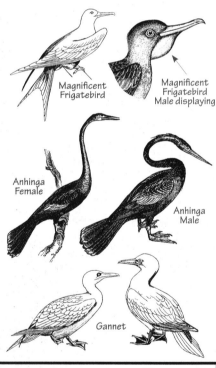

Magnificent Frigatebird

Magnificent Frigatebird Male displaying

Anhinga Female

Anhinga Male

Gannet

GREBES

These birds resemble Loons but their toes are not connected by webs. Their toes have a lump of skin that extends when the foot is on the propulsive push and then folds back on the return stroke. These birds live on prairie lakes.

Grebe Tracks

Red Necked Grebe

Crested Grebe

Clarke's Grebe

PETRELS SHEARWATER FULMARS

Sooty Shearwater

Cory's Shearwater

Black Capped Petrel

Fulmer Petrel Head

Fulmer Petrel

Fulmer Petrel Leg

AMERICAN BITTERN

Tropic Bird

Blue-footed Booby

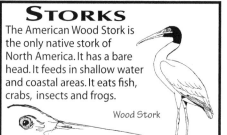

Red-footed Booby

PELICAN

Pelicans can hold from a gallon to three gallons of food and water in their bills.

CORMORANT

Cormorant Skull

Double-crested Cormorant

Great Cormorant

Red-faced Cormorant

Crested Cormorant

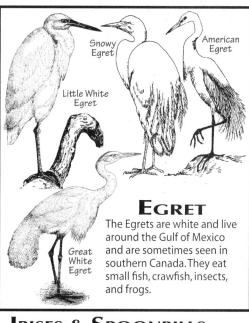

Florida Cormorant

STORKS

The American Wood Stork is the only native stork of North America. It has a bare head. It feeds in shallow water and coastal areas. It eats fish, crabs, insects and frogs.

Wood Stork

FLAMINGO

They eat mollusks, shrimps, worms, insects, algae and other foods found in the water.

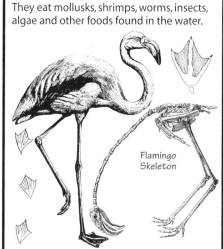

Flamingo Skeleton

HERONS

Golden Crowned Night Heron

Great Blue Heron

Little Blue Heron

Night Heron

Night Heron

Great White Egret

Snowy Heron

Heron in flight.

EGRET

Snowy Egret

American Egret

Little White Egret

The Egrets are white and live around the Gulf of Mexico and are sometimes seen in southern Canada. They eat small fish, crawfish, insects, and frogs.

IBISES & SPOONBILLS

They are similar to storks but their bills are soft and leathery rather than hard and horny.
The family has two groups:
Ibis - has long, thin, down-curved bills.
Spoonbill - has a spoon-shaped bill.

White Ibis

Roseate Spoonbill

Roseate Spoonbill

MERGANSERS, DUCKS, GEESE & SWANS

MERGANSERS, DUCKS, GEESE & SWANS

This family has the majority of larger waterfowl in North America. They are swimming birds with four toes and only two webs. To eat, they strain the water through their bills.

Ducks: Have a rapid wing beat.
Geese: Have larger wings and a slower powerful wing beat.
The difference between Duck and Mergansers is that ducks have flattened bills and Mergansers have narrow bills. Teals are the smallest of ducks.

Duck Foot

Surface feeding duck foot.

Surface duck feeding bill.

Wood Duck Tracks

Redhead Duck

Harlequin Duck

Goldeneye Duck

Ruddy Duck

Wood Duck and Nest: Male duck in front and the nest is in the hole in the tree trunk. Duckling in hole looking out.

Mallard Duck

Common Scoter

White-winged Scoter

Great Scaup

Shoveler Duck Bill

Pintailed Duck

Northern Pintail Duck

Shoveler Duck

Black Scoter

Gadwall Duck

Eider Duck Bill

Surf Scoter

Duck bill is flat when compared to merganser's bill.

Eider Duck

Eider Duck

Mallard Bill

Mallard Duck Female

Mallard Duck Male

Mallard Duck

Goose taking flight.

MERGANSER

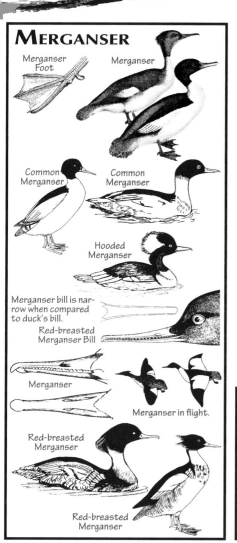

Merganser Foot

Merganser

Common Merganser

Common Merganser

Hooded Merganser

Merganser bill is narrow when compared to duck's bill.

Red-breasted Merganser Bill

Merganser

Merganser in flight.

Red-breasted Merganser

Red-breasted Merganser

Canada Goose
The escape.

Hooded Merganser

Why certain migrating birds fly in a "V" formation

The lead bird flaps its wings and disturbs the air leaving a wind eddy behind it. Heavy birds (as geese) take advantage of these eddies by flying in a "V" formation. This gives additional support from the wake of the bird immediately ahead. Quite often you see a "V" reforming and the leader of the group changing position to take a rest.

GEESE

Geese are similar to ducks but are larger, have flattened bodies and longer legs. They have a strong low frequency flight.

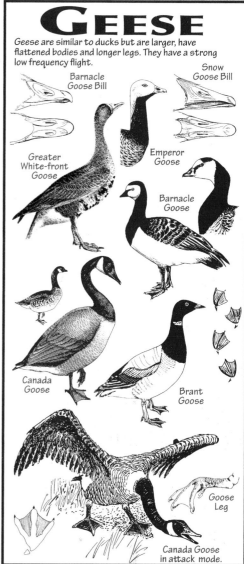

Barnacle Goose Bill

Snow Goose Bill

Greater White-front Goose

Emperor Goose

Barnacle Goose

Canada Goose

Brant Goose

Goose Leg

Canada Goose in attack mode.

Bewick's Swan

Black Swan

Swan in flight.

Whistling Swan Bill

Swans

Swans fly with their necks extended forward (like the crane). But they do not have the long protruding legs of the cranes.

SWAN

Tundra Swans

Observing waterfowl from a blind.

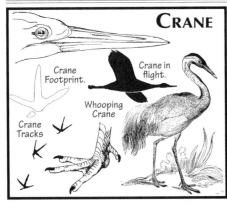

CRANE

Crane Footprint.

Crane in flight.

Whooping Crane

Crane Tracks

CURLEW

Curlew Track

Curlew Foot

Bristle-thighed Curlew

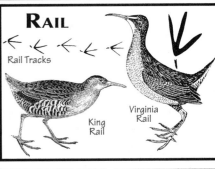

RAIL

Rail Tracks

King Rail

Virginia Rail

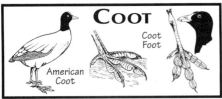

COOT

Coot Foot

American Coot

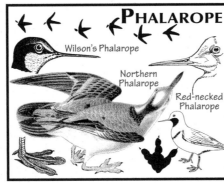

AVOCET

American Avocet

European Avocet

Avocet Foot & Head

GOODWIT

Hudsonian Goodwit

Goodwit Tracks

LAPWING

Lapwing

TURNSTONE

Black Turnstone

Turnstone

PHALAROPE

Wilson's Phalarope

Northern Phalarope

Red-necked Phalarope

PLOVER

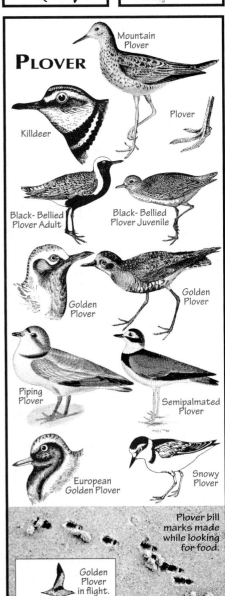

Mountain Plover

Plover

Killdeer

Black-Bellied Plover Adult

Black-Bellied Plover Juvenile

Golden Plover

Golden Plover

Piping Plover

Semipalmated Plover

European Golden Plover

Snowy Plover

Plover bill marks made while looking for food.

Golden Plover in flight.

GALLINULE

Purple Gallinule

Gallinule Foot

STILT

Black-necked Stilt

GREAT SKUA

WHIMBREL

JAEGER

SANDERLING

Tracks

OYSTERCATCHER

SHORE BIRDS

Dowitcher

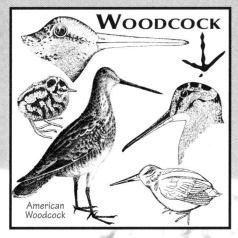

WOODCOCK

American Woodcock

BLACK GUILLEMOT

Summer
Winter

STILT

Black-necked Stilt

PUFFIN

TERN

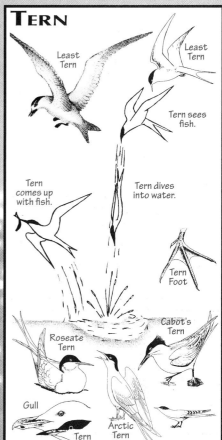

Least Tern
Least Tern
Tern sees fish.
Tern comes up with fish.
Tern dives into water.
Tern Foot
Cabot's Tern
Roseate Tern
Gull
Arctic Tern
Tern

WILLET

SKIMMER

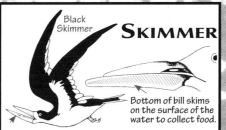

Black Skimmer
Bottom of bill skims on the surface of the water to collect food.

SNIPE

Common Snipe
Great Solitary Snipe
Wilson's Snipe
Red-brested Snipe

MURRES

SANDPIPER

Solitary Sandpiper Flying
Solitary Sandpiper Head
Solitary Sandpiper
Red Backed Sandpiper
Least Sandpiper
Purple Sandpiper
Marsh Sandpiper
Greater Yellowlegs
Upland Sandpiper

GULL

Bonaparte's Gull
Franklin Gull
Laughing Gull
Ring-billed Gull
Red-billed Gull
Common Gull
Great Black-backed Gull
Gull's Tracks
Herring Gull
Herring Gull Wing
Jaeger
Gull
Tern

REPTILES & AMPHIBIANS

Reptiles: (snakes, alligators, turtles, lizards) are covered with scales which protect them and reduce the loss of moisture.
Amphibians: (frogs, toads, salamanders) have a thin skin and have to have access to water or humidity. They are cold-blooded and the temperature of their bodies is the same as their surroundings. When it gets cooler they can be seen sunning themselves on rocks.

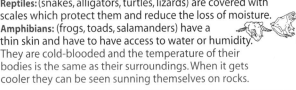

Adrien and Friend

LIFE CYCLE OF A FROG

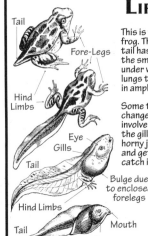

Fourth Stage
This is the final stage between tadpole and small frog. The metamorphosis is almost complete but the tail has not been completely absorbed. At this stage the small frogs will leap ashore. They have lost their under water respiratory system and will use their lungs to breathe. The skin will always be respiratory in amphibians.

Third Stage
Some three months after hatching, the tadpoles change into little frogs, and this metamorphosis involves many changes. The tail begins to shorten, the gills are absorbed and the gill clefts close up, the horny jaws are lost, the eyes become more prominent and get lids, the tongue becomes muscular enough to catch insects, etc.

Second Tadpole Stage
The hind limbs bud out at the root of the tail. The fore limbs start to grow at the same time but are retained by the gill chamber until they are fully formed.

First Tadpole Stage
A few days after hatching from an egg.

Labels: Tail, Fore-Legs, Hind Limbs, Eye, Gills, Tail, Bulge due to enclosed forelegs, Hind Limbs, Tail, Mouth, Eye

ALLIGATOR

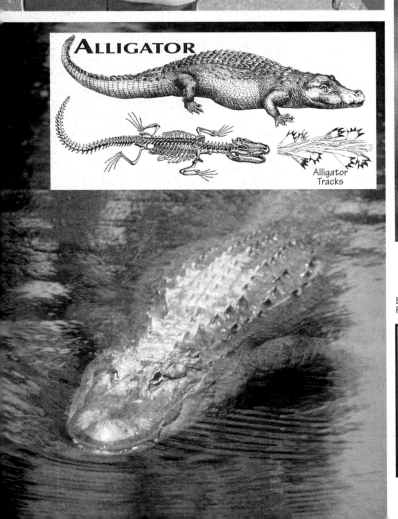

Alligator Tracks

FROGS

Giant Water Bug catching a Leopard Frog.

A Water Tiger looks like inoffensive brown stems. It extends it legs and rapidly swims and catches the tadpole by hold it with its legs and biting it with its jaws.

Bull Frog Track

FROG & TOAD EGGS
Toad's eggs are laid in strings.

Frog's eggs laid in a jelly like mass.

FROG CATCHING INSECT
Tongue shoots out above the insect.

Insect

Common Frog
Ear Drum

Hump

The drum of the ear, flush with the skin, is seen behind the eye. The double hump on the back shows where the hip is attached to the last free vertebra. The size of the foot can be seen.

← Large Foot

LEOPARD FROG

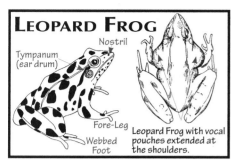

Nostril
Tympanum (ear drum)
Fore-Leg
Webbed Foot

Leopard Frog with vocal pouches extended at the shoulders.

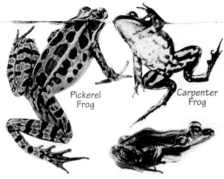

Pickerel Frog
Carpenter Frog

Wiggle fingers of one hand.

Catch with second hand.

CATCHING A FROG

TOAD CATCHING INSECT

The sticky tongue is attached to the front of the mouth instead of in the back. It can extend two inches, in an exceedingly rapid movement.

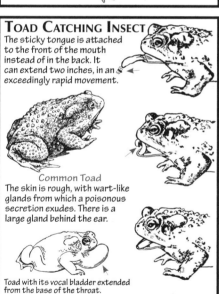

Common Toad
The skin is rough, with wart-like glands from which a poisonous secretion exudes. There is a large gland behind the ear.

Toad with its vocal bladder extended from the base of the throat.

A: Draws feet up.

B: Pushes away with its webbed feet open.

C: Glides along.

Back-swimmers pounce upon tadpoles and suck their blood.

Frog Swimming
A frog does not use its arms to swim, but holds them close to its side, and swims by kicking its long legs and webbed feet.

Frog Skeleton

FROGS

Frogs are amphibians. Frogs, when compared to salamanders, are unusual because they lack tails as adults and their legs are more suited to jumping because they have long jumping hind legs. Oxygen can pass through their highly permeable skin. This unique feature allows frogs to "breathe" largely through their skin and when on land they breathe through their nose and lungs. Due to their permeable skin, frogs are often semi-aquatic or inhabit humid areas, but move easily on land.

FROG OR TOAD?

Members of the anuran family Bufonidae are called true toads, but many species from other families are also called toads. "Toads" are usually identifies by their "look"- squat with warty bumpy dry skin. The use of the term "frog" in common names usually refers to species that are aquatic or semi-aquatic with smooth and/or moist skins, and the term "toad" generally refers to species that tend to be terrestrial with dry, warty skin. A distinction is often made between frogs and toads on the basis of their appearance, caused by the convergent adaptation among so-called toads to dry environments.

ALLIGATORS

American alligators are found in the Southeast US. They live in freshwater environments, such as ponds, marshes, wetlands, rivers, lakes, and swamps, as well as brackish environments. Large male alligators are solitary territorial animals. Smaller alligators can often be found in large numbers close to each other. They are capable of short bursts of speed, especially in very short lunges. They may kill larger prey by grabbing it and dragging it into the water to drown. Alligators and crocodiles both live in Southern Florida.

ALLIGATOR OR CROCODILE?

Alligators: Wider and shorter head, and a more U-shaped than V-shaped snout. The alligator's upper jaw is wider than its lower jaw, and the teeth in the lower jaw fit into small depressions in the upper jaw.

Crocodiles: The upper and lower jaws are the same width, and teeth in the lower jaw fall along the edge or outside the upper jaw when the mouth is closed. When the crocodile's mouth is closed, the large fourth tooth in the lower jaw fits into a constriction in the upper jaw. React aggressively and are for the most part more aggressive, than alligators, in their natural habitat

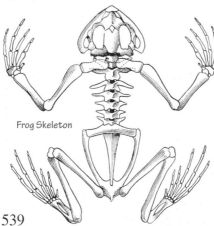

Frog Skeleton

539

TREE FROGS

Tree frogs have "toe pads" to help grip vertical surfaces. These pads, located on the ends of the toes, do not work by suction. Rather, the surface of the pad consists of interlocking cells, with a small gap between adjacent cells. When the frog applies pressure to the moist toe pads, the interlocking cells grip irregularities on the substrate. This allows the frog to grip smooth surfaces, and does not function when the pads are excessively wet.

Reduce Water Loss
This is the water-conserving position of some tree frogs. This position involves the frog lying with its toes and fingers tucked under its body and chin with no gap between the body and substrate.

Singing
The air from the lungs forced through the throat vocal pouch.

Gripping Toes

Gray Tree Frog
Has adhesive toe pads to help it climb vertically. It can change colors depending on the temperature, light intensity, or humidity. Only 1-2 inches long.

SALAMANDER

Northern Red Salamander

Red Backed Salamander
Found below an old board. There are land Isopods ("Wood Lice" or "Sow Bugs") in this moist area with the salamanders. The Wood Lice are actually land-living crustaceans.

Salamander
Are amphibians with slender bodies, short noses, and long tails. Most salamanders have four toes on their front legs and five on their rear legs. Their moist skin usually makes them reliant on habitats in or near water, or under some protection (e.g., moist ground), often in a wetland. Some salamander species are fully aquatic throughout life, some take to the water intermittently, and some are entirely terrestrial as adults. Unique among vertebrates, they are capable of regenerating lost limbs, as well as other body parts. Salamanders have a unique escape tactic – their tail will drop off and wriggle around for a little while, and the they will either run away or stay still enough to not be noticed while the predator is distracted.

Yellow Eyed Salamander

Rough-skinned Newt

Taricha newts of western North America are particularly toxic. The Rough-skinned newt of the Pacific Northwest produces more than enough toxin to kill an adult human.

NEWT
Is a relative of salamanders. Many newts produce toxins in their skin secretions as a defense mechanism against predators. Most newts can be safely handled, provided that the toxins they produce are not ingested or allowed to come in contact with mucous membranes, or breaks in the skin. After handling, proper hand-washing techniques should be followed due to the risk from the toxins they produce and bacteria they carry, such as salmonella.

LIZARD

Collared Lizard

LIZARDS
Lizards are reptiles related to snakes. Lizards typically have limbs and external ears, while snakes lack both these characteristics. Lizards have excellent color vision that is used to locate prey.

Lizard Skeleton

Gila Monster Tracks

Gila Monster
This is one of the two most venomous lizards in the world. It is the only poisonous lizard in North America.

RATTLESNAKES
Rattlesnakes are native to the Americas, with the large majority of species in the American Southwest and Mexico and their range extends north into Canada. Rattlesnakes consume mice, rats, small birds and other small animals. They subdue their prey with a venomous bite. The venom will immediately stun or kill typical prey. Rattlers are known to strike at distances up to nearly their body length.

RATTLESNAKES BITES
If the rattlesnake is not cornered or threatened, it will usually attempt to flee from encounters with humans. Bites often occur when humans startle the snake or provoke it. Those bitten while provoking rattlesnakes have usually underestimated the range and speed with which a coiled snake can strike.

RATTLE
The rattle is used as a warning device when threatened. The rattle consists of hollow beads which are actually modified scales from the tail tip. The first bead is the "button." Every time the snake sheds its skin, a new rattle segment is added. The rattling sound is created by the dried skin in the rattle segment.

Rattle Segments

CORAL SNAKE

Remember the ditty:
*"Red on yellow will kill a fellow;
Red on black, venom will lack"*

- This snake is very colorful with bright red, yellow and black bands completely encircling the body. It is usually 30" long, thin and has a small head.
- Note that the red band is next to the yellow. This is important as there are many similar colored snakes, but the coral snake is the only one with the red adjacent to the yellow band. This potential for confusion underscores the importance of seeking care for any snakebite (unless positive identification of a non-poisonous snake can be made).
- It is very rare and lives in Florida and the desert of the Southwest. It will only bite when mishandled.

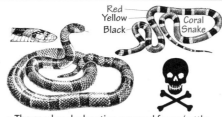

Red
Yellow
Black
Coral Snake

- The coral snake has tiny grooved fangs (rattlesnakes have hollow fangs) at the rear of its mouth and injects its venom with its teeth. A chewing motion is used to inject the venom. Because of its small mouth, teeth and limited jaw expansion, it usually bites on a small extremity such as the foot, hand, or a finger. After the bite, you will see tiny punctures or scratch marks.

Coachwhip Snake

AVOIDING RATTLESNAKES BITES

- Do not lift stones, logs or other possible hiding places before moving the object with a stick or a properly protected foot (with a heavy high boot).
- Do not gather firewood during the dark. When picking it up follow the same precautions as above.
- Do not reach into holes in the ground, trees or cacti even if a bird has just flown into it.
- Remember that rattlesnakes are usually in the shade on hot days and due to their camouflage colors are hard to detect.
- Be very observant when walking along a path and even more when walking through low bushes.
- Rattlers can be found in trees, bushes and they can swim.
- Rattlers are found at altitudes up to 11,000 feet in the southwest and up to 14,500 feet in Mexico.
- Always watch the ground even if you are photographing game birds in the sky.
- If you are walking single file and the leader has passed a point it does not mean that there are no snakes on the path. He might just have disturbed it and it might bite a person further down the line.
- If mountaineering, do not reach above your head for a hand hold. Avoid placing your hands in or near a crevice into which you cannot see.
- Avoid walking below rock ledges.

- A snake might enter your boat while you are traveling. Do not panic, he only wants to rest. Remove him with your paddle.
- When you hear the rattle, do not move, until you see the snake as you might walk into its range. If you back away make sure that you do not back into another snake.
- Do not step over logs step on them, so that you can see what is lurking on the other side, and only then step down.
- Look around your seating area before you sit down.
- Rattlers usually only attack moving objects.
- Pitch your tent in a clearing and make sure that a rattler will not crawl into your boots, clothing or backpack. Do not camp near rock piles or deep brush.
- Do not play with dead rattlesnakes as the head has been known to bite 1/2 an hour after it was removed from the body. Bury the head.

PROTECTIVE CLOTHING

- Protect your feet and legs by wearing heavy boots or thick puttees. The material should be impenetrable and should rise up to the knee.
- Wear your pants over your boots as the loose pant legs will provide added protection.
- If you rock climb wear heavy gauntlet-type gloves.

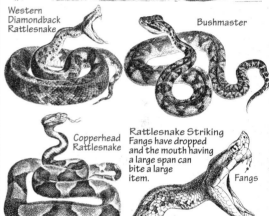

Western Diamondback Rattlesnake

Bushmaster

Copperhead Rattlesnake

Rattlesnake Striking
Fangs have dropped and the mouth having a large span can bite a large item.

Fangs

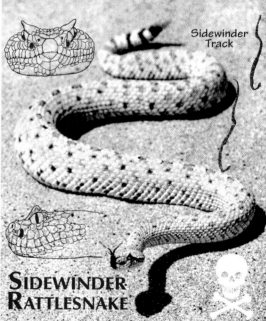

Sidewinder Track

SIDEWINDER RATTLESNAKE

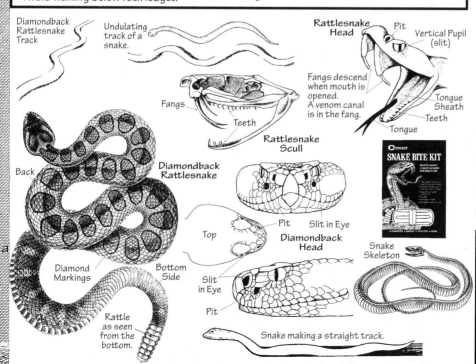

Diamondback Rattlesnake Track

Undulating track of a snake.

Rattlesnake Head

Pit

Vertical Pupil (slit)

Fangs descend when mouth is opened. A venom canal is in the fang.

Tongue Sheath

Teeth

Tongue

Fangs

Teeth

Rattlesnake Scull

SNAKE BITE KIT

Back

Diamondback Rattlesnake

Pit

Slit in Eye

Top

Diamondback Head

Snake Skeleton

Diamond Markings

Bottom Side

Slit in Eye

Pit

Rattle as seen from the bottom.

Snake making a straight track.

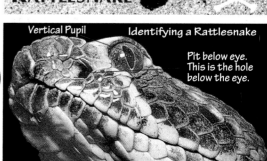

Vertical Pupil

Identifying a Rattlesnake

Pit below eye. This is the hole below the eye.

ANIMAL TRACKS

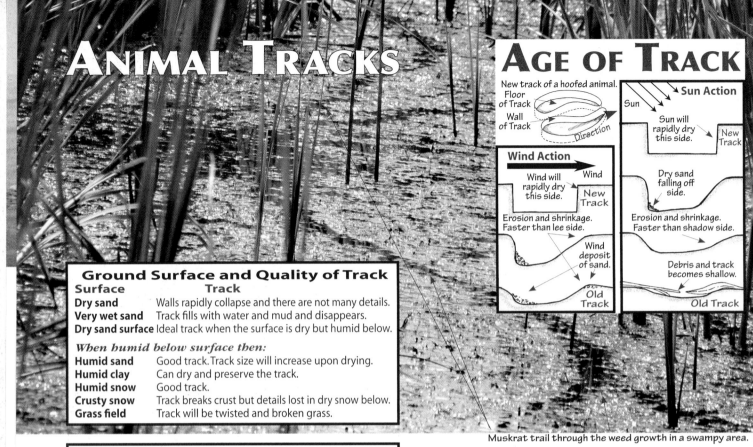

AGE OF TRACK

New track of a hoofed animal.
Floor of Track
Wall of Track
Direction

Sun Action
Sun
Sun will rapidly dry this side.
New Track
Dry sand falling off side.
Erosion and shrinkage. Faster than shadow side.
Debris and track becomes shallow.
Old Track

Wind Action
Wind
Wind will rapidly dry this side.
New Track
Erosion and shrinkage. Faster than lee side.
Wind deposit of sand.
Old Track

Muskrat trail through the weed growth in a swampy area.

Ground Surface and Quality of Track

Surface	Track
Dry sand	Walls rapidly collapse and there are not many details.
Very wet sand	Track fills with water and mud and disappears.
Dry sand surface	Ideal track when the surface is dry but humid below.

When humid below surface then:

Humid sand	Good track. Track size will increase upon drying.
Humid clay	Can dry and preserve the track.
Humid snow	Good track.
Crusty snow	Track breaks crust but details lost in dry snow below.
Grass field	Track will be twisted and broken grass.

Sun, Wind & Rain Effect on a Track

Weather	Surface	Impact on Track
Sun	Sand	Rapidly dry track and cause sides to fall.
	Snow	Melt snow, enlarge hole, and obliterate details.
	Rock	Wet footprint will dry it in a few minutes.
Rain	Sand	Wash out track.
	Snow	Obliterate track.
	Rock	No track will be made.
Wind	Sand	Dry track and cause sides to fall. Leave sand and other debris deposits in cavity.
	Snow	Drift snow across the track.
	Rock	Wet footprint will dry it in a few minutes.

Brown Creeper track in mud.

Tracks made by animals "age" due to the action of weather and other tracks being made over them. A track is made by the pressure of the weight of the animal on the ground and this pressure usually breaks the surface exposing humid soil or a lower layer of snow. As soon as a track is made the weather will start acting (aging) on the track. If frost crystals have formed on the track after a cold night, the track was made before the frost. If there is no frost, the track is recent. A fresh track in snow will have a crisp curl with snow particles kicked in the direction of movement. A track is old when evaporation or blown snow have dulled the crispness. Aging happens in a few hours as the sun dries the dew, frost, or humidity from a dirt track, and the edges start to crumble.

TRACKING
Page 304
ANIMAL TRACKS

The story of an animal passing through a meadow is left by its tracks. Tracks consist of bent blades of grass, gnawed bone, broken seeds, the dragged body or tail, and the foot print of the animal.

All prints of an animal are not the same as they depend upon:

- The age of the animal.
- The movement of the animal - walking, running, bounding.
- The material it is walking on - sand, mud, clay, grass, or snow.
- The season - some animals have extra fur on their paws in the winter.
- The age of the track.

When you see a track:

- Choose a well-defined area of the track.
- Study the track to determine the direction of travel, the forefoot and hind foot pattern.
- Are there any body rub points as a dragged tail, dragged foot, or dragged fur of the body?
- Is the animal running, hopping, walking, trotting, or just meandering?

THREE TYPES OF TRACKS

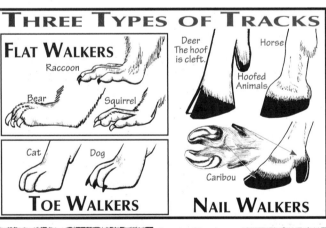

FLAT WALKERS
Raccoon
Bear
Squirrel

Deer The hoof is cleft.
Horse
Hoofed Animals
Caribou

TOE WALKERS
Cat
Dog

NAIL WALKERS

Looking for Tracks
Tracks are found on undisturbed sand, dusty roads, riverbeds, snow, and grass in areas where animals travel for water or food.

Deer hoof track that has partially dried. Note that the print is less distinct and the cleft mark of the hoof is hardly visible.

Deer hoof track that is still humid. Note that the print is distinct and the cleft mark of the hooves is visible.

ARCTIC HARE SKY JUMPING

Can jump up to 6 feet.

Wolf chasing snowshoe hare.

COTTONTAIL MAKING TRACKS

Rabbit starts a leap with its hind legs leaving the ground.

In the air the rabbit's legs will reposition themselves to prepare to land and start the next leap.

Front legs will first make contact with the ground. When looking at the tracks you will see that the front leg's print will be behind the hind leg's print.

The hind legs touch the ground and the next bound starts.

A cluster is called a 'set'.

Straddle - the width of a track.

A 'leap' is the distance between the toe and heel of two following sets.

Hind

Front

Snowshoe Hare

Cottontail

Cottontail Sitting

Hind Print

Front Print

Cottontail Track

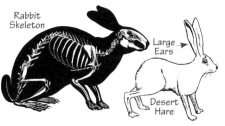

Rabbit Skeleton

Large Ears

Desert Hare

Cottontail Rabbit Jumping

HARE

Hare Jumping

RABBIT

SNOWSHOE HARE

HOARY MARMOT

Hind

Fore

MOUSE

Wood Mouse

Jumping Mouse

Deer Mouse Hopping

Meadow Mouse Running

White-foot Deer Mouse

Meadow Mouse Walking

Meadow Mouse

PORCUPINE

A Fisher hunting a porcupine. Because the fisher cannot attack the porcupine through the needles on its back it digs a tunnel in the snow and attacks the porcupine's stomach which has no needle protection.

Fisher

Porcupine

RACCOON

Hind

Fore

Running

Walking

Fore

Hind

Raccoon

Forefoot with "fingers" used for climbing and washing food.

Hind

Southern Flying Squirrel

PIKA

RAT

Hind

Tail Mark

Kangaroo Rat

Kangaroo Rat

Norway Rat

Rat Running

Fore

Hind

Wood Rat

Rat Walking

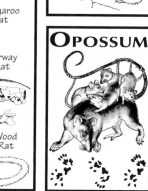

OPOSSUM

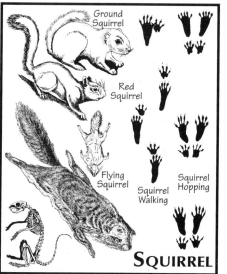

Ground Squirrel

Red Squirrel

Flying Squirrel

Squirrel Walking

Squirrel Hopping

SQUIRREL

547

SKUNK

Skunk Running

Skunk Walking

Hind
Fore

CHIPMUNK

Incisor Teeth adapted for cutting.

Hind

Front

WOODCHUCK

Fore

Hind

Woodchuck Walking

COLLARED LEMMING

EASTERN MOLE

MUSKRAT

Fore

Hind

Tail

PRAIRIE VOLE / MEADOW VOLE

Prairie Vole

VOLE

Meadow Vole

BATS

Vampire Bat Skeleton

Desert Bat

Big Brown Bat catching an insect.

Little Brown Bat

Long-eared Bat

Large Canine Teeth

Position of a bat holding onto a wall.

CAT

Cat Track

Claw
Ligament
Tendon

Cat claw in normal retracted position.

Domestic Cat

CAT CLAW

Down
Ligament
Tendon

Ligament keeps the claw raised. The cat has to make its claw tendon lower the claw.

Fore

Hind

BEAVER

Incisor Teeth adapted for cutting.

From the tracks you can see that the beaver is not made for walking. Its whole body drags. The feet are crossed. The beaver is built for swimming as shown from its webbed hind feet and its powerful tail.

Line made from the body and fur dragging.

Front foot has fingers to manipulate pieces of wood and mud when dam-building.

Hind foot webbed for swimming.

Beavers will cut trees along streams where they build their houses and dams. The trees usually fall towards the stream bank because trees have a heavier growth on the exposed sunny side.

DOG

Domestic Dog Track

Hind
Fore

Domestic Dog Track
Notice how it drags its toes when taking a step. This is especially visible in snow.

A fresh track in snow will have a crisp curl with snow particles kicked in the direction of movement.

COYOTE

Hind   Fore

BADGER

Badger Trotting

Badger Walking

The front feet have large claws because the badger is an animal that digs for animals in their dens.

Forefoot

Fore   Hind

WOLF

Wolf Walking

Fore   Hind

Wolves chasing a fisher.

Wolf Pack

LYNX

Winter Tracks

Lynx Hind Paw

ERMINE

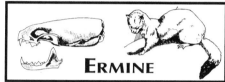

FISHER

Fisher looking for mice under the snow.

Fisher watching from a tree.

MARTEN

Hopping

Walking

MINK

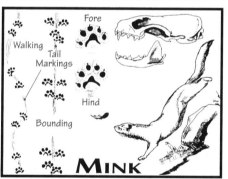

Walking

Tail Markings

Fore

Hind

Bounding

Otter Walking

Otters are very playfull, especially on an otter slide.

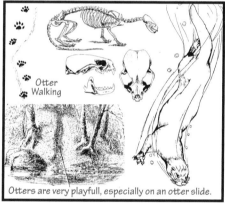

FOX

Red Fox Hunting

Arctic Fox (Summer/Winter)

Arctic Fox Foot Print

Digital Pad

Claw

Palmar Pad

Dew Claw

Right Hind   Right Fore

Fore   Hind

Fox Skull

Red Fox Tracks

WOLVERINE

Fore

Hind

Walking

Wolverine planning an attack on a herd of deer.

WEASEL

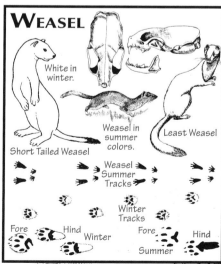

White in winter.

Weasel in summer colors.

Least Weasel

Short Tailed Weasel

Weasel Summer Tracks

Winter Tracks

Fore   Hind   Winter

Fore   Hind

Summer

Swift Fox Hunting
Province of Alberta Museum

HORSE

Superficial Layers of Muscles of a Horse

Would be similar to other hoofed animals - and four legged animals.

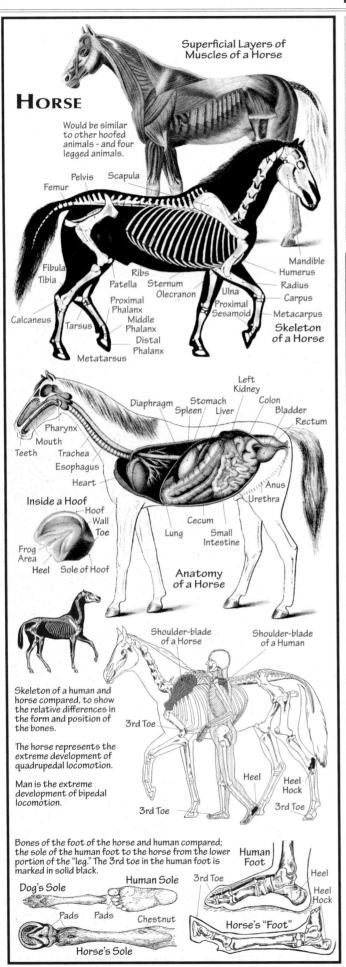

Skeleton of a Horse

- Pelvis
- Scapula
- Femur
- Mandible
- Humerus
- Radius
- Fibula
- Tibia
- Ribs
- Patella
- Sternum
- Olecranon
- Ulna
- Proximal Sesamoid
- Carpus
- Metacarpus
- Calcaneus
- Tarsus
- Proximal Phalanx
- Middle Phalanx
- Distal Phalanx
- Metatarsus

Anatomy of a Horse

- Pharynx
- Mouth
- Teeth
- Trachea
- Esophagus
- Heart
- Diaphragm
- Stomach
- Spleen
- Liver
- Left Kidney
- Colon
- Bladder
- Rectum
- Anus
- Urethra
- Cecum
- Lung
- Small Intestine

Inside a Hoof

- Hoof
- Wall
- Toe
- Frog Area
- Heel
- Sole of Hoof

Skeleton of a human and horse compared, to show the relative differences in the form and position of the bones.

The horse represents the extreme development of quadrupedal locomotion.

Man is the extreme development of bipedal locomotion.

- Shoulder-blade of a Horse
- Shoulder-blade of a Human
- 3rd Toe
- Heel
- Heel Hock
- 3rd Toe
- 3rd Toe

Bones of the foot of the horse and human compared; the sole of the human foot to the horse from the lower portion of the "leg." The 3rd toe in the human foot is marked in solid black.

- Human Foot
- 3rd Toe
- Heel
- Heel Hock
- Human Sole
- Dog's Sole
- Pads
- Pads
- Chestnut
- Horse's Sole
- Horse's "Foot"

MUSK OX

ELK

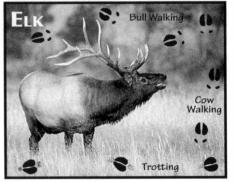

- Bull Walking
- Cow Walking
- Trotting

PRONGHORN ANTELOPE

- Walking
- Galloping

MOUNTAIN SHEEP (BIGHORN)

- Hind
- Bounding
- Fore
- Walking

Province of Alberta Museum

WILD PIG

- Fore
- Boar (male)
- Hind

MOUNTAIN GOAT

- Bounding
- Walking

DALL SHEEP

Dall Sheep Intermediate Coloration

Dall Sheep

Stone Sheep

Mountain Sheep

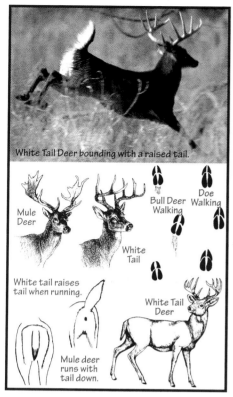

White Tail Deer bounding with a raised tail.

Mule Deer

White Tail

Bull Deer Walking

Doe Walking

White tail raises tail when running.

White Tail Deer

Mule deer runs with tail down.

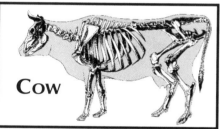

Cow

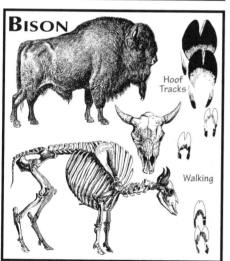

Bison

Hoof Tracks

Walking

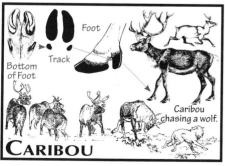

Foot

Track

Bottom of Foot

Caribou chasing a wolf.

Caribou

50 Dangerous Animals

Bears Cougars Moose

N.H. Fish & Game Department © 1999

BRAKE FOR MOOSE
IT COULD SAVE YOUR LIFE

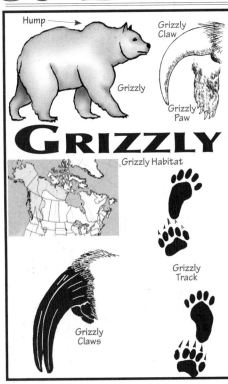

Hump

Grizzly

Grizzly Claw

Grizzly Paw

GRIZZLY

Grizzly Habitat

Grizzly Track

Grizzly Claws

GRIZZLY OR BROWN BEAR

The unpredictable bear! (Ursus Arctos)

Habitat: Open tundra close to forested areas and forest meadows in forested areas.

Size: Adults stands 7 feet tall

Weight: Adult males   600-800 lbs,
              Adult females   300 lbs

Food: Berries, nuts, tubers, honey, grass, wood fiber, insects, small and large mammals, mushrooms, spawning fish, frogs, dead animals.

General Behavior: Peaceful, secretive, very savage when aggravated.

Agitation Sounds: Pop jaw, woof, and possibly yawn. Major stress - foam at mouth.

Agitation Body Movement: Basic strategy is to look big. Grizzly will judge the situation and attack or run.

Attack Strategy: When attacking it makes a direct charge. Utters a deep roar and charges by running in lopping bounds then rises up (all 7 ft), bites the head or neck and shakes while clawing the victim.

Tree Climbing: Has large claws so climbing is difficult. Will climb to get hiker's caches.

Sleeping Area: On ground as too heavy (as an adult) for trees and shallow depressions in ground.

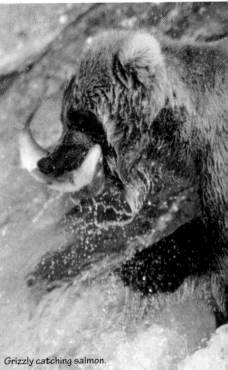

Grizzly catching salmon.

BLACK BEAR

Black Bear

BLACK BEAR

Ursus Americanus

Habitat: In forested foothills and mountains in proximity to food and heavy cover.

Size: Adults range from 5 feet long.

Weight: Adult males   400 lbs
              Adult females   220 lbs
              One year old   75 lbs

Food: Berries, nuts, tubers, honey, grass, wood fiber, insects, small mammals, mushrooms, spawning fish, frogs, dead animals.

General Behavior: Very clever, inquisitive, playfull.

Agitation Sounds: Popping sound with jaws, slap the ground, possibly yawn. Major stress foam at mouth.

Agitation Body Movement: Basic strategy is to look big. Stand sideways with hair on neck and back standing.

Attack Strategy: Stalks by zigzagging behind trees and bushes while approaching the prey. First might stand to smell the air, might stalk the prey and charge with speeds up to 30 mph. Bites and claws victims.

Tree Climbing: Excellent climber. Can easily climb 30 feet.

Sleeping Area: On ground or on limbs in trees.

Black bear shedding it's fur in the summer.

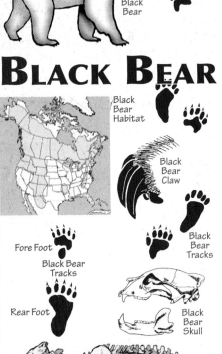

Black Bear Habitat

Black Bear Claw

Fore Foot

Black Bear Tracks

Rear Foot

Black Bear Tracks

Black Bear Skull

Black Bear Skeleton

Polar Bear

Polar bear entering tent.

POLAR BEAR

Thalarctos maritimus

Habitat: Coastline, ice flows, and Arctic water.

Size: Adults stand 8-10 feet tall.

Weight:
Adult males	500-1000 lbs
Adult females	400-600 lbs

Food: Rarely eats vegetation, carnivore - ringed seals, young walrus. It can smell a carcass that is miles away.

General Behavior: Silent plodder, fierce fighter, variable personality.

Agitation Sounds: Hisses, low growl, possibly yawn. Major stress - foam at mouth.

Attack Strategy: Uses its white coat as camouflage. It will even cover its black nose with its paw! It uses stealth of moving between ice blocks while approaching its prey. Moves into the wind so that its prey does not smell it. It will even slide along the ice while pushing itself with its hind legs, like swimming. When it is within 30 ft of the prey it bounds forwards and seizes the front of the body.

Tree Climbing: Does not climb trees but is very agile in its icy environment.

Sleeping Area: Dens that are dug in snow, dirt, ice field or shoreline. These sites are lined with moss or lichen.

POLAR BEAR ATTACK

Polar bears are great, stealthy, and patient hunters. They have an attack strategy. The most dangerous are the young that have just left their mothers at approximately 2 1/2 years old. Not being expert hunters they are always very hungry. They are curious and will investigate anything unusual.

It is important that you see the bear before it sees you because it will go into stealth mode and be on top of you before you have time to defend yourself. A single unarmed human has a marginal chance of survival. Always carry bear spray and a firearm if possible. Inuit usually have dogs near their dwellings to sound an alarm.

POLAR BEAR POISONING

Poisoning from eating polar bear liver and kidneys. If butchering the animal for survival, attention should be paid to not cutting into these organs. The poisonous ingredients seems to be a very high concentration of vitamin A. If unintentional poisoning has occurred, some symptoms are: a frontal headache, nausea, vomiting, abdominal pain, diarrhea, drowsiness. Death from this poisoning in a healthy person is rare.

Polar Bear

POLAR BEAR

Polar Bear Habitat

Polar Bear Paws

Polar Bear Tracks

HIKING IN BEAR COUNTRY

HIKING IN BEAR COUNTRY

- Get information on recent bear activity.
- With the reduction of bear habitat, there are increased chances of encountering a bear.
- Bears usually avoid people.
- Be sensitive to your surroundings - watch for bear indicators: scratch piles, tracks, droppings.
- Watch when going around blind corners, going over the crest of a hill, dark wooded patches.
- Watch where you camp or rest - look for bear markings. Also remember that you look smaller when you sit or lie down.
- Watch for noisy streams and changes in wind directions that may mask your sound and scent.
- Avoid scented wipes, soaps, deodorants, and cosmetics.
- Most encounters are by surprise - so make noise, talk, or sing while hiking to avoid startling a bear. Use bear bells. A bear looks slow and clumsy but can show surprising speed - up to 30 mph.
- Avoid hiking alone. Hike in small groups. Bears have not been known to attack groups of more than 4 people. Hike close together. Hike during daylight hours only.
- Try to hike with the wind to your back.
- Sleep in a tent for a tent serves as a psychological barrier to a bear. It will sniff around the tent and most likely not do anything.
- Approach known bear territory by traveling upwind - so that the bears will smell your presence and have time to leave.
- Avoid approaching recently killed or partially covered dead animals (deer or elk) as they might be bear kill.
- Be extra prudent when the wind is in your face as the bear ahead of you will not get a warning of your presence.

Avoid thick brush and be watchful when traveling off trail. If you can't avoid traveling through brush, try to walk with the wind at your back so your scent will warn bears of your presence.

BEAR PRESENCE INDICATORS

- Watch for areas that might be of interest to bears - berry patches, areas with rotten tree stumps. If flowers are missing their heads, it means a bear has passed by.
- Bears like to travel on game trails, saddles between hill ridges, and along streams.
- Carcasses of animals buried below mounds of branches, grass, dirt - with scavenger birds as crows, jays, and magpies fluttering about. These are caches made by bears. They are very protective of these reserves and you should not stay in the area. You will probably smell the odor of the carcass. Bears usually sleep near their caches.
- Bear territorial claw and bite marks on trees and posts. Also hair from rubbing against trees.
- Bark stripped off trees by the bear to access the soft inner layer of wood.
- Holes dug for: tubers, insects, small animals.
- Actual signs - scratch piles, tracks, droppings, damaged tree stumps, turned over rocks, peeled or rubbed trees. Bear droppings consist of partly digested food as grass, leaves, wood, fruits, hair, broken bones.
- Grizzly scat is 2 inches in diameter.

Log turned over by a bear looking for grub

Black bear scratch marks on tree trunk.

BEAR PRESENCE

TRAVEL IN GROUPS

When sighting a bear stay close together to look as big as possible. The bear will see this as one large something and not attack. The group should not break up and run as the bear will choose one person to follow until it catches the victim, usually the slowest or weakest. This is what bears do when they will attack a herd of deer.

The old joke...
When hiking - make sure that your partner is a slower runner than you are.

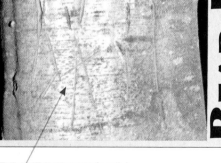

Bear Rub

WARNING

BEAR

FREQUENTING AREA

Removal of this sign may result in INJURY to others and is punishable by law.

THERE IS NO GUARANTEE OF YOUR SAFETY WHILE HIKING OR CAMPING IN BEAR COUNTRY

Hiking with Children

- Children should stay in plain sight close to and in front of group.
- Children should never approach bears, especially cubs.
- When in bear country, youngsters should always be supervised even when playing.
- Petting, feeding, or posing for a photo with bears or near them is a definite NO.

DO NOT

- Cook or keep food, garbage, cooking clothing near your tent.
- Cooking smoke should not drift over the tent.
- Get greasy hands on the tent flaps.
- Camp next to or in a berry patch, or other food source.
- Camp near a bear path.
- Bring backpack into tent as it might have food odors. Leave it with the flap open further from the tent.
- Cook in your tent - even if it is raining.
- Bury garbage as the odors might attract a bear when the next group uses the site.

CHOICE OF SITE

- Camp in the open so you can see any bear movement - especially with black bears as they will sneak up behind cover.
- In grizzly country camp near a tree for an emergency or in the open to see your surrounding.
- Store food in a tree at least 100 feet downwind from tent.

Do

- Wash with odorless soap after cooking and eating.
- If in group, camp close together.

Dogs & Cats & Camping

- Do not leave your vehicle when there are bears at the roadside and keep your windows rolled up.
- Do not bring an animal on a hiking trip.
- Do not leave a pet tied up while you are swimming as the smell and noise of a tied up pet, producing stressful sounds, will attract bears.
- Do not leave dog food in a bowl next to the tent.
- Do not hike alone with a dog as they might (will!!) rouse a bear's curiosity.

Bears Climbing Trees... Yes!!

- Adult grizzlies cannot climb trees as their claws are too long and not curved enough. Young grizzlies have difficulty climbing but can climb trees if the branches starting near ground level are spaced like rungs of a ladder. A grizzly can reach 10' while standing.
- Black bears have short curved claws so they are excellent climbers.
- Never climb tree - unless you can go high enough over 40' or in a tree that a black bear might feel is not strong enough.

Sitka Spruce: Ideal bear ladder

Black Bear Short claws: Good climber.

Grizzly Long claws: Difficult to climb.

To Reduce Bear Activity

- Camp in open areas away from thick cover, trails, and the bear's cache.
- Try to use dried food for low odor.
- Don't leave food unprotected.
- Store garbage in cans with tight-fitting lids. Keep camp clean. Wash dishes and dispose of food scrapes right after eating.
- Minimize odors as they will attract small animals that are of interest to bears.
- Make sure all camping gear is free of food odors.
- Never store food or smelly clothing in a tent. Do not sleep in the same clothing you wore when you cooked.
- Store food by hanging it from a rope between two trees. The rope should be 10 feet above the ground and the bag should be at least 4' from the tree trunk. Do the same if hanging game.
- Cook 100 yards and downwind from where you sleep. Do the same if hanging game.
- Do not hike with odorous food like bacon, sausage, fish, cheese, etc. Freeze dried foods are good as their packaging is nearly odor free.
- Avoid cooking food that might be of special interest to bears - bacon, sausage, piece of fish.
- After fishing dispose of fish entrails by puncturing the air bladder (so they will not float) and drop them offshore in deep water or burn them in a very hot fire. Avoid getting any fishy liquids on your clothing or body.

Information in this chapter is based upon various National Park Service publications and other data.

Bear's Favorite Berry
Canadian Buffaloberry
Shepherdia Canadensis

Season: Ripens late July to mid-August.
Habitat: Open woods, especially forests of lodgepole pine.

You have to be able to recognize this plant as they might indicate the presence of bears. Buffaloberries are the most important food for bears when the berries are ripe. Any trails with these berries will probably have bears so make as much noise as possible to indicate your presence.

Structure: It is a woody shrub, up to 5 ft high.
Leaves: dark green, oval leaves 3/4-3.5 inches long, arranged in an opposite manner.
Berries: Translucent and 1/4 inch in diameter, and vary from bright red to orange (occasionally yellow).
Range: Throughout Rockies, more common on eastern slopes.

Buffaloberry Flower

Buffaloberry

Food Storage - Bear Country

- Use animal-resistant food storage boxes. Never leave food or trash when leaving a camp site.
- Bear-resistant containers will keep out rodents as well as bears. Hang the container in a tree at least 100 yards (30m) downwind of your tent or, if a tree is not available, tie it to a rock or log to keep the container from rolling away.
- If you do not have a bear-resistant container, suspend the food in a bag. Plastic bags are best as they help seal in the food odors. A plastic coated material bag is the best as it would also partially protect against rodents. The bag should be suspended at a location that is visible from a distance so that you can see if a bear is loitering around.
- Suspend the bag between two trees so that it is at least 10 feet (3m) from the ground and at least 4 feet (1.2 m) from the trunks.
- Do not contaminate sleeping gear or clothing with food odors.
- No food or food container should be kept in the tent.
- Bears are not the only animals attracted by food and equipment. Deer will trample with their hooves. Ravens and crows will peck at plastic or cloth bags to access stored food. Mice, skunks, and raccoons will gnaw and tear through packs.

CAMP SANITATION

- A camp should be free of odors. Avoid cooking fragrant foods as bacon, fish, and meat in general.
- Never cook or eat in or near your tent. Do not burn remnants of food in the fire as it will leave odors.
- Wash dishes right after eating - do not use soap in the streams or lakes and dispose of all gray water far away from any natural water.
- Hang and store garbage along with your food and personal effects.

SLEEPING

- It is safer to sleep in a tent: it is a physical barrier.
- Do not sleep in clothing with food or sweaty odors. You might smell like an all dressed hamburger! Hang odorous clothing further away from the camp.

Fishing in Bear Country

- Store game, meat, and fish as carefully as you store your food.
- With fish entrails, puncture the air bladders before disposing of them at least 100 ft off shore in deep water. Do not dispose of them by burying near the camp, in the campfire (unless they are completely charred to ashes), or in a toilet.

Other Precautions

- Urine odors attract wildlife as urine is used as a territorial marker. Use toilets when available or urinate on rocks, snow or bare ground.
- Do not camp in an area where you find a dead animal. It might be a bear's cache.

Polar Bear

NIGHT BEAR ATTACK
- Never hike in bear territory at night, early mornings or dusk.
- If in group camp close together.
- Be careful when leaving the tent at night.
- Take care in choosing a camp site.
- Keep pepper spray in tent.

BEAR IN CAMP
In general bears that enter a camp should be considered as being DANGEROUS. They have possibly lost their fear of humans due to their eating human garbage or food.

If the bear is close you will hear hard breathing and continued sniffling. When a bear walks over rocks there are scratching sounds of its claws. Bears claws are not retractable as a cat's.

- You hear sounds of marauding around the camp site. Check from the tent, with a flashlight, to see if it is a bear, a small animal, or only one of your camping partners. Keep your pepper spray on hand.
- The bear probably is inspecting the cooking area. Make a lots of noise to scare the bear away. If the bear is within 15 feet use your pepper spray and it will probably leave.
- If you can safely reach your escape tree you might climb it - otherwise stay in the tent.
- Do not stay in the campsite for the following night.

BEAR ENTERS TENT...
You should know the attack characteristics of the attacking bear... this is hard to figure out in the dark!
Black bears usually once they attack - will continue the attack. Grizzly's have a more of a hit and run approach. They attack, bite, paw... and leave. In either case you have to yell - bang pots and pans - use pepper spray - shine lights into its eyes - make sure that the bear knows that you are human as you know the bear is looking for food - so do not play dead.
If the bear collapses the tent over you there is the additional problem that the tent envelopes you and the bear might not recognize you as a human.

REASONS FOR BEAR ATTACKS
- Protect its cubs
- Protection of cached food
- Surprise, confusion, and fear
- Space invaded
- Travel route or exit blocked
- Defensive action
- Sees the victim as prey

Black Bear and Cub

BEAR - SMELL & SIGHT
Bears have an excellent sense of smell - but their eye sight is marginal.

BEARS MOST DANGEROUS...
- During years of drought as this will reduce the berry crop.
- In the fall, especially after a dry summer, as the bears have to build up their body fat for hibernation.

GRIZZLY SUDDEN ENCOUNTER...
Sudden encounter sow with cubs - consider running to tree or play dead if cannot reach tree. If the tree is not at hand - remember the grizzly can outrun you - it is more prudent to play dead

YOUNG GRIZZLIES
Are dangerous as having been abandoned by their mother, are not good hunters, and live in marginal food areas due to pressure from larger bears. They roam and forage for food at campsites getting to associate food with humans.

HUNTING DANGERS
- In some areas of Alaska bears have learnt that a gun shot means potential food and will actually go towards the location of the sound. Be aware of this when approaching and cleaning the kill. Have your partner stand guard.
- Leave carcass in the open if you will return the next day. Approach cautiously as a bear might already have taken possession or partially covered the carcass. If so, abandon the carcass and leave immediately.
- Having a rifle should not give you false confidence in your security. To shoot a bear, the bullet has to be well placed which is hard to do when it is charging you at 30 mph and it might take several bullets.

A Visitor at Night

TWO TYPES OF BEAR CHARGES
The following does not apply to all bears as each bear has its own hunting experience and personality.

Ears up during charge... not decided.
Ears down... decided.

BLUFF ATTACK... YOU WISH!
Bear does not want to fight so they usually bluff charge to make you leave the area.
- Ears will be up.
- Does not necessarily make a direct charge and might veer back and forth while advancing.
- Charge has a looping gate with feet moving in a very fast walk type run.
- Bear will veer of at the last minute and possibly run away.

REAL ATTACK
The closer to the bear when surprised the increased odds of a real charge.
- Ears will be pinned back. Like a dog getting into a fight. Head low.
- Full speed charge direct on victim.
- Feet will be moving in unison (both front feet up at the same time).
- Will stare directly at victim as if measuring distance to coordinate a pounce.
- Makes no sound but might roar just before striking.

NEVER FEED WILD ANIMALS...
- Will associate humans with food.
- Will become dependant on humans for food.
- Animals approaching cars for food will get killed.
- Might become aggressive if not fed.

Grizzly checking the air for odors.

Grizzly Scat

Grizzly on Alert!

PEPPER SPRAY

Pepper spray is a deterrent and should not give you a false sense of security in bear country. The bear might not be happy getting sprayed... actually get really mad! Be prepared for a reaction. Restrictions apply in Canada.

- Only used at the time of an attack... not as an anti-bear deodorant!!
- Buy biggest container available. Do not worry about the weight. Leave something else at home.
- Range of fog blast of up to 30 ft. To maximize the pressure of the aerosol use short blasts. Ideally the wind should be behind you.

Limitations: Wind is blowing towards you the spray will not carry very far and you might get the returning mist. Heavy vegetation, heavy rain might wash the spray down.

- Carry pepper spray container in an easily accessible holster. Attacks can be unexpected and the speed of your reaction might be very important. Keep pepper spray always next to you and in tent at night.

EFFECTS OF PEPPER SPRAY

- Dilates the capillaries of the eye causing temporary blindness.
- Restricts breathing by causing mucous membrane to swell.
- Disorients and induces choking (temporary restricted breathing), coughing and nausea.
- If the mist blows back on you... you will know how the bear feels - stinging watery eyes, difficult choking breathing, loss of muscle strength, and temporary loss of coordination.

Read the manufacturer's instructions before going on hike. Check for the low temperature characteristics of your pepper spray. Follow storage instructions.

BEAR SEES YOU FROM...

Long Range *(approximately 300 Feet)*

- Do not run.
- Try to back off, slowly.
- Do not make direct eye contact. Eye contact could be perceived as a threat and provoke a charge.
- If the bear stands upright or moves closer... it might not be an aggressive act but only to detect smells in the air.
- Stay upwind so that the bear will know you are a human.
- Back off in a direction where you can seek shelter if required.

At this stage the bear will usually lose interest and go about what it was doing or wander away. *Read the information on stalking bear.*

Medium Range *(60 - 250 feet)*

- At this distance the objective is to make sure that you look large and the bear knows that you are human. So yell, clap your hands and wave your arms. Raise your jacket to make yourself as large as possible.
- Slowly back away towards shelter or up slope to look taller. Try not to show fear.
- As always avoid eye contact. But you realize that the bear has eyed you and possibly ambles off into the brush.

Stalking Bear: At this point you might have lost sight of the bear - do not relax - but keep backing away. The bear might be stalking you from behind the bushes or over the crest of a hill - this might be the case if the bear is in a predatory mood and trying to get a better view or attack position. Also watch behind your back. A young inexperienced bear might stalk humans - having no knowledge of humans. You should be prepared to defend yourself.

Close Range *(50 - a few feet)*

This is when you see their small beady eyes! You know that you are a potential meal.

- Leave your backpack on as it might help protect your back and neck. Throw a hat to distract it.
- If you have pepper spray judge the direction of the breeze - hopefully it is not blowing into your face.
- You should know the projection distance of your spray (usually 20 - 30 ft) to judge when to release the spray to form a cloud that the bear will enter during the charge. Start spraying at 40 feet and the bear will run into the pepper cloud. Note that the bear might be running at over 30 mph. Start yelling at the same time.
- Throw sticks, rocks, etc. - but do not look too small when you bend over to pick up the projectiles.
- If you have no spray or weapon try to look as large as possible (raising your jacket above your head) start to talk calmly and stand your ground.

BEAR HAS NOT SEEN YOU

- Immediately QUIETLY leave the area while making no abrupt moves.
- Do not cut off the bear's escape route.

Decision has to be made if you want to proceed on planned route...

- If any doubts turn back on path and plan another hike.
- Sows with cubs are very protective - change route, hike somewhere else.
- If bear has no cubs and you want to proceed on planned route - make a wide detour (hundreds of yards) downwind from the bear. Take the bear's direction of travel into consideration.

GRIZZLY ATTACK

- Direct charge.
- Swats with its paws, bites head or neck and then leaves if it is not in a predatory mood.

BLACK BEAR ATTACK

- Zigzag undercover stalking attack.
- Puts you in a "bear hug" while biting, scratching and tearing flesh.
- Will continue attacking so you have to fight back.

The extent of injury depends upon...
Defensive attack: you have intruded into its territory or cubs are present - the bear will attack but not have the objective to kill. It will swat and bite but not necessarily go for the neck or head.
Offensive attack: the bear is hungry and it intends to kill. It will go for the neck and head.

GRIZZLY ACTION - ATTACK SEQUENCE

Not Aggressive: rears on hind legs - it wants to see what is happening
Aggression: Standing on four legs may show aggression by...

- swinging head from side to side.
- making popping sounds or opening and closing its mouth while clacking its teeth.
- Running to a downwind position so that it can smell the intruder.

If threatened or predatory...
- A grizzly will flee or...
- A grizzly will attack - to judge the potential ferocity of a charge observe the position of the ears - as with dogs. The further they slope back the more serious. Also watch for hair rising on back of neck and back. A growl might precede an attack.

In the case of a grizzly attack...

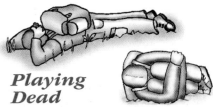

Playing Dead

- Play dead by lying flat on your stomach with legs spread out, cover neck with interlaced fingers of both hands, and have elbows covering face. The legs are spread out to prevent bear from rolling you over.
- Do not attempt to run as the bear can outrun you and the action of you running will trigger the bear's predatory instinct.
- If bear rolls you over keep on rolling so that you will again land on your stomach.
- At this point the bear might get bored and leave. Do not move until you are sure it has left. It might only be lying nearby and resting.
- If the bear starts to lick your wounds - you know it is serious and you will have to fight. Try hitting it on its snout or poking a stick or finger in its eyes.

In the case of a black bear attack...

- Do not play dead.
- Fight - hit snout, try to poke stick in eye, throw dirt or rocks into eyes, do anything...
- Do not climb tree nor run. Black bears can climb trees - very fast!! Climbing a tree might not help.

NEVER RUN... EXCEPT...

Never run from a bear - except if you are sure that you can reach a spot of safety before it reaches you - a bear can run over 30 mph.

COUGAR
COUGAR MOUNTAIN LION

Larger than the lynx and the bobcat. Cougars are primarily nocturnal creatures and, even when active in daylight, they are secretive and rarely seen. They favor dense forest and brush that provides good stalking cover while hunting. Cougars also take advantage of steep canyons and rock outcrops to remain hidden.

Although few people ever see this elusive cat in the wild, sighting and encounters in the national parks have increased in recent years.

They have great leaping power, as their hind legs are longer than their forelegs. Cougars are entirely capable of lethal attacks on people, and predatory attacks by cougars have occurred across the western U.S. and southwestern Canada over at least the last 50 years. Some incidents occur when people behave in a manner that resembles a cougar's normal prey. Expanding development and subdivisions into cougar habitat, particularly in areas with high deer populations, and residents who leave pet food or small pets or other animals outdoors at night seem to be factors that contribute to increased frequencies of cougar attacks.

CHILDREN & COUGARS
Cougars might be especially attracted to children because of their small size, erratic movement, and high pitched voices. They might not realize they are humans and not prey. Explain the dangers of cougars to children and have them play in groups when outside. Make sure they are indoors by dusk.

- At home consider getting a dog as an early-warning system. A dog can see, smell, and hear a cougar sooner then we can. Dogs offers little deterrent value but may distract a cougar from attacking a human.
- Keep children close to you while hiking, and do not allow them to run ahead or lag behind on the trail.
- Pick them up if you see fresh signs of a cougar.
- Consider minimizing shrubs around the house.

PETS & COUGARS
- Do not leave pet food outdoors as it will attract small wildlife which might attract cougars.
- Roaming pets are easy prey they should be kept indoors at night.

A pet's stand-off !!

COUGAR SAFETY
- Never approach a cougar, especially if feeding.
- Cougars are unpredictable, but will normally avoid a confrontation.
- Give a cougar an escape route.
- Hike in a group. Particularly in areas where cougars have been sighted, avoid hiking alone.
- Make enough noise to not surprise a cougar.
- Cougar kittens are usually well hidden. Do not approach or attempt to pick them up. Leave them immediately. The female will strongly defend her young.
- Avoid loitering around dead animals as they might be a cougar's food cache.
- Watch for cougar tracks, scat and markings.
- Keep a clean camp. • Leave pets at home.
- Pets running free may provoke a cougar, and then lead it to you.
- Be alert to the surroundings.
- Jogging is not recommended. People running or moving rapidly may be at higher risk.
- A walking stick makes a useful weapon.

ENCOUNTERING A COUGAR
- Stop. Do not run.
- Running may trigger a cougar's attack instinct.
- Immediately pick up small children. Children might get scared and the rapid movement or cries might cause the cougar to attack.
- Stay calm. Talk to the cougar in a confident voice.
- Stand upright, do not sit or bend over.
- Do not try to crouch and hide.
- Spread your arms, open your coat to look as large as possible.
- Do not approach the animal, back away slowly.
- Maintain eye contact with the cougar, and attempt to slowly back away.

COUGAR ACTS AGGRESSIVELY
- Be assertive. If approached, wave your arms, shout, and throw sticks or rocks at it.
- Convince the cougar that you are a threat and not a meal.
- Do not turn your back or take your eyes off the cougar.

COUGAR ATTACK
A cougar attack is an unlikely event and, by taking the mentioned precautions, you can reduce the chances even further.
- Fight back aggressively using anything - cameras, sticks, fishing rods, etc.
- Report any sighting of a cougar in a national park as soon as possible.

Cougar Encounters
• On Sunday, July 11, a cougar approached a group of five people, while they were hiking through the woods after fishing along the Quinault River. The group remained calm, shouted at the cougar, while one member of the group waved his fishing rod at the animal. The cougar retreated after several minutes.
• On Friday, July 16, a man photographing along a gravel bar on the river heard several sounds behind him. Turning towards the sound, he saw a cougar running towards him. The man shouted, waved his camera gear and a tripod at the animal. The cougar stopped about 10 –15 feet from the man and after several minutes, retreated. The man saw the cougar several more times as he returned to his car, which was parked at the Graves Creek stock camp. US National Park Service

Adult Weight: 85 to 180 pounds.
Length: 6 - 8 feet when including the tail which makes up about one-third of its total length.
Food: mice, raccoons, elk, but deer are their preferred prey. It is capable of killing a moose.
Dens: recesses on ledges, tree hollows on steep slopes, under fallen logs, and between rocks.

Cougar

Stalking

Trotting

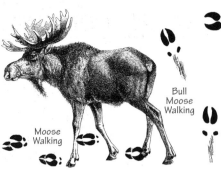

The Newfoundlander News 1895

1 THE RUN...

Making a Run for it: Upon hearing the note of an angry 'musky' moose bull reaching their ear, both sank slowly to the ground, quickly disencumbered themselves of their backpacks, and proceeded to contemplate an escape. On came the stag confronting the two men. A magnificent animal, snorting with rage, pawing up the stiff soil until showers of debris fell over his broad brown back. He presented a perfect picture of evil fury incarnate. Thereupon, as though recognizing their helplessness, the enraged animal immediately charged, so that both men were driven to make a hasty retreat.

2 THE TREE...

The Tree: Presently Alfred, hard pressed by the stag, made a run of about fifty yards to a juniper tree in the open, which he climbed in hot haste. In this instance the resemblance was heightened by the fact that the tree was not quite upright, but leaned over at a noticeable angle. To the horror of both men, as Alfred climbed higher to avoid the blows from the forefeet of the stag, delivered with lightning like rapidity, the slender tree began to slowly bend downwards beneath his weight. Inch by inch, lower and lower, the tree swayed and bent with Alfred's weight - slowly towards the irate animal, which pounded away at the bark just below the his feet. It was evidently only a question of a few moments, when the man would be at the mercy of the stag when doubtlessly he would he torn by the dagger like tines of the spreading antlers and, perhaps, pounded out of all resemblance of human form by the terrible splayed hoofs, with their knife like edges.

3 THE DUEL...

The Duel: Upon seeing Alfred in mortal danger, his brother, Harry came out of hiding to wage a duel to the death with the fierce animal - a duel in which a victory meant the deliverance of his brother from a terrible fate, and defeat the certain destruction of both of them. Quickly drawing his long hunter's knife from the scabbard which hung from his belt, he advanced boldly, with the bright steel glistening in his left hand. When he was halfway to the tree the caribou charged down upon him with a hoarse bellowing roar which was dreadful to hear. Fortunately the Harry was practiced in quick movements, and managed to dodge the first deadly rush. Then came a period during which man and beast hovered round one another, fencing for an opening, and when at length the two combatants closed the man managed to hold on to one horn with his right hand, while he tried to stab the beast in the neck with his other arm.

The vast strength of the stag - at this season of the year in the prime condition and frenzied with rage was too much for him, and he was thrown to the ground. Harry feel on his back and receiving some nasty thrusts from the sharp tines of the brow antlers. But never for a moment did he relax his hold on the horn; and he remembered a trick he had learned in his youth for throwing domestic cattle. With his right hand pulling on the left horn of the stag he twisted the nose up thus exerting a telling leverage on the animal's neck.

In the mêlée, however, his knife fell to the ground, leaving him unarmed.

His brother, dropped from the yielding tree, and, after recovering the hunting knife, ran to his side. Locked together in a fearful trial of strength, man and stag, striving desperately for the mastery, went swaying this way and that, until, with one supreme effort, Harry sent the great stag down on his knees, while Alfred kept stabbing away in the vicinity of the ribs, making only a small incision as the blade of the knife was not long enough to reach the vital organs. Finally, with one desperate drawing cut, he passed the sharp blade across the throat. After this the great beast plunged heavily forward on the bloodstained moss, while his life slowly ebbed away in a red stream, and Harry, breathless, but only slightly hurt, rose from that perilous battleground.

MEET A MOOSE

Trotting Moose

Bull Moose Walking

Moose Walking

Weight: 1000 lbs
Size: four times the size of a big white-tailed deer.
Shoulder Height: 6 ft.
Moose are active at dusk and dawn.

MOOSE MEETS CAR

At night a car's headlights shine through the legs of a moose which are hard to see because their legs are the same color as the background - especially at night. The belly of a moose fits nicely over the hood of a car and upon impact the belly will slide along the hood into the windshield possibly injuring the occupants of the front set. Do not attempt to make a moose standing on a highway move as it might attack your car.

AVOIDING MOOSE ATTACKS

- Aggressive when approached by humans. They are large and very powerful and can "plow" through the underbrush.
- Moose cows are very aggressive, in late spring and early summer, while protecting their calves. Never walk between a cow moose and its calf.
- During the fall breeding season the bulls are very aggressive. You might be seen as being the competition.
- Very agitated when dogs bark at them. Moose see dogs as being wolves who are their mortal enemies. Never hike or camp with a dog in moose country.
- If you encounter a moose on a path give it a lot of room - back off and change direction.

MOOSE IN URBAN AREAS

- If you see a moose resting in the shade or munching on some fruit - do not approach - as it might get stressed and get aggressive.
- Do not feed the moose as it will relate humans to food and get aggressive if not offered food in its next encounter with a human.
- If you see a moose in the yard take children and dogs inside and keep them quiet. Do not try to chase the moose away nor block its escape route. If you have large picture windows draw the curtains so that it does not look like an escape route. The moose might get aggressive if it sees a reflection of itself.

HOW MOOSE ATTACKS

Moose when threatened might choose to fight. Adult bulls can use their lethal rack of antlers in an attack. Moose usually attack with their front feet kicking forward, knocking over the victim, and then stomping and kicking.

MOOSE ATTACK SEQUENCE

- Can try to warn you with a bluff charge.
- Slowly walking towards you - this is dangerous - you are in its space and you are the intruder.
- If ears lay back, stomping the ground, hair rising on its shoulder hump, or swinging its head you know its time to leave. If it licks its lips your departure is overdue.
- As a moose is not a predator like a cougar or bear - you can run from a moose. It might chase you but usually not too far.
- Look for an obstacle to hide behind or climb a tree. If hiding behind a tree make sure it is heavy enough to resist a moose's attack.
- If knocked over curl up in a fetal position protecting your head - do not move.
- The moose might have made a run at you and continued running or it might stop to stomp and kick - do not move - show no aggression.
- Only get up when you are sure the moose has left - it may renew its attack!

INSECTS & ARTHROPODS

Insects are similar to other arthropods by:
- Having jointed legs
- Having a hard exoskeleton (the outside hard skin acts as a skeleton)

Insects differ from other arthropods because:
- They have six legs
- They usually have wings

THREE PARTS OF INSECTS

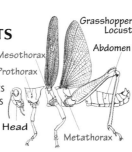

Grasshopper Locust

Mesothorax, Prothorax, Abdomen, Head, Metathorax

Head: has the mouth, antennae, & eyes. The mouth can either bite (fire ant), chew (termite), or suck liquids (as butterflies or mosquitoes). The antennae can be sensors to physical objects (as for feeling items), respond to chemical odors (food or sexual stimulus).

Thorax: is in three parts - *prothorax, mesothorax, metathorax* (see the grasshopper exploded view). These parts have three pairs of jointed legs attached and sometimes have wings attached. The legs are all jointed but can serve different functions on different insects - they can jump, be diggers (mole cricket), catch prey (praying mantis), swim (backswimmer), make music (crickets). If an insect has wings it might - fly, glide after a jump, glide from a higher elevation (insect is too heavy or mis-shaped to start flying from the ground surface), be a protective shell, reflect the sun, store air bubbles for diving in the water (aquatic bugs).

Abdomen: consists of hard segments (11) that can usually flex like an accordion. There might be outgrowths on the end of the abdomen and even a stinging mechanism.

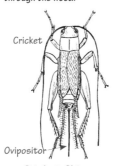

Ichneumon Wasp

Ovipositor

This long needle-like tail is used by the female to drill into wood to deposit an egg on a beetle grub inside a tree trunk. It senses the presence of the grub by the vibrations from the grub while it is gnawing through the wood.

Cricket

Ovipositor

Cricket Chirp
Male crickets chirp by running the top of one wing along the teeth at the bottom of the other wing. This is done while the cricket holds the wings up and open, so that the wing membranes acts as an acoustical sail.

INSECTS & INSECT-BORNE DISEASES

Common insects such as flies, mosquitoes, lice, ticks, and mites carry many of our most serious diseases such as typhoid fever, dysentery, malaria, brain fever, and yellow fever. Every possible means should be used to avoid the contamination of food by flies and bites of mosquitoes and other insects. If you have no screening, bed net, insecticides, or repellents it is difficult to keep insects away.

- Protect food and beverages from flies and other vermin.
- Cover the body to reduce exposure to mosquitoes, especially after dark.
- When available, take a suppressive drug to prevent malaria.
- Keep free of lice. • Promptly remove ticks.

CRICKETS

Snowy Tree Cricket
The female snowy tree cricket inserts her eggs into a raspberry cane.

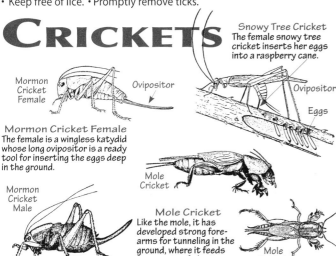

Mormon Cricket Female

Ovipositor

Ovipositor

Eggs

Mormon Cricket Female
The female is a wingless katydid whose long ovipositor is a ready tool for inserting the eggs deep in the ground.

Mole Cricket

Mormon Cricket Male

Mole Cricket
Like the mole, it has developed strong forearms for tunneling in the ground, where it feeds upon roots of plants.

Mole Cricket

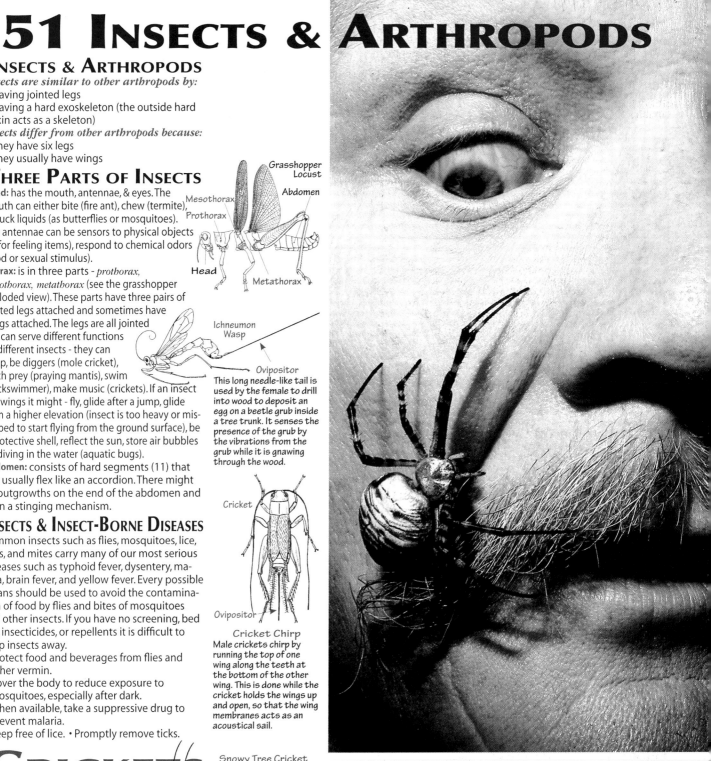

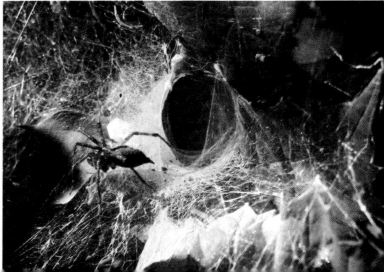

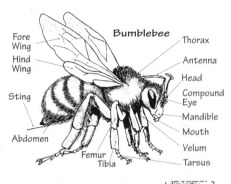

Fore Wing
Hind Wing
Sting
Abdomen
Bumblebee
Thorax
Antenna
Head
Compound Eye
Mandible
Mouth
Velum
Tarsus
Femur
Tibia

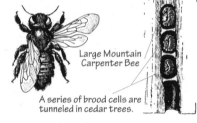

Large Mountain Carpenter Bee

A series of brood cells are tunneled in cedar trees.

Ichneumon Wasp

Ovipositor
See page 559

Wasp

Hornet

Honey Bee Worker on a honey comb. the pollen can be seen on its hind feet.

Baldface Hornet nest in a spruce tree. The nest is paper-like and can be up to three feet tall with entrance at the bottom. The nest consists of a number of horizontal layers, one below the other completely enclosed by a paper-like envelope as a covering.

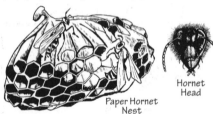

Paper Hornet Nest

Hornet Head

KILLER BEES

The threat of killer bees ("African bees") has been greatly exaggerated, but they have arrived in the United States. African bees are more aggressive than the European bees. The European honey bee is less aggressive as they live in well protected hollow trees and other cavities. They do not have to protect their nests so they do not have to be aggressive and sting as frequently to protect their home.

African bees come from arid regions, making nests in the open on tree branches and in holes in the ground; their nests are vulnerable to attack and they have to fight any potential predator. For this reason they are easily provoked and highly defensive. The alarm scent from one worker might trigger the defensive action of hundreds or thousands of fellow bees. African bees respond more quickly, stay agitated longer, and chase enemies further than European bees. The sting of a single African bee is no more dangerous than that of other honey bees but the massive attack of hundreds of bees and hundreds of stings can prove fatal. African honey bees do not store large amounts of honey and they use more cells to raise their young. This causes the hive population to grow very rapidly and the bees swarm more frequently. Absconding is when all bees in a hive permanently leave due to some major disturbance. African honey bees have a tendency to abandon their nests. African honey bees escaped from a research area in Brazil in 1957 and reached the southern United States in 1990.

The African bees overwhelm European bees and even steal their honey. African drones mated with European bees and the following generations retained their aggressive characteristics. Referring to African bees as "Killer Bees" gives a false impression because they only sting to defend their hive or swarm. Stinging incidents involving many bees is not common.

IDENTIFICATION

African bees look like other honey bees but they are slightly smaller, weigh less, and have shorter stingers and forewings. They are more nervous in their hives and fly farther and in a more zigzag pattern than European bees.

Precautions

- People can coexist with the African honey bee by learning about the bee's behavior and being alert to their presence.
- The main danger is in encountering a wild colony that might be swarming.
- Watch for potential nesting areas: stone walls, underground holes, bird houses, discarded tires, empty flower pots, etc.
- If under attack, leave as quickly as possible (release any attached animals). Enter a car or building. If no shelter is available run behind bushes, trees, a fence or other obstacle that blocks the bees' line of vision.
- If you have numerous stings see a doctor as soon as possible, especially if you feel dizzy and have difficulty breathing.

Honey Bee

BEE & WASP CHARACTERISTICS

	Bee	Wasp (includes hornets)
Coat	furry	little or no hair
Legs	not visible while flying	two hind legs visible while flying
Waist	wider and thorax hairy	usually slender to thin
Pollen baskets	yes	none
Behavior	gentle	usually aggressive
Food	nectar from flowers	varies from other insects, sugary drinks, human food, meat
Sting	kills the bee as it continues to pump and the stinger is barbed and stays embedded	smooth stinger retracts and can sting again
Living structure	large colonies in wax based honeycomb (honey bee) and Bumblebee in small cavities in the soil	small (yellow jacket, paper wasp) or large paper nests (hornet, bald-faced hornet hung in protected areas
Sting pain perception:	wasp is considered as having a more pain full sting	

Worker feeding Yellowjacket Hornet queen

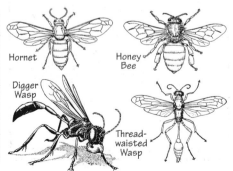

Hornet

Honey Bee

Digger Wasp

Thread-waisted Wasp

YELLOW JACKET STING PREVENTION

This also applies to all wasps/hornets. Bees are not as aggressive as wasps/bornets and only sting once as the barbed stinger gets embedded in the victims skin.

WASPS IN AREA OR LANDING ON YOU

- Never swing or strike at it or run away since quick movements often provoke attack and painful stings.
- When a wasp is near you, slowly raise your hands to protect your face remain calm and stationary for a while and then move away very slowly. Wasps and bees can fly about six to seven miles per hour so you cannot outrun them.
- Avoid stepping on any wasp nest that might be in the ground near you.
- Never crush a wasp or bee near you as this will release a venom which could incite nearby yellowjackets into a frenzied attack.
- Wasps and bees rarely sting in a enclosed environment as a house or car. They just look for an open window to escape - so open the windows and they will leave.
- When mowing the lawn or making much noise might infuriate any wasps in the area and lead to an attack.
- If eating outdoors keep the food well covered as the odor can attract yellowjackets. See adjacent "Wasp Diversion".
- If outdoors do not wear or use strongly scented perfume or perfumed products e.g. hair spray, suntan lotion, aftershave lotions, heavy-scented soaps, shampoos.
- Avoid shiny and colorful objects and clothing.
- If there are hypersensitive persons in your hiking group make sure that they are always part of the group and do not wander off. If stung they will need prompt attention as they might have a shock-like or fainting reaction to a sting.

After Being Stung
- Use a treatment as per the instructions of an Insect Sting Kit.
- Immediately apply a poultice of a meat tenderizer to the wound to reduce the pain if wound is not too deep.
- Sensative people should get medical attention as soon as possible.

Grasshopper

If camping or eating outdoors keep the food well covered as the odor can attract yellowjackets. As a protective measure you can lure them by hanging a rotting fish upwind from the site - this will attract the wasps downwind. By placing water in a container below the fish any wasps that fly too close to the reflecting surface will drown.

Rotting Fish

Water

WASP DIVERSION

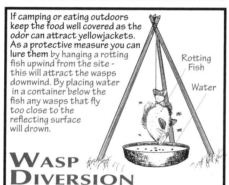

Grasshopper laying eggs in the ground. A grasshopper will lay two to four hundred eggs in a dozen or more pods.

Pods of Eggs

STINGING APPARATUS OF WASP

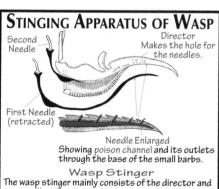

Second Needle

Director Makes the hole for the needles.

First Needle (retracted)

Needle Enlarged
Showing poison channel and its outlets through the base of the small barbs.

Wasp Stinger
The wasp stinger mainly consists of the director and two needles. The director pierces the skin and then the delicate needles with barbs slide into the hole to inject the poison. The poison comes from a poison sac.

Wasps (including hornets) have a lance-like stinger without barbs (small) and can sting repeatedly whereas honey bees have a barbed stinger, that gets embedded in the victim, and thus sting only once.

Yellowjacket Wasp

GRASSHOPPER : LOCUST

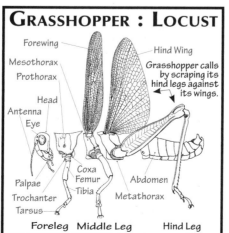

Forewing
Mesothorax
Prothorax
Head
Antenna
Eye
Palpae
Trochanter
Tarsus

Coxa
Femur
Tibia

Hind Wing

Grasshopper calls by scraping its hind legs against its wings.

Abdomen
Metathorax

Foreleg   Middle Leg   Hind Leg

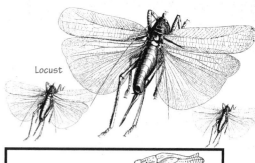

Locust

LOCUST MOLTING

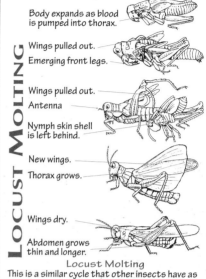

Body expands as blood is pumped into thorax.

Wings pulled out.
Emerging front legs.

Wings pulled out.
Antenna

Nymph skin shell is left behind.

New wings.
Thorax grows.

Wings dry.

Abdomen grows thin and longer.

Locust Molting
This is a similar cycle that other insects have as their skeleton is the outside shell. To grow larger they have to shed the outside shell.

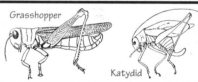

Grasshopper

Katydid

Lesser Locust Growth Cycle

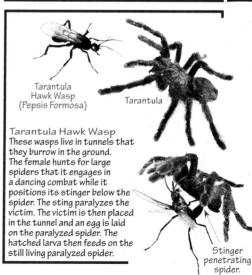

Tarantula Hawk Wasp (Pepsis Formosa)

Tarantula

Tarantula Hawk Wasp
These wasps live in tunnels that they burrow in the ground. The female hunts for large spiders that it engages in a dancing combat while it positions its stinger below the spider. The sting paralyzes the victim. The victim is then placed in the tunnel and an egg is laid on the paralyzed spider. The hatched larva then feeds on the still living paralyzed spider.

Stinger penetrating spider.

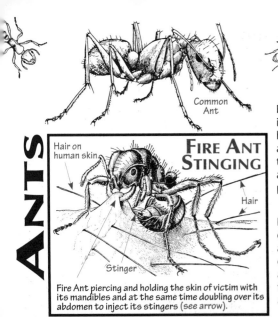

Common Ant

ANTS

FIRE ANT STINGING

Fire Ant piercing and holding the skin of victim with its mandibles and at the same time doubling over its abdomen to inject its stingers (see arrow).

Hair on human skin

Hair

Stinger

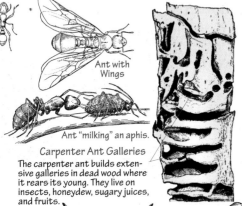

Ant eggs underneath a sun heated rock. During hot summer days worker ants bring ant eggs from the nest to warm beneath large sun heated rocks.

Ant with Wings

Ant "milking" an aphis.

Carpenter Ant Galleries
The carpenter ant builds extensive galleries in dead wood where it rears its young. They live on insects, honeydew, sugary juices, and fruits.

FIRE ANTS
National Park Service & additional information.

VENOM STING

Fire ants are so called because their venom, injected by a stinger like a wasp's, creates a burning sensation. They are also active and aggressive, swarming over anyone or anything that disturbs their nest. An encounter with a fire ant nest can leave a lasting memory of burning pain, followed by tiny, itching pustules.

RECREATIONAL DANGERS

Because of this, and occasional stories of animals or people killed by multiple stings, people fear fire ants. In some areas infested with certain species of fire ants, playgrounds, parks, and picnic areas lie abandoned, unused because of the presence of fire ants. It is often difficult to put up or take down a tent without being stung by angry fire ants.

FIRE ANT STINGS

In infested areas, fire ant stings occur more frequently than bee, wasp, hornet, and yellowjacket stings. Stepping on a mound is almost unavoidable when walking in heavily infested areas. Furthermore, many mounds are not easily seen, with many lateral tunnels extending several feet away from the mound just beneath the soil surface. Ants defend these tunnels as part of their mound. A person who stands on a mound or one of its tunnels, or who leans against a fence post included in the defended area, can have hundreds of ants rush out to attack. Typically, the ants can be swarming on a person for 10 or more seconds before they grab the skin with their mandibles, double over their abdomens, and inject their stingers.

Multiple stings are common, not only because hundreds of ants may have attacked, but because individual ants can administer several stings. Each sting usually results in the formation of a pustule within 6 to 24 hours. The majority of stings are uncomplicated, but secondary infections may occur if the pustule is broken, and scars may last for several months. Severe infections requiring skin grafting or amputation have been known to occur.

Some people experience a generalized allergic reaction to a fire ant sting. The reaction can include hives, swelling, nausea, vomiting, and shock. People exhibiting these symptoms after being stung by fire ants should get medical attention immediately. Death can occur in hypersensitive people. Individuals who are allergic to fire ant toxins may require desensitization therapy.

IDENTIFICATION

Red Imported Fire Ant (*Solenopsis invicta*): Introduced from South America, this species is the number one fire ant pest wherever it occurs. It builds mounds that are, on average, 10"-24" in diameter and 18" high. It is associated with disturbed habitats, mostly created by humans, and is abundant in old fields, pastures, lawns, roadsides and many other open sunny areas. In areas where grass is periodically cut, mounds are flush with the ground and are hard to see. This species is rarely found in mature forests and other areas with heavy shade, unless part of the area has been disturbed by fire or storms. *It is now found throughout most of the southeastern United States and west into Texas.*

Black Imported Fire Ant (*Solenopsis richteri*): It is very similar to the red imported fire ant. It is currently limited to a small area of northern Mississippi and Alabama.

Southern Fire Ant (*Solenopsis xyloni*): It is a native species that occurs from North Carolina south to northern Florida, along the Gulf Coast and west to California. Colonies may be observed as mounds or more commonly may be constructed under the cover of stones, boards, and other objects or at the base of plants. These ants also nest in wood or the masonry of houses, especially around heat sources such as fireplaces. Nests often consist of loose soil with many craters scattered over 2 to 4 square feet. In dry areas nests may be along streams, arroyos, and other shaded locations where soil moisture is high.

Fire Ant (*Solenopsis geminata*): It is a native species sometimes called the tropical fire ant. *This ant ranges from South Carolina to Florida and west to Texas.* Very similar to the southern fire ant, it usually nests in mounds constructed around clumps of vegetation, but may also nest under objects or in rotting wood.

MONITORING FOR FIRE ANTS

The first step is to identify the species of fire ants in the area. Population monitoring for fire ant control generally consists of determining the number of active mounds in a particular unit area. Any mound where at least three ants are observed after mound disturbance should be considered active. Heavily infested fields can contain over 100 active mounds per acre.

RED WOOD-ANT NEST
Debris of heaped-up fir needles and twigs.

Ant Nurseries (larva)

Main Galleries

CARPENTER ANTS

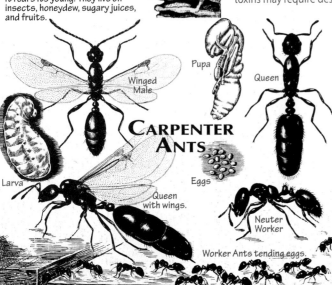

Winged Male

Pupa

Queen

Larva

Eggs

Queen with wings.

Neuter Worker

Worker Ants tending eggs.

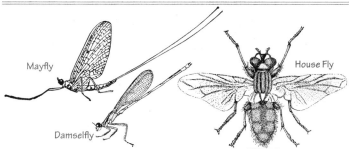

Mayfly

Damselfly

House Fly

DIFFERENCE BETWEEN BUTTERFLIES & MOTHS

BUTTERFLY

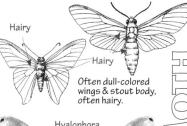

Clubbed Antennae

Often very colorful wings & Slender smooth body

Smooth

MOTH

Antennas are feather-like or threadlike.

Hairy

Hairy

Often dull-colored wings & stout body, often hairy.

LICE, FLEAS & MITES

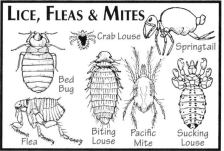

Crab Louse

Springtail

Bed Bug

Flea

Biting Louse

Pacific Mite

Sucking Louse

Black Fly

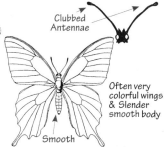
When butterflies rest their wings are held upright. Moths flatten their wings when resting.

Hyalophora Cecropia Moth

Hairy

CADDISFLY
MAYFLY

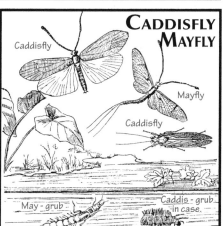

Caddisfly

Mayfly

Caddisfly

May - grub

Caddis - grub in case.

Sandfly

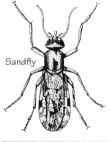

Monarch Butterfly Caterpillar changing into a pupa (chrysalis).

A — Button of Silk made by caterpillar.
A Larva hanging from a leaf.

B — Shedded Skin
B The covering of a larva is shed and the formed pupa is revealed.

C — Cremaster
C The cremaster feeling about for the button of silk on the surface above.

D — Button of Silk
D Chrysalis totally formed.

The chrysalis is covered with a silky cocoon.

Moths flatten their wings when resting.

COCKROACH

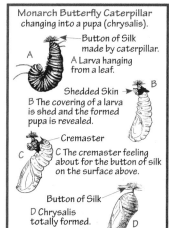

Eye

Antenna

Prothorax

Front Wing

Cerci

Styles
Male Cockroach

German Cockroach

LIFE OF A GNAT

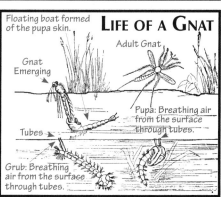

Floating boat formed of the pupa skin.

Adult Gnat

Gnat Emerging

Pupa: Breathing air from the surface through tubes.

Tubes

Grub: Breathing air from the surface through tubes.

Butterfield Caterpillar

Girdle of silk

Bare Butterfly Chrysalis Swallowtail Butterfly with the chrysalis held by a button and a girdle of silk.

Button

Six "true" feet. These actually act as feet.

Cushion feet at middle of the body.

Two cushion feet at tail. it will hang from these feet when it forms a pupa.

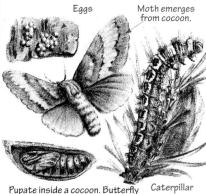

Eggs

Moth emerges from cocoon.

Pupate inside a cocoon. Butterfly does not have a cocoon but a hard surfaced chrysalis.

Caterpillar

LIFE OF DRAGONFLY

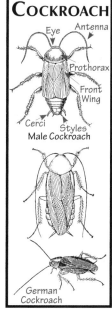

Mature Dragonfly

Dragonfly creeping out of its grub skin.

Crumpled Wings

Old legs gripping stem.

Old Exoskeleton

Grub

Dragonfly wriggling out of old body. Its body is still soft - but it will soon dry and form a firm exoskeleton (the outside skeleton of an insect as it has no internal skeleton). Blood will pump into crumpled wings to give them a rigid form.

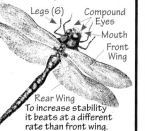

Legs (6)

Compound Eyes

Mouth

Front Wing

Rear Wing
To increase stability it beats at a different rate than front wing.

Tent Caterpillar Moth (larvae)
As a caterpillar they live in colonies in a silky tent like structure. The caterpillars leave silk trails when they move about - in this way a colony builds the tent like structure and the individual caterpillars spin a silk trail when they spread over a branch.

INSECT IDENTIFIER

Bark Beetle

Engelmann Spruce Beetle

Ground Beetle

Ground Beetle

Bean Leaf Beetle

Colorado Potato Beetle

Japanese Beetle

Tortoise Beetle

Larder Beetle

May Beetle

Strawberry Leaf Beetle

Lacebug

Pales Weevil

Striped Blister Beetle

Sweet Potato Weevil

Squash Bug

White-fringe Beetle

Weevil

Two Spotted Ladybug

Chinch Bug

Western Hemlock Strainer
It is a very small beetle that constructs individual cells for rearing its young in timber trees.

Western Hemlock Strainer

Rove Beetle

Spotted Cucumber Beetle

Buffalo Treehopper

Thrips

Aphid

Stinkbug

Harlequin Bug

Say's Stinkbug

Junebug + Larva

Vegetable Weevil

Sawfly

Lacewing

Termite

Termite

Red Chafer

Horsefly

Hornfly

Tse Tse Fly

Earwig

Silverfish

Leafhopper

Longhorne Beetle

Praying Mantis

Praying Mantis

Female

Male

Buffalo Gnat

Stonefly

Springtail

Dobsonfly

Cicada

Cicada Flying

Oriental Fruit Fly

Horse Fly

Chalcidfly

Psocid

Blowfly

Blowfly

Mediterranean Fruit Fly

Drone Fly
It mimics the honey bee in color, size, and actions.

Tomato Hornworm

Beyer's Scarab

Flesh Fly

Squash Vine Borer

Stablefly

Stripped Horse Fly

Darkling Beetles
These beetles are found in hot dry regions. They are active during the twilight and night hours and feed on fungi and dry or decomposing organic matter - including body parts.

Fleshfly

Pomacefly

Crane Fly

Firefly

564

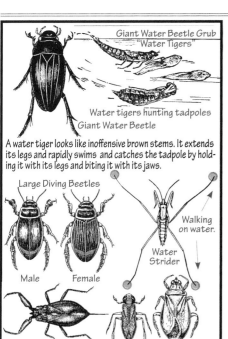

Giant Water Beetle Grub "Water Tigers"

Water tigers hunting tadpoles

Giant Water Beetle

A water tiger looks like inoffensive brown stems. It extends its legs and rapidly swims and catches the tadpole by holding it with its legs and biting it with its jaws.

Large Diving Beetles

Walking on water.

Male   Female

Water Strider

Giant Water Bug   Water Boatman   Toe Biter

DIVING BEETLES & WATER BUGS

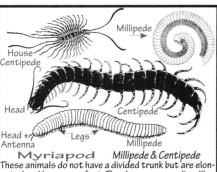

Millipede

House Centipede

Head

Centipede

Head + Antenna   Legs   Millipede

Myriapod   Millipede & Centipede

These animals do not have a divided trunk but are elongated and have many feet. They have an accordion-like body structure with legs attached to each hardened segment. Millipedes have two pairs of legs attached to each segment and centipedes only have one pair at each segment. The centipedes have a pair of poison claws that can inflict a nasty bite that can cause vomiting and fever in humans.

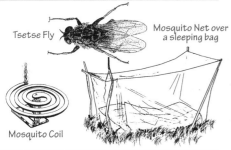

Tsetse Fly

Mosquito Net over a sleeping bag

Mosquito Coil

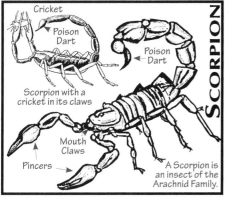

Cricket

Poison Dart

Poison Dart

Scorpion with a cricket in its claws

Mouth Claws

Pincers

A Scorpion is an insect of the Arachnid Family.

SCORPION

ARACHNID
Spiders, Scorpions, Ticks, Mites
Differ from insects because...

- The bodies of arachnid are divided into *two* parts not *three* parts as with insects.
- Have no antennae
- Have 8 legs and not 6 as insects.

Head + Thorax: Called the *cephalothorax* are fused together, no antennae, have a pair of jaw-like appendages in front of the mouth. The four pairs of jointed legs are attached to the cephalothorax which are used for walking. There are another two pairs of appendages attached to the cephalothorax - as mentioned above, the jaw-like appendages used for feeding and a second pair of pedipalps (small feet or claws (scorpion)) - used for catching prey, in mating.

Abdomen: the abdomen might be one piece (spider) or segmented and have a tail-like extension (scorpion).

Garden Spider

Garden Spider Web

Foot of Spider

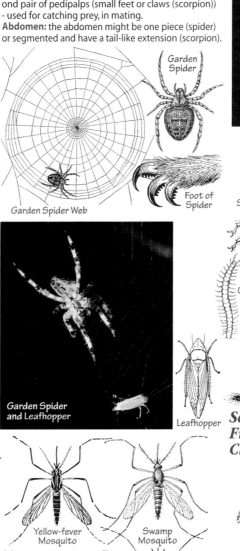

Garden Spider and Leafhopper

Leafhopper

Yellow-fever Mosquito

Swamp Mosquito

Salt-marsh Mosquito

Common Malaria Mosquito

Southern House Mosquito

Common Western Mosquito

Anopheles Mosquito

Culex Mosquito

INSECT REPELLENT

STING-EZE

Crab Spider catching bee.

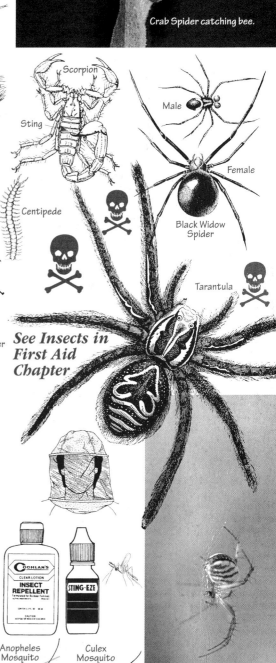

Scorpion

Sting

Centipede

Male

Female

Black Widow Spider

Tarantula

See Insects in First Aid Chapter

Barn Spider

52 Edible Plants

Plants were an important ingredient of the Indian diet. They used over 250 species of wild fruit to round off their diet. Indians migrated and established summer settlements around the different harvesting seasons of plants and berries. This chapter gives you information on the location and traditional use of a selection of edible North American plants. Take every opportunity to see the plants in their natural habitat. Eating plants provides you with energy and calorie-giving carbohydrates.

All parts of a plant are not necessarily edible.

PARTS OF PLANT
Roots & Underground Parts
Tubers: They are found below the ground and are cooked or roasted. Example is the potato.

Roots & Rootstock: Roots are rich in starch, are usually several feet long, and are not swollen like tubers. Rootstock are underground stems which can be several inches thick, short, and pointed. Examples are bulrush roots and stems, water plantain, and cattail.

Bulbs: All bulbs are high in starch content and, with the exception of the wild onion, are more palatable if they are cooked. Examples are the wild onion, and wild tulip.

Shoots & Stems
Edible shoots grow very similarly to asparagus. Most are better when parboiled for 10 minutes, the water drained off, and reboiled until tender. Example is bamboo and ferns.

Nuts
Nuts are among the most nutritious of all plant foods and contain valuable protein. Examples are walnut, hazelnut, chestnut, and acorn.

Leaves
Leaves can be eaten raw or cooked. Do not cook them too long as the vitamins will be destroyed. Leaves can also be dried to make tea. Examples are water lettuce, dock, sorrel, chicory, arctic willow, and rhubarb.

Seeds & Grain
The seeds of all cereals and most grasses are rich in oils and plant protein. Grains can be stored and ground into flour. Examples are rice, corn, and sunflowers.

Fruit
There are many edible fruits from berries, grapes, figs, to apples.

Bark
The inner bark, the layer next to the wood, can be eaten raw, cooked or dried and ground into a flour.

TABLE OF MEDICINAL PLANTS & USAGE

Plant	Action	Indication
Alfalfa	Source of vit. A,C,E,K and minerals as calcium, potassium, phosphorus and iron	To prevent a a lack of vitamins A,C,E,K.
Artichoke	Helps bile evacuation, diuretic	Liver disorders
Balm	Antispasmodic, sedative	Depressive states
Bearberry	Diuretic	Cystitis
Black Radish	Helps bile evacuation	Galibladder disorder
Boldo	Liver stimulant	Liver pains
Burdock	Diuretic	Skin eruptions, rheumatism
Cascara Sagrada	Mild laxative	Constipation
Chamomile	Sedative	Acidity, heartburns
Dandelion	Helps bile evacuation, diuretic	Constipation, muscular rheumatism
Devil's Claw	Anti-inflammatory	Arthritis, rheumatism
Fennel	Carminative	Flatulence
Flowering Oat	Antidepressant	Melancholy, depression
Ginseng	Reputed as being an aphrodisiac	Neuralgia
Hop	Sedative	Insomnia
Lindenbark	Diuretic	Digestive disorders
Mountain Grape	Helps bile evacuation	Helps bile secretion
Nettle	Anti-hemorrhagic, known to have hypo-glycemic properties	Skin eruptions, infantile eczema
Passion Herb	Sedative, antispasmodic	Insomnia, hysteria
Patience	Mild laxative	Constipation, chronic skin disease
Primrose	Mild diuretic, sedative	Insomnia, hysteria
Sage	Astringent, antiseptic	Pharyngitis, gingivitis
Sarsaparilla	Anti-rheumatism	Skin problems, rheumatism
Senna	Laxative	Constipation
Walnut Tree Bark	Laxative	Constipation
Willow	Anti-inflammatory, antiseptic	Flu and respiratory catarrh
Valerian	Sedative	Insomnia, migraine

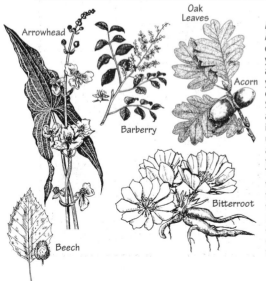

Acorn *(Querus)* Found: US & Southern Canada. Acorns (from oak trees) are one of the major foods of the forest and all are edible. Some are bitter and you can remove the bitterness by boiling the shelled acorns in water until the water become yellow. (This yellow liquid can be further boiled to increase its concentration, to use it to dye cotton, wool or leather.) Slowly dry the acorns in a cast iron frying pan or in a stove. Dried acorns can be eaten whole or ground into a flour and baked. Roast and grind acorns and use them as a coffee substitute. If the ground acorns are mixed with cocoa and sugar it makes a beverage that will stop diarrhea and act as a general tonic. To remove the bitterness from acorns the Indians would bury them in a muddy swamp and retrieve them the following year. Crushed fresh oak leaves will promote the healing of wounds.

Bitterroot *(Lewisia)* Found: In valleys of the mountainous areas of temperate North America. Roots: collected during the spring. Remove the outer rind and boil it in water. The dried roots can be used as filler in soups.

Arrowhead *(Sagittaria)* Found: US, Mexico & Southern Canada. Edible tubers at end of the roots. Can eat them raw but cooking removes their bitterness. They are picked after midsummer. They are found at the edge of slow flowing or still water. They can be picked by scraping a stick in the water, below the plants and the tubers will float to the surface.

Barberry *(Berberis Vulgaris)* Found: Temperate North America. Berries: can be used to make a drink, jelly or jam. All parts of plant, except the berries, are poisonous. Roots and wood: boiled to make a dye for wool, leather, cotton.

Beech *(Fagus)* Found: in humid cool areas, southern, central and eastern states up to southern eastern Canada. Nuts: eaten raw are sweet and very nutritious. Can be roasted and ground into substitute coffee. Inner Bark: can be dried and ground to make flour for emergency bread. Sawdust of wood: can be boiled in water, dried, and added to flour to make bread.

52 EDIBLE PLANTS

Birch *(Betula Pendula)* Found: Most of Temperate North America. Bark: used as paper to make canoes, to cover shelter, water basins, torches etc. Inner bark: eaten raw, cut into strips, cooked and eaten as noodles or spaghetti. Spring sap: boiled as maple syrup. Young leaves: They can be dried and used to make a tea that is used for urinary infections and for kidney stones. The leaves can be used for invigorating baths.

Black Walnut *(Juglans-Nigre)* Found: Eastern US. Nuts: are sweet and very nutritious in protein, fatty oil, carbohydrates, phosphorus, potassium, vitamin A, thiamin, riboflavin, niacin. The outer green shell is used for medicinal purposes. Husks of walnuts: can be boiled to make an indelible brown dye.

Blackberry See Raspberry

Blueberry *(Vaccinium, Gaylussacia)* Found: All over the US & Canada (including the Arctic) Berries: are edible (They can be confused with huckleberries -which are also edible). They can be cooked, frozen or dried.

Buffalo Berry *(Shepherdia)* Found: US (except in South West) & Canada (including Arctic) Berry: eaten raw and cooked but is bitter if picked before the first frost.

Bunchberry *(Cornus)* Found: Area north of California and north of New Jersey to Alaska and the Arctic islands. Berries: eaten raw or cooked. They are rather bland in taste and should be added to other fruit.

Burdock *(Artium)* Found: US & Southern Canada. Leaf stems: peel and cook until tender. The burdock stems can be used to make excellent rope (See Rope Chapter). The roots of wintering plants are collected before flowering for medicinal purposes.

Butternut *(Juglans)* Found: Eastern United States and Canada Nuts: very nutritious and contain protein, fat, carbohydrates and iron. Sap: can be collected in spring and boiled like maple syrup.

Cattail *(Typha)* Found: US & Southern Canada. Roots: Peeled roots can be eaten raw or cooked. They are an excellent survival food as they can be extracted from the ground if not too frozen. Roots can be dried and ground into flour. Young stems: can be peeled and eaten raw (called Cossack asparagus). Heads: when green can be cooked and eaten as corn. When they are full of pollen they can be scraped and used as a flour substitute. When the heads are ripe and have become fluffy this fluff can be used as an insulation against the cold (under your jacket, as duvet covers, or for pillows).

Chia-Sage *(Salvia)* Found: South Western United States. Seeds: can be ground into flour. Can be eaten dry or drink mixture of seeds and water. Seeds are very nutritious.

Chicory *(Chichorium Intybus)* Found: West Coast. Roots: roasted as a coffee substitute (this coffee was used in Europe during the Second World War). Leaves: can be used for salads. They contain calcium, phosphorus, iron, potassium, vitamins A and C. In herbal medicine the dried roots are used in tea form as a tonic, mild diuretic, and laxative.

Chokecherry *(Prunus)* Found: North America. Berries: eaten raw, cooked or used for wines. Do not eat pits or leaves as they are poisonous.

Chufa *(Cyperus, Earth Almonds)* Found: North America. Tubers: can be eaten raw. Dried and ground can be used as flour. Roasted can be ground and used as a coffee substitute.

Clover *(Trifolium Pratense)* Found: Temperate North America. Leaves: can be eaten raw as salads or steamed as spinach. Roots: can be eaten with salad dressing. Flowers: can be used as a moth repellent. Can be eaten raw in a salad. Dried seed-filled flowers can be used to make bread. An infusion from the flowers is used to treat bronchitis, coughs, hoarseness, diarrhea, and chronic skin conditions. Externally they can be used as a bath preparation to treat rashes, burns, and sores.

Common Chickweed *(Stellaria Alsine)* Found: North America - moist areas. Leaves: for salad when young. When mature as a filler in stews. Can be cooked in the same way as spinach. Leaves as an anti-scorbutic.

Cowslip *(Caltha)* Found: Northern North America. Are edible when cooked to remove the poisonous glucoside. Do not use unless you are prepared to follow the required procedure and can distinguish Cowslip from some poisonous look alike - water hemlock and white hellebore.

Cranberry *(Vaccinium)* Found: Throughout North America, north of Virginia to Oregon. Berries: picked after the first frost. They should be stored in cloth sacks in a cool spot to reduce the risk of molding. They can be cooked with sugar to form a sauce to be used with meats, etc. When dried they can be crushed and then regenerated for cooking by adding water.

Daisy *(Bellis Perennis)* Found: North America. Young leaves: eaten raw as a salad. Flower: can be dried to make tea.

Dandelion *(Taraxacum Officinale)* Found: North America. Root: can be boiled in salt water and eaten. They can be roasted and ground to make a coffee substitute. An infusion made of dried roots will stimulate the appetite and aid digestion. Flowers and buds: eaten as a salad. They can be used to make an excellent wine. Stems and young leaves: eaten as a salad. Plants contain vitamin A, calcium, sodium, potassium, ascorbic acid, riboflavin.

Dill *(Anethum Graveolens)* Found: North America where it has escaped from gardens. Flowering stems: used in cooking or flavoring preserved food.

Dock *(Rumex)* Found: North America. Greens: can be eaten like spinach (raw, cooked, pureed). Tastes like lemon. Seeds: can be dried and ground into flour. The plant is very rich in vitamin C, vitamin A and potassium.

Birch · Black Walnut · Blackberry · ARCTIC WILLOW · Edible Shoots · Edible inner bark. · Bunchberry · Blueberry · Butternut · Common Clover · Burdock · Cattail · Chia-Sage · Butternut · Cattail Root · Buffalo Berry · Chokecherry · Dandelion · Chicory · Chickweed · Dock · Cowslip · Dill · Chufa · Cranberry · Daisy

BAMBOO · Edible Shoots · Hollow bamboo stem to make water vessel.

PRICKLY PEAR CACTUS · Yellow Flower · Edible Pulp · Edible Fruit

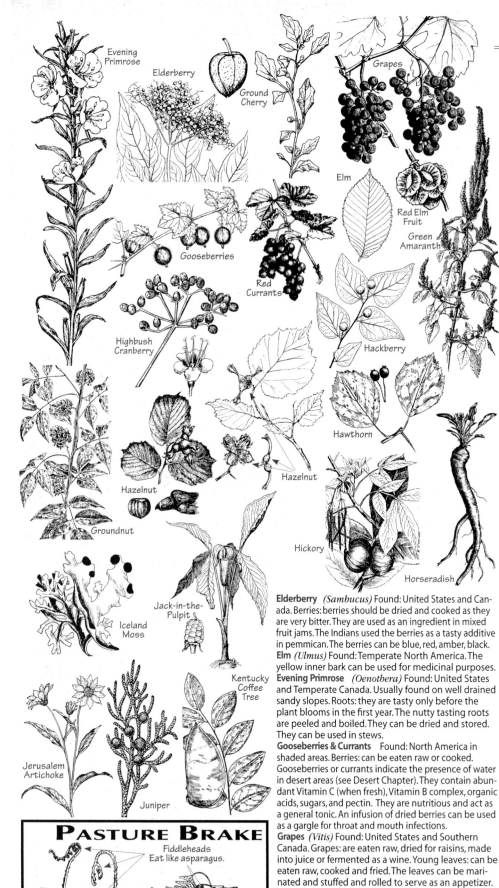

Southern Canada. Tubers on roots: look like potatoes and can be eaten raw or cooked. When cooked they should be eaten hot for the best flavor. The tubers are found just below the surface and a stick can be used to probe and remove them. Seeds: are in bean-like pods and can be cooked in salty water, as peas.

Hackberry *(Celtis)* Found: North America. Berries: can be eaten raw. Pits: the white kernels in the pits can be eaten and taste like dates. The dried pits can be ground and used as flavoring on wild game.

Hawthorn *(Crataegus Laevigata)* Found: United States and Southern Canada. Fruit: looks like tiny apples. Colors can be reddish, yellow, black or bluish. They can be eaten fresh or dried to be ground and mixed with pemmican. The fruit makes excellent jams and jellies. The fruit contains flavonoid glycosides, organic acids, tannins, an essential oil, Vitamin C, B complex, and pectin.

Hazelnut *(Corylus Avellana)* Found: North America. Nut: the nut can be eaten raw or mixed into salads, etc. Do not pack them in plastic bags as they have to breath during storage. They contain up to 60% fatty oils, plus proteins, sugars, and vitamins. Leaf: as a tea it has diuretic properties. Externally has been used in a bath to treat slow-healing wounds.

Hickory *(Carya)* Found: North America - different trees of this family live in different areas of North America. Hickory nuts (this includes the Pecan): these nuts are very nutritious and can be eaten raw or added to other dishes (pecan pie). Liquor: made by pounding the whole nut (including shells) until it is a powder. Add water. Let ferment until you have a thick milky colored oily liquid. Try it - you might like it!

Highbush Cranberry *(Viburnum)* Found: US & Canada. Berries: are a very important survival food in the winter as they remain frozen on the branches. These berries can be eaten off the branch or cooked and eaten as a compote. They are very rich in vitamin C.

Horseradish *(Armoracia)* Found: North America. Leaves: cooked, steamed or baked in salty water and served as spinach with oil or butter. Roots: grate the roots and add lemon to produce horseradish which you can use to season bland food (usually cooked meats). The roots are nutritious and contain calcium, phosphorous, iron, potassium and ascorbic acid. Horseradish roots can be cooked, the liquid cooled and drinking small quantities at a time will help bowel movements. Do not use large doses as it may irritate the digestive track.

Iceland Moss *(Cetraria Islandica)* Found: Northern US up to Alaska & Northern Canada. It is a lichen and not a moss. This is an edible lichen that is a multifaceted food. To prepare the Iceland Moss, it should be soaked in two changes of water and then dried. The soaking removes the bitter tasting organic acid. After drying crush the lichen into a powder. This powder can be stored in a dry dark location and used as required. When gently boiled and cooked it makes a nutritious jelly. It is used in folk medicine for its nutritive properties and for treating chest ailments. The Indians mixed the powder with water or milk and lightly heated it to produce a porridge-like substance. You can mix the powder with flour to bake bread. The powder can be added to soups or stews. An excellent and easily obtainable survival food

Jack-in-the-Pulpit *(Arisaema)* Found: Eastern North America from Florida to the Canadian Maritime provinces. Roots: it is very important to remove the acridness by drying the fresh roots. It might take a month to dry naturally. When dry the roots can be eaten like chips. If the roots are pulverized the powder can be added to wheat flour.

Jerusalem Artichoke *(Helianthus)* Found: US & Central Canada - grows in damp but not wet areas. Tubers: should be dug after first frost. By removing the skin you can eat the tubers raw. To cook them simmer them in water and remove the skin. Serve the same way as potatoes.

Juniper *(Juniperus)* Found: North America. Berries: can be eaten raw. Can be dried and ground to use as a tasty flour additive. They can be roasted and ground to make a coffee substitute. Do not eat too many berries as they are a diuretic and might irritate your kidneys. Twigs: use berry-less twigs to make juniper tea if you want a high concentration of vitamin.

Kentucky Coffee Tree *(Gymnocladus)* Found: United States, New York State to Oklahoma. Seeds: roasted and ground for a coffee substitute. Can be roasted and eaten like nuts.

Elderberry *(Sambucus)* Found: United States and Canada. Berries: berries should be dried and cooked as they are very bitter. They are used as an ingredient in mixed fruit jams. The Indians used the berries as a tasty additive in pemmican. The berries can be blue, red, amber, black.

Elm *(Ulmus)* Found: Temperate North America. The yellow inner bark can be used for medicinal purposes.

Evening Primrose *(Oenothera)* Found: United States and Temperate Canada. Usually found on well drained sandy slopes. Roots: they are tasty only before the plant blooms in the first year. The nutty tasting roots are peeled and boiled. They can be dried and stored. They can be used in stews.

Gooseberries & Currants Found: North America in shaded areas. Berries: can be eaten raw or cooked. Gooseberries or currants indicate the presence of water in desert areas (see Desert Chapter). They contain abundant Vitamin C (when fresh), Vitamin B complex, organic acids, sugars, and pectin. They are nutritious and act as a general tonic. An infusion of dried berries can be used as a gargle for throat and mouth infections.

Grapes *(Vitis)* Found: United States and Southern Canada. Grapes: are eaten raw, dried for raisins, made into juice or fermented as a wine. Young leaves: can be eaten raw, cooked and fried. The leaves can be marinated and stuffed and rolled to serve as an appetizer. Roots: are poisonous.

Green Amaranth *(Amaranthus)* Found: Temperate North America. Leaves: cooked as spinach. They contain vitamin A, vitamin C, vitamin B's, thiamin, riboflavin and niacin.

Ground Cherry *(Physalis)* Found: United States and Southern Canada. Fruit: can be eaten raw or cooked into jams. When picking leave them in their paper-like shells so that they can mature.

Groundnut *(Apios)* Found: Florida, New Mexico to

PASTURE BRAKE

Fiddleheads Eat like asparagus.

Edible Rootstalk

52 Edible Plants

Kinnikinic *(Arctostaphylos)* Found: Northern Region of North America. Berries: eaten raw or cooked. Young leaves: tea made to cleanse the kidneys. Leaves: cure and dry, cut up and use as a tobacco.

Knotweed *(Polygonum)* Found: US & Canada. Roots: are tubers that can be roasted or boiled. Young shoots: cooked in boiling salted water and seasoned as asparagus. Long shoots: peel and cook.

Labrador Tea *(Ledum)* Found: Northern US & Canada. Mainly in wet areas. Leaves: dry and use for tea.

Lamb's Quarter *(Chenopodium)* Found: North America on former farmlands. Leaves: can be eaten as a spinach. Seeds: dried and ground for flour or can be cooked in water as a porridge. Very nutritious containing calcium, vitamin A, thiamin, riboflavin, and niacin.

Lettuce Saxifrage *(Saxi Frage)* Found: North America. Young leaves: for salads. Leaves: cooked as a soup or in a frying pan, with bacon, as a substitute for eggs.

Live-Forever *(Sedum)* Found: North America. Young leaves: as a salad. Leaves: cooked in a stew. Tubers: can be added to salads.

Maple *(Acer)* Found: North America. Seeds: remove covering and can be eaten raw or cooked. Can be dried and stored. Young leaves: these are rich in sugar and can be eaten raw, in a salad, or cooked and added to stews. Sap: make syrup and sugar. Inner bark: eaten raw or cooked after being cut into spaghetti like strips. To make maple syrup. Cut a 'V' into a tree and drill a 2" deep hole and insert a spout. Hammer a nail above the 'V' and hang the pail from this nail.

May Apple *(Podophyllum)* Found: Quebec, Ontario to Florida. Fruit: eaten raw, as a juice or an uncooked jam. Roots, stems, leaves are poisonous.

Milkweed *(Asclepias)* Found: US & Southern Canada. Young sprouts: when up to 7" long are cooked and eaten as asparagus. Young leaves and young flower buds: can be boiled or steamed. To remove the bitter milky sap bring the plant to a boil in water twice and discard the water each time.

Mountain Ash *(Sorbus)* Found: US & Canada. The tree prefers wet soil. Berries: can be eaten fresh or dried and ground into flour. They can also be cooked as jams and marmalades. They can make an excellent bittersweet wine.

Mountain Sorrel *(Oxyria)* Found: In North America at higher elevations, in the southern areas, and at lower levels in the Arctic. Young leaves: in sandwiches. Leaves: chewed raw as a thirst quencher and can be used in salads or cooked as spinach. Older leaves: can be used to give body to soup. This plant is very rich in vitamin C.

Mulberry *(Morus)* Found: US & Southern Ontario. Berries: can be eaten raw or prepared for juice. Young twigs: can be eaten raw or cooked.

Mustard *(Brassica)* Found: US & Southern Canada. Seeds: as a spice for salads, seasoning, soups, stews. Can be used to prepare table mustard (crush seeds, add vinegar or white wine to make paste. You can also add paprika, pepper, garlic). Flowers: cook and eat as broccoli. They are very rich in vitamin A. Leaves: cook as spinach. Leaves contain large quantities of calcium, phosphorous, iron, potassium, vitamin A, thiamin, riboflavin, niacin, vitamin C.

Nettles *(Urtica)* Found: North America. Young leaves: can be boiled or steamed and eaten as a spinach. They are very rich in protein. In survival situations you can eat nettle leaves and they will be a cornerstone of your diet. You could even be imaginative and cook nettles with some exotic foods such as insects and slugs.

New Jersey Tea *(Ceanothus)* Found: Eastern North America Southern Canada to Florida. Young leaves: green or dried for tea. The leaves are caffeine free. The best tea is made from dry leaves.

Orach *(Atriplex)* Found: US & Southern Canada: grows along the coast in wet marshlands. Leaves: as a salad or steamed as a spinach. Seeds: eaten raw or dried and ground into a flour.

Papaw *(Asimina)* Found: US to Southern Ontario. Fruit: raw or cooked has a very special taste which one has to get used to. It is an excellent source of nutrients. The fruit can be gathered green and ripened in the sun.

Partridge Berry *(Mitchella)* Found: Eastern Atlantic Coast Berry: They stay on the plants all winter, so are an excellent survival food. Usually found in pine forests.

Indians gathering maple-sap in the Canadian woods.
Placing wood spigot
Sap from tree.
Boiling sap to make syrup.   Collecting sap in wood container.   Carrying sap.

Knotweed
Kinnikinic
Lamb's Quarter
Labrador Tea
New Jersey Tea
Mountain Sorrel
Live-Forever
Pin Cherry
Mountain Ash
Mustard
Papaw
Nettles
Milkweed Seeds
May Apple
Orach
Milkweed
Lettuce Saxifrage
Sugar Maple
Pine
Pasture Brake
Mulberry
Partridge Berry

Pasture Brake *(Pteridium)* Found: North America. Young ferns are called "fiddle heads": can be eaten raw or steamed. Do not eat too many raw because the thiaminate enzyme, which is destroyed by cooking, will eliminate vitamin B from your body.

Pin Cherry *(Prunus)* Found: Southern Canada to South Dakota. Cherry: eaten raw or cooked as a jelly. Eating raw cherries will quench your thirst and they are nutritional.

Pine *(Pinus)* Found: North America. Young needles: can be chewed and have nutritional value. Spring inner bark: can be eaten raw or cooked. To cook cut the bark lengthwise into strips and cook like spaghetti. Can be dried and ground into flour and used to bake bread.

PINE NUTS

Pine Cone
Shell
Pine Nut removed from shell.

569

53 POISONOUS PLANTS

Poison Ivy

Poison Oak

Poison Ivy

Poisonous Plant Information

The purpose of this chapter is to remind the reader that there are a number of poisonous plants in the wild. This is not a definitive guide on this topic. Also, due consideration and observation have to be made before any plant is consumed. The reader should read a specialized book on this topic and obtain expert botanical advice.

The effect of a poisonous plant is hard to quantify. Some plants require much contact or consumption for an effect; others require a small quantity to cause death. Individuals have different tolerances when coming into contact or consuming poisonous plants.

COMMON POISONOUS PLANTS
How Poisonous Plants Affect You
Poisonous plants can be divided into three classes - categorized by how they usually transmit their poison.

Contact: These are plants that are poisonous to the touch. They might cause skin irritation or dermatitis. Examples are such plants as poison ivy, poison oak, and poison sumac.

Ingestion: These are plants that are poisonous to the touch only when parts of them are eaten. Examples include poison hemlock, nightshade, Jimson weed, some mushrooms, and other plants.

Inhalation or Absorption: These enter the body by being inhaled or absorbed through the skin.

Some factors to consider...
- Some plants, such as poison ivy, are poisonous to some individuals while they are harmless to others.
- The strength of toxins and their effect upon an individual may vary as to the growing conditions and subspecies of the individual plant. Individuals might have different reactions and levels of resistance to the toxins in the plants.
- The amount of contact with the plant required to cause allergic reactions might vary per individual or type of plant.

Poison Ivy

PLANTS POISONOUS TO TOUCH
POISON IVY *(Rhus radicans)*
POISON OAK *(Rhus toxicodendron)*
Location: North America, Bermuda & Bahamas
Found: Nearly everywhere but mostly along fences and stone walls.

Description: Poison Ivy is a common plant. It is a vine that is especially abundant in rocky places, where it sometimes crowds out all other vegetation. In other places it twines about trees, fences, and the like, making a dense mass of vegetation through which one who is susceptible to the poison of the plant cannot pass with safety. The flowers are rather inconspicuous and occur in loose clusters. The fruits are whitish or cream-colored, and are hard and do not have a hairy surface. The leaves are composed of three rather broad leaflets, the two lateral leaflets being smaller than the terminal one. The oil the poison ivy plant often causes an irritation of the skin.
- Poison Oak is usually a shrub but can climb trees. Leaves are lobed and resemble oak leaves. Fruit is hairy.
- Poison Ivy & Poison Oak: leaves alternate, composed of three leaflets borne on a long stem. Leaves are dark, waxy green above and light, more fuzzy beneath. Fruit stays on plant all winter and spring.

Caution: Over half the population is allergic to Poison Ivy and Poison Oak. The urushiol oil in Poison Ivy and Poison Oak cause the red rash. Can poison on contact and the poison can be carried by smoke if plants are burned. Poison causes inflammation, spreading blisters and scabs 4 to 24 hours after contact. May cause temporary blindness. Wash all items that were in contact with the plants.

Treatment: Within 5 minutes of exposure wash affected area with *a lot of cold water* - warm water enhances penetration of the oil. The poison is an oil that does not dissolve in water but the water wash dilutes the oil - to make it less active. To stop the itching, use calamine lotion which cools the skin and distracts your skin from the itching sensation. Calamine lotion leaves a dry crust on the skin which absorbs the oozing liquid. Apply three or four times a day and stop applying when oozing stops. *See the doctor for a more detailed instructions.*

POISON SUMAC *(Rhus Vernix)*
Location: Maine to Florida, west to Minnesota, Missouri & Louisiana.
Found: Only in wet, acidy soil swamps
Description: Poison Sumac tree or shrub grows to height of 25 ft. Trunk diameter to 6 ft, coarse and gray bark. The leaves are numerous leaflets arranged opposite each other along a common axis. In this species there is always an odd number of leaflets, usually seven to thirteen. The flowers are clustered together loosely and are greenish white and rather inconspicuous. The fruit is globular and nearly white, and is prominent after the leaves have fallen from the plant. Stays on plant all winter.
Caution: *Whole plant very poisonous.*
The plant is probably our most dangerous poisonous species. Leaves have a brilliant color therefore attracting amateur collectors.

As the plant is tall, it usually affects the face and head (poison ivy usually the feet and legs). Poison sumac differs from poison ivy in that it is not a climber and in that it has seven to thirteen leaflets instead of three. The effect of poisoning by this plant is very similar to that by poison ivy.

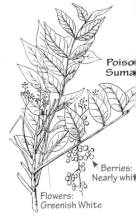

Poison Sumac

Berries: Nearly white

Flowers: Greenish White

DEATH LILY, DEATH CAMAS
(Zygadenus Venenosus)
Location: Western North America.
Found: A spring and summer plant in fields. Individual plants or in large groups.
Description: Death Lily leaves are grasslike, long, narrow, and bent, so much resembling the leaves of grass that they are not recognized. Flowers are numerous, small, about 1/4" in diameter, six petals, yellowish or greenish white, some having a green heart shaped structure in them.
Caution: All of the plant is poisonous with the seeds being more toxic.

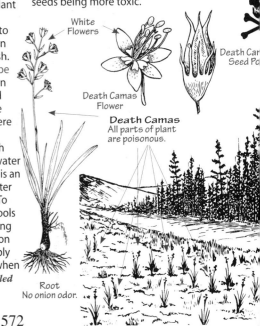

White Flowers

Death Camas Flower

Death Camas Seed Pod

Death Camas
All parts of plant are poisonous.

Root
No onion odor.

53 POISONOUS PLANTS

WATER HEMLOCK (*Cicuta Maculata*)

Location: Throughout North America.

Found: In swampy areas.

Description: This plant is often mistaken for some other plant and is eaten unintentionally (eaten for artichoke). The roots of water hemlock secrete a yellowish, pungent oil - not the case of artichoke. In artichoke, the roots are attached to the parent plant at the narrower end and by spring are usually separated by decay, while in water hemlock, the roots are clustered with the larger ends together and remain near each other. The leaves of water hemlock are two or three times pinnate, the lower ones being on long stems. The leaflets have notched margins, are about three times as long as broad, and are comparatively long pointed. The fruits are about one eighth of an inch long and are borne in the characteristic compound umbel.

Caution: All parts of this plant are poisonous. A small piece of the root may kill an adult. The poisoning is painful and can cause intense stomach pains, delirium, tremors, salivation, and death.

Water Hemlock

Purple-Streaked

Poison Hemlock: This member of the parsley family grows to a height of two to six feet. It grows frequently in moist waste places and has a root stalk which resembles a sweet potato in shape. The stems are hollow and are coarsely spotted with red splashing. The leaves of poison hemlock are large, many times compound, and widely spreading. The stalks of the leaves, or petioles, clasp the stem with a very pronounced sheath. The leaflets are comparatively small and are acutely and deeply cut on the margins. The flowers are white and are clustered terminally in a dense compound. It is supposed that it was a tincture of poison hemlock that Socrates drank.

...rts are poison-especially ...ootstalk. The ...talk has air ...bers

Poison Hemlock

Purple-Streaked

...ow ...em

Poison Hemlock is similar to Water Hemlock but has lacy leaves and white flowers. It grows in open areas throughout North America.

Deep yellow flowers.

Golden Alexanders

PLANTS POISONOUS TO INGEST

Plants not poisonous to the touch, but poisonous if eaten.

Nightshade: is particularly noticeable in fall, when the vines, laden with bright red berries, are conspicuous along the roadsides. The leaves are characteristic, being lobed or cleft at the base and appearing to be composed of one large leaflet with two smaller leaflets at the base. Some species of nightshade have blue flowers. The whole plant, except the flowers and fruits, has a deep greenish color, often with a slight purplish tinge. The fruits hang in rather loose clusters and are juicy.

Black Nightshade: is very closely related to bittersweet. It is not, however, a climber and the leaves are of a different type. The fruits, too, differ in being nearly globose and dark blue or black in color. The flowers closely resemble those of bittersweet, but are white in color and much like potato blossoms. The leaves are somewhat diamond-shaped, with deep notches toward the end, They are usually full of holes made by insects or by fungous diseases. The poison of this plant is usually deadly.

Virginia Creeper: is a member of the vine family. It is not a particularly poisonous plant, but the fruits, which appear tempting, often cause a severe sickness if eaten. As is suggested by the names, the plant is a climber. The characteristic leaves are composed of five leaflets radiating from a common stem, or petiole. The fruit is dark blue or black, globular, and in abruptly angled clusters. The plant is very common and is used as decor.

Jimson Weed: is another member of the nightshade family. Like the black nightshade, it is not a climber. The leaves are large and are shaped much like the leaf of the red oak, although they are much thicker and are usually perforated with holes. They are deep green above and pale green beneath. The flowers are large, funnel-shaped, and of a creamy white color. The capsule, or fruit, is coated with prickles and resembles somewhat the capsule of a poppy. The whole plant is poisonous.

Golden Alexanders: This member of the parsley family is found commonly in meadows and woods. It differs from the other species mentioned in having deep yellow flowers, which are borne in a compact umbel. The leaves are comparatively short, while the leaflets are comparatively broad. The fruits are about 1/4 inch long and rather slender.

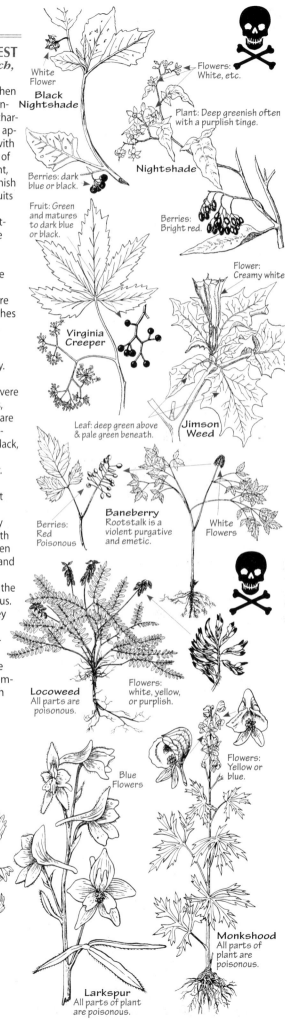

White Flower

Black Nightshade

Flowers: White, etc.

Plant: Deep greenish often with a purplish tinge.

Nightshade

Berries: dark blue or black.

Berries: Bright red.

Fruit: Green and matures to dark blue or black.

Flower: Creamy white

Virginia Creeper

Leaf: deep green above & pale green beneath.

Jimson Weed

Berries: Red Poisonous

Baneberry Rootstalk is a violent purgative and emetic.

White Flowers

Locoweed All parts are poisonous.

Flowers: white, yellow, or purplish.

Seed Pods

Yellow Flower

Blue Flowers

Flowers: Yellow or blue.

Lupine All parts of the plant are poisonous.

Buttercup Leaves of plant are poisonous.

Larkspur All parts of plant are poisonous.

Monkshood All parts of plant are poisonous.

Development of Amanita Vernus

Universal Veil

Cross Section

Button Stage

Universal Veil

Universal Veil Breaking Up

Remnants of Universal Veil

Remnants of Universal Veil

Pileus

Gills

Veil

Volva or Cup

POISONOUS OR EDIBLE ??

Edible mushrooms often have similar looking species that can be very poisonous. If you collect mushrooms for food you should be able to recognize the characteristics of the members of the Amanita group and other poisonous mushrooms of your area. Three of the Amanita species cause the majority of fatalities every year.

To identify any mushroom you require all the parts including the base touching or in the ground. Use a knife to extract mushrooms. Most mushrooms are very fragile so your specimen has to be fresh and undamaged. This chapter outlines the popular Common Field Mushroom and compares its characteristics to the poisonous members of the Amanita Family.

There are many other poisonous mushrooms.

GROWTH OF A MUSHROOM

Mushrooms first appear on the surface of the ground, on the bark of trees, or on other surfaces in the form of small, solid balls (buttons), which gradually enlarge and shoot up into a stem, or stipe, bearing at its summit an umbrella cap, or pileus, which is at first closed around the stalk like a closed umbrella and then expands more or less widely according to the species.

BUTTON

When small and just beginning to open, the growth is called a button. The young buttons arise from a complicated mass of fine, colorless threads in the ground (called spawn), in logs, dung, or other substances.

MATURE MUSHROOM

After the button has fully formed it may develop into a mature mushroom very rapidly. Development of the button from the spawn usually takes considerable time - weeks, months, or even years may elapse before the spawn comes to the surface and forms the button.

MUSHROOM IS FRUIT OF SPAWN

The mushroom on the ground is the fruit of the spawn in the ground. All the absorption and assimilation of food, all the purely vegetative functions, are performed by the spawn, while the mushroom, is a fruit like an apple. It is the reproductive body that produces the spores (microscopic dust-like bodies, which correspond in function to seeds).

SPORES FALLING TO GROUND.

FLY AGARIC VOLVA (CUP)

ANGEL OF DEATH VOLVA (CUP)

IDENTIFICATION OF AMANITA MUSHROOMS

AREA OF GROWTH

- They grow on the ground in or at the edge of forests. They also occur on lawns with scattered trees. They grow in the United States and Canada.

BUTTON STAGE

- The universal veil completely covers the button.
- The universal veil and a partial veil is visible when the button is split lengthwise.
- The universal veil can break in different ways so that the resulting pattern can vary.

Universal Veil

Button

OPENED STAGE

- The veils break when the button expands. Spots or flattened membrane from the outer veil will remain on the cap. The veil can easily break off.
- A cuplike volva from the veil fragments remains at the base. Some of the cups on the volva are not open but might be a series of ridges. The volva might remain in the ground when the mushroom is removed. The volva can wither away with age and remnants can be found around the stem base. The cuplike volva is a distinguishing characteristic of the Amanita family.

Universal Veil Breaking

Spots

- The inner veil will break and remains as a ring or skirt on the stem below the cap. This ring can be poorly formed and may be hard to see or not be there. The ring is a distinguishing characteristic of the Amanita family.

Spots

Ring

Volva

- Always check for the cuplike base and ring.

OTHER FEATURES

- Amanita mushrooms are beautiful.
- Gills are pure white or cream colored.
- Gills do not touch or just touch stem and are of unequal length.
- Stem separates cleanly and easily from cap.
- Spore is white.

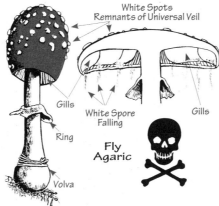

White Spots
Remnants of Universal Veil

Gills

White Spore Falling

Gills

Ring

Fly Agaric

Volva

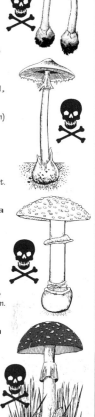

Amanita Phalloides Death Cap

Color: Cap greenish-olive to yellowish.
Cap: 2-6 inches (5-15 cm)
Stem: Lighter color than cap
Volva: Large
Gills: White
Flesh: White
MOST POISONOUS

Amanita Virosa Destroying Angel, Angel of Death

Color: Completely pure white.
Cap: More conical. 2-8" (5-20 cm)
Stem: Scaly
Volva: Large
Gills: White
Smell: Sweet pungent odor.
DEADLY POISON
Northeastern states and eastern Canada. Also in the Pacific Northwest.

Amanita Pantherina Panther Cap

Color: Cap brownish with pure white specks which can wash off.
Cap: 2-4 inches (5-10 cm)
Stem: White and thick.
Gills: White
Veil: Pure White
Gills: White
VERY POISONOUS
Causes coma-like sleep and delirium.

Amanita Muscaria Fly Agaric

Color: Cap red with white spots. The spots can wash off in the rain.
Cap: 3-10 inches (7.5-25 cm)
Stem: White with rings of white to yellow warts at the base.
Gills: White
POISONOUS
There is also a yellow form in eastern America found under pine trees. The red variety is found under pine and birch trees in the west.

Amanita Fulva Tawny Grisette

Color: Cap shiny brownish orange to light orange-yellow. Ribbed cap edge. The spots can wash off in the rain.
Cap: 2-4 inches (5-10 cm)
Stem: Slender, fragile stalk, NO RING.
Gills: White
NOT RECOMMENDED
Forests and clearings throughout America. On lawns summer & fall.

Fly Agaric

Pileus (cap) is often a shining white, but may be of any shade, from a pale dull yellow to olive, and when wet is more slimy than the field mushroom or the fly agaric.

No distinct scales, and only occasionally a few membranous patches on the pileus.

Gills are white.

Stalk is longer and slenderer in proportion to the diameter of the pileus than in either the fly agaric or the field mushroom, and is buried rather deep in the soil or dead leaves, so that it often happens that the bulb is broken off and left behind when the fungus is gathered.

Stalk is white having a large ring like the fly agaric, and is hollow, or, when young, is loosely filled with cottony threads, which soon disappear.

Base of the stalk differs from that of the fly agaric in being more bulbous and in having the upper part of the bulb bordered by a sac-like membrane, called the volva. The volva, is often of considerable size, but more frequently it is reduced to a membranous rim.

Deadly Agaric, Death Cap
(Amanita Phalloides)

Where: Rather common and grows singly in woods and on the borders of fields, rarely appearing in lawns, and is not preeminently an inhabitant of grassy pastures, like the field mushroom.

Soil: Prefers a damper and less sandy soil than the fly agaric.

Fly Agaric

Pileus (cap) is polished with prominent, angular, warty scales, which can be easily scraped off.

Color from a brilliant yellow to orange and a deep red, the yellow and orange being more common.

Stalk is white, and there is a large, membranous collar, which hangs down from the upper part of the stem.

Differs from the field mushroom in having gills which are always white, never pink or purple, and in having a hollow stem which is bulbous (volva) at the base and clothed with irregular, fringy scales on all the lower part.

When compared to the field mushroom it is difficult to conceive how anyone who has ever seen a common mushroom could mistake the fly agaric for the common field mushroom. It is often collected by mistake on the supposition that it is the field mushroom.

Edible or Not Edible?

To classify a mushroom as edible or not, do not trust in any simple rules or general formulae. The only way to identify a species is by assessing ALL the characteristics. Establish the environment and the best season for the mushroom you are looking for, and look for mushrooms as often as possible. Note the location where you found the mushroom(s) and establish its environment. Make sure that your sample is complete. Study it for a few days while referring to guide books making sure that every feature listed is identified on your sample. Then see a mushroom expert to see if your identification is correct.

Difference between Field Mushrooms & Fly Agaric, Deadly Agaric

All three species are pleasant to the taste, showing that one can not infer that a species is not poisonous because the taste is agreeable. The fly agaric has scarcely any odor. The other two species have odors of their own, which are difficult to describe.

Pileus (cap) which is not covered with wart-like scales.

Gills are brownish purple when mature.

Common Field Mushrooms

A nearly cylindrical stalk which is not hollow; with a ring near the middle. Stalk is generally shorter than the breadth of the pileus and comparatively stout.

Common Mushroom

- Has a pileus (cap) which is not covered with wart-like scales and averages from 3-4 inches in width.
- Gills are brownish purple when mature.
- A nearly cylindrical stalk which is not hollow; with a ring near the middle. Stalk is generally shorter than the breadth of the pileus and comparatively stout.
- Without a bulbous base sheathed by a membrane or by scales.
- The pileus remains convex for a long time, and does not become quite flat-topped until old.
- The body is firm and solid.

The pileus (cap) of the field mushroom has been described as smooth and without scales. Varieties are not infrequently found in which the surface is more or less flocculent (like tufts of wool) and with flat, tufted scales. The scales are not prominent, and are not at all like the large, angular warts on the fly agaric, which can be easily scraped off the otherwise smooth surface. The scales of field mushroom varieties are formed by the breaking up of the surface into a sort of fringe, which can not be pulled off without tearing the pileus.

Fly Agaric

- Has a pileus marked with prominent warts.
- The pileus, at first oval and convex, soon becomes flat and attains a breadth of 6-8 inches and sometimes more.
- Gills always white.
- Stalk, with a large ring around the upper part, and hollow or cottony inside, but solid at the base, where it is bulbous and scaly.
- The stalk has a length equal to or slightly exceeding the breadth of the pileus, and is comparatively slenderer than in the field mushroom, but nevertheless rather stout.
- The body is less firm than in the field mushroom.

Deadly Agaric, Death Cap

- Has a pileus without distinct warts.
- The pileus is thinner than that of the field mushroom, and, from being rather bell-shaped when young, becomes gradually flat-topped with the center a little raised. In width it is intermediate between the two preceding species.
- Stalk usually are longer than the width of the pileus, and the habit is slenderer than in the two preceding species.
- Gills always white.
- Hollow stalk, with a large ring, and a prominent bulb at the base, whose upper margin is membranous or bag-like.

Mushroom Poisoning

No case of mushroom poisoning should ever be regarded lightly. In ANY case of mushroom poisoning, medical assistance should be summoned immediately. As a First-Aid measure, the stomach and intestines should be emptied by inducing vomiting or administering purgatives or an enema.

Parts of mushrooms vomited up, or the remains of the dish eaten should be preserved so that the species responsible for the poisoning can be identified. If any fresh mushrooms of the original gathering remain they would be still more useful for this purpose.

A PARTIAL list of possible poison indicators.

- Avoid fungi when in the button or unexpanded stage; also those in which the flesh has begun to decay, even if only slightly.
- Avoid all fungi which have stalks with a swollen base surrounded by a sac-like or scaly envelope, especially if the gills are white.
- Avoid fungi having a milky juice, unless the milk is reddish.
- Avoid fungi in which the cap, or pileus, is thin in proportion to the gills, and in which the gills are nearly all of equal length, especially if the pileus is bright colored.
- Avoid all tube-bearing fungi in which the flesh changes color when cut or broken or where the mouths of the tubes are reddish, and in the case of other tube-bearing fungi, experiment with caution.
- Fungi which have a sort of spider web or flocculent ring round the upper part of the stalk should in general be avoided.

Types of Mushroom Poisoning

Most Poisonous: *Amanita Phalloides:* 90% of the recorded deaths from fungus poisoning have been caused by species of this group.

- The folly of the superstition that a mushroom that peels is safe is well illustrated here because these Amanita species peel readily.
- Are so deadly that even small amounts may prove fatal.
- The danger is increased by the fact that there is apparently no unpleasant taste and no symptoms are manifested until 8 to 12 hours, or sometimes even longer, after the mushrooms are eaten. By this time the poison has been absorbed into the blood stream and the usual procedures such as pumping out the stomach are of no avail.

Symptoms: There are severe abdominal pains, vomiting, cold sweats, diarrhea and excessive thirst. After persisting for some time the symptoms usually subside for a while and then recur more intensely; the liver is affected as well as the nervous system. There may be delirium, deep coma, and finally death. The patient suffers great pain.

A. Muscaria & A. Pantherina Poisoning
The symptoms usually appear soon after eating the mushrooms, within one-half to four hours.

Symptoms: The most characteristic symptoms are nervous excitement, hallucinations and behavior suggesting alcoholic intoxication. This may be followed by coma and sometimes death, although the percentage of recovery from this type of poisoning is much greater than with the *A. phalloides* type. *A. pantherina* is considered to be more dangerous than *A. muscaria*.

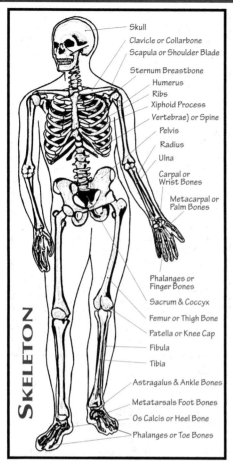

Skull
Clavicle or Collarbone
Scapula or Shoulder Blade
Sternum Breastbone
Humerus
Ribs
Xiphoid Process
Vertebrae) or Spine
Pelvis
Radius
Ulna
Carpal or Wrist Bones
Metacarpal or Palm Bones
Phalanges or Finger Bones
Sacrum & Coccyx
Femur or Thigh Bone
Patella or Knee Cap
Fibula
Tibia
Astragalus & Ankle Bones
Metatarsals Foot Bones
Os Calcis or Heel Bone
Phalanges or Toe Bones

SKELETON

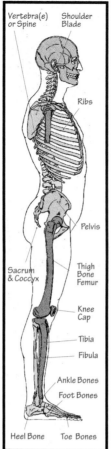

Vertebra(e) or Spine
Shoulder Blade
Ribs
Pelvis
Sacrum & Coccyx
Thigh Bone Femur
Knee Cap
Tibia
Fibula
Ankle Bones
Foot Bones
Heel Bone
Toe Bones

THE SKELETON - BONES

The skeleton, which gives the body its shape and keeps us upright, has 206 bones. These bones are connected by joints. Some bones do not move relative to the adjacent bones (fixed joint) while others have freely moveable joints that have great dexterity.

MUSCLES

Muscles produce the movements of the body. Muscles are made up of parallel interlocking fibers that are from a fraction of an inch (few millimeters) to nearly a yard (30 cm) long. Most of the muscles are attached to a tendon or skin. The body has over 600 muscles.

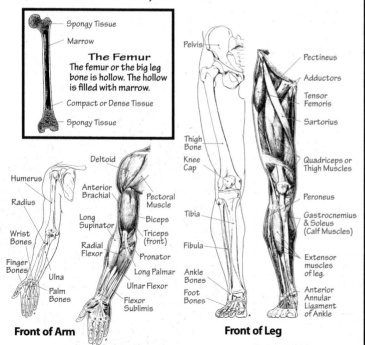

Spongy Tissue
Marrow

The Femur
The femur or the big leg bone is hollow. The hollow is filled with marrow.

Compact or Dense Tissue
Spongy Tissue

Pelvis
Thigh Bone
Knee Cap
Tibia
Fibula
Ankle Bones
Foot Bones

Pectineus
Adductors
Tensor Femoris
Sartorius
Quadriceps or Thigh Muscles
Peroneus
Gastrocnemius & Soleus (Calf Muscles)
Extensor muscles of leg.
Anterior Annular Ligament of Ankle

Deltoid
Humerus
Radius
Anterior Brachial
Pectoral Muscle
Long Supinator
Biceps
Triceps (front)
Radial Flexor
Pronator
Long Palmar
Ulnar Flexor
Flexor Sublimis
Wrist Bones
Finger Bones
Ulna
Palm Bones

Front of Arm

Front of Leg

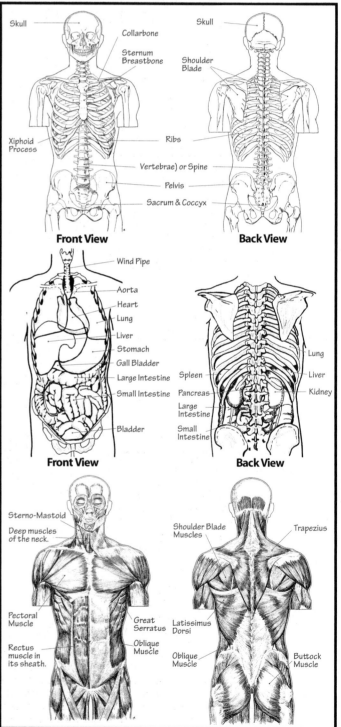

Skull
Collarbone
Sternum Breastbone
Xiphoid Process
Ribs
Vertebrae) or Spine
Pelvis
Sacrum & Coccyx

Front View

Skull
Shoulder Blade
Ribs
Vertebrae) or Spine
Pelvis
Sacrum & Coccyx

Back View

Wind Pipe
Aorta
Heart
Lung
Liver
Stomach
Gall Bladder
Large Intestine
Small Intestine
Bladder

Front View

Lung
Liver
Kidney
Spleen
Pancreas
Large Intestine
Small Intestine

Back View

Sterno-Mastoid
Deep muscles of the neck.
Pectoral Muscle
Rectus muscle in its sheath.
Great Serratus
Oblique Muscle

Shoulder Blade Muscles
Trapezius
Latissimus Dorsi
Oblique Muscle
Buttock Muscle

SKULL

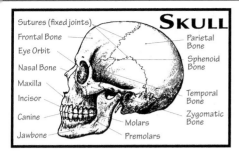

- Sutures (fixed joints)
- Frontal Bone
- Eye Orbit
- Nasal Bone
- Maxilla
- Incisor
- Canine
- Jawbone
- Parietal Bone
- Sphenoid Bone
- Temporal Bone
- Zygomatic Bone
- Molars
- Premolars

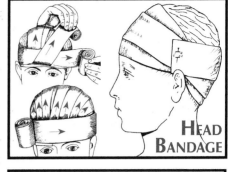

HEAD BANDAGE

REEF KNOT (SQUARE KNOT)

To securely tie the ends of a bandage a reef knot should be used. The knot should be placed where it will not cause any discomfort to the injured person or a pad should be placed between the knot and the body. The tieing of a reef Knot can be confused with a Granny Knot.

Note that the Granny Knot is not stable and has a tendency to slip so should not be used.

Reef Knot

Reef Knot Used to Tie Bandage
Note the difference from a Granny Knot. The ends will point in the same direction as the bandage.

Injured Shoulder

Place the base of the bandage under the hand.

Reef Knot Pinned

TRIANGULAR SLING

Sling raises and rests the hand. It can be used for a fractured collar bone or to rest the arm or hand. Place the victim's forearm across the chest with the fingers point towards the shoulder. The palm resting on the breast bone.

TRIANGULAR BANDAGE

This is the most useful format for a first aid bandage. The ends should always be tied with a reef knot. The illustration shows how to fold this format to give you different widths.

A: Half fold used for slings.
B: Fold used to cover large areas and as a first bandage.
C: Upper layer fastening bandage or for restricted areas.
D: Narrow fold used For tying and tourniquets.

GRANNY KNOT

The Granny Knot is very similar to the Reef Knot but should not be used as it has a tendency to slip and unravel. When a bandage is tied with a Granny knot it will look untidy with the ends being perpendicular to the direction of the bandage.

Granny Knot

Ends of bandage in a Granny Knot do not lie in the direction of the bandage.

Do not use the Granny Knot to tie bandages.

Triceps Muscle

Biceps Muscle

Radius

Ulna

Hand Bones

Reef Knot

Pin

ARM SLING

An arm sling is extremely useful as it can be used for injuries to the shoulder, arm, elbow, and hand. The application is very simple and it can be made of any lightweight material available. Apply as in the illustration. The reef knot should be tied in the hollow point of the shoulder in the area of the collar bone. This location will reduce the rubbing of the knot on the skin. Gently raise the injured arm into the sling position.

Applying Roller Bandage

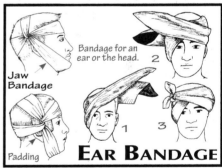

Jaw Bandage

Bandage for an ear or the head.

Padding

EAR BANDAGE

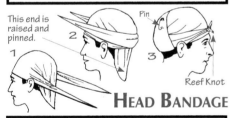

This end is raised and pinned.

Pin

Reef Knot

HEAD BANDAGE

SPLINT TIE

When securing a splint a narrow bandage can be folded double and passed around the limb and splint. Then one end is inserted through the loop forming a double bandage and it is tied, with a reef knot, to the free end.

One end of bandage passed through loop.

See Chapter on Knots.

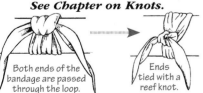

Both ends of the bandage are passed through the loop.

Ends tied with a reef knot.

The same as the Splint Tie but both ends of the bandage are passed, in opposite directions, through the loop and then knotted with a reef knot on the outside.

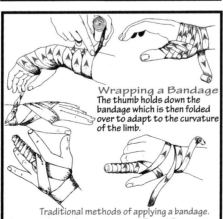

Wrapping a Bandage
The thumb holds down the bandage which is then folded over to adapt to the curvature of the limb.

Traditional methods of applying a bandage.

BANDAGING ADJACENT TO SKIN SURFACES

If two parts of the body are being bandaged together, separate skin surfaces with absorbent material to prevent irritation and pressure. Examples of such surfaces are toes, fingers, ear and scalp, arm and trunk.

Greek warrior applying a bandage during the Trojan War. From a ancient Greek plate. 300-400 BC

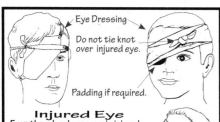

Eye Dressing

Do not tie knot over injured eye.

Padding if required.

Injured Eye
Even though only one eye is injured, both eyes should be bandaged. As both eyes move together, any movement of the uninjured eye would cause the same movement and further damage to the injured eye.

EYE BANDAGE
The middle of a narrow folded bandage is placed diagonally across the injured eye. Sterile clean padding is placed on the injured eye. The bandage is then wound around the head and knotted. Do not tie the knot over the injured eye.

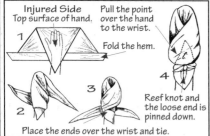

1

2 — Wrap bandage over the wrist.

3

Drape bandage over palm.

Wrap over palm.

4

Wrap over palm.

5

6 — Tie a reef knot on wrist.

Sequence of applying a hand or palm bandage.

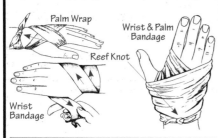

Palm Wrap

Wrist & Palm Bandage

Reef Knot

Wrist Bandage

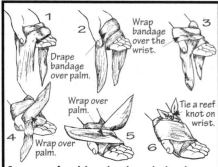

Injured Side
Top surface of hand.

Pull the point over the hand to the wrist.

Fold the hem.

1

2

3

4

Reef knot and the loose end is pinned down.

Place the ends over the wrist and tie.

HAND BANDAGE
Place an open bandage, as in the illustration, on the uninjured side of the hand.

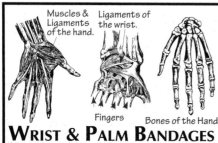

Muscles & Ligaments of the hand.

Ligaments of the wrist.

Fingers

Bones of the Hand

WRIST & PALM BANDAGES
Palm is placed on the middle of a narrow bandage. Cross the bandage as in the illustration leaving the thumb free. Tie the bandage around the wrist with a reef knot. See adjacent illustrations.

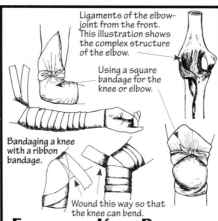

Ligaments of the elbow-joint from the front. This illustration shows the complex structure of the elbow.

Using a square bandage for the knee or elbow.

Bandaging a knee with a ribbon bandage.

Wound this way so that the knee can bend.

ELBOW OR KNEE BANDAGE
This method can be used to put a bandage on the elbow or knee. Place the point of the bandage in the middle of the thigh or arm, turn a fold at the base of the bandage the same way as in the hand bandage.

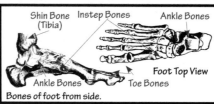

Shin Bone (Tibia) Instep Bones Ankle Bones

Foot Top View

Ankle Bones   Toe Bones

Bones of foot from side.

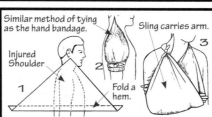

Similar method of tying as the hand bandage.

Sling carries arm.

Injured Shoulder

2   Fold a hem.

1

3

Methods of Dressing Shoulder
After applying a bandage for wounds of an upper limb, the limb should always be supported by a sling.

Shoulder & Lesser Shoulder Bandage

Shoulder Bandage
Shoulder is bandaged and weight is carried by the sling.

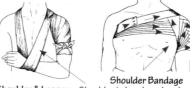

Large Arm Sling

Small Arm Sling

Collar & Cuff Sling

* See the Knot Chapter for the Clove Hitch

Apply a loose bandage to the wrist. Use a clove hitch* to tie the knot as it will not tighten around the wrist.

Pass a support bandage through the wrist bandage and fasten it around the neck. Using a reef knot, tie the bandage.

SHOULDER BANDAGE
Apply a square bandage, to an injured shoulder, the same way as in tying the Hand Bandage on this page. Apply an arm sling to support the weight of the injured shoulder.

US Military Procedure of Assessing Emergency Medical Treatment

Problem: *A patient with an unknown injury under field conditions. To perform primary and secondary patient surveys by examining (look, listen, and feel) the patient to determine probable injury or illness.*

Should ONLY be used by a qualified person.

Primary Survey of the Patient
A Talk to the patient to determine the extent of injuries and the level of consciousness.
B Check the patient's pulse, preferably the carotid.
C Check the patient's breathing.
- Look for a rise and fall of the chest.
- Listen for the escape of air from the patient's mouth or nose by placing your ear next to the patient's mouth and nose.
- Feel the exchange of air at the mouth or nose with your ear at the same time as you are listening for the air exchange.
D Look the patient over quickly and carefully to determine if there is any arterial bleeding to be controlled or other life threatening injuries to be taken care of immediately.
Caution: *A quick, but complete check of the immediate area should be made to remove or reduce hazards to your life and the patient's life such as live electrical wires that are exposed, spilled gas, fire, etc.*
Note: *This examination should be performed by a person with the required medical training. Life threatening problems that are found in the primary survey are treated first and then the secondary survey is conducted.*
Secondary Survey of the Patient
Caution: *Care must be taken so that injuries are not aggravated.*
A Examine the scalp. Part the hair to look and feel for: • Bleeding • Fractures
B Examine the facial area. Look for obvious injuries as well as blood and/or cerebrospinal fluid at ears and/or nose.
C Examine the neck for obvious injuries as well as for possible internal injuries such as a cervical fracture.
D Examine the chest for injuries.
- Look for abnormal movement, color and appearance on one side of the body, face, limb etc. that does not appear on the other as well as bleeding.
- Feel the area for abnormal movement.
E Examine the abdominal region for spasms, tenderness, bleeding, rigidity, & protruding organs.
F Examine the pelvic region for fractures and bleeding.
G Examine the extremities for fractures, dislocations, paralysis, loss of feeling, pain, and/or bleeding.
H Examine the buttocks for fractures & bleeding.
Caution: *Before rolling the patient over, check to make sure there are no spinal injuries. Treatment may range from treating life-threatening conditions to observation. It is possible (and a part of medical practice) for one person to survey a patient and another person to follow up with the actual treatment.*

BRUISING
Bruising might occur during a fall or when bumping into something. It might damage the tissue and muscles under the skin. There might be swelling and pain when touched or pressure is applied.

First Aid
Wrap the affected area with a bandage with a soft pad to reduce the risk of it being inadvertently touched.

Bandage for an abrasion on front of the leg.

SPRAINS

In a sprain the ligaments of a joint are torn by a sudden twist or wrench. The joint is very painful when moved, and there can be considerable swelling. A deep bruise may gradually appear. A bad sprain is hard to distinguish from a fracture.

FIRST AID

Seek medical help. Treat the injury as a fracture if there is any doubt if the injury is a sprain or a fracture. Wrap sprained joint in a heavy bandage. Rest the limb in a comfortable elevated position. Treatment depends upon the pain and disability.

ANKLE OR KNEE SPRAINS

A severely sprained ankle or knee may require rest with the foot elevated for two or three days before the swelling begins to diminish. Ice should be applied every four to six hours for up to 2 days. Wrap the sprained area with an elastic bandage when the swelling has fallen. Firmly apply the bandage without constricting the circulation of the blood. If the bandage is affecting the blood flow the limb below the bandage will swell and be bluish in color. Reapply the bandage less tightly. The injured person should be encouraged to exercise his limb by bearing his weight on it.

FINGER SPRAINS

Treatment is similar as for a knee with the rest, cooling, bandaging, and exercise.

SPRAIN OR FRACTURE?

It is very difficult to be sure whether a joint is merely sprained or a bone is broken. If the pain and swelling of a sprain do not disappear within a few days, keep on resting the part, applying splints if necessary. Do not let the patient use the limb. Minor sprains do not have to be rested but should be bandaged. The joint should be used as usual short of causing pain.

FRACTURED COLLAR BONE

After a collar bone fracture the arm on the injured side is partially helpless and the injured person will support it at the elbow with his hand. Also incline head towards the injured side.

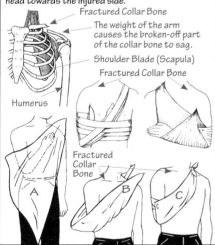

Fractured Collar Bone

The weight of the arm causes the broken-off part of the collar bone to sag.

Shoulder Blade (Scapula)

Fractured Collar Bone

Humerus

Fractured Collar Bone

A   B   C

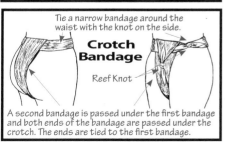

Tie a narrow bandage around the waist with the knot on the side.

Crotch Bandage

Reef Knot

A second bandage is passed under the first bandage and both ends of the bandage are passed under the crotch. The ends are tied to the first bandage.

FRACTURES
TYPES OF FRACTURES
CLOSED FRACTURE

A closed fracture is a break in the bone without a break in the overlying skin. In a closed fracture there may be tissue damage beneath the skin. Even though an injury may be a dislocation or sprain, it should be considered as a closed fracture for purposes of applying first aid.

OPEN FRACTURE

An open fracture is a break in the bone as well as in the overlying skin. The broken bone may have come through the skin. An open fracture can be contaminated and is subject to infection.

Signs & Symptoms of a Fracture

A fracture is easily recognized when the bone is protruding through the skin, the body part is in an unnatural position, or the chest wall is caved in. Other indications of a fracture are tenderness or pain when light pressure is applied to the injured part and swelling as well as discoloration of the skin at the site of the injury. A deep, sharp pain when the victim attempts to move the part is also a sign of a fracture. Do not, however encourage the victim to move a part in order to identify a fracture as movement of the part would cause further damage to surrounding tissue and promote shock. If you are not sure whether or not a bone is fractured, treat the injury as a fracture.

Purpose of Immobilizing a Fracture

A body part which contains a fracture must be immobilized to prevent the razor-sharp edges of the bone from moving and cutting tissue, muscle, blood vessels, and nerves. Furthermore, immobilization greatly reduces pain and helps to prevent or control shock. In a closed fracture, immobilization keeps bone fragments from causing an open wound which could become contaminated and possibly infected. Immobilization is accomplished by splinting.

SIGNS OF A BROKEN BONE

- Swelling   • Pain
- Difficulty in moving injured part.
- Broken bone might protrude through skin.
- Misalignment or deformity of the injured part.
- There can be internal injuries.

Do not move injured person unless in a dangerous location.

Fractures (broken bones) can cause total disability or death. Usually they can be treated so that there is complete recovery. Recovery usually depends upon the first aid received before moving the victim. The basic splinting principle is to immobilize the joints above and below any fracture.

Using a soft padding as a temporary support for a fracture.

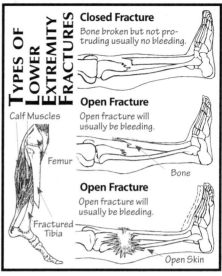

Closed Fracture
Bone broken but not protruding usually no bleeding.

Open Fracture
Open fracture will usually be bleeding.

Calf Muscles

Femur

Bone

Open Fracture
Open fracture will usually be bleeding.

Fractured Tibia

Open Skin

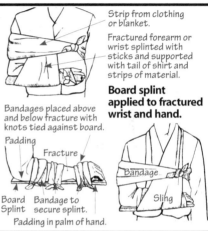

Strip from clothing or blanket.

Fractured forearm or wrist splinted with sticks and supported with tail of shirt and strips of material.

Board splint applied to fractured wrist and hand.

Bandages placed above and below fracture with knots tied against board.

Padding

Fracture

Bandage

Board Splint   Bandage to secure splint.

Padding in palm of hand.

Sling

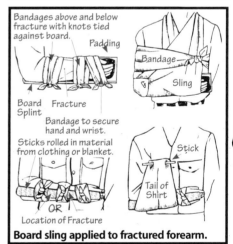

Bandages above and below fracture with knots tied against board.

Padding

Bandage

Board Splint   Fracture

Sling

Bandage to secure hand and wrist.

Sticks rolled in material from clothing or blanket.

Stick

Tail of Shirt

OR

Location of Fracture

Board sling applied to fractured forearm.

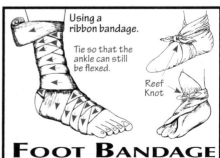

Using a ribbon bandage.

Tie so that the ankle can still be flexed.

Reef Knot

FOOT BANDAGE

Place foot in the middle of the bandage with the point of the bandage in front of the toes. Fold the sides of the bandage over the foot and around the leg and tie.

FRACTURES

FRACTURES

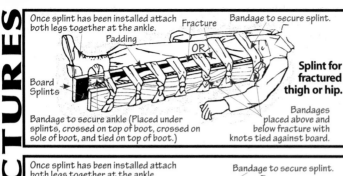

Once splint has been installed attach both legs together at the ankle.
Padding
Fracture
Bandage to secure splint.
Board Splints
Bandage to secure ankle (Placed under splints, crossed on top of boot, crossed on sole of boot, and tied on top of boot.)
Bandages placed above and below fracture with knots tied against board.

Splint for fractured thigh or hip.

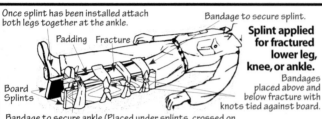

Once splint has been installed attach both legs together at the ankle.
Padding
Fracture
Bandage to secure splint.
Board Splints
Bandage to secure ankle (Placed under splints, crossed on top of boot, crossed on sole of boot, and tied on top of boot.)
Bandages placed above and below fracture with knots tied against board.

Splint applied for fractured lower leg, knee, or ankle.

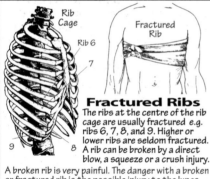

Use a rolled carpet or cloth rolled on a stick as a support. Place the support between the legs and wrap bandages around both legs to immobilize the injured leg.

Tie knots on side of uninjured leg.

Temporary support to immobilize a fractured leg.

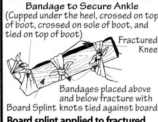

Bandage to Secure Ankle
(Cupped under the heel, crossed on top of boot, crossed on sole of boot, and tied on top of boot)

Fractured Knee

Bandages placed above and below fracture with Board Splint knots tied against board.

Board splint applied to fractured or dislocated knee.

Fractured Ribs

Rib Cage
Rib 6
7
9
8
Fractured Rib

The ribs at the centre of the rib cage are usually fractured e.g. ribs 6, 7, 8, and 9. Higher or lower ribs are seldom fractured. A rib can be broken by a direct blow, a squeeze or a crush injury. A broken rib is very painful. The danger with a broken or fractured rib is the possible injury to the lungs.

Board Splints
Bandages above fracture.
Fracture
Bandages below fracture.
Padding
Knots tied against board.
Bandages to immobilize arm.

Board splints applied to fractured arm or elbow when elbow is not bent.

Compound Fracture

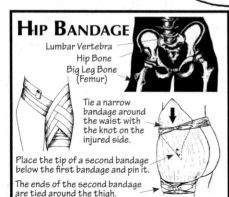

HIP BANDAGE

Lumbar Vertebra
Hip Bone
Big Leg Bone (Femur)

Tie a narrow bandage around the waist with the knot on the injured side.

Place the tip of a second bandage below the first bandage and pin it.

The ends of the second bandage are tied around the thigh.

Upper Body Immobilization

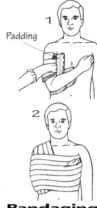

1
Padding

2

Bandaging Adjacent Skin Surfaces

If two parts of the body are being bandaged together, separate skin surfaces with absorbent material to prevent irritation and pressure. Examples of such surfaces are toes, fingers, ear and scalp, arm and trunk.

MATERIAL FOR EMERGENCY SPLINT

Cover Blankets
Drapes, curtains, clothing, or rugs.

Padding
Bed sheets, rags, leafy vegetation, soft clothing, bandages, and moss.

Bandages
Belt, tie, scarf, tape, large handkerchief, strips of shirt or light pants, stockings. Narrow material such as wire or cord should not be used to secure a splint in place.

Splints
Suitable-sized pieces of wood, rolled cardboard, rugs, rolled newspapers, sticks, or broom handles.

Wound Dressing
Any clean material such as handkerchiefs, strips of shirt, curtains or bed sheets. Place the cleanliest absorbent material closest to the wound especially if there is an open fracture.

Slings
Slings may be improvised by using the tail of a coat or shirt, belts, and pieces torn from such items as clothing and blankets. The triangular bandage is ideal.

RULES FOR SPLINTING

If the fracture is open, first stop the bleeding, then apply a dressing and bandage as you would for any other wound.

- Apply the proven principle "Splint them where they lie". This means to splint the fractured part before any movement is attempted and without any change in the position of the fractured part. If a bone is in an unnatural position or a joint is bent, do not try to straighten it. If a joint is not bent, do not try to bend it.
- Collect appropriate splinting material and padding for the body area involved.
- Apply a splint so that the joint above the fracture and the joint below the fracture are immobilized.
- Use padding between the injured part and the splint to prevent undue pressure and further injury to tissue, blood vessels, and nerves. This is especially important at the crotch, in the armpit, and in places where the splint comes in contact with bony parts such as the elbow, wrist, fingers, knee, and ankle joint.
- Bind the splint with bandages at several points above and below the fracture, but do not bind so tightly to interfere the flow of the blood. At least two binding points above and two below. No bandage should be applied across the fracture. Tie bandages that the knot is against the splint, and tie them with a square knot (reef knot). *See Knot Chapter.*
- Use a sling to support a splinted arm which is bent at the elbow, a fractured elbow which is bent, a sprained arm, and an arm with a painful wound.

HOW TO RESPOND TO A FRACTURE
Call for medical help.

- Check pulse and breathing *(if any irregularities administer CPR).*
- Watch for signs of shock. Keep injured person warm, lying down, and calm until medical help arrives.
- Do not give food or liquids.
- Do not try to exert pressure on suspected broken bone or have patient "try out" the injury.
- If bleeding, place cloth (clean if possible) on wound and exert gentle pressure to stop bleeding.

SPLINTS

- First aid splints are not used to "set" fractures but to relieve pain by giving rest to the injured limb and to prevent the broken bone from piercing the skin.
- By splinting you will avoid additional damage to the bone, muscles, arteries, veins, or nerves.
- If no splints are available use an uninjured part of the body as a temporary support.
- Use an uninjured leg for the leg or the chest for the injured arm.
- The skin should be well protected by padding. Tight string, cord, wire, etc., can cause serious damage to the skin if it presses or rubs.
- Knots, in particular, should never be in direct contact with the bare skin.

Some fracture articles & illustrations based on EFMB Study Guide, Department of Military Medicine, US Army

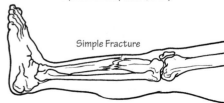

Simple Fracture

HEEL PAIN

Badly fitting shoes might cause a bruising or inflammation of the ligaments from undue strain. To relieve the strain on the Achilles tendon place something under the heel to raise it so that the back of the shoe does not cut into the tendon. You might also consider hammering to soften the back upper lip of the shoe if it cuts into the heel.

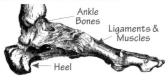

Ankle Bones
Ligaments & Muscles
Heel

Ligaments & Muscles of the Foot
This illustrates the complexity of the movement in the foot and why a well fitting boot or shoe is so important.

CRAMP

A cramp is a muscle spasm which occurs if the blood circulation is impaired or if the muscle is over exerted. It usually occurs in the leg and may develop when swimming in cold water. It can happen when you are immobile in a 'cramped' position. You might have a sudden attack during sleep.
See article on "Heat Illness" page 589.

TREATMENT OF CRAMP

Put the affected muscles in a stretched position while vigorously kneading the limb.
Calf muscle:
Straighten the knee and bend the foot up.
Front of the leg:
Bend the knee and push the foot downward.

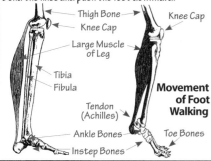

Thigh Bone
Knee Cap
Knee Cap
Large Muscle of Leg
Tibia
Fibula
Tendon (Achilles)
Ankle Bones
Toe Bones
Instep Bones

Movement of Foot Walking

DISLOCATED JAW

Usually caused by a big yawn. The jaw freezes in a forward position, and cannot move.
Make sure there is no broken bone.

Try to replace the bone:
• Wind a piece of handkerchief around each of your thumbs. This will serve as padding.
• The person should be sitting and facing you. Remove any dentures. Press steadily downwards while moving your protected thumbs along the teeth of the lower jaw as far back into the mouth as possible. While pressing downwards with your thumbs slightly raise the chin with your palms and the jaw will suddenly fall back in place.
• Keep thumbs were well protected.
• The person should not to try to open his mouth wide as a dislocation will almost certainly reoccur.

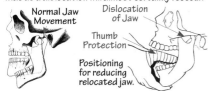

Normal Jaw Movement
Dislocation of Jaw
Thumb Protection
Positioning for reducing relocated jaw.

HEART

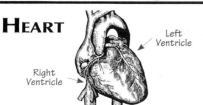

Left Ventricle
Right Ventricle

DISLOCATION OF A JOINT

A dislocation is an injury to a joint in which bones making the joint have slipped or moved out of their usual position relative to one another. A dislocation is very painful. The joint will not be able to be moved and will be "stuck" in an abnormal position. Sometimes it may prove difficult to ascertain if it is a dislocation or a fracture in the area of the joint. It is possible that both have occurred.

First Aid

• Generally, do not attempt to re-place the bones. Keep the injured part as found or place it in a less painful position.
• Treat the injury as a fracture by making a well-padded splint.

Splint for a dislocated finger.

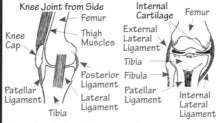

Knee Joint from Side
Femur
Knee Cap
Thigh Muscles
Posterior Ligament
Patellar Ligament
Lateral Ligament
Tibia

Internal Cartilage
Femur
External Lateral Ligament
Tibia
Fibula
Patellar Ligament
Internal Lateral Ligament

Knee-Cap Dislocation
Can happen from a blow to the knee area.

Slipped Knee
Displacement of the internal cartilage from between the ends of the bones.

TO TREAT SCRAPES

After a scrape occurs: Remove all splinters and foreign objects using clean tweezers. Wash the wound with warm water and soap. Cover the wound with sterile dressing. If an infection occurs see a doctor.

CONTROLLING EXTERNAL BLEEDING
PRESSURE OVER WOUND

Direct pressure can be applied with the fingers or hand or by using a bandage that is wound fairly tightly. This tight winding should be only temporary, to reduce the flow of the blood, and then should be cut (to reduce the pressure) but not removed as the wound will be disturbed. Place a new bandage over first.

PRESSURE ON A MAJOR ARTERY

Pressure is applied on a major artery leading to the wound. This will slow the rate of flow of the blood but medical assistance will be required to close the cut.
See Pressure Point page 584.

APPLY A TOURNIQUET

A tourniquet is rarely necessary and can cause harm to injured extremities.
See Tourniquet page 585.

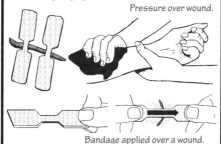

Pressure over wound.

Bandage applied over a wound.

NICK OR SCRAPES

The gentle ooze which occurs when you slightly cut your finger or nick yourself shaving is known as capillary bleeding. It stops by itself or upon the application of a small dressing and is of no consequence but should be kept clean to avoid infection.

COMMON BLEEDING

Is a welling up of the blood from the depths of the wound in a slow steady stream. The blood comes from numerous blood vessels, except large arteries, of all sizes that have been severed. Usually it is not dangerous but it may look alarming. It can be controlled by a firm dressing.

LARGE ARTERY BLEEDING

If a large artery is damaged, bleeding may be severe. The blood spurts from the wound in a pulsating stream and several pints may be lost in a few minutes. This is the type of bleeding which can endanger life, but is fairly rare.
See Pressure Points page 584.

SEVERE ARTERIAL BLEEDING

Immediately apply direct pressure with the thumbs and fingers over that part of the wound from which the blood is coming. Continue pressure, while a suitable pad and bandage are being found, will help to reduce the flow of blood pending the application of a pad and firm bandaging. On the very rare occasion when these measures fail, and it is obvious that the wound is continuing to bleed, a tourniquet should be applied.
See article on Tourniquets page 585.

EFFECTS OF SEVERE BLEEDING

When bleeding is severe, or moderate and continuous, the whole body is affected. The presence of internal bleeding can be assumed by observing symptoms, as indicated below, without any blood being visible.

SYMPTOMS OF SEVERE BLEEDING

The immediate effect is shock. With additional bleeding the shock gradually becomes worse and eventually the patient becomes very restless, aimlessly moving his arms and legs. Breathing becomes hurried and labored, with sighing or gasping for air. Check the pulse every 15 minutes to judge the amount of bleeding. If the pulse rate continues to increase this indicates continued bleeding.

BLEEDING

Capillary
A slow steady oozing.

Bleeding from Artery
It sprays and is bright red.

Flow from Vein
Steady dark red or reddish-blue flow.

Intensity of blood flow from a wound depends upon the source of the blood.

PRESSURE POINTS
To reduce bleeding

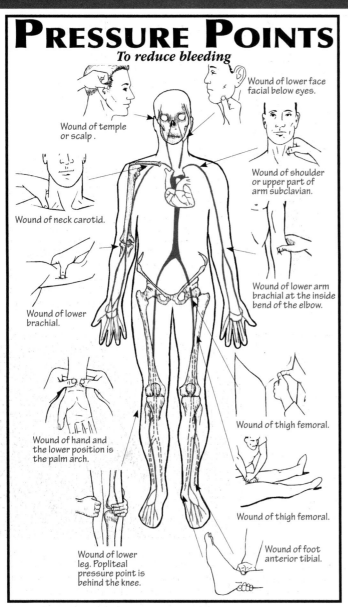

Wound of temple or scalp.

Wound of lower face facial below eyes.

Wound of neck carotid.

Wound of shoulder or upper part of arm subclavian.

Wound of lower brachial.

Wound of lower arm brachial at the inside bend of the elbow.

Wound of hand and the lower position is the palm arch.

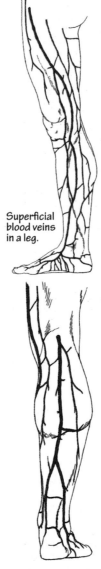

Superficial blood veins in a leg.

Wound of thigh femoral.

Wound of thigh femoral.

Wound of lower leg. Popliteal pressure point is behind the knee.

Wound of foot anterior tibial.

FIRST AID
FOR COMMON BLEEDING
The following is an outline of first aid but medical attention should be obtained immediately.

- If bleeding is from the area of the mouth the victim should be laid on his side or sit with his head tilted forwards, so that the blood does not drain into his mouth or nose and choke him.
- Lay the victim down and raise the bleeding area or limb (as long as it is not fractured) above the level of the heart. This might slow or stop the flow of the blood.
- The victim with a wound on one side of his body should be laid with the wound on the upper side.
- Remove the clothing from the spot that is bleeding. Stop the bleeding by applying a sterilized dressing or clean padding large enough to cover the wound. Firmly apply a bandage over the dressing. The bandage should not be too tight as the area of the wound area will swell during the next few hours.
- With severe bleeding, the bandage must initially be tight. Once the bleeding subsides cut through the layers of the original bandage (without disturbing the wound) and apply a new loose bandage over the original.
- If blood soaks and seeps through the original bandage do not remove the original bandage but place a larger dressing over the original. Apply the new bandage on a larger area over new dressing but apply it more firmly than the first bandage. More layers might be required.
- Immobilize the injured part with a sling and splints if necessary.
- Victim might be in shock if the wound is severe and there has been loss of blood.

BULLET / METAL PROJECTILE INJURY
Wounds caused by a bullet or metal fragment may have an exit wound which is usually larger than the entry wound. The projectile on passing through the body might have broken a bone, cut an artery or damaged a vital organ. The projectile might hit a bone and deflect into the body, causing internal damage, making it difficult to remove the fragment. *See a doctor.*

CHEST WOUND
Superficial Wound: If minor can be treated as a regular wound.
Deep Wound: A deep wound might be penetrating the lungs and require specialized immediate first aid. A lung penetrating wound will produce the sound of air coming from the lungs. The victim will be in a state of shock and find breathing very difficult. Try to prevent the air from passing through the wound.
See a doctor immediately.

NOSE BLEEDING
Bleeding is common after a blow to the nose or if you have a head cold and are continually blowing your nose. It is rarely dangerous.
Treatment: Keep your head up and sit upright, preferably in a cool spot or in a draft. Do not breath through the nose but use the mouth. The nose can be pinched below the nose bone until the bleeding stops. Avoid blowing your nose.

HEAD INJURIES
Head injuries should not be ignored.
Swelling after a Bump
Apply an ice pack to reduce swelling and find the reason for the swelling. *See a doctor.*

BLEEDING SCALP WOUND
Much blood goes to the head to maintain the brain so that head wounds bleed profusely. Raise the head and shoulders to slow the bleeding and place a sterile dressing over the wound. When bleeding has slowed wrap a bandage around the head to keep the bandage in place. Strands of hair can be tied together to act as a suture. *See Pressure Points above. See a doctor.*

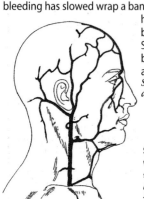

Superficial blood veins in head showing the danger points for bleeding.

To establish the presence of a pulse.

Lightly place two fingers on the air pipe below the chin. Slide the fingers into the grove between the air pipe and the muscle below the ear and jaw bone. At this point you should feel the blood pulse of the carotid artery.

BLACK EYE
A "black eye" occurs when the eye area has been bruised. The white of the eye might be partially red from a broken blood vessel. The eyelid and surrounding area may swell so that the eye cannot be opened. This condition will clear with time.
Treatment: As the black eye is a bruise there are no preventive measures. To reduce the pain and the swelling use an ice compress held in place with a bandage. Remove the compress after six hours or you might cause a minor local trench foot like condition. *See Trench Foot article.*

APPLYING A TOURNIQUET

Tourniquet (Constrictive Bandage)

Because of the potential adverse effects of tourniquets and difficulty in their proper application, use of a tourniquet to control bleeding of the extremities is indicated only if direct pressure is not effective or possible and if the first aid provider has proper training in tourniquet use.

American Heart Association 2010

Some comments on tourniquet application:

Rule 1 A tourniquet should be just tight enough to control the bleeding. If too tight it may damage the nerves and tissue in the limb and may cause unnecessary pain. A finger should be able to pass between the bandage and the skin.

Rule 2 A tourniquet must be loosened after 15 minutes as permanent damage and gangrene of the limb, may result. If additional bleeding occurs retighten the bandage for an additional 15 minutes. Gradually loosen the tourniquet to see if bleeding has stopped or what minimal pressure is required. If bleeding has stopped, then loosen the tourniquet but keep it in place so that it can be reapplied.

Rule 3 Do not cover a tourniquet with clothing, bandage or splint as it might be forgotten. Keep the limb cool and exposed. A blanket can be placed on the victim.

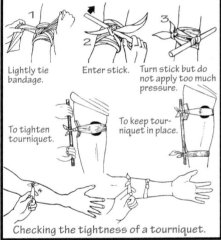

1. Lightly tie bandage.
2. Enter stick.
3. Turn stick but do not apply too much pressure.

To tighten tourniquet.

To keep tourniquet in place.

Checking the tightness of a tourniquet.

APPLYING PRESSURE TO STOP BLEEDING

FIRST AID FOR WOUNDS

If no qualified person is present see a doctor.

- Never wash the wound. Except in a case of a dog bite *(page 610)* also see article on acid burns *(page 595 & adjacent)*.
- Never try to remove metal fragments or pieces of glass unless they are superficial and can be easily lifted out.
- Never put antiseptic into the wound.
- Never touch the wound with your fingers.
- Remove any superficial fragments of metal or glass only with gauze or a dressing covering your finger and thumb, or with sterilized forceps if readily available.
- Never leave the wound exposed to the air.

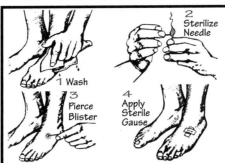

1. Wash
2. Sterilize Needle
3. Pierce Blister
4. Apply Sterile Gause

TREATING A BLISTER

If a blister is in a non abrasive area let it gradually disappear. If you are hiking and a large blister forms in an area where it will break.

- Clean blister area with soap and water.
- Puncture edge of blister with a sterilized needle.
- Press liquid out through the puncture point by gradually pressing the fluid towards the puncture point.
- Apply a sterile gauze pad and adhesive.
- Replace the gauze pad if it gets wet from the blister liquids.

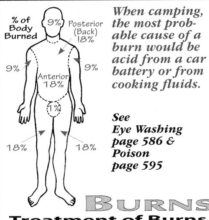

% of Body Burned

Posterior (Back) 18%

9%

9% Anterior 18% 9%

1%

18% 18%

When camping, the most probable cause of a burn would be acid from a car battery or from cooking fluids.

See Eye Washing page 586 & Poison page 595

BURNS

Treatment of Burns

See a doctor. This is only an outline.

- Minimize the effects of the shock by giving fluids, about half a cup at a time as more might cause vomiting.
- A burn is considered to be an open wound and infection should be prevented. To prevent infection apply sterile dressing to cover the burned area before the victim is moved.
- Do not attempt to pull off any clothing that may be stuck. Use scissors to cut it away, but leave the pieces that are stuck.
- Try not to touch the surface of a burn with your fingers.
- Do not break or prick blisters.
- Reassure the patient, and treat with extreme gentleness.

Burns: Acids & Alkalis

Acids or Alkalis can cause a severe burn:

- Immediately flood the affected area with water even without removing the clothing. The water should be flushed gently not to affect the damaged skin.
- Keep on flushing with water while removing the contaminated clothing.
- Continue washing injury with water.
- Get medical attention.

Acid burns: wash with a one tablespoonful to one pint of water solution of sodium bicarbonate.

Alkali burns: wash with a solution of one unit of vinegar to six units of water.

REMOVE A SPLINTER

- Wash your hands and area around the splinter with soap and water.
- Sterilize a needle and tweezers.
- Slide the needle under the splinter to raise it, and remove it with the tweezers.
- Wash the area.
- If the skin is infected do not remove the splinter but see a doctor. If the splinter is very deep see a doctor.

If a doctor is not available and the splinter has infected the area, soak in warm water until the infection drains. The splinter surfaces and is easy to remove. See a doctor if required.

To Sterilize a Needle

To sterilize a needle boil it in water for 10 minutes or heat until red over a gas flame, match, or electric burner. Remove the black carbon deposit with sterile gauze.

Scalds of the Mouth & Throat

If some ice is available, give the victim several pieces to suck on or drinks of ice cold water. *Get medical attention.*

Kayak Roll

CLOTHING ON FIRE

- Do not allow the victim to run around as this will provide additional oxygen for the flames.
- Lie the victim down on the ground immediately with the flames on the upper side.
- Pour water on the victim and thoroughly soak the clothing. Do not do this if the victim is saturated with gasoline, oil or paraffin.
- If water is not available smother the flames with a blanket, rug, coat, etc. Wrap it around the victim to smother the flames, pressing the material against the body, to limit the access of air.
- Do all you can to prevent the victim's face and hands from being burned and take care of your own.
- When the flames have been put out, get medical attention. A qualified person should give treatment for shock.

Roll victim on the ground.

Cover victim with a blanket so that the flame lacks oxygen to burn.

Do not cover with a synthetic material blanket as it might be very flammable. Use cotton or wool.

FOREIGN BODY IN EYE

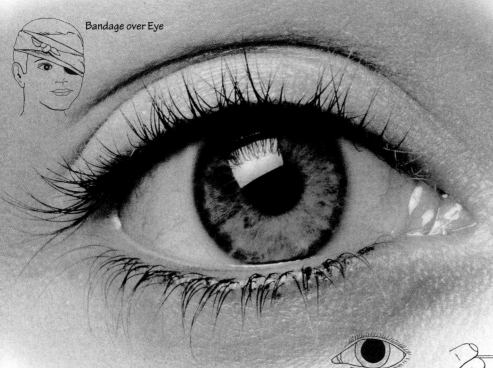

Bandage over Eye

OBJECT BELOW THE UPPER EYE LID

This procedure should be done by a qualified person.

With the patient looking down, gently grasp the lashes of the upper lid and pull the lid forward so that tears or to wash out the particle. If this does not help pull the upper lid forward, push the lower lid under it, and the lashes of the lower lid brushing the under surface of the upper lid, may dislodge the particle. Try this once or twice. Have the patient blow his nose, this sometimes shifts the foreign body to where it can be seen and removed.

If this has not removed the foreign body, place the patient on a seat. Ask the patient to look down. Place a dull stick, match stick, narrow spoon handle or similar object horizontally on top of the upper lid. Take the upper eyelashes with the finger and thumb of your other hand and pull them upwards over the match. This turns the upper lid inside out, and you should hold it in this position while you remove the foreign body. Gently replace the lid in position by pulling down on the eye lashes.

Pupil Dilated

Pupil Constricted

Match stick or a wooden applicator.

Gently grasp the lashes of the upper lid...

2

Foreign Body

1

Foreign Body

3

Turning the upper lid with a wooden applicator.

WASHING EYE

If a chemical enters the eye flush the eye Immediately with large quantities of water. Keep flushing for at least twenty minutes especially if it is an alkali in the eye.

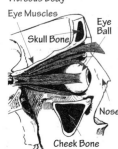

Washing Eye

Place a soft bandage over the eye and see a doctor immediately.

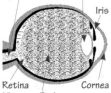

Optic Nerve | Crystalline
Iris
Retina
Vitreous Body | Cornea

Eye Muscles
Skull Bone
Eye Ball
Nose
Cheek Bone

REMOVING FOREIGN BODY

Sand, dust, bits of wood can be blown or rubbed into your eye. There is a danger that the particle might scratch the surface or become embedded in the eye. Do not rub the eye.

The following procedure should be done by a qualified person.

• Wash your hands and inspect the eye.
• If the object is below the lower lid: Pull down the lower eyelid and ask the patient to look up. If a foreign body can be seen, gently brush it with a corner of a piece of clean linen or paper tissue, towards the inner angle of the eye and then out of the eye. Do not use dry cotton as it might leave some particles behind.
• If the object is below the upper lid see the adjacent article.
• If particle can not be found by the above procedures shine a light at different angles to check the cornea. If you see the particle wash the eye with clean water. Do not touch eye. If the particle does not come off it might be embedded in the cornea. Should all attempts fail, keep the eyes* covered, with a dry dressing, and obtain medical assistance as soon as possible. (*both eyes move when looking)

ELECTRICAL BURNS

Electrical burns do not look too serious but a large area of tissue under a small skin wound can have been destroyed.

Electrical burns usually leave two spots on the body, one where the current enters and one where the current exits. Both spots should be covered with a dry, sterile dressing and the victim should be taken to the hospital immediately. Electrical burns can occur when power lines fall, from lightning, home wiring, etc.

FALLEN POWER LINES

Power lines by themselves are not dangerous as long as the object touching them is not grounded. You can see birds sitting on power lines and not getting a shock. If something touches a "hot" power line and at the same time is standing on the wet ground he is "grounded", the circuit is completed and the electricity will flow through the person giving him an electric shock.
• Do not touch electrical equipment while standing on wet ground. Do not remove the third prong (ground) on a plug. Make sure that the "ground" in a wall receptacle is active.
• Be careful when digging in an area where there are buried power lines as a metal shovel might cut through the insulation and produce an electric shock.
• Be careful when cutting a live wire as the flash from the ends of the wire, when it flips free or because of the wire cutters, may cause severe burns.

Symbol that should be posted near high voltage areas.

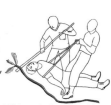

Lifting a body off a cable.

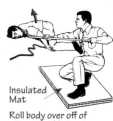

Insulated Mat

Roll body over off of exposed cable.

FALLEN POWER LINES ON A CAR

If a power line has fallen across a car assume that the line is live. The rubber tires of the car form a satisfactory insulation between the fallen wire and the ground. The people in the car are safe as long as they do not touch the metal frame of the car and the ground - at the same time. By touching the ground and car at the same time a person would bypass the insulation of the car's tires. The person should stay in the car if help is on its way. If the car is on fire, in a dangerous location, or if no help is on the way then the occupants can jump clear of the car making sure that they are not touching the car and the ground at the same time.

Body Temperature

- The body temperature is taken with a clinical thermometer which is made of a little glass tube with a fine bore containing mercury.
- A body thermometer is usually graduated from 95°F (35°C) to 110°F (43.3°C). Each degree is subdivided into fifths by small lines, and each fifth is equal to 0.2°F.
- The average normal temperature of the body is 98.4°F (36.9°C) indicated by an arrow.
- Shake down the thermometer, below 96°F (35.6°C), each time before using.

Take Body Temperature

- Before taking the temperature shake down the thermometer, below 96°F (35.6°C), each time before using.
- Take the temperature under the tongue with the lips closed, but not between the teeth. It should remain there for at least three minutes. Do not take the temperature by the mouth for 20 minutes after drinking a hot beverage.
- Take a reading in the armpit if the patient is restless or unconscious. Keep the thermometer in the dry armpit for five minutes. Keep the arm across the patient's chest while taking the temperature.

Temperature above 99.4°F (37.4°C) is suspect.

Between 100°F (37.8°C) to 102°F (38.9°C), a moderate fever.

Above 102°F (38.9°C), a high fever.

Feverish illness if temperature does not rise much above 104°C (40°C).

Early morning temperature of an adult may be between 96°F (35.6°C) and 98.4°F (36.9°C).

Body Temperature & Fever

	F°	C°	
Fatal (usually)	110°	43.3°	💀
	109°	42.8°	
	108°	42.2°	
Dangerous Fever	107°	41.7°	☠
	106°	41.1°	
High Fever	105°	40.6°	
	104°	40.0°	
	103°	39.4°	
Moderate Fever	102°	38.9°	
	101°	38.3°	
	100°	37.8°	
Healthy	99°	37.2°	
	98°	36.7°	
	97°	36.1°	
	96°	35.6°	
Weakness	95°	35.0°	

Wind Chill

The wind chill is based on the rate of heat loss from exposed skin caused by combined effects of wind and cold. As winds increase, heat is carried away from the body at a faster rate, driving down both the skin temperature and eventually the internal body temperature. Animals are also affected by wind chill. While exposure to low wind chills can be life threatening to both humans and animals alike, the only effect that wind chill has on inanimate objects, such as vehicles, is that it shortens the time that it takes the object to cool to the actual air temperature (it cannot cool the object down below that temperature).

Avoid Over-exertion: such as shoveling heavy snow, pushing a car, or walking in deep snow. The strain from the cold and the hard labor may cause a heart attack. Sweating could lead to a chill and hypothermia.

Windchill Factor

- To obtain the windchill factor take the actual temperature of your surroundings.
- Estimate the speed of the wind by looking at the characteristics outlined on the *Beaufort Wind Scale; page 430.* Take the temperature and apply both parameters to the Wind Chill Chart.

Windchill & Winter Travel

30°F and below
Alert group to the potential for cold injuries.
25°F and below
Check that group has sufficiently warm winter clothing. Provide warm-up tents or areas and hot beverages.
0°F and below
Inspect the group for cold injuries. Discourage smoking.
-13°F and below
Initiate the buddy system by having members of the group check each other for cold injuries.
-25°F and below
Plan to curtail all but essential travel or outdoor activity especially in wind exposed areas.

Windchill Index gives the equivalent temperature of the cooling power of wind on exposed flesh.

To Read a Windchill Chart

Look at the column headed with your actual "Temperature in Calm Air (°F)" and look at the horizontal line with your "Wind Speed MPH". The intersection of the column and line will indicate your "Windchill Factor".
For example: with a wind speed of 15 mph and the "temperature in calm air" of 10°F, the windchill factor temperature is -7°F.

Frostbite

Frostbite is a condition in which the skin, and sometimes deeper tissues, actually become frozen. Common areas of frostbite are the nose, cheeks, ears, fingers, and toes. Frostbite is similar to a skin burn.

Signs of Frostbite

The area initially might have a painful pinprick sensation and then become cold, hard, and numb. The freezing can occur quite suddenly especially if it is windy and the skin exposed.
Splotches of opaque pale and yellowish-white areas appear on the exposed skin. These areas gradually get hard and freeze. If they are not covered and warmed they will spread. Check the extremities, the ears, tips of fingers, nose, toes and cheeks. The defensive measure of the body getting cold is to withdraw blood from its extremities, to keep the vital organs warm, which will let the extremities freeze. Touch the exposed areas and if there is no feeling immediately enter a warm area or if not possible cover the frozen skin so that it can gradually thaw out. If traveling alone, check your face in a mirror and watch for white yellow splotches on your skin. Frozen skin remains unchanged until it thaws when it becomes inflamed. The damage depends upon the degree of freezing. Do not touch the frozen area and let it thaw out from the heat within your body. The highest risk of frostbite is when you do not realize the windchill factor is very high so that the actual temperature is much lower due to the wind.

How to Avoid Frostbite

Know the temperature, the windchill factor, and wear the correct clothing before going out. Leave no skin exposed. Wear mitts and not gloves, baklava with a face cover, boots that are well insulated and not too tight. Watch for any discoloration of the skin on yourself and your fellow travelers.

Frostbite - See a doctor...
Enter a warm area and take a warm (not hot) bath. If a bath is not possible wrap the victim in a warm blanket and place his hands in his armpits.

- All tight clothing, including boots and socks, should be removed. Clothing frozen onto the body should be thawed by immersion in warm water. Avoid damaging the frozen skin.
- Frostbitten parts should be warmed by immersion in warm water (temperature 100°F, 37.8°C). If warm water is not readily available exposure the body to warm air. Do not, expose skin directly to an open fire. Do not massage frozen area, rub the skin, or apply snow to the skin.
- Give hot drinks or soup. Do not give any alcohol.
- Do not prick or break blisters. Do not aggressively move the injured extremities or limbs.

Wind Chill Chart

Frostbite Times: ☐ 30 Minutes · ☐ 10 Minutes · ☐ 5 Minutes

Wind Speed (MPH) \ Temperature (°F) in Calm Air	40	35	30	25	20	15	10	5	0	-5	-10	-15	-20	-25	-30	-35	-40	-45
5	36	31	25	19	13	7	1	-5	-11	-16	-22	-28	-34	-40	-46	-52	-57	-63
10	34	27	21	15	9	3	-4	-10	-16	-22	-28	-35	-41	-47	-53	-59	-66	-72
15	32	25	19	13	6	0	-7	-13	-19	-26	-32	-39	-45	-51	-58	-64	-71	-77
20	30	24	17	11	4	-2	-9	-15	-22	-29	-35	-42	-48	-55	-61	-68	-74	-81
25	29	23	16	9	3	-4	-11	-17	-24	-31	-37	-44	-51	-58	-64	-71	-78	-84
30	28	22	15	8	1	-5	-12	-19	-26	-33	-39	-46	-53	-60	-67	-73	-80	-87
35	28	21	14	7	0	-7	-14	-21	-27	-34	-41	-48	-55	-62	-69	-76	-82	-89
40	27	20	13	6	-1	-8	-15	-22	-29	-36	-43	-50	-57	-64	-71	-78	-84	-91
45	26	19	12	5	-2	-9	-16	-23	-30	-37	-44	-51	-58	-65	-72	-79	-86	-93
50	26	19	12	4	-3	-10	-17	-24	-31	-38	-45	-52	-60	-67	-74	-81	-88	-95
55	25	18	11	4	-3	-11	-18	-25	-32	-39	-46	-54	-61	-68	-75	-82	-89	-97
60	25	17	10	3	-4	-11	-19	-26	-33	-40	-48	-55	-62	-69	-76	-84	-91	-98

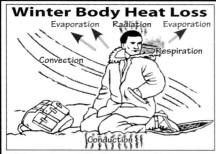

Winter Body Heat Loss
Evaporation · Radiation · Evaporation
Respiration
Convection
Conduction

BODY HEAT LOSS

By understanding heat loss we can learn how to prevent or avoid hypothermia. Body heat is lost by Radiation, Conduction, and Convection.

Radiation

The major form of heat loss which is the direct transfer of heat from our body by heat waves to the air. To reduce this transfer we wear clothing and protect ourselves in shelters such as tents or snow trenches.

The head has many blood vessels to heat and feed the brain. If uncovered, at 40°F (4°C), up to 50% of the body's heat loss is through the head. At 5°F (-15°C) the loss is 75%. If there is a high windchill factor the heat loss is higher and much more rapid. For this reason a hat should be warn to keep the body warm.

Conduction

Conduction is caused by the transfer of heat to an adjacent colder medium. This medium can be the adjacent air, the cold seat you are sitting on, etc. To reduce conduction wear clothing with many pores or air pockets e.g. wool or down fill. Solids such as ice, metal, snow and cold water against bare skin are very high conductors of heat and cause high and rapid heat loss.

Cold water heat loss is the most dramatic because water will wet clothing, filling the insulating air pockets, and this will accelerate heat loss from the body.

Clothing can get wet from the outside but if the clothing does not breath, absorb or transmit humidity from the body you will soon get clammy and wet especially if you are exerting yourself. For this reason many people recommend natural fibers such as wool and cotton as they have many pores and a higher wicking factor to absorb humidity.

Convection

Is the removal of heat from the body by the motion of the surrounding air. This is a minor factor if there is no wind but with wind the exposed skin will be affected by the windchill factor.

Respiration

Warm air is exhaled with your breath. Limit heat loss by breathing through your nose. This is especially true at high elevations where, to obtain more oxygen, there is more frequent and labored breathing.

TRENCH FOOT

Trench Foot is called "Trench Foot" because this condition was a common occurrence during the First World War. Combatants, on both sides of the conflict, lived and fought in wet trenches for months on end.

BODY HEAT PRODUCTION

Production of Heat by the Body

You should have no problem with hypothermia if your body can continue to produce sufficient heat to complement the heat loss the cold. If the heat loss exceeds heat production you are a candidate for hypothermia.

Body Heat Production

The body combines fuel (food that you have eaten) with oxygen to produce heat.

Three types of body heating:

Basal Heat Production: This is the basic production of heat for a sedentary person. This heat production is partly controlled by the thyroid gland and cannot respond very fast to an emergency, e.g. heat loss, thus leading to hypothermia.

Thermo-regulatory (Shivering): This form of heat production, which is involuntary, responds to a drop in body temperature. This response is in the form of shivering which can increase the heat production by up to three times the basal rate. Heat production by shivering is not very productive. It can be stopped by putting on more clothing or getting out of the cold.

Exercise: A well planned activity in a survival situation can be very productive.

- Hiking uphill with a load can increase heat production up to six times the basal rate. Hiking is very productive in producing body heat. This activity, performed by a healthy adult, might be sustained for an hour or two and is recommended if you know where you are and how far away the shelter is. If you are not sure of your location or destination it might be better to use your energy to develop heat by building a shelter and fire which will last the night.

- Heavy exertion, where you can produce heat up to ten times the basal rate, can be maintained for 10 minutes by a healthy adult. This should only be done if you are 100% sure of your destination and a proper shelter can be reached in that time. Make sure that your clothing is well ventilated to release humidity. At the end of this heavy exertion, if you are not in a warm dry shelter, fatigue and humid clothing can lead to hypothermia.

Clothing

Wet clothing loses heat by conduction and evaporation. If your clothing is totally waterproof (rubber or dense nylon) water, humidity or water vapor from the body cannot escape and you will soon become humid and cold.

CAUSES OF HYPOTHERMIA

A person weakened by lack of food, has a low energy level, is not well dressed, or does not have a strong will to live is a prospect for hypothermia.

The major conditions are:
- Cold (even temperatures as 32°F-50°F (0°C-10°C)).
- Wind. • Being wet or in very high humidity.

Optimum Body Temperature

Human body temperature is nearly 98°F (37°C) and any major deviation up or down can cause problems. The uncovered body will start to shiver at approximately 95°F (35°C). Shivering is an automatic body reaction to cold that is intended to move the muscles to produce more heat. When a body gets cold there is an automatic defense mechanism that reduces the flow of blood to the extremities (toes, fingers, etc.) and tries to heat the vital life sustaining body organs - heart, lungs, brain. Hypothermia is the drop of the vital core temperature of the body. This condition is a major threat to life. 85% of wilderness deaths are caused by hypothermia.

Body Nutrition

Food is our source of fuel to keep our bodies warm.
Carbohydrates: e.g. sugar, are instant sources of energy as they are quickly burned by the body. Consuming small amounts at regular intervals will provide energy for the outdoors.
Proteins & Fat: burn more slowly but are required by the body and protein is important for its staying power.

TREATING HYPOTHERMIA

- Get the victim out of adverse weather into a shelter that is dry and not in the wind. If the victim is in the water get him out as soon as possible.
- Replace wet clothing with dry clothing or put him in a dry sleeping bag. You might even consider joining the victim in the sleeping bag.
- Give the victim some warm liquid or soup. This will help increase the core temperature from the inside. A more rapid way to heat the inside of the body is to have victim inhale steam from boiling water as it will heat the heart and lungs. Make sure that he is not too close to the source of the steam as he might be scalded and damage the lungs and airway.
- Do not give alcohol as it will open the blood vessels near the skin which will dissipate heat and less heat will be available for the key body organs.
- *Get medical help.*

TRENCH FOOT

Feet, legs, arms or hands immersed for hours in cold water, wet boots or mud, at temperatures below 50°F (10°C), the nerves, blood vessels, and skin will gradually be damaged. Trench foot injuries can occur at any point on the windchill chart and is much more likely to occur than frostbite especially during extended travel in a wet environment. The longer the stay, the colder the temperature, the greater the damage to the tissue. North of latitude 50° the Atlantic and Pacific waters are cold enough to cause injuries in winter and summer months.

Cause

Wet/damp feet (socks and boots) for several hours or days with the temperature being below 50°F (10°C).

Signs of Trench Foot

Long immersion in water can be painful. The long term problem is that the body adapts to the pain. The condition getting worse without being noticed or treated. In half an hour the exposed part becomes red and numb and it is difficult to move the toes or fingers. Within three hours the limb is slightly swollen. The swelling will increase especially if the limb is hanging down. If the immersion ends and the limbs can be warmed and dried this initial damage will quickly disappear. If the exposure to humidity and cold lasts several days swelling of ankles, wrists, and feet will occur. There will also be blisters or dark patches and the skin will crack.

First Aid

Remove clothing and keep the victim warm and dry. *Get medical help.*

STAGES OF HYPOTHERMIA

Shivering

This is the first indication that there is a small drop in the core temperature of the body and that heat loss from the body exceeds heat production. Shivering will start at a core temperature just below 98.6°. This is the first sign of a mild hypothermia and the person will start to be in a withdrawn state. This is a warning that heat loss should be reduced. If your core temperature is 91°F-95°F (33°C-35°C) you will have:

- Intense shivering. Trembling hands.
- Difficulty in speaking, memory lapse, become forgetful, lack concentration, cannot think logically, and becomes indecisive.
- Exhaustion and drowsiness.
- Loss of coordination, stumbling, falling, and inability to use hands.

Accidents from the lack of coordination can occur. You might have an accident on the trail, not be able to build a shelter, put up your tent or unroll your sleeping bag. These are early stages of hypothermia and hopefully you have a partner who will recognize these symptoms and prepare a shelter, build a fire and give you some carbohydrates.

Tense Muscular Rigidity

This is the second stage in hypothermia when the core temperature drops to 86°-91°F (30°-33°C) and shivering decreases but your muscles become tense and rigid. Your thinking will be impaired, you cannot speak but you can still walk. The fact that you have stopped shivering should tell you that your core temperature is still falling. At 90°F (32°C) or lower the heart beat can fall to three or four beats a minute. With increased hypothermia the healthy beat will disappear and ventricular fibrillation will occur. The person should be treated in a clinic even if he looks dead as the heartbeat can be extremely low and breathing undetectable.

Body's Gradual Failure

Below 86°F (30°C), depending upon your personal physical condition, the body chemistry begins to change and major problems can occur:

- Pulse and respiration slow down.
- May fall into a coma.
- Behavior becomes uncoordinated and irrational and can evolve into lethargy, e.g. a person sitting down to die of heat loss. You will require assistance to stop the continued falling of the core temperature.

Unconsciousness

The core temperature below 80°F (27°C) will result in a deep unconsciousness.

- Reflexes will be dramatically reduced. Breathing is difficult
- Heartbeat will be erratic and the pulse weaker.
- Cardiac arrhythmias may be noted.

If you are warmed up at this stage your core temperature will continue falling and nothing can be done in a wilderness survival situation.

Death

Around 78°F (25°C) the respiratory and cardiovascular systems fail. This is followed by pulmonary edema and ventricular fibrillation and then cardiac standstill.

TO PREVENT HYPOTHERMIA

- stay dry
- avoid cold
- get rest
- avoid wind
- eat well
- stay active
- Have warm dry clothing available. Natural insulation might be available in the wilderness.
- Travel with an emergency space blanket.
- Do not be strong-headed and attempt to complete a challenging excursion.
- Turn back, seek shelter, avoid hypothermia.
- Find shelter and heat when you still have enough energy left. Build your shelter when your mind is still lucid. • Avoid perspiring.

EXTREME HEAT CONDITIONS

Temperatures that hover 10°F or more above the average high temperature for the region and last for several weeks are defined as extreme heat. Humid or muggy conditions, which add to the discomfort of high temperatures, occur when a "dome" of high atmospheric pressure traps hazy, damp air near the ground. Excessively dry and hot conditions can provoke dust storms and low visibility. Droughts occur when a long period passes without any substantial rainfall. A heat wave combined with a drought is a very dangerous situation.

EMERGENCY INFORMATION

1 Heat kills by pushing the human body beyond its limits. Under normal conditions, the body's internal thermostat produces perspiration that evaporates and cools the body. However, in extreme heat and high humidity, evaporation is slowed and the body must work extra hard to maintain a normal temperature.

2 Most heat disorders occur because the victim has been overexposed to heat or has over exercised for his or her age and physical condition. Other conditions that can induce heat-related illnesses include stagnant atmospheric conditions and poor air quality.

3 A prolonged drought can have a serious economic impact on a community. Increased demand for water and electricity may result in shortages of resources. Moreover, food shortages may occur if agricultural production is damaged or destroyed by a loss of crops or livestock.

HEAT ILLNESS

Are caused by the surrounding heat especially when humid.
- *Heatstroke (sunstroke).*
- *Heat exhaustion.* • *Heat cramps.*

You should be able to recognize the symptoms, know the treatment and how to avoid these heat illnesses. You might save a life.
Heatstroke and heat exhaustion are mainly due to the excessive loss of fluid and salt from continuous sweating or overexertion in a hot climate. This fluid and salt must be continually replaced.

- Heat illness can be expected when the wet bulb temperature is above 90°F (32.2°C), or the dry bulb temperature is above 110°F (43.3°C).*
- With much exertion the body can lose up to 2 quarts of fluids per hour in hot and humid environments.

*See Weather Chapter

HOW BODY DISSIPATES HEAT

Because men sweat more than women, men are more susceptible to heat illness because they become more quickly dehydrated.

US Army Water Requirement Guidelines

Activity	Typical Duties	Quarts Per Person Per Day	
		< 105°F (41°C)	105°F (41°C)+
Light	Desk work, Radio operating, Guard duty.	6	10
Moderate	Route march on level ground.	7	11
Heavy	Forced marches, Route march with heavy loads, Digging in.	9	13

US Army Acclimatization Schedule

Hours of work that may be performed in a minimum period of acclimatization.

Day	Less than 105°F (41°C)		More than 105°F (41°C)	
	AM	PM	AM	PM
1	1 hr	1 hr	1 hr	1 hr
2	1.5	1.5	1.5	1.5
3	2	2	2	2
4	3	3	2.5	2.5
5	regular duty	3	3	
6	regular duty	regular duty		

HEAT ILLNESSES

ILLNESS	CAUSE	SYMPTOMS	FIRST AID
Heat Exhaustion	Excessive loss of water and salt.	Cool moist skin, profuse sweating. Headache, dizziness, vomiting, weakness, rapid pulse and breathing. May be slight rise in temperature.	Heat cramps are relieved by replacing the salt lost from body. Place individual in cool outer clothing. Give all water slowly in the form of 0.1% saline solution. If cramps are very severe individual should be sent to a hospital.
Heat Cramps	Excessive loss of salt from body.	Severe cramps in limbs, back and/or abdomen, following exposure to heat. Body temperature remains normal.	Move patient to cool shaded place. Remove outer clothing. Elevate feet or message legs above the cramp area. Give all water that can be drunk in form of 0.1% saline solution. Get medical attention.
Heat Stroke	Collapse of body cooling mechanism.	Hot dry skin. Headache, mental confusion, and bizarre behavior, dizziness, weakness and rapid breathing and pulse. High temperature (106°F+). May be unconscious.	Medical emergency. Seek medical aid immediately. The lowering of the patient's body temperature as rapidly as possible is the most important objective in the treatment of heat stroke. Move individual to shaded area. Remove clothing. Sprinkle or bathe patient with cool water and fan to increase cooling effect. Massage trunk, arms, and legs. If evacuating to a hospital continue treatment on way.

US Army Heat Illness Guideline

An individual who has already had a heat stroke or severe case of heat exhaustion is more likely to fall sick again than one who has not suffered from these illnesses. An individual who has already been affected should be subsequently exposed to potential heat stress with caution.

Symptoms to Distinguish Between Salt Depletion and Water Depletion

Symptoms	Salt Depletion	Water Depletion
Duration of symptoms	3-5 days	1 day
Thirst	seldom	prominent
Fatigue	prominent	seldom
Cramps	prominent	none
Vomiting	prominent	none
Weakness	progressive	acute

EXCESSIVE HEAT

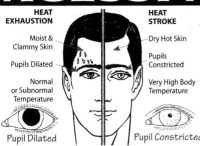

HEAT EXHAUSTION | HEAT STROKE
- Moist & Clammy Skin — Dry Hot Skin
- Pupils Dilated — Pupils Constricted
- Normal or Subnormal Temperature — Very High Body Temperature
- Pupil Dilated — Pupil Constricted

PRECAUTIONS AGAINST HEAT ILLNESS

- Avoid heavy exertion if not acclimatized to the heat or humidity.
- Eat fruits and vegetables to have an additional source of salt.
- Increase the movement of the air as it helps the natural cooling system of the body. Wear light colored loose fitting cotton clothing.
- Increase water consumption to at least 8 pints (5 L) per day. Drink small quantities of water at frequent intervals to avoid an increase in sweating.
- Increase salt intake. Use 2 salt tablets with a quart of water, four times daily. If table salt is used take a level teaspoonful (5 ml) dissolved in a quart of water every morning and evening. Add extra salt to the food. Extra salt will reduce fatigue and listlessness common to hot and humid climates. Use the Urine Test outlined on next page to check for salt deficiency.
- Avoid exposure to the sun during the hottest part of the day. Wear a wide-brimmed hat. From time to time douse the head with cold water. Do not remove your shirt as it helps to retain the sweat that cools your body. Keep your body covered at all times.
- Noon meals should be light. Eat the more substantial meals in the evening. Avoid caffeine (coke, tea and coffee).
- If working take frequent rests and drink a lot of fluids. Avoid alcohol.
- Bathe frequently as clean skin helps sweating. Do not use too much skin cream as it clogs the pores. Keep your clothing clean and dry to avoid fungal infection.
- If you have any of the symptoms of Heat Illness get medical help.

HOT WEATHER LEG CRAMPS

Loss of potassium, sodium, and salt might cause leg cramps in hot weather. This loss causes cramps that are spasmodic painful contractions of muscles, usually in the leg. To reduce the probability of these cramps eat well balanced meals rich in potassium and sodium. Foods to eat are eggs, liver, chicken, milk, citrus fruits, bananas and dark green leafy vegetables. The victim of an attack should rest in a cool area and drink a saline solution or lemonade. Avoid cramps by warming up before any strenuous activity.

During an attach stretch out the muscle while massaging above the painful area to increase the flow of blood.

People living in urban areas may be at greater risk from the effects of a prolonged heat wave than people living in rural regions. In urban areas there is a lack of trees and grass and the asphalt streets and dark roofs retain heat. An increased health problem can occur when stagnant atmospheric conditions trap pollutants in urban areas, thus adding contaminated air to excessively hot temperatures.

HEATSTROKE (SUNSTROKE)

Heatstroke can occur after a few hours of exposure to intense heat, but usually after a few days or weeks of exposure as in a heat wave or holiday in the tropics. People from temperate climates who have not had a chance to acclimatize are at a higher risk of being affected. The problem of heat is increased when combined with strenuous activities.

Heatstroke is caused by the failure of the brain in regulating the heat mechanism of the body which will cause a cessation of sweating (cooling).

- The initial symptoms are a feeling of weakness, nausea and headache (symptoms which are typical of heat exhaustion). Its appearance is usually sudden.
- Onset is very rapid. Immediate attention is required as a heatstroke is dangerous to life.

A heatstroke is characterized by:
- The skin being dry, flushed and burning and sweating will stop.
- Person appears feverish. Lack of coordination.
- Nausea and vomiting.
- Have a headache.
- Restlessness and mental confusion.

This may lead to:
- Respiration rate will rise.
- The pulse rate is high even up to 160.
- Twitching and cramps of the muscles will occur.
- Body temperature can be between 105°-110°F (40.5°-43.3°C).
- Delirium, collapse, convulsions, and coma will lead to death.

The patient's temperature will be at 105°F (40.5°C) and can go to 110°F (43.3°C) before death occurs. Medical attention is required if the initial stages of heatstroke are suspected.

HEAT CRAMP

Heat cramps are caused by the loss of salt when there is excessive sweating. The lack of salt will affect the muscles of the abdomen and limbs giving severe and painful cramps. There may be vomiting. Cramps may be a side affect of heat exhaustion.

Treatment

The victim should lie down. If there are abdominal cramps apply a hot water bottle and massage the cramped muscles. Give the victim saline water of a 1/4 teaspoon of salt in a quart of water. The victim should rest for at least 12 hours before resuming any strenuous activities. In the victim continues the activities causing the sweating he should increase his water and salt intake to reduce the risk of cramps.
See Hot Weather Leg Cramps; adjacent article.

TREATMENT OF HEATSTROKE
Immediately Cool the Patient

Cooling the patient is the very important in treating a heatstroke and should be carried out immediately. *Continually* watch the fall of the temperature as prolonged exposure to cold might cause hypothermia. Reduce the temperature of the patient to below 100°F (37.8°C) as soon as possible. Move patient to a cool place and strip naked. Cover with a wet sheet and massage vigorously with a cold cloth and ice cubes. If you have a fan direct its airflow over the wet sheets. The fan increases the cooling by evaporation. If available, immerse the patient in a tub of ice cold water. At 100°F (37.8°C) natural body sweating usually resumes. Keep the patient in a cool spot and watch for symptoms of hypothermia. Continually take the temperature and if it begins to rise resume the cooling treatment.

Urgently get medical help.
Replace Lost Body Fluid & Salt

- Have patient drink a saline water mixture of a teaspoon of table salt (or 8 salt tablets) per pint of water. The patient can also drink water or fruit juices.
- In general the patient should have at least 8 pints of saline or other fluid in 24 hours.
- The patient, upon recovering, should be covered with a light dry blanket and kept in a cool spot for a week. Make sure that he drinks sufficient water. Watch for any signs of a relapse.

HEAT EXHAUSTION

Excessive sweating in hot climates causes dehydration (loss of body fluids) and loss of salt. The use of alcohol, vomiting, diarrhea, or other loss of body fluids will increase a persons exposure to heat exhaustion. *The loss of salt and water unbalances the body fluids which results in a series of symptoms called heat exhaustion.* Usually caused by extreme physical exertion in hot and humid areas to which a person lacks acclimatization. Its effect accumulates over a prolonged period if the physical activities are maintained.

Symptoms

Thirst, listlessness, loss of appetite, ashen skin, dizziness, cool clammy sweating skin, nausea and vomiting and mild muscular heat cramps. Concentration is difficult. The heart may race with the pulse at 100 beats per minute. The temperature may be below normal or slightly raised. Fainting may occur the victim might even become unconscious. Prickly Heat (see article) is also a form of heat exhaustion. *Get medical help.*

Treatment

Keep patient in a cool well ventilated area. Loosen and wet the clothing. Administer water to which a level teaspoonful of table salt (or 8 salt tablets) per pint has been added. Have the person rest for at least 24 hours while still drinking a saline solution. Add salt to light food.

SUN SAFETY & UV RADIATION

Positive Effects: Positive effects of UV radiation include warmth, light, photosynthesis in plants, and vitamin D synthesis in the body. UV radiation gives a positive mood in people and kills bacterial and fungal growth. In the desert where washing is difficult it is good to air your clothing in the sun.

Negative Effects: Overexposure to UV radiation has adverse health effects. Overexposure to UV radiation is the primary environmental risk factor in the development of diseases of the eye, immune suppression, and skin cancers (Basal Cell, Squamous Cell Cancers, and Melanoma). Children are most at risk for overexposure to UV radiation.

Eye Damage: "Snow Blindness" a "burning" of the eye surface from extended exposure to bright sunlight. The effect usually disappear within a couple of days, but may lead to further complications later in life. Cataracts of the eye might also be caused by unprotected exposure to strong sunlight.

Photo aging 'Wrinkles': Chronic overexposure to the sun changes the texture and weakens the elastic properties of the skin. The epidermis, which is the outer layer of the skin, thickens, becomes leathery, and wrinkles as a result of sun skin exposure.

SUNBURN

- For minor burns, apply cold cream, talcum powder or mineral oil to relieve the pain.
- If badly burned and blistered apply cold compresses of water, whole milk, or a saline solution. An effective saline solution would be one teaspoon of salt to a pint of cool water.

A severe sunburn should be treated by a doctor to avoid infection.

Prevention

- Keep the body covered. Especially if your skin is very sensitive and has not previously been exposed to the sun.
- The body should be gradually exposed to the sun. Initially at 15 minute intervals per day (including cloudy days). Increase the exposure 5 - 10 minutes a day until it is less sensitive. Cloudy days can cause sunburns.
- Apply a high rated sunscreen but to minimize any risk of skin cancer keep your body covered and wear a wide brimmed hat.

DISLODGING A FOREIGN OBJECT FROM THE RESPIRATORY TRACK OF A YOUNG CHILD

The young child can be laid prone with the head downwards over the knee and given three or four sharp slaps between the shoulders to dislodge the foreign body. If the child is light enough you can hold the child up by the legs and then slap three or four times between the shoulders.

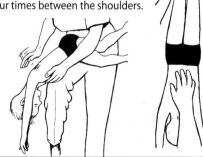

PRICKLY HEAT

Occurs when it is hot with high humidity. It is a rash of tiny red pimples which is extremely itchy and irritating.

It affects any part of the body but most common in areas where tight fitting clothing does not let the body breath and sweat and humidity build up. This impairs the sweat glands and they do not function properly. Prickly heat might occur on the forehead below a cap, on the back below a backpack, or below a pant waistline. If the area is not washed and dried a minor rash can develop into septic spots or boils. If very humid it can occur on areas exposed to the sun such as the forearms and hands. There might be some of the symptoms of heat illness.

Treatment

Try to avoid the rash by taking frequent showers. Clothing worn should be light, loose, porous and washed frequently. Place a cotton towel between your nylon backpack and your back when traveling on hot humid days. When stopping on a hike let the humid clothing dry in the sun. This will reduce the possibility of fungal growth.

If you have a rash bathe frequently every day in cold water, dry well, and put on clean clothing (preferably clean loose cotton garments). During showers avoid the use of soap or rubbing the affected parts. After a shower pat the affected area dry and apply some calamine which will dry to a fine powder. Avoid creams that will clog pores.

EXCESSIVE HEAT

US Army Salt Requirement Guidelines	
Addition of table salt to produce 0.1% salt solution	
Table Salt	**Amount of Water**
1/4 spoon (3.7 ml)	1 quart canteen (625 ml)
1 1/3 level mess kit spoons	5 gallon can (19 L)
9 level mess kit spoons (0.3 lb)	36 gallon bag (136 L)
1 lb (450 g)	100 gallon tank (379 L)
1 level canteen cup	250 gallons (946 L)

SALT REQUIREMENTS

URINE SALT TEST PAPERS

To test for excessive salt loss place a salt test paper in a urine sample or pass urine on to it and watch for the color change.

If normal the color becomes bright yellow. If salt is immediately required the paper will take a long time to change, be incomplete or not change at all.

The paper is light sensitive and should be stored in the dark. If unexposed it is brick red, when exposed to light it becomes harder and the color becomes like chocolate and then slate colored. The paper is sensitive to the salty sweat on the hands, which might cause it to change, handle with care.

Take salt tablets only if specified by your physician.

Persons on salt-restrictive diets should check with a physician before increasing salt intake.

Dangers of Sun Exposure
Types of Ultraviolet Radiation

Type	Effect	Long Term Effects
UVA	No pain	Penetrates the deepest layers of the skin. Linked to skin cancer and photo aging. UV exposure is cumulative during your life.
UVB	Burns skin	The body protects itself by producing pigment melanin which produces a tan. Over exposure produces a burn which shows that the defence mechanism has been overwhelmed.
UVC		Filtered out by the ozone layer.

CHILD DROWNING

Pool submersions involving children happen quickly. A child can drown in the time it takes to answer a phone. 75% of the victims had been missing from sight for 5 minutes or less. Survival depends on rescuing the child quickly and restarting the breathing process, even while the child is still in the water. Seconds count in preventing death or brain damage. Child drowning is a silent death. There's no splashing to alert anyone that the child is in trouble. If a child is missing, check the pool first. Seconds count in preventing death or disability. Go to the edge of the pool and scan the entire pool, bottom and surface, as well as the pool area.

SEQUENCE OF EVENTS IN A DROWNING

- A problem occurs
- This is followed by panic and loss of control
- Inefficient breathing, retention or deprivation of air
- Decreased buoyancy
- Exhaustion
- Drowning or cardiac arrest

Cold Water Death

Water in May, June and July is still cold. Body temperature, in the water, might drop 6°- 8°F which affects rational thinking. Studies indicate that if a person remains immobile in the water his probability of rescue is increased 30%. Swimming increases the loss of core heat by 35% to 50% as opposed to remaining still.

DROWNING SURVIVAL DEPENDS UPON

- Speed of rescue
- Knowledge of artificial resuscitation... by the rescuer and rapid application and persistence with resuscitation efforts. Extended efforts have saved many victims.
- Immediate clearing of the airway... by turning the victim on his stomach or lowering his head.
- Immediate use of artificial ventilation & cardiopulmonary resuscitation (CPR), if required.
- Will of the victim to recover.
- The type of water and under what conditions the accident occurred. The possibility of hypothermia, etc.

GUARD AGAINST DROWNING...

You can greatly reduce the chances of you or your children becoming drowning or near-drowning victims by following a few simple safety tips:

- Whenever young children are swimming, playing, or bathing in water, make sure an adult is constantly watching them. The supervising adult should not read, play cards, talk on the phone, mow the lawn, or do any other distracting activity while watching children.
- Never swim alone or in unsupervised places. Teach children to always swim with a buddy.
- Keep small children away from buckets containing liquid: 5-gallon industrial containers are a particular danger. Be sure to empty buckets when household chores are done.
- Never drink alcohol during or just before swimming, boating, or water skiing. Never drink alcohol while supervising children. Teach teenagers about the danger of drinking alcohol and swimming, boating, or water skiing.
- Respect the "power" of water.
- Learn to swim and understand the water environment.
- Do not swim alone or without a life guard present. Follow the beach safety rules.
- If swimming underwater tell a friend as you might need help if you get tangled in debris, blackout or have cramps.
- Beware of cold water as it might cause cramps or immersion hypothermia.
- Watch for flash floods on dry riverbeds and high tide areas when pitching camp for the night. Listen for any unusual sounds as they might foretell a flash flood from a distant storm.
- When attempting to rescue a potential drowning victim throw a flotation device, rope, or extend a stick. Avoid jumping into the water especially if you are a weak swimmer or water conditions are unpredictable.

TO PREVENT CHOKING...

Never chew gum or eat while swimming, diving, or playing in water.

CHECK EYE PUPIL

Pupil that constricts to light. — Dilated Pupil

To verify the effectiveness of your CPR check the pupils of the eyes from time to time.
- Pupils that constrict when exposed to light indicate adequate oxygenation and blood flow to the brain.
- Pupils that remain dilated and do not react to light indicate that serious brain damage may be imminent or may have occurred. Dilated pupils, but still reacting, are a less ominous sign.

TIPS: OPEN WATER

- Know the local weather conditions and forecast before swimming or boating. Listen to weather forecasts, have a barometer, watch for a change in the direction of the wind or waves, and learn how to read the clouds for major changes in weather.
- Thunderstorms and strong winds can be extremely dangerous to swimmers and boaters.
- Restrict activities to designated swimming areas, which are usually marked by buoys.
- Be cautious, even with lifeguards present.
- Watch where you dive especially if you do not know the depth or what debris is at the bottom.
- Use U.S. Coast Guard-approved personal flotation devices (life jackets) when boating, regardless of distance to be traveled, size of boat, or swimming ability of boaters.
- Stay with a capsized boat or debris and if possible attach yourself to it.
- Remember that open water usually has limited visibility, and conditions can sometimes change from hour to hour. Currents are often unpredictable - they can move rapidly and quickly change direction. A strong water current can carry even expert swimmers far from shore.
- Watch for dangerous waves and signs of rip currents - water that is discolored, unusually choppy, foamy, or filled with debris.
- If you are caught in a rip current, swim parallel to the shore. Once you are out of the current, swim toward the shore.
- Be careful when fording streams.

COLD WATER DEATH
(Immersion Hypothermia)

Drowning can be caused by water in the lungs or by immersion hypothermia which is the same as hypothermia on land. In cold water the unprotected body chills rapidly and as its temperature falls the victim becomes numb, unconscious, and slides below the water. See Hypothermia as outlined on page 121, 181, 199, 588, 589. The exposed body in water below 20°C (68°F) cannot maintain its normal functions and the pulse slows, breathing and, heartbeat is erratic and death follows. Clothing reduces heat loss. Wet clothing does not retain the insulation loft of dry clothing but it reduces the water's convection currents on the body. Clothed and not moving in the water will help reduce heat loss. Swimming and movement increases heat loss. If the victim is not recovered in a short time he will succumb to hypothermia. Cold water death can occur when falling through the ice.

Treatment

Rewarm the victim in a hot bath or remove all the wet clothing, dry the body, and wrap it in a warm blanket. Offer some hot drinks. Artificial resuscitation might be required. "Drowning victims" might be revived by rewarming.

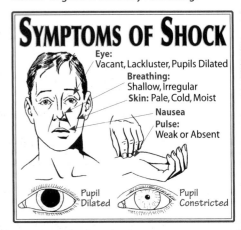

SYMPTOMS OF SHOCK

Eye: Vacant, Lackluster, Pupils Dilated
Breathing: Shallow, Irregular
Skin: Pale, Cold, Moist
Nausea
Pulse: Weak or Absent

Pupil Dilated — Pupil Constricted

In 2010 the American Heart Association updated its guidelines for CPR with chest compressions. The major change is the change of the sequence in performing CPR...
TO... Circulation, Airway, Breathing (CAB)
FROM... Airway, Breathing, Circulation (ABC)

This change emphasizes the restoration of blood circulation with chest compressions. This action will help to keep blood flowing through the heart and the brain.

FIRST if possible Call 911...
Check the victim for unresponsiveness. If the person is not responsive and not breathing or not breathing normally. Call 911 and return to the victim. In most locations the emergency dispatcher can assist you with CPR instructions.

SECOND... PUMP
If the victim is still not breathing normally, coughing or moving, begin chest compressions. Push down in the center of the chest 2 inches 30 times. Pump hard and fast at the rate of at least 100/ minute, faster than once per second.

THIRD... BLOW
Tilt the head back and lift the chin. Pinch nose and cover the mouth with yours and blow until you see the chest rise. Give 2 breaths. Each breath should take 1 second. CONTINUE WITH 30 PUMPS AND 2 BREATHS UNTIL HELP ARRIVES
NOTE: This ratio is the same for one-person & two-person CPR. In two-person CPR the person pumping the chest stops while the other gives mouth-to-mouth breathing.

ESTABLISH PRESENCE OF A PULSE

Lightly place two fingers on the air pipe below the chin. Slide the fingers into the grove between the air pipe and the muscle below the ear and jaw bone. At this point you should feel the blood pulse of the carotid artery.
See Pressure Points: page 584.

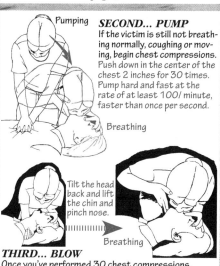

Pumping

SECOND... PUMP
If the victim is still not breathing normally, coughing or moving, begin chest compressions. Push down in the center of the chest 2 inches for 30 times. Pump hard and fast at the rate of at least 100/ minute, faster than once per second.

Breathing

Tilt the head back and lift the chin and pinch nose.

Breathing

THIRD... BLOW
Once you've performed 30 chest compressions, open the person's airway using the head-tilt, chin-lift maneuver. Tilt the head back and lift the chin. Pinch nose and cover the mouth with yours and blow until you see the chest rise. Give 2 breaths. Each breath should take 1 second. CONTINUE WITH 30 PUMPS AND 2 BREATHS UNTIL HELP ARRIVES.

LOCATING PRESSURE POINT FOR CHEST COMPRESSION

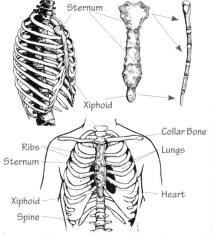

Sternum

Xiphoid

Collar Bone
Ribs
Sternum
Lungs
Xiphoid
Heart
Spine

If pressure is not applied vertical to the ground you might fracture ribs, the sternum or may lacerate the heart. The vertical position distributes the pressure, that you exert, over all the ribs at the same time. Control the application of pressure. Do not use a jabbing motion as it can not be effectively controlled. Jabbing motions risk producing fractures of the ribs and sternum.

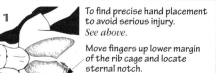

1 To find precise hand placement to avoid serious injury. *See above.*

Move fingers up lower margin of the rib cage and locate sternal notch.

Finger on sternum head.

2

3

Place heel of hand closest to head of sternum next to, but not covering, the finger. Place the second hand on first.

HAND PLACEMENT FOR CHEST COMPRESSIONS
Location of the heart is slightly to the left of the middle of the chest between the sternum and the spine. Rhythmic pressure-and-relaxation applied to the lower half of the sternum compresses the heart and produces artificial circulation.

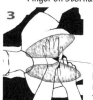

Position of Hands
The heel of only one hand is in contact with the sternum. The second hand is on top of the first hand.

CHEST COMPRESSIONS
100 compressions a minute.

Keep elbows straight with shoulders directly above hands.

See adjacent articles for hand placement.

Using your upper body weight (not just your arms) as you push straight down on the chest for depth of at least 2 inches. Pushing hard at a rate of at least 100 compressions a minute.

Place victim on flat firm surface and kneel next to victim for stability.

OPENING THE AIRWAY: HEAD TILT MANEUVERS

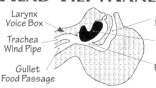

Larynx Voice Box
Trachea Wind Pipe
Gullet Food Passage
Nasal Passage
Tongue
Pharynx Passage for food + air.

When the victim is laid flat on the ground the tongue might block the airway (Pharynx).

Tongue

It is essential that the air passage from mouth to lungs be open.

Jaw-Thrust Maneuver
Neck raised forehead tilted backwards and tongue moves to open the airway.

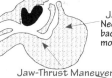

Jaw-Thrust Maneuver

Tilt victim's head back as far as possible. Sometimes the victim might start breathing spontaneously.

Head Tilt- Neck Lift Maneuver
The best way to tilt the head backwards is by placing a hand on the victim's forehead and pressing down as far as possible with the palm. The second hand can be used to apply a neck lift or chin lift.

Head Tilt-Jaw Lift Maneuver
Pull the jaw and pushing the forehead will assure the opening of the airway.

One of these maneuvers usually works to free the airway. If not, pull the jaw forward (this can be done quite forcefully) while pushing on the forehead.
Do not press on the soft tissue below the chin as it might obstruct the airway.

HEIMLICH MANEUVER FOR CHOKING

A choking victim cannot speak and has difficulty breathing needs immediate help. Do not slap the victim's back - the problem might get worse.
- Stand behind the victim and wrap your hands around the victim's waist.
- Clasp your hands together with your thumbs towards the victim - just below the rib cage and above the navel - as in the illustration.
- Do not squeeze the rib cage.
- Give quick upward abdominal thrusts.
- Repeat until object is expelled. If unresponsive use the Ventilation Method (see in Drowning).

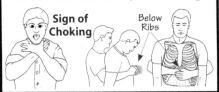

Sign of Choking   Below Ribs

Tie   Tied Crawl

CARRY AN INJURED PERSON

JACKET METHOD

Fold two or three shirts or field jackets so that the lining is on the outside. Button them up with the sleeves inside. Pass a pole through each sleeve.

Jacket Litter

CHAIR USED AS A LITTER

The patient can be attached to a chair with a belt. The carrier at the head position should first tilt the chair back.
The carrier at the leg position can bend his knees, keeping his body straight, and then pick up the legs of the chair.

OPEN BLANKET LITTER

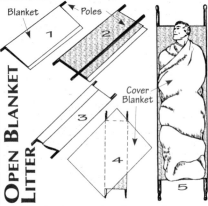

Blanket   Poles

Cover Blanket

- The blanket is spread on the ground.
- One pole is laid across the center of the blanket which is then folded over it.
- The second pole is placed across the center of the new fold.
- The blanket is folded over the second pole as over the first.
- The free end of the blanket is attached.

LITTER BEARERS

Litter bearers are ordinarily grouped into squads of four for carrying patients. The fatigue of long carries should be shared by the group of at least four people.

General Rules for Litter Bearers
- In moving a patient, the litter bearers must make every movement deliberately and as gently as possible. The command STEADY should be used to prevent undue haste and other irregular movements.
- The rear bearers should watch the movements of the front bearers and time their movements with them to insure easy and steady progress.
- The litter should be kept as level as possible at all times even when crossing obstacles such as ditches.
- As a general rule, the patient should be carried on the litter feet first except when going uphill or upstairs when the head should be forward. If the patient has a fracture of the lower extremity (or for any reason beneficial to the patient), he should be carried uphill or upstairs feet foremost and downhill or downstairs head foremost to prevent the weight of the body from pressing upon the injured part.

IMPROVISING A LITTER

Many objects and materials may be used to make improvised litters in an emergency. The usual way to make a litter is with a blanket, shelter tent, or poncho and poles about 7 feet (2 m) long.

Oar Litter

FLAT SURFACE METHOD

Use any flat-surfaced object of suitable size, such as cots, window shutters, doors, benches, ladders, boards, or poles tied together. Pad the litter if possible.

Door Flat Surface Litter

POSITIONING VICTIM FOR LIFTING

The first step in manual carries is to position the victim who is to be lifted. If victim is conscious, tell him how he is being positioned and transported. This will reduce his fear of movement and gain his cooperation. It may be necessary to roll the victim onto his abdomen or his back depending upon the position in which he is lying and a particular method of carry to be used.

Four Hand Seat Carry

Blanket Pull

Two Hand Seat Carry

Fore and Aft Carry

Maintain body temperature while planning transport.

PIGGY BACK

A simple method of carrying a person is only useful when he is conscious and able to hold onto the carrier with his arms round the carrier's neck.

TWO-HAND SEAT CARRY

The two-hand seat carry is used in carrying a patient for a short distance and to place a patient on a litter

THREE HANDED SEAT

Handy method of carrying a patient. One arm and hand of one of the helpers is left free and can be used either to support an injured leg or as a back support for the patient.

FOUR HAND SEAT CARRY

Two men holding each other's wrists form a four hand seat with which to carry a patient. A conscious patient supports himself with his arms around the shoulders of his helpers. This carry is especially useful in transporting the patient with a head or foot injury for a moderate distance or to place him on a litter or vehicle.

ORDINARY MAN HANDLING

A patient may be carried by two helpers without a "seat" being formed by their hands. One arm of each helper supports the back and shoulders and their hands hold the patient's thighs. The patient can help to support himself with his hands on the shoulders of the helpers sufficiently firmly in place to prevent movement, but not so tightly as to interfere with the circulation of the blood in the limb.

TWO-MAN SUPPORTING CARRY

Can be used in transporting both conscious and unconscious patients. If a patient is taller than the bearers, it may be necessary for the bearers to lift the legs and let them rest on their forearms.

TWO-MAN ARMS CARRY

Useful in carrying a patient for a moderate distance and for placing a patient on a litter. To lessen fatigue, the bearers should carry the patient as high and close to their chests as possible. In extreme emergencies, when there is no time to obtain a litter, this manual carry is the safest one for transporting a patient with a back injury. Two additional bearers should be used to keep the patient's head and legs in alignment with his body.

FORE-AND-AFT CARRY

The fore-and-aft carry is a useful two-man carry for transporting the patient a long distance. One helper supports the patient under his arms and the other under his knees. The taller of the two bearers should position himself at the head of the patient. By altering this carry so that both bearers face the patient, it is also useful for placing a patient on a litter.

FIREMAN'S CARRY

The fireman's carry is one of the easiest ways for one individual to carry another. After the unconscious patient has been properly positioned, he is raised from the ground, supported and placed in the carrying position.

Piggy Back   Fireman's Carry

NON-CORROSIVE POISONS

It is essential to immediately get the poison out of the victim's stomach. This should not be done with corrosive poisons.

Encourage Vomiting: If conscious tickle the back of the throat with the fingers. A mixture of two tablespoonfuls of salt in a glassful of warm water can induce vomiting. After vomiting have the victim drink water, milk, or tea to help dilute any remaining poison.

Get medical attention.

CORROSIVE POISONS

The victim should not be made to vomit.
Strong corrosive poisons usually leave a yellowish, black or grey stain on the contact point with the body. If it has been swallowed the pain will be intense and the victim will be in a state of shock.

FOR CORROSIVE POISONS

Do not know poison: Have victim drink a large quantity of cold water or milk. Then the victim should drink a mixture of raw eggs or flour and water.
Acid: Give the victim a mild alkali to neutralize the acid. This mild alkali can be half a tablespoon of bicarbonate of soda in a cup of water or a tablespoonful of stomach powder in a cup of water. Follow this with a pint of water.
Alkali: Give the victim a mild acid to neutralize the Alkali. This can be two tablespoons of vinegar in a glass of water. Lemon or lime juice can be mixed with an equal part of water.

SWALLOWED POISONS

These affect the digestive track and will cause vomiting, abdominal pain, and diarrhea. These poisons can be poisonous berries, contaminated food, poisonous mushrooms, etc..
Some swallowed poisons might have a delayed reaction as they will only act after they have been absorbed by the blood and then affect the nervous system. Some of these poisons can be sedative tablets, excessive alcohol, and cyanide.

Treatment
Get medical help.
The following is only an outline.
Prompt treatment is essential. Find the source of the poison. If the victim is conscious he might indicate the source. If unconscious, there might be some telltale signs: a bottle, partially eaten food, etc. which might indicate the source of poisoning. Telephone hospital poison unit for help.

TETANUS

Make sure that your anti-tetanus shot is up to date especially if you live in the country.
The incubation period is usually 2 to 8 days and sometimes up to 3 weeks. Tetanus (Lock-Jaw) is a disease that enters the body through a wound or scratch. The germ, a microbe that is usually found in soil fertilized with manure, is common in nature. Tetanus is characterized by painful muscular contractions and spasms starting in the jaw and neck muscles and soon spreads to the back and upper body. Muscular spasms become more frequent with the victim having a sardonic grin during an attack. If untreated exhaustion, heart failure, and death might occur or the spasms become less frequent and the victim recovers. The mortality rate is high.
Get medical help immediately.

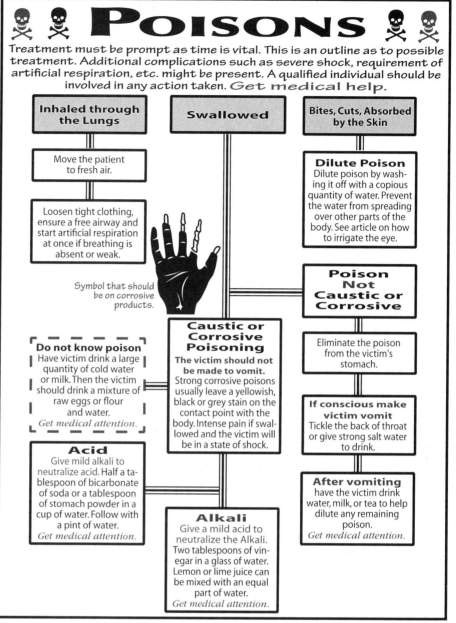

☠ ☠ POISONS ☠ ☠

Treatment must be prompt as time is vital. This is an outline as to possible treatment. Additional complications such as severe shock, requirement of artificial respiration, etc. might be present. A qualified individual should be involved in any action taken. *Get medical help.*

Inhaled through the Lungs

Move the patient to fresh air.

Loosen tight clothing, ensure a free airway and start artificial respiration at once if breathing is absent or weak.

Symbol that should be on corrosive products.

Swallowed

Do not know poison
Have victim drink a large quantity of cold water or milk. Then the victim should drink a mixture of raw eggs or flour and water.
Get medical attention.

Acid
Give mild alkali to neutralize acid. Half a tablespoon of bicarbonate of soda or a tablespoon of stomach powder in a cup of water. Follow with a pint of water.
Get medical attention.

Caustic or Corrosive Poisoning
The victim should not be made to vomit.
Strong corrosive poisons usually leave a yellowish, black or grey stain on the contact point with the body. Intense pain if swallowed and the victim will be in a state of shock.

Alkali
Give a mild acid to neutralize the Alkali. Two tablespoons of vinegar in a glass of water. Lemon or lime juice can be mixed with an equal part of water.
Get medical attention.

Bites, Cuts, Absorbed by the Skin

Dilute Poison
Dilute poison by washing it off with a copious quantity of water. Prevent the water from spreading over other parts of the body. See article on how to irrigate the eye.

Poison Not Caustic or Corrosive

Eliminate the poison from the victim's stomach.

If conscious make victim vomit
Tickle the back of throat or give strong salt water to drink.

After vomiting
have the victim drink water, milk, or tea to help dilute any remaining poison.
Get medical attention.

CANNED FOOD

Examine all tin cans that have been stored. If storing tin cans, date them and consume the oldest first. The ends of untainted tin cans are usually concave or flat. When you press the end and it moves in and out this means that the can has lost its vacuum and should be thrown away. When a tin is opened and the contents has an abnormal color and/or an unusual odor do not consume the contents. When the ends bulge out (convex) suspect a problem of decomposition.
Do not eat.

SMALLPOX *(Variola Major)*

Was a highly contagious disease characterized by fever, a vesicular and pustular eruption, and a high mortality rate. At one time, smallpox accounted for 10% of all deaths in the world. The global eradication of smallpox was officially announced in 1979, marking one of the greatest achievements of modern medicine. By 1985, less than ten years after the last reported case, routine vaccination against smallpox was abandoned throughout the world.

MOTION SICKNESS

Occurs usually in a confined space, with the body subject to acceleration or erratic movement, when the visual reference contact with the outside horizon is not available. What actually happens is that the balance center of the inner ear sends signals of movement (the movement of the vehicle) to the brain while the eye sees the inside of the vehicle (outside not visible as in a ship's or airplane's cabin or if you are reading a book while the car is moving) as standing still.
Symptoms: dizziness, fatigue, nausea & vomiting.
Prevention: Find a place of less movement or face fore ward and look out of a window to re-establish a true horizon. Some medications are available - *see a doctor.*

TRAVELER'S DIARRHEA

The most common cause is the Escherichia coli bacteria. This bacteria is in your digestive tract and helps your intestines in the digestion process. Foreign strains of the bacteria can give you diarrhea by producing a toxin that prevents your intestines from absorbing the water ingested in the form of fluid and food. This will cause runny stools and you might feel nausea, possibly have cramps and a slight fever. Drink a lot of water as it will help you avoid dehydration.

How to Avoid Traveler's Diarrhea

- When traveling in underdeveloped areas avoid uncooked vegetables, salads, fruits that cannot peel, under cooked meat, raw shellfish and ice cubes made from local water.
- Dishes and cutlery have to be cleaned with purified water.
- Drink carbonated water that has been sealed in bottles or cans.
- See Finding Water and Summer Hiking Chapters on the purification of water.
- Drink acidic drinks like orange juice and colas as these will reduce the bacteria count.

If you have any medical side effects (e.g. red or black stools, fever, abdominal bloating, vomiting) immediately see a doctor. A severe diarrhea can cause excessive fluid and salt loss. This can lead to dehydration, electrolyte imbalance, shock, and possible death.

Natural remedies if no alternatives:

Clay: Type of clay containing kaolin can be eaten. It is found on river banks.

Ash: Brew ash from a fire or burned, pulverized bone fragments into a tea.

Tannic acid: Use a tea with tannic acid as it will stop muscular contractions of the intestines. Brew a tea of acorns, the bark of oak trees or other hardwoods.

Blackberry root: Boil as a tea. *See Edible Plant Chapter.*

Plantain: Make into a tea as the leaves are strongly astringent.

Apple peels: Cook the peels and drink the liquid.

Blueberries: Five or six blueberries will cure diarrhea. If you eat too many blueberries you will become constipated.

COCCIDIOIDOMYCOSIS

Coccidioides immitis

Infection usually presents as influenza-like illness with fever, cough, headaches, rash, and myalgias.

Region: Soils in semiarid areas, (primarily in the "lower Sonoran life zone"). Endemic in the southwestern United States, parts of Mexico and South America.

Transmission: Inhalation of airborne arthroconidia after disturbance of soil by humans or natural disasters (e.g., wind storms & earthquakes).

Risk groups: Persons in areas with endemic disease who have occupations exposing them to dust (e.g., construction or agricultural workers, and archeologists). High risk groups are African-Americans and Asians, pregnant women during the third trimester, and immunocompromised persons.

BLASTOMYCOSIS

Symptoms: Usually presents as a flu-like illness with fever, chills, productive cough, myalgia, arthralgia and pleuritic chest pain.

Source: Moist soil enriched with decomposing organic debris. Endemic in parts of the south-central, south-eastern and mid-western US.

Transmission: Inhalation of airborne conidia (spores) after disturbance of contaminated soil.

Risk Groups: Persons in areas with endemic disease with exposures to wooded sites (e.g., farmers, forestry workers, hunters, and campers).

LISTERIOSIS

Listeriosis, a serious infection caused by eating food contaminated with the bacterium Listeria monocytogenes, has recently been recognized as an important public health problem in the United States. The disease affects primarily pregnant women, newborns, and adults with weakened immune systems. It can be avoided by following a few simple recommendations.

Symptoms: A person with listeriosis has fever, muscle aches, and sometimes gastrintestinal symptoms such as nausea or diarrhea. If infection spreads to the nervous system, symptoms such as headache, stiff neck, confusion, loss of balance, or convulsions can occur.

Source of Listeria

Listeria monocytogenes is found in soil and water. Vegetables can become contaminated from the soil or from manure used as fertilizer. Animals can carry the bacterium without appearing ill and can contaminate foods of animal origin such as meats and dairy products. The bacterium has been found in a variety of raw foods, such as uncooked meats and vegetables, as well as in processed foods that become contaminated after processing, such as soft cheeses and cold cuts at the deli counter. Unpasteurized (raw) milk or foods made from unpasteurized milk may contain the bacterium. Listeria is killed by pasteurization, and heating procedures used to prepare ready-to-eat processed meats should be sufficient to kill the bacterium; however, unless good manufacturing practices are followed, contamination can occur after processing.

Prevention: The general guidelines recommended for the prevention of listeriosis are similar to those used to help prevent other food borne illnesses, such as salmonellosis.

- Thoroughly cook raw food from animal sources, such as beef, pork, or poultry.
- Wash raw vegetables thoroughly before eating.
- Keep uncooked meats separate from vegetables and from cooked foods and ready-to-eat foods.
- Avoid raw (unpasteurized) milk or foods made from raw milk.
- Wash hands, knives, and cutting boards after handling uncooked foods.
- Left-over foods or ready-to-eat foods, such as hot dogs, should be cooked until steaming hot before eating.

Adapted from the CDC.

HISTOPLASMOSIS

Histoplasmosis is a disease caused by the fungus *Histoplasma capsulatum.* Its symptoms vary greatly, but the disease primarily affect the lungs. Occasionally, other organs are affected.

Region of risk: H. capsulatum is common in the eastern and central United States. The fungus has been found in poultry house litter, caves, areas harboring bats, and in bird roosts.

Infection: H. capsulatum grows in soil and material contaminated with bat or bird droppings. Spores become airborne when contaminated soil is disturbed. Breathing the spores causes infection. The disease is not transmitted from an infected person to someone else.

Symptoms: Most infected persons have no apparent ill effects. The acute, benign respiratory disease is characterized by respiratory symptoms, a general ill feeling, fever, chest pains, and a dry or nonproductive cough.

Precautions to reduce risk of exposure:

Avoid areas that may harbor the fungus, e.g., accumulations of bird or bat droppings.

Adapted from the CDC.

SCHISTOSOMIASIS

Schistosomiasis, also known as bilharzia, is a disease caused by parasitic worms. Although schistosomiasis is not found in the United States, 200 million people are infected worldwide. Infection occurs when your skin comes in contact with contaminated fresh water in which certain types of snails that carry schistosomes are living.

Fresh water becomes contaminated by Schistosoma eggs when infected people urinate or defecate in the water. The eggs hatch, and if certain types of snails are present in the water, the parasites grow and develop inside the snails. The parasite leaves the snail and enters the water where it can survive for about 48 hours. Schistosoma parasites can penetrate the skin of persons who are wading, swimming, bathing, or washing in contaminated water. Within several weeks, worms grow inside the blood vessels of the body and produce eggs. Some of these eggs travel to the bladder or intestines and are passed into the urine or stool.

Symptoms: Within days after becoming infected, you may develop a rash or itchy skin. Fever, chills, cough, and muscle aches can begin within 1-2 months of infection. Most people have no symptoms at this early phase of infection.

Risk factors: If you live in or travel to areas where schistosomiasis occurs and your skin comes in contact with fresh water from canals, rivers, streams, or lakes, you are at risk of getting schistosomiasis. American areas of risk are: Brazil, Suriname, Venezuela, Antigua, Dominican Republic, Guadeloupe, Martinique, Montserrat, Saint Lucia (risk is low).

Prevent schistosomiasis:

- Avoid swimming or wading in fresh water when you are in countries in which schistosomiasis occurs. Swimming in the ocean and in chlorinated swimming pools is generally thought to be safe.
- **Drink safe water.** Because there is no way to make sure that water coming directly from canals, lakes, rivers, streams or springs is clean safe, you should either boil water for 1 minute or filter water before drinking it. Boiling water for at least 1 minute will kill any harmful parasites, bacteria, or viruses present. Iodine treatment alone WILL NOT GUARANTEE that water is safe and free of all parasites.
- Bath water should be heated for 5 minutes at 150°F. Water held in a storage tank for at least 48 hours should be safe for showering.
- Vigorous towel drying after an accidental, very brief water exposure may help to prevent the Schistosoma parasite from penetrating the skin. You should NOT rely on vigorous towel drying to prevent schistosomiasis.

SPOROTRICHOSIS

Sporotrichosis is a fungal infection caused by a fungus called *Sporothrix schenckii*. It usually infects the skin. Persons handling thorny plants, sphagnum moss, or baled hay are at increased risk of getting sporotrichosis. Outbreaks have occurred among nursery workers handling sphagnum moss, rose gardeners, children playing on baled hay, and greenhouse workers handling bayberry thorns contaminated by the fungus. It enters the skin through small cuts or punctures from thorns, barbs, pine needles, or wires. It is not spread from person to person.

Symptom: The first symptom is usually a small painless bump resembling an insect bite. It can be red, pink, or purple in color. The first nodule may appear any time from 1 to 12 weeks after exposure to the fungus. Usually the nodules are visible within 3 weeks after the fungus enters the skin. The bump (nodule) usually appears on the finger, hand, or arm where the fungus first enters through a break on the skin. This is followed by one or more additional bumps or nodules which open and may resemble boils. Eventually lesions look like open sores (ulcerations) and are very slow to heal. The infection can spread to other areas of the body. *See a doctor.*

Prevention: wear gloves and long sleeves when handling wires, rose bushes, hay bales, conifer (pine) seedlings, or other materials that may cause minor skin breaks. It is also advisable to avoid skin contact with sphagnum moss.

LIFEBOAT & RAFT AILMENTS

Ailments can develop because of exposure to saltwater, wind, sun, heat and cold, and shortage of water.

SALT WATER PROBLEMS

Cracking skin: Skin gets covered with a fine layer of salt from salt water spray. To reduce this problem cover your skin with suntan lotion or soft paraffin wax. If exposed to direct sunlight do not use skin oils as baby oil or butter as you might get a severe sunburn.

Salt water boils: Prolonged salt water spray exposure might lead to salt water boils. Do not squeeze or prick them. Do not remove excess liquid from boils that burst. Bad looking boils should be covered with a dressing.

LACK OF DRINKING WATER

Dry mouth: A common problem which can be relieved by rinsing your mouth with drinking water. You can suck a button or a piece of metal such as a coin. You can chew gum or grease the inside of the mouth with butter or fat.

Urination problems: Urination will be dark and possibly thick as not much water is being consumed. If there is difficulty in passing urine dangle your hand in the sea. This might be of some help.

SUN & WIND EXPOSURE

Cracked & parched lips: These should be smeared with soft paraffin.

Cracked skin: Due to dryness from exposure to the sun and wind. Can be helped by rubbing soft paraffin wax on the skin.

Eye inflammation: Caused by sunburn, wind, fuel oil contamination, or sun glare. Apply soft paraffin wax to the upper and lower eyelids. Make some emergency slit sunglasses. See Inuit sunglasses. These sunglasses will dramatically reduce the intensity of the sun's glare, the salt spray settling in the sensitive eye area, and reduce the drying action of the wind. Bandage eyes if painful and bloodshot.

MOTION SICKNESS

- A slight feeling of listlessness with a headache.
- A dry mouth.
- Sense of nausea in the stomach.
- Repeated vomiting due to the continual motion of a small boat. It might also have been caused by having swallowed oil or salt water. After severe vomiting lie down and keep warm.
- Feeling of wretchedness and mental depression.

Motion sickness is caused by the movement of the liquids in the inner ear that confuse the balance sensory devices producing a loss of balance and gastrointestinal disturbances. A victim should try to drink as much as possible (but not alcohol), and should eat a little at frequent intervals. See a doctor who can prescribe seasickness tablet and use them before it occurs.

ADRIFT: SHORT TIME

People adrift in lifeboats or rafts need warmth, cover from the sun and ocean spray, dry clothing, water, and some food. If survivors had been immersed for a short time in relatively warm water they should be given a warm bath and dry clothing.

ADRIFT: MANY DAYS

If survivors experienced a shortage of food and water, they will be weak, demoralized, and at some stage of hypothermia if exposed to the elements. Treat for hypothermia if required. Give them warm drinks which they should not drink too fast as they might vomit. Food in the form of soup and bread should be given sparingly. Any food should be easy to digest.

OTHER PROBLEMS

Constipation: Bowel movements are limited because of the lack of food. Do not use laxatives.

Swollen legs: Swollen legs are common and will clear up after a few days on land.

Other ailments of exposure are...
Heat exposure, Frostbite, Hypothermia, Trench Foot, etc.

FUEL OIL CONTAMINATION

Swallowing fuel oil and salt water might produce vomiting and coughing from oil and water in the stomach and lungs. Eyes might be sore form the oil and salt water mixture. These problems will usually clear up. To clean the skin take a bath with a mild soap. Treat the eyes by applying some soft wax to the eyelids. Drink some warm milk with honey or sweet tea to help soothe the stomach. *Get medical attention especially if there are wounds.*

CHAPPED SKIN OR LIPS

Exposure to cold winds, salt water, or washing in cold weather without adequate drying of the skin, will cause cracks on the backs of the hands, the feet, lips, or ears. There is often much irritation and pain.

Treatment

Avoid this problem by using a cream or smearing the skin with soft paraffin and keeping warm. Wear the appropriate clothing to protect the skin.

INSECT STINGS

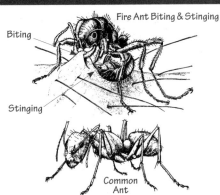
Fire Ant Biting & Stinging
Biting
Stinging
Common Ant

Burying yourself in beach sand to avoid the swarms of mosquitoes.

YELLOW JACKETS, BEES, HORNETS, WASPS *(Hymenoptera)*

- These insects inject venom under the skin.
- The sting produces a few minutes of fierce burning, followed by redness and itching at the point of the sting. A welt may form and subside in 3 or 4 hours. Should be normal within 24 hours.

Honey bee: Stings only once as the barbed stinger will stay embedded in the skin. Remove the stinger as soon as possible as the venom sac will continue to pump for two to three minutes driving the venom deeper into the skin. The best way to remove the stinger is to scrape it out with a fingernail as this will avoid squeezing the venom sac.

Bumble bees, wasps, hornets & yellow jackets: have smooth stingers and so can sting numerous times. If a yellow jacket is squashed and the venom sac is broken, the chemical scent given off will attract other yellow jackets so don't stick around!

Treatment

A victim stung in the mouth or throat should be given ice to suck and immediately sent to a hospital, as rapid swelling may occur; this may obstruct breathing.

- Wash the sting area with water and soap.
- If stinger and venom sac remains in the wound scrape them out with your fingernail or knife blade. Wash the sting area again.

Avoid Hymenoptera Stings

- Destroy all nests around houses or do not camp in their proximity. Watch for old stumps and holes in the ground.
- Avoid scented soaps, lotions, shampoo, perfumes, avoid floral prints and bright colors. Basically do not look or smell like a flower.
- When camping keep food covered until served and pack leftovers. Keep the garbage disposal area far from the camp. Avoid eating melons as they attract Hymenoptera.
- Do not act aggressively with insects. Be calm or slowly back away. Do not try to swat it.
- Consume vitamin B (thiamin), on days of potential insect activity. The smell of the vitamin secreted through the skin might keep them away.
- Wear light colored clothing - white, grey, or khaki.

REDUCE THE PAIN & ITCHING

- Sprinkle some meat tenderizer on some gauze and apply to the sting for 30 minutes. Instead of tenderizer you can use ice, cold compresses, calamine or other soothing lotions.
- Apply an alkaline lotion such as a strong solution of sodium bicarbonate (baking soda). 1 tablespoonful to 1 pint of water.
- Itching may also be relieved by applying a mixture of baking soda and ammonia (a few drops of household cleaning ammonia).
- Wash the sting area with soap and water.
- Wash with an antiseptic (to relieve pain).
- Apply ice pack or ice cubes.
- Rub an Aspirin tablet on wet sting area (do not use if allergic to aspirin).
- Dab household ammonia on spot.
- Apply mud to sting area and cover with bandage. Keep in place until dry.

Symptoms of an Allergic Reaction

If there is an allergic reaction to a sting see a doctor immediately.

Some symptoms are: Labored breathing, difficulties in swallowing, constricted chest, abdominal pain, nausea, state of confusion, vomiting, weakness, blurriness, rapid fall of blood pressure, collapse, incontinence, unconsciousness.

Five per cent of people are allergic to the venom of the bee, wasp or ant. A person who is allergic to bee stings should carry a "bee sting kit" which can be used after being stung. A bee can sting only once but wasps, hornets, ants can sting or bite repeatedly.

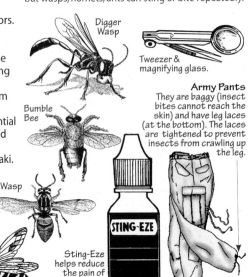
Digger Wasp
Tweezer & magnifying glass.
Army Pants They are baggy (insect bites cannot reach the skin) and have leg laces (at the bottom). The laces are tightened to prevent insects from crawling up the leg.
Bumble Bee
Sting-Eze helps reduce the pain of an insect sting.
STING-EZE

Hornet
Honey Bee
Wasp
Bumble Bee
Wasp
Hornet

REDUCE EXPOSURE TO BITING INSECTS

- Stay away from breeding areas. Usually slow flowing or stagnant bodies of water.
- Avoid areas with high grass or dense vegetation.

Insure that you:

- Have a good bed net.
- Your immunizations are current.
- Laundry and bathing facilities are available.
- Shirt is buttoned. • Sleeves are rolled down.
- Pants tucked inside boots.
- Have clean clothing. • Use insect repellent.
- Bathe or shower regularly.
- Take malaria pills if prescribed.

Preventing Skin Infections

Bathe frequently. If showers or baths are not available, wash the following with a wash cloth every daily.

- Your genital area. • Your armpits.
- Your feet and between toes.
- Other areas where you sweat or that become wet such as: between thighs or (for females) under the breasts.

Keep the Skin Dry

- Use foot powder on your feet, especially if you have had previous fungal infections on the feet.
- Use talcum powder in areas where wetness is a problem, such as: between the thighs or (for females) under the breasts.

Wear Proper Clothing

- Wear loose fitting clothing as this allows for better ventilation. Tight fitting clothing reduces blood circulation and ventilation.
- Do not wear nylon or silk undergarments; cotton undergarments are more absorbent and allow the skin to dry.

For Females

- Wash your genital area each day.
- Do not use perfumed soaps or feminine deodorants in the field as they cause irritation and attract insects.
- Do not douche unless directed by a doctor.
- Drink extra fluids, even when it is not hot. Some individuals do not drink enough fluid and tend to hold their urine due to the lack of privacy. Urinary tract infections are one of the most frequent medical problems females face in the field. Drinking extra fluids will help prevent these infections.

US Army Insect Bar *(Bed Net)*

An insect bar should be used in all malaria areas. You must take care not to come in contact with the net as insects can bite through it.

There are places in the tropics where 20% of the US troops have become ill with malaria as the result of being exposed to mosquitoes for one night without the protection of an insect bar.

Insect articles partially based on EFMB Study Guide, Department of Military Medicine, US Army

INSECT-BORNE DISEASES

The term insects in this book refers to mosquitoes, flies, fleas, lice ticks, mites, chiggers spiders, and scorpions which are properly called arthropod.

Insects affect the health of human beings:
- By transmitting disease. • By injecting venom.
- By invading living tissue. • By annoyance.

The principal insect-borne diseases include some of the most common and most serious epidemics of mankind such as malaria, plague, yellow fever, and the typhus fevers. They are most common in the tropics but may occur in most parts of the world.

Principal Insect-Borne Diseases

Disease	Insect
Dengue fever	Mosquito
Encephalitis (sleeping sickness)	Mosquito
Filariasis *(elephantiasis)*	Mosquito
Malaria	Mosquito
Yellow fever	Mosquito
Typhus fever (epidemic)	Body louse
Rocky Mountain spotted fever	Tick
Bubonic plague	Flea
Typhus fever (Murine)	Flea
Scrub typhus	Larval mite (chigger)
Leishmanissis	Sand fly *(Phlebotomus)*
Sand fly fever *or* Phlebotomus fever	Sand fly *(Phlebotomus)*
Onchocerciassis	Black fly (buffalo gnat)
Chagas' disease	Conenosed bug (kissing bug)

METHODS OF TRANSMISSION

Disease agents are transmitted by insects in two general ways...

Mechanical Transmission: Is when the disease organisms are picked up on the body or the legs of the insect and are then deposited on food, drink or open sores. An example of this method is the transfer of typhoid or dysentery organisms from fecal matter.

Biological Transmission: Is when the insect becomes infected with an organism by biting a diseased human or animal. The organism develops in the body of the insect which later is transmitted to a susceptible individual by a bite. This occurs in the case of malaria or less commonly by contamination of chafed skin with the body juices or feces of the carrier, as in the case of louse-borne typhus. Certain species of bees, wasps, scorpions and spiders inject poisons which can produce symptoms of varying severity.

Insect Annoyance

When gnats, mosquitoes, flies and other pests become sufficiently numerous they can affect the health and morale of a person.

Control Measures

Control measures are directed primarily toward the source of infection (human beings and animals) and toward the transmitting insect. The sources of infection are controlled through personal hygiene, surveillance, isolation, quarantine, and treatment. The transmitting insects are controlled through the practice of sanitation. Individual protective measures and chemical measures.

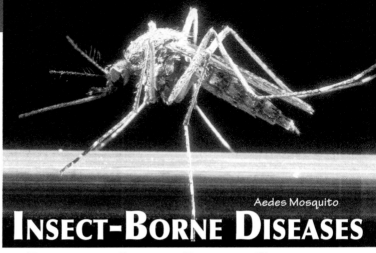

Aedes Mosquito

INSECT-BORNE DISEASES

CHOOSING INSECT REPELLENTS

Insect repellents are available in various forms and concentrations. Aerosol and pump-spray products are intended for skin applications as well as for treating clothing. Liquid, cream, lotion and stick products enable direct skin application. Products with a low concentration of active ingredient may be appropriate for situations where exposure to insects is minimal. Higher concentration of active ingredient may be useful in highly infested areas, or with insect species which are more difficult to repel. And where appropriate, consider non chemical ways to deter biting insects - screens, netting, long sleeves, and slacks.

USING INSECT REPELLENTS SAFELY

- Repellents should be applied only to exposed skin and/or clothing (as directed on the product label). Do not use under clothing.
- Never use repellents over cuts, wounds, or irritated skin.
- Don't apply to eyes and mouth, and apply sparingly around ears. When using sprays do not spray directly onto face; spray on hands first and then apply to face.
- Do not allow children to handle this product, and do not apply to children's hands. When using on children, apply to your own hands and then put it on the child.
- If you suspect that you or your child are reacting to an insect repellent, discontinue use, wash treated skin and then call your local poison control center. Show the doctor the repellent used.
- Do not spray in enclosed areas. Avoid breathing a repellent spray, and do not use it near food.
- Use just enough repellent to cover exposed skin and/or clothing. Heavy application and saturation is unnecessary for effectiveness; if biting insects do not respond to a thin film of repellent, apply a bit more.
- After returning indoors, wash treated skin with soap and water or bathe. This is particularly important when repellents are used repeatedly in a day or on consecutive days. Also, wash treated clothing before wearing it again.
- Follow use directions carefully, use only the amount directed, at the time and under the conditions specified, and for the purpose listed. For example, if you need a tick repellent, make sure that the product label lists this use. If ticks are not listed, the product may not be formulated for this use.

INSECT BITES & CHILDREN

Protect your children from mosquito bites. Have them wear long-sleeved shirts and long pants; apply insect repellent to exposed skin. Mosquitoes that transmit malaria bite between dusk and dawn. Use insect repellents that contain DEET. *See caution below.*

DEET Repellent Precautions

- Always use according to label directions.
- Use only when outdoors and wash skin after coming indoors.
- Do not breathe in, swallow, or get it in the eyes.
- Do not put on wounds or broken skin.

DEET is toxic when ingested. High concentrations applied to skin may cause blistering. Rare cases of encephalopathy in children, some fatal, have been reported after cutaneous exposure. Other neurologic side effects also have been reported. Toxicity did not appear to be dose-related in many cases and these may have been idiosyncratic reactions in predisposed individuals. However, a dose-related effect leading to irritability and impaired concentration and memory has been reported.

Natural Mosquito Repellents

- Wet clothing is preferred over dry.
- Clothing with perspiration is more attractive than wet clothing.
- Mosquitoes appear to prefer the color blue.

PROTECTION AGAINST BITING INSECTS

If you do not have any insect repellent.

You might want to try:
- Smoking up the camp - insects do not like smoke.
- Mud plaster: Plaster mud on exposed surfaces of skin during travel. This will hurt, when the mud dries, if the mud is applied too thick.
- Birch bark: Place thin sheets of bark below thin socks and below T-shirts etc.
- Install your tent in a windy area so that pests get blown away.

Tent with Mosquito Net

Citronella Candle

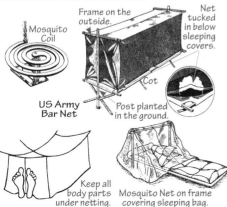

Net tucked in below sleeping covers.

Frame on the outside.

Mosquito Coil

Cot

US Army Bar Net

Post planted in the ground.

Keep all body parts under netting.

Mosquito Net on frame covering sleeping bag.

Mosquito Net over a swamp bed

Mosquito Net on frame covering sleeping bag.

Mosquito Gazebo

Mosquito Net head cover.

Insect Repellent

Application of ointment

Water Surface

Mosquito pupa in a test tube.

Culex mosquito laying eggs.

INSECTICIDE INJURY
In Case of an Emergency

First determine what the person was exposed to and what part of the body was affected before you take action, since taking the right action is as important as taking immediate action. If the person is unconscious, having trouble breathing, or having convulsions, give the indicated first aid immediately. Call 911 or your local emergency service. If these symptoms are not noticeable, contact your local Poison Control Center, physician, 911 or your local emergency service and follow their directions.

POISON FIRST AID GUIDELINES

Poison in eye: Eye membranes absorb pesticides faster than any other external part of the body. Eye damage can occur in a few minutes with some types of pesticides. If poison splashes into an eye, hold the eyelid open and wash quickly and gently with clean running water from the tap or a gentle stream from a hose for at least 15 minutes. If possible, have someone contact a Poison Control Center while the victim is being treated. Do not use eye drops, chemicals, or drugs in the wash water.
Poison on skin: If pesticide splashes on the skin, drench area with water and remove contaminated clothing. Wash skin and hair thoroughly with soap and water. Later discard contaminated clothing or thoroughly wash it separately from other laundry.
Inhaled poison: Carry or drag victim to fresh air immediately. If proper protection is unavailable, call the Fire Department. Loosen victim's tight clothing. Open doors and windows to prevent fumes from poisoning others.
Swallowed poison: Induce vomiting ONLY if the emergency personnel on the phone tell you to do so. It will depend on what the victim has swallowed; some petroleum products, or caustic poisons can cause serious damage if vomited.

PROTECTION: MOSQUITOES & OTHER ARTHROPOD

Exposure to arthropod bites can be minimized by modifying patterns of activity or behavior. Some mosquitoes are most active in twilight periods at dawn and dusk or in the evening. Avoidance of outdoor activity during these periods may reduce risk of exposure. Mosquitoes prefer wet clothing. Clothing with perspiration is more attractive than wet clothing. They appear to prefer the color blue.

Vector-borne Infections

A vector-borne infection is an infection that is transmitted (carried) by an insect. The insect itself is not sick but it carries the infection in the liquid that it transmits by biting a human or other animal. Vectors can be mosquitoes, ticks, fleas, mites, etc.

GENERAL PREVENTIVE MEASURES

The principal approach to prevention of vector-borne diseases is avoidance.
Place: Tick- and mite-borne infections characteristically are diseases of "place;" whenever possible, known foci of disease transmission should be avoided. Although many vector-borne infections can be prevented by avoiding rural locations, certain mosquito- and midge-borne arboviral and parasitic infections are transmitted around human residences and in urban locations.
Transmitted seasonally: Most vector-borne infections are transmitted seasonally, and simple changes in itinerary may greatly reduce risk for acquiring certain infections. Exposure to arthropod bites can be minimized by modifying patterns of activity or behavior.
Twilight periods: Some vector mosquitoes are most active in twilight periods at dawn and dusk or in the evening. Avoidance of outdoor activity during these periods may reduce risk of exposure.
Clothing: Wearing long-sleeved shirts, long pants, and hats will minimize areas of exposed skin. Shirts should be tucked in. Repellents applied to clothing, shoes, tents, mosquito nets, and other gear will enhance protection. When exposure to ticks or mites is a possibility, pants should be tucked into socks and boots should be worn; sandals should be avoided. Permethrin-based repellents applied as directed *(see below)* will enhance protection.
Remove ticks: During outdoor activity and at the end of the day, travelers should inspect themselves and their clothing for ticks. Ticks are detected more easily on light-colored or white clothing. Prompt removal of attached ticks may prevent infection.
Bed netting: When accommodations are not adequately screened or air-conditioned, bed nets are essential to provide protection and comfort. Bed nets should be tucked under mattresses and can be sprayed with repellent. Aerosol insecticides and mosquito coils may help to clear rooms of mosquitoes; however, some coils may contain DDT and should be used with caution.

MOSQUITO-BORNE DISEASES & THEIR CONTROL

Mosquitoes are found all over the world. In the tropics and sub tropics they breed throughout the year. In the sub-Arctic regions they appear in tremendous numbers during the brief summer season. Most of the disease-carrying mosquitoes are found in milder climates and in the tropics. Different types of mosquitoes transmit different diseases. The three most common types of mosquitoes which transmit disease are *Anopheles, Aedes,* and *Culex.* Each of these types consist of many species.

MOSQUITO-BORNE DISEASES

There are many diseases transmitted by mosquitoes. Some of the more important ones are malaria, yellow fever, dengue fever, encephalitis, and filariasis. Of these diseases, malaria is the greatest threat in normal travel. It is important to know that antimosquito measures is the major weapon against this group of diseases. Drugs are available for the suppression and cure of malaria and a vaccine for the prevention of yellow fever. Overuse of drugs have made some insect-borne diseases immune to their use.

MALARIA

Malaria is rare in the United States but it is common in most tropical, subtropical, and semitropical areas of the world. Malaria is caused by a microscopic parasite carried by the *Anopheles* mosquito. This parasite destroys the blood cells and causes chills, fever, weakness, and anemia. Unless the disease is treated promptly and properly, it may cause death from damage to the brain. The only sure way of preventing malaria is to avoid the bites of infected mosquitoes.

Fight Mosquitoes by:

- Empty standing water in old tires, cemetery urns, buckets, plastic covers, toys, or any other container where "wrigglers" and "tumblers" live.
- Empty and change the water in bird baths, fountains, wading pools, rain barrels, and potted plant trays at least once a week if not more often.
- Drain or fill temporary pools with dirt. Keep swimming pools treated and circulating and rain gutters unclogged.
- Use mosquito repellents when necessary and follow label directions and precautions closely.
- Use head nets, long sleeves and long pants if you venture into areas with high mosquito populations, such as salt marshes.
- If there is a mosquito-borne disease warning in effect, stay inside during the evening when mosquitoes are most active.
- Make sure window and door screens are "bug tight."
- Replace your outdoor lights with yellow "bug" lights.

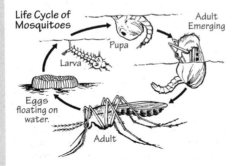

Life Cycle of Mosquitoes
Pupa
Adult Emerging
Larva
Eggs floating on water.
Adult

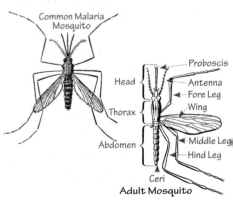

Common Malaria Mosquito
Proboscis
Antenna
Fore Leg
Wing
Head
Thorax
Abdomen
Middle Leg
Hind Leg
Ceri
Adult Mosquito

MOSQUITO TYPES

Anopheles

Anopheles mosquitoes primarily bite during the period from dusk to dawn. They may bite during the daylight hours in an area which is heavily shaded or in a dark room. Normally, most species will breed in any collection of water and some species breed only in tree holes. The larvae lie parallel to the surface of the water. The adults usually rest and feed with the body at an angle of 45° to the surface.

Aedes

Aedes mosquitoes bite in daylight. They breed in fresh, stagnant, or brackish water. *Aedes aegypti*, one of the most important disease transmitters, breed almost entirely in old tires, cans, and other similar manufactured containers. The adults rest and feed with their body parallel to the surface.

Culez

Culez mosquitoes. Depending upon the species may bite at any time of day or night. They are commonly found in fresh or stagnant water in and about buildings as well as swamps, ditches, street gutters, and other water containing areas. The common house mosquitoes found in the United States are members of this group. The adults rest and feed parallel to the surface as the *Aedes*.

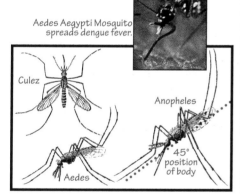

Aedes Aegypti Mosquito spreads dengue fever.

Culez

Anopheles

45° position of body

Aedes

DENGUE FEVER

Dengue is primarily a disease of the tropics. Dengue viruses are transmitted during the feeding process by the Aedes aegypti, a domestic, day-biting mosquito that prefers to feed on humans. These mosquitoes are found near human habitations and are often present indoors.
Symptoms: Dengue fever is characterized by sudden onset, high fever, severe headaches, joint and muscle pain, nausea/vomiting, and rash. The rash may appear 3–4 days after the onset of fever. Infection is diagnosed by a blood test that detects the presence of the virus or antibodies. The illness may last up to 10 days, but complete recovery can take 2–4 weeks. Dengue is commonly confused with other infectious illnesses such as influenza, measles, malaria, typhoid, leptospirosis, and scarlet fever. The symptoms of dengue can be treated with bed rest, fluids, and medications to reduce fever; aspirin should be avoided. Travelers should alert their physician of any fever illnesses occurring within 3 weeks after leaving an endemic area. There is no vaccine for dengue fever; therefore, the traveler should avoid mosquito bites by remaining in well screened or air-conditioned areas. Travelers to tropical areas are advised to use mosquito repellents on skin and clothing, to bring aerosol insecticides to use indoors, and use bed nets. The risk of dengue is generally higher in urban areas.

MALARIA

Malaria is a serious, sometimes fatal, disease caused by a parasite.
Large areas of Central and South America, Haiti and the Dominican Republic), Africa, are considered malaria-risk areas. About 1,200 cases of malaria are diagnosed in the United States each year. Most cases in the United States are travelers returning from malaria-risk areas.

Contracting Malaria

Humans get malaria from the bite of a malaria-infected mosquito (vector). When a mosquito bites an infected person, it ingests microscopic malaria parasites found in the person's blood. The malaria parasite must grow in the mosquito for a week or more before infection can be passed to another person. If, after a week, the mosquito then bites another person, the parasites go from the mosquito's mouth into the person's blood. The parasites then travel to the person's liver, enter the liver's cells, grow and multiply. During this time when the parasites are in the liver, the person has not yet felt sick. The parasites leave the liver and enter red blood cells; this may take as little as 8 days or as many as several months. Once inside the red blood cells, the parasites grow and multiply. The red blood cells burst, freeing the parasites to attack other red blood cells. Toxins from the parasite are also released into the blood, making the person feel sick. If a mosquito bites this person while the parasites are in his or her blood, it will ingest the tiny parasites. After a week or more, the mosquito can infect another person. Each year in the United States, a few cases of malaria result from blood transfusions, are passed from mother to fetus during pregnancy, or are transmitted by locally infected mosquitoes.

Signs & Symptoms of Malaria

For most people, symptoms begin 10 days to 4 weeks after infection, although a person may feel ill as early as 8 days or up to 1 year later. Symptoms of malaria include fever and flu-like illness, including shaking chills, headache, muscle aches, and tiredness. Nausea, vomiting, and diarrhea may also occur. Malaria may cause anemia and jaundice (yellow coloring of the skin and eyes) because of the loss of red blood cells. Infection with one type of malaria, P. falciparum, if not promptly treated, may cause kidney failure, seizures, mental confusion, coma, and death.
Any traveler who becomes ill with a fever or flu-like illness while traveling and up to 1 year after returning home should immediately seek professional medical care. You should tell your health care provider that you have been traveling in a malaria-risk area.

TO PREVENT MALARIA

- Visit your health care provider 4-6 weeks before foreign travel for any necessary vaccinations and a prescription for an antimalarial drug. Take your antimalarial drug exactly on schedule without missing doses.
- Prevent mosquito and other insect bites. Use DEET insect repellent on exposed skin and flying insect spray in the room where you sleep.
- Wear long pants and long-sleeved shirts, especially from dusk to dawn. This is the time when mosquitoes that spread malaria bite.
- Sleep under a mosquito bed net that has been dipped in permethrin insecticide if you are not living in screened or air-conditioned housing.

WEST NILE ENCEPHALITIS (WNE)

"*Encephalitis*" means an inflammation of the brain and can be caused by viruses and bacteria, including viruses transmitted by mosquitoes. WNE is an infection of the brain caused by West Nile virus which is closely related to St. Louis encephalitis virus.

Bite of Mosquito

People get WNE by the bite of a mosquito (primarily one of the *Culex* species) that is infected with West Nile virus. Mosquitoes become infected when they feed on infected birds, which may circulate the virus in their blood for a few days. After an incubation period of 10 days to 2 weeks, infected mosquitoes can then transmit West Nile virus to humans and animals while biting to take blood.
WNE is NOT transmitted from person-to-person.
Hunters & Wild Game: A hunter should follow the usual precautions when handling wild animals. Outdoors apply insect repellents to clothing and skin, according to label instructions. Wear gloves when handling and cleaning animals to prevent blood exposure to bare hands. *Cook meat thoroughly.*

Symptoms of WNE

Most infections are mild and symptoms include fever, headache, and body aches, often with skin rash and swollen lymph glands. More severe infection may be marked by headache, high fever, neck stiffness, stupor, disorientation, coma, tremors, convulsions, muscle weakness, paralysis and, rarely, death. The incubation period in humans is 3 to 15 days.

Prevention

- Stay indoors at dawn, dusk, and in the early evening.
- Wear long-sleeved shirts & long pants whenever outdoors.
- Empty water from outside objects such as bird baths, old tires and any containers in which water accumulates and where mosquitoes may breed.
- Apply insect repellent sparingly to exposed skin. Repellents may irritate the eyes and mouth, so avoid applying repellent to the hands of children.
- Spray clothing with repellents containing permethrin or DEET, as mosquitoes may bite through thin clothing. Be sure to read and follow the manufacturer's direction of use.

Note: Vitamin B and "ultrasonic" devices are NOT effective in preventing mosquito bites.

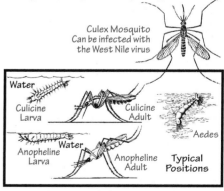

Culex Mosquito Can be infected with the West Nile virus

Water
Culicine Larva
Culicine Adult
Aedes
Water
Anopheline Larva
Anopheline Adult
Typical Positions

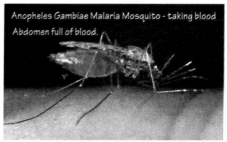

Anopheles Gambiae Malaria Mosquito - taking blood Abdomen full of blood.

ROCKY MOUNTAIN SPOTTED FEVER

LYME DISEASE

Transmission: Lyme disease is spread by the bite of the deer tick. The tick normally feeds on the white-footed mouse, white-tailed deer, other mammals, and birds, is responsible for transmitting Lyme disease bacteria to humans. On the Pacific Coast, the bacteria are transmitted to humans by the western black-legged tick, and in the southeastern states possibly by the black-legged tick. The ticks are much smaller than common dog and cattle ticks. In their larval and nymphal stages, they are no bigger than a pinhead. Adult ticks are slightly larger.

Ticks & Humans: Ticks can attach to any part of the human body but often attach to the more hidden and hairy areas such as the groin, armpits, and scalp. Ticks transmit Lyme disease to humans during the nymph stage. The nymphs, small and hard to see, typically have ample time to feed and transmit the infection (ticks are most likely to transmit infection after approximately 2 or more days of feeding). Adult ticks can transmit the disease, but since they are larger and more likely to be removed from a person's body within a few hours, they are less likely than the nymphs to have sufficient time to transmit the infection. Adult ticks are most active during the cooler months of the year, when outdoor activity is limited. Ticks search for host animals from the tips of grasses and shrubs (not from trees) and transfer to animals or persons that brush against vegetation. Ticks only crawl; they do not fly or jump. Ticks feed on blood by inserting their mouth parts (not their whole bodies) into the skin of a host animal. They are slow feeders: a complete blood meal can take several days. As they feed, their bodies slowly enlarge.

Description: Lyme disease most often presents with a characteristic "bull's-eye" rash, erythema migrans, accompanied by nonspecific symptoms such as fever, malaise, fatigue, headache, muscle aches, and joint aches. The incubation period is typically 7 to 14 days but may be as short as 3 days and as long as 30 days. Some infected individuals have no recognized illness, or manifest only non-specific symptoms such as fever, headache, fatigue, and myalgia. The signs of early disseminated infection usually occur days to weeks after the appearance of a solitary lesion. Lyme disease is intermittent swelling and pain of one or a few joints, usually large, weight-bearing joints such as the knee. Some patients develop sleep disturbance, fatigue, personality changes, etc. Lyme disease is rarely, if ever, fatal. *Campers, hikers, outdoor workers, and others who frequent wooded, brushy, and grassy places are commonly exposed to ticks, and this may be important in the transmission of Lyme disease in some areas.*

Dime and a Deer Tick

Adults

Young

Centimeters

1 2

Deer Tick

TICKS

AVOIDING TICKS & LYME DISEASE

Lyme disease has become the leading tick-borne illness in the U.S. The deer tick is the species that most often transmits Lyme disease. With proper precautions, Lyme disease is preventable.

• Deer ticks are most active from April through October, so exercise additional caution when venturing into tick country.
• When in a tick-infested area, a good prevention is an insect repellent. Consider using a product designed to be applied to clothing rather than your skin. An insect repellent with DEET and/or permethrin can be used. Follow instructions in the use of these and other repellents.
• Tuck pants cuffs into boots or socks, and wear long sleeves and light-colored clothing which makes it easier to spot ticks.
• Stay to the center of hiking paths, and avoid grassy and marshy woodland areas.
• Avoid contact with wild animals and birds (including bird's nests) in tick endemic areas.
• Inspect yourself and your children for clinging ticks after leaving an infested area. Deer ticks are hard to see-nymphs are dot-sized; adults, smaller than a sesame seed. If you discover a tick feeding, do not panic: studies indicate that an infected tick does not usually transmit the Lyme organism during the first 24 hours.

If you suspect Lyme disease or its symptoms, contact your doctor immediately.

Head of Needle

Adult Deer Tick

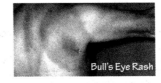

Bull's Eye Rash

Tweezers to remove ticks.

Rocky Mountain Wood Tick

TO REMOVE ATTACHED TICKS

1 Use fine-tipped tweezers or shield your fingers with a tissue, paper towel, or rubber gloves. Avoid removing ticks with bare hands.
2 Grasp the tick as close to the skin surface as possible and pull upward with steady, even pressure. Do not twist or jerk the tick; this may cause the mouthparts to break off and remain in the skin. If this happens, remove mouthparts with tweezers.

1

Do not squeeze, crush, or puncture the body of the tick.

2

Grasp the tick as close to the skin surface as possible and pull upward with steady, even pressure.

3 Do not squeeze, crush, or puncture the body of the tick because its fluids (saliva, body fluids, gut contents) may contain infectious organisms.
4 After removing the tick, thoroughly disinfect the bite site and wash your hands with soap and water.
5 To help your doctor make an accurate diagnosis save the tick for identification in case you become ill. Place the tick in a plastic bag and put it in your freezer.

ROCKY MOUNTAIN SPOTTED FEVER (RMSF)

RMSF is the most severe and most frequently reported rickettsial illness in the United States. The disease is caused by *Rickettsia rickettsii*, a species of bacteria that is spread to humans by ixodid (hard) ticks. The organism is transmitted by the bite of an infected tick. The American dog tick and Rocky Mountain wood tick are the primary vectors. The incubation period is about 5-10 days after a tick bite.

SIGNS & SYMPTOMS

Initial symptoms may include fever, nausea, vomiting, muscle pain, lack of appetite and severe headache. Later signs and symptoms include rash, abdominal pain, joint pain, and diarrhea. Three important components of the are fever, rash, and a previous tick bite, although one or more of these components may not be present. RMSF can be a severe illness, and the majority of patients are hospitalized. It occurs throughout the United States during the months of April through September.

Prevention: In persons exposed to tick-infested habitats, prompt careful inspection and removal of crawling or attached ticks is an important method of preventing disease. It may take several hours of attachment before organisms are transmitted from the tick to the host.

• Wear light-colored clothing to allow you to see ticks that are crawling on your clothing.
• Tuck your pant legs into your socks so that ticks cannot crawl up the inside of your pant legs.
• Apply repellents to discourage tick attachment. Repellents containing permethrin can be sprayed on boots and clothing, and will last for several days. Repellents containing DEET can be applied to the skin, will last only a few hours before reapplication is necessary. Use DEET with caution on children. Application of large amounts of DEET on children has been associated with adverse reactions.
• Conduct a body check upon return from potentially tick-infested areas by searching your entire body for ticks. Remove any tick you find on your body.
• Parents should check their children for ticks - especially in the hair. Ticks may be carried into the household on clothing and pets.

Tick Removal: When you are in the woods, check yourself and your companions at least twice a day for ticks. If you do find a tick on yourself, remove it immediately with tweezers. Gently grasp the tick as close as possible to your skin and slowly pull it away. If tweezers are not available, fingers covered with tissue paper can be used. Do not attempt to remove the tick with Vaseline, hot objects such as matches or cigarettes, or by other methods. After handling ticks, be sure to wash your hands thoroughly with soap and water.

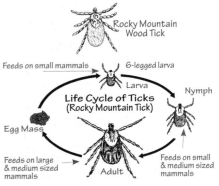

Rocky Mountain Wood Tick

Feeds on small mammals

6-legged larva

Larva

Nymph

Life Cycle of Ticks (Rocky Mountain Tick)

Egg Mass

Feeds on large & medium sized mammals

Adult

Feeds on small & medium sized mammals

TICKS

Ticks occur most commonly in the tropic, sub tropic, and temperate zones; but they have also been collected in the arctic and subarctic zones. They are divided into two groups: hard ticks and soft ticks. The hard tick has a hard shield on its back and the mouthparts can be seen from above. The soft tick has no shield over its back, its body is soft, and the mouthparts can be seen only from below.

Tick-Borne Diseases: Ticks are the vectors and reservoirs of several diseases. Hard ticks are known to transmit Rocky Mountain spotted fever and other typhus-like fevers, tularemia (rabbit fever), and Q fever. Moreover, the females. of certain species are capable of causing a condition known as tick paralysis. Several species of Soft ticks transmit the disease organism of relapsing fever. When tick bites are numerous the skin may become badly inflamed and infected.

Methods of Transmission: The tick becomes infected with the disease organism when it feeds on an infected animal. It can then transmit this disease to man if it feeds on him later. Both the hard and the soft ticks can also pass the germs of several diseases on to their off spring through the egg, so that future generations of ticks are already infected when they hatch from the egg.

LIFE CYCLE OF TICKS

The life cycle of ticks is not the same for all species. Some species have a one-host cycle; that is, the tick does not leave its host until it reaches the adult stage. Others have several hosts; the tick will feed on one animal, then drop off to enter the next stage of its life cycle and later attack another animal to obtain a blood meal. The life cycle of a tick consists of four stages: egg, larva (seed ticks), nymph, and adult. Below is shown the life cycle of the Rocky Mountain spotted fever, tick *Dermacentor andersoni*.

Eggs: The fully engorged female deposits eggs on the ground in masses of from 100 to 10,000 or more. The incubation period requires about 35 days.

Larvae (Seed Ticks): The larvae have six legs. The young larvae climb upon grass and brush and await the passing of animals. The disturbance caused by animal or man moving through the area causes the seed tick to reach out with its forelegs. Should an animal or man brush by the vegetation on which the larval or "seed tick" is waiting, the tick grabs at the fur or the clothing and thus transfers itself to the host. Here it feeds for a few days and then drops off to molt to its next form, called nymph.

Nymphs: The six-legged larval forms transform into eight-legged nymphal forms, which become active and climb upon plants and vegetation; if fortunate (not for host - might be you!), they become attached to some animal on which they will feed for approximately one week. After engorgement, they drop to the ground. During the next two months they change into the adult-stage. Usually the hot weather prevents the adults from attaching to a new host and they remain inactive until the following spring. If the nymphs have not found a host during the summer they may survive another season before feeding.

Adults: The adults, both male and female, become active in the early spring when the weather turns warm. They also climb upon vegetation and await the passing of animals. Large animals, including man, are the usual hosts of adult ticks. The males and females mate on the animal; and after feeding for a week or two, the females drop to the ground, seek out a crevice in rocks or under debris, digest their blood meal, deposit their eggs, and die. It usually requires two years to complete a tick's life cycle, but it may last as long as three or four years.

CONTROL OF TICKS

Out in the open, ticks are very difficult to control with insecticides. A certain amount of local control can be accomplished by clearing away brush and vegetation and keeping animals out of the area. Within buildings, insecticide sprays and dusts have been used successfully for the control of dog ticks. Personal protective measures, such as the use of chemical repellents and protective clothing, are very effective.

CONTROL OF BREEDING AREAS

The control of large breeding areas involves the application of chemicals to the areas in order to destroy all stages of the ticks-, as well as the control or removal of animal hosts. Cattle that may be grazing in these areas should be dipped periodically in insecticide solutions.

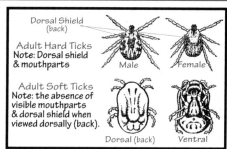

Dorsal Shield (back)
Adult Hard Ticks
Note: Dorsal shield & mouthparts
Male Female
Adult Soft Ticks
Note: the absence of visible mouthparts & dorsal shield when viewed dorsally (back).
Dorsal (back) Ventral

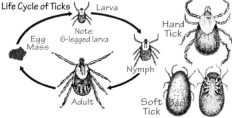

Life Cycle of Ticks Larva
Egg Mass Note: 6-legged larva Hard Tick
Nymph
Adult Soft Tick

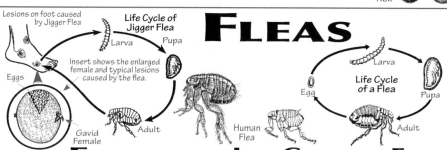

Lesions on foot caused by Jigger Flea
Life Cycle of Jigger Flea
Larva Pupa
Insert shows the enlarged female and typical lesions caused by the flea.
Eggs
Gavid Female Adult

FLEAS

Life Cycle of a Flea
Egg Larva Pupa
Human Flea Adult

FLEAS

Fleas are of medical importance because they produce irritating bites and transmit serious diseases. The fleas which attack man live chiefly on cats, dogs, and rodents. When man is in close association with these animals, conditions are ideal for the occurrence of flea-borne diseases. In areas where rats and other rodents abound, the rat and flea problem demands particular attention.

Flea-Borne Diseases: Rodent fleas are responsible for the transmission of bubonic plague and endemic (murine) typhus. Various rodents, principally rats and ground squirrels, are sources of infection from which fleas pick up the disease organisms and transmit them to man. When the normal rodent hosts are unavailable, rodent fleas will readily attack man. Some fleas harbor the cyst stage of a small tapeworm and if accidentally swallowed by man they will cause tapeworms to develop in his digestive tract. Other fleas (chigoe or jigger flea) attack the bare feet, usually between the toes and on the soles of the feet, where they cause painful swelling and inflammation.

Method of Transmission: In the case of plague, the flea feeds on a rodent which is infected with plague. The plague germs then multiply in the stomach of the flea. After a period of time a mass of blood and germs is formed which blocks the flea's digestive tract. Thereafter, when the flea attempts to feed, the blood meal cannot break through this obstruction but is forced back through the mouth by the struggle of the insect and is returned to the victim, carrying with it living plague germs from the fleas fore-gut. Plague germs are also passed in the feces of the flea and may enter the host if rubbed into skin abrasions at the site of the flea bite. Under certain conditions the organism may be coughed out from the lungs of pneumatic type cases and then breathed in by persons near the patient. The germs causing endemic typhus are transmitted in the feces and crushed bodies of fleas in the same manner as is louse-borne typhus.

LIFE CYCLE OF FLEAS

Fleas go through four stages of development: egg, larva, pupa, and adult.

Egg: Flea eggs are small, glistening white, and are laid in the debris of rodent nests or in places where cats and dogs sleep. The adult female lays from 2 to 18 eggs at one time and during her life may lay 400 eggs or more. Depending upon temperature and humidity, the egg stage lasts from 2 to 12 days.

Larva: Flea larvae are tiny worm-like creatures. They feed in the debris of the nest of their hosts, such as rats, squirrels, cats, dogs, etc. The larval stage may last from 9 to 200 or more days, depending on temperature, humidity, and the availability of suitable food.

Pupa: Mature larvae spin cocoons and pupate inside of them. The pupal stage takes from seven days to over a year to complete. The length of time required to pupate depends upon temperature and humidity.

Adult: The wingless adult fleas are flattened from side to side and have strong, spiny legs which enable them to move rapidly among the hairs or feathers of their host and to jump great distances, (the human flea can jump as far, as 13 inches). Their mouthparts are fitted for piercing the skin and sucking blood. Adult fleas are parasitic on warm-blooded animals.

Habits: Although fleas have certain host preferences, they will readily transfer the feed on different animals, including man. This makes them important in the transmission of disease from animal to man. Both male and female forms occur on the host, and eggs are deposited and fall off on the ground or into burrows, nests, or shelters. The adult females require a blood meal before egg laying.

Control of Fleas: Fleas are controlled by applying insecticides either to the animal hosts or to the infested areas.

Fleas

These small wingless insects can be extremely dangerous. In some areas they can transmit the plague to man after feeding on plague-ridden rodents.

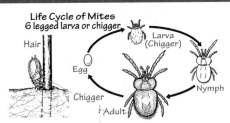

PLAGUE

PLAGUE

Plague is usually transmitted to humans by the bites of infected rodent fleas. Persons and animals that visit places where rodents have recently died from plague risk getting the disease from flea bites.

Persons also can become directly infected through handling infected rodents, rabbits, or wild carnivores that prey on these animals, when plague bacteria enter through breaks in the person's skin. House cats also are susceptible to plague. Infected cats become sick and may directly transmit plague to persons who handle or care for them. Also, dogs and cats may bring plague-infected fleas into the home. Inhaling droplets expelled by the coughing of a plague-infected person or animal (especially house cats) can result in plague of the lungs (plague pneumonia). Transmission of plague pneumonia from person to person is uncommon but sometimes results in dangerous epidemics that can quickly spread.

PLAGUE: DIAGNOSIS

Swollen lymph glands caused by plague bacteria (bubonic plague).

Diagnosis: The typical sign of the most common form of human plague is a swollen and very tender lymph gland, accompanied by pain. Bubonic plague should be suspected when a person develops a swollen gland, fever, chills, headache, and extreme exhaustion, and has a history of possible exposure to infected rodents, rabbits, or fleas.

A person usually becomes ill with bubonic plague 2 to 6 days after being infected. When bubonic plague is left untreated, plague bacteria invade the bloodstream. As the plague bacteria multiply in the bloodstream, they spread rapidly throughout the body and cause a severe and often fatal condition. Infection of the lungs with the plague bacterium causes the pneumonic form of plague, a severe respiratory illness. The infected person may experience high fever, chills, cough, and breathing difficulty and may expel bloody sputum. If plague patients are not given specific antibiotic therapy, the disease can progress rapidly to death. About 14% (1 in 7) of all plague cases in the United States are fatal.

Black Tailed Prairie Dog

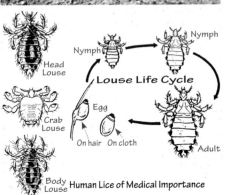

Head Louse

Nymph

Nymph

Louse Life Cycle

Egg

On hair   On cloth

Adult

Crab Louse

Body Louse   *Human Lice of Medical Importance*

BEDBUGS

BEDBUGS

Bedbugs survive wherever they can live in close association with man. In some persons their bite produces marked swellings and considerable irritation, while in others not the slightest inconvenience may be caused.

Egg: The female deposits eggs in batches of from 10 to 50, in convenient crevices in mattresses, bedsteads, and bedsprings, and in cracks of floors and walls. The eggs are yellowish white and visible to the naked eye. One female may lay as many as 500 eggs. Depending upon the temperature, the egg stage lasts from 7 to 30 days.

Nymphs: The nymphs look very much like the adult, except that they are smaller. The nymphal stage may last from 40 days to many months. The nymphs molt five times before reaching maturity, the average period between molting being eight days. Ordinarily they take but one meal between molts.

Adults: The adults have flattened bodies which permit them to crawl into narrow crevices. A nasty, pungent odor is noticeable where bedbugs are abundant. Adults may live up to four months without food. Under ordinary room temperature normally fed bedbugs may live as long as a year. A temperature of 100°F+ will kill them.

Habits: Bedbugs feed at night. During the day they hide in cracks and crevices and often can be found in the seams of mattresses or in the bedsprings. Very active at night, bedbugs will travel considerable distances to attack a sleeping person. They are timid and will retreat to the nearest hiding place at the slightest disturbance.

Control: Bedbugs are easily controlled with chemicals. The general issue residual spray is very effective. It is applied to walls, cracks, and crevices on the inside of buildings to a height of from five to six feet. Bed frames are sprayed particularly the undersides, joints, and cracks where bedbugs like to hide. The surplus spray should be allowed to fall on the wall behind the beds. Mattresses are sprayed on both sides and on the ends, seams, tufts, and crevices receiving special attention. For big jobs a three-man team is needed: one man to do the spraying, the other two to turn over each mattress and remove it after it has been sprayed. If no equipment for spraying is available, the solution may be applied with a paint brush. A slight moistening of the surface is all that is required. The insecticide acts slowly; but when the above procedures are followed practically all of the bedbugs will be dead within 24 hours. There should be no smoking or fire in the building during the spraying, and the barracks should be aired out for about four hours following the treatment. While doing the spraying, operating personnel should wear suitable masks, or respirators, and rubber gloves.

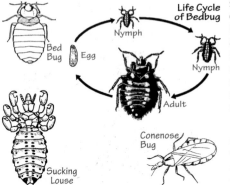

Bed Bug   Egg

Nymph

Nymph

Life Cycle of Bedbug

Nymph

Adult

Conenose Bug

Sucking Louse

Life Cycle of Mites

6 legged larva or chigger

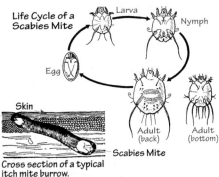

Hair

Egg

Larva (Chigger)

Chigger

Adult

Nymph

CHIGGER MITES

Chiggers are found in low damp places covered with vegetation such as tall grass and weeds. The larva of chiggers attach themselves to the body by sticking their mouth into the follicle (holes through which hair grow) of hair. They inject enzymes and feed upon human cells. After a few hours there will be extreme itching and small red welts will appear. To remove the chiggers lather several times with soap. Place a cold pack on affected area to relieve the stinging feeling.

Life Cycle of a Scabies Mite

Larva

Nymph

Egg

Adult (back)

Adult (bottom)

Skin

Scabies Mite

Cross section of a typical itch mite burrow.

CHAGAS' DISEASE - CONENOSE BUG ADULTS

Chagas' disease continues to be among the most important diseases in the tropics and sub tropics of North and South America.

The protozoan is carried in the hind gut of the conenose bug and passed to humans and other mammals while the insect feeds on blood. However, the disease organisms are not passed through the bite, but rather through the feces of the bug, which defecates on the victim's skin during blood feeding. The protozoans are then transferred from the insect feces to the host via scratching of the skin or entry into the conjunctiva of the eye or the mucosa of the nose or mouth. The site of infection, which is the most apparent external sign of the disease, is characterized by a unilateral swelling on the face or eyelid, or other site on the body. Once in the human blood stream, the incubation period is about 1 to 2 weeks. Then, moderate to high fever and edema of the body may occur. In some cases, nervous disorders occur, especially in small children. After four weeks, if the victim survives, the disease stabilizes and enters a long equilibrium phase known as the chronic phase. During this phase, which may last 10-20 years after the initial infection, the trypanosomes invade and destroy cardiac, integumentary, and nervous tissue. The victim may develop cardiopathy, chronic digestive lesions, and neurological disorders. Patients with severe chronic disease may ultimately die as a result of heart failure.

CONENOSE BUG ADULTS

Conenose bug adults and nymphs bite their victims at night. During the day, the bugs hide in cracks of poorly constructed homes and in the thatches of grass hut roofs.

SANDFLIES
(Phlebotomus Species)

Resemble small gnats and are common in many warm countries, although they are rare in the US.

Diseases Transmitted: Sandflies, transmit sandfly fever (pappataci fever) a disease present in the coastal regions of the Mediterranean. They may also transmit a form of oriental sore as well as serious diseases.

Habits: Sandflies are active at night, in the evening, and at dawn; they usually avoid wind, sun, and full daylight but are attracted to artificial light. They travel in short hops from their breeding areas but rarely migrate farther than 50 yards in buildings, sandflies seldom travel above the first floor. They attack man at the wrist, ankles, or any exposed part of the body, and will readily bite through thin socks. Their bite is painful and may result in marked irritation. They breed in dark places, eaves, crevices, stone embankments, crumbling ruins, earth fissures, and stony rubble. Although the larvae require damp breeding media, too much moisture will kill them.

Control: Sandflies are very sensitive to residual insecticides. In areas where there has been extensive residual spraying against mosquitoes for the control of malaria, sandflies likewise have been eliminated. Their habit of frequenting only the lower floor of buildings can sometimes be used to advantage by moving personnel to upper floor levels. Repellents, also, give protection against attacks by this pest.

Egg: The adult female deposits its eggs at the water line of aquatic plants, logs, and rocks, usually in swift-flowing streams, in masses of from 300 to 500. Breeding may also occur in roadside ditches or in more slowly running streams. Hatching requires from 5 to 30 days, depending on the temperature.

Larva: The emerged larvae are cylindrical and, when fully matured, are from 10 to 15 mm. in length. They attach themselves to objects in the stream and feed on small Crustacea, Protozoa, and Algae. The larval period lasts from 3 to 10 weeks. At the end of the larval period they spin a basket-like cocoon in which pupation takes place. These cocoons are attached to rocks or other objects in shallow water.

Pupa: In some species the Pupal period is short- not more than five or six days; in others it may last from three to five weeks.

Adult: The adults emerge and seek a blood meal. They may be found long distances away from their breeding area, apparently seeking a host. Their life history from egg to adult ranges from two to four months.

BLACKFLY

The bite of a blackfly is very painful and irritating. All exposed parts of the body are subject to attack. The extreme pain, intense itching, and the resultant local swelling with occasional severe complications indicate the presence of an active venom. Animals often die from the bites of these flies. The most important disease transmitted by blackflies is onchocerciasis - a disease of Central America and Africa.

BLACKFLIES (BUFFALO GNATS)

Blackflies (differ from Blackfly) are from 1 to 5 mm. Their common name is derived from their characteristic humpback appearance. They are particularly abundant in the north temperate and sub-arctic zones and often appear in great swarms during the late spring and early summer in hilly sections where swiftly flowing streams provide well-aerated water for larval development.

STABLEFLY

The stablefly also called biting housefly and dogfly, looks like a housefly but has piercing mouthparts and is a severe biter of man and animals. Like the housefly, it has four stages of development in its life history. Along coastal areas, where it breeds in sea grass washed up on sheltered beaches along, the coast, it is often a very serious pest. Inland, the stablefly breeds in barnyard manures that contain large quantities of decaying hay, in waste feed, in litter beneath feeding troughs, under piled hay or peanut litter left in the fields. Stableflies are best controlled by treating their breeding places with insecticides. Spreading manure and litter before it becomes infested and in such a way that it drys quickly will also prevent fly breeding.

Insect repellent: provides effective protection for man or animals against the bites of stableflies. It may be applied to clothing and also to the face, neck, hands, and ankles, just as for mosquitoes.

NO-SEE-UMS

These are small, biting midges (from 1 to 3 mm. in length) which are extremely annoying and can pass through the mesh of ordinary window screens. They are commonly found in the tropics and sub tropics and in the arctic during the short summer months. Some species breed in salt marshes where the larvae feed upon dead crabs and small fish left in wet soil. Other species breed in rot-holes of trees, and the larvae feed upon decaying insects usually present in those locations. When the adults emerge they are attracted to light and will feed upon warm-blooded animals.

Control of No-see-ums

Screening: Only a fine mesh (0.0334 inch) can keep them out. Ordinary screening can be made midge proof by frequent painting with insecticide.

Insecticides & Repellents: Use as for mosquitoes.

EYE GNATS

Gnats are small flies which crawl about the nose, mouth, and eyes and are annoying to both man and livestock. Gnats feed readily on serum exuding from wounds or lacerated surfaces and may be responsible for spreading serious eye infections. They have a wide distribution and are most common in the milder climates.

Control: Breeding of gnats can be controlled by the proper disposal of human wastes and by plowing and exposing infested soil to sun and air. Drying infested soil is very important in the control of breeding places of gnats. A repellent for mosquitoes also affords protection from gnats and should be applied after sundown to exposed parts of the body. One application should be made at sundown and another upon retiring.

Jar Traps: will help to reduce the gnat nuisance around camps and buildings, but their value as a practical means of control is questionable. These traps consist of a 1/2 gallon glass jar fitted with very fine (60- to 80- in. mesh) screen wire cones The jars are laid on their sides in the forks of trees or in other shady places. Bait inside the jar consists of a cube of liver, about one in inch square, with a small amount of water added to keep the liver from drying out.

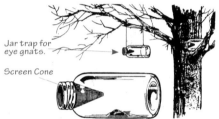

Jar trap for eye gnats.

Screen Cone

Eye Gnat Trap   Wet liver or other meat.

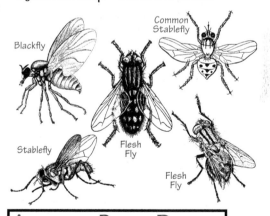

Blackfly

Common Stablefly

Stablefly

Flesh Fly

Flesh Fly

ARACHNID-BORNE DISEASES
(Ticks, Mites, Spiders)

Ticks, mites, spiders, and scorpions are commonly referred to as insects. Technically, however, they belong to the class Arachnida, whereas true insects belong to the class Insecta.

Arachnids differ from insects in their body structure as follows:

Arachnida
(Ticks, Mites, Spiders, Scorpions)
- Antennae absent
- Four pairs of legs in adult stage.
- Body divided into one or two parts.

Insecta
(Flies, Fleas, Mosquitoes, etc.)
- Antennae present.
- Three pairs of legs in adult stage.
- Body divided into three parts.

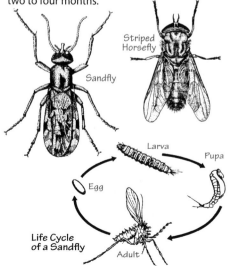

Striped Horsefly

Sandfly

Larva

Pupa

Egg

Life Cycle of a Sandfly

Adult

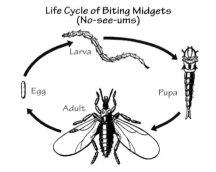

Life Cycle of Biting Midgets (No-see-ums)

Larva

Egg

Pupa

Adult

Diamondback Rattlesnake

Tail with Rattle

There are approximately 50,000 snake bites in the United States annually. 7,000 of these are caused by poisonous snakes with approximately 15 fatalities per year.

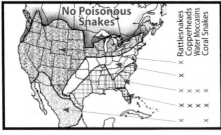

NORTH AMERICAN POISONOUS SNAKES

PIT VIPERS *(Crotalidae)*

Include rattlesnakes, copperheads and cotton-mouths (water moccasins). Pit vipers get their common name from a small "pit" between the eye and nostril. The pit is a heat sensing organ that allows the snake to strike a warm target even in the dark. They have a triangular head and the pupil of the eye is vertical and slit-like. They deliver venom through two fangs. When striking the snake opens its mouth wide and the fangs are pulled down and penetrate the target. About 99% of the venomous bites in this country are from pit vipers.

Mojave rattlesnakes or canebrake rattlesnakes: carry a neurotoxic venom that can affect the brain or spinal cord.

Copperheads: on the other hand, have a milder and less dangerous venom that sometimes may not require antivenin treatment.

COBRA FAMILY: CORAL SNAKES *(Elapidae)*

There are two species of coral snakes found chiefly in the Southern states. Related to the much more dangerous Asian cobras and kraits, coral snakes have small mouths and short teeth, which give them a less efficient venom delivery than pit vipers. People bitten by coral snakes lack the characteristic fang marks of pit vipers, sometimes making the bite hard to detect. Coral snake toxic venom affects the nervous system. Though coral snakebites are rare in the US - only about 25 a year by some estimates - the snake's neurotoxic venom can be dangerous.

SIMILAR L◉◉KING SNAKES

Some nonpoisonous snakes, such as the **scarlet king snake**, mimic the bright red, yellow and black coloration of the coral snake. This potential for confusion underscores the importance of seeking care for any snakebite (unless positive identification of a nonpoisonous snake can be made). *The bites of both pit vipers and coral snakes can be effectively treated with antivenin. But other factors, such as time elapsed since being bitten and care taken before arriving at the hospital, also are critical.*

Red
Yellow
Black
Coral Snake

IDENTIFY A CORAL SNAKE

Remember the ditty:
"Red on yellow will kill a fellow
Red on black, venom will lack"

- This snake is very colorful with bright red, yellow and black bands completely encircling the body.
- Note that the red band is next to the yellow. This is important as there are many similar colored snakes but the coral snake is the only one with the red adjacent to the yellow band.
- It is very rare and lives in Florida and the desert of the Southwest. It will only bite when mishandled.
- The amount of venom injected is directly related to the size of the snake and the length of time it holds on to the victim.
- The coral snake has tiny fangs at the rear of its mouth and injects its venom with its teeth. A chewing motion is used to inject the venom. Because of its small mouth, teeth and limited jaw expansion it usually bites on a small extremity such as the foot, hand, or a finger. After the bite you will see tiny punctures or scratch marks.
- The Coral snake bites and holds.
- The initial symptoms are a slight burning pain and mild local swelling at the wound. After a few minutes additional symptoms will occur: the victim will begin to lose control of all reflexes, blurring of vision, drooping eyelids, slurred speech, drowsiness, sweating, increased salivation, difficulty in breathing and nausea.

Coral Snake Head

Coral Snake Bites
Pull the snake off immediately as the Coral snake fangs are relatively small, and they have to work at getting venom into the wound. Therefore, the faster the snake is removed the less venom is injected.

No Poisonous Snakes

Rattlesnakes
Copperheads
Water Moccasins
Coral Snakes

SNAKE BITES

The majority of snakes in North America are not poisonous. The main poisonous ones belong to the viper and cobra families. Sea snakes of the Indian and Pacific Oceans are almost all poisonous. Harmless snakes have no poisonous fangs and inflict a bite with two roughly parallel rows of small tooth marks.

Top of Mouth   Bottom of Mouth   **Harmless Snake Bite**

Poisonous snakes, have two large fangs, and sometimes smaller ones behind. They inflict a bite which have two main punctures (from the fangs) and some small marks.

Fangs
Fang Marks   Top of Mouth   Bottom of Mouth
Poisonous Snake Bite

A poisonous snake bite is painful and a swelling develops around the bite. There can be symptoms of shock, faintness, vomiting and a difficulty in breathing.

Fer de Lance Rattlesnake Striking
Fangs have dropped and the mouth having a large span can bite a large animal.

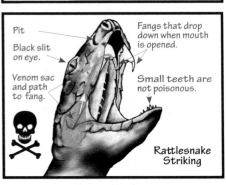

Pit
Black slit on eye.
Venom sac and path to fang.

Fangs that drop down when mouth is opened.

Small teeth are not poisonous.

Rattlesnake Striking

SNAKE BITES

FIRST AID : SNAKEBITES

Over the years, snakebite victims have been exposed to all kinds of slicing, freezing and squeezing as stopgap measures before receiving medical care. Some of these approaches, like cutting into a bite and attempting to suck out the venom, have largely fallen out of favor. "In the past five or 10 years, there's been a backing off in first aid from really invasive things like making incisions," says Arizona physician David Hardy, M.D., who studies snakebite epidemiology. "This is because we now know these things can do harm and we don't know if they really change the outcome."

Many health-care professionals embrace just a few basic first-aid techniques. According to the American Red Cross, these steps should be taken.

- Wash the bite with soap and water.
- Immobilize the bitten area and keep it lower than the heart.
- *Get medical help.*

"The main thing is to get to a hospital and don't delay," says Hardy. "Most bites don't occur in real isolated situations, so it is feasible to get prompt [medical care]." Some medical professionals, along with the American Red Cross, cautiously recommend two other measures:

- If a victim is unable to reach medical care within 30 minutes, a bandage, wrapped two to four inches above the bite, may help slow venom. The bandage should not cut off blood flow from a vein or artery. A good rule of thumb is to make the band loose enough that a finger can slip under it.
- A suction device may be placed over the bite to help draw venom out of the wound without making cuts. Suction instruments often are included in commercial snakebite kits.

Parts of the Snake Bite information was adapted from an article by John Henkel: FDA

TREATMENT DRAWBACKS

Antivenins have been in use for decades and are the only effective treatment for some bites. "Antivenins have a fairly good safety record," says Don Tankersley, deputy director of FDA's division of hematology. "There are sometimes reactions to them, even life-threatening reactions, but then you're treating a life-threatening situation. It's clearly a case of weighing the risks versus the benefits."

People previously treated with antivenin for snakebites probably will develop a lifelong sensitivity to horse products (used to make antivenin). To identify these and other sensitive patients, hospitals typically obtain a record of the victim's experience with snakebites or horse products. Hospitals also perform a skin test that quickly shows any sensitivity. Certain venomous snakebites may be treated without using antivenin. This is usually a judgment call the doctor makes based on the snake's size and other factors, which normally involves close monitoring of patients in a medical facility. "In some areas, such as desert areas, most rattlesnakes are small and don't have as potent a venom," says Edward L. Hall, M.D., a Thomasville, Ga., trauma surgeon who treats snakebites. "You might get by with those patients in not using antivenin." But with other snakes, Hall says, antivenin can be a lifesaver. For example, the Eastern diamondback rattlesnake - found in large quantities in the region of Georgia where Hall practices medicine and in other Southern states from the Carolinas to Louisiana - can reach six feet in length and deliver a potent payload of venom. "It's an enormously dangerous bite that requires very aggressive treatment (with antivenin) or the patient will die," Hall says.

RATTLESNAKES

All rattlesnakes are poisonous. Rattlesnakes inject their venom from their fangs and their poison is a blood-destroying poison (different from the coral snake). Their dens are usually on the south side of rocky areas. The rocks act as a heat collector which keep the cold-blooded snakes warm especially at night. Be careful in shady areas during a hot day as rattlesnakes avoid the heat by hiding behind rocks, below bushes, behind debris, in your clothing or behind your backpack. They travel at night when it is cooler.

To protect against rattlesnakes (and all snakes):
- Never put your feet or hands in areas that you cannot see.
- Wear heavy high boots, long loose pants.
- Walk in open areas.
- Be cautious and alert when climbing rocks.
- Stay out of tall grass unless you wear thick leather boots, and remain on hiking paths as much as possible.
- At night use a flash light.

IF YOU HEAR THE RATTLE

A rattlesnake does not always rattle before striking.
- If you hear a rattle - **freeze.**
- Try to locate the snake by slowly moving your head.
- Slowly retreat. When you see the snake, make sure there is only one snake.

... Make no sudden movements.

RATTLESNAKE STRIKE RANGE

The striking distance of a rattlesnake is from half the snake's body length to the length of the snake's body. The Western Diamondback can strike at its full length from an uncoiled position and can actually leave the ground while striking.

Snake Bites
85% of bites are below the knee.
Wear boots and/or heavy baggy pants if possible.

A RATTLESNAKE BITE

- Remain calm - Remember that there is an excellent chance for survival, and in most cases there is plenty of time.
- Swelling can progress rapidly, so rings, watches and bracelets should be removed.
- Look for the actual fang bite (these are two fangs, one on each side of the mouth).
- If venom has been injected there will be intense, burning pain and swelling around the holes.
- Swelling will occur within a few minutes to an hour.
- Bite location will discolor and become painful.
- The victim might go into a state of shock.
- Further symptoms: numbness, breathing problems, nausea, and temporary blindness.

If possible, kill the snake and take the reptile to a hospital for identification as the venom treatment may vary between different snakes.

TREATING VENOMOUS SNAKE BITES

Every state but Maine, Alaska and Hawaii is home to at least one of 20 domestic poisonous snake species. A bite from one of these, in which the snake may inject varying degrees of toxic venom, should always be considered a medical emergency.

Some experts say that because victims can't always positively identify a snake, they should seek prompt care for any bite, though they may think the snake is nonpoisonous. Even a bite from a so-called "harmless" snake can cause an infection or allergic reaction in some people. Medical professionals sometimes disagree about the best way to manage poisonous snakebites. Some physicians hold off on immediate treatment, opting for observation of the patient to gauge a bite's seriousness. Procedures such as fasciotomy, a surgical treatment of tissue around the bite, have some supporters. But most often, doctors turn to the antidote to snake venom - antivenin - as a reliable treatment for serious snakebites.

Parts of the Snake Bite information was adapted from an article by John Henkel: FDA

HOW NOT TO Treat A SNAKEBITE

Though U.S. medical professionals may not agree on every aspect of what to do for snakebite first aid, they are nearly unanimous in their views of what NOT to do.

Among their recommendations...
- No ice or any other type of cooling on the bite. Research has shown this to be potentially harmful.
- No tourniquets. This cuts blood flow completely and may result in loss of the affected limb.
- No electric shock. This method is under study and has yet to be proven effective. It could harm the victim.
- No incisions in the wound. Such measures have not been proven useful and may cause further injury.

Arizona physician David Hardy, M.D., says part of the problem when someone is bitten is the element of surprise. "People often aren't trained in what to do, and they are in a panic situation." He adds that preparation - which includes knowing in advance how to get to the nearest hospital - could greatly reduce anxiety and lead to more effective care.

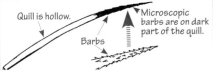

Quill is hollow. Microscopic barbs are on dark part of the quill. Barbs

PORCUPINE QUILLS

These quills can become embedded in your skin. As with a fish hook the quills are barbed and can only travel one way. If a quill is left in the body, with muscle action, it can migrate through the host part and reemerge on the other side. If a vital organ is on its route this travel through the body can be fatal. To remove quills pull them out, as close to the skin as possible, with a pair of pliers. Pull them out straight without wiggling back and forth so that the tip is not broken off.

GILA MONSTER

This is one of the two most venomous lizards in the world. It is the only poisonous lizard in North America. The monster will not bite you unless it is handled. It is very rare so it should not be killed or disturbed. It lives in the Southwest.

CONSTIPATION

Constipation is the difficulty in passage or ir-regularity of the bowel movement. Side affects can include stomach discomfort, headache, loss of appetite, discomfort and listlessness.
A change of diet or environment might result in temporary irregularity. It can be caused by an irregular life-style. It might indicate the onset of appendicitis if there is abdominal pain or fever.
See a doctor.

Treatment

• Porridge, bread, fruit, or vegetables gives bulk to the stool. Find a vegetable or fruit that might help you establish a regular stool, possibly carrots, prunes etc.
• See the chapter on Edible Plants for more ideas.
• Drinking a cup hot water might help.
• Avoid the regular use of purgative as they will lose their effectiveness.
• If the constipation is not relieved by these measures, then it may be necessary to use a soap and water enema. *See a doctor.*

FISH HOOK PIERCING BODY

If the fish hook and barb has completely pen-etrated the skin consider pushing the hook through the skin and then cut off the hook at the barb or at the shank and remove it.
If the hook is only partially in the skin try to re-move it. If it is not possible see a doctor. Before going to the doctor washed the wound with alcohol and cover the hook with a bandage to stop it from moving. Do not move the muscle, near the penetration area, as it might cause the barb to enter further. If you are in the wil-derness you might consider pushing the hook through and proceed as above. Let the wound bleed to eliminate any infecting organisms and foreign particles. Cover the wound with sterile dressing and see a doctor.
If the hook has been lodged on the face or eye apply sterile dressing and see a doctor.
A treble hook penetration is more complicated and in most cases requires surgical removal. If the hook is rusty or contaminated there might be an infection or tetanus. See page 595.

If the hook and barb has entered the body consider pushing the hook through the skin and cutting off the barb. See a doctor.

If barb has not entered too far the hook can be pulled out.

A   B   C   Pliers

DOG BITES

• Encourage bleeding for a short time by bathing the bitten area in hot water to with some antiseptic. Apply a clean dressing.
• The dog may be suffering from rabies *(hydro-phobia)*, and special treatment is necessary. Ra-bies should be suspected if the dog was acting abnormally. Abnormal activities as irrationally snapping at objects and persons, barking wildly, has its tongue hanging out with quantities of frothy saliva. The dog is often partly paralyzed.

First Aid

The patient should get medical attention as soon as possible for antirabies treatment. Try to keep access to the dog for further testing if required.
Animal Bites
Immediately wash with water to remove animal saliva then spend 5 to 10 minutes cleansing the wound with water and soap.
See RABIES next column.

RABIES *(Hydrophobia)*

Human symptoms of rabies can appear from 10 days to up to two years after the bite. Rabies, or hydrophobia, is caused by an organism which enters the blood as the result of a bite by an animal suffering from the disease. Once rabies has developed it is invariably fatal.
A doctor has to be seen and an antirabies treatment has to be followed as soon as possible.

Identify Animals with Rabies
Types of Rabies

Furious rabies: An animal is vicious and agitated, it then gets paralyzed and dies.
Dumb rabies: Animal looks paralytic.
The most common symptom is when an animal is not following its normal behavior. Some indicators might be: animals losing their fear of humans, animals not following their normal liv-ing patterns e.g. bats flying during the daytime.
If you have any indication or fear of infection see a doctor.
Watch for other infections as tetanus, swelling, etc. that might occur after an animal bite.

DANGERS OF RABBIT FEVER

The Tularemia germ can be fatal if it gets into an open scratch or wound. Wear gloves when clean-ing a wild rabbit or work a heavy soap lather into your skin before opening the body. The soap film will protect your skin. Thoroughly wash your hands when finished. Do not hunt slow sluggish rabbits. Wait 2 or 3 weeks after a heavy frost be-fore hunting for rabbit. Cook all rabbits until well done. The rabbit fever germ can be destroyed by intensive heat. Be careful when trapping as you will not know the health of the rabbit. *Page 343.*

Terebra Shell

Cone Shell Walking

Cone Shell

Snails that Bite
The bite can cause acute pain, swelling, paralysis, blindness, and possible death in a few hours.

CONE SHELLS *Conidae*

Cone-shaped shells that have a smooth sur-face and elongated shape. They live between rocks and crevices in coral reefs, and along rocky shores in tropical areas. They look harm-less but have tiny very sharp teeth. Upon bit-ing they inject an extremely poisonous venom. This fast acting venom can cause extreme pain, then swelling, paralysis, blindness, and possible death within hours. Do not handle any cone shells - no matter how attractive they look.

TEREBRA SHELLS *Terebridae*

These shells are found in both temperate and tropical waters. They are similar to cone shells but much thinner and longer. They poison in the same way as cone shells, but their venom is not as poisonous.

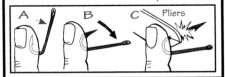

I hope you are enjoying this book -
it has taken over three years to write.
Paul Tawrell

Notes

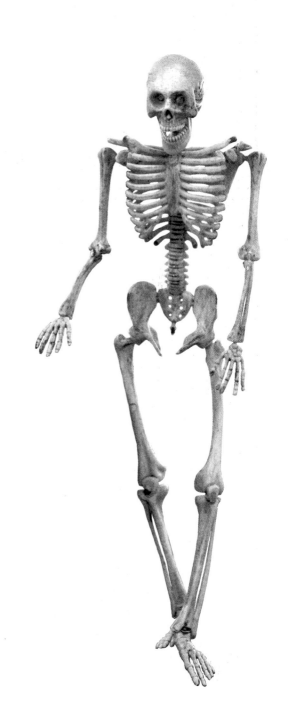

Author's Acknowledgments

This book is an accumulation of knowledge on camping, wilderness travel, and related information on the outdoors. Many sources were used including material from: Oxford University Press: R. L. Peterson, The Mammals of Eastern Canada, © 1966. Adapted illustrations of animals by permission. Provincial Museum of Alberta for photographs. The U.S. Government and the U.S. Military Services for the diversity of research they perform to give us a better understanding of the effect of nature and its phenomena upon us.

I would like to thank my mother, Melita Fechner, for teaching, Arlene Berg for a sharp eye, Dagmar & Klaus Jenett for many years of help, Emilia Cinca for being patient, Herman Lawetz for his help, the late Donald Curley, the great Nova Scotia artist, for his true to life nature paintings, Charles Banal for vision, Patricia Morse & Stacy Young for tumbling numbers, Dominique Dhin for keeping the Northern numbers, George Sand for providing foresight, Klements Bayer for his kindness, CB/CP for being the first to see the light, Emilia Cinca for Photoshopping, Barbara Black for keeping the ticker going, Metric Carolina Slowinska, Brian Curtis for keeping the Macs humming, my goddaughter Mathilde Borsenberger for tickling frogs and her son and also my godson, Adrien Tergny for having fun and Axel Tergny for learning.

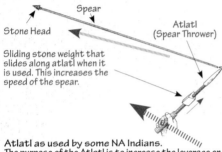

Spear

Stone Head

Atlatl
(Spear Thrower)

Sliding stone weight that slides along atlatl when it is used. This increases the speed of the spear.

Atlatl as used by some NA Indians.
The purpose of the Atlatl is to increase the leverage on hurling the spear. It gives a greater range and accuracy comparable to the bow at shorter distances.

Acknowledgement of the source of images used in this book. The letters adjacent to the page number are based upon the position of the image on the page as per the chart on the bottom left of this page. The publisher has tried to give credit to all images used - but could inadvertently have left out some credits - which will be included in future printings of this book.

US Government: NOAA (NSSL, NWS, NURP, NERR: 60A;126N;128A; 129H;147L;148I;151BF;152A;209P,D;212A,E;213P;217E;220P;229I; 381D;383P;390E;433L;439D,H,L,J,P;441H,J;442M;443N;445A,F,G,H,L; 446D,O,P,K;451P,L,H,F;452M;453D,H;454M,N;455M,L,D;456A,M;457 H;458A,D,E,I,J,H;459D,H,H,L,P;460AM;461D;462I;465D;467D,H,C,PM; 468M,P;469D,H,P,I;471G,D,J;475M,P;476M,P;477D;478A,B,D,E,M; 479G,H,K,L;480D;493J,F,E;494E,L;495K,C,G;497D;498P;499M,C,D,L; 500I,M,D;501A,B,F,J,N,M;510MNOP;511GHKLOP;513E;513P; 514CD,KLOPMN;515H,CD,EFG,IJMN;516;517;518;519;544;545. Araya 144E; John Bortniak 13D;124N;213M,L;244FJ;250I;272A,E ,I,J;334FG;390E;425D;450A,E;478J. Julia Brownlee 47GH. Evans 498E;515P. Grant W. Goodge 442A;480H. Golden 130P;470C. David K. Hoadley 144A. Mary Hollinger NODC 446I;501L. Ralph F. Kresge 442E,J,H. Leighline 247M. Meyer 249JN;250M,P. Cynthia McFee 478N. Mieremet 383L. Muller 310E. Harley D. Nygren 271P. Oxley 448M. Hubert A. Paton 128FJ. Pawlowski 72P. Grady Tuell 448E;470H. Walton 228B. NHRSA 16C;122M,N. NASA 57;75A;141;212I;217D,H;252G;263D;373E;375H;378A;384A; 385M,D;386A,B;388H;389A;423D;428E,K;430O;433O;432J;472. CDC 464E;602FG,M. FEMA12M;477M. Dept of Interior 78M;410A; 411H,P;412A,E,I,N,P,L;413A,P;414A,E,MO;416A,E,I,M,P. US Geological Survey29A;46M;378;379E,F,I,J. US Coast Guard 130A. USFWS 501D. Duane Raver/USFWS 502E;503D,H,LP;504ABEIMGK P;505BFJN,DHLP,K;506AEIM,B,O;507E,J,B,F,G,H,NO;508A,O,AE,BF,G K;509B,O,F,HLP.

Marius Barbeau 254L;255IM. Brunton 223P;363M;365NLOP; 390A,AE. Emilia Cinca 5H;561B;624P. Mark Ciufo 424A. Coleman24A;31M;53P;143P;316A;316M. Corel/Allan Fournier 524C;524C,I,P,N;526A,M,N;527M;529H;530D,H,K;531I;532A;533I ,M;535N;536I;550D. Donald Curley 103-104;115-116;265. John Hatch 268B;269D. National Wild Turkey Federation528H. Ortovox 241M. Cerasela Popa510A;513D. Provincial Museum of Alberta 328;527C;549P;550K. Pyle 51P. Société Canadienne D'Histoire Naturelle 524M. South Dakota Tourism 230A. Stearns 361D;361H. Thommen 375K. Hy Watson 31A;330A;332M. Wyeth 95A;590D.

Publisher's Acknowledgments

The publisher would like to thank the following companies for the use of illustrations and material from their promotional material:

Brunton — Binoculars, etc.
Camping Gaz — Camping stoves.
Coghlan's — Selection of outdoor accessories.
Coleman — Camping accessories.
Eureka! — Tents. • Gerber Knives.
G & V Snowshoes — Snowshoes.
Katadyn — Water purifiers. • Browning Fishing.
Kelty — Backpacks. • Opinel Knives.
Leatherman Tool — Multipurpose tools.
MAG Instrument — Flashlights.
MSR — Camping stoves. Water purifiers.
Optimus — Camping accessories.
Orthovox — Avalanche equipment,
PentaPure — Water purifiers. • Pur Water purifiers.
Petzl — Head lamps. • Stearns Water purifiers
Silva Compass — Compasses.
Swiss Army Brand — Compasses.
Wenger SA — Swiss Army knives.
World Famous Sales of Canada — Outdoor accessories, tents, snowshoes, & sleeping bags.
Outbound Products — Outdoor accessories, tents, and sleeping bags.

All Brand Names and Trademarks mentioned in this book belong to their respective companies. We regret if there has been an oversight and a company's name has been omitted from the above list.

A	B	C	D
E	F	G	H
I	J	K	L
M	N	O	P

Grid for the illustration coordinates.
Example:
Page IJ;

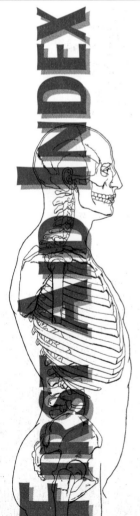

INDEX

Mathilde tickling a frog.

A-Frame tent of a surveying party.

A moose hunting camp with a lean-to shelter and reflecting fire.

Beach Shelter
Built of driftwood.
The roof of the shelter slopes down towards the water. This is to deflect the incoming wind.

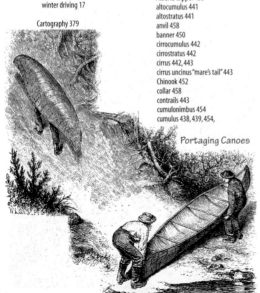

Portaging Canoes

Spearing Eels at night with a torch.

Hail 445
Hantavirus (HPS) 606

Hurricane (boats) 131

Indians hunting mountain sheep in the Rocky Mountains.

A moose "running down a tree."
In this way a moose can feed on the branches.
If attacked by a moose do not climb a small tree!

Indian Tumpline leather carrying strap.

Suspended in a strainer.

Rafting through a strainer.

Beaching a boat during a storm.

Running Rapids

Lining a canoe.

Rocky Mountain Sheep

Indians calling moose.

Mountain sheep jumping over a precipice.

Fishing for trout at night using torches.

Notes

STANDARD CONVERSIONS

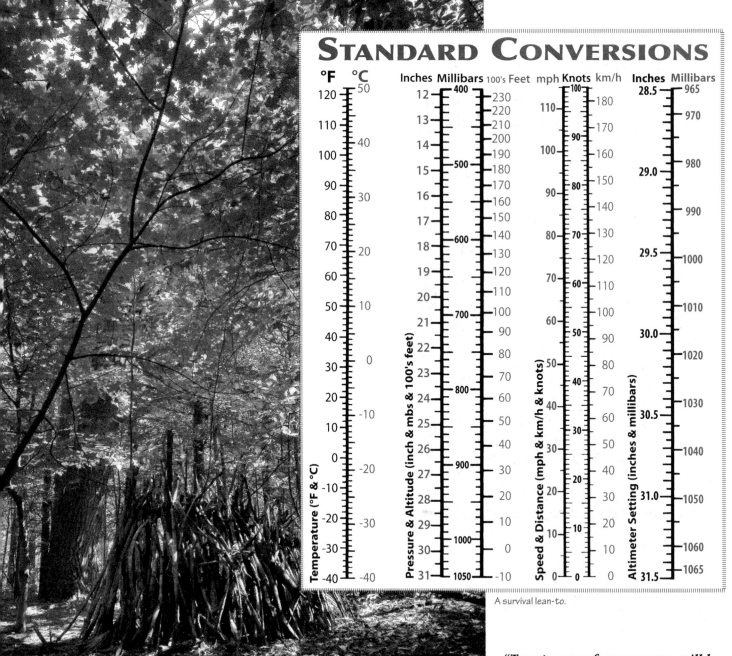

A survival lean-to.

> "Twenty years from now you will be more disappointed by the things that you didn't do than by the ones you did do. So throw off the bowlines. Sail away from the safe harbor. Catch the trade winds in your sails. Explore. Dream. Discover."
> *Mark Twain*

You only see what you know.
Goethe

The objective of this book is to help you understand the outdoors - so that you can have a great time and appreciate nature's intricate beauty.

The author's favorite car - a VW Thing 1974

PAUL TAWRELL
ACTIVE MEMBER:
OUTDOOR WRITERS ASSOCIATION OF AMERICA
OUTDOOR WRITERS OF CANADA

Notes